PRINCIPLES OF ECONOMICS

FOURTH EDITION

Dirk Mateer

University of Texas at Austin

Lee Coppock

University of Virginia

100

W. W. NORTON & COMPANY

Celebrating a Century of Independent Publishing

W. W. Norton & Company has been independent since its founding in 1923, when William Warder Norton and Mary D. Herter Norton first published lectures delivered at the People's Institute, the adult education division of New York City's Cooper Union. The firm soon expanded its program beyond the Institute, publishing books by celebrated academics from America and abroad. By midcentury, the two major pillars of Norton's publishing program—trade books and college texts—were firmly established. In the 1950s, the Norton family transferred control of the company to its employees, and today—with a staff of five hundred and hundreds of trade, college, and professional titles published each year—W. W. Norton & Company stands as the largest and oldest publishing house owned wholly by its employees.

Printed in Canada.

Editor: Eric Svendsen
Assistant Editor: Mia Davis
Managing Editor: Marian Johnson
Developmental Editor: Kurt Norlin
Project Editor: Layne Broadwater
Production Manager: Richard Bretan
Media Editor: Meg Leary
Associate Media Editor: Arielle Holstein
Media Editorial Assistant: Lily Edgerton
Managing Editor, College Digital Media: Kim Yi
Digital Project Editor: Rachel Mayer
Ebook Producer: Sophia Purut
Marketing Research and Strategy Manager: Ashley Sherwood
Marketing Strategy Manager: Alex Ottley
Director of College Permissions: Megan Schindel
College Permissions Specialist: Elizabeth Trammell
Photo Editor: Ted Szczepanski
Photo Researcher: Dena Digilio Betz
Art Director: Rubina Yeh
Text Design: Jen Montgomery
Cover Design and "Snapshot" Infographics: Kiss Me I'm Polish
Composition: Graphic World
Manufacturing: Transcontinental Printing

Permission to use copyrighted material is included on p. A-11.

ISBN 978-0-393-89206-2

W. W. Norton & Company, Inc., 500 Fifth Avenue, New York, NY 10110-0017
wwnorton.com

W. W. Norton & Company Ltd., 15 Carlisle Street, London W1D 3BS

1 2 3 4 5 6 7 8 9 0

In memory of our editor, Jack Repcheck, whose zest for life was contagious. Thanks for believing in us and challenging us to share our passion for economic education with others.

D.M. and L.C.

BRIEF CONTENTS

CONTENTS

PART II The Role of Markets

PART III The Theory of the Firm

8 Business Costs and Production 250

9 Firms in a Competitive Market 280

PART IV Labor Markets and Earnings

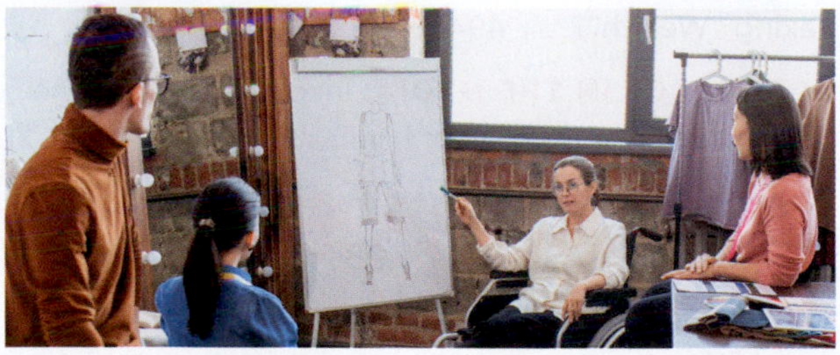

PART V Special Topics in Microeconomics

PART VI Macroeconomic Basics

PART VII The Long and Short of Macroeconomics

PART VIII Fiscal Policy

PART IX Monetary Policy

PART X International Economics

PREFACE

We are teachers of principles of economics. That is what we do. We each teach principles of microeconomics and macroeconomics to over a thousand students a semester, every single semester, at the University of Texas at Austin and the University of Virginia. To date, we have taught over 60,000 students.

We decided to write our own text for one big reason. We simply were not satisfied with the available texts and felt strongly that we could write an innovative book to which dedicated instructors like us would respond. It's not that the already available texts were bad or inaccurate; it's that they lacked an understanding of what we, as teachers, have learned through fielding the thousands of questions that our students have asked us over the years. We do not advise policymakers, but we do advise students, and we know how their minds work.

For instance, there really was no text that showed an understanding for where students consistently trip up (for example, cost curves) and therefore provided an additional example or, better yet, a worked exercise. There really was no text that was careful to reinforce new terminology and difficult sticking points with explanations in everyday language. There really was no text that leveraged the fact that today's students are key participants in the twenty-first-century economy and that used examples and cases from markets in which they interact all the time (such as the markets for cell phones, social networking sites, computing devices, and online booksellers).

What our years in the classroom have brought home to us is the importance of meeting students where they are. This means knowing their cultural touchstones and trying to tell the story of economics with those touchstones in mind. In our text, we meet students where they are through *resonance* and *reinforcement*. In fact, these two words are our mantra—we strive to make each topic resonate and then make it stick through reinforcement.

Whenever possible, we use student-centered examples that resonate with students. For instance, many of our examples refer to jobs that students often hold and businesses that often employ them. If the examples resonate, students are much more likely to dig into the material wholeheartedly and internalize key concepts. This revision process is not new to us; every time a new term begins, we update our course materials. What you see in the Fourth Edition of this book is a reflection of current economic theory, the contributions of students (past and present), and the changes in society around us. As professional instructors, we have an unfailing commitment to reach every student who crosses our paths and equip them for success. This book, like our classrooms, reflects this goal.

When we teach, we try to create a rhythm of reinforcement in our lectures that begins with the presentation of new material, is followed by a concrete example and then a reinforcing device, and then closes with a "make it stick" moment. We do this over and over again. We have tried to bring that rhythm to the book. We believe strongly that this commitment to reinforcement works. To give an example, in our chapter "Oligopoly and Strategic Behavior," while presenting the crucial yet difficult subject of game theory, we work through the concept of the prisoner's dilemma at least six different ways.

No educator is happy with the challenge we all face to motivate our students to read the assigned text. No matter how effective our lectures are, if our students are not reinforcing those lectures by reading the assigned text chapters, they are only partially absorbing the key takeaways that properly trained citizens need in order to thrive in today's world. A second key motivation for us to undertake this ambitious project was the desire to create a text that students would read, week in and week out, for the entire course. By following our commitment to resonance and reinforcement, we are confident that we have written a text that's a good read for today's students. So good, in fact, that we believe students will read entire chapters and actually enjoy them. Many users of the first three editions have indicated that this is the case.

What do we all want? We want our students to leave our courses having internalized fundamentals that they will remember for life. The fundamentals (such as understanding incentives, opportunity cost, and thinking at the margin) will help them to make better choices in the workplace, in their personal investments, in their long-term planning, in their voting, and in all their critical choices. The bottom line is that they will live more fulfilled and satisfying lives if we succeed. The purpose of this text is to help all of us succeed in this quest.

What does this classroom-inspired, student-centered text look like?

A Simple Narrative

First and foremost, we keep the narrative simple. We always bear in mind all those office-hour conversations with students where we searched for some way to make sense of this foreign language—for them—that is economics. It is incredibly satisfying when you find the right expression, explanation, or example that creates the "Oh, now I get it . . ." moment with your student. We have filled the narrative with those successful "now I get it" passages.

Real-World, Relatable Examples and Cases That Resonate

Nothing makes this material stick for students like good examples and cases that they relate to, and we have peppered our book with them. They are part of the narrative, set off with an Economics in the Real World heading. We further feature Economics in the Media boxed examples that use scenes from movies and TV shows that illustrate economic concepts. One of us has written the book (literally!) on economics in the movies, and we have used these clips year after year to make economics stick with students.

In addition, we have continued to work hard to create a text that represents the student population. Economics as a discipline is less diverse than many other fields of study, and that's something we've been trying to change, at the ground level, for decades. How do we do this? We listen to our students in our office hours, through email and informal conversations, and by observing the level of engagement in our classrooms. We also go out of our way to reach out and help those in need to learn and feel welcome. We hope you get this same feeling when you read this book! The style of writing is clear but intentionally conversational—the photos and captions are designed to draw you in, just as a lecture would. Take a quick read or flip through the pages, and you will see what we mean.

How much would you pay to avoid sitting in traffic?

ECONOMICS IN THE REAL WORLD

EXPRESS LANES USE DYNAMIC PRICING TO EASE CONGESTION

Metro Washington, D.C., is notorious for traffic, especially on the Capital Beltway (Interstate 495). New express lanes keep traffic moving by using dynamic pricing which adjusts tolls based on real-time traffic conditions.
manage the quantity demanded and keeps motorists mo
express-lane tolls can range from as low as $0.20 per mil
approximately $1.25 per mile in some sections during ru
rates are designed to ensure that the express lanes do no
ists thus have a choice: pay more to use the express lanes
regular lanes and arrive later. The decision about wheth
about opportunity cost. High-opportunity-cost motorist
lanes, while others with lower opportunity costs avoid th

Because dynamic prices become part of a motorist's i
motorists to weigh the costs and benefits of driving into
the dynamic pricing of express lanes causes motorists to
terms of the time when they drive. High-demand times,
ning rush, see higher tolls for using the express lanes an
lar lanes. Faced with either sitting in traffic (if they don't
more to enter the express lanes at peak-demand times, n
the Beltway at off-peak times. Since drivers internalize t
the dynamic toll prices even more precisely, the traffic fl
of the day so the existing road capacity is used more effic

Opportunity cost
Marginal thinking

· ECONOMICS *in the* MEDIA ·

The Crypto Bowl

The 2022 Super Bowl featured so many ads for cryptocurrency and related services that *Fortune* magazine dubbed the event the "Crypto Bowl." Many of the ads played on viewers' FOMO, or "fear of missing out," if they hadn't already gotten in on the crypto action.

One unintentionally hilarious ad featured Matt Damon comparing crypto investors to adventurers and pioneers like Magellan and the Wright brothers. "Fortune favors the brave," he intoned, as a crew of crypto-astronauts prepared for liftoff. One look at the past ups and downs of, say, Bitcoin will tell you that anyone buying crypto is likely in for a wild ride. Whether fortune will reward the move is anyone's guess. A few online retailers, like Shopify and Overstock.com, have started accepting crypto as payment. At present, though, cryptocurrencies are still mostly

Matt Damon, financial advisor?

what will happen with these currencies in the long run. Ads may promote cryptocurrencies as investment opportunities, but the ads are being paid for mostly by

Applying Economic Decision-Making through Problem-Solving

Most instructors in this course want students to learn to think like economists and to apply economic principles to their decision-making. This text shares this goal. To get students thinking about economics, we open each chapter with a scenario to illustrate a popular concept or to point out a misconception. Students come to our classes with a number of strongly held beliefs about economics and the economy, so we begin each chapter recognizing that fact and then establishing what we will do to illuminate and clarify that subject area. Then, in each chapter, several Practice What You Know features allow students to self-check their comprehension while also laying the foundation for the step-by-step problem-solving required for the end-of-chapter study problems. And throughout the text, key equations are used, and the five core foundations of economics (incentives, trade-offs, opportunity cost, marginal thinking, and trade creates value) are reinforced with a special icon to ensure that students are constantly connecting the dots.

Incentives
Trade-offs
Opportunity cost
Marginal thinking
Trade creates value

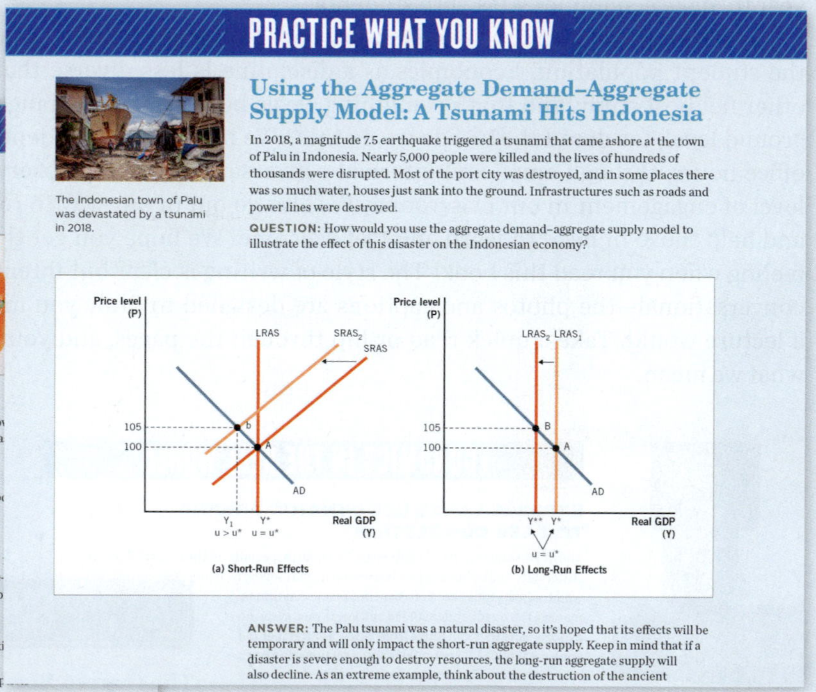

PRACTICE WHAT YOU KNOW

Using the Aggregate Demand–Aggregate Supply Model: A Tsunami Hits Indonesia

The Indonesian town of Palu was devastated by a tsunami in 2018.

In 2018, a magnitude 7.5 earthquake triggered a tsunami that came ashore at the town of Palu in Indonesia. Nearly 5,000 people were killed and the lives of hundreds of thousands were disrupted. Most of the port city was destroyed, and in some places there was so much water, houses just sank into the ground. Infrastructures such as roads and power lines were destroyed.

QUESTION: How would you use the aggregate demand–aggregate supply model to illustrate the effect of this disaster on the Indonesian economy?

ANSWER: The Palu tsunami was a natural disaster, so it's hoped that its effects will be temporary and will only impact the short-run aggregate supply. Keep in mind that if a disaster is severe enough to destroy resources, the long-run aggregate supply will also decline. As an extreme example, think about the destruction of the ancient

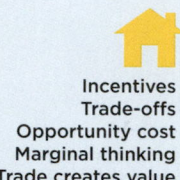

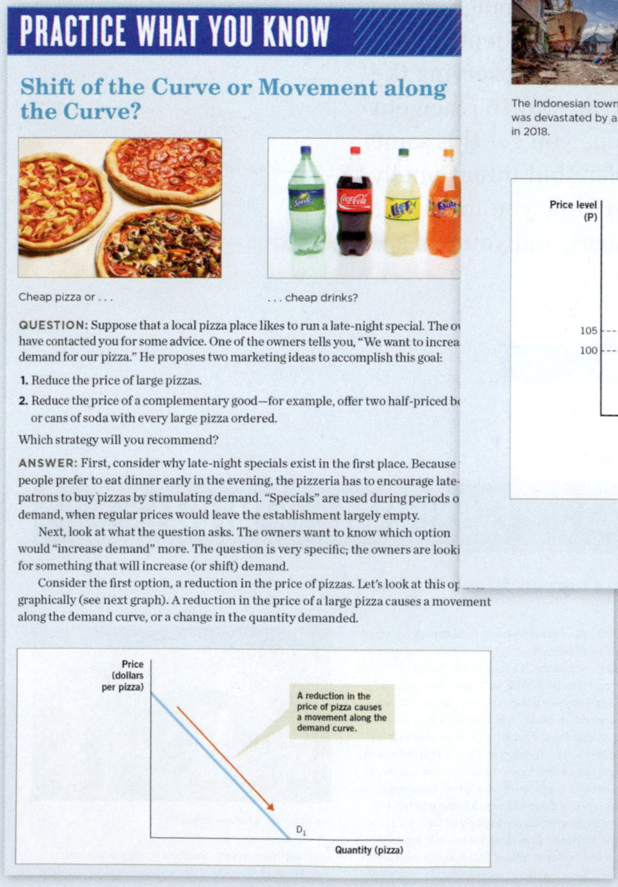

PRACTICE WHAT YOU KNOW

Shift of the Curve or Movement along the Curve?

Cheap pizza or . . .

. . . cheap drinks?

QUESTION: Suppose that a local pizza place likes to run a late-night special. The ov have contacted you for some advice. One of the owners tells you, "We want to increa demand for our pizza." He proposes two marketing ideas to accomplish this goal:

1. Reduce the price of large pizzas.
2. Reduce the price of a complementary good—for example, offer two half-priced b or cans of soda with every large pizza ordered.

Which strategy will you recommend?

ANSWER: First, consider why late-night specials exist in the first place. Because people prefer to eat dinner early in the evening, the pizzeria has to encourage late- patrons to buy pizzas by stimulating demand. "Specials" are used during periods o demand, when regular prices would leave the establishment largely empty.

Next, look at what the question asks. The owners want to know which option would "increase demand" more. The question is very specific; the owners are looki for something that will increase (or shift) demand.

Consider the first option, a reduction in the price of pizzas. Let's look at this op graphically (see next graph). A reduction in the price of a large pizza causes a movement along the demand curve, or a change in the quantity demanded.

Updated Big-Picture Pedagogy in the NEW Norton Illumine Ebook

Since today this book is normally used by students in an ebook format, its ebook comes with new features specifically designed for beginning students. To help students stay focused on the big ideas of each chapter while continuing to emphasize critical thinking, we use several unique features. First, we introduce students to the objectives in each chapter in the form of Big Questions that students will explore rather than memorize. Throughout each chapter, the ebook provides dynamic learning opportunities and conceptual reinforcement via interactive activities, Data Snapshots, and Check Your Understanding assessment questions. Then, we come back to the Big Questions in the conclusion to the chapter with Answering the Big Questions.

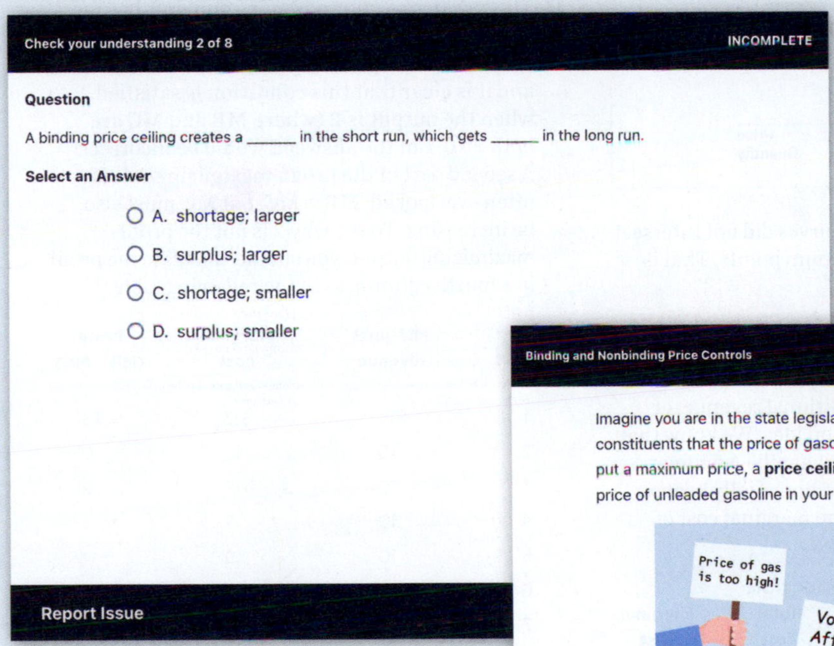

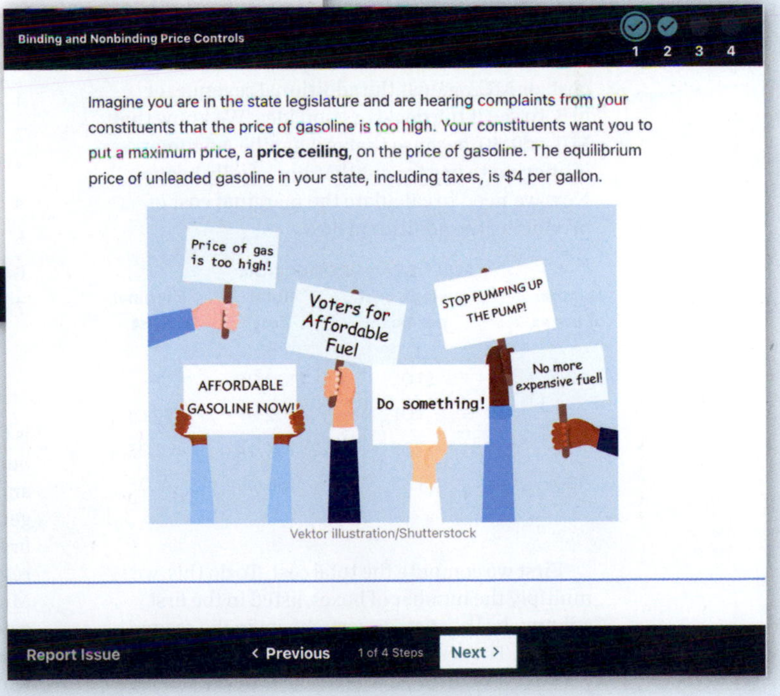

Solved-Problems Pedagogy

Last but certainly not least, we conclude each chapter with a selection of fully solved problems. These problems show students how to approach material they will see in homework, quizzes, and tests.

Solved Problems

6. Here is the corrected graph with the errors struck out and some explanation below.

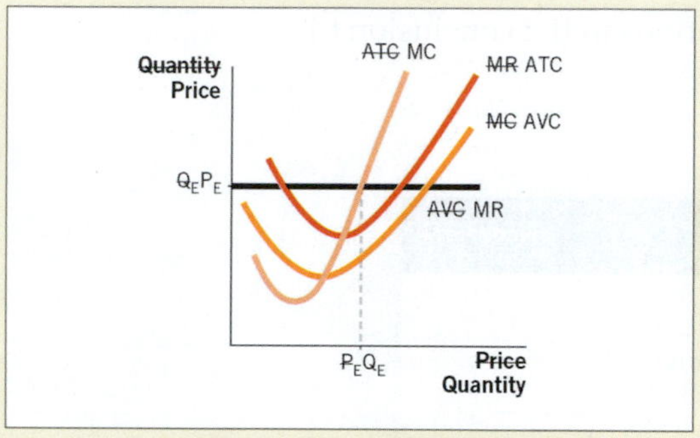

Also, the ATC and AVC curves did not intersect the MC curve at their minimum points. That is corrected here.

11. This problem requires marginal thinking. We know the profit-maximizing rule, MR = MC. Here all we need to do is compare the additional cost, or MC, against the additional revenue, or MR, to see if the deal is a good idea. We know that MR = \$1.50, because that is what the customer is offering to pay for another box of jelly beans. Now we need to calculate the marginal cost of producing the additional box.

JELLY BEAN PRODUCTION

Number of boxes	Average cost per box	Total cost	Marginal cost
100	\$1.00	\$100.00	–
101	1.01	102.01	\$2.01
102	1.02	104.04	2.03
103	1.03	106.09	2.05

First we compute the total cost. To do this, we multiply the number of boxes, listed in the first column, by the average cost, shown in the second column. The results are shown in the third column.

Next we find the marginal cost. Recall that the marginal cost is the amount it costs to produce one more unit. So we subtract the total cost of producing 101 boxes from the total cost of producing 100 boxes. For 101 boxes, MC = \$102.01 – \$100.00, or \$2.01. Because MR – MC is \$1.50 – \$2.01, producing the 101st box would create a loss of \$0.51. Therefore, at a price of \$1.50, your firm should not produce the 101st box.

13. This problem confounds many students because if you've memorized only one thing from this chapter, it is the profit-maximizing rule, MR = MC, and it is clear that this condition is satisfied when the output is 2 (where MR and MC are both \$10). But the answer 2 would be incorrect. A second part of the profit-maximizing rule is often overlooked: MR = MC, but MC must also be increasing. To see why 2 is not the profit-maximizing output, you should calculate the profit in a fourth column, as in the following table:

Output	Marginal revenue	Marginal cost	Profit (MR – MC)
1	\$10	\$13	– \$3
2	10	10	0
3	10	8	2
4	10	7	3
5	10	9	1
6	10	11	–1
7	10	14	–4

Profit is maximized at an output of 5, but why is this the case? Marginal cost is declining until output reaches 4, at which point the MR = \$10 and MC = \$7. So when the fourth unit is sold, it generates \$3, and the firm is profitable for the first time. By the fifth unit, MC is rising but remains less than MR, so the profit rises. However, MC is higher than MR for the sixth unit, which causes profits to decline. The reason 2 is *not* the profit-maximizing output is that MC is falling, which means that the firm is at the point where additional output is just becoming profitable.

Principles of Microeconomics—Hallmarks and Updates to the Fourth Edition

When we wrote the First Edition of *Principles of Microeconomics*, we decided to follow the traditional structure found in most texts. Though every chapter is critical, we believe that those covering supply and demand, elasticity, and production costs are the *most* fundamental, since so many other insights and takeaways build on them. We tried triply hard to reinforce these chapters with extra examples and opportunities for self-assessment.

Enthusiastic feedback has told us that our readers are happy with the organization of the book, so in this edition we continue to focus our updates on elements that we believe add tremendous value. We did a big rethink on every example in the textbook, updating and changing examples so that they are relatable, inclusive, culturally relevant, and interesting, and so the reader is engaged. This involved updating text content, features boxes, images, and illustrations. We took a hard look at many chapters, considering where we might introduce the work of different economists, especially women and people of color, who are often not well represented in principles texts. In trying to be relatable to a varied student body, we always looked for places where we could make sure every reader finds themselves represented repeatedly throughout the book.

The Fourth Edition has of course had many improvements, both to reflect changes in today's economy and also the input of close to 60 reviewers. For example, we have updated and simplified Snapshots, and now call out certain Snapshots as Data Snapshots. These Data Snapshots are paired with special data exercises available in the ebook and on our website, helping students better understand this material and practice their data skills.

A sampling of specific updates to the text includes new and revised material featuring the research of economists like Joan Robinson, Elinor Ostrom, Emily Oster, Susan Dynarski, Rachel Griffith, Aurelie Ouss, and Ulrike Malmendier, among others. There are new and updated media examples featuring *Shark Tank, Chef, Breaking Bad, Crazy Rich Asians, Superior Donuts, Mad Men, Superstore, Captain America: Civil War, Last Week Tonight with John Oliver, Worth It, Inside Out, The Onion, Planet Money* and the YouTube channels Veritasium and College Humor. And our updated examples feature new data on the relationship between educational attainment and pay; a full explanation of the gender wage gap, along with a study on why the gender gap exists at Uber; how universities can send signals to increase minority applications; bias and real estate appraisals; and a figure showing gender differences among the most common jobs. We dug deeper to give our students the best data so that they can become more informed.

One hallmark of this textbook that is not found anywhere else in the principles markets remains: this text includes a separate chapter on price discrimination. We have done this because the digital economy has made price discrimination much more common than it ever was before, so what was once a fun but somewhat marginal topic is no longer marginal. What's more, students really relate to it because they experience it in many of the markets in which they participate—for example, college sporting events.

We also place a stand-alone consumer theory chapter toward the end of the volume, but that does not mean that we consider it an optional chapter. We have learned that there is tremendous variation among instructors for when to present this material in the course, and we wanted to allow for maximum flexibility.

Principles of Macroeconomics—Hallmarks and Updates to the Fourth Edition

Principles of Macroeconomics follows the traditional structure found in most texts, including chapters on GDP, unemployment, and inflation. But it also contains several chapters on new topics that reflect the latest thinking and priorities in macroeconomics. First, at the end of the unit on macroeconomic basics, we have an entire chapter on financial markets, including coverage of securitization and mortgage-backed securities. Economic growth is presented before coverage of the short run, and we have two chapters devoted to the topic. The first focuses on the facts of economic growth. It discusses in largely qualitative terms how nations like South Korea and Singapore can be so wealthy while nations like North Korea and Liberia are so impoverished. The second chapter on growth presents the Solow model in very simple terms. We've included this chapter to highlight the importance of growth and modeling. That said, it is optional and can be skipped by those instructors who have time for only one chapter on growth.

Coverage of the short run includes a fully developed chapter on the aggregate demand–aggregate supply model, and a second chapter that uses this key model to analyze—essentially side by side—the Great Depression, the Great Recession, and the coronavirus recession. We feel this is a very effective way of presenting several of the key debates within economics, as well as showing different applications of the AD/AS model.

Finally, we have written a unique chapter on the federal budget, which has allowed us to discuss at length the controversial topic of entitlements and the foreign ownership of U.S. national debt.

Of course, the world has changed since the last edition was published. The Fourth Edition has been driven by the need to explain these changes and by feedback from almost 60 reviewers. Reviewers continue to note how important it is to clearly frame and ground concepts at the start of each chapter. In the Fourth Edition, we continue to use and have updated the large photographs, sometimes multiple ones, in the openers to draw students in. Over the last few years, we have seen the rise of inflation, spikes and drops in unemployment, and major new fiscal and monetary policy initiatives. The Fourth Edition covers all of these. Further, we continue to update the money and Federal Reserve material—in particular, our section on excess reserves and how the Fed now uses interest on reserve balances to affect the federal funds rate. Based upon extensive reviews, we do retain coverage of older tools of the Fed as needed material for students and the money multiplier, too. We have added important new material on topics like spending during the coronavirus recession, why recessions occur, the savings rate in America, and understanding cryptocurrencies.

In addition to these changes and addressing a concern in the discipline, this text features the voices and roles of a diverse group of economists, including people like Carol Graham, Dambisa Moyo, Valerie Ramey, Esther Duflo, Caren Gaffney, and Cecilia Rouse. We continue to fine-tune our aggregate demand–aggregate supply chapter as well as our appendix on the aggregate expenditures model.

Of course, we have updated the examples in the book, including new features with examples from *Dune, The Fast and the Furious,* the Crypto Bowl, and the band BTS. We now call out certain Snapshots as Data Snapshots, which are paired with special data exercises available in the ebook and on our website, helping students better understand this material and practice their data skills.

By far and away, most of our student readers are using an ebook version of this text. Because of this, we have developed many new features available through our ebook that improve the experience and learning process. Read on to learn more about it.

Supplements and Media

This text comes with robust support. Most can be accessed electronically either at digital.wwnorton.com/prineco4 or by locating this title's catalog page at wwnorton.com.

NORTON ILLUMINE EBOOK

The new Norton Illumine Ebook is the ideal platform for today's multimodal learners. Each chapter includes dynamic, interactive learning opportunities embedded directly into the ebook platform so that students grasp concepts quickly and apply them as they learn. Features of the new ebook include:

Check Your Understanding Questions

Each Big Question concludes with two Check Your Understanding questions about the most important concepts in that section. These questions provide students with an opportunity to reflect on and correct any misunderstandings before moving on in their reading, and the answer-specific feedback gives students automatic feedback to coach them toward the correct answer. The questions are also trackable by completion, meaning that instructors can make the reading truly assignable as part of the overall grade.

Data Snapshots

These dynamic maps, charts, and graphs ask students to interact with real data to make predictions and explore on their own time. They help students gain some practice and experience with basic data.

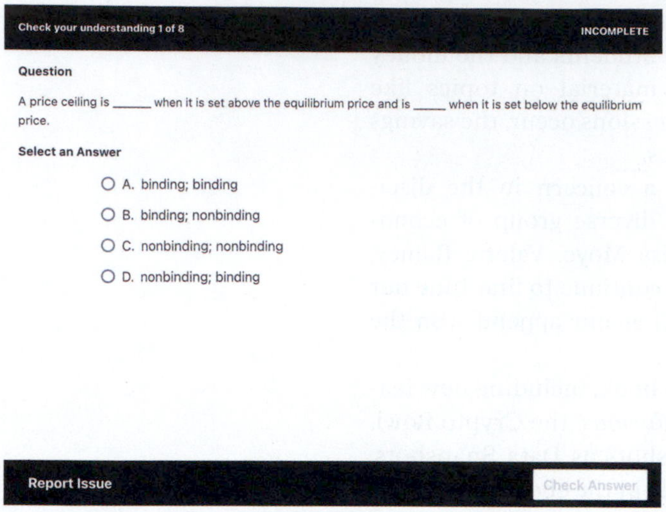

Check your understanding 1 of 8
INCOMPLETE
Question
A price ceiling is ______ when it is set above the equilibrium price and is _____ when it is set below the equilibrium price.
Select an Answer
A. binding; binding
B. binding; nonbinding
C. nonbinding; nonbinding
D. nonbinding; binding
Report Issue
Check Answer

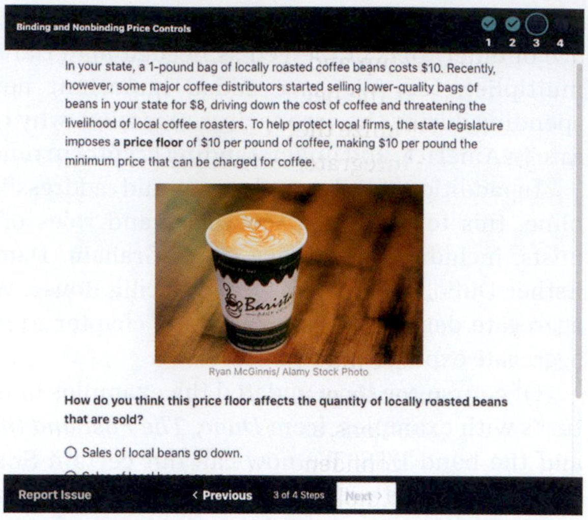

Binding and Nonbinding Price Controls
1 2 3 4
In your state, a 1-pound bag of locally roasted coffee beans costs $10. Recently, however, some major coffee distributors started selling lower-quality bags of beans in your state for $8, driving down the cost of coffee and threatening the livelihood of local coffee roasters. To help protect local firms, the state legislature imposes a price floor of $10 per pound of coffee, making $10 per pound the minimum price that can be charged for coffee.
Ryan McGinnis/ Alamy Stock Photo
How do you think this price floor affects the quantity of locally roasted beans that are sold?
Sales of local beans go down.
Report Issue
Previous
3 of 4 Steps
Next

Interactives

The Fourth Edition of *Principles of Economics* contains 20 interactives throughout the ebook. These embedded activities ask students to make predictions and work with concepts, developing their economic intuition and demonstrating that economic thinking is practiced by people in all walks of life.

SMARTWORK

Smartwork for *Principles of Economics* is an online learning environment that helps instructors meet the teaching goal of connecting concepts and showing applications. Richly varied questions and intuitive functionality give users the flexibility to create the type of learning that works best for their students. Try a demo of the following features at digital.wwnorton.com/prineco4.

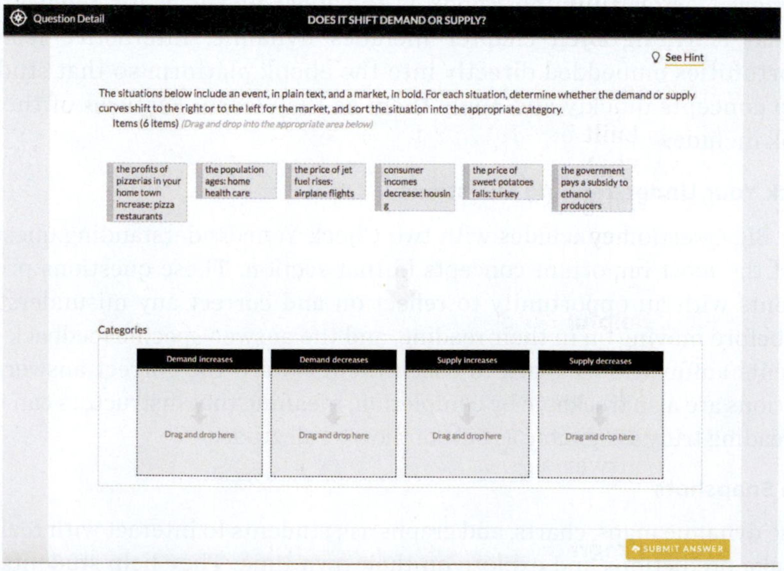

DOES IT SHIFT DEMAND OR SUPPLY?

Smartwork Norton's easy-to-use homework system designed to integrate with your LMS.

Easy to Launch, Easy to Assign in Your Learning Management System

Simple course setup and intuitive student registration minimize administrative headaches at the beginning of the semester. Instructors can use prebuilt activities or customize their own assignments and questions to suit their needs. Smartwork also integrates with campus learning management systems, so that student grades flow automatically to the instructor's LMS course.

Trusted Economics Tools and Content

Smartwork teaches students not only how to solve problems but also how to problem-solve, connecting concepts to learned skills through varied applications. Smartwork includes interactives based on real-world economic scenarios, "Office Hours" video tutorials presented in the learning moment, analytical and interactive graphing questions, and application problems. Rich answer-specific feedback builds students' confidence and economic skills. Questions are book specific, matching the terminology and conventions that students see in their textbook. They were developed in collaboration with instructors actively teaching with the Mateer and Coppock textbook. Norton also has implemented a three-fold Smartwork reviewing process to ensure maximum clarity and accuracy: First, all new questions were reviewed by instructors in the course; second, those questions' functionality and language were tested by undergraduate students; and third, the editorial team analyzed performance data from every question in the question bank to ensure that all questions were functioning and being used as intended.

Rich Performance Reports

Intuitive performance reports for both individual students and entire classes help instructors gauge student comprehension and adjust their teaching accordingly.

INQUIZITIVE

InQuizitive is Norton's award-winning, easy-to-use adaptive learning tool that personalizes the learning experience for students and helps them master—and retain—key learning objectives.

Play with a Purpose

Gaming elements built into InQuizitive engage students and motivate them to keep working. Students wager points on every question based on their confidence level and gain additional points for high success rates and on bonus questions. They can improve their grade by continuing to work questions in InQuizitive.

Active Learning, Helpful Feedback

InQuizitive includes a variety of question types beyond basic multiple choice. Image-click, numeric entry, and various graph interpretation questions build economic skills and better prepare students for lecture, quizzes, and exams. Rich answer-specific feedback helps students understand their mistakes.

Easy to Use, and Integrates with Your Campus LMS

Instructors can set up InQuizitive for their students in less than 5 minutes. Students can access InQuizitive on tablet devices as well as on computers,

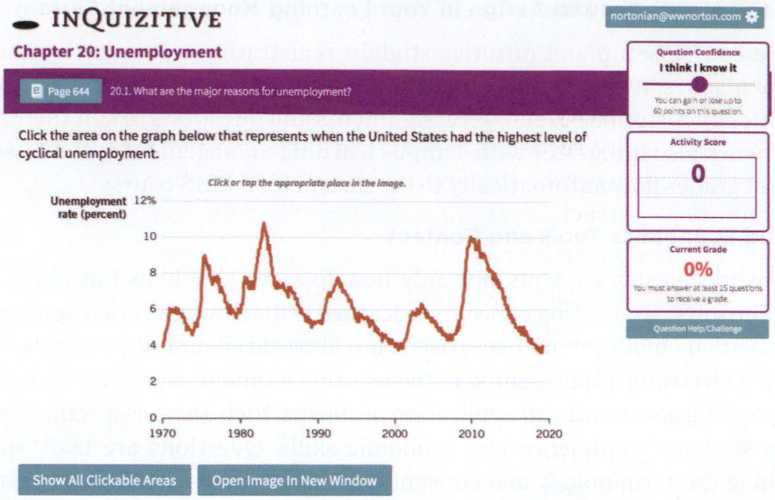

Inquizitive offers adaptive quizzing with gamelike features.

making it easy to study on the go. InQuizitive integrates with campus learning management systems; when integration is enabled, grades flow automatically to campus LMS gradebooks. A single sign-on between the LMS and Norton digital products simplifies student access.

RESOURCES FOR YOUR LMS

Bring tutorial videos, assessment, and other online teaching resources directly into your new or existing online course with the Resources for Your LMS (RLMS). The file is easily customizable and available for all major learning management systems, including Blackboard, Desire2Learn, Moodle, and Canvas.

The RLMS file for *Principles of Economics* includes:

- Office Hours video tutorials
- Economics in the Media Videos
- Interactives
- Interactive Scratch Paper modules
- Flashcards
- Links to the ebook, InQuizitive, and Smartwork

NORTON TEACHING TOOLS— THE "ULTIMATE GUIDE" TO TEACHING IS NOW FULLY SEARCHABLE AND ACCESSIBLE ONLINE!

The Norton Teaching Tools database is much more than an instructor's manual; it is at-your-service support. It includes 1,000= teaching tips each for micro- and macroeconomics from the classrooms of the authors and other innovative instructors. It can help instructors, both new and experienced, incorporate best-teaching practices and find inspiring ideas for enlivening their lectures.

The tips in the Norton Teaching Tools include:

- Core Skills Pathway activities that put students into their future career for the day, requiring them to apply the concepts from the course, economic data, and other principles skills to workplace decisions.

- Think-pair-share activities to promote small-group discussion and active learning
- "Recipes" for in-class activities and demonstrations that include descriptions of the activity, required materials, estimated length of time, estimated difficulty, recommended class size, and instructions. Improved and ready-to-use worksheets are also available for select activities, now with additional instructions to make them easier to use in class.
- Clicker questions and questions designed for other classroom signaling systems
- Ideas for music examples that can be used as lecture starters
- Suggestions for additional real-world examples to engage students
- An expanded Taking It Online appendix in each chapter that shows how class-tested teaching ideas can be adapted to online teaching environments
- Writing to Learn tips that give instructors short (one-page or less) paper prompts with ideas for potential student responses
- Worksheets and exercises to help you introduce and utilize the Federal Reserve's FRED economic data site in class.

Each chapter ends with solutions to the unsolved end-of-chapter problems in the textbook.

All these tips and resources can be searched and filtered by a number of criteria, such as topic, chapter, key word, media format, and resource type. Instructors can even save their favorite assets to a list, so they don't need to hunt for them each time they revisit.

To access the Norton Teaching Tools, visit digital.wwnorton.com/prineco4 or locate this title's catalog page at wwnorton.com

OFFICE HOURS VIDEO TUTORIALS

This collection of 66 videos brings the office-hours experience online. Each video explains a fundamental concept. Videos were developed and filmed working with the authors as well as a new team of presenters.

Perfect for online courses, each Office Hours video tutorial is succinct (90 seconds to 2 minutes in length) and mimics the office-hours experience. The videos focus on topics that are typically difficult to explain just in writing (or over email), such as shifting supply and demand curves.

The Office Hours videos have been incorporated throughout the Smartwork online homework system as video feedback for questions, integrated into the ebook, and included in the RLMS file.

ECONOMICS IN THE MEDIA VIDEOS

Accompanying the book's popular Economics in the Media features, these new 2-minute videos demonstrate the economic concepts underpinning many popular movies and TV shows. Some examples are supply shocks in the movie *Dune*, game theory in *Crazy Rich Asians*, and demand shift in *Guardians of the Galaxy*.

NORTON TESTMAKER

Norton Testmaker brings Norton's high-quality testing materials online. Using more than 8,000 questions—1,690 of them revised for the Fourth

Edition—you can create assessments from anywhere with an Internet connection, without downloading files or installing specialized software. Search and filter test bank questions by chapter, type, difficulty, learning objectives, and other criteria. You can also customize questions to fit your course. Then, easily export your tests to Microsoft Word or Common Cartridge files for import into your LMS.

PRESENTATION TOOLS

Norton offers a variety of presentation tools so that new instructors and veteran instructors alike can find the resources that are best suited for their teaching style.

Enhanced Lecture PowerPoint Slides

NEW Revised lecture PowerPoints now also use key images from the text to convey complex economic concepts. All slides are supported with complete lecture notes. These comprehensive, lecture-ready slides are perfect for new instructors and instructors who have limited time to prepare for lecture. The slides include elements such as images from the book, stepped-out versions of in-text graphs, additional examples not included in the chapter, and clicker questions.

Student Note-taking Slides

This resource is a trimmed-down version of the lecture slides with instructor notes removed for instructors who prefer slides that are more visual and with limited bullets. These are great for posting to the LMS for students to download for note-taking during lecture.

Art Slides and Art JPEGs

For instructors who simply want to incorporate in-text art into their existing slides, all art from the book (tables, graphs, photos, and Snapshot infographics) is available in both PowerPoint and .jpeg formats. Stepped-out versions of in-text graphs and Snapshot infographics are also provided and optimized for screen projection.

LEECOPPOCK.COM

This blog serves as a one-stop-shop for all the "econ news you can use." Here you will find timely economic data, graphics, and teaching materials you will need to keep your course fresh and topical.

DIRKMATEER.COM

Visit dirkmateer.com to find a library of hundreds of recommended movie and TV clips and links to online video sources to use in class.

ACKNOWLEDGMENTS

We would like to thank the literally hundreds of fellow instructors who have helped us refine both our vision and the actual words on the page for four editions of this text.

Our reviewers and advisors from focus groups:
Mark Abajian, California State University, San Marcos
Teshome Abebe, Eastern Illinois University
Casey R. Abington, Northwest Missouri State University
Charity-Joy Acchiardo, University of Arizona
Rebecca Achee Thornton, University of Houston
Mehdi Afiat, College of Southern Nevada
Carlos Aguilar, El Paso Community College
Clelia Aguirre, Miami Dade College
Seemi Ahmad, State University of New York, Dutchess
Abdullah Al-Bahrani, Northern Kentucky University
Frank Albritton, Seminole State College
Rashid Al-Hmoud, Texas Tech University
Farhad Ameen, Westchester Community College
Christian Anderson, College of the Sequoias
Giuliana Andreopoulos, William Paterson University
Tom Andrews, West Chester University
Becca Arnold, San Diego Mesa College
Giant Aryani, Collin College
Lisa Augustyniak, Lake Michigan College
Dennis Avola, Bentley University
Roberto Ayala, California State University, Fullerton
Nahata Babu, University of Louisville
Philip Baca, New Mexico Military Institute
Sahar Bahmani, University of Wisconsin, Parkside
Linda Bailey-Mcweeney, Baruch College
Diana Bajrami, Diablo Valley College
Ron Baker, Millersville University
Saad Bakir, Alabama State University
Mihajlo Balic, Harrisburg Area Community College
Kuntal Banerjee, Florida Atlantic University
Gyanendra Baral, Oklahoma City Community College
Ryan Baranowski, Coe College
Ruth Barney, Edison Community College
David Barrus, Brigham Young University, Idaho
Clare Battista, California Polytechnic State University
Jude Bayham, Washington State University
Mary Beal-Hodges, University of North Florida
Michael Bech, University of Southern Denmark
Stacie Beck, University of Delaware
Eric Beckman, Delta College, University Center Campus
Q Beckman, Delta College
Christian Beer, University of North Carolina, Wilmington
Jodi Beggs, Northeastern University
Richard Beil, Auburn University
Ari Belasen, Southern Illinois University
Doris Bennett, Jacksonville State University
Karen Bernhardt-Walther, The Ohio State University
Joel Beutel, Delta College
Prasun Bhattacharjee, East Tennessee State University
Richard Bilas, College of Charleston
Benjamin Blair, Columbus State University
Kelly Blanchard, Purdue University
Wesley Blundell, California State University, East Bay
Inácio Bo, Boston College
Michael Bognanno, Temple University
Antonio Bojanic, California State University, Sacramento
David Boldt, University of West Georgia
Michael Bonnal, University of Tennesse, Chattanooga
Heather Bono, University of West Georgia
Andrea Borchard, Hillsborough Community College
Feler Bose, Alma College
Inoussa Boubacar, University of Wisconsin, Stout
Donald Boudreaux, George Mason University
Austin Boyle, Penn State
Jared Boyd, Henry Ford Community College
Elissa Braunstein, Colorado State University
Elizabeth Breitbach, University of Southern California
Kristie Briggs, Creighton University
Gregory Brock, Georgia Southern University
Stacey Brook, University of Iowa
Bruce Brown, California State Polytechnic University, Pomona
John Brown, Clark University
Vera Brusentsev, Swarthmore College
Laura Maria Bucila, Texas Christian University
Bryan Buckley, Northeastern State University
Benjamin Burden, Temple College
Richard Burkhauser, Cornell University
Whitney Buser, Young Harris College
W. Jennings Byrd, Troy University
Joseph Calhoun, Florida State University
Charles Callahan, State University of New York, Brockport
Douglas Campbell, University of Memphis
Giorgio Canarella, University of Nevada, Las Vegas

Laura Carolevschi, Winona State University
Nancy Carter, Kilgore College
Michael Casey, University of Central Arkansas
Amber Casolari, Riverside Community College
Nevin Cavusoglu, James Madison University
Valbona Cela, TriCounty Technical College
Semih Cekin, Texas Tech University
Rebecca Chambers, University of Delaware
Jason Chang, California Polytechnic State University, Pomona
Myong-Hun Chang, Cleveland State University
June Charles, North Lake College
Gregory Chase, Liberty University
Sanjukta Chaudhuri, University of Wisconsin, Eau Claire
Parama Chaudhury, University College of London
Chuiping Chen, American River College
Shuo Chen, State University of New York, Geneseo
Monica Cherry, State University of New York, Buffalo
Larry Chisesi, University of San Diego
Kenneth Christianson, Binghamton University
Christopher Clarke, University of Houston
David L. Cleeton, Illinois State University
Marcelo Clerici-Arias, Stanford University
Steve Cobb, University of North Texas
John Colletti, North Central College
Kristen Collett-Schmitt, University of Notre Dame
Rhonda Collier, Portland Community College
Simon Condliffe, West Chester University
Christopher K. Coombs, Louisiana State University
Michael Coon, Hood College
Gary Cooper, University of Minnesota
William Cooper, University of Kentucky
Doug Copeland, Johnson County Community College
Joab Corey, University of California, Riverside
Carlos Cortinhas, University of Exeter
Allen Coson, East Los Angeles College
Chad D. Cotti, University of Wisconsin, Oshkosh
Richard Cox, Arizona State University
Erik Craft, University of Richmond
Antoinette Criss, University of South Florida
Zachary Cronin, Hillsborough Community College
Glynice Crow, Wallace State Community College
Patrick Crowley, Texas A&M University, Corpus Christi
Sarah E. Culver, University of Alabama at Birmingham
Norman Cure, Macomb Community College
Damian Damianov, University of Texas, Pan American
Morassa Danai, California State University, Fullerton
Alexander Danel, University of Virginia
Ribhi Daoud, Sinclair Community College
Patrick Dolenc, University of Massachusetts, Amherst
John Donahue, Estrella Mountain Community College
Oswaldo Donoso, Lone Star College, North Harris
Kacey Douglas, Mississippi State University
Whitney Douglas-Buser, Young Harris College
Chelsea Dowell, Upper Iowa University
Alissa Dubnicki
William Dupor, The Ohio State University
Grace Eau, Georgia State University
Renee Edwards, Houston Community College
Harold W. Elder, University of Alabama
Diantha Ellis, Abraham Baldwin Agricultural College
Harry Ellis, University of North Texas
Amani Elobeid, Iowa State University
Tisha Emerson, Baylor University
Lucas Englehardt, Kent State University
Michael Enz, Framingham State University
Erwin Erhardt, University of Cincinnati
Jonathan Ernest, Clemson University
Mary Ervin, El Paso Community College
Molly Espey, Clemson University
Jose Esteban, Palomar Community College
Sarah Estelle, Hope College
Patricia Euzent, University of Central Florida
Brent Evans, Mississippi State University
Carolyn Fabian Stumph, Indiana University–Purdue University, Fort Wayne
Leila Farivar, The Ohio State University
Ben Fitch-Fleischmann, University of Oregon
Va Nee Van Fleck, California State University, Fresno
Oscar Flores, Minnesota State University, Moorhead
Robert Foran, Miami Dade College
Cynthia Foreman, Clark College
Michael Forney, Austin Community College
Irene Foster, George Washington University
Roger Frantz, San Diego State University
Shelby Frost, Georgia State University
Gnel Gabrielyan, Washington State University
Craig Gallet, California State University, Sacramento
Susan Garrigan-Piela, Hudson Valley Community College
Wayne Geerling, University of Texas at Austin
Karl Geisler, Idaho State University
Elisabetta Gentile, University of Houston
Erin George, Hood College
Menelik Geremew, Texas Tech University
Linda Ghent, Eastern Illinois University
Dipak Ghosh, Emporia State University
Edgar Ghossoub, University of Texas at San Antonio
J. Robert Gillette, University of Kentucky
Gregory Gilpin, Montana State University
Joana Girante, Arizona State University
Lisa Gloege, Grand Rapids Community College
Robert Godby, University of Wyoming
John Goddeeris, Michigan State University
Rajeev Goel, Illinois State University
Bill Goffe, State University of New York, Oswego
Michael Gootzeit, University of Memphis
Aspen Gorry, Clemson University
Richard Gosselin, Houston Community College
Paul Graf, Indiana University, Bloomington
Alan Green, Stetson University
Barbara Grey, Brown Foundation
Natalia Grey, Southeastern Missouri State University
Daniel Grossman, West Virginia University
Jeremy Groves, Northern Illinois University
Felicia Guity, Seattle Central Community College

Sheryl Hadley, Johnson County Community College
Gail Hayne Hafer, St. Louis Community College
Dan Hamermesh, University of Texas at Austin
Gabriela Q. Hamilton, Hillsborough Community College-Dale Mabry Campus
Mehdi Haririan, Bloomsburg University
Oskar Harmon, University of Connecticut
David Harrington, The Ohio State University
David Harris, Benedictine College
Darcy Hartman, The Ohio State University
Jenny Hawkins, Case Western Reserve University
John Hayfron, Western Washington University
Beth Haynes, East Tennessee State University
Jill Hayter, East Tennessee State University
Densie Hazlett, Whitman College
Phil Heap, James Madison University
Douglas Heiwig, Ivy Tech Community College
Marc Hellman, Oregon State University
Amy Henderson, St. Mary's College Maryland
Jessica Hennessey, Furman State
Wayne Hickenbottom, University of Texas at Austin
Mike Hilmer, San Diego State University
John Hilston, Eastern Florida State College
Bradley K. Hobbs, Clemson University
Ashley Hodgson, St. Olaf College
Adam Hoffer, University of Wisconsin, La Crosse
Jan Höffler, University of Göttingen
Lora Holcombe, Florida State University
Suneye Holmes, Spelman College
Charles Holt, University of Virginia
James Hornsten, Northwestern University
Nancy Howe, Hudson Valley Community College
Gail M. Hoyt, University of Kentucky
Yu-Mong Hsiao, Campbell University
Alice Hsiaw, College of the Holy Cross
Yu Hsing, Southeastern Louisiana University
Amanda Hughey, University of Delaware
Brad R. Humphreys, West Virginia University
Greg W. Hunter, California State Polytechnic University, Pomona
Rebecca Innerarity, Angelina College
Miren Ivankovic, Anderson University
Oleg Ivashchenko, University of Albany
Meredith Jackson, Snead State Community College
Sarah Jenyk, Youngstown State University
Michal M. Jerzmanowski, Clemson University
Sichao Jiang, University of Oregon
Rebecca L. Johannsen, Pasadena City College
Kristen Johnson, Metropolitan State University of Denver
Paul Johnson, University of Alaska, Anchorage
David Kalist, Shippensburg University of Pennsylvania
Mustafa Karakaplan, Oregon State University
Nicholas Karatjas, Indian University of Pennsylvania
Reza Karim, Des Moines Area Community College
Hossein Kazemi, Stonehill College
Janis Kea, West Valley College
Michael Kelley, Oakwood University
Sukanya Kemp, University of Akron
Carrie B. Kerekes, Florida Gulf Coast University
Frank Kim, University of San Diego
Sandra Kinel, Monroe Community College
Linda Kinney, Shepherd University
Vivian Kirby, Kennesaw State University
Ara Khanjian, Ventura College
Jennifer Klein, University of Colorado Boulder
Colin Knapp, University of Florida
Mary Knudson, University of Iowa
Brian Koralewski, Suffolk County Community College, Ammerman
Dmitri Krichevskiy, Elizabethtown College
Lone Grønbæk Kronbak, University of Southern Denmark
Paul Kubik, DePaul University
Daniel Kuester, Kentucky State University
Jean Kujawa, Lourdes University
Sunita Kumari, Eastern Florida State College
Sylvia Kuo, Brown University
MAJ James Lacovara, United States Military Academy at West Point
Becky Lafrancois, Colorado School of Mines
Ermelinda Laho, LaGuardia Community College
Bree Lang, University of California, Riverside
David Lang, California State University, Sacramento
Ghislaine Lang, San Jose State University
Nancy Lang, Northern Kentucky University
Carsten Lange, California State Polytechnic University, Pomona
Tony Laramie, Merrimack College
Paul Larson, University of Delaware
Teresa Laughlin, Palomar College
Jason Lee, University of California, Merced
Logan Lee, University of Oregon
Jenny Lehman, Wharton County Junior College
Mike Leonard, Kwantlen Polytechnic
Tesa Leonce, Columbus State University
Phillip Letting, Harrisburg Area Community College, Harrisburg
Amy Leung, Cosumnes River College
Eric Levy, Florida Atlantic University
Herman Li, University of Nevada, Las Vegas
Ishuan Li, Minnesota State University, Mankato
Carlos Liard-Murier, Central Connecticut State University
Daniel Lin, American University
Jaclyn Lindo, University of Hawaii, Manoa
Charles Link, University of Delaware
Delores Linton, Tarrant County College
Arthur Liu, East Carolina University
Bo Liu, Southern New Hampshire University
Weiwei Liu, Saginaw Valley State University
Xuepeng Liu, Kennesaw State University
Monika Lopez-Anuarbe, Connecticut College
Heriberto Lozano, Mississippi State University
Josephine Lugovskyy, University of Kansas
Ed Lukco, Ohio State University at Marion and Ohio Dominican University
Brian Lynch, Lake Land College
Martin Ma, Brigham Young University-Idaho
Lynn MacDonald, St. Cloud State University

Zachary Machunda, Minnesota State University, Moorhead
Bruce Madariaga, Montgomery College
Brinda Mahalingam, University of California, Riverside
Chowdhury Mahmoud, Concordia University
David Mahon, University of Delaware
Mark Maier, Glendale Community College
Lucy Malakar, Lorain County Community College
Len Malczynski, University of New Mexico
Ninos Malek, San Jose State University
Margaret Malixi, California State University, Bakersfield
Khawaja Mamun, Sacred Heart University
Nimantha Manamperi, St. Cloud University
Amber Mann, Corretta Scott King High School
Sonia Mansoor, Westminster College
Fady Mansour, Columbus State University
Farhad Mansourian, Crafton Hills College
Daniel Marburger, Arkansas State University
Emily Marshall, Dickinson College
Kerry Martin, Wright State University
Erika Martinez, University of South Florida
Jim McAndrew, Luzerne County Community College
Michael McAvoy, State University of New York, Oneonta
Kate McClain, University of Georgia
Myra McCrickard, Bellarmine University
Cara McDaniel, Arizona State University
Justin McDonald, State College of Florida, Manatee–Sarasota
Scott McGann, Grossmont College
Christopher McIntosh, University of Minnesota, Duluth
Craig McLaren, University of California, Riverside
Kris McWhite, University of Georgia
Shah Mehrabi, Montgomery College
Mark Melichar, Tennessee Technical University
Diego Mendez-Carbajo, Illinois Wesleyan University
Evelina Mengova, California State University, Fullerton
William G. Mertens, University of Colorado, Boulder
Charles Meyrick, Housatonic Community College
Frannie Miller, Texas A&M University
Laurie Miller, University of Nebraska, Lincoln
Edward L. Millner, Virginia Commonwealth University
Ida Mirzaie, The Ohio State University
Kaustav Misra, Saginaw Valley State University
Kara Mitchell, Belmont University
Michael A. Mogavero, University of Notre Dame
Mehdi Mohaghegh, Norwich University
Conor Molloy, Suffolk County Community College
Moon Moon Haque, University of Memphis
Francis Mummery, Fullerton College
Sheena Murray, University of Colorado, Boulder
Yolunda Nabors, Tennessee Technological University
Max Nagiel, Daytona State University
Mark Nair, Amarillo College
Mijid Naranchimeg, Central Connecticut State University
Mike Nelson, Oregon State University
Gibson Nene, University of Minnesota, Duluth
Carla Nietfeld, Miami University
Boris Nikolaev, University of South Florida
Jasminka Ninkovic, Emory University
Caroline Noblet, University of Maine
Daniel Norgard, Normandale Community College
Stephen Norman, University of Washington, Tacoma
Leah Norris, Midlands Technical College
Farrokh Nourzad, Marquette University
Grace O, Georgia State University
Ichiro Obara, University of California, Los Angeles
Fola Odebunmi, Cypress College
Vincent Odock, State University of New York, Orange
Constantin Ogloblin, Georgia Southern University
Lee Ohanian, University of California, Los Angeles
Paul Okello, Tarrant County College
Gregory Okoro, Georgia Perimeter College, Clarkston Campus
Ifeakandu Okoye, Florida A&M University
Neal Olitsky, University of Massachusetts, Dartmouth
Martha Olney, University of California, Berkeley
EeCheng Ong, National University of Singapore
Stephen Onyeiwu, Allegheny College
Sandra Orozco-Aleman, Mississippi State University
Lynda Marie Ortega, Saint Phillip's College
Christopher Otrok, University of Missouri
Stephanie Owings, Fort Lewis College
Caroline Padgett, Francis Marion University
Jennifer Pakula, Saddleback College
Kerry Pannell, DePauw University
Pete Parcells, Whitman College
Darshak Patel, University of Kentucky
Lawrence Paye, Houston Community College, Northeast College, Northline Campus
R. Scott Pearson, Charleston Southern University
Jodi Pelkowski, Wichita State University
Faye Peng, University of Wisconsin, Richland
Erica Perdue, Virginia Polytechnic Institute and State University
Andrew Perumal, University of Massachusetts, Boston
Brian Peterson, Central College
Dorothy Peterson, Washington University
Michael Petrowsky, Austin Community College
Van T.H. Pham, Salem State University
Rinaldo Pietrantonio, West Virginia University
Inna Pomorina, Bath Spa University
Steve Price, Butte College
Irina Pritchett, North Carolina State University
Guangjun Qu, Birmingham—Southern College
Jason Query, Western Washington University
Gabriela Quevado, Hillsborough Community College
Sarah Quintanar, University of Arkansas at Little Rock
Aleksander Radisich, Glendale Community College
Tobi Ragan, San Jose State University
Robi Ragan, Mercer University
Nahreen Rahman, University of Cincinnati
Mona Ray, Morehouse College
Ranajoy Ray-Chaudhuri, The Ohio State University
Mitchell Redlo, Monroe Community College
Tracy Regan, Boston College
Dawn Renninger, Penn State Altoona
Ann Rhoads, Delaware State University
Jennifer Rhoads, St. Catharine University

Samual Riewe, Sonoma State University
Matthew Rolnick, City College of New York
Leanne Roncolato, American University
Debasis Rooj, Northern Illinois University
Brian Rosario, American River College
Ildiko Roth, North Idaho College
Matthew Rousu, Susquehanna University
Jason Rudbeck, University of Georgia
Nicholas G. Rupp, East Carolina University
Anne-Marie Ryan-Guest, Normandale Community College
Martin Sabo, Community College of Denver
Hilary Sackett, Westfield State University
Mariana Saenz-Ayala, Georgia Southern University
Shrawantee Saha, College of St. Benedict
Ravi Samitamana, Daytona State College
Rolando Sanchez, Northwest Vista College
Allen Sanderson, University of Chicago
Jeff Sarbaum, University of North Carolina, Greensboro
Naveen Sarna, Northern Virginia Community College
Supriya Sarnikar, Westfield State University
Noriaki Sasaki, McHenry County College
Stefania Scandizzo, University of Maryland
Thomas Scheiding, University of Hawaii-West Oahu
Douglas Schneiderheinze, Lewis & Clark Community College
Jessica Schuring, Central College
Robert Schwab, University of Maryland
James Self, Indiana University, Bloomington
Sean Severe, Drake University
Sheikh Shahnawaz, California State University, Chico
Gina Shamshak, Goucher College
Neil Sheflin, Rutgers University
Brandon Sheridan, North Central College
Dorothy R. Siden, Salem State College
Cheri Sides, Lane College
Joe Silverman, Mira Costa College
Scott Simkins, North Carolina A&T State University
Robert Simonson, Minnesota State University, Mankato
Michael C. Slagel, College of Southern Idaho
Brian Sloboda, University of Phoenix
Gordon Smith, Anderson University
Kara Smith, Belmont University
John Solow, University of Iowa
Robert Sonora, Fort Lewis Collge
Todd Sorensen, University of California, Riverside
Maria Sorokina, West Virginia University
Christian Spielman, University College London
Denise Stanley, California State University, Fullerton
Leticia Starkov, Elgin Community College
Kalina Staub, University of North Carolina, Chapel Hill
Tesa Stegner, Idaho State University
Rebecca Stein, University of Pennsylvania
Joe Stenard, Hudson Valley Community College
Heather Stephens, California State University, Long Beach
Liliana Stern, Auburn University
Joshua Stillwagon, University of New Hampshire
Burak Sungu, Miami University
Paul Suozzo, Centralia College
Dan Sutter, Troy University
Omari Swinton, Howard University
David Switzer, St. Cloud Sate University
Vera Tabakova, East Carolina University
Ariuna Taivan, University of Minnesota, Duluth
Yuan Emily Tang, University of California, San Diego
Anna Terzyan, Loyola Marymount University
David Thomas, Ball State University
Henry Thompson, Auburn University
James Tierney, Pennsylvania State University
Aleksander Tomic, Macon State College
Suzanne Toney, Savannah State University
Mehmet Tosun, University of Nevada, Reno
Steve Trost, Virginia Polytechnic Institute and State University
Mark Trueman, Macomb College
Melissa Trussell, College of Coastal Georgia
Phillip Tussing, Houston Community College
Nora Underwood, University of Central Florida
Gergory B. Upton, Jr., Louisiana State University
Mike Urbancic, University of Oregon
Jesus Valencia, Slippery Rock University
Robert Van Horn, University of Rhode Island
Va Nee Van Vleck, California State University, Fresno
Adel Varghese, Texas A&M University
Marieta Velikova, Belmont University
Tatsuma Wada, Wayne State University
Jaime Wagner, University of Nebraska, Lincoln
Anne Walker, Boise State University
Will Walsh, Samford University
Yongqing Wang, University of Wisconsin, Waukesha
Mark V. Wheeler, Western Michigan University
Thomas White, Assumption College
Katie Wick, Abilene Christian University
Johnathan Wight, University of Richmond
Eric Wilbrandt, Auburn University
Nick Williams, University of Cincinnati
Douglas Wills, University of Washington, Tacoma
Ann Wimmer, Iowa Lakes Community College
Kafu Wong, University of Hong Kong
Kelvin Wong, University of Minnesota
Ken Woodward, Saddleback College
Jadrian Wooten, Virginia Polytechnic and State University
Ranita Wyatt, Paso-Hernando State College
Justin Yarvis, University of Arizona
Erin Yetter, University of Arizona
Kuzey Yilmaz, Cleveland State University
Young-Ro Yoon, Wayne State University
Anne York, Meredith College
Han Yu, Southern Connecticut State University
Kristen Zaborski, State College of Florida
Arindra Zainal, Oregon State University
Erik Zemljic, Kent State University
Tianwei Zhang, University of Georgia
Ying Zhen, Wesleyan College
Dmytro Zhosan, Glendale Community College
Alex Zhylyevskyy, Iowa State University
Kent Zirlott, University of Alabama

We would also like to thank our media authors, who worked tirelessly to create engaging tools and resources for the Fourth Edition. Our heartfelt thanks to Casey Abington (Northwest Missouri State University): Smartwork, Norton Teaching Tools; Whitney Buser (Georgia Institute of Technology): Interactive Activities; Jonathan Ernest (Case Western Reserve University): Smartwork; Wayne Geerling (University of Texas at Austin): Norton Teaching Tools; Alexander Hill (Arizona State University): Check Your Understanding Questions; Kim Holder (University of West Georgia): Norton Teaching Tools; Teresa Laughlin (Palomar College): Office Hour Videos, Interactive Activities; Lucy Malakar (Lorain County Community College and College of the Sequoias): Check Your Understanding Questions; Kris McWhite (Piedmont University): Check Your Understanding Questions; Yolunda Nabors (Tennessee Tech University): InQuizitive; Carla Nietfeld (Miami University-Ohio): Check Your Understanding Questions; Matthew Roelofs (Western Washington University): Check Your Understanding Questions; Hillary Sackett (Westfield State University): Norton Teaching Tools; Melissa Trussell (College of Coastal Georgia): Check Your Understanding Questions, Office Hour Videos; Erin Yetter (University of Arizona): Norton Teaching Tools.

All of the individuals above helped us to improve the text and ancillaries, but a smaller group of them have offered us extraordinary insight and support. In particular, we want to recognize Alicia Baik (University of Virginia), Jodi Beggs (Northeastern University), Dave Brown (Penn State University), Jennings Byrd (Troy University), Douglas Campbell (University of Memphis), Shelby Frost (Georgia State University), Wayne Geerling (University of Texas at Austin), Karl Geisler (Idaho State University), Paul Graf (Indiana University), Oskar Harmon (University of Connecticut), Jill Hayter (East Tennessee State University), Phil Heap (James Madison University), John Hilston (Brevard Community College), Kim Holder (University of West Georgia), Todd Knoop (Cornell College), Katie Kontak (Bowling Green State University), Brendan LaCerda (University of Virginia), Paul Larson (University of Delaware), David Mahon (University of Delaware), Lucy Malakar (Lorain County Community College and College of the Sequoias), Kerry Martin (Wright State University), Kris McWhite (Piedmont University), Ida Mirzaie (The Ohio State University), Yolunda Nabors (Tennessee Technical University), Charles Newton (Houston Community College), Boris Nikolaev (University of South Florida), J. Brian O'Roark (Robert Morris University), Andrew Perumal (University of Massachusetts, Boston), Irina Pritchett (North Carolina State University), Robi Ragan (Mercer University), Matt Rousu (Susquehanna College), Tom Scheiding (University of Hawaii-West Oahu), Brandon Sheridan (North Central College), Clair Smith (Saint John Fisher College), James Tierney (Penn State University), Phillip Tussing (Houston Community College), Nora Underwood (University of Central Florida), Joseph Whitman (University of Florida), Erin Yetter (University of Arizona), Erik Zemljic (Kent State University), and Zhou Zhang (University of Virginia).

We would also like to thank our partners at W. W. Norton & Company, on all four editions, who have been as committed to this text as we've been. They have been a pleasure to work with and we hope that we get to work together for many years. We like to call them Team Econ: Melissa Atkin, Hannah Bachman, Jack Borrebach, Rich Bretan, Layne Broadwater, Miryam Chandler, Cassie del Pilar, Mia Davis, Laura Dragonette, Lily Edgerton, Christina Fuery, Sam Glass, Arielle

Holstein, Jeannine Hennawi, John Kresse, Meg Leary, Pete Lesser, Sasha Levitt, Lindsey Osteen, Alex Ottley, Eric Pier-Hocking, Jack Repcheck, Victoria Reuter, Spencer Richardson-Jones, Carson Russell, Nicole Sawa, Megan Schindel, Ashley Sherwood, Eric Svendsen, Elizabeth Trammel, Janise Turso, and Stefani Wallace. Our development editors, Becky Kohn, Steve Riglosi, and Kurt Norlin, were a big help, as were our copy editors, Laura Sewell, Alice Vigliani, Janet Greenblatt, and Carla Barnwell. The visual appeal of the book is the result of our photo researchers, Dena Digilio Betz, Nelson Colón, and Ted Szczepanski, and the design teams at W. W. Norton and Kiss Me I'm Polish: Jen Montgomery, Debra Morton-Hoyt, Tiani Kennedy, Rubina Yeh, Agnieszka Gasparska, Andrew Janik, and Annie Song.

Finally, we would like to thank Kaitlyn Amos for the help she provided generating photo ideas. Thanks to all.

ABOUT THE AUTHORS

Dirk Mateer is a senior lecturer at the University of Texas at Austin, and an award-winning instructor. He has been featured in the "Great Teachers in Economics" series and he was also the inaugural winner of the Economic Communicator contest sponsored by the Association of Private Enterprise Education. Previously, while he was at Penn State, he received the George W. Atherton Award, the university's highest teaching award, and was voted the best overall teacher in the Smeal College of Business by the readers of *Critique Magazine*. Then, at the University of Arizona, he received the best large-class lecture award in the Eller College of Management and in 2021 won the Kenneth G. Elzinga Distinguished Teaching Award from the Southern Economic Association. He founded the *Journal of Economics Teaching* in 2015 in order to create a peer-reviewed journal dedicated to innovative instruction in economics. He is also the author of *Economics in the Movies* (Cengage, 2014).

Lee Coppock is a professor and undergraduate director in the Department of Economics at the University of Virginia, where he has taught more than 15,000 students in principles of macroeconomics. He has received several teaching awards, including the 2017 Kenneth G. Elzinga Distinguished TeachingAward from the Southern Economics Association and the 2018 UVA Alumni Distinguished Professor Award. Before teaching at UVA, Professor Coppock taught for nine years at Hillsdale College, where he honed his skills in small classes of 10–15 students, giving him an understanding of each student's point of view. Now teaching more than 1,000 students in a class, he applies what he learned in those small classes through participation, captivating imagery, and relevant stories that draw students' attention.

PRINCIPLES OF ECONOMICS

FOURTH EDITION

PART I

Introduction

CHAPTER

01

Five Foundations of Economics

Economics Is About More Than Money.

Have you ever thought about what it would be like to have a money tree in your backyard? Imagine walking outside, picking cash off the branches, and using it to buy whatever you desired. If that sounds too good to be true, it is—and not just because money doesn't grow on trees. The problem is, if money did grow on trees, it wouldn't be scarce. Everyone would have their own money tree, and therefore they wouldn't have any reason to give you something in return for the greenbacks you waved in front of them. You'd have all the money you could possibly want, and yet in practical terms it would be worthless. You couldn't give it away.

But is money what we really care about, anyway? No. What we care about is what we can use money to acquire: the actual goods and services that make our lives more enjoyable. Economist Carol Graham, who studies "the economics of happiness," makes the point that happiness is about a lot more than just how much people earn.

For starters, *predictability* of income matters. Many people regularly go through periods of unemployment. Even when these folks are working, uncertainty about the future subtracts from their happiness. Other people's incomes are on a smoother track: these folks are relatively poor when young, earn more and build up savings during middle age, and then draw down those savings once they retire. For

A money tree sounds awesome, but be careful what you wish for. Other people are going to want one, too.

the most part, these people avoid the happiness-undermining effects of financial uncertainty.

Then there's the matter of where you live. New York City is way more expensive than Charlottesville, Virginia, or Austin, Texas (where your authors live). On the other hand, New York has cultural opportunities that for some people justify the high cost of living. The moral? Clearly there is more to human happiness than simply how much money you make.

This textbook provides the tools you need to fill in more of the picture and make your own assessments about the economy. What other discipline helps you discover how the world works, how to be an informed citizen, and how to make day-to-day decisions? Economics can improve your understanding of the stock market and help you make better decisions. If you are concerned about the future of Social Security, this textbook explains how it works. If you are interested in learning more about the economics of health care and some of the challenges it faces, the answers are here.

In New York's pricey Greenwich Village, money doesn't grow on trees. The people living here do make a lot more money than most people, though. So do the residents of Miami Beach and Beverly Hills. Does that make them happier? Not necessarily.

In this chapter, you will learn about five foundations of economics—incentives, trade-offs, opportunity cost, marginal thinking, and the principle that trade creates value. You will find that many of the more complex problems presented later in the text are based on these foundations, either singly or in combination. Think of this chapter as a road map that provides a broad overview of your first journey into economics.

· BIG QUESTIONS ·

- What is economics?
- What are five foundations of economics?

What Is Economics?

Economists study how decisions are made. Examples of economic decisions include whether you should buy or lease a car, sublet your apartment, or buy that Gibson guitar you've been eyeing. And just as individuals must choose what to buy within the limits of their income, society as a whole must determine what to produce from its limited set of resources.

Of course, life would be a lot easier if we could have whatever we wanted whenever we wanted it. Unfortunately, life does not work that way. Our wants and needs are practically unlimited, but the resources available to satisfy these wants and needs are always limited. The term used to describe the limited nature of society's resources is **scarcity**.

Even the most abundant resources, like the water we drink and the air we breathe, are not always abundant enough everywhere to meet the wants and needs of every person. So how do individuals and societies make decisions about scarce resources? This is the basic question economists seek to answer. **Economics** is the study of how individuals and societies allocate their limited resources to satisfy their practically unlimited wants.

Scarcity
refers to the inherently limited nature of society's resources, given society's unlimited wants and needs.

Economics
is the study of how individuals and societies allocate their limited resources to satisfy their practically unlimited wants.

Microeconomics and Macroeconomics

The study of economics is divided into two subfields: microeconomics and macroeconomics. **Microeconomics** (micro) is the study of the individual units that make up the economy, such as households and businesses. **Macroeconomics**

Microeconomics
is the study of the individual units that make up the economy.

Macroeconomics
is the study of the overall aspects and workings of an economy.

Water is scarce . . .

. . . and so are diamonds!

(macro) is the study of the overall aspects and workings of an economy, such as inflation (an overall increase in prices), growth, employment, interest rates, and the productivity of the economy. To understand the difference, consider a worker who gets laid off and becomes unemployed. Is this an issue that would be addressed in microeconomics or macroeconomics? The question seems to fit parts of both definitions. The worker is an individual, which is micro, but employment is one of the broad areas of concern for the economy as a whole, which is macro. However, because only one worker is laid off, this is a micro issue. When many workers are laid off, the result is a higher unemployment rate across the entire economy. Then the issue is broad enough to be studied by macroeconomists. However, macroeconomics is more than just an aggregation of microeconomics. Macroeconomists examine, among other things, government policies regarding the federal budget and money supply, the reasons for inflation and unemployment, economic growth, international trade, and government borrowing—topics that are too complex to be understood using only microeconomic analysis.

What Are Five Foundations of Economics?

Incentives
Trade-offs
Opportunity cost
Marginal thinking
Trade creates value

The study of economics can be complicated, but we can make it very accessible by breaking it down into a set of component parts. The five foundations presented here are key components of economics. They are a bit like the natural laws of physics or chemistry. Almost every economic subject can be analyzed through the prism of one of these foundations. By mastering the five foundations, you will be on your way to succeeding in this course and thinking like an economist. The five foundations of economics are:

- Incentives
- Trade-offs
- Opportunity cost
- Marginal thinking
- Trade creates value

ECONOMICS *in the* MEDIA

Scarcity

NATION JUST WANTS TO BE SAFE, HAPPY, RICH, COMFORTABLE, ENTERTAINED AT ALL TIMES

A short video on the satirical website *The Onion* describes a fictitious report from the Pew Research Center about what Americans want and expect from life. After a graphic details how practically all Americans would like to be everything from "safe" to "romantically fulfilled," the video segues to interviews with individuals whose "all I want" lists range from the endearing (a big, happy dog) to the quirky (a new Wes Anderson movie), the unrealistic (quick and easy weight loss), and the impossible ("I don't want to die").

We live in a world of scarcity. But that alone doesn't explain why we're unable to meet everyone's wants. Couldn't we just redistribute goods and services more evenly, to satisfy everyone? No chance, because our wants exceed our needs, and when all our wants are met, we come up with new ones. Many people spend their lives trying to "keep up with the Joneses." This isn't all bad, because competitive drive causes people to work longer and harder, which makes the economy more productive. At the same time, when we purchase one good, we have less to spend on other goods we also desire, and therefore we face trade-offs and opportunity costs.

Based on a fictitious report on the satirical website *The Onion*, this graphic shows what Americans want. Of course, part of the joke is that this is not far from the truth for most of us, right?

Each of these five foundations reappears throughout the book and enables you to solve complex problems. Every time you encounter one of the five concepts, you will see an icon of a house in the margin. As you become more adept at economic analysis, you will often use two or more of these foundational ideas to understand the economic world around you.

Incentives

When you are faced with making a decision, you usually make the choice that you think will most improve your situation. In making your decision, you respond to **incentives**—factors that motivate you to act or exert effort. For example, your choice to study for an exam you have tomorrow, instead of spending the evening with your friends, is based on your belief that doing well on the exam will provide a greater benefit. You have an incentive to study because you know that an A in the course will raise your grade-point average and make you a more

Incentives are factors that motivate a person to act or exert effort.

PRACTICE WHAT YOU KNOW

Microeconomics and Macroeconomics: The Big Picture

Decide whether each of the following statements identifies a microeconomic issue or a macroeconomic issue.

STATEMENT: The personal savings rate averages more than 10% of income.

ANSWER: The personal savings rate is a statistic based on the average amount each household saves as a percentage of income. As such, it is a broad measure of savings that describes a macroeconomic issue.

STATEMENT: Maya was laid off from her job and is currently unemployed.

ANSWER: Maya's personal financial circumstances constitute a microeconomic issue, because she is an individual worker.

STATEMENT: Apple decides to open 100 new stores.

ANSWER: Even though Apple is a very large corporation, and 100 new stores will create many new jobs, Apple's decision is a microeconomic issue because it is best understood as part of an individual firm's competitive strategy.

STATEMENT: The government passes a jobs bill designed to stabilize the economy during a recession (an economic downturn).

ANSWER: You might be tempted to ask how many jobs are created, but that information is not relevant to answering this question. The key part of the statement refers to "stabilize the economy during a recession," which is an example of the government taking an active role in managing the overall workings of the economy. Therefore, it is a macroeconomic issue.

This mosaic illustrates the difference between micro and macro. The tiny tiles represent many individual decisions. The economy as a whole is the composite we "see" when we look at the entire picture.

attractive candidate on the job market when you are finished with school. We can further divide incentives into two paired categories: positive and negative, and direct and indirect.

POSITIVE AND NEGATIVE INCENTIVES *Positive incentives* encourage action by offering rewards or payments. For example, end-of-year bonuses motivate employees to work hard throughout the year, higher oil prices cause suppliers to extract more oil, and tax rebates encourage citizens to spend more money. *Negative incentives* discourage action by providing undesirable consequences or punishments. For instance, the fear of receiving a speeding ticket keeps motorists from driving too fast, higher oil prices might spur some consumers to use less oil, and the dread of a trip to the dentist motivates people to brush their teeth regularly. In each case, we see that incentives spur individuals to action.

Conventional wisdom tells us that "learning is its own reward," but try telling that to most students. Teachers are aware that incentives, both positive and negative, create additional interest among their students to learn the course material. Positive incentives include bonus points, gold stars, public praise, and extra credit. Many students respond to these encouragements by studying more. However, positive incentives are not enough. Suppose your instructor never gave any grade lower than an A. Your incentive to participate actively in the course, do assignments, or earn bonus points would be small. For positive incentives to work, they generally need to be coupled with negative incentives. This is why instructors require students to complete assignments, take exams, and write papers. Students know that if they do not complete these requirements, they will get a lower grade, or perhaps even fail the class.

DIRECT AND INDIRECT INCENTIVES Incentives can also be direct or indirect. For instance, if one gas station lowers its prices, it most likely will get business from customers who would not usually stop there. This is a *direct incentive*. Lower gasoline prices also work as an *indirect incentive*, because lower prices might encourage consumers to use more gas.

Direct incentives are easy to recognize. "Cut my grass and I'll pay you $30" is an example of a direct incentive. Indirect incentives are more difficult to recognize. But learning to recognize them is one of the keys to mastering economics. For instance, consider the indirect incentives at work in some government assistance programs. Almost everyone agrees that societies should provide a safety net for those without employment or whose income isn't enough to meet their basic needs. In other words, a society has a direct incentive to alleviate suffering caused by poverty. But how does a society provide this safety net without taking away the incentive to work? If the amount a person receives is higher than the amount that person can hope to make from a job, there is far less incentive to go back to work. In fact, there is an incentive not to. This situation creates an *unintended consequence*, where assistance originally meant as a safety net could start to be seen as a permanent source of income.

Policymakers have the tough task of deciding how to balance such conflicting incentives. Budget planners and legislators could decide to reduce benefits, but this decision might leave some people without enough to live on. For this reason, many government programs specify limits on the amount of time people can receive benefits. Ideally, this limit allows the welfare programs to continue meeting people's basic needs while creating incentives that encourage recipients to search for a job and acquire skills that will help them get a job. We'll learn more about welfare issues in Chapter 15.

During the coronavirus pandemic, the government added $600 a week to unemployment payments. Was this an expansion of the safety net, or an incentive not to work?

ECONOMICS IN THE REAL WORLD

WHY ARE THERE SO MANY DASHBOARD CAMERAS IN RUSSIA?

Let's look at an example of how incentives operate in the real world and how they can produce surprising consequences. Compared to the United States, Russia is quite a dangerous place to drive (see Figure 1.1). On top of the collisions that occur due to chaotic traffic conditions, insurance scammers regularly stage accidents. To protect themselves against scammers, most Russian motorists have dashcams, which provide video evidence of a driver's innocence in court. The fact that so many Russian drivers are willing to invest in dashcams strongly suggests that the benefits of having a cam exceed the cost.

In the United States, and in most other countries where there are fewer annual deaths (and accidents) per vehicle, staged accidents are much less common, and consequently dashcams are much less prevalent.

INCENTIVES AND INNOVATION Incentives also play a vital role in innovation, the engine of economic growth. An excellent example is Steve Jobs. He and the company he founded, Apple, held over 300 patents at the time of his death in 2011.

In the United States, the patent system and copyright laws guarantee inventors a specific period of time in which they have the exclusive right to sell their work. This system encourages innovation by creating a powerful financial

FIGURE 1.1

Global Status Report on Safety

Compared to the United States, Russia is quite a dangerous place to drive. Widespread insurance scamming in Russia has led most motorists to install dashcams. The fact that insurance scammers exist is an unintended consequence of mandated insurance, especially in Russia where the rules of the road and safe driving are often ignored.

Country	Annual deaths per 100,000 vehicles
Russia	53.4
Europe	19.0
United States	12.9
Australia	7.3

Source: See, WHO, ed., "Global Status Report on Road Safety 2015" (2015).

reward for creativity. Without patents and copyright laws, inventors would bear all the costs, and almost none of the rewards, for their efforts. Why would firms invest in research and development or artists create new music if others could immediately copy and sell their work? To reward the perspiration and inspiration required for innovation, society allows patents and copyrights to create the right incentives for economic growth.

In recent years, new forms of technology have made the illegal sharing of copyrighted material quite easy. As a result, illegal downloads of books, music, and movies are widespread. When writers, musicians, actors, and studios cannot effectively protect what they have created, they earn less. So illegal downloads reduce the incentive to produce new content. Will the next Oprah work so hard? Or the next John Legend or Tyler Perry? Will the next Leigh Bardugo (author of the *Shadow and Bone* books) hone her writing craft so diligently if there is so much less financial reward for success? Is the "I want it for free" culture causing the truly gifted to be less committed to their craft, thus depriving society of excellence? Maintaining the right rewards, or incentives, for hard work and innovation is essential for making sure that inventors and other creative people are compensated for their creativity and vision. Some see services like Spotify, Apple Music, and SoundCloud as the answer. While streaming services are now very successful, the amount artists receive is still far lower than it used to be.

INCENTIVES ARE EVERYWHERE One very powerful incentive is saving time. You can test out your time-savings skills when you walk across campus to a class. An app will give you a detailed route and an estimated time of arrival, but your app won't know the local shortcuts. Sometimes the shortcuts everyone takes are through buildings or along dirt paths. Sometimes all you have to do is crowdsource the best route by following others. The paths worn into greens by students' feet will show you how to get across campus as quickly as possible.

Understanding incentives, from positive to negative and direct to indirect, is the key to understanding economics. If you remember only one concept from this course, it should be that incentives matter.

Incentives

Taking a shortcut saves time.

"Baby shark, doo doo doo doo . . ." What might have been achieved in the time it has taken to watch the Baby Shark Dance video over 10 billion times?

Trade-Offs

In a world of scarcity, each and every decision incurs a cost. Even time is a scarce resource; after all, there are only 24 hours in a day. So deciding to play *Animal Crossing* now means you won't be able to read one of the Harry Potter books until later. More generally, doing one thing often means you will not have the time, resources, or energy to do something else. Similarly, paying for a college education can require spending tens of thousands of dollars that might be used elsewhere instead.

Trade-offs

Understanding the trade-offs that exist in life can completely change how you view the world. Let's look at Pinkfong's catchy melody "Baby Shark." The video for this song has been viewed over 10 billion times on YouTube, making it the most watched video of all time. Imagine what could have been accomplished if people had used that time differently. Consider the trade-offs. "Baby Shark" is 2 minutes and 16 seconds long, which means that more than 370 million hours have been spent watching the video. That's over 40,000 years! In the same amount of time, 16 Burj Khalifas (one of the world's tallest buildings, constructed with over 22 million total hours of human labor) could have been built, or the entire contents of the English Wikipedia entered—22 times over! (On the plus side, to be fair, millions of weary caregivers have used the catchy tune to "buy" a few minutes of rest.)

People who don't understand economics sometimes ignore the trade-offs that are natural in a world of scarcity. They unconsciously assume that we can (as individuals or a group) have more of everything we want. But in fact, decision-making generally involves trade-offs. For example, if you decide to increase your time allotment for studying economics, you will need to give up something else: you might study less for other courses, work fewer hours at your job, or spend less time on social media. That is, there is a trade-off between higher economics grades and other things you desire. As a nation, we may wish to increase subsidies to college education, or to increase international aid, or to strengthen our national defense. Economists are the ones who then ask: What about the trade-offs?

For a recent example, take the Coronavirus Aid, Relief, and Economic Security (CARES) Act, which was passed by Congress with overwhelming bipartisan support and signed on March 27, 2020. This $2.2 trillion relief package provided financial assistance for American workers, families, and small businesses, and preserved jobs in American industries. But what could all that money have bought instead, if we'd spent it differently? Well, we could have created 1.5 million state-of-the-art hospital beds. Or we could have built 440 brand-new NFL stadiums, or given every citizen a check for $6,728, or created 550,000 one-megawatt solar farms, or hired 700,000 K–12 teachers for 50 years each. You get the point.

Ultimately, thinking about trade-offs means that we will make more informed decisions about how to use our scarce resources.

Opportunity Cost

Opportunity cost

The existence of trade-offs requires making hard decisions. Trade-offs are about having to give something up, while opportunity cost quantifies "what" or "how much" is being given up. Choosing one thing means giving up something else. Suppose you receive two invitations for the same Saturday—the first to spend the day hiking and the second to go to a concert. No matter which event you choose, you have to sacrifice the other option. In this example, you can think of the cost of going to the concert as the lost opportunity to go on the hike. Likewise, the cost of going hiking is the lost opportunity to go to the concert. No matter what choice you make, there is an opportunity cost, or next-best alternative, that must be sacrificed. **Opportunity cost** is the highest-valued alternative that must be sacrificed to get something else.

Opportunity cost is the highest-valued alternative that must be sacrificed to get something else.

Every time we make a choice, we experience an opportunity cost. The key to making the best possible decision is to minimize your opportunity cost by selecting the option that gives you the largest benefit. If you prefer going to a concert, you should go to the concert. What you give up (the hike) has less value to you than the concert, so it represents an opportunity cost.

The hiking/concert choice is a simple and clear example of opportunity cost. Usually, it takes deliberate effort to see the world through the opportunity cost prism. But it is a worthwhile practice because it will help you make better decisions. For example, imagine you are a small business owner. Your financial officer informs you that you have had a successful year and made a sizable profit. So everything is good, right? Not so fast. An economist will tell you to ask yourself, "Could I have made *more* profit doing something else?" Good economic thinkers ask this question all the time. "Could I be using my time, talents, or energy on another activity that would be even more profitable for me?"

Profits on an official income statement are only part of the story, because they only measure how well a business does relative to the bottom line. Accountants cannot measure what *might* have been better. For example, suppose you had decided not to open a new store. A few months later, a rival opened a very successful store in the same location you had considered. Your profits were good for the year, but if you had opened the new store, your profits could have been even better. So when economists talk about opportunity cost, they are assessing whether the alternatives are

In *Animal Crossing*, money really does grow on trees, but you must bury a bag of Bells and wait for this to happen, an example of opportunity cost.

Alicia Keys knew that the key to her success in music was a record deal.

Opportunity cost

better than what you are currently doing, which considers a larger set of possible outcomes.

For example, in the chapter opener, we mused about having a money tree. It turns out that money trees really do exist—in the virtual world. In *Animal Crossing*, Nintendo's breakout title of the 2020 pandemic, the player must bury a bag of Bells (the game's currency) using a golden shovel. After the tree has fully grown, it will bloom with three bags of Bells at amounts dependent on how much was initially buried. In this simple example, there is still an opportunity cost—what might have been done with the bag of Bells instead of growing a Bell tree! Planting a Bell tree today increases your future income, but you forgo the opportunity to spend Bells now.

Back in the real world, Alicia Keys understands opportunity cost. A high school valedictorian, she was enrolled at Columbia University but left when she signed a contract with Columbia Records. Keys defied the usual wisdom about staying in school and completing her degree, because finishing school would have meant passing up an opportunity that might not come her way again. Given her success, it's hard to fault her decision. If she had completed her degree, she may have missed the opportunity to become the star we know today.

PRACTICE WHAT YOU KNOW

The Opportunity Cost of Attending College

Spending thousands on college expenses? You could be working instead!

QUESTION: What is the opportunity cost of attending college?

ANSWER: When people think about the cost of attending college, they usually think of tuition, room and board, course materials, and travel-related expenses. While those expenses are often a part of going to college, they are not its full cost. The opportunity cost is the next-best alternative that is sacrificed. This opportunity cost—or what you potentially could have done if you were not in college—includes the lost income you could have earned working a full-time job. If you consider the cost of attending college plus the forgone income lost while in college, you can see that college is an awfully expensive proposition. Setting aside the question of how much more you might have to pay for room and board at college rather than elsewhere, consider the cost of tuition, which can be $40,000 or more at many of the nation's most expensive colleges. Add that out-of-pocket expense to the forgone income from a full-time job that might pay $40,000 a year, and your four years in college can easily cost over a quarter of a million dollars.

CHALLENGE QUESTION: Alicia Keys honed her stage presence in small venues until she became famous. But for every Alicia Keys, there are thousands of other singer-songwriters who never made it big. What advice would you give to someone wrestling with the decision to leave college?

ANSWER: The question is tricky. We can't know the future, and staying in college and leaving college both have opportunity costs. By staying, you forgo the opportunity to try new things and, perhaps, discover in the process something else you excel at. However, leaving means a college degree will not be part of your résumé. Making decisions when there is uncertainty about how the future will unfold is what makes choices difficult, because there are opportunity costs in both directions.

ECONOMICS IN THE REAL WORLD

HOW LONG WOULD YOU WAIT IN LINE ON BLACK FRIDAY TO SAVE $300?

A few years ago in Beaumont, California, Vicky Torres and Juanita Alva were first in line to secure a large-screen television at Best Buy during the Black Friday Sale. The TV they wanted was advertised at $199. Let's say that was a markdown from $499. How many hours would you wait in line to save $300? Two hours? Five? Ten? How about 500 hours? That's how long the two women waited, because they arrived *three weeks* early. By all accounts they enjoyed their time waiting, spending their days talking to strangers and taking turns saving each other's spots in line overnight. However, there's an opportunity cost here that makes Vicky and Juanita's decision puzzling. Think of the many trade-offs they faced: missed sleep, time they could have spent with friends and family, and the time they could be working instead of waiting in line, to name just a few. It is hard to justify the women's choices using marginal analysis. Saving $300 by spending 500 hours makes their time worth 60 cents an hour. They could have spent 30 hours working an extra job at $10 an hour and each earned enough money to purchase the TV at full price—and still had 470 hours to do other things. In short, they don't seem to have been aware of the opportunity cost of waiting in line.

How long would you wait in line to save $300?

Marginal Thinking

The process of systematically evaluating a course of action is called economic thinking. **Economic thinking** involves a purposeful evaluation of the available opportunities to make the best decision possible. In this context, economic thinkers use a process called *marginal analysis* to break down decisions into smaller parts. Often, the choice is not between doing and not doing something, but between doing more or less of something. For instance, if you take on a part-time job while in school, you probably wrestle with the question of how many hours to work. If you work a little more, you can earn additional income. If you work a little less, you have more time to study. Working more has a tangible benefit (more money) and a tangible cost (lower grades). All of this should sound familiar from our earlier discussion about trade-offs. The work-study trade-off affects how much money you have and what kind of grades you earn.

Economic thinking requires a purposeful evaluation of the available opportunities to make the best decision possible.

An economist would say that your decision—weighing how much money you want against the grades you want—is a decision at the *margin*. What exactly does the word "margin" mean as used in economics? In economics, **marginal thinking** requires decision-makers to evaluate whether the benefit of one more unit of something is greater than its cost. Understanding how to analyze decisions at the margin is essential to thinking like a good economist.

Marginal thinking requires decision-makers to evaluate whether the benefit of one more unit of something is greater than its cost.

For example, have you ever wondered why people vacuum, dust, scrub the bathrooms, clean out their garages, and wash their windows, but leave the dust bunnies under the refrigerator? The answer lies in thinking at the margin. Moving the refrigerator out from the wall to clean requires a significant effort for a small benefit. Guests who enter the kitchen can't see under the refrigerator. So

Marginal thinking

most of us ignore the dust bunnies and just clean the visible areas of our homes. In other words, when economists say you should think at the margin, what they really mean is that you should weigh the costs and benefits of your actions and choose to do the things with the greatest payoff. For most of us, that means being willing to live with dust bunnies. The *marginal cost* of cleaning under the refrigerator (or on top of the cabinets or even behind the sofa cushions) is too high, and the added value of making the effort, or the *marginal benefit*, is too low to justify the additional cleaning.

Trade

Markets bring buyers and sellers together to exchange goods and services.

Imagine trying to find food in a world without grocery stores. The task of getting what you need to eat each day would require visiting many separate locations. Many centuries ago, this need to bring buyers and sellers together was met by weekly markets, or bazaars, in central locations like town squares. **Markets** bring buyers and sellers together to exchange goods and services. As commerce spread throughout the ancient world, trade routes developed. Markets grew from infrequent gatherings, where exchange involved trading goods and services for other goods and services, into more sophisticated systems that use cash, credit, and other financial instruments. Today, when we think of markets, we often think of eBay or Craigslist. For instance, if you want to find a rare Hot Wheels Black Panther Movie Die-Cast Vehicle, an excellent place to look is eBay, which allows users to search for just about any product, bid on it, and then have it sent directly to their home.

Trade creates value

The **circular flow diagram** shows how goods, services, and resources flow through the economy.

THE CIRCULAR FLOW When we consider all the trade that occurs in an economy, it is helpful to use a **circular flow diagram**. This shows how goods, services, and resources flow through the economy via commerce between households and firms. Households are made up of consumers, as we usually picture them. Firms are businesses. Households desire the goods and services produced by firms, but to produce those goods and services, firms require the resources owned by households. The circular flow diagram illustrates the movement of goods, services, and resources that results when firms and households do business with each other.

In the circular flow in Figure 1.2, households are on the right and firms on the left. Households buy goods and services from firms in product markets, at the top of the diagram. This is the kind of transaction you undertake all the time: when you buy groceries or school supplies, you purchase these in product markets, from firms. But households are also sellers, in that they provide the inputs or resources that firms use to produce their output. These transactions take place in resource markets, at the bottom of the diagram. When you put in time at your job and get a paycheck in return, that is a resource market transaction.

The red arrows that form the clockwise inner loop show goods and services flowing from firms to households across the top of the circle and resources flowing from households to firms across the bottom. Goods, services, and resources are paid for with *funds*. The green arrows forming the outer loop show how funds flow in the opposite direction of whatever they are paying for. Each loop is closed. On the inside, resources go into the production of goods and services, which in turn go into sustaining households so they can continue to provide firms with resources. On the outside, funds are transferred from households'

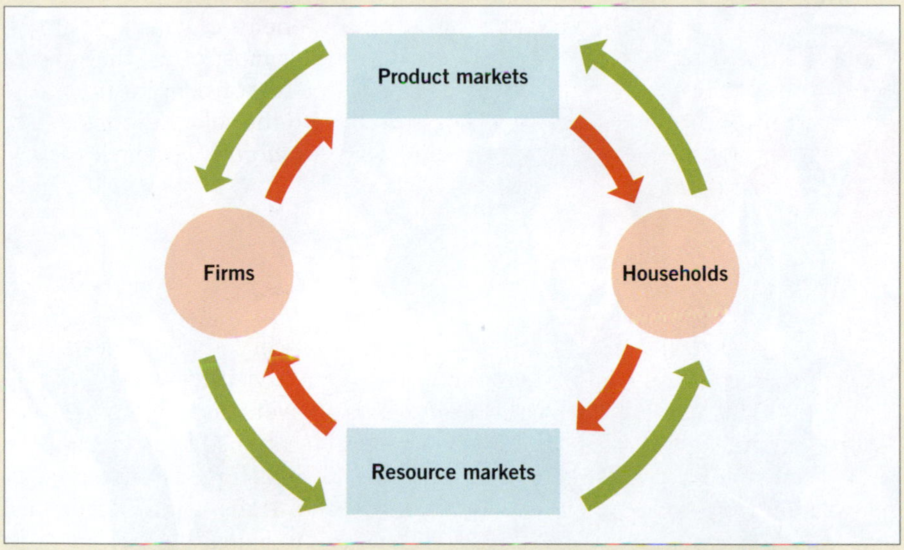

FIGURE 1.2

The Circular Flow

The circular flow of goods and services appears as the red inner loop, and the circular flow of funds to purchase goods and services appears as the green outer loop.

bank accounts to firms' accounts as payment for goods and services, and then return to households as payment for resources.

Consider a simple example. Let's say you spend $1,000 on a new Dell computer. You trade for your computer in a product market, and Dell gets the $1,000: this takes place in the top half of the circular flow diagram. Then Dell uses the $1,000 to pay its workers' wages and other suppliers for the use of resources. This happens in the bottom half of the diagram. In the end, the funds make the complete circuit back to households.

This simple circular flow diagram leaves out some details. For one thing, government is an important player in any economy. Funds flow into and out of governments, which participate in both the product and resource markets. In addition, households and firms also interact with foreign firms and households. We consider the roles of government and foreign firms and households later in the text, but for now, this simple circular flow diagram serves as a schematic summary of how households and firms interact through trade in an economy.

TRADE CREATES VALUE **Trade** is the voluntary exchange of goods and services between two or more parties.

Trade
is the voluntary exchange of goods and services between two or more parties.

Voluntary trade among rational individuals creates value for everyone involved. Imagine you are on your way home from class and you want to pick up a gallon of milk. You know that milk will be more expensive at a convenience store than at the grocery store 5 miles away, but you are in a hurry to study for your economics exam and are willing to pay up to $5 for the convenience of getting the milk quickly. At the store, you find that the price is $4 and you happily purchase the milk. This ability to buy for less than the price you are willing to pay provides a positive incentive to make the purchase. But what about the seller? If the store owner paid $3 to buy the milk from a supplier, and you are willing to pay the $4 price she has set in order to make a profit, the store owner has an incentive to sell. This simple voluntary transaction has made both of you better off.

Incentives
Trade creates value

Our economy depends on specialization.

Comparative advantage refers to the situation where an individual, business, or country can produce at a lower opportunity cost than a competitor can.

By fostering the exchange of goods, trade helps to create additional growth through specialization. **Comparative advantage** refers to the situation in which an individual, business, or country can produce at a lower opportunity cost than a competitor can. Comparative advantage harnesses the power of specialization, a topic we discuss in more detail in Chapter 2. As a result, it is possible to be a physician, teacher, or plumber and not worry about how to do everything yourself. The physician becomes proficient at dispensing medical advice, the teacher at helping students, and the plumber at fixing leaks. The physician and the teacher call the plumber when they need work on their plumbing. The teacher and the plumber see the doctor when they are sick. The physician and the plumber entrust their children's education to the teacher.

The same process is at work among businesses. For instance, Starbucks specializes in making coffee, Honda in making automobiles. You would not want to get your morning cup of joe at Honda any more than you would want to buy a car from Starbucks!

On a broader scale, specialization and trading of services exist at the international level as well. Some countries have highly developed workforces capable of managing and solving complex processes. Other countries have large pools of relatively unskilled labor. As a result, businesses that need skilled labor gravitate to countries where they can easily find the workers they need. Likewise, firms with production processes that rely on unskilled labor look for employees in less developed countries, where workers are paid less. By harnessing the power of increased specialization, global companies and economies create value through increased production and growth.

However, globalized trade is not without controversy. When goods and jobs are free to move across borders, not everyone benefits equally, nor should we expect this outcome. Consider the case of a U.S. worker who loses her job when her position is outsourced to a call center in India. The jobless worker now has to find new employment—a process that requires significant time and energy. In contrast, the new position in the call center in India provides a job

SNAPSHOT

Five Foundations of Economics

In this book, we study five foundations of economics—incentives, trade-offs, opportunity cost, marginal thinking, and the principle that trade creates value. Once you have mastered these five concepts, even complex economic processes can be reduced to smaller, more easily understood parts. If you keep these foundations in mind, you'll find that understanding economics is rewarding and fun.

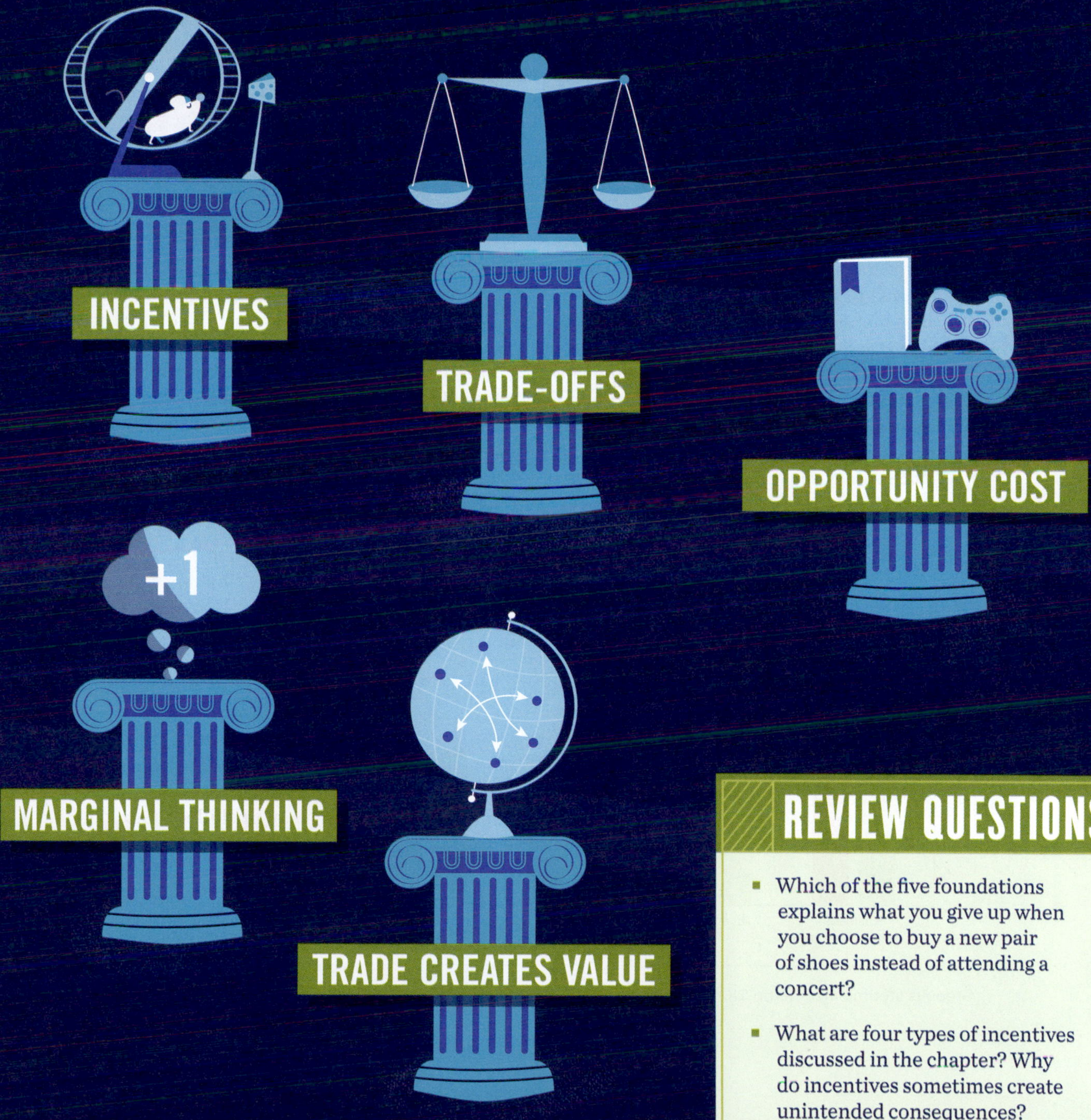

REVIEW QUESTIONS

- Which of the five foundations explains what you give up when you choose to buy a new pair of shoes instead of attending a concert?
- What are four types of incentives discussed in the chapter? Why do incentives sometimes create unintended consequences?

ECONOMICS *for* LIFE

So You Wanna Be a Billionaire? Study Economics

- Economics majors are more likely to become billionaires than majors in any other subject.
- Economics majors, on average, make $3.4 million in career earnings.
- Economics majors are also top performers on the Law School Admission Test.

Travie McCoy and Bruno Mars collaborated on the mega-hit "Billionaire." Little did they know that majors in economics are most likely to make the Forbes 400, a list of the richest people in the United States. In this graphic, we report the six majors that produce the highest number of billionaires and cross-reference those findings with projected lifetime earnings to give you a sense of how much the average college graduate with one of these degrees is likely to earn. We've intentionally used lifetime earnings, since they are a better indicator of financial well-being than the typical starting salary ranges you might be more familiar with. It is how much money you make over your entire career that matters.

Majoring in economics gives you the best chance of becoming a billionaire.

The financial rewards are nice, but that's not the only reason to choose economics. Economics majors are also versatile in other ways: they are top performers on the LSAT (Law School Admission Test) and are in demand as policy experts, consultants, and forecasters.

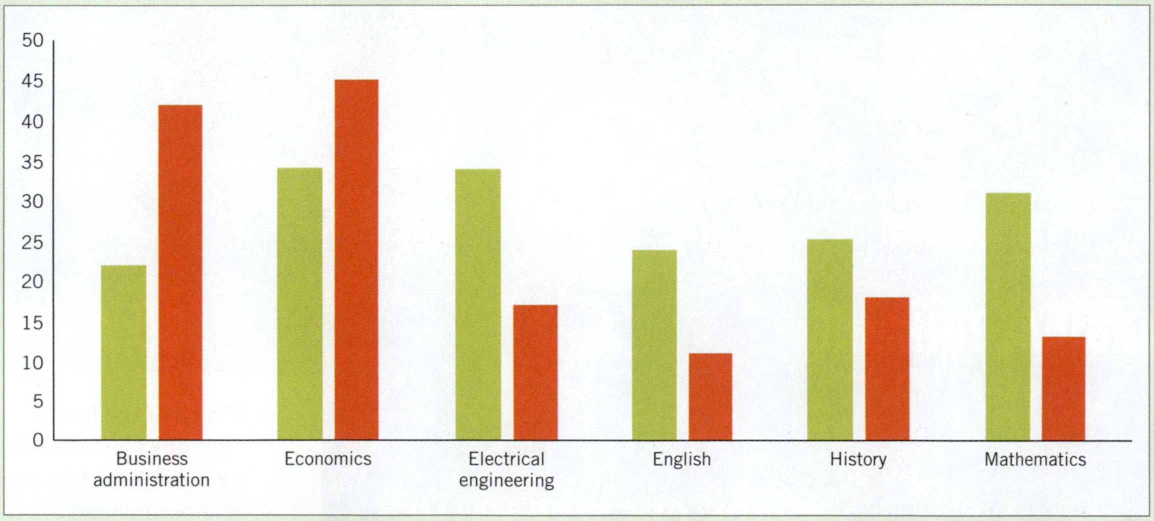

Green is lifetime income (in $100,000s) and red is the number of billionaires in the Forbes 400.

and an income that improve the life of another worker. Also, the U.S. firm enjoys the advantage of being able to hire lower-cost labor elsewhere. The firm's lower costs often translate into lower prices for domestic consumers. None of those advantages make the outsourcing of jobs any less painful for affected workers, but outsourcing is an important component of economic growth in the long run.

Conclusion

Economists ask, and answer, big questions about life. This is what makes the study of economics so fascinating. Understanding how an entire economy functions may seem like a daunting task, but it is not nearly as difficult as it sounds. Remember when you learned to drive? At first, everything was difficult and unfamiliar. But as you probably found, becoming a good driver is just a matter of mastering a few key principles, and then, with a little experience under your belt, you can drive any car on the road. In the same way, once you have learned the fundamentals of economics, you can use them to analyze almost any problem. In the next chapter, we use the ideas developed in this chapter to explore trade in greater depth. ✷

- ANSWERING *the* BIG QUESTIONS -

What is economics?

- Economics is the study of how people allocate their limited resources to satisfy their practically unlimited wants. Because of the limited nature of society's resources, even the most abundant resources are not always plentiful enough everywhere to meet the wants and needs of every person. So how do individuals and societies make decisions about how to use the scarce resources at their disposal? This is the basic question economists seek to answer.

What are five foundations of economics?

Five foundations of economics are incentives, trade-offs, opportunity cost, marginal thinking, and the principle that trade creates value.

- Incentives are important because they help explain how rational decisions are made.
- Trade-offs exist when a decision-maker has to choose a course of action.
- Each time we make a choice, we experience an opportunity cost, or a lost chance to do something else.
- Marginal thinking requires a decision-maker to weigh the extra benefits against the extra costs.
- Trade creates value because participants in markets are able to specialize in the production of goods and services they have a comparative advantage in making.

CHAPTER PROBLEMS

Concepts You Should Know

circular flow diagram (p. 18)
comparative advantage (p. 20)
economics (p. 7)
economic thinking (p. 17)
incentives (p. 9)
macroeconomics (p. 7)
marginal thinking (p. 17)
markets (p. 18)
microeconomics (p. 7)
opportunity cost (p. 15)
scarcity (p. 7)
trade (p. 19)

Questions for Review

1. How would you respond if your instructor gave daily quizzes on the course readings? Are these quizzes a positive incentive or a negative incentive?
2. Explain why many seniors often earn lower grades in their last semester before graduation. (**Hint:** This is an incentive problem.)
3. What is the opportunity cost of reading this textbook?
4. Evaluate the following statement: "Trade is like football: one team wins and the other loses."

Study Problems *(✱ solved at the end of the section)*

✱ 1. What role do incentives play in each of the following situations? Are there any unintended consequences?
   a. You learn you can resell a ticket to next week's homecoming game for twice what you paid.
   b. A state government announces a "sales tax holiday" for back-to-school shopping during one week each August.
2. Compare your standard of living with that of your parents when they were the age you are now. Ask them or somebody you know around their age to recall where they were living and what they owned. How has the well-being of the typical person changed over the last 25 years? Explain your answer.
3. By referencing events in the news or something from your personal experiences, describe one example of each of the five foundations of economics discussed in this chapter.

✱ 4. Suppose that Colombia is good at growing coffee but not very good at making computer software and that Canada is good at making computer software but not very good at growing coffee. If Colombia decided only to grow coffee and Canada only to make computer software, would both countries be better off or worse off? Explain. Can you think of a similar example from your life?
5. After some consideration, you decide to hire someone to help you move from one apartment to another. Wouldn't it be cheaper to move yourself? Do you think the choice to hire someone is a rational choice? Explain your response.

✱ 6. When a town gets snowed in for a couple of days—the urban legend goes—the local hospital is likely to see a boost in births nine months later. In other words: blizzards might be prime baby-making time. Explain, using *economic* reasoning, why snowstorms may indeed cause an uptick in births nine months down the road.
7. In *A Star is Born* (2018), Ally faces a tough choice. Should she go on a long-planned concert tour of Europe, or should she stay home with her husband, Jack, who just got out of rehab and will relapse without her? Either way, there will be a cost. When Ally stays home, Jack blames himself for her decision to put her singing career on hold. Instead of coming to her local concert, he commits suicide. The movie ends with Ally's heartfelt rendition of a song Jack wrote for her before he died, "I'll Never Love Again." (You can watch the official video on YouTube.) What trade-offs are you facing in your life right now? How do you decide which trade-offs are acceptable?

✷ **8.** We have talked about how trade creates value. Use the information in each example below to compute the total value created in each exchange:

   a. Patrick bought an orange pen from Jill for $2.00. Patrick would have been willing to pay $2.50 for the pen, and Jill would have been willing to sell the pen for $1.25.

   b. Hillary found a car on Craigslist for which she would have been willing to pay up to $10,000. The car's owner, Jason, needed to sell the car right away and would have accepted $6,000. The price they agreed on was $7,500.

9. What concept best explains why you wouldn't want to make your own clothes completely from scratch and instead will normally prefer to buy them from a retailer?

Solved Problems

1. a. Because your tickets are worth more than you paid for them, you have a direct positive incentive to resell them.

   b. The "sales tax holiday" is a direct positive incentive to buy more clothes during the back-to-school period. An unintended consequence of this policy is that fewer purchases are likely to be made both before and after the tax holiday.

4. If Colombia decided to specialize in the production of coffee, it could trade coffee to Canada in exchange for computer software. This process illustrates gains from specialization and trade. Both countries have a comparative advantage in producing one particular good. Colombia has ideal coffee-growing conditions, and Canada has a workforce that is more adept at writing software. Since both countries specialize in what they do best, they are able to produce more value than they could produce by trying to make both products on their own.

6. The situation has changed the incentives people face. In other words, the perceived costs and benefits of their choices have changed. Inclement weather makes it more costly to go outside; thus, more people will choose to stay home and engage in at-home activities.

8. a. In this example, Patrick is better off by $0.50, because he was willing to pay $2.50 but paid just $2.00. And Jill is better off by $0.75, because she would have accepted $1.25 but received $2.00. So the total value created is the additional value to Patrick ($0.50) plus the additional value to Jill ($0.75), which sums to $1.25.

   b. The value added for Jason is $1,500, which is the difference between the minimum price he would have accepted ($6,000) and the price he received ($7,500). The value added for Hillary is $2,500, which is the difference between the maximum price she would have paid ($10,000) and the price she actually paid ($7,500). In total, $1,500 + $2,500 = $4,000 in new value was created through the exchange.

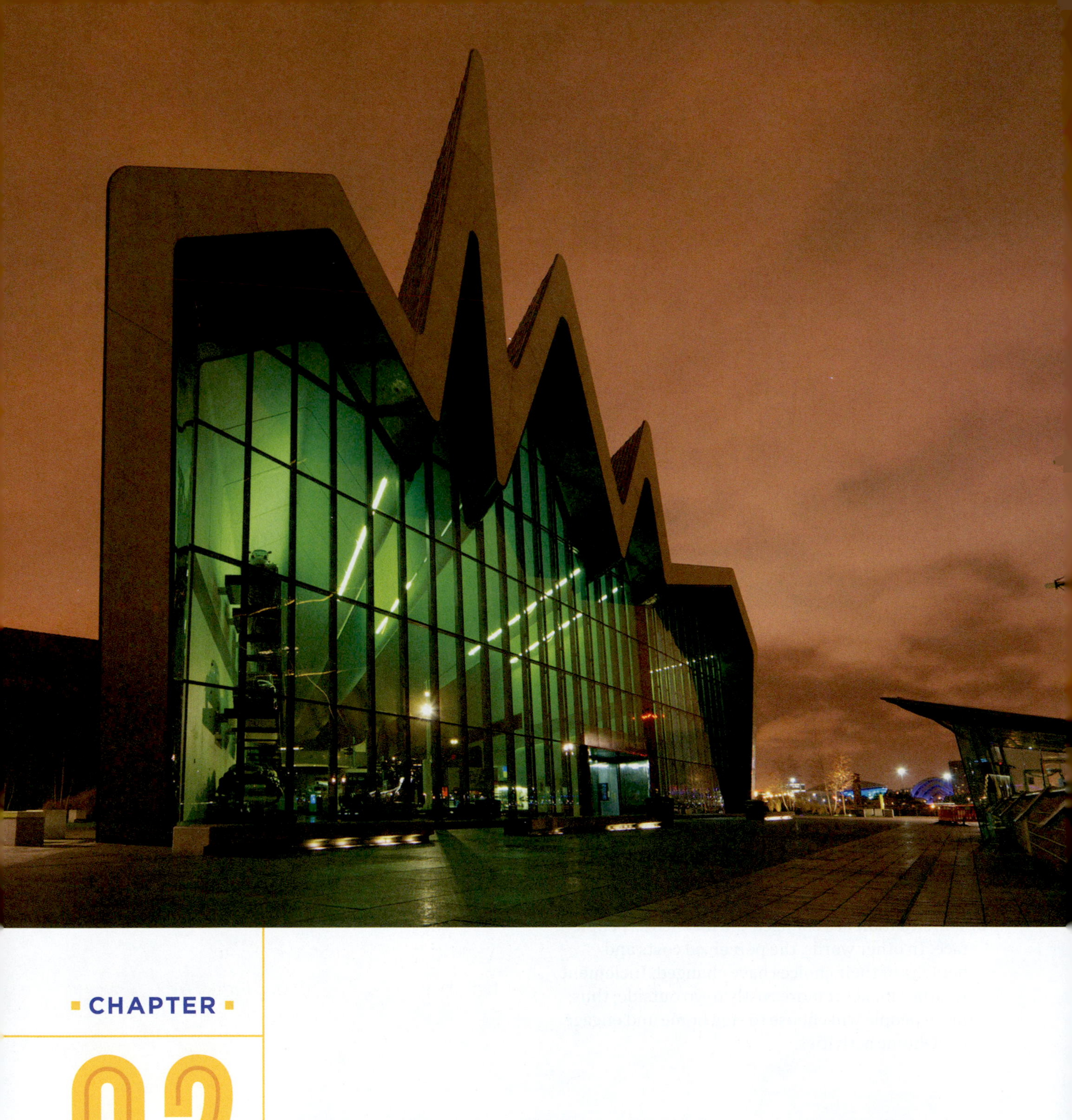

CHAPTER

02

Model Building and Gains from Trade

When People Trade, Both Sides Normally Win.

It's only common sense that trade benefits both parties. After all, if it's voluntary, both sides must be getting something out of it. But there's more to the story: we can quantify the extent to which trade makes each side better off. We do this by establishing how much more productive a person can become through trade, given that trade allows people to specialize in what they're good at. That's what we're going to learn about in this chapter.

Consider the interaction between a contractor and an architect. They each have a vital role to play in the building process. The architect designs the plans to the buyer's specifications. The contractor is an expert at bringing the architect's design to fruition by organizing the equipment, supplies, and labor to complete the project on time. The architect is the creative genius and the contractor is a genius at managing the construction workflow. The architect understands how to design plans that pass engineering tests and meet building codes. The contractor understands the supply chain. By specializing, each becomes more productive and gets their part of the project done faster, trading their expertise and time for monetary payment.

In 2004, Zaha Hadid became the first woman to win the Pritzker Architecture Prize. To turn her visions into reality, she had to work with many different, specialized construction contractors. The results could be stunning, like this museum in Scotland.

To help understand how trade works, we will develop our first economic model, the production possibilities frontier, so we can explore the more nuanced reasons why trade creates value.

· BIG QUESTIONS ·

- How do economists study the economy?
- What is a production possibilities frontier?
- What are the benefits of specialization and trade?
- What is the trade-off between having more now and having more later?

How Do Economists Study the Economy?

Economics is a social science that uses the scientific method to develop *economic models*. To create these models, economists make many assumptions to simplify reality. These models help economists understand the key relationships that drive economic decisions.

The Scientific Method in Economics

Veritasium is a YouTube channel with over 8 million subscribers. It is dedicated to the scientific exploration of counterintuitive results. In 2021, Veritasium's creator, Derek Muller, posted a video titled "A Physics Prof Bet Me $10,000 I'm Wrong." The video shows Muller driving a wind-powered vehicle directly downwind—and going faster than the wind that's pushing him.

Xyla Foxlin built a model to settle a $10,000 bet.

A UCLA physics professor believed that what the video supposedly showed was impossible. According to him, the video footage could be explained by factors like gusting winds with variable speeds and different wind speeds at different heights above the ground. The professor bet Muller $10,000 that the Veritasium result would not hold up under careful testing.

To settle the bet, Muller asked engineer Xyla Foxlin (a YouTuber in her own right) to build small-scale models

The scientific method was used to determine whether this wind-powered vehicle could really travel faster than the wind itself.

and test them under controlled conditions. Muller believed, based on a mathematical analysis, that even after the factors the professor proposed were eliminated, faster-than-wind travel could still occur. Foxlin's models confirmed that a wind-driven vehicle traveling directly downwind can indeed exceed the speed of the wind behind it! The professor, graciously, paid up.

Economists work in much the same way as the Veritasium team: they use the scientific method to answer questions about observable phenomena and to explain how the world works. The scientific method consists of four steps:

- First, researchers observe a phenomenon that interests them.
- Next, based on these observations, researchers develop a *hypothesis*, which is a proposed explanation for the phenomenon.
- Then they construct a model to test the hypothesis.
- Finally, they look for opportunities to test how well the model (which is based on the hypothesis) works. After collecting data, they use statistical methods to verify, revise, or refute the hypothesis.

The economist's laboratory is the world around us, and it ranges from the economy as a whole to the decisions made by firms and individuals. As a result, economists cannot always design experiments to test their hypotheses. Often, they must gather historical data or wait for real-world events to take place—such as the Great Recession (economic downturn) of 2007–2009 or the coronavirus pandemic of 2020—to better understand the economy. When real-world events meet the criteria of an experiment designed to test a hypothesis, we have what's called a *natural* experiment.

Positive and Normative Analysis

As scientists, economists strive to approach their subject with objectivity. They want to understand how the world actually works. It might be nice, for example, if everyone were perfectly altruistic, but the reality is that most people favor their own interests and those of people close to them. For economists, this is a fact to be dealt with, not something to be wished away.

A **positive statement** can be tested and validated; it describes "what is."

A **normative statement** is an opinion that cannot be tested or validated; it describes "what ought to be."

To be as objective as possible, economists deploy positive analysis. A **positive statement** can be tested and validated. Each positive statement can be thought of as a description of "what is." For instance, the statement "The unemployment rate is declining" is a positive statement, because it can be tested by gathering data and shown to be true or false.

In contrast, a statement about "what ought to be" is a **normative statement** that cannot be empirically tested or validated. For instance, the statement "An unemployed worker should receive financial assistance to help make ends meet" is a matter of opinion. One can reasonably argue that financial assistance to the unemployed is a socially beneficial anti-poverty measure. However, some argue that financial unemployment assistance provides the wrong incentives. If the assistance is enough to meet basic needs, workers may end up spending more time unemployed than they otherwise would.

Incentives

Of course, policy decisions eventually have to be made by somebody, one way or the other. Just remember that when we talk about what is "best" or what "should happen," we are in the realm of differing viewpoints, based on values, beliefs, and opinions.

PRACTICE WHAT YOU KNOW

Positive versus Normative Statements

QUESTION: Which of the following statements are positive and which ones are normative?

1. Winters in Arkansas are too cold.
2. Everyone should work at a bank to learn the true value of money.
3. The current exchange rate is 0.7 British pounds per U.S. dollar.
4. On average, people save 15% on insurance when they switch to Geico.
5. The best way to prepare for a pandemic is to stock up on masks.
6. University of Virginia graduates earn more than Duke University graduates.
7. Wyoming reported fewer COVID-19 deaths than any other state.
8. The average January temperature in Fargo, North Dakota, is 56°F.

ANSWERS

1. The phrase "too cold" is a matter of opinion. This is a normative statement.
2. While working at a bank might give someone an appreciation for the value of money, the word "should" indicates an opinion. This is a normative statement.
3. This is a positive statement. You can look up the current exchange rate and verify if this statement is true or false.
4. Geico made this claim in one of its commercials. It is a positive statement because it is a testable claim. If you had the data from Geico, you could determine if the statement were correct or not.
5. This sounds like a true statement, or at least a very sensible one. However, the word "best" makes it an opinion. This is a normative statement.

(CONTINUED)

6. You can look up the data and see which university's graduates earn more. This is a positive statement.
7. You can look up the data and determine whether the statement is accurate or not. This is a positive statement.
8. This is a positive statement, but the statement is wrong. North Dakota is much colder than that in January. The statement can be verified (in this case, proved wrong) by climate data.

CHALLENGE QUESTIONS: Some statements aren't simple declarative sentences but instead take the form of hypotheticals. Are the following hypotheticals positive or normative?

9. If Steph Curry makes 50% of his two-point shots and 40% of his three-point shots, his effective field goal percentage comes out higher than 50%, since this statistic weighs three-point shots more than two-point shots.
10. If Steph Curry makes 40% of his three-point shots, he should shoot only three-pointers.
11. If you earn a college degree, you may earn less income than someone who only completes high school.
12. If you earn a college degree, you should share what you learned with the less fortunate.

ANSWERS

9. This hypothetical statement is mathematically verifiable, so the statement is positive.
10. This is a hypothetical statement in which the second part is an opinion, so the statement is normative.
11. This statement is factually verifiable, so the statement is positive.
12. The second part of this statement is an opinion, so the statement is normative.

NBA star Steph Curry has made three-pointers his trademark.

Economic Models

Thinking like an economist means learning how to analyze complex issues and problems. Many economic topics, such as international trade, Social Security, job loss, and inflation, are complicated. To analyze these phenomena and to determine the effect of various government policy options related to them, economists use economic models, which are simplified versions of reality. Models help us analyze the components of the economy.

CETERIS PARIBUS Let's return to the example of the wind-powered vehicle driven by Veritasium creator Derek Muller. Using a small-scale model on a treadmill, engineer Xyla Foxlin was able to alter a single variable—for example, propeller size—while keeping other factors, such as wheel size and treadmill speed, the same. Changing one variable while holding everything else constant involves a concept known as ***ceteris paribus***, from the Latin meaning "other things being equal" or "all else equal."

Ceteris paribus [*pronounced KETeris PAReebus*] means "other things being equal" or "all else equal" and is used to build economic models. It allows economists to examine a change in one variable while holding everything else constant.

The *ceteris paribus* assumption is central to model building. If Foxlin had changed many design elements on the wind-powered model simultaneously and found that the new version worked better, she would have had no way of knowing which change was responsible for the improved performance. For this reason, engineers generally modify only one design element at a time and test only that one element before testing additional elements.

Like Foxlin, economists start with a simplified version of reality. They build models, change one variable at a time, and ask whether the change in the variable has a positive or negative impact on performance. Perhaps the best-known economic model is supply and demand, which we study in Chapter 3.

Endogenous factors are the variables that are inside a model.

Exogenous factors are the variables that are outside a model.

ENDOGENOUS VERSUS EXOGENOUS FACTORS Models must account for factors we can control (*endogenous*) and factors we can't (*exogenous*). Factors that are accounted for inside the model are **endogenous factors**. Foxlin's treadmill setup allowed her to control as many endogenous factors as possible, including wind speed, wheel size, propeller size, propeller pitch, and gear ratio.

Factors beyond our control—outside the model—are **exogenous factors**. The wind gusts that the UCLA professor thought could explain the faster-than-wind travel in the video were an exogenous factor. They made experiments with a full-sized wind vehicle more challenging.

Building an economic model is remarkably similar to the process Foxlin used. We need to be mindful of three factors: (1) what we include in the model, (2) the assumptions we make when choosing what to include in the model, and (3) the outside conditions that can affect the model's performance. In the case of the wind-driven vehicle, the design was an endogenous factor, because it was within the designer's control. In contrast, the weather (wind, air pressure, and other atmospheric conditions) was an exogenous factor, because it could not be controlled.

Because the world is a complex place, a model that works perfectly on a treadmill may not perform reliably when it is exposed to the elements. If we add more exogenous variables, or factors we cannot control—for example, wind and rain—to test our model's performance, the test becomes more realistic, but at the same time, the outcome becomes less predictable.

In the early 2000s, some investors believed that real estate prices could only rise.

THE IMPORTANCE OF ASSUMPTIONS When we build a model, we need to make choices about which variables to include. Ideally, we would like to include all the important variables inside the model and exclude all the variables that can safely be ignored. Then we have made reasonable simplifying assumptions. Excluding the wrong variables, on the other hand, can lead to spectacular failures. So can making *false* assumptions. An excellent example is the financial crisis and Great Recession that began in December 2007.

In the years leading up to the crisis, banks sold and repackaged mortgage-backed investments under the faulty assumption that real estate prices will always rise. This assumption seemed perfectly reasonable in a world where real estate prices were rising annually. Unfortunately, the assumption turned out to be false. From 2007 to 2008, real estate prices fell dramatically. Because of one faulty assumption, the entire financial market teetered on the edge of collapse. Shocks, be they financial or pandemic-related, often defy the usual logic. Contrary to conventional wisdom, the real estate market did not crater during the pandemic, but instead it skyrocketed in 2020–2021, as the pandemic caused people to hunker down and invest more in their homes.

Throughout this textbook we will assume that firms and households are rational benefit-maximizers who both respond to incentives predictably and thoughtfully consider the costs and benefits of their actions. Rationality is a cornerstone of most economic theory. It's a simplifying assumption, and in Chapter 17 we will see how it sometimes fails in real life, but for the most part we treat it as "true enough."

ECONOMICS IN THE REAL WORLD

ECONOMISTS INVESTIGATE: ARE CRIMINAL SENTENCES FAIR?

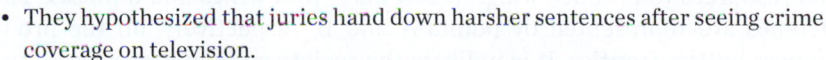

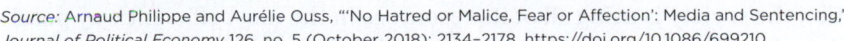

If media coverage influences the length of criminal sentences, is that fair?

Ideally, the outcome of a criminal trial should depend only on the evidence at hand, not on irrelevant events outside the courtroom. But is that how things work in practice? In France, economists Arnaud Philippe and Aurélie Ouss obtained some unexpected, unsettling results when they examined the impact of television news coverage of crimes on juries' sentencing decisions.

Philippe and Ouss used the scientific method. Specifically: they focused on something of interest, namely the potential influence of crime stories in the media on juries' sentencing deliberations.

- They hypothesized that juries hand down harsher sentences after seeing crime coverage on television.
- They constructed a model, in the form of a mathematical function, relating juries' exposure to crime coverage to the length of jail sentences.
- They collected data on television broadcasts and the length of jail sentences and used the model to determine the relationships between these two data sets.

Philippe and Ouss found that in France, coverage of crime on television leads to longer sentences for those convicted of a misdeed. What is particularly interesting is that the coverage on TV does not need to be related to the specific case a jury is hearing. If the media covers a story about *any* crime the day before a verdict, the average sentence handed down by a jury is, on average, 3 months longer than if there is no media coverage.

Here is something else that's interesting: while juries were found to be influenced by what they saw on the evening news, judges were not. If a sentence was decided by a judge rather than by a jury, there was no discernable difference in the length of a sentence.

Source: Arnaud Philippe and Aurélie Ouss, "'No Hatred or Malice, Fear or Affection': Media and Sentencing," *Journal of Political Economy* 126, no. 5 (October 2018): 2134–2178, https://doi.org/10.1086/699210.

What Is a Production Possibilities Frontier?

Now it's time to learn our first economic model. However, before you go on, you might want to review the appendix on graphing at the end of this chapter. Graphs are a key tool in economics because they display the relationship between two variables. Your ability to read a graph and understand the model it represents is crucial to learning economics.

Trade-offs

In Chapter 1, we learned that economics is about the trade-offs individuals and societies face every day. For instance, you may frequently have to decide between spending more time studying or hanging out with your friends, either in person or online. The more time you study, the less time you have for your friends. Similarly, a society has to determine how to allocate its resources. The decision to build new roads will mean that there is less money available for new schools, and vice versa.

A **production possibilities frontier (PPF)** is a model that illustrates the combinations of outputs a society can produce if all of its resources are being used efficiently.

A **production possibilities frontier (PPF)** is a model that illustrates the combinations of outputs a society can produce if all of its resources are being used efficiently. An outcome is considered *efficient* when resources are fully utilized and potential output is maximized. To preserve *ceteris paribus,* we assume that the technology available for production and the quantity of resources remain fixed, or constant. These assumptions allow us to model trade-offs more clearly.

Let's begin by imagining a society that produces only two goods—pizza and chicken wings. This may not seem like a very realistic assumption, since a real economy produces millions of different goods and services, but this approach helps us understand trade-offs by keeping the analysis simple.

Figure 2.1 shows the production possibilities frontier for our simplified two-product society. Remember that the number of people and the total resources in this two-product society are fixed. If the economy uses all of its resources to produce pizza, it can produce 100 pizzas and 0 wings. If it uses all of its resources to produce wings, it can make 300 wings and 0 pizzas. These outcomes are represented by points A and B, respectively, on the production possibilities frontier. It is unlikely the society will choose either of these extreme outcomes, because it is human nature to enjoy variety.

If our theoretical society decides to spend some of its resources producing pizzas and some of its resources making wings, its economy will end up with a combination of pizza and wings somewhere along the PPF between points A and B. At point C, for example, the society would deploy its resources to produce 70 pizzas and 90 wings. At point D, the combination would be 50 pizzas and 150 wings. Each point along the production possibilities frontier represents a possible set of outcomes the society can choose if it uses all of its resources efficiently.

Notice that some combinations of pizza and wings cannot be produced because not enough resources are available. Our theoretical society would enjoy point E, but given the available resources, it cannot produce that output level. Points beyond the production possibilities frontier are desirable but not feasible with the available resources and technology.

At any combination of wings and pizzas along the production possibilities frontier, the society is using all of its resources in the most efficient way possible. But what about point F and any other points located in the shaded region? These points represent outcomes inside the production possibilities frontier,

FIGURE 2.1

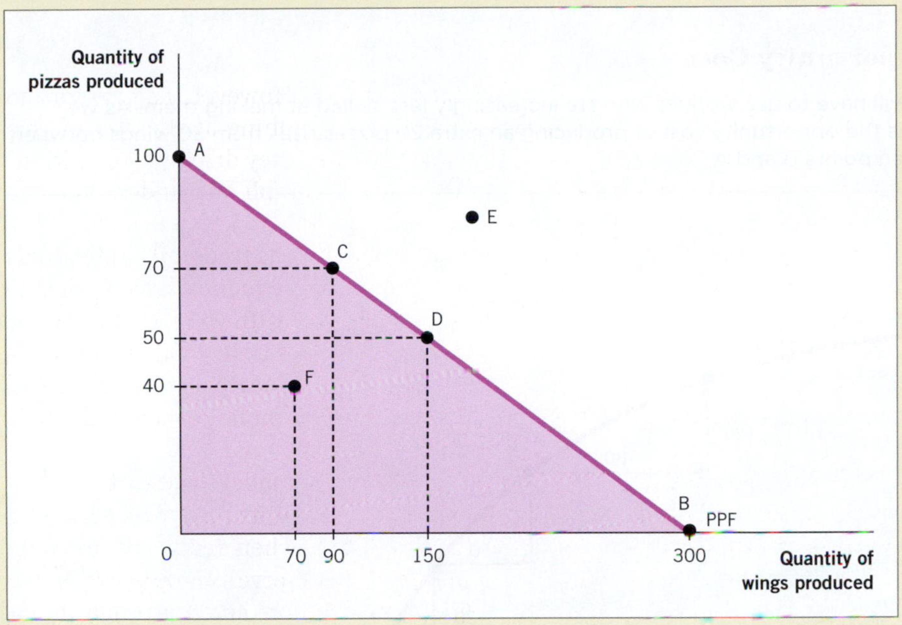

The Production Possibilities Frontier for Pizza and Chicken Wings

The production possibilities frontier (PPF) shows the trade-off between producing pizza and producing wings. Any combination of pizza and wings is possible along, or inside, the line. Combinations of pizza and wings beyond the production possibilities frontier—for example, at point E—are not possible with the current set of resources. Point F and any other points located in the shaded region are inefficient.

and they indicate an inefficient use of the society's resources. Consider, for example, the labor resource. If employees spend many hours at work surfing the Web instead of doing their jobs, the output of pizza and wings will drop, and the outcome will no longer be efficient. As long as workers use all of their time efficiently, they will produce an efficient amount of pizza and wings, and output will lie somewhere on the PPF.

Whenever society is producing on the production possibilities frontier, the only way to get more of one good is to accept less of another. Because an economy operating at a point on the frontier will be efficient, every point on the frontier represents full-capacity output. But a society may favor one point over another because it prefers that combination of goods. For example, in our theoretical two-good society, if wings suddenly become more popular, the movement from point C to point D will represent a desirable trade-off. The society will produce 20 fewer pizzas (decreasing from 70 to 50) but 60 additional wings (increasing from 90 to 150).

Trade-offs

The Production Possibilities Frontier and Opportunity Cost

Because our two-good society produces only pizza and wings, the trade-offs that occur along the production possibilities frontier represent the opportunity cost of producing one good instead of the other. As we saw in Chapter 1, an opportunity cost is the highest-valued alternative given up to pursue another course of action. As Figure 2.1 shows, when society moves from point C to point D, it gives up 20 pizzas; this is the opportunity cost of producing more wings. The movement from point D to point C has an opportunity cost of 60 wings.

Opportunity cost

FIGURE 2.2

The Law of Increasing Opportunity Cost

To make more pizzas, the society will have to use workers who are increasingly less skilled at making them. As we move up along the PPF, the result is the opportunity cost of producing an extra 20 pizzas rises from 30 wings between points D and C to 80 wings between points B and A.

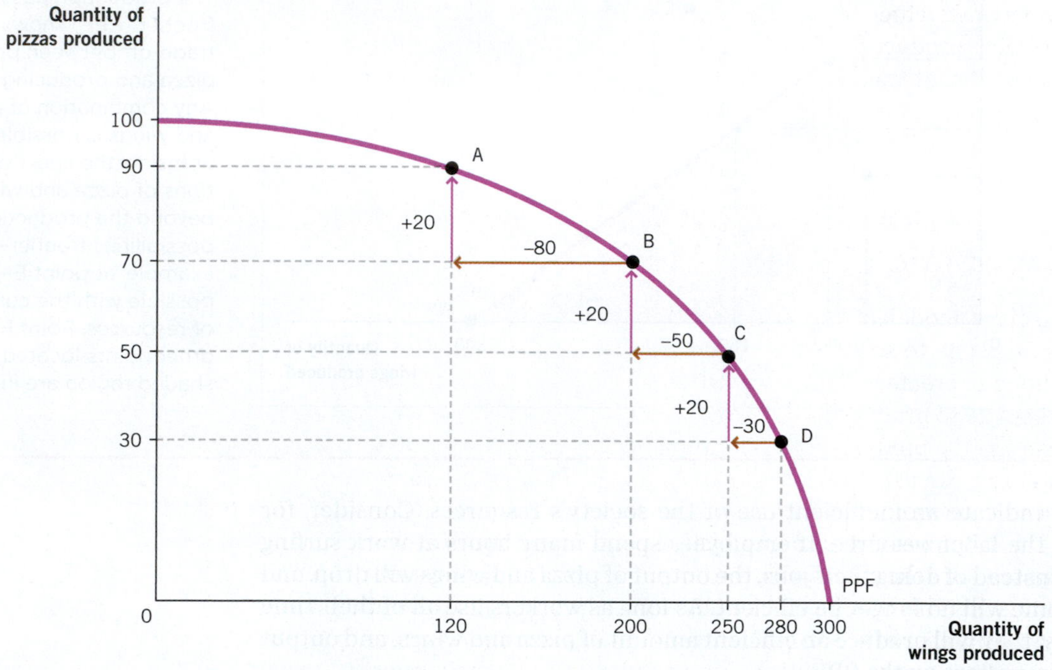

Until now, we have assumed a constant trade-off between the number of pizzas and the number of wings produced. However, not all resources in our theoretical society are perfectly adaptable for use in making pizza and wings. Some workers are good at making pizza, and others are not so good. When the society tries to make as many pizzas as possible, it will be using both types of workers. That is, to get more pizzas, the society will have to use workers who are increasingly less skilled at making them. For this reason, pizza production will not expand at a constant rate. You can see this effect in the new production possibilities frontier in Figure 2.2; it is bowed outward rather than a straight line.

Because resources are not perfectly adaptable, production does not expand at a constant rate. For example, to produce 20 extra pizzas, the society can move from point D (30 pizzas) to point C (50 pizzas). But moving from point D (280 wings) to point C (250 wings) means giving up 30 wings. So moving from point D to point C has an opportunity cost of 30 wings.

Now suppose that the society decides it wants even more pizzas and moves from point C (50 pizzas) to point B (70 pizzas). Now the opportunity cost of 20 more pizzas is 50 wings, because wing production declines from 250 to

200. If the society decides that 70 pizzas are not enough, it can expand pizza production from point B (70 pizzas) to point A (90 pizzas). Now the society gives up 80 wings. Notice that as we move up along the PPF from point D to point A, the opportunity cost of producing an extra 20 pizzas rises from 30 wings to 80 wings. This higher opportunity cost reflects the increased trade-off necessary to produce more pizzas.

A bowed-out production possibilities frontier reflects the increasing opportunity cost of production. Figure 2.2 illustrates the **law of increasing opportunity cost**, which states that the opportunity cost of producing a good rises as a society produces more of it. Changes in relative cost mean that a society faces a significant trade-off if it tries to produce an extremely large amount of a single good.

The **law of increasing opportunity cost** states that the opportunity cost of producing a good rises as a society produces more of it.

The Production Possibilities Frontier and Economic Growth

So far, we have modeled the production possibilities frontier based on the resources available to society at a particular moment in time. However, most societies hope to create economic growth. *Economic growth* is the process that enables a society to produce more output in the future.

We can use the production possibilities frontier to explore economic growth. For example, we can ask what would happen to the PPF if our two-good society develops a new technology that increases productivity. Suppose that a new pizza assembly line improves the pizza production process and that the new assembly line does not require the use of more resources—it simply redeploys the resources that already exist. This development would allow the society to make more pizza with the same number of workers. Or it would allow the same amount of pizza to be made with fewer workers than previously. Either way, the society has expanded its resource base. Figure 2.3 shows this change as a shift in the PPF.

With the new technology, it becomes possible to produce 120 pizzas using the same number of workers and in the same amount of time it previously took to produce 100 pizzas. Although the ability to produce wings has not changed, the new pizza-making technology expands the production possibilities frontier outward from PPF_1 to PPF_2. It is now possible for the society to move from point A to point B, where it can produce more of both goods (80 pizzas and 220 wings). Why can the society produce more of both? Because the improvement in pizza-making technology—the assembly line—allows a redeployment of the labor force that also increases the production of wings. Improvements in technology make point B possible.

The production possibilities frontier will also expand if the population grows. A larger population means more workers to make pizza and wings. Figure 2.4 illustrates what happens when the society adds workers to help produce pizza and wings. With more workers, the society can produce more pizzas and wings than before. The PPF curve shifts from PPF_1 to PPF_2, expanding up along the *y* axis and out along the *x* axis. Like improvements in technology, additional resources expand the frontier and allow the society to reach a point—in this case, point C—that was not possible before. The extra workers have pushed the entire frontier out—not just one end of it, as the pizza assembly line did.

FIGURE 2.3

A Shift in the Production Possibilities Frontier

A new pizza assembly line that improves the productive capacity of pizza makers shifts the PPF upward from PPF_1 to PPF_2. More pizzas can be produced. Comparing points A and B, you can see that the enhanced pizza-making capacity also makes it possible to produce more wings at the same time.

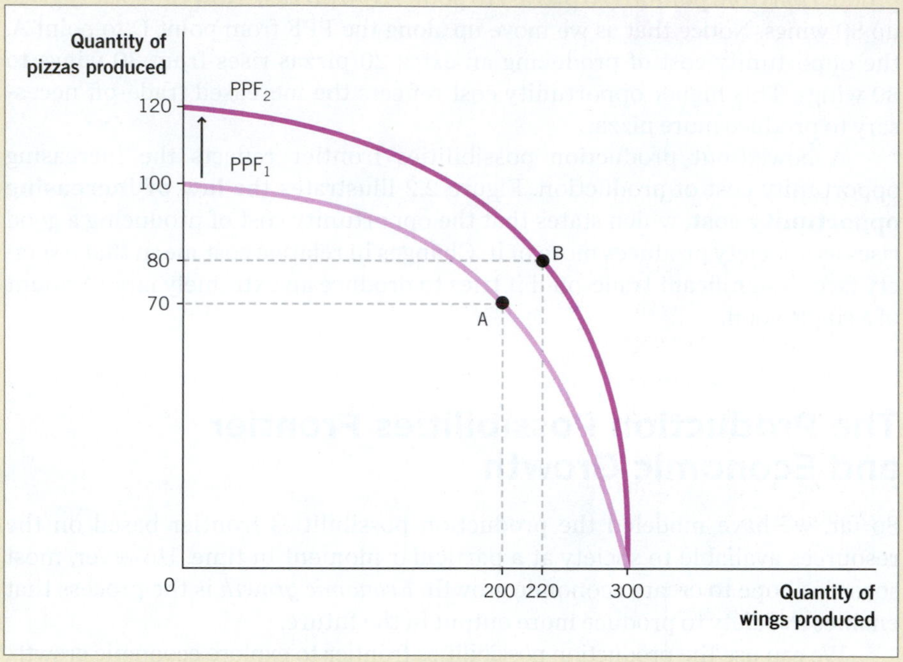

FIGURE 2.4

More Resources and the Production Possibilities Frontier

When more resources (such as additional workers) are available for the production of either pizza or wings, the entire PPF shifts upward and outward. This shift makes point C, along PPF_2, possible.

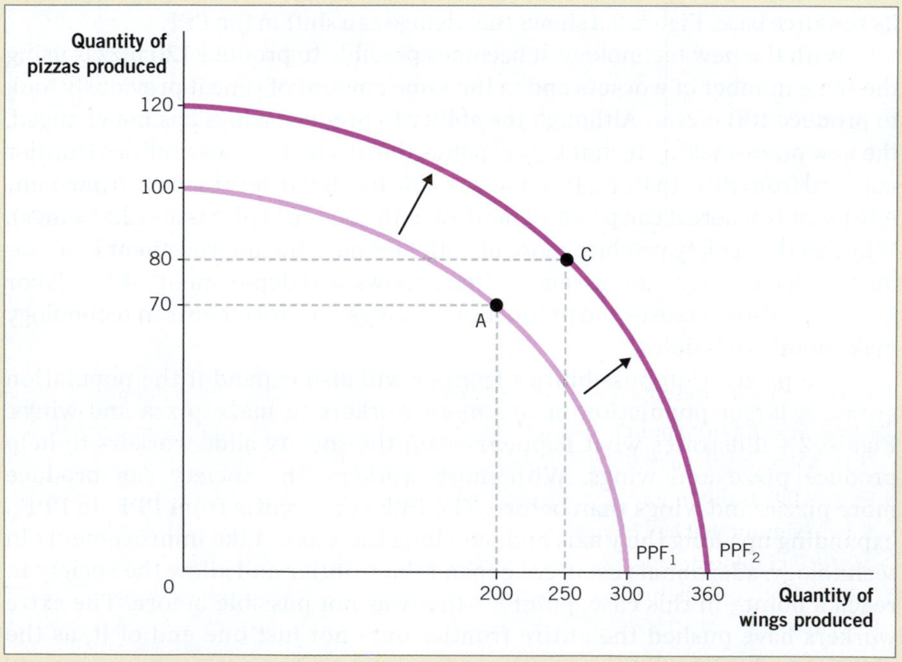

PRACTICE WHAT YOU KNOW

The Production Possibilities Frontier: Bicycles and Cars

There is a trade-off between making bicycles and making cars.

QUESTION: Are the following statements true or false? Base your answers on the PPF shown below.

1. Point A represents possible numbers of cars and bicycles that can be sold.
2. The movement along the curve from point A to point B shows the opportunity cost of producing more bicycles.
3. If society experiences a substantial increase in unemployment, the PPF shifts inward.
4. If an improved process for manufacturing cars is introduced, the entire PPF will shift outward.
5. If society is operating on the PPF, it is possible to produce more cars and bicycles simultaneously.

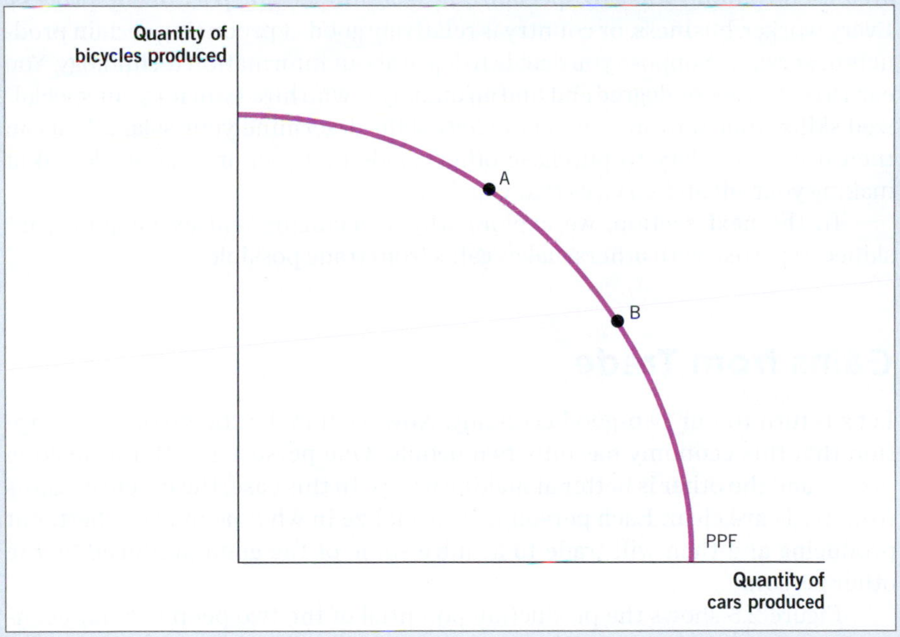

ANSWERS

1. False. Point A represents the number of cars and bicycles that can be *produced*, not sold.
2. False. Moving from point A to point B shows the opportunity cost of producing more cars, not more bicycles.
3. False. Higher unemployment does not shift the curve inward, because the PPF is the maximum that can be produced when all resources are being used efficiently. More unemployment would locate society at a point inside the PPF, because some people who could help produce more cars or bicycles would not be working.

(CONTINUED)

4. False. The PPF will shift outward along the car axis, but it will not shift upward along the bicycle axis.
5. False. Since society is operating on the PPF, all resources are already in use. This means that it is impossible to simultaneously produce more cars and bicycles, given the resource constraint in place. However, if we relax the resource constraint, by adding more labor or capital, then the PPF can move outward and allow for a simultaneous increase in both goods.

What Are the Benefits of Specialization and Trade?

Specialization is the limiting of one's work to a particular area.

We have seen that improving technology and adding resources make an economy more productive. A third way to create gains for society is through specialization and trade. **Specialization** is the limiting of one's work to a particular area. Determining what to specialize in is an important part of the process. Every worker, business, or country is relatively good at producing certain products or services. Suppose you decide to learn about information technology. You earn a certificate or degree and find an employer who hires you for your specialized skills. Your information technology skills determine your salary. You can then use your salary to purchase other goods that you are not so skilled at making yourself and services that you desire.

In the next section, we explore why specializing and exchanging your skilled expertise with others makes gains from trade possible.

Gains from Trade

Trade creates value

Let's return to our two-good economy. Now we'll make the further assumption that this economy has only two people. One person is better at making pizzas, and the other is better at making wings. In this case, the potential gains from trade are clear. Each person will specialize in what he or she is better at producing and then will trade to acquire some of the good produced by the other person.

Figure 2.5 shows the production potential of the two people in our economy, Gwen and Blake. From the table at the top of the figure, we see that if Gwen devotes all of her work time to making pizzas, she can produce 60 pizzas. If she does not spend any time on pizzas, she can make 120 wings. In contrast, Blake can spend all his time on pizzas and produce 24 pizzas or all his time on wings and produce 72 wings.

The graphs illustrate the amount of pizza and wings each person produces daily. Wing production is plotted on the *x* axis, pizza production on the *y* axis. Each production possibilities frontier is drawn from the data in the table at the top of the figure.

Trade-offs

Because the production possibilities frontiers here are straight, not bowed, Gwen and Blake each face a *constant* trade-off between producing pizza and producing wings. Gwen produces 60 pizzas for every 120 wings; this means her trade-off between producing pizza and producing wings is fixed

FIGURE 2.5

The Production Possibilities Frontier with No Trade

(a) If Gwen cannot trade with Blake, she chooses to produce 40 pizzas and 40 wings, because she likes both foods equally.
(b) If Blake cannot trade with Gwen, he chooses to produce 18 pizzas and 18 wings, because he likes both foods equally.

Person	Daily production Pizzas	Wings
Gwen	60	120
Blake	24	72

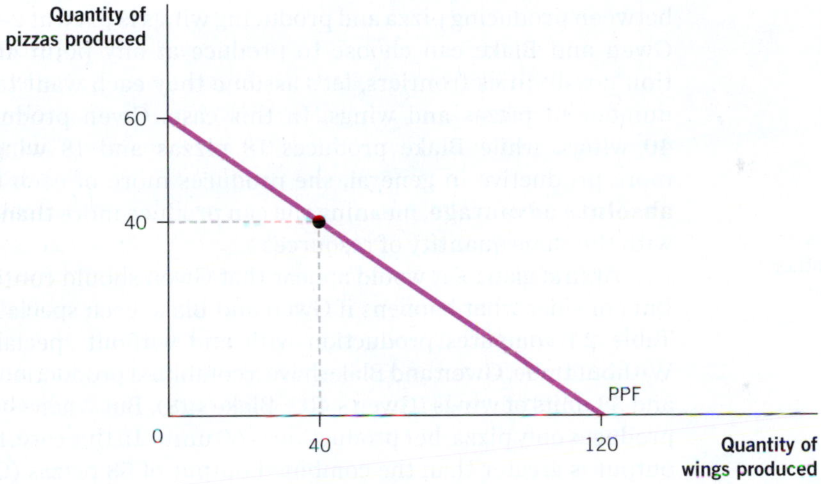

(a) Gwen

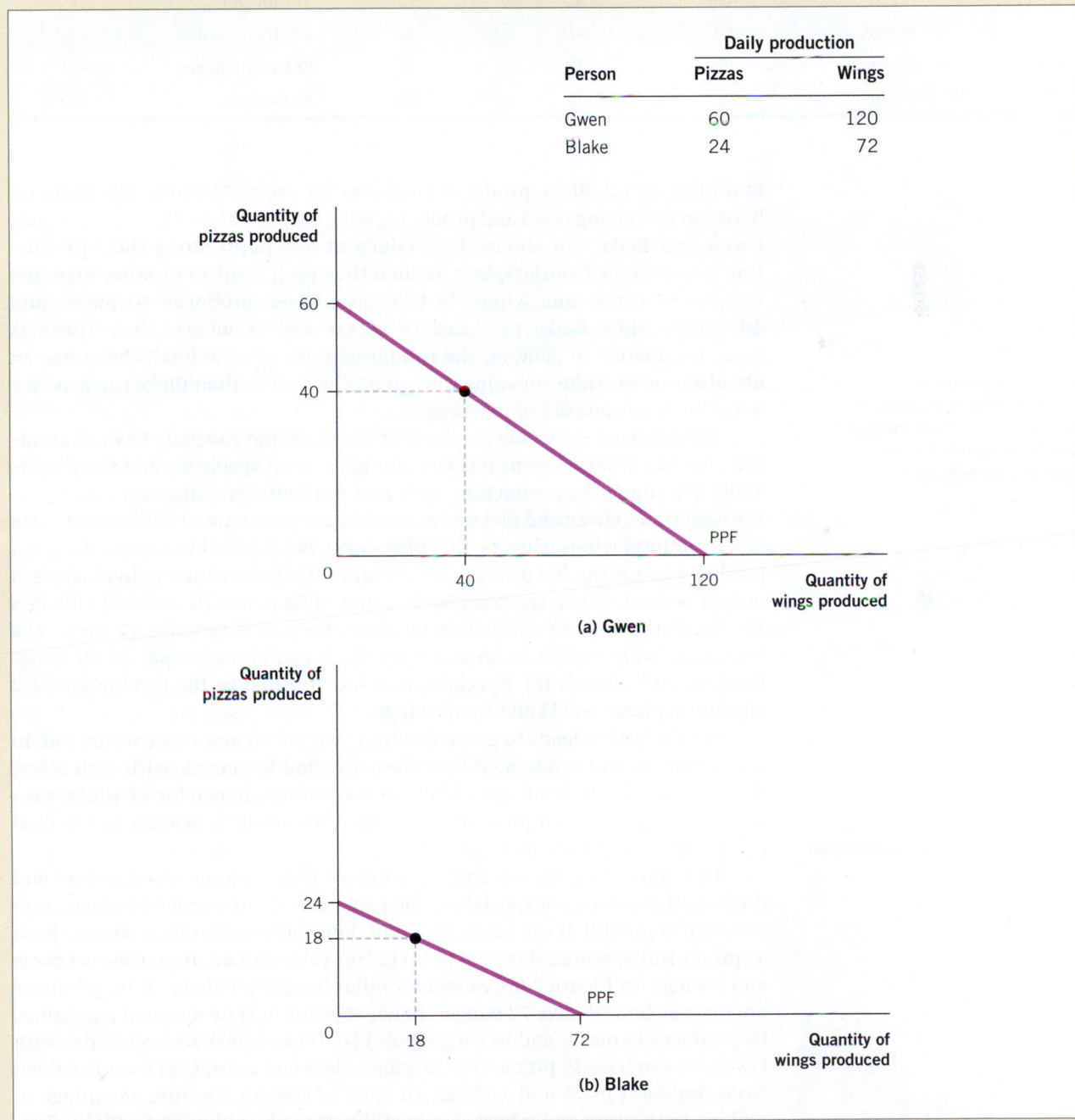

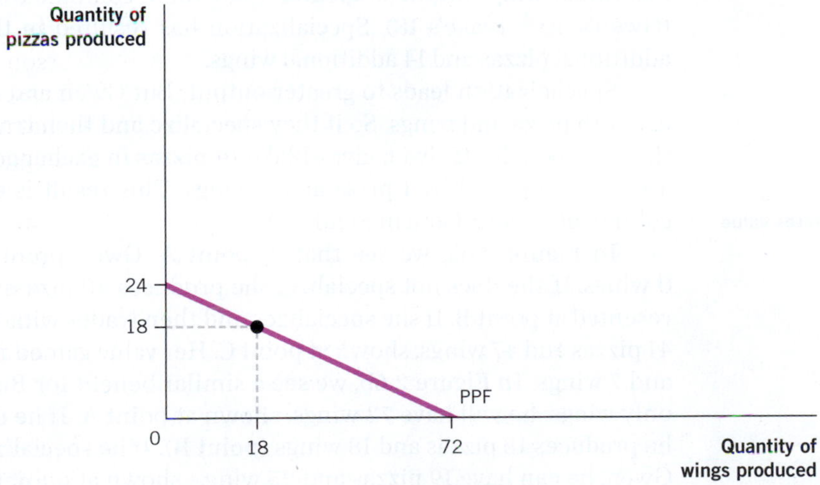

(b) Blake

TABLE 2.1

The Gains from Trade

Person	Good	Without trade: Production	Without trade: Consumption	With specialization and trade: Production	With specialization and trade: Consumption	Gains from trade
Gwen	Pizza	40	40	60	41 (keeps)	+1
	Wings	40	40	0	47 (from Blake)	+7
Blake	Pizza	18	18	0	19 (from Gwen)	+1
	Wings	18	18	72	25 (keeps)	+7

at 60:120, or 1:2. Blake produces 24 pizzas for every 72 wings. His trade-off between producing pizza and producing wings is fixed at 24:72, or 1:3. Because Gwen and Blake can choose to produce at any point along their production possibilities frontiers, let's assume they each want to produce an equal number of pizzas and wings. In this case, Gwen produces 40 pizzas and 40 wings, while Blake produces 18 pizzas and 18 wings. Since Gwen is more productive in general, she produces more of each food. Gwen has an **absolute advantage**, meaning she can produce more than Blake can produce with the same quantity of resources.

Absolute advantage refers to one producer's ability to make more than another producer with the same quantity of resources.

At first glance, it would appear that Gwen should continue to work alone. But consider what happens if Gwen and Blake each specialize and then trade. Table 2.1 compares production with and without specialization and trade. Without trade, Gwen and Blake have a combined production of 58 units of pizza and 58 units of wings (Gwen's 40 + Blake's 18). But when Gwen specializes and produces only pizza, her production is 60 units. In this case, her individual pizza output is greater than the combined output of 58 pizzas (Gwen's 40 + Blake's 18). Similarly, if Blake specializes in wings, he is able to make 72 units. His individual wing output is greater than their combined output of 58 wings (Gwen's 40 + Blake's 18). Specialization has resulted in the production of 2 additional pizzas and 14 additional wings.

Specialization leads to greater output. But Gwen and Blake would like to eat both pizza and wings. So if they specialize and then trade with each other, they will benefit. If Gwen gives Blake 19 pizzas in exchange for 47 wings, they are each better off by 1 pizza and 7 wings. This result is evident in the final column of Table 2.1 and in Figure 2.6.

Trade creates value

In Figure 2.6a, we see that at point A, Gwen produces 60 pizzas and 0 wings. If she does not specialize, she produces 40 pizzas and 40 wings, represented at point B. If she specializes and then trades with Blake, she can have 41 pizzas and 47 wings, shown at point C. Her value gained from trade is 1 pizza and 7 wings. In Figure 2.6b, we see a similar benefit for Blake. If he produces only wings, he will have 72 wings, shown at point A. If he does not specialize, he produces 18 pizzas and 18 wings (point B). If he specializes and trades with Gwen, he can have 19 pizzas and 25 wings, shown at point C. His value gained from trade is 1 pizza and 7 wings. In spite of Gwen's absolute advantage in making both pizza and wings, she is still better off trading with Blake. This amazing result occurs because of specialization. When Gwen and Blake spend their time on what they do best, they are able to produce more collectively and then divide the gain.

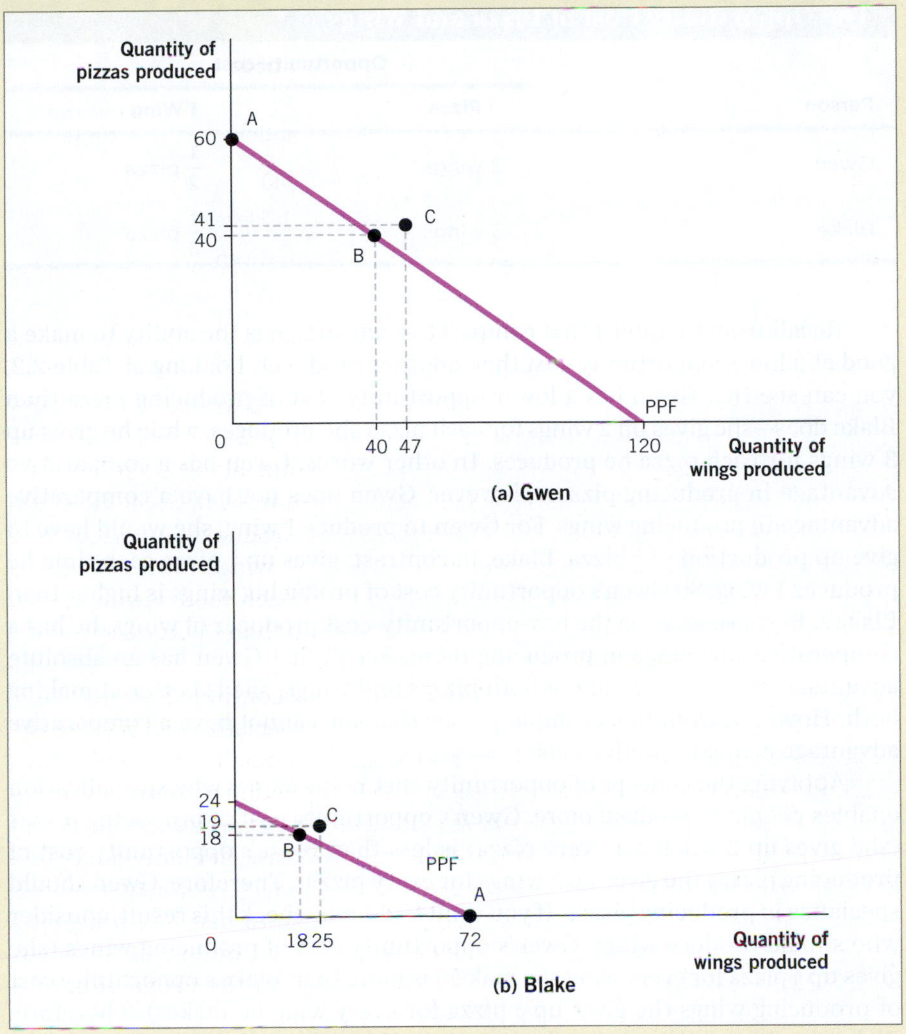

FIGURE 2.6

The Production Possibilities Frontier with Trade

(a) If Gwen produces only pizza, she will have 60 pizzas, shown at point A. If she does not specialize, she will produce 40 pizzas and 40 wings (point B). If she specializes and trades with Blake, she will have 41 pizzas and 47 wings (point C). (b) If Blake produces only wings, he will have 72 wings (point A). If he does not specialize, he will produce 18 pizzas and 18 wings (point B). If he specializes and trades with Gwen, he can have 19 pizzas and 25 wings (point C).

Comparative Advantage

Opportunity cost

We have seen that specialization enables workers to enjoy gains from trade. The concept of opportunity cost provides us with a second way of validating the principle that trade creates value. Recall that opportunity cost is the highest-valued alternative that is sacrificed to pursue something else. Looking at Table 2.2, you can see that in order to produce 1 more pizza, Gwen must give up producing 2 wings. We can say that the opportunity cost of 1 pizza is 2 wings. We can also reverse the observation and say that the opportunity cost of one wing is $\frac{1}{2}$ pizza. In Blake's case, each pizza he produces means giving up the production of 3 wings. In other words, the opportunity cost for him to produce 1 pizza is 3 wings. In reverse, we can say that when he produces 1 wing, he gives up $\frac{1}{3}$ pizza.

TABLE 2.2

The Opportunity Cost of Pizza and Wings

	Opportunity cost	
Person	**1 Pizza**	**1 Wing**
Gwen	2 wings	$\frac{1}{2}$ pizza
Blake	3 wings	$\frac{1}{3}$ pizza

Recall from Chapter 1 that comparative advantage is the ability to make a good at a lower opportunity cost than another producer. Looking at Table 2.2, you can see that Gwen has a lower opportunity cost of producing pizza than Blake does—she gives up 2 wings for each pizza she produces, while he gives up 3 wings for each pizza he produces. In other words, Gwen has a comparative advantage in producing pizzas. However, Gwen does not have a comparative advantage in producing wings. For Gwen to produce 1 wing, she would have to give up production of $\frac{1}{2}$ pizza. Blake, in contrast, gives up $\frac{1}{3}$ pizza each time he produces 1 wing. So Gwen's opportunity cost of producing wings is higher than Blake's. Because Blake is the low-opportunity-cost producer of wings, he has a comparative advantage in producing them. Recall that Gwen has an absolute advantage in the production of both pizzas and wings; she is better at making both. However, from this example we see that she cannot have a comparative advantage in making both goods.

Applying the concept of opportunity cost helps us see why specialization enables people to produce more. Gwen's opportunity cost of producing pizzas (she gives up 2 wings for every pizza) is less than Blake's opportunity cost of producing pizzas (he gives up 3 wings for every pizza). Therefore, Gwen should specialize in producing pizzas. If you want to double-check this result, consider who should produce wings. Gwen's opportunity cost of producing wings (she gives up $\frac{1}{2}$ pizza for every wing she makes) is more than Blake's opportunity cost of producing wings (he gives up $\frac{1}{3}$ pizza for every wing he makes). Therefore, Blake should specialize in producing wings. When Gwen produces only pizzas and Blake produces only wings, their combined output is 60 pizzas and 72 wings.

Finding the Right Price to Facilitate Trade

Opportunity cost

We have seen that Gwen and Blake will do better if they specialize and then trade. But how many wings should it cost to buy a pizza? How many pizzas for a wing? In other words, what trading price will benefit both parties? To answer this question, we need to return to opportunity cost. For context, think of the process you likely went through when trading lunch food with friends in grade school. Perhaps you wanted a friend's apple and he wanted a few of your Oreos. If you agreed to trade three Oreos for the apple, the exchange benefited both parties, because you valued your three cookies less than your friend's apple, and your friend valued your three cookies more than his apple.

In our example, Gwen and Blake will benefit from exchanging a good at a price that is lower than the opportunity cost of producing it. Recall that Gwen's opportunity cost is 1 pizza per 2 wings, or half a pizza per wing. This means

ECONOMICS in the MEDIA

Specialization

HOW TO MAKE A $1,500 SANDWICH IN ONLY SIX MONTHS

This video on the YouTube channel How to Make Everything features a YouTuber who takes building a sandwich from scratch to new lengths. We're not talking about going to the store and getting the needed ingredients. We're talking 100% do-it-yourself: growing the vegetables, evaporating seawater for salt, milking a cow and using the milk to make cheese, slaughtering a chicken for the protein, and grinding wheat to make bread flour. It is all quite fascinating to watch. At the end he taste tests the sandwich. "Not bad" he says, "not bad for six months of my time"—and then he puts his head down on the table.

How long would it take you to make a sandwich from scratch?

When you decide to forgo specialization and comparative advantage, you're effectively turning back the clock on economic progress and living like our ancestors did. Without any help, we end up doing everything ourselves. When that happens, we are not getting the benefits of comparative advantage. So the next time you think to yourself, I can do this on my own, think again.

Sandwiches only take a few minutes to make, precisely because in a modern economy we rely on others to make the component parts we want. You can even get your sandwich brought to your door by someone who specializes in food delivery. That's amazing, when you think about it.

Trade creates value

that any exchange where she can get a wing for less than half a pizza will be beneficial to her, because she ends up with more pizza and wings than she had without trade. Blake's opportunity cost is 1 pizza per 3 wings, so any trade where he can get a pizza for less than three wings will be beneficial to him. For trade to be mutually beneficial, the exchange ratio must fall between Gwen's opportunity cost ratio of 1:2 (0.50) and Blake's opportunity cost ratio of 1:3 (0.33). Outside of that range, either Gwen or Blake will be better off without trade, because the trade will not be attractive to both parties. In the example shown in Table 2.3, Gwen trades 19 pizzas for 47 wings. The ratio of 19:47 (0.40) falls between Gwen's and Blake's opportunity cost ratios and is therefore advantageous to both of them.

As long as the terms of trade fall between the trading partners' opportunity costs, the trade benefits both sides. But if Blake insists on a trading ratio of 1 wing for 1 pizza, which would be a good deal for him, Gwen will refuse to trade because she will be better off producing both goods on her own. Likewise, if Gwen insists on receiving 4 wings for every pizza she gives to Blake, he will refuse to trade with her because he will be better off producing both goods on his own.

TABLE 2.3

Gaining from Trade

Person	Opportunity cost	Ratio
Gwen	1 pizza equals 2 wings	1:2 = 0.50 pizza per wing
Terms of trade	19 pizzas for 47 wings	19:47 = 0.40 pizza per wing
Blake	1 pizza equals 3 wings	1:3 = 0.33 pizza per wing

PRACTICE WHAT YOU KNOW

Opportunity Cost

QUESTION: Imagine that you are planning to visit your family in Chicago. You can take a train or a plane. The plane ticket costs $300, and traveling by air takes 2 hours each way. The train ticket costs $200, and traveling by rail takes 12 hours each way. Which form of transportation should you choose?

ANSWER: The key to answering the question is learning to value time. The simplest way to do this is to calculate the cost savings of taking the train and compare that with the value of the time you would save if you took the plane.

Cost savings with train	Round-trip time saved with plane
$300 − $200 = $100	24 hours − 4 hours = 20 hours
(plane) − (train)	(train) − (plane)

Will you travel by plane or by train?

A person who takes the train can save $100, but it will cost 20 hours to do so. At an hourly rate, the savings would be $100/20 hours = $5 per hour. If you value your time at exactly $5 an hour, you will be indifferent between plane and train travel (that is, you will be equally satisfied with both options). If your time is worth more than $5 an hour, you should take the plane. If your time is worth less than $5 an hour, you should take the train.

It is important to note that this approach to calculating opportunity cost gives us a more realistic answer than simply observing ticket prices. The train has a lower ticket price, but very few people ride the train instead of flying, because the opportunity cost of their time is worth more to them than the difference in the ticket prices. Opportunity cost explains why most business travelers fly—it saves valuable time. Good economists learn to examine the full opportunity cost of their decisions, which must include both the financials and the cost of time.

Opportunity cost

We have examined this question by holding everything else constant (that is, applying the principle of *ceteris paribus*). In other words, at no point did we discuss possible side issues such as the fear of flying, sleeping arrangements on the train, comparisons of comfort and personal space, or anything else that might be relevant to someone making the decision.

ECONOMICS IN THE REAL WORLD

WHY JASON MOMOA USES BODYGUARDS

Jason Momoa is a giant of a man—6′4″, 235 pounds, and ripped. He is best known as the actor who played the fearsome warlord Khal Drogo on *Game of Thrones* and who starred in the movie *Aquaman*. Given his size and strength, you might think that Momoa is the last person who would need two bodyguards. But despite the fact that he could likely defend himself better than two ordinary bodyguards, they were hired to protect him, even though next to him, they look like *they* need the protecting! Let's examine the situation to see if this was a wise decision.

Momoa has an absolute advantage in both acting and being a great bodyguard. But as we have seen, an absolute advantage doesn't mean that Momoa should do both tasks himself. When you are paid millions of dollars to act, the time spent interacting with *paparazzi* is time lost earning money—a substantial opportunity cost. The bodyguards, with a much lower opportunity cost of their time, have a comparative advantage in dealing with pesky photographers and overzealous fans—so Momoa made a smart decision to hire them!

Does Aquaman need bodyguards, or do the bodyguards need Aquaman?

Opportunity cost

What Is the Trade-Off between Having More Now and Having More Later?

So far, we have examined short-run trade-offs. In looking at our wings–pizza trade-off, we were essentially living in the moment. But both individuals and society as a whole must weigh the benefits available today (the short run) with those available tomorrow (the long run). In the **short run**, we make decisions that reflect our immediate or short-term wants, needs, or limitations. In the short run, consumers can partially adjust their behavior. In the **long run**, we make decisions that reflect our wants, needs, and limitations over a much longer time horizon. In the long run, consumers have time to fully adjust to market conditions.

The **short run** is the period in which we make decisions that reflect our immediate or short-term wants, needs, or limitations. In the short run, consumers can partially adjust their behavior.

The **long run** is the period in which we make decisions that reflect our needs, wants, and limitations over a long time horizon. In the long run, consumers have time to fully adjust to market conditions.

Many of life's important decisions are about the long run. We must decide where to live, whether and whom to marry, whether and where to go to college, and what type of career to pursue. Getting these decisions right is far more important than simply deciding how many wings and pizzas to produce. For instance, the decision to save money requires giving up something you want to buy today for the benefit of having more money available in the future. Similarly, if you decide to go to a party tonight, you benefit today, while staying home to study creates a larger benefit at exam time. We are constantly making decisions that reflect this tension between today and tomorrow—eating a large piece of cake or a healthy snack, taking a nap or exercising at the gym, buying a jet ski or purchasing stocks in the stock market. Each of these decisions is a trade-off between the present and the future.

Trade-offs

ECONOMICS *in the* MEDIA

Opportunity Cost

XBOX OR PLAYSTATION?

In *The Big Bang Theory,* Sheldon wants to buy either a new Xbox or a new PlayStation. He explains to his girlfriend, Amy, over dinner that because each system has many advantages, it is hard to choose. Eventually, he settles on an Xbox, but after picking one up at the store, he begins to have second thoughts. He starts by recalling decisions from his past that in hindsight were poor choices: he bought a Betamax instead of a VHS player, an HD-DVD player instead of a Blu-ray player, and a Zune instead of an iPod. Sheldon puts the Xbox back, because he doesn't want to experience regret.

Seeing that Sheldon is unable to choose, Amy intervenes and offers to buy him both systems! Problem solved, right? Not quite, because Sheldon only has one slot open on his entertainment system. Amy counters that she'll buy him a new entertainment center, only to have Sheldon respond, "Which one?" because he knows he won't be able to make that choice easily, either! Hours later, we see Sheldon and Amy lying on the floor while Sheldon is still deciding. Eventually the store closes and they are forced to come back another day.

Which would you choose, an Xbox or a PlayStation?

We may not be as indecisive as Sheldon, but we face the same basic problem all the time. When you buy a new phone, rent a new apartment, buy a new outfit, go out to eat, or decide where to go to college, you give up your next-best option. The more important the decision and the better the alternatives, the harder the choice becomes. In those situations, the choice involves a high opportunity cost. If the choice is trivial or the second-best option isn't appealing, the choices we make involve low opportunity costs.

Consumer Goods, Capital Goods, and Investment

Consumer goods are produced for present consumption.

Capital goods help produce other valuable goods and services in the future.

We have seen that the trade-off between the present and the future is evident in the tension between what we consume now and what we plan to consume later. Any good that is produced for present consumption is a **consumer good**. These goods help to satisfy our needs or wants now. Food, entertainment, and clothing are all examples of consumer goods. **Capital goods** help in the production of other valuable goods and services in the future. Capital goods are everywhere. Roads, factories, trucks, and computers are all capital goods.

Education is a form of capital. The time you spend earning a college degree makes you more attractive to future employers. When you decide to go to college instead of working, you are investing in your *human capital*. **Investment** is the process of using resources to create or buy new capital.

Investment
is the process of using resources to create or buy new capital.

Because we live in a world with scarce resources, every investment in capital goods has an opportunity cost of forgone consumer goods. For example, if you decide to buy a new laptop, you cannot use the money to travel over spring break. Similarly, a firm that decides to invest in a new factory to expand future production is unable to use that money to hire more workers now.

The decision between whether to consume or to invest has a significant impact on economic growth in the future, or long run. What happens when society chooses to produce many more consumer goods than capital goods? Figure 2.7a shows the result. When relatively few resources are invested in producing capital goods in the short run, very little new capital is created. Because new capital is a necessary ingredient for economic growth in the future, the long-run production possibilities curve expands only a small amount.

What happens when society chooses to plan for the future by producing more capital goods than consumer goods in the short run? Figure 2.7b shows the result. With investment in new capital, the long-run production possibilities curve expands outward much more.

Trade-offs

All societies face the trade-off between spending today and investing for tomorrow. Thailand and Peru are good examples of emerging global economies investing in the future. Over the last 20 years, the citizens of these countries have invested significantly more in capital goods than have the citizens of wealthier nations in North America and Europe. Not surprisingly, economic growth rates in Thailand and Peru are much higher than they are in more developed countries. Part of the difference in these investment rates can be explained by the fact that the United States and Europe already have large capital stocks per capita (per person) and therefore have less to gain from operating at point B in Figure 2.7b than developing countries do. Thailand clearly prefers point B at this stage of its economic development, but point B is not necessarily better than point A. Developing nations, such as Thailand, are sacrificing the present for a better future, while many developed countries,

Study now . . .

. . . play later.

FIGURE 2.7

Investing in Capital Goods and Promoting Growth

(a) When a society chooses point A in the short run, very few capital goods are created. Because capital goods are needed to enhance future growth, the long-run PPF_2 expands, but only slightly. (b) When a society chooses point B in the short run, many capital goods are created, and the long-run PPF_2 expands significantly.

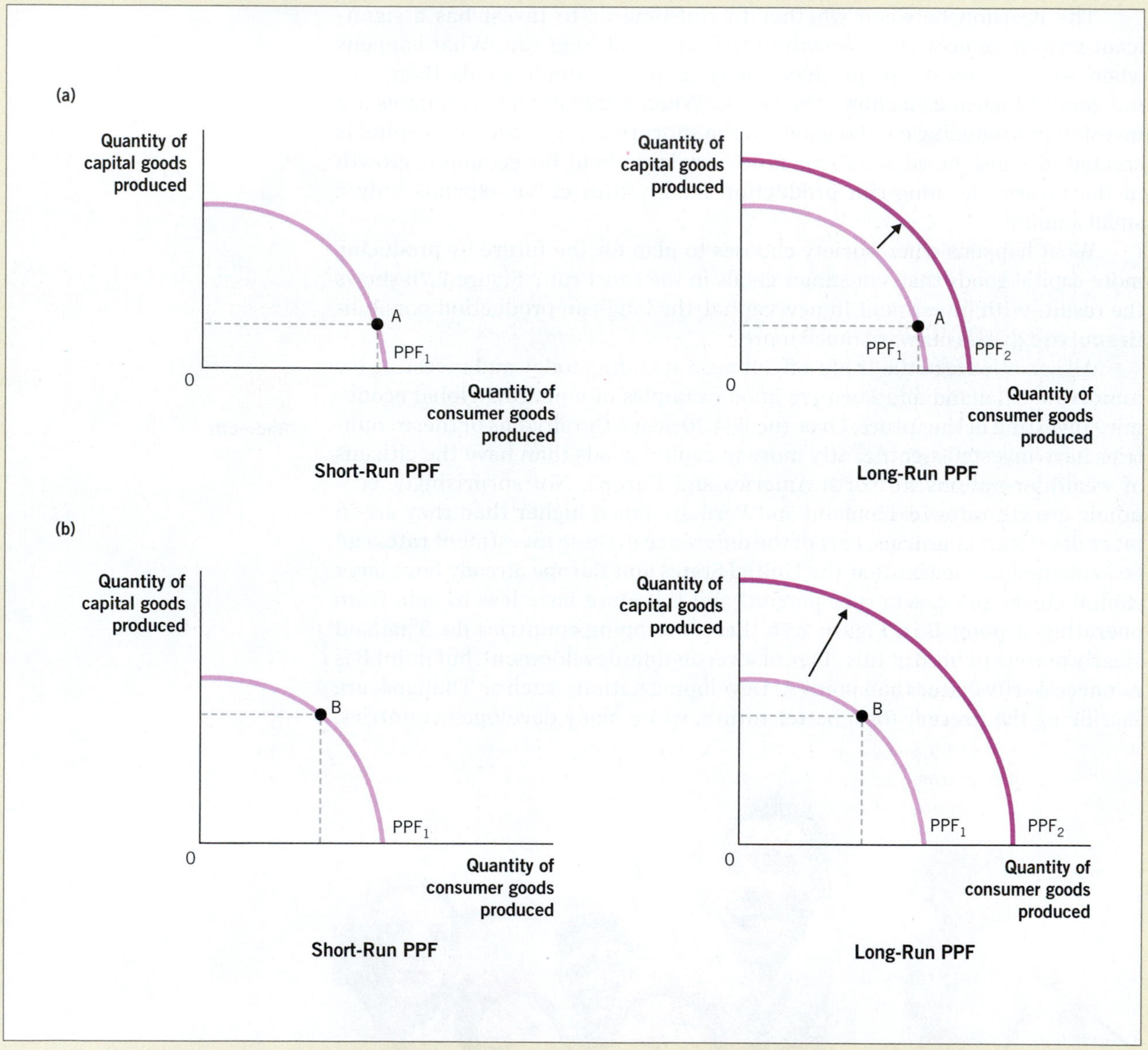

ECONOMICS in the MEDIA

The Trade-Off between the Short Run and the Long Run

CHEF

In this 2014 movie, Carl Casper is the longtime head chef of Gauloises, a Southern California restaurant. Carl wants to try out new menu ideas, but the owner insists that he stick to the old favorites Gauloises is known for. One day, Carl has had enough. After a Twitter fight with a renowned food critic escalates into a physical confrontation, Carl is free to pursue a new dream: serving home-style Cuban food out of a food truck! Restoring the old truck costs him a lot of time and money but gives him great joy. Eventually, through a social media campaign, Carl's backstory and passion for cooking become widely known, and the truck becomes a destination for foodies. This time, the food critic raves about Carl's food and offers to bankroll a new restaurant where Carl will have full control of the menu. As the film ends, Carl's new restaurant is a success, and his personal relationships are restored, too.

Owning a food truck can pay long-run dividends.

The movie illustrates the trade-off between enjoying consumer goods in the short run and investing in capital goods in the long run. Carl's choice to give up a secure, well-paying position and start over from scratch was not easy. Fixing up a used food truck and crisscrossing the country to boost his profile was an expensive and risky endeavor. However, the plan gave Carl artistic control over the food he served, and his creative talents allowed his venture to flourish. Investing in a food truck is like choosing point B in Figure 2.7b. Investing now will allow the production possibilities frontier to grow over time, affording Carl a better life in the long run.

such as the United States, take a more balanced approach to weighing current needs against future growth. For Thai workers, this trade-off typically means longer work hours and higher savings rates than their U.S. counterparts can claim, despite far lower average salaries for the Thai workers. In contrast, U.S. workers have much more leisure time and more disposable (spendable) income, a combination that leads to much higher rates of consumption in the United States.

PRACTICE WHAT YOU KNOW

No pain, no gain.

Trade-Offs

QUESTION: Your friend is fond of saying he will study later. He eventually does study, but he often doesn't get quite the grades he had hoped for because he doesn't study enough. Every time this happens, he says, "It's only one exam." What advice would you give him about trade-offs?

ANSWER: Your friend doesn't understand long-run trade-offs. You could start by reminding him that each decision has a consequence at the margin and also later in life. The marginal cost of not studying enough is a lower exam grade. To some extent, your friend's reasoning is correct. How well he does on one exam over four years of college is almost irrelevant. The problem is that many poor exam scores have a cumulative effect over the semesters. If your friend graduates with a 2.5 GPA instead of a 3.5 GPA because he did not study enough, his employment prospects will be significantly diminished.

Marginal thinking

ECONOMICS IN THE REAL WORLD

Incentives

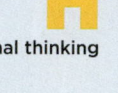

How long would you stay, if each minute costs you 12 cents?

ZIFERBLAT CAFÉ UNDERSTANDS INCENTIVES

Ziferblat is a small but growing café chain with locations in the UK and Eastern Europe. Their slogan is "Everything is free inside; except the time you spend." Unlike most cafés, which charge for the items you order, Ziferblat charges 8 pence a minute (about $7.00 per hour), and everything (Wi-Fi, dozens of brands of tea and coffee, biscuits, and cakes) is included.

In most cafés the scarcest resource is table space. The reason is that once a customer purchases something, they are allowed to sit as long as they want. Ziferblat has solved the "squatting" problem that plagues other cafés by giving each customer a clock that charges them based on how long they stay. This nontraditional pricing structure creates an incentive to take time into account, by raising the cost of staying after you have finished your refreshment.

Ziferblat is a good example of voluntary trade. Customers can use Ziferblat for a quick bite or beverage and also use it as a shared office or meeting space. Ziferblat sets a price per minute that allows it to make a profit, and customers are willing to pay for the comforts provided. That's a win-win exchange.

Conclusion

Trade creates value

The simple, yet powerful idea that trade creates value has far-reaching consequences for how we should organize our society. Since we all win when voluntary trade takes place, creating opportunities for more trades to take place between consumers and producers and across countries enriches all of our lives.

We have developed our first model, the production possibilities frontier. This model illustrates the benefits of trade and also enables us to describe ways

· ECONOMICS *for* LIFE ·

Why Men Should Do More Housework

- **Men spend, on average, 50 minutes per day less than women on household chores.**
- **If labor in the household is allocated in a gender-neutral way, output-per-hour increases by 5.4%.**
- **Reducing the amount of time talented women spend doing household chores helps them earn pay equal to their male counterparts.**

When men share chores equally, it's good for all of us.

According to the U.S. Census Bureau's American Time Use Survey, the division of household chores falls disproportionately on females. It turns out that this imbalance is a contributor to the wage gap that exists between men and women (more on that in Chapter 15). Researchers at the National Bureau of Economic Research, a private nonprofit organization, found that women earn less than men do because they are less willing to work jobs that require long hours. The researchers determined that if labor in the household is allocated in a gender-neutral way, this increases output-per-hour by 5.4%, as people make better use of their time, given their respective skills. Freeing up talented women from household chores also helps them earn pay equal to that of their male counterparts.

The life lesson is clear here. When partners both work outside the home, they should each pull their weight by spending equal amounts of time completing chores at home. Each partner should specialize in the chores they are comparatively good at, enabling the other partner to do likewise.

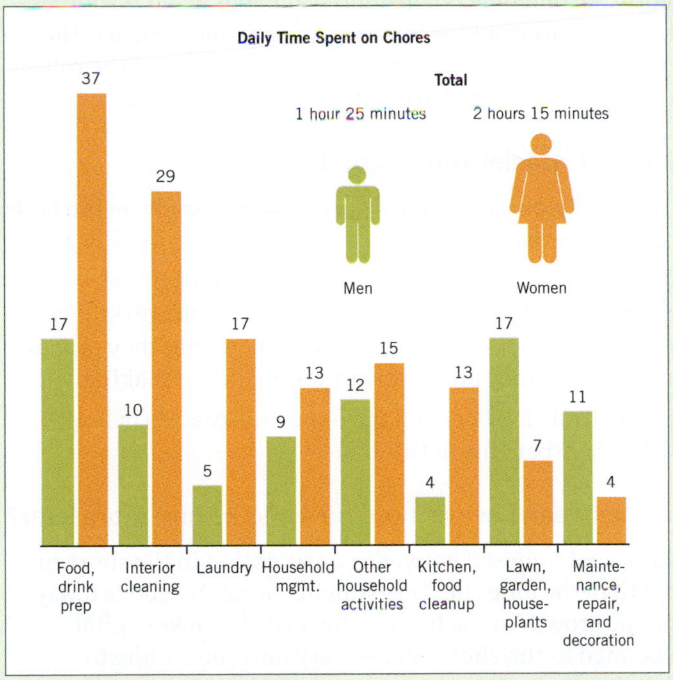

Women on the average spend more of their time than men do on household activities. Households that break up tasks more based on skill increase household labor output per hour by 5.4%. This earns the family more money. If women participated in the economy identically to men, one report estimates it would add $28 trillion, or 26%, to the annual global economy.

Sources: NBER Study, 2017, https://www.nber.org/system/files/working_papers/w23636/w23636.pdf; McKinsey Global Institute, 2015, www.mckinsey.com/featured-insights/employment-and-growth/how-advancing-womens-equality-can-add-12-trillion-to-global-growth.

Opportunity cost
Trade creates value

to grow the economy. Trade and growth rest on a more fundamental idea—specialization. When producers specialize, they focus their efforts on those goods and services for which they have the lowest opportunity cost and they trade with others who are good at making something else. To have something valuable to trade, each producer, in effect, must find its comparative advantage. As a result, trade creates value and contributes to an improved standard of living in society. ✷

· ANSWERING *the* BIG QUESTIONS ·

How do economists study the economy?

- Economists design hypotheses (proposed explanations) and then test them by collecting real data. The economist's laboratory is the world around us.
- A good model should be simple, flexible, and useful for making accurate predictions. A model is both more realistic and harder to understand when it involves many variables. To keep models simple, economists often use the concept of *ceteris paribus*, or "all else equal." Maintaining a positive (as opposed to normative) framework is crucial for economic analysis because it allows decision-makers to observe the facts objectively.

What is a production possibilities frontier?

- A production possibilities frontier (PPF) is a model that illustrates the combinations of outputs a society can produce if all of its resources are being used efficiently. An outcome is considered efficient when resources are fully utilized and potential output is maximized. Economists use the PPF to illustrate trade-offs and to explain opportunity costs and the role of additional resources and technology in creating economic growth.

What are the benefits of specialization and trade?

- Society is better off if individuals and firms specialize and trade on the basis of the principle of comparative advantage.
- Parties that are better at producing goods and services than all their potential trading partners (and thus hold an absolute advantage) still benefit from trade. Trade allows them to specialize and trade what they produce for other goods and services they are relatively less skilled at making.
- As long as the terms of trade fall between the opportunity costs of both trading partners, the trade benefits both sides.

What is the trade-off between having more now and having more later?

- All societies face a crucial trade-off between consumption in the short run and economic growth in the long run. Investments in capital goods today help to spur economic growth in the future. However, because capital goods are not consumed in the short run, society must be willing to sacrifice how well it lives today in order to have more later.

CHAPTER PROBLEMS

Concepts You Should Know

absolute advantage (p. 42)
capital goods (p. 48)
ceteris paribus (p. 31)
consumer goods (p. 48)
endogenous factors (p. 32)
exogenous factors (p. 32)
investment (p. 49)
law of increasing opportunity cost (p. 37)
long run (p. 47)
normative statement (p. 30)
positive statement (p. 30)
production possibilities frontier (PPF) (p. 34)
short run (p. 47)
specialization (p. 40)

Questions for Review

1. What is a positive economic statement? What is a normative economic statement? Provide an example of each (other than those given in the chapter).

2. Is it important to build completely realistic economic models? Explain your response.

3. Draw a production possibilities frontier curve. Illustrate the set of points that is feasible, the set of points that is efficient, the set of points that is inefficient, and the set of points that is not feasible.

4. Why does the production possibilities frontier bow out?

5. Does having an absolute advantage mean that you should undertake to produce everything on your own? Why or why not?

6. What criteria would you use to determine which of two workers has a comparative advantage in performing a task?

7. Why does comparative advantage matter more than absolute advantage for trade?

8. What factors are most important for economic growth?

Study Problems *(✱ solved at the end of the section)*

✱ **1.** Michael and Angelo live in a small town in Italy. They work as artists. Michael is the more productive artist. He can produce 10 small sculptures each day but only 5 paintings. Angelo can produce 6 sculptures each day but only 2 paintings.

	Output per day	
	Sculptures	**Paintings**
Michael	10	5
Angelo	6	2

a. What is the opportunity cost of a painting for each artist?
b. Based on your answer in part (a), who has a comparative advantage in producing paintings?
c. If the two men decide to specialize, who should produce the sculptures and who should produce the paintings?

✱ **2.** The following table shows scores a student can earn on two upcoming exams according to the amount of time devoted to study:

Hours spent studying for economics	Economics score	Hours spent studying for history	History score
10	100	0	40
8	96	2	60
6	88	4	76
4	76	6	88
2	60	8	96
0	40	10	100

a. Plot the production possibilities frontier.
b. Does the production possibilities frontier exhibit the law of increasing relative cost?
c. If the student wishes to move from a grade of 60 to a grade of 88 in economics, what is the opportunity cost?

3. Think about comparative advantage when answering this question: Should your professor, who has highly specialized training in economics, take time out of his or her teaching schedule to mow the lawn? Defend your answer.

✷ 4. Are the following statements positive or normative?

   a. My dog weighs 75 pounds.
   b. Dogs are required by law to have rabies shots.
   c. You should take your dog to the veterinarian once a year for a checkup.
   d. Chihuahuas are cuter than bulldogs.
   e. Leash laws for dogs are a good idea because they reduce injuries.

5. How does your decision to invest in a college degree add to your human capital? Use a projected production possibilities frontier for 10 years from now to compare your life with and without the college degree.

✷ 6. Suppose that an amazing new fertilizer doubles the production of potatoes. How would this invention affect the production possibilities frontier for an economy that produces only potatoes and carrots? Would it now be possible to produce more potatoes *and* more carrots or only more potatoes?

7. Suppose that a politician tells you about a plan to create two expensive but necessary programs to build more production facilities for solar power and wind power. At the same time, the politician is unwilling to cut any other programs. Use the production possibilities frontier graph below to explain if the politician's proposal is possible.

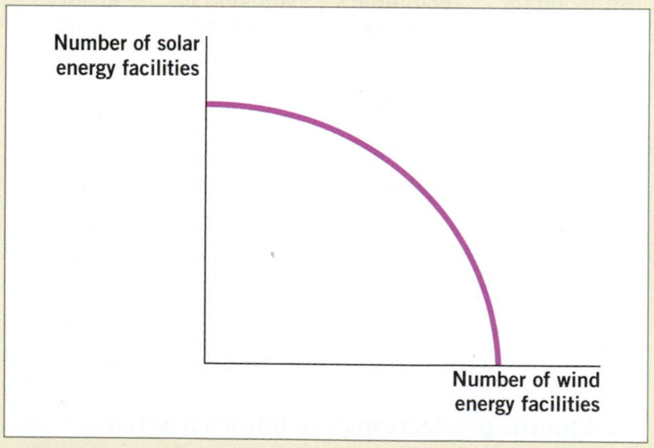

✷ 8. Two siblings, David and Alexis Rose, enjoy baking bread and making apple pie. Alexis takes 2 hours to bake a loaf of bread and 1 hour to make a pie. David takes 4 hours to bake a loaf of bread and 4 hours to make a pie.

   a. What are David's and Alexis's opportunity costs of baking bread?
   b. Who has the absolute advantage in making bread?
   c. Who has a comparative advantage in making bread?
   d. If David and Alexis both decide to specialize to increase their joint production, what should David produce? What should Alexis produce?
   e. The price of a loaf of bread can be expressed in terms of an apple pie. If David and Alexis are specializing in production and decide to trade with each other, what range of ratios of bread and apple pie would allow both parties to benefit from trade?

9. Where would you plot unemployment on a production possibilities frontier? Where would you plot full employment on a production possibilities frontier? Now suppose that in a time of crisis everyone pitches in and works much harder than usual. What happens to the production possibilities frontier?

10. Read the poem "The Road Not Taken," by Robert Frost. What line(s) in the poem capture the opportunity cost of decision-making?

✷ 11. Suppose that you must decide between attending an Ariana Grande concert or a Selena Gomez concert. The concerts are at the same time on the same evening, so you cannot see both. You love Ariana Grande and would pay as much as $200 to see her perform. Tickets to her concert are $135. You are not as big a Selena Gomez fan, but a friend has just offered you a free ticket to the concert. If you decide to take the free ticket to see Selena Gomez, what is your opportunity cost?

✷ 12. In this chapter we have seen that the PPF could be bowed-out or a straight line.

   a. Provide an example of two goods where the PPF would be bowed-out.
   b. Provide an example of two goods where the PPF would be a straight line.

c. It also turns out that the PPF can bow in. This occurs when the production process produces economies of scale, which means that it is possible to make *more* of each good as production expands. Can you think of two goods where the PPF would be bowed-in?

13. Barrville is a country that produces either all dumbbells, or all sandals, or a combination of the two.

a. Draw a production possibilities frontier and label the *x* and *y* axes appropriately.

b. Place a point that shows where the country would be operating if a recession hits and companies are laying off workers. Label this point B.

c. Place a point that shows an unattainable point under the current situation. Label this point C.

d. If a point is unattainable now, will it always be unattainable? If you write that it can be attainable, what would cause it to become attainable?

Solved Problems

1. a. Michael's opportunity cost is 2 sculptures for each painting he produces. How do we know this? If he devotes all of his time to sculptures, he can produce 10. If he devotes all of his time to paintings, he can produce 5. The ratio 10:5 is the same as 2:1. Michael is therefore twice as fast at producing sculptures as he is at producing paintings. Angelo's opportunity cost is 3 sculptures for each painting he produces. If he devotes all of his time to sculptures, he can produce 6. If he devotes all of his time to paintings, he can produce 2. The ratio 6:2 is the same as 3:1.

b. For this question, we need to compare Michael's and Angelo's relative strengths. Michael produces 2 sculptures for every painting, and Angelo produces 3 sculptures for every painting. Because Michael is only twice as good at producing sculptures, his opportunity cost of producing each painting is 2 sculptures instead of 3. Therefore, Michael is the low-opportunity-cost producer of paintings.

c. If they specialize, Michael should paint and Angelo should sculpt. You might be tempted to argue that Michael should just work alone, but if Angelo does the sculptures, Michael can concentrate on the paintings. This is what comparative advantage is all about.

2. a.

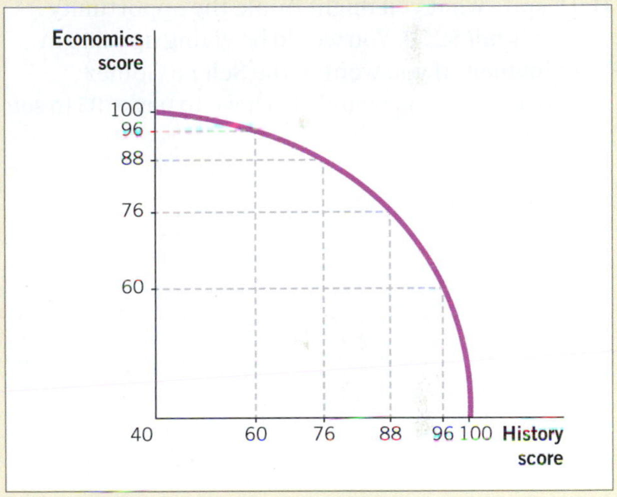

b. Yes, because it is not a straight line.

c. The opportunity cost is that the student's grade falls from 96 to 76 in history.

4. a. positive
b. positive
c. normative
d. normative
e. normative

6. A new fertilizer that doubles potato production will shift the entire PPF out along the potato axis but not along the carrot axis. Nevertheless, the

added ability to produce more potatoes means that less acreage will have to be planted in potatoes and more land can be used to produce carrots. This makes it possible to produce more potatoes and carrots at many points along the production possibilities frontier. Figure 2.3 has a nice illustration if you are unsure how this process works.

8. a. Alexis gives up 2 pies for every loaf she makes. David gives up 1 pie for every loaf he makes.

b. Alexis

c. David

d. David should make the bread and Alexis the pies.

e. Alexis makes 2 pies per loaf and David makes 1 pie per loaf. Any trade between 2:1 and 1:1 would benefit them both.

11. Despite what you might think, the opportunity cost is *not* \$200. You would be giving up \$200 in enjoyment if you went to the Selena Gomez concert, but you would also have to pay \$135 to see Ariana Grande, whereas the Selena Gomez ticket is free. The difference between the satisfaction you would have experienced at the Ariana Grande concert (\$200) and the amount you must pay for the ticket (\$135) is the marginal benefit you would receive from her concert. That amount is \$200 – \$135 = \$65. You are not as big a Selena Gomez fan, but the ticket is free. As long as you think the Selena Gomez concert is worth more than \$65, you will get a larger marginal benefit from seeing Selena Gomez perform than from seeing Ariana Grande perform. Therefore, the opportunity cost of using the free ticket is \$65.

12. a. tattoos and (in-ground) swimming pools

b. left shoes and right shoes

c. The cost of producing some goods goes down as production increases. Computers, automobiles, and fast food are good examples. For such goods, the PPF would bow in.

APPENDIX

02A Graphs in Economics

Many students try to understand economics without taking the time to learn how to read and interpret graphs. This approach is shortsighted. You can "think" your way to the correct answer in a few cases, but the models we build and illustrate with graphs are designed to help analyze the tough questions, where your intuition can lead you astray.

Economics is fundamentally a quantitative science. That is, economists often solve problems by finding a numerical answer. For instance, economists determine the unemployment rate, the inflation rate, the growth rate of the economy, prices, costs, and much more. Economists also like to compare present-day numbers with numbers from the immediate past and historical data. Throughout your study of economics, you will find that many data-driven topics—for example, financial trends, transactions, the stock market, and other business-related variables—naturally lend themselves to graphic display. You will also find that many theoretical concepts are easier to understand when depicted visually in graphs and charts.

Economists also find that graphing can be a powerful tool when attempting to find relationships between different sets of variables. For example, the production possibilities frontier model presented in this chapter involves the relationship between the production of pizza and the production of chicken wings. The graphical presentations make this relationship, the trade-off between pizza and wings, much more vivid.

In this appendix, we begin with simple graphs involving a single variable. We then move to graphs that consist of two variables.

Graphs That Consist of One Variable

There are two common ways to display data with one variable: bar graphs and pie charts. A **variable** is a quantity that can take on more than one value. Let's look at the market share of the largest carbonated-beverage companies. Figure 2A.1 shows the data in a bar graph. On the vertical (y) axis is the market share held by each firm. On the horizontal (x) axis are the three largest firms (Coca-Cola Co., PepsiCo Inc., and Keurig Dr Pepper) and a separate category for the remaining firms, called "Others." Coca-Cola Co. has the largest market

A **variable** is a quantity that can take on more than one value.

FIGURE 2A.1

Bar Graphs

Each firm's market share in the beverage industry is represented by the height of the bar.

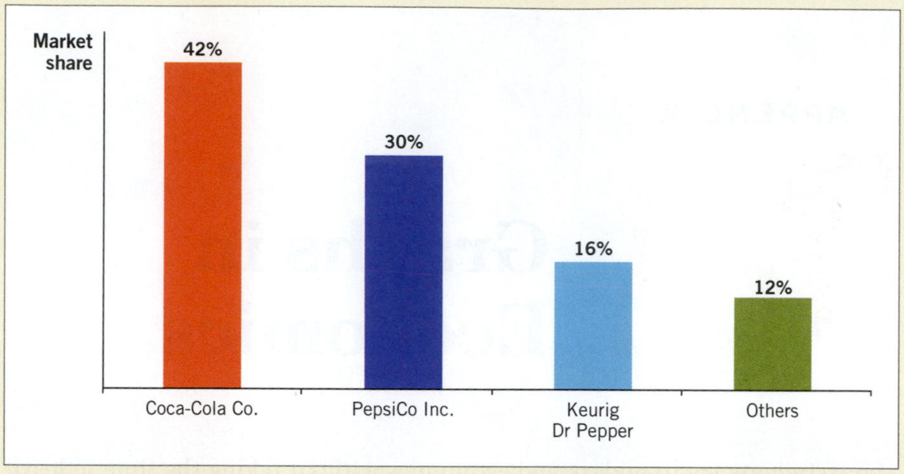

FIGURE 2A.2

Pie and Treemap Charts

Each firm's market share in the beverage industry is represented by the size of the pie slice or the chunk of the overall shape.

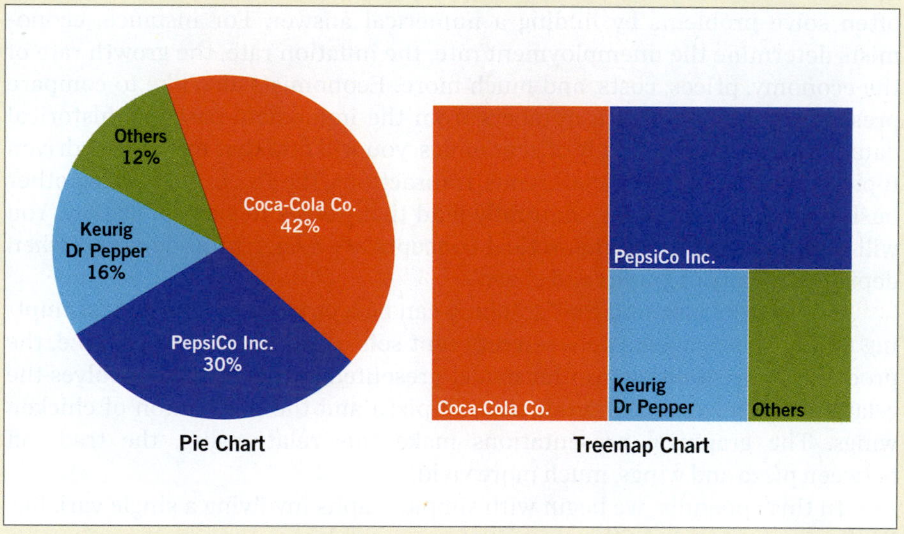

share of the U.S. market at 42%, followed by PepsiCo Inc. at 30%, and Keurig Dr Pepper at 16%. The height of each firm's bar represents its market-share percentage. The combined market share of the other firms in the market is 12%.

Figure 2A.2 illustrates the same data from the beverage industry on pie and treemap charts. Now the market share is expressed as the size of the pie slice or chunk of the overall rectangle for each firm.

The information in a bar graph and a pie chart is the same, so does it matter which visualization you use? Bar graphs are particularly good for comparing sizes or quantities, while pie charts are generally better for illustrating proportions (parts of a whole).

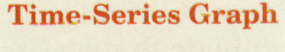

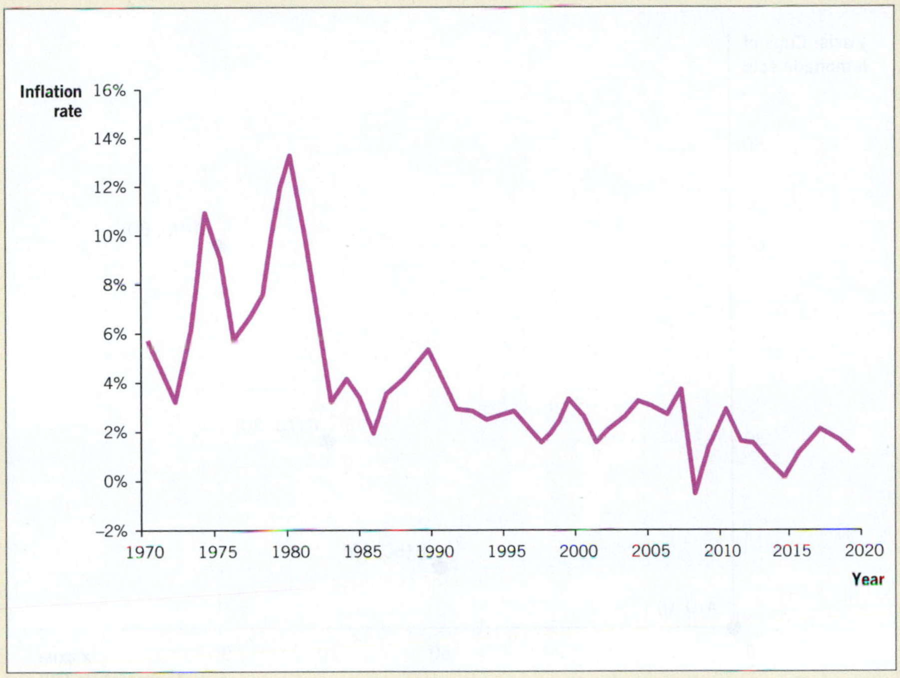

FIGURE 2A.3

Time-Series Graph

In a time-series graph, you immediately get a sense of when the inflation rate was highest and lowest, the trend through time, and the amount of volatility in the data.

Time-Series Graphs

A time-series graph displays information about a single variable across time. For instance, if you want to show how the inflation rate has varied over a certain period of time, you could list the annual inflation rates in a lengthy table, or you could illustrate each point as part of a time series in a graph. Graphing the points makes it possible to quickly determine when inflation was highest and lowest without having to scan through the entire table. Figure 2A.3 illustrates this point.

Graphs That Consist of Two Variables

Sometimes, understanding graphs requires you to visualize relationships between two economic variables. Each variable is plotted on a coordinate system, or two-dimensional grid. The coordinate system allows us to map a series of ordered pairs that show how the two variables relate to each other. For instance, suppose we examine the relationship between the amount of lemonade sold and the air temperature, as shown in Figure 2A.4.

The air temperature is graphed on the *x* axis (horizontal) and cups of lemonade sold on the *y* axis (vertical). Within each ordered pair (*x*, *y*), the first value, *x*, represents the value along the *x* axis and the second value, *y*, represents the value along the *y* axis. For example, at point A, the value of *x*, or the

FIGURE 2A.4

Plotting Points in a Coordinate System

Within each ordered pair (*x*, *y*), the first value, *x*, represents the value along the *x* axis, and the second value, *y*, represents the value along the *y* axis. The combination of all the (*x*, *y*) pairs is known as a scatterplot.

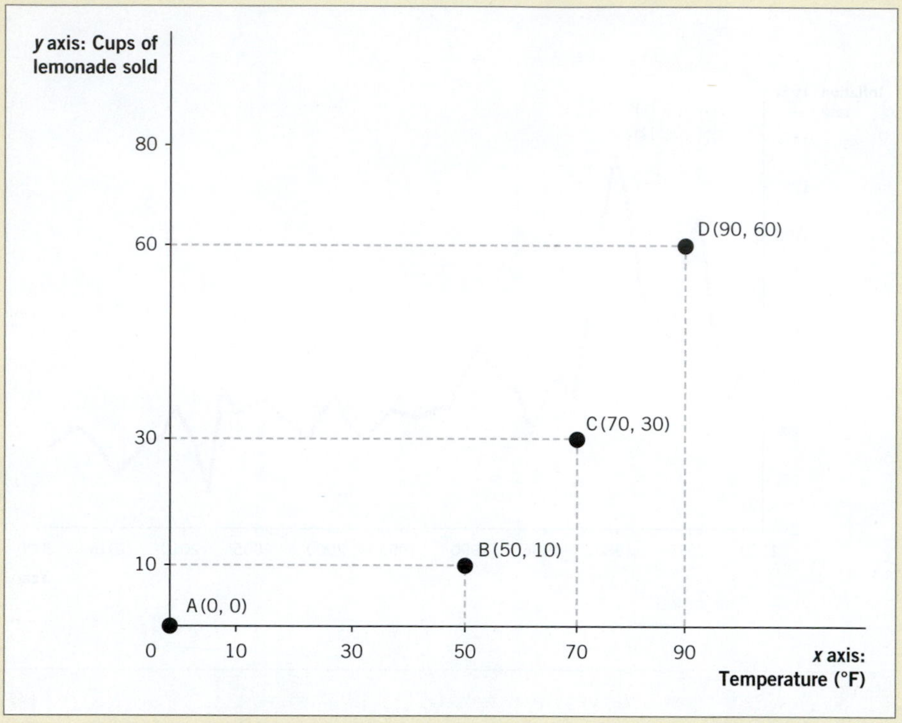

temperature, is 0 and the value of *y*, or the amount of lemonade sold, is also 0. No one would want to buy lemonade when the temperature is that low. At point B, the value of *x*, the air temperature, is 50°F, and the value of *y*, the number of cups of lemonade sold, is 10. By the time we reach point C, the temperature is 70°F and the amount of lemonade sold is 30 cups. Finally, at point D, the temperature has reached 90°F, and 60 cups of lemonade are sold.

A **scatterplot** is a graph that shows individual (*x*, *y*) points.

Positive correlation occurs when two variables move in the same direction.

Negative correlation occurs when two variables move in opposite directions.

The graph you see in Figure 2A.4 is known as a **scatterplot**; it shows the individual (*x*, *y*) points in a coordinate system. Note that in this example, the amount of lemonade sold rises as the temperature increases. When the two variables move together in the same direction, we say there is a **positive correlation** between them (see Figure 2A.5a). Conversely, if we graph the relationship between hot chocolate sales and temperature, we find they move in opposite directions; as the temperature rises, hot chocolate consumption goes down (see Figure 2A.5b). This data set reveals a **negative correlation**, which occurs when two variables, such as cups of hot chocolate sold and temperature, move in opposite directions. Economists are ultimately interested in using models and graphs to make predictions and test theories, and the coordinate system makes both positive and negative correlations easy to observe.

Figure 2A.5 illustrates the difference between a positive correlation and a negative correlation. Figure 2A.5a shows the same information as Figure 2A.4. When the temperature increases, the quantity of lemonade sold increases as well. However, in Figure 2A.5b we have a very different set of ordered pairs. As the temperature increases, the quantity of hot chocolate sold falls. We can see this relationship by starting with point E, where the temperature is 32°F

FIGURE 2A.5

Positive and Negative Correlations

(a) This graph displays the positive relationship, or correlation, between lemonade sales and higher temperatures.
(b) This graph displays the negative relationship, or correlation, between hot chocolate sales and higher temperatures.

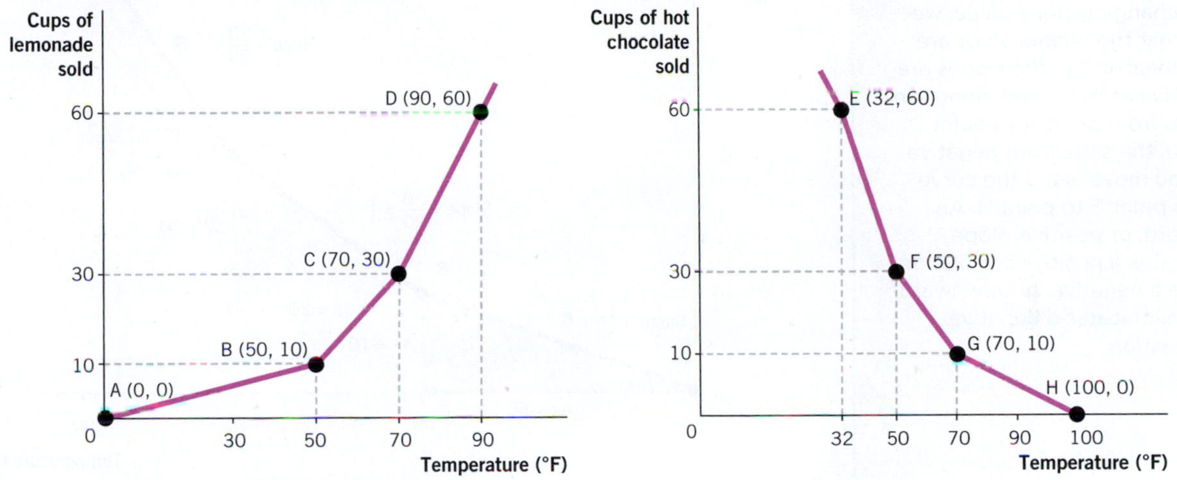

(a) Positive Correlation

(b) Negative Correlation

and hot chocolate sales are 60 cups. At point F, the temperature rises to 50°F, but hot chocolate sales fall to 30 cups. At point G, the temperature is 70°F and hot chocolate sales are down to 10 cups. The purple line connecting points E–H illustrates the negative correlation between hot chocolate sales and temperature, because the line is downward sloping. This relationship contrasts with the positive correlation in Figure 2A.5a, where lemonade sales rise from point A to point D and the line is upward sloping. But what exactly is slope?

The Slope of a Curve

A key element in any graph is the **slope**, or the rise along the *y* axis (vertical) divided by the run along the *x* axis (horizontal). The *rise* is the amount the vertical distance changes. The *run* is the amount the horizontal distance changes.

Slope
refers to the change in the rise along the *y* axis (vertical) divided by the change in the run along the *x* axis (horizontal).

$$\text{Slope} = \frac{\text{change in } y}{\text{change in } x}$$

A slope can have a positive, negative, or zero value. A slope of zero—a straight horizontal line—indicates that there is no change in *y* for a given change in *x*. The slope can also be positive, as it is in Figure 2A.5a, or negative, as it is in Figure 2A.5b. Figure 2A.6 highlights the changes in *x* and *y* between the points

FIGURE 2A.6

Positive and Negative Slopes

Notice that in both panels the slope changes value from point to point. Because of this changing slope value, we say that the relationships are nonlinear. In (a), the slopes are positive as you move along the curve from point A to point D. In (b), the slopes are negative as you move along the curve from point E to point H. An upward, or positive, slope indicates a positive correlation, while a negative, or downward, slope indicates a negative correlation.

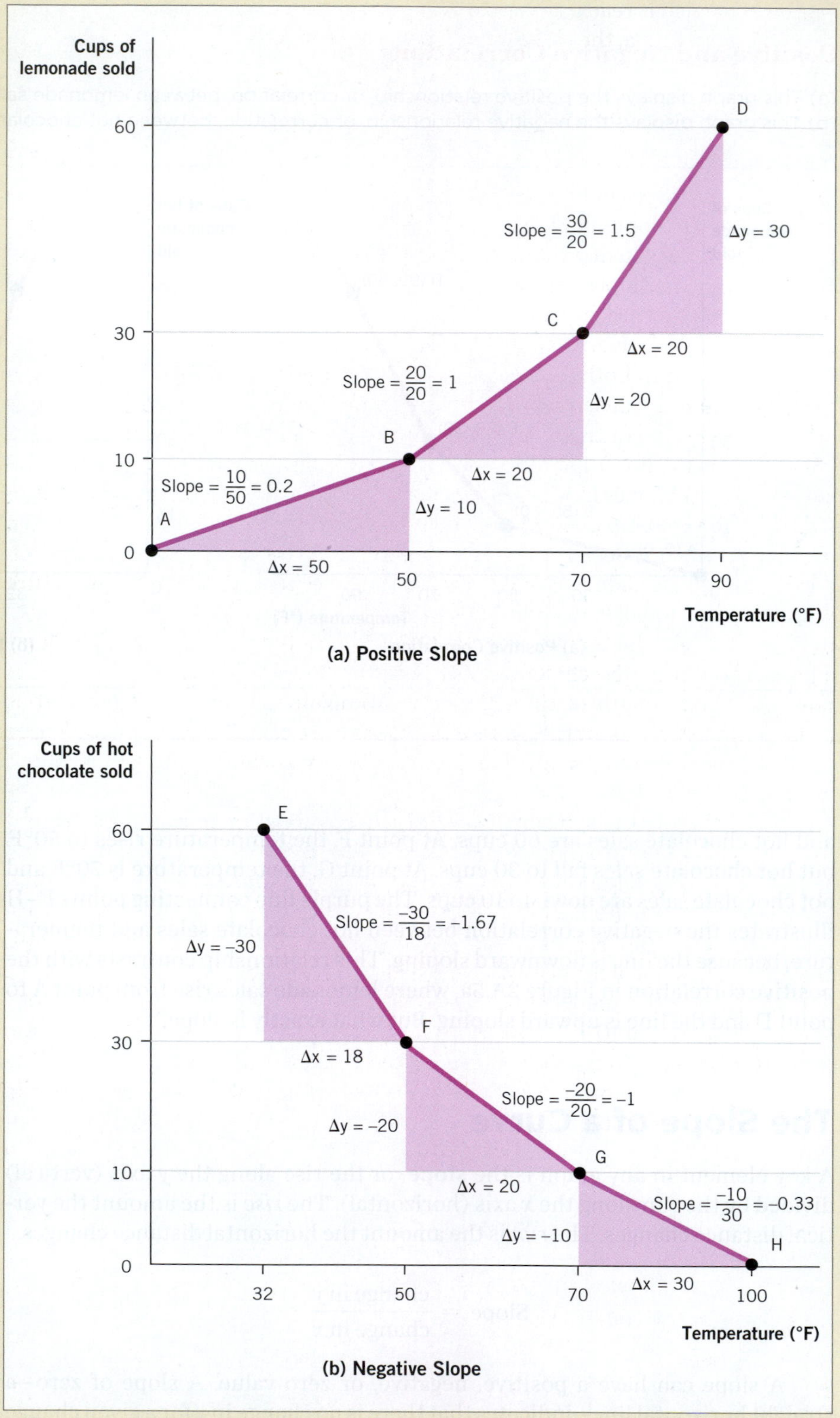

on Figure 2A.5. (The change in a variable is often notated with a Greek delta symbol, Δ, which is read as "change in.")

In Figure 2A.6a, the slope from point B to point C is

$$\text{Slope} = \frac{\text{change in } y}{\text{change in } x} = \frac{30 - 10 \text{ or } 20}{70 - 50 \text{ or } 20} = 1$$

All of the slopes in Figure 2A.6 are tabulated in Table 2A.1.

Each of the slopes in Figure 2A.6a is positive, and the values slowly increase from 0.2 to 1.5 as you move along the curve from point A to point D. However, in Figure 2A.6b, the slopes are negative as you move along the curve from point E to point H. An upward, or positive, slope indicates a positive correlation, while a downward, or negative, slope indicates a negative correlation.

Notice that in both panels of Figure 2A.6, the slope changes values from point to point. Because of this changing slope, we say that the relationships are *nonlinear*. (In contrast, the relationship is *linear* when the slope does not change along the line.) The slope tells us something about how responsive consumers are to changes in temperature. Consider the movement from point A to point B in Figure 2A.6a. The change in y is 10, while the change in x is 50, and the slope (10/50) is 0.2. Because zero indicates no change and 0.2 is close to zero, we can say that lemonade customers are not very responsive as the temperature rises from 0°F to 50°F. However, they are much more responsive from point C to point D, when the temperature rises from 70°F to 90°F. At point D, lemonade consumption—the change in y—rises from 30 to 60 cups, and the slope is now 1.5. The strength of the positive relationship is much stronger, and as a result, the curve is much steeper, or more vertical. This part of the curve contrasts with the movement from point A to point B, where the curve is flatter, or more horizontal.

We can apply the same analysis to Figure 2A.6b. Consider the movement from point E to point F. The change in y is –30, the change in x is 18, and the slope is –1.7. This value represents a strong negative relationship, so we would say that hot chocolate customers were quite responsive; as the temperature rose from 32°F to 50°F, they cut their consumption of hot chocolate by 30 cups. However, hot chocolate customers are not very responsive from point G to point H, where the temperature rises from 70°F to 100°F. In this case, consumption falls from 10 cups to 0 cups and the slope is –0.3. The strength of the negative relationship is much weaker (closer to zero), and as a result, the line is much flatter, or more horizontal. This part of the curve contrasts with the movement from point E to point F, where the curve is steeper, or more vertical.

TABLE 2A.1

Positive and Negative Slopes

(a)		(b)	
Points	**Slope**	**Points**	**Slope**
A to B	0.2	E to F	–1.7
B to C	1.0	F to G	–1.0
C to D	1.5	G to H	–0.3

Formulas for the Area of a Rectangle and a Triangle

Sometimes, economists interpret graphs by examining the area of different sections below a curve. Consider the demand for Bruegger's Bagels shown in Figure 2A.7. The demand curve (labeled D) has a downward slope, which tells us that when the price of bagels falls, consumers will buy more bagels. (We will learn more about demand curves in Chapter 3.) But this curve also can tell us about the revenue the seller receives—one of the most important considerations for the firm. In this case, let's assume that the price of each bagel is \$0.60 and Bruegger's sells 4,000 bagels each week. We can illustrate the total amount of Bruegger's revenue by shading the area bounded by the number of sales and the price—the green rectangle in the figure. In addition, we can identify the surplus benefit consumers receive from purchasing bagels; the blue triangle shows this amount. Because many buyers are willing to pay more than \$0.60 per bagel, we can visualize the "surplus" consumers get from Bruegger's Bagels by highlighting the blue triangular area under the demand curve and above the price of \$0.60.

To calculate the area of a rectangle, we use the formula

$$\text{Area of a rectangle} = \text{height} \times \text{base}$$

In Figure 2A.7, the green rectangle is the amount of revenue that Bruegger's Bagels receives when it charges \$0.60 per bagel. The total revenue is $\$0.60 \times 4{,}000$, or \$2,400.

FIGURE 2A.7

Working with Rectangles and Triangles

We can determine the area of the green rectangle by multiplying the height by the base. This gives us $\$0.60 \times 4{,}000$, or \$2,400 for the total revenue earned by Bruegger's Bagels. We can determine the area of a triangle by using the formula $\frac{1}{2} \times \text{height} \times \text{base}$. This gives us $\frac{1}{2} \times \$0.60 \times 4{,}000$, or \$1,200 for the area of consumer surplus.

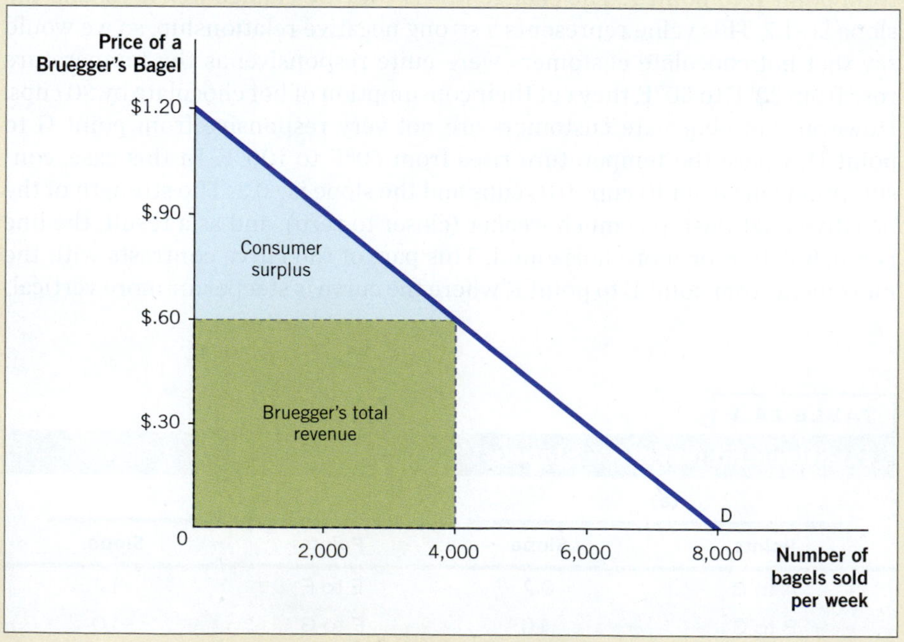

To calculate the area of a triangle, we use the formula

$$\text{Area of a triangle} = \tfrac{1}{2} \times \text{height} \times \text{base}$$

In Figure 2A.7, the blue triangle represents the amount of surplus consumers get from buying bagels. The amount of consumer surplus is $\frac{1}{2} \times \$0.60 \times 4{,}000 = \$1{,}200$. Note that the value of the height, \$0.60, comes from reading the *y* axis: \$1.20 at the top of the triangle − \$0.60 at the bottom of the triangle = \$0.60.

Cautions in Interpreting Numerical Graphs

In Chapter 2, we utilized *ceteris paribus,* which entails holding everything else around us constant (unchanged) while analyzing a specific relationship. Suppose that you omitted an important part of the relationship. What effect would this omission have on your ability to use graphs as an illustrative tool? Consider the relationship between sales of lemonade and sales of bottles of suntan lotion. The graph of the two variables would look something like Figure 2A.8.

FIGURE 2A.8

Graph with an Omitted Variable

What looks like a strongly positive correlation is misleading. What underlying variable is causing lemonade and suntan lotion sales to rise? The demand for both lemonade and suntan lotion rises because the temperature rises.

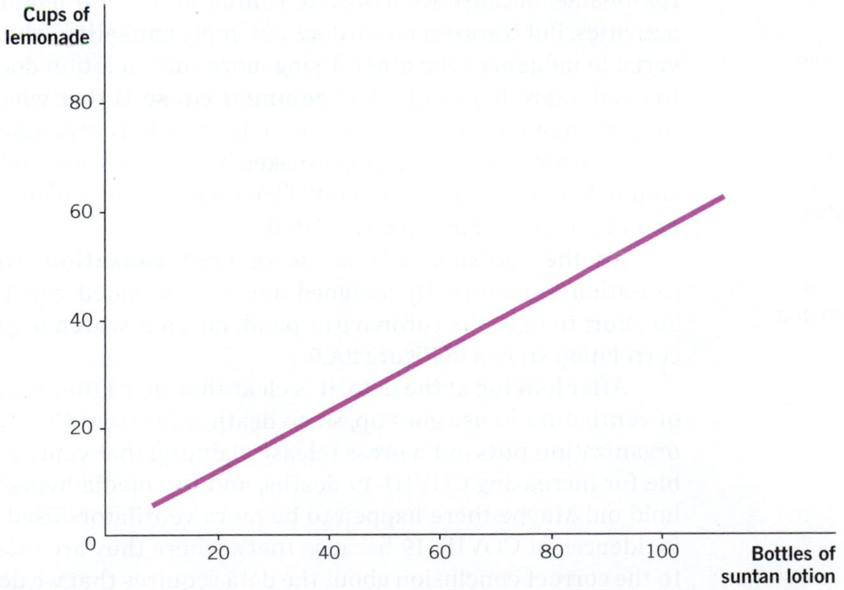

FIGURE 2A.9

Reverse Causation

COVID-19 deaths are associated with having more ventilators in use in a given area. But the ventilators are part of the treatment for the disease, not the cause of it. Suggesting that more ventilators in use causes more deaths from COVID-19 would be a mistake—an example of reverse causation.

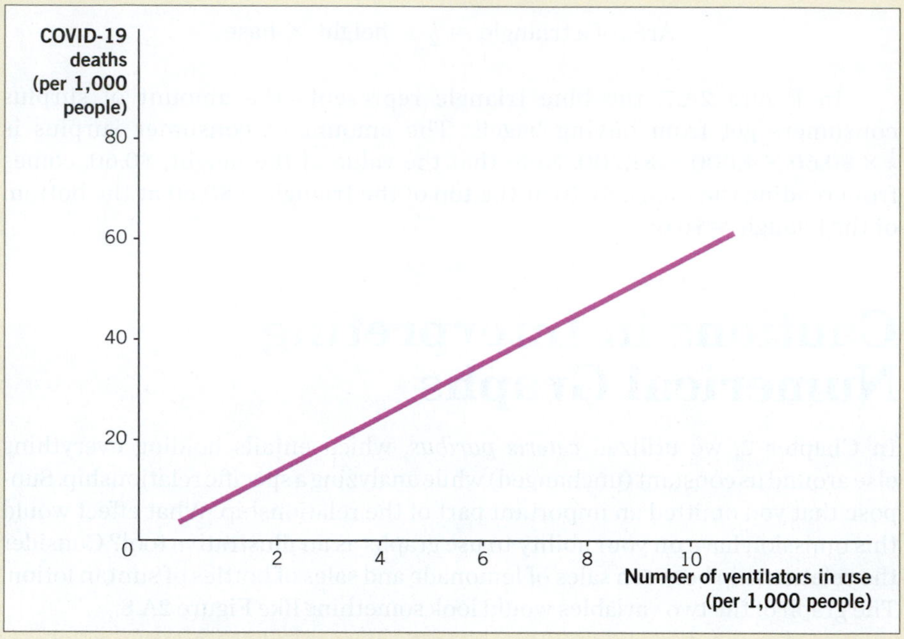

Looking at Figure 2A.8, you would not necessarily know that it is misleading. However, when you stop to think about the relationship, you quickly recognize that the graph is deceptive. Because the slope is positive, the graph indicates a positive correlation between the number of bottles of suntan lotion sold and the amount of lemonade sold. At first glance this relationship seems reasonable, because we associate suntan lotion and lemonade with summer activities. But the association does not imply **causality**, which occurs when one variable influences the other. Using more suntan lotion does not cause people to drink more lemonade. The **common cause** is that when it is hot outside, more suntan lotion is used and more lemonade is consumed. In this case, the causal factor is heat! The graph makes it look like the number of people using suntan lotion affects the amount of lemonade being consumed, when in fact the two variables are not directly related.

Causality occurs when one variable influences another.

A **common cause** is a single cause responsible for two phenomena observed to correlate with each other.

Reverse causation occurs when causation is incorrectly assigned among associated events.

Another possible mistake is **reverse causation**, which occurs when causation is incorrectly assigned among associated events. Suppose that in an effort to fight the coronavirus pandemic, a research organization notes the correlation shown in Figure 2A.9.

After looking at the data, it is clear that (per 1,000 people) as the number of ventilators in use goes up, so do death rates from COVID-19. The research organization puts out a press release claiming that ventilator use is responsible for increasing COVID-19 deaths, and the media hypes the discovery. But hold on! Maybe there happen to be more ventilators used in areas with high incidences of COVID-19 because that's where they are most needed. Coming to the correct conclusion about the data requires that we do more than simply look at the correlation.

APPENDIX PROBLEMS

Concepts You Should Know

causality (p. 68)
common cause (p. 68)
negative correlation (p. 62)
positive correlation (p. 62)
reverse causation (p. 68)
scatterplot (p. 62)
slope (p. 63)
variable (p. 59)

Study Problems (✱ *solved at the end of the section*)

1. The following table shows the price and the quantity demanded of apples (per week).

Price per apple	Quantity demanded
$0.25	10
$0.50	7
$0.75	4
$1.00	2
$1.25	1
$1.50	0

a. Plot the data provided in the table into a graph.
b. Is the relationship between the price of apples and the quantity demanded negative or positive?

✱ **2.** In the following graph, calculate the value of the slope if the price rises from $20 to $40.

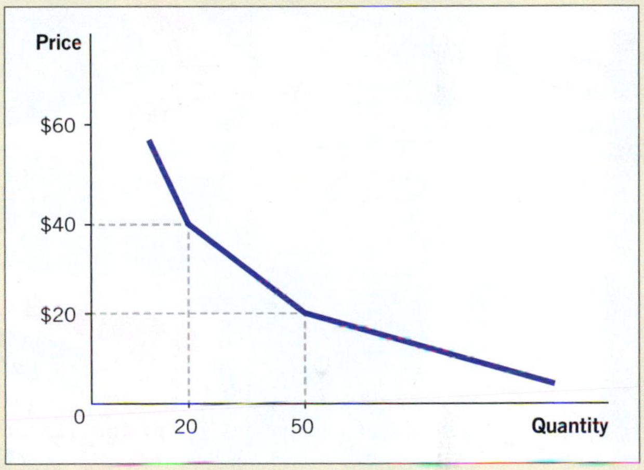

3. Explain the logical error in the following sentence: "As ice cream sales increase, the number of people who drown increases sharply. Therefore, ice cream causes drowning."

4. Of the following relationships, which are the result of a common cause or reverse causation?

a. Increased dash cam use causes more accidents to happen.
b. Increased sales of life jackets lead to more shark attacks.
c. When people wear sandals more often, it's because they're wearing shorts more often.

Solved Problem

2. The slope is calculated by using the formula:

$$\text{Slope} = \frac{\text{change in } y}{\text{change in } x} = \frac{\$40 - \$20}{20 - 50} = \frac{\$20}{-30} = -0.6667$$

MARKET

PART II

The Role of MARKETS

CHAPTER

03

The Market at Work: Supply and Demand

Buyers and Sellers Together Determine the Price of the Good.

What do Starbucks, Nordstrom, and Amazon have in common? If you guessed that they all have headquarters in Seattle, that's true. But even more interesting is that each company supplies a product much in demand by consumers. Starbucks supplies coffee from coast to coast and seems to be everywhere someone wants a cup of coffee. Nordstrom, a giant retailer with hundreds of department stores, supplies fashion apparel to meet a broad spectrum of individual demand, from the basics to designer collections. Amazon delivers online products to customers all over the world. When stores had to close during the COVID-19 pandemic, demand for Amazon products grew even more.

Notice the two recurring words in the previous paragraph: "supply" and "demand." Sometimes buyers set the price—through live auctions, on eBay, or at shopgoodwill.com. Other times, sellers set the price and then adjust it based on how well an item sells and how much inventory remains. Buyers and sellers each influence both prices and quantities traded, so that these end up being determined by how buyers' and sellers' price-versus-quantity calculations interact.

This chapter describes how markets work and discusses the nature of competition. To shed light on the process, we introduce the formal model of demand and supply. We begin

In-person holiday shopping isn't the same as before COVID-19. Consumer demand is moving away from Black Friday in-store specials toward online shopping, whether Cyber Monday discounts or others throughout the season. Retailers like Target and Walmart are shifting their promotions and supplies accordingly.

by looking at demand and supply separately. Then we combine them to see how they interact to establish the market price and determine how much is produced and sold.

· BIG QUESTIONS ·

- What are the fundamentals of markets?
- What determines demand?
- What determines supply?
- How do supply and demand interact to create equilibrium?

What Are the Fundamentals of Markets?

In a **market economy**, resources are allocated among households and firms with little or no government interference.

The **invisible hand** is a phrase coined by Adam Smith to refer to the unobservable market forces that guide resources to their highest-valued use.

Markets bring trading partners together to create order out of chaos. Companies supply goods and services, and customers want to obtain the goods and services that companies supply. In a **market economy**, resources are allocated among households and firms with little or no government interference. Adam Smith, the founder of modern economics, described the dynamic best: "It is not from the benevolence of the butcher, the brewer, or the baker, that we expect our dinner, but from their regard to their own interest." In other words, producers earn a living by selling the products consumers want. Consumers are also motivated by self-interest; they must decide how to use their money to select the goods they need or want the most. This process, which Adam Smith called the **invisible hand**, guides resources to their highest-valued use.

Peak season is expensive . . .

The exchange of goods and services in a market economy happens through prices that are established in markets. Those prices change according to the level of demand for a product and how much is supplied. For instance, hotel rates near Disney World are reduced in the fall when demand is low, and they peak in March when spring break occurs. If spring break takes you to a ski resort instead, you will find lots of company and high prices. But if you are looking for an outdoor adventure during the summer, ski resorts have plenty of lodging available at great rates. Or take your average college town. It will have plenty of affordable hotel rooms available on a normal weekend. But on graduation weekend? Not so much.

Unexpected events can disrupt the normal pricing calculus. As COVID-19 swept the United States, Disney World shut down, ski resorts closed runs, and college graduations went virtual. Suddenly, hotels struggled to attract customers at regular, off-season prices. The story was the same in the restaurant and travel industries.

Why does all of this happen? Supply and demand tell the story. We begin our exploration of supply and demand by looking at where they interact—in markets. A firm's degree of control over the market price is the distinguishing feature between *competitive markets* and *imperfect markets*.

. . . but off-season is a bargain.

Competitive Markets

Buyers and sellers of a specific good or service come together to form a market. Formally, a *market* is a collection of buyers and sellers of a particular product or service. The buyers create the demand for the product, while the sellers produce the supply. The interaction of the buyers and sellers in a market establishes the price and the quantity produced of a particular good or the amount of a service offered.

Trade creates value

Markets exist whenever goods and services are exchanged. Some markets are online, and others operate in traditional "brick and mortar" stores. Pike Place Market in Seattle is a collection of markets spread across 9 acres. For over a hundred years, it has brought together buyers and sellers of fresh, organic, and specialty foods. Because there is a large number of buyers and sellers for each type of product, we say that the markets at Pike Place are competitive. A **competitive market** is one in which there are so many buyers and sellers that each has only a small impact on the market price and output. In fact, the impact is so small that it is negligible.

A **competitive market** exists when there are so many buyers and sellers that each has only a small (negligible) impact on the market price and output.

At Pike Place Market, like other local markets, the goods sold by each vendor are similar. Because each buyer and seller is just one small part of the whole market, no single buyer or seller has any influence over the market price. These two characteristics—similar goods and many participants—create a highly competitive market in which the price and quantity sold of a good are determined by the market rather than by any one person or business.

To understand how competition works, let's look at sales of salmon at Pike Place Market. On any given day, dozens of vendors sell salmon at this market. If a single vendor is absent or runs out of salmon, the quantity supplied that day will not change significantly—the remaining sellers will have no trouble filling the void. The same is true for those buying salmon. Customers will have no trouble finding salmon at the remaining vendors. Whether a particular salmon buyer decides to show up on a given day makes little difference when hundreds of buyers visit the market each day. No single buyer or seller has any appreciable influence on the price of salmon. As a result, the market for salmon at Pike Place Market is a competitive one.

One of many vendors at Pike Place Market.

The EdgeWalk atop the CN Tower in Toronto is a one-of-kind attraction.

Imperfect Markets

Markets are not always fully competitive. British economist Joan Robinson wrote that in imperfect competition, "a certain difficulty arises [because] the individual demand curve for the product of each of the firms . . . will depend to some extent upon the price policy of the others."* Accordingly, we define these **imperfect markets** as markets in which either the buyer or the seller can influence the market price. For example, the CN Tower in Toronto affords an iconic view of the city. Not surprisingly, the cost of taking the elevator to the top of the building is not cheap. But many customers buy the tickets anyway, because they have decided that the view is worth the price. The managers of the CN Tower can set a high price for tickets because there is no other place in Toronto with such a great view. Once at the top, you can also take the EdgeWalk, a dizzying, hands-free trip around the top of the tower's main pod, 116 stories above the ground. Of course, you'll have to pay extra. From this example, we see that when sellers produce goods and services that are different from their competitors', they gain some control, or leverage, over the price they charge. The more unusual the product being sold, the more control the seller has over the price. When a seller has some control over the price, we say that the market is imperfect. Specialized products, such as popular video games, front-row concert tickets, or dinner reservations at a trendy restaurant, give the seller substantial pricing power. **Market power** is a firm's ability to influence the price of a good or service by exercising control over its demand, supply, or both.

An **imperfect market** is one in which either the buyer or the seller can influence the market price.

Market power is a firm's ability to influence the price of a good or service by exercising control over its demand, supply, or both.

In between the highly competitive environment at the Pike Place Market and markets characterized by a lack of competition, such as the CN Tower with its one-of-a-kind attraction, there are many other types of markets. Some, like the market for fast-food restaurants, are highly competitive but sell products that are not identical. Other businesses—for example, Comcast Cable—function like monopolies because they are the only provider of a service in a geographic area. A **monopoly** exists when a single company supplies the entire market for a particular good or service. We'll talk a lot more about different market structures, such as monopoly, in later chapters. But even in imperfect markets, the forces of supply and demand significantly influence producer and consumer behavior. For the time being, we'll keep our analysis focused on supply and demand in competitive markets.

A **monopoly** exists when a single company supplies the entire market for a particular good or service.

What Determines Demand?

Demand exists when an individual or group wants something badly enough to pay or trade for it. How much an individual or group actually buys depends on the price of the good or service. In economics, the amount of a good or service that buyers are willing and able to purchase at the current price is known as the **quantity demanded**.

The **quantity demanded** is the amount of a good or service that buyers are willing and able to purchase at the current price.

When the price of a good increases, consumers often respond by purchasing less of the good or buying something else. For instance, many consumers who would buy salmon at $5 per pound would likely buy something else if the price of salmon rose to $20 per pound. Therefore, as price goes up, quantity

*Joan Robinson, *The Economics of Imperfect Competition* (London: Macmillan, 1933).

PRACTICE WHAT YOU KNOW

Markets and the Nature of Competition

QUESTION: Which of the following are competitive markets? How will each firm price its products, and how much market power does each firm have?

1. gas stations at a busy interstate exit
2. a firm that develops a vaccine for a new disease
3. a fresh produce stand at a farmers' market

Is this a competitive market?

ANSWERS

1. Because each gas station sells the same product and competes for the same customers, they often charge the same price. This is a competitive market. However, gas stations also differentiate themselves by offering conveniences such as fast food, clean restrooms, ATM machines, and so forth. The result is that individual stations have some market power.
2. The firm has something that people need and other sellers can't provide. The developer can charge whatever customers will pay, without worrying about rivals offering the same vaccine at a lower price. This is not a competitive market.
3. Because consumers can buy fresh produce in season from many stands at a farmers' market, individual vendors have very little market pricing power. They must charge the same price as other vendors in order to attract customers. This is a competitive market.

demanded goes down. Similarly, as price goes down, quantity demanded goes up. This negative (opposite) relationship between the price and the quantity demanded is the law of demand. The **law of demand** states that, all other things being equal, the quantity demanded falls when the price rises, and the quantity demanded rises when the price falls. The law of demand holds true over a wide range of goods and settings.

Trade creates value

The **law of demand** states that, all other things being equal, quantity demanded falls when the price rises, and rises when the price falls.

The Demand Curve

A table that shows the relationship between the price of a good and the quantity demanded is known as a **demand schedule**. To discuss this idea (and to take a break from fish markets), let's introduce a new hypothetical involving action hero and former athlete Dwayne "The Rock" Johnson. The Rock gets a lot of bumps and bruises in his active career, and Table 3.1 shows The Rock's hypothetical demand schedule for healing crystals. When the price is $20.00 or more per crystal, The Rock will not purchase any crystals. However, below $20.00, the amount The Rock purchases is negatively related to the price. For instance, at a price of $10.00, The Rock demands 4 crystals. If the price rises to $12.50, he demands 3 crystals. Every time the price increases, The Rock buys fewer crystals. In contrast, every time the price falls, he buys more. If the price falls to zero, The Rock would demand 8 crystals. That is, even if the crystals are free, there is a limit to his demand because he would grow tired of using the crystals.

A **demand schedule** is a table that shows the relationship between the price of a good and the quantity demanded.

Incentives

TABLE 3.1

The Rock's Demand for Healing Crystals

Price of healing crystals	Number demanded
$20.00	0
17.50	1
15.00	2
12.50	3
10.00	4
7.50	5
5.00	6
2.50	7
0.00	8

A **demand curve** is a graph of the relationship between the prices in the demand schedule and the quantity demanded at those prices.

The numbers in The Rock's demand schedule from Table 3.1 are plotted on a graph in Figure 3.1, known as a demand curve. A **demand curve** is a graph of the relationship between the prices in the demand schedule and the quantity demanded at those prices. For simplicity, the demand "curve" is often drawn as a straight line. Economists always place the independent variable, which is the price, on the *y* (vertical) axis and the dependent

FIGURE 3.1

The Rock's Demand Curve for Healing Crystals

The Rock's demand curve for healing crystals plots the data from Table 3.1. When the price of a crystal is $10.00, he buys 4. If the price rises to $12.50, The Rock reduces the quantity he buys to 3. The figure illustrates the law of demand by showing a negative relationship between price and the quantity demanded.

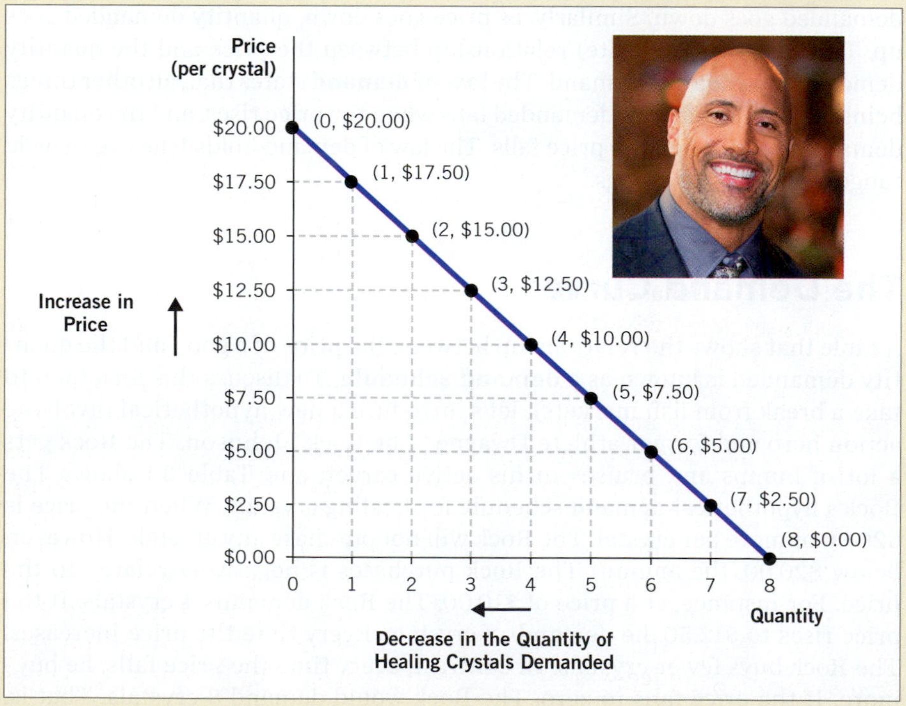

variable, which is the quantity demanded, on the x (horizontal) axis. The relationship between the price and the quantity demanded produces a downward-sloping curve. In Figure 3.1, we see that as the price rises from $0.00 to $20.00 along the y axis, the quantity demanded decreases from 8 to 0 along the x axis.

Market Demand

So far, we have studied individual demand, but a market is composed of many different buyers. In this section, we examine the collective demand of all of the buyers in a given market.

The **market demand** is the sum of all the individual quantities demanded by each buyer in a market at each price. During a typical day, thousands of individuals buy healing crystals. However, to make our analysis simpler, let's assume that our market consists of only two buyers, The Rock and Emma Stone, each of whom enjoys using healing crystals. Figure 3.2 shows individual demand schedules for the two people in this market, a combined market demand schedule, and the corresponding graphs. At a price of $10, Emma buys 2 crystals, while The Rock buys 4. To determine the market demand curve, we add Emma's 2 to The Rock's 4 for a total of 6 crystals. As you can see in the table within Figure 3.2, by adding Emma's demand and The Rock's demand, we arrive at the total (that is, combined) market demand. Any demand curve shows the law of demand with movements along (up or down) the curve that reflect the effect of a price change on the quantity demanded of the good or service. Only a change in price can cause a movement along a demand curve.

Market demand
is the sum of all the individual quantities demanded by each buyer in the market at each price.

Shifts of the Demand Curve

We have examined the relationship between price and quantity demanded. This relationship, described by the law of demand, shows us that when price changes, consumers respond by altering the amount they purchase. But in addition to price, many other variables influence how much of a good or service is purchased. For instance, news about the possible risks or benefits associated with the consumption of a good or service can change overall demand.

Suppose the government issues a nationwide safety warning that cautions against eating mango because of a recent discovery of *Listeria* bacteria in some mangoes. The government warning would cause consumers to buy fewer mangoes at any given price, and overall demand would decline. Looking at Figure 3.3, we see that an overall decline in demand will cause the entire demand curve to shift to the left of the original curve, from D_1 to D_2. Note that though the price remains at $5 per mango, demand has moved from 6 mangoes to 3. Figure 3.3 also shows what does *not* cause a shift of the demand curve: the price. The orange arrow alongside D_1 indicates that the quantity demanded will rise or fall in response to a price change. *A price change causes a movement along a given demand curve, but it cannot cause a shift of the demand curve.*

FIGURE 3.2

Calculating Market Demand

To calculate the market demand for healing crystals, we add Emma Stone's quantity demanded and The Rock's quantity demanded.

Price of healing crystals	Emma's demand	The Rock's demand	Combined market demand
$20.00	0	0	0
17.50	0	1	1
15.00	1	2	3
12.50	1	3	4
10.00	2	4	6
7.50	2	5	7
5.00	3	6	9
2.50	3	7	10
0.00	4	8	12

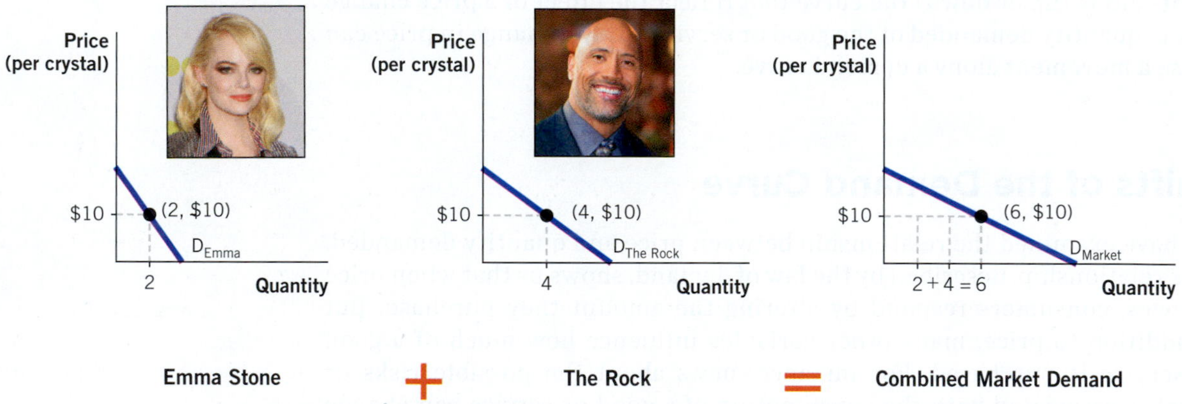

Purchasing power is the value of your income expressed in terms of how much you can afford.

Incentives

A decrease in overall demand shifts the demand curve to the left. What happens when a variable causes overall demand to increase? Suppose that the news media have just announced the results of a medical study indicating that a mango contains a natural substance that lowers cholesterol. Because of the newly discovered health benefits of the mango, overall demand for it will increase. This increase in demand shifts the demand curve to the right, from D_1 to D_3, as Figure 3.3 shows.

FIGURE 3.3

A Shift of the Demand Curve

When the price changes, the quantity demanded changes along the existing demand curve, as indicated by the orange arrow. A shift of the demand curve, indicated by the black arrows, occurs when something other than price changes.

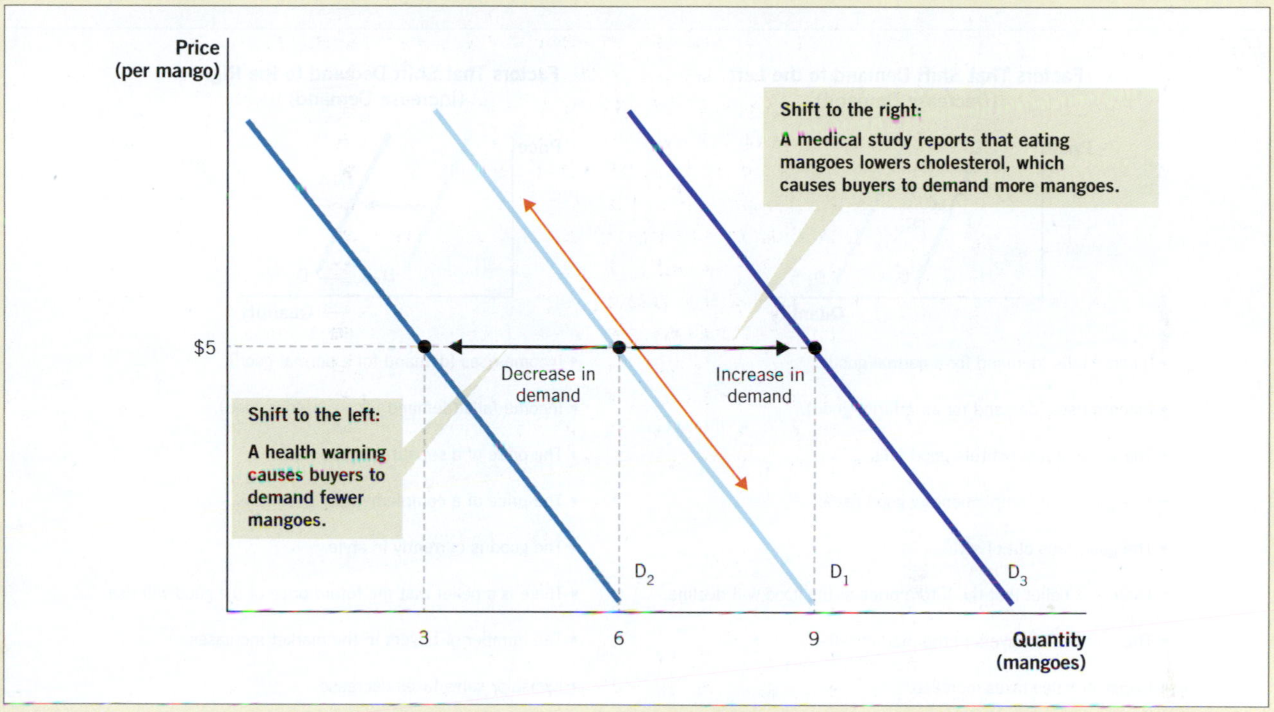

In our mango example, we saw that demand shifted because of changes in consumers' tastes and preferences. However, many different variables can shift demand. These include changes in buyers' income, the price of related goods, changes in buyers' tastes and preferences, price expectations, the number of buyers, and taxes.

Figure 3.4 provides an overview of the variables, or factors, that can shift demand. The easiest way to keep all of these elements straight is to ask yourself a simple question: Would this change cause me to buy more or less of the good? If the change reduces how much you would buy at any given price, you shift the demand curve to the left. If the change increases how much you would buy at any given price, you shift the curve to the right.

CHANGES IN BUYERS' INCOME When your income goes up, you have more to spend. Assuming that prices don't change, individuals with higher incomes are able to buy more of what they want. Similarly, when your income declines, your **purchasing power**, or how much you can afford, falls. In either case, your income affects your overall demand.

If a new medical study indicates that eating more mango lowers cholesterol, would this finding cause a shift in demand, or a movement along the demand curve?

FIGURE 3.4

Factors That Shift the Demand Curve

The demand curve shifts to the left when a factor decreases demand. The demand curve shifts to the right when a factor increases demand. (*Note:* A change in price does not cause a shift. Price changes cause movements along the demand curve.)

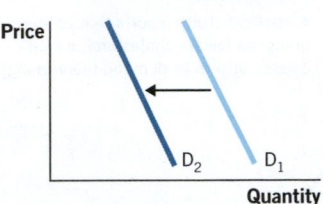

Factors That Shift Demand to the Left (Decrease Demand)

- Income falls (demand for a normal good).
- Income rises (demand for an inferior good).
- The price of a substitute good falls.
- The price of a complementary good rises.
- The good falls out of style.
- There is a belief that the future price of the good will decline.
- The number of buyers in the market falls.
- Excise or sales taxes increase.
- Subsidies to consumers decrease.

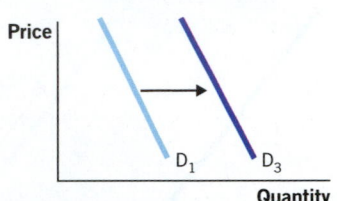

Factors That Shift Demand to the Right (Increase Demand)

- Income rises (demand for a normal good).
- Income falls (demand for an inferior good).
- The price of a substitute good rises.
- The price of a complementary good falls.
- The good is currently in style.
- There is a belief that the future price of the good will rise.
- The number of buyers in the market increases.
- Excise or sales taxes decrease.
- Subsidies to consumers increase.

Consumers buy more of a **normal good** as income rises, holding all other factors constant.

An **inferior good** is one where demand declines as income rises.

When economists look at how consumers spend, they often differentiate between two types of goods: normal and inferior. Consumers will buy more of a **normal good** as their income goes up (assuming all other factors remain constant). An example of a normal good is a meal at a restaurant. When income goes up, the demand for restaurant meals increases and the demand curve shifts to the right. Similarly, if income falls, the demand for restaurant meals goes down and the demand curve shifts to the left.

While consumers with an increased income may purchase more of some things, the additional purchasing power will mean they purchase fewer inferior goods. An **inferior good** is one where demand declines as income rises. Examples include rooms in boardinghouses, as opposed to one's own apartment or house, and hamburgers and ramen noodles, as opposed to filet mignon. As income goes up, consumers buy less of an inferior good because they can afford something better. Within a specific product market, you can often find examples of inferior and normal goods in the form of different brands.

THE PRICE OF RELATED GOODS Another factor that can shift the demand curve is the price of related goods. Certain goods directly influence the demand for other goods. **Complements** are two goods that are used together. **Substitutes** are two goods that are used in place of each other.

Complements are two goods that are used together. When the price of a complementary good rises, the quantity demanded of that good falls and the demand for the related good goes down.

Substitutes are two goods that are used in place of each other. When the price of a substitute good rises, the quantity demanded of that good falls and the demand for the related good goes up.

Consider this pair of complements: smartphones and phone cases. What happens when the price of one of the complements—say, the smartphone—rises? As you would expect, the quantity demanded of the smartphone goes down. The demand for its complement, the phone case, also goes down because people are not likely to use one without the other.

Substitute goods work the opposite way. When the price of a substitute good increases, the quantity demanded declines, and the demand for the alternative good increases. For example, if the price of the PlayStation 4 goes up and the price of Microsoft's Xbox remains unchanged, the demand for Xbox will increase while the quantity demanded of the PS4 will decline.

CHANGES IN TASTES AND PREFERENCES Fashion goes in and out of style quickly. Walk into Nordstrom or another clothing retailer, and you will see that fashion changes from season to season and year to year. For instance, what do you think of Crocs? They first became popular in 2006 and are still a common sight today, but they cycle in and out of fashion, so it is safe to assume that in a few years they will once again go out of style. While something is popular, demand increases. As soon as it falls out of favor, you can expect demand for it to decrease. Tastes and preferences can change quickly, and this fluctuation alters the demand for a particular good.

Though changes in fashion trends are usually purely subjective, other changes in preferences are the result of new information about the goods and services we buy. Recall our example of shifting demand for mangoes as the result of either the *Listeria* infection or new positive medical findings. This is one example of how information can influence consumers' preferences. Contamination would cause a decrease in demand because people would no longer want to eat mangoes. In contrast, if people learn that eating mangoes lowers cholesterol, their demand for the fruit will go up.

PRICE EXPECTATIONS Have you ever waited to purchase a sweater because warm weather was right around the corner and you expected the price to come down? Conversely, have you ever purchased an airline ticket well in advance because you figured that the price would rise as the flight filled up? In both cases, expectations about the future influenced your current demand. If we expect a price to be higher tomorrow, we are likely to buy more today to beat the price increase. The result is an increase in current demand. Likewise, if you expect a price to decline soon, you might delay your purchases to try to get a lower price in the future. An expectation of a lower price in the future will therefore decrease current demand.

Are these Crocs stylish or fit for the dumpster? It depends on consumers' tastes in fashion at the time.

· ECONOMICS *in the* MEDIA ·

Peter Quill's Orb Auction

In *Guardians of the Galaxy*, treasure hunter Peter Quill recovers a mysterious orb from ancient ruins on the planet Morag. But when he delivers the orb to The Broker, who hired him, Quill reveals that someone else is after it, too: Ronan, a hulking blue-faced alien famed for his ruthlessness. Frightened, The Broker now wants nothing to do with the orb. Meanwhile, however, others are showing interest. The orb, you see . . .

Well, you should watch the film. Suffice it to say, a lot of people are after that orb. Besides Ronan, there's The Collector, and there's Thanos, a world-destroying supervillain, as well as Thanos's adopted daughters, Gamora and Nebula.

Peter Quill quickly learns that demand for the orb is high.

Once Quill learns the secret of the orb, he cooks up a plan to sell it to the highest bidder. Busy dodging blaster shots, Quill isn't exactly thinking about economics. But if he were, he'd tell you that with more and more buyers trying to acquire the orb, the demand curve is shifting to the right, as shown in the figure. The shift should result in a higher price. Of course, this being an action thriller set in space, Quill's plan is bound to hit some speed bumps.

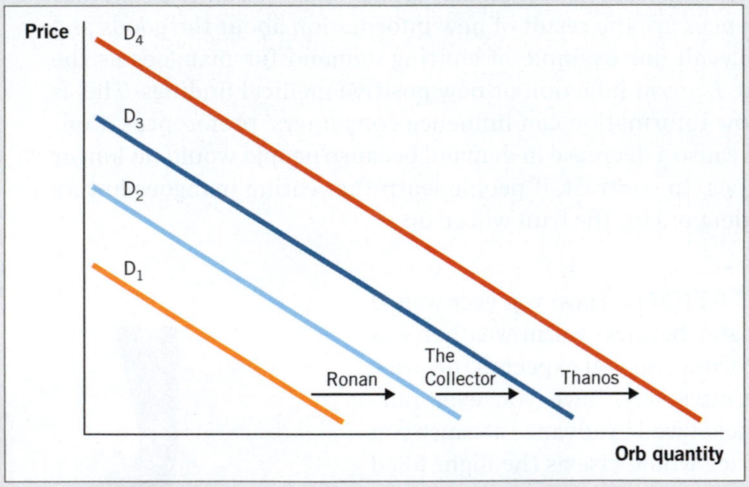

THE NUMBER OF BUYERS Recall that the market demand curve is the sum of all individual demand curves. Therefore, another way for market demand to increase is for more individual buyers to enter the market. The United States adds 3 million people each year to its population through immigration and births. All those new people have needs and wants, just as the

PRACTICE WHAT YOU KNOW

Shift of the Curve or Movement along the Curve?

Cheap pizza or . . .

. . . cheap drinks?

QUESTION: Suppose that a local pizza place likes to run a late-night special. The owners have contacted you for some advice. One of the owners tells you, "We want to increase the demand for our pizza." He proposes two marketing ideas to accomplish this goal:

1. Reduce the price of large pizzas.
2. Reduce the price of a complementary good—for example, offer two half-priced bottles or cans of soda with every large pizza ordered.

Which strategy will you recommend?

ANSWER: First, consider why late-night specials exist in the first place. Because most people prefer to eat dinner early in the evening, the pizzeria has to encourage late-night patrons to buy pizzas by stimulating demand. "Specials" are used during periods of low demand, when regular prices would leave the establishment largely empty.

Incentives

Next, look at what the question asks. The owners want to know which option would "increase demand" more. The question is very specific; the owners are looking for something that will increase (or shift) demand.

Consider the first option, a reduction in the price of pizzas. Let's look at this option graphically (see next graph). A reduction in the price of a large pizza causes a movement along the demand curve, or a change in the quantity demanded.

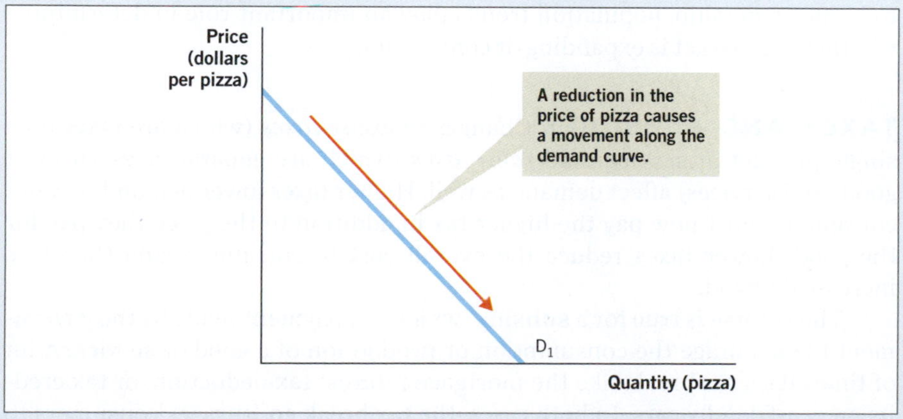

(CONTINUED)

Now consider the second option, a reduction in the price of a complementary good. Let's look at this option graphically (next graph). A reduction in the price of a complementary good (for example, soda) causes the entire demand curve to shift. This is the correct answer, because the question asks which marketing idea would increase (or shift) demand more.

Incentives

Recall that a reduction in the price of a complementary good shifts the demand curve to the right. The other answer, cutting the price of pizzas, causes a movement along the existing demand curve, which does not increase demand.

If you move along a curve instead of shifting it, you will analyze the problem incorrectly.

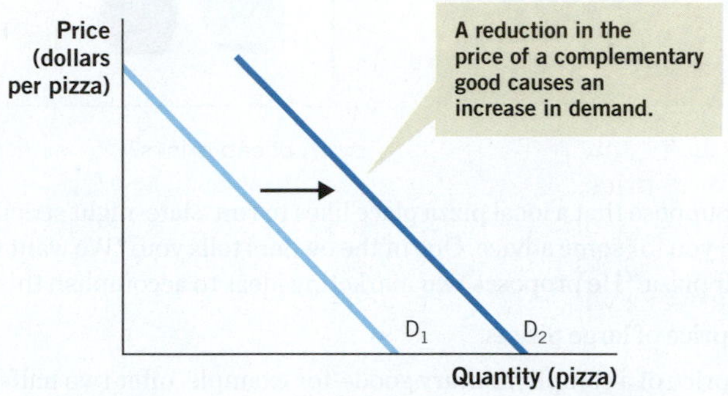

existing population of 325 million does. Collectively, the new people add about 1% to the overall size of many existing markets on an annual basis.

The number of buyers also varies by age. Consider two markets—one for baby products (such as diapers, high chairs, and strollers) and the other for health care (including medicine, cancer treatments, hip replacement surgery, and nursing facilities). In countries with aging populations—for example, in Japan, where the birthrate has plummeted over several generations—the demand for baby products will decline and the demand for health care will expand. In other words, demographic changes in society are another source of shifts in demand. In many markets, ranging from movie theater attendance to home ownership, population trends play an important role in determining whether the market is expanding or contracting.

Incentives

TAXES AND SUBSIDIES Changes in *excise taxes* (which are taxes on a single product or service) and *sales taxes* (which are general taxes on most goods and services) affect demand as well. Higher taxes lower demand because consumers must now pay the higher tax in addition to the price they pay for the good. Lower taxes reduce the overall cost to consumers and therefore increase demand.

A **subsidy** is a payment made by the government to encourage the consumption or production of a good or service.

The reverse is true for a **subsidy**, which is a payment made by the government to encourage the consumption or production of a good or service. A lot of times it's a tax break, like the mortgage interest tax deduction, or tax credits on eco-friendly cars. In both cases, the tax break encourages consumers to purchase more of the subsidized good.

What Determines Supply?

Even though we have learned a great deal about demand, our understanding of markets is incomplete without also analyzing supply. Let's go back to Seattle's Pike Place Market and focus on the behavior of producers selling goods there.

We have seen that with demand, price and output are *negatively related*. That is, they move in opposite directions. With supply, however, the price level and quantity supplied are *positively related*. That is, they move in the same direction. For instance, few producers would sell salmon if the market price were $2.50 per pound, but many would sell it at a price of $20.00 per pound. (At $20.00, producers earn more profit than they do at a price of $2.50.) The **quantity supplied** is the amount of a good or service that producers are willing and able to sell at the current price. Higher prices cause the quantity supplied to increase. Conversely, lower prices cause the quantity supplied to decrease.

The **quantity supplied** is the amount of a good or service producers are willing and able to sell at the current price.

When price increases, producers often respond by offering more for sale. As price goes down, quantity supplied also goes down. This direct positive relationship between price and quantity supplied is the law of supply. The **law of supply** states that, all other things being equal, the quantity supplied increases when the price rises, and the quantity supplied falls when the price falls. This law holds true over a wide range of goods and settings.

The **law of supply** states that, all other things being equal, the quantity supplied of a good rises when the price of the good rises, and falls when the price of the good falls.

The Supply Curve

A **supply schedule** is a table that shows the relationship between the price of a good and the quantity supplied. The supply schedule for salmon in Table 3.2 shows how many pounds of salmon Sol Amon, owner of Pure Food Fish, would sell each month at different prices. (Pure Food Fish is a fish stand that sells all kinds of freshly caught seafood.) When the market price is $20.00 per pound, Sol is willing to sell 800 pounds. At $12.50, Sol's quantity offered is 500 pounds. If the price falls to $10.00, he offers 400 pounds. Every time the price falls, Sol offers less salmon. This means he is constantly adjusting the amount he offers.

A **supply schedule** is a table that shows the relationship between the price of a good and the quantity supplied.

TABLE 3.2

Pure Food Fish's Supply Schedule for Salmon

Price of salmon (per pound)	Pounds of salmon supplied (per month)
$20.00	800
17.50	700
15.00	600
12.50	500
10.00	400
7.50	300
5.00	200
2.50	100
0.00	0

FIGURE 3.5

Pure Food Fish's Supply Curve for Salmon

Pure Food Fish's supply curve for salmon plots the data from Table 3.2. When the price of salmon is $10.00 per pound, Pure Food Fish supplies 400 pounds. If the price rises to $12.50 per pound, Pure Food Fish increases its quantity supplied to 500 pounds. The figure illustrates the law of supply by showing a positive relationship between price and the quantity supplied.

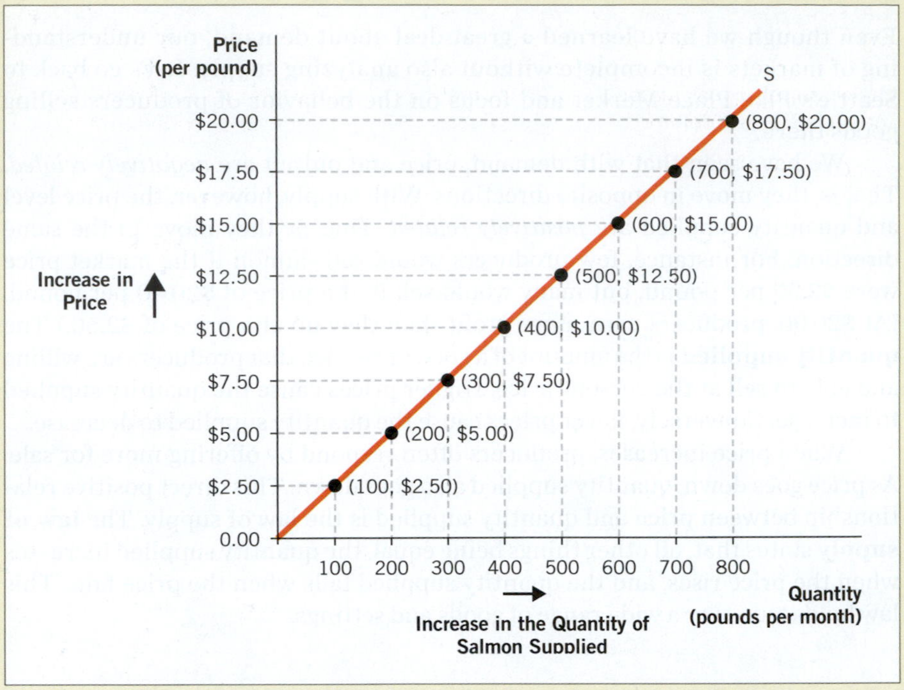

As the price of salmon falls, so does Sol's profit from selling it. Because Sol's livelihood depends on selling seafood, he has to find a way to compensate for the lost income. So he might offer more cod instead.

Sol and the other seafood vendors must respond to price changes by adjusting what they offer for sale in the market. This is why Sol offers more salmon when the price rises and less salmon when the price declines.

A **supply curve** is a graph of the relationship between the prices in the supply schedule and the quantity supplied at those prices.

When we plot the supply schedule in Table 3.2, we get the supply curve shown in Figure 3.5. A **supply curve** is a graph of the relationship between the prices in the supply schedule and the quantity supplied at those prices. As you can see in Figure 3.5, this relationship produces an upward-sloping curve. Sellers are more willing to supply the market when prices are high, because this higher price generates more profits for the business. The upward-sloping curve means that the slope of the supply curve is positive, which illustrates a direct (positive) relationship between the price and the quantity offered for sale. For instance, when the price of salmon increases from $10.00 per pound to $12.50 per pound, Pure Food Fish will increase the quantity it supplies to the market from 400 pounds to 500 pounds.

Incentives

Market Supply

Market supply is the sum of the quantities supplied by each seller in the market at each price.

Sol Amon is not the only vendor selling fish at the Pike Place Market. The **market supply** is the sum of the quantities supplied by each seller in the market at each price. However, to make our analysis simpler, let's assume

FIGURE 3.6

Calculating Market Supply

Market supply is calculated by adding together the quantity supplied by individual vendors. The total quantity supplied, shown in the last column of the table, is illustrated in the market supply graph below.

Price of salmon (per pound)	City Fish's supply (per month)	Pure Food Fish's supply (per month)	Combined market supply (pounds of salmon)
$20.00	200	800	1000
17.50	175	700	875
15.00	150	600	750
12.50	125	500	625
10.00	100	400	500
7.50	75	300	375
5.00	50	200	250
2.50	25	100	125
0.00	0	0	0

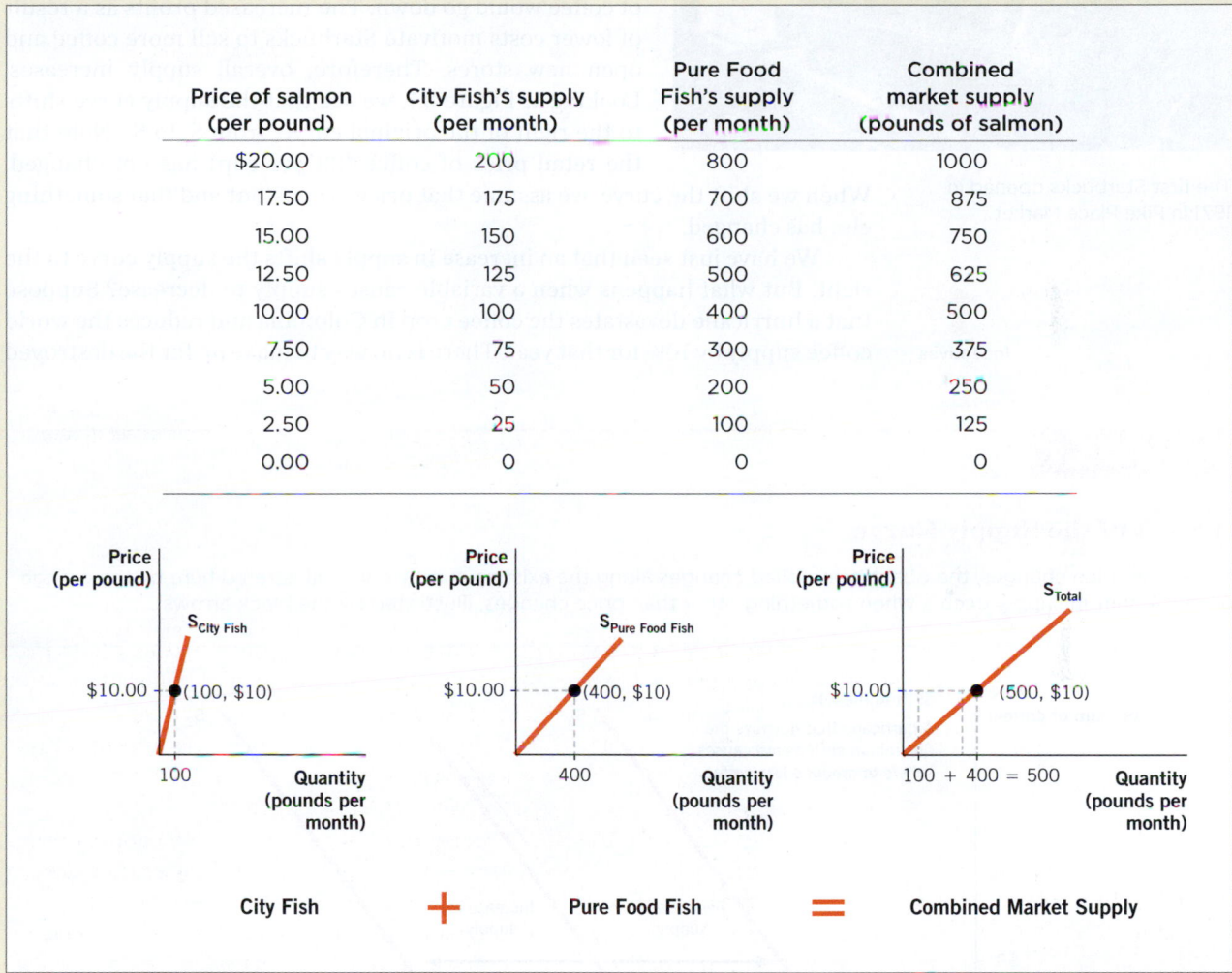

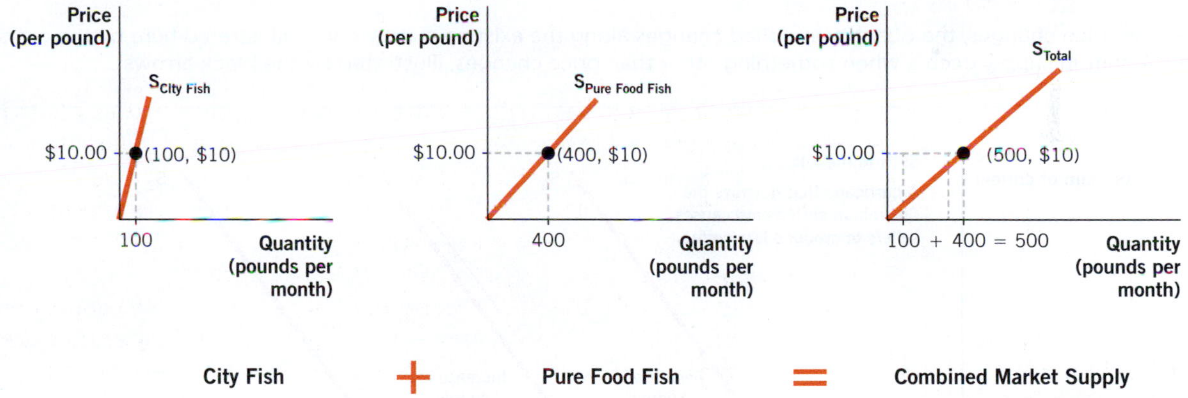

that our market consists of just two sellers, City Fish and Pure Food Fish, each of which sells salmon. Figure 3.6 shows supply schedules for those two fish sellers and the combined, total-market supply schedule and the corresponding graphs.

Looking at the supply schedule (the table within the figure), you can see that at a price of $10.00 per pound, City Fish supplies 100 pounds of salmon, while Pure Food Fish supplies 400 pounds. To determine the total market supply, we add City Fish's 100 pounds to Pure Food Fish's 400 pounds for a total market supply of 500 pounds.

The first Starbucks opened in 1971 in Pike Place Market.

Shifts of the Supply Curve

When a variable other than the price changes, the entire supply curve shifts. For instance, suppose that beverage scientists at Starbucks discover a new way to brew a richer coffee at half the cost. The new process would increase the company's profits because its costs of supplying a cup of coffee would go down. The increased profits as a result of lower costs motivate Starbucks to sell more coffee and open new stores. Therefore, overall supply increases. Looking at Figure 3.7, we see that the supply curve shifts to the right of the original curve, from S_1 to S_2. Note that the retail price of coffee ($3 per cup) has not changed. When we shift the curve, we assume that price is constant and that something else has changed.

Incentives

We have just seen that an increase in supply shifts the supply curve to the right. But what happens when a variable causes supply to decrease? Suppose that a hurricane devastates the coffee crop in Colombia and reduces the world coffee supply by 10% for that year. There is no way to make up for the destroyed

FIGURE 3.7

A Shift of the Supply Curve

When the price changes, the quantity supplied changes along the existing supply curve, illustrated here by the orange arrow. A shift in supply occurs when something other than price changes, illustrated by the black arrows.

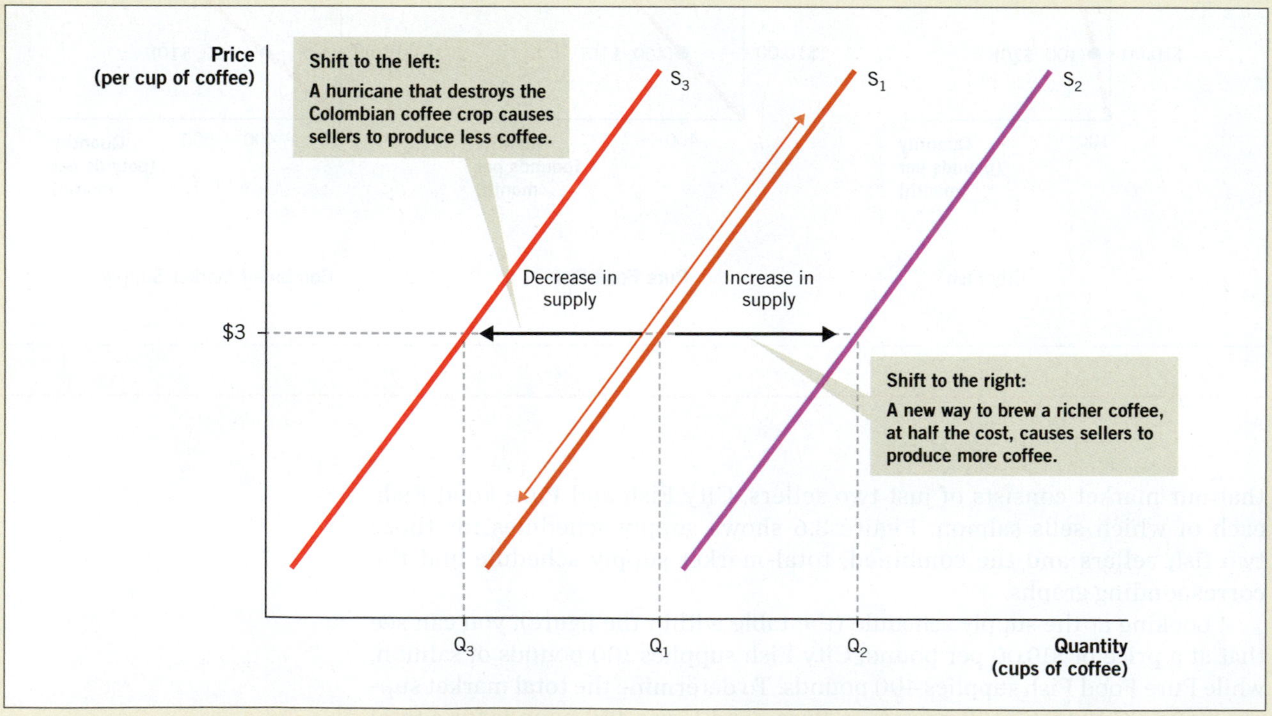

coffee crop, and for the rest of the year at least, the quantity of coffee supplied will be less than the previous year. This decrease in supply shifts the supply curve in Figure 3.7 to the left, from S_1 to S_3.

Many variables can shift supply, but Figure 3.7 also reminds us of what does *not* cause a shift in supply: the price. Recall that price is the variable that causes the supply curve to slope upward. The orange arrow alongside S_1 indicates that the quantity supplied will rise or fall in response to a price change. *A price change causes a movement along the supply curve, not a shift in the curve.*

Factors that shift the supply curve include the cost of inputs, changes in technology or the production process, taxes and subsidies, the number of firms in the industry, and price expectations. Figure 3.8 provides an overview of these variables that shift the supply curve. The easiest way to keep them straight is to ask yourself a simple question: Would the change cause a business to produce more of the good or less of the good? If the change would reduce the amount of a good or service a business is willing and able to supply at every given price, the supply curve shifts to the left. If the change would increase the amount of a good or service a business is willing and able to supply at every given price, the supply curve shifts to the right.

THE COST OF INPUTS Inputs are resources used in the production process. Inputs may include workers, equipment, raw materials, buildings, and capital goods. Each of these resources is critical to the production process.

Inputs
are resources used in the production process.

FIGURE 3.8

Factors That Shift the Supply Curve

The supply curve shifts to the left when a factor decreases supply. The supply curve shifts to the right when a factor increases supply. (*Note*: A change in price does not cause a shift. Price changes cause movements along the supply curve.)

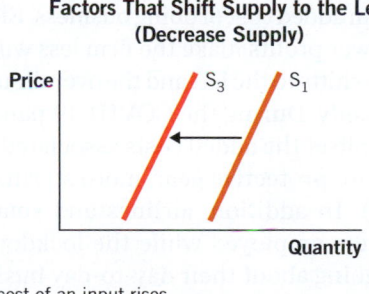

Factors That Shift Supply to the Left (Decrease Supply)

- The cost of an input rises.
- Business taxes increase or subsidies decrease.
- The number of sellers decreases.
- The price of the product is anticipated to rise in the future.
- Capital or resource destruction (e.g., damage caused by a hurricane).

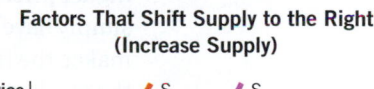

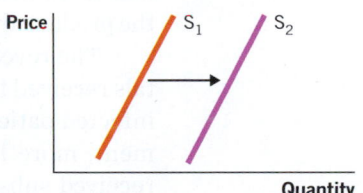

Factors That Shift Supply to the Right (Increase Supply)

- The cost of an input falls.
- Business taxes decrease or subsidies increase.
- The number of sellers increases.
- The price of the product is expected to fall in the future.
- The business deploys more efficient technology.

Baristas' wages make up a large share of the cost of selling coffee.

When the cost of inputs changes, so does the seller's profit. If the cost of inputs declines, profits improve. Improved profits make the firm more willing to supply the good. So, for example, if Starbucks is able to purchase coffee beans at a significantly reduced price, it will want to supply more coffee. Conversely, higher input costs reduce profits. For instance, at Starbucks, the salaries of Starbucks store employees (or baristas, as they are commonly called) are a large part of the production cost. An increase in the minimum wage would require Starbucks to pay its workers more. This higher minimum wage would raise the cost of making coffee and make Starbucks less willing to supply the same amount of coffee at the same price.

CHANGES IN TECHNOLOGY OR THE PRODUCTION PROCESS *Technology* encompasses knowledge that producers use to make their products. An improvement in technology enables a producer to increase output with the same resources or to produce a given level of output with fewer resources. For example, if a new espresso machine works twice as fast as the old machine, Starbucks could serve its customers more quickly, reduce long lines, and increase its sales. As a result, Starbucks would be willing to produce and sell more espressos at each price in its established menu. In other words, if the producers of a good discover a new and improved technology or a better production process, there will be an increase in supply. That is, the supply curve for the good will shift to the right.

TAXES AND SUBSIDIES Taxes placed on suppliers are an added cost of doing business. For example, if property taxes are increased, the cost of doing business goes up. A firm may attempt to pass along the tax to consumers through higher prices, but higher prices will discourage sales. So, in some cases, the firm will simply have to accept the taxes as an added cost of doing business. Either way, a tax makes the firm less profitable. Lower profits make the firm less willing to supply the product; thus, the supply curve shifts to the left and the overall supply declines.

The reverse is true for a subsidy. During the COVID-19 pandemic, hospitals received federal subsidies to offset the added costs associated with treating infected patients (more tests, more protective gear, more sterilizing of equipment, more laundry, and so on). In addition, airlines and small businesses received subsidies to keep workers employed while the lockdown prevented people from traveling and from going about their day-to-day business at work. As a result, more essential workers remained employed, compared to what would have happened without the subsidies.

THE NUMBER OF FIRMS IN THE INDUSTRY We saw that an increase in total buyers (population) shifts the demand curve to the right. A similar dynamic happens with an increase in the number of sellers in an industry. Each additional firm that enters the market increases the available supply of a good. In graphic form, the supply curve shifts to the right to reflect the increased

ECONOMICS IN THE REAL WORLD

WHY DO THE PRICES OF NEW ELECTRONICS ALWAYS DROP?

The first personal computers (PCs) released in the 1980s cost as much as $10,000. Today, you can purchase a laptop computer for less than $500. When a new technology emerges, prices are initially very high and then tend to fall rapidly. The first PCs profoundly changed the way people could work with information. Before the PC, complex programming could be done only on large mainframe computers that often took up an entire room. But at first only a few people could afford a PC. What makes emerging technology so expensive when it is first introduced and so inexpensive later in its life cycle? Supply tells the story. Advances in manufacturing methods lead to an increased willingness to supply, and therefore the supply curve shifts out. When the supply expands, there is both an increase in the quantity sold and a lower price.

Technological progress is also driving newer markets, like the market for custom shoes. 3D printing makes it possible for anyone to go online, or enter information at a kiosk in a store, and order shoes that are 100% customized. You can design the uppers, insoles, and tread however you like, and in about an hour, your shoes will be printed for you. If your two feet are slightly different sizes, you will get two different-size insoles, to match your feet perfectly. Fully customized 3D printed shoes are still pretty pricey (about $300), but the price is dropping rapidly as the process becomes more efficient and designers build templates that make it easier for customers to get exactly what they want. As the technology continues to improve, the supply curve will continue to shift out. With time, customized shoes may eventually become so cheap that almost everyone will be able to afford them easily—just like computers today!

Why did consumers pay $5,000 for this?

production. By the same reasoning, if the number of firms in the industry decreases, the supply curve shifts to the left.

Changes in the number of firms in a market are a regular part of business. For example, if a new pizza joint opens up nearby, more pizzas can be produced, and supply expands. Conversely, if a pizzeria closes, the number of pizzas produced falls and supply contracts.

PRICE EXPECTATIONS A seller who expects a higher price for a product in the future may wish to delay sales until a time when the product will bring a higher price. For instance, florists know that the demand for roses spikes on Valentine's Day and Mother's Day. Because of higher demand, they can charge higher prices. To be able to sell more flowers during the times of peak demand, many florists work longer hours and hire temporary employees. These actions allow them to make more deliveries, so supply increases.

Likewise, the expectation of lower prices in the future will cause sellers to offer more while prices are still relatively high. This effect is particularly noticeable in the electronics sector, where newer—and much better—products are constantly being developed and released. Sellers know that their current offerings will soon be replaced by something better and that consumer demand for the existing technology will then plummet. This means that prices typically fall when a product has been on the market for a time. Because producers know that the price will fall, they supply as many of the current models as possible before the next wave of innovation cuts the price they can charge.

PRACTICE WHAT YOU KNOW

I scream, you scream, we all scream for ice cream.

Ice Cream: Supply and Demand

QUESTION: Which one of the following will increase the demand for ice cream?

a. a decrease in the price of the butterfat used to make ice cream

b. a decrease in the price of ice cream

c. an increase in the price of the milk used to make ice cream

d. an increase in the price of frozen yogurt, a substitute for ice cream

ANSWER: If you answered b, you made a common mistake. A change in the price of a good cannot change overall market demand; it can only cause a movement along an existing curve. So, as important as price changes are, they are not the right answer. Instead, you need to look for an event that shifts the entire curve.

Choices a and c refer to the prices of butterfat and milk. Because these are the inputs of production for ice cream, a change in their prices will shift the supply curve, not the demand curve. That leaves choice d as the only possibility. Choice d is correct because the increase in the price of frozen yogurt will cause consumers to substitute away from frozen yogurt and toward ice cream. This shift in consumer behavior will result in an increase in the demand for ice cream even though its price remains the same.

(CONTINUED)

QUESTION: Which one of the following will decrease the supply of chocolate ice cream?

a. a medical report finding that consuming chocolate prevents cancer

b. a decrease in the price of chocolate ice cream

c. an increase in the price of chocolate, an ingredient used to make chocolate ice cream

d. an increase in the price of whipped cream, a complementary good

ANSWER: We know that b cannot be the correct answer because a change in the price of the good cannot change supply; it can only cause a movement along an existing curve. Choices a and d would both cause a change in demand without affecting the supply curve. That leaves choice c as the only possibility. Chocolate is a necessary ingredient in the production process. Whenever the price of an input rises, profits are squeezed. The result is a decrease in supply at the existing price.

How Do Supply and Demand Interact to Create Equilibrium?

We have examined supply and demand separately. Now it is time to see how the two interact. The real power of supply and demand analysis is in how well it predicts prices and output in the entire market.

Supply, Demand, and Equilibrium

Let's consider the market for salmon again. This example meets the conditions for a competitive market because the salmon sold by one vendor is essentially the same as the salmon sold by another, and there are many individual buyers.

In Figure 3.9, we see that when the price of salmon fillets is $10 per pound, consumers demand 500 pounds and producers supply 500 pounds. This situation is represented graphically at point E, known as the point of **equilibrium**, where the demand curve and the supply curve intersect. At this point, the two opposing forces of supply and demand are perfectly balanced.

Equilibrium occurs at the point where the demand curve and the supply curve intersect.

Notice that at $10 per pound, the quantity demanded equals the quantity supplied. At this price, and only this price, the entire supply of salmon in the market is sold. Moreover, every buyer who wants salmon is able to find some and every producer is able to sell his or her entire stock. We say that $10 is the **equilibrium price** because the quantity supplied equals the quantity demanded. The equilibrium price is also called the *market-clearing price*, because this is the only price at which no surplus or shortage of the good exists. Similarly, there is also an **equilibrium quantity** at which the quantity supplied equals the quantity demanded (in this example, 500 pounds). When the market is in equilibrium, we sometimes say that *the market clears* or that *the price clears the market*.

The **equilibrium price** is the price at which the quantity supplied is equal to the quantity demanded. It is also known as the *market-clearing price*.

The **equilibrium quantity** is the amount at which the quantity supplied is equal to the quantity demanded.

The equilibrium point has a special place in economics because movements away from that point throw the market out of balance. The equilibrium process is so powerful that it is often referred to as the **law of supply and demand**, the idea that market prices adjust to bring the quantity supplied and the quantity demanded into balance.

The **law of supply and demand** states that the market price of any good will adjust to bring the quantity supplied and the quantity demanded into balance.

FIGURE 3.9

The Salmon Market

At the equilibrium point, E, quantity supplied and quantity demanded are perfectly balanced. At prices above the equilibrium price, a surplus exists. At prices below the equilibrium price, a shortage exists.

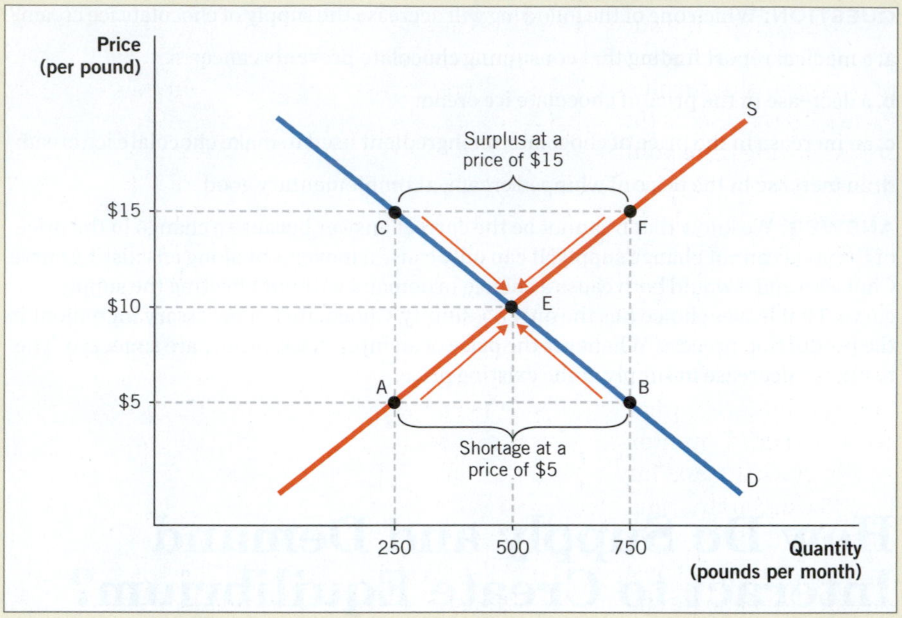

SHORTAGES AND SURPLUSES How does the market respond when it is not in equilibrium? Let's look at two other prices for salmon shown on the *y* axis in Figure 3.9: $5 per pound and $15 per pound.

At a price of $5 per pound, salmon is quite attractive to buyers but not very profitable to sellers. The quantity demanded is 750 pounds, represented by point B on the demand curve (D). However, the quantity supplied, which is represented by point A on the supply curve (S), is only 250 pounds. So at $5 per pound there is an excess quantity of $750 - 250 = 500$ pounds demanded. This excess demand creates disequilibrium in the market.

A **shortage** occurs whenever the quantity supplied is less than the quantity demanded. A shortage is also called *excess demand.*

When there is more demand for a product than sellers are willing or able to supply, we say there is a shortage. A **shortage**, or *excess demand*, occurs whenever the quantity supplied is less than the quantity demanded. In our case, at a price of $5 per pound of salmon, there are three buyers for each pound. New shipments of salmon fly out the door, providing a strong signal for sellers to raise the price. As the market price increases in response to the shortage, sellers continue to increase the quantity they offer. You can see the increase in quantity supplied on the graph in Figure 3.9 by following the upward-sloping arrow from point A to point E. At the same time, as the price rises, buyers demand an increasingly smaller quantity, represented by the arrow from point B to point E along the demand curve. Eventually, when the price reaches $10 per pound, the quantity supplied and the quantity demanded are equal. The market is in equilibrium.

What happens when the price is set above the equilibrium point—say, at $15 per pound? At this price, salmon is quite profitable for sellers but not very attractive to buyers. The quantity demanded, represented by point C on the demand curve, is 250 pounds. However, the quantity supplied, represented by point F on the supply curve, is 750 pounds. In other words, sellers provide 500 pounds more than buyers wish to purchase. This excess supply creates disequilibrium in the market. Any buyer who is willing to pay $15 for a pound of salmon can find some because there are 3 pounds available for every customer. A **surplus**, or *excess supply*, occurs whenever the quantity supplied is greater than the quantity demanded.

A **surplus** occurs whenever the quantity supplied is greater than the quantity demanded. A surplus is also called *excess supply*.

When there is a surplus, sellers realize that salmon has been oversupplied, giving them a strong signal to lower the price. As the market price decreases in response to the surplus, more buyers enter the market and purchase salmon. Figure 3.9 represents this situation on the demand side by the downward-sloping arrow moving from point C to point E along the demand curve. At the same time, sellers reduce output, represented by the arrow moving from point F to point E on the supply curve. As long as the surplus persists, the price will continue to fall. Eventually, the price reaches $10 per pound. At this point, the quantity supplied and the quantity demanded are equal and the market is in equilibrium again.

In competitive markets, surpluses and shortages are resolved through the process of price adjustment. Buyers who are unable to find enough salmon at $5 per pound compete to find the available stocks; this competition drives the price up. Likewise, businesses that cannot sell their product at $15 per pound must lower their prices to reduce inventories; this desire to sell all inventory drives the price down.

Every seller and buyer has a vital role to play in the market. Venues like the Pike Place Market bring buyers and sellers together. Amazingly, market equilibrium occurs without the need for government planning to ensure an adequate supply of the goods consumers want or need. You might think that a decentralized system would create chaos, but nothing could be further from the truth. Markets work because buyers and sellers can rapidly adjust to changes in prices. These adjustments bring balance. When markets were suppressed in communist countries during the twentieth century, shortages were commonplace, in part because there was no market price system to signal that additional production was needed.

In summary, Figure 3.10 provides four examples of what happens when either the supply curve or the demand curve shifts. As you study these examples, you should develop a sense for how price and quantity are affected by changes in supply and demand. When one curve shifts, we can make a definitive statement about how price and quantity will change.

In Appendix 3A, we consider what happens when supply and demand change at the same time. There you will discover the challenges in simultaneously determining price and quantity when more than one variable changes.

PRACTICE WHAT YOU KNOW

Bacon: Supply and Demand

QUESTION: Suppose that the government decides to subsidize bacon producers. What is the impact on the equilibrium market price and output?

ANSWER: In order to answer this question, you first need to determine whether the supply curve or the demand curve shifts in response to the subsidy. Since the subsidy is given to the bacon producers, the supply curve shifts out. The end result is that the market price falls to P_2 and the market output increases to Q_2.

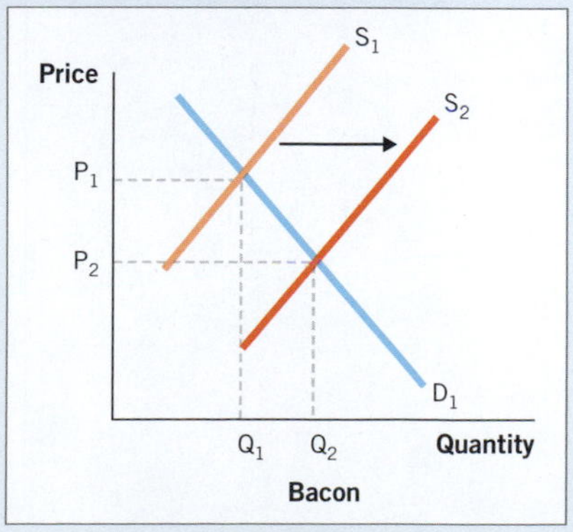

(CONTINUED)

CHALLENGE QUESTION: Is the statement in the meme true or false?

ANSWER: By now you should know that a price decrease causes a change in the quantity demanded, not a change in demand. Therefore, you might be tempted to judge the meme false. But if you did, you would be wrong! Let's see why. The first step is recognizing that bacon and eggs are complements. Therefore, a reduction in the price of the one increases the demand for the other. Recall that a reduction in the price of a complementary good shifts the demand curve to the right. The second step is to look at this graphically (see the graphs below). Using the color-coded letters, we see that (B_1) the price drop on bacon causes an increase in the quantity demanded of bacon (a slide along the existing demand curve) and (E_2) since consumers buy more bacon than before, this increases the demand for eggs (demand shifts to the right) in the egg market. At the same time, (E_1) the price drop on eggs causes an increase in the quantity demanded of eggs (a slide along the existing demand curve) and (B_2) since consumers buy more eggs than before, this increases the demand for bacon (demand shifts to the right) in the bacon market. We model this by showing the two related markets, bacon and eggs, side by side so you can see how a price reduction of the related goods increases the "demand for each other." Since both curves shift out, the meme is true.

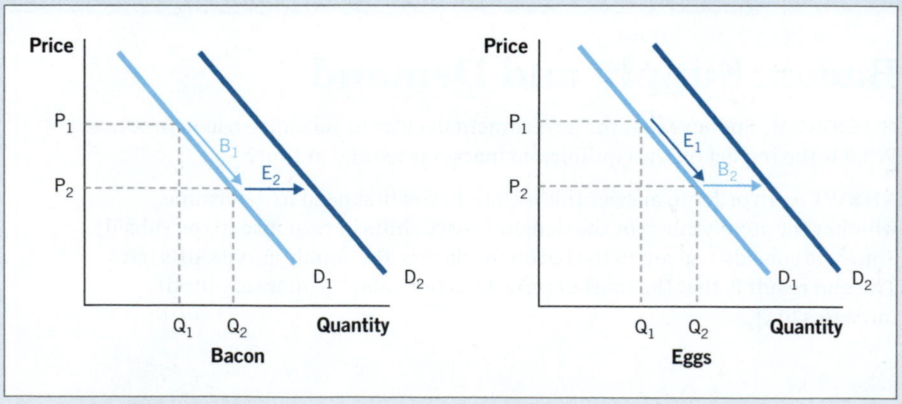

FIGURE 3.10

Price and Quantity When Either Supply or Demand Changes

Change | **Illustration** | **Impact on price and quantity**

1. Demand increases; supply does not change.

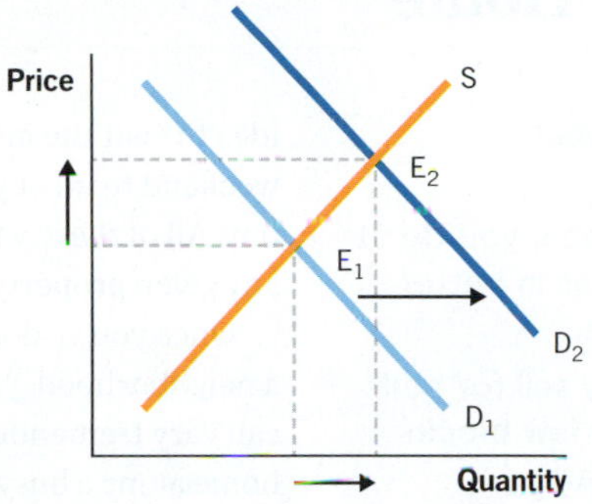

The demand curve shifts to the right. As a result, the equilibrium price and the equilibrium quantity increase.

2. Supply increases; demand does not change.

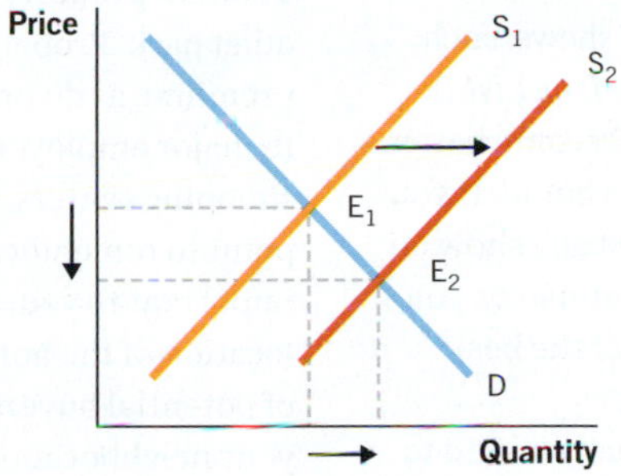

The supply curve shifts to the right. As a result, the equilibrium price decreases and the equilibrium quantity increases.

3. Demand decreases; supply does not change.

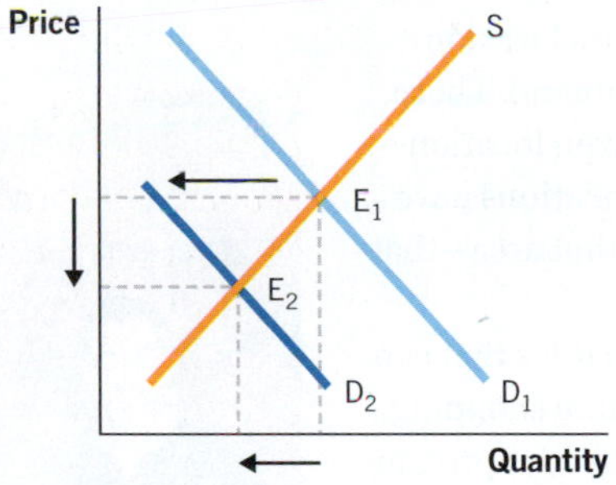

The demand curve shifts to the left. As a result, the equilibrium price and the equilibrium quantity decrease.

4. Supply decreases; demand does not change.

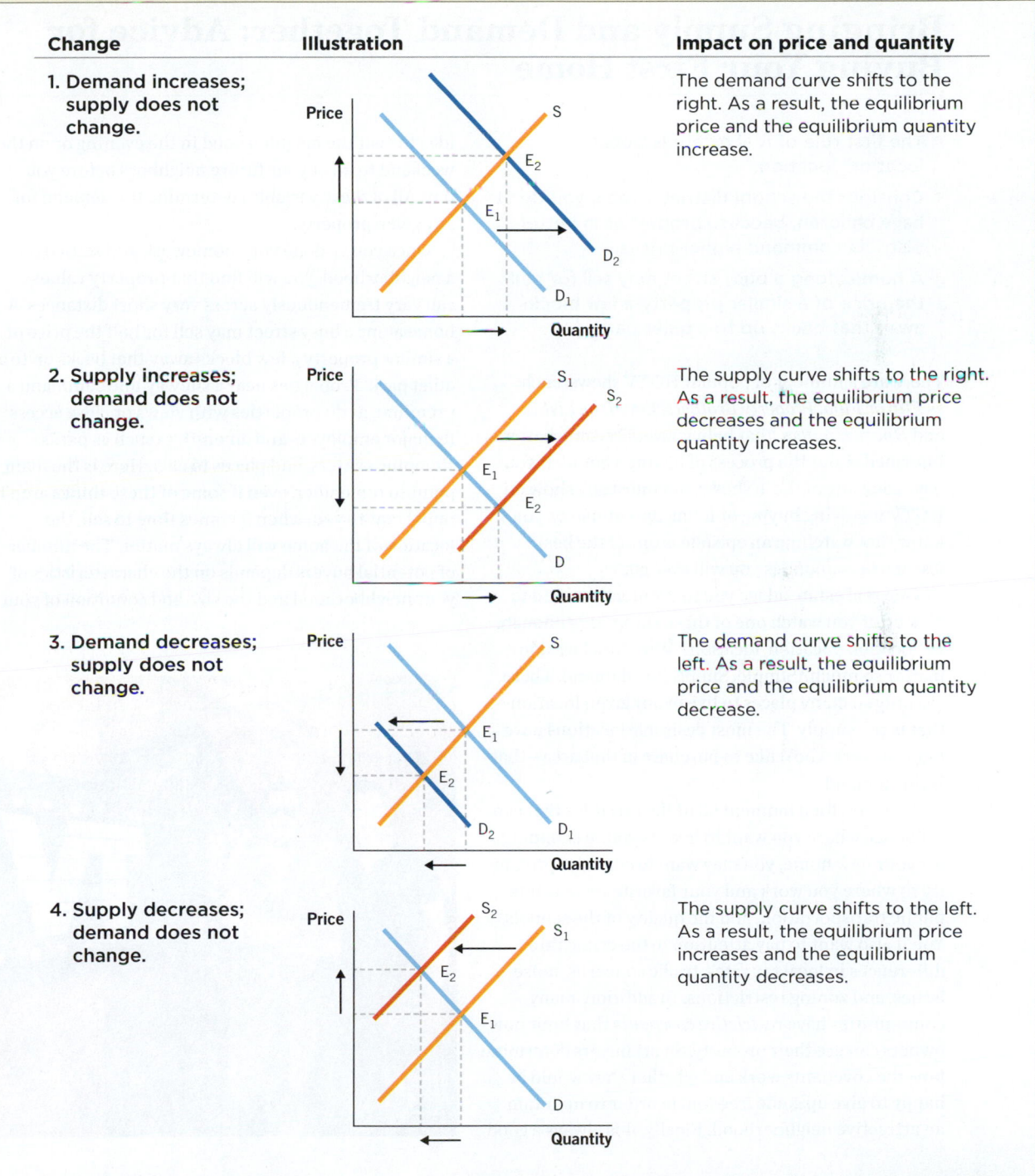

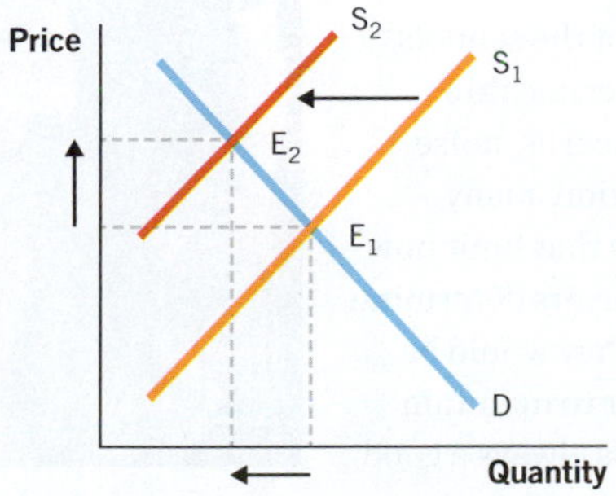

The supply curve shifts to the left. As a result, the equilibrium price increases and the equilibrium quantity decreases.

ECONOMICS *for* LIFE

Bringing Supply and Demand Together: Advice for Buying Your First Home

- The first rule of real estate is "location, location, location."
- Consider the school district, even if you don't have children, because properties in better districts command higher prices.
- A home along a busy street may sell for half the price of a similar property a few blocks away that backs up to a quiet park.

There are a number of popular HGTV shows, such as *Flip or Flop*, *Property Brothers*, *Love It or List It*, and *House Hunters*, that help viewers become better informed about the process of buying a home. If you have seen any of these shows, or almost any show on HGTV involving buying or fixing up a property, you know that watching an episode is one of the best lessons in economics you will ever get.

One real estate adage you're eventually bound to pick up, if you watch one of these shows long enough, is "location, location, location." Why does location matter so much? Simple. Supply and demand. There are only so many places to live in any given location—that is the supply. The most desirable locations have many buyers who'd like to purchase in that area—that is the demand.

Consider for a moment all of the variables that can influence where you want to live. As you're shopping for your new home, you may want to consider proximity to where you work and your favorite restaurants, public transportation, and the quality of the schools. You'll also want to pay attention to the crime rate, differences in local tax rates, traffic concerns, noise issues, and zoning restrictions. In addition, many communities have *restrictive covenants* that limit how owners can use their property. Smart buyers determine how the covenants work and whether they would be happy to give up some freedom in order to maintain an attractive neighborhood. Finally, it is always a good idea to visit the neighborhood in the evening or on the weekend to meet your future neighbors before you buy. All of these variables determine the demand for any given property.

Once you've done your homework and settled on a neighborhood, you will find that property values can vary tremendously across very short distances. A home along a busy street may sell for half the price of a similar property a few blocks away that backs up to a quiet park. Properties near a subway line command a premium, as do properties with views or close access to major employers and amenities (such as parks, shopping centers, and places to eat). Here is the main point to remember, even if some of these things aren't important to you: when it comes time to sell, the location of the home will always matter. The number of potential buyers depends on the characteristics of your neighborhood and the size and condition of your

(CONTINUED)

property. If you want to be able to sell your home easily, you'll have to consider not only where you want to live now but who might want to live there in the future.

All of this discussion brings us back to supply and demand. The best locations are in short supply and high demand. The combination of low supply and high demand causes property values in those areas to rise. Likewise, less desirable locations have lower property values because demand is relatively low, and the supply is relatively high. Because first-time buyers often have wish lists that far exceed their budgets, considering the costs and benefits will help you find the best available property.

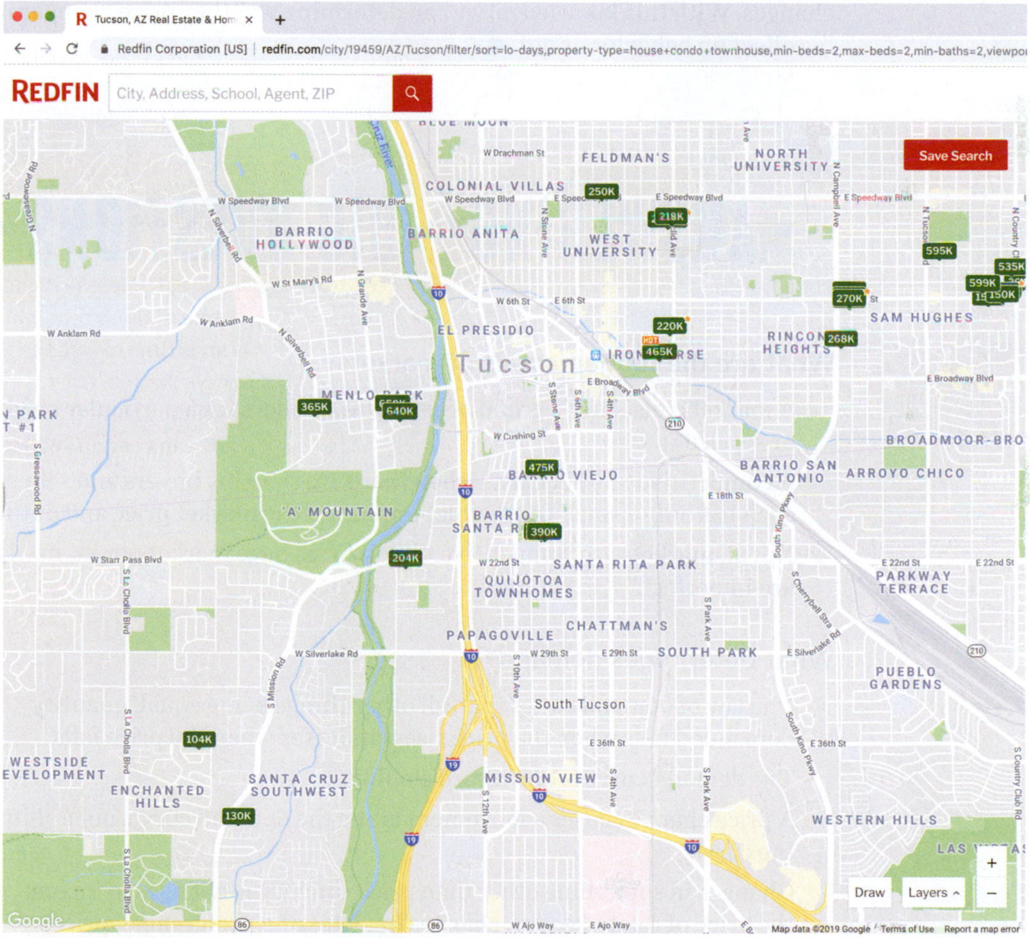

Location Matters

This graphic shows listings for prices of 2-bedroom, 2-bath houses on the market in Tuscon, Arizona. Prices range from $104K to $640K. What are some rules of thumb to remember?

Conclusion

Five years from now, if someone asks you what you remember about your first course in economics, you will probably respond with two words: "supply" and "demand." These two forces allow us to model market behavior through prices. Supply and demand help establish the market equilibrium, or the price at which quantity supplied and quantity demanded are in balance. At the equilibrium point, every good and service produced has a corresponding buyer who wants to purchase it. When the market is out of equilibrium, either a shortage or surplus exists. This condition persists until buyers and sellers have a chance to adjust the quantity they demand and the quantity they supply, respectively.

In the next chapter, we extend our understanding of supply and demand by examining how sensitive, or responsive, consumers and producers are to price changes. With this knowledge, we can determine whether price changes have a big effect on behavior or not. ✷

ANSWERING *the* BIG QUESTIONS

What are the fundamentals of markets?

- A market consists of a group of buyers and sellers for a particular product or service.
- A competitive market exists when there are so many buyers and sellers that each has only a small (negligible) impact on the market price and output.
- Not all markets are competitive. When firms have market power, markets are imperfect.

What determines demand?

- The law of demand states that, all other things being equal, quantity demanded falls when the price rises, and rises when the price falls.
- The demand curve is downward sloping.
- A price change causes a movement along the demand curve, not a shift of the curve.
- Changes in something other than price (including changes in income, the price of related goods, changes in tastes and preferences, price expectations, the number of buyers, and taxes) shift the demand curve.

What determines supply?

- The law of supply states that, all other things being equal, the quantity supplied of a good rises when the price of the good rises, and falls when the price of the good falls.

- The supply curve is upward sloping.
- A price change causes a movement along the supply curve, not a shift of the curve.
- Changes in something other than price (the cost of inputs, changes in technology or the production process, taxes and subsidies, the number of firms in the industry, and price expectations) shift the original supply curve.

How do supply and demand interact to create equilibrium?

- Supply and demand work together in a market-clearing process that leads to equilibrium, the balancing point between the two forces. The market-clearing price and output are determined at the equilibrium point.
- When the price is above the equilibrium point, a surplus exists, and inventories build up. Suppliers lower their price in an effort to sell the unwanted goods. The process continues until the equilibrium price is reached.
- When the price is below the equilibrium point, a shortage exists, and inventories are depleted. Suppliers raise the price until the equilibrium point is reached.

CHAPTER PROBLEMS

Concepts You Should Know

competitive market (p. 75)
complements (p. 83)
demand curve (p. 78)
demand schedule (p. 77)
equilibrium (p. 95)
equilibrium price (p. 95)
equilibrium quantity (p. 95)
imperfect market (p. 76)
inferior good (p. 82)
inputs (p. 91)
invisible hand (p. 74)
law of demand (p. 77)
law of supply (p. 87)
law of supply and demand (p. 95)
market demand (p. 79)
market economy (p. 74)
market power (p. 76)
market supply (p. 88)
monopoly (p. 76)
normal good (p. 82)
purchasing power (p. 81)
quantity demanded (p. 76)
quantity supplied (p. 87)
shortage (p. 96)
subsidy (p. 86)
substitutes (p. 83)
supply curve (p. 88)
supply schedule (p. 87)
surplus (p. 97)

Questions for Review

1. What is a competitive market, and why does it depend on the existence of many buyers and sellers?
2. Why does the demand curve slope downward?
3. Does a price change cause a movement along a demand curve or a shift of the entire curve? What factors cause the entire demand curve to shift?
4. Describe the difference between inferior goods and normal goods. Give an example of each type of good.
5. Why does the supply curve slope upward?
6. Does a price change cause a movement along a supply curve or a shift of the entire curve? What factors cause the entire supply curve to shift?
7. Describe the process that leads a market toward equilibrium.
8. What happens in a competitive market when the price is above the equilibrium price? Below the equilibrium price?
9. What roles do shortages and surpluses play in the market?

Study Problems *(✱solved at the end of the section)*

1. Which of these is endogenous in the supply and demand model?
   a. price
   b. income
   c. quantity
   d. cost of labor
2. For each of the following scenarios, determine if there is an increase or a decrease in demand for the good in *italics*.
   a. The price of *oranges* increases.
   b. The cost of producing *tires* increases.
   c. Samantha Brown, who is crazy about *air travel*, gets fired from her job.
   d. A local community has an unusually wet spring and a subsequent problem with mosquitoes, which can be deterred with *citronella*.
   e. Many motorcycle enthusiasts enjoy riding without *helmets* (in states where this is not prohibited by law). The price of new motorcycles rises.
3. For each of the following scenarios, determine if there is an increase or a decrease in supply for the good in *italics*.
   a. The price of *silver* increases.
   b. Growers of *tomatoes* experience an unusually good growing season.
   c. New medical evidence reports that consumption of *organic products* reduces the incidence of cancer.
   d. The wages of low-skilled workers, a resource used to help produce *clothing*, increase.
   e. The price of movie tickets, a substitute for *streaming video rental at Amazon*, goes up.

4. Are laser pointers and cats complements or substitutes? (Not sure? Search for videos of cats and laser pointers online.) Discuss.

✷ **5.** The market for ice cream has the following demand and supply schedules:

Price (per quart)	Quantity demanded (quarts)	Quantity supplied (quarts)
$2	100	20
3	80	40
4	60	60
5	40	80
6	20	100

a. What are the equilibrium price and equilibrium quantity in the ice cream market? Confirm your answer by graphing the demand and supply curves.

b. If the actual price is $3 per quart, what would drive the market toward equilibrium?

6. Are Hot Cheetos and Takis complements or substitutes for each other? (For inspiration, try Googling "Hot Cheetos & Takis" by Y.N.RichKids.)

7. The Seattle Mariners baseball team wishes to determine the equilibrium price for seats for each of the next two seasons. The supply of seats at the ballpark is fixed at 45,000.

Price (per seat)	Quantity demanded in year 1	Quantity demanded in year 2	Quantity supplied
$25	75,000	60,000	45,000
30	60,000	55,000	45,000
35	45,000	50,000	45,000
40	30,000	45,000	45,000
45	15,000	40,000	45,000

Draw the supply curve and each of the demand curves for years 1 and 2.

✷ **8.** Demand and supply curves can also be represented with equations. Suppose that the quantity demanded, Q_D, is represented by the following equation:

$$Q_D = 90 - 2P$$

The quantity supplied, Q_S, is represented by the equation

$$Q_S = P$$

a. Find the equilibrium price and quantity. (**Hint:** Set $Q_D = Q_S$ and solve for the price, P, and then plug your result back into either of the original equations to find Q.)

b. Suppose that the price is $20. Determine Q_D and Q_S.

c. At a price of $20, is there a surplus or a shortage in the market?

d. Given your answer in part (c), will the price rise or fall in order to find the equilibrium point?

✷ **9.** Let's take a look at two real-world episodes in the market for gasoline and try to figure out why the price fluctuates so much.

a. In the spring of 2020, during the COVID-19 lockdown, the price of regular gasoline in the United States plummeted to $1.75 per gallon. Use the supply and demand model to determine which curve shifted and what happened to the equilibrium price of gasoline. For this part of the question, assume no other changes in the market for gasoline.

b. By the summer of 2021, the price of regular gasoline in the United States had bounced back and was hovering around $3.20 per gallon. Use the supply and demand model to determine which curve shifted and then what happened to the equilibrium price of gasoline. For this part of the question, assume no other changes in the market for gasoline.

c. Imagine that instead of falling at the start of the COVID-19 lockdown, the price of gasoline had risen sharply in 2020 and then come back down in 2021. What would the explanation for that have looked like?

✷ **10.** If the price of alcohol decreases, what happens to the demand for red Solo (plastic) cups?

11. Consider the market for the Samsung Galaxy S21.

a. Scenario 1: Using a supply and demand graph, show what will happen to the current equilibrium price and quantity of Galaxy S21s if people expect the price of S21s to fall in the future.

b. Scenario 2: Now, using a second supply and demand graph, show instead what will happen to the equilibrium price and quantity of S21s if the price of the iPhone 13 falls. In your answer, assume that the S21 and iPhone 13 are substitutes in consumption.

c. Scenario 3: You observe that the price of S21s increases. Can you definitively conclude that there has been an increase in demand? If not, what besides an increase in demand could explain the price increase?

✷ **12.** One of the responses completes this list of things that shift the supply curve: technology, expectations, the number of sellers, and ___________. Identify the correct answer and also explain why the other three responses are incorrect.

a. the price of related goods
b. income
c. the cost of inputs
d. the price

Solved Problems

5. a. The equilibrium price is $4, and the equilibrium quantity is 60 quarts. The next step is to graph the curves, as shown here.

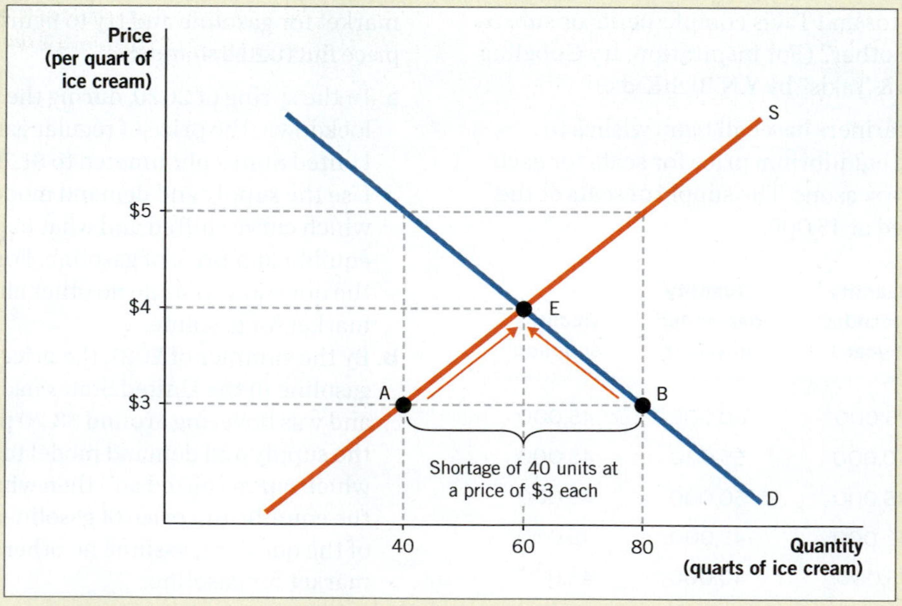

b. A shortage of 40 quarts of ice cream exists at $3 (quantity demanded is 80 and the quantity supplied is 40); therefore, there is excess demand. Ice cream sellers will raise their price as long as excess demand exists—that is, as long as the price is below $4. It is not until $4 that the equilibrium point is reached and the shortage is resolved.

8. a. The first step is to set $Q_D = Q_S$. Doing so gives us $90 - 2P = P$. Solving for price, we find that $90 = 3P$, or $P = 30$. Once we know that $P = 30$, we can plug this value back into either of the original equations, $Q_D = 90 - 2P$ or $Q_S = P$. Beginning with Q_D, we get $90 - 2(30) = 90 - 60 = 30$, or we can plug it into $Q_S = P$, so $Q_S = 30$. Because we get a quantity of 30 for both Q_D and Q_S, we know that the price of $30 is correct.

b. In this part, we plug $20 into Q_D. Doing so yields $90 - 2(20) = 50$. Now we plug $20 into Q_S. Doing so yields 20.

c. Because $Q_D = 50$ and $Q_S = 20$, there is a shortage of 30 quarts.

d. Whenever there is a shortage of a good, the price will rise in order to find the equilibrium point.

9. a. The reduction in private travel and commercial vehicle traffic led to a negative, or leftward, shift in the demand curve for gasoline. Assuming that the supply curve did not move, the equilibrium price of gasoline had to fall.

b. As lockdowns ended and the economy recovered, people resumed their normal travel habits, commuting to work and going on vacations. Commercial vehicle traffic returned to normal, as well. The demand curve shifted rightward again, driving the price of gasoline back up.

c. The only reasonable explanation for a sudden rise in the price of gasoline would have been a disruption of supply, due perhaps to labor shortages at oil pumps and refineries, or to a shortage of tanker-truck drivers. Prices would have come back down as those workers returned to their jobs. In reality, any such disruptions were small compared to the shift on the demand side.

10. Because alcohol and Solo cups are complements, the key here is to recall that a change in the price of a complementary good shifts the demand curve for the related good. Lower alcohol prices will cause consumers to purchase more alcohol and therefore demand more Solo cups. In other words, the entire demand curve for Solo cups shifts to the right.

12. a. The price of related goods is a demand shifter, so it is incorrect.

b. Income is a demand shifter, so it is incorrect.

c. The cost of inputs is a supply shifter, so it is correct.

d. The price causes a movement along the supply curve, so it is incorrect.

APPENDIX

03A

Changes in Both Demand and Supply

We have considered what would happen if supply *or* demand changes. But life is often more complex than that. To provide a more realistic analysis, we need to examine what happens when supply and demand both shift at the same time.

Suppose that a major drought hits the northwestern United States. The water shortage reduces both the amount of farmed salmon and the ability of wild salmon to spawn in streams and rivers. Figure 3A.1a shows the ensuing decline in the salmon supply, from S_1 progressively leftward, represented by the dotted supply curves. At the same time, a medical journal reports that people who consume at least 4 pounds of salmon a month live five years longer than those who consume an equal amount of cod. Figure 3A.1b shows the ensuing rise in the demand for salmon, from D_1 progressively rightward, represented by the dotted demand curves. This scenario leads to a twofold change. Because of the water shortage, the supply of salmon shrinks. At the same time, new information about the health benefits of eating salmon causes demand for salmon to increase.

It is impossible to predict exactly what happens to the equilibrium point when both supply and demand are shifting. We can, however, determine a region where the resulting equilibrium point must reside.

In this situation, we have a simultaneous decrease in supply and increase in demand. Since we do not know the magnitude of the supply reduction or demand increase, the overall effect on the equilibrium quantity cannot be determined. This result is evident in Figure 3A.1c, as illustrated by the purple region. The points where supply and demand cross within this area represent the set of possible new market equilibria. Because each of the possible points of intersection in the purple region occurs at a price greater than $10 per pound, we know that the price must rise. However, the left half of the purple region produces equilibrium quantities that are lower than 500 pounds of salmon, while the right half of the purple region results in equilibrium quantities that are greater than 500. Therefore, the equilibrium quantity may rise, fall, or stay the same if both shifts are of equal magnitudes.

The world we live in is complex, and often more than one variable will change simultaneously. In such cases, it is not possible to be as definitive as when only one variable—supply or demand—changes. You should think of the new equilibrium not as a single point but as a range of outcomes represented by the purple area in Figure 3A.1c. Therefore, we cannot be exactly sure at what point the new price *and* new quantity will settle. For a closer look at four possibilities, see Figure 3A.2, where E_1 equals the original equilibrium point and the new equilibrium (E_2) lies somewhere in the purple region.

FIGURE 3A.1

A Shift in Supply and Demand

When supply and demand both shift, the resulting equilibrium can no longer be identified as an exact point. We can see this effect in (c), which combines the supply shift in (a) with the demand shift in (b). When supply decreases and demand increases, the result is that the price must rise, but the equilibrium quantity can either rise or fall, or stay the same if both shifts are of equal magnitudes.

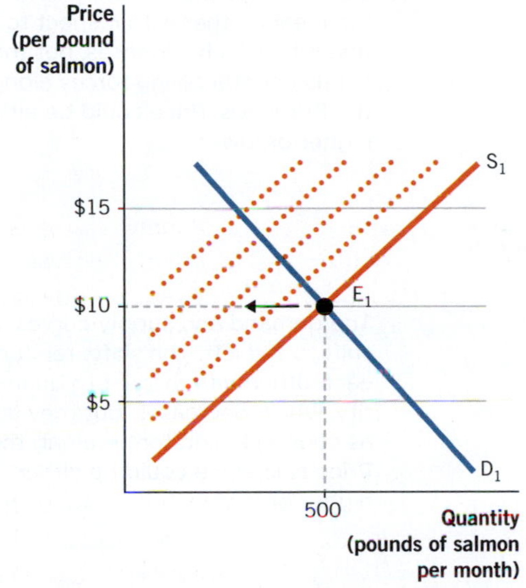

(a) A Fall in the Supply of Salmon

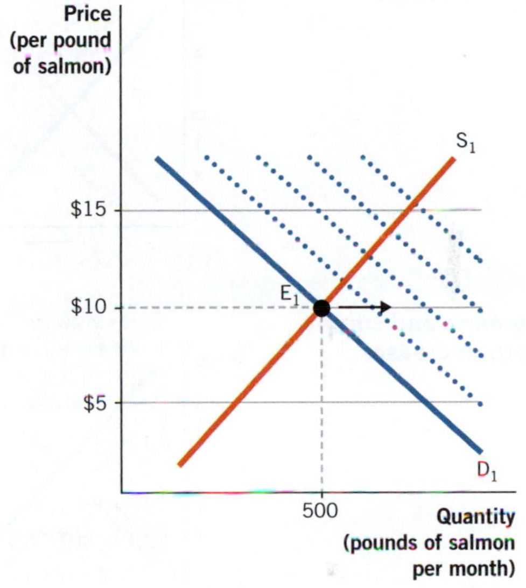

(b) A Rise in the Demand for Salmon

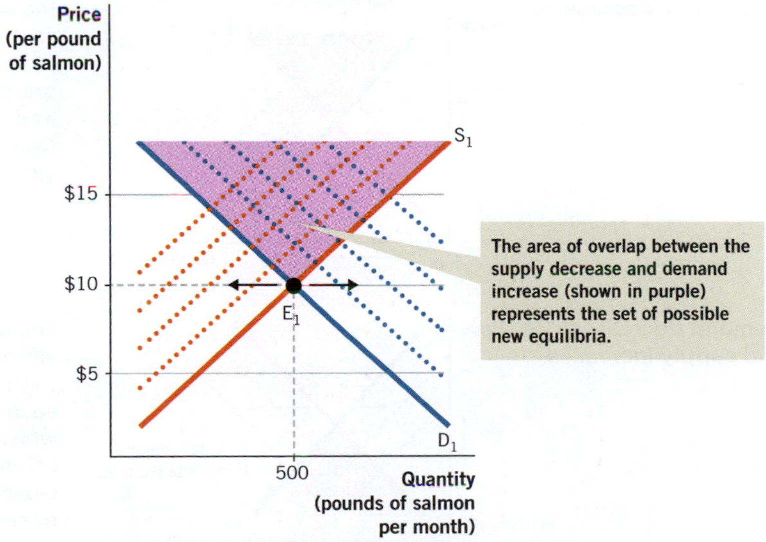

(c) Possible Equilibria after Supply Decreases and Demand Increases

FIGURE 3A.2

Price and Quantity When Demand and Supply Both Change

Change	Illustration	Impact on price and quantity
1. Demand and supply both increase.	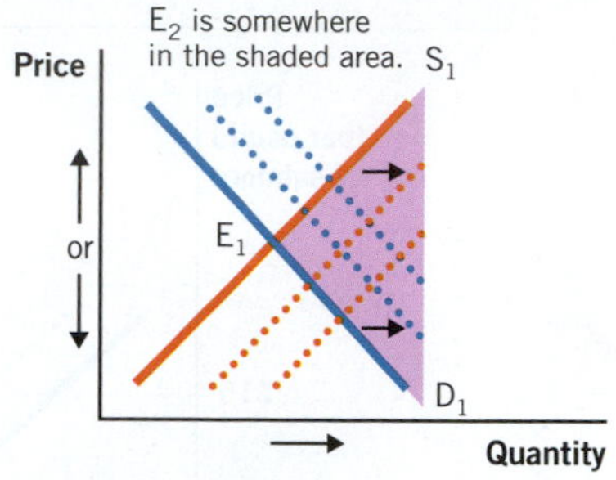	The demand and supply curves shift to the right. The shifts reinforce each other with respect to quantity, which increases, but they act as countervailing forces along the Price axis. Price could be either higher or lower.
2. Demand and supply both decrease.	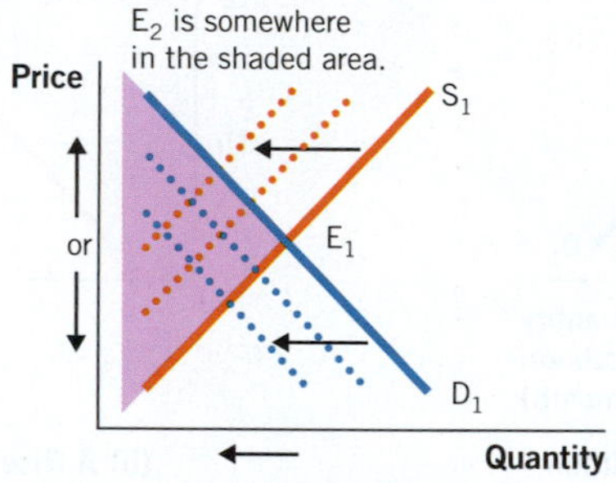	The demand and supply curves shift to the left. The shifts reinforce each other with respect to quantity, which decreases, but they act as countervailing forces along the Price axis. Price could be either higher or lower.
3. Demand increases and supply decreases.	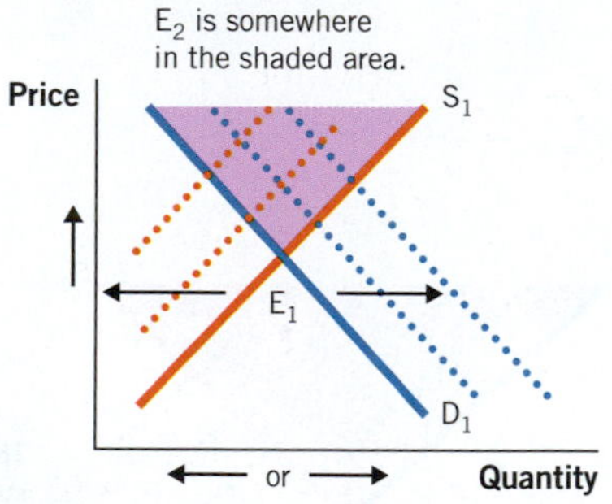	The demand curve shifts to the right and the supply curve shifts to the left. The shifts reinforce each other with respect to price, which increases, but they act as countervailing forces along the Quantity axis. Quantity could be either higher or lower.
4. Demand decreases and supply increases.	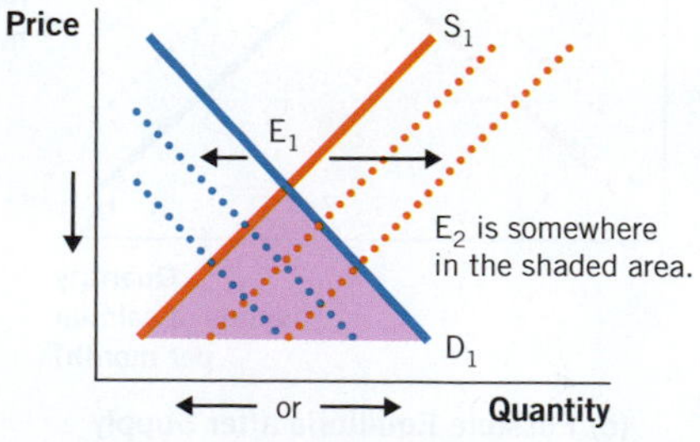	The demand curve shifts to the left and the supply curve shifts to the right. The shifts reinforce each other with respect to price, which decreases, but they act as countervailing forces along the Quantity axis. Quantity could be either higher or lower.

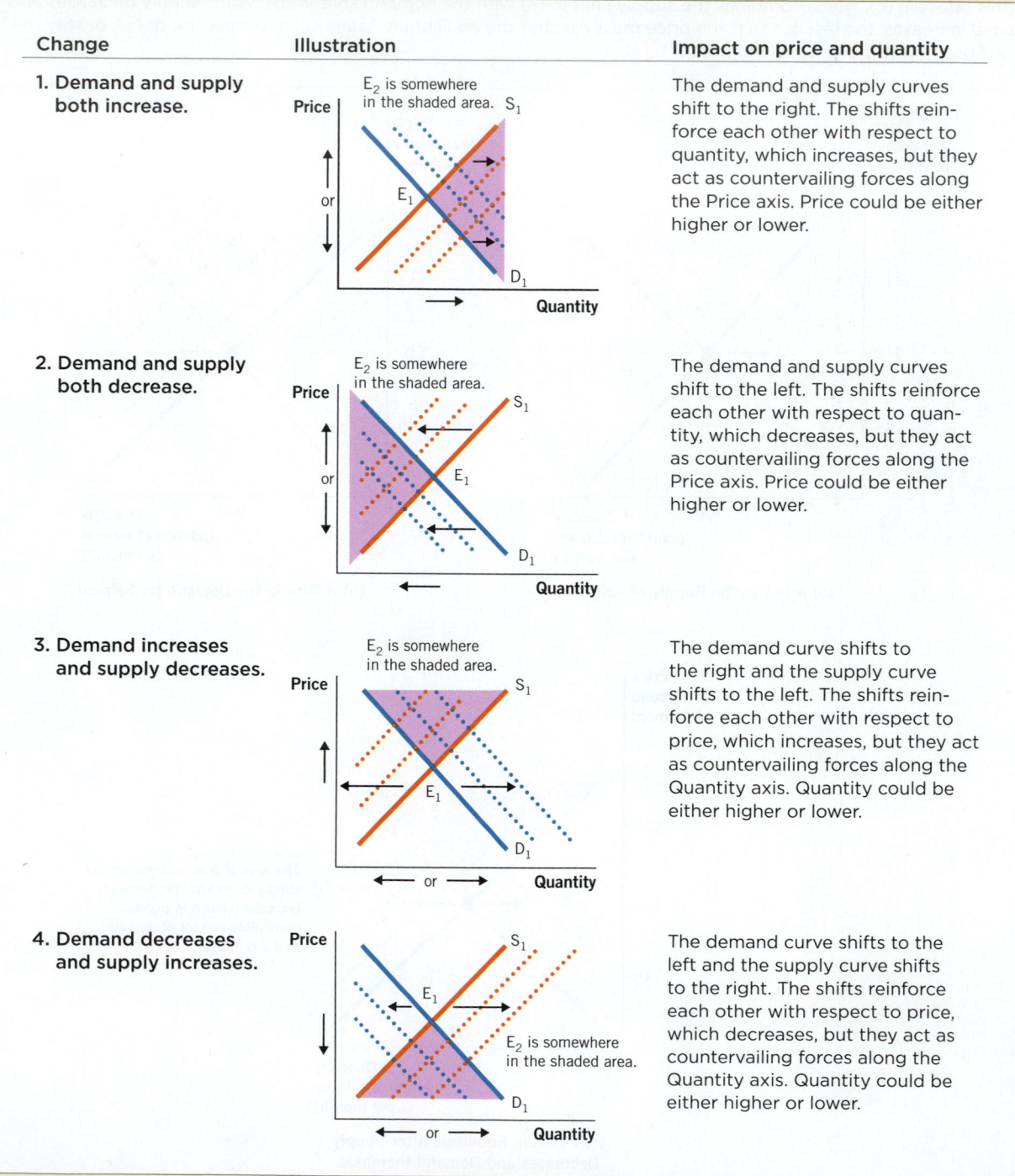

PRACTICE WHAT YOU KNOW

When Supply and Demand Both Change: Electric Vehicles (EVs)

QUESTION: At lunch, two friends are engaged in a heated argument. Their exchange goes like this:

The first friend begins, "The supply of EVs and the demand for EVs will both increase. I'm sure of it. I'm also sure the price of EVs will go down."

The second friend replies, "I agree with the first part of your statement, but I'm not sure about the price. In fact, I'm pretty sure that EV prices will rise."

They go back and forth endlessly, each unable to convince the other, so they turn to you for advice. What do you say to them?

ANSWER: Either of your friends could be correct. In this case, supply and demand both shift out to the right, so we know that the quantity bought and sold will increase. However, an increase in supply would normally lower the price, and an increase in demand would typically raise the price. Without knowing which of these two effects on price is stronger, you can't predict how price will change. The overall price will rise if the increase in demand is larger than the increase in supply. However, if the increase in supply is larger than the increase in demand, prices will fall. But your two friends don't know which condition will be true—so they're locked in an argument that neither can win. As an aside, Tesla came out with its priciest models first and is working its way down the affordability scale, which suggests that it is betting on EV prices going down over time.

Electric vehicles are becoming increasingly common.

ECONOMICS IN THE REAL WORLD

HEAT DOME ECONOMICS

In 2021, an unprecedented atmospheric heat dome brought record temperatures to the Pacific Northwest. Portland reached 116 degrees, Seattle topped out at 108, and Quillayute, Washington, on the Pacific coast, reached 110—an astonishing 45 degrees above average. But the effect was even stronger north of the border. Lytton, British Columbia, reached 121 degrees, breaking the previous temperature record for all of Canada by a whopping 8 degrees. To put this into perspective: it was hotter in Lytton than has ever been recorded in Las Vegas, 1,000 miles to the south.

The economic effects of the 2021 heat dome provide a textbook example of a positive demand shock and negative supply shock (a "shock" is an unexpected event) hitting at the same time.

First, the positive demand shock. It is easy to understand. Unprecedented heat dramatically increased (that's why we say "positive") the demand for electricity in the Pacific Northwest, because much more electricity than usual was needed to cool homes.

Second, the negative supply shock. It turns out that excessive heat also stresses the existing electric grid, leading to rolling blackouts, thus lowering (that's why we say "negative") supplies of electricity to cool homes. Just when people needed electricity the most, it was in short supply.

Third, the complication. The extreme temperatures worsened the already dry conditions throughout the Pacific Northwest. Because this area relies on hydroelectric power more than any other part of the country, the heat dome made it even harder for supply to meet peak demand in the future. As you can probably guess, "even harder" quickly translates into "even more expensive."

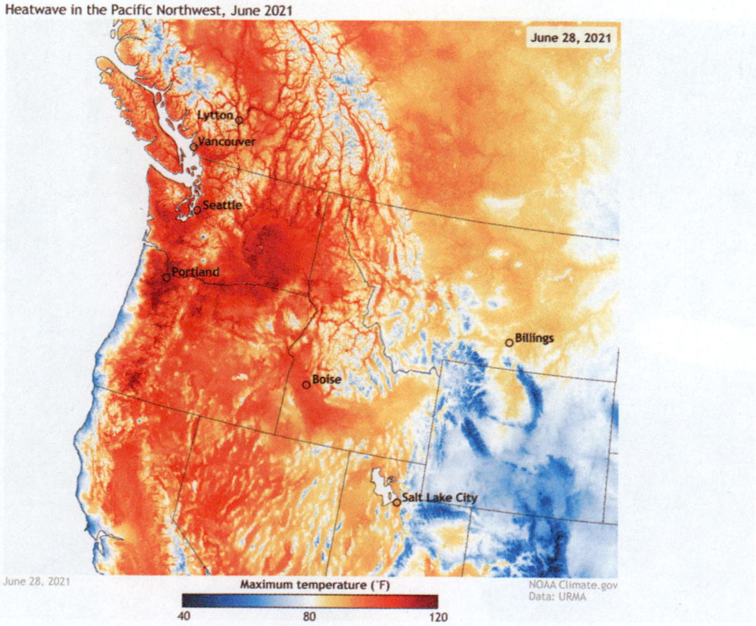

The heat dome is coming. Do you have air conditioning?

· APPENDIX PROBLEMS ·

Questions for Review

1. What happens to price and quantity when supply and demand change at the same time?
2. Is there more than one potential equilibrium point when supply and demand change at the same time? Explain.

Study Problems (*solved at the end of the section)

* 1. Assume that, over time, consumer incomes generally increase but also that technological advancements in oil extraction lead to lower prices of crude oil (the primary input for gasoline).
   a. If consumer incomes increase by significantly more than input prices fall, what happens to both the price and quantity of gasoline?
   b. If, instead, consumer incomes increase relatively less than input prices fall, what happens to the price and quantity of gasoline?

2. Every Valentine's Day, the price of roses spikes. Using your understanding of the factors that shift both demand and supply, draw the equilibrium in the rose market on January 31 and then draw the new equilibrium that occurs on February 14.

Solved Problem

1. a. The increase in consumer income increases demand and shifts the demand curve to the right. The decrease in input prices increases supply and shifts the supply curve to the right. Equilibrium quantity unequivocally increases. The demand shift is relatively larger, so price also increases.
   b. Again, we see that the increase in consumer income increases demand and shifts the demand curve to the right; and the decrease in input prices increases supply and shifts the supply curve to the right. Equilibrium quantity increases. But in this question, the demand shift is relatively smaller, so price falls.

CHAPTER

04

Elasticity

The Rebound Effect

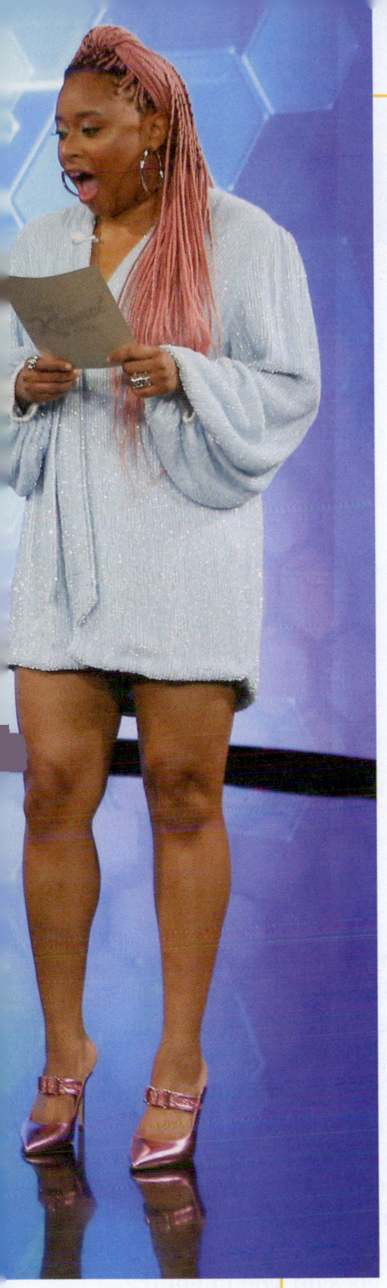

An important factor in how far a ball rebounds or responds when dropped is how elastic it is. An inflated basketball is more responsive or elastic than a tennis ball and therefore will rebound higher. A dropped bowling ball only "gives" a little and hits the ground with a thud and very little rebound. A snowball thrown at a tree smacks it with a "splat" and is almost totally inelastic.

Economists use the idea of elasticity in a similar way, to describe responsiveness to a change in market conditions. In the previous chapter, we learned that demand and supply regulate economic activity by responding to the interests of buyers and sellers through prices. A higher price causes the quantity supplied to rise and the quantity demanded to fall. A lower price causes the quantity supplied to fall and the quantity demanded to rise. How strongly the quantity consumed or produced responds to a change in the price is its *elasticity*. High elasticity means a large, very responsive change in quantity, while low elasticity means a small change. So the change in price is like the drop height of a ball, and the change in quantity is like the rebound height.

This is an important concept in economics. Understanding elasticity helps us to determine the impact of government policy on the economy, to vote more intelligently, and even to make wiser day-to-day decisions.

Zaila Avant-garde demonstrates her feel for basketball elasticity to *Jimmy Kimmel Live!* guest host Phoebe Robinson. Zaila is a Guinness World Record holder for her dribbling skills (and a National Spelling Bee champion, too). Visualizing how balls bounce differently can help you understand the concept of elasticity in economics!

· BIG QUESTIONS ·

- What is the price elasticity of demand, and what are its determinants?
- How do changes in income and the prices of other goods affect elasticity?
- What is the price elasticity of supply?
- How do the price elasticities of demand and supply relate to each other?

What Is the Price Elasticity of Demand, and What Are Its Determinants?

Trade-offs

Many things in life are replaceable, or have substitutes: boyfriends and girlfriends come and go, and people stream videos instead of going out to a movie. Pasta fans may prefer linguini to spaghetti or angel hair, but all three taste about the same and can be substituted for one another in a pinch. With goods like pasta, where consumers can easily purchase a substitute, we think of demand as being *responsive*. That is, a small change in price will likely cause many people to switch from one good to another.

In contrast, many things in life are irreplaceable or have few good substitutes. Examples include electricity and a hospital emergency room visit. A significant rise in price for either of these items would probably not cause you to consume a smaller quantity. If the price of electricity goes up, you might try to cut your usage somewhat, but you would probably not start generating your own power. Likewise, you could try to treat a serious medical crisis without a

How much do each of these different objects rebound off the ground?

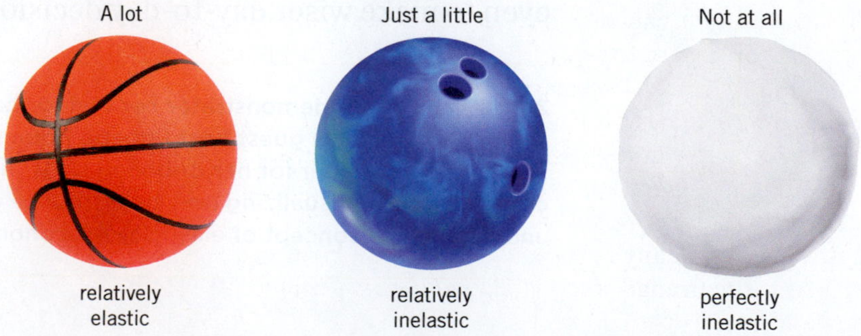

visit to the ER—but the consequences of making a mistake would be enormous. In these cases, we say that consumers are *unresponsive*, or unwilling to change their behavior, even when the price of the good or service changes.

Elasticity is a measure of the responsiveness of buyers and sellers to changes in price or income. Elasticity is a useful concept because it allows us to measure *how much* consumers and producers change their behavior when either price or income changes. In the next section, we look at the factors that determine the price elasticity of demand.

Elasticity
is a measure of the responsiveness of buyers and sellers to changes in price or income.

Determinants of the Price Elasticity of Demand

The law of demand tells us that as price goes up, quantity demanded goes down, and as price goes down, quantity demanded goes up. In other words, there is a negative relationship between the price of a good and the quantity demanded. Elasticity allows us to measure how much the quantity demanded changes in response to a change in price. If the quantity demanded changes significantly as a result of a price change, then demand is *elastic*. If the quantity demanded changes a small amount as a result of a price change, then demand is *inelastic*.

The **price elasticity of demand** measures the responsiveness of quantity demanded to a change in price. For instance, if the price of a sweatshirt with a college logo rises by $10 and the quantity demanded falls by a large amount (say, half), we'd say that the demand for those sweatshirts is elastic. But if the $10 rise in price results in very little or no change in the quantity demanded, the demand for the sweatshirts is inelastic.

The **price elasticity of demand** measures the responsiveness of quantity demanded to a change in price.

Five determinants play a crucial role in influencing whether demand will be elastic or inelastic: the existence of substitutes, the share of the budget spent on a good, whether the good is a necessity or a luxury good, how broadly defined the market is, and time.

THE EXISTENCE OF SUBSTITUTES The most important determinant of price elasticity is the number of substitutes available. When substitutes are plentiful, market forces tilt in favor of the consumer. For example, imagine that an unexpected freeze in Florida reduces the supply of oranges. As a result, the supply of orange juice shifts to the left (picture the supply curves we discussed in Chapter 3). Because demand remains unchanged, the price of orange juice rises. However, the consumer of orange juice can find many good substitutes. Because cranberries, grapes, and apple crops are unaffected by the Florida freeze, prices for juices made from those fruits remain constant. This situation leads to a choice: a consumer can continue to buy orange juice at a higher price or choose to pay a lower price for a fruit juice that may not be his first choice but is nonetheless acceptable. Faced with higher orange juice prices, some consumers will switch. How quickly this switch takes place, and to what extent consumers are willing to replace one product with another, determines whether demand is elastic or inelastic. Because many substitutes for orange juice exist, the demand for orange juice is elastic, or responsive to price changes.

Your friend's band is replaceable.

Beyoncé is irreplaceable.

What if there are no good substitutes? There is no amusement park quite like Disney. Where else can you see all your favorite Disney characters? Nowhere! Because the experience is unique, the number of close substitutes is small. Therefore, demand is more inelastic, or less responsive to price changes.

To some degree, the price elasticity of demand depends on consumer preferences. For instance, sports fans are often willing to shell out big bucks to follow their passions. Amateur golfers can play the same courses that professional golfers do. But the opportunity to golf where the professionals play does not come cheaply. A round of golf at the Tournament Players Club at Sawgrass, a famous course in Florida, costs close to $300. Why are some golfers willing to pay that much? For an avid golfer with the financial means, the experience of living out the same shots seen on television tournaments is worth $300. In this case, demand is inelastic—the avid golfer does not view other golf courses as good substitutes. However, a less enthusiastic golfer, or one without the financial resources, is happy to golf on a less expensive course even if the pros don't play it on TV. When less expensive golf courses serve as good substitutes, the price tag makes demand elastic. Ultimately, whether demand is inelastic or elastic depends on the buyer's preferences and resources.

Incentives

THE SHARE OF THE BUDGET SPENT ON THE GOOD Despite our example of an avid and affluent golfer willing to pay a premium fee to play at a famous golf course, in most cases price is a critical element in determining what we can afford and what we choose to buy. If you plan to purchase an 80-inch-screen TV, which can cost as much as $2,000, you will probably be willing to take the time to find the best deal. Because of the high price, even a small percentage discount can cause a relatively large change in consumer demand. A 10% off sale may not sound like much, but when purchasing a big-ticket item like a TV, it can mean hundreds of dollars in savings. In this case, the willingness to shop for the best deal indicates that the price matters, so demand is elastic.

Demand is much more inelastic for inexpensive items on sale. For example, if a candy bar is discounted 10%, the price falls by pennies. The savings from switching candy bars is not enough to make a difference in what you can afford elsewhere. Therefore, the incentive to switch is small. Most consumers still buy their favorite candy because the price difference is so insignificant. In this case, demand is inelastic because the savings gained by purchasing a less desirable candy bar are small in comparison to the consumer's budget.

Saving 10% on this purchase amounts to a few pennies.

NECESSITIES VERSUS LUXURY GOODS A big-screen TV and a candy bar are both luxury goods. You don't need to have either one. But some goods are necessities. For example, you have to pay your rent and water bill, purchase gasoline for your car, and eat. When consumers purchase a necessity, they are generally thinking about the need, not the price. When the need trumps the price, we expect demand to be relatively inelastic. Therefore, the demand for things like cars, textbooks, and heating oil all tend to have inelastic demand.

Saving 10% on this purchase adds up quickly.

WHETHER THE MARKET IS BROADLY OR NARROWLY DEFINED The more broadly we define a market for a good, the harder it is to live without. For instance, demand for housing in general is quite inelastic because without some form of housing you'd be living on the street. However, the demand for a particular apartment or house is much more price sensitive because you don't need to live in *that* exact place. Therefore, a good falling into a narrowly defined category, such as Crest toothpaste, will have more elastic demand than a broadly defined category, such as toothpaste, which has more inelastic demand.

TIME AND THE ADJUSTMENT PROCESS When the market price changes, consumers and sellers respond. But that response does not remain the same over time. As time passes, both consumers and sellers are able to find substitutes. To understand these different market responses, when considering elasticity economists consider time in three distinct periods: the *immediate run*, the *short run*, and the *long run*.

This is *not* the time to try and find cheap gas.

In the **immediate run**, there is no time for consumers to adjust their behavior. Consider the demand for gasoline. When the gas tank is empty, you have to stop at the nearest gas station and pay the posted price. Filling up as soon as possible is more important than driving around searching for the lowest price. Inelastic demand exists whenever price is secondary to the desire to attain a certain amount of the good. So in the case of an empty tank, the demand for gasoline is inelastic.

But what if your tank is not empty? The **short run** is a period of time when consumers can partially adjust their behavior (in this case, can search for a good deal on gas). In the short run, we make decisions that reflect our immediate or short-term wants, needs, or limitations. When consumers have some time to make a purchase, they gain flexibility. They can shop for lower prices at the pump, carpool to save gas, or even change how often they drive. In the short run, flexibility reduces the demand for expensive gasoline and makes consumer demand more elastic.

Finally, if we relax the time constraint completely, it is possible to use even less gasoline. The **long run** is a period of time when consumers have time to fully adjust to market conditions. In the long run, we make decisions that reflect our wants, needs, and limitations over a long time horizon. If gasoline prices are high in the long run, consumers can relocate closer to work and purchase fuel-efficient cars. These changes further reduce the demand for gasoline. As a result of the flexibility that additional time gives the consumer, the demand for gasoline becomes more elastic.

We have looked at five determinants of elasticity—substitutes, the share of the budget spent on the good, necessities versus luxury goods, whether the

In the **immediate run**, there is no time for consumers to adjust their behavior.

The **short run** is a period of time when consumers can partially adjust their behavior. In the short run, we make decisions that reflect our immediate or short-term wants, needs, or limitations.

The **long run** is a period of time when consumers have time to fully adjust to market conditions. In the long run, we make decisions that reflect our wants, needs, and limitations over a long time horizon.

TABLE 4.1

Developing Intuition for the Price Elasticity of Demand

Example	Discussion	Overall elasticity
Football tickets for a true fan 	Being able to watch a game in person and go to pregame and postgame tailgates is a unique experience. For many fans, the experience of going to the game has few close substitutes. In addition, this is a narrowly defined experience. Therefore, the demand is relatively inelastic.	Tends to be relatively inelastic
Assigned textbooks for a course in your major 	The information inside a textbook is valuable. Substitutes such as older editions and free online resources are not exactly the same. As a result, most students buy the required course materials. Acquiring the textbook is more important than the price paid; therefore, the demand is inelastic. The fact that a textbook is needed in the short run (for a few months while taking a class) also tends to make the demand inelastic.	Tends to be inelastic
A slice of pizza from Domino's 	In most locations, many pizza competitors exist, so there are many close substitutes. The presence of so much competition tends to make the demand for a narrowly defined brand of pizza elastic.	Tends to be elastic
A Yellow Kia Soul 	There are many styles, makes, and colors of cars to choose from. With large purchases, consumers are sensitive to smaller percentages of savings. Moreover, people typically plan their car purchases many months or years in advance. The combination of all these factors makes the demand for any narrowly defined model relatively elastic.	Tends to be relatively elastic

market is broadly or narrowly defined, and time. Each is significant, but the number of substitutes tends to be the most influential factor and dominates the others. Table 4.1 will help you develop your intuition about how different market situations influence the overall elasticity of demand.

Computing the Price Elasticity of Demand

Until this point, our discussion of elasticity has been descriptive. However, to apply the concept of elasticity in decision-making, we need to view it more quantitatively. For example, if the owner of a business is trying to decide whether to put a good on sale, he or she needs to estimate how many new customers would purchase it at the sale price. If a government is considering a new tax, it needs to know how much revenue that tax will generate. These are questions about elasticity that we can evaluate by using a mathematical formula.

PRACTICE WHAT YOU KNOW

Price Elasticity of Demand

Umbrella
GRÖSSBY
blue/yellow
$4.99
Rainy day special
$2.50
Offer valid on GRÖSSBY umbrella only.
IKEA

Take a look at this IKEA advertisement and think about the determinants of the price elasticity of demand.

QUESTION: Do you think IKEA's "Rainy day special" price makes sense?

ANSWER: Let's start by figuring out whether the demand for umbrellas is elastic or inelastic when it is raining. The GRÖSSBY umbrella is quite inexpensive even at full price, so the purchase would represent only a small share of a consumer's budget. That would tend to make the demand inelastic. Also, when do you need an umbrella? When it's raining, of course! Consumers without umbrellas need them immediately, and that also tends to make demand inelastic. Finally, how many good substitutes are there for an umbrella? A raincoat or poncho, maybe, but it's a lot harder for two people to share a raincoat than an umbrella. The lack of good substitutes is another factor that tends to make demand inelastic. On rainy days, then, demand is even more inelastic than usual. If IKEA decided to charge more and raised the price of the GRÖSSBY on rainy days, instead of lowering it, the store would have increased revenues. From a short-run revenue perspective, the rainy day special does not make any sense. Instead, IKEA's pricing strategy seems designed to build long-run brand loyalty—something we will discuss in more detail in Chapter 12.

THE PRICE ELASTICITY OF DEMAND FORMULA Let's begin with an example of a pizza shop. Consider an owner who is trying to attract more customers. For one month, he lowers the price of a pizza by 10% and is pleased to find that sales jump by 30%.

Here is the formula for the price elasticity of demand (E_D):

$$\text{price elasticity of demand} = E_D = \frac{\text{percentage change in the quantity demanded}}{\text{percentage change in price}} \qquad \textbf{(EQUATION 4.1)}$$

Using the data from the example, we calculate the price elasticity of demand as follows:

$$\text{price elasticity of demand} = E_D = \frac{30\%}{-10\%} = -3$$

The price elasticity of demand, −3 in this case, is expressed as a coefficient (3) with a specific sign (it has a minus sign in front of it). The coefficient tells us how much the quantity demanded has changed (30%) compared with the price change (−10%). In this case, the percentage change in the quantity demanded is three times the percentage change in the price. Whenever the percentage change in the quantity demanded is larger than the percentage change in price, the demand is elastic. In other words, the price drop made a big difference in how much pizza consumers purchased from the pizza shop. If the opposite occurs and a price drop makes a small difference in the quantity that consumers purchase, demand is inelastic (see Table 4.2).

· ECONOMICS *in the* MEDIA ·

Price Elasticity of Demand

THE BIG BANG THEORY

The Mystic Warlords of Ka'a (an obvious spoof of Magic: The Gathering) is a fictional trading card game that Sheldon, Leonard, Raj, and Howard all enjoy playing. Howard complains about the release of a new expansion pack called Wild West Witches:

RAJ: Hey, look, the new Warlords of Ka'a expansion pack is out.

HOWARD: A new one? Unbelievable. They just keep making up more cheesy monsters, slapping them on cards, and selling them at 25 bucks a pop.

RAJ: Stuart, settle an argument for us. Who would win, Billy the Kid or the White Wizard?

STUART: If I tell you that, I'm robbing you of the hours of fun you could have for the magical, rootin' tootin' low price of $24.95.

RAJ: I'll take one.

HOWARD: Mmm, make it two.

LEONARD: I hate all of you and myself. Three.

STUART: I'll ring it up. Like shooting nerds in a barrel.

Analysis: Expansion packs allow players of Mystic (and other role-playing games) the opportunity to improve the deck of cards with which they play the game. Because all of the guys are smart and competitive, new expansion packs make Mystic more challenging to play and also increases the chance of winning when you play against others who do not have the latest cards. The demand for new expansion packs is quite inelastic because the purchase is made in the short run, the share of the budget that each guy spends on the item ($25) is relatively small, and the number of available substitutes for cards with new powers is effectively zero.

Howard considers buying an expansion pack.

The negative (minus) sign in front of the coefficient is equally important. Recall that the law of demand describes a negative relationship between the price of a good and the quantity demanded; when price rises, the quantity demanded falls. The E_D coefficient reflects this negative relationship with a negative sign. In other words, the pizza shop drops its price and consumers buy more pizza. Because the price of pizza and consumer purchases of pizza generally move in opposite directions, the sign of the price elasticity of demand is almost always negative.

THE MIDPOINT METHOD Our earlier calculation was simple because we looked at the change in price and the change in the quantity demanded from only one direction—that is, from a high price to a lower price and from the corresponding lower quantity demanded to the higher quantity demanded. However, the complete—and proper—way to calculate elasticity is from both directions. Consider the following demand schedule for pizza:

Price	Quantity demanded
$12	20
6	30

Let's calculate the elasticity of demand. If the price drops from $12 to $6—a drop of 50%—the quantity demanded increases from 20 to 30—a rise of 50%. Plugging the percentage changes into the E_D formula yields

$$\text{price elasticity of demand} = E_D = \frac{50\%}{-50\%} = -1.0$$

But if the price rises from $6 to $12—an increase of 100%—the quantity demanded falls from 30 to 20, or decreases by 33%. Plugging the percentage changes into the E_D formula yields

$$\text{price elasticity of demand} = E_D = \frac{-33\%}{100\%} = -0.33$$

This result occurs because percentage changes are usually calculated by using the initial value as the base, or reference point. In this example, we worked the problem two ways: by using $12 as the starting point and dropping the price to $6, and then by using $6 as the starting point and increasing the price to $12. Even though we are measuring elasticity over the same range of values, the percentage changes are different.

To avoid this problem, economists use the *midpoint method,* which gives the same answer for the elasticity no matter what point you begin with. Equation 4.2 uses the midpoint method to express the price elasticity of demand. While this equation looks more complicated than Equation 4.1, it is not. The midpoint method merely specifies how to plug in the initial and ending values for price and quantity to determine the percentage changes. Q_1 and P_1 are the initial values, and Q_2 and P_2 are the ending values.

$$E_D = \frac{\text{change in Q} \div \text{average value of Q}}{\text{change in P} \div \text{average value of P}} \qquad \textbf{(EQUATION 4.2)}$$

$$= \frac{(Q_2 - Q_1) \div [(Q_1 + Q_2) \div 2]}{(P_2 - P_1) \div [(P_1 + P_2) \div 2]}$$

The change in the quantity demanded, $(Q_2 - Q_1)$, and the change in price, $(P_2 - P_1)$, are each divided by the average of the initial and ending values, or $[(Q_1 + Q_2) \div 2]$ and $[(P_1 + P_2) \div 2]$.

The midpoint method is the preferred method for solving elasticity problems. To see why, let's return to our pizza demand example.

If the price rises from \$6 to \$12, the quantity demanded falls from 30 to 20. Here the initial values are $P_1 = \$6$ and $Q_1 = 30$. The ending values are $P_2 = \$12$ and $Q_2 = 20$. Using the midpoint method,

$$E_D = \frac{(20 - 30) \div [(30 + 20) \div 2]}{(\$12 - \$6) \div [(\$6 + \$12) \div 2]} = \frac{-10 \div 25}{\$6 \div \$9} = -0.60$$

If the price falls from \$12 to \$6, quantity demanded rises from 20 to 30. This time, the initial values are $P_1 = \$12$ and $Q_1 = 20$. The ending values are $P_2 = \$6$ and $Q_2 = 30$. Using the midpoint method,

$$E_D = \frac{(30 - 20) \div [(20 + 30) \div 2]}{(\$6 - \$12) \div [(\$12 + \$6) \div 2]} = \frac{10 \div 25}{-\$6 \div \$9} = -0.60$$

When we calculated the price elasticity of demand from \$6 to \$12 using \$6 as the initial point, $E_D = -0.33$. Moving in the opposite direction, from \$12 to \$6, made \$12 the initial reference point and $E_D = -1.0$. The midpoint method splits the difference and uses \$9 and 25 pizzas as the midpoints. This approach makes the calculation of the elasticity coefficient the same, –0.60, no matter what direction the price moves. Therefore, economists use the midpoint method to standardize the results.

So, using the midpoint method, we arrive at an elasticity coefficient of –0.60, which is between 0 and –1. What does that number mean? In this case, the percentage change in the quantity demanded is less than the percentage change in the price. Whenever the percentage change in the quantity demanded is smaller than the percentage change in price, we say that demand is inelastic. In other words, the price drop does not make a big difference in how much pizza consumers purchase from the pizza shop. When the elasticity coefficient is less than –1, the opposite is true, and demand is elastic.

Graphing the Price Elasticity of Demand

Visualizing elasticity graphically helps us understand the relationship between elastic and inelastic demand. Figure 4.1 shows elasticity graphically. As demand becomes increasingly elastic, or responsive to price changes, the demand curve flattens. The range of elasticity runs from perfectly inelastic through perfectly elastic.

For many pet owners, the demand for veterinary care is perfectly inelastic.

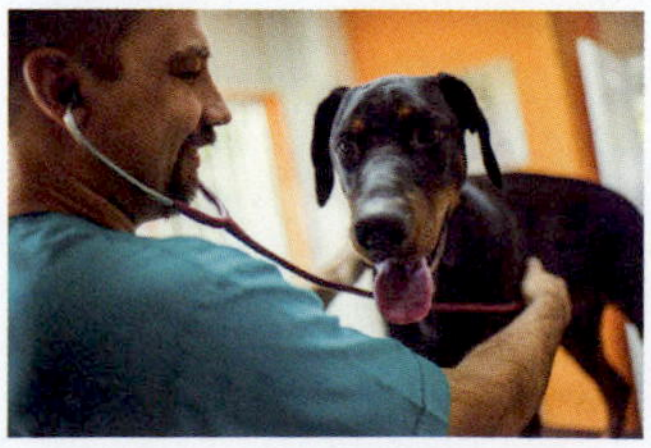

PERFECTLY INELASTIC DEMAND Figure 4.1, panel (a), depicts the price elasticity for pet care. Many pet owners report that they would pay any amount of money to help their sick or injured pet get better. For these pet owners, the demand curve is a vertical line. If you look along the quantity axis in panel (a), you will see that the quantity of pet care demanded (Q_D) remains constant no matter what it costs. At the same time, the price increases from P_0 to P_1. We can calculate the price elasticity coefficient as follows:

$$E_{\text{pet care}} = \frac{\text{percentage change in } Q_D}{\text{percentage change in P}} = \frac{0}{\text{percentage change in P}} = 0$$

When zero is in the numerator, we know that the answer will be zero no matter what we find in the denominator. This conclusion makes sense. Many pet owners will try to help their pet feel better no matter what the cost, so we can say that their demand is *perfectly inelastic*. This means that the value of E_D will always be zero. (Of course, pet care is not perfectly inelastic, because there is certainly a price beyond which some pet owners would not or could not pay; but for illustrative purposes, let's say that pet care *is* perfectly elastic.) As you continue reading this section, refer to Table 4.2 on page 128 to help you keep track of the different types of elasticity.

The demand for electricity is relatively inelastic.

RELATIVELY INELASTIC DEMAND Moving on to panel (b) of Figure 4.1, we consider the demand for electricity. Whereas many pet owners will not change their consumption of health care for their pet no matter what the cost, consumers of electricity will modify their use of electricity in response to price changes. When the price of electricity goes up, they will use less, and when the price goes down, they will use more. Because living without electricity is not practical, using less is a matter of making relatively small lifestyle adjustments—buying energy-efficient light bulbs or adjusting the thermostat a few degrees. As a result, the demand curve in panel (b) is relatively steep, but not completely vertical as in panel (a).

When the change on the quantity axis is small compared with the change on the price axis, the price elasticity is *relatively inelastic*. Plugging these changes into the elasticity formula, we get

$$E_{\text{electricity}} = \frac{\text{percentage change in } Q_D}{\text{percentage change in P}} = \frac{\text{small change}}{\text{large change}}$$

Recall that the law of demand describes a negative relationship between price and quantity demanded. Therefore, the changes along the price and quantity axes will always be in opposite directions. A price elasticity of zero tells us there is no change in the quantity demanded when price changes. So when demand is relatively inelastic, the price elasticity of demand must be relatively close to zero. The easiest way to think about this scenario is to consider how a 10% increase in electric rates affects most households. How much less electricity would you use? The answer for most people would be a little less, but not 10% less. You can adjust your thermostat, but you still need electricity to run your appliances and lights. When the price changes more than quantity changes, there is a larger change in the denominator. Therefore, the price elasticity of demand is between 0 and −1 when demand is relatively inelastic.

The demand for apples is relatively elastic.

RELATIVELY ELASTIC DEMAND In Figure 4.1, panel (c), we consider apples. Because there are many good substitutes for apples, the demand for apples is *relatively elastic*. The flexibility of consumer demand for apples is illustrated by the degree of responsiveness we see along the quantity axis relative to the change exhibited along the price axis. We can observe this responsiveness by noting that a relatively elastic demand curve

The demand for a $10 bill is perfectly elastic.

is flatter than an inelastic demand curve. So whereas perfectly inelastic demand shows no change in demand with an increase in price, and relatively inelastic demand shows a small change in quantity demanded with an increase in price, relatively elastic demand shows a relatively large change in quantity demanded with an increase in price. Placing this information into the elasticity formula gives us

$$E_{\text{apples}} = \frac{\text{percentage change in } Q_D}{\text{percentage change in P}} = \frac{\text{large change}}{\text{small change}}$$

Now the numerator—the percentage change in Q_D—is large, and the denominator—the percentage change in P—is small. E_D is less than −1. Recall that the sign must be negative, because there is a negative relationship between price and the quantity demanded. As the price elasticity of demand moves farther away from zero, the consumer becomes more responsive to a price change. Because many other fruits are good substitutes for apples, a small change in the price of apples will have a large effect on the quantity demanded.

PERFECTLY ELASTIC DEMAND Figure 4.1, panel (d), provides an interesting example: the demand for a $10 bill. Would you pay $11.00 to get a $10 bill? No. Would you pay $10.01 for a $10 bill? Still no. However, when the price drops to $10.00, you will probably become indifferent (that is, you will be equally satisfied with paying $10.00 for the $10 bill or not making the trade). The real magic here occurs when the price drops to $9.99. How many $10 bills would you buy if you could buy them for $9.99 or less? The answer: as many as possible! This is exactly what happens in currency markets, where small differences among currency prices around the globe motivate traders to buy and sell large quantities of currency and clear a small profit on the difference in exchange rates. This extreme form of price sensitivity is illustrated by a perfectly horizontal demand curve, which means that demand is *perfectly elastic*. Solving for the elasticity yields

$$E_{\$10\text{ bill}} = \frac{\text{percentage change in } Q_D}{\text{percentage change in P}} = \frac{\text{nearly infinite change}}{\text{very small (\$0.01) change}}$$

We can think of this very small price change, from $10.00 to $9.99, as having essentially an unlimited effect on the quantity of $10 bills demanded. Traders go from being uninterested in trading at $10.00 to seeking to buy as many $10 bills as possible when the price drops to $9.99. As a result, the price elasticity of demand approaches negative infinity (−∞).

UNITARY ELASTICITY There is a fifth type of elasticity, not depicted in Figure 4.1. *Unitary elasticity* describes the situation in which elasticity is neither elastic nor inelastic. This situation occurs when E_D is exactly −1, and it happens when the percentage change in price is exactly equal to the percentage change in quantity demanded. This characteristic of unitary elasticity will be important when we discuss the connection between elasticity and total revenue later in this chapter. You're probably wondering what an example of a unitary

FIGURE 4.1

Elasticity and the Demand Curve

For any given price change across two demand curves, demand will be more elastic on the flatter demand curve than on the steeper demand curve. In (a), the demand is perfectly inelastic, so the price does not matter. In (b), the demand is relatively inelastic, so the price is less important than the quantity purchased. In (c), the demand is relatively elastic, so the price matters more than quantity. In (d), the demand is perfectly elastic, so price is all that matters.

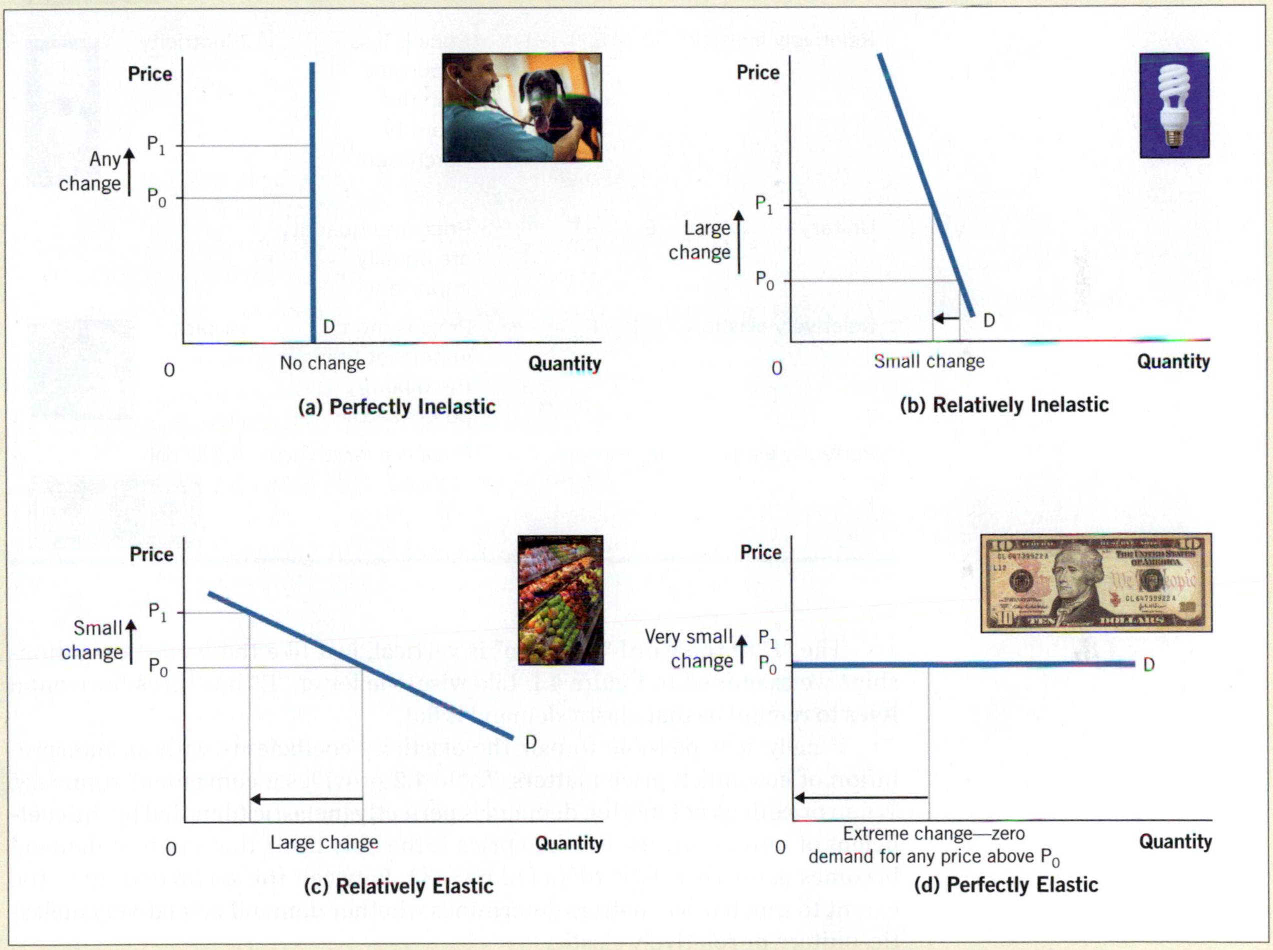

good would be. Relax. It is impossible to find a good that has a price elasticity of exactly −1 at all price points. It is enough to know that unitary demand represents the crossover from elastic to inelastic demand.

PRICE ELASTICITY OF DEMAND: A SUMMARY Now that you have had a chance to look at all four panels in Figure 4.1, here is a handy trick you can use to keep the difference between inelastic and elastic demand straight.

I = inelastic and **E** = elastic

TABLE 4.2

The Relationship between Price Elasticity of Demand and Price

Elasticity	E_D coefficient	Interpretation	Example in Figure 4.1
Perfectly inelastic	$E_D = 0$	Price does not matter.	Saving your pet 
Relatively inelastic	$0 > E_D > -1$	Price is less important than the quantity purchased.	Electricity 
Unitary	$E_D = -1$	Price and quantity are equally important.	
Relatively elastic	$-1 > E_D > -\infty$	Price is more important than the quantity purchased.	Apples 
Perfectly elastic	$E_D \to -\infty$	Price is everything.	A $10 bill 

The "I" in the word "inelastic" is vertical, just like the inelastic relationships we examined in Figure 4.1. Likewise, the letter "E" has three horizontal lines to remind us that elastic demand is flat.

Finally, it is possible to pair the elasticity coefficients with an interpretation of how much price matters. Table 4.2 provides a convenient summary. When price does not matter, demand is perfectly inelastic (denoted by the coefficient of zero). Conversely, when price is the only thing that matters, demand becomes perfectly elastic (denoted by $-\infty$). Between these two extremes, the extent to which price matters determines whether demand is relatively inelastic, unitary, or relatively elastic.

TIME, ELASTICITY, AND THE DEMAND CURVE We have already seen that increased time makes demand more elastic. Figure 4.2 shows this result graphically. When the price rises from P_1 to P_2, consumers cannot avoid the price increase in the immediate run, and demand is represented by the perfectly inelastic demand curve, D_1. For example, if your gas tank is almost empty, you must purchase gas at the new, higher price. Over a slightly longer time horizon—the short run—consumers are more flexible and drive less in order to buy less gasoline. Demand rotates to D_2, and in the short run consumption declines to Q_2. In the long run, when consumers have time to purchase a more fuel-efficient vehicle or move closer to work, demand rotates to D_3 and gas purchases fall even further. As the demand curve continues to flatten, the quantity demanded falls to Q_3.

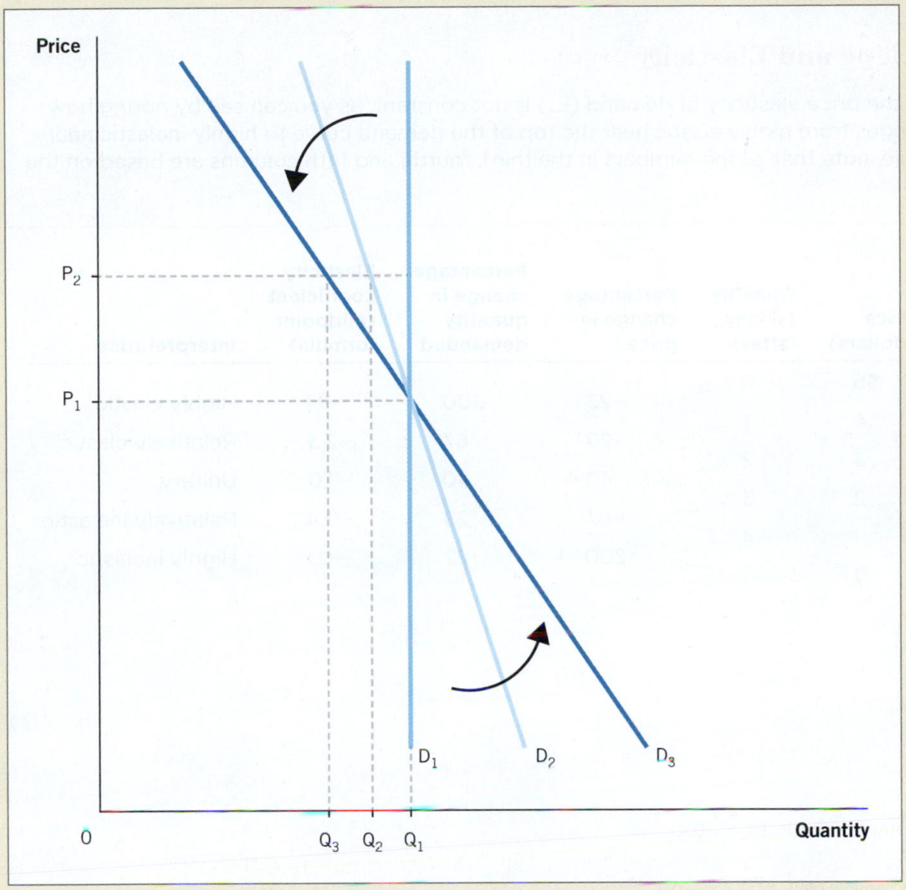

FIGURE 4.2

Elasticity and the Demand Curve over Time

Demand becomes more elastic over time. When the price rises from P_1 to P_2, consumers are unable to avoid the price increase in the immediate run (D_1). In the short run (D_2), consumers become more flexible and consumption declines to Q_2. Eventually, in the long run (D_3), there is time to make lifestyle changes that further reduce consumption. As a result, the demand curve continues to flatten and the quantity demanded falls to Q_3 in response to the higher price.

SLOPE AND ELASTICITY In this section, we pause to make sure that you understand what you are observing in the figures. The demand curves shown in Figures 4.1 and 4.2 are straight lines, and therefore they have a constant slope, or steepness. (A refresher on slope is found in the appendix to Chapter 2.) So, looking at Figures 4.1 and 4.2, you might think that slope is the same as the price elasticity. But slope does not equal elasticity.

Consider, for example, a trip to Starbucks. Would you buy a tall skinny latte if it costs $10? How about $7? What about $5? Say you decide to buy the skinny latte because the price drops from $5 to $4. In this case, a small price change, a drop from $5 to $4, causes you to make the purchase. You can say that the demand for skinny lattes is relatively elastic. Now look at Figure 4.3, which shows a demand curve for skinny lattes. At $5 the consumer purchases zero lattes, at $4 she purchases one latte, at $3 she purchases two, and she continues to buy one additional latte with each $1 drop in price. As you progress downward along the demand curve, price becomes less of an inhibiting factor, and as a result, the price elasticity of demand slowly becomes more inelastic. Notice that the slope of a linear demand curve is constant. However, when we calculate the price elasticity of demand between the various points in Figure 4.3, it becomes clear that demand is increasingly inelastic as we move

FIGURE 4.3

The Difference between Slope and Elasticity

Along any straight demand curve, the price elasticity of demand (E_D) is not constant, as you can see by noting how the price elasticity of demand changes from highly elastic near the top of the demand curve to highly inelastic near the bottom of the curve. In the table, note that all the numbers in the third, fourth, and fifth columns are based on the midpoint formula.

Price (dollars)	Quantity (skinny lattes)	Percentage change in price	Percentage change in quantity demanded	Elasticity coefficient (midpoint formula)	Interpretation
$5	0				
4	1	−22	200	−9.1	Highly elastic
3	2	−29	67	−2.3	Relatively elastic
2	3	−40	40	−1.0	Unitary
1	4	−67	29	−0.4	Relatively inelastic
0	5	−200	22	−0.1	Highly inelastic

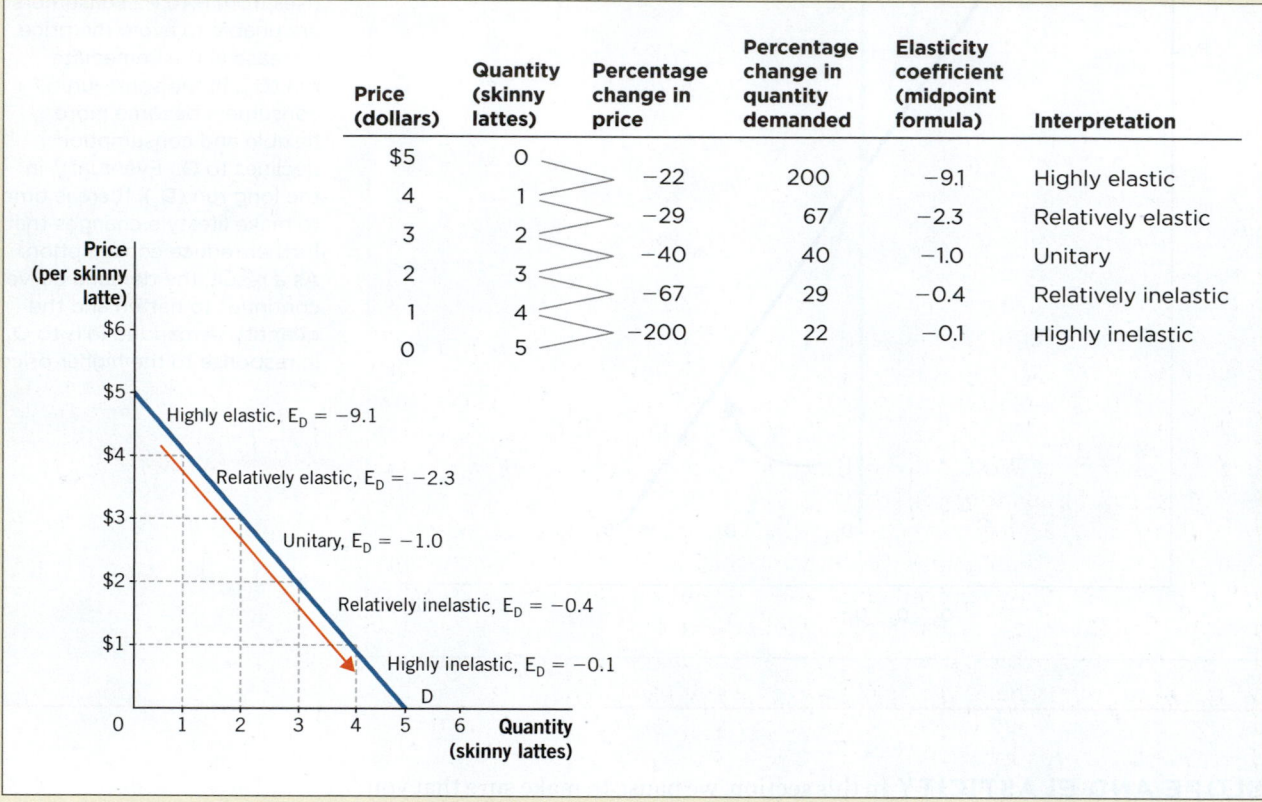

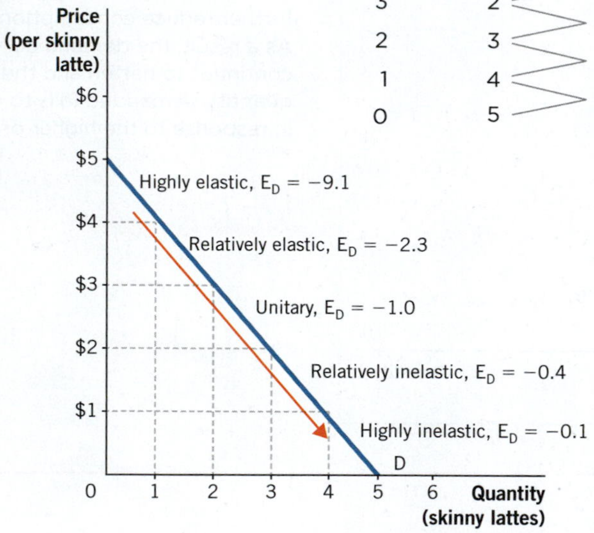

down the demand curve. You can see this in the change in E_D; it steadily increases from −9.1 to −0.1.

Perfectly inelastic demand would exist if the elasticity coefficient reached zero. Recall that a value of zero means that there is no change in the quantity demanded as a result of a price change. Therefore, values close to zero reflect inelastic demand, while those farther away from zero reflect more elastic demand.

Price Elasticity of Demand and Total Revenue

Understanding the price elasticity of demand for the product you sell is important when running a business. Consumer responsiveness to price changes determines whether a firm would be better off raising or lowering its price for

TABLE 4.3

The Price Elasticity of Demand and Total Revenue

Price (P) (per skinny latte)	Quantity (Q) (skinny lattes)	Total revenue P × Q	Percentage change in price	Percentage change in quantity	Elasticity coefficient	Interpretation
$5	0	$0				
			−22	200	−9.1	Highly elastic
4	1	4				
			−29	67	−2.3	Relatively elastic
3	2	6				
			−40	40	−1.0	Unitary
2	3	6				
			−67	29	−0.4	Relatively inelastic
1	4	4				
			−200	22	−0.1	Highly inelastic
0	5	0				

a given product. In this section, we explore the relationship between the price elasticity of demand and a firm's total revenue.

But first we need to understand the concept of total revenue. **Total revenue** is the amount that a firm receives from the sale of goods and services. Total revenue for a particular good is calculated by multiplying the price of the good by the quantity of the good that is sold. Table 4.3 reproduces the table from Figure 4.3 (with numbers based on the midpoint formula) and adds a column for the total revenue. We find the total revenue by multiplying the price of a tall skinny latte by the quantity purchased.

Total revenue is the amount that a firm receives from the sale of goods and services. Total revenue for a particular good is calculated by multiplying the price of the good by the quantity of the good that is sold.

After calculating total revenue at each price, we can look at the column of elasticity coefficients to determine the relationship. When we link revenues with the price elasticity of demand, a trade-off emerges. (This trade-off occurs because total revenue and elasticity relate to price differently. Total revenue involves multiplying the price by the quantity, while elasticity involves dividing the percentage change in quantity demanded by the percentage change in price.) Total revenue is zero when the price is too high ($5 or more) and when the price is too low ($0). Between these two extremes, prices from $1 to $4 generate positive total revenue.

Trade-offs

Consider what happens when the price drops from $5 to $4. At $4, the first latte is purchased. Total revenue is $4 × 1 = $4. This is also the range at which the price elasticity of demand is highly elastic. As a result, lowering the price increases revenue. Revenue continues to increase when the price drops from $4 to $3. Now two lattes are sold, so the total revenue rises to $3 × 2 = $6. At the same time, demand remains elastic. We thus conclude that when demand is elastic, lowering the price will increase total revenue. This relationship is shown in panel (a) of Figure 4.4. By lowering the price from $4 to $3, the business has generated $2 more in revenue. But to generate this extra revenue, the business has lowered the price from $4 to $3 and therefore has given up $1 for each unit it sells. This lost revenue is represented by the red area under the demand curve in panel (a).

When the price drops from $3 to $2, the total revenue stays at $6. This result occurs because demand is unitary, as shown in panel (b). This special condition exists when the percentage price change is exactly offset by an equal percentage change in the quantity demanded. In this situation, revenue remains constant. At $2, three lattes are purchased, so the total revenue is $2 × 3, which is the same as it was when the price was $3. As a result, we can

FIGURE 4.4

(a) The Total Revenue Trade-Off When Demand Is Elastic

In the elastic region of the demand curve, lowering the price will increase total revenue. The gains from increased purchases, shown in the light green area, are greater than the losses from a lower purchase price, shown in the red area. The green area is part of the total revenue that exists at both prices.

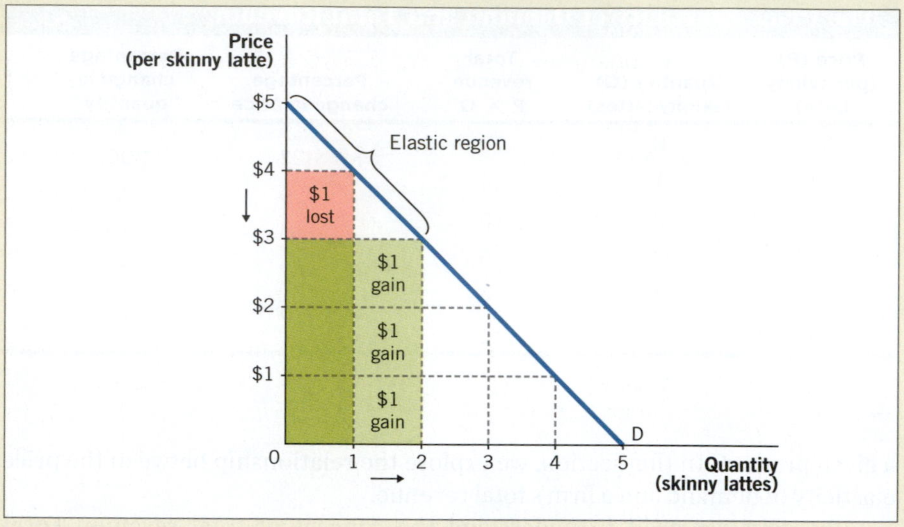

(b) . . . When Demand Is Unitary

When demand is unitary, lowering the price will no longer increase total revenue. The gains from increased purchases, shown in the light green area, are equal to the losses from a lower purchase price, shown in the red area.

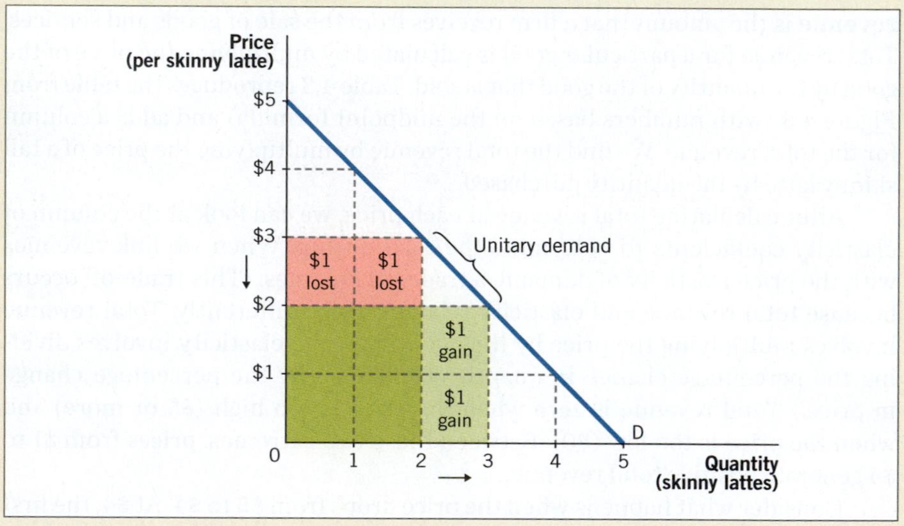

(c) . . . When Demand Is Inelastic

In the inelastic region of the demand curve, lowering the price will decrease total revenue. The gains from increased purchases, shown in the light green area, are smaller than the losses from a lower purchase price, shown in the red area.

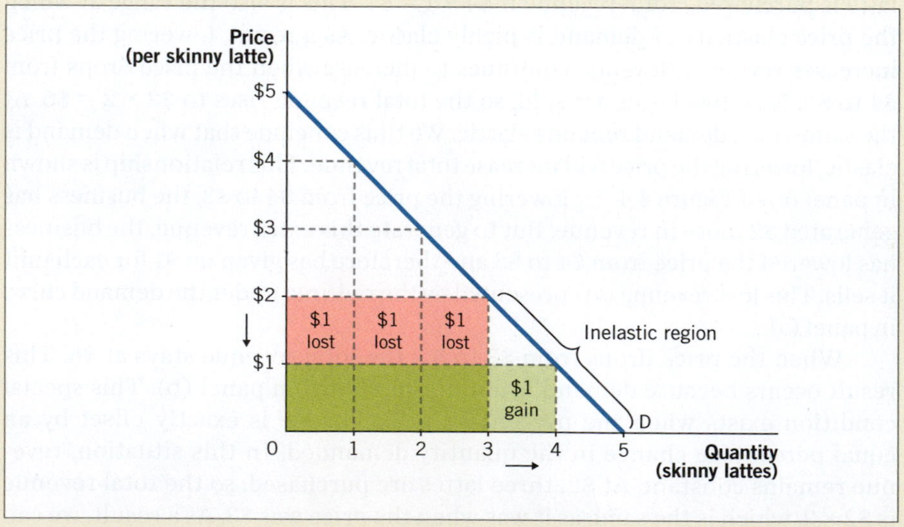

see that total revenue has reached a maximum. Between $3 and $2, the price elasticity of demand is unitary. This finding does not necessarily mean that the firm will operate at the unitary point. Maximizing profit, not revenue, is the ultimate goal of a business, and we have not yet accounted for costs in our calculation of profits.

Once we reach a price below unitary demand, we move into the realm of inelastic demand, shown in panel (c). When the price falls to $1, total revenue declines to $4. This result occurs because the price elasticity of demand is now relatively inelastic, or price insensitive. Even though the price is declining by $1, price is increasingly unimportant; as you can see by the light green square, lowering the price to $1 does not spur a large increase in consumption.

As we see in panel (c), at a price of $2, three units are sold and total revenue is $\$2 \times 3 = \$6$. When the price falls to $1, four units are sold, so the total revenue is now $\$4 \times 1 = \$4$. By lowering the price from $2 to $1, the business has lost $2 in extra revenue because it does not generate enough extra revenue from the lower price. Lowering the price from $2 to $1 causes a loss of $3 in existing sales revenue (the red boxes). At the same time, it generates only $1 in new sales (the light green box), so the net change is a loss of $2.

In this analysis, we see that once the demand curve enters the inelastic area, lowering the price decreases total revenue. This outcome is unambiguously bad for a business. The lower price brings in less revenue and requires the business to produce more goods. Because making goods is costly, it does not make sense to lower prices into the region where revenues decline. We can be sure that no business will intentionally operate in the inelastic region of the demand curve because it will earn less profit.

ECONOMICS IN THE REAL WORLD

PRICE ELASTICITY OF DEMAND: SMOKING VERSUS VAPING

Economists studying the United States and other high-income countries generally find that the price elasticity of demand for tobacco cigarettes lies in a relatively narrow range, from −0.25 to −0.50. This implies that if tobacco cigarette prices rise by 10%, tobacco cigarette smoking will fall by between 2.5 and 5%. But similar studies of e-cigarettes produce values ranging from −0.56 to −0.80, indicating that demand is more elastic.

How much less would you vape if the price rose 10%?

Incentives

It makes sense that e-cigarette users would be more price-sensitive than tobacco smokers, since many users of e-cigarettes are trying to quit smoking altogether. An increase in the price of e-cigarettes will induce some users to switch to the cold-turkey method. It will also, unfortunately, cause other users to go back to tobacco.

PRACTICE WHAT YOU KNOW

Is the demand for a sandwich elastic or inelastic?

Price Elasticity of Demand

The following two questions ask you to compute price elasticity of demand. Before we do the math, ask yourself whether the price elasticity of demand for sandwiches or the antibiotic amoxicillin is elastic.

QUESTION: A deli manager decides to lower the price of a featured sandwich from \$3 to \$2, and she finds that sales during the week increase from 240 to 480 sandwiches. Is demand elastic?

ANSWER: Consumers were flexible and bought significantly more sandwiches in response to the price drop. Let's calculate the price elasticity of demand (E_D) using Equation 4.2. Recall that

$$E_D = \frac{(Q_2 - Q_1) \div [(Q_1 + Q_2) \div 2]}{(P_2 - P_1) \div [(P_1 + P_2) \div 2]}$$

Plugging in the values from the question yields

$$E_D = \frac{(480 - 240) \div [(240 + 480) \div 2]}{(\$2 - \$3) \div [(\$3 + \$2) \div 2]} = \frac{240 \div 360}{-\$1 \div \$2.50}$$

Therefore, $E_D = -1.67$. This means that if the price decreases by 1%, the quantity of sandwiches consumed will increase by 1.67%.

Whenever the price elasticity of demand is less than −1, demand is elastic: the percentage change in the quantity demanded is greater than the percentage change in price. This outcome is exactly what the store manager expected. But sandwiches are just one option for a meal; there are many other choices, such as salads, burgers, and chicken—all of which cost more than the now-cheaper sandwich. Therefore, we should not be surprised that there is a relatively large percentage increase in sandwich purchases by price-conscious customers.

Is the demand for amoxicillin elastic or inelastic?

QUESTION: A local pharmacy manager decides to raise the price of a 50-pill prescription of amoxicillin (an antibiotic) from \$8 to \$10. The pharmacy tracks the sales of amoxicillin over the next month and finds that sales decline from 1,500 boxes to 1,480. Is demand elastic?

ANSWER: First, let's consider the potential substitutes for amoxicillin. To be sure, it's possible to substitute other drugs, but they might not be as effective. Therefore, most patients prefer to use the drug prescribed by their doctor. Also, in this case the cost of the drug is relatively small. Finally, patients' need for amoxicillin is a short-run consideration. They want the medicine now so they will get better! All three factors would lead us to believe that the demand for amoxicillin is relatively inelastic. Let's find out if the data confirm that intuition.

The price elasticity of demand using the midpoint method is

$$E_D = \frac{(Q_2 - Q_1) \div [(Q_1 + Q_2) \div 2]}{(P_2 - P_1) \div [(P_1 + P_2) \div 2]}$$

(CONTINUED)

Plugging in the values from the question yields

$$E_D = \frac{(1480 - 1500) \div [(1500 + 1480) \div 2]}{(\$10 - \$8) \div [(\$8 + \$10) \div 2]}$$

Simplifying produces this equation:

$$E_D = \frac{-20 \div 1490}{\$2 \div \$9}$$

Therefore, $E_D = -0.06$. If the price increases by 1%, the quantity of amoxicillin purchased will drop by just 0.06%.

Recall that an E_D near zero indicates that the price elasticity of demand is highly inelastic, which is what we suspected. The price increase does not cause consumption to fall very much. If the store manager was hoping to bring in a little extra revenue from the sales of amoxicillin, his plan is successful. Before the price increase, the business sold 1,500 units at \$8, so total revenue was \$12,000. After the price increase, sales decrease to 1,480 units, but the new price is \$10, so total revenue is now \$14,800. Raising the price of amoxicillin has helped the pharmacy make an additional \$2,800 in total revenue.

CHALLENGE QUESTION: Now suppose that the local pharmacy manager decides to raise the price of a 50-pill prescription of amoxicillin from \$8 to \$40, instead of just to \$10. Again, the pharmacy tracks the sales, and this time it finds that sales decline from 1,500 boxes all the way down to 50 boxes. Is demand still elastic?

ANSWER: Plugging in the values from the question using the midpoint method yields

$$E_D = \frac{(50 - 1500) \div [(1500 + 50) \div 2]}{(\$40 - \$8) \div [(\$8 + \$40) \div 2]}$$

Simplifying produces

$$E_D = \frac{-1450 \div 775}{\$32 \div \$24}$$

Therefore $E_D = -1.41$. So, if the price increases by 1%, the quantity of amoxicillin purchased will drop by 1.41%.

An E_D value below -1 represents relatively elastic demand. At this point, the price increase has clearly backfired. Total revenue has gone from \$12,000 (1,500 boxes at \$8 each) down to 50 boxes × \$40 per box = \$2,000. Raising the price of amoxicillin to a point where demand is elastic has cost the pharmacy \$10,000 in total revenue. This is a vivid reminder that the elasticity of demand steadily becomes more elastic as the price rises.

SNAPSHOT

Price Elasticity of Demand

Determining the price elasticity of demand for a product or service involves calculating the responsiveness of quantity demanded to a change in the price. The chart below gives the actual price elasticity of demand for ten common products and services. Remember, the number is always negative because of the negative relationship between price and the quantity demanded. Why is price elasticity of demand important? It reveals consumer behavior and allows for better pricing strategies by businesses.

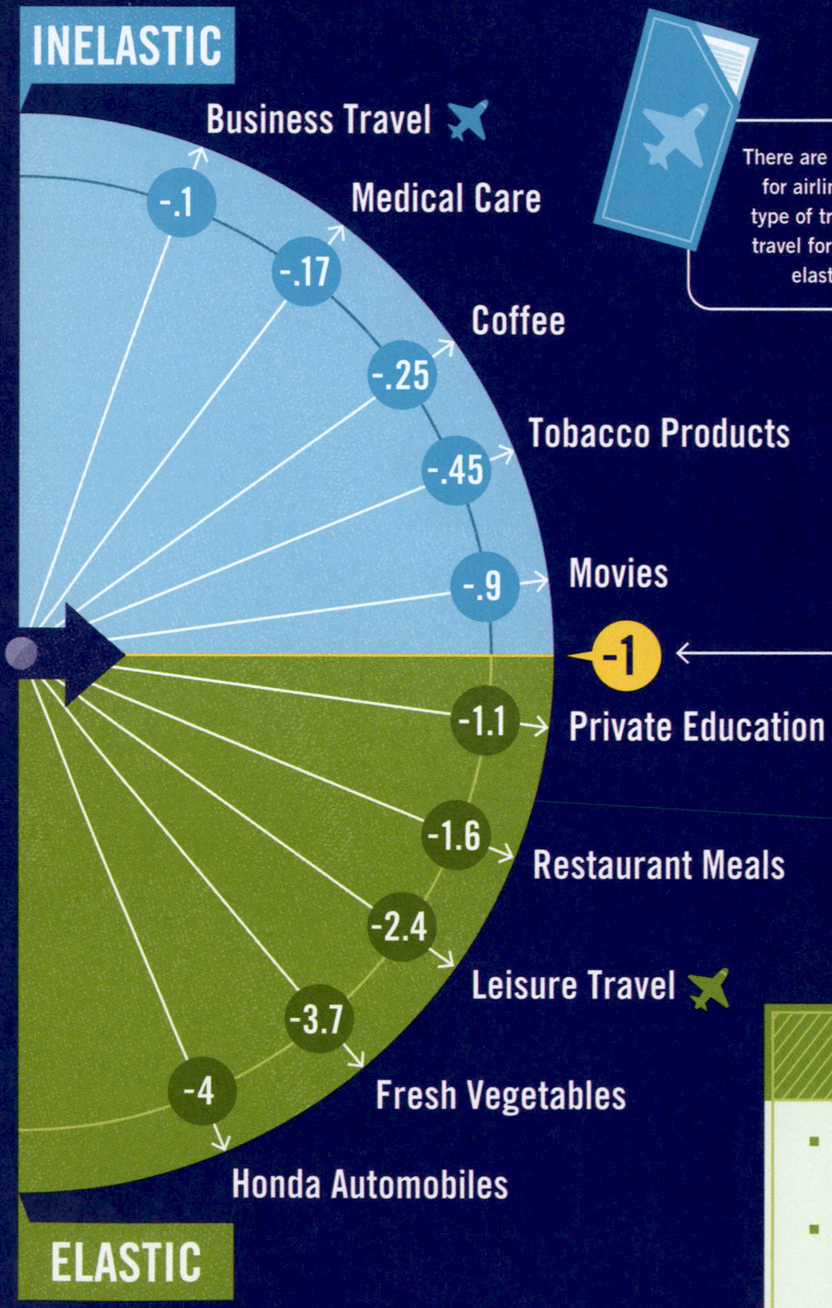

There are two very different elasticity values for airline travel. The relatively inelastic type of travel includes business travel and travel for an emergency, and the relatively elastic type is travel for pleasure.

An inelastic product or service is not highly responsive to a price change and has an elasticity value between 0 and -1. Between the inelastic and elastic regions, demand is unitary and equal to -1. A relatively elastic product or service is highly responsive to a price change and has an elasticity value less than -1.

REVIEW QUESTIONS

- Why is demand for coffee relatively inelastic?
- For business owners, why is it important to understand whether demand for their products is elastic or inelastic?

· ECONOMICS *in the* MEDIA ·

Price Elasticity of Demand and Total Revenues

SHARK TANK: VURTEGO POGO

Do you increase revenue by lowering or raising prices?

The answer, according to economist Charity-Joy Acchiardo, is that "it all depends on the price elasticity of demand for your product or service." Acchiardo is one of the creators of econshark.com, a website dedicated to dissecting the economic principles on display in the popular TV show *Shark Tank*. In one episode, Brian Spencer is looking for an investment from the Sharks so he can mass-market his amazingly cool, extreme-sport pogo stick, the "Vurtego Pogo." However, Shark Robert Herjavec questions whether high-end pogo sticks are a good fit for the mass market. Spencer's current price of $330, Robert feels, is too low for a specialty product like a high-performance pogo stick, but too high for the mass market. The other Sharks agree. They urge Spencer to raise his price and concentrate on dominating the niche he's carved out for himself. Spencer leaves the Shark Tank empty-handed but realizing that he's been given good advice. When something is cool and there is nothing else exactly like it on the market, people are willing to pay more to buy one. Translation: when demand is inelastic, don't price your product too low.

How much would you pay to be able to do flips on a pogo stick?

How Do Changes in Income and the Prices of Other Goods Affect Elasticity?

We have seen how consumer demand responds to changes in the price of a single good. In this section, we examine how responsive demand is to changes in income and to price changes in other goods.

Income Elasticity

Changes in personal income can have a large effect on consumer spending. After all, the money in your pocket influences not only how much you buy, but also the types of purchases you make. A consumer who is low on money may opt to buy a cheap generic product, while someone with a little extra cash can afford to upgrade. The grocery store aisle reflects different shoppers' budgets. Store brands and name products compete for shelf space. Lower-income shoppers can choose the store brand to save money, while more affluent shoppers can choose their favorite brand-name product without worrying about the purchase price. The **income elasticity of demand** (E_I) measures how a change in income affects spending. It is calculated by dividing the percentage change in the quantity demanded by the percentage change in personal income:

The **income elasticity of demand** (E_I) measures how a change in income affects spending.

(EQUATION 4.3)

$$E_I = \frac{\text{percentage change in the quantity demanded}}{\text{percentage change in income}}$$

Unlike the price elasticity of demand, which is negative, the income elasticity of demand can be positive or negative. When a higher level of income enables the consumer to purchase more, the goods that are purchased are *normal goods*, a term we learned in Chapter 3. Because the demand for normal goods goes up with income, they have a positive income elasticity; a rise in income causes a rise in the quantity demanded. For instance, if you receive a 20% pay raise and you decide to pay an extra 10% on your cable TV bill to add HBO, the resulting income elasticity is positive, because 10% divided by 20% is 0.5. Whenever a good is normal, the result is a positive income elasticity of demand, and purchases of the good rise as income expands and purchases of the good fall as income falls.

Normal goods fall into two categories: *necessities* and *luxuries*. Goods that people consider necessities generally have income elasticities between 0 and 1. For example, expenditures on items such as clothing, electricity, and gasoline are unavoidable, and consumers at any income level must buy them no matter what. Although purchases of necessities will increase as income rises, they do not rise as fast as the increase in income does. Therefore, as income increases, spending on necessities will expand at a slower rate than the increase in income.

Rising income enables consumers to enjoy significantly more luxuries, producing an income elasticity of demand greater than 1 for luxuries. For instance, a family of modest means may do their own lawn mowing and other outdoor maintenance. However, as the family's income rises, they can afford a lawn care service and can devote their time to something else.

Clothing purchases expand with income.

In Chapter 3, we saw that *inferior goods* are those that people will choose not to purchase when their income goes up. Inferior goods have a negative income elasticity, because as income expands, the demand for these goods declines. We see this effect in Table 4.4 with the example of macaroni and cheese, an inexpensive meal. As a household's income rises, the family is able to afford healthier food and more variety in its meals. Consequently, the number of times that mac and cheese is purchased declines. The decline in consumption indicates that mac and cheese is an inferior good, as reflected in the negative sign of the income elasticity.

Cross-Price Elasticity

A lawn care service is a luxury good.

Now we will look at how a price change in one good can affect the demand for a related good. For instance, if you enjoy pizza, the choice between ordering from Domino's or Pizza Hut is influenced by the price of both goods. The **cross-price elasticity of demand** (E_C) measures the percentage change in the quantity demanded of one good to the percentage change in the price of a related good:

$$E_C = \frac{\text{percentage change in the quantity demanded of one good}}{\text{percentage change in the price of a related good}}$$

(EQUATION 4.4)

The **cross-price elasticity of demand** (E_C) measures the percentage change in the quantity demanded of one good to the percentage change in the price of a related good.

Consider how two goods are related. If the goods are substitutes, a price rise in one good will cause the quantity demanded of that good to decline. At the same time, because consumers can purchase the substitute good for the same price as before, demand for the substitute good will increase. When the price of Domino's pizza rises, consumers will buy more pizza from Pizza Hut. This means that the cross-price elasticity of demand is positive.

Trade-offs

The opposite is true if the goods are complements. In that case, a price increase in one good will make the joint consumption of both goods more expensive. Therefore, the consumption of both goods will decline. For example, a price increase for turkeys will cause the quantity demanded of both turkey and gravy to decline, and a price decrease for turkeys will cause the quantity demanded of both turkey and gravy to increase. This means that the cross-price elasticity of demand is negative.

What if there is no relationship between two goods? For example, if the price of basketballs goes up, that price increase probably will not affect the quantity demanded of bedroom slippers. In this case, the cross-price elasticity is neither positive nor negative; it is zero. Table 4.5 lists cross-price elasticity values according to type of good.

TABLE 4.4

Income Elasticity

Type of good	Subcategory	E_I coefficient	Example	
Inferior		$E_I < 0$	Macaroni and cheese	
Normal	Necessity	$0 < E_I < 1$	Milk	
Normal	Luxury	$E_I > 1$	Diamond ring	

TABLE 4.5

Cross-Price Elasticity

Type of good	E_c coefficient	Example
Substitutes	$E_C > 0$	Pizza Hut and Domino's  
No relationship	$E_C = 0$	A basketball and bedroom slippers  
Complements	$E_C < 0$	Turkey and gravy  

PRACTICE WHAT YOU KNOW

Cross-Price Elasticity of Demand

To learn how to calculate cross-price elasticity, let's consider enjoying the soft drink Mr. Pibb with Red Vines candy. If you have never tried this combination, you should!

QUESTION: Suppose that the price of a 2-liter bottle of Mr. Pibb falls from $1.49 to $1.29. In the week immediately preceding the price drop, a local store sells 60 boxes of Red Vines. After the price drop, sales of Red Vines increase to 80 boxes. What is the cross-price elasticity of demand for Red Vines when the price of Mr. Pibb falls from $1.49 to $1.29?

ANSWER: The cross-price elasticity of demand using the midpoint method is

$$E_C = \frac{(Q_{RV2} - Q_{RV1}) \div [(Q_{RV1} + Q_{RV2}) \div 2]}{(P_{MP2} - P_{MP1}) \div [(P_{MP1} + P_{MP2}) \div 2]}$$

Notice that there are now additional subscripts to denote that we are measuring the percentage change in the quantity demanded of good RV (Red Vines) in response to the percentage change in the price of good MP (Mr. Pibb).

Plugging in the values from the example yields

$$E_C = \frac{(80 - 60) \div [(60 + 80) \div 2]}{(\$1.29 - \$1.49) \div [(\$1.49 + \$1.29) \div 2]}$$

Simplifying produces

$$E_C = \frac{20 \div 70}{-\$0.20 \div \$1.39}$$

Solving for E_C gives us a value of −1.99. The result's negative value confirms our intuition that two goods that go well together are complements, since a 1% decrease in the price of Mr. Pibb causes consumers to buy almost 2% more Red Vines.

Have you tried Mr. Pibb and Red Vines together?

ECONOMICS IN THE REAL WORLD

TENNIS, ANYONE?

How much would you be willing to pay for court time?

Are you a casual tennis player or passionate about your game? The answer to that question helps us understand a real-life elasticity experiment.

In 2011, the New York City Parks Department doubled the prices paid by tennis players between the ages of 18 and 61. Single-pay passes for an hour of court time jumped from $7 to $15, while season passes rose from $100 to $200.

Far fewer tennis permits were sold under the new prices, according to data from the Parks Department. Sales of season passes for most players slipped by 40%, with 7,400 sold in 2011 as compared to 12,400 in 2010. Sales of one-day passes took a big hit as well, dropping by nearly a third from more than 40,000 for the 2010 season to 27,000.

Type of pass	Price in 2010	Price in 2011	Passes sold in 2010	Passes sold in 2011	Total revenue in 2010 (in millions)	Total revenue in 2011 (in millions)	E_D
One-day	$7	$15	40,000	27,000	$0.28	$0.41	−0.53
Annual	100	200	12,400	7,400	1.24	1.48	−0.75
Total					**$1.52**	**$1.89**	

We calculated the price elasticity of demand, E_D, using the midpoint formula. Because the coefficients for the one-day and annual passes are between 0 and −1, we know that demand is relatively inelastic at these prices. We also know that when demand is inelastic and prices increase, total revenue should increase, and that is exactly what happened. Tennis court revenues increased from $1.52 million in 2010 to $1.89 million in 2011.

As you might guess, many tennis players in New York City were quite upset with the sudden price increase. However, the data show that many tennis players decided to keep playing rather than quit. This result shouldn't surprise you too much. Tennis is good exercise, a social experience, and a hobby that many people enjoy. While the price increases were dramatic on a percentage basis (they doubled!), the increase in price is a relatively small part of most New Yorkers' budgets. Because there are not many good substitutes for tennis available in New York City, we'd expect many to continue playing, as the data confirmed.

Sources: Authors' calculations; data from Matt McCue, "Tennis Fees Ace Out Many," *Wall Street Journal*, August 5, 2012, https://www.wsj.com/articles/SB10000872396390443687504577564933033308176.

PRACTICE WHAT YOU KNOW

Yummy, or all you can afford?

Income Elasticity

QUESTION: A college student eats ramen noodles twice a week and earns $300 a week working part-time. After graduating, the student earns $1,000 a week and eats ramen noodles once every other week , or 0.5 time a week. What is the student's income elasticity?

ANSWER: The income elasticity of demand using the midpoint method is

$$E_I = \frac{(Q_2 - Q_1) \div [(Q_1 + Q_2) \div 2]}{(I_2 - I_1) \div [(I_1 + I_2) \div 2]}$$

Plugging in the values from the question yields

$$E_I = \frac{(0.5 - 2.0) \div [(2.0 + 0.5) \div 2]}{(\$1000 - \$300) \div [(\$300 + \$1000) \div 2]}$$

Simplifying yields

$$E_I = \frac{-1.5 \div 1.25}{\$700 \div \$650}$$

Therefore, $E_I = -1.1$. If income increases by 1%, the quantity of ramen purchased will drop by 1.1%.

The income elasticity of demand is positive for normal goods and negative for inferior goods. Therefore, the negative coefficient indicates that ramen noodles are an inferior good over this person's range of income—in this example, between $300 and $1,000 per week. This result should confirm your intuition. The higher postgraduation income enables the student to substitute away from ramen noodles and toward other meals that provide more nourishment and enjoyment.

What Is the Price Elasticity of Supply?

The **price elasticity of supply** is a measure of the responsiveness of the quantity supplied to a change in price.

Like consumers, sellers are sensitive to price changes. However, the determinants of the price elasticity of supply are substantially different from the determinants of the price elasticity of demand. The **price elasticity of supply** is a measure of the responsiveness of the quantity supplied to a change in price.

In this section, we examine how much sellers respond to price changes. For instance, if the market price of gasoline increases, how will oil companies respond? The answer depends on the elasticity of supply. Oil must be refined into gasoline. If it is difficult for oil companies to increase their output of gasoline significantly, the quantity of gasoline supplied will not increase much even if the price increases a lot. In this case, we say that supply is inelastic, or unresponsive. However, if the price increase is small and suppliers respond by offering significantly more gasoline for sale, then supply is elastic. We would expect to observe this outcome if it is easy to refine oil into gasoline.

When supply is not able to respond to a change in price, we say it is inelastic. Think of an oceanfront property in Southern California. The amount of land next to the ocean is fixed. If the price of oceanfront property rises, the supply of land cannot adjust to the price increase. In this case, the supply is perfectly inelastic and the price elasticity of supply is zero. Recall that a price elasticity coefficient of zero means that quantity supplied does not change as price changes.

What would it take to own a slice of paradise?

When the supplier's ability to make quick adjustments is limited, the elasticity of supply is less than 1. For instance, when a cellular network becomes congested, it takes suppliers a long time to provide additional capacity. They have to build new cell towers, which requires the purchase of land and additional construction costs. In contrast, a local hot dog vendor can easily add another cart in relatively short order. As a result, for the hot dog vendor, supply is elastic, with an elasticity coefficient that is greater than 1.

Table 4.6 examines the price elasticity of supply (E_s). Recall the law of supply, which states that there is a direct relationship between the price of a good and the quantity that a firm supplies. As a result, the percentage change in the quantity supplied and the percentage change in price move in the same direction. The E_s coefficient reflects this direct relationship with a positive sign.

Determinants of the Price Elasticity of Supply

When we examined the determinants of the price elasticity of demand, we saw that consumers have to consider the number of substitutes, how expensive the item is compared to their overall budget, whether the good is a necessity or

TABLE 4.6

A Closer Look at the Price Elasticity of Supply

Elasticity	E_s coefficient	Example	
Perfectly inelastic	$E_s = 0$	Oceanfront land	
Relatively inelastic	$0 < E_s < 1$	Cell phone tower	
Relatively elastic	$E_s > 1$	Hot dog vendor	

a luxury, and the amount of time they have to make a decision. Time and the adjustment process are also key elements in determining the price elasticity of supply. However, there is a critical difference: the degree of flexibility that producers have in bringing their product to the market quickly.

The Flexibility of Producers

When a producer can quickly ramp up output, supply tends to be elastic. One way to maintain flexibility is to have spare production capacity. Extra capacity enables producers to quickly meet changing price conditions, so supply is more responsive, or elastic. The ability to store the good is another way to stay flexible. Producers who have stockpiles of their products can respond more quickly to changes in market conditions. For example, De Beers, the international diamond conglomerate, stores millions of uncut diamonds. As the price of diamonds fluctuates, De Beers can quickly change the quantity of diamonds it offers to the market. Likewise, hot dog vendors can relocate quickly from one street corner to another or add carts if demand is strong. However, many businesses cannot adapt to changing market conditions quickly. For instance, a golf course cannot easily add nine new holes to meet additional demand. This constraint limits the golf course owner's ability to adjust quickly, preventing the owner from quickly increasing the supply of golfing opportunities as soon as the fee changes.

Time and the Adjustment Process

In the immediate run, businesses are stuck with what they have on hand. For example, a pastry shop that runs out of chocolate glazed doughnuts cannot bake more instantly. As we move from the immediate run to the short run and a price change persists through time, supply—just like demand—becomes more elastic. For instance, a golf resort may be able to squeeze extra production out of its current facility by staying open longer hours or moving tee times closer together, but those short-run efforts will not match the production potential of adding another golf course in the long run.

Figure 4.5 shows how the two determinants of supply elasticity are mapped onto the supply curve. In the immediate run, the supply curve is vertical (S_1). A vertical curve tells us that there is no responsiveness when the price changes. As producers gain additional time to make adjustments, the supply curve rotates from S_1 (the immediate run) to S_2 (the short run) to S_3 (the long run). Like the demand curve, the supply curve becomes flatter through time. The only difference is that the supply curve rotates clockwise; in contrast, as we saw in Figure 4.2, the demand curve rotates counterclockwise. With both supply and demand, the most important thing to remember is that more time allows for greater adjustment, so the long run is always more elastic.

CALCULATING THE PRICE ELASTICITY OF SUPPLY We can use a simple formula to calculate the price elasticity of supply. Doing so is useful when a business owner must decide how much to produce at various prices. The elasticity of supply measures how quickly the producer is able to change production in response to changes in price. When supply is elastic, producers

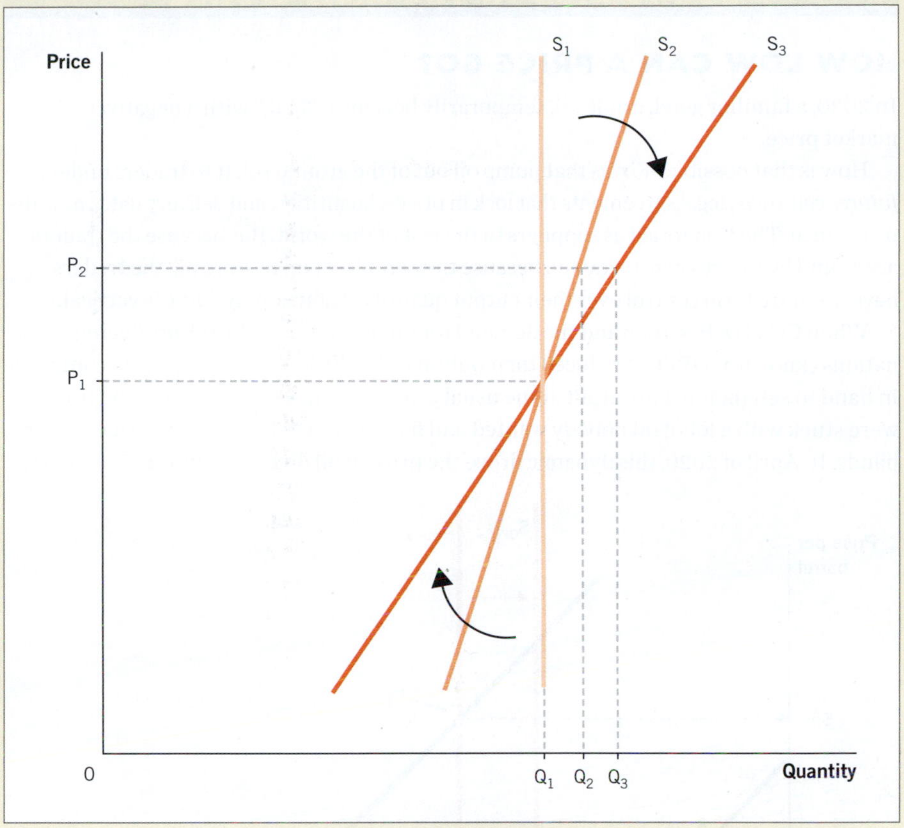

FIGURE 4.5

Elasticity and the Supply Curve

Increased flexibility and more time make supply more elastic. When price rises from P_1 to P_2, producers are unable to expand output immediately and the supply curve remains at Q_1 in the immediate run. In the short run (S_2), the firm becomes more flexible and output expands to Q_2. Eventually, in the long run (S_3), the firm is able to produce even more, and it moves to Q_3 in response to higher prices.

are able to quickly adjust production. If supply is inelastic, production tends to remain roughly constant, despite large swings in price.

Here is the formula for the price elasticity of supply (E_S):

$$E_S = \frac{\text{percentage change in the quantity supplied}}{\text{percentage change in the price}}$$

(EQUATION 4.5)

Consider how the manufacturer of Solo cups might respond to an increase in demand that causes the cups' market price to rise. The company's ability to change the amount it produces depends on the flexibility of the manufacturing process and the length of time needed to ramp up production. Suppose that the price of the cups rises by 10%. The company can increase its production by 5% immediately, but it will take many months to expand production by 20%. What can we say about the price elasticity of supply in this case? Using Equation 4.5, we can take the percentage change in the quantity supplied immediately (5%) and divide that by the percentage change in price (10%). This calculation gives us $E_S = 0.5$, so if the price increases by 1%, the quantity supplied will increase by 0.5%, which signals that supply is relatively inelastic. However, with time the firm is able to increase the quantity supplied by 20%. If we divide 20% by the percentage change in the price (10%), we get $E_S = 2.0$, which indicates that supply is relatively elastic in the long run.

How would the manufacturer of Solo cups respond to a price increase in the short run and in the long run?

ECONOMICS IN THE REAL WORLD

What happens to the price of oil when refineries have no availability?

HOW LOW CAN A PRICE GO?

In 2020, a familiar good, crude oil, temporarily became a "bad," with a negative market price.

How is that possible? Firms that pump oil out of the ground sell it to traders under *futures contracts*, legal agreements that lock in prices, quantities, and delivery dates months in advance. The traders act as suppliers to the rest of the world. But because the traders are bound by futures contracts, and because they aren't set up to store oil, the traders have no short-term control over their output quantity. Their supply curve is vertical.

When COVID-19 struck and the demand for oil plummeted, the oil-producing nations (known as OPEC+) reduced their output only a little. After all, they had contracts in hand to sell their usual output at the usual price, around $50 per barrel. The traders were stuck with a lot of oil nobody wanted and had to pay customers to take it off their hands. In April of 2020, this dynamic drove the price of oil down to minus $37 per barrel!

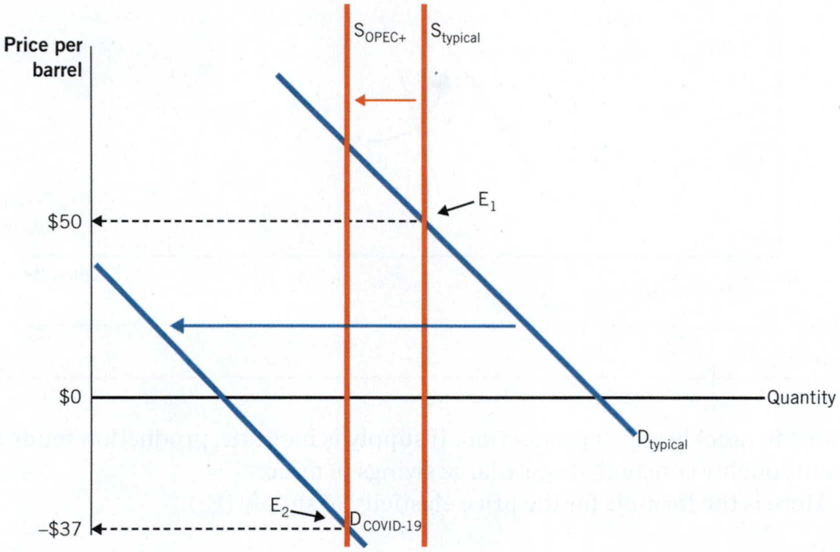

How Do the Price Elasticities of Demand and Supply Relate to Each Other?

The interplay between the price elasticity of supply and the price elasticity of demand allows us to explain more fully how the economy operates. With an understanding of elasticity at our disposal, we can conduct a much richer and deeper analysis of the world around us.

For instance, suppose that we are concerned about what will happen to the price of oil as economic development spurs additional demand in China and India. An examination of the determinants of the price elasticity of supply quickly confirms that oil producers have a limited ability to adjust production in response to rising prices. Oil wells can be uncapped to meet rising demand, but it takes years to bring the new capacity online. Moreover, storing oil reserves, while possible, is expensive. Therefore, the short-run supply of oil is quite inelastic. Figure 4.6 shows the combination of inelastic supply-side production constraints in the short run and the inelastic short-run demand for oil (D_1).

An increase in global demand from D_1 to D_2 will create significantly higher prices (from $50 to $90 per barrel) in the short run. This result occurs because increasing oil production is difficult in the short run. Therefore, the short-run supply curve (S_{SR}) is relatively inelastic. In the long run, though, oil producers are able to bring more oil to the market when prices are higher, so the supply curve rotates clockwise (to S_{LR}), becoming more elastic, and the market price falls to $80 per barrel (point E_3). (Note that we are using an arbitrary price for a barrel of oil. The price of oil has swung widely over the last decade, making it difficult to predict.)

What does this example tell us? It reminds us that the interplay between the price elasticity of demand and the price elasticity of supply determines the magnitude of the resulting price change. We cannot observe demand in isolation without also considering how supply responds. Similarly, we cannot simply think about the short-run consequences of demand and supply shifts; we also must consider how prices and quantity will vary in the long run. Armed with this knowledge, you can begin to see the power of the supply and demand model to explain the world around us.

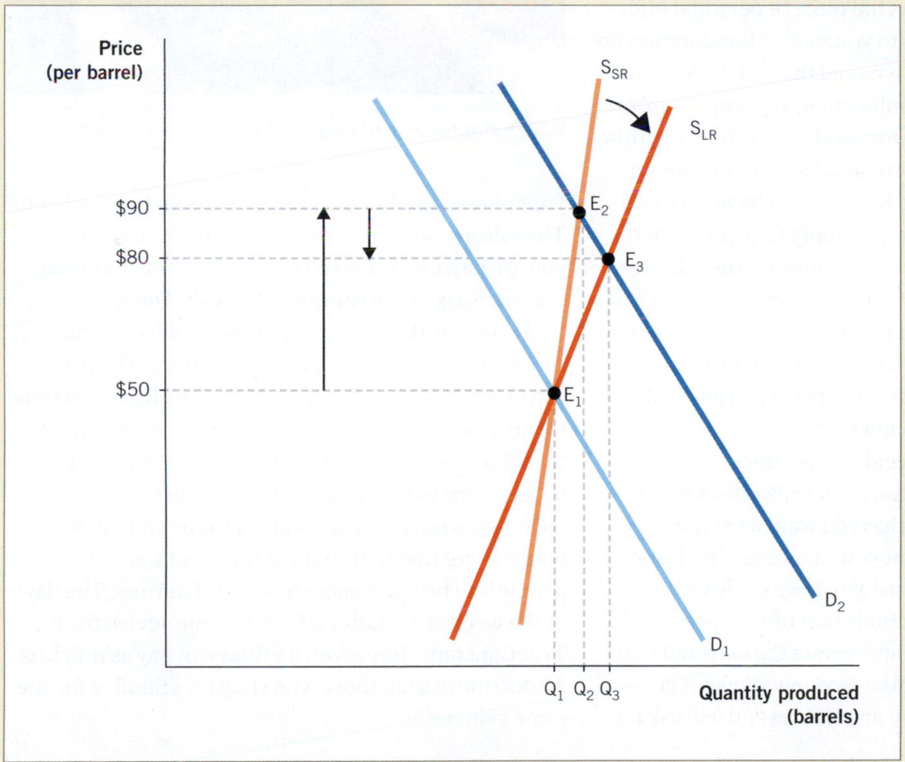

FIGURE 4.6

A Demand Shift and the Consequences for Short- and Long-Run Supply

When an increase in demand causes the price of oil to rise from $50 to $90 per barrel, initially producers are unable to expand output very much—production expands from Q_1 to Q_2. However, in the long run, as producers expand their production capacity, the price will fall to $80 per barrel.

· ECONOMICS *for* LIFE ·

Price Elasticity of Supply and Demand: Buying Your First Car

- Never buy a car on your first visit. Walking away shows that your demand is elastic and gives you a bargaining advantage.
- Don't give salespeople information about your budget or allow them to run your credit.
- Shop when prices tend to be lower (end of the month, end of the model year, on a Sunday).

Watch out for shady negotiation practices.

When you buy a car, your knowledge of price elasticity can help you negotiate the best possible deal.

Recall that three of the determinants of price elasticity of demand are (1) the share of the budget, (2) the number of available substitutes, and (3) the time you have to make a decision.

Let's start with your budget. You should have one in mind, but don't tell the salesperson what you are willing to spend; that is a vital piece of personal information you want to keep to yourself. If the salesperson suggests that you look at a model that is too expensive, just say that you are not interested. You might reply, "Buying a car is a stretch for me; I've got to stay within my budget." If the salesperson asks indirectly about your budget by inquiring whether you have a particular monthly payment in mind, reply that you want to negotiate over the invoice price once you decide on a vehicle. Never negotiate on the sticker price, which is the price you see in the car window, because it includes thousands of dollars in markup. You want to make it clear to the salesperson that the price you pay matters to you—that is, your demand is elastic.

Taking your time to decide is also important. Never buy a car the first time you walk onto a lot. If you convey the message that you want a car immediately, you are saying that your demand is inelastic. If the dealership thinks that you have no flexibility, the staff will not give you their best offer. Instead, tell the salesperson that you appreciate the help and that you will be deciding over the next few weeks. A good salesperson will know you are serious and will ask for your phone number or email address and contact you. The salesperson will sweeten the deal if you indicate you are narrowing down your choices and his or her dealership is in the running. You wait. You win.

Also know that salespeople and dealerships have times when they want to move inventory. The price elasticity of supply is at work here as well. A good time to buy is when the dealer is trying to move inventory to make room for new models (the autumn months), because prices fall for end-of-the-model-year close-outs. Likewise, many sales promotions and sales bonuses are tied to the end of the month, so sales-people will be more eager to sell at that time. The day of the week also matters. Here is some advice from TrueCar.com: "Buyers on a Friday can pay as much as $2,000 more than those who shop on a Sunday for the same vehicle."

PRACTICE WHAT YOU KNOW

Elasticity: Trick or Treat Edition

How much would you spend on a Halloween pumpkin?

QUESTION: An unusually bad growing season leads to a small pumpkin crop. What will happen to the price of pumpkins as Halloween approaches? Use elasticity to explain your answer.

ANSWER: The demand for pumpkins peaks in October and rapidly falls after Halloween. Purchasing a pumpkin is a short-run decision to buy a unique product that takes up a relatively small share of the consumer's budget. As a result, the price elasticity of demand for pumpkins leading up to Halloween tends to be quite inelastic. At the same time, a small crop causes the entire supply curve to shift left. As a result, the market price of pumpkins rises. Because the demand is relatively inelastic in the short run and the supply of pumpkins is fixed, we expect the price to rise significantly. After Halloween, the price of any remaining pumpkins falls, because demand declines dramatically.

Conclusion

Incentives

Do sellers charge the highest price possible? We can now address this misconception definitively: no. Sellers like higher prices in the same way consumers like lower prices, but that does not mean that sellers will charge the highest price possible. At very high prices, consumer demand is quite elastic. Therefore, a seller who charges too high a price will not sell much. As a result, firms learn that they must lower their price to attract more customers and maximize their total revenue.

The ability to determine whether demand and supply are elastic or inelastic enables economists to calculate the effects of personal, business, and policy decisions. When you combine the concept of elasticity with the supply and demand model from Chapter 3, you get a very powerful tool. In subsequent chapters, we use elasticity to refine our models of economic behavior and make our results more realistic. ✷

· ANSWERING *the* BIG QUESTIONS ·

What is the price elasticity of demand, and what are its determinants?

- The price elasticity of demand is a measure of the responsiveness of quantity demanded to a change in price.
- Demand will generally be more elastic if there are many substitutes available, if the item accounts for a large share of the consumer's budget, if the item is a luxury good, if the market is more narrowly defined, or if the consumer has plenty of time to make a decision.

- Economists categorize time in three distinct periods: (1) the immediate run, when there is no time for consumers to adjust their behavior; (2) the short run, when consumers can adjust, but only partially; and (3) the long run, when consumers have time to fully adjust to market conditions.
- The price elasticity of demand is calculated by dividing the percentage change in the quantity demanded by the percentage change in price. A value of zero indicates that the quantity demanded does not respond to a price change; if the price elasticity is zero, demand is said to be perfectly inelastic. When the price elasticity of demand is between 0 and −1, demand is inelastic. If the price elasticity of demand is less than −1, demand is elastic. When price elasticity is exactly −1, the item has unitary elasticity.

How do changes in income and the prices of other goods affect elasticity?

- The income elasticity of demand measures how a change in income affects spending. Normal goods have a positive income elasticity. Inferior goods have a negative income elasticity.
- The cross-price elasticity of demand measures the responsiveness of the quantity demanded of one good to a change in the price of a related good. Positive values for the cross-price elasticity mean that the two goods are substitutes, while negative values indicate that the two goods are complements. If the cross-price elasticity is zero, then the two goods are not related to each other.

What is the price elasticity of supply?

- The price elasticity of supply is a measure of the responsiveness of the quantity supplied to a change in price. Supply will generally be more elastic if producers have flexibility in the production process and ample time to adjust production.
- The price elasticity of supply is calculated by dividing the percentage change in the quantity supplied by the percentage change in price. A value of zero indicates that the quantity supplied does not respond to a price change; if the price elasticity of supply is zero, supply is said to be perfectly inelastic. When the price elasticity of supply is between 0 and 1, demand is relatively inelastic. If the price elasticity of supply is greater than 1, supply is elastic.

How do the price elasticities of demand and supply relate to each other?

- The interplay between the price elasticity of demand and the price elasticity of supply determines the magnitude of the resulting price change.

CHAPTER PROBLEMS

Concepts You Should Know

cross-price elasticity of demand (p. 139)
elasticity (p. 117)
immediate run (p. 119)
income elasticity of demand (p. 138)
long run (p. 119)
price elasticity of demand (p. 117)
price elasticity of supply (p. 142)
short run (p. 119)
total revenue (p. 131)

Questions for Review

1. Define the price elasticity of demand.
2. What are the four determinants of the price elasticity of demand?
3. Give an example of a good that has elastic demand. What is the value of the price elasticity if demand is elastic? Give an example of a good that has inelastic demand. What is the value of the price elasticity if demand is inelastic?
4. What is the connection between total revenue and the price elasticity of demand? Illustrate this relationship along a demand curve.
5. Explain why slope is different from elasticity.
6. Define the price elasticity of supply.
7. What are the two determinants of the price elasticity of supply?
8. Give an example of a good that has elastic supply. What is the value of the price elasticity if supply is elastic? Give an example of a good that has an inelastic supply. What is the value of the price elasticity if supply is inelastic?
9. Give an example of a normal good. What is the income elasticity of a normal good? Give an example of a luxury good. What is the income elasticity of a luxury good? Give an example of a necessity. What is the income elasticity of a necessity? Give an example of an inferior good. What is the income elasticity of an inferior good?
10. Define the cross-price elasticity of demand. Give an example of a good with negative cross-price elasticity, another with zero cross-price elasticity, and a third with positive cross-price elasticity.

Study Problems *(✱ solved at the end of the section)*

✱ 1. If the government decided to impose a 50% tax on gray T-shirts, would this policy generate a large increase in tax revenues or a small increase? Use elasticity to explain your answer.

✱ 2. College logo T-shirts priced at $15 sell at a rate of 25 per week, but when the bookstore marks them down to $10, it finds that it can sell 50 T-shirts per week. What is the price elasticity of demand for the logo T-shirts?

3. Black Friday, the day after Thanksgiving, is the largest shopping day of the year. Do the early shoppers, who often wait in line for hours in the cold to get doorbuster sale items, have elastic or inelastic demand? Explain your response.

4. If a 20% increase in price causes a 10% drop in the quantity demanded, is the price elasticity of demand for this good elastic, unitary, or inelastic?

5. Characterize the demand for each of the following goods or services as perfectly elastic, relatively elastic, relatively inelastic, or perfectly inelastic.
   a. a lifesaving medication
   b. photocopies at a copy shop, when all competing shops charge 10 cents per copy
   c. a fast-food restaurant located in the food court of a shopping mall
   d. the water you buy from your local utility company

6. A local paintball business receives a total revenue of $8,000 a month when it charges $10 per person and $9,600 in total revenue when it charges $6 per person. Over that range of prices, does the business face elastic, unitary, or inelastic demand?

7. At a price of $200, a cell phone company manufactures 300,000 phones. At a price of $150, the

company produces 200,000 phones. What is the price elasticity of supply?

8. Do customers who visit convenience stores at 3 a.m. have a price elasticity of demand that is more elastic or less elastic than those who visit at 3 p.m.?

* 9. A worker eats at a restaurant once a week. He then gets a 25% raise. As a result, he decides to eat out twice as much as before and have frozen samosas for dinner once every other week instead of once per week. Determine the income elasticity of demand for eating at a restaurant and for having frozen samosa dinners.

10. The cross-price elasticity of demand between Fenty Beauty and Kylie Cosmetics is 2.0. What does that coefficient tell us about the relationship between these two stores?

11. An amusement park is considering lowering its fees in order to increase its total revenue. Under what conditions will the fee reduction achieve its goal?

12. A private university notices that in-state and out-of-state students seem to respond differently to tuition changes.

Tuition	Quantity demanded (in-state applicants)	Quantity demanded (out-of-state applicants)
$10,000	6,000	12,000
15,000	5,000	9,000
20,000	4,000	6,000
30,000	3,000	3,000

As the price of tuition rises from $15,000 to $20,000, what is the price elasticity of demand for in-state applicants and also for out-of-state applicants?

* 13. The TV show *Extreme Couponing* features coupon users who go to extraordinary measures to save money on their weekly purchases. The show follows these coupon users throughout the week as they assemble coupons and scout out stores to see which have the best deals, and then follows them to the store for the big buy. Do extreme "couponers" have extremely elastic demand or extremely inelastic demand? Explain. (*Note:* If you are unfamiliar with the show, you can Google it and watch a segment.)

14. Suppose a hotel raises the price of the bottled water in the minibar in each room from $3 to $5. The hotel tracks the number of customers who buy the bottled water and finds that consumption drops from 1,000 bottles a week to 900 bottles. Is demand elastic or inelastic? Explain.

15. Americans bought 143 billion gallons of gas in 2016 when the price was $2.25. Back in 2012, when the price was $3.64, they bought 133 billion gallons. Is the demand for gasoline elastic, unitary, or inelastic?

16. In 2018, the Atlanta Falcons football team moved to a new stadium. As part of this move, they dropped their stadium's food and beverage prices 50% versus prices at the old stadium. In order for this pricing strategy to work, the Falcons must believe that consumer demand is ________. Explain your answer.

Solved Problems

1. To answer this question, we need to consider the price elasticity of demand. The tax is only on gray T-shirts. This means that T-shirt customers who buy other colors can avoid the tax entirely—which means that the demand for gray T-shirts is relatively elastic. Not many gray T-shirts will be sold, so the government will generate only a small increase in revenues from the tax.

2. Plugging into the formula for E_D gives us

$$E_D = \frac{(50 - 25) \div [(25 + 50) \div 2]}{(10 - 15) \div [(15 + 10) \div 2]} = -1.67$$

9. In this question a worker gets a 25% (or 0.25) raise, so we can use this information in the denominator when determining the income elasticity of demand. We are not given the percentage change for the meals out, so we need to plug in how often the worker ate out before (once a week) and the amount he eats out after the raise (twice a week) into the numerator.

Plugging into E_I gives us

$$E_I = \frac{(2 - 1) \div [(1 + 2) \div 2]}{0.25}$$

Simplifying yields

$$E_I = \frac{1 \div 1.5}{0.25}$$

Therefore, $E_I = 2.67$.

The income elasticity of demand for eating at a restaurant is positive for normal goods. Therefore, eating at a restaurant is a normal good. This result should confirm your intuition.

Let's see what happens with frozen samosas once the worker gets the 25% raise. Now he cuts back on the number of frozen dinners from once a week to once every other week. This information is plugged into the numerator, while the 25% change in income, or 0.25, is plugged into the denominator.

Plugging into E_I gives us

$$E_I = \frac{(0.5 - 1) \div [(1 + 0.5) \div 2]}{0.25}$$

Simplifying yields

$$E_I = \frac{-0.5 \div 0.75}{0.25}$$

Therefore, $E_I = -2.67$.

The income elasticity of demand for having frozen samosas is negative. Therefore, the frozen dinners are an inferior good. This result should confirm your intuition.

13. The show is called *Extreme Couponing* for a reason. Ordinary people don't spend more than 20 hours a week trying to find the best deals on grocery items, scouting stores, comparing prices, and make purchases based solely on what's on sale. The persons featured in the show are obsessive about saving money. When the price you pay is the most important determinant of what you buy, demand is extremely elastic.

CHAPTER

05 Market Outcomes and Tax Incidence

Taxes on Firms Affect Consumers.

Many people believe that when the government taxes businesses, consumers catch a break because firms pay the tax. If only life worked that way! As this chapter explains, who actually pays the tax often is quite different from the party that is legally responsible for making the tax payment.

Gasoline prices are a common and visible sign of the market at work. It is hard not to notice when gasoline prices rise or fall, because every gas station posts its prices prominently. But there are a few things you might not know. First, in the United States, gasoline taxes are paid by the seller and not displayed at the pump. Second, gasoline taxes vary significantly from state to state, and they vary wildly from country to country. Residents of Saudi Arabia pay some of the lowest gasoline prices in the world, while the Dutch have to put up with the world's third-highest gas prices. This occurs because the governments of certain oil-rich countries, such as Saudi Arabia, subsidize gasoline so that their citizens pay less than the market price. In countries where gasoline is subsidized, consumers drive their cars everywhere, mass transportation is largely unavailable, and there is less concern for fuel efficiency. As you might imagine, the opposite is true in countries with high gasoline taxes, like the Netherlands, where consumers drive less, use public transportation more often, and tend to purchase fuel-efficient vehicles.

In countries with high gasoline taxes, close to $50 of every fill-up can be for taxes. However, in Saudi Arabia, gasoline taxes are almost nonexistent and gasoline is less expensive than bottled water.

What do gasoline taxes and subsidies around the world have in common? They are all folded into the price you see at the pump, which might lead you to believe that the seller is paying all of the tax or receiving the entire subsidy. Nothing could be further from the truth. The firm will try to pass along the tax to consumers in the form of higher prices. Likewise, in countries with subsidies, the firm must pass along lower prices to consumers. After reading this chapter, you will understand how this process works.

We begin this chapter by discussing consumer and producer surplus, two concepts that illustrate gains from trade. These concepts help us measure the efficiency of markets and the effects of taxation. Then we examine how taxation creates distortions in economic behavior by altering the incentives people and firms face when consuming and producing goods that are taxed.

· BIG QUESTIONS ·

- What are consumer surplus and producer surplus?
- When is a market efficient?
- Why do taxes create deadweight loss in otherwise efficient markets?

Trade creates value

What Are Consumer Surplus and Producer Surplus?

Welfare economics is the branch of economics that studies how the allocation of resources affects economic well-being.

Markets create value by bringing together buyers and sellers so that consumers and producers can mutually benefit from trade. **Welfare economics** is the branch of economics that studies how the allocation of resources affects economic well-being. In this section, we develop two concepts that help us measure the value markets create: *consumer surplus* and *producer surplus*.

In competitive markets, the equilibrium price is simultaneously low enough to attract consumers and high enough to encourage producers. This balance between demand and supply enhances the *welfare* (well-being) of society. That is not to say that society's welfare depends solely on markets. People also find satisfaction in many nonmarket settings, including spending time with families and friends, doing hobbies, and helping with charity work. We incorporate aspects of personal satisfaction into our economic model in Chapter 16. For now, let's focus on how markets enhance human welfare.

These characters from *Money Heist* want to earn consumer and producer surplus.

Consumer Surplus

Consider three students: Sergio, Silene, and Raquel. They need to take a class in basic economics. Like students everywhere, each of them has a maximum price he or she is willing to pay for a new economics textbook. Sergio has a keen interest in financial matters, and he is prepared to invest quite a bit of money in a new book. Silene is extremely conscientious but on a tighter budget than Sergio and also not quite so committed to that particular class. Raquel is a high achiever and is also successful in her outside life. Table 5.1 shows the value each student places on the textbook. This value, called the **willingness to pay**, is the maximum price a consumer will pay for a good or service. The willingness to pay is also known as the *reservation price*. In an auction or a negotiation, the willingness to pay, or reservation price, is the price beyond which the consumer decides to walk away from the transaction.

Willingness to pay also known as the *reservation price*, is the maximum price a consumer will pay for a good or service.

Consider what happens when the price of the book is $151. If Sergio purchases the book at $151, he pays $49 less than the $200 maximum he was willing to pay. He values the textbook at $49 more than the purchase price, so buying the book makes him better off.

Consumer surplus is the difference between the willingness to pay for a good (or service) and the price paid to get it. While Sergio gains $49 in consumer surplus, a price of $151 is more than either Silene or Raquel is willing to pay. Because Silene is willing to pay only $150, if she purchases the book she will experience a consumer loss of $1. Raquel's willingness to pay is $100, so if she buys the book for $151 she will experience a consumer loss of $51. Whenever the price is greater than the willingness to pay, a rational consumer will decide not to buy.

Consumer surplus is the difference between the willingness to pay for a good (or service) and the price paid to get it.

TABLE 5.1

Willingness to Pay for a New Economics Textbook

Buyer	Willingness to pay
Sergio	$200
Silene	150
Raquel	100

FIGURE 5.1

Demand Curve for an Economics Textbook

The demand curve has a step for each additional textbook purchase. As the price goes down, more students buy the textbook.

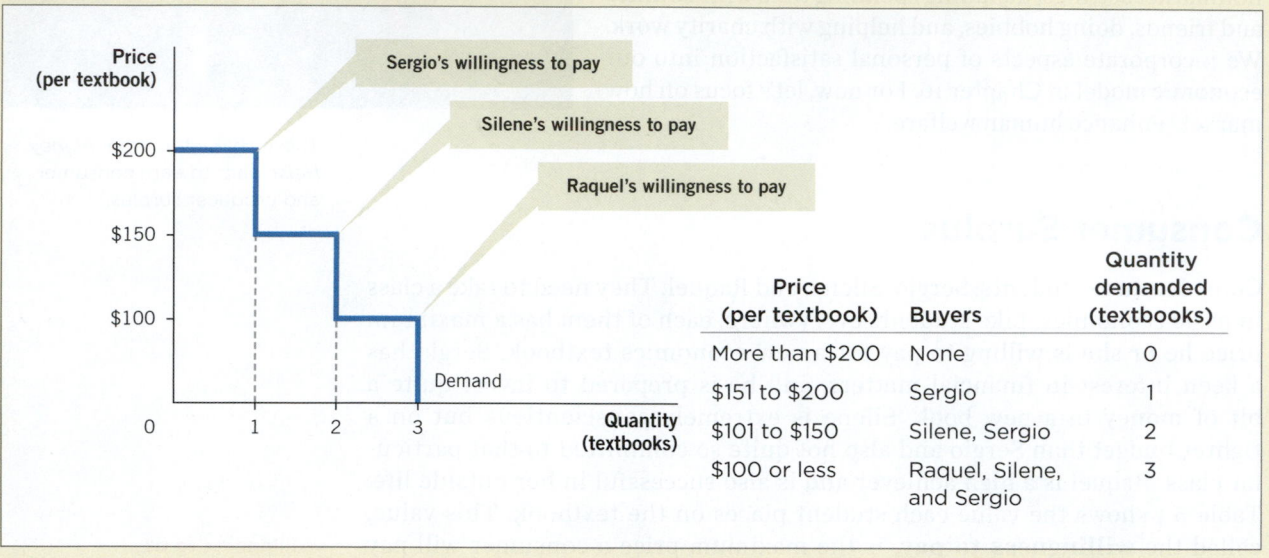

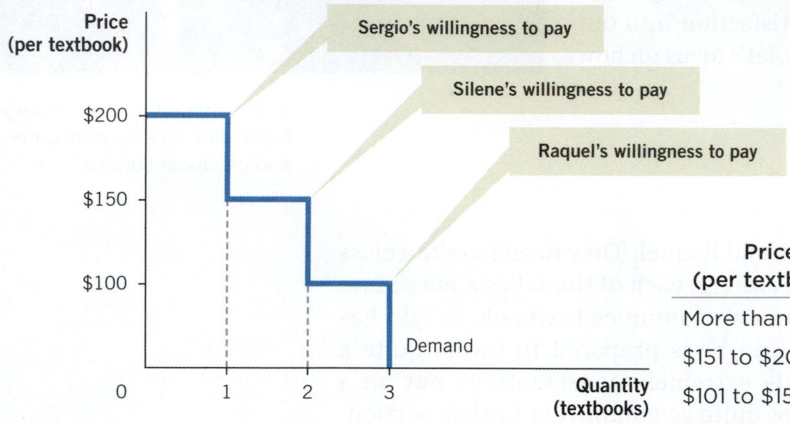

Price (per textbook)	Buyers	Quantity demanded (textbooks)
More than $200	None	0
$151 to $200	Sergio	1
$101 to $150	Silene, Sergio	2
$100 or less	Raquel, Silene, and Sergio	3

Using Demand Curves to Illustrate Consumer Surplus

In the previous section, we discussed consumer surplus as a dollar amount. We can illustrate it graphically with a demand curve. Figure 5.1 shows the demand curve drawn from the data in Table 5.1. Notice that the curve looks like a staircase with three steps—one for each additional textbook purchase. Each point on a market demand curve corresponds to a specific number of units sold.

At any price above $200, none of the students wants to purchase a textbook. This relationship is evident on the *x* axis where the quantity demanded is 0 at a price of $200. At any price between $151 and $200, Sergio is the only buyer, so the quantity demanded is 1. At prices between $101 and $150, Sergio and Silene are both willing to buy the textbook, so the quantity demanded is 2. Finally, if the price is $100 or less, all three students are willing to buy the textbook, so the quantity demanded is 3. As the price falls, the quantity demanded increases.

We can measure the total extent of consumer surplus by examining the area under the demand curve for each of our three consumers, as shown in Figure 5.2. In panel (a), the price is $175, and only Sergio decides to buy. Because his willingness to pay is $200, he is better off by $25, which is his consumer surplus. The light blue area under the demand curve and above the price represents the benefit Sergio receives from purchasing a textbook at a price of $175.

FIGURE 5.2

Determining Consumer Surplus from a Demand Curve

(a) At a price of $175, Sergio is the only buyer, so the quantity demanded is 1. (b) At a price of $125, Sergio and Silene are both willing to buy the textbook, so the quantity demanded is 2.

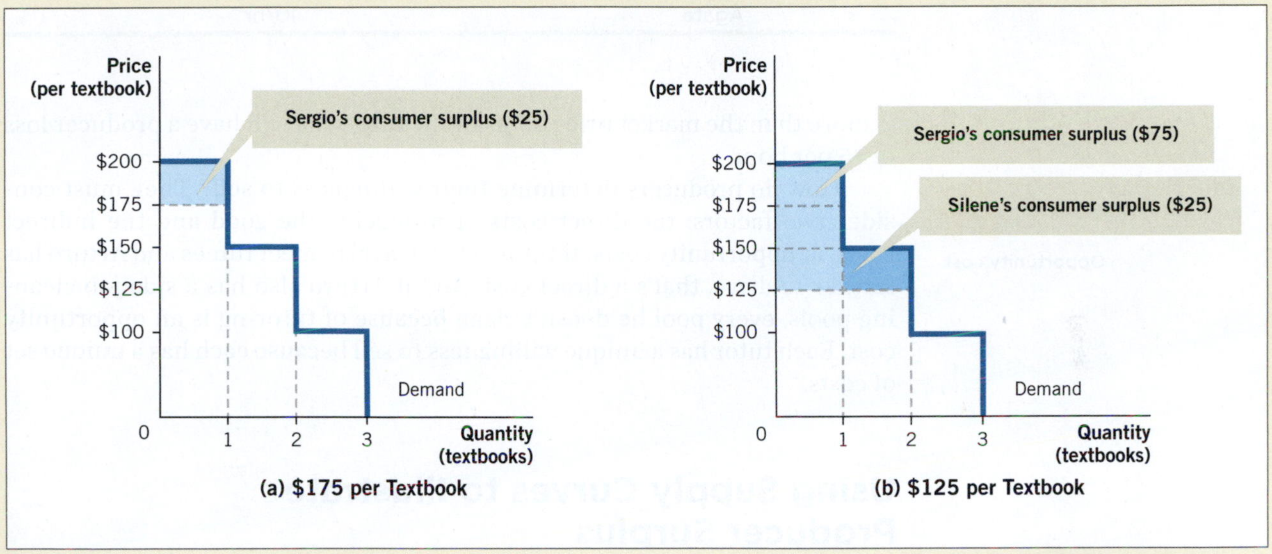

When the price drops to $125, as shown in panel (b), Silene also decides to buy a textbook. Now the total quantity demanded is 2. Silene's willingness to pay is $150, so her consumer surplus, represented by the darker blue area, is $25. However, since Sergio's willingness to pay is $200, his consumer surplus rises from $25 to $75. So a textbook price of $125 raises the total consumer surplus from $25 at a price of $200 to $75 + $25 = $100. In other words, lower prices create more consumer surplus in this market—and in any other.

Producer Surplus

Sellers also benefit from market transactions. In this section, three other students, Ágata, Mónica, and Arturo, discover that they are good at economics and decide to go into the tutoring business. They do not want to provide this service for free, but each has a different minimum price. The **willingness to sell** is the minimum price a seller will accept to sell a good or service. Table 5.2 shows each tutor's willingness to sell their services.

Willingness to sell is the minimum price a seller will accept to sell a good or service.

Consider what happens at a tutoring price of $25 per hour. Because Ágata is willing to tutor for $10 per hour, every hour she tutors at $25 per hour earns her $15 more than her willingness to sell. This extra $15 per hour is her producer surplus. **Producer surplus** is the difference between the willingness to sell a good or service and the price the seller receives. Mónica is willing to tutor for $20 per hour and earns a $5 producer surplus for every hour she tutors at $25 per hour. Finally, Arturo's willingness to tutor, at $30 per hour,

Producer surplus is the difference between the willingness to sell a good (or service) and the price the seller receives.

TABLE 5.2

Willingness to Sell Tutoring Services

Seller	Willingness to sell
Arturo	$30/hr
Mónica	20/hr
Ágata	10/hr

is more than the market price of $25. If he tutors, he will have a producer loss of $5 per hour.

Opportunity cost

How do producers determine their willingness to sell? They must consider two factors: the direct costs of producing the good and the indirect costs, or opportunity costs. If tutors must travel to meet tutees and Arturo has farther to drive, that's a direct cost. And if Arturo also has a side job cleaning pools, every pool he doesn't clean because of tutoring is an opportunity cost. Each tutor has a unique willingness to sell because each has a unique set of costs.

Using Supply Curves to Illustrate Producer Surplus

Continuing our example, the supply curve in Figure 5.3 shows the relationship between the price for an hour of tutoring and the number of tutors who are willing to sell their services. As you can see on the supply schedule (the table within the figure), at any price less than $10 per hour, no one wants to tutor. At prices between $10 and $19 per hour, Ágata is the only tutor, so the quantity supplied is 1. Between $20 and $29 per hour, Ágata and Mónica are willing to tutor, so the quantity supplied rises to 2. Finally, if the price is $30 or more, all three coworkers are willing to tutor, so the quantity supplied is 3. As the price they receive for tutoring rises, the number of tutors increases from 0 to 3.

What do these relationships between price and quantity supplied tell us about producer surplus? Let's turn to Figure 5.4. By examining the area above the supply curve, we can measure the extent of producer surplus. In panel (a), the price of an hour of tutoring is $15. At that price, only Ágata decides to tutor. Since she would be willing to tutor even if the price were as low as $10 per hour, she is $5 per hour better off tutoring. Ágata's producer surplus is represented by the light red area between the supply curve and the price of $15. Because Mónica and Arturo do not tutor when the price is $15 per hour, they do not receive any producer surplus. In panel (b), the price for tutoring is $25 per hour. At this price, Mónica also decides to tutor. Her willingness to tutor is $20, so when the price is $25 per hour, her producer surplus is $5 per hour, represented by the darker red area. Since Ágata's willingness to tutor is $10, at $25 per hour her producer surplus rises to $15 per hour. By looking at the shaded boxes in panel (b), we see that an increase in the rates for tutoring raises the combined producer surplus of Ágata and Mónica to $15 + $5 = $20 per hour.

FIGURE 5.3

Supply Curve for Economics Tutoring

The supply curve has three steps, one for each additional coworker who is willing to tutor. Progressively higher prices will induce more coworkers to become tutors.

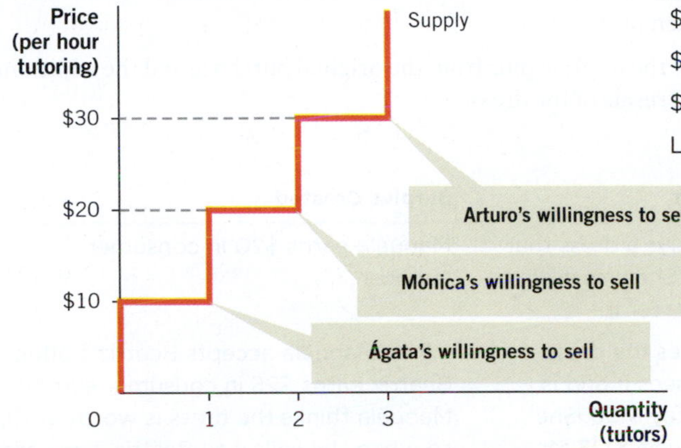

Price (per hour tutoring)	Sellers	Quantity supplied (tutors)
$30 or more	Ágata, Mónica, Arturo	3
$20 to 29	Ágata, Mónica	2
$10 to 19	Ágata	1
Less than $10	None	0

FIGURE 5.4

Determining Producer Surplus from a Supply Curve

(a) The price of an hour of tutoring is $15. At this price, only Ágata decides to tutor. (b) The price for tutoring is $25 per hour. At this price, Mónica also decides to tutor.

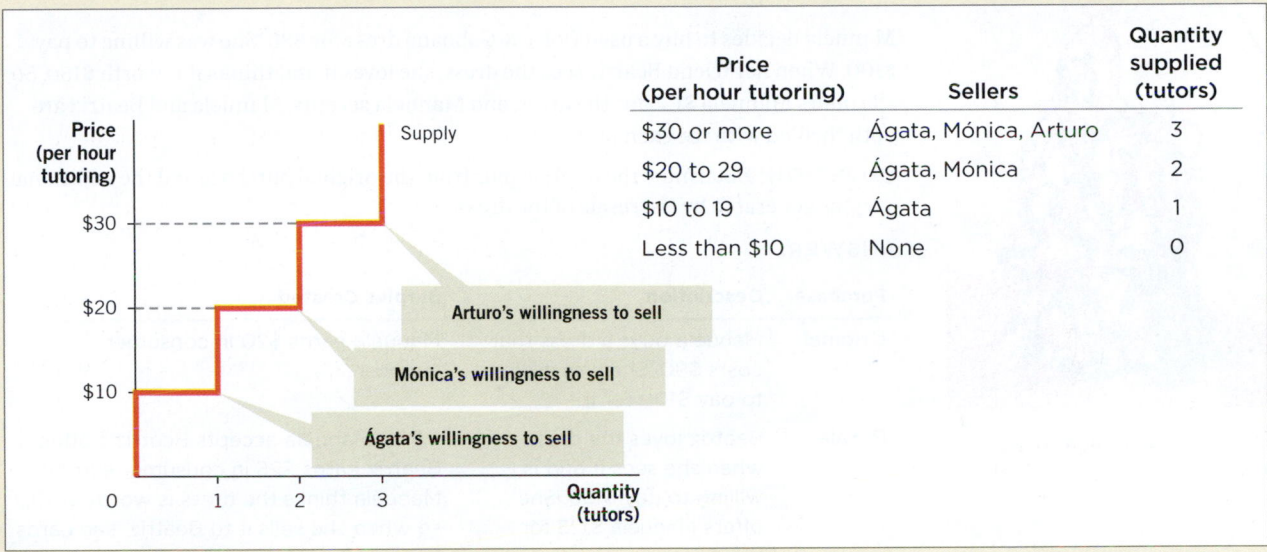

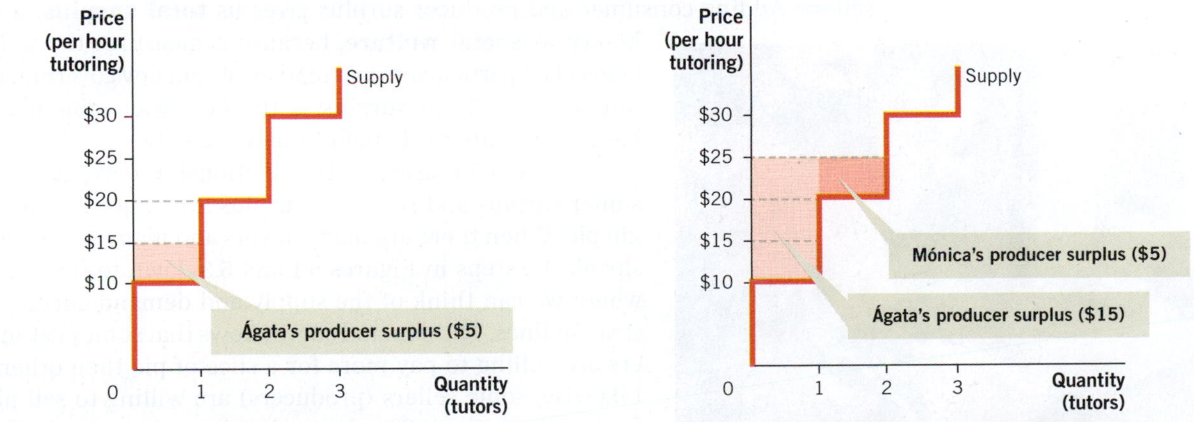

(a) $15 per Hour Tutoring

(b) $25 per Hour Tutoring

PRACTICE WHAT YOU KNOW

Cardi B looking regal in a D&G dress.

Consumer and Producer Surplus: Trendy Fashion

Manuéla decides to buy a used Dolce & Gabbana dress for $80. She was willing to pay $100. When her friend Beatriz sees the dress, she loves it and thinks it is worth $150. So she offers Manuéla $125 for the dress, and Manuéla accepts. Manuéla and Beatriz are both thrilled with the exchange.

QUESTION: Determine the total surplus from the original purchase and the additional surplus generated by the resale of the dress.

ANSWER:

Purchase	Description	Surplus Created
Original	Manuéla buys a dress that costs $80. She was willing to pay $100 for it.	Manuéla earns $20 in consumer surplus.
Resale	Beatriz loves the dress when she sees it and is willing to pay $150. She offers Manuéla $125 for the dress.	When Manuéla accepts Beatriz's offer, Beatriz earns $25 in consumer surplus. Manuéla thinks the dress is worth $100, so when she sells it to Beatriz, she earns $25 in producer surplus.

Total surplus, also known as **social welfare**, is the sum of consumer surplus and producer surplus. It measures the well-being of all participants in a market, absent any government intervention.

When Is a Market Efficient?

We have seen how consumers benefit from lower prices and how producers benefit from higher prices. When we combine the concepts of consumer and producer surplus, we can build a complete picture of the welfare of buyers and sellers. Adding consumer and producer surplus gives us **total surplus**, also known as **social welfare**, because it measures the well-being of all participants in a market, absent any government intervention. Total surplus is the best way economists have to measure the benefits markets create.

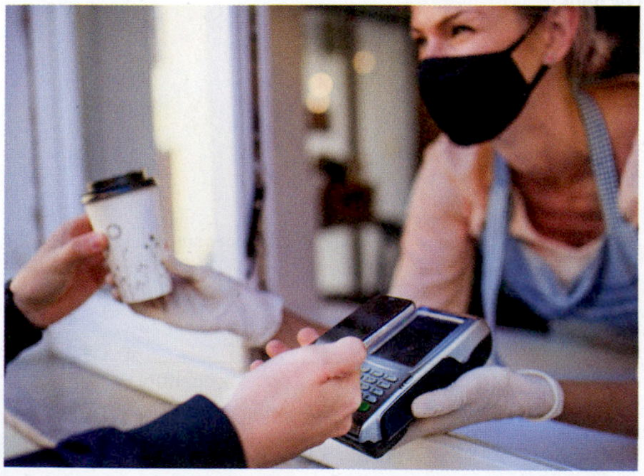

The buyer and seller each benefit from this exchange.

Figure 5.5 illustrates the relationship between consumer surplus and producer surplus for a slice of pumpkin pie. When there are many buyers and many sellers, we shrink the steps in Figures 5.1 and 5.3 down to the point where we can think of the supply and demand curves as straight lines. The demand curve shows that some customers are willing to pay more for a slice of pie than others. Likewise, some sellers (producers) are willing to sell pie for less than others. The demand and supply curves in this section are drawn as straight lines (as opposed to the stair-steps we have seen so far), since we will now assume there are a large number of buyers and sellers in each market.

FIGURE 5.5

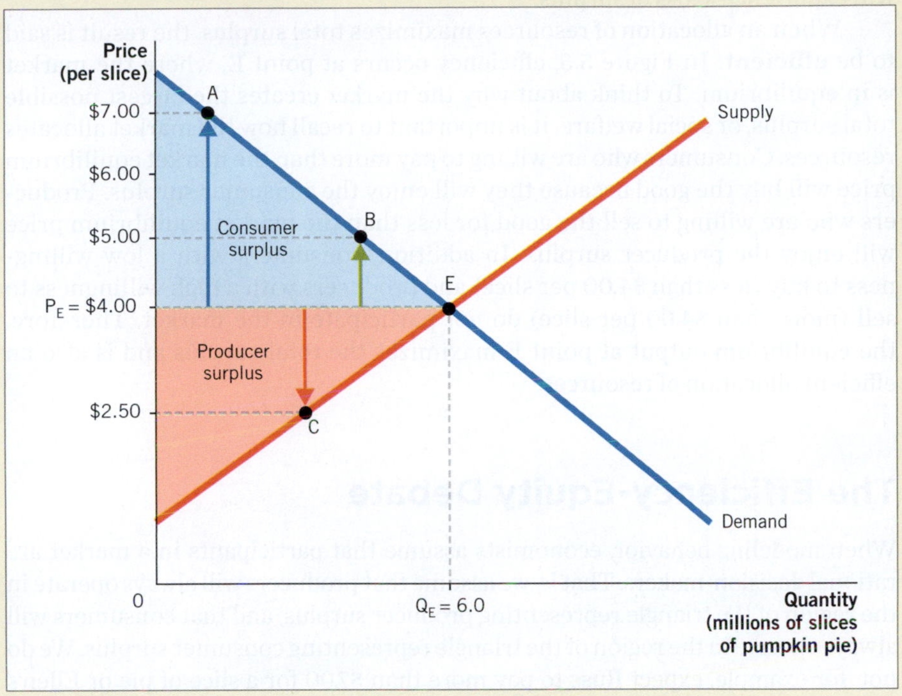

Consumer and Producer Surplus for Pumpkin Pie

Consumer surplus is the difference between the willingness to pay along the demand curve and the equilibrium price, P_E. It is illustrated by the blue triangle. Producer surplus is the difference between the willingness to produce along the supply curve and the equilibrium price. It is illustrated by the red triangle.

Trade creates value

Let's say that Russ is willing to pay $7.00 for a slice of pie, but when he gets to the store he finds it for $4.00. The difference between the price he is willing to pay, represented by point A, and the price he actually pays, represented by E (the equilibrium price), is $3.00 in consumer surplus, as indicated by the blue arrow showing the distance from $4.00 to $7.00. Russ's friend Audrey is willing to pay $5.00 for a slice of pie, but, like Russ, she finds it for $4.00. Therefore, she receives $1.00 in consumer surplus, as indicated by the green arrow at point B showing the distance from $4.00 to $5.00. In fact, all consumers who are willing to pay more than $4.00 are better off when they purchase the slice of pie at $4.00. We can show this total area of consumer surplus on the graph as the blue triangle bordered by the demand curve, the *y* axis, and the equilibrium price (P_E). At every point in this area, consumers who are willing to pay more than the equilibrium price for pie are better off.

Continuing with Figure 5.5, to identify producer surplus we follow a similar process. Suppose that Ellen's Bakery is willing to sell pumpkin pie for $2.50 per slice, represented by point C. Because the equilibrium price is $4.00, the business makes $1.50 per slice in producer surplus, as indicated by the red arrow at point C showing the distance from $4.00 to $2.50. If we think of the supply curve as representing the costs of many different sellers, we can calculate the total producer surplus as the red triangle bordered by the supply curve, the *y* axis, and the equilibrium price. The blue triangle (consumer surplus) and the red triangle (producer surplus) describe the increase in total surplus, or social welfare, created by the production and exchange of the good at the equilibrium price. At the equilibrium quantity of 6 million slices of pie, output and consumption reach the largest possible combination of producer and consumer surplus. In the region of the graph beyond 6 million units, buyers and sellers will experience a loss of surplus.

An outcome is **efficient** when an allocation of resources maximizes total surplus.

When an allocation of resources maximizes total surplus, the result is said to be **efficient**. In Figure 5.5, efficiency occurs at point E, where the market is in equilibrium. To think about why the market creates the largest possible total surplus, or social welfare, it is important to recall how the market allocates resources. Consumers who are willing to pay more than the market equilibrium price will buy the good because they will enjoy the consumer surplus. Producers who are willing to sell the good for less than the market equilibrium price will enjoy the producer surplus. In addition, consumers with a low willingness to buy (less than $4.00 per slice) and producers with a high willingness to sell (more than $4.00 per slice) do not participate in the market. Therefore, the equilibrium output at point E maximizes the total surplus and is also an efficient allocation of resources.

The Efficiency-Equity Debate

When modeling behavior, economists assume that participants in a market are rational decision-makers. That is, we assume that producers will always operate in the region of the triangle representing producer surplus, and that consumers will always operate in the region of the triangle representing consumer surplus. We do not, for example, expect Russ to pay more than $7.00 for a slice of pie or Ellen's Bakery to sell pie for less than $2.50 per slice. In other words, for the market to work efficiently, voluntary instances of consumer loss must be rare. We assume that self-interest helps to ensure that all participants benefit from an exchange.

Trade creates value

However, the fact that both parties benefit from an exchange does not mean that both parties benefit equally. Economists are also interested in the distribution of the gains. **Equity** refers to the fairness of the distribution of benefits among the members of a society. In a world where no one cared about equity, only efficiency would matter, and no particular division would be preferred. Another way of thinking about fairness versus efficiency is to consider a pie. If our only concern is efficiency, we will simply want to make sure that none of the pie goes to waste. But if we care about equity, we will also care about how the pie is divvied up, perhaps making sure that everyone gets a bite of the pie or at least has access to the pie.

Equity refers to the fairness of the distribution of benefits among the members of a society.

Efficiency only requires that the pie get eaten. Equity is a question of how the pie gets divided.

ECONOMICS *in the* MEDIA

Efficiency versus Equity

SUPERSTORE

In an early episode of the TV series *Superstore*, the pharmacy is hit with a rush of people who want flu shots. The problem is, supply can't keep up with demand. Soon, the pharmacy is down to one remaining dose, with dozens of customers still waiting. Each of them believes they "need" that last flu shot the most. Should the last dose go to the next person in line, or the pregnant woman, or the teacher? Who is most deserving? This is the kind of problem where equity issues come into play.

During the COVID-19 pandemic, society faced a similar problem when vaccines became available. In the United States, the first doses went to healthcare workers and elderly long-term-care residents. Everyone else had to wait their turn. Equity is ultimately a normative consideration, and reasonable people might disagree about who is most deserving. Efficiency, on the other hand, is just about making sure that available resources are used and not wasted. All efficiency requires at the *Superstore* pharmacy is that the last flu shot go to somebody, and not be thrown away.

In our first look at consumer and producer surplus, we have assumed that markets produce efficient outcomes. But in the real world, efficient outcomes are not guaranteed. Markets also fail; their efficiency can be compromised in a number of ways. We discuss market failure in much greater detail in subsequent chapters. For now, all you need to know is that failure can occur.

PRACTICE WHAT YOU KNOW

Total Surplus: How Would Lower Consumer Income Affect Airbnb and Its Customers?

Does less consumer income affect total surplus?

QUESTION: If a drop in consumer income occurs, what will happen to the consumer surplus that travelers and vacationers using Airbnb enjoy? What will happen to the producer surplus Airbnb receives? Illustrate your answer by shifting the demand curve and labeling the old and new areas of consumer and producer surplus.

(CONTINUED)

ANSWER: Because the rooms rented through Airbnb are normal goods, a drop in consumer income shifts the demand curve (D) to the left. In graph (b), the black arrow shows the shift. When you compare the area of consumer surplus (in blue) before and after the drop in consumer income, you can see that consumer surplus shrinks. Producer surplus (in red) also shrinks.

Your intuition might already confirm what the graphs tell us. Because consumers have less income, they book fewer rooms—so consumer surplus falls. Likewise, because fewer customers book rooms, Airbnb does less business—so producer surplus falls. This result is also evident in graph (b), because $Q_2 < Q_1$.

CHALLENGE QUESTION: Now let's add an additional consideration. Suppose that due to COVID-19, Airbnb also faces higher management costs at the same time that consumer income drops. (Think about the costs associated with developing and overseeing new cleaning protocols.) Will consumer and producer surplus continue to shrink in size or rebound?

ANSWER: Higher producers' costs will cause the supply curve to shift left. If you look at the second panel, you can visualize how a leftward shift in the supply curve will cause the new equilibrium to occur at a price above P_2 and the new equilibrium quantity to be less than Q_2. Since the overall quantity supplied shrinks, the areas of consumer and producer surplus will shrink as well.

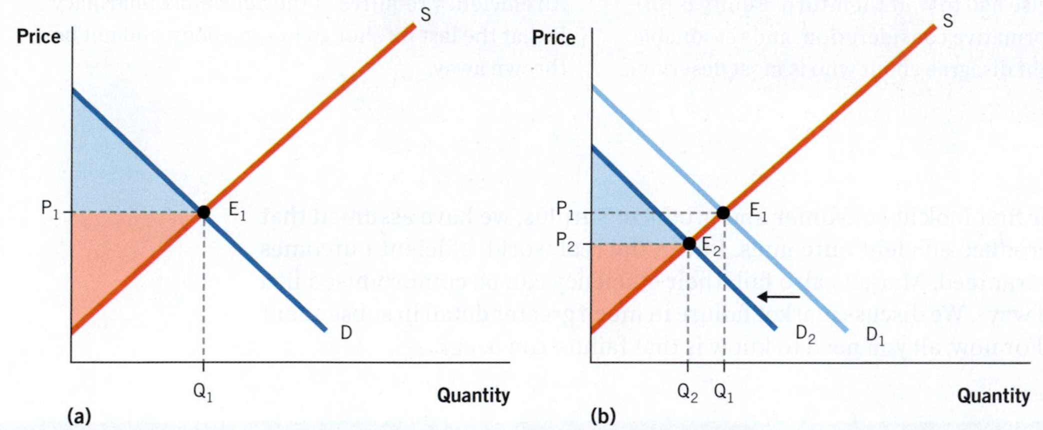

Why Do Taxes Create Deadweight Loss in Otherwise Efficient Markets?

Taxes provide many benefits. Taxes help to pay for many of society's needs—public transportation, schools, police, the court system, and the military, to name just a few. Most of us take these services for granted, but without taxes it would be impossible to pay for them. How much do all of these services cost?

When you add all the federal, state, and local government budgets in the United States, you get over $6 trillion a year in taxes!

Spending tax dollars incurs opportunity costs, because the money could have been used in other ways. In this section, we use the concepts of consumer and producer surplus to explain the effect of taxation on social welfare and market efficiency. Taxes come in many sizes and shapes. There are taxes on personal income, payroll, property, corporate profits, sales, and inheritance, for example. Fortunately, we do not have to examine the entire tax code all at once. In the pages that follow, we explore the impact of taxes on social welfare by looking at one of the simplest taxes, the *excise tax*.

Opportunity cost

Tax Incidence

Economists want to know how taxes affect the choices that consumers and producers make. When a tax is imposed on an item, do buyers switch to alternative goods that are not taxed? How do producers respond when the products they sell are taxed? Because taxes cause prices to rise, they can affect how much of a good or service is bought and sold. This outcome is especially evident with **excise taxes**, which are taxes levied on a particular good or service. For example, all 50 states levy excise taxes on cigarettes, but the amount assessed varies tremendously. In New York, cigarette taxes are over $4.00 per pack, while in a handful of tobacco-producing states (including Virginia and North Carolina), the excise tax is less than $0.50 per pack. Overall, excise taxes, such as those on cigarettes, alcohol, and gasoline, account for less than 4% of all tax revenues. But because we can isolate changes in consumer behavior that result from taxes on one item, excise taxes help us understand the overall effect of a tax.

Excise taxes are taxes levied on a particular good or service.

In looking at the effect of a tax, economists are also interested in the **incidence** of taxation, which refers to the burden of taxation on the party who pays the tax. To understand this idea, consider a $1.00 tax on milk purchases. We consider two cases: a tax placed directly on buyers and a tax placed directly on sellers.

Incidence refers to the burden of taxation on the party who pays the tax through higher prices, regardless of whom the tax is actually levied on.

EXAMPLE 1: TAX ON BUYERS Each time a consumer buys a gallon of milk, the cash register adds $1.00 in tax. This means that to purchase the milk, the consumer must be willing to pay the price of the milk plus the $1.00 tax.

The result of the $1.00 tax on milk is shown in Figure 5.6. Because of the tax, consumers' willingness to pay for milk goes down, and the demand curve shifts down from D_1 to D_2. Why does the demand curve shift? The extra cost makes consumers less likely to buy milk at every price, which causes the entire demand curve to shift down. The intersection of the new demand curve (D_2) with the existing supply curve (S) creates a new equilibrium price of $3.50 ($E_2$), which is $0.50 lower than the original price of $4.00 per gallon. But even though the base price is lower, consumers are still worse off. Because they must also pay part of the $1.00 tax, the total price to them rises to $4.50 per gallon. Many students mistakenly believe that the new equilibrium price will be $5.00, but that would only be the case if demand were perfectly inelastic. We will take a look at that scenario shortly.

Why do we place excise taxes on cigarettes . . .

. . . and gasoline?

FIGURE 5.6

A Tax on Buyers

After the tax, the new equilibrium price (E_2) is \$3.50, but the buyer must also pay \$1.00 in tax. Therefore, despite the drop in equilibrium price, the buyer still pays more for a gallon of milk: \$4.50 instead of the original equilibrium price of \$4.00. A similar logic applies to the producer. Because the new equilibrium price after the tax is \$0.50 lower, the producer shares the tax incidence equally with the buyer in this example. The consumer pays \$0.50 more, and the seller nets \$0.50 less.

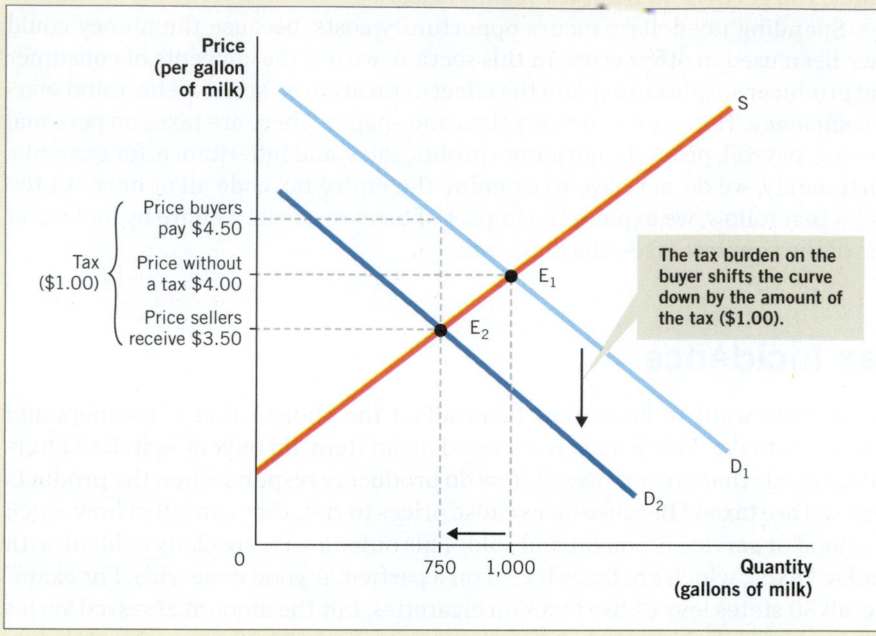

At the same time, because the new equilibrium price after the tax is \$0.50 lower than it was before the tax, the producer splits the tax incidence with the buyer. The producer receives \$0.50 less, and the buyer pays \$0.50 more.

The tax on milk purchases also affects the amount sold in the market, which we also see in Figure 5.6. Because the after-tax equilibrium price (E_2) is lower, producers of milk reduce the quantity they sell to 750 gallons. Therefore, the market for milk becomes smaller than it was before the good was taxed.

Excise taxes are rarely levied on consumers because these taxes are highly visible. If you were reminded that you have to pay a \$1.00 tax every time you buy a gallon of milk, it would be hard for you to ignore the tax. As a result, politicians often prefer to place the tax on the seller.

EXAMPLE 2: TAX ON SELLERS Now let's look at what happens when the \$1.00 tax on milk is placed on sellers. Figure 5.7 shows the result. First, look at the shift in the supply curve. Why does it shift? The \$1.00-per-gallon tax on milk lowers willingness to sell, which causes producers to offer less milk at every price level. As a result, the entire supply curve shifts up in response to the tax that milk producers owe the government. The intersection of the new supply curve (S_2) with the existing demand curve creates a new equilibrium price (E_2) of \$4.50 per gallon—which is \$0.50 higher than the original equilibrium price of \$4.00 (E_1). Many students mistakenly believe that the new equilibrium price will be \$5.00, but again, that would only be the case if supply were perfectly inelastic. This higher equilibrium price occurs because the seller passes part of the tax increase along to the buyer in the form of a higher price. However, the seller is still worse off. After the tax, the new equilibrium price is \$4.50 per

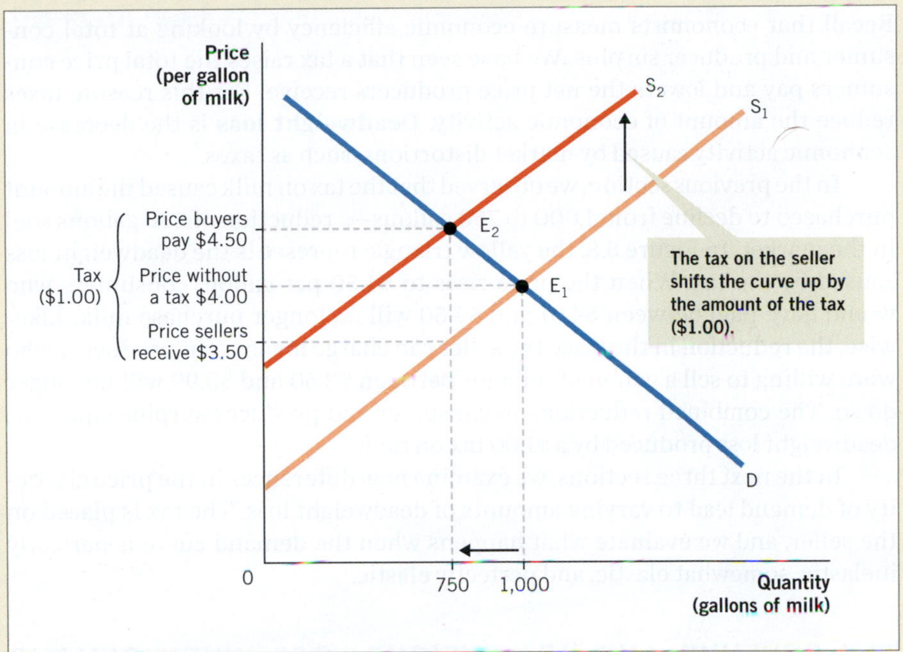

FIGURE 5.7

A Tax on Sellers

After the tax, the new equilibrium price (E_2) is $4.50, but $1.00 must be paid in tax to the government. Therefore, despite the rise in price, the seller nets only $3.50. Similar logic applies to the consumer. Because the new equilibrium price after the tax is $0.50 higher, the consumer shares the $1.00-per-gallon tax incidence equally with the seller. The consumer pays $0.50 more, and the seller nets $0.50 less.

gallon, but $1.00 goes as tax to the government. Therefore, despite the rise in price, the seller nets only $3.50 per gallon, which is $0.50 less than the original equilibrium price.

The tax also affects the amount of milk sold in the market. Because the new equilibrium price after the tax is higher, consumers reduce the quantity demanded from 1,000 gallons to 750 gallons.

SO WHO BEARS THE INCIDENCE OF THE TAX? It's important to notice that the result in Figure 5.7 looks much like that in Figure 5.6 because it does not matter whether a tax is levied on the buyer or the seller. The tax places a wedge of $1.00 between the price buyers ultimately pay ($4.50) and the net price sellers ultimately receive ($3.50), regardless of who is actually responsible for paying the tax.

Continuing with our milk example, when the tax was levied on sellers, they were responsible for collecting the entire tax ($1.00 per gallon), but they transferred $0.50 of the tax to the consumer by raising the market price to $4.50. Similarly, when the tax was levied on consumers, they were responsible for paying the entire tax, but they essentially transferred $0.50 of it to producers, because the market price fell to $3.50. Therefore, we can say that the incidence of a tax is independent of whether it is levied on the buyer or the seller. However, depending on the price elasticity of supply and demand, the tax incidence need not be shared equally, as we will see later. All of this means that the government doesn't get to determine whether consumers or producers bear the tax incidence—the market does!

Deadweight Loss

Deadweight loss is the decrease in economic activity caused by market distortions.

Recall that economists measure economic efficiency by looking at total consumer and producer surplus. We have seen that a tax raises the total price consumers pay and lowers the net price producers receive. For this reason, taxes reduce the amount of economic activity. **Deadweight loss** is the decrease in economic activity caused by market distortions, such as taxes.

In the previous section, we observed that the tax on milk caused the amount purchased to decline from 1,000 to 750 gallons—a reduction of 250 gallons sold in the market. In Figure 5.8, the yellow triangle represents the deadweight loss caused by the tax. When the price rises to $4.50 per gallon, consumers who would have paid between $4.01 and $4.50 will no longer purchase milk. Likewise, the reduction in the price the seller can charge means that producers who were willing to sell a gallon of milk for between $3.50 and $3.99 will no longer do so. The combined reductions in consumer and producer surplus equal the deadweight loss produced by a $1.00 tax on milk.

In the next three sections, we examine how differences in the price elasticity of demand lead to varying amounts of deadweight loss. The tax is placed on the seller, and we evaluate what happens when the demand curve is perfectly inelastic, somewhat elastic, and perfectly elastic.

How do phone companies get away with all the added fees per month? Answer: inelastic demand.

TAX REVENUE AND DEADWEIGHT LOSS WHEN DEMAND IS INELASTIC In Chapter 4, we saw that necessary goods and services—for example, water, electricity, and phone service—have highly inelastic demand. These goods and services are often taxed. For example, consider all the taxes associated with your cell phone bill: sales tax, city tax, county tax, federal excise

FIGURE 5.8

The Deadweight Loss from a Tax

The yellow triangle represents the deadweight loss caused by the tax. When the price rises, all consumers who would have paid between $4.01 and $4.50 no longer purchase milk. Likewise, the reduction in revenue the seller receives means that producers who were willing to sell a gallon of milk for between $3.50 and $3.99 will no longer do so.

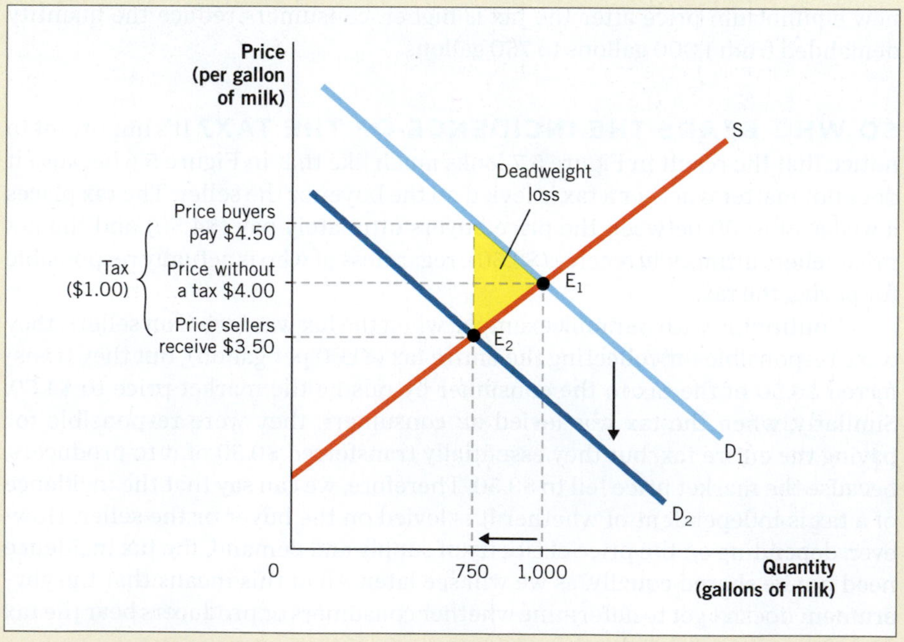

ECONOMICS *in the* MEDIA

Is Soda Demand Elastic or Inelastic?

PARKS AND RECREATION: SODA TAX

Leslie Knope, who serves on the Pawnee city council in the TV series *Parks and Recreation*, has to decide whether to vote for a citywide tax on sugary soda drinks. Leslie wants to understand both sides of the issue, so she meets with Pawnee Restaurant Association spokeswoman Kathryn Pinewood to discuss the city's growing drink sizes. Leslie is concerned about the obesity problem in Pawnee, so she is horrified to learn that the sodas come in 64-, 128- and 512-ounce containers. She can't imagine why anyone would want so much soda. Kathryn won't allow Leslie to drag her into that discussion and instead touts the incredible value for consumers. Kathryn also argues that the tax would mean lost jobs in the local restaurant industry. Leslie and Kathryn, though on opposite sides, agree on this much: if passed, the tax will have a negative effect on the quantity demanded.

Since this episode first aired in 2012, soda taxes have been implemented throughout Mexico (2014) and in a number of major U.S. cities (San Francisco, Chicago, and Philadelphia). Researchers studied the impact of the sugary drink tax in Mexico and found that a 10% increase in the price of sweetened sugar beverages was associated with an 11.6% decrease in quantity consumed.* That translates into a price elasticity of demand of −1.16 (slightly elastic). For proponents of soda taxes, this indicates that even a relatively small increase in price will meaningfully reduce consumption and lessen obesity.

Mexico's sugary drink tax cut consumption by about 12%.

*M. A. Colchero, J. C. Salgado, M. Unar-Munguía, M. Hernández-Ávila, and J. A. Rivera-Dommarco, "Price Elasticity of the Demand for Sugar Sweetened Beverages and Soft Drinks in Mexico," *Economics & Human Biology*, vol. 19 (December 2015): 129–137, https://doi.org/10.1016/j.ehb.2015.08.007.

tax, and annual regulatory fees. In addition, many companies add surcharges, including activation fees, local-number portability fees, telephone number pooling charges, emergency 911 service, directory assistance, telecommunications relay service surcharges, and cancellation fees. Of course, there is a way to avoid all these fees: don't use a cell phone! However, many people today feel that cell phones are a necessity. Cell phone providers and government agencies take advantage of consumers' strongly inelastic demand by tacking on these extra charges.

Figure 5.9 shows the result of a tax on products with perfectly inelastic demand, such as phone service—something people feel they need to have no matter what the price. For our purposes, the demand for access to a phone (either a landline or a cell phone) can be considered perfectly inelastic. Recall that whenever demand is perfectly inelastic, the demand curve is vertical. Panel (a) shows the market for phone service before the tax. The blue rectangle

FIGURE 5.9

A Tax on Products with Almost Perfectly Inelastic Demand

(a) Before the tax, the consumer enjoys the consumer surplus (C.S.) shaded in blue, and the producer enjoys the producer surplus (P.S.) shaded in red. (b) After the tax, the incidence, or the burden of taxation, is borne entirely by the consumer. A tax on a good with perfectly inelastic demand, such as phone service, represents a transfer of welfare from consumers to the government, as reflected by the reduced size of the blue rectangle in (b) and the creation of the green tax revenue rectangle between P_1 and P_2.

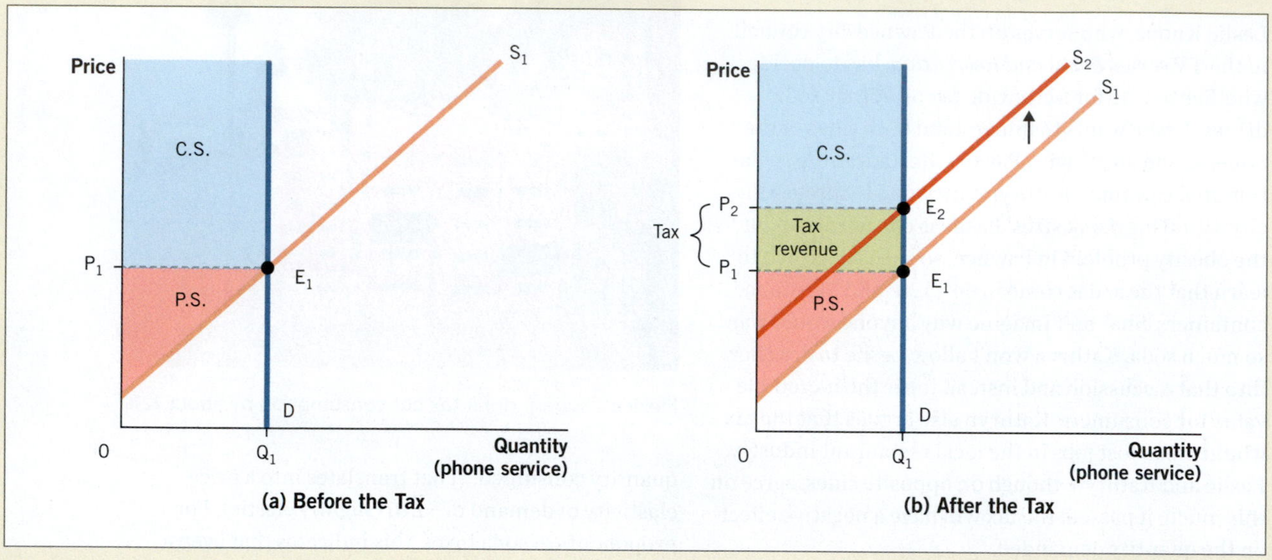

represents consumer surplus (C.S.), and the red triangle represents producer surplus (P.S.). Now imagine that a tax is levied on the seller, as shown in panel (b). The supply curve shifts from S_1 to S_2. The shift in supply causes the equilibrium point to move from E_1 to E_2 and the price to rise from P_1 to P_2, but the quantity supplied, Q_1, remains the same. We know that when demand is perfectly inelastic, a price increase does not alter how much consumers purchase. So the quantity demanded remains constant at Q_1 even after the government collects tax revenue equal to the green rectangle.

There are two reasons why the government may favor excise taxes on goods with almost perfectly (or highly) inelastic demand. First, because these goods do not have substitutes, the tax will not cause consumers to buy less. Thus, the revenue from the tax will remain steady. Second, because the number of transactions, or quantity demanded (Q_1), remains constant, there will be no deadweight loss. As a result, the yellow triangle we observed in Figure 5.8 disappears in Figure 5.9 because the tax does not alter the efficiency of the market. Looking at Figure 5.9, you can see that the same number of transactions exist in panels (a) and (b); the total surplus, or social welfare, is equal in both panels. You can also see this equality by comparing the full shaded areas in both panels. The sum of the blue area of consumer surplus and the red area of producer surplus in panel (a) is equal to the sum of the consumer surplus, producer surplus, and tax revenue in panel (b). The green area in panel (b) is subtracted entirely from the blue rectangle in panel (a), which indicates that the surplus is redistributed from consumers to the government. But society overall enjoys the same total surplus (even though some of this surplus is now in the form of a tax). Thus, we see that when demand is perfectly inelastic, the incidence, or the burden of taxation, is borne entirely by the consumer. A tax on a good with almost perfectly inelastic demand represents a transfer of welfare from consumers of the good to the government, reflected by the reduced size of the blue rectangle in panel (b).

TAX REVENUE AND DEADWEIGHT LOSS WHEN DEMAND IS MORE ELASTIC Now consider a tax on a product with more elastic demand, such as milk, the subject of our earlier discussion. The demand for milk is price sensitive, but not overly so. This elasticity is reflected in a demand curve with a typical slope as shown in Figure 5.10. Let's compare the after-tax price, P_2, in panel (b) of Figures 5.9 and 5.10. When demand is perfectly inelastic, as it is in panel (b) of Figure 5.9, the price increase from P_1 to P_2 is absorbed entirely by consumers. But in panel (b) of Figure 5.10, because demand is flatter and therefore more sensitive to price, suppliers must absorb part of the tax themselves (from P_1 to P_3). Thus, the net price they charge, P_3, is less than what they received when the good was not taxed. In addition, the total tax revenue generated (the green area) is not as large in panel (b) of Figure 5.10 as in panel (b) of Figure 5.9 because as the price of the good rises to P_2, some consumers no longer buy it and the quantity demanded falls from Q_1 to Q_2.

FIGURE 5.10

A Tax on Products with More Elastic Demand

(a) Before the tax, the consumer enjoys the consumer surplus (C.S.) shaded in blue, and the producer enjoys the producer surplus (P.S.) shaded in red. (b) A tax on a good for which demand and supply are both somewhat elastic will cause a transfer of welfare from consumers and producers to the government, the revenue shown as the green rectangle. It will also create deadweight loss (D.W.L.), shaded in yellow, because the quantity bought and sold in the market declines (from Q_1 to Q_2).

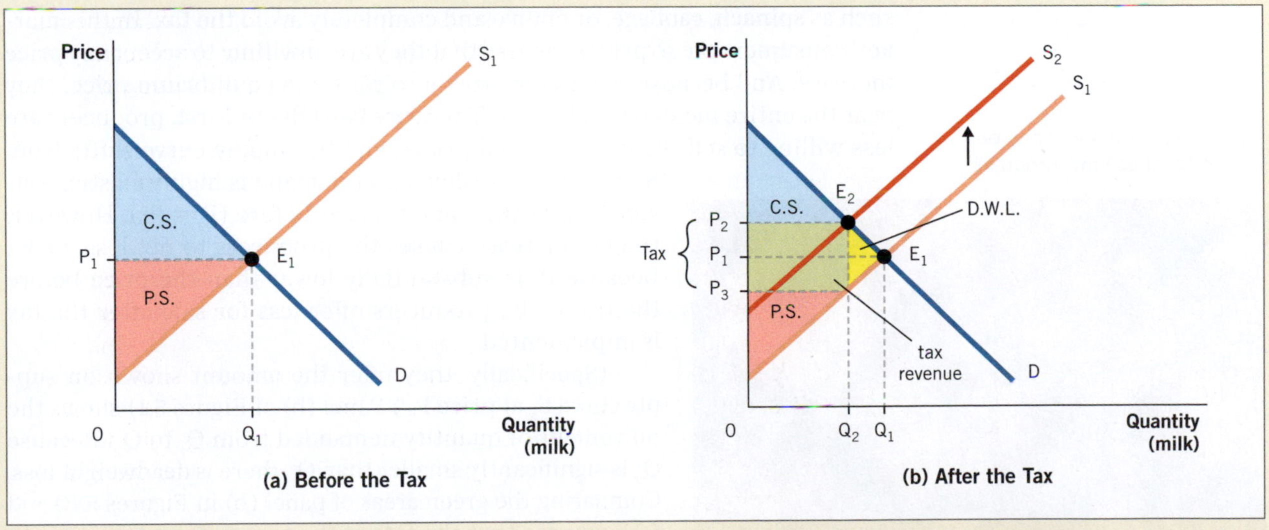

Notice that both consumer surplus (C.S., the blue triangle) and producer surplus (P.S., the red triangle) in Figure 5.10, panel (b), are smaller after the tax. Because the price rises after the tax increase (from P_1 to P_2), those consumers with a relatively low willingness to pay for the good are priced out of the market. Likewise, sellers with relatively high costs of production will stop producing the good, because the price they net after paying the tax drops to P_3. The total reduction in economic activity, the change from Q_1 to Q_2, is the deadweight loss (D.W.L.) indicated by the yellow triangle.

A tax on a good for which demand and supply are both somewhat elastic will cause a transfer of welfare from consumers and producers of the good to the government. At the same time, because the quantity bought and sold in the market declines, deadweight loss is created. Another way of seeing this result is to compare the red and blue areas in Figure 5.10, panel (a), with the red and blue areas in panel (b) of Figure 5.10. The sum of the consumer surplus and producer surplus in panel (a) is greater than the sum of the consumer surplus, tax revenue, and producer surplus in panel (b) because the deadweight loss in panel (b) is no longer a part of the surplus. Therefore, the total surplus is lower, which means that the efficiency of the market is smaller. The tax is no longer a pure transfer from consumers to the government, as was the case in Figure 5.9 with perfectly inelastic demand.

TAX REVENUE AND DEADWEIGHT LOSS WHEN DEMAND IS HIGHLY ELASTIC We have seen the effect of taxation when demand is inelastic and somewhat elastic. What happens when demand is highly elastic? For example, a customer who wants to buy fresh lettuce at a produce market will find many local growers charging the same price and many varieties to choose from. If one of the vendors decides to charge $1 per pound above the market price, consumers will stop buying from that vendor. They will be unwilling to pay more when they can get the same product from another grower at a lower price. In other words, their demand is highly elastic.

Figure 5.11 shows the result of a tax on lettuce, a good with highly elastic demand. After all, when lettuce is taxed, consumers can switch to other greens such as spinach, cabbage, or endive and completely avoid the tax. In this market, consumers are so price sensitive that they are unwilling to accept any price increase. And because sellers are unable to raise the equilibrium price, they bear the entire incidence of the tax. There are two effects. First, producers are less willing to sell the product at all prices, and the supply curve shifts from S_1 to S_2. Because consumer demand is highly elastic, consumers pay the same price as before ($P_1 = P_2$). However, the tax increase causes the producers to net less, or P_3. Because P_3 is substantially lower than the price before the tax, or P_2, producers offer less for sale after the tax is implemented.

How much would you pay per pound for these mushrooms?

(Specifically, they offer the amount shown on supply curve S_2 at price P_2.) Panel (b) of Figure 5.11 shows the movement of quantity demanded from Q_1 to Q_2. Because Q_2 is significantly smaller than Q_1, there is deadweight loss. Comparing the green areas of panel (b) in Figures 5.10 and 5.11, you see that the size of the tax revenue continues to shrink. There is an important lesson here for policymakers.

FIGURE 5.11

A Tax on Products with Highly Elastic Demand

(a) Before the tax, the producer enjoys the producer surplus (P.S.) shaded in red. (b) When consumer demand is highly elastic, consumers pay the same price after the tax as before. But they are worse off because less is produced and sold; the quantity produced moves from Q_1 to Q_2. The result is deadweight loss (D.W.L.), as shown by the yellow triangle. The total surplus, or efficiency of the market, is much smaller than before. The size of the tax revenue (shaded in green) is also noticeably smaller in the market with highly elastic demand.

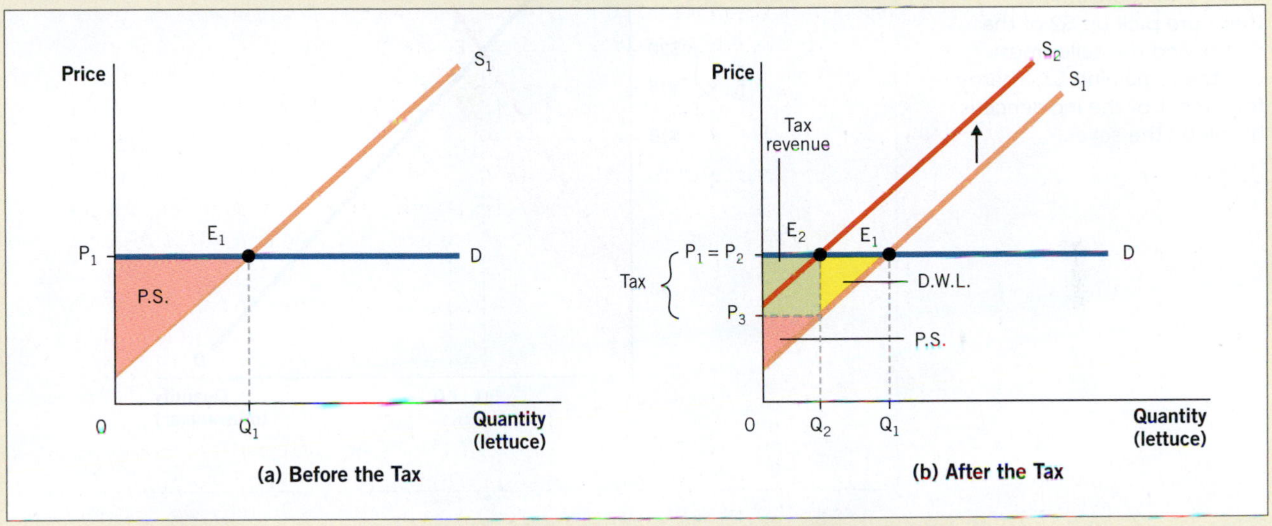

They should tax goods with relatively inelastic demand (if the goal is to generate tax revenue or minimize efficiency losses). Doing so will not only lessen the deadweight loss of taxation, but also generate larger tax revenues for the government.

INTERACTION OF DEMAND ELASTICITY AND SUPPLY ELASTICITY

The incidence of a tax is determined by the relative steepness of the demand curve compared with the supply curve. When the demand curve is steeper (more inelastic) than the supply curve, consumers bear more of the incidence of the tax. When the supply curve is steeper (more inelastic) than the demand curve, suppliers bear more of the incidence of the tax. Also, whenever the supply and/or demand curves are relatively steep, deadweight loss is minimized.

Let's explore an example in which we consider how the elasticity of demand and elasticity of supply interact. Suppose that a $5-per-pound tax is placed on shiitake mushrooms. Given the information in Figure 5.12, we will compute the incidence, deadweight loss, and tax revenue from the tax.

Let's start with the incidence of the tax. After the tax is implemented, the market price rises from $18 per pound (at E_1) to $20 per pound (at E_2). But since sellers must pay $5 per pound to the government, they keep only $15. Tax incidence measures the share of the tax paid by buyers and sellers, so we need to compare the incidence of the tax paid by each party. Because the

FIGURE 5.12

A Realistic Example

A \$5-per-pound tax is placed on mushroom suppliers, driving the equilibrium price up from E_1 (\$18) to E_2 (\$20). Notice that the price rises by only \$2. Consumers therefore pick up \$2 of the \$5 tax and the seller must pay the remaining \$3. Therefore, most of the incidence is borne by the seller.

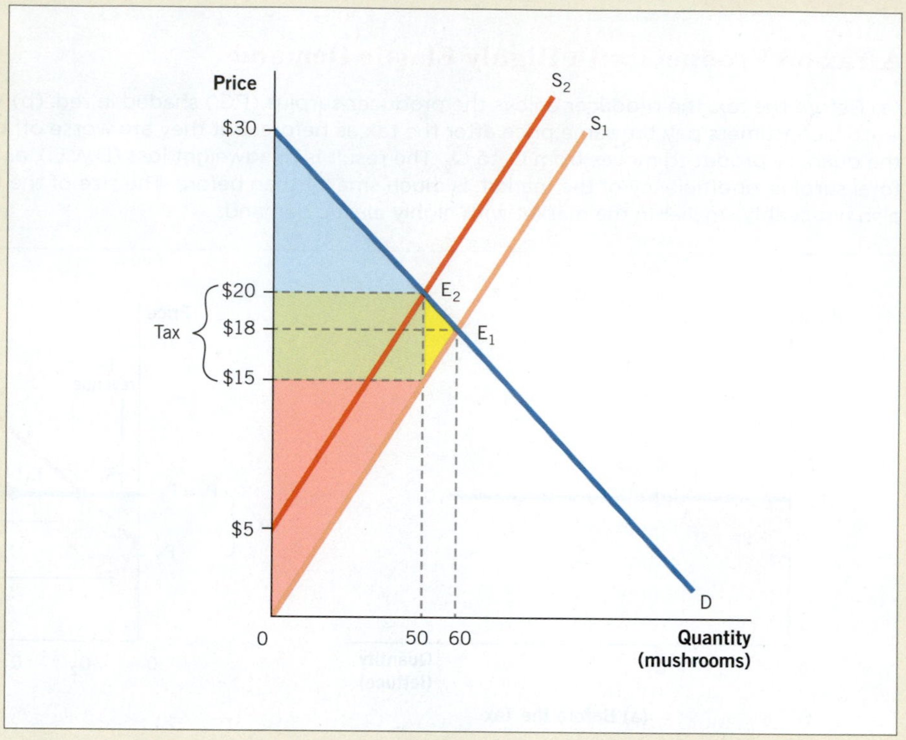

market price rises by \$2 (from \$18 to \$20), buyers are paying \$2 of the \$5 tax, or $\frac{2}{5}$. Because the amount the seller keeps falls by \$3 (from \$18 to \$15), sellers are paying \$3 of the \$5 tax, or $\frac{3}{5}$. Notice that the demand curve is slightly more elastic (flatter) than the supply curve; therefore, sellers have a limited ability to raise their price.

Now let's determine the deadweight loss caused by the tax—that is, the decrease in economic activity. Deadweight loss is represented by the decrease in the total surplus found in the yellow triangle in Figure 5.12. To compute the amount of the deadweight loss, we need to determine the area of the triangle:

(EQUATION 5.1) $$\text{area of a triangle} = \frac{1}{2} \times \text{base} \times \text{height}$$

The triangle in Figure 5.12 is sitting on its side, so its height is $60 - 50 = 10$, and its base is $\$20 - \$15 = \$5$.

$$\text{deadweight loss} = \frac{1}{2} \times 10 \times \$5 = \$25$$

This means that \$25 worth of mushroom sales will not take place because of the tax.

ECONOMICS IN THE REAL WORLD

DISTORTIONS

"Snowbirds" love to escape harsh winters (and high taxes).

Did you know that five states have no sales tax, and seven states have no income tax? One state, Alaska, has no sales *or* income tax! And even if you include property taxes, which are relatively high in Alaska, it still has the lowest combined tax incidence of any state. A household earning $69,000 per year (the national median) will pay, on average, almost $8,500 per year in state taxes in New York, and less than half that in Alaska—just over $3,500.

Of course, not everyone can pick up and move to Alaska. But sometimes there are easier opportunities to game the system. For example, if your job is in Portland, Oregon, you can live in nearby Vancouver, Washington. In exchange for a 15-minute work commute, you get to pay no state income taxes, because you're a Washington resident, and at the same time you can avoid sales taxes by doing your shopping in Portland. Win-win!

Incentives

Then there are the "snowbirds," as they're called—retirees who maintain a legal residence in a low-tax, southern state like Florida, Texas, or Arizona and live there during the winter, but during the summer escape the heat by traveling back to New York, Illinois, or Oregon, where the taxes are much higher but the snowbirds don't have to pay them.

In maintaining their domiciles in the low-tax states, the snowbirds are responding to the incentive structure created by having different tax codes in different states. It is, of course, inefficient to travel a large distance twice a year to avoid paying taxes. Taxation creates distortions by altering the incentives people and firms face and therefore altering their economic behavior. When taxes vary from state to state, the amount of distortion, which we think of as deadweight loss, depends on how flexible households and firms are in relocating from one state to another. The deadweight loss is a lot greater for the snowbirds than for the residents of Vancouver, Washington.

Source: G. Brian Davis, "States with the Lowest Overall Tax Burden (Income, Property & Sales)," Moneycrashers.com, April 27, 2021, https://www.moneycrashers.com/states-lowest-overall-tax-burden/.

Finally, what is the tax revenue generated by the tax? In Figure 5.12, the tax revenue is represented by the green-shaded area, which is a rectangle. We can calculate the tax revenue by determining the area of the rectangle:

$$\text{area of a rectangle} = \text{base} \times \text{height} \qquad \textbf{(EQUATION 5.2)}$$

The height of the tax revenue rectangle is the amount of the tax ($5), and the number of units sold after the tax is 50 (the base).

$$\text{tax revenue} = \$5 \times 50 = \$250$$

Balancing Deadweight Loss and Tax Revenues

Up to this point, we have kept the size of the tax increase constant. Doing so enabled us to examine the impact of the elasticity of demand and supply on deadweight loss and tax revenues. But what happens when a tax is high enough to significantly alter consumer or producer behavior? For instance, in 2002, the

Republic of Ireland instituted a tax of 15 euro cents on each plastic bag in order to curb litter and encourage recycling. Since the cost of production of each plastic bag is just a few pennies, a 15-euro-cent tax is enormous by comparison. As a result, consumer use of plastic bags quickly fell by over 90%. Thus, the tax was a major success because the government achieved its goal of curbing litter. In this section, we consider how consumers respond to taxes of different sizes, and we determine the relationship between the size of a tax, the deadweight loss, and tax revenues.

Figure 5.13 shows the market response to a variety of tax increases. The five panels in the figure begin with a reference point, panel (a), where no tax is levied, and progress toward panel (e), where the tax rate becomes so extreme that it curtails all economic activity.

As taxes rise, so do prices. You can trace this price rise from panel (a), where there is no tax and the price is P_1, all the way to panel (e), where the extreme tax causes the price to rise to P_5. At the same time, deadweight loss (D.W.L.) also rises. You can see this increase by comparing the sizes of the yellow triangles. The trade-off is striking. Without any taxes, deadweight loss does not occur. But as soon as taxes are in place, the market equilibrium quantity demanded begins to decline, moving from Q_1 to Q_5. As the number of transactions (quantity demanded) declines, the area of deadweight loss rapidly expands.

Incentives
Trade-offs

When taxes are small, as in panel (b), the tax revenue (green rectangle) is large relative to the deadweight loss (yellow triangle). However, as we progress through the panels, this relationship slowly reverses. In panel (c), the size of

PRACTICE WHAT YOU KNOW

What is the optimal tax rate?

Deadweight Loss of Taxation: The Politics of Tax Rates

Imagine that you and two friends are discussing the politics of taxation. One friend, who is fiscally conservative, argues that tax rates are too high. The other friend, who is more progressive, argues that tax rates are too low.

QUESTION: Is it possible that both friends are right?

ANSWER: Surprisingly, the answer is yes. When tax rates become extraordinarily high, the amount of deadweight loss dwarfs the amount of tax revenue collected. Fiscal conservatives often note that taxes inhibit economic activity. They advocate lower tax rates and limited government involvement in the market, preferring to minimize the deadweight loss on economic activity—see panel (b) in Figure 5.13. However, progressives prefer somewhat higher tax rates than fiscal conservatives, because a moderate tax rate—see panel (c)—generates more tax revenue than a small tax does. The additional revenues that moderate tax rates generate can fund more government services.

Trade-offs

Therefore, a clear trade-off exists between the size of the public (government) sector and market activity. Depending on how you view the value created by markets versus the value added through government provision, there is ample room for disagreement about the best tax policy.

FIGURE 5.13

Examining Deadweight Loss and Tax Revenues

The panels show that increased taxes result in higher prices. Progressively higher taxes lead to more deadweight loss (D.W.L.), but higher taxes do not always generate more tax revenue, as evidenced by the reduction in tax revenue that occurs when tax rates become too large in panels (d) and (e).

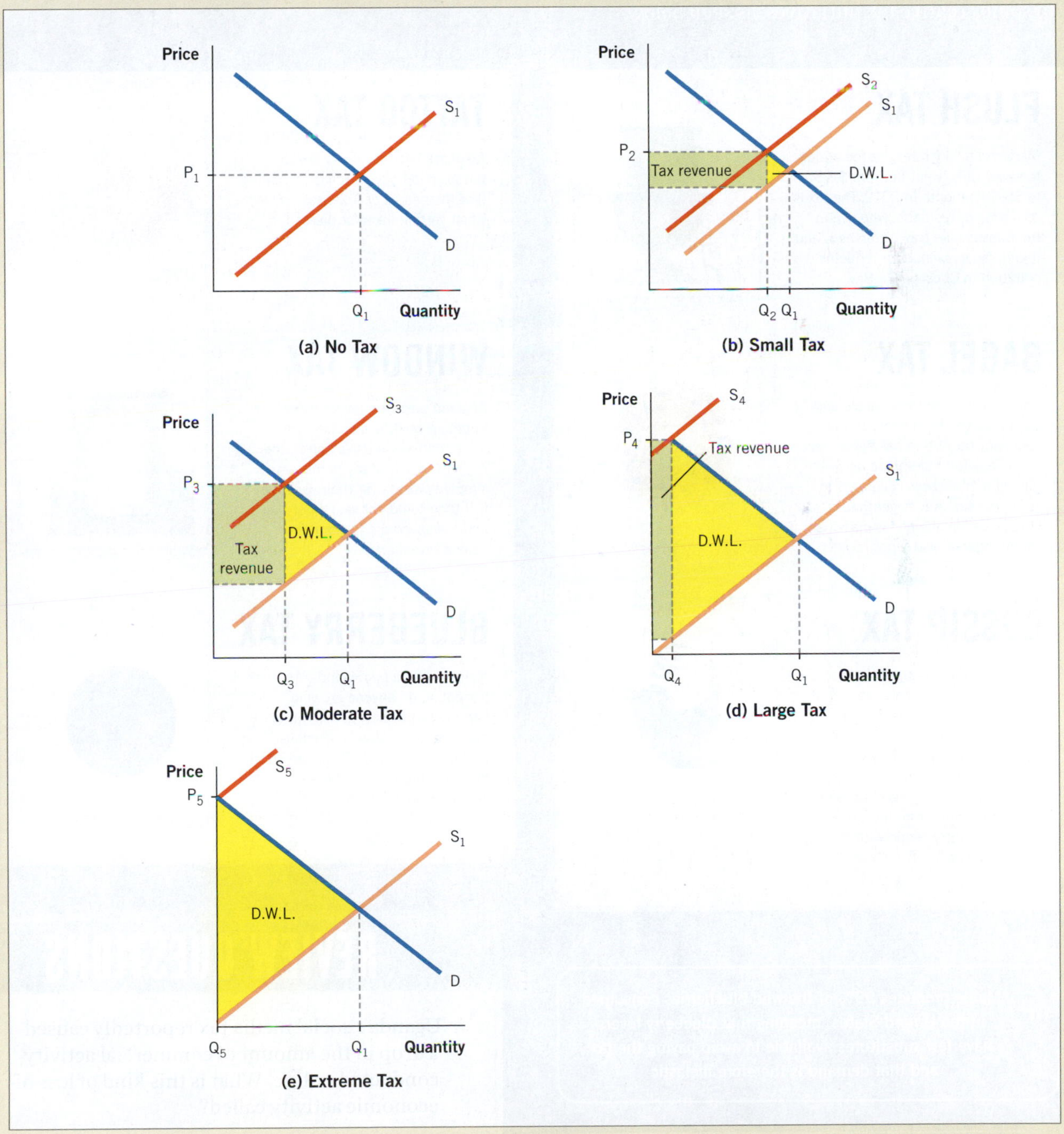

SNAPSHOT

Unusual Taxes

Governments tax their citizens for a variety of reasons. Often it's to raise revenue. Sometimes, taxes are levied to influence citizens' behavior. Occasionally, both of these reasons are in play. These two motivations have led to some creative tax initiatives, as seen below.

FLUSH TAX

Maryland's "flush tax," a fee added to sewer bills, went up from $2.50 to $5.00 a month in 2012. The tax is paid only by residents who live in the Chesapeake Bay Watershed, and it generates revenue for reducing pollution in Chesapeake Bay.

BAGEL TAX

New Yorkers love their bagels and cream cheese from delis. In the state, any bagel that has been sliced or has any form of spread on it (like cream cheese) is subject to an 8-cent tax. Any bagel that is purchased "unaltered" is classified as unprepared and is not taxed.

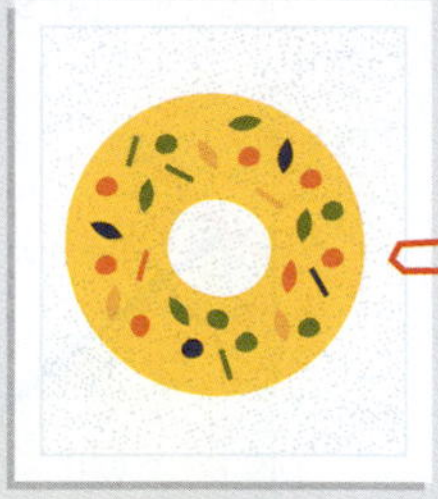

GOSSIP TAX

In 2018, Uganda passed a "social media tax" of 200 shillings (about $0.05) per day on anyone using online services like Facebook, WhatsApp, and Twitter. President Yoweri Museveni declared that Internet messaging platforms encourage gossip, and that the revenue from the tax would help the country "cope with the consequences."

TATTOO TAX

Arkansas imposes a 6% tax on tattoos and body piercings, meaning that the people of Arkansas pay extra when getting inked or pierced.

WINDOW TAX

England passed a tax in 1696 targeting wealthy citizens—the more windows in one's house, the higher the tax. Many homeowners simply bricked over their windows. But they could not seal all of them, and the government did indeed collect revenue.

BLUEBERRY TAX

Maine levies a penny-and-a-half tax per pound on anyone growing, handling, processing, selling, or purchasing the state's delicious wild blueberries. The tax is an effort to make sure that the blueberries are not overharvested.

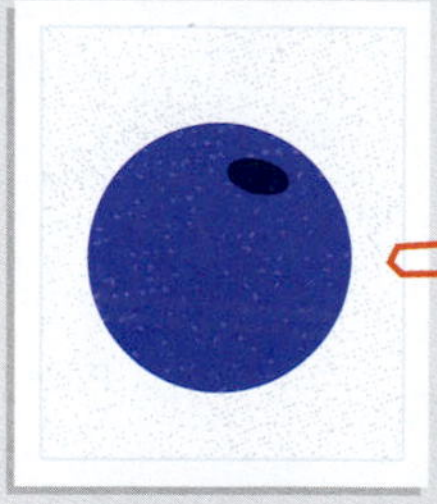

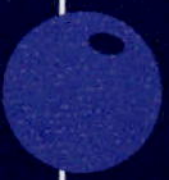

Maine produces 99% of the wild blueberries consumed in the United States, meaning that blueberry lovers have few substitutes available to avoid paying the tax and that demand is therefore inelastic.

Marylanders are being taxed on a negative externality, which we cover in Chapter 7.

REVIEW QUESTIONS

- Uganda's social media tax reportedly caused a drop in the amount of commercial activity conducted online. What is this kind of loss of economic activity called?
- Do you think the New York bagel tax is an effective tool to raise government revenue? Think about how the tax may or may not affect the purchasing behavior of New Yorkers.

the tax revenue remains larger than the deadweight loss. In panel (d), however, the magnitude of the deadweight loss is far greater than the tax revenue. The size of the tax in panel (d) is creating a significant cost in terms of economic efficiency. Finally, panel (e) shows an extreme case in which all market activity ceases as a result of the tax. Because nothing is produced and sold, there is no tax revenue.

Conclusion

The government largely taxes goods that have inelastic demand, which means that firms are able to transfer most of the tax incidence to consumers through higher prices.

In the first part of this chapter, we learned that society benefits from unregulated markets because they generate the largest possible total surplus. However, society also needs the government to provide an infrastructure for the economy. The taxation of specific goods and services gives rise to a form of market failure called deadweight loss, which reflects reduced economic activity. Thus, any intervention in the market requires a deep understanding of how society will respond to the incentives created by the legislation. In addition, unintended consequences can affect the most well-intentioned tax legislation and, if the process is not well thought through, can cause inefficiencies with far-reaching consequences. None of this means that taxes are undesirable. Rather, society must balance (1) the need for tax revenues and the programs those revenues help fund with (2) trade-offs in the market. ✷

Incentives
Trade-offs

· ECONOMICS *for* LIFE ·

Excise Taxes Are Almost Impossible to Avoid

- Excise taxes are placed on specific products.
- Excise taxes are typically levied on goods with inelastic demand.
- A typical household of four pays over $1,000 in excise taxes annually.

Excise taxes are everywhere.

The federal government collected $83 billion in excise taxes in 2017. Excise taxes are placed on many different products, making them almost impossible to avoid. They also have the added advantages of being easy to collect, hard for consumers to detect since the producer is responsible for paying the tax, and easier to enact politically than other types of taxes. You'll find federal excise taxes on many everyday household expenses—what you drink, the gasoline you purchase, plane tickets, and much more. Let's add them up over the course of a typical year.

1. **Gasoline (and Diesel).** 18.4 cents per gallon (and 24.4 cents per gallon), generating $41 billion to help finance the interstate highway system.
2. **Cigarettes.** $1.01 per pack, generating $10 billion for the general federal budget.
3. **Air travel.** 7.5% of the base price of the ticket plus $4 per flight segment, generating $14 billion for the Transportation Security Administration and the Federal Aviation Administration.
4. **Alcohol.** 5 cents per can of beer, 21 cents per bottle of wine, and $2.14 per bottle of spirits, generating $10 billion for the general federal budget.

These four categories account for $75 billion in excise taxes. You could still avoid the taxman with this simple prescription: don't drink, don't travel, and don't smoke. Where does that leave you? Way out in the country somewhere far from civilization. Since you won't be able to travel to a grocery store, you'll need to live off the land, grow your own crops, and hunt or fish.

But there is still one last federal excise tax to go.

5. **Hunting and fishing.** Taxes range from 3 cents for fishing tackle boxes to 11% for archery equipment, generating over $1 billion for fish and wildlife services.

Living off the land and avoiding taxes just got much harder, and that's the whole point. The government taxes products with relatively inelastic demand because most people will still purchase them after the tax is in place. As a result, avoiding excise taxes isn't practical.

Excise taxes are everywhere.

· ANSWERING *the* BIG QUESTIONS ·

What are consumer surplus and producer surplus?

- Consumer surplus is the difference between the willingness to pay for a good or service and the price that is paid to get it. Producer surplus is the difference between the price the seller receives and the price at which the seller is willing to sell the good or service.
- Total surplus (social welfare) is the sum of consumer and producer surplus that exists in a market.

When is a market efficient?

- Markets maximize consumer and producer surplus, provide goods and services to buyers who value them most, and reward sellers who can produce goods and services at the lowest cost. As a result, markets create the largest amount of total surplus possible.
- Whenever an allocation of resources maximizes total surplus, the result is said to be efficient. However, economists are also interested in the distribution of the surplus. Equity refers to the fairness of the distribution of the benefits within the society.

Why do taxes create deadweight loss in otherwise efficient markets?

- Deadweight loss occurs because taxes increase the purchase price, which causes consumers to buy less and producers to supply less. Deadweight loss can be lessened by taxing goods or services that have inelastic demand or supply.
- Economists are also concerned about the incidence of taxation. Incidence refers to the burden of taxation on the party who pays the tax through higher prices, regardless of whom the tax is actually levied on. The incidence is determined by the balance between the elasticity of supply and the elasticity of demand.

CHAPTER PROBLEMS

Concepts You Should Know

consumer surplus (p. 157)
deadweight loss (p. 170)
efficient (p. 164)
equity (p. 164)
excise taxes (p. 167)
incidence (p. 167)
producer surplus (p. 159)
social welfare (p. 162)
total surplus (p. 162)
welfare economics (p. 156)
willingness to pay (p. 157)
willingness to sell (p. 159)

Questions for Review

1. Explain how consumer surplus is derived from the difference between the willingness to pay and the market equilibrium price.
2. Explain how producer surplus is derived from the difference between the willingness to sell and the market equilibrium price.
3. Why do economists focus on consumer and producer surplus and not on the possibility of consumer and producer loss? Illustrate your answer on a supply and demand graph.
4. How do economists define efficiency?
5. What type of goods should be taxed in order to minimize deadweight loss?
6. Suppose that the government taxes a good that has very elastic demand. Illustrate what will happen to consumer surplus, producer surplus, tax revenue, and deadweight loss on a supply and demand graph.
7. What happens to tax revenues as tax rates increase?

Study Problems *(* solved at the end of the section)*

1. A college student enjoys eating pizza. Her willingness to pay for each slice is shown in the following table:

Number of pizza slices	Willingness to pay (per slice)
1	$6
2	5
3	4
4	3
5	2
6	1
7	0

   a. If pizza slices cost $3 each, how many slices will she buy? How much consumer surplus will she enjoy?
   b. If the price of slices falls to $2, how much consumer surplus will she enjoy?

2. A cash-starved town decides to impose a $6 excise tax on T-shirts sold. The following table shows the quantity demanded and the quantity supplied at various prices.

Price per T-shirt	Quantity demanded	Quantity supplied
$19	0	60
16	10	50
13	20	40
10	30	30
7	40	20
4	50	10

   a. What are the equilibrium quantity demanded and the quantity supplied before the tax is implemented? Determine the consumer and producer surplus before the tax.

b. What are the equilibrium quantity demanded and quantity supplied after the tax is implemented? Determine the consumer and producer surplus after the tax.

c. How much tax revenue does the town generate from the tax?

3. Andrew pays $30 to buy a potato cannon, a cylinder that shoots potatoes hundreds of feet. He was willing to pay $45. When Andrew's friend Nick learns that Andrew bought a potato cannon, he asks Andrew if he will sell it for $60, and Andrew agrees. Nick is thrilled, since he would have paid Andrew up to $80 for the cannon. Andrew is also delighted. Determine the consumer surplus from the original purchase and the additional surplus generated by the resale of the cannon.

4. If the government wants to raise tax revenue, which of the following items are good candidates for an excise tax? Why?

a. granola bars
b. cigarettes
c. toilet paper
d. automobile tires
e. bird feeders

* **5.** If the government wants to minimize the deadweight loss of taxation, which of the following items are good candidates for an excise tax? Why?

a. bottled water
b. prescription drugs
c. oranges
d. batteries
e. luxury cars

6. A new medical study indicates that boba tea helps prevent cancer. If the demand for boba tea increases, what will happen to the size of the consumer surplus and producer surplus? Illustrate your answer by shifting the demand curve appropriately and labeling the new and old areas of consumer and producer surplus.

7. Use the following graph to answer questions a–f.

a. What area represents consumer surplus before the tax?
b. What area represents producer surplus before the tax?
c. What area represents consumer surplus after the tax?
d. What area represents producer surplus after the tax?
e. What area represents the tax revenue after the tax?
f. What area represents the deadweight loss after the tax?

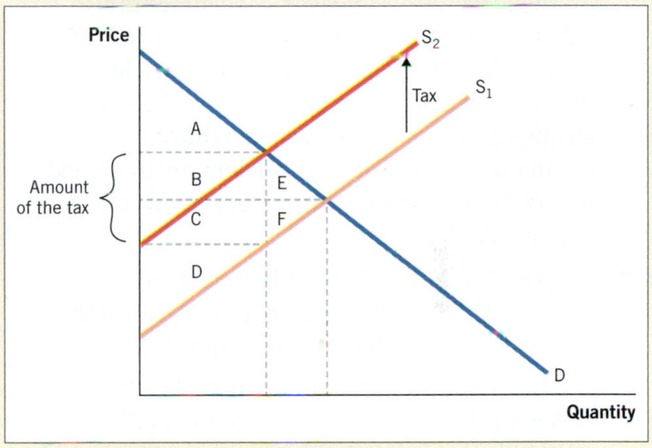

8. The cost of many electronic devices has fallen appreciably since they were first introduced. For instance, computers, cell phones, microwave ovens, and calculators not only provide more functions but also do so at a lower cost. Illustrate the impact of lower production costs on the supply curve. What happens to the size of the consumer surplus and producer surplus? If consumer demand for cell phones is relatively elastic, who is likely to benefit the most from the lower production costs?

9. Suppose that the demand for a concert, Q_D, is represented by the following equation, where P is the price of concert tickets and Q is the number of tickets sold:

$$Q_D = 2500 - 20P$$

The supply of tickets, Q_S, is represented by the equation

$$Q_S = -500 + 80P$$

a. Find the equilibrium price and quantity of tickets sold. (**Hint:** Set $Q_D = Q_S$ and solve for the price, P, and then plug the result back into either of the original equations to find Q_E.)
b. Carefully graph your result from part a.

c. Calculate the consumer surplus at the equilibrium price and quantity. (**Hint:** Because the area of consumer surplus is a triangle, you will need to use the formula for the area of a triangle, $\frac{1}{2} \times$ base $\times$ height, to solve the problem.)

10. In this chapter, we focused on the effect of taxes on social welfare. However, governments also subsidize goods, making them cheaper to buy or sell. How would a $2,000 subsidy on the purchase of a new hybrid car impact the consumer surplus and producer surplus in the hybrid-car market? Use a supply and demand diagram to illustrate your answer. Does the subsidy create deadweight loss?

∗ **11.** Suppose that a new $50 tax is placed on each new cell phone sold. Use the information in the following graph to answer these questions.

a. What is the incidence of the tax?

b. What is the deadweight loss of the tax?

c. What is the amount of tax revenue generated?

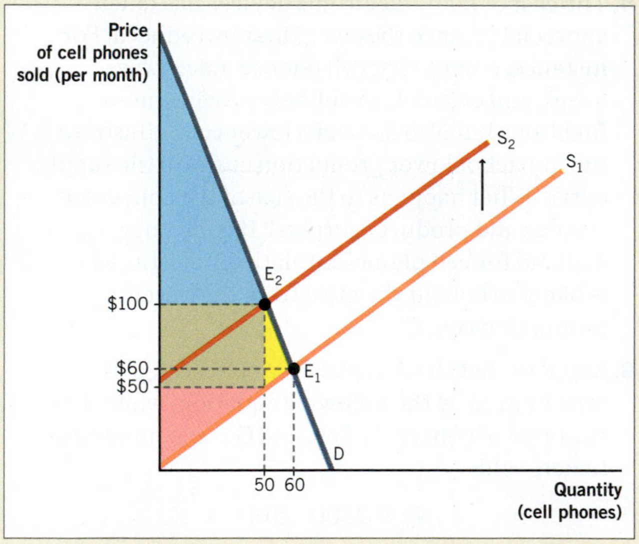

∗ **12.** A well-known saying goes, "Honesty is not only morally right, it is also highly efficient." Explain why firms that practice honesty generate more social welfare than firms that practice dishonesty.

13. We defined deadweight loss as the decrease in economic activity caused by market distortions. One place where we see deadweight loss is during Halloween's trick-or-treat. Children of all ages return home with bags of candy, some of which they love and some of which they don't care for. A lot of candy ends up uneaten. In this context, we can think of uneaten candy as not being distributed effectively by the market; therefore, deadweight loss occurs. What ways can you think of to improve how candy is given away during trick-or-treat so that children would receive more candies they enjoy? Provide three possible solutions.

∗ **14.** Assume that a $0.25/gallon tax on milk causes a loss of $300 million in consumer and producer surplus and creates a deadweight loss of $75 million. From this information, we know that the tax revenue from the tax is __________.

∗ **15.** For each of three potential buyers of avocados, the table displays the willingness to pay for the first three avocados of the day. Assume Carri, Carina, and Carlos are the only three buyers of avocados.

	First avocado	Second avocado	Third avocado
Carri	$2.00	$1.50	$0.75
Carina	1.50	1.00	0.80
Carlos	0.75	0.25	0.00

If the market price of avocados increases from $0.70 to $1.40, what is the change in total consumer surplus?

16. Suppose that the government imposes a $2 tax on consumers of donuts. What will happen to the market price?

Solved Problems

5. a. Many good substitutes are available: consumers can drink tap water, filtered water, or other healthy beverages instead of bottled water. Therefore, bottled water is not a good candidate for an excise tax.

b. Taxing prescription drugs will generate significant revenues without reducing sales much, if at all. There is almost no deadweight loss because consumers have few, if any, alternatives. Thus, prescription drugs are a good candidate for an excise tax.

c. Consumers can select many other fruits to replace oranges. The deadweight loss will be quite large. Therefore, oranges are not a good candidate for an excise tax.

d. Without batteries, many devices won't work. The lack of substitutes makes demand quite inelastic, so the deadweight loss will be small. Thus, batteries are an excellent candidate for an excise tax.

e. Wealthy consumers can spend their income in many ways. They do not have to buy luxury cars. As a result, the tax will create a large amount of deadweight loss. Therefore, luxury cars are a poor candidate for an excise tax.

11. a. After the tax is implemented, the market price rises from \$60 to \$100; but because sellers must pay \$50 to the government, they net only \$50. Tax incidence measures the share of the tax paid by buyers and sellers. Because the market price rises by \$40 (from \$60 to \$100), buyers are paying \$40 of the \$50 tax, or $\frac{4}{5}$. Because the net price falls by \$10 (from \$60 to \$50), sellers are paying \$10 of the \$50 tax, or $\frac{1}{5}$.

b. The deadweight loss is represented by the decrease in the total surplus found in the yellow triangle. To compute the amount of the deadweight loss, we need to determine the area inside the triangle. The area of a triangle is found by taking $\frac{1}{2}$ × base × height. The triangle is sitting on its side, so the height of the triangle is 10 (60 − 50) and the base is \$50 (\$100 − \$50). Hence the deadweight loss is $\frac{1}{2} \times 10 \times \$50 = \$250$.

c. The tax revenue is represented by the green area. You can calculate the tax revenue by multiplying the amount of the tax (\$50) by the number of units sold after the tax (50), which equals \$2,500.

12. For markets to benefit both the buyer and the seller, both parties must have accurate information about the good. We learned that an efficient allocation maximizes total surplus. Think about how dishonesty disrupts trade. Suppose a seller misrepresents the qualities of the good she is selling. A consumer buys the good and finds it to be defective or undesirable. As a result, the consumer does not get any consumer surplus from the transaction. In this case, total surplus is less than it otherwise would be. In addition, the consumer will no longer purchase from the dishonest seller, which means that potential gains from trade in the future will be lost as well.

14. The tax revenue is the lost consumer surplus plus the lost producer surplus minus the deadweight loss. Therefore, the answer is \$300M − \$75M = \$225M.

15. When avocados are \$0.70, Carri buys three and receives (\$2.00 + \$1.50 + \$0.75 − \$0.70 × 3 =) \$2.15 in consumer surplus, and Carina buys three and receives (\$1.50 + \$1.00 + \$0.80 − \$0.70 × 3 =) \$1.20 in consumer surplus. Carlos buys one and receives (\$0.75 − \$0.70 =) \$0.05 in consumer surplus. Totaling the combined consumer surplus gives us \$2.15 + \$1.20 + \$0.05 = \$3.40.

After the price rises to \$1.40, Carri buys two and receives (\$2.00 + \$1.50 − \$1.40 × 2 =) \$0.70 in consumer surplus, and Carina buys one and receives (\$1.50 − \$1.40 =) \$0.10 in consumer surplus. Carlos no longer buys avocados. Totaling the combined consumer surplus gives us \$0.70 + \$0.10 = \$0.80.

Therefore, the change in consumer surplus is \$0.80 − \$3.40 = −\$2.60.

CHAPTER

06

Price Controls

Price Controls Cause Surpluses and Shortages.

Nineteen-year-old Monica Savaleta is just like a lot of us, but she lives in Caracas, Venezuela, where the prices charged for basic necessities are typically strictly regulated. On the surface this sounds like an intriguing idea. Lower prices for essential items, like rice and sugar, means that those items are more affordable for everyone, right? Unfortunately, nothing in life is free. Sure, Venezuelan supermarkets sell food staples at prices that are often kept low not just by law but also through government subsidies. But the reality is that to buy those products you must wait in line for many hours, with no assurance that there will be any left when it's your turn to roam the aisles.

Meanwhile, market profiteers called *bachaqueros* do sell commodities like rice and sugar—for more than $5 a pound, a tremendous expense for a typical Venezuelan earning the minimum wage, equivalent to about $50 month. Monica is faced with two bad choices: wait in line at the supermarkets, or pay the bachaqueros. "I've been waiting in line since 3 a.m. and have only managed to get two tubes of toothpaste," she says. "If I buy from the bachaqueros, my whole salary is blown on three kilos of rice."*

Price controls are not a new idea. The first recorded attempt to regulate prices was 4,000 years ago in ancient Babylon, when King Hammurabi decreed how much corn

*Flora Charner and Rachel Clarke, "Venezuela: Where Flour, Pasta, and Milk Can Cost a Month's Pay," CNN.com, last modified August 2, 2016, http://edition.cnn.com/2016/08/02/americas/venezuela-food-prices/index.html.

In recent years, price controls in Venezuela have made it harder for stores to keep basic necessities in stock. Here, shoppers in the nation's capital, Caracas, wait their turn to enter a supermarket and hope to find at least a few of the items they came for.

a farmer could pay for a cow. Similar attempts to control prices occurred in ancient Egypt, Greece, and Rome. Each attempt ended badly. History has shown us that price controls generally do not work. Why? Because they disrupt the normal functioning of the market. Yet they are tried time and again, as seen in the frequent calls for price controls during the COVID-19 pandemic. By the end of this chapter, you will understand why price controls are rarely the win-win propositions that legislators often claim. To help you understand why price controls lead to disequilibrium in markets, this chapter focuses on the two most common types of price controls: *price ceilings* and *price floors*.

· BIG QUESTIONS ·

- When do price ceilings matter?
- What effects do price ceilings have on economic activity?
- When do price floors matter?
- What effects do price floors have on economic activity?

When Do Price Ceilings Matter?

Price controls attempt to set prices through government regulations in the market.

A **price ceiling** is a legally established maximum price for a good or service.

Price controls attempt to set prices through government regulations in the market. In most cases, and certainly in the United States, price controls are enacted to ease perceived burdens on society. A **price ceiling** creates a legally established maximum price for a good or service. In the next section, we consider what happens when a price ceiling is in place. Price ceilings create many unintended effects that policymakers rarely acknowledge.

Understanding Price Ceilings

To understand how price ceilings work, let's try a simple thought experiment. Suppose that most prices are rising as a result of *inflation*, an overall increase in prices. The government is concerned that people with low incomes will not be able to afford to eat. To help the disadvantaged, legislators pass a law stating that no one can charge more than $0.50 for a loaf of bread. (Note that this price ceiling is about one-third the typical price of a loaf of generic white bread.) Does the new law accomplish its goal? What happens?

The law of demand tells us that if the price drops, the quantity that consumers demand will increase. At the same time, the law of supply tells us that the quantity supplied will fall because producers will be receiving lower profits for their efforts. This combination of increased quantity demanded and reduced quantity supplied will cause a shortage of bread.

On the demand side, consumers will want more bread than is available at the legal price. There will be long lines for bread, and many people will not be able to get the bread they want. On the supply side, producers will look for ways to maintain their profits. They can reduce the size of each loaf they produce. They can also use cheaper ingredients, thereby lowering the quality of their product, and they can stop making fancier varieties.

In addition, illegal markets will develop. For instance, in 2014 Venezuela instituted price controls on flour, which has led to severe shortages of bread. In this real-life example, many people who do not want to wait in line for bread or who do not obtain it despite waiting in line will resort to illegal means to obtain it. In other words, sellers will go "underground" and charge higher prices to customers who want bread. Table 6.1 summarizes the likely outcomes of price controls on bread.

Long lines for bread in Venezuela.

Incentives

TABLE 6.1

A Price Ceiling on Bread

Question	Answer / Explanation	Result	
Will there be more bread or less bread for sale?	Consumers will want to buy more because the price is lower (the law of demand), but producers will manufacture less (the law of supply). The net result will be a shortage of bread.		Empty shelves
Will the size of a typical loaf change?	Because the price is capped at $0.50 per loaf, manufacturers will try to maintain profits by reducing the size of each loaf.		No more giant loaves
Will the quality change?	Because the price is capped, producers will use cheaper ingredients, and many expensive brands and varieties will no longer be profitable to produce. Thus the quality of available bread will decline.		Focaccia bread will disappear
Will the opportunity cost of finding bread change?	The opportunity cost of finding bread will rise. Consumers will spend significant resources going from store to store to see if a bread shipment has arrived and waiting in line for a chance to get some.		Bread lines will become the norm
Will people have to break the law to buy bread?	Because bread will be hard to find and people will still need it, an illegal market will develop. Those selling and buying on these markets will be breaking the law.		Bread dealers in illegal markets will help reduce the shortage

If you can touch the ceiling, you can't go any higher. A binding price ceiling stops prices from rising.

The Effect of Price Ceilings

Now that we have some understanding of how a price ceiling works, we can transfer that knowledge into the supply and demand model for a deeper analysis of how price ceilings affect the market. To explain when price ceilings matter in the short run, we examine two types of price ceilings: nonbinding and binding. Both are set by law, but only one actually makes a difference to prices.

NONBINDING PRICE CEILINGS The effect of a price ceiling depends on the level at which it is set relative to the equilibrium price. When a price ceiling is above the equilibrium price, we say it is *nonbinding*. Figure 6.1 shows a price ceiling of $2.00 per loaf in a market where $2.00 is above the equilibrium price (P_E) of $1.00. All prices at or below $2.00 (the green area) are legal. Prices above the price ceiling (the red area) are illegal. But because the market equilibrium (E) occurs in the green area, the price ceiling does not influence the market; it is nonbinding. As long as the equilibrium price remains below the price ceiling, price will continue to be regulated by supply and demand.

BINDING PRICE CEILINGS When a price ceiling is below the market price, it creates a binding constraint that prevents supply and demand from clearing the market. In Figure 6.2, the price ceiling for bread is set at $0.50 per loaf. Because $0.50 is well below the equilibrium price of $1.00, the price ceiling is *binding*. Notice that at a price of $0.50, the quantity demanded (Q_D) is greater than the quantity supplied (Q_S); in other words, a shortage exists. Shortages typically cause prices to rise, but the imposed price ceiling prevents that from happening. A price ceiling of $0.50 allows only the prices in the green area. The market cannot reach the equilibrium point E at $1.00 per loaf because it is located above the price ceiling, in the red area.

Incentives

The illegal price is also set by supply and demand. Because prices above $0.50 are illegal, sellers are unwilling to produce more than Q_S. Because a shortage exists, this market will form in response to the shortage. Here, purchasers can illegally resell what they have just bought at $0.50 for far more than what they just paid. Because the supply of legally produced bread is Q_S, the intersection of the vertical dashed line that reflects Q_S with the demand curve D_{SR} at point $E_{illegal}$ establishes a market price ($P_{illegal}$) at $2.00 per loaf for illegally sold bread. The market price is substantially more than the market equilibrium price (P_E) of $1.00. As a result, the price in these illegal markets eliminates the shortage caused by the price ceiling. However, the price ceiling has created two unintended consequences: a smaller quantity of bread supplied (Q_S is less than Q_E), and a higher price for those who purchase it there.

Price Ceilings in the Long Run

In the long run, supply and demand become more elastic, or flatter. Recall from Chapter 4 that when consumers have additional time to make choices, they find more ways to avoid high-priced goods and more ways to take advantage of low prices. Additional time also gives producers the opportunity to produce more

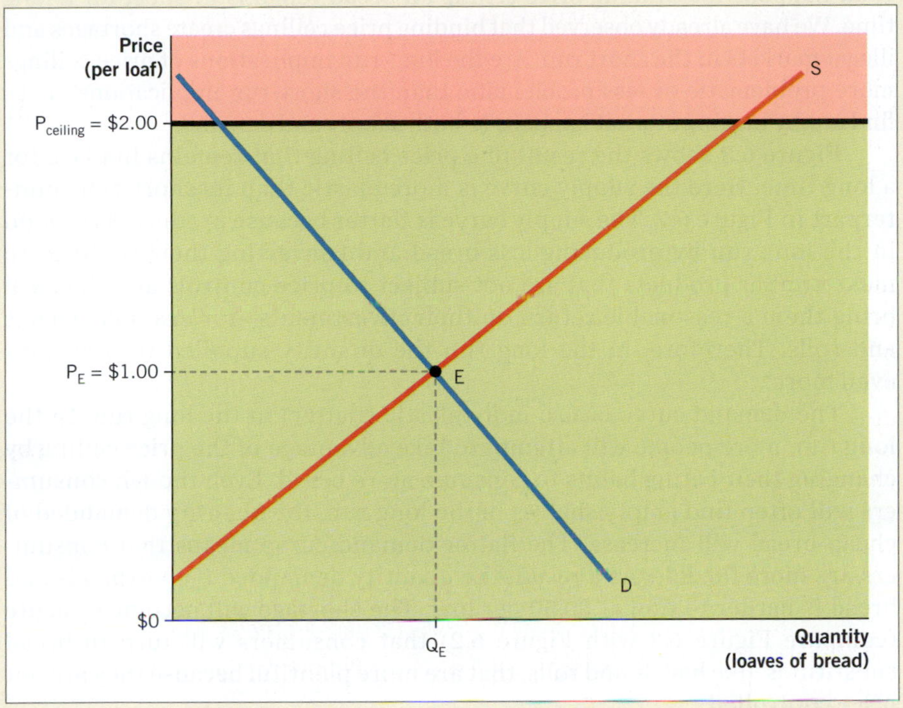

FIGURE 6.1

A Nonbinding Price Ceiling

The price ceiling ($2.00) is set above the equilibrium price ($1.00). Because market prices are set by the intersection of supply (S) and demand (D), as long as the equilibrium price is below the price ceiling, the price ceiling is nonbinding and has no effect.

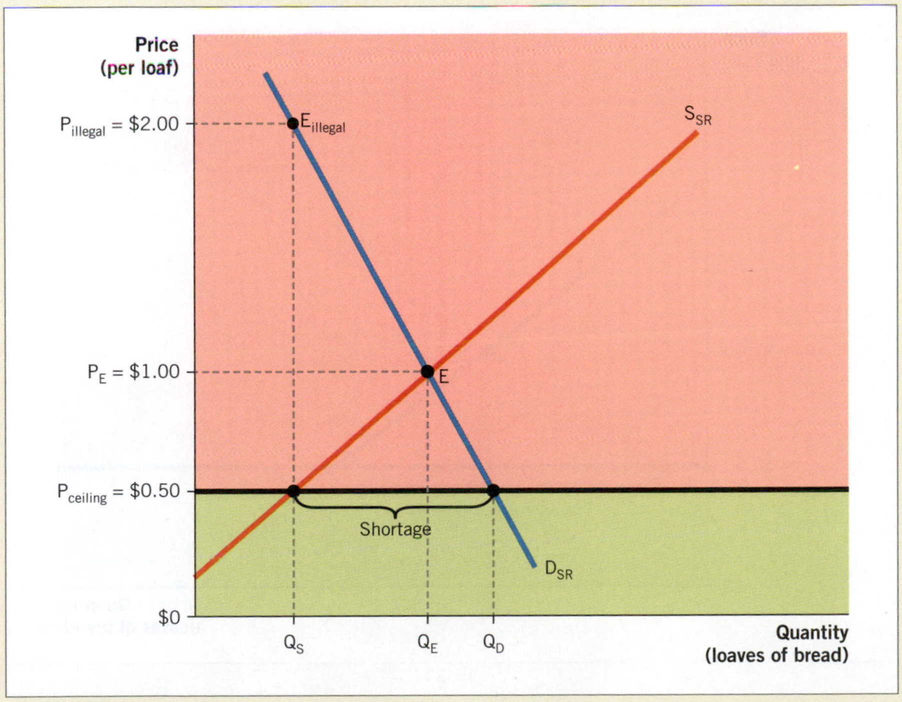

FIGURE 6.2

The Effect of a Binding Price Ceiling in the Short Run

A binding price ceiling prevents sellers from increasing the price and causes them to reduce the quantity they offer for sale. As a consequence, prices no longer signal relative scarcity. Consumers desire to purchase the product at the price ceiling level, which creates a shortage in the short run (SR); many will be unable to obtain the good. As a result, those who are shut out of the market will turn to other means to acquire the good, establishing an illegal market for it at a higher, illegal price.

when prices are high and less when prices are low. In this section, we consider what happens if a binding price ceiling on bread remains in effect for a long time. We have already observed that binding price ceilings create shortages and illegal markets in the short run. Are the long-run implications of price ceilings more problematic or less problematic than the short-run implications? Let's find out by looking at what happens to both supply and demand.

Figure 6.3 shows the result of a price ceiling that remains in place for a long time. Here the supply curve is more elastic than its short-run counterpart in Figure 6.2. The supply curve is flatter because producers respond in the long run by producing less bread and converting their facilities to make similar products that are not subject to price controls and that will bring them a reasonable return on their investments—for example, bagels and rolls. Therefore, in the long run the quantity supplied (Q_S) shrinks even more.

The demand curve is also more elastic (flatter) in the long run. In the long run, more people will attempt to take advantage of the price ceiling by changing their eating habits to consume more bread. Even though consumers will often find empty shelves in the long run, the quantity demanded of cheap bread will increase. The flatter demand curve means that consumers are more flexible. As a result, the quantity demanded (Q_D) expands and bread is harder to find at $0.50 per loaf. The shortage will become so acute (compare Figure 6.3 with Figure 6.2) that consumers will turn to bread substitutes, like bagels and rolls, that are more plentiful because they are not price controlled.

FIGURE 6.3

The Effect of a Binding Price Ceiling in the Long Run

In the long run (LR), increased elasticity on the part of both producers and consumers makes the shortage larger than it was in the short run. Consumers adjust their demand to the lower price and want more bread. Producers adjust their supply and make less of the unprofitable product. As a result, the product becomes progressively harder to find.

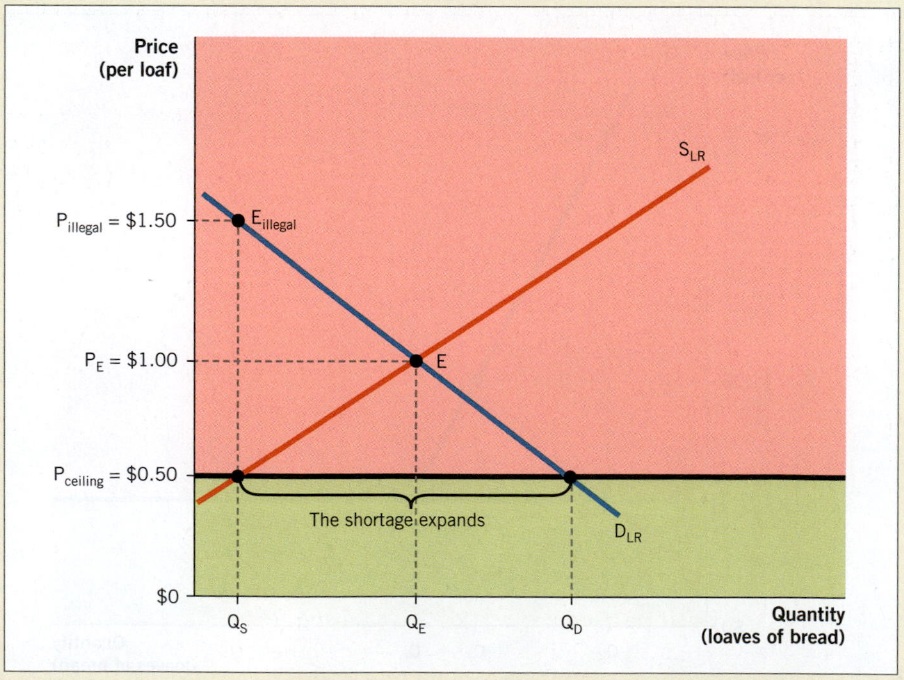

ECONOMICS in the MEDIA

Price Ceilings

SLUMDOG MILLIONAIRE

The Dharavi slum in Mumbai is the setting for *Slumdog Millionaire*.

The setting for the Academy Awards' Best Picture of 2008 is Mumbai, India. Eighteen-year-old Jamal Malik is an Indian Muslim who is a contestant on the Indian version of *Who Wants to Be a Millionaire?* Dharavi, where the film is set, is a Mumbai slum about half the size of New York's Central Park. Over 1 million people call Dharavi home. Malik is one question away from the grand prize. However, he is detained by the authorities, who suspect him of cheating because they cannot comprehend how a "slumdog" could know all the answers. The movie beautifully chronicles the events in Jamal's life that provided him with the answers. Jamal, contrary to the stereotype of the people that live in the Dharavi slum, is intelligent, entrepreneurial, and fully capable of navigating life in the 21st century.

Rent controls have existed in Mumbai since 1947. Under the Rents, Hotel and Lodging House Rates Control Act, the government placed a cap on the amount of rent a tenant pays to a landlord. This limit has remained virtually frozen despite the consistent rise in market prices over time. As economists, we know that this policy will create excess demand. Renters are lined up for housing, and therefore, landlords can offer substandard accommodations and still have many takers. When this process continues for generations, as it has in Mumbai, the cumulative effect is that many buildings are unsafe to live in.

Price ceilings set the regulated price below the market equilibrium price determined by supply and demand. As a result, there is an increase in the quantity demanded. At the same time, since the price that landlords can charge is below the market equilibrium price, many landlords have left the apartment market to sell and invest elsewhere. As a consequence, the supply of rental units is reduced over time, which leads to long wait lists for apartments. Since the quantity demanded exceeds the quantity supplied, some landlords also impose additional requirements on potential tenants, leading to discrimination against certain groups of people.

Increased elasticity on the part of producers and consumers magnifies the unintended consequences we observed in the short run. Therefore, products subject to a price ceiling become progressively harder to find in the long run and the illegal market continues to operate. However, in the long run our bread consumers will choose substitutes for this expensive bread, leading to somewhat lower prices in the long run.

PRACTICE WHAT YOU KNOW

Price Ceilings: Ridesharing

Desperately need a Lyft? Better hope there's one available!

QUESTION: Surge pricing is the practice of raising prices during periods of increased demand, sometimes for just a few hours at a stretch. Suppose that users of rideshare services, such as Lyft and Uber, persuade Congress to ban surge pricing when emergencies are declared. How will this policy affect the number of people who can use ridesharing in times of crisis?

ANSWER: The price that makes quantity supplied equal to quantity demanded is now illegal, because of the binding price ceiling. As a result, there will be a shortage of drivers willing to supply their service. Because rideshare drivers control when and where they choose to work, many will choose to stay home or work other areas not affected by the emergency. Consumers seeking a ride in the affected areas will turn to taxi cabs, buses and other forms of mass transit, but those services are also likely to be disrupted. In sum, the supply of available transportation options will dwindle. So the answer to the question is that fewer people will be able to get a rideshare, and this problem will be most acute in the worst-hit areas.

What Effects Do Price Ceilings Have on Economic Activity?

We have seen the logical repercussions of a hypothetical price ceiling on bread and the incentives it creates. Now let's use supply and demand analysis to examine two real-world price ceilings: *rent control* and *price gouging laws*.

Rent Control

Rent control is a price ceiling that applies to the market for apartment rentals.

Under **rent control**, a local government caps the price of apartment rentals to keep housing affordable. While this goal may be laudable, rent control doesn't work. In fact, it doesn't help the low-income residents of a city find affordable housing or gain access to housing at all. In addition, these policies contribute to dangerous living conditions.

Mumbai, India, provides a chilling example of what can happen when rent controls are applied over an extended period. In Mumbai, many rent-controlled buildings have become dilapidated. Every monsoon season, several of these buildings fall—often with tragic consequences. Because the rent that property owners are permitted to charge is so low, they have less income to use for maintenance on the buildings. They cannot make a reasonable profit and afford to maintain the buildings properly. As a result, rent control policies have led to the decay of many apartment buildings. Similar controls have caused the same problem in cities worldwide.

To understand how a policy can backfire so greatly, let's look at the history of rent control in New York City. In 1943, in the midst of World War II, the federal government established the Emergency Price Control Act. The act was designed to keep inflation in check during the war, when many essential commodities were scarce. After the war, the federal government ended price controls, but New York City continued rent control. Today, there are about 22,000 fully rent-controlled apartments in New York City, where tenants essentially pay the same rents as in the 1970s. On top of that, roughly 50% of all New York City apartments have rents that increase but are "stabilized" by when and how much a landlord can raise the rent.

Does this abundance of apartments with rent controls mean that less affluent households can easily find a cheap place to live? Hardly. When a fully rent-controlled unit is vacated, the property is generally no longer subject to rent control, but laws allow the tenants to pass those apartments from generation to generation, which keeps the apartments in the rent control program. Because so many rent-controlled apartments are inherited, rent control no longer even remotely serves its original purpose of helping low-income households. In the words of Curbed.com, a website that specializes in these markets, rent control is the "golden ticket" of New York real estate.

Many apartment buildings in Mumbai, India, are dilapidated as a result of rent control laws.

Even the rent-stabilized apartments enable a person to get a discounted apartment that "does not depend on your income level, the apartment size, how many people live there, or any other needs-based factors."* A 2019 *Wall Street Journal* study found those that benefited were "more affluent, white residents of Manhattan."† In multiple studies, different forms of rent control have been shown to decrease the landlord's interest in upkeep, discourage the creation of new rental housing (for fear of it being controlled), and increase conversion to condominium housing, when possible, which lowers overall rental stock.

Incentives

In the end, this attempt to make housing more affordable in New York City has, ironically, made it harder to obtain. It is a factor that has encouraged the building of upscale properties rather than low-income units, and it has created a set of behaviors among landlords that is inconsistent with the affordability that rent control was designed to address. Figure 6.4 shows why rent control fails.

*Emily Nonko, "New York Apartment Guide: Rent Control vs. Rent Stabilization," Curbed, January 3, 2020, https://ny.curbed.com/2017/8/28/16214506/nyc-apartments-housing-rent-control.

†Josh Barbanel, "Wealthy, Older Tenants in Manhattan Get Biggest Boost from Rent Regulations," *Wall Street Journal*, June 12, 2019, https://www.wsj.com/articles/wealthy-older-tenants-in-manhattan-get-biggest-boost-from-rent-regulations-11560344400.

FIGURE 6.4

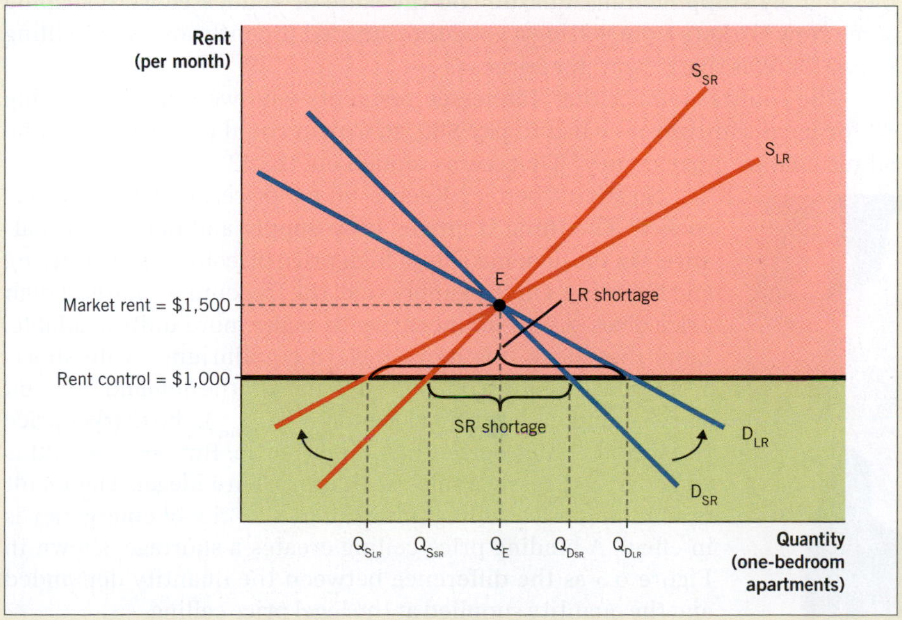

Rent Control in the Short Run and the Long Run

Because rent-controlled apartments are vacated slowly, the quantity supplied contracts in the short run and the supply curve become more elastic in the long run. Demand also becomes more elastic in the long run, causing the quantity demanded to rise. The combination of fewer units available to rent and more consumers looking to find rent-controlled units leads to a larger shortage in the long run.

As with any binding price ceiling, rent control causes a shortage because the quantity demanded in the short run ($Q_{D_{SR}}$) is greater than the quantity supplied in the short run ($Q_{S_{SR}}$). The combination of fewer available units and more consumers looking for rent-controlled units leads to a larger shortage in the long run.

Price Gouging

Price gouging laws place a temporary ceiling on the prices that sellers can charge during times of emergency.

Another kind of price control, **price gouging laws**, place a temporary ceiling on the prices that sellers can charge during times of emergency. Over 30 U.S. states have laws against price gouging. The intent is to keep people in desperate circumstances from being charged an arm and a leg for basic, essential goods. But like all price controls, price gouging laws have unintended consequences. Just ask Matt Colvin.

Colvin, who lives in Chattanooga, Tennessee, makes a nice living by finding things he can buy cheaply from out-of-the-way sources and selling them at a higher price on Amazon. Think sneakers, pet toys, and anything trendy. (This kind of exploitation of price differences is called *arbitrage*.) When the coronavirus pandemic struck, Colvin saw the opportunity to start hoarding hand sanitizer and face masks early on. Soon after, demand exploded, and Colvin was selling those goods at a huge markup. Bottles of hand sanitizer went for as much as $80. However, there was a declared health emergency, and Colvin was in clear violation of price gouging laws. Amazon shut down his business, and he eventually donated his remaining inventory to local charities.

Incentives

Now, was that a good thing? At the time, those bottles of hand sanitizer were more badly needed in places like New York City, where the outbreak was raging, than in rural Tennessee, where conditions weren't so bad. Colvin was making the rounds of country stores, buying sanitizer, and charging the prevailing market price. This was basically what he had always done, with the law's blessing. By stopping him, Amazon and the state of Tennessee were keeping some New Yorkers from getting a good they needed urgently and were willing to pay for. Was that a "win" for fairness?

The counterpoint is that Tennessee residents who were used to paying $3 for hand sanitizer now had to pay $80, so Colvin could earn what even he admitted was "crazy money." That seems repugnant, right?

Demand for hand sanitizer soared in many cities as COVID-19 became prevalent.

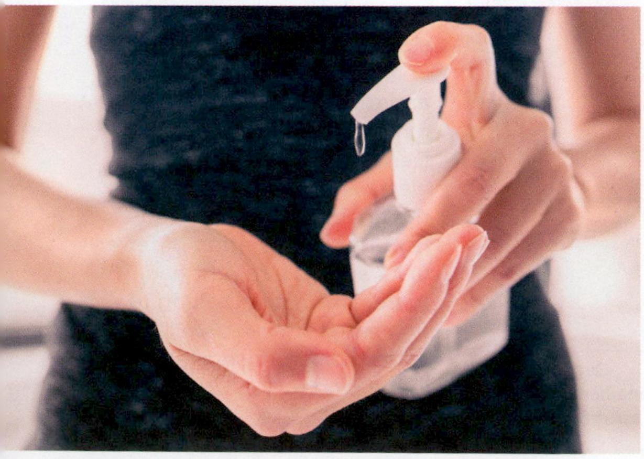

So what's better? Keep a lid on prices, or let them skyrocket? The thing is, prices keep supply and demand in balance. On the demand side, a high price discourages overbuying and hoarding. On the supply side, the freedom to charge a high price gives sellers an incentive to make more units available. Laws that block this move toward equilibrium create shortages. Figure 6.5 illustrates the dynamic. If the demand for hand sanitizer increases during a pandemic (D_{after}), the market price rises from $3 per bottle to $80 per bottle. But because $80 is considered excessive, sales at that price are illegal. The result is a binding price ceiling for as long as a state of emergency is in effect. A binding price ceiling creates a shortage, shown in Figure 6.5 as the difference between the quantity demanded and the quantity supplied at the legal price ceiling.

FIGURE 6.5

Price Gouging

Price gouging laws serve as a nonbinding price ceiling during normal times. However, when a natural disaster strikes, price gouging laws go into effect. In our example, the demand curve for hand sanitizer shifts to the right as a result of the emergency, causing the new equilibrium price (E_{after}) to rise above the legal limit. The result is a shortage. When the emergency is lifted, the market demand returns to normal, and the temporary shortage created by price gouging legislation is eliminated.

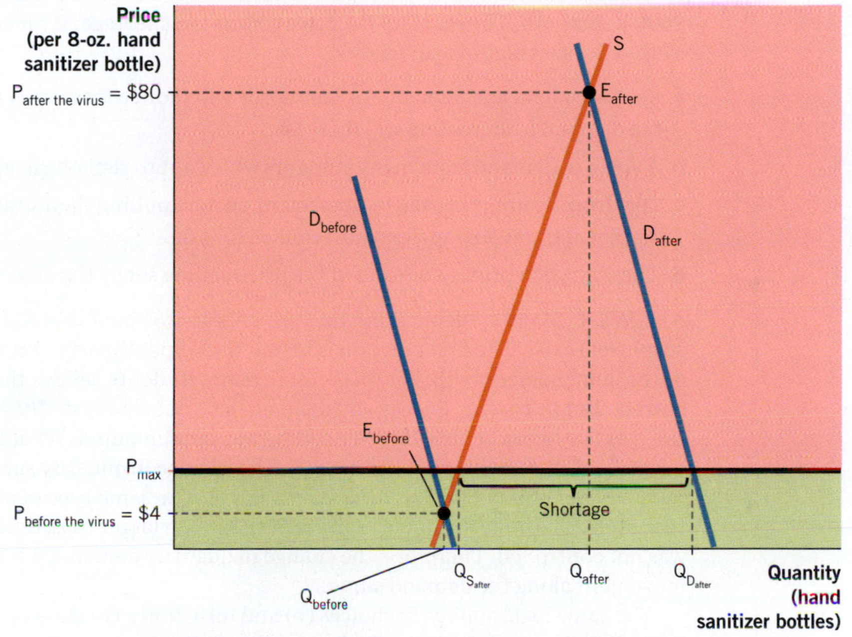

For a time, then, the normal ability of supply and demand to ration the available hand sanitizer is wiped away. Because more people demand hand sanitizer after the emergency than before it, those who don't get to the store soon enough are out of luck. When the emergency is lifted and the market returns to normal, the temporary shortage created by price gouging laws will be eliminated.

This does not mean that price gouging laws are automatically bad policy. After all, there is a limit to what we are willing to allow in the free market. (See Chapter 18, which talks about the market in human organs.) But from an economic point of view, price gouging laws are mostly downside.

When Do Price Floors Matter?

A **price floor** creates a legally established minimum price for a good or service. The minimum wage law is an example of a price floor in the market for labor. Like price ceilings, price floors create many unintended effects that policymakers rarely acknowledge. However, unlike price ceilings, price floors result from

A **price floor** is a legally established minimum price for a good or service.

PRACTICE WHAT YOU KNOW

Price Ceilings: Student Rental Apartments

Here is a question that often confuses students.

QUESTION: Imagine that a city council decides that the market price for student rental apartments is too high. It passes a law that establishes a rental price ceiling of $600 per month. The result of the price ceiling is a shortage. Which of the following has caused the shortage of apartments?

a. Both suppliers and demanders. Landlords will reduce the supply of apartments, and the demand from renters will increase.

b. A spike in demand from many students who want to rent cheap apartments.

c. The drop in supply caused by apartment owners pulling their units off the rental market and converting them into condos for sale.

d. The change in price as a result of the price ceiling set by the city council.

ANSWER: Many students think that markets are to blame when shortages (or surpluses) exist. The first reaction is to find the culpable party—either the supplier or the demander, or both. For this reason, many students believe that choice (a) is correct. But be careful. Supply and demand have not changed—they are exactly the same as they were before the price ceiling was implemented. What has changed is the quantity of apartments supplied at $600. This change in quantity supplied is represented by a movement along the existing supply curve. The same type of analysis applies to renters. The quantity demanded at $600 is much larger than it was when the price was not controlled. Therefore, the change in quantity demanded is represented by a movement along the demand curve.

The same logic applies to choices (b) and (c). Choice (b) states that there is a spike in student demand caused by the lower price. But price cannot cause a shift in the demand curve; it can only cause a movement along a curve. Likewise, choice (c) states that apartment owners supply fewer units for rent. The fact that fewer apartments are available at $600 per month would be represented by a movement along the apartment supply curve.

So we are left with choice (d), which is the correct answer. There is only one change in market conditions: the city council has passed a new price ceiling law. A binding price ceiling disrupts the market's ability to reach equilibrium. Therefore, we can say that the change in the price as a result of the price ceiling has caused the shortage.

the political pressure of suppliers to keep prices high. Most consumers prefer lower prices when they shop, so the idea of a law that keeps prices high may sound like a bad one to you. However, if you are selling a product or service, you might think that legislation to keep prices high is a very good idea. For instance, many states establish minimum prices for milk. As a result, milk prices are higher than they would be if supply and demand set the price.

In this section, we follow the same progression that we did with price ceilings. We begin with a simple thought experiment. Once we understand how price floors work, we use supply and demand analysis to examine the short- and long-run implications for economic activity.

Understanding Price Floors

To understand how price floors affect the market, let's try a thought experiment. Suppose that a politician suggests we should encourage dairy farmers to produce more milk so that supplies will be plentiful and everyone will get enough calcium. To accomplish these goals, the government sets a price floor of $6 per gallon—about twice the price of a typical gallon of fat-free milk—to make production more attractive to milk producers. What repercussions should we expect?

First, more milk will be available for sale because the higher price will cause dairies to increase the quantity that they supply. At the same time, because consumers must pay more, the quantity demanded will fall. The result will be a surplus of milk. Because every gallon of milk that is produced but not sold hurts the dairies' bottom line, sellers will want to lower their prices enough to get as many sales as possible before the milk goes bad. But the price floor will not allow the market to respond, and sellers will be stuck with milk that goes to waste. They will be tempted to offer illegal discounts in order to recoup some of their costs.

What happens next? Because the surplus cannot be resolved through lower prices, the government will try to help equalize the quantity supplied and the quantity demanded through other means. It can do so in one of two ways: by restricting the supply of the good or by stimulating additional demand. Both solutions are problematic. If production is restricted, dairy farmers will not be able to generate a profitable amount of milk. Likewise, stimulating additional demand is not as simple as it sounds. Let's consider how these government programs work with other crops.

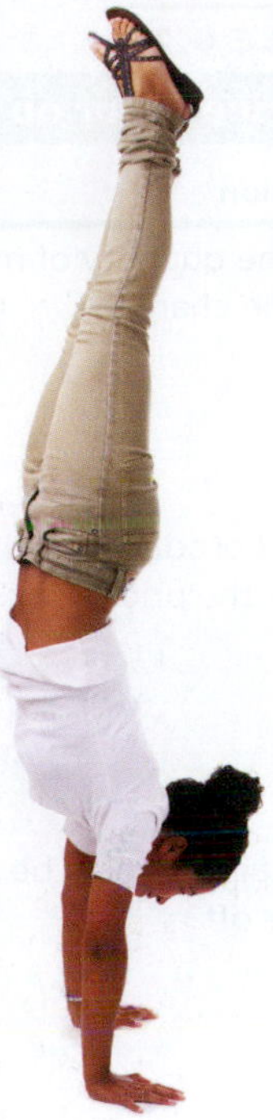

If you're doing a handstand, you need the floor for support. A binding price floor keeps prices from falling.

In many cases, the government purchases surplus agricultural production, most notably with corn, soybeans, cotton, and rice. Once the government buys the surplus production, it often sells the surplus below cost to developing countries to avoid wasting the crop. This strategy has the unintended consequence of making it cheaper for consumers in these developing nations to buy excess agricultural output from developed nations like the United States than to have local farmers grow the crop. International treaties ban the practice of dumping surplus production, but it continues under the guise of humanitarian aid. This practice makes little economic sense, but it continues to exist because it often makes political sense. Table 6.2 summarizes the result of our price floor thought experiment using milk.

Got milk? Maybe not, if there's a price floor.

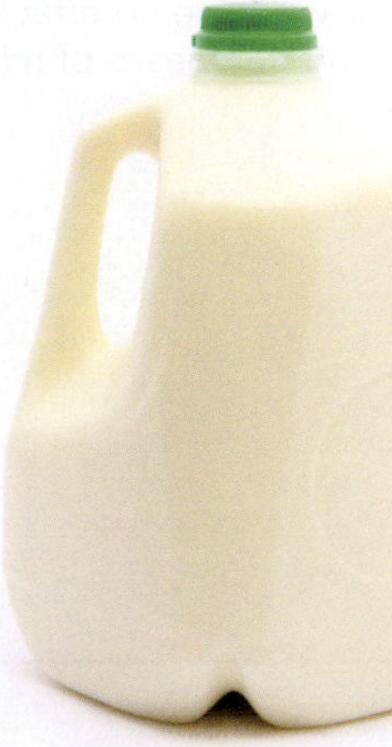

The Effect of Price Floors

We have seen that price floors create unintended consequences. Now we will use the supply and demand model to analyze how price floors affect the market. We look at the short run first.

NONBINDING PRICE FLOORS Like price ceilings, price floors can be binding or nonbinding. Figure 6.6 illustrates a nonbinding price floor of $2 per gallon on milk. As you can see, at $2 the price floor is below the equilibrium price (P_E), so the price floor is nonbinding. Because the actual market price is above the legally established minimum price (P_{floor}), the price floor does not prevent the market from reaching equilibrium at point E. Consequently, the price floor

TABLE 6.2

A Price Floor on Milk

Question	Answer / Explanation	Result	
Will the quantity of milk for sale change?	Consumers will purchase less because the price is higher (the law of demand), but producers will manufacture more (the law of supply). The net result will be a surplus of milk.		There will be a surplus of milk
Would producers sell below the price floor?	Yes. A surplus of milk would give sellers a strong incentive to undercut the price floor to avoid having to discard leftover milk.		Illegal discounts will help reduce the milk surplus
Will dairy farmers be better off?	Not if they have trouble selling what they produce.		There might be a lot of spoiled milk

FIGURE 6.6

A Nonbinding Price Floor

Under a nonbinding price floor, price is regulated by supply and demand. Because the price floor ($2) is below the equilibrium price ($3), the market will voluntarily charge more than the legal minimum. Therefore, this nonbinding price floor will have no effect on sales and purchases of milk.

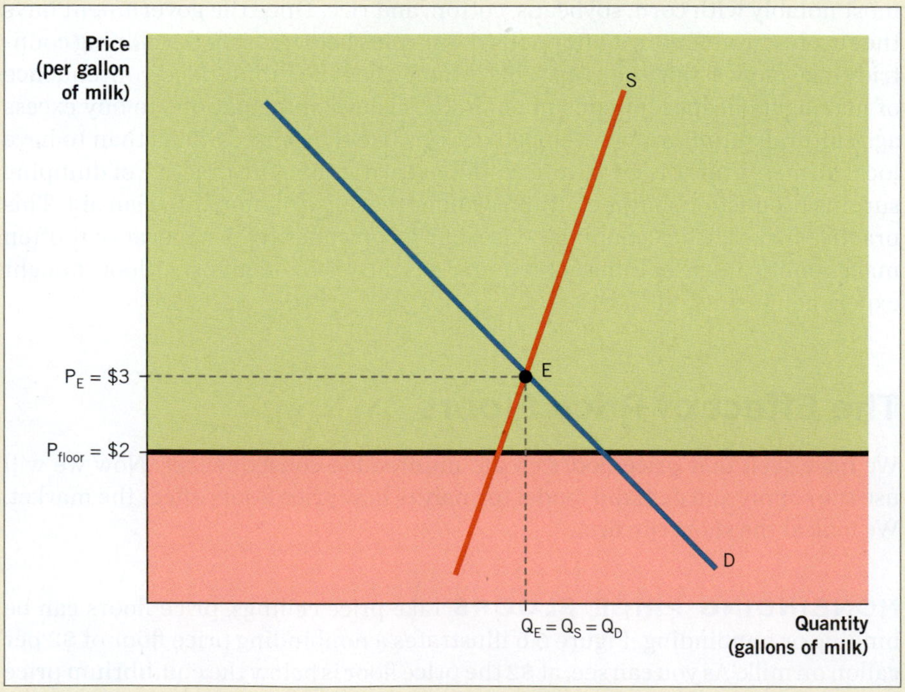

has no impact on the market. As long as the equilibrium price remains above the price floor, price is determined by supply and demand.

Full shelves signal a market at equilibrium.

BINDING PRICE FLOORS For a price floor to have an impact on the market, it must be set above the market equilibrium price. In that case, it is a binding price floor. With a binding price floor, the quantity supplied will exceed the quantity demanded. Figure 6.7 illustrates a binding price floor in the short run. Continuing our example of milk prices, at $6 per gallon the price floor is above the equilibrium price of $3. Market forces always attempt to restore the equilibrium between supply and demand at point E. So we know that there is downward pressure on the price. At a price floor of $6, we see that $Q_{S_{SR}} > Q_{D_{SR}}$. The difference between the quantity supplied and the quantity demanded is the surplus. Because the market's price adjustment mechanism is not permitted to work, sellers find themselves holding unwanted inventories of milk. To eliminate the surplus, which will spoil unless it is sold, an illegal market may develop with prices substantially below the legislated price. At a price ($P_{illegal}$) of $2, this market eliminates the surplus that the price floor caused. However, the price floor has created two unintended consequences: a smaller demand for milk ($Q_{D_{SR}} < Q_{E_{SR}}$) and an illegal market to eliminate the glut.

Incentives

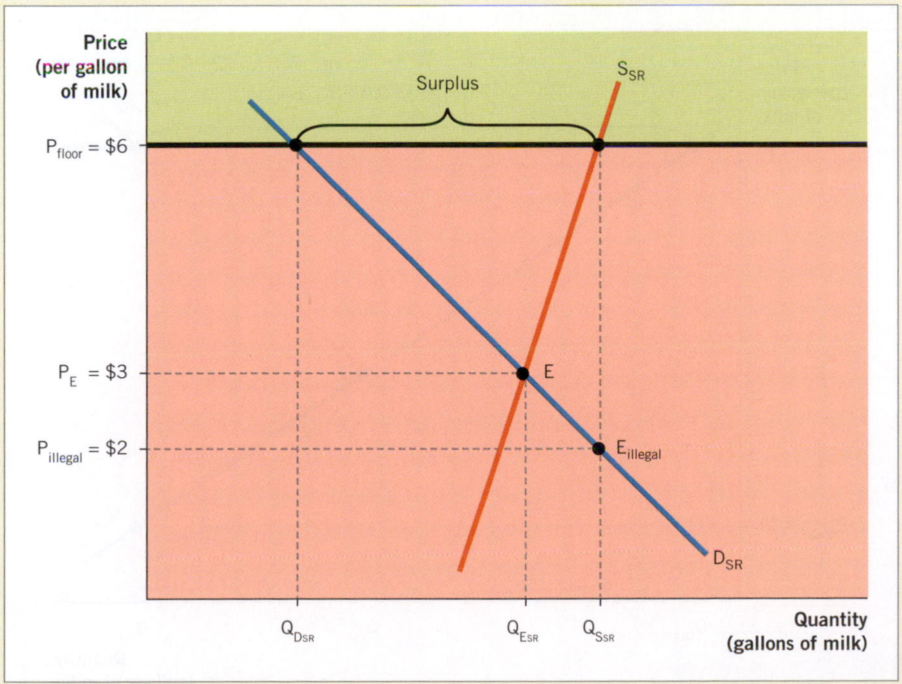

FIGURE 6.7

A Binding Price Floor in the Short Run

A binding price floor creates a surplus, which has two unintended consequences: (1) a smaller quantity demanded than the equilibrium quantity ($Q_{D_{SR}} < Q_{E_{SR}}$) and (2) a lower, illegal price to eliminate the glut of the product.

Price Floors in the Long Run

Once price floor legislation is passed, it can be politically difficult to repeal. What happens if a binding price floor on milk stays in effect for a long time? To answer that question, we need to consider elasticity. We have already observed that in the short run, binding price ceilings cause shortages and that illegal markets follow.

Figure 6.8 shows a price floor for milk that remains in place well past the short run. The long run gives consumers a chance to find milk substitutes—for example, products made from soy, rice, or almond that are not subject to the price floor—at lower prices. This added consumer flexibility makes the long-run demand for milk more elastic. As a result, the demand curve depicted in Figure 6.8 is more elastic than its short-run counterpart in Figure 6.7. The supply curve also becomes flatter (more elastic) because firms (dairy farms) are able to produce more milk by acquiring additional land and production facilities. Therefore, a price floor ($6) that remains in place over time causes the supply and demand curves to become more elastic, magnifying the surplus.

What happens to supply? In the long run, producers are more flexible and therefore supply is more elastic. The pool of potential milk producers rises as other closely related businesses retool their operations to supply more milk. The flatter supply curve in Figure 6.8 reflects this flexibility. As a result, $Q_{S_{LR}}$ expands and becomes much larger than it was in Figure 6.7. The increased elasticity on the part of both producers and consumers makes the surplus larger in the long run and magnifies the unintended consequences we observed in the short run.

FIGURE 6.8

The Effect of a Binding Price Floor in the Long Run

When a price floor is left in place over time, supply and demand both become more elastic. The result is a larger surplus ($Q_{S_{LR}} > Q_{D_{LR}}$) in the long run. Because sellers are unable to sell all that they produce at $6 per gallon, an illegal market develops to eliminate the glut of milk.

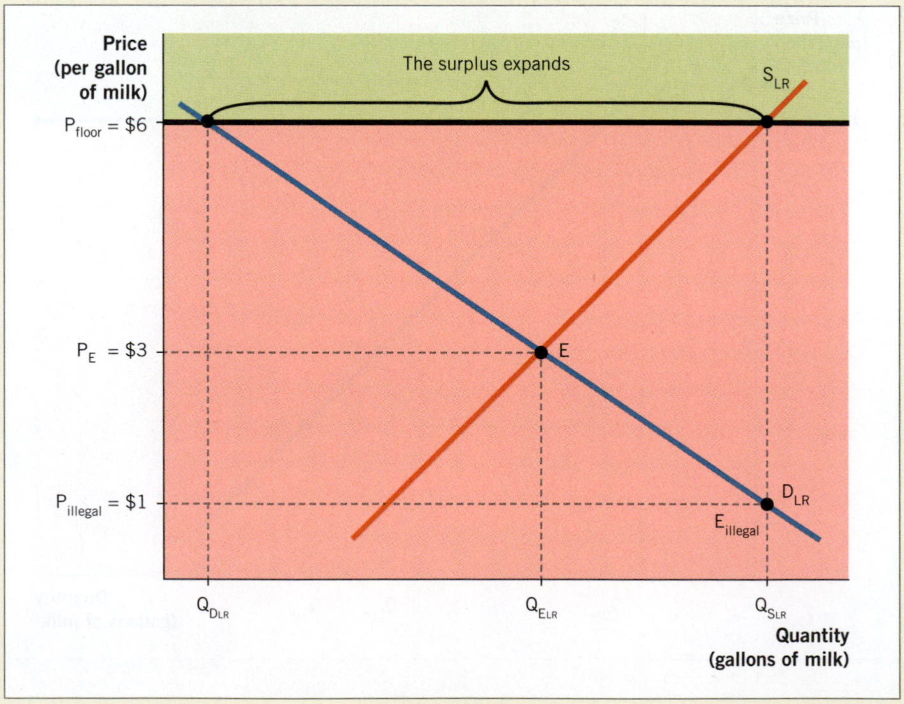

PRACTICE WHAT YOU KNOW

Price Floors: Fair-Trade Coffee

Would fair-trade coffee producers benefit from a price floor?

Opportunity cost

Fair-trade coffee is sold through organizations that purchase directly from growers. The coffee is usually sold for a higher price than standard coffee. The goal is to promote more humane working conditions for the coffee pickers and growers. Fair-trade coffee has become more popular but still accounts for a small portion of all coffee sales, in large part because it is substantially more expensive to produce.

QUESTION: Suppose that the price of a 1-pound bag of standard coffee is $8 and the price of a 1-pound bag of fair-trade coffee is $12. Congress decides to impose a price floor of $10 per pound on all 1-pound bags of coffee. What will most likely happen?

ANSWER: Fair-trade producers typically sell their product at a higher price than mass-produced coffee brands. Therefore, a $10 price floor is binding for inexpensive brands like Folgers but nonbinding for premium coffees, which include fair-trade sellers. The price floor will reduce the price disparity between fair-trade coffee and mass-produced coffee.

To see how the market will respond, consider a fair-trade coffee producer who charges $12 per pound and a mass-produced brand that sells for $8 per pound. A price floor of $10 reduces the difference between the price of fair-trade coffee and the inexpensive coffee brands, which now must sell for $10 instead of $8. The consumer's opportunity cost of choosing fair-trade coffee is now lower. Therefore, some consumers of the inexpensive brands will opt for fair-trade coffee instead. As a result, fair-trade producers will benefit indirectly from the price floor. Thus, the answer to the question is that more people will buy fair-trade coffee because of this price floor policy.

CHALLENGE QUESTION: Suppose the price floor is set at $12. What will most likely happen?

ANSWER: Now that the price floor is set at $12, the price differential between fair-trade and standard coffee no longer exists. Most consumers will switch to fair-trade coffee, since it's a cost-free way to feel ethical. In the short run, this will result in a shortage of fair-trade coffee, as producers struggle to keep up with demand. However, in the long run, we would expect producers of fair-trade coffee to expand production.

· ECONOMICS *in the* MEDIA ·

The Opportunity Cost of Higher Prices

College Humor created a short YouTube video, "Buy Food Ethically, Unless It's Too Hard," that illustrates the trade-offs people face when they make purchases at a local farmer's market. The people in the video have the best of intentions: they want to save the environment, eat healthier, and support local growers. But they admit they don't always buy at the farmer's market, despite their stated intentions. One of the primary reasons they don't go there as often as they would like to is the price. Each person is young and socially conscious, but prices matter to them as well, and that, combined with the inconvenience of going to the farmer's market, means they rarely go. The video illustrates a very important point: prices matter, whether those prices are naturally set in the market or artificially set through price controls.

Do you buy your produce at the farmer's market?

Trade-offs
Incentives

What Effects Do Price Floors Have on Economic Activity?

We have seen the logical repercussions of a hypothetical price floor on milk and the incentives it creates. Now let's use supply and demand analysis to examine two real-world price floors: *minimum wage laws* and *sugar subsidies.*

The Minimum Wage

The **minimum wage** is the lowest hourly wage rate that firms may legally pay their workers.

The **minimum wage** is the lowest hourly wage rate that firms may legally pay their workers. Minimum wage workers can be skilled or unskilled and experienced or inexperienced. The common thread is that these workers, for a variety of reasons, lack better prospects.

A minimum wage functions as a price floor. Figure 6.9 shows the effect of a binding minimum wage. Note that the wage, or the cost of labor, on the *y* axis ($10 per hour) is the price that must be paid. However, the market equilibrium wage ($7), or W_E, is below the minimum wage. The minimum wage prevents the market from reaching W_E at E (the equilibrium point) because only the

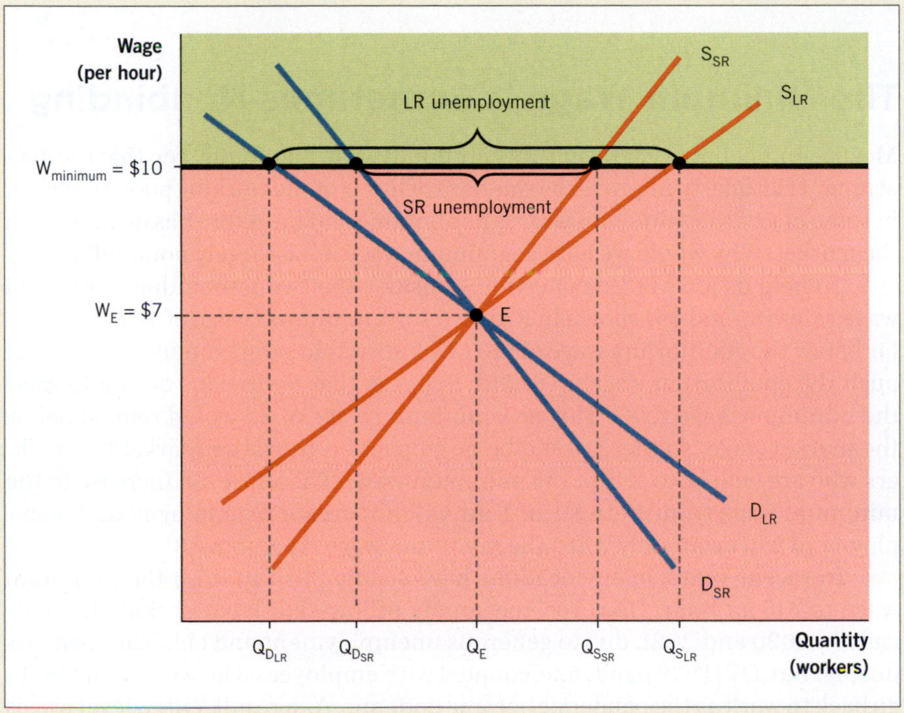

FIGURE 6.9

Price Floors and a Binding Minimum Wage Market in the Short Run and Long Run

A binding minimum wage is a price floor above the current equilibrium wage, W_E. At $10 per hour, the number of workers willing to supply their labor (S_{SR}) is greater than the demand for workers (D_{SR}). The result is a surplus of workers (which we recognize as unemployment). Because the supply of workers and demand for workers both become more elastic in the long run, unemployment expands ($Q_{S_{LR}} > Q_{D_{LR}}$).

wages in the green area are legal. The minimum wage raises the cost of hiring workers. Therefore, a higher minimum wage will lower the quantity of labor demanded. At the same time, firms will look for ways to substitute capital for workers. As a result, a binding minimum wage results in unemployment in the short run because $Q_{S_{SR}} > Q_{D_{SR}}$.

Businesses generally want to keep costs down, so in the long run they will try to reduce the amount they spend on labor. They might replace workers with machinery, shorten work hours, offer reduced customer service, or even relocate to countries that do not have minimum wage laws. As we move past the short run, more people will attempt to take advantage of higher minimum wages. Like firms, workers will adjust to the higher minimum wage over time. Some workers who might have decided to go to school full-time or remain retired or who simply want some extra income will enter the labor market because the minimum wage is now higher. As a result, minimum wage jobs will become progressively harder to find and unemployment will increase. The irony is that in the long run, the minimum wage, just like any other price floor, has created two unintended consequences: a smaller demand for workers by employers ($Q_{D_{LR}}$ is significantly less than Q_E) and a larger supply of workers ($Q_{S_{LR}}$) looking for jobs.

Incentives

Proponents of minimum wage legislation are aware that it often creates unemployment. To address this problem, they support investment in training, education, and the creation of government jobs programs to provide more work opportunities. While jobs programs increase the number of minimum wage jobs, training and additional education enable workers to acquire skills needed for jobs that pay more than the minimum wage. Economists generally believe that education and training programs have longer-lasting benefits to society as a whole because they enable workers to obtain better-paying jobs on a permanent basis.

The Minimum Wage Is Sometimes Nonbinding

Most people believe that raising the minimum wage is a simple step that the government can take to improve the standard of living of the working poor. However, in some places the minimum wage is nonbinding and therefore has no impact on the market. Why would we have a minimum wage if it is largely nonbinding?

To help us answer this question, consider the two nonbinding minimum wage rates ($7 and $9) shown in Figure 6.10. A minimum wage of $7 per hour is far below the equilibrium wage of $10 ($W_E$), so at that point supply and demand push the equilibrium wage up to $10. Suppose that politicians decide to raise the minimum wage to $9. This new minimum wage of $9 would remain below the market wage, so there would be no impact on the labor market for workers who are willing to accept the minimum wage. Therefore, an increase in the minimum wage from $7 to $9 an hour will not create unemployment. Unemployment will occur only when the minimum wage rises above $10.

In recent years, many locations have seen a push to raise the minimum wage to $15 an hour. However, the supply of low-skill labor shrank dramatically in 2020 and 2021, due to generous unemployment and childcare benefits during the COVID-19 pandemic, coupled with employees who were reluctant to go back to work as the pandemic became endemic. As a result, entry-level wages for low-skill workers are now above $15 in several metropolitan areas. In these

FIGURE 6.10

A Nonbinding Minimum Wage

An increase in the minimum wage from $7 to $9 remains nonbinding. Therefore, it will not change the demand for labor or the unemployment rate. If the minimum wage rises above the market wage, unemployment will occur.

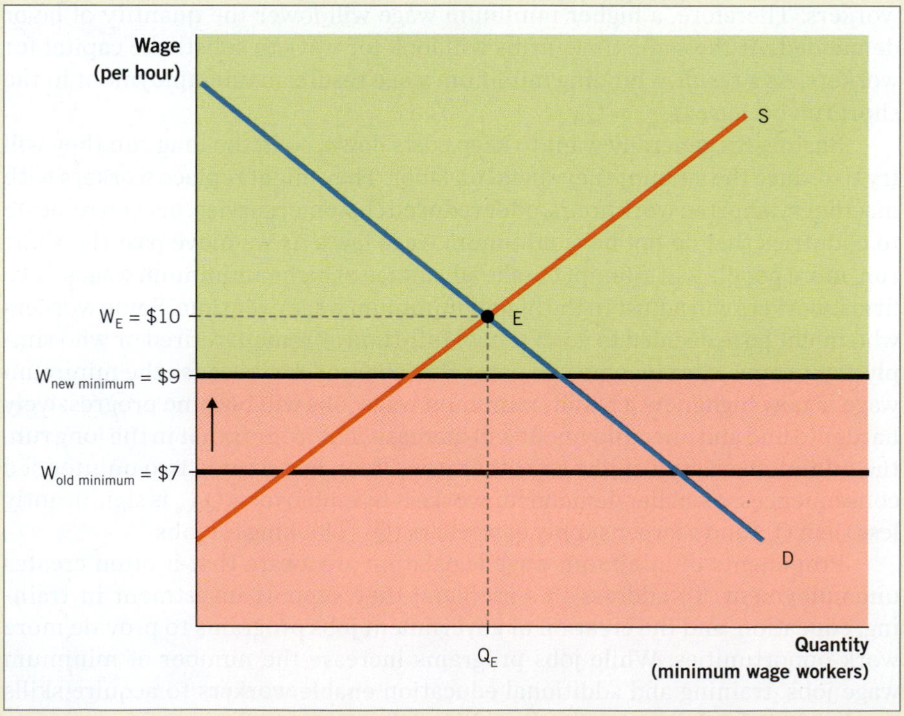

DATA SNAPSHOT

Minimum Wage: Always the Same?

A minimum wage is a price floor, a price control that doesn't allow prices—in this case the cost of labor—to fall below an assigned value. Although the media and politicians often discuss the minimum wage in the United States as if there is only one minimum wage, there are numerous minimum wages in the USA. In states where the state minimum wage is not the same as the federal minimum wage, the higher of the two wage rates takes effect.

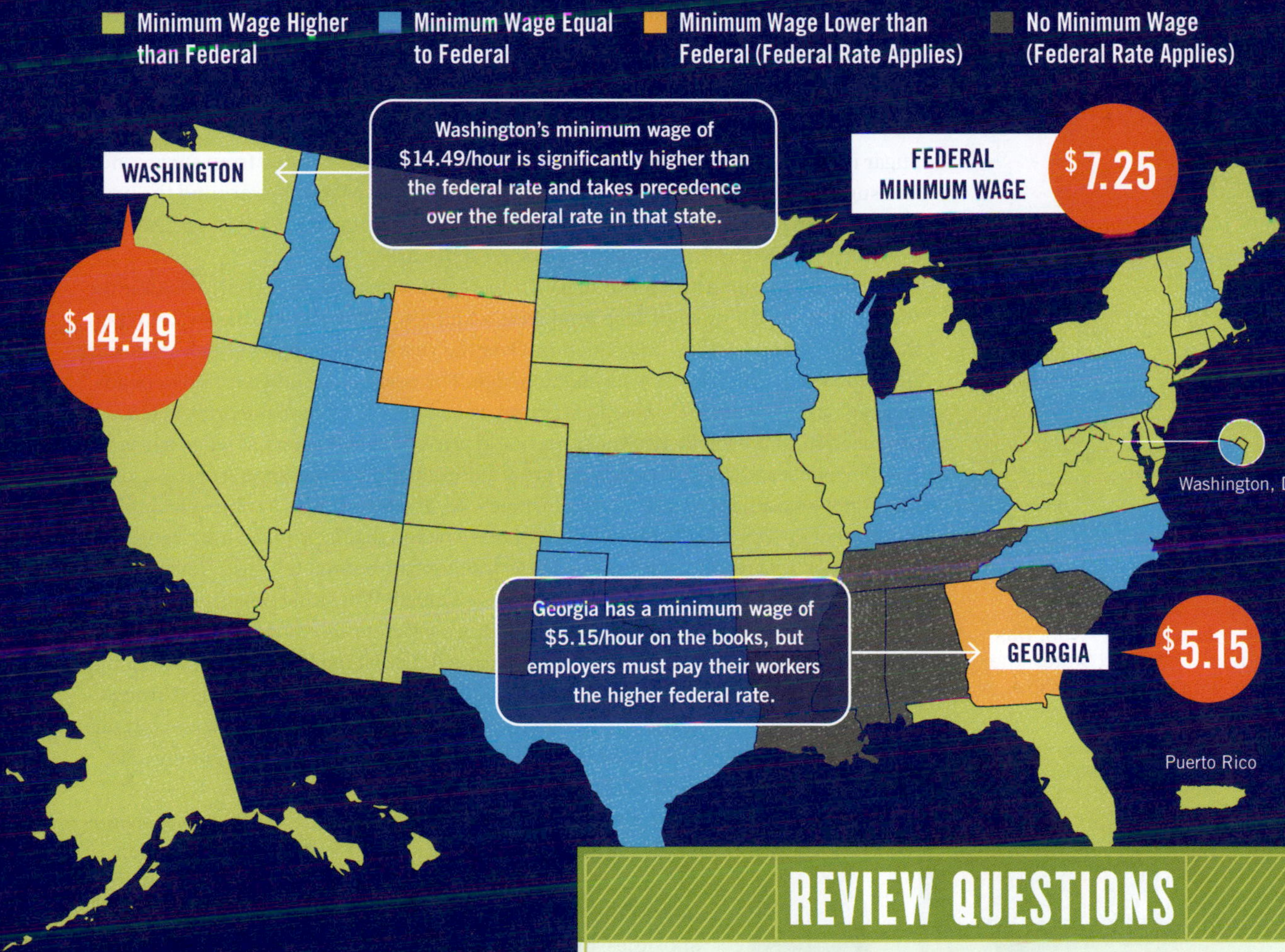

HIGHEST MINIMUM WAGES, 2022

District of Columbia	$15.20
Washington	$14.49
Massachusetts	$14.25
California	$14.00

Source: U.S. Department of Labor.

REVIEW QUESTIONS

- Suppose you live in Oklahoma and are looking for a job. The state minimum wage rate is $7.25/hour, the federal minimum wage rate is $7.25/hour, and the market equilibrium wage for the job is $8.00/hour. What wage will you be paid? Are the state and national minimum wages binding or non-binding price floors?
- Suppose Wisconsin increases its minimum wage from $7.25/hour, which is below the market wage for low-skill labor, to $11.00/hour, which is above the market wage. Using supply and demand curves, show how this might increase the number of unemployed workers.

places, a $15 minimum wage will be nonbinding. San Francisco, for example, adopted a $15 minimum wage in 2018, but as of 2021, the average starting wage for low-skill jobs in that city is $17.80.

That's not to say that efforts to raise the minimum wage in other places will have the same impact as in San Francisco. In many parts of the United States, the minimum wage is binding. Note, also, that when a minimum wage is binding and causes some unemployment, this does not automatically mean that low-wage workers are harmed overall. If enough low-wage workers stay employed when the minimum wage is increased, the total payroll that workers receive can still increase, even though some workers will have lost their jobs.

ECONOMICS IN THE REAL WORLD

WHY IS SUGAR SO EXPENSIVE IN THE UNITED STATES?

Sugar is one of life's small pleasures. It can be extracted and refined from sugarcane and sugar beets, two crops that can be grown in a variety of climates around the world. Sugar is both plentiful and cheap. As a result, Americans enjoy a lot of it—an average of over 100 pounds of refined sugar per person each year!

We would consume a lot more sugar if it were not subject to price controls. After the War of 1812, struggling sugarcane producers asked the government to pass a tariff (tax) that would protect domestic production. Over the years, price supports of all kinds have served to keep domestic sugar production high. The result is an industry that depends on a high price to survive. Under the current price-support system, the price of U.S.-produced sugar is roughly two times the world price. This situation has led to a bizarre set of incentives whereby U.S. farmers grow more sugar than they should and use land that is not well suited to the crop. For instance, sugarcane requires a subtropical climate, but most of the U.S. crop is grown in Louisiana, a region that is prone to hurricanes in the summer. As a result, many sugarcane crops there are completely lost. Have farmers turned to other, more locally suited crops? Not so much! What's happened is that frost-resistant strains have been developed that will grow farther inland, at colder locations.

Incentives

Why do farmers persist in growing sugarcane in Louisiana? The answer lies in the political process: sugar growers have effectively lobbied to keep prices high through tariffs on foreign imports. Because lower prices would put many U.S. growers out of business and cause the loss of many jobs, politicians have given in to their demands.

Meanwhile, the typical sugar consumer is largely oblivious to the political process that sets the price floor. It has been estimated that the sugar subsidy program costs consumers over $1 billion a year. To make matters worse, thanks to corn subsidies, high-fructose corn syrup has become a cheap alternative to sugar and is often added to processed foods and soft drinks. In 1980, Coca-Cola replaced sugar with high-fructose corn syrup in its U.S. factories to reduce production costs. However, Coca-Cola continues to use sugarcane in many Latin American countries because it is cheaper there. Research shows that high-fructose corn syrup causes a metabolic reaction that makes people who ingest it more inclined to obesity. This is an example of an unintended consequence that few policymakers could have imagined.

Which of these is the *real* thing? The Coke on the right, with high-fructose corn syrup, was made in the United States; the other, with sugar, was made in Mexico.

PRACTICE WHAT YOU KNOW

How Would Price Controls Affect Internet Access?

In today's Internet age, four degrees of separation are all that stand between you and the rest of the world.

Price of Internet	Connections demanded (millions of units)	Connections supplied (millions of units)
$60	10.0	62.5
50	20.0	55.0
40	30.0	47.5
30	40.0	40.0
20	50.0	32.5
10	60.0	25.0

QUESTION: What are the equilibrium price and equilibrium quantity of Internet service?

ANSWER: First, look at the table to see where quantity supplied and quantity demanded are equal. At a price of $30, consumers purchase 40 million units and producers supply 40 million units. Therefore, the equilibrium price is $30 and the equilibrium quantity is 40 million. At any price above $30, the quantity supplied exceeds the quantity demanded, so there is a surplus. The surplus gives sellers an incentive to cut the price until it reaches the equilibrium point, E. At any price below $30, the quantity demanded exceeds the quantity supplied, so there is a shortage. The shortage gives sellers an incentive to raise the price until it reaches the equilibrium point, E.

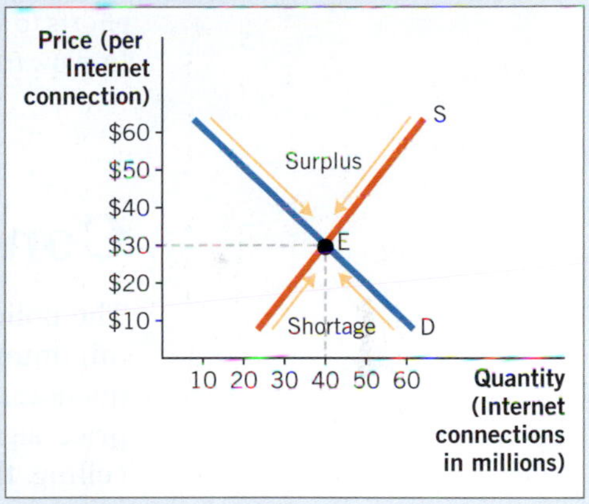

QUESTION: Suppose that providers convince the government that maintaining high-speed access to the Internet is an important element of technology infrastructure. As a result, Congress approves a price floor at $10 above the equilibrium price to help companies provide Internet service. How many people are able to connect to the Internet?

ANSWER: Adding $10 to the market price of $30 gives us a price floor of $40. At $40, consumers demand 30 million connections. Producers provide 47.5 million connections. The result is a surplus of 17.5 million units (shown in the graph). A price floor means that producers cannot cut the price below that point to increase the quantity that consumers demand. As a result, only 30 million units are sold. So only 30 million people connect to the Internet.

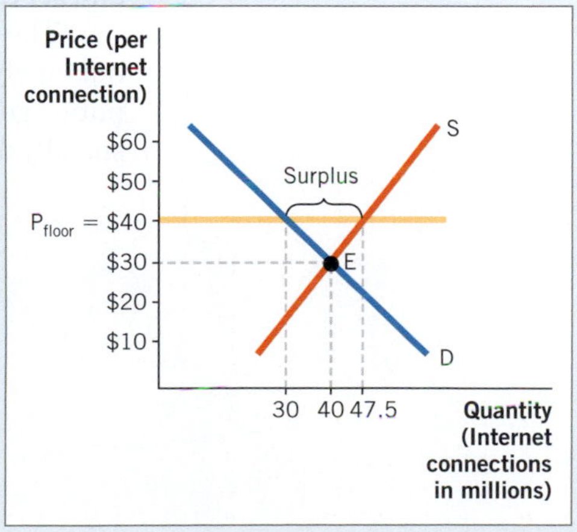

(CONTINUED)

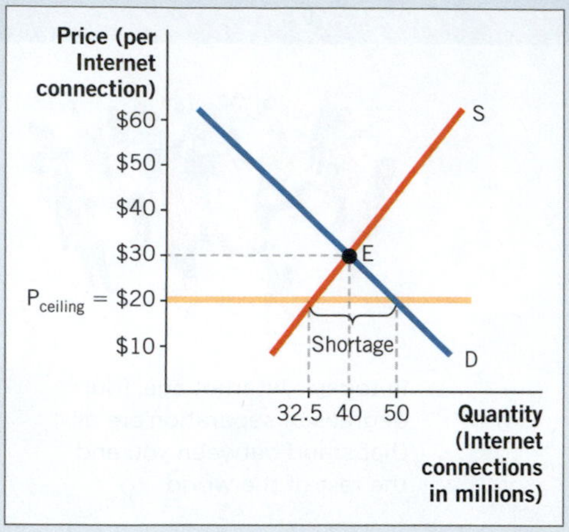

QUESTION: When consumers realize that fewer people are purchasing Internet access, they demand that the price floor be repealed and a price ceiling be put in its place. Congress acts immediately to remedy the problem, and a new price ceiling is set at $10 below the market price. Now how many people are able to connect to the Internet?

ANSWER: Subtracting $10 from the market price of $30 gives us a price ceiling of $20. At $20 per connection, consumers demand 50 million connections. However, producers provide only 32.5 million connections. The result is a shortage of 17.5 million units (shown in the graph). A price ceiling means that producers cannot raise the price, which will cause an increase in the quantity supplied. As a result, only 32.5 million units are sold, so only 32.5 million people connect to the Internet.

QUESTION: Which provides the greatest access to the Internet: free markets, price floors, or price ceilings?

ANSWER: With no government intervention, 40 million connections are sold. Once the price floor is established, 30 million people have an Internet connection. Under the price ceiling, 32.5 million people have an Internet connection. Despite legislative efforts to satisfy both producers and consumers of Internet service, the best solution is to allow free markets to allocate the good.

Conclusion

The policies presented in this chapter—rent control, price gouging laws, the minimum wage, and agricultural price controls—create unintended consequences. Attempts to control prices should be viewed cautiously. When the price signal is suppressed through a binding price floor or a binding price ceiling, the market's ability to allocate goods and services is diminished, surpluses and shortages develop and expand through time, and obtaining goods and services becomes difficult.

The role of markets in society has many layers, and we've only just begun our analysis. In the next chapter, we consider two cases—externalities and public goods—in which the unregulated market produces an output that is not socially desirable. ✷

· ECONOMICS *for* LIFE ·

Price Gouging: Disaster Preparedness

- Set aside money in a long-term emergency fund.
- Keep a simple disaster supply kit.
- Safeguard your financial and legal records.

Will you be ready if disaster strikes?

In this chapter, we saw how economists analyze pricing during disasters. However, economists look at the broad picture, too, to see the greater societal impact of the event. In 2017, a team of economists—Leah Platt Boustan, Matthew Kahn, Paul Rhode, and Maria Lucia Yanguas—analyzed all 10,000 natural disasters that occurred in the U.S. from 1920 to 2010. They found that locations that had experienced severe disasters had lower home prices, more people leaving the area, and higher poverty rates. Rents were lower in these areas too, also driven by lower overall demand.*

The study further observed that the rate of disasters is increasing. In the 2010s, there were 115 declared disasters causing $1 billion in damage, more than double the 55 declared disasters of this size (inflation adjusted) during each of the two previous decades. Practically, this means it's a good idea to be prepared for these events. During a disaster, shortages of essential goods and services become widespread. In the more than 30 states where price gouging laws are on the books, merchants are prevented from charging unusually high prices. If you live in one of these states, cash alone can't save you. You will have to survive on your own for a time before help arrives and communication channels are restored.

"[It was] a little bit of a pandemonium," Orlando-area resident Diane Williams said, describing shoppers' efforts to stock up on supplies just before Hurricane Irma struck Florida in 2017. "It's just that everybody is panicked, so they are preparing, which is wise, but it's just, like, crazy."†

Taking measures to prepare for a disaster reduces the likelihood of injury, loss of life, and property damage far more than anything you can do after a disaster strikes. An essential part of disaster planning should include financial planning. Let's begin with the basics. Get adequate insurance to protect your family's health and property; plan for the possibility of job loss or disability by building a cash reserve; and safeguard your financial and legal records. It is also important to set aside extra money in a long-term emergency fund. Nearly all financial experts advise saving enough money to cover your expenses for six months. Most households never come close to reaching this goal, but don't let that stop you from trying.

Preparing a simple disaster supply kit is also a must. Price gouging laws make it important to stock a bunch of stuff, because you can't rely on just having cash on hand to buy what you need on short notice. Keep enough water, nonperishable food, sanitation supplies, batteries, medications, and cash on hand for three days. Often, the power is out after a disaster, so you cannot count on ATMs or banks to be open. These measures will help you to weather the immediate impact of a disaster.

---

*Leah Platt Boustan, Matthew E. Kahn, Paul W. Rhode, and Maria Lucia Yanguas, "The Effect of Natural Disasters on Economic Activity in U.S. Counties: A Century of Data," (NBER Working Paper Series 23410, National Bureau of Economic Research, Cambridge, MA, May 2017, revised June 2020), https://www.nber.org/papers/w23410.

†"Irma Eyes the U.S.: 'Everybody Is Panicked'; Shelves Empty; Gas Pumps Run Dry," Offthegridnews.com, September 7, 2017, https://www.offthegridnews.com/current-events/irma-eyes-the-u-s-everybody-is-panicked-shelves-empty-gas-pumps-run-dry/.

ANSWERING *the* BIG QUESTIONS

When do price ceilings matter?

- A price ceiling is a legally imposed maximum price. When the price is set below the equilibrium price, the quantity demanded will exceed the quantity supplied. The result is a shortage. Price ceilings matter when they are binding (below the equilibrium price).

What effects do price ceilings have on economic activity?

- Price ceilings create two unintended consequences: a smaller quantity supplied of the good (Q_S) and a higher price for consumers who turn to illegal markets.

When do price floors matter?

- A price floor is a legally imposed minimum price. The minimum wage is an example of a price floor. If the minimum wage is set above the equilibrium wage, a surplus of labor will develop. However, if the minimum wage is nonbinding, it will have no effect on the market wage. Thus, price floors matter when they are set above the equilibrium price.

What effects do price floors have on economic activity?

- Price floors lead to many unintended consequences, including surpluses, the creation of illegal markets, and artificial attempts to bring the market back into balance. For example, proponents of a higher minimum wage are concerned about finding ways to alleviate the resulting surplus of labor, or unemployment.

CHAPTER PROBLEMS

Concepts You Should Know

minimum wage (p. 206)
price ceiling (p. 190)
price controls (p. 190)
price floor (p. 199)
price gouging laws (p. 198)
rent control (p. 196)

Questions for Review

1. Does a binding price ceiling cause a shortage or a surplus? Provide an example to support your answer.
2. Does a nonbinding price floor cause a shortage or a surplus? Provide an example to support your answer.
3. Will a surplus or a shortage caused by a price control become smaller or larger over time? Explain.
4. Are price gouging laws an example of a price floor or a price ceiling?
5. What will happen to the market price when a price control is nonbinding?
6. Why do most economists oppose attempts to control prices? Why does the government attempt to control prices anyway in a number of markets?

Study Problems (* solved at the end of this section)

* 1. Imagine that the community you live in decides to enact a rent control of $700 per month on every one-bedroom apartment. Using the following table, determine the market price and equilibrium quantity without rent control. How many one-bedroom apartments will be rented after the rent control law is passed?

Monthly rent	Quantity demanded	Quantity supplied
$600	700	240
700	550	320
800	400	400
900	250	480
1,000	100	560

Source: https://www.census.gov/data/tables/2017/demo/supplemental-poverty-measure/poverty-thresholds.html.

2. Suppose that the federal government places a binding price floor on chocolate. To help support the price floor, the government purchases all of the leftover chocolate that consumers do not buy. If the price floor remains in place for a number of years, what do you expect to happen to each of the following?
   a. quantity of chocolate demanded by consumers
   b. quantity of chocolate supplied by producers
   c. quantity of chocolate purchased by the government
3. Suppose that a group of die-hard sports fans are upset about the high price of tickets to many games. As a result of their lobbying efforts, a new law caps the maximum ticket price to any sporting event at $50. Will more people be able to attend the games? Explain your answer. Will certain teams and events be affected more than others? Provide examples.

4. Many local governments use parking meters on crowded downtown streets. However, the parking spaces along the street are typically hard to find because the metered price is often set below the market price. Explain what happens when local governments set the meter price too low. Why do you think the price is set below the market-clearing price?

5. Imagine that local suburban leaders decide to enact a minimum wage. Will the community lose more jobs if the nearby city votes to increase the minimum wage to the same rate? Discuss your answer.

* 6. Examine the following graph, showing the market for low-skilled laborers.

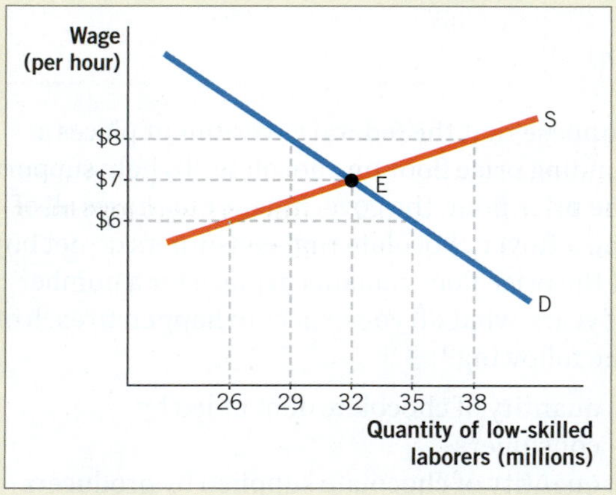

How many low-skilled laborers will be unemployed when the minimum wage is $8 an hour? How many low-skilled workers will be unemployed when the minimum wage is $6 an hour?

7. Demand and supply curves can be represented with equations. Suppose that the demand for low-skilled labor, Q_D, is represented by the following equation, where W is the wage rate:

$$Q_D = 53{,}000{,}000 - 3{,}000{,}000W$$

The supply of low-skilled labor, Q_S, is represented by the equation

$$Q_S = -10{,}000{,}000 + 6{,}000{,}000W$$

a. Find the equilibrium wage. (**Hint:** Set $Q_D = Q_S$ and solve for the wage, W.)

b. Find the equilibrium quantity of labor. (**Hint:** Now plug the value you got in part (a) back into Q_D or Q_S. You can double-check your answer by plugging the answer from part (a) into both Q_D and Q_S to see that you get the same result.)

c. What happens if the minimum wage is $8? (**Hint:** Plug W = 8 into both Q_D and Q_S.) Does this minimum wage cause a surplus or a shortage?

d. What happens if the minimum wage is $6? (**Hint:** Plug W = 6 into both Q_D and Q_S.) Does this minimum wage cause a surplus or a shortage?

8. Most of us would agree that movie theater popcorn is outrageously priced. Why don't price gouging laws result in arrests and prosecutions of theater operators and other firms that charge prices far beyond the actual cost of production?

* 9. More than 5,000 people in the United States die each year because they cannot find a suitable kidney donor. Under U.S. law, citizens cannot sell their spare kidney, which effectively means that there is a price ceiling on the sale of kidneys equal to $0. What do you think would happen to the number of deaths caused by kidney failure each year if the law prohibiting the sale of kidneys were repealed?

* 10. Scotland has introduced price floors on alcohol as a public health measure. Higher alcohol prices will lower sales, which would seem to hurt producers. If you were a producer in Scotland, would you necessarily be against this proposal?

11. Suppose the equilibrium rent for one-bedroom apartments in your neighborhood is $1,000 per month. If the government imposes a rent ceiling of $750 per month, what will happen to the number of one-bedroom apartments rented out each month?

a. It will increase, since more people will want to rent apartments when they are cheaper.
b. It will decrease, since fewer landlords will want to rent out their apartments when they can't charge as much.
c. It will not change, since the rent control is set below the equilibrium rent.
d. None of the above

* 12. Suppose the government imposes a minimum wage that is above the equilibrium wage. Will workers be better off or worse off?

Solved Problems

1. The equilibrium price occurs where the quantity demanded is equal to the quantity supplied. This equilibrium occurs when $Q_D = Q_S = 400$. When the quantity is 400, the monthly rent is $800. Next, the question asks how many one-bedroom apartments will be rented after a rent control law limits the rent to $700 a month. When the rent is $700, the quantity supplied is 320 apartments. It is also worth noting that the quantity demanded when the rent is $700 is 550 units, so there is a shortage of $550 - 320 = 230$ apartments once the rent control law goes into effect.

6. The first question asks how many low-skilled laborers will be unemployed when the minimum wage is $8 an hour. The quantity demanded is 29 million, and the quantity supplied is 38 million. The result is 38 million − 29 million = 9 million unemployed low-skilled workers.

The next question asks how many low-skilled workers will be unemployed when the minimum wage is $6 an hour. Because $6 an hour is below the market equilibrium wage of $7, it has no effect. In other words, a $6 minimum wage is nonbinding, and therefore no unemployment is caused.

9. Despite the repugnant nature of organ sales, there is no doubt that a price exists that would alleviate the kidney shortage and save lives. Under the current system, market prices are unable to identify people who would sell their spare kidney and match those sellers with the people who would be willing to buy a kidney. In the absence of a legal market, illegal markets have arisen to bring buyers and sellers together. The market price for a kidney here ($250,000) is far higher than the market equilibrium price ($20,000) that economists estimate would exist if organ sales were legal.

10. If demand for alcohol is relatively inelastic, a price floor could increase revenues for most suppliers.

12. This is an empirical question. Low-wage workers may be better off, if enough of them keep their jobs and subsequently earn a higher wage, compared to the number of workers who lose their jobs and become unemployed.

CHAPTER

07

Market Inefficiencies: Externalities and Public Goods

Should We Eliminate All Pollution?

We would all agree that it's important to protect the environment. So when we face pollution and other environmental degradation, should we eliminate it? If your first thought is "yes, always," you're not alone. After all, there's only one Earth, and we'd better get tough on environmental destruction wherever we find it, whatever it takes. Right?

It's tempting to think this way, but the prescription comes up short as a useful social policy. No one wants to go back to the way it was when businesses were free to dump their waste anywhere they chose. Further, researchers at organizations like the Environmental Protection Agency and the American Lung Association report that the United States' nonwhite population and those of lower socioeconomic status experience more harm from pollution than the white and well-off.* However, it is also impractical to eliminate all pollution. Some amount of environmental damage is inevitable whenever we extract resources, manufacture goods, fertilize croplands, or power our electrical grid—all activities that are integral to modern society. But how do we figure

*"Disparities in the Impact of Air Pollution," American Lung Association, updated April 20, 2020, https://www.lung.org/clean-air/outdoors/who-is-at-risk/disparities.
Ihab Mikati, Adam F. Benson, Thomas J. Luben, Jason D. Sacks, Jennifer Richmond-Bryant, "Disparities in Distribution of Particulate Matter Emission Sources by Race and Poverty Status," *American Journal of Public Health* 108, no. 4 (April 2018): pp. 480–485.

This outflow looks like lava flow from Mount Kilauea in Hawaii, but it's slag from a nickel refinery in Ontario, Canada. Every few hours, another load gets dumped. No doubt we'd like to make the growing heap of black waste go away. But are we willing to do without the jobs the factory provides? For an economist, deciding what to do about pollution isn't as easy as it may at first seem.

out what the "right" level of pollution is, and decide what kind of impact is acceptable? And how do we get there? How do we examine the tension between social costs and benefits and try to ensure that participants in markets are fully accounting for both?

In the preceding chapters, we saw that markets provide many benefits and that they typically work because participants pursue their own self-interests. But sometimes markets need a helping hand. For example, some market exchanges harm innocent bystanders, and some trades are not efficient because the ownership of property is not clearly defined or actively enforced. To help explain why markets do not always operate efficiently, this chapter explores two important concepts: externalities and the differences between private and public goods.

· BIG QUESTIONS ·

- What are externalities, and how do they affect markets?
- What are private goods and public goods?
- What are the challenges of providing nonexcludable goods?

What Are Externalities, and How Do They Affect Markets?

Externalities are the costs or benefits of a market activity that affect a third party.

Market failure occurs when there is an inefficient allocation of resources in a market.

We have seen that buyers and sellers benefit from trade. But what about the effects trade might have on bystanders? **Externalities**, or the costs and benefits of a market activity that affect a third party, often lead to undesirable consequences. **Market failure** occurs when there is an inefficient allocation of resources in a market. Externalities are a type of market failure. For example, in 2010, an offshore oil rig in the Gulf of Mexico operated by British Petroleum (BP) exploded, causing millions of barrels of oil to spill into the water and resulting in over $40 billion in damage. Even though both BP and its customers benefit from the production of oil, others along the Gulf Coast had their lives severely disrupted. Industries and communities dependent on high environmental quality, like tourism and fishing, were hit particularly hard by the costs of the spill.

For a market to work as efficiently as possible, two things must happen. First, each participant must be able to evaluate the **internal costs** of participation—the costs that only the individual participant pays. For example, when we choose to drive somewhere, we typically consider our internal (also known as personal) costs—the time it takes to reach our destination, the amount we pay for gasoline, and what we pay for routine vehicle maintenance. Second, for a market to work efficiently, the external costs must also be paid. **External costs** are the costs of a market activity imposed on people who are not participants in that market. In the case of driving, the congestion and pollution our cars create are external costs. Economists define **social costs** as the sum of the internal costs and external costs of a market activity.

Internal costs are the costs of a market activity paid only by an individual participant.

External costs are the costs of a market activity imposed on people who are not participants in that market.

Social costs are the sum of the internal costs and external costs of a market activity.

In this section, we consider some of the mechanisms that encourage consumers and producers to account for the social costs of their actions.

The Third-Party Problem

An externality exists whenever an internal cost (or benefit) diverges from a social cost (or benefit). For example, manufacturers who make vehicles and consumers who purchase them benefit from the transaction, but making and using those vehicles lead to externalities—including air pollution and traffic congestion—that adversely affect others. A **third-party problem** occurs when those not directly involved in a market activity experience negative or positive externalities.

A **third-party problem** occurs when those not directly involved in a market activity experience negative or positive externalities.

If a third party is adversely affected, the externality is negative. For example, a negative externality occurs when the number of vehicles on the roads causes air pollution. Negative externalities present a challenge to society because it is difficult to make consumers and producers take responsibility for the full costs of their actions. For example, drivers typically consider only the internal costs (their own costs) of reaching their destination. Likewise, manufacturers generally prefer to ignore the pollution they create, because addressing the problem would raise their costs without providing them with significant direct benefits.

In general, society would benefit if all consumers and producers considered both the internal and external costs of their actions. Given most people feel this expectation is unlikely to happen, governments design policies that create incentives for firms and people to limit the amount of pollution they emit.

Incentives

An effort by the city government of Washington, D.C., shows the potential power of this approach. Like many communities throughout the United States, the city instituted a 5-cent tax on every plastic bag a consumer picks up at a store. While 5 cents may not sound like much of a disincentive, shoppers have responded by switching to cloth bags or reusing plastic ones. In Washington, D.C., the number of plastic bags used every month fell from 22.5 million in 2009 to 3 million in 2018, significantly reducing the amount of plastic waste entering landfills in the process.

Not all externalities are negative, however. For instance, education creates a large positive externality for society beyond the benefits to individual students, teachers, and support staff. A more knowledgeable workforce benefits employers looking for qualified employees and is more efficient and productive than an uneducated workforce. And because local businesses experience a positive externality from a well-educated local community, they have a stake in the educational process.

A good example of the synergy between local business and higher education is California's Silicon Valley, which is home to many high-tech companies and Stanford University. As early as the late nineteenth century, Stanford's

Many of the most successful businesses associated with Stanford have made large donations to the university.

Large cruise ships may be causing parts of Venice's lagoon to break down.

leaders felt that the university's mission should include fostering the development of self-sufficient local industry. After World War II, Stanford encouraged faculty and graduates to start their own companies, which led to the creation of Hewlett-Packard, Bell Labs, and Xerox. A generation later, this nexus of high-tech firms gave birth to leading software and Internet firms like 3Com, Adobe, Facebook, and Snapchat, and—more indirectly—Cisco, Apple, and Alphabet.

Recognizing the benefits they received, many of the most successful businesses associated with Stanford have donated large sums to the university. For instance, the Hewlett Foundation gave $400 million to Stanford's endowment for the humanities and sciences and for undergraduate education—an act of generosity that highlights the positive externality Stanford University had on Hewlett-Packard.

And sometimes, a small silver of good comes from a large negative externality. Consider Venice, which typically has 25 million visitors a year. Modern cruise ships traversing the Guidecca Canal into Venice's lagoon tower over the buildings, and, critics say, the waves from the ships have been accelerating the erosion of the city's 14th-century buildings, which are built on shallow and unstable mudbanks. These tourists spend a lot of money in Venice though, and local businesses have fought to keep the big ships coming into the lagoon. However, COVID-19, a very large externality, halted cruise ship travel during the pandemic, and severely slowed it for the near future. With this income stopping anyway, opponents had a window to suggest alternatives and emphasize that keeping cruise ships out of the lagoon would help preserve Venice's status as a World Heritage site. In August of 2021, Italy moved to ban large cruise ships from sailing into the city center. They will be diverted to the industrial port of Marghera, whereas smaller cruise ships can continue to reach the heart of the city.

The **social optimum** is the price and quantity combination that would exist if there were no externalities.

When oil refineries are permitted to pollute the environment without any limitations, they are likely to overproduce.

CORRECTING FOR NEGATIVE EXTERNALITIES In this section, we explore ways to correct for negative externalities. To do so, we use supply and demand analysis to understand how the externalities affect the market. Let's begin with supply and compare the difference between what market forces produce and what is best for society in the case of an oil refinery. A refinery converts crude oil to gasoline. This complex process generates many negative externalities, including the release of pollutants into the air and the dumping of waste by-products.

Figure 7.1 illustrates the contrast between the market equilibrium and the social optimum in the case of an oil refinery. The **social optimum** is the price

FIGURE 7.1

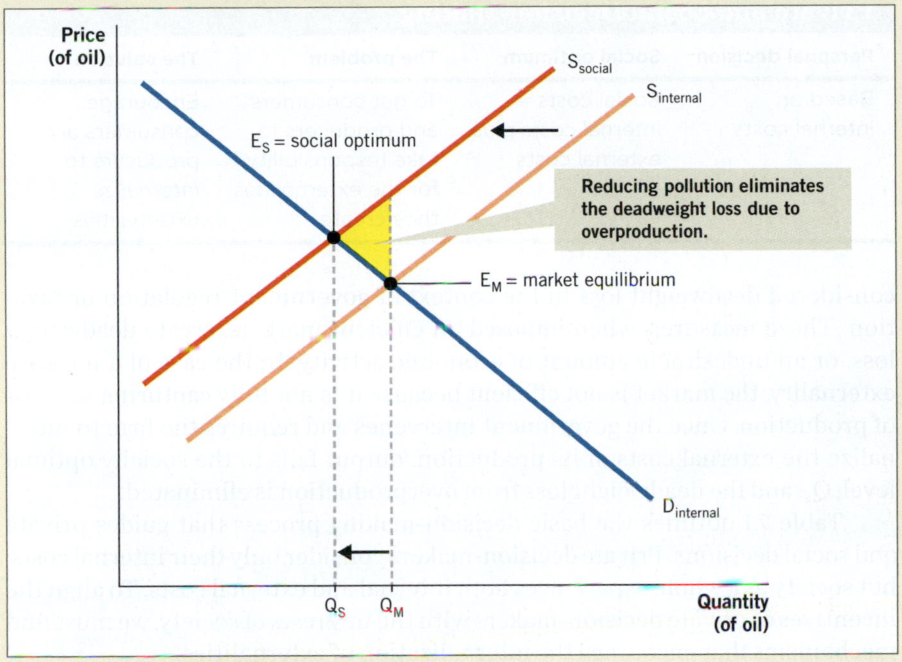

Negative Externalities and Social Optimum

When a firm is required to internalize the external costs of production, the supply curve shifts to the left, pollution is reduced, and output falls to the socially optimal level, Q_S. The deadweight loss that occurs from overproduction is eliminated.

and quantity combination that would exist if there were no externalities. The supply curve $S_{internal}$ represents how much the oil refinery will produce if it does not have to pay for the negative consequences of its activity. In this situation, the market equilibrium, E_M, accounts only for the internal costs of production.

When a negative externality occurs, the government may be able to restore the social optimum by requiring externality-causing market participants to pay for the cost of their actions. In this case, there are three potential solutions. First, the refinery can be required to install pollution abatement equipment or change production techniques to reduce emissions and waste by-products. Second, the government can levy a tax on the refinery as a disincentive to produce. Finally, the government can require the firm to pay for any environmental damage it causes. Each solution forces the firm to **internalize** the externality, meaning that the firm must take into account the external costs (or benefits) to society that occur as a result of its actions.

Incentives

Firms **internalize** an externality when they take into account the external costs (or benefits) to society that occur as a result of their actions.

Having to pay the costs of imposing pollution on others reduces the amount of the pollution-causing activity. This result is evident in the shift of the supply curve to S_{social}. The new supply curve reflects a combination of the internal and external costs of producing the good. Because each corrective measure requires the refinery to spend money to correct the externality and therefore increases overall costs, the willingness to sell the good declines, or shifts to the left. The result is a social optimum at a lower quantity, Q_S, than at the market equilibrium quantity demanded, Q_M. The trade-off is clear. We can reduce negative externalities by requiring producers to internalize the externality. However, doing so does not come without cost. Because the supply curve shifts to the left, the quantity produced is lower and the price rises. In the real world, there is always a cost.

Trade-offs

In addition, when an externality occurs, the market equilibrium creates deadweight loss, as shown by the yellow triangle in Figure 7.1. In Chapter 5, we

TABLE 7.1

Private and Social Decision-Making

Personal decision	Social optimum	The problem	The solution
Based on internal costs	Social costs = internal costs plus external costs	To get consumers and producers to take responsibility for the externalities they create	Encourage consumers and producers to *internalize* externalities

considered deadweight loss in the context of government regulation or taxation. These measures, when imposed on efficient markets, create deadweight loss, or an undesirable amount of economic activity. In the case of a negative externality, the market is not efficient because it is not fully capturing the cost of production. Once the government intervenes and requires the firm to internalize the external costs of its production, output falls to the socially optimal level, Q_S, and the deadweight loss from overproduction is eliminated.

Table 7.1 outlines the basic decision-making process that guides private and social decisions. Private decision-makers consider only their internal costs, but society as a whole experiences both internal and external costs. To align the incentives of private decision-makers with the interests of society, we must find mechanisms that encourage the internalization of externalities.

How much would you pay to avoid sitting in traffic?

ECONOMICS IN THE REAL WORLD

EXPRESS LANES USE DYNAMIC PRICING TO EASE CONGESTION

Metro Washington, D.C., is notorious for traffic, especially on the Capital Beltway (Interstate 495). New express lanes keep traffic moving by using dynamic pricing, which adjusts tolls based on real-time traffic conditions. Dynamic pricing helps manage the quantity demanded and keeps motorists moving at highway speeds. I-495 express-lane tolls can range from as low as $0.20 per mile during less busy times to approximately $1.25 per mile in some sections during rush hour. The higher rush-hour rates are designed to ensure that the express lanes do not become congested. Motorists thus have a choice: pay more to use the express lanes and arrive faster, or use the regular lanes and arrive later. The decision about whether to use the express lanes is all about opportunity cost. High-opportunity-cost motorists regularly drive the express lanes, while others with lower opportunity costs avoid the express lanes.

Because dynamic prices become part of a motorist's internal costs, they cause motorists to weigh the costs and benefits of driving into congested areas. In addition, the dynamic pricing of express lanes causes motorists to make marginal adjustments in terms of the time when they drive. High-demand times, such as the morning and evening rush, see higher tolls for using the express lanes and also longer waits in the regular lanes. Faced with either sitting in traffic (if they don't pay the toll) or being charged more to enter the express lanes at peak-demand times, many motorists attempt to use the Beltway at off-peak times. Since drivers internalize the external costs as a result of the dynamic toll prices even more precisely, the traffic flow spreads out over the course of the day so the existing road capacity is used more efficiently.

Opportunity cost
Marginal thinking

CORRECTING FOR POSITIVE EXTERNALITIES

Positive externalities, such as vaccines, are the result of economic activities that have benefits for third parties. As with negative externalities, economists use supply and demand analysis to compare the efficiency of the market with the social optimum. This time, we focus on the demand curve. Consider a person who gets a flu shot. When the vaccine is administered, the recipient is immunized, which creates an internal benefit. But there is also an external benefit. Because the recipient likely will not come down with the flu, fewer other people will catch the flu and become contagious, which helps to protect even those who do not get flu shots. Therefore, we can say that vaccines provide a positive externality to the rest of society.

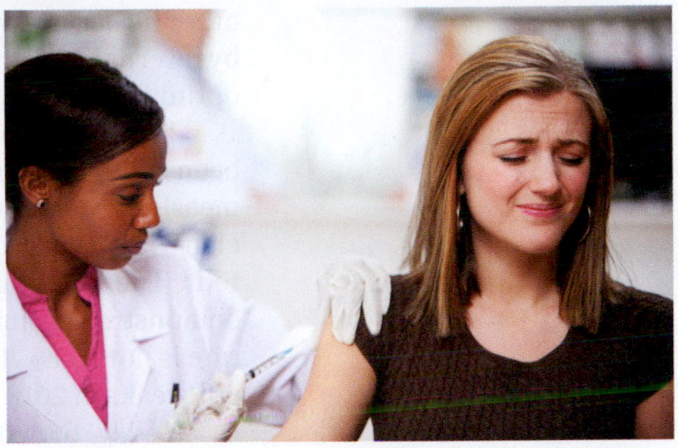

Vaccines offer both internal and external benefits.

Why do positive externalities exist in the market? Using our example of flu shots, there is an incentive for people in high-risk groups to get vaccinated for the sake of their own health. In Figure 7.2, we capture this internal benefit in the demand curve labeled $D_{internal}$. However, the market equilibrium, E_M, only accounts for the internal benefits of individuals deciding whether to get vaccinated. To maximize the health benefits for everyone, public health officials need to find a way to encourage people to consider the external benefit of their vaccination, too. For instance, making flu shots mandatory for hospital staff and

FIGURE 7.2

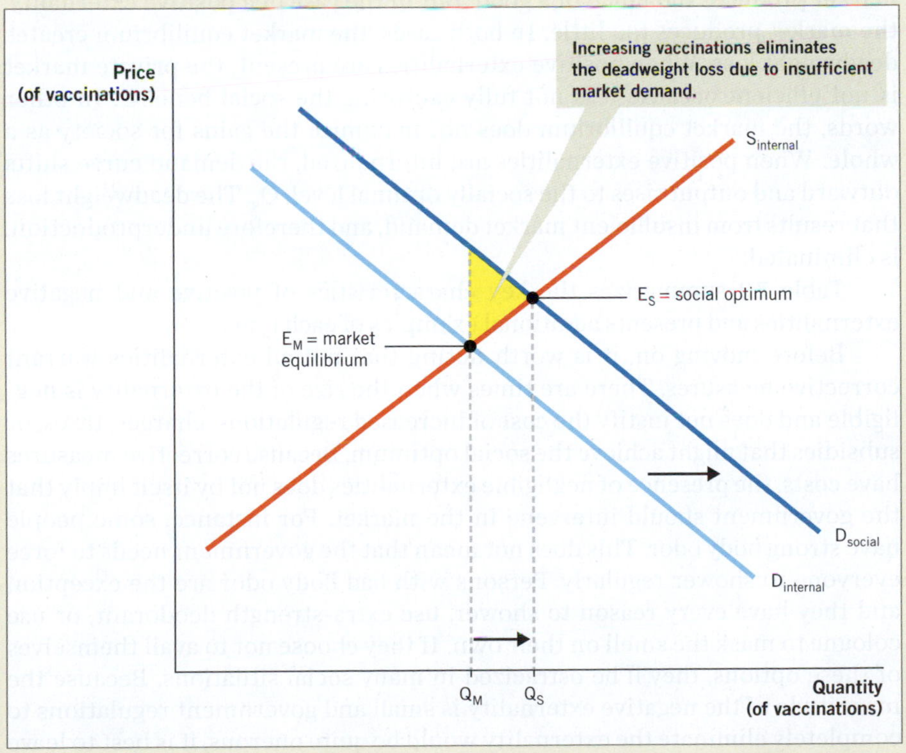

Positive Externalities and Social Optimum

The subsidy encourages consumers to internalize the externality. As a result, consumption moves from the market equilibrium (Q_M) to a social optimum at a higher quantity (Q_S), vaccinations increase, and the deadweight loss from insufficient market demand is eliminated.

other healthcare workers produces positive benefits for all members of society, by internalizing the externality, and helps nudge the market toward the socially optimal number of vaccinations.

Despite the benefits, however, vaccination rates in the United States have been steadily falling for years. The lower vaccination rate led to an outbreak of measles at Disneyland in California in late 2014, where it was believed a foreign visitor introduced the disease and unvaccinated children were exposed to it. The outbreak eventually spread to six U.S. states, Mexico, and Canada—demonstrating just how quickly measles can spread when the vaccination rate is not 100%. This disease continues to be a problem worldwide, with major outbreaks in 2018 in places like Algeria, Greece, and Indonesia.

Today, the coronavirus pandemic is a much more pressing public health threat than measles. When a vaccine becomes available, it would make sense for the government to offer a subsidy, or price break, to encourage people to get vaccinated. The subsidy lowers the price to individuals but increases the demand for vaccines, which raises the overall market price.

Governments routinely provide free or reduced-cost vaccines to those most at risk from flu and to their caregivers. Because the subsidy enables consumers to spend less money, their willingness to get the vaccine increases, shifting the demand curve in Figure 7.2 from $D_{internal}$ to D_{social}. The social demand curve reflects the sum of the internal and external benefits of getting the vaccination. In other words, the subsidy encourages consumers to internalize the externality. As a result, the output moves from the market equilibrium quantity demanded, Q_M, to a social optimum at a higher quantity, Q_S.

Incentives

Markets do not handle externalities well. With a negative externality, the market produces too much of a good. But in the case of a positive externality, the market produces too little. In both cases, the market equilibrium creates deadweight loss. When positive externalities are present, the private market is not efficient because it is not fully capturing the social benefits. In other words, the market equilibrium does not maximize the gains for society as a whole. When positive externalities are internalized, the demand curve shifts outward and output rises to the socially optimal level, Q_S. The deadweight loss that results from insufficient market demand, and therefore underproduction, is eliminated.

Table 7.2 summarizes the key characteristics of positive and negative externalities and presents additional examples of each type.

Before moving on, it is worth noting that not all externalities warrant corrective measures. There are times when the size of the externality is negligible and does not justify the cost of increased regulations, charges, taxes, or subsidies that might achieve the social optimum. Because corrective measures have costs, the presence of negligible externalities does not by itself imply that the government should intervene in the market. For instance, some people have strong body odor. This does not mean that the government needs to force everyone to shower regularly. Persons with bad body odor are the exception and they have every reason to shower, use extra-strength deodorant, or use cologne to mask the smell on their own. If they choose not to avail themselves of these options, they'll be ostracized in many social situations. Because the magnitude of the negative externality is small and government regulations to completely eliminate the externality would be quite onerous, it is best to leave well enough alone.

TABLE 7.2

A Summary of Externalities

		Negative externalities		Positive externalities
Definition		Costs borne by third parties		Benefits received by third parties
Examples		Oil refining creates air pollution.	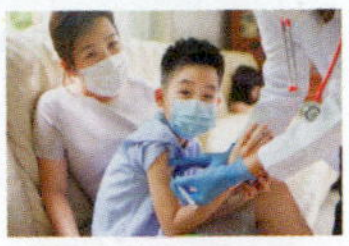	Flu shots prevent the spread of disease.
		Traffic congestion causes all motorists to spend more time on the road waiting.		Education creates a more productive workforce and enables citizens to make more informed decisions for the betterment of society.
		Airports create noise pollution.		Restored historic buildings enable people to enjoy beautiful architectural details.
Corrective measures		Taxes or charges		Subsidies or government provision

PRACTICE WHAT YOU KNOW

Externalities: Fracking

What the frack?

In 2003, energy companies began using a process known as hydraulic fracturing, or fracking, to extract underground reserves of natural gas in certain states, including Pennsylvania, Texas, West Virginia, and Wyoming. Fracking involves injecting water, chemicals, and sand into rock formations more than a mile deep. The process releases the natural gas that is trapped in those rocks, allowing it to escape up the well. The gas comes to the surface along with much of the water and chemical mixture, which now must be disposed of. Unfortunately, the chemicals in the mix make the water toxic. Consequently, as fracking has expanded to more areas, controversy has grown about the potential environmental effects of the process.

QUESTION: What negative externalities might fracking generate?

ANSWER: People who live near wells worry about the pollutants in the water mixture and their potential to leach into drinking-water supplies. Additionally, the drilling of a well is a noisy process. Drilling occurs 24 hours a day for a period of a few weeks. This noise pollution affects anyone who lives close by. Another issue is that the natural gas has to be trucked away from the well. Additional truck traffic can potentially damage local roads and cause even more pollution.

(CONTINUED)

QUESTION: What positive externalities might fracking generate?

ANSWER: Fracking has brought economic growth to the areas where it is occurs. The resulting jobs have employed many people, providing them with a good income. Local hotels and restaurants have seen an increase in business as temporary employees move from one area to another. As permanent employees take over the operation of a well, housing prices climb as a result of increasing demand, which benefits local homeowners.

What Are Private Goods and Public Goods?

Property rights give the owner the ability to exercise control over a resource.

The presence of externalities reflects a divide between the way markets operate and the social optimum. What creates this divide? The answer is often related to property rights. **Property rights** give the owner the ability to exercise control over a resource. When property rights are not clearly defined, resources can be mistreated. For instance, because no one owns the air, manufacturing firms often emit pollutants into it.

Incentives

To understand why firms sometimes overlook their actions' effects on others, we need to examine the role of property rights in market efficiency. When property rights are poorly established or not enforced effectively, the wrong incentives come into play. The difference is apparent when we compare situations in which people do have property rights. Private owners have an incentive to keep their property in good repair because they bear the costs of fixing what they own when it breaks or no longer works properly. For instance, if you own a personal computer, you will probably protect your investment by treating it with care and dealing with any problems immediately. However, if you access a public computer terminal in a campus lab or library and find that it is not working properly, you will most likely ignore the problem and simply look for another computer that is working. The difference between solving the problem and ignoring it is crucial to understanding why property rights matter.

Private Property

Private property provides an exclusive right of ownership that allows for the use, and especially the exchange, of property.

One way to minimize externalities is to establish well-defined private property rights. **Private property** provides an exclusive right of ownership that allows for the use, and especially the exchange, of property. This right creates incentives to maintain, protect, and conserve property and to trade with others. Let's consider these four incentives in the context of automobile ownership.

1. *The incentive to maintain property.* Car owners have an incentive to maintain their vehicles. Routine maintenance, replacement of worn parts, and repairs keep the vehicle safe and reliable. In addition, a well-maintained car can be sold for more than one in poor condition.

Incentives

2. *The incentive to protect property.* Owners have an incentive to protect their vehicles from theft or damage. They protect their property by using alarm systems, locking the doors, and parking in well-lit areas.

3. *The incentive to conserve property*. Car owners also have an incentive to extend the usable life of their automobiles by limiting the number of miles they put on their cars each year.

4. *The incentive to trade with others*. Car owners have an incentive to trade with others because they may profit from the transaction. Suppose someone offers to buy your car for $5,000 and you think it is worth only $3,000. Because you own the car, you can do whatever you want with it. If you decline to sell, you will incur an opportunity cost: you will be giving up $5,000 to keep something you value at $3,000. There is no law requiring you to sell your vehicle, so you *could* keep the car—but you probably won't. Why? Because private property gives you as the owner an incentive to trade for something better in the market.

Opportunity cost

The incentives to maintain, protect, and conserve property help to ensure that owners keep their private property in good shape. The fourth incentive, to trade with others, helps to ensure that private property is held by the person with the greatest willingness to pay for it.

THE COASE THEOREM In 1960, Nobel Prize–winning economist Ronald Coase argued that establishing private property rights can close the gap between internal costs and social costs.

Consider an example involving two adjacent landowners, one who raises cattle and another who grows wheat. Because neither landowner has built a fence, the cattle wander onto the neighboring land to eat the wheat. Coase concluded that in this situation, both parties are responsible for the dilemma. He arrived at that conclusion by considering two possible scenarios.

The first scenario supposes that the wheat farmer has the legal right to expect cattle-free fields. In this scenario, the cattle rancher is liable for the damage caused to the wheat farmer. If the damage is costly and the rancher is liable, the rancher will build a fence to keep the cattle in rather than pay for the damage they cause. The fence internalizes the negative externality and forces the rancher to bear the full cost of the damage. If the cost of the damage to the crop is much smaller than the cost of building a fence, then the rancher is more likely to compensate the wheat farmer for his losses rather than build the fence.

What if the wheat farmer does not have the legal right to expect cattle-free fields? In this scenario, the cattle rancher is not liable for any damages his cattle cause to the wheat farmer. If the damage to the nearby wheat field is large and the rancher is *not* liable, the wheat farmer will build a fence to keep the cattle out. The fence internalizes the negative externality and forces the wheat farmer to bear the full cost of the damage. If the amount of damage is smaller than the cost of a fence, the farmer may accept occasional damage as the lower-cost option.

From comparing these two scenarios, Coase determined that whenever the externality is large enough to justify the expense, the externality gets internalized. As long as the property rights are fully specified (and there are no barriers to negotiations), either the cattle rancher or the wheat farmer will build a fence. The fence will keep the cattle away from the wheat, remove the externality, and prevent the destruction of property.

Selling a car, an exchange of private property, benefits both the owner and the buyer.

If the cattle find the wheat, whose problem is that?

A fence internalizes the externality.

The **Coase theorem** states that if there are no barriers to negotiations, and if property rights are fully specified, interested parties will bargain to correct externalities.

With these scenarios in mind, we can now appreciate the **Coase theorem**, which states that if there are no barriers to negotiations, and if property rights are fully specified, interested parties will bargain privately to correct externalities. As a result, the assignment of property rights under the law gives each party an incentive to internalize any externalities. If it is difficult to bargain (because the costs of reaching an agreement are too high), private parties will be unable to internalize the externality between themselves. Therefore, the Coase theorem also suggests that private solutions to externality problems are not always possible, implying a prominent role for government in solving complex externality issues.

To think about the case for a government role, consider the difference between the example of a rancher and a farmer with adjacent land and the example of a community-wide problem such as pollution. With two landowners, a private solution should be possible because the parties can bargain with each other at a low cost. With pollution, though, so many individuals are affected that the polluting company cannot afford to bargain with each one. Because bargaining costs are high in the case of pollution, an intermediary, like the government, is often necessary to ensure that externalities are internalized.

Private and Public Goods

When we think of private goods, most of us imagine something that we enjoy, like a sandwich or a favorite jacket. When we think of public goods, we think of goods provided by the government, like roads, the post office, and the military. The terms "private" and "public" typically imply ownership or production, but that is not the criterion economists use to categorize private and public goods. To understand the difference between private and public goods, you need to know whether a good is excludable, rival in consumption, or both. An **excludable good** is one for which access can be limited to paying customers. A **rival good** is one that cannot be enjoyed by more than one person at a time.

An **excludable good** is one for which access can be limited to paying customers.

A **rival good** is a good that cannot be enjoyed by more than one person at a time.

A **private good** has two characteristics: it is excludable and rival in consumption.

PRIVATE GOODS A **private good** is both excludable and rival in consumption. For instance, a sandwich is excludable because you must purchase it before you can eat it. Also, a sandwich is rival; only one person can eat it. These two characteristics, excludability and rivalry, allow the market to work efficiently in the absence of externalities. Consider a sandwich shop. The business makes sandwiches because it knows it can sell them to consumers. Likewise, consumers are willing to buy sandwiches because that is a food they enjoy. Because the producer gets to charge a price and the consumer gets to acquire a rival good, the stage is set for mutual gains from trade.

Trade creates value

PUBLIC GOODS Markets have no difficulty producing purely private goods, like sandwiches, because in order to enjoy them you must first purchase them. But when was the last time you paid to see a fireworks display? Hundreds of thousands of people view many of the nation's best fireworks displays, but only a small percentage of them pay admission to get a preferred seat. Fireworks displays are a **public good** because (1) they are consumed by more than one person and (2) it is difficult to exclude nonpayers. Because consumers cannot be easily forced to pay to observe fireworks, they may desire more of the good than is typically supplied. As a result, a market economy underproduces fireworks displays and many other public goods.

A sandwich is a private good.

Public goods are often underproduced because people can get them without paying for them. This means that public goods, like externalities, also result in market failure. Consider Joshua Bell, one of the most famous violinists in the world. The day after giving a concert in Boston for which patrons paid $100 a ticket, he decided to reprise the performance in a Washington, D.C., subway station and just ask for donations.* Any passerby could listen to the music—it did not need to be purchased to be enjoyed. In other words, it was nonexcludable and nonrival in consumption. But because it is impossible for a street musician to force bystanders to pay, it is difficult for the musician—even one as good as Joshua Bell—to make a living. Suppose he draws a large crowd and the music creates $500 worth of enjoyment among the audience. At the end of the performance, he receives a loud round of applause and then motions to the donation basket. A number of people come up and donate, but when he counts up the contributions, he finds only $30—the actual amount he earned while playing in the Metro.

Public goods are consumed by more than one person, and nonpayers are difficult to exclude.

Why did Joshua Bell receive $30 when he created many times that amount in value? This phenomenon, known as a **free-rider problem**, occurs whenever people receive a benefit they do not pay for. A street musician provides a public good and must rely on the generosity of the audience to contribute. If very few people contribute, many potential musicians will not find it worthwhile to perform. We tend to see very few street performances because free-riding lowers the returns to performing, and the private equilibrium amount of street performances is undersupplied in comparison to the social optimum. When payment cannot be linked to production or consumption, the efficient quantity is not produced.

A **free-rider problem** occurs whenever someone receives a benefit without having to pay for it.

*This really happened. The *Washington Post* and Bell conducted an experiment to test the public's reaction to performances of "genius" in unexpected settings. Our discussion here places the event in a hypothetical context. For the real-life result, see Gene Weingarten, "Pearls before Breakfast," *Washington Post*, April 8, 2007, https://www.washingtonpost.com/lifestyle/magazine/pearls-before-breakfast-can-one-of-the-nations-great-musicians-cut-through-the-fog-of-a-dc-rush-hour-lets-find-out/2014/09/23/8a6d46da-4331-11e4-b47c-f5889e061e5f_story.html.

Would everyone wear a mask in public spaces if they were provided for free?

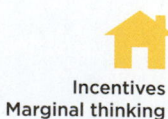

Street performances are just one example of a public good subject to free-riding. Other examples are streetlights, clean air, and national defense. A particularly timely example is the wearing of masks to prevent contagion. For some people—young and fit, or old but stubborn—the cost and inconvenience of donning a mask day after day outweigh the benefits, especially if everyone *else* is wearing one. Yet if a lot of people opt out of mask-wearing, everyone is at increased risk, including the young, the fit, and the stubborn. One way to influence this behavior might be for the government to pony up the cost of free masks for everyone and then make mask-wearing mandatory, with noncompliance punishable by a fine, like speeding or illegal parking. The cost burden would fall on all taxpayers but especially on violators, and the free-rider problem would be practically eliminated.

Most people agree that government should provide certain public goods for society, including national defense, the interstate highway system, and medical and science-related research to fight pandemics. In each case, public-sector provision helps to eliminate the free-rider problem and create the socially optimal level of activity.

ECONOMICS IN THE REAL WORLD

GROUP WORK

Perhaps you've taken a class where group work is required. These assignments are valuable opportunities to develop a skill businesses are looking for in potential employees: the ability to work as a team to accomplish a task. However, group work in class or in the workplace creates an environment for the free-rider problem. In many groups, one of the members doesn't put in the time or effort to complete the project. This person realizes he or she will get the benefit of the group grade without incurring the full cost. You may think that this behavior is lazy or inconsiderate, and it is, but it is nonetheless quite rational. The question for the free-rider is whether his or her actions will marginally affect the group's grade. Does the cost of completing part of the project justify what is likely to be only a small change in the grade earned by every member in the group? If the work raises the group's grade from a B- to a B, the free-rider may find

Incentives
Marginal thinking

that it is too costly to participate. To avoid the free-rider problem, teachers often ask the group to grade each group member's contribution to the group's overall output, and this determines the part of the project grade attributed to individual effort. The hope is that this system will give free-riders the incentive to pull their own weight.

CLUB GOODS AND COMMON-RESOURCE GOODS There are two additional types of goods we have not yet introduced. Because club goods and common-resource goods have characteristics of both private and public goods, the line between private provision and public provision is often blurred.

A **club good** is nonrival in consumption and excludable. Streaming services such as Netflix, Hulu, and Disney+ are examples. Streamed content is an excludable good, because you must pay to receive it, but it is nonrival in consumption because there is no cap on how many subscribers can watch at the same time. Because customers who wish to enjoy club goods can be excluded, markets typically provide these goods. However, once a streaming service is in place, the cost of adding customers is low. Firms are motivated to maximize profits, not the number of people they serve, so the market price is higher, and the output is lower, than what society desires.

A **common-resource good** is rival in consumption but nonexcludable. King crab in the Bering Sea off Alaska is an example. Because any particular crab can be caught by only one boat crew, the crabs are a rival resource. At the same time, exclusion is not possible because any boat crew that wants to brave the elements can catch crab.

"How much would it cost to see a sunset if God decided to charge for it?"

We have seen that the market generally works well for private goods. In the case of public goods, the market generally needs a hand. In between, club and common-resource goods illustrate the tension between the private and public provision of many goods and services. Table 7.3 summarizes the four types of goods we have discussed.

A **club good** has two characteristics: it is nonrival in consumption and excludable.

A **common-resource good** has two characteristics: it is rival in consumption and nonexcludable.

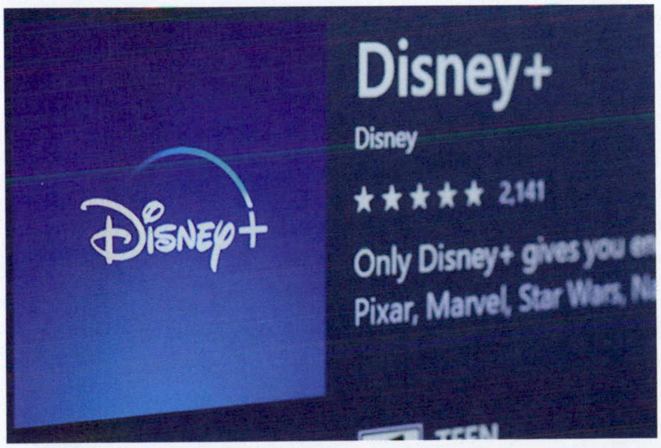

Streaming services are club goods.

Alaskan king crab is a common-resource good.

TABLE 7.3

The Four Types of Goods

		Consumption: Rival	Consumption: Nonrival
Excludable?	Yes	*Private goods* are rival and excludable: sandwiches, watches, automobiles. 	*Club goods* are nonrival and excludable: streaming services, education, country clubs. 
Excludable?	No	*Common-resource goods* are rival and nonexcludable: Alaskan king crab, a large shared popcorn at the movies, congested roads. 	*Public goods* are nonrival and nonexcludable: street performers, national defense, tsunami warning systems. 

PRACTICE WHAT YOU KNOW

Are Parks Public Goods?

Many goods have the characteristics of a public good, but few goods meet the exact definition.

QUESTION: Are parks public goods?

ANSWER: We tend to think of public parks as meeting the necessary requirements to be a public good. But not so fast. Have you been to any of America's top national parks on a peak summer weekend? Most parks have limited parking capacity, which makes them rival. In addition, most national and state parks require an admission fee—translation: they are excludable. Therefore, public parks do not meet the exact definition of a public good.

Not surprisingly, there are many good examples of private parks that maintain, protect, and conserve the environment alongside their public counterparts. For instance, Meteor Crater is a privately owned and operated park in Arizona that showcases an extremely well-preserved meteor strike. The United States is dotted with private parks that predate the establishment of the national park system. Like their public counterparts, private parks are also not public goods.

Meteor crater in Arizona

CHALLENGE QUESTION: Suppose you have pitched your tent at a campsite with a lovely view, when another party comes along and prepares to pitch their tent where it will block your view. They explain that the ground is conveniently level and soft in the spot they chose. What could be done about this, assuming that people have a right to pitch their tent wherever they want? What would the solution be if, instead, whoever arrived first had a right, by park rules, to an unobstructed view?

ANSWER: To answer this question, we recall the Coase theorem. In the first case, you could offer the other party money to shift to an acceptable if less comfortable part of their campsite. In the second case, they could offer you money as compensation for your loss of view so they can pitch their tent where they want.

What Are the Challenges of Providing Nonexcludable Goods?

Understanding the four types of goods provides a solid foundation for understanding the role of markets and the government in society. Next, we consider some of the special challenges that arise in providing nonexcludable goods.

Cost-Benefit Analysis

To help make decisions about providing public goods, economists turn to **cost-benefit analysis**, a process used to determine whether the benefits of providing a public good outweigh the costs. Costs are usually easier to quantify than benefits. For instance, if a community puts on a Fourth of July celebration, it will have to pay for the fireworks and labor involved in setting up the event. Barring unusual factors, like a risk of fire or disease transmission, the costs are a known quantity. But benefits are difficult to quantify. Because people do not need to pay to see the fireworks, it is hard to determine how much benefit the community receives. If asked, people might misrepresent the social benefit in two ways. First, some residents who value the celebration highly might claim that the fireworks bring more benefit than they actually do, because they want the community fireworks to continue. Second, those residents who dislike the crowds and noise might understate the benefit of the fireworks, because they want the fireworks to cease. Since there is no way to know how truthful people are when responding to a questionnaire, the actual social benefit of a fireworks show is hard to measure.

Cost-benefit analysis is a process that economists use to determine whether the benefits of providing a public good outweigh the costs.

Because people do not pay to enjoy public goods, and because the government provides them without charging a direct fee, determining the socially optimal amount typically takes place through the political system. Generally speaking, elected officials do not get reelected if the populace believes they have not done a good job with their cost-benefit analyses.

Figuring out the social benefit of a fireworks display is quite difficult.

ECONOMICS IN THE REAL WORLD

INTERNET PIRACY

The digitization of media, along with the speed with which it can be transferred across the Internet, has made the protection of *intellectual property rights* (that is, the protection of patents, copyrights, and trademarks) very difficult to enforce. Many countries either do not have strict copyright standards or fail to enforce them. The result is an illegal market filled with bootlegged copies of movies, music, and other media.

Because digital "file sharing" is so common these days, you might not fully understand the harm that occurs. Piracy is an illegal form of free-riding. Every song and every movie that is transferred takes away royalties that would have gone to the original artist or the studio. After all, producing content is expensive, and violations of copyright law prevent businesses from making a fair return on their investments. However, consumers of content don't often see it this way. Some believe that breaking the copyright encryption is fair game because they "own" the object in question or bought it legally or got it from a friend. The reality is different. One reason copyright law exists is to limit free-riding. When copyrights are fully specified and enforced across international boundaries, content creators receive compensation for their efforts. But if copyrights are routinely violated, revenues to private businesses will decline and the amount of music and movies produced will decrease. In the long run, artists will produce less and society will suffer. (For other benefits of copyright law, see Chapter 10.)

Incentives

Think about the relationship between artists and the public as reciprocal: each side needs the other. In that sense, the music you buy or the movie you watch is not a true public good, but more of a club good. Copyright laws make the good excludable but nonrival. For this reason, some people will always have an incentive to violate copyright law, artists and studios will insist on ever more complicated encryption methods to protect their interests, and for the betterment of society as a whole, the government will have to enforce copyright law to prevent widespread free-riding.

Common Resources and the Tragedy of the Commons

The **tragedy of the commons** occurs when a common-resource good becomes depleted.

Common resources often give rise to the **tragedy of the commons**, a situation that occurs when a common-resource good becomes depleted. The term "tragedy of the commons" refers to a phenomenon ecologist Garrett Hardin wrote about in the magazine *Science* in 1968. Hardin described the hypothetical use of a common pasture shared by local herders in a pastoral community. Herders know that intensively grazed land will be depleted and that this depletion is very likely to happen to common land. Knowing that the pasture will be depleted creates a strong incentive for individual herders to bring their animals to the pasture as much as possible while it is still green, because every other herder will be doing the same thing. Each herder has the same incentive to overgraze, which quickly makes the pasture unusable. The overgrazing is a negative externality brought about by poorly designed incentives and the absence of clearly defined private property rights.

Incentives

Even though the concept of common ownership sounds ideal, it can be a recipe for resource depletion and economic disaster. Common ownership, unlike private ownership, leads to overuse. With a system of private property rights, an owner can seek damages in the court system if his property is damaged or destroyed. But the same cannot be said for common property, because joint ownership allows any party to use the resource as he or she sees fit. This situation creates incentives to use the resource now rather than later and to neglect it. In short, common property leads to abuse and depletion of the resource.

Consider global warming. Scientific evidence clearly links increasing amounts of CO_2 (carbon dioxide) in the atmosphere and global warming. This negative externality is caused by some but borne jointly by everyone. Because large CO_2 emitters consider only the internal costs of their actions and ignore the social costs, the amount of CO_2 released, and the corresponding increase in global warming, is larger than optimal. The air, a common resource, is being "overused" and degraded.

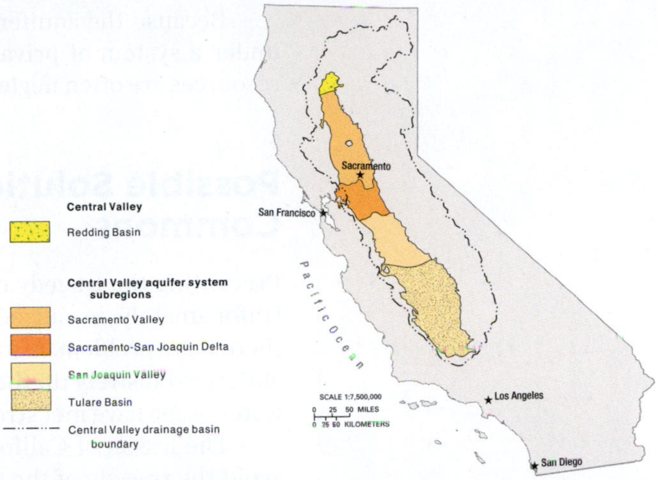

The aquifers in California's Central Valley, shown in the U.S. Geological Survey Map, are badly depleted.

Private property rights give owners an incentive to maintain, protect, and conserve their property and to transfer it if someone else values it more than they do. How are those incentives different under a system of common ownership? Let's examine a real-world example of the tragedy of the commons: California's aquifiers. Aquifiers are massive, natural underground reservoirs, replenished by rainfall percolating down into the ground. For years, California has been pumping water from its aquifers, mainly for agricultural use, at an unsustainable rate. As the aquifers are drained, the land has sunk down in places to partially fill the space left by the removed water. Scientists call this settling of soil subsidence. When it happens, the aquifers lose water-holding capacity, and generally, the damage is permanent.*

So now, California is not only using water at an unsustainable rate but has a reduced natural capacity to store water from rain and snowfall. Why did this happen? Well, consider the incentives associated with common property in the context of the aquifers.

Incentives

1. *An incentive to neglect.* No one owns the aquifers. As a result, for most of the last century, little attention was paid to aquifer depletion. Only when wells started running dry, and surface canals stopped flowing properly because of subsidence, did most people begin to realize that the state had a big and growing problem on its hands.
2. *An incentive to overuse.* California's main agricultural region, the great Central Valley, is fertile but arid, so crops are watered using groundwater. But even if farmers know that the current overall pumping rate is unsustainable, conservation on the part of an individual farmer is hard to motivate if other farmers use whatever water is left behind. Because the aquifer is a finite resource, there is an incentive to use as much water as you can.

*Ellen Hanak, Caitrin Chappelle, and Thomas Harter, "Groundwater in California," Public Policy Institute of California, May 2017, https://www.ppic.org/publication/groundwater-in-california.

Because the aquifer is a common resource, the incentives we discussed under a system of private ownership do not apply. With common property, resources are often neglected and overused.

Possible Solutions to the Tragedy of the Commons

Preventing the tragedy of the commons requires planning and coordination. Unfortunately, in our aquifer example, officials were slow to recognize that there was a problem. Also, because many communities in the Central Valley rely almost exclusively on the aquifer for all their water needs, attempts to reduce water usage have met strong political resistance.

The lesson of California's aquifers is a powerful reminder that efforts to avoid the tragedy of the commons must begin before a problem develops. For example, tiered pricing of water can provide strong incentives to curb water usage. Likewise, sustainable practices, such as watering overnight, can reduce evaporation. Planting drought-tolerant crops also helps reduce water usage. Sustainable practices like these help avoid the tragedy of the commons.

Incentives

Nobel-winning economist Elinor Ostrom examined how some commons are sustainably managed without government, despite the tragedy of the commons and free-rider problems. She understood many of the problems we face today. "[N]o one communicates, everyone acts independently, no attention is paid to the effects of one's actions, and the costs of trying to change the structure of the situation are high."* Her advice was for individuals to communicate often with one another, in order to develop shared norms from which intuitional arrangements would naturally arise to address common-resource dilemmas.

Can the misuse of a common resource be foreseen and prevented? If predictions of rapid global warming are correct, our analysis points to a number of solutions to minimize the tragedy of the commons. Businesses and individuals can be discouraged from producing emissions through carbon pricing, which charges firms by the ton for the CO_2 they put into the atmosphere. This policy encourages parties to internalize the negative externality, because carbon pricing acts as an internal cost that must be considered before creating carbon pollution.

Cap and trade is an approach used to curb pollution by creating a system of emissions permits that are traded in an open market.

Another solution, known as **cap and trade**, is an approach to emissions reduction that has received much attention lately. The idea behind cap and trade policy is to encourage carbon producers to internalize the externality by establishing markets for tradable emissions permits. As a result, a profit motive is created for some firms to purchase, and others to sell, emissions permits. Under cap and trade, the government sets a *cap*, or limit, on the amount of CO_2 that can be emitted. Businesses and individuals are then issued permits to emit a certain amount of carbon each year. Also, permit owners may *trade* permits. In other words, companies that produce fewer carbon emissions can sell the permits they do not use. By establishing property rights that control emissions permits, cap and trade causes firms to

Trade creates value

*Elinor Ostrom, *Governing the Commons: The Evolution of Institutions for Collective Action* (New York: Cambridge University Press, 1990).

internalize externalities and to seek out methods that lower emissions. Global warming is an incredibly complex process, but cap and trade policy is one tangible step that minimizes free-riding, creates incentives for action, and promotes a socially efficient outcome.

Cap and trade is a good idea, but there are issues that must be overcome to make it work effectively. For example, cap and trade presumes that nations can agree on and enforce emissions limits, but international agreements have proved difficult to negotiate. Without binding international agreements, nations that adopt cap and trade policies will experience higher production costs, while nations that ignore them—and free-ride in the process—will benefit.

What is the best way to curb global warming?

ECONOMICS IN THE REAL WORLD

THE GREAT PACIFIC GARBAGE PATCH

The Great Pacific Garbage Patch is an immense swirl of floating debris in the central North Pacific Ocean, the vast majority of which are plastics from microscopic to large sizes. It was first discovered in 1988 and is roughly twice the size of Texas! One would think that an environmental calamity of that scale would prompt significant intervention. That has not happened, because no one person or country "owns" the open Pacific. When trash makes its way out to sea from the shorelines of the Philippines, Vietnam, China, Japan, South and North Korea, Russia, Canada, the United States, and Mexico, it all eventually ends up in the Garbage Patch.

The Great Pacific Garbage Patch is an extreme example of the tragedy of the commons. Its tragedy is especially striking because many people care deeply about marine quality. The tragedy occurs because no one individual, group, or country has the means to solve the problem independently. Even if you and I, and all our friends, consciously make sure we never let any trash enter the ocean, this won't stop debris from elsewhere. Likewise, if Japan unilaterally decided to filter the outflow from all its rivers before entering the ocean, debris from other countries would still litter the garbage patch. Complicating matters, once in the ocean the debris is hard to detect from satellites and even harder to collect and dispose of properly. The only real solution would be a cooperative agreement among all North Pacific Rim nations to filter ocean-bound debris. That's a very expensive proposition to a problem in a location so remote that it is out of sight, and therefore, out of mind.

Can anything be done to clean up the Great Pacific Garbage Patch?

PRACTICE WHAT YOU KNOW

Common Resources: Why Do Tailgaters Trash Parking Lots?

Tailgating can be one of the best parts of attending a big game or concert. You enjoy a great time with your friends and take in the action, leaving quickly afterward with little concern about the trash left behind. Consider this example: In 2014, country artist Luke Bryan played at Heinz Field in Pittsburgh. No doubt his fans care about the environment, but they absolutely trashed the parking lot. It was so bad, it made the local news. On the plus side, some city officials said the trash wasn't as bad as the Kenny Chesney concert the year before!

Why don't these tailgaters make a "concerted" effort to clean up?

QUESTION: What economic concept explains why so many people left so much trash behind?

ANSWER: Tailgaters brought snacks, drinks, cups, napkins, and all kinds of things to party before the concert, so a lot of trash was generated. Would you throw your trash on your driveway? Of course not. But otherwise conscientious individuals often don't demonstrate the same concern for public property. As a public space, the Heinz Field parking lot is subject to the tragedy of the commons. No one person can keep the lot clean, so overuse and littering occur. The effects of littering can be especially apparent when 50,000 people fill a stadium at one time.

Conclusion

Trade-offs

Although it's tempting to believe that the appropriate response to pollution is always to eliminate it, this belief is a misconception. As with all things, there are trade-offs. When pollution is taxed or regulated, business activity declines. It's possible to eliminate too much pollution, forcing businesses to shut down, creating undesirably high prices for anything from groceries to gasoline to electronics, and all in all creating an enormous deadweight loss to society. When you think about pollution like an environmental economist, you realize that eliminating pollution would create benefits and also costs. A truly "green" environment without any pollution would leave most people without enough "green" in their wallets. Therefore, the goal for pollution isn't zero, because the cost of attaining zero pollution outweighs the benefit.

In this chapter, we have considered two types of market failure: externalities and public goods. When externalities and public goods exist, the market does not provide the socially optimal amount of the good or service. One solution is to encourage businesses to internalize externalities. The government can aid the process through taxes and regulations that force producers to account for the negative externalities they create. Similarly, subsidies can spur the production of activities that generate positive externalities.

ECONOMICS *in the* MEDIA

Tragedy of the Commons

SOUTH PARK AND WATER PARKS

If you have ever been to a water park or community pool, you know that the staff checks the pH of the water regularly to make sure it is clean. However, in an episode of *South Park*, everyone is peeing in Pi Pi's water park. The resulting pee concentration ends up being so high that it triggers a disaster-movie-style cataclysm, unleashing a flood of pee that destroys the place.

Why did this happen? Because each person looked at all the water and thought it wouldn't matter if *he* or *she* peed in it. But when *everyone* thought the same way, the water quality was affected. This led to the tragedy of the commons, in which the overall water quality became degraded. Pee-ew.

Thankfully, the real world is cleaner than South Park.

Likewise, public goods present a challenge for the market. Free-riding leads to the underproduction of goods that are nonrival and nonexcludable. Because not enough is produced privately, one solution is to eliminate free-riding by making involvement compulsory through taxation or regulation. A second problem occurs whenever goods are nonexcludable, as is the case with common-resource goods. This condition gives rise to the tragedy of the commons and can lead to the overuse of valuable resources. ✷

· ECONOMICS *for* LIFE ·

Buying Used Can Be Good for Your Wallet and for the Environment

- When you buy used you don't pay the "new" price markup.
- When you buy used you extend the usable life of a product, which is good for the environment.
- Some items are available for significant discounts soon after they are first sold.

Many people often spend their hard-earned money buying new, when choices to buying *almost* new instead are available. While some customers are willing to pay a premium for that "new" feeling, if you avoid that price markup for untouched goods, you'll usually save money *and* extend the usable life of a product. Here are a few ideas.

1. **Thrift-shop clothing**. Why would you buy something that immediately drops in value by 70%? When you buy new clothes at a retail store, you'll rarely get even a third of it back if you need to sell it at a consignment store or garage sale. Pick up bargains on lightly used clothing at your local thrift store instead.
2. **Sports equipment**. Let the enthusiasts buy the latest equipment. When they tire of it and switch to the newest golf clubs or buy a new kayak, you can swoop in and save big bucks. Play It Again Sports is a retailer that sells new and used equipment side-by-side so you can decide for yourself if new is worth the price difference.
3. **Video game consoles and games**. You can buy used and pay half price or less. The catch is you'll have to wait. But the good news is that you'll never find out that your expensive new system isn't as exciting as advertised. Waiting means better information *and* lower prices. That's how you find a good deal.

Listen to Macklemore's "Thrift Shop" advice: "It was 99 cents!"

4. **Automobiles**. The average new car can lose as much as 20% of its value during the first year after purchase. For a $30,000 car, that means $6,000 in lost value. Let someone else take that hit and buy a used vehicle instead.
5. **Tools and yard equipment**. Think twice before heading to the hardware store. Many tools like hammers and shovels are designed to last. Used tools might not look shiny-new, but they work just as well.

Every time you buy used, you extend the usable life of a product, which helps maximize the value society gets from its resources. These examples also illustrate the benefit of private property: recall that owners have incentives to (1) maintain, (2) protect, and (3) conserve the products they own so that they can (4) maximize the value when they sell them.

ANSWERING *the* BIG QUESTIONS

What are externalities, and how do they affect markets?

- An externality exists whenever an internal cost (or benefit) diverges from a social cost (or benefit). Third parties can experience negative or positive externalities from market activity. Externalities are a type of market failure, which occurs when there is an inefficient allocation of resources in a market.
- Social costs are the sum of an activity's internal costs and external costs.
- When a negative externality exists, government can restore the social optimum by discouraging economic activity that harms third parties. When a positive externality exists, government can restore the social optimum by encouraging economic activity that benefits third parties.
- An externality is internalized when decision-makers must pay for the externality created by their participation in the market.

What are private goods and public goods?

- Private goods (or private property) ensures that owners have an incentive to maintain, protect, and conserve their property and also to trade it with others.
- A public good has two characteristics: it is nonexcludable and nonrival in consumption. Public goods give rise to the free-rider problem and result in the underproduction of the good in the market. Public goods give rise to market failure.

What are the challenges of providing nonexcludable goods?

- Economists use cost-benefit analysis to determine whether the benefits of providing a particular good outweigh the costs, but benefits can be hard to determine.
- Under a system of common property, the incentive structure encourages neglect and overuse.

CHAPTER PROBLEMS

Concepts You Should Know

cap and trade (p. 238)
club good (p. 233)
Coase theorem (p. 230)
common-resource good (p. 233)
cost-benefit analysis (p. 235)
excludable good (p. 230)
external costs (p. 221)
externalities (p. 220)
free-rider problem (p. 231)
internal costs (p. 221)
internalize (p. 223)
market failure (p. 220)
private good (p. 230)
private property (p. 228)
property rights (p. 228)
public good (p. 231)
rival good (p. 230)
social costs (p. 221)
social optimum (p. 222)
third-party problem (p. 221)
tragedy of the commons (p. 236)

Questions for Review

1. Does the market overproduce or underproduce when third parties enjoy positive externalities? Show your answer on a supply and demand graph.
2. Is it possible to use bargaining to solve externality problems involving many parties? Explain your reasoning.
3. Describe all of the ways in which externalities can be internalized.
4. Does cost-benefit analysis apply to public goods only? If yes, why? If not, name situations in which economists would use cost-benefit analysis.
5. What is the tragedy of the commons? Give an example that is not in the chapter.
6. What are the four incentives of private property? How do they differ from the incentives found in common property?
7. Give an example of a good that is nonrival in consumption and nonexcludable. What do economists call goods that share these characteristics?

Study Problems (*✱ solved at the end of the section)*

1. Many cities have noise ordinances that impose especially harsh fines and penalties for early-morning and late-evening disturbances. Explain why these ordinances exist.
2. Indicate whether the following activities create a positive or negative externality:
   - **a.** Late-night road construction begins on a new bridge. As a consequence, traffic is rerouted past your house while the construction takes place.
   - **b.** An excavating company pollutes a local stream with acid rock.
   - **c.** A homeowner whose property backs up on a city park enjoys the sound of kids playing soccer.
   - **d.** A student uses her cell phone discreetly during class.
   - **e.** You and your friends volunteer to plant wildflowers along the local highway.
3. Indicate whether the following are private goods, club goods, common-resource goods, or public goods:
   - **a.** a pork tamale
   - **b.** an MLS soccer match between Austin FC and DC United
   - **c.** a fireworks show
   - **d.** a swimming pool
   - **e.** a vaccination for the flu
   - **f.** streetlights
4. Can you think of a reason why making cars safer would create negative externalities? Explain.
5. Which of the following activities give rise to the free-rider problem?
   - **a.** recycling programs
   - **b.** biking
   - **c.** studying for an exam
   - **d.** riding a bus

✷ **6.** The students at a crowded university have trouble waking up before 10 a.m., and most work jobs after 3 p.m. As a result, there is a great deal of demand for classes between 10 a.m. and 3 p.m., and classes before and after those hours are rarely full. To make matters worse, the university has a limited amount of classroom space and faculty. As a result, not every student can take classes during the most desirable times. Building new classrooms and hiring more faculty are not options. The administration asks for your advice about the best way to solve the problem of demand during the peak class hours. What advice would you give?

7. Two roommates are opposites. One enjoys playing *Modern Warfare* with his friends all night. The other likes to get to bed early for a full 8 hours of sleep. If Ronald Coase is right, the roommates have an incentive to solve the noise externality issue themselves. Name at least two solutions that will internalize, or eliminate, the externality.

✷ **8.** Two companies, Toxic Waste Management and Sludge Industries, both pollute a nearby lake. Each firm dumps 1,000 gallons of goo into the lake every day. As a consequence, the lake has lost its clarity and the fish are dying. Local residents want to see the lake restored. But Toxic Waste's production process depends heavily on being able to dump the goo into the lake. It would cost Toxic Waste $10 per gallon to clean up the goo it generates. Sludge can clean up its goo at a cost of $2 per gallon.

a. If the local government cuts the legal goo emissions in half for each firm, what are the costs to each firm to comply with the law? What is the total cost to both firms in meeting the goo-emissions standard?

b. Another way of cutting goo emissions in half is to assign each firm tradable pollution permits that allow 500 gallons of goo to be dumped into the lake every day. Under this approach, will each firm still dump 500 gallons of goo? Would the firms be willing to trade permits with one another?

9. A study finds that leaf blowers make too much noise, so the government imposes a $10 tax on the sale of every unit to correct for the social cost of the noise pollution. The tax completely internalizes the externality. Before the corrective tax, Blown Away Manufacturing regularly sold blowers for $100. After the tax is in place, the consumer price for leaf blowers rises to $105.

a. Describe the impact of the tax on the number of leaf blowers sold.

b. What is the socially optimal price to the consumer?

c. What is the private market price?

d. What net price is Blown Away receiving after it pays the tax?

10. In most areas, developers are required to submit an environmental impact study before work can begin on a new construction project. Suppose that a commercial developer wants to build a new shopping center on an environmentally protected piece of property that is home to a rare three-eyed toad. The shopping complex, if approved by the local planning commission, will cover 10 acres. The planning commission wants the construction to go forward because the shopping complex means additional jobs for the local community, but it also wants to be environmentally responsible. One member of the commission suggests that the developer relocate the toads. She describes the relocation process as follows: "The developer builds the shopping mall and agrees to create 10 acres of artificial toad habitat elsewhere." Will this proposed solution make the builder internalize the externality? Explain.

✷ **11.** Describe the difference between the way an environmental economist thinks about policy and the way an environmentalist thinks about policy. (**Hint:** Recall the difference between positive economics and normative economics from Chapter 2.)

12. If a company pollutes the water and transactions costs are high, which of the following makes the most economic sense?

a. All parties connected with the pollution should negotiate.

b. The company should be allowed to pollute.

c. The company should be liable for the damages it causes.

d. The company should go out of business.

13. A homeowner is piling debris near his lot line. It would be $300 worth of trouble to put it elsewhere. The next-door neighbor is worried that the unsightly debris drops $5,000 from the market value of the home she's trying to sell.

    a. How might the two parties voluntarily resolve this conflict?

    b. If the local homeowners' association prohibits debris piles, how is the dispute likely to get resolved? Is this a socially beneficial solution?

* 14. Does antibiotic use entail an external cost or an external benefit?

* 15. Suppose Heesun lives alone. She has two pet hamsters; she likes the hamsters because they are cute. But cleaning their cage every day is a hassle. In this case, Heesun's hamsters entail

    a. an external cost.

    b. an external benefit.

    c. neither an external cost nor an external benefit.

16. A cattle rancher and a wheat farmer own adjacent properties. The accompanying table identifies the annual profit received by each party in the event there is, or there is not, a fence. If there is no fence, one can be installed and maintained at an annual cost of $15,000.

	Fence	No fence
Cattle rancher	$40,000	$50,000
Wheat farmer	50,000	20,000

If legal rights are assigned to the wheat farmer so that the cattle rancher is liable for any damage caused by her cattle to the wheat crop, will the cattle rancher build a fence? What if instead, the cattle rancher is not liable, but the two can negotiate?

Solved Problems

6. A flat-fee congestion charge is a good start, because this charge would reduce the quantity demanded between 10 a.m. and 3 p.m., but such a fee is a blunt instrument. Making the congestion charge dynamic (or varying the price by the hour) will encourage students to move outside the window with the most popular class times in order to pay less. For instance, classes between 11 a.m. and 2 p.m. would have the highest fee. Classes between 10 and 11 a.m. and between 2 and 3 p.m. would be slightly discounted. Classes between 9 and 10 a.m. and between 3 and 4 p.m. would be cheaper still, and those earlier than 9 a.m. and after 4 p.m. would be the cheapest. By altering the price of different class times, the university would be able to offer classes at less popular times and fill them up regularly, thus efficiently using its existing resources.

8. a. If the local government cuts the legal goo emissions in half for each firm, Toxic Waste will cut its goo by 500 gallons at a cost of $10 per gallon, for a total cost of $5,000. Sludge Industries will also cut its goo by 500 gallons; at $2 per gallon, the cost is $1,000. The total cost to both firms in meeting the goo-emissions standard is $5,000 + $1,000 = $6,000.

    b. It costs Toxic Waste $10 per gallon to clean up its goo. It is therefore more efficient for Toxic to buy all 500 permits from Sludge—which enables Toxic to dump an additional 500 gallons in the lake and saves the company $5,000 minus the price it pays to Sludge for its permits. At the same time, Sludge could decide not to dump any goo in the lake. Because it costs Sludge $2 per gallon to clean up its goo, it will have to pay $1,000 unless it sells its permits to Toxic, in which case it might actually make a profit. Because Toxic is saving more than it costs Sludge to clean up the goo, the two sides have an incentive to trade the permits.

11. Thinking like an economist requires one to consider the marginal benefits and the marginal costs of every policy. This perspective allows environmental economists to assess whether a particular

policy will create enough benefits to outweigh the costs. It is this positive (dispassionate) perspective that causes an environmental economist to argue that the optimal rate of pollution is above zero. In contrast, an environmentalist sees policy solutions through a normative lens. Environmentalists weigh the benefits of protecting the environment much more heavily than the costs and therefore advocate for policies that protect the environment even when the costs are quite high.

14. Antibiotics create both an external cost and an external benefit. There is external cost because overuse makes bacteria more resistant to future treatment, and an external benefit because the use of antibiotics helps to slow the spread of bacteria.

15. The correct answer is c. There is no third party, so there is no negative or positive externality.

PART III

The Theory of THE FIRM

CHAPTER

08

Business Costs and Production

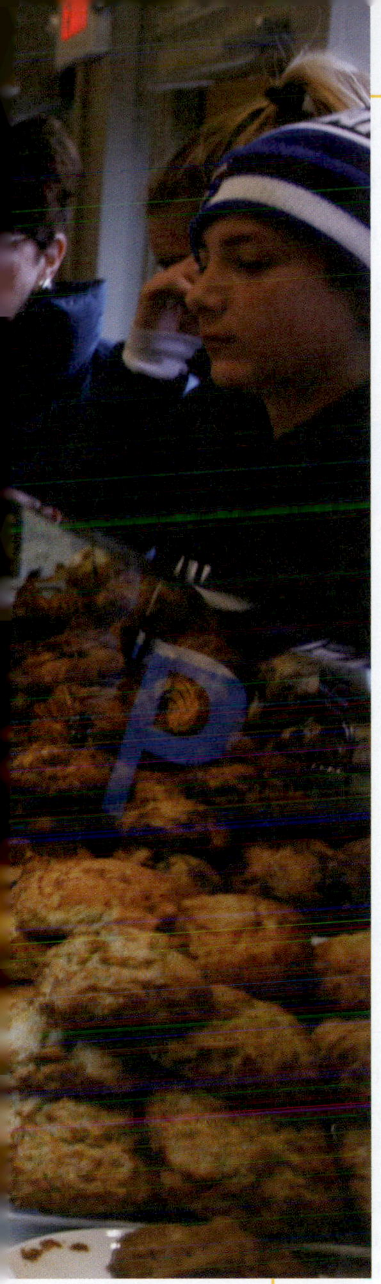

Do Larger Firms Always Have a Cost Advantage Over Their Smaller Rivals?

Walmart, the nation's largest retailer, leverages its size to get price breaks on bulk purchases from its suppliers. People commonly believe that this kind of leverage enables larger firms to operate at lower costs than smaller firms do. It is true that large firms have broader distribution networks, and they benefit from more specialization and automation compared with their smaller competitors. However, not all industries enjoy lower costs with additional sales the way retailers do. Even Walmart, known for its very low prices, can be undercut by online outlets that have lower costs and therefore lower prices. In other words, larger firms do not always have the lowest costs.

Some products are especially unsuited to mass production. Consider pastries. The thing is, there's no cost-effective way to mass-produce fresh custard tarts and filled croissants. They have to be baked locally, in small batches, and sold quickly before they go soggy or stale. Because independent bakeries excel at that kind of operation, they have no trouble offering their wares at competitive prices, and at a quality equal to or better than that of the chain shops. Even growing chains like Paris Baguette and Tous les Jours (both founded and hugely popular in South Korea) make sure to advertise how they make their products locally, every day.

We begin the chapter with an examination of costs and how they relate to production. After we understand the basics, we consider how firms can keep their costs low in the

The baker is happy, because she knows there's nothing the big national chains can do that she can't. Making pastries is a craft, not a factory process.

long run by choosing a scale of operation that best suits their needs. By the end of this chapter, you will appreciate the importance of cost and understand why smaller and more nimble firms are sometimes able to undercut the prices of larger franchises.

· BIG QUESTIONS ·

- How are profits and losses calculated?
- How much should a firm produce?
- What costs do firms consider in the short run and the long run?

The first McDonald's—much like the one pictured here—opened in San Bernardino, California, in 1940.

How Are Profits and Losses Calculated?

To determine the potential profits of a business, the first step is to look at how much it will cost to run it. Consider a McDonald's restaurant. While you are probably familiar with the products McDonald's sells, you may not know how an individual franchise operates. For one thing, the manager at a McDonald's must decide how many workers to hire and how many to assign to each shift. Other managerial decisions involve the equipment needed and what supplies to have on hand each day—everything from hamburger patties to paper napkins. In fact, behind each purchase a consumer makes at McDonald's, there is a complicated symphony of delivery trucks, workers, and managers.

For a company to be profitable, it is not enough to provide products consumers want. It must simultaneously manage its costs. In this section, we discuss how profits and costs are calculated.

Calculating Profit and Loss

Total revenue is the amount a firm receives from the sale of goods and services.

Total cost is the amount a firm spends to produce and/or sell goods and services.

A **profit** results when total revenue is higher than total cost.

The simplest way to determine profit or loss is to calculate the difference between revenue and expenses (costs). The **total revenue** of a business is the amount the firm receives from the sale of goods and services. In the case of McDonald's, the total revenue is determined by the number of items sold and their prices. **Total cost** is the amount a firm spends to produce and/or sell goods and services. To determine total cost, the firm adds the individual costs of the resources used in producing and/or selling the goods. A **profit** occurs whenever total revenue is higher than total cost. A **loss** occurs whenever total revenue is less than total cost. We can express this relationship as an equation:

A **loss** results when total revenue is less than total cost.

$$\textbf{profit (or loss)} = \text{total revenue} - \text{total cost} \quad \textbf{(EQUATION 8.1)}$$

To calculate total revenue, we look at the dollar amount the business takes in over a specific period. For instance, suppose that in a given day McDonald's sells 1,000 hamburgers for $1.00 each, 500 orders of large fries for $2.00 each, and 100 shakes for $2.50 each. The total revenue is the sum of all of these values, or $2,250. The profit is therefore $2,250 (total revenue) minus the total cost.

Calculating costs, however, is a little more complicated than calculating revenue; we don't simply tally the cost of making each hamburger, order of large fries, and shake. Total cost has two parts—one that is visible and one that is largely invisible. In the next section, we will see that determining total costs is part art and part science.

Explicit Costs and Implicit Costs

Economists break costs into two components: explicit costs and implicit costs. **Explicit costs** are tangible out-of-pocket expenses. To calculate explicit costs, we add every expense incurred to run the business. For example, in the case of a McDonald's franchise, the weekly supply of hamburger patties is one explicit cost; the owner receives a bill from the meat supplier and has to pay it. **Implicit costs** are the costs of resources already owned, for which no out-of-pocket payment is made. Implicit costs are also opportunity costs, because the use of owned resources means that the next-best alternative use is forgone.

Explicit costs are tangible out-of-pocket expenses.

Implicit costs are the costs of resources already owned, for which no out-of-pocket payment is made.

Let's consider an example. Purchasing a McDonald's franchise costs about $1 million; this is an explicit cost. However, there is also a high opportunity cost—the next-best possibility for investing $1 million. That money could have earned interest in a bank, been used to start a different business, or been invested in the stock market. Each alternative is an implicit cost.

Implicit costs are hard to calculate and easy to miss. For example, it is difficult to determine how much an investor could have earned from an alternative activity. Is the opportunity cost the 1% interest they might have earned by

TABLE 8.1

Examples of a Firm's Explicit and Implicit Costs

Explicit costs	Implicit costs
The electricity bill	The labor of an owner who works for the company but does not draw a salary
Advertising in the local newspaper	The opportunity cost of the capital invested in the business
Employee wages	The use of the owner's car, computer, or other personal equipment to conduct company business

Opportunity cost

placing the money in a bank, the 10% possibly earned in the stock market, or potentially much larger gains from investing in a different business? We can be sure there is an opportunity cost for owner-provided capital, but we can never know exactly how much that might be.

In addition to the opportunity cost of capital, implicit costs include the opportunity cost of the owner's labor. Often, business owners do not pay themselves a direct salary. However, because they could have been working somewhere else, it is reasonable to consider the fair value of the owner's time—income the owner could have earned by working elsewhere—as part of the business's costs.

To fully account for all the costs of doing business, we must calculate the explicit costs, determine the implicit costs, and add them together:

(EQUATION 8.2) **total cost** = explicit costs + implicit costs

A simple way of thinking about the distinction between explicit costs and implicit costs is to consider someone who wants to build a bookcase. Suppose that Jane purchases \$30 in materials and takes half a day off from work, where she normally earns \$12 an hour. After 4 hours, she completes the bookcase. Her explicit cost is \$30, but her total cost is much higher because she also gave up 4 hours of work at \$12 an hour. Her implicit cost is therefore \$48. When we add the explicit cost (\$30) and the implicit cost (\$48), we get Jane's total cost (\$78).

Table 8.1 shows examples of a firm's explicit and implicit costs.

Accounting Profit versus Economic Profit

Now that you know about explicit and implicit costs, we can refine our definition of profit. In fact, there are two types of profit—accounting profit and economic profit.

Accounting profit is calculated by subtracting the explicit costs from total revenue.

A firm's **accounting profit** is calculated by subtracting only the explicit costs from total revenue. Accounting figures permeate company reports, quarterly and annual statements, and the media.

(EQUATION 8.3) **accounting profit** = total revenues − explicit costs

As you can see, accounting profit does not take into account the implicit costs of doing business. To calculate the full cost of doing business, we need to consider both implicit and explicit costs. Doing so yields a firm's economic profit. **Economic profit** is calculated by subtracting both the explicit and the implicit costs from total revenue. Economic profit gives a more complete assessment of how a firm is doing.

Economic profit is calculated by subtracting both the explicit costs and the implicit costs from total revenue.

economic profit = total revenues − (explicit costs + implicit costs) **(EQUATION 8.4)**

Simplifying Equation 8.4 gives us

economic profit = accounting profit − implicit costs **(EQUATION 8.5)**

Therefore, economic profit is always less than accounting profit.

The difference in accounting profits among various types of firms can be misleading. For instance, if a company with $1 billion in assets reports an annual profit of $10 million, we might think it is doing well. After all, wouldn't you be happy to make $10 million in a year? However, that $10 million is only 1% of the $1 billion the company holds in assets. As Table 8.2 shows, a 1% return is far less than the typical return available in a number of other places, including the stock market, bonds, or a savings account at a financial institution.

If the return on $1 billion in assets is low compared with what an investor can expect to make elsewhere, the firm with the $10 million accounting profit actually has a negative economic profit. For instance, if the firm had invested the $1 billion in a savings account, according to Table 8.2 it would have earned 2% on $1 billion—that is, $20 million. In that case,

economic profit = accounting profit − implicit costs
= $10 million − $20 million
= − $10 million

As you can see, economic profit can be negative, since the negative dollar amount is a loss. If a business has an economic profit, its revenues are larger than the combination of its explicit costs and implicit costs. Likewise, a business has an economic loss when its revenues are smaller than the combination of its explicit and implicit costs. The difficulty in determining economic profit lies in calculating the tangible value of implicit costs.

TABLE 8.2

Historical Rates of Return in Stocks, Bonds, and Savings Accounts, 1928–2018

Financial instrument	Historical average rate of return since 1928 (adjusted for inflation)
Stocks	8%
Bonds	3
Savings account at a financial institution	2

Source: Federal Reserve database in St. Louis (FRED) and author's adjustments. Data from 1928 to 2018.

PRACTICE WHAT YOU KNOW

Accounting Profit versus Economic Profit: Calculating Summer Job Profits

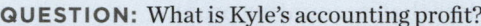

How much economic profit do you make from painting?

Kyle is a college student who works during the summer to pay for tuition. Last summer he worked at a fast-food restaurant and earned \$2,500. This summer he is working as a painter and will earn \$4,000. To do the painting job, Kyle had to spend \$200 on supplies.

QUESTION: What is Kyle's accounting profit?

ANSWER: accounting profit = total revenues − explicit cost
= \$4,000 − \$200 = \$3,800

QUESTION: If working at the fast-food restaurant was Kyle's next-best alternative, how much economic profit will Kyle earn from painting?

ANSWER: To calculate economic profit, we need to subtract the explicit and implicit costs from the total revenue. Kyle's total revenue from painting will be \$4,000. His explicit costs are \$200 for supplies, and his implicit cost is \$2,500—the salary he would have earned in the fast-food restaurant. So Kyle's

economic profit = total revenue − explicit cost + implicit cost
= \$4,000 − (\$200 + \$2,500) = \$1,300

QUESTION: Suppose that Kyle can get an internship at an investment bank. The internship provides a stipend of \$3,000 and tangible work experience that will help him get a job after graduation. Should Kyle take the painting job or the internship?

ANSWER: The implicit costs have changed because Kyle now has to consider the \$3,000 stipend and the increased chance of securing a job after graduation versus what he can make painting houses. Calculation of economic profit from painting is now

economic profit = \$4,000 − (\$200 + \$3,000) = \$800

So at this point, Kyle's economic profit from painting would be only \$800. But this number is incomplete. There is also the value of the internship experience. If Kyle wants to work in investment banking after graduation, then this decision is a no-brainer. He should take the internship—that is, unless some investment banks value painting houses more than work experience!

How Much Should a Firm Produce?

Every business must decide how much to produce. In this section, we describe the factors that determine output, and we explain how firms use inputs to maximize their production. Because it is possible for a firm to produce too little or too much, we must also consider when a firm should stop production.

ECONOMICS *in the* MEDIA

Keeping Costs Down

INCREDIBLES 2

The 2018 sequel to *The Incredibles* opens where the original left off, with the Incredible family fighting to stop The Underminer. By now, all superheroes have been forced into hiding by public outrage over the collateral damage that the crime-fighting Supers habitually leave in their wake. Enter Winston Deavor, the head of a major telecommunications company. Not long after the Supers were banned, robbers broke into the Deavor mansion and shot his father. Winston always believed that if the Supers had been allowed to continue helping people, his father would still be alive. So when he and his sister inherited the company, they decided to create a campaign to bring back the superheroes.

Winston Deavor explains why he wants Elastigirl to fight the villains while Mr. Incredible stays home with the kids.

To do this, Winston wants to change the public's perception by filming a superhero saving the day. He wants Elastigirl to lead the campaign, because a cost-benefit analysis by his sister determined that Elastigirl is able to solve crimes with far less damage than her husband, Mr. Incredible. That leaves the big guy in the role of stay-at-home dad. Elastigirl changes public opinion about the Supers as she defeats the villains, because she is adept at minimizing property damage and loss of life. Good economists do likewise, by keeping costs as low as possible while getting the job done.

The Production Function

For a firm to earn an economic profit, it must produce a product that consumers want. This product is the firm's **output**. A firm should produce an output that is consistent with the largest possible economic profit.

Output is the product the firm creates.

The firm must also control its costs. To do so, the firm must use resources efficiently. There are three primary **factors of production**: labor, land, and capital. Each factor of production is an *input*, or a resource used in the production process to generate the firm's output. *Labor* consists of workers, *land* consists of the geographical location used in production, and *capital* consists of all the resources the workers use to create the final product. Consider McDonald's as an example. The labor input includes managers, cashiers, cooks, and janitorial staff. The land input includes the land on which the McDonald's building sits. The capital input includes the building itself, the equipment used, the parking lot, the signs, and all the hamburger patties, buns, fries, ketchup, and other foodstuffs.

Factors of production are the inputs (labor, land, and capital) used in producing goods and services.

The **production function** describes the relationship between the inputs a firm uses and the output it creates.

To keep costs down in the production process, a firm needs to find the right mix of these inputs. The **production function** describes the relationship between the inputs a firm uses and the output it creates. As we saw at the beginning of the chapter, the manager of a McDonald's must make many decisions about inputs. If she hires too little labor, some of the land and capital will be underutilized. Likewise, with too many workers and not enough land or capital, some workers will not have enough to do to stay busy. For example, suppose that only a single worker shows up at McDonald's one day. This employee will have to do all the cooking; bag up the meals; handle the register, the drive-through, and the drinks; and clean the tables. This single worker, no matter how productive, will not be able to keep up with demand. Hungry customers will grow tired of waiting and take their business elsewhere.

When a second worker shows up, the two employees can begin to specialize in what they do well. Recall that specialization and comparative advantage lead to higher levels of output (see Chapter 2). Therefore, individual workers will be assigned to tasks that match their skills. For example, one worker can take the orders, fill the bags, and get the drinks. The other can work the grill area and drive-through. When a third worker comes on, the specialization process can extend even further. Specialization and division of labor are key to the way McDonald's operates. Production per worker expands as long as additional workers become more specialized and there are enough capital resources to keep each worker occupied.

McDonald's needs the correct amount of labor to maximize its output.

When only a few workers share capital resources, the resources each worker needs are readily available. But what happens when the restaurant is very busy? The manager can hire more staff for the busiest shifts, but the amount of space for cooking and the number of cash registers, drink dispensers, and tables in the seating area are fixed. Because the added employees have less capital to work with, beyond a certain point the additional labor will not continue to increase the restaurant's output at the same rate as it did at first. You might recognize this situation if you have ever waited in a fast-food drive-through line at lunchtime. Even though the kitchen bustles with busy employees, they can't keep up with the orders. Only so many meals can be produced in a short time and in a fixed space; some customers have to wait.

The restaurant must also maintain an adequate supply of materials. If a shipment is late and the restaurant runs out of patties, sales (and total revenue) will decrease. The manager must therefore (1) decide how many workers to hire for each shift and (2) manage the inventory of supplies.

Let's look more closely at the manager's decision about how many workers to hire. On the left side of Figure 8.1, we see what happens when workers are added. When the manager adds one worker, output goes from 0 meals to 5 meals. Going from one worker to two workers increases total output to 15 meals. The second worker has increased the number of meals produced from 5 to 15, an increase of 10 meals. This increase in output is the **marginal product**, which is the change in output associated with one additional unit of an input.

Marginal product is the change in output associated with one additional unit of an input.

(EQUATION 8.6) **marginal output** = (output from n input units) − (output from $n-1$ input units)

In this case, the change in output (10 additional meals) divided by the increase in input (1 worker) gives us a marginal product of 10 ÷ 1, or 10. Because

FIGURE 8.1

The Production Function and Marginal Product

(a) Total output rises rapidly in the green zone from zero to three workers, rises less rapidly in the yellow zone between three and eight workers, and falls in the red zone after eight workers. (b) The marginal product of labor rises in the green zone from zero to three workers, falls in the yellow zone from three to eight workers but remains positive, and becomes negative after eight workers. Notice that the marginal product becomes negative after total output reaches its maximum at eight workers. As long as marginal product is positive, total output rises. Once marginal product becomes negative, total output falls.

Marginal thinking

Number of workers	Total output (number of meals served per hour)	Marginal product of labor
0	0	
1	5	5
2	15	10
3	30	15
4	42	12
5	52	10
6	60	8
7	65	5
8	67	2
9	64	−3
10	56	−8

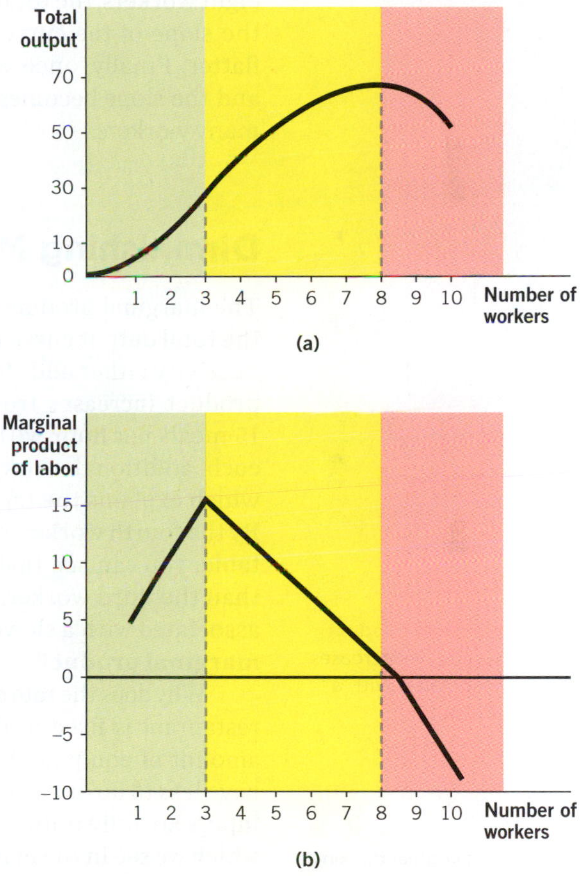

the table in Figure 8.1 adds one worker at a time, the marginal product is just the increase in output shown in the third column. Conversely, for any given number of workers, the total output is the sum of the individual workers' marginal products.

Marginal thinking

Looking down the three columns, we see that the total output continues to expand, and it keeps growing through eight workers. But after the first three workers, the rate of increase in the marginal product slows down. Why? The gains from specialization are slowly declining. With the ninth worker (going from 8 to 9), we see a negative marginal product. Once the cash registers, drive-through, grill area, and other service stations are fully staffed, there is not much for an extra worker to do. Eventually, extra workers will get in the way or distract other workers from completing their tasks.

The graphs on the right side of Figure 8.1 show (a) total output and (b) marginal product of labor. The graph of total output in (a) uses data from the second column of the table. As the number of workers goes from 0 to 3 on the *x* axis, total output rises at an increasing rate from 0 to 30. The slope of the total output curve rises until it reaches three workers at the first dashed vertical line. Between three workers and the second dashed vertical line at eight workers, the total output curve continues to rise, though at a slower rate; the slope of the curve is still positive, but the curve becomes progressively flatter. Finally, once we reach the ninth worker, total output begins to fall and the slope becomes negative. At this point, it is not productive to have so many workers.

Diminishing Marginal Product

The marginal product curve in panel (b) of Figure 8.1 explains the shape of the total output curve in panel (a). Consider that each worker's marginal productivity either adds to or subtracts from the firm's overall output. Marginal product increases from 5 meals served per hour with the first worker to 15 meals per hour with the third worker. From the first worker to the third, each additional worker leads to increased specialization and teamwork, which explains the rapid rise—from 0 to 30 meals—in the total output curve. By the fourth worker, marginal product begins to decline. Looking back to the table, you can see that the fourth worker produces 12 extra meals—3 fewer than the third worker. The point at which successive increases in inputs are associated with a slower rise in output is known as the point of **diminishing marginal product**.

Diminishing marginal product occurs when successive increases in inputs are associated with a slower rise in output.

Why does the rate of output slow? In our example, the size of the McDonald's restaurant is fixed in the short run. Because the size of the building and the amount of equipment do not increase, at a certain point additional workers have less to do or can even interfere with the output of other workers. After all inputs are fully utilized, additional workers cause marginal product to decline, which we see in the marginal product curve in Figure 8.1, panel (b).

Marginal thinking

What does diminishing marginal product tell us about the firm's labor input decision? Turning again to the two graphs, we see that in the green area, as the number of workers increases from zero to three, the marginal product and total output also rise. But when we enter the yellow zone with the fourth worker, we reach the point of diminishing marginal product where the curve starts to decline. Total output continues to rise, though at a slower rate. Finally, in the red zone, which we enter with the ninth worker, marginal product becomes negative and total output declines. No rational manager would hire more than eight workers in this scenario, because doing so would cause total output to drop.

A common mistake when considering diminishing marginal product is to assume that a firm should stop production as soon as marginal product starts to fall. This is not necessarily true. "Diminishing" does not mean "negative."

There are many times when marginal product is declining but still relatively high. In our example, diminishing marginal product begins with the fourth worker. However, that fourth worker still produces 12 extra meals. If McDonald's can sell those 12 additional meals for more than it pays the fourth worker, the company's profits will rise.

What Costs Do Firms Consider in the Short Run and the Long Run?

Production is one part of a firm's decision-making process. If you have run even a simple business—for example, mowing lawns—you know that it requires decision-making. How many lawns do you want to be responsible for? Should you work on different lawns at the same time or specialize by task, with one person doing all the mowing and another taking care of the trimming? These are the kinds of production-related questions every firm must address. The other major component of production is cost. Should you invest in a big industrial-size mower? How much gasoline will you need to run your mowers? What does it cost to hire someone to help get the work done? These are some of the cost-related concerns firms face. Each one may seem like a small decision, but the discovery process that leads to the answers is crucial.

PRACTICE WHAT YOU KNOW

Diminishing Returns: Snow Cone Production

It's a hot day, and customers are lined up for snow cones at your small stand. The following table shows your firm's short-run production function for snow cones.

Number of workers	Total output of snow cones per hour
0	0
1	20
2	50
3	75
4	90
5	100
6	105
7	100
8	90

(CONTINUED)

How many workers are too many? Use marginal product to decide.

QUESTION: When does diminishing marginal product begin?

ANSWER: You have to be careful when calculating this answer. Total output is maximized when you have six workers, but diminishing marginal return begins before you hire that many workers. Look at the following table, which includes a third column showing marginal product.

Number of workers	Total output of snow cones per hour	Marginal product
0	0	
		20
1	20	
		30
2	50	
		25
3	75	
		15
4	90	
		10
5	100	
		5
6	105	
		−5
7	100	
		−10
8	90	

Marginal thinking

The marginal product is highest when you hire the second worker. After that, each subsequent worker you hire has a lower marginal product. Therefore, the answer to the question is that diminishing marginal product begins after the second worker.

Every firm, whether just starting out or already well established and profitable, can benefit by assessing how much to produce and how to produce it more efficiently. In addition, production and cost considerations are different in the short run and in the long run. We begin with the short run because the majority of firms are most concerned with making the best short-run decisions, and then we extend our analysis to the long run, where planning ahead plays a central role.

Costs in the Short Run

All firms experience some costs that are unavoidable in the short run. These unavoidable costs—for example, a lease on space or a contract with a supplier—are a large part of short-run costs. In the short run, costs can be variable or fixed.

Variable costs change with the rate of output.

Variable costs change with the rate of output. Let's see what this means for a McDonald's and further simplify our example by assuming that the McDonald's produces only Big Macs. In this case, the variable costs include the number of workers the firm hires; the electricity the firm uses; cleaning supplies and other consumables; the all-beef patties, special sauce, and other ingredients needed to create the Big Macs; and the packaging. These items are variable costs because the restaurant doesn't need them unless it has customers. The amount of these resources varies with the amount of output the restaurant produces. You might be thinking that a firm should decide to produce at an output where its average variable costs are lowest, but be careful—you don't have all the facts yet. In Chapter 9, we add demand to our analysis to determine how much the firm should produce. For now, we stay focused on the cost side.

Fixed costs are unavoidable; they do not vary with output in the short run. For instance, no matter how many Big Macs the McDonald's sells, most of the costs associated with the building remain the same and the business must pay for them. These fixed costs—also known as *overhead*—include rent, insurance, and property taxes.

Fixed costs are unavoidable; they do not vary with output in the short run. Fixed costs are also known as overhead.

INTERPRETING TABULAR DATA Every business must be able to determine how much it costs to provide the products and services it sells. Table 8.3 lists many different ways to measure the costs associated with business decisions.

Let's begin with total variable cost (TVC) in column 2 and total fixed cost (TFC) in column 3. Notice that when output—the quantity (Q) of Big Macs produced per hour—is 0, total variable cost starts at $0 and rises with production at an uneven rate, depending on output and the cost of the ingredients that go into each Big Mac. We attribute this increase in TVC to the simple fact that additional workers and other inputs are needed to generate additional output. In contrast, total fixed cost starts at $100, even when output is 0, and remains constant as output rises. As already noted, fixed costs include overhead expenses such as rent, insurance, and property taxes. For simplicity, we assume that this amount is $100 a day. When we add fixed cost and variable cost together, we get total cost (TC), listed in column 4: TC = TVC + TFC.

TABLE 8.3

Measuring Costs

(1)	(2)	(3)	(4)	(5)	(6)	(7)	(8)
Quantity (Q = Big Macs produced per hour)	Total variable cost	Total fixed cost	Total cost	Average variable cost	Average fixed cost	Average total cost	Marginal cost
Abbreviation:	TVC	TFC	TC	AVC	AFC	ATC	MC
Formula:			TVC + TFC	TVC ÷ Q	TFC ÷ Q	TC ÷ Q or AVC + AFC	ΔTVC ÷ ΔQ or ΔTC ÷ ΔQ
0	$0.00	$100.00	$100.00				
10	30.00	100.00	130.00	$3.00	$10.00	$13.00	$3.00
20	50.00	100.00	150.00	2.50	5.00	7.50	2.00
30	65.00	100.00	165.00	2.17	3.33	5.50	1.50
40	77.00	100.00	177.00	1.93	2.50	4.43	1.20
50	87.00	100.00	187.00	1.74	2.00	3.74	1.00
60	100.00	100.00	200.00	1.67	1.67	3.34	1.30
70	120.00	100.00	220.00	1.71	1.43	3.14	2.00
80	160.00	100.00	260.00	2.00	1.25	3.25	4.00
90	220.00	100.00	320.00	2.44	1.11	3.55	6.00
100	300.00	100.00	400.00	3.00	1.00	4.00	8.00

Average variable cost (AVC) is determined by dividing total variable cost by the output.

Columns 5 and 6 enable us to determine the cost of producing a Big Mac by examining the average cost of production. **Average variable cost (AVC)**, in column 5, is the total variable cost divided by the output produced: AVC = TVC ÷ Q. Notice that the average variable cost declines until 60 Big Macs are produced at an average variable cost of $1.67, which is the lowest average variable cost. Why should we care about AVC? Because it can be a useful signal. In this case, total variable costs in column 2 always rise, but the average variable cost falls until 60 Big Macs are produced.

Average fixed cost (AFC) is determined by dividing total fixed cost by the output.

Average fixed cost (AFC), listed in column 6, is calculated by dividing total fixed cost by the output: AFC = TFC ÷ Q. Because total fixed cost is constant, dividing these costs by the output means that as the output rises, the average fixed cost declines. In other words, higher output levels spread out the total fixed cost across more units. As Table 8.3 shows, average fixed cost is lowest at an output of 100 Big Macs, where

$$AFC = TFC \div Q$$
$$AFC = \$100 \div 100$$
$$AFC = \$1$$

What does this example tell a business that wants to lower its costs? Because overhead costs such as rent cannot be changed, the best way to lower average fixed costs is to raise output.

Average total cost (ATC) is the sum of average variable cost and average fixed cost.

Average total cost (ATC), shown in column 7, is calculated by adding the AVC and AFC. It can also be calculated by dividing total cost by quantity (TC ÷ Q). Let's look at the numbers to get a better understanding of what average total cost tells us. Even though the average variable cost rises from $1.67 to $1.71 after 60 Big Macs are produced, the average fixed cost is still falling, from $1.67 to $1.43. The decline in average fixed cost is enough to pull the average total cost down to $3.14. Eventually, increases in variable cost overwhelm the cost savings achieved by spreading fixed cost across more production. We can see this result if we compare the average total costs of making 70 Big Macs and 80 Big Macs.

For 70 Big Macs:

$$ATC = AVC + AFC$$
$$ATC = \$1.71 + \$1.43 = \$3.14$$

For 80 Big Macs:

$$ATC = AVC + AFC$$
$$ATC = \$2.00 + \$1.25 = \$3.25$$

At 80 Big Macs, the average variable cost rises from $1.71 to $2.00. And the average fixed cost falls from $1.43 to $1.25. Therefore, the rise in average variable cost—$0.29—is higher than the fall in average fixed cost—$0.18. ATC therefore rises, removing the benefit of higher output.

INTERPRETING DATA GRAPHICALLY Now that we have walked through the numerical results in Table 8.3, it is time to visualize the cost relationships with graphs. Figure 8.2 shows a graph of total cost curves (a) and the relationship between the marginal cost curve and the average cost curves (b).

In panel (a) of Figure 8.2, we see that although the total cost curve continues to rise, the rate of increase in total cost is not constant. For the first 50 Big Macs, the total cost rises at a decreasing rate, reflecting the gains of specialization and comparative advantage that come from adding workers who concentrate on specific tasks. After 50 Big Macs, diminishing marginal product causes the total cost curve to rise at an increasing rate. Because a McDonald's restaurant has a fixed capacity, producing more than 50 Big Macs requires a significantly higher investment in labor, and those workers do not have any additional space to work in—a situation that makes the total cost curve rise more rapidly at high production levels. The total cost (TC) curve is equal to the sum of the total fixed cost and total variable cost curves, as shown in panel (a). Total fixed cost (TFC) is constant, so it is the total variable cost (TVC) that gives the TC curve its shape.

Marginal thinking

But that is not the most important part of the story. Any manager at McDonald's can examine total costs. Likewise, she can look at the average cost and compare that information with the average cost at other local businesses. But neither the total cost of labor nor the average cost will tell her anything about the cost of making additional units—that is, Big Macs.

A manager can make even better decisions by looking at marginal cost. The **marginal cost (MC)** is the increase in cost that occurs from producing one

Marginal cost (MC) is the increase in cost that occurs from producing one additional unit of output.

FIGURE 8.2

The Cost Curves

(a) The total variable cost (TVC) dictates the shape of the total cost (TC) curve. After 50 Big Macs, diminishing marginal product causes the total cost curve to rise at an increasing rate. Notice that the total fixed cost curve (TFC) stays constant, or flat. (b) The marginal cost curve (MC) reaches its minimum before average variable cost (AVC) and average total cost (ATC). Marginals always lead the average variable and average total costs either up or down. Average fixed cost (AFC), which has no variable component, continues to fall with increased quantity, because total fixed costs are spread across more units.

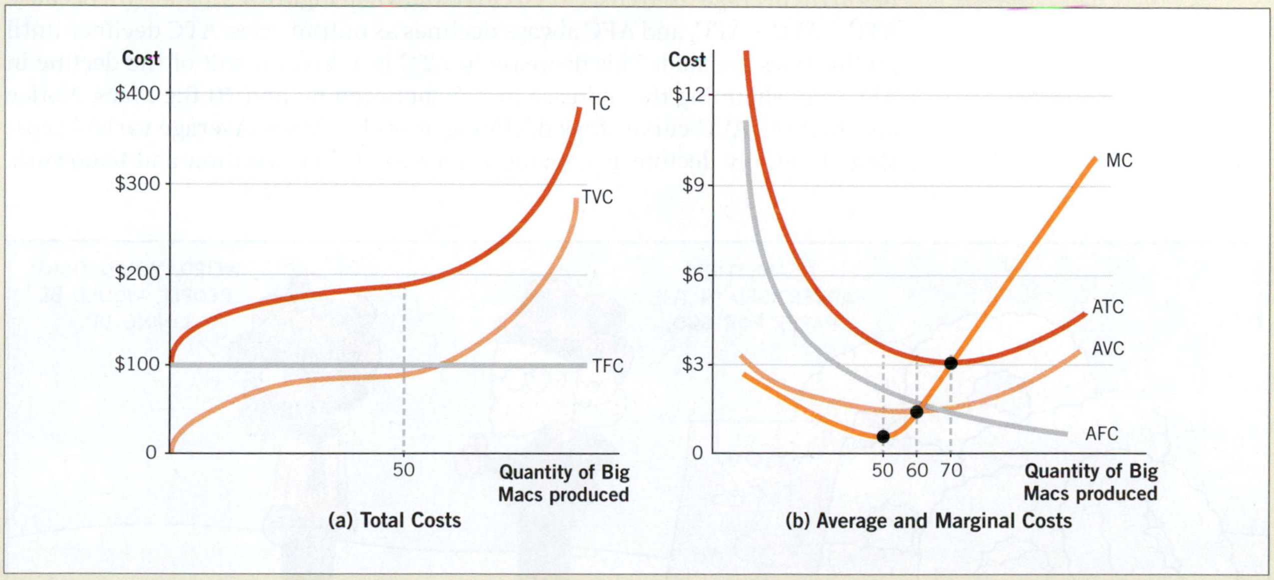

additional unit of output. (In column 8 of Table 8.3, this relationship is shown as the change in TVC divided by the change in quantity produced, where "change" is indicated by Δ [the Greek letter delta]).

(EQUATION 8.7) **marginal cost** = (cost of producing n units) − (cost of producing $n-1$ units)

For example, in planning the weekly work schedule, the manager has to consider how many workers to hire for each shift. She wants to hire additional workers when the cost of doing so is less than the expected boost in profits. In this situation, it is essential to know the marginal cost, or extra cost, of hiring one more worker.

In Table 8.3, marginal cost (MC) falls to a minimum of $1.00 when between 40 and 50 Big Macs are produced. Notice that the minimum MC occurs at a lower output level than average variable cost (AVC) and average total cost (ATC) in panel (b) of Figure 8.2. When output is less than 50 Big Macs, marginal cost is falling because over this range of production the marginal product of labor is increasing due to better teamwork and more specialization. After the fiftieth Big Mac, MC rises, acting as an early warning that average variable and total costs will soon follow suit. Why would a manager care about the marginal cost of the last few units being produced more than the average total cost of producing all the units? Because marginal cost helps the manager decide if making one more unit of output will increase profits or not!

Marginal thinking

The MC curve reaches its lowest point before the lowest point of the AVC and ATC curves. For this reason, a manager who is concerned about rising costs would look to the MC curve as a signal that average total cost will eventually increase as well. Once marginal cost begins to increase, it continues to pull down average variable cost until sales reach 60 Big Macs. After that point, MC is above AVC, and AVC begins to rise as well. However, ATC continues to fall until 70 Big Macs are sold. Note that the MC curve intersects the AVC and ATC curves at the minimum point along both curves.

Why does average total cost fall while MC and AVC are rising? The answer lies in the average fixed cost (AFC) curve shown in Figure 8.2, panel (b). Because ATC = AVC + AFC, and AFC always declines as output rises, ATC declines until 70 Big Macs are sold. This decrease in ATC is a direct result of the decline in AFC overwhelming the increase in AVC between 60 and 70 Big Macs. Notice also that the AVC curve stops declining at 60 Big Macs. Average variable cost should initially decline as a result of increased specialization and teamwork.

ECONOMICS in the MEDIA

Costs in the Short Run

RAMSAY'S KITCHEN NIGHTMARES

In this series, renowned chef Gordon Ramsay visits struggling restaurants and tries to help them turn things around. In one particularly memorable episode, Ramsay visits a fancy French restaurant in Scotland. He quickly discovers that no less than seven cooks make marginal changes to each dish before it is ready to be served. We see one cook trimming some fat, another adding a garnish, and so on, until the last cook carefully inspects the final product before it goes out. While each of the cooks contributes value, the head chef is oblivious to the cost of their labor and also to what all that extra prep time costs in terms of lost table rollover. You may have heard that too many cooks spoil the broth, but that's not the problem here. The cooks are all adding value—only, not enough to cover the cost of having them on the payroll. Too many cooks . . . means lower profits.

One chef is plenty—especially when it's Gordon Ramsay.

Marginal thinking

However, at some point the advantages of continued specialization are overtaken by diminishing marginal product, and average variable cost begins to rise. The transition from falling costs to rising costs is of particular interest because as long as average total cost is declining, the firm can lower its costs by increasing its output.

Once the marginal cost in Table 8.3 rises above the average total cost, the average total cost begins to rise as well. This result is evident if we compare the average total cost of making 70 Big Macs ($3.14) and 80 Big Macs ($3.25) with the marginal cost ($4.00) of making those extra 10 Big Macs. Since the marginal cost ($4.00) of making Big Macs 71 through 80 is higher than the average total cost at 70 ($3.14), the average total cost of making 80 Big Macs goes up (to $3.25).

Marginal cost always leads (or pulls) average variable cost and average total cost along. The MC eventually rises above the average total cost because of diminishing marginal product. Because the firm has to pay a fixed wage in our McDonald's example, the cost to produce each hamburger increases as each worker's output decreases.

Note that there is one "average" curve that the marginal cost does not affect: average fixed cost. Notice that the AFC curve in panel (b) of Figure 8.2 continues to fall even though marginal cost eventually rises. The AFC curve declines with increased output. Because McDonald's has $100.00 in fixed costs each day, we can determine the average fixed cost by dividing the total fixed cost ($100.00) by the number of Big Macs sold. When 10 Big Macs are sold, the average fixed cost is $10.00 per Big Mac, but this value falls to $1.00 per Big Mac if 100 burgers are sold. Because McDonald's is a high-volume business that relies on low costs to compete, being able to produce enough Big Macs to spread out the firm's fixed costs is essential.

Costs in the Long Run

We have seen that in the short run, businesses have fixed costs and fixed capacities. In the long run, all costs are variable and can be renegotiated. Thus, firms have more control over their costs in the long run, which enables them to reach their desired level of production. One way firms can adjust in the long run is by changing the **scale**, or size, of the production process. If the business is expected to grow, the firm can ramp up production. If the business is faltering, it can scale back its operations. This flexibility enables firms to avoid a situation of negative marginal product. Economists refer to the quantity of output that minimizes the average total cost in the long run as the **efficient scale**.

Scale
refers to the size of the production process.

The **efficient scale** is the output level that minimizes average total cost in the long run.

A long-run time horizon allows a business to choose a scale of operation that best suits its needs. For instance, if a local McDonald's is extremely popular, in the short run the manager can only hire more workers or expand the restaurant's hours to accommodate more customers. However, in the long run all costs are variable; the manager can add drive-through lanes, increase the number of registers, expand the grill area, and so on.

Building more than one house at a time would represent economies of scale.

The absence of fixed factors in the long-run production process means that we cannot explain total costs in the long run in the same way we explained short-run costs. Short-run costs are a reflection of diminishing marginal product, whereas long-run costs are a reflection of scale and the cost of providing additional output. Because diminishing marginal product is no longer relevant in the long run, one might assume that costs would fall as output expands. However, this is not necessarily the case. Depending on the industry and the prevailing economic conditions, long-run costs can rise, fall, or stay approximately the same.

THREE TYPES OF SCALE In this section, we describe three different scenarios for a firm in the long run. A firm may experience *economies of scale*, *diseconomies of scale*, or *constant returns to scale*. Let's consider each of these in turn.

If output expands and long-run average total costs decline in the long run, a business experiences **economies of scale**. National homebuilders, such as Toll Brothers, provide a good example of economies of scale. All builders, whether they are local or national, do the same thing—they build houses. Each builder needs lumber, concrete, excavators, electricians, plumbers, roofers, and many more specialized workers or subcontractors. A big company, such as Toll, is able to hire many specialists and also buy the equipment it needs in bulk. As a result, Toll can manufacture the same home as a local builder but at a much lower cost.

Economies of scale
occur when long-run average total costs decline as output expands.

But bigger isn't always better! Sometimes a company grows so large that coordination problems make costs rise. For example, as an enterprise expands its scale, it might require more managers, highly specialized workers, and a coordination process to pull everything together. As the layers of management expand, the coordination process can break down. For this reason, a larger firm can become less effective at holding down long-run average total costs and experience **diseconomies of scale**, or higher costs as output expands in the long run.

Would you rather see the ER's doctor du jour or your own physician?

The problem of diseconomies of scale is especially relevant in the service sector of the economy. For example, large regional hospitals have many layers of bureaucracy. These added management costs and infrastructure expenses can make medical care more expensive beyond a certain point. If you are not convinced, ask yourself why large cities have many smaller competing hospitals rather than one centralized hospital. The answer becomes obvious: bigger doesn't always mean less expensive (or better)!

When long-run average total costs remain constant even as output expands in the long run, we say that the firm has **constant returns to scale**. For example, large national restaurant chains like Panda Express, which specializes in Chinese cuisine, compete with local Chinese restaurants. In each case, the local costs to hire workers and build the restaurant are the same. Panda Express does have a few advantages; for example, it can afford to advertise on national television and buy food in bulk. But Panda Express also has more overhead costs for its many layers of management. Constant returns to scale in the bigger chain mean that a small local Chinese restaurant will have approximately the same menu prices as its bigger rivals.

Diseconomies of scale occur when long-run average total costs rise as output expands.

Constant returns to scale occur when long-run average total costs remain constant as output expands.

ECONOMICS IN THE REAL WORLD

ECONOMIES OF SCALE: BUC-EE'S

If you want proof that everything really *is* bigger in Texas, take a look at Buc-ee's, a chain of roadside convenience stores headquartered in the Lone Star State. Many locations have over 100 gasoline pumps. Inside each Buc-ee's you will find souvenirs, a BBQ station, a wall filled with sodas of all sorts, custom Buc-ee's clothing, and much more. The world's largest single convenience store is a Buc-ee's, with 68,000 square feet of floor space. The world's longest car wash, also at a Buc-ee's, treats customers to a 255-foot journey down the conveyer belt. That's only 45 feet short of a football field.

No one seems to mind all the hubbub. Quite the opposite: people are drawn to Buc-ee's because it's not like every other gas station/convenience store. Prices are reasonable, not outrageous. Buc-ee's was able to achieve economies of scale in its operation by making the road-trip-stop experience unique.

Everything's bigger in Texas!

LONG-RUN COST CURVES Now it is time to illustrate the long-run nature of cost curves. We have seen that increased output may not always lead to economies of scale. Average total costs can decline, be constant, or rise with output. Figure 8.3 illustrates each of the three scale possibilities graphically.

Will you find lower prices at Panda Express or your local Chinese restaurant?

The long-run average total cost curve (LRATC) is actually a composite of many short-run average total cost curves (SRATC), which appear as the faint U-shaped dashed curves drawn in gray. By visualizing the short-run cost curves at any given output level, we can develop a composite of them to create the LRATC curve, which comprises all the short-run cost curves the firm may choose to deploy in the long run. In the long run, the firm is free to choose any of its short-run curves, so it always picks the output/cost combination that minimizes costs.

In the long run, there are three distinct possibilities: economies of scale, constant returns to scale, and diseconomies of scale. At first, each LRATC curve exhibits economies of scale as a result of increased specialization, the utilization of mass production, bulk purchasing power, and increased automation. The main question in the long run is whether the cost curve will continue to decline, level off, or rise. In an industry with economies of scale at high output levels—for example, homebuilding—the cost curve continues to decline, and the most efficient output level is always the largest output: the purple curve in Figure 8.3. In this situation, we would expect only one large firm to dominate

FIGURE 8.3

Costs in the Long Run

In the long run, there are three distinct possibilities: the long-run average total cost curve (LRATC) can exhibit economies of scale (the purple curve), constant returns to scale (the red curve), or diseconomies of scale (the orange curve).

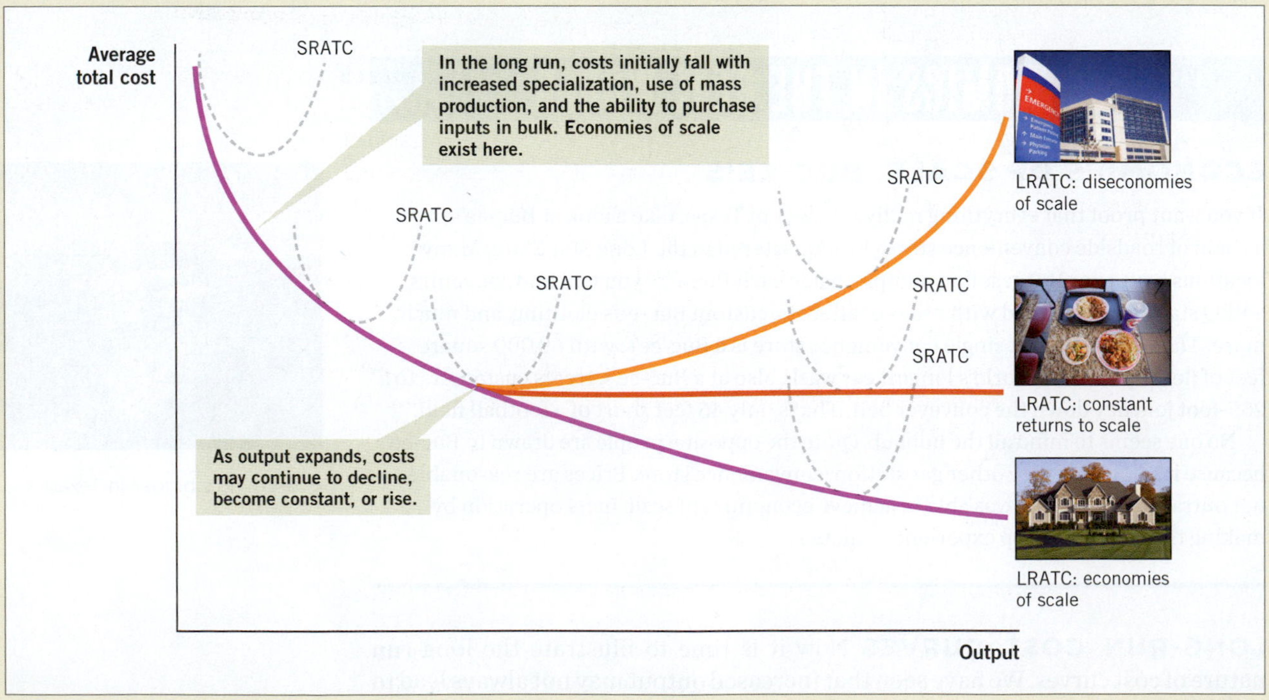

ECONOMICS *in the* MEDIA

Economies of Scale

THE BIG BANG THEORY: THE WORK SONG NANOCLUSTER

In an episode of the long-running TV series *The Big Bang Theory*, Penny decides to make flower barrettes in her spare time to supplement her pay as a waitress. When Sheldon stops by, she decides to take advantage of his analytical skills to help her with her business. What transpires can only be described as the best explanation of business costs you'll ever see.

As Sheldon explains to Penny: "If you took advantage of modern marketing techniques and optimized your manufacturing process, you might make this a viable business." They get to work and Sheldon starts timing how long it takes Penny to make a flower barrette. It takes her 12 minutes and 17 seconds, and Penny seems quite happy until Sheldon says, "That's 4.9 Penny Blossoms per hour. Based on your cost of materials and your wholesale selling price, you'll effectively be paying yourself $5.19 a day. There are children in a sneaker factory in Indonesia who outearn you." To increase Penny's productivity, he suggests they create an assembly line to lower the cost of manufacturing the barrettes, and they begin working together to make the Penny Blossoms, even singing a rhythmic work song to increase their productivity. Together they can now make each Penny Blossom in under 3 minutes!

Creating flower barrettes by hand in your apartment misses out on economies of scale.

At this point, Leonard, Howard, and Raj enter Penny's apartment and start to ask questions about what is going on. Everyone quickly realizes they will have to expand the scale of the operation to fully optimize the production process to lower costs even further. The result is that you see the production process evolve from a small-scale operation in Penny's apartment in the short run to a sophisticated large-scale enterprise in the long run. All of this is done in one very funny 22-minute episode.

Costs are defined in a number of ways, but marginal cost plays the most crucial role in a firm's cost structure. By observing what happens to marginal cost, you can understand changes in average cost and total cost. This simple fact explains why economists place so much emphasis on marginal cost. Going forward, a solid grasp of marginal analysis will help you understand many of the most important concepts in microeconomics.

Marginal thinking

You now understand the cost, or supply side, of business decisions. However, to provide a complete picture of how firms operate, we still need to examine how markets work. Costs are only part of the story, and in the next chapter we take a closer look at profits.

the industry because large firms have significant cost advantages. However, in an industry with constant returns to scale—for example, restaurants—the cost curve flattens out: the red line. Once the curve becomes constant, firms of varying sizes can compete equally with one another because they have the same costs. Finally, in the case of diseconomies of scale—for example, big-city hospitals—bigger firms have higher costs: the orange curve.

ECONOMICS IN THE REAL WORLD

ECONOMIES OF SCALE

Even when there are economies of scale, expanding isn't a guarantee of success. Costs are bound to increase, and they must be managed carefully. Also, marketing and distribution have to go smoothly to make sure that all that additional output actually generates additional sales revenue.

China's third-largest bike share company, Bluegogo, went out of business in 2017, when it expanded too rapidly and ran out of the cash needed to keep going. Bluegogo's chief executive said he had been "filled with arrogance" and believed that all they had to do was flood the market with bikes and people would use them.

Many firms mistakenly believe that expanding will make them more profitable. Bluegogo's two main rivals, Ofo and Mobike, followed the same strategy but survived because they generated more revenues. What does it look like when firms expand too rapidly? Check out this bicycle scrap pile, littered with broken shared bicycles that the companies would rather discard than fix.

Bike share graveyard in Xiamen, China, a testament to the perils of expanding too quickly.

PRACTICE WHAT YOU KNOW

Marginal Cost: The True Cost of Admission to Universal Studios

You and your family visit Orlando for a week. While there, you decide to go to Universal Studios. When you arrive, you notice that each family member can buy a day pass for $115 or a two-day pass for $150. Your parents are concerned about spending too much,

(CONTINUED)

so they decide to calculate the average cost of a two-day pass to see if it is a good value. The average cost is $150 ÷ 2, or $75 per day. Their math is correct, but something you learned in economics tells you they are not thinking about this situation in the correct way.

QUESTION: What concept can you apply to make the decision clearer?

ANSWER: Tell your parents about *marginal cost*. The first day costs $115, but the marginal cost of going back to the park on the second day is only the extra cost per person, or $150 − $115, which equals $35. Your parents still might not want to spend the extra money, but spending only an extra $35 for a second day makes it an attractive value. Someone who does not appreciate economics might think the second day costs an extra $75 because that is the average cost, but the average cost is misleading. Looking at marginal cost is the best way to weigh these two options. By the way, if you want a three-day pass the price is $170, making the marginal cost of the third day just $170 − $150, which equals $20. That sounds ridiculously low, but the incremental increase in the price is low because no matter how much you like Harry Potter, a third straight day in the same theme park becomes repetitive quickly.

Is one day enough to see Hogwarts?

Marginal thinking

CHALLENGE QUESTION: Suppose you are considering a single-day three-park pass to Universal Studios, Islands of Adventure, and Volcano Bay. The price for the three-park pass is $170. If you value Universal Studios at $140, Islands of Adventure at $30, and Volcano Bay at $20, should you buy the three-park pass instead of the single-day pass to just Universal Studios?

ANSWER: The total value of the three-park pass to you is $140 + $30 + $20 = $190, which is more than enough to justify the expense of the park hopper ticket ($170), since you'd earn $20 in consumer surplus. However, you'd earn more consumer surplus if you purchased the day pass to just Universal Studios, since $140 − $115 = $25 in consumer surplus. That means you are better off sticking just with Universal Studios, since the price of the three-park pass provides less consumer surplus.

Conclusion

Do larger firms have lower costs? Not always. When diseconomies of scale occur, average total costs will rise with output. This result contradicts the common misconception that bigger firms have lower costs than their smaller competitors. Simply put, sometimes a leaner firm with less overhead can beat its larger rivals on cost. ✷

· ECONOMICS *for* LIFE ·

"The Family Firm": How Much Does It Cost to Raise a Child?

- Raising a child costs about $250,000.
- Families that have three or more children spend an average of 22% less on each child.
- These costs force trade-offs.
- Consider using a "mission-first" approach to make decisions.

Opportunity cost

Raising a child is one of life's most rewarding experiences, but it can be very expensive. According to the U.S. Department of Agriculture, the cost for a middle-income, two-parent family to raise a child from birth to age 18 is about $250,000 (not including college). That includes everything from food, clothing, and medical care to entertainment and a share of the family home and vehicles. For perspective, the median U.S. home value in 2021 was $275,000.

What if a family has more than one child? You wouldn't necessarily multiply the cost by 2 or 3, because there are economies of scale in raising more children. For example, the children might share a bedroom and wear hand-me-downs. Also, the family can purchase food in bulk. Families that have three or more children manage to spend an average of 22% less on each child.

Trade-offs

The cost of raising children also forces families to make trade-offs. In many households, both parents must work, or work longer hours. When one parent steps out of the workforce, the household loses a paycheck. In addition, time away from the workplace lowers the stay-at-home parent's future earning power.

Raising a child is an expensive proposition in both the short run and the long run. But don't let this discourage you; it is also one of the most rewarding personal investments you will ever make. More importantly, there are large benefits to society as well, as economist Nancy Folbre, author of *Valuing Children: Rethinking the Economics of the Family,* notes. "When you raise children, they grow up to become workers and taxpayers and participants in an economic system that reproduces itself over time." This has large implications for how the costs of raising children should be distributed among parents and society.

In the TV show *One Day at a Time* (2017–2020), Penelope Alvarez navigates the challenges of being a single mother.

Emily Oster, economist and author of *The Family Firm,* adds that the "mission-first" or "values-driven" approach that small businesses often use when making decisions can also help tackle and prioritize the many questions and decisions that families face. Especially as children age and decisions can become more complicated, families need to take a more business-like approach. Oster emphasizes that parents should think about how even small daily decisions have major impacts on the family's overall goals. These decisions need to be made with the big picture in mind. Oster notes in one interview about the book: "We sometimes make small decisions thinking, 'Oh, that's just a small decision, you know, oh, I'm going to let my kid [play] soccer. And that's just a little thing.' But then sometimes you wake up and you realize that four nights a week you're sitting at the soccer field watching your kid play soccer when actually you'd like to be sitting down for family dinner." In other words, it's far better to weigh the full implications of each choice up front and see if this supports the goals of the family as a whole.*

*Nancy Folbre, *Valuing Children: Rethinking the Economics of the Family* (Cambridge, MA: Harvard University Press, 2010); Emily Oster, *The Family Firm: A Data-Driven Guide to Better Decision Making in the Early School Years* (New York: Penguin Press, 2021); Elise Hu, "Get Your Family Running More Smoothly with Tricks from Running Small Businesses," Life Kit, NPR, August 9, 2021, https://www.npr.org/2021/08/06/1025447008/emily-oster-the-family-firm-decision-making-parenting.

· ANSWERING *the* BIG QUESTIONS ·

How are profits and losses calculated?

- Profits and losses are determined by calculating the difference between expenses (total cost) and total revenue.
- There are two types of profit: economic profit and accounting profit. If a business has an economic profit, its revenue is larger than the combination of its explicit and implicit costs.
- Economists break costs into two components: explicit costs, which are easy to calculate, and implicit costs, which are hard to calculate. Because economic profit accounts for implicit costs, the economic profit is always less than the accounting profit.

How much should a firm produce?

- A firm should produce an output that is consistent with the largest possible economic profit.
- To maximize profit, firms must effectively combine land, labor, and capital in the right quantities.
- In any short-run production process, a point of diminishing marginal product will occur at which additional units of a variable input no longer generate as much output as before. Diminishing marginal product is a result of fixed inputs (such as capital and land) in the short run.
- Marginal cost (MC) is the key variable in determining a firm's cost structure. The MC curve always leads the average total cost (ATC) and average variable cost (AVC) curves up or down.

What costs do firms consider in the short run and the long run?

- In the short run, firms consider variable and fixed costs, as well as marginal cost. Firms also consider average variable cost (AVC), average fixed cost (AFC), and average total cost (ATC).
- With the exception of the average fixed cost (AFC) curve, which always declines, short-run cost curves are U-shaped. All variable costs initially decline due to increased specialization. At a certain point, the advantages of continued specialization give way to diminishing marginal product, and the MC, AVC, and ATC curves begin to rise.
- Long-run costs are a reflection of scale. Firms can experience diseconomies of scale, economies of scale, or constant returns to scale, depending on the industry.

CHAPTER PROBLEMS

Concepts You Should Know

accounting profit (p. 254)
average fixed cost (AFC) (p. 264)
average total cost (ATC) (p. 264)
average variable cost (AVC) (p. 264)
constant returns to scale (p. 269)
diminishing marcginal product (p. 260)
diseconomies of scale (p. 269)
economic profit (p. 255)
economies of scale (p. 268)
efficient scale (p. 268)
explicit costs (p. 253)
factors of production (p. 257)
fixed costs (p. 263)
implicit costs (p. 253)
loss (p. 253)
marginal cost (MC) (p. 265)
marginal product (p. 258)
output (p. 257)
production function (p. 258)
profit (p. 252)
scale (p. 268)
total cost (p. 252)
total revenue (p. 252)
variable costs (p. 262)

Questions for Review

1. What is the equation for the profit (or loss) of a firm?
2. Why is economic profit a better measure of profitability than accounting profit? Give an example.
3. What role does diminishing marginal product play in determining the ideal mix of labor and capital a firm should use?
4. Describe what happens to the total product of a firm when marginal product is increasing, decreasing, and negative.
5. Explain why marginal cost is the glue that connects average variable cost and average total cost.
6. Compare the short-run and long-run cost curves. In a few sentences, explain their differences.
7. Name examples of industries that illustrate each of the following: economies of scale, constant returns to scale, and diseconomies of scale. Think creatively; do not use the textbook examples.

Study Problems *(✱ solved at the end of this section)*

1. The following table shows a short-run production function for laptop computers. Use the data to determine where diminishing product begins.

Number of workers	Total output of laptop computers
0	0
1	40
2	100
3	150
4	180
5	200
6	205
7	200
8	190

2. A street vendor who sells churros has the cost structure described below. The firm's fixed costs are $25 per day. Calculate the firm's average fixed costs, average variable costs, average total costs, and marginal costs.

Output (churros per day)	Total cost of output
0	$25
100	75
200	115
300	150
400	175
500	190
600	205
700	225
800	250

* **3.** A firm is considering changing its plant size, so it calculates the average cost of production for various plant sizes, shown below. If the firm is currently using plant size C, is the firm experiencing economies of scale, diseconomies of scale, or constant returns to scale?

Plant size	Average total cost
A (smallest)	$10,000
B	9,500
C	9,000
D	8,800
E	8,800
F (largest)	8,900

4. True or false?

a. The AFC curve can never rise.
b. Diminishing marginal product is a long-run constraint that prevents lower costs.
c. The MC curve intersects the AVC and ATC curves at the minimum point along both curves.
d. Accounting profit is smaller than economic profit.
e. Total cost divided by output is equal to marginal cost.

5. Digital media distributed over the Internet often have marginal costs of zero. For instance, people can download music and movies instantly through many providers. Do these products exhibit economies, diseconomies, or constant returns to scale?

6. An airline has a marginal cost per passenger of $30 on a route from Boston to Detroit. At the same time, the typical fare charged is $300. The planes that fly the route are usually full, yet the airline claims that it loses money on the route. How is this possible?

7. Many amusement parks offer two-day passes at dramatically discounted prices. If a one-day pass costs $40 but the two-day pass costs $50, what is the average cost for the two-day pass? What is the marginal cost of the second day pass?

* **8.** Suppose that you own a yard care business. You have your own mower, flatbed truck, and other equipment. You are also the primary employee. Why might you have trouble calculating your profits? (**Hint:** Think about the difference between accounting profits and economic profits.)

9. Use the information provided in the following table to fill in the blanks.

Output	Total fixed cost	Total variable cost	Total Fixed cost	Average fixed cost	Average variable cost	Average total cost	Marginal cost
0	$500	$0	$500	____	____	____	
1	500	200	____	____	____	____	____
2	____	____	800	____	____	____	____
3	____	____	875	____	____	____	____
4	____	____	925	____	____	____	$25
5	____	____	____	$100	____	____	____
6	____	450	____	____	____	____	____

10. If you are a fan of cold dessert treats, you'll recognize that the production process at Cold Stone Creamery differs a great deal from frozen yogurt places. At Cold Stone you give the server your order and the mix-ins you want, and the server creates your treat for you. This process is labor intensive. At a frozen yogurt place, you pick up a cup, choose your flavor from the self-serve machine, serve it yourself, and add in your own mix-ins. You put your creation on a scale and the worker then rings you up. This process is capital intensive. Given this information, which type of frozen dessert business will have the lower marginal cost of production?

11. Take a look at the table in Problem 9. What is happening to the marginal cost as more and more units are produced? Can you think of an industry where this might be expected?

✷ **12.** All else equal, when the marginal product of labor is falling, the marginal cost of producing output

a. is falling.
b. is rising.
c. could be rising or falling.

Solved Problems

3. The key to solving this problem is recognizing the direction of change in the average total cost. If the firm were to switch to a smaller plant, like B, its average total cost would rise to $9,500. Because the smaller plant would cost more, plant C is currently enjoying economies of scale. When we compare the average total cost of C ($9,000) to D ($8,800), it continues to fall. Because the average total cost is falling from B to D, we again know that the firm is experiencing economies of scale.

8. When calculating your costs for the mower, truck, and other expenses, you are computing your explicit costs. Subtracting the explicit costs from your total revenue will yield the accounting profit you have earned. However, you still do not know your economic profit because you haven't determined your implicit costs. Because you are the primary employee, you also have to add in the opportunity cost of the time you invest in the business. You may not know exactly what you might have earned doing something else, but you can be sure it exists—this is your implicit cost. Implicit costs are the reason you may have trouble computing your profits. You might show an accounting profit only to discover that what you thought you made was less than you could have made by doing something else. If that is the case, your true economic profit is actually negative.

12. When the marginal product of labor is falling, the marginal cost of production is rising, since each worker is becoming less productive and therefore each unit requires more labor to produce.

CHAPTER

09

Firms in a Competitive Market

Why Do Firms Charge the Price They Do?

You want to send your mom flowers for Mother's Day, but when you check out the price of an arrangement from your favorite local florist, Doug's Flower Cottage, you have an attack of sticker shock. Why in the world are flowers so expensive?

Let's consider things from Doug's point of view, though. Growing flowers is labor-intensive, since they must be carefully tended and then harvested by hand. Being highly perishable, they then must be shipped rapidly, under refrigeration, to the point of sale. Doug must charge enough to cover all the costs associated with getting the flowers to his shop. He then must cover the expense of storing the flowers, again under refrigeration, and the spoilage loss of those that go unsold. Doug also must pay the staff he relies on to market, design, and sell arrangements and deliver them on time. So while flower delivery might seem expensive to the consumer, Doug is just charging the market rate and can't go lower, due to his many behind-the-scenes costs. He might wish he could charge more, but since there are many florists, all of whom sell essentially the same services, competition drives prices down, which limits any one firm's ability to charge as much as it would like.

Such a lovely sight! But a lot of money probably went into this gorgeous display. These flowers may well have been grown in Colombia or Ecuador, the main foreign suppliers to the U.S. flower market. Getting them to the shop was not cheap.

In this chapter and the next four, we look in more detail at how markets work, the profits firms earn, and how market forces determine the price a firm can charge for its product or service. We begin our examination of *market structure*, or how individual firms are interconnected, by looking at the conditions necessary to create a competitive market. Although few real markets achieve the ideal market structure described in this chapter, this model provides a good starting point for understanding other market structures.

Our analysis of competitive markets shows that when competition is widespread, firms have little or no control over the price they can charge, and they make little or no economic profit. Thus, in competitive markets, firms are completely at the mercy of market forces that set the price. Let's find out why.

• BIG QUESTIONS •

- How do competitive markets work?
- How do firms maximize profits?
- What does the supply curve look like in perfectly competitive markets?

How Do Competitive Markets Work?

Competitive markets exist when there are so many buyers and sellers that each one has only a small impact on the market price and output. Recall that in Chapter 3 we used the example of the Pike Place Market, where each fish vendor sells similar products. Because each fish vendor is small relative to the whole market, no single firm can influence the market price. It doesn't matter where you buy salmon because the price is the same or very similar at every fish stall. When buyers are willing to purchase a product anywhere, sellers have no control over the price they charge. These two characteristics—similar goods and many participants—create a highly competitive market where the price and quantity sold are determined by the market conditions rather than by any one firm.

In competitive markets, buyers can expect to find consistently low prices and a wide availability of the good they want. Firms that produce goods in competitive markets are known as price takers. A **price taker** has no control over the price set by the market. It "takes"—that is, accepts—the price determined by the overall supply and demand conditions that regulate the market. One of the reasons why firms are price takers is that each seller is small compared to the overall market. This means that any individual seller's decision (to either increase or decrease production) has no impact on the market price.

A **price taker** has no control over the price set by the market. It "takes" (accepts) the price determined from the overall supply and demand conditions that regulate the market.

Competitive markets have another important feature: new competitors can easily enter the market. If you want to open a copy shop, all you have to do is rent store space and several copy machines. There are no licensing or regulatory obstacles in your way. Likewise, there is very little to stop competitors from leaving the market. If you decide to shut down your business, you can lock the doors, return the equipment you rented, and move on to do something else. When barriers to entry into a marketplace are low, new firms are free to compete with existing businesses, which ensures the existence of competitive markets and low prices. Table 9.1 summarizes the characteristics of competitive markets.

Real-life examples of competitive markets usually fall short of perfection. Markets that are almost perfectly competitive, shown in Table 9.2, include the stock market, farmers' markets, online ticket auctions, and currency trading. Of all the market structures, perfect competition has the most benefits to society, because it maximizes combined consumer surplus and producer surplus (as we saw in Chapter 5). The more imperfectly competitive a market is, the lower is the total of the two types of surplus and the less beneficial it is to society overall.

In the next section, we examine the profits competitive firms make. After all, profits motivate firms to produce a product, so knowing how a business can make the most profit is central to understanding how competitive markets work.

TABLE 9.1

Characteristics of Competitive Markets

- Many sellers
- Similar products
- Free entry and exit
- Price taking
- Every firm is small

TABLE 9.2

Almost Perfect Markets

Example	How it works	Reality check
Stock market 	Millions of shares of stocks are traded every day on various stock exchanges, and generally the buyers and sellers have access to real-time information about prices. Because most of the traders represent only a small share of the market, they have little ability to influence the market price.	Because of the volume of shares that they control, large institutional investors, like Pacific Investment Management Company (PIMCO), manage billions of dollars in funds. As a result, they are big enough to influence the market price.
Farmers' markets 	In farmers' markets, sellers are able to set up at little or no cost. Many buyers are also present. The gathering of numerous buyers and sellers of similar products causes the market price for similar products to converge toward a single price.	Many produce markets do not have enough sellers to achieve a perfectly competitive result. With fewer vendors, individual sellers can often set their prices higher.
Online ticket auctions 	The resale market for tickets to major sporting events and concerts involves many buyers and sellers. The prices for seats in identical sections end up converging quickly toward a narrow range.	Some ticket companies and fans get special privileges that enable them to buy and sell blocks of tickets before others can enter the market.
Currency trading 	Hundreds of thousands of traders around the globe engage in currency buying and selling on any given day. Because all traders have very good real-time information, currency trades in different parts of the world converge toward the same price.	Currency markets are subject to intervention on the part of governments that want to strategically alter the prevailing price of their currency.

ECONOMICS IN THE REAL WORLD

AALSMEER FLOWER AUCTION

The world's largest flower auction takes place in Aalsmeer, a small town in the Netherlands. Each week, producers sell over 100 million flowers there. In fact, over one-third of all the flowers sold in the world pass through Aalsmeer. Because the Aalsmeer market serves thousands of buyers and sellers, it is one of the best examples of a competitive market you will ever find. The supply comes from approximately 6,000 growers worldwide. More than 2,000 buyers attend the auction to purchase flowers.

Aalsmeer uses a method known as a Dutch auction to determine the price for each crate of flowers sold. Most people think of an auction as a situation in which two or more individuals try to outbid each other. However, in Aalsmeer that process is reversed. As each crate of flowers goes on sale, the price on a huge board starts at 100 euros and then goes down until the lot is sold. This special kind of auction was invented here, and it is a very efficient way of getting the highest price out of the buyer who wants the lot the most.

At Aalsmeer, individual buyers and sellers are small compared with the overall size of the market. In addition, the flowers offered by one seller are almost indistinguishable from those offered by the other sellers. As a result, individual buyers and sellers have no control over the price set by the market.

The Aalsmeer flower market is almost perfectly competitive.

How Do Firms Maximize Profits?

All firms, whether they are active in a competitive market or not, attempt to maximize profits. Making a profit requires that a firm have a thorough grasp of its costs and revenues. In the previous chapter, we learned about the firm's cost structure. In this section, we examine its revenues. Combining the firm's revenues with its costs enables us to determine how much profit the firm makes.

Profits are a key goal of almost every firm, but they don't always materialize. Sometimes, firms experience losses instead of profits, so we also explore whether a firm should shut down or continue to operate in order to minimize its losses. Once we fully understand the firm's decision-making process, we will better comprehend how the entire market functions. To make this process

PRACTICE WHAT YOU KNOW

Price Takers: Your Local Food Truck Lot

Your instructor asks you to find an example of a competitive market nearby. Your friend suggests that you consider a food truck lot near your campus.

QUESTION: Do the food trucks each meet the definition of a price taker, thereby signaling a competitive market?

ANSWER: A lot full of food trucks is a lot full of choices. Whether it's burgers, BBQ, or chicken; Mexican, Chinese, Thai, or Indian food; grilled, steamed, or deep-fried—you name it, and there's probably a truck that has it. But typically, the prices are all pretty comparable. A single serving of burger and fries will cost about the same as chicken pad Thai. Is this enough to make a food truck a price taker? Not quite. Each truck has some market power, because it serves different food, enabling the more popular vendors to charge somewhat more.

While the trucks are not price takers, the drinks (both fountain drinks and bottled water) that they sell are essentially the same. Any customer who is only interested in getting something to drink has a highly competitive market to choose from.

Are these food trucks price takers?

ECONOMICS *in the* MEDIA

Competitive Markets

THE SIMPSONS: MR. PLOW

Homer's great idea is about to melt away.

In this episode, Homer buys a snowplow and goes into the snow removal business. After a few false starts, his business, Mr. Plow, becomes a huge success. Every snowy morning, he looks out the window and comments about "white gold."

The episode illustrates each of the factors that go into making a competitive market. Businesses providing snow removal all offer the same service. Because there are many buyers (homeowners) and many businesses (the "plow people"), the market is competitive.

However, Homer's joy, profits, and notoriety are short-lived. Soon his friend Barney buys a bigger plow and joins the ranks of the "plow people." Barney's entry into the business shows how easy it is for competitors to enter the market. Then Homer, who has begun to get lazy and rest on his success, wakes up late one snowy morning to find all the driveways in the neighborhood already plowed. A nasty battle over customers ensues.

When firms can easily enter the market, any positive economic profit a firm enjoys in the short run will dissipate in the long run, due to increased competition. As a result, we can say that this *Simpsons* episode shows a market that is not just competitive; it is perfectly competitive.

easier, throughout this section we refer to Mr. Plow (from the *Simpsons* episode mentioned in the Economics in the Media box above) to examine the choices every business must make. We look at the price Mr. Plow (Homer Simpson) charges and how many driveways he clears, and then we compare his revenues to his costs to determine whether he is maximizing his profit.

The Profit-Maximizing Rule

Let's imagine how much revenue Mr. Plow will make if the competitive price is \$10 for each driveway he clears. Table 9.3 shows how much profit he might make if he clears up to 10 driveways. As we learned in Chapter 8, total profit (column 4) is determined by taking the total revenue (column 2) and subtracting the total cost (column 3). Mr. Plow's profits start out at −\$25 because even if he does not clear any driveways, he incurs a fixed cost of \$25 to rent a snowplow each day. To recover the fixed cost, he needs to generate revenue by clearing driveways. As Mr. Plow clears more driveways, the losses (the negative numbers) shown in column 4 gradually contract; he begins to earn a profit by the time he plows 6 driveways.

What does Table 9.3 tell us about Mr. Plow's business? Column 4 shows the company's profits (π) at various output (Q) levels. Profit reaches a maximum of \$10 at 8 driveways. From looking at this table, you might suppose that the firm can make a production decision based on the data in the profit column. However, firms don't work this way. The total profit (or loss) is typically determined after the fact. For example, Homer may have to fill up with gas at the end of the day, buy new tires for his plow, or purchase liability insurance. His accountant will take his receipts and deduct each expense to determine his accounting profit. This process takes time. An accurate understanding of Homer's profits may have to wait until the end of the quarter, or even the year, in order to fully account for all the irregular expenses associated with running a business. This means that the information found in the profit column is not available until long after the business decisions have been made. So, in day-to-day operations, the firm needs another way to make production decisions.

The key to determining Mr. Plow's profits comes from understanding the relationship between marginal revenue (column 5) and marginal cost (column 6). The **marginal revenue** is the change (Δ) in total revenue when the firm produces one additional unit of output. So, looking down column 5, we see that for every driveway Mr. Plow clears, he makes \$10 in extra revenue. The marginal cost (column 6) is the change (Δ) in total cost when the firm produces one additional unit. Column 7 calculates the difference between the marginal revenue (column 5) and marginal cost (column 6).

Marginal thinking

Marginal revenue is the change in total revenue a firm receives when it produces one additional unit of output.

In Chapter 8, we saw that to understand cost structure, a firm focuses on marginal cost. The same is true on the revenue side. To make a good decision on the level of investment, Mr. Plow must use marginal analysis. Looking at column 7, we see that for output levels at or below 8, MR − MC is positive, as

TABLE 9.3

Calculating Profits for Mr. Plow

(1)	(2)	(3)	(4)	(5)	(6)	(7)
Quantity (Q = driveways cleared)	Total revenue	Total cost	Total profit	Marginal revenue	Marginal cost	Change (Δ) in profit
Abbreviation:	TR	TC	π	MR	MC	$\Delta\pi$
Formula:	P × Q		TR − TC	ΔTR	ΔTC	MR − MC
0	\$0	\$25	−\$25			
				\$10	\$9	\$1
1	10	34	−24			
				10	7	3
2	20	41	−21			
				10	5	5
3	30	46	−16			
				10	3	7
4	40	49	−9			
				10	2	8
5	50	51	−1			
				10	3	7
6	60	54	6			
				10	7	3
7	70	61	9			
				10	9	1
8	80	70	10			
				10	25	−15
9	90	95	−5			
				10	50	−40
10	100	145	−45			

indicated by the numbers in green. Expanding output to 8 driveways adds to profits. But as Mr. Plow services more driveways, the marginal cost rises dramatically. For instance, Mr. Plow may have to seek driveways farther away and thus incur higher transportation costs for those additional customers. Whatever the cause, increased marginal cost (column 6) eventually overtakes the constant marginal revenue (column 5), causing MR − MC to go negative (shown in red in column 7).

If you already own a truck and a plow, starting your own snowplow business is inexpensive.

Recall that we began our discussion by saying that a firm can't wait for the yearly, or even quarterly, profit statements to make production decisions. By examining the marginal impact, shown in column 7, a firm can make good day-to-day operational decisions. Each time it snows, Mr. Plow has to decide whether or not to clear more driveways. For instance, if he is plowing 4 driveways, he may decide to work a little harder the next time it snows and plow one more. At 5 driveways, his profits increase by $8. Since he enjoys making this extra money, he could expand again from 5 to 6 driveways. This time, he makes an extra $7 in profit. From 6 to 7 driveways, he earns $3 more in profit, and from 7 to 8 driveways he earns $1 in profit. However, when Mr. Plow expands beyond 8 driveways, he discovers that at 9 driveways he loses $15. This loss would cause him to scale back his efforts to a more profitable level of output.

Marginal thinking

Marginal thinking helps Mr. Plow discover the production level at which his profits are maximized. The **profit-maximizing rule** states that profit maximization occurs when a firm expands output as long as marginal revenue is greater than marginal cost, stopping as close to MR = MC as practical. According to the MR = MC rule, production should stop at the point at which profit opportunities no longer exist. In the case of Mr. Plow, he should stop adding new driveways once he reaches 8.

The **profit-maximizing rule** states that profit maximization occurs when a firm chooses the quantity of output that equates marginal revenue and marginal cost, or MR = MC.

Deciding How Much to Produce in a Competitive Market

We have observed that a firm in a highly competitive market is a price taker; it has no control over the price set by the market. Because all snow removal companies provide the same service, they must charge the price determined by the overall supply and demand conditions that regulate that particular market.

To better understand these relationships, we can look at them visually. In Figure 9.1, we use the MR and MC data from Table 9.3 to illustrate the profit calculation. For reference, we also include the average total cost curve. Recall from Chapter 8 that the marginal cost curve (MC, shown in orange) always crosses the average total cost curve (ATC) at the lowest point. Figure 9.1 illustrates the relationship between the marginal cost curve (MC) and the marginal revenue curve (MR). Because the price (P) Mr. Plow charges is constant at $10, marginal revenue is horizontal. Unlike MR, MC at first decreases and then rises due to diminishing marginal product. Therefore, the firm wants to expand production as long as MR is greater than MC, and it will stop production at the quantity where MR = MC = $10. When Q = 8, MR = MC and profits are maximized. At quantities beyond 8, the MC curve is above the MR curve. Marginal cost is higher than marginal revenue, and the firm's profits fall.

FIGURE 9.1

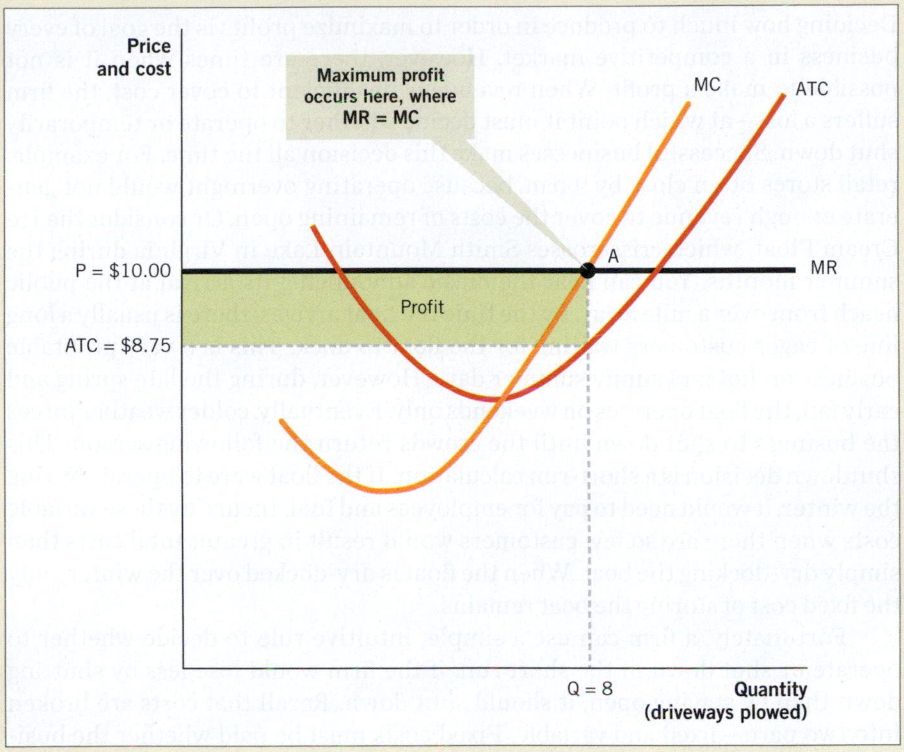

Profit Maximization

Mr. Plow uses the profit-maximizing rule to locate the point at which marginal revenue equals marginal cost, or MR = MC. This point determines the ideal output level, Q. The firm takes the price from the market; price is shown as the horizontal MR curve at P = $10.00. Because the price charged is higher than the average total cost curve along the dashed line at quantity Q, the firm makes the economic profit shown in the green rectangle.

Note that we can use the profit-maximizing rule, MR = MC, to identify the most profitable output in a two-step process:

1. Locate the point at which the firm will maximize its profits: MR = MC. This is the point labeled A in Figure 9.1.
2. Look for the profit-maximizing output: move down the vertical dashed line to the *x* axis at point Q. Any quantity greater than or less than Q would result in lower profits.

Once we know the profit-maximizing quantity, we can determine the average cost of producing Q units. From Q, we move up along the dashed line until it intersects with the ATC curve. From that point, we move horizontally until we come to the *y* axis. Doing so tells us the average cost of making 8 units. Because the total cost in Table 9.3 is $70 when 8 driveways are plowed, dividing 70 by 8 gives us $8.75 for the average total cost. We can calculate Mr. Plow's profit rectangle from Figure 9.1 as follows:

$$\text{profit} = (\text{price} - \text{ATC [along the dashed line at quantity Q]}) \times \text{Q}$$

This equation gives us $(10 - 8.75) \times 8 = \$10$, which is the profit we see in Table 9.3, column 4, in red. Because the MR is the price, and because the price is higher than the average total cost, the firm makes the profit visually represented in the green rectangle.

The Firm in the Short Run

Deciding how much to produce in order to maximize profits is the goal of every business in a competitive market. However, there are times when it is not possible to make a profit. When revenue is insufficient to cover cost, the firm suffers a loss—at which point it must decide whether to operate or temporarily shut down. Successful businesses make this decision all the time. For example, retail stores often close by 9 p.m. because operating overnight would not generate enough revenue to cover the costs of remaining open. Or consider the Ice Cream Float, which crisscrosses Smith Mountain Lake in Virginia during the summer months. You can hear the music announcing its arrival at the public beach from over a mile away. By the time the float arrives, there is usually a long line of eager customers waiting for the float to dock. This is a very profitable business on hot and sunny summer days. However, during the late spring and early fall, the float operates on weekends only. Eventually, colder weather forces the business to shut down until the crowds return the following season. This shutdown decision is a short-run calculation. If the float were to operate during the winter, it would need to pay for employees and fuel. Incurring these variable costs when there are so few customers would result in greater total costs than simply dry-docking the boat. When the float is dry-docked over the winter, only the fixed cost of storing the boat remains.

Fortunately, a firm can use a simple, intuitive rule to decide whether to operate or shut down in the short run: if the firm would lose less by shutting down than by staying open, it should shut down. Recall that costs are broken into two parts—fixed and variable. Fixed costs must be paid whether the business is open or not. Because variable costs are incurred only when the business is open, if it can make enough to cover its variable costs—for example, employee wages and the cost of the electricity needed to run the lighting—it will choose to remain open. Once the variable costs are covered, any extra money goes toward paying the fixed costs.

A business should operate if it can cover its variable costs, and it should shut down if it cannot. Figure 9.2 illustrates the decision using cost curves. As long as the firm's marginal revenue curve (MR) is greater than the minimum point on the average variable cost curve (AVC)—the green and yellow areas—the firm will choose to operate. (Note that the MR curve is not shown in Figure 9.2. The shaded areas in the figure denote the range of potential MR curves that are profitable and those that cause a loss.) Recalling our example of the Ice Cream Float, you can think of the green area as the months during the summer when the business makes a profit and the yellow area as the times during spring and fall when the float operates even though it is incurring a loss (because the loss is less than if the float were to shut down entirely). Finally, if the MR curve falls below the AVC curve—the red area—the firm should shut down. Table 9.4 summarizes these decisions.

The Ice Cream Float, a cool idea on a hot day at the lake.

To make the shutdown decision more concrete, imagine that the Ice Cream Float's minimum ATC (average total cost) is $2.50 and its minimum AVC is $2.00. During the summer, when many customers line up on the dock waiting for it to arrive, it can charge more than $2.50 and earn a substantial profit. However, as the weather cools,

FIGURE 9.2

When to Operate and When to Shut Down

If the MR (marginal revenue) curve is above the minimum point on the ATC (average total cost) curve, the Ice Cream Float will make a profit (shown in green). If the MR curve is below the minimum point on the ATC curve ($2.50) but above the minimum point on the AVC (average variable cost) curve ($2.00), the float will operate at a loss (shown in yellow). If the MR curve is below the minimum point on the AVC curve ($2.00), the float will temporarily shut down (shown in red).

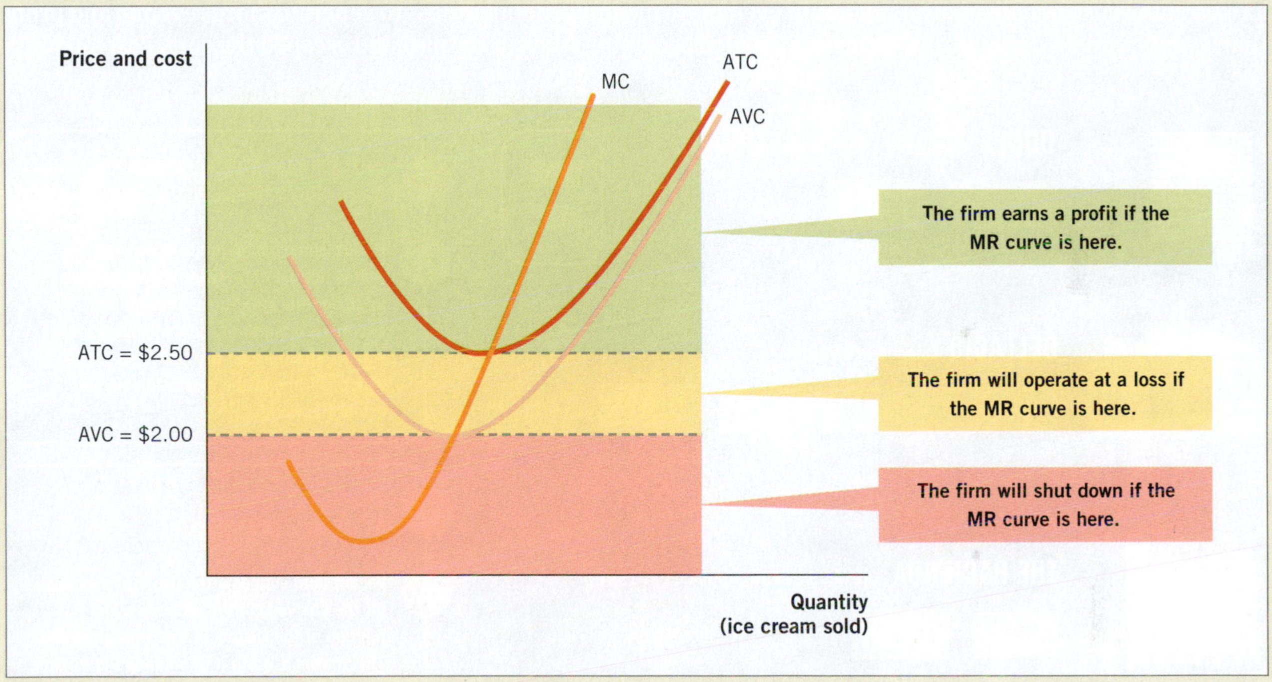

TABLE 9.4

Profit and Loss in the Short Run

Condition	In words	Outcome
P > ATC	The price is greater than the average total cost of production.	The firm makes a profit.
ATC > P > AVC	The average total cost of production is greater than the price the firm charges, but the price is greater than the average variable cost of production.	The firm will operate to minimize loss.
AVC > P	The price is less than the average variable cost of production.	The firm will temporarily shut down.

DATA SNAPSHOT

The Sunk Cost Fallacy

Have you ever wondered why buildings that are structurally stable are imploded? Look no further than Las Vegas, a city in the middle of nowhere that now attracts 40 million visitors a year. In order to keep up, Las Vegas must continually reinvent itself. That's why old casinos regularly make way for new ones—that, and the fact that newer casinos generate way more revenue than legacy hotels. Rather than keeping older structures, Las Vegas developers looked at the cost-benefit analysis and built even more magnificent buildings* to generate more revenue and profits than ever before. In doing so, Las Vegas has avoided becoming stuck in the past and escaped the sunk cost fallacy.

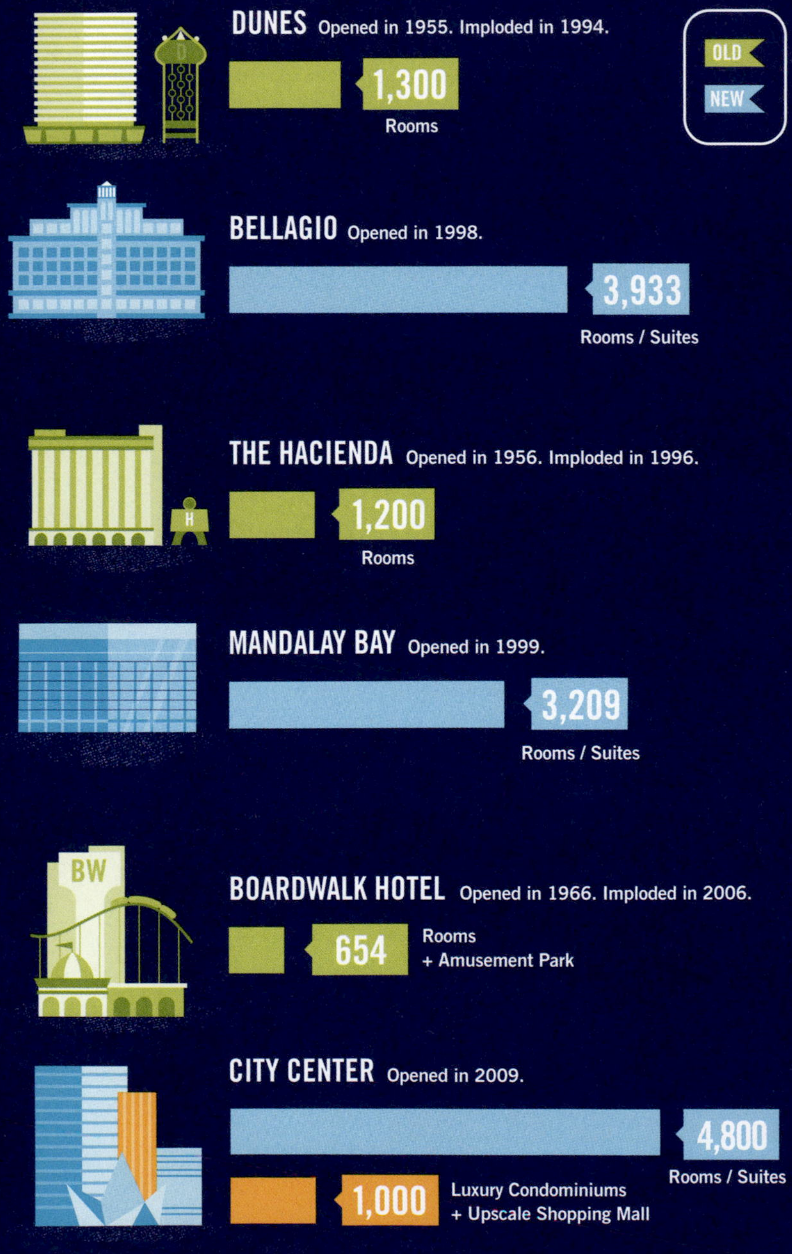

Q WHY DIDN'T THE DEVELOPERS REFURBISH THE OLDER HOTELS RATHER THAN DESTROY THEM?

A Refurbishing can be quite expensive, but that is not the only reason the developers imploded the structures. There is an enormous opportunity cost to having too small a structure on the Las Vegas Strip, which is some of the most valuable real estate the world.

Q WHY DIDN'T THE DEVELOPERS BUILD ON VACANT LAND NEARBY?

A Vacant land sounds attractive, but a location off the Las Vegas Strip receives a tiny fraction of the visitors of the Strip properties. This makes it worth it to implode the existing structure and build back bigger and better to attract more customers than before.

Q HERE IS ANOTHER QUESTION TO HELP YOU THINK ABOUT SUNK COSTS: DO YOU WEAR YOUR CLOTHES UNTIL THEY ARE COMPLETELY WORN OUT OR REPLACE THEM SOONER?

A Wearing worn out clothes is something a lot of us do, but there comes a point when most of us donate or discard the old clothes in order to look your best. Buying new clothes is one way we overcome the sunk cost fallacy.

REVIEW QUESTIONS

- Why does this graph use the number of hotel rooms as a comparison?
- Use the idea of sunk costs to analyze switching majors in college.

* We look at the number of rooms before and after demolition, but the casino size and square footage in each newer development also increased by approximately that same proportion.

fewer people want ice cream. The Ice Cream Float still has to crisscross the lake to make sales, burning expensive gasoline and paying employees to operate the vessel. If the Ice Cream Float is to keep its revenues high, it needs customers; but cooler weather suppresses demand. If the Ice Cream Float charges $2.25 in the fall, it can make enough to cover its average variable cost of $2.00, but not enough to cover its average total cost of $2.50. Nevertheless, it will continue to operate because it makes enough in the yellow region to pay part of its fixed cost. Finally, it reaches a point at which the price drops below $2.00. Now the business is no longer able to cover its average variable cost. At this point, it shuts down for the winter. It does this because operating when MR is very low causes the business to incur a larger loss.

The Firm's Short-Run Supply Curve

Cost curves provide a detailed picture of a firm's willingness to supply a good or service. We have seen that when the MR curve is below the minimum point on the AVC curve, the firm shuts down and production, or output, falls to zero. In other words, when revenues are too low, no supply is produced. For example, during the winter, the Ice Cream Float is dry-docked, so the supply curve does not exist. However, when the firm is operating, it bases its output decisions on the marginal cost. Recall that the firm uses the profit-maximizing rule, or MR = MC, to determine how much to produce. The marginal cost curve is therefore the firm's short-run supply curve as long as the firm is operating.

Marginal thinking

Figure 9.3 shows the Ice Cream Float's short-run supply curve. In the short run, diminishing marginal product causes the firm's costs to rise as the quantity produced increases. This is reflected in the shape of the firm's short-run supply

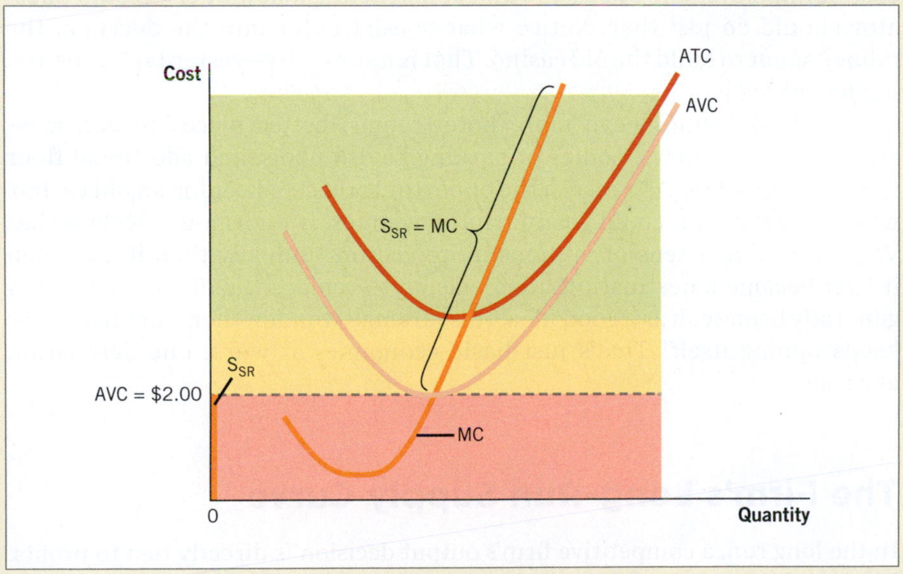

FIGURE 9.3

The Firm's Short-Run Supply Curve

The short-run supply curve (S_{SR}) and marginal cost curve (MC) are equivalent when the price is above the minimum point on the average variable cost curve (AVC). Below that point, the firm shuts down and no supply exists.

In Las Vegas, casino implosions come with fireworks.

curve, shown in orange. The supply curve is upward sloping above the minimum point on the AVC curve. Below the minimum point on the AVC curve, the short-run supply curve is vertical at a quantity of zero, indicating that a willingness to supply the good does not exist below a price of $2.00. At prices above $2.00, the firm will offer more for sale as the price increases.

Sunk Costs

Sunk costs are unrecoverable costs that have been incurred as a result of past decisions.

Unrecoverable costs that have been incurred as a result of past decisions are known as **sunk costs**. They represent money that has already been spent, no matter what comes next, and that therefore should have no bearing on future decisions. This is known as the principle of sunk costs. It's the "What's done is done" rule, applied to economics.

To see the sunk-costs principle at work, consider the transformation of the Las Vegas Strip over the last 50 years. Most of the iconic casinos built along the Strip in the early days have been imploded and built back—bigger, grander, and with the latest amenities. This is despite the fact that the buildings that were imploded had been built at considerable expense and were still structurally sound and perfectly serviceable.

Why would a business destroy a usable asset? Why wouldn't casino owners add on to an existing casino or refurbish it instead? To understand the implosion phenomenon, we need to use marginal thinking. If demolishing an old casino and replacing it with a new casino creates a marginal benefit large enough to pay for the marginal cost of imploding the old casino and constructing a new one, a casino operator should do just that. Notice what doesn't enter into the decision: the money spent to build the old casino. That is a sunk cost—yesterday's expense, irrelevant today.

Marginal thinking

Modern casinos have more hotel rooms, better places to eat, massive venues for shows, oodles of parking, lavish pools, and additional floor space for gamblers. As a result, the opportunity cost of keeping an old casino, when a new casino could easily triple revenues, is enormous. Because Las Vegas now draws tens of millions more visitors annually than it did when it first became a destination, the decision to replace the older casinos has generally been seen as a good idea. It is no small wonder, then, that Las Vegas keeps upping itself! That's just basic economics at work, one detonation at a time.

Opportunity cost

The Firm's Long-Run Supply Curve

In the long run, a competitive firm's output decision is directly tied to profits. Because the firm is flexible in the long run, all costs are variable. As a result, the firm's long-run supply curve exists only when the firm expects to cover its total

PRACTICE WHAT YOU KNOW

The Profit-Maximizing Rule: Show Me the Money!

What is the rule for making the most profit?

Here is a question that often confuses students.

QUESTION: At what point does a firm maximize profits: where the profit per additional unit is greatest, or where marginal revenue equals marginal cost?

ANSWER: Each answer sounds plausible, so the key is to think about each one in a concrete way. To help do that, we will refer back to the Mr. Plow data in Table 9.3. Making a large profit per unit sounds great. However, if the firm stops production when the profit per unit peaks—at \$8 in column 7—it will fail to realize the additional profits, namely \$7, then \$3, and then \$1 in column 7, that come from continuing to produce until MR = MC. The correct answer is where marginal revenue equals marginal cost. A firm maximizes profits where MR = MC, because at this point all profitable opportunities are exhausted. If Mr. Plow clears 8 driveways, his profit on the additional driveway is \$1. If he clears 9 driveways, his profit on the additional driveway is −\$15, because the marginal cost of clearing that ninth driveway, \$25, is greater than the \$10 he earns in marginal revenue.

costs of production (because otherwise the firm would go out of business—that is, exit the market).

Returning to the Ice Cream Float example, recall that the boat shuts down over the winter instead of going out of business because demand is low but is expected to return. If for some reason the crowds do not come back, the float would go out of business. Turning to Figure 9.4, we see that at any point below the minimum point, \$2.50, on the ATC curve, the float will experience a loss. Because firms are free to enter or exit the market in the long run, no firm will willingly produce in the market if the price is less than average total cost ($P < ATC$). As a result, no supply exists below \$2.50. However, if price is greater than average total cost ($P > ATC$), the float expects to make a profit and thus will continue to produce.

The firm's long-run supply curve, shown in Figure 9.4 in orange, is upward sloping above the minimum point on the ATC curve, which is denoted by ATC on the *y* axis. The supply curve is vertical at a quantity of zero, indicating that a willingness to supply the good does not exist below a price of \$2.50. In the long run, a firm that expects price to exceed ATC will continue to operate, because the conditions for making a profit seem favorable. In contrast, a firm that does not expect price to exceed ATC should cut its losses and exit the market. Table 9.5 outlines the long-run decision criteria.

So far, we have examined the firm's decision-making process in the short run in the context of revenue versus cost, which has enabled us to determine the profit each firm makes. However, a single firm represents only a small part of the overall supply in a competitive market. In the next section, we develop the short-run and long-run market supply curves.

FIGURE 9.4

The Firm's Long-Run Supply Curve

The long-run supply curve (S_{LR}) and marginal cost curve (MC) are equivalent when the price is above the minimum point on the average total cost curve (ATC). Below that point, the firm shuts down and no supply exists.

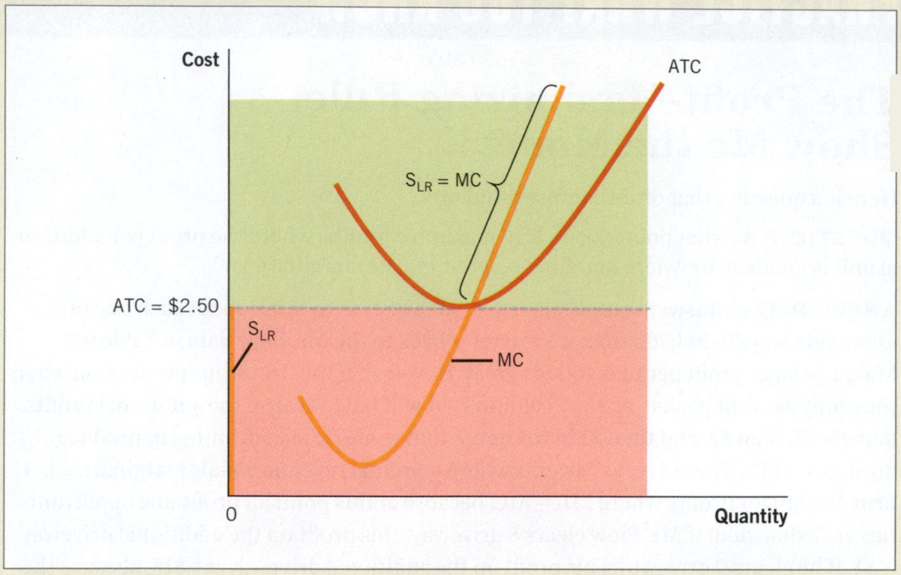

TABLE 9.5

The Long-Run Shutdown Criteria

Condition	In words	Outcome
P > ATC	The price is greater than the average total cost of production.	The firm makes a profit.
P < ATC	The price is less than the average total cost of production.	The firm should shut down.

ECONOMICS IN THE REAL WORLD

IS OFFICE WEAR GONE FOR GOOD? THE SHORT RUN VERSUS THE LONG RUN

What happens if your customers do not return? What if you simply had a bad idea to begin with, and the customers never arrived in the first place?

When the long-run profit outlook is bleak, a firm is better off going out of business. This is a normal part of the ebb and flow of a market economy. Around the year 1900, there were thousands of companies that made "buggy whips," small whips used by drivers of horse-drawn carriages. Today, few buggy whip makers remain; however, lots of companies now make auto parts.

COVID-19 has set off a similar upheaval in the clothing industry. Men's Wearhouse, Jos. A. Bank, Brooks Brothers, Ann Taylor, and LOFT all filed for bankruptcy in 2020, in order to restructure their operations and their debts. These mainstay business attire brands are victims of a change in demand. With Zoom meetings the norm, white-collar workers no longer feel the need to dress to impress. That's terrible news for retailers who specialize in upscale office wear.

To be clear, COVID-19 alone didn't cause all these bankruptcies. The trend toward increasingly casual attire in the workplace has been going on for years. That puts those struggling retailers in a tough spot. They might hope that after suffering through some months of losses, they will emerge from bankruptcy better positioned to serve customers returning to stores as the pandemic subsides. But the transformation of the workplace, by casualization and now by work-from-home practices, may be permanent. In that case, some of those bankrupt retailers are probably better off just going out of business now, instead of postponing the inevitable at the cost of more red ink.

The workplace of tomorrow?

To complicate matters, if demand for dressy clothing does rebound, there is no guarantee that traditional brick-and-mortar retailers will win the future. It is more likely that online retailers will be the first choice of many shoppers. In a free market, the only real guarantee is that things change.

What Does the Supply Curve Look Like in Perfectly Competitive Markets?

We have seen that a firm's willingness to supply a good or service depends on whether the firm is making a short-run or long-run decision. In the short run, a firm may choose to operate at a loss to recover a portion of its fixed costs. In the long run, there are no fixed costs, so a firm is willing to operate only if it expects the price it charges to cover total costs.

However, the supply curve for a single firm represents only a small part of the overall supply in a competitive market. We now turn to market supply and develop the short-run and long-run market supply curves.

The Short-Run Market Supply Curve

A competitive market consists of a large number of identical sellers. Because an individual firm's supply curve is equal to its marginal cost curve, if we add together all the individual supply curves in a market, we arrive at the short-run market supply curve. Figure 9.5 shows the short-run market supply curve in a two-firm model consisting of Mr. Plow and the Plow King. At a price of $10, Mr. Plow is willing to clear 8 driveways (Q_A) and the Plow King is willing to clear 20 driveways (Q_B). When we sum the output of the two firms, we get a total market supply of 28 driveways (Q_{market}), seen in the third graph.

The Long-Run Market Supply Curve

Recall that a competitive market is one in which a large number of buyers seek a product many sellers offer. Competitive markets are also characterized by easy entry and exit. Existing firms and entrepreneurs decide whether to enter

FIGURE 9.5

Short-Run Market Supply

The market supply is determined by summing the individual supplies of all the firms in the market. Although we have only shown this process for two firms, Mr. Plow and Plow King, the process extends to any number of firms in a market.

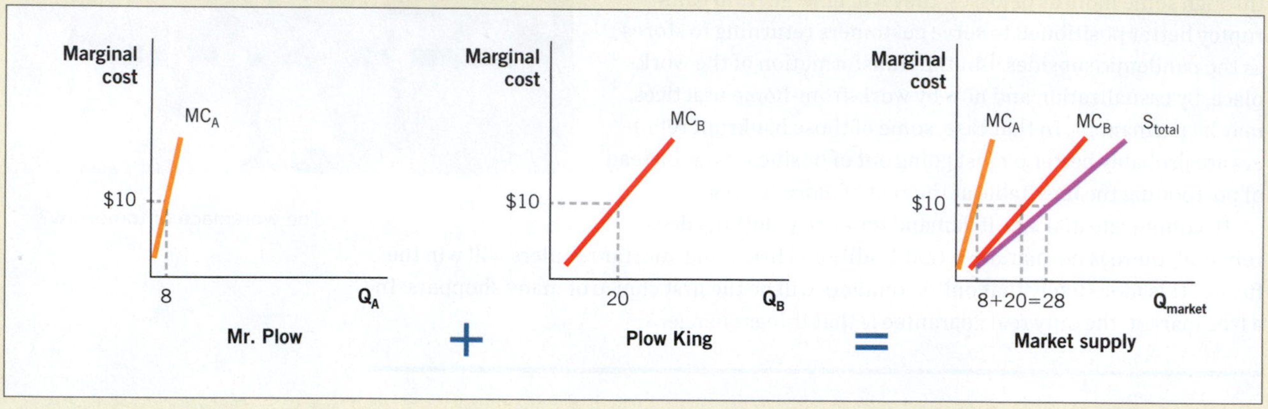

and exit a market based on incentives. When existing firms are enjoying profits, there is an incentive for them to produce more and also for entrepreneurs to enter the market. The result is an increase in the quantity of the good supplied. Likewise, when existing firms are experiencing losses, there is an incentive for them to exit the market; then the quantity supplied decreases.

Incentives

Entry and exit have the combined effect of regulating the amount of profit a firm can hope to make in the long run. As long as profits exist, the quantity supplied will increase because existing firms expand production or other firms enter the market. When losses exist, the quantity supplied will decrease because existing firms reduce production or other firms exit the market. So both profits and losses signal a need for an adjustment in market supply. In other words, profits and losses act as signals for resources to enter or leave a market. **Signals** convey information about the profitability of various markets.

The **signals** of profits and losses convey information about the profitability of various markets.

The only time an adjustment does not take place is when participants in the market make zero economic profit. In that case, the market is in long-run equilibrium. Existing firms and entrepreneurs are not inclined to enter or exit the market; the adjustment process that occurs through price changes ends.

The benefit of a competitive market is that profits guide existing firms and entrepreneurs to produce more goods and services that society values. Losses encourage firms to exit and move elsewhere. Without profits and losses acting as signals for firms to enter or exit the market, resources will be misallocated and surpluses and shortages will occur.

Figure 9.6 captures how entry and exit determine the market supply. The profit-maximizing point of the individual firm in panel (a), MR = MC, is located at the minimum point on the ATC curve. The price (P = min. ATC) that existing firms receive is just enough to cover costs, so profits are zero. As a result, new firms have no incentive to enter the market and existing firms have no reason to leave. At all prices above P = min. ATC, firms will earn a profit (the green area), and at all prices below P = min. ATC, firms will experience a loss

FIGURE 9.6

The Long-Run Market Supply Curve and Entry and Exit

Entry into the market and exit from it force the long-run price to be equal to the minimum point on the average total cost curve (ATC). At all prices above P = min. ATC, firms will earn a profit (the green area), and at all prices below P = min. ATC, firms will experience a loss (the red area). For this reason, the long-run supply curve (S_{LR}) must be horizontal at price P = min. ATC. If the price was any higher or lower, firms would enter or exit the market, and the market could not be in a long-run equilibrium.

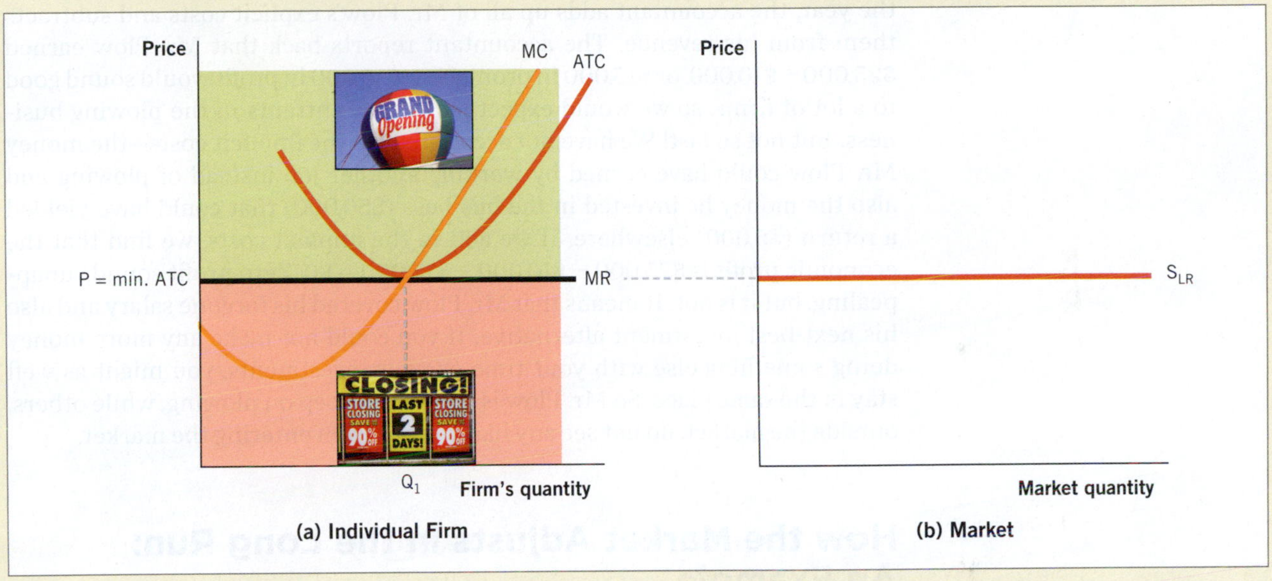

(the red area). This picture is consistent for all markets with free entry and exit; zero economic profit occurs at only one price, and that price is the lowest point of the ATC curve.

At this price, the supply curve in panel (b) must be a horizontal line at P = min. ATC. If the price were any higher, firms would enter, supply would increase, and price would be forced back down to P = min. ATC. If the price were any lower, firms would exit, supply would decrease, and price would be forced up to P = min. ATC. Because we know that these adjustments will have time to take place in the long run, the long-run supply curve must also be equal to P = min. ATC to satisfy the demand that exists at this price.

A REMINDER ABOUT ECONOMIC PROFIT Now that you have learned how perfect competition affects business profits in the long run, you may not think that a competitive market is a desirable environment for businesses seeking to earn profits. After all, if a firm cannot expect to make an economic profit in the long run, why bother? It's easy to forget the distinction between accounting profit and economic profit. Firms enter a market when they expect to be reasonably compensated for their investment. And they leave a market when the investment does not yield a satisfactory result. Economic profit is determined by deducting the explicit and implicit costs from total revenue. The remaining examples (graphs) in this chapter focus on our benchmark, economic profit. Therefore, firms are willing to stay in perfectly competitive markets in the long run when they are breaking even because they are being reasonably compensated for the explicit expenses they have incurred and also for the implicit expenses—like the opportunity costs of other business ventures—they would expect to incur elsewhere.

Opportunity cost

For example, if Mr. Plow has the explicit and implicit costs shown in Table 9.6, we can see the distinction between accounting profit and economic profit more clearly. Mr. Plow has a revenue of $25,000 during the year.

If Mr. Plow asks his accountant how much the business earned during the year, the accountant adds up all of Mr. Plow's explicit costs and subtracts them from his revenue. The accountant reports back that Mr. Plow earned $25,000 − $10,000, or $15,000 in profit. Now $15,000 in profit would sound good to a lot of firms, so we would expect many new entrants in the plowing business. But not so fast! We have not accounted for the implicit costs—the money Mr. Plow could have earned by working another job instead of plowing and also the money he invested in the business ($50,000) that could have yielded a return ($5,000) elsewhere. If we add in the implicit costs, we find that the economic profit is $25,000 − $10,000 − $15,000 = $0. Zero profit sounds unappealing, but it is not. It means that Mr. Plow covered his forgone salary and also his next-best investment alternative. If you could not make any more money doing something else with your time or your investments, you might as well stay in the same place. So Mr. Plow is content to keep on plowing, while others, outside the market, do not see any likely profit from entering the market.

How the Market Adjusts in the Long Run: An Example

We have seen that profits and losses may exist in the short run; in the long run, the best the competitive firm can do is earn zero economic profit. This section looks in more detail at the adjustment process that leads to long-run equilibrium.

We begin with the market in long-run equilibrium, shown in Figure 9.7. Panel (a) represents an individual firm operating at the minimum point on its ATC curve. In long-run equilibrium, all firms are operating as efficiently as possible. Because the price is equal to the average cost of production,

TABLE 9.6

Mr. Plow's Economic Profit and the Entry or Exit Decision

Explicit costs per year	
Payment on the loan on his snowplow	$7,000
Gasoline	2,000
Miscellaneous equipment (shovels, salt)	1,000
Implicit costs	
Forgone salary	$10,000
The forgone income that the $50,000 invested in the business could have earned if invested elsewhere	5,000
Total cost	$25,000

FIGURE 9.7

A Competitive Market in Long-Run Equilibrium

When a market is in long-run equilibrium, the short-run supply curve (S_{SR}) and short-run demand curve (D_{SR}) intersect along the long-run supply curve (S_{LR}). At this point, the price the firm charges is equal to the minimum point along the average total cost curve (ATC). The existing firms in the market earn zero economic profit, and there is no incentive for firms to enter or exit the market.

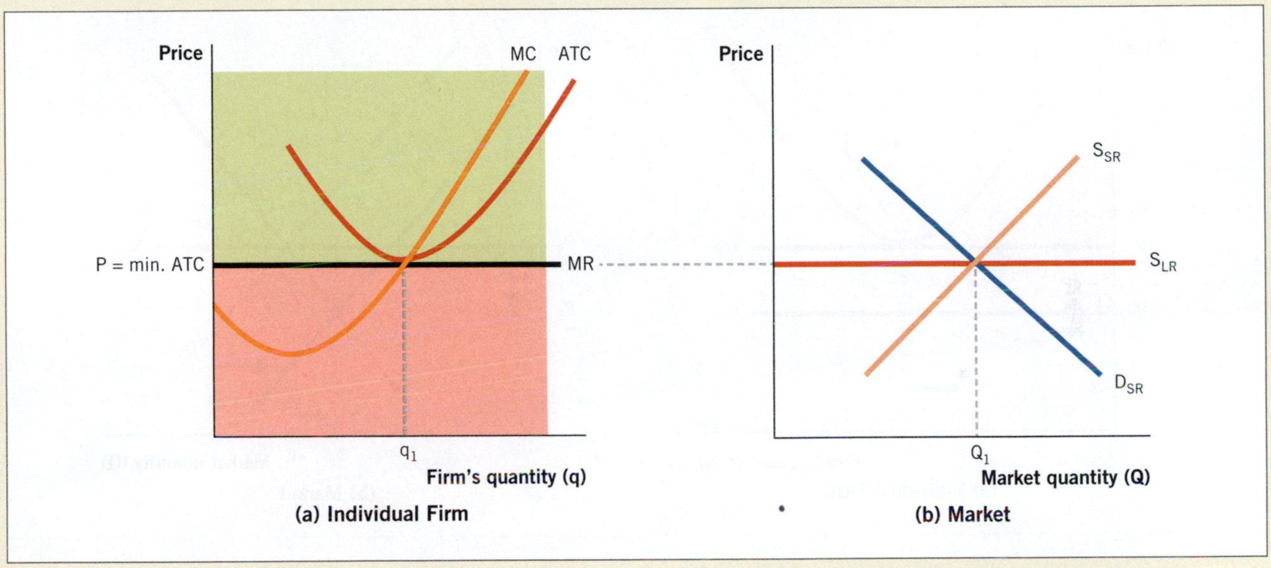

economic profit for the firm is zero. In panel (b), the short-run supply curve (S_{SR}) and the short-run demand curve (D_{SR}) intersect along the long-run supply curve (S_{LR}), so the market is also in equilibrium. But if the short-run supply curve and demand curve happened to intersect above the long-run supply curve, then the price would be higher than the minimum point on the ATC curve. The result would be short-run profits, indicating that the market is not in long-run equilibrium. And if the short-run supply curve and demand curve intersected below the long-run supply curve, then the price would be lower than the minimum point on the ATC curve. In that case, the result would be short-run losses.

Now suppose that demand declines, as shown in Figure 9.8. In panel (b), we see that the market demand curve shifts from D_1 to D_2. When demand falls, the equilibrium point moves from point A to point B. The price drops to P_2 and the market output drops to Q_2. The firms in this market take their price from the market, so the new marginal revenue curve shifts down from MR_1 to MR_2 at P_2 in panel (a). Because the firm maximizes profits where MR = MC, the firm will produce an output of q_2. When the output is q_2 the firm's costs, C_2, are higher than the price it charges, P_2, so it experiences a loss equal to the red area in panel (a). In addition, because the firm's output is lower, it is no longer producing at the minimum point on its ATC curve, so the firm is not as efficient as before.

Firms in a competitive market can exit the market easily. Some will do so to avoid further losses. Figure 9.9 continues the example from Figure 9.8. It shows that as firms exit, the market supply contracts from S_{SR1} to S_{SR2} and the market

FIGURE 9.8

The Short-Run Adjustment to a Decrease in Demand

A decrease in demand causes the price to fall in the market, as shown by the movement from D_1 to D_2 in panel (b). Because the firm is a price taker, the price it can charge falls to P_2. As we see in panel (a), the intersection of MR_2 and MC occurs at q_2. At this output level, the firm incurs the short-run loss shown by the red area in (a).

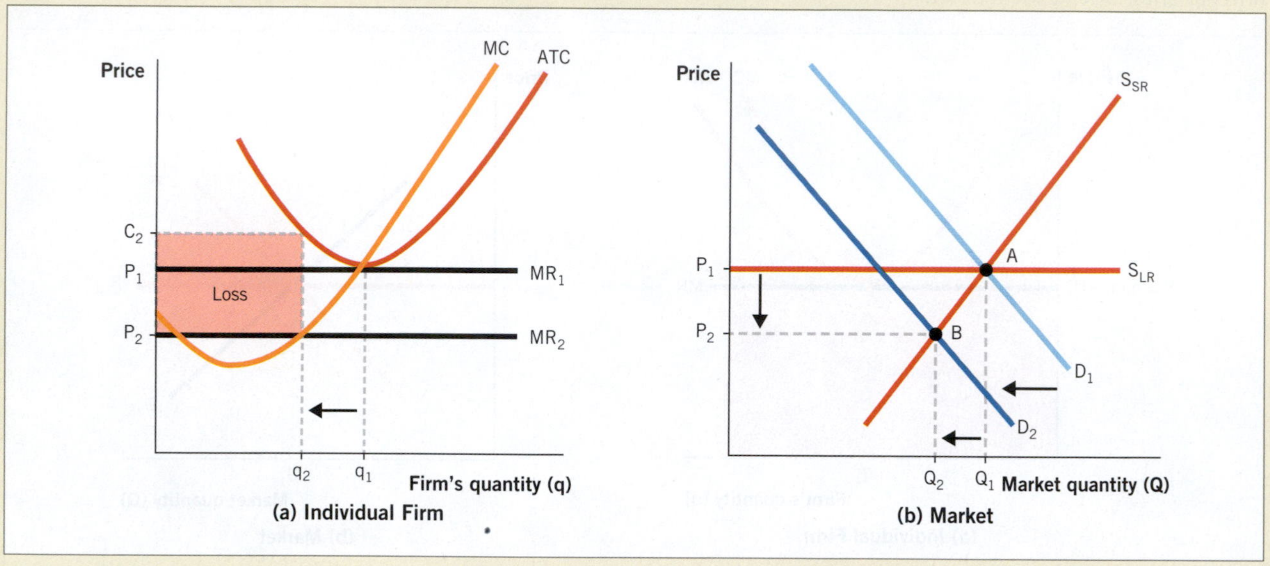

What does it take to produce more avocados?

equilibrium moves from point B to point C. At point C, the price rises back to P_1 and the market output drops to Q_3. The firms that remain in the market no longer experience a short-run loss, because MR_2 returns to MR_1 and costs fall from C_2 to C_1. The end result is that the firm is once again efficient, and economic profit returns to zero.

For example, suppose there is a decline in demand for avocados due to a false rumor that links the fruit to a salmonella outbreak. The decline in demand causes the price of avocados to drop. As a consequence, avocado producers experience negative economic profit—generating curves like the ones shown in Figure 9.8. In response to the negative profit, some avocado growers will exit the market, the avocado trees will be sold for firewood, and the land will be converted to other uses. With fewer avocados being produced, the supply will contract. Eventually, the smaller supply will cause the price of avocados to rise until a new long-run equilibrium is reached at a much lower level of output, as shown in Figure 9.9.

MORE ON THE LONG-RUN SUPPLY CURVE To keep the previous example as simple as possible, we assumed that the long-run supply curve was horizontal. However, this is not always the case. There are two reasons why the long-run supply curve may slope upward. First, some resources needed to produce the product may only be available in limited supplies. As firms try to expand production, they must bid to acquire those resources—a move that

FIGURE 9.9

The Long-Run Adjustment to a Decrease in Demand

Short-run losses cause some firms to exit the market. Their exit shifts the market supply curve to the left in panel (b) until the price returns to long-run equilibrium at point C. Price is restored to P_1 and the MR_2 curve in panel (a) shifts up to MR_1. At P_1 the firm is once again earning zero economic profit.

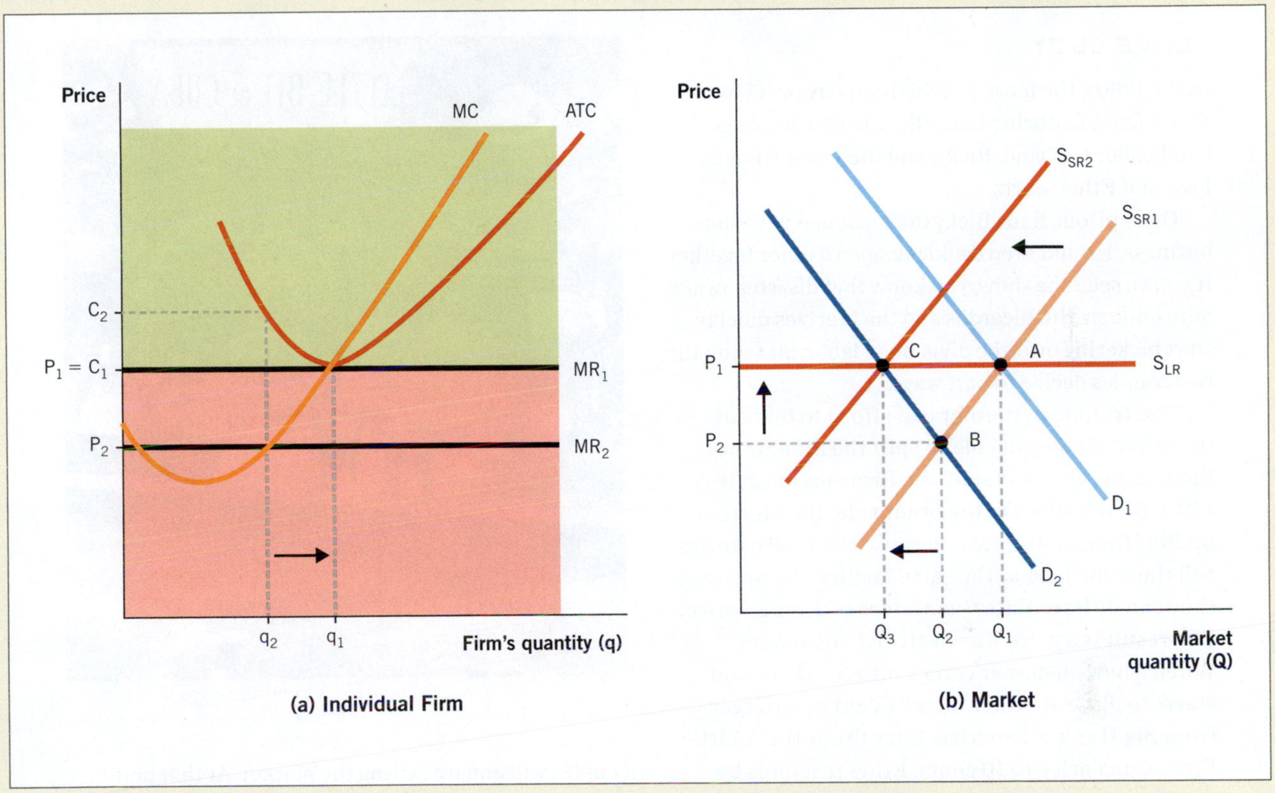

causes the average total cost curve to rise. For instance, an avocado grower who wants to plant more trees must acquire more land. Because avocados require well-drained soil and long growing seasons with frost-free winters, not all land is perfectly suited to growing them. The limited supply of land will cause the price of producing more avocados to rise, which will cause the supply curve to be positively sloped.

A second reason the long-run supply curve may be upward sloping is the opportunity cost of the labor used in producing the good. If you want to produce more avocados, you will need more workers to pick the fruit. Hiring extra workers will mean finding people who are both willing and capable. Some workers are better than others at picking avocados, and some workers have higher opportunity costs. As your firm attempts to expand production, it must increase the wage it pays to attract additional help or accept new workers who are not quite as capable. Either way you slice it, the result is higher costs, which would be reflected in an upward-sloping long-run supply curve.

Opportunity cost

ECONOMICS *in the* MEDIA

Entry and Exit

I LOVE LUCY

In the 1950s, the most-watched comedy on TV was *I Love Lucy*, featuring Lucy Ricardo and her singer-bandleader husband, Ricky, and their best friends, Fred and Ethel Mertz.

One episode finds Ricky disillusioned with show business. He and Fred decide to open a diner together. If you've seen the show, you know that disaster awaits. Sure enough, the Ricardos and the Mertzes quickly start bickering over the division of labor, and soon the two couples decide to part ways.

The trouble is, neither can afford to buy out the other. So they decide to split the diner down the middle! On their side, the Ricardos operate A Little Bit of Cuba. On the other side, the Mertzes set up Big Hunk of America. Because the rival eateries sell the same food at the same facility, the only way they can differentiate themselves is through price. The result is a price war to attract customers. When a new customer comes into the diner and starts to place an order for a 15-cent hamburger from Big Hunk of America, Lucy drops the A Little Bit of Cuba price to 10 cents. Ethel responds by going down to 5 cents. The two continue lowering the price until Ethel drops her price all the way down to 1 cent! Problem: even in the 1950s, a penny didn't cover the marginal cost of making a hamburger.

Neither the Ricardos nor the Mertzes can stay in business selling one-cent burgers, so one of the couples will end up exiting the market. At that point, the remaining couple should be able to charge more. But if they end up making a profit, that profit will encourage entrepreneurs to enter the market. As the supply of hamburgers expands, the market price will be driven back down. Because we live in an economically dynamic world, prices are always moving toward long-run equilibrium.

This discussion simply means that higher prices are necessary to induce suppliers to offer more for sale. None of it changes the basic ideas we have discussed throughout this section. The entry and exit of firms ensure that the market supply curve is much more elastic in the long run than in the short run.

PRACTICE WHAT YOU KNOW

Long-Run Profits: How Much Can a Firm Expect to Make?

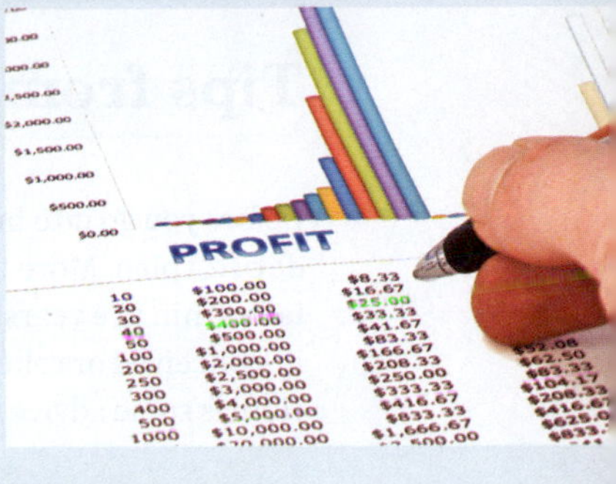

Calculating profits.

QUESTION: True or false? "If firms in an industry are making economic profits, other firms will enter."

ANSWER: In the long run, a firm in a perfectly competitive market earns zero economic profit, so the opportunity in the short run to enjoy positive economic profits will cause existing firms to increase output and new firms to enter the market. The statement is true.

CHALLENGE QUESTION: The company you work for reported in its annual stockholder meeting that it made $1 million in profits last year. Should you invest?

ANSWER: The profit in the example is accounting profit. We don't know how large the firm is. If the firm had $5 million in assets, $1 million would represent a 20% return—which would be excellent. However, if the firm had $100 million in assets, the rate of return would only be 1%—which is poor. Economists are concerned with the rate of return adjusting for the implicit cost of the resources used. Recall that the stock market rises, on average, 8% a year. To account for this, when economists speak of profits, they adjust the accounting profits downward for the implicit costs of doing business. For instance, let's take 8% off of the two hypothetical returns; 20% becomes a 12% return over the firm's next best alternative, and that's why this outcome is "excellent." But when you subtract 8% from 1%, you get a return of −7%, which will drive firms out of the market. The firm could have used its assets more successfully by deploying them elsewhere.

So the answer to the question, "Should you invest?" is that it depends on the amount of economic profit—not the accounting profit—the firm expects to make going forward. Even then, you must be mindful about competition from other firms entering the market, since that will drive economic profits down to zero in the long run. Perhaps more pertinently, investing in a market characterized by no long-run economic profits should give you pause. In the next few chapters we will focus on imperfect competition. Firms with market power, barriers to entry, and differentiated products are able to consistently earn economic profits. That's where the smart investors look.

Conclusion

In competitive markets, where firms are at the mercy of market forces that set the price, individual firms have no control over the price because they sell the same products as their competitors. In addition, profits and losses help regulate economic activity in competitive markets and promote economic efficiency. Profits reward producers for producing a good that is valued more highly than the resources used to produce it. Profits encourage entry into a market. Likewise, losses penalize producers who operate inefficiently or produce goods consumers do not want. Losses encourage exit from the market. The process of entry and exit ensures that resources flow into markets that are undersupplied and away from markets where too many firms exist.

· ECONOMICS *for* LIFE ·

Tips from the Sharks for Becoming a Millionaire

Before you go into business for yourself, you need to devise a plan. More than 80% of all small businesses fail within five years, because the businesses were ill-conceived or relied on unrealistic sales projections. Here is some advice from stars of *Shark Tank*:

- **Barbara Corcoran:** "Every business is born out of an individual's intense passion and a real need to succeed, so you'll need enough passion to get started, but also enough to get through the intense 12-hour days when the chips are down and everything and everyone seems against you."
- **Mark Cuban:** "You've got to be good at something and not only be good at it, but you've got to love it, and then you're willing to work and do whatever it takes. Then, if you're fortunate, that turns into something that creates wealth for you."
- **Lori Greiner:** "Make sure you are hands-on and the one driving things because no one will care about your business like you do. Be involved in all details and be aggressive at attaining your goals and know how to pivot when necessary."
- **Kevin O'Leary:** "If you can afford to take a risk and you're young enough, either start your own company or be involved with one where you're racking up equity."
- **Robert Herjavec:** "You've got to go back to the basics. Find a need, solve a problem, and most importantly, make sure you have a customer. If those things are in place, and you have the ability to scale, now we're talking. It's going to be incredibly hard work. Harder than you've ever imagined, but it's the best time in America to start a business. The time is now!"
- **Daymond John:** "Go out there and do something that you really, really love, even if it's not something you went to school for. Find out what your passion is. I can't guarantee that you're ever going to make a dollar doing anything, but do something that you absolutely love and you're going to look back over the years and say that you enjoyed life."

The Sharks may have a scary-sounding name, but they're rooting for you to succeed.

Source: Kim Lachance Shandrow, "All 7 *Shark Tank* Stars Share Tips on How to Become a Millionaire," *Entrepreneur*, July 12, 2016, https://www.entrepreneur.com/slideshow/278607.

In this chapter, we studied competitive markets to establish a benchmark that will help us understand how other market structures compare with this ideal. In the next few chapters, we explore imperfect markets, which provide a significant contrast with the results we have just seen. The closer a market is to meeting the criteria of perfect competition, the better the result for consumers and society in general.

ANSWERING *the* BIG QUESTIONS

How do competitive markets work?

- The firms in competitive markets sell similar products. Firms are also free to enter and exit the market whenever they wish.
- A price taker has no control over the price it receives in the market.
- In competitive markets, the price and quantity produced are determined by market forces instead of by the firm.

How do firms maximize profits?

- A firm maximizes profits by expanding output until marginal revenue is equal to marginal cost (MR = MC, or the profit-maximizing rule). The profit-maximizing rule is a condition for stopping production at the point where profit opportunities no longer exist.
- The firm should shut down in the short run if the price it receives does not cover its average variable costs. Because variable costs are incurred only when operating, if a firm can make enough to cover its variable costs in the short run, it will choose to continue to operate.
- In the long run, the firm should go out of business if it cannot cover its average total costs.

What does the supply curve look like in perfectly competitive markets?

- Profits and losses act as signals for firms to enter or leave a market. As a result, perfectly competitive markets drive economic profit to zero in the long run.
- The entry and exit of firms ensure that the market supply curve in a competitive market is much more elastic in the long run than in the short run.

CHAPTER PROBLEMS

Concepts You Should Know

marginal revenue (p. 287)
price taker (p. 283)
profit-maximizing rule (p. 288)
signals (p. 298)
sunk costs (p. 294)

Questions for Review

1. What are the necessary conditions for a perfectly competitive market to exist?
2. Describe the two-step process used to identify the profit-maximizing level of output.
3. Under what circumstances will a firm have to decide whether to operate or to shut down?
4. What is the difference between the decision to go out of business and the decision to shut down?
5. How do profits and losses act as signals that guide producers to use resources to make what society wants most?
6. What are sunk costs? Give an example from your own experience.
7. Why do competitive firms earn zero economic profit in the long run?

Study Problems (*✱ solved at the end of this section*)

1. Using the definition of a price taker as your guide, explain why each of the following industries does not meet the definition.
   a. the pizza delivery business
   b. the home improvement business
   c. cell phone companies
   d. cereal producers
2. A local business sells kebabs for $3 each. It has the following cost and output structure per hour:

Output (kebabs per hour)	Total cost (per hour)
0	$60
10	90
20	110
30	120
40	125
50	135
60	150
70	175
80	225

   a. Calculate the total revenue for the business at each rate of output.
   b. Calculate the total profit for the business at each rate of output.
   c. Is the business operating in the short run or the long run?
   d. Calculate the profit-maximizing rate of output using the MR = MC rule. (**Hint:** First compute the marginal revenue and marginal cost from the table.)
3. Determine whether the following statements are true or false. Explain your answers.
   a. A firm will make a profit when the price it charges exceeds the average variable cost of the chosen output level.
   b. To maximize profits in the short run, a firm must minimize its costs.
   c. If economic profit is positive, firms will exit the market in the short run.
   d. A firm that receives a price greater than its average variable cost but less than its average total cost should shut down.

4. In the following table, fill in the blanks. After you have completed the entire table, determine the profit-maximizing output.

Output	Price	Total revenue	Marginal revenue	Total cost	Marginal cost	Total profit
1	$20	____	____	$40	____	−$20
2	____	____	____	50	____	____
3	____	____	____	60	____	____
4	____	____	____	65	$5	____
5	____	____	____	85	____	____
6	____	$120	____	120	____	____

5. Use the graph to answer the questions that follow.

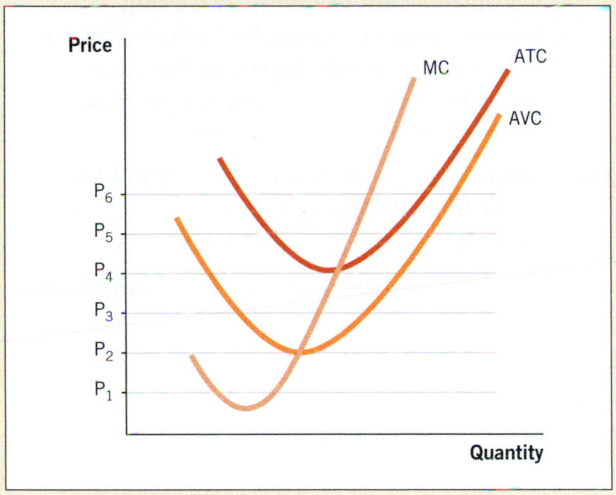

a. At what prices is the firm making an economic profit, breaking even, and experiencing an economic loss?
b. At what prices would the firm shut down?
c. At what prices does the firm's short-run supply curve exist? At what prices does the firm's long-run supply curve exist?

✳ 6. Identify as many errors as you can in the following graph.

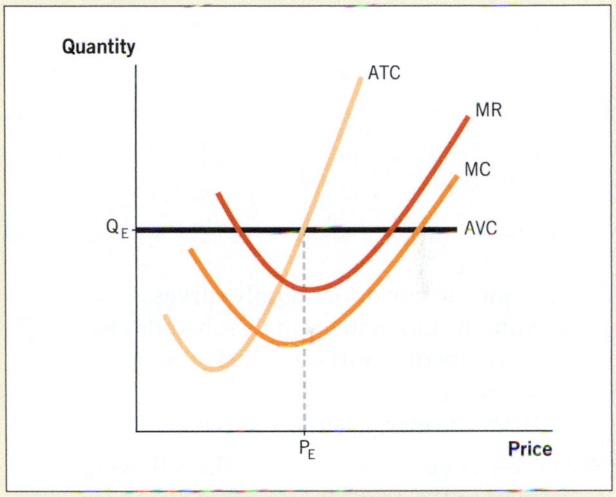

7. A firm is experiencing a loss of $5,000 per year. The firm has fixed costs of $8,000 per year.
a. Should the firm operate in the short run or shut down?
b. If the situation persists into the long run, should the firm stay in the market or go out of business?
c. Now suppose that the firm's fixed costs are $2,000. How would this level of fixed costs change the firm's short-run and long-run decisions?

8. Three students at the same school hear about the success of cookie delivery businesses on college campuses. Each student decides to open a local

service. The individual supply schedules are shown below.

	QUANTITY SUPPLIED		
Delivery charge	Esra	Remzi	Camilo
$1	2	3	6
2	4	6	7
3	6	9	8
4	8	12	9
5	10	15	10
6	12	18	11

a. Draw the individual supply curves.
b. Sum the individual supply schedules to compute the short-run market supply schedule.
c. Draw the market supply curve.

9. Do you agree or disagree with the following statement? "A profit-maximizing, perfectly competitive firm should select the output level at which the difference between the marginal revenue and marginal cost is the greatest." Explain your answer.

10. Barney's snow removal service is a profit-maximizing, competitive firm. Barney clears driveways for $10 each. His total cost each day is $250, and half of his total costs are fixed. If Barney clears 20 driveways a day, should he continue to operate or shut down? If this situation persists, will Barney stay in the market or exit?

* **11.** Suppose you are the owner of a firm producing jelly beans. Your production costs are shown in the following table. Initially, you produce 100 boxes of jelly beans per time period. Then a new customer calls and places an order for an additional box of jelly beans, requiring you to increase your output to 101 boxes. She offers you $1.50 for the additional box. Should you produce it? Why or why not?

JELLY BEAN PRODUCTION

Number of boxes	Average cost per box
100	$1.00
101	1.01
102	1.02
103	1.03

12. In which of the following examples does the decision-maker avoid the sunk cost fallacy?

a. You pay $10 to see *Furious 10* but realize 15 minutes into the film that the plot and acting are truly terrible, so you leave immediately.
b. You sign up for a year-long membership at a local fitness center. You tire of the club visits quickly, but still go regularly to make sure you get the most out of your membership.
c. A construction company builds a new bridge, but soon afterwards the traffic flow unexpectedly increases. The new bridge must be replaced before it needs repairs.

* **13.** Determine the profit-maximizing output level from the following table. The firm has no fixed costs in this example, only variable costs.

Output	Marginal revenue	Marginal cost
1	$10	$13
2	10	10
3	10	8
4	10	7
5	10	9
6	10	11
7	10	14

14. Which of the following statements are true? Explain your reasoning.

a. The marginal cost curve passes through the lowest points of the ATC, AVC, and AFC curves.
b. The quantity for which MR = MC is the quantity for which the profit rectangle's area is maximized.
c. The AVC curve can be derived from the MC curve.
d. The AFC curve always slopes downward.

Solved Problems

6. Here is the corrected graph with the errors struck out and some explanation below.

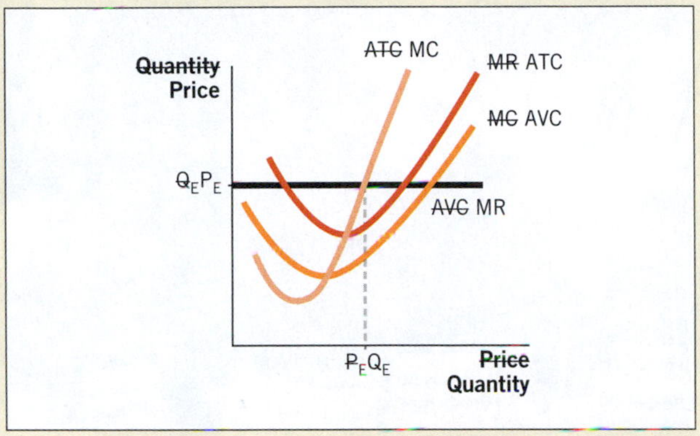

Also, the ATC and AVC curves did not intersect the MC curve at their minimum points. That is corrected here.

11. This problem requires marginal thinking. We know the profit-maximizing rule, MR = MC. Here all we need to do is compare the additional cost, or MC, against the additional revenue, or MR, to see if the deal is a good idea. We know that MR = $1.50, because that is what the customer is offering to pay for another box of jelly beans. Now we need to calculate the marginal cost of producing the additional box.

JELLY BEAN PRODUCTION

Number of boxes	Average cost per box	Total cost	Marginal cost
100	$1.00	$100.00	—
101	1.01	102.01	$2.01
102	1.02	104.04	2.03
103	1.03	106.09	2.05

First we compute the total cost. To do this, we multiply the number of boxes, listed in the first column, by the average cost, shown in the second column. The results are shown in the third column.

Next we find the marginal cost. Recall that the marginal cost is the amount it costs to produce one more unit. So we subtract the total cost of producing 101 boxes from the total cost of producing 100 boxes. For 101 boxes, MC = $102.01 − $100.00, or $2.01. Because MR − MC is $1.50 − $2.01, producing the 101st box would create a loss of $0.51. Therefore, at a price of $1.50, your firm should not produce the 101st box.

13. This problem confounds many students because if you've memorized only one thing from this chapter, it is the profit-maximizing rule, MR = MC, and it is clear that this condition is satisfied when the output is 2 (where MR and MC are both $10). But the answer 2 would be incorrect. A second part of the profit-maximizing rule is often overlooked: MR = MC, but MC must also be increasing. To see why 2 is not the profit-maximizing output, you should calculate the profit in a fourth column, as in the following table:

Output	Marginal revenue	Marginal cost	Profit (MR − MC)
1	$10	$13	− $3
2	10	10	0
3	10	8	2
4	10	7	3
5	10	9	1
6	10	11	− 1
7	10	14	− 4

Profit is maximized at an output of 5, but why is this the case? Marginal cost is declining until output reaches 4, at which point the MR = $10 and MC = $7. So when the fourth unit is sold, it generates $3, and the firm is profitable for the first time. By the fifth unit, MC is rising but remains less than MR, so the profit rises. However, MC is higher than MR for the sixth unit, which causes profits to decline. The reason 2 is *not* the profit-maximizing output is that MC is falling, which means that the firm is at the point where additional output is just becoming profitable.

CHAPTER

10

Understanding Monopoly

Monopolies Have Market Power.

In this chapter, we explore another market structure: monopoly. Monopolists enjoy market power for their specific product, but they cannot force consumers to purchase what they are selling. By the law of demand, when a monopolist charges more, people buy less. If demand is low enough, a monopolist may even experience a loss instead of a profit. But on the other hand, when demand is high, and on top of that is inelastic, a monopolist is sometimes able to earn massive profits.

Sometimes monopolies literally hold the power of life and death. An illness called cystic fibrosis (CF) affects about one in 3,000 newborns. It scars the lungs and shortens life expectancy by decades. A new drug, Trikafta, manufactured by Vertex Pharmaceuticals, effectively manages the disease in most CF patients. There's just this catch: Trikafta treatment costs over $300,000 per year, and *only* Vertex makes it. Demand for Trikafta is substantial and highly inelastic. Should drug companies like Vertex be allowed to charge what the market will bear for drugs they develop and have patents on? What are the consequences if the government interferes with their profit making?

In 2019, Vertex Pharmaceuticals and Great Britain's National Health Service were haggling over the price of lifesaving medication for children with cystic fibrosis. These protesters gathered to voice their anger over the slow progress of negotiations.

While pure monopolies are unusual, it is important to study this market structure, because many markets exhibit some form of monopolistic behavior. Google, the National Football League, the United States Postal Service (for first-class mail), and some small-town businesses are all examples of monopoly. The typical result of monopoly is higher prices and less output than we find in a competitive market.

In this chapter, we explore the conditions that give rise to monopolies, how they work, and what can be done about the problems they create.

· BIG QUESTIONS ·

- How are monopolies created?
- How much do monopolies charge, and how much do they produce?
- What are the problems with, and solutions for, monopoly?

How Are Monopolies Created?

As we explained in Chapter 3, a monopoly exists when a single seller supplies the entire market for a particular good or service. Two conditions enable a single seller to become a monopolist. First, the firm must have something unique to sell—that is, something without close substitutes. Second, it must have a way to prevent potential competitors from entering the market.

Monopolies occur in many places and for several different reasons. For example, companies that provide natural gas, water, and electricity are all examples of monopolies that occur naturally because of economies of scale. But monopolies can also occur when the government regulates the amount of competition. For example, trash pickup, street vending, taxicab rides, and ferry service are often licensed by local governments. These licenses have the effect of limiting competition and creating **monopoly power**, which is a measure of a monopolist's ability to set the price of a good or service.

A monopolist operates in a market with high **barriers to entry**, which are restrictions that make it difficult for new firms to enter a market. As a result, monopolists have no competition nor any immediate threat of competition.

Monopoly power is a measure of a monopolist's ability to set the price of a good or service.

Barriers to entry are restrictions that make it difficult for new firms to enter a market.

High barriers to entry insulate the monopolist from competition, which means that many monopolists enjoy long-run economic profits. There are two types of barriers to entry: natural barriers and government-created barriers. Let's look at each.

Natural Barriers

Some barriers exist naturally within the market. These include control of resources, problems in raising capital, and economies of scale.

CONTROL OF RESOURCES The best way to limit competition is to control a resource that is essential in the production process. This extremely effective barrier to entry is hard to accomplish. But if you control a scarce resource, other competitors will not be able to find enough of it to compete. For example, China controls about 70 percent of the world's known reserves of rare-earth metals, elements essential for electronics manufacturing. With its tight grip on the world market for rare earths, it's no wonder that China in the past has taken advantage of its dominance by threatening to restrict exports in trade disputes. China is also the only country capable of processing rare earths, so even those that are mined in the United States must be sent to China to be turned into usable form. This has allowed Chinese corporations, many of which are state-owned, to achieve dominance in the rare-earth metals market.

PROBLEMS IN RAISING CAPITAL Monopolists are usually very big companies that have grown over an extended period. Even if you had a wonderful business plan, it is unlikely that a bank or a venture-capital company would lend you enough money to start a business that could compete effectively with a well-established company. For example, if you wanted to design a new operating system to compete with Microsoft and Apple, you would need tens of millions of dollars to fund your start-up. Lenders provide capital for business projects when the chance of success is high, but the chance of a new company successfully competing against an entrenched monopolist is not high. Consequently, raising capital to compete effectively is difficult.

ECONOMIES OF SCALE In Chapter 8, we saw that economies of scale occur when long-run average costs fall as production expands. Low unit costs and the low prices that follow give some larger firms the ability to drive rivals out of business. For example, imagine a market for electric power where companies compete to generate electricity and deliver it through their own grids. In such a market, it would be technically possible to run competing sets of wire to every home and business in the community, but the cost of installation and the maintenance of separate lines to deliver electricity would be both prohibitive and impractical. Even if a handful of smaller electric companies could produce electricity at the same cost, each would have to pay to deliver power through its own grid. This system would be highly inefficient.

In an industry that enjoys large economies of scale, production costs per unit continue to fall as a firm expands. Smaller rivals then have much higher average costs that prevent them from competing with a larger company. As a result, firms in the industry tend to combine over time. These mergers lead to

A **natural monopoly** occurs when a single large firm has lower costs than any potential smaller competitor.

the creation of a **natural monopoly**, which occurs when a single large firm has lower costs than any potential smaller competitor.

Government-Created Barriers

The creation of a monopoly can be either intentional or an unintended consequence of a government policy. Government-enforced statutes and regulations, such as laws and regulations covering licenses and patents, limit the scope of competition by creating barriers to entry.

LICENSING In many instances, it makes sense to give a single firm the exclusive right to sell a good or service. To minimize negative externalities, governments occasionally establish monopolies, or near monopolies, through licensing requirements. For example, in some communities, trash collection is licensed to a single company. The rationale usually involves economies of scale, but there are additional factors to consider. Because firms cannot collect trash without a government-issued operating license, opportunities to enter the business are limited, which leaves consumers with a one-size-fits-all level of service. This outcome is the opposite of what we'd expect to see in a competitive market, where there would be many varieties of service at different price points.

Licensing also creates an opportunity for corruption. In fact, in many parts of the world, bribery is so common that it often determines which companies receive licenses in the first place.

PATENTS AND COPYRIGHT LAW Another area in which the government fosters monopoly is that of patents and copyrights. For example, when musicians create a new song and copyright their work, they earn royalties over the life of the copyright. The copyright is the government's assurance that no one else can play or sell the work without the artist's permission. Similarly, when a pharmaceutical company develops a new drug, the company receives a patent under which it has the exclusive right to market and sell the drug for as long as the patent is in force.

By granting patents and copyrights to developers and inventors, the government creates monopolies. Patents and copyrights create stronger incentives to develop new drugs and produce new music than would exist if market competitors could immediately copy inventions. The social benefits of patent law can be enormous. In 2020, firms in the United States and around the world were racing to develop vaccines for the COVID-19 virus. Imagine how different the picture would be if vaccines couldn't be patented. After the patent or copyright expires, rivals can mimic the invention. This new competition opens up the market and provides dual benefits: wider access to the innovation and more sellers—both of which are good for consumers in the long run.

Incentives

Nonetheless, many economists wonder if patents and copyrights are necessary or have unintended consequences. Sometimes copyright holders benefit more from exposure than from exercising their right to charge consumers. For example, when a music video goes viral on YouTube, the exposure causes many people to buy the original artist's work. Consider Justin Bieber. He managed to leverage his YouTube fame into a successful album launch, concert tours, and appearance fees that might never have occurred if a music studio had tightly

TABLE 10.1
The Characteristics of Monopolies
• One seller
• A unique product without close substitutes
• High barriers to entry
• Price making

controlled his sound while he was an emerging artist. Conversely, Taylor Swift refused to allow her music on Spotify from 2014 to 2017, because she felt the service did not properly compensate her and all the other people involved in creating the music. Other artists, such as Chance the Rapper, have ditched record labels entirely and release their own music independently. The point to remember is that copyright protection gives artists the right to decide how to distribute their work and what price to charge. It also gives them the ability to litigate when their work is stolen, illegally downloaded, or improperly used.

Taylor's fans wanted her *to stay, stay, stay* but there was a *blank space* on Spotify for three years.

Though market-created and government-created barriers occur for different reasons, they have the same effect—they create monopolies. Table 10.1 summarizes the key characteristics of monopolies. In the next section, we examine how the monopolist determines the price it charges and how much to produce, explaining the term "price making" listed in Table 10.1.

ECONOMICS IN THE REAL WORLD

PFIZER'S LIPITOR

Lipitor is the best-selling drug of all time. Pfizer corporation spent millions of dollars developing the drug and bringing it to the market. Lipitor is highly effective in lowering blood cholesterol. It was also highly profitable for Pfizer, generating over $11 billion in annual revenues before the patent ran out in 2011. Lipitor is now available in an inexpensive generic formulation at a price that is 80% lower than the original patent-protected price. Even after the patent expired, many customers continued to ask for Lipitor—not the generic—so brand recognition and customer loyalty represent another entry barrier.

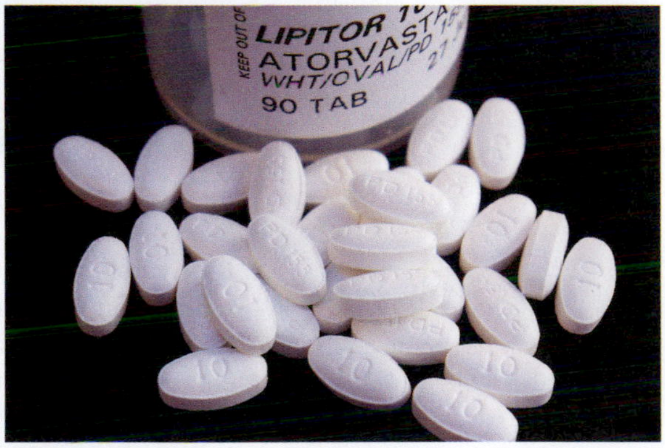

Do you want fries with that cholesterol medication?

Would Lipitor have been developed without patent protection? Probably not. Pfizer would have had little incentive to incur the cost of developing a cholesterol treatment if other companies could immediately copy the drug. In this case, society benefits because of the twofold nature of patents: they give firms the incentive to innovate, but they also limit the amount of time the patent is in place (20 years from the time of filing), thereby guaranteeing that competitive forces will govern long-run access to the product.

Incentives

ECONOMICS *in the* MEDIA

Characteristics of Monopoly

THE OFFICE: PRINCESS UNICORN

Dwight Schrute buys up all of the Princess Unicorn dolls in local stores. As the Christmas holidays approach and parents become more desperate to find the dolls for their children, Dwight plans to sell his dolls marked way, way up—to $200. Toby wants to buy a doll for his daughter, Sasha, and is delighted to learn that Dwight has a stash he is selling, because now Toby has a chance to be a hero to his daughter. But he waits too long and learns that Dwight sold his last doll to Darryl. Distraught, Toby approaches Darryl, explains that he promised a doll to Sasha, and starts crying. Darryl decides to let Toby have the prized doll for $400, double what Darryl paid.

Dwight has a good understanding of the elements that create monopoly power. He is the sole seller in his area, and he has a uniquely desirable product without close substitutes. That gives him monopoly power and the ability to raise the price he charges. Darryl also understands economics. He sees that Toby is desperate (has very inelastic demand) for the last doll and doubles Dwight's already high price.

FA-LA-LA-LA-LA, LA-LA, KA-CHING!

How Much Do Monopolies Charge, and How Much Do They Produce?

A **price maker** has some control over the price it charges.

Both monopolists and firms in a competitive market seek to earn a profit. However, a monopolist is the sole provider of its product and holds market power. Thus, monopolists are price makers. A **price maker** has some control over the price it charges. As you learned in Chapter 9, a firm in a competitive market is a price taker.

We can see the difference between price takers and price makers graphically in Figure 10.1. The demand curve for the product of a firm in a competitive market, shown in panel (a), is horizontal. When individual firms are price takers, they have no control over what they charge. In other words, demand is perfectly elastic—or horizontal—because every firm sells the same product. Demand for an individual firm's product exists only at the price determined by the market, and each firm is such a small part of the market that it can sell its entire output without lowering the price.

In contrast, because a monopolist is the only firm—the sole provider—in the industry, the demand curve for its product, shown in panel (b), constitutes the market demand curve. But the demand curve is downward sloping, which limits the monopolist's ability to make a profit. The monopolist would like to exploit its market power by charging a high price to many customers. However, the law of demand, which identifies a negative relationship between price and quantity demanded, dictates otherwise. Unlike the horizontal demand curve of a firm in a competitive market, the downward-sloping demand curve of the monopolist has many price-output combinations. If market demand is inelastic, a monopolist will choose a higher price. When market demand is more elastic, a monopolist will choose a lower price. As a result, monopolists must search for the profit-maximizing price and output.

PRACTICE WHAT YOU KNOW

Monopoly: Can You Spot the Monopolist?

Monopoly profits!

Here are three questions to test your understanding of the conditions necessary for monopoly power to arise.

QUESTION: Is Amazon a monopolist?

ANSWER: Amazon is the nation's largest bookseller, with sales that dwarf those of its nearest retail rival, Barnes & Noble. Amazon is also by far the nation's leader in e-commerce with online sales that exceed the combined total of Walmart, Apple, Macy's, Home Depot, Best Buy, Costco, Nordstrom, Gap, and Target! Amazon's outsize market share, however, does not make it a monopolist. It still faces intense competition.

QUESTION: Is the only hairdresser in a small town a monopolist?

ANSWER: For all practical purposes, yes. He or she sells a unique service with inelastic demand. Because the nearest competitor is in the next town, the local hairdresser enjoys significant monopoly power. At the same time, the town's size limits potential competitors from entering the market, because the small community may not be able to support two hairdressers. Once one hairdresser is in place, a potential rival looks at the size of the market in the small town, calculates how many people he or she could expect to serve, and deduces that the potential revenue is too small to justify entrance into this market.

CHALLENGE QUESTION: Which of these four firms do you think the government might, with good reason, allow to operate as a monopolist?

a. Tesla

b. Pacific Gas and Electric

c. Twitter

d. Walmart

ANSWER: The correct answer is B. Gas and electric companies are natural monopolies that have lower costs of production when they scale up. Dividing a natural monopolist into two or more smaller firms would drive costs significantly higher. Governments allow firms with significant economies of scale to remain monopolists and, as we shall learn, regulate the prices the firms can charge, to ensure that consumers are not gouged. Tesla, Walmart, and Twitter would, of course, like to be monopolists, too, but there is no compelling reason why society would be better off with just one large manufacturer of electric vehicles, or just one department store, or just one social media outlet.

ECONOMICS *in the* MEDIA

Barriers to Entry

FORREST GUMP

If shrimping were easy, everyone would do it.

In this 1994 movie, Tom Hanks's character, Forrest Gump, keeps his promise to his deceased friend, Bubba, to go into the shrimping business after leaving the army. Forrest invests $25,000 in an old shrimp boat, but the going is tough—he catches only a handful of shrimp because of the competition for space in the shrimping waters. So Forrest tries naming his boat for good luck and brings on a first mate, Lieutenant Dan, who unfortunately is less knowledgeable and resourceful than Forrest. The fledgling enterprise continues to struggle, and eventually Forrest decides to pray for shrimp. Soon after, Forrest's boat, the *Jenny*, is caught out in the Gulf of Mexico during a hurricane. Miraculously, the *Jenny* makes it through the storm while the other shrimp boats, all anchored in the harbor, are destroyed. Boom! Forrest has a short-run monopoly.

The film suggests that Forrest's good luck—being in the right place at the right time—explains how he became a millionaire. But is Forrest's case realistic? Let's consider the situation in real-world economic terms.

Remember, Forrest was able to enter the business simply by purchasing a boat. To be sure, he will catch more shrimp in the short run, while the other boats are docked for repairs. However, once the competitors' boats return, they will resume catching shrimp, and Forrest's short-run profits will disappear. The reason we can be so confident of this result is that shrimping, with low barriers to entry and an undifferentiated product, is an industry that closely mirrors a perfectly competitive market. So when profits exist, new entrants will expand the supply produced and profits will return to the break-even level. Having Forrest become a "millionaire" makes for a good movie, but none of the elements are in place to suggest that he could attain a permanent monopoly. Forrest does not control an essential resource; the other shrimp captains will have little difficulty raising capital to repair their boats; and the economies of scale in this situation are small.

FIGURE 10.1

Comparing the Demand Curves of Perfectly Competitive Firms and Monopolists

(a) Firms in a competitive market face a horizontal demand curve. (b) Because the monopolist is the sole provider of the good or service, the demand for its product constitutes the industry—or market—demand curve, which is downward sloping. So while the perfectly competitive firm has no control over the price it charges, the monopolist gets to search for the profit-maximizing price and output.

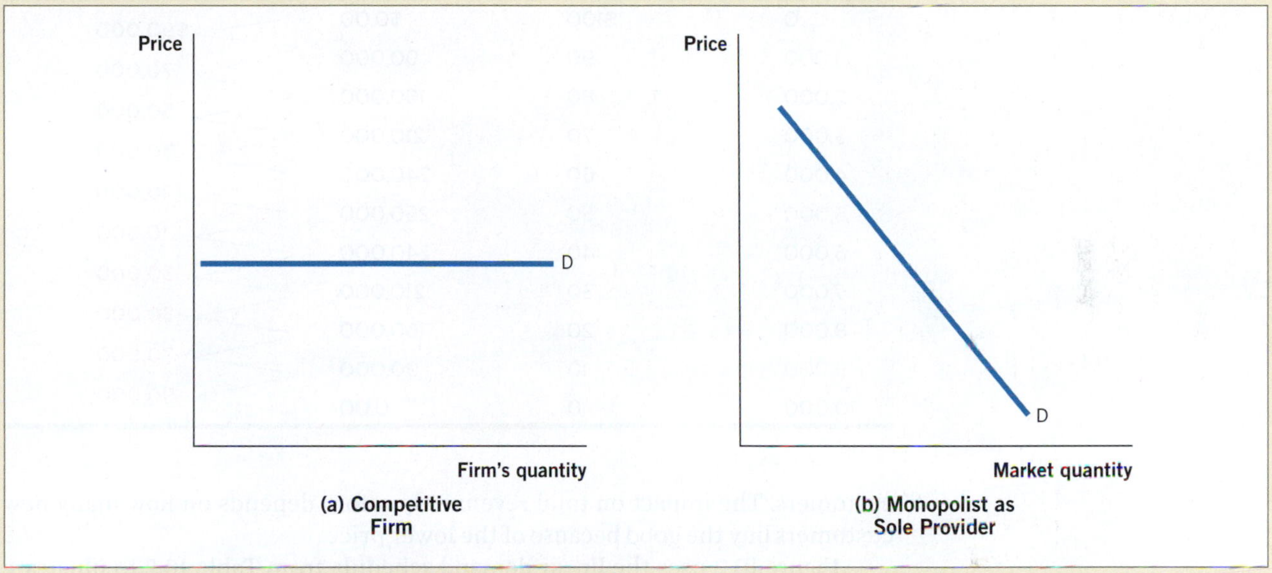

The Profit-Maximizing Rule for the Monopolist

A competitive firm can sell all it produces at the existing market price. But a monopolist, because of the downward-sloping demand curve, must search for the most profitable price. To maximize profits, a monopolist can use the profit-maximizing rule we introduced in Chapter 9: MR = MC. For the price-taking firm, MR is just the market price, full stop. For the monopolist, however, there's a calculation involved.

Table 10.2 shows the marginal revenue for a cable company that serves a small community. Notice the negative relationship between output (quantity of customers) and price in columns 1 and 2: as the price goes down, the quantity of customers goes up. Total revenue is calculated by multiplying output by price (TR = Q × P). At first, total revenue rises as the price falls. Once the price becomes too low ($40), total revenue begins to fall. As a result, the total revenue in column 3 initially rises to $250,000 before it begins to fall off. The final column, marginal revenue, shows the change (Δ) in total revenue. Here we see positive (though falling) marginal revenue associated with prices between $100 and $50 (see the green dollar amounts in column 4). Below $50, marginal revenue becomes negative (see the red dollar amounts in column 4).

Marginal thinking

The change in total revenue reflects the trade-off a monopolist encounters in trying to attract additional customers. To gain additional sales, the firm must lower its price. But the lower price is available to both new and existing

Trade-offs

TABLE 10.2

Calculating the Monopolist's Marginal Revenue

(1) Quantity of customers	(2) Price of service	(3) Total revenue	(4) Marginal revenue per 1,000 customers
(Q)	(P)	(TR)	(MR)
Formula:		Q × P	Δ TR
0	$100	$0.00	
			$90,000
1,000	90	90,000	
			70,000
2,000	80	160,000	
			50,000
3,000	70	210,000	
			30,000
4,000	60	240,000	
			10,000
5,000	50	250,000	
			−10,000
6,000	40	240,000	
			−30,000
7,000	30	210,000	
			−50,000
8,000	20	160,000	
			−70,000
9,000	10	90,000	
			−90,000
10,000	0	0.00	

customers. The impact on total revenue therefore depends on how many new customers buy the good because of the lower price.

Figure 10.2 uses the linear demand schedule from Table 10.2 to illustrate the two separate effects that determine marginal revenue. First, there is a *price effect,* which reflects how the lower price affects revenue. If the price of service drops from $70 to $60, each of the 3,000 existing customers saves $10, and the firm loses $10 × 3,000, or $30,000 in revenue, represented by the red area on the graph. But dropping the price also has an *output effect,* which reflects how the lower price affects the number of customers. Because 1,000 new customers buy the product (that is, cable service) when the price drops to $60, revenue increases by $60 × 1,000, or $60,000, represented by the green area. The output effect ($60,000) is greater than the price effect ($30,000). When we subtract the $30,000 in lost revenue (the red rectangle) from the $60,000 in revenue gained (the green rectangle), the result is $30,000 in marginal revenue at an output level between 3,000 and 4,000 customers.

Lost revenues associated with the price effect are always subtracted from the revenue gains created by the output effect. Now let's think of this data at the individual level. Because the firm adds 1,000 new customers, the marginal revenue per customer—$30,000 ÷ 1,000 new customers—is $30. Notice that this marginal revenue is less than the price, $60, that the firm charges. Because there is a price effect whenever the price drops, the marginal revenue curve lies below the demand curve. Therefore, in Figure 10.2, the *y* intercept is the same for the demand and marginal revenue curves and the *x* intercept of the MR curve is half of the demand curve's.

At high price levels—where demand is elastic—the price effect is small relative to the output effect. As the price drops, demand slowly becomes more inelastic. The output effect diminishes and the price effect increases. In other words, as the price falls, it becomes harder for the firm to acquire enough new

FIGURE 10.2

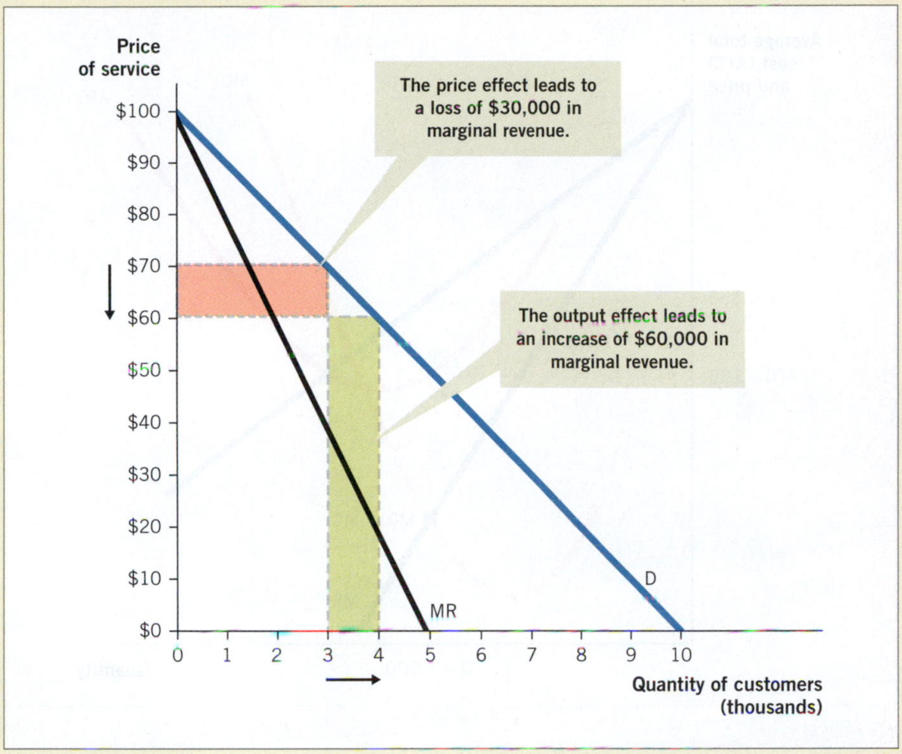

The Marginal Revenue Curve and the Demand Curve

A price drop has two effects. (1) Existing customers now pay less—this is the price effect. (2) New customers decide to purchase the good for the first time—this is the output effect. The relative size of the two effects, as shown by the red and green rectangles, determines whether the firm is able to increase its revenue by lowering its price. In this case, marginal revenue increases by $30,000.

customers to make up for the difference in lost revenue. Eventually, the price effect becomes larger than the output effect. This means that the marginal revenue curve will have the same *y* intercept as the demand curve and be twice as steep. As a result, marginal revenue becomes negative and dips below the *x* axis, as shown by the MR curve in Figure 10.2. When the marginal revenue is negative, the firm cannot maximize profit. This outcome puts an upper limit on the amount the firm will produce. This outcome is evident in Table 10.2: once the price becomes too low, the firm's marginal revenue is negative.

Marginal thinking

DECIDING HOW MUCH TO PRODUCE In Chapter 9, we explored the profit-maximizing rule for a firm in a competitive market. This rule also applies to a monopolist: marginal revenue should be equal to marginal cost. However, there is one big difference: a monopolist does not charge a price equal to marginal revenue.

Figure 10.3 illustrates the profit-maximizing decision-making process for a monopolist. We use a two-step process to determine the monopolist's profit:

1. Locate the point at which the firm will maximize its profits: MR = MC.
2. Set the price: from the point at which MR = MC, determine the profit-maximizing output, Q. From Q, move up along the dashed line until it intersects with the demand curve (D). From that point, move horizontally until you come to the *y* axis. This point on the *y* axis tells us the price (P)

FIGURE 10.3

The Monopolist's Profit Maximization

The firm uses the profit-maximizing rule to locate the point at which MR = MC. This condition determines the ideal output level, Q. Because the price (which is determined by the demand curve) is higher than the average total cost curve (ATC) along the dashed line at quantity Q, the firm makes the profit shown in the green area.

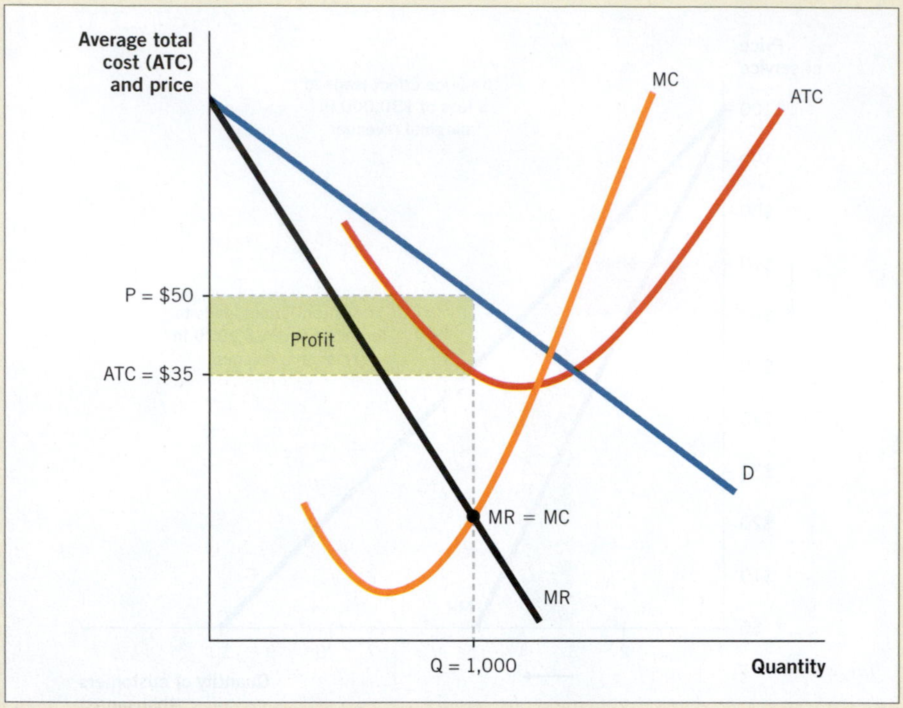

the monopolist should charge. Notice that the monopolist's price (P) is greater than MC (P > MC). This result differs from the competitive outcome, where P = MC.

Using this two-step process, we can determine the monopolist's profit. Locate the average total cost, ATC, of making Q units along the vertical dashed line. From that point, move horizontally until you come to the *y* axis. This point tells us the average total cost of making Q units. The difference between the price and the average total cost multiplied by Q tells us the profit (or loss) the firm makes. Any time the U-shaped ATC curve dips below the downward-sloping demand curve, D, there is a way to earn positive economic profits.

Because the price (P = $50) is higher than the average total cost (ATC = $35), the firm makes the profit shown in the green rectangle. For example, a profit-maximizing veterinarian will choose the point where MR = MC, and that means that the vet will serve 1,000 customers. Because the price at Q is $50 and the average total cost is $35, total profits are 1,000 × ($50 − $35) = $15,000.

Table 10.3 summarizes the differences between a competitive market and a monopoly. The competitive firm must take the price established in the market. If it does not operate efficiently, it cannot survive. Nor can it make an economic profit in the long run. The monopolist operates very differently. Because high barriers to entry limit competition, the monopolist may be able to earn long-run profits by restricting output. It operates inefficiently from society's perspective, and it has significant market power.

TABLE 10.3

The Major Differences between a Monopoly and a Competitive Market

Competitive market	Monopoly
Many firms	One firm
Cannot earn long-run economic profits	May earn long-run economic profits
Has no market power (is a price taker)	Has significant market power (is a price maker)
Produces an efficient level of output (because P = MC)	Produces less than the efficient level of output (because P > MC)

ECONOMICS IN THE REAL WORLD

THE BROADBAND MONOPOLY

Is there only one provider in your area?

Many markets in the United States have only a single high-speed Internet provider. The technology race strongly favors cable transmission over competing telephone lines. Internet access is provided by telephone companies using aging copper wiring, whereas cable companies use the latest fiber-optic technology. When it comes to truly high-speed Internet access, cable companies benefit from considerable barriers to entry. In many places, Comcast and Charter, the two largest cable companies in the United States by far, effectively own access to the Internet and can price their services accordingly.

The cable monopoly on high-speed Internet access affects both consumers and businesses. First, consumers increasingly need more bandwidth to stream movies, view YouTube, and load media-rich web sites. A slow connection can make surfing the Internet a chore. In other words, consumer demand is high and very inelastic. Second, businesses rely on bandwidth to maintain web sites and provide services to customers. Streaming services such as Netflix, Amazon Prime, and Hulu Plus, which deliver content over the Internet, rely on access to a relatively affordable broadband Internet connection. Therefore, businesses also have high demand that is quite inelastic. For this reason, many people argue that relatively inexpensive access to the Internet is crucial if it is to continue as an engine of economic growth. Without competition, access will remain expensive.

Our dependence on the Internet invites a larger question. Where only one provider controls the bandwidth, should the government have a role in providing the infrastructure, or cables, in order to allow greater (or less expensive) access? This is a concern in metropolitan areas served by only one Internet provider. Meanwhile, small rural communities may have no Internet access at all. For example, it is estimated that more than 25 million people in rural areas remain off the grid. Cable companies wouldn't make enough profit to connect these low-density areas, making it more difficult for their residents to participate in today's economy. The unfeasibility of having separate infrastructure for every would-be Internet provider makes this an example of a natural monopoly, a topic we'll take up toward the end of the chapter.

PRACTICE WHAT YOU KNOW

Is there a key profit takeaway?

Monopoly Profits: How Much Do Monopolists Make?

QUESTION: A monopolist always earns ____ economic profit.

a. a positive

b. zero

c. a negative

d. We cannot be sure about the profit a monopolist makes.

ANSWERS:

a. Incorrect. A monopolist is a price maker with considerable market power. This situation usually leads to a positive economic profit.

b. Incorrect. Zero economic profit exists in competitive markets in the long run. Because a monopolist, by definition, does not operate in competitive markets, it is protected from additional competition that would drive its profit to zero.

c. Incorrect. Whoa there! Negative profit? There is absolutely no reason to think that would happen. Monopolists sell a unique product without close substitutes in a market that is insulated from competitive pressures.

d. Correct. Because a monopolist benefits from barriers that limit the entry of competitors into the market, we would expect an economic profit. However, this outcome is not guaranteed. Monopolies do not control the demand for the product they sell. Consequently, in the short run the monopolist may experience a loss (if demand is low).

What Are the Problems with, and Solutions for, Monopoly?

Monopolies can adversely affect society by restricting output and charging higher prices than sellers in competitive markets do. This activity causes monopolies to operate inefficiently, provide less choice, promote an unhealthy form of competition known as *rent seeking* (addressed in a later section), and make economic profits that fail to guide resources to their highest-valued use. Recall that market failure occurs when there is an inefficient allocation of resources in a market. Once we have examined the problems with monopoly, we will turn to the potential solutions to the problems of monopoly.

The Problems with Monopoly

Monopolies result in an inefficient level of output, provide fewer choices to consumers, and encourage monopoly firms to lobby for government protection. Let's look at each of these concerns.

INEFFICIENT OUTPUT AND PRICE From an efficiency standpoint, the monopolist charges too much and produces too little. This result is evident in Figure 10.4, which shows what happens when a competitive market (denoted by the subscript C) ends up being controlled by a monopolist (denoted by the subscript M).

First, imagine a competitive fishing industry in which each boat catches a small portion of the fish, as shown in panel (a). Each firm is a price taker that must charge the market price. In contrast, panel (b) depicts pricing and output decisions for a monopoly fishing industry when it confronts the same cost structure as presented in panel (a). When a single firm controls the entire fishing ground, it is the sole supplier, so the supply curve becomes the monopolist's marginal cost curve. To set its price, it considers the downward-sloping demand and marginal revenue curves that serve the entire market. Therefore, it sets marginal revenue equal to marginal cost. The result is a smaller output than the competitive industry ($Q_M < Q_C$) and a higher price ($P_M > P_C$). The smaller output level is not efficient. In addition, the price the monopolist charges, P_M, is significantly above the marginal cost at the profit-maximizing level of output.

Figure 10.5 captures the deadweight loss (see Chapter 5) of the monopoly. The monopolist charges too high a price and produces too little of the product, so some consumers who would benefit from a competitive market lose out.

FIGURE 10.4

When a Competitive Industry Becomes a Monopoly

(a) In a competitive industry, the intersection of supply and demand determines the price (P_C) and quantity (Q_C). (b) When a monopolist controls an entire industry, the supply curve becomes the monopolist's marginal cost curve. The monopolist uses MR = MC to determine its price (P_M) and quantity (Q_M). As a result, the monopolist charges a higher price and produces a smaller output than when an entire industry is populated with competitive firms.

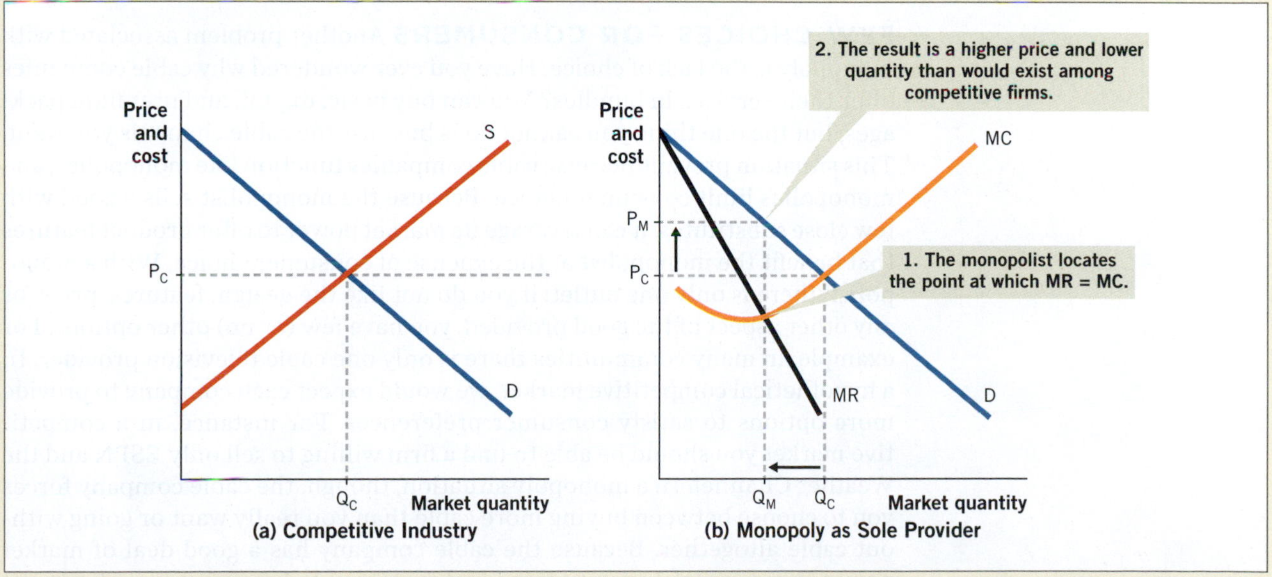

FIGURE 10.5

The Deadweight Loss of Monopoly

Because the profit-maximizing monopolist produces an output of Q_M, an amount that is less than Q_C, the result is the deadweight loss shown in the yellow triangle. The blue rectangle is the consumer surplus transferred to the monopolist.

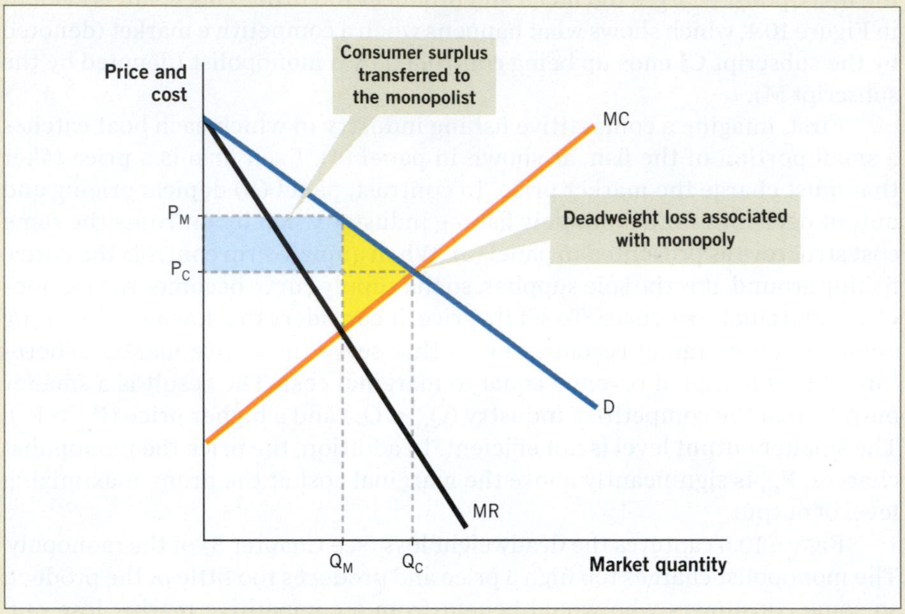

Because the demand curve (the willingness to pay) is greater than the marginal cost between output levels Q_M and Q_C, society would be better off if output expanded to Q_C. But a profit-maximizing monopolist will limit output to Q_M. The result, a deadweight loss equal to the area of the yellow triangle, is inefficient for society. Consumer surplus is also transferred to the monopolist, as shown in the blue rectangle.

FEW CHOICES FOR CONSUMERS Another problem associated with monopoly is the lack of choice. Have you ever wondered why cable companies offer their services in bundles? You can buy basic, digital, and premium packages, but the one thing you cannot do is buy just the cable channels you want. This situation prevails because cable companies function like monopolies, and monopolies limit consumer choice. Because the monopolist sells a good with few close substitutes, it can leverage its market power to offer product features that benefit the monopolist at the expense of consumer choice. With a monopolist, there is only one outlet: if you do not like the design, features, price, or any other aspect of the good provided, you have few (or no) other options. For example, in many communities there is only one cable television provider. In a hypothetical competitive market, we would expect each company to provide more options to satisfy consumer preferences. For instance, in a competitive market you should be able to find a firm willing to sell only ESPN and the Weather Channel. In a monopoly situation, though, the cable company forces you to choose between buying more cable than you really want or going without cable altogether. Because the cable company has a good deal of market power, it can restrict your options and force you to buy more in order to get

Would you rather watch the Weather Channel . . .

. . . or SportsCenter?

what you want. This is a profitable strategy for the company but a bad outcome for consumers.

RENT SEEKING The term **rent seeking** was coined by Anne Krueger in 1974. It refers to the attempt to gain monopoly power through the political process, by using lobbying and other means to secure legal monopoly rights. Throughout this text, we have seen the desirable effects of competition: lower prices, increased efficiency, and enhanced service and quality. However, rent seeking is a form of competition that produces an undesirable result. When firms compete to become monopolists, there is one winner, without any of the benefits usually associated with competition.

Rent seeking occurs when resources are used to secure monopoly rights through the political process.

Consider Intuit corporation and its flagship product, TurboTax, which millions of Americans use every year to file their taxes electronically. For years, Intuit lobbied the U.S. government not to let people file directly with the IRS online, for free. Intuit didn't want the competition. Of course, all that lobbying cost money, but the expense was worth it to protect Intuit's revenue stream. Even after finally agreeing to offer free e-filing through TurboTax to eligible filers, Intuit deliberately made that feature of the software hard to find. The company's response to complaints about its shady behavior was—you guessed it—more lobbying, to protect its position. This is a general rule: when lobbying is more profitable than creativity and productivity, typically companies that can afford to will prefer to lobby. If the lobbying succeeds, society can be adversely affected.

Trade creates value

A former steel plant in Bethlehem, Pennsylvania.

Solutions to the Problems of Monopoly

We have learned that monopolies do not produce as much social welfare as competitive markets do. As a result, public policy approaches attempt to address this problem. The policy solutions include breaking up the monopoly, reducing trade barriers, and regulating markets.

PRACTICE WHAT YOU KNOW

Problems with Monopoly: Coffee Consolidation

A community has many competing coffee shops.

QUESTION: How can we use the market demand curve to illustrate the consumer surplus and producer surplus created by a competitive market?

When companies compete, consumers win.

ANSWER:

In a competitive market, supply and demand determine the price and quantity. In the figure, consumer surplus is represented by the blue area. Producer surplus is represented by the red area.

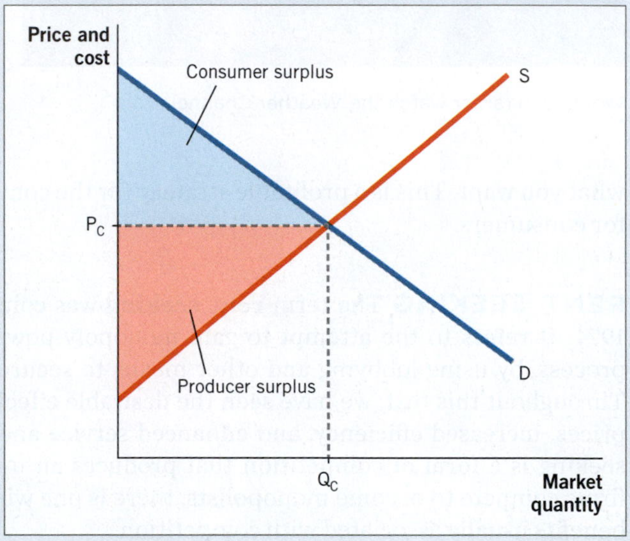

QUESTION: Now imagine that all the independent coffee shops combine under one fictional franchise, known as Harbucks. How can we create a new graph that illustrates the consumer surplus, producer surplus, and deadweight loss that occur when a monopolist takes over the market?

ANSWER:

In this figure, we see that the consumer surplus has shrunk, the producer surplus has increased, and the higher price charged by Harbucks creates deadweight loss. Allowing a monopolist to capture a market does not benefit consumers and is inefficient for society.

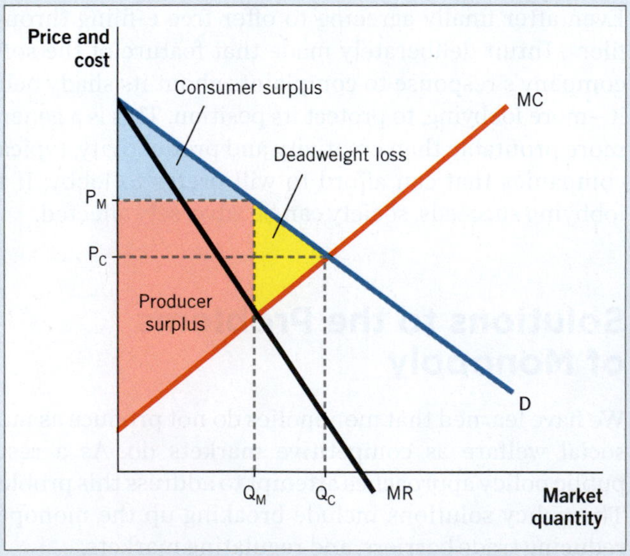

· ECONOMICS *in the* MEDIA ·

Monopoly Power

BREAKING BAD

Breaking Bad is widely regarded as one of the greatest television series of all time. It tells the story of Walter White, a depressed high school chemistry teacher diagnosed with lung cancer who turns to crime to secure his family's financial future before he dies. Together with a former student, Jesse Pinkman, the two produce and sell methamphetamine. Walt is the chemist who makes the best crystal meth in town. Jesse has the contacts Walt needs to sell it. Together, the two begin a long journey to take over the meth market in Albuquerque, New Mexico.

In one scene Jesse is enthused about how well they are doing and says, "Gonna be some mad cheddar, yo. Cheddar, Mr. White. Fat stacks, dead presidents, cash money. Gonna own this city."

Walt immediately responds, "We're not charging enough."

JESSE: "What?

WALT: "You corner the market, then raise the price. Simple economics."

Walt understands that you have to corner the market before you can raise your price.

BREAKING UP THE MONOPOLY Eliminating deadweight loss and restoring efficiency can be as simple as promoting competition. From 1913 until 1982, AT&T had a monopoly on the delivery of telephone services in the United States. As the years passed, however, it became progressively harder for AT&T to defend its position that having a single provider of phone services was good for consumers. By the early 1980s, AT&T was spending over $300 million to fend off antitrust lawsuits from the states, the federal government, and many private firms. The AT&T monopoly ended in 1982, when enormous pressure from the government led the company to split into eight smaller companies. Suddenly, AT&T had to compete to survive. The newly competitive phone market forced each of the phone companies to expand the services it offered—and sometimes even lower its prices—to avoid losing customers. For example, rates on long-distance calls, which were quite high before the break-up, plummeted.

Incentives

From this example, we see that the government can help to limit monopoly outcomes and restore a competitive balance. The government can accomplish this goal through antitrust legislation. Antitrust laws are designed to prevent monopoly practices and promote competition. The government has exercised control over monopoly practices since the passage of the Sherman Act in 1890, and the task currently falls to the Department of Justice. We discuss these regulations at greater length in Chapter 13.

REDUCING TRADE BARRIERS Countries use *tariffs*, which are taxes on imported goods, as a trade barrier to prevent competition and protect domestic business. However, any barrier—whether a tariff, a quota, or a prohibition—limits the possible gains from trade. For monopolists, trade barriers prevent rivals from entering their territory. For example, imagine that Florida could place a tariff on California oranges. For every California orange sold in Florida, the seller would have to pay a fee. Florida orange producers might like this tariff because it would limit competition from California. But California growers would cry foul and reciprocate with a tariff on Florida oranges. Growers in both states would be happy, but consumers would be harmed. For example, if a damaging freeze in Florida depleted the crop, Florida consumers would have to pay more than the demand-driven price for imported oranges from California. If, in contrast, Florida had a bumper crop, the tariff would keep prices artificially high, and much of the extra harvest would go to waste.

The United States has achieved tremendous growth by limiting the ability of individual states to place import and export restrictions on goods and services. The Constitution reads, "No State shall, without the consent of Congress, lay any imposts or duties on imports or exports." Rarely have so few words been more profound. With this simple law in place, states must compete on equal terms.

Reducing trade barriers creates more competition, lessens the influence of monopoly, and promotes the efficient use of resources. For example, prior to 1994, private air carriers accounted for less than 0.5% of the air traffic in India. In 1994, Indian airspace was opened to allow private airlines to operate scheduled service. This move forced the state-owned Air India to become more competitive. These changes in Indian aviation policies had the effect of raising the share of private airline operators in domestic passenger carriage to over 85% by 2018. Air India—which once controlled the market—has fallen to third place.

Reduced barriers to competition have transformed India's airline industry.

REGULATING MARKETS In the case of a natural monopoly, it is not practical to harness the benefits of competition. Consider the economies of scale that utility companies experience. Breaking up a company that provides natural gas, water, or electricity would result in higher production costs. For instance, a second water company would have to build infrastructure to each residence or business in a community. Having redundant water lines with only a fraction of the customers would make the delivery of water extremely expensive, such that the final price to the consumer, even with competition, would be higher. Therefore, keeping the monopoly intact is the best option. In this situation, policymakers might attempt to create a more efficient outcome and maximize society's welfare by regulating the monopolist's prices. Theoretically, this process would be straightforward. However, the reality is that few regulators are experts in the fields of electricity, natural gas, water, and other regulated industries, so they often lack sufficient knowledge to make the regulations work as designed.

When a natural monopoly exists, the government may choose to use the marginal cost pricing rule, P = MC, to generate the greatest welfare for society. Because the price is determined along the demand curve, setting P = MC guarantees that the good or service will be produced as long as the willingness to pay exceeds the additional cost of production. Figure 10.6 shows the difference in pricing and profits for a regulated monopoly and an unregulated natural monopoly. Recall that a natural monopoly is characterized by economies of scale, which we can idealize as a constant marginal cost that leads to a steadily dropping ATC curve, as in Figure 10.6.

To maximize profits, an unregulated monopolist sets MR = MC and produces quantity Q_M at a price of P_M. Because P_M is greater than the average total cost of producing Q_M units, or C_M, the monopolist earns the profit shown in

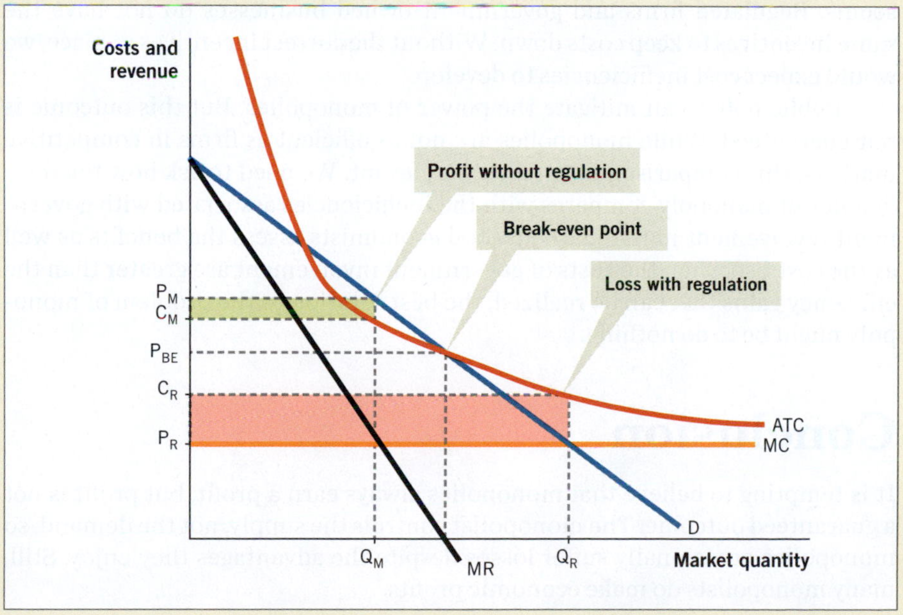

FIGURE 10.6

The Regulatory Solution for Natural Monopoly

An unregulated monopolist uses the profit-maximizing rule MR = MC and earns a small profit, shown in the green rectangle. If the monopolist is regulated using the marginal cost pricing rule, P = MC, it will experience the loss shown in the red rectangle.

Marginal thinking

the green rectangle. If the firm is regulated and the price is set at marginal cost, regulators can set P = MC, and the output expands to Q_R. (The subscript R denotes the regulated monopolist.) In this example, because the cost of production is subject to economies of scale, the cost falls from C_M to C_R and generates a large improvement in efficiency. The regulated price, P_R, is lower than the unregulated monopolist's price, P_M, and production increases. As a result, consumers are better off.

But what happens to the monopolist? It loses money in the amount of the red rectangle because the average total costs under the marginal cost pricing solution, C_R, are higher than the price allowed by regulators, P_R. This outcome is problematic because a firm that suffers losses will go out of business. That outcome is not desirable from society's standpoint, because the consumers of the product will be left without it. There are three possible solutions. First, to make up for the losses incurred at the higher output level, C_R, the government could subsidize the monopolist in order to achieve the socially efficient level of production. Second, the regulated price could be set at P_{BE}, where the ATC crosses the D curve, so that the firm breaks even; we can think of this as the second-best solution. Third, the government could own and operate the business in lieu of the private firm. This solution, however, has its own challenges, as we explore in the next section.

A CAVEAT ABOUT GOVERNMENT OVERSIGHT Firms with a profit motive have an incentive to minimize the costs of production, because lower costs translate directly into higher profits. If a firm's managers do a poor job reining in costs, they will be fired. The same cannot be said about government managers, or bureaucrats. Government employees are rarely let go, regardless of their performance. As a result, the government oversight and management of monopolies is problematic because there are fewer incentives to keep costs in check.

Incentives

Consequently, the marginal cost pricing rule is not as effective as it first seems. Regulated firms and government-owned businesses do not have the same incentives to keep costs down. Without the correct incentives in place, we would expect cost inefficiencies to develop.

Public policy can mitigate the power of monopolies. But this outcome is not guaranteed. While monopolies are not as efficient as firms in competitive markets, this comparison is not always relevant. We need to ask how the inefficiency of monopoly compares with the inefficiencies associated with government involvement in the market. Good economists assess the benefits as well as the costs, so when the costs of government involvement are greater than the efficiency gains that can be realized, the best solution to the problem of monopoly might be to do nothing.

Conclusion

It is tempting to believe that monopolies always earn a profit, but profit is not a guaranteed outcome. The monopolist controls the supply, not the demand, so monopolies occasionally suffer losses despite the advantages they enjoy. Still, many monopolists do make economic profits.

· ECONOMICS *for* LIFE ·

Playing Monopoly Like an Economist

- Buy and trade properties with others. Recall that trade is one of our Five Foundations.
- Some properties are landed on far more frequently than others. Buy or trade for them.
- If you obtain a monopoly, develop it as quickly as possible.

Apply some basic economic principles, and you can win big.

In the game Monopoly, you profit only by taking from other players. The assets of its world are fixed in number. The best player drives others into bankruptcy and is declared the winner only after gaining control of the entire board.

Here is some advice on how to play the game like an economist.

- Remember that a monopoly is built on trade. You are unlikely to acquire a monopoly by landing on the color groups you need. Instead, you have to trade properties in order to acquire the ones you need. Because every player knows this, acquiring the last property to complete a color group is nearly impossible. Your competitors will never willingly hand you a monopoly unless they get something of great value in return.
- Don't wait to trade until it is obvious what you need. Instead, try to acquire as many properties as you can in order to gain trading leverage as the game unfolds. Always pick up available properties if no other player owns one of the same color group; purchase properties that will give you two or three of the same group; or purchase a property if it blocks someone else from completing a set.
- Think about probability. Mathematicians have determined that Illinois Avenue is the property most likely to be landed on and that B&O is the best railroad to own. Know the odds, and you can weigh the risks and rewards of trade better than your opponents. This is just like doing market research before you buy. Being informed matters in Monopoly and in business.
- When you get a monopoly, develop it quickly. Build three houses as quickly as you can, but don't build a fourth house or put a hotel on your property—the returns to those additional investments are not worth the price.
- Finally, if you gain the upper hand and have a chance to bankrupt a player from the game, do it. Luck plays a key role in Monopoly, as it does in life. Although it may sound harsh, eliminating a competitor moves you one step closer to winning the game.

The decisions you make while playing Monopoly are all about cost-benefit analysis. You have limited resources and only so many opportunities to use them to your advantage. The skilled player understands how to weigh the values of tradable properties, considers the risk-return proposition of every decision, manages money effectively, and eliminates competitors when given a chance.

In this chapter, we examined the monopoly model and, along the way, compared the results under monopoly with the results of the competitive model that we developed in the previous chapter. While competitive markets generally yield welfare-enhancing outcomes for society, monopolies often do the opposite. Because monopolists do not produce an efficient outcome, government often seeks to limit monopoly outcomes and promote competitive markets.

Competitive markets and monopoly are market structures at opposite extremes. Indeed, we rarely encounter the conditions necessary for either a pure monopoly or a perfectly competitive market. Most economic activity takes place between these two alternatives. In the upcoming chapters, we examine monopolistic competition and oligopoly—two markets that constitute the bulk of the economy. Fortunately, if you understand the market structures at the extremes, understanding the middle ground is straightforward. As we move forward, we will deploy the same tools we used to examine monopoly in order to understand monopolistic competition (Chapter 12) and oligopoly (Chapter 13).

ANSWERING *the* BIG QUESTIONS

How are monopolies created?

- Monopoly is a market structure characterized by a single seller that produces a well-defined product with no good substitutes.
- Monopolies operate in a market with high barriers to entry, the chief source of market power.
- Monopolies are created when a single seller supplies the entire market for a particular good or service.

How much do monopolies charge, and how much do they produce?

- Monopolists are price makers who may earn long-run economic profits.
- Like perfectly competitive firms, a monopolist tries to maximize its profits. To do so, it uses the profit-maximizing rule, MR = MC, to select the optimal price and quantity combination of a good or service.

What are the problems with, and solutions for, monopoly?

- From an efficiency standpoint, the monopolist charges too much and produces too little. Because the monopolist's output is smaller than the output that would exist in a competitive market, monopolies lead to deadweight loss.
- Government grants of monopoly power encourage rent seeking, or the use of resources to secure monopoly rights through the political process.

- There are three potential solutions to the problem of monopoly. First, the government may break up firms that gain too much market power in order to restore a competitive market. Second, the government can promote open markets by reducing trade barriers. Third, the government can regulate a monopolist's ability to charge excessive prices.
- When the costs of government involvement in regulating a monopoly are greater than the efficiency gains that can be realized, it is better to leave the monopolist alone.

· CHAPTER PROBLEMS ·

Concepts You Should Know

barriers to entry (p. 314)
monopoly power (p. 314)
natural monopoly (p. 316)
price maker (p. 318)
rent seeking (p. 329)

Questions for Review

1. Describe the difference between a monopoly and a natural monopoly.
2. What are barriers to entry, and why are they crucial to the creation of potential long-run monopoly profits? Give an example of a barrier that can lead to monopoly.
3. Explain why a monopolist is a price maker but a perfectly competitive firm is a price taker.
4. Why is a monopolist's marginal revenue curve less than the price of the good it sells?
5. What is the monopolist's rule for determining the profit-maximizing output? What two steps does the monopolist follow to maximize profits?
6. Why does a monopolist operate inefficiently? Draw a demand curve, a marginal revenue curve, and a marginal cost curve to illustrate the deadweight loss from monopoly.
7. Why is it difficult to regulate a natural monopoly?

Study Problems *(✱ solved at the end of the section)*

1. In the figure below, identify the price the monopolist will charge and the output the monopolist will produce. How do these two decisions on the part of the monopolist compare with the efficient price and output?

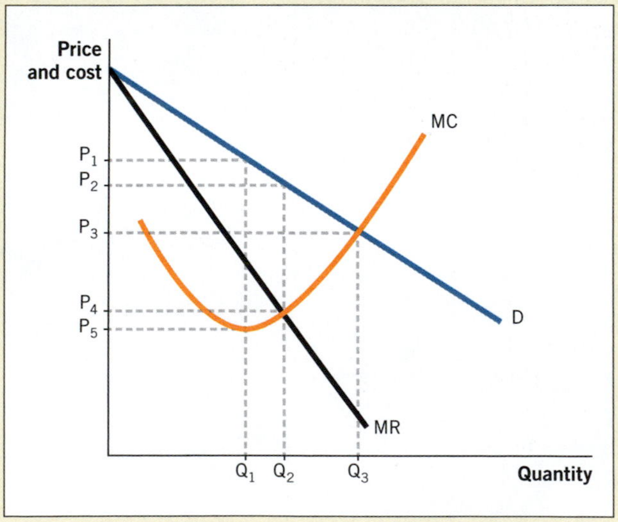

2. Which of the following could be considered a monopolist?
   a. your local water company
   b. Boeing, a manufacturer of airplanes
   c. Brad Pitt
   d. Walmart
   e. the only gas station along a 100-mile stretch of road
3. A monopolist has the following fixed and variable costs:

Price	Quantity	Fixed cost	Variable cost
$10	0	$8	$0
9	1	8	5
8	2	8	8
7	3	8	10
6	4	8	11
5	5	8	13
4	6	8	16
3	7	8	20
2	8	8	25

At what level of output will the monopolist maximize profits?

4. The year is 2278, and the starship *Enterprise* is running low on dilithium crystals, which are used to regulate the matter-antimatter reactions that propel the ship across the universe. Without the crystals, space-time travel is not possible. If there is only one known source of dilithium crystals, are the necessary conditions met to establish a monopoly? If the crystals are government owned or regulated, what price should the government set for them?

* **5.** If demand falls, what is likely to happen to a monopolist's price, output, and economic profit?

* **6.** A new musical group called The Incentives cuts a debut single. The record company determines a number of price points for the group's first single, "The Big Idea."

Price per download	Quantity of downloads
$2.99	25,000
1.99	50,000
1.49	75,000
0.99	100,000
0.49	150,000

The record company can produce the song with fixed costs of $10,000 and no variable cost.

a. Determine the total revenue at each price. What is the marginal revenue as the price drops from one level to the next?
b. What price would maximize the record company's profits? How much would the company make?
c. If you were the agent for The Incentives, what signing fee would you request from the record company? Explain your answer.

7. Recalling what you have learned about elasticity, what can you say about the connection between the price a monopolist chooses to charge and whether or not demand is elastic, unitary, or inelastic at that price? (**Hint:** Examine the marginal revenue curve of a monopolist. The fact that marginal revenue becomes negative at low prices implies that a portion of the demand curve cannot possibly be chosen.)

8. A small community is served by five independent gas stations. Gasoline is a highly competitive market. Use the market demand curve to illustrate the consumer surplus and producer surplus created by the market. Now imagine that the five independent gas stations are all combined under one franchise. Create a new graph that illustrates the consumer surplus, producer surplus, and deadweight loss after the monopolist enters the market.

9. A local community bus service charges $2.00 for a one-way fare. The city council is thinking of raising the fare to $2.50 to generate 25% more revenue. The council has asked for your advice as a student of economics. In your analysis, be sure to break down the impact of the price increase into the price effect and the output effect. Explain why the city council's estimate of the revenue increase is likely to be overstated. Use a graph to illustrate your answer.

10. Suppose that a monopolist's marginal cost curve shifts upward. What is likely to happen to the price the monopolist charges, the quantity it produces, and the profit it makes? Use a graph to illustrate your answer.

11. Suppose a firm collects $60 in revenues when it sells four units, $70 in revenues when it sells five units, and $75 when it sells six units. You can infer that the firm is

a. perfectly competitive.
b. either a perfectly competitive firm or a monopolist.
c. a monopolist.

✷ 12. Suppose Ambika, a graduate student in economics, tutors undergraduates to supplement her income as a teaching assistant. Ambika might tutor nine students each week. Their reservation prices for tutoring are given in the following table.

Each tutoring session lasts an hour. If the opportunity cost of Ambika's time is \$20 per hour, and if she must charge each student the same price, how many students should she tutor each week? What price should she charge? What will be her economic profit?

Student	Reservation price
A	\$50
B	46
C	42
D	38
E	34
F	30
G	26
H	22
I	18

Solved Problems

5. The following graph shows a monopolist making a profit:

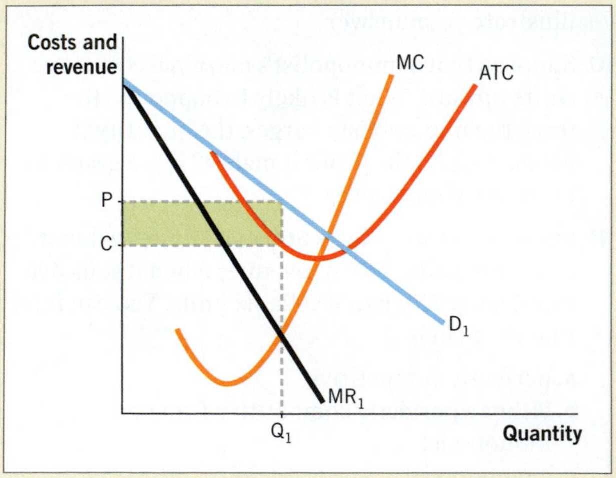

Now we show what happens if demand falls:

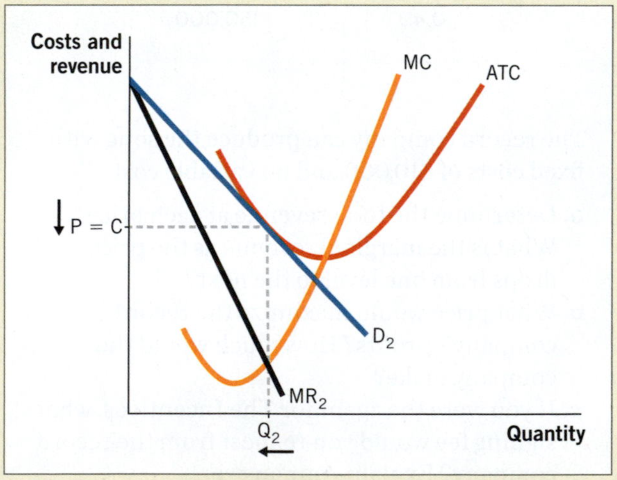

Lower demand causes the price to fall, the output to decline, and the profit to disappear.

6. a.

Price per download	Downloads	Total revenue	Marginal revenue
$2.99	25,000	$74,750	$74,750
1.99	50,000	99,500	24,750
1.49	75,000	111,750	12,250
0.99	100,000	99,000	–12,750
0.49	150,000	73,500	–25,500

b. Because marginal costs are $0, the firm would maximize its profits at $1.49. The company would make $111,750 – $10,000, or $101,750.

c. The company makes $101,750 from production, so as the agent you could request any signing fee up to that amount. Because determining a fee is a negotiation and both sides have to gain from trade, as the agent you should argue for a number close to $100,000, and you should expect the firm to argue for a much smaller fee.

12. She should tutor four students (students A–D). The marginal revenue of tutoring student D is $26, which is greater than Ambika's opportunity cost, but the marginal revenue of tutoring student E is only $18, which is less than Ambika's opportunity cost. So Ambika should stop at student D. She should charge $38, which is student D's reservation price. At this price, her economic profit will be 4($38) – 4($20) = $72.

Student	Reservation price	Total revenue	Marginal revenue
A	$50	$50	$50
B	46	92	42
C	42	126	34
D	38	152	26
E	34	170	18
F	30	180	10
G	26	182	2
H	22	176	–6
I	18	162	–14

CHAPTER

11

Price Discrimination

Charging Different Prices to Different People Isn't Automatically a Bad Thing.

Have you ever wondered why private colleges have high sticker prices and then offer tuition discounts to some students but not others? And why theaters charge more for adults than for children, when everyone sees the same movie? In these examples, some customers pay more and others pay less. Is this practice unfair? Well, think of it this way: everyone's paying a price they're willing to pay, and nearly everyone is still enjoying some consumer surplus. Anyway, two-tiered pricing usually works to the advantage of people who need a financial break, and in the big picture there are net social benefits, in the form of greater market efficiency.

Discounts for college students are a prime example. Here's a rundown of companies that will give you a price break if you can prove you're a student:

- clothing retailers like J. Crew, Eastern Mountain Sports, and TopShop
- tech companies such as Apple, Microsoft, Adobe, and MathWorks (makers of MATLAB)
- entertainment companies like Cinemark, Major League Baseball, museums, and most ski resorts and amusement parks
- travel and transportation companies such as Greyhound, Amtrak, many hotel brands, and some air carriers

College students win big with price discrimination—your student I.D. gets you hundreds of discounts.

- your favorite news publications, like the *New York Times* or the *Economist* (!)
- auto insurance (if you have good grades)
- all the major cell phone carriers
- last, but certainly not least: many national restaurant chains and almost all local restaurants

In this chapter, we examine many real-life pricing situations and how businesses can make additional profits if they charge different prices to different groups of customers. The study of *price discrimination* adds a layer of complexity to the simple models of perfect competition and monopoly. A thorough understanding of how price discrimination works is especially useful as we complete our study of market structure with monopolistic competition and oligopoly in the next two chapters.

· BIG QUESTIONS ·

- What is price discrimination?
- How is price discrimination practiced?

What Is Price Discrimination?

Price discrimination occurs when a firm sells the same good or service at different prices to different groups of customers.

Price discrimination occurs when a firm sells the same good or service at different prices to different groups of customers. The difference in price is not related to differences in cost. Although "price discrimination" sounds like something illegal, in fact it is beneficial to both sellers and buyers. When a firm can charge more than one price, markets work more efficiently. Because price-discriminating firms typically charge a "high" and a "low" price, some consumers are able to buy the product at a low price. Of course, firms are not in business to provide goods at low prices; they want to make a profit. Price discrimination enables them to make more money by dividing their customers into at least two groups: those who get a discount and others who pay more.

We have seen that in competitive markets, firms are *price takers*. If a competitive firm attempts to charge a higher price, its customers will likely buy elsewhere. To practice price discrimination, a firm must be a *price maker*; it must have some market power before it can charge more than one price. Both monopolies and nonmonopolistic companies use price discrimination to earn higher profits. Common examples of price discrimination are movie theater tickets, restaurant menus, college tuition, airline reservations, discounts on academic software, and coupons.

Conditions for Price Discrimination

For price discrimination to take place, two conditions must be met. First, there must be at least two different types of buyers. Second, the firm must be able to prevent resale of the product or service. Let's look at each in turn.

DISTINGUISHING GROUPS OF BUYERS To price-discriminate, a firm must be able to distinguish groups of buyers with different price elasticities of demand. Under those conditions, the firm faces a downward-sloping demand curve for its product, instead of a horizontal one. This gives the firm market power. Firms can generate additional revenues by charging more to customers with inelastic demand and less to customers with elastic demand. For instance, many restaurants offer lower prices, known as "early-bird specials," to people who eat dinner early. Who are these customers? Many, such as retirees and families with children, are on a limited budget. These early diners not only have lower demand but also represent demand that is more elastic; they eat out only if the price is low enough.

Trade-offs

Early-bird specials work for restaurants by separating customers into two groups: one that is price sensitive and another that is willing to pay full price. This strategy enables the restaurants to serve more customers and generate additional revenue.

PREVENTING RESALE For price discrimination to be a viable strategy, a firm must also be able to prevent resale of the product or service. In some cases, preventing resale is easy. For example, airlines require that electronic tickets match the passenger's government-issued photo ID. This system prevents a passenger who received a discounted fare from reselling it to another passenger who would be willing to pay more. The process works well for airlines and enables them to charge more to groups of flyers with more inelastic demand, such as business travelers. It also works well for restaurants offering early-bird specials, because the restaurants can easily distinguish between customers who arrive in time for the specials and those who arrive later.

One Price versus Price Discrimination

A business that practices price discrimination would prefer to differentiate every customer by selling the same good or service at a price unique to that customer—a situation known as **perfect price discrimination**. To achieve this result, a business would have to know exactly what any particular customer would be willing to pay and charge him or her exactly that price. Many jewelry stores and automobile dealerships attempt to practice perfect price discrimination by posting high sticker prices and then bargaining with each customer to

Perfect price discrimination occurs when a firm sells the same good or service at a unique price to every customer.

reach a deal. When you enter a jewelry store or a vehicle showroom, the salesperson tries to determine the highest price you are willing to pay. Then he or she bargains with you until that price is reached.

In practice, perfect price discrimination is hard to implement, so most firms instead settle for charging two or three prices based on sorting customers into a few easily identified groups. To see how this works, let's look at a hypothetical example. Consider two airlines, Flat Earth Air and Discriminating Fliers. Each airline has a monopoly on the route it flies, and each faces the same market demand curves and marginal costs. What happens if one of the airlines price-discriminates but the other does not?

In Figure 11.1, Flat Earth Air charges the same price to every passenger, while Discriminating Fliers uses two different price structures. To keep our example easy to work with, the marginal cost (MC) is set at $100, shown as a horizontal line.

Flat Earth Air sets its price by using the profit-maximizing rule, MR = MC. It charges $300 for every seat and serves 100 customers (that is, passengers).

FIGURE 11.1

One Price versus Price Discrimination

(a) A firm that charges a single price uses MR = MC to earn a profit. (b) When a firm price-discriminates, it takes in more profit than a firm that charges a single price. The discriminating firm increases its revenue by charging some customers more and other customers less, as shown in the green areas. The increase in profit is partly offset by the loss of revenue from existing customers who receive a lower price, as shown in the red area.

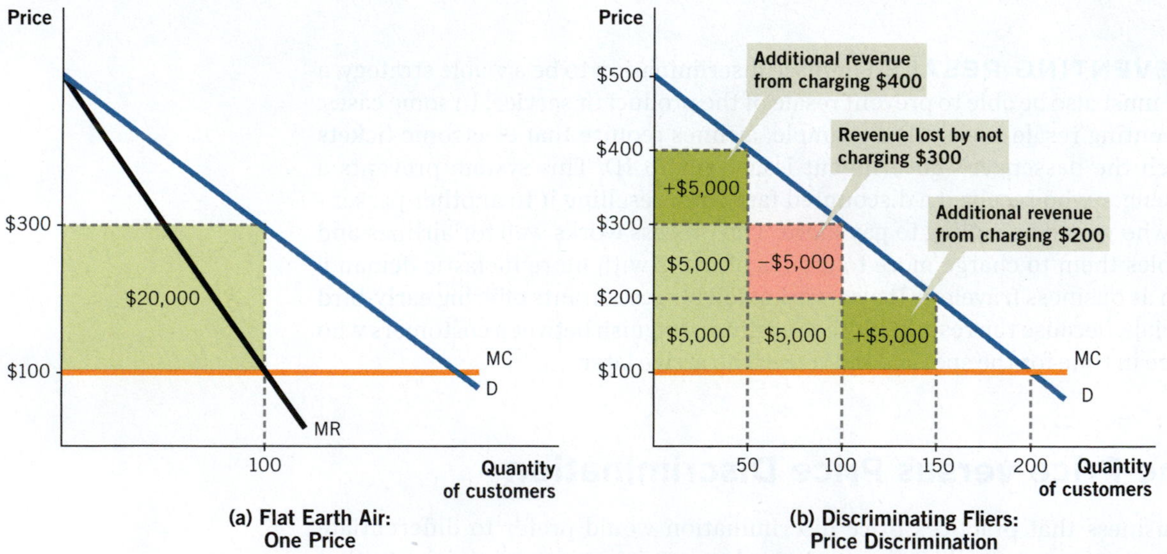

(a) Flat Earth Air: One Price

(b) Discriminating Fliers: Price Discrimination

Because the marginal cost is $100, every passenger who gets on the plane generates $200 in producer surplus. The profit, represented by the green rectangle in panel (a), is $200 × 100, or $20,000. At 100 passengers, this airline has done everything it can to maximize profits at a single price. At the same time, there are plenty of unsold seats in the plane, which can hold 200 passengers (even while leaving the middle row empty for social distancing). Those unfilled seats represent a lost opportunity to earn additional revenue. As a result, airlines typically try to fill the plane by discounting the price of some seats. And this is precisely what Discriminating Fliers does.

Airlines offer lower fares if you are willing to take the red-eye.

Discriminating Fliers experiments with two prices, as shown in panel (b). Let's look at the reasoning behind these two prices. Because the firm faces a downward-sloping demand curve, the airline cannot sell every available seat on the plane at the higher price. So it saves a number of seats, in this case 50, for last-minute bookings to capture customers with less flexibility who are willing to pay $400. These are travelers with inelastic demand, such as those who travel for business. The airline offers the rest of the seats at a low price, in this case $200, to capture customers with more elastic demand. The challenge for the airline is to make sure that the people who are willing to pay $400 do not purchase the $200 seats. So it makes the low fare available to customers who book far in advance, because these customers are typically more flexible and shop for the best deal. It is common for a businessperson who needs to visit a client to make flight arrangements just days before the meeting, which precludes purchasing a $200 ticket weeks in advance. The customers who book early fill the seats that would otherwise be empty if the airline had charged only one price, as Flat Earth Air does. We can see this outcome by comparing the total number of passengers under the two strategies. Discriminating Fliers, with its two-price strategy, serves 50 passengers who pay $400 and 100 additional passengers who pay $200. Flat Earth Air's single price of $300 brings in only 100 passengers.

Marginal thinking

The net effect of price discrimination is apparent in the shaded areas of panel (b). By charging two prices, Discriminating Fliers generates more profit. The high price, $400, generates additional revenue equal to the upper dark green rectangle—$5,000—from passengers who must pay more than the $300 charged by Flat Earth Air. Discriminating Fliers also gains additional revenue with its low price of $200. The less-expensive tickets attract passengers with more elastic demand, such as college students, vacationers, and retirees. The low-price tickets generate $5,000 in revenue, as shown by the lower dark green rectangle.

Some customers would have paid Discriminating Fliers more if the airline had charged a single price. Customers willing to pay $300 can acquire tickets on Discriminating Fliers for $200. The red rectangle represents the lost profit, equal to $5,000. The $10,000 in revenue represented by the dark green rectangles more than offsets the $5,000 in lost profit represented by the red rectangle. The airline that price-discriminates, depicted in panel (b), generates a profit of $25,000. The airline that charges a single price, depicted in panel (a), generates a profit of $20,000.

· ECONOMICS *in the* MEDIA ·

Price Discrimination

LEGALLY BLONDE

In this 2001 film, Reese Witherspoon stars as Elle Woods, who defies others' expectations by attending Harvard Law School. Believing that her boyfriend is about to propose to her, Elle and two friends go shopping to find the perfect dress for the occasion. They enter an exclusive boutique and start trying on dresses.

The saleswoman comments to another associate, "There's nothing I love more than a dumb blonde with daddy's plastic." She grabs a dress off the clearance sale rack and removes the "special sale" tag. Approaching Elle, she says, "Did you see this one? We just got it in yesterday." Elle fingers the dress, then the price tag, and looks at the saleswoman with excitement.

ELLE: "Is this a low-viscosity rayon?"

SALESWOMAN: "Uh, yes—of course."

ELLE: "With half-loop topstitching on the hem?"

SALESWOMAN (smiling a lie): "Absolutely. It's one of a kind."

(Elle hands the dress back to her, no longer pretending to be excited.)

ELLE: "It's impossible to use a half-loop topstitch on low-viscosity rayon. It would snag the fabric. And you didn't just get this in, because I remember it from the June *Vogue* a year ago, so if you're trying to sell it to me at full price, you picked the wrong girl."

Do you know how to get the best price? Elle does!

The scene is a wonderful example of an attempt at price discrimination gone wrong. Unbeknownst to the saleswoman, Elle is majoring in fashion merchandising in college and knows more about fashion than the saleswoman does. Her effort to cheat Elle fails miserably.

What makes the scene powerful is the use of stereotypes. When merchants attempt to price-discriminate, they look for clues to help them decide whether the buyer is willing to pay full price or needs an incentive, or discount, to make a purchase. In this case, the saleswoman misjudges Elle, assuming she is an uninformed buyer with highly inelastic demand. Consequently, her strategy backfires.

Price discrimination boosts profits under normal circumstances, but it also gives a firm more flexibility when things get crazy. For example, commercial airlines actually use sophisticated revenue management algorithms to change ticket prices instantly, trying to get the highest price possible for each customer. However, these algorithms rely on a predictable marketplace, and COVID-19 put them into a tailspin. Normally, airlines know from past data how many passengers will want to fly from, let's say, Tucson to Houston on a Saturday in April. In April 2020, that number was 90% less than what the airlines were used to seeing.

How would that kind of collapse in demand play out in our textbook example? Discriminating Fliers and Flat Earth Air would both want to institute dramatic price cuts, to keep the quantity consumed from dropping to zero. Discriminating Fliers has the advantage over Flat Earth Air, though, because it gets to experiment with lowering two different prices to fill empty seats. Flat Earth Air, which charges every customer the same price, is unable to differentiate between its customers. Consequently, its revenues will end up being lower than those earned by Discriminating Fliers.

The Welfare Effects of Price Discrimination

Price discrimination is profitable for the companies that practice it. But it also increases the welfare of society. How, you might ask, can companies make more profit and also benefit consumers? The answer: because a price discriminator charges a high price to some and a low price to others, more consumers are able to buy the good.

To illustrate this point, let's imagine an airline, Perfect Flights, that is able to perfectly price-discriminate. Perfect Flights charges each passenger a price exactly equal to what that passenger is willing to pay. As a result, some customers pay more and others pay less than they would under a single-price system. This outcome is evident in Figure 11.2, where a profit-maximizing firm charges $300. At this price, the firm captures the profit in the light green rectangle, B.

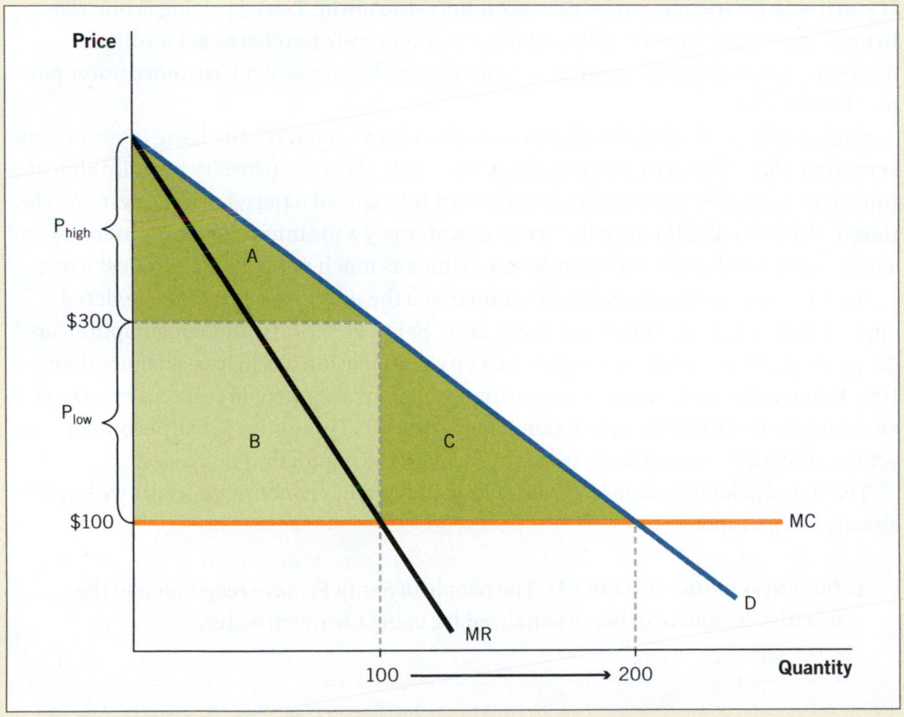

FIGURE 11.2

Perfect Price Discrimination

If the firm charges one price, the most it can earn is the profit in the light green rectangle. However, if a firm is able to perfectly price-discriminate, it can pick up the additional profit represented by the green triangles.

However, Perfect Flights charges each passenger a price based on his or her willingness to pay. Therefore, it earns significantly more profit. By charging higher prices (P_{high}) to those willing to pay more than $300, the firm is able to capture the additional profit in the upper dark green triangle, A. Likewise, by charging lower prices (P_{low}) to those not willing to pay $300, the firm is able to capture the additional profit in the lower dark green triangle, C. As a result, Perfect Flights is making more money and serving more customers.

Marginal thinking

By charging a different fare to every customer, Perfect Flights can also increase the quantity of tickets sold to 200. This strategy yields two results worth noting. First, in the long run, a perfectly competitive firm would charge a price just equal to marginal cost. In the case of Perfect Flights, the last customer who gets on the plane will pay an extraordinarily low price of $100—the price you might find in a competitive market. Second, this outcome mirrors the result of a government-regulated monopolist that uses the marginal cost pricing rule, P = MC, to enhance social welfare. Perfect Flights is therefore achieving the efficiency of a competitive market while also producing the output a regulated monopolist would choose. This strategy provides the firm with the opportunity to convert the area consisting of the two green triangles into more profit. In other words, the process maximizes the quantity sold. The efficiency of the market improves, and the firm generates more profit.

ECONOMICS IN THE REAL WORLD

SANTA FE, NEW MEXICO: USING NEGATIVE INCENTIVES AS PRICE DISCRIMINATION

Incentives

Tiered pricing encourages water conservation.

If you live in an arid climate, water rationing is the norm. Tiered pricing is one way to encourage water conservation. In most markets, bulk purchases get a volume discount. But as a way of encouraging water rationing, those who use more water pay much more for it.

Santa Fe, New Mexico, decided to use economics to address the issue of water conservation. Fifteen years ago, facing an acute water shortage (the city literally almost ran out of water), Santa Fe's city government introduced a tiered pricing system. The tiered system makes the heaviest users of water pay a premium for water used beyond a minimum. The heaviest users pay three times as much per gallon as modest users.

An article in the *New York Times* summarized the program's effects: "The tiered approach has worked as intended. Since 2001, Santa Fe's total water consumption has dropped by a fifth, even as the high desert city's population has increased more than 10%. When water costs more as its consumption increases, people respond exactly as an economics textbook would dictate: They use less."* This policy is truly economics in action, with a 20% reduction in water use even as the population increases!

The tiered pricing system involves several important economic concepts we have already learned about:

1. *Incentives matter* (Chapter 1). The people of Santa Fe have responded to the negative incentive of being penalized for using too much water.

*Nelson D. Schwartz, "Water Pricing in Two Thirsty Cities: In One, Guzzlers Pay More, and Use Less," *New York Times*, May 6, 2015, https://www.nytimes.com/2015/05/07/business/energy-environment/water-pricing-in-two-thirsty-cities.html.

2. *Internalizing the externality* (Chapter 7). Before 2001, heavy water users were affecting everyone in Santa Fe by creating periodic water shortages, but they did not have to pay extra for their actions. By paying much more for their water now, the heavy users are internalizing (paying for) the externality.
3. *Tragedy of the commons* (Chapter 7). Santa Fe has avoided a tragedy-of-the-commons scenario where all the water runs dry.
4. *The welfare effects of price discrimination* (this chapter). Dividing groups by their willingness to pay is beneficial to society, and that is what the Santa Fe water pricing system has achieved.

COMPARING PERFECT PRICE DISCRIMINATION WITH PERFECT COMPETITION AND MONOPOLY To understand the welfare effects of perfect price discrimination, we can compare the consumer and producer surplus in three scenarios: a competitive market, a market in which a monopolist charges a single price, and a market characterized by perfect price discrimination. The results, shown in Table 11.1, are derived by examining Figure 11.2.

In a perfectly competitive market, there are no barriers to entry and no firm has market power. In the long run, the price will be equal to the marginal cost. In our example of airline ticket prices, the price is driven down to $100. At this price, 200 tickets are sold. The entire area above the marginal cost curve (A + B + C) is consumer surplus, because the willingness to pay—as determined along the demand curve—is at least as great as the price. Because the ticket price is the same as the marginal cost, the producer surplus is zero. Because every customer who is willing to pay $100 or more can find a ticket, there is no deadweight loss. Under perfect competition, the market structure clearly favors consumers.

Marginal thinking

A monopoly holds substantial market power, so the firm in this scenario sets a price using the profit-maximizing rule, MR = MC, without having to worry about competition driving the price down to marginal cost. The monopolist's profit-maximizing price, or $300 in Figure 11.2, is higher than the $100 price under perfect competition. This higher price reduces the amount of consumer surplus to triangle A and creates a producer surplus equal to rectangle B. In addition, because the number of tickets sold falls to 100, there is now deadweight loss equal to triangle C. Economic activity associated with triangle C no longer exists, and the total welfare of society is now limited to A + B. From this analysis, we see that monopoly causes a partial transfer of consumer surplus to producers and a reduction in total welfare for society.

TABLE 11.1

The Welfare Effects of Perfect Price Discrimination

	Perfect competition	A monopolist that charges a single price	Perfect price discrimination
Consumer surplus	A + B + C	A	0
Producer surplus	0	B	A + B + C
Deadweight loss	0	C	0
Total welfare	A + B + C	A + B	A + B + C

In our third scenario, a firm that can practice perfect price discrimination is able to charge each customer a price exactly equal to the price that customer is willing to pay. This strategy enables the firm to convert the entire area of consumer surplus that existed under perfect competition into producer surplus (A + B + C). For the firm to capture the entire area of available consumer surplus, it must lower some prices all the way down to marginal cost. At that point, the number of tickets sold returns to 200, the market is once again efficient, and the deadweight loss disappears. Perfect price discrimination transfers the gains from trade from consumers to producers, but it also yields maximum efficiency.

Marginal thinking

Note that these examples give us a better understanding of what economists mean when they use the word "perfect" in connection with a market. It can mean that consumer surplus is maximized, as it is under perfect competition, or that producer surplus is maximized, as it is under perfect price discrimination. It does not specify an outcome from a particular perspective; instead, *perfect* describes any market process that produces no deadweight loss. If society's total welfare is maximized, economists do not distinguish whether the benefits accrue to consumers or producers. It is also important to note that while we compare the perfectly competitive result with the monopoly result and the result under perfect price discrimination as if those were the only three possible outcomes, those results are the extremes. Actual firms fall on a spectrum somewhere between these outcomes.

ECONOMICS IN THE REAL WORLD

OUTLET MALLS—IF YOU BUILD IT, THEY WILL COME

Have you ever noticed that outlet malls along major roadways are often located a considerable distance from large population centers? Moreover, every item at an outlet mall can be found closer to home. The same clothes, shoes, and kitchenware are available nearby.

Incentives

Logic tells us it would be more convenient to shop locally and forgo the time and hassle of getting to an outlet center. But that is not how many shoppers feel.

Discount shopping is a big deal. How big? Potomac Mills, 30 miles south of Washington, D.C., is Virginia's most popular attraction, with nearly 23 million visitors a year. (That figure rivals the number of annual visitors to Disney World's Magic Kingdom!)

How far would you drive to visit an outlet mall?

Outlet shopping is an example of price discrimination at work. Traditional malls are usually situated in urban settings and offer a wide variety of choices, but not necessarily low prices. If you want convenience, the local shopping mall is right around the corner. But if you want a bargain, shopping at a traditional local mall is not the best way to go.

What makes outlets so attractive are the discounts. Bargain hunters have much more elastic demand than their traditional mall-shopping counterparts who desire convenience. Moreover, the difference in the price elasticity of demand between these two groups means that traditional malls can more easily charge full price, while outlets must discount their merchandise to attract customers. The difference between these two groups of customers gives merchants a chance to price-discriminate on the basis of location—which is another way of separating customers into two groups and preventing resale at the same time. Retailers can therefore earn additional profits through price discrimination, while price-sensitive consumers can find lower prices at the outlets.

It is noteworthy that the convenience of finding discounts online threatens not only the traditional malls but also the outlets. When savvy shoppers can simply click to find the best deal, will they continue to drive to the outlets? Online retailers that have built user-friendly web sites with fast shipping and a seemingly endless list of products—think Amazon—are building platforms that many shoppers prefer to in-person shopping. Internet shopping also facilitates price discrimination. Cookies that record your search history can be used to influence the price you are offered, in effect enabling firms to discover a price closer to your willingness to pay. Online retailers also track whether you arrive at their address on a Mac or PC and what operating system you use. Did you know that many web sites routinely place more expensive products higher up in the search results if you are a Mac user? That's another example of price discrimination, but this time groups are differentiated based on the gadgets they use.

Opportunity cost

PRACTICE WHAT YOU KNOW

Price Discrimination: Taking Economics to New Heights

How much would you pay to fly in a helicopter?

Consider the table below, which shows seven potential customers who are interested in taking a 30-minute helicopter ride. The helicopter has room for eight people, including the pilot. The cost to the helicopter company of taking on each additional passenger is $5.

Customer	Maximum willingness to pay	Age
Amelia	$80	66
Orville	70	34
Wilbur	40	17
Neil	50	16
Sally	60	9
Mae	100	49
Charles	20	9

QUESTION: If the company can charge only one price, what should it be?

ANSWER: First, create an ordered array of the customers, from those willing to pay the most to those willing to pay the least.

If the firm charges $100, only Mae will take the flight. When the firm drops the price to $80, Mae and Amelia both buy tickets, so the total revenue (TR) is 80 × 2, or $160. Successively lower prices result in higher total revenue from the first five customers.

(CONTINUED)

Customer	Maximum willingness to pay	Price	TR	MR
Mae	$100	$100	$100	$100
Amelia	80	80	160	60
Orville	70	70	210	50
Sally	60	60	240	30
Neil	50	50	250	10
Wilbur	40	40	240	−10
Charles	20	20	140	−100

The firm will benefit from lowering its price as long as the marginal revenue is greater than the marginal cost, $5. When the price is $50, five customers get on the helicopter, for a total of $250 in revenue. Adding the fifth passenger brings in $10 in marginal revenue. The marginal revenue for the sixth passenger is negative, so $50 is the best possible price to charge. Because each of the five passengers has a marginal cost of $5, the company makes $250 − (5 × $5) or $225 in profit.

QUESTION: If the company could charge two prices, what should they be, and who would pay them?

ANSWER: First, arrange the customers in two distinct groups: adults and children.

Adult customers	Willingness to pay	Age	Price	TR	MR
Mae	$100	49	$100	$100	$100
Amelia	80	66	80	160	60
Orville	70	34	70	210	50

Young customers	Willingness to pay	Age	Price	TR	MR
Sally	$60	9	$60	$60	$60
Neil	50	16	50	100	40
Wilbur	40	17	40	120	20
Charles	20	9	20	80	−40

As you can see, two separate prices emerge. For adults, profits are maximized at a price of $70. For children, total profits are maximized at $40. The company should charge $70 to the adult customers, which brings in $70 × 3, or $210 in total revenue. The company should charge $40 for each child under the age of 18, which brings in $40 × 3, or $120.

Price discrimination earns the company $210 + $120 − (6 × $5), or $300 in profit. This is a $75 improvement over charging a single price. In addition, six passengers are now able to get on the helicopter, instead of only five under the single-price model. Of course, leaving nine-year-old Charles on the ground by himself isn't a great idea! Let's hope there's an adult friend or relative who was planning to sit the ride out.

How Is Price Discrimination Practiced?

Price discrimination is one of the most interesting topics in economics because each example is slightly different from the others. In this section, we take a closer look at real-world examples of price discrimination at movie theaters and on college campuses. Movie theaters and college campuses would like to achieve perfect price discrimination, but it simply isn't possible to know each customer's exact willingness to pay. As you will see, price discrimination takes many forms—some that are easy to describe and others that are more nuanced.

Price Discrimination at the Movies

Have you ever gone to the movies early so you can pay less for tickets? Movie theaters price-discriminate based on the time of day, age, student status, and whether or not you buy snacks. Let's examine these pricing techniques to see if they are effective.

PRICING BASED ON THE TIME OF THE SHOW Why are matinees priced less than evening shows? To encourage customers to attend movies during the afternoon, theaters discount ticket prices for matinees. This strategy makes sense because customers who can attend matinees (retirees, people on vacation, and those who do not work during the day) either have less demand or are more flexible, or price elastic. Work and school limit the options for many other potential customers. As a result, theaters discount matinee prices to encourage moviegoers who have elastic demand and are willing to watch at a less-crowded time. Movie theaters also discount the price of matinee shows because they pay to rent films on a weekly basis, so it is in their interest to show a film as many times as possible during a given week. Because the variable cost of being open during the day is essentially limited to paying a few employees relatively low wages, the theater can make additional profits even with a relatively small audience. On weekends, matinees also offer a discount to families that want to see a movie together—adding yet another layer of price discrimination.

Theaters charge two different prices based on showtime because they can easily distinguish between inelastic-demand customers and price-sensitive customers who have the flexibility to watch a matinee. Those with inelastic demand have less-flexible schedules and must pay higher ticket prices to attend in the evening.

Even if you're at the matinee because your demand is highly elastic, be considerate of people who really want to watch the movie.

PRICING BASED ON AGE OR STUDENT STATUS Why are there different movie prices for children, seniors, students, and everyone else? This is a complex question. Income does not fully explain the discounts that the young, the old, and students receive. Movie attendance is highest among 13- to 24-year-olds and declines thereafter with age. Given the strong demand among teenagers, it is not surprising that "child" discounts are phased out at most theaters by age 12. But did you know that most "senior"

YOUR ORDER

Child Seat: B4	$7.98
Child Seat: B5	$7.98
Child Seat: B2	$7.98
Child Seat: B3	$7.98
Adult Seat: B7	$8.73
Adult Seat: B6	$8.73
Subtotal	$49.38
Payment Processing Fee	$9.00
Your Total	**$58.38**

When theaters add a "convenience" fee to orders, this is price discrimination.

discounts begin before age 65? In some places, senior discounts start at age 50. Now you might think that because people in their 50s tend to be at the peak of their earning power, discounting ticket prices for them would be a bad move. However, because interest in going to the movies declines with age, the "senior" discount actually provides an incentive for a population that might not otherwise go to a movie theater. However, as we have seen, age-based price discrimination does not always work perfectly. Theaters do not usually ask for proof of age, and it may be hard to tell the difference between a child who is just under 12 and one who is over 12. Nonetheless, price discrimination works well enough to make age or student status a useful revenue-generating tool. Empty seats represent lost revenue, so it makes sense to price-discriminate through a combination of high and low prices.

CONVENIENCE FEES Movie theaters, like other large venues, will charge you a convenience fee (usually a few dollars) to reserve a seat in advance and skip waiting in line to get your ticket at the door. But if you don't care so much where you sit and are willing to wait in line, you can avoid that fee. This is another way theaters price-discriminate. The optional convenience fee enables them to attract both the customers who like to go to the movies in style and those who count their pennies.

Price Discrimination on Campus

Colleges and universities are experts at price discrimination. Think about tuition. Some students pay the full sticker price, while others enjoy a free ride. Some students receive the in-state rate, while out-of-state students pay substantially more. And once you get to campus, discounts for students are everywhere. In this section, we consider the many ways in which colleges and universities differentiate among their students.

TUITION Price discrimination begins before you ever set foot on campus, with the Free Application for Federal Student Aid (known as the FAFSA) that most families complete. The form determines eligibility for federal aid. Families that qualify are eligible for grants and low-interest loans, which effectively lower the tuition cost for low- and medium-income families. Therefore, the FAFSA enables colleges to separate applicants into two groups based on income. Because many colleges also use the FAFSA to determine eligibility for their own institutional grants of aid, the FAFSA makes it possible for colleges to precisely target grants and loans to the students who need the most financial help.

Many state institutions of higher education have a two-tiered pricing structure. In-state students get a discount on the tuition, while out-of-state students pay a much higher rate. Part of the difference is attributable to state subsidies that are intended to make in-state institutions more affordable for residents. In-state students pay less because their parents have been paying taxes to the state, often for many years, and the state then uses some of those tax dollars to support its system of higher education. However, in-state subsidies only partially explain the difference in pricing. Out-of-state tuition is higher than it would be if all students paid the same price because out-of-state students are generally less sensitive to price than in-state students.

Resort or college? Sky-high tuition and room and board are one way to help pay for a beautiful campus.

This two-tiered pricing structure creates two separate groups of customers with distinctly different elasticities of demand. Students choose an out-of-state college or university because they like what that institution has to offer more than the institutions in their home state. It might be that a particular major or program is more highly rated at the out-of-state school. Whatever the reason, they are willing to pay more for the out-of-state school. Therefore, out-of-state students have a much more inelastic demand. Colleges know this and price their tuition accordingly. Conversely, in-state students often view the opportunity to attend a nearby college as the most economical decision. Because price is a big factor in choosing an in-state institution, it is not surprising that in-state demand is more elastic.

Selective private colleges also play the price discrimination game by advertising annual tuition and other expenses that exceed $60,000. With price discrimination, the "sticker" price is often discounted. Depending on how much the college wants to encourage a particular student to attend, it can discount the tuition all the way to zero. This strategy enables selective private colleges to price-discriminate by offering scholarships based on financial need, while also guaranteeing placements for the children of wealthy alumni and others willing to pay the full sticker price.

Colleges and universities also use "early decision" and campus visits to determine how eager you are to attend. That information is a measure of your price elasticity of demand. At the margin, students who commit to an early decision have more inelastic demand than those who only apply for regular admission. This is yet another way colleges fine-tune student aid packages based on observed behavior.

ECONOMICS IN THE REAL WORLD

TARGETED COMMUNICATION ALLOWS COLLEGES TO SELECTIVELY PRICE-DISCRIMINATE

In practice, price discrimination can be hard to achieve. Take college applications, for instance. A University of Michigan study* found that many qualified low-income students were not applying to elite schools, even when they would receive significant financial aid to lower their costs. Why not? Apparently, many of these students found the application process intimidating, especially because of all the complex financial aid paperwork, and—key point—they incorrectly thought they had a low chance of being

*Susan Dynarksi, C. J. Libassi, Katherine Michelmore, and Stephanie Owen, "Closing the Gap: The Effect of a Targeted, Tuition-Free Promise on College Choices of High-Achieving. Low-Income Students," NBER Working Paper Series, No. 25349, December 2018, revised June 2020, https://doi.org/10.3386/w25349.

SNAPSHOT

Now Playing: Economics!

Have you ever gone to the movies early so you can pay less for tickets? Movie theaters price- discriminate based on the time of the movie and the age of the customer. In order to practice price discrimination, theaters must be able to identify different groups of moviegoers, where each group has a different price elasticity of demand.

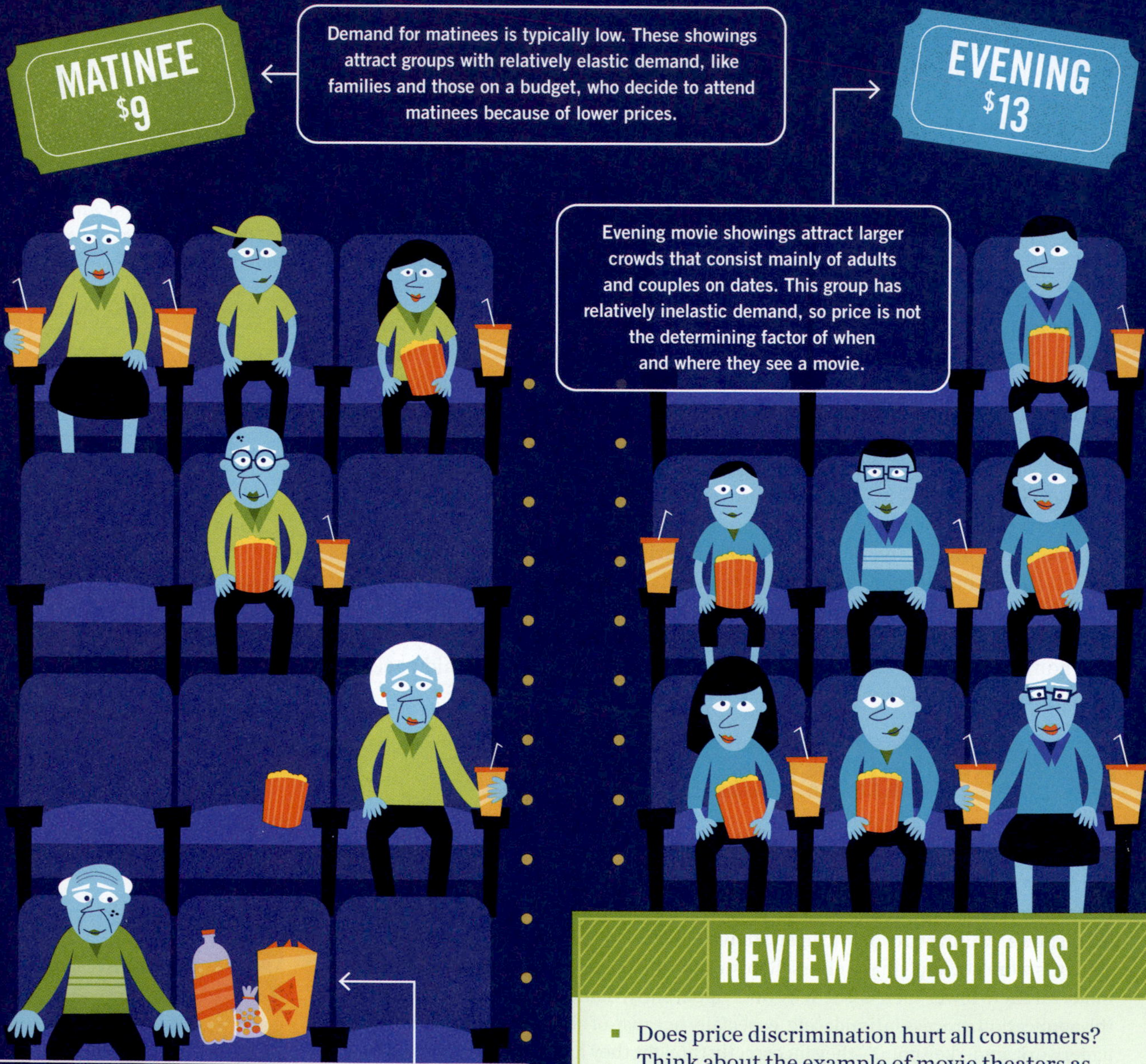

MATINEE $9
Demand for matinees is typically low. These showings attract groups with relatively elastic demand, like families and those on a budget, who decide to attend matinees because of lower prices.
EVENING $13
Evening movie showings attract larger crowds that consist mainly of adults and couples on dates. This group has relatively inelastic demand, so price is not the determining factor of when and where they see a movie.

The concession counter also generates profit for the movie theater. The high prices mean that patrons who are price–conscious (having relatively elastic demand) skip the counter or smuggle in their own snacks, while those who are more concerned about convenience than price (having relatively inelastic demand) buy snacks at the counter.

REVIEW QUESTIONS

- Does price discrimination hurt all consumers? Think about the example of movie theaters as you craft your response.
- Your local movie theater is thinking about increasing ticket prices for just the opening day of a blockbuster movie. How would you explain the economics behind this price increase?

accepted. On paper, there was price discrimination, but elite schools weren't getting enough takers.

The obvious solution was better communication. For the study, several thousand high-achieving, low-income students were sent letters telling them up front that if they applied to UM, they would be admitted and would receive a full, four-year scholarship. Giving the students this information early in their decision process made a huge difference. In the targeted group, the number of students who applied and ultimately enrolled more than doubled. Here's the takeaway: price-discriminating works best when combined with effective marketing. In this case, the outcome was a win for the students who took the offer; for the university, which made progress toward its enrollment goals; and for society at large.

STUDENT DISCOUNTS The edge of campus is a great place to look for price discrimination. Local bars, eateries, and shops all want college students to step off campus, so student discounts are the norm. Why do establishments offer student discounts? Think about the average college student. Price matters to that student. Knowing this, local merchants in search of college customers can provide student discounts without lowering their prices across the board. This means they can charge more to their regular clients while providing the necessary discounts to get college students to make the trek off campus.

Price discrimination also occurs at entertainment venues near a college campus. For example, students typically receive discounts for campus activities like concerts and sporting events. Because students generally have elastic demand, price discrimination provides greater student access to events than charging a single price does.

PRACTICE WHAT YOU KNOW

Price Discrimination in Practice: Everyday Examples

QUESTION: Test your understanding by thinking about the examples below. Are they examples of price discrimination?

a. **Retail coupons.** Programs such as discount coupons, rebates, and frequent-buyer plans appeal to customers willing to spend time pursuing a deal.

b. **Using Priceline to make hotel reservations.** "Naming your price" on Priceline.com is a form of haggling that enables users to get hotel rooms at a discount. Hotels negotiate with Priceline to fill unused rooms while still advertising the full price on their web sites.

c. **The 1-2-3 Menu at McDonald's.** Customers who order off the 1-2-3 Menu get a variety of smaller menu items for $1, $2, or $3 each.

During 2020, COVID-19 was the worst of times, but you could make the best of it by downloading the Burger King app.

(CONTINUED)

ANSWERS:

a. **Retail coupons.** Affluent customers generally do not bother with the hassle of clipping, sending in, and keeping track of coupons because they value their time more than the small savings. However, customers with lower incomes usually take the time to get the discount. This means that coupons, rebates, and frequent-buyer programs do a good job of price-discriminating.

b. **Using Priceline to make hotel reservations.** Priceline enables hotels to divide their customers into two groups: those who don't want to be bothered with haggling and those who value the savings enough to justify the time spent negotiating. This is a good example of price discrimination.

c. **The 1-2-3 Menu at McDonald's.** Anyone can buy off the 1-2-3 Menu at any time. Because McDonald's does not force customers to do anything special in order to get the deal, this is not price discrimination.

CHALLENGE QUESTION: For two weeks at the outset of the coronavirus pandemic, customers who downloaded Burger King's app were entitled to two free kids' meals with any purchase. Are discounts for app users a form of price discrimination?

ANSWER: Downloading the app was a hoop to jump through. Customers who did that got the two free kids' meals, while customers who didn't bother with the app missed out. Any retailer can use this method to divide customers into two groups: those with elastic demand (willing to download an app to get a deal) and those with inelastic demand (they'd rather not hassle with the app). Don't be distracted by the fact that anyone can download the app. Most people won't go to the trouble, and that is what makes price discrimination possible.

ECONOMICS IN THE REAL WORLD

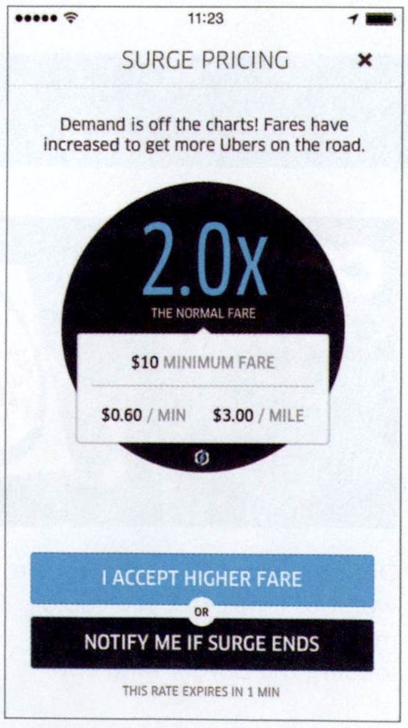

Pay or wait for the surge to end.

UBER AND LYFT: SURGE PRICING

When ride-sharing companies impose "surge pricing" during times of peak demand for rides and/or a low supply of drivers, what is going on? It's supply and demand at work, of course. But look closer. Surge pricing is a way to divide ride-share customers into at least two distinct groups, with different elasticities of demand. In short, surge pricing is a form of price discrimination.

Uber is completely up front about this. As the company explains on its web site, anything from rush hour to bad weather to a special event can increase the demand for rides. When this demand hits Uber's app, its algorithm calculates a new, higher price. The new price does two things. First, it lures more drivers onto the road. That's the supply side of the dynamic. But second, some riders will choose to pay the higher price, while others, as Uber puts it, "will choose to wait a few minutes to see if the rates go back down."* That's price discrimination on the demand side.

The price discrimination is customer-driven and completely voluntary. Suppose you're trying to catch a ride to the beach when the prices surge. If you accept the higher fare, it means your demand is relatively inelastic. Maybe you have friends waiting, or

*Uber.com, "How Surge Pricing Works," https://www.uber.com/us/en/drive/driver-app/how-surge-works/.

· ECONOMICS *in the* MEDIA ·

Price Discrimination

JURASSIC PARK

Early on in the original *Jurassic Park* film, there's a discussion about the price of admission to the live-dinosaur theme park. "We can charge anything we want," muses the investors' lawyer, "two thousand a day, ten thousand a day, and people will pay it." Hammond, the park's visionary founder, objects: "This park was not meant to cater only for the super-rich. Everyone in the world has the right to enjoy these animals." The lawyer doesn't see a problem. "Sure. They will. We'll have a coupon day or something."

The ingenious thing about offering coupons, and about price discrimination in general, is that it would generate more total revenue for the firm while simultaneously increasing the number of visitors who are able to take in the park. The lawyer understands that some people's demand for dino-safaris is highly inelastic, but if that is the only market segment the park attracts, there may be times (off-season) when they can generate additional revenue by lowering the price to a separate group of tourists whose demand is more price-sensitive.

How much would you be willing to pay to see a real-life dinosaur in the wild?

Opportunity cost

maybe you're just impatient. On the other hand, if you wait for the surge to end, or if you just catch a bus instead, it means you care more about the price than the time you would save. Translation: your demand is elastic.

Ride-share customers display different degrees of price sensitivity all the time. The algorithm doesn't care, but because you and I do, we willingly separate ourselves into different groups, and thereby participate in Uber or Lyft's practice of price discrimination.

Conclusion

The word "discrimination" has negative connotations, but not when combined with the word "price." Charging different prices to different groups of customers results in more economic activity and is more efficient than charging a single price across the board. Under price discrimination, many consumers pay less than they would if a firm had charged a single price, while other consumers

· ECONOMICS for LIFE ·

Gender-Based Price Discrimination

On average, across the five industries surveyed, one report found that women paid:

- 7% more for toys and accessories.
- 4% more for children's clothing.
- 8% more for adult clothing.
- 13% more for personal care products.
- 8% more for senior/home health care products.

Throughout this chapter, we considered the shopping experience in the context of price discrimination. Here we focus on how firms separate men and women into different groups by making cosmetic changes to the products they sell.

In a report prepared for the New York City Department of Consumer Affairs, author Anna Bessendorf and her team compared nearly 800 products with clear male and female versions from more than 90 brands sold at two dozen New York City retailers, both online and in stores.

The report found that women frequently paid more than men for the same products. Specifically, the report found that women's products cost 7% more than similar products for men. To minimize differences between men's and women's items, Bessendorf's team selected products with male and female versions that were very similar in branding, appearance, materials, construction, and/or marketing. In all but five of the 35 product categories analyzed, products for female consumers were priced higher than those for male consumers. Across the entire sample, the report found that women's products cost more 42% of the time, while men's products cost more only 18% of the time.

Why would firms charge more for the female version of a product? The answer is price discrimination.

Why do the same jeans cost $50 more for women?

When different groups (males and females) have different price elasticities of demand, price discrimination allows a firm to earn more revenue. In most of the products surveyed, females had more inelastic demand, which translates into higher prices for them in the marketplace compared to males.* If you are not happy about gender-based pricing there is a potential workaround: buy the comparable male product. Is a pink razor really something you have to have when a similar blue razor sells for less?

*Anna Bessendorf, New York City Department of Consumer Affairs, "From Cradle to Cane: The Cost of Being a Female Consumer," December 2015, https://www1.nyc.gov/assets/dca/downloads/pdf/partners/Study-of-Gender-Pricing-in-NYC.pdf.

will pay more because their demand is more inelastic. But overall, total social welfare increases, and the amount of deadweight loss in society is reduced.

Price discrimination also helps us understand how many markets actually function, because instances of perfectly competitive markets and monopoly are rare. ✷

- ANSWERING *the* BIG QUESTIONS -

What is price discrimination?

- Price discrimination occurs when firms can identify different groups of customers with varying price elasticities of demand and can prevent resale among their customers.
- A firm must have some market power before it can charge more than one price.

How is price discrimination practiced?

- Under price discrimination, some consumers pay a higher price and others receive a discount. Price discrimination is profitable for the firm, reduces deadweight loss, and leads to a higher output level.

CHAPTER PROBLEMS

Concepts You Should Know

perfect price discrimination (p. 345)

price discrimination (p. 344)

Questions for Review

1. What two challenges must a price maker overcome to effectively price-discriminate?
2. Why does price discrimination improve the efficiency of the market?
3. Why is preventing resale a key to successful price discrimination?
4. If perfect price discrimination reduces consumer surplus to zero, how can this situation lead to the most socially desirable level of output?

Study Problems *(✱ solved at the end of the section)*

1. Seven potential customers are interested in seeing a movie. Because the marginal cost of admitting additional customers is zero, the movie theater maximizes its profits by maximizing its revenue.

Customer	Maximum willingness to pay	Age
Allison	$8	66
Becky	11	34
Charlie	6	45
David	7	16
Erin	6	9
Franco	10	28
Grace	9	14

   a. What price would the theater charge if it could charge only one price?
   b. If the theater could charge two prices, what prices would it choose? Which customers would pay the higher price, and which would pay the lower price?
   c. How much profit does the theater make when it charges only one price? How much profit does the theater make if it price-discriminates?

2. Which of the following are examples of price discrimination? Explain your answers.
   a. A cell phone carrier offers unlimited calling on the weekends for all of its customers.
   b. Tickets to the student section for all basketball games are $5.
   c. A restaurant offers a 20% discount for customers who order dinner between 4 and 6 p.m.
   d. A music store has a half-price sale on last year's guitars.
   e. A well-respected golf instructor charges each customer a fee just under the customer's maximum willingness to pay for lessons.

3. At many amusement parks, customers who enter after 4 p.m. receive a steep discount on the price of admission. Explain how this practice is a form of price discrimination.

4. Name three products for which impatience on the part of the consumer enables a firm to price-discriminate.

✱ 5. Prescription drug prices in the United States are often substantially higher than in Canada, the United Kingdom, and India. Today, pharmacies in these countries fill millions of low-cost prescriptions through the mail to U.S. citizens. Given that the pharmaceutical industry cannot prevent the resale of these drugs, are the industry's efforts to price-discriminate useless? Explain your answer.

✱ 6. Metropolitan Opera tickets are the most expensive on Saturday night. There are often a very limited number of "student rush tickets," with which a lucky student can wind up paying $20 for a $250 seat. The student rush tickets are available first-come, first-served. Why does the opera company offer these low-cost tickets? How does it benefit from this practice? Why are students, and not other groups of customers, offered the discounted tickets?

* **7.** Have you ever tipped a restaurant host in order to bypass a long wait and get a table more quickly? Would this be an example of price discrimination? Why or why not? Discuss.

8. Orbitz, the travel web site, routinely offers PC and Apple users different search results. Apple users typically have higher-priced hotels show up on the top page of the results, while PC users are presented with somewhat lower prices. Is Orbitz practicing price discrimination? Discuss.

* **9.** When Subway customers pay less per inch for footlong subs than they pay per inch for a six-inch sub, is this price discrimination or not?

* **10.** If an app uses geolocation to understand where you are and offers different prices based on your location, is this price discrimination or not?

Solved Problems

5. Buying prescription drugs outside the United States is increasingly common. Because the pharmaceutical companies charge three to four times more for drugs sold domestically than they do in most other countries, it would seem that the drug industry's efforts to price-discriminate aren't working, but that is not true. Not everyone fills their prescriptions from foreign sources; only a small fraction of U.S. customers go to that much effort. Because most U.S. citizens still purchase the more expensive drugs here, the pharmaceutical companies are benefiting from price discrimination, even though some consumers manage to navigate around their efforts.

6. The Met hopes to sell all of its $250 tickets, but not every show sells out and some tickets become available at the last minute. The student rush tickets benefit both the opera company and the students: the company can fill last-minute seats, and the students, who have elastic demand and low income, get a steep discount. The Met is able to price-discriminate, because the rush tickets require a student ID. Other groups of operagoers are therefore unable to buy the rush tickets. This practice effectively separates the customer base into two groups: students and nonstudents. Students make ideal rush customers because they are more willing to change their plans in hopes of obtaining last-minute tickets than other groups. Some opera companies also open up the rush tickets to seniors, another group that is easy to identify and generally has significant flexibility.

7. As a college student you probably don't have a lot of money to tip the restaurant host. But if you do have the money, it would make sense to tip the host. Here is why: First, your tip gets you seated sooner and avoids the wait time. Time is money, so you save right there. Second, the host has an incentive to let tippers in sooner, and that's not just good for the host. It is also good for the business because tippers have much more inelastic demand, which translates into customers who spend more while dining. So the host is actually separating customers into two groups: tippers with inelastic demand and nontippers with much more elastic demand. Third, the restaurant wins because when tippers with inelastic demand get tables faster, the restaurant makes more revenue.

9. Anyone could conceivably get the better deal, but only those with big appetites or a willingness to eat leftovers will choose a footlong. Those with smaller appetites are stuck paying more per inch for a six-inch sub. Since Subway can differentiate between those with big and smaller appetites by the size of sandwich they order, this is a form of price discrimination based on making a "bulk" purchase.

10. This is a form of price discrimination, and like all price discrimination efforts it will generate more revenue. Companies can use your location to raise or lower the price shown on the app. For instance, in 2018 Burger King offered its app users a free Whopper if they happened to be near a McDonald's!

CHAPTER

12 Monopolistic Competition and Advertising

Advertising and Product Differentiation Are Notable Features of Monopolistic Competition.

If you drive down a busy street, you will find many competing businesses, often right next to one another. These competing firms advertise heavily. The temptation is to see advertising as driving up the price of a product without any benefit to the consumer. However, in markets where competitors sell slightly differentiated products, advertising enables firms to inform their customers about new products and services. Yes, costs rise, but consumers also gain information to help make purchasing decisions.

Consumers also benefit from added variety, and we all get a product that's pretty close to our vision of a perfect good—no other market structure delivers that outcome. Consider MOD pizza. Founded in 2008, MOD has grown to over 500 restaurants throughout the United States and the United Kingdom. How did MOD break into an already crowded pizza market? By doing pizza differently. Instead of offering a selection of traditional Italian-style pies, MOD gives customers the freedom to choose unlimited toppings at a set price, from a wide assortment of fresh items. Once you've selected your "modifications," MOD fires the pizza, and it is ready in three minutes. In other words, MOD made pizza even better!

What do you like on your pizza? MOD probably has you covered. Do you want just sliced tomatoes and basil? If not, what about carrots and bean sprouts? Or double bacon? Or baby broccoli? Poblano chilies, anyone? Take your pick.

In this chapter, we look at *monopolistic competition,* a widespread market structure that has features of both competitive markets and monopoly. We also explore the benefits and disadvantages of advertising, which is prevalent in markets with monopolistic competition.

BIG QUESTIONS

- What is monopolistic competition?
- What are the differences among monopolistic competition, competitive markets, and monopoly?
- Why is advertising prevalent in monopolistic competition?

What Is Monopolistic Competition?

Some consumers prefer the fries at McDonald's, while others may crave a salad at Panera Bread or the chicken at KFC. Each fast-food establishment has a unique set of menu items. The different products in fast-food restaurants give each seller a small degree of market power. This combination of market power and competition is typical of the market structure known as monopolistic competition. Indeed, **monopolistic competition** is characterized by low barriers to entry, many different firms, and product differentiation. **Product differentiation** is the process firms use to make a product more attractive to potential customers. Firms use product differentiation to contrast their product's unique qualities with competing products. The differences, which we will examine in detail, can be minor and can involve subtle changes in packaging, quality, availability, and promotion. Or the differences can be very significant. For example, some soup companies specialize in organic soups, which the consumers they are targeting would find an extremely important characteristic.

Monopolistic competition is a type of market structure characterized by low barriers to entry, many different firms, and product differentiation.

Product differentiation is the process firms use to make a product more attractive to potential customers.

How does monopolistic competition compare with other market structures we have studied? As Table 12.1 shows, monopolistic competition falls between competitive markets and monopoly in terms of the number of sellers, the types of products sold, and competing firms' ability to enter and exit the market.

We have seen that firms in competitive markets do not have any market power. As a result, buyers can expect to find consistently low prices and wide availability. And we have seen that monopolies charge more and restrict the availability of a good or service. In markets that are monopolistically competitive, firms sell differentiated products. This differentiation gives the

TABLE 12.1

Competitive Markets, Monopolistic Competition, and Monopoly

Competitive markets	Monopolistic competition	Monopoly
Many sellers	Many sellers	One seller
Similar products	Differentiated products	A unique product without close substitutes
Free entry and exit	Low barriers to entry and exit	Significant barriers to entry and exit

monopolistic competitor some market power, though not as much as a monopolist, which controls the entire market. Monopolistically competitive firms have a small amount of market power that enables them to search for the most profitable price.

To understand how monopolistic competition works, we begin with a closer look at product differentiation.

Product Differentiation

Monopolistically competitive firms create some market power through product differentiation. Differentiation can occur in a variety of ways, including style or type, location, and quality.

STYLE OR TYPE A trip to a mall is a great way to see product differentiation firsthand. For example, you will find many clothing stores, each offering a unique array of styles and types of clothing. Some stores, such as Abercrombie & Fitch, carry styles that attract younger customers. Others, such as Talbots, appeal to older shoppers. Clothing stores can also vary by the type of clothing they sell, specializing in apparel such as business clothing, plus sizes, or sportswear. Each store hopes to attract a specific type of customer.

When you're ready for lunch at the mall, you can go to the food court, where many different places to eat offer a wide variety of choices. Where you decide to eat is a matter of your personal preferences and the price you are willing to pay. Like most consumers, you will select the place that gives you what you want while providing the best value for your money. Consumers' differing tastes make it possible for a wide range of food vendors to compete side by side with rivals who provide many good substitutes.

LOCATION Many businesses attract customers because of their convenient location. Gasoline stations, dry cleaners, barber shops, and car washes provide products and services that customers tend to choose on the basis of convenience of location rather than price. When consumers prefer to save time and to avoid the inconvenience of shopping for a better deal, a firm with a more convenient location will have some pricing power. As a result, producers who sell very similar products can generate some market power by locating their businesses along routes most customers use to go to and from work or in other areas where customers frequently travel.

Would you like your Mexican food cheaper . . .

. . . or fresher?

QUALITY Firms also compete on the basis of quality. For instance, if you want Mexican food, you can go to Taco Bell, which is inexpensive and offers food cooked in advance. In contrast, at Moe's Southwest Grill the food is freshly prepared and, as a result, more expensive. This form of product differentiation serves consumers quite well. Budget-conscious consumers can feast at Taco Bell, while those with a larger budget and a taste for higher-quality Mexican food can consider Moe's as another option.

PRACTICE WHAT YOU KNOW

Is Hollister a monopolistic competitor?

Product Differentiation: Would You Recognize a Monopolistic Competitor?

QUESTION: Which of the following is a monopolistic competitor?

a. a local apple farm that grows Red Delicious apples

b. Hollister, an apparel store

c. your local water company

ANSWERS:

a. Because Red Delicious apples are widely available at grocery stores, this local apple farm does not have a differentiated product to sell. In addition, it has many competitors that grow exactly the same variety of apples. This apple farm is part of a competitive market; it is not a monopolistic competitor.

b. Hollister has a slightly different mix of clothes than competitors Abercrombie & Fitch and American Eagle Outfitters. This differentiation gives the brand some pricing power. Hollister is a good example of a monopolistically competitive firm.

c. Because water is essential and people cannot easily do without it, the local water company has significant monopoly power. Moreover, purifying and distributing water are subject to economies of scale. Your local water company is definitely a monopolist, not a monopolistic competitor.

What Are the Differences among Monopolistic Competition, Competitive Markets, and Monopoly?

Monopolistic competition occupies a place between competitive markets, which produce an efficient output at low prices, and monopoly, which produces an inefficient output at high prices. To help explain whether monopolistic competition is desirable or not, we consider the outcomes that individual firms can achieve when facing monopolistic competition in the short run and in the long run. Once you understand how monopolistic competition works, we will be able to compare the long-run equilibrium result with that of competitive markets and then determine if monopolistic competition is efficient.

Monopolistic Competition in the Short Run and the Long Run

A monopolistically competitive firm sells a differentiated product and for this reason has some market power. Recall that in perfect competition, each firm sells the same product, so competitors' products are perfect substitutes, which means that demand is perfectly elastic (flat). In monopolistic competition, each competitor provides a differentiated product, so competitors' products are imperfect substitutes for one another, which means that demand is relatively elastic (less flat), but still flatter (more elastic) than monopoly. Like a monopolist, the monopolistic competitor uses the profit-maximizing rule, MR = MC, and locates the corresponding point on its demand curve to determine the best price to charge and the best quantity to produce. Whether the firm earns a profit, experiences a loss, or breaks even is a function of other firms entering and exiting the market. Recall that entry and exit do not take place in the short run. In the long run, however, firms are free to enter an industry when they see a potential for profits or leave if they are making losses. Therefore, entry and exit regulate how much profit a firm can make in the long run.

Marginal thinking

Suppose you own a Hardee's fast-food restaurant in Asheville, North Carolina. Your business is doing well and making a profit. Then one day a Five Guys opens up across the street. Some of your customers will try Five Guys and switch, while others will still prefer your fare. But your profit will take a hit. Whether or not you stay in business will depend on how much business you lose. To understand how a business owner makes the decision to keep operating or to shut down, we now turn to the short-run and long-run implications of monopolistic competition.

MONOPOLISTIC COMPETITION IN THE SHORT RUN Figure 12.1 depicts a firm, like Hardee's, in a monopolistically competitive environment. In panel (a), the firm makes a profit. Panel (b) shows the same firm incurring a loss after a new competitor, like Five Guys, opens nearby. In each case, the firm uses the profit-maximizing rule to determine the best price to charge by locating the point at which marginal revenue equals marginal cost. This calculation

FIGURE 12.1

The Monopolistically Competitive Firm in the Short Run

In this figure, we see how a single monopolistically competitive firm may make a profit or incur a loss depending on the demand conditions it faces. Notice that the marginal cost curve (MC) and average total cost curve (ATC) are identical in both panels because we are considering the same firm. The only functional difference is the location of the demand curve (D) and marginal revenue curve (MR). The demand in (a) is high enough for the firm to make a profit. In (b), however, there is not enough demand, so the firm experiences a loss.

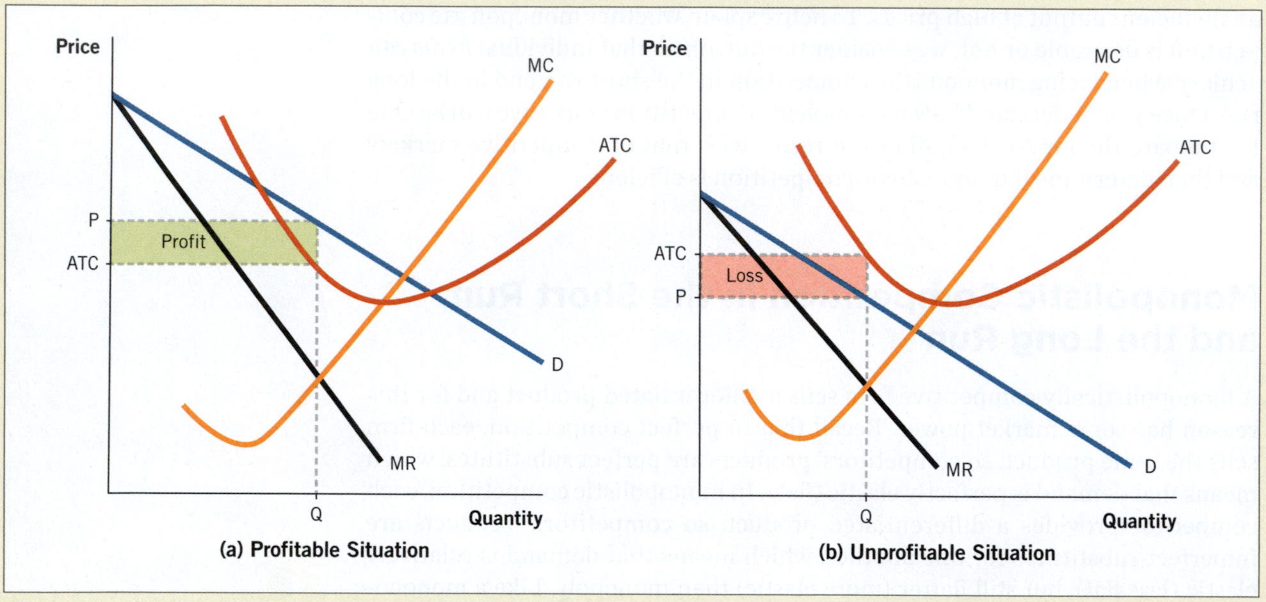

establishes the profit-maximizing output (Q) along the vertical dashed line. The firm determines the best price to charge (P) by following the dashed horizontal line from the demand curve to the vertical axis.

In panel (a), we see that because price is greater than average total cost (P > ATC), the firm makes a short-run economic profit. The situation in panel (b) is different. Because P < ATC, the firm experiences a short-run economic loss. What accounts for the difference? Because we are considering the same firm, the marginal cost (MC) and average total cost (ATC) curves are identical in both panels. The only functional difference is the location of the demand (D) and marginal revenue (MR) curves. The demand in panel (a) is high enough for the firm to make a profit. In panel (b), however, there is not enough demand; perhaps too many customers have switched to the new Five Guys. So even though the monopolistic competitor has some market power, if demand is too low, the firm may not be able to price its product high enough to make a profit.

MONOPOLISTIC COMPETITION IN THE LONG RUN In the long run, when firms can easily enter and exit a market, competition will drive economic profit to zero. This dynamic should be familiar to you from our previous discussions of competitive markets. If a firm is making an economic profit, that profit attracts new entrants to the business. Then the larger supply of competing firms will cause the demand for an individual firm's product to contract. Eventually, as more firms enter the market, it is no longer possible for existing firms to make an economic profit. A reverse process unfolds in the case of a market experiencing a loss. In this case, some firms exit the industry. Then consumers have fewer options to choose from, and the remaining firms experience an increase in demand. Eventually, demand increases to the point at which firms no longer experience a loss.

Figure 12.2 shows the market after the long-run adjustment process takes place. Price (P) is just equal to the average total cost of production (ATC) at the profit-maximizing rate of output (Q). At this point, firms are earning zero economic profit, as noted by P = ATC along the vertical axis; the market reaches a long-run equilibrium at the point where there is no reason for firms to enter or exit the industry. Note that the demand curve is drawn *tangent* to the average total cost curve (touching at one place). If demand were any larger, the result would look like panel (a) in Figure 12.1 and firms would experience an economic profit. Conversely, if demand were any lower, the result would look like panel (b) in Figure 12.1 and firms would experience an economic loss. Where entry and exit exist, profits and losses are not possible in the long run. In this way, monopolistic competition resembles a competitive market.

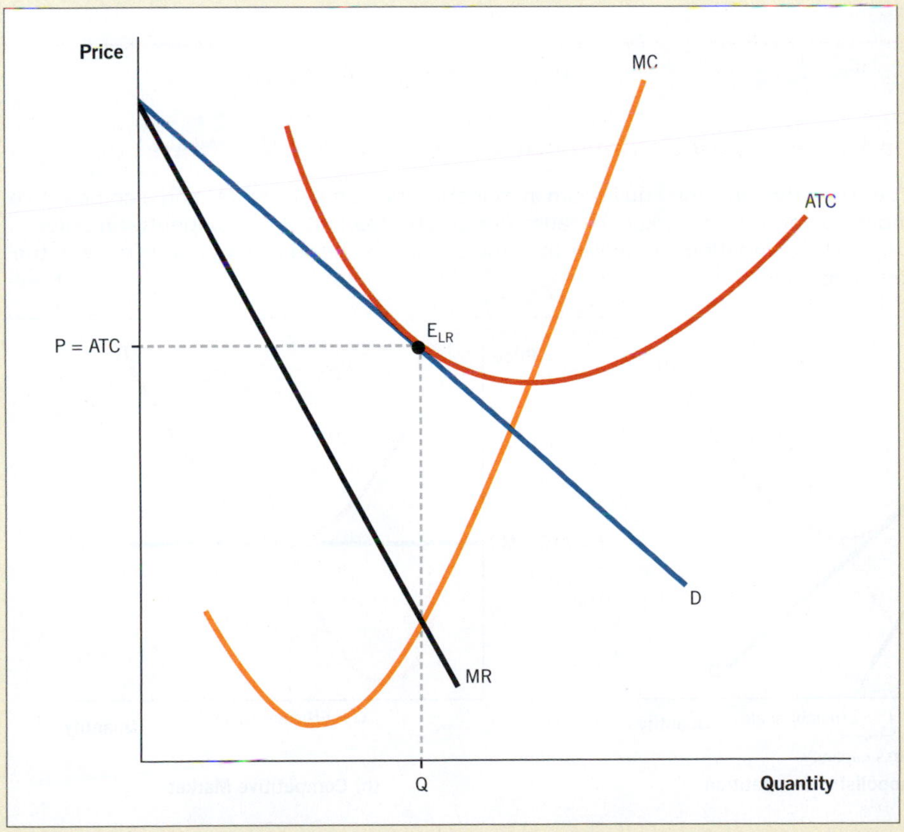

FIGURE 12.2

The Monopolistically Competitive Firm in the Long Run

Entry and exit cause short-run profits and losses to disappear in the long run, which means that the price charged (P) must be equal to the average total cost (ATC) of production. At this point, firms are earning zero economic profit, as noted by P = ATC along the vertical axis. The market reaches a long-run equilibrium (E_{LR}) at the point where there is no reason for firms to enter or exit the industry.

Incentives

Returning to our example of Hardee's, the firm's success will attract attention and encourage rivals, like Five Guys, to enter the market. As a result, the short-run profits that Hardee's enjoys will erode. As long as profits occur in the short run, other competitors will be encouraged to enter, while short-run losses will prompt some existing firms to close. The dynamic nature of competition guarantees that long-run profits and losses are not possible.

Monopolistic Competition and Competitive Markets

We have seen that monopolistic competition and competitive markets are similar; both market structures drive economic profit to zero in the long run. But monopolistic competitors enjoy some market power, which is a crucial difference. In this section, we compare pricing and output decisions in these two market structures. Then we look at issues of scale and output.

THE RELATIONSHIP BETWEEN PRICE, MARGINAL COST, AND LONG-RUN AVERAGE COST Monopolistically competitive firms have some market power, which enables them to charge slightly more than firms in competitive markets. Figure 12.3 compares the long-run equilibrium between monopolistic competition and a competitive market. Turning first to the firm in a market characterized by monopolistic competition, shown in panel (a),

FIGURE 12.3

The Long-Run Equilibrium in Monopolistic Competition and Competitive Markets

There are two primary differences between the long-run equilibrium in monopolistic competition (a) and a competitive market (b). First, monopolistic competition produces markup, because P is greater than MC. In a competitive market, P = MC. Second, the output in monopolistic competition is smaller than the efficient scale. In a competitive market, the firm's output is equal to the most efficient scale.

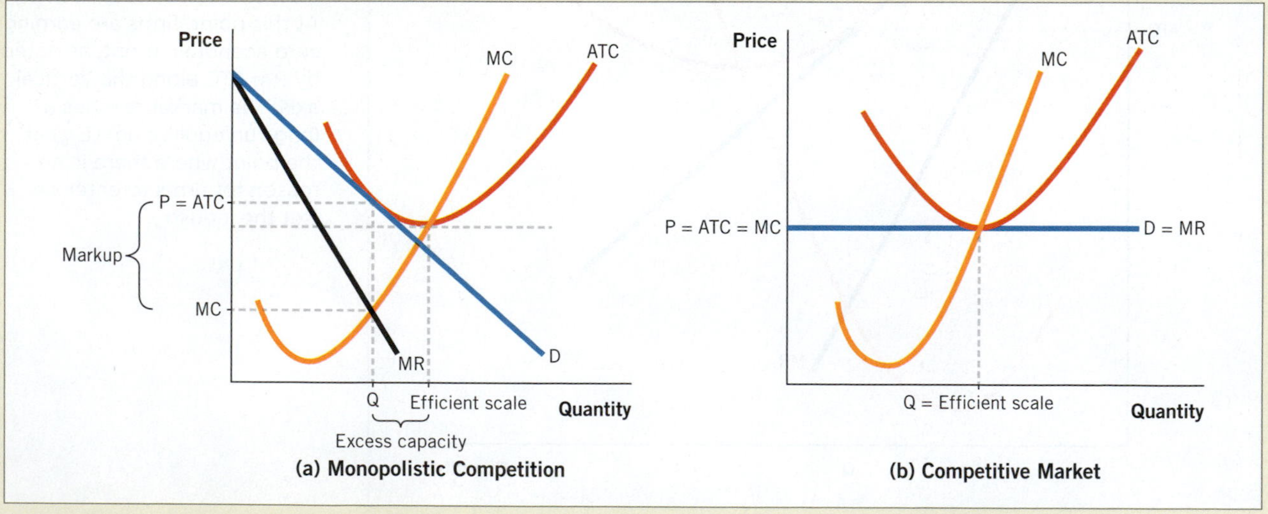

notice that the price (P) is greater than the marginal cost (MC) of making one more unit. The difference between P and MC is known as the markup. **Markup** is the difference between the price the firm charges and the marginal cost of production.

Markup
is the difference between the price the firm charges and the marginal cost of production.

A markup is possible when a firm enjoys some market power. Products such as bottled water, cosmetics, prescription medicines, eyeglass frames, brand-name clothing, restaurant drinks, and greeting cards all have hefty markups. Let's focus on bottled water. In most cases, it costs just pennies to produce a bottle of water, but you're unlikely to find it for less than $1; there is a lot of markup on every bottle! Some firms differentiate their product by marketing their water as the "purest" or the "cleanest." Other companies use special packaging. While the marketing of bottled water is unquestionably a successful business strategy, the markup means that consumers pay more. You can observe this result in panel (a) of Figure 12.3, where the price under monopolistic competition is higher than the price in a competitive market, shown in panel (b).

Next, look at the ATC curves in both panels. Because a monopolistic competitor has a downward-sloping demand curve, the point of tangency between the demand curve and the ATC curve is different from the point of tangency in a competitive market. The point where P = ATC is higher under monopolistic competition. Panel (b) shows the demand curve just tangent to the ATC curve at ATC's lowest point in a competitive market. Consequently, we can say that monopolistic competition produces higher prices than a competitive market does. If this result seems odd to you, recall that entry and exit do not ensure the lowest possible price, only that the price is equal to the average total cost of production. In a competitive market, where the demand curve is horizontal, the price is always the lowest possible average total cost of production. This is not the case under monopolistic competition. However, the price in monopolistic competition often reflects quality; cheap food is cheap for a reason. Firms may charge more for higher-quality food, but there will still be zero economic profit.

SCALE AND OUTPUT When a firm produces at an output level smaller than the output level needed to minimize average total costs, we say it has **excess capacity**. Turning back to panel (a) of Figure 12.3, we see excess capacity in the difference between Q and the efficient scale.

Excess capacity
occurs when a firm produces at an output level smaller than the output level needed to minimize average total costs.

This result differs from what we see in panel (b) of Figure 12.3 for a competitive market. In a competitive market, the profit-maximizing output is equal to the most efficient scale of operation. This result is guaranteed because each firm sells an identical product and must therefore set its price equal to the minimum point on the average total cost curve. If, for instance, a corn farmer tried to sell a harvest for more than the prevailing market price, the farmer would not find any customers. In contrast, a monopolistic competitor in a food hall enjoys market power because some customers prefer its product, which enables food hall vendors to charge more than the lowest average total cost. Therefore, under monopolistic competition, the profit-maximizing output is less than the minimum efficient scale. Monopolistically competitive firms have the capacity to produce more output at a lower cost. But if they produced more, they would have to lower their price. Because a lower price decreases the firm's marginal revenue, it is more profitable for the monopolistic competitor to operate with excess capacity.

Perrier has a distinctive look—but how different is it from other mineral water?

Monopolistic Competition, Inefficiency, and Social Welfare

Monopolistic competition produces a higher price and a lower level of output than a competitive market does. Recall that we looked at efficiency as a way to determine whether a firm's decisions are consistent with an output level beneficial to society. Does monopolistic competition display efficiency?

In Figure 12.3, panel (a), we observed that a monopolistic competitor has costs slightly above the lowest possible cost. So the average total costs of a monopolistically competitive firm are higher than those of a firm in a competitive market. This result is not efficient. To achieve efficiency, the monopolistically competitive firm could lower its price to what we would find in competitive markets. However, because a monopolistic competitor's goal is to make a profit, there is no incentive for the firm to lower its price. Every monopolistic competitor has a downward-sloping demand curve, so the demand curve cannot be tangent to the minimum point along the average total cost curve, as seen in panel (a).

Markup is a second source of inefficiency. We have seen that, for a monopolistically competitive firm at the profit-maximizing output level, $P > MC$ by an amount equal to the markup. The price reflects the consumer's willingness to pay, and this amount exceeds the marginal cost of production. A reduced markup would benefit consumers by lowering the price and decreasing the spread between the price and the marginal cost. If the firm did away with the markup entirely and set $P = MC$, the output level would benefit the greatest number of consumers. However, this result would not be practical. At the point where the greatest efficiency occurs, the demand curve would be below the average total cost curve and the firm would lose money. It is unreasonable to expect a profit-seeking firm to pursue a pricing strategy that would benefit its customers at the expense of its own profit.

What if the government intervened on behalf of the consumer? Increased efficiency could be achieved through government regulation. After all, the government regulates monopolists to reduce market power and restore social welfare. Couldn't the government do the same in monopolistically competitive markets? Yes and no! It is certainly possible, but not desirable. Monopolistically competitive firms have a limited amount of market power, so they cannot make a long-run economic profit like monopolists do. In addition, regulating the prices that firms in a monopolistically competitive market can charge would put many of them out of business. Bear in mind we are talking about firms in markets like the fast-food industry. Doing away with a significant percentage of these firms would mean fewer places for consumers to grab a quick bite. The remaining restaurants would be more efficient, but with fewer restaurants the trade-off for consumers would be less convenience and fewer choices.

Trade-offs

Regulating monopolistic competition through marginal cost pricing, or setting $P = MC$, would also create a host of problems like those we discussed for monopoly. A good proportion of the economy consists of monopolistically competitive firms, so the scale of the regulatory effort would be enormous. And because implementing marginal cost pricing would result in widespread losses, the government would need to find a way to subsidize the regulated firms to keep them in business. Because the only way to fund these subsidies would be higher taxes, the inefficiencies present in monopolistic competition do not warrant government action.

VARYING DEGREES OF PRODUCT DIFFERENTIATION We have seen that products sold under monopolistic competition are more differentiated than those sold in a competitive market and less differentiated than those sold under monopoly. At one end of these two extremes we have competitive markets where firms sell identical products, have no market power, and face a perfectly elastic demand curve. At the other end we have a monopolist that sells a unique product without good substitutes and faces a steep downward-sloping demand curve indicative of highly inelastic demand. What about the firm that operates under monopolistic competition?

Figure 12.4 illustrates two monopolistic competitors with varying degrees of product differentiation. Firm A enjoys significant differentiation. High levels of differentiation occur when the firm has an especially attractive location, style, type, or quality of product that is in high demand among consumers and that competitors cannot easily replicate. H&M, Urban Outfitters, and Abercrombie & Fitch are good examples. Consumers have strong brand loyalty for the clothes these firms sell, so the demand curve is quite inelastic. The relatively steep slope of the demand curve means that the point of tangency between the demand curve (D) and the average total cost curve (ATC) occurs at a high price, which produces a large amount of excess capacity. In contrast,

FIGURE 12.4

Product Differentiation, Excess Capacity, and Efficiency

The difference in product differentiation is represented by the steepness (elasticity) of the demand curve, since the demand curve for firm A enjoys more product differentiation. As a result, it has more excess capacity and is less efficient. Firm B sells a product that is only slightly different from its competitors'. In this case, consumers have only weak preferences about which firm to buy from, and consumer demand is elastic. The results are a small amount of excess capacity and a more efficient result.

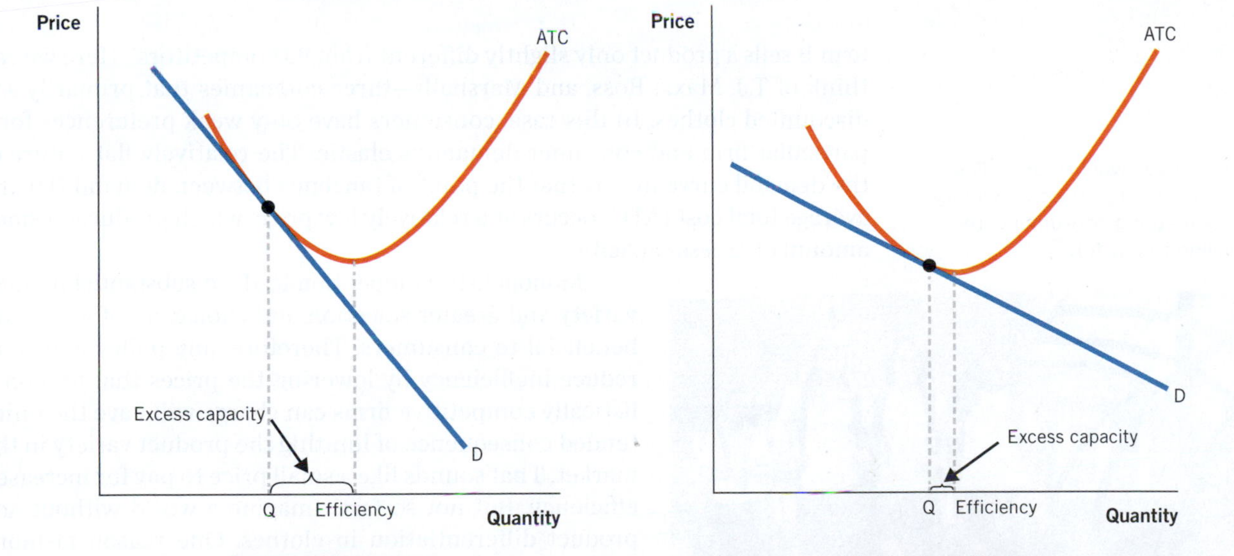

Firm A: More Product Differentiation | **Firm B: Less Product Differentiation**

ECONOMICS in the MEDIA

Product Differentiation

SUPERIOR DONUTS

On the CBS sitcom *Superior Donuts,* Arthur is an old-school doughnut shop owner who runs the place with the help of a young employee, Franco. One day a new customer, Sofia, comes in and starts asking general questions about the neighborhood and how the shop operates. It turns out Sofia was doing recon, trying to gauge whether or not she should park her food truck out front! When she shows up a few minutes later, Arthur is incensed but Sofia doesn't care. She pops a few coins in a parking meter and opens her truck for business.

Which do you prefer—an organic breakfast bowl or a donut?

Sofia sells organic breakfast dishes at a much higher price point than Superior Donuts, so customers now have a second choice of where to eat. More importantly, since barriers to entering the market are low and the products served are differentiated, this is a great example of how monopolistically competitive markets work to provide consumers with variety and reasonable prices.

firm B sells a product only slightly different from its competitors'. Here we can think of T.J. Maxx, Ross, and Marshalls—three companies that primarily sell discounted clothes. In this case, consumers have only weak preferences for a particular firm and consumer demand is elastic. The relatively flat nature of the demand curve means that the point of tangency between demand (D) and average total cost (ATC) occurs at a relatively low price, which produces a small amount of excess capacity.

Would you want to dress like this every day? Product variety is something consumers are willing to pay for.

Monopolistic competition leads to substantial product variety and greater selection and choice, all of which are beneficial to consumers. Therefore, any policy efforts to reduce inefficiency by lowering the prices that monopolistically competitive firms can charge will have the unintended consequence of limiting the product variety in the market. That sounds like a small price to pay for increased efficiency. But not so fast! Imagine a world without any product differentiation in clothes. One reason fashions go in and out of style is the desire among consumers to express their individuality. Therefore, consumers are willing to pay a little more for product variety in order to look different from everyone else.

PRACTICE WHAT YOU KNOW

Markup: Punch Pizza versus Pizza Hut

Punch Pizza uses wood-fired ovens.

QUESTION: Punch Pizza is a small upscale chain in Minnesota that uses wood-fired ovens. In contrast, Pizza Hut is a large national chain. Which pizza chain would have a greater markup on each pizza?

ANSWER: If you ask people in the Twin Cities about their favorite pizza, you will find a cultlike following for Punch Pizza. That loyalty translates into inelastic demand. Punch Pizza claims to make the best Neapolitan pie. Fans of this style of pizza gravitate to Punch Pizza for the unique texture and flavor. In contrast, Pizza Hut competes in the middle of the pizza market and has crafted a taste that appeals to a broader set of customers. Pizza Hut's customers can find many other places that serve a similar product, so these customers are much more price sensitive.

The marginal cost of making pizza at both places consists of the dough, the toppings, and wages for labor. At Pizza Hut, pizza assembly is streamlined for efficiency. Punch Pizza is more labor intensive, but its marginal cost is still relatively low. The prices at Punch Pizza are much higher than at Pizza Hut. As a result, the markup—or the difference between the price charged and the marginal cost of production—is greater at Punch Pizza than at Pizza Hut.

Marginal thinking

CHALLENGE QUESTION: If there's a higher markup for Punch Pizza, and therefore a higher economic profit, won't this attract new entrants?

ANSWER: Since barriers to entry into a monopolistically competitive market are relatively low, new firms will enter. As the supply expands, the market price drops and the demand for any particular pizza place becomes more elastic. This means that Punch Pizza's markup shrinks. So even though Punch Pizza is in an enviable position for now, competition will eventually reduce the price to a point where Punch Pizza earns zero economic profits—as is the case in every market where firms are free to enter.

Why Is Advertising Prevalent in Monopolistic Competition?

Advertising is a fact of daily life. It is also a means by which companies compete and therefore a cost of doing business in many industries. In the United States, advertising expenditures account for approximately 2% of all economic output annually. Worldwide, advertising expenses are a little less—about 1% of global economic activity. While the percentages are small in relative terms, in absolute terms worldwide advertising costs are over half a trillion dollars each year. Is this money well spent? Or is it a counterproductive contest that increases cost without adding value for the consumer? In this section, we will find that the answer is a little of both. Let's start by seeing who advertises.

This Dairy Queen sign was a clever way to advertise during the coronavirus shortage.

Why Firms Advertise

No matter the company or slogan, the goal of advertising is to drive additional demand for the product being sold. Advertising campaigns use a variety of techniques to stimulate demand. In each instance, advertising is designed to highlight an important piece of information about the product (and remember the name of the company!). Table 12.2 shows how this process works. For instance, the FedEx slogan "The World on Time" conveys reliability and punctual service. Some customers who use FedEx are willing to pay a premium for overnight delivery because the company has differentiated itself from its competitors—UPS, DHL, and (especially) the United States Postal Service.

A successful advertising campaign will change the demand curve in two dimensions: it will shift the demand curve to the right and alter its shape. Turning to Figure 12.5, we see this change. First, the demand curve shifts to the right in response to the additional demand created by the advertising. Second, the demand curve becomes more inelastic, or slightly more vertical. This change in shape happens because advertising has highlighted features that make the product attractive to specific customers who are now more likely to want it. Because demand is more inelastic after advertising, the firm increases its market power and can raise its price.

In addition to increasing demand, advertising conveys information that consumers may find helpful in matching their preferences. Advertising tells us about the price of the goods offered, the location of products, and the introduction of new products. Firms also use advertising as a competitive mechanism to underprice one another. Finally, an advertising campaign signals quality. Firms that run expensive advertising campaigns are making a significant investment in their product. It is highly unlikely that a firm would spend a great deal on advertising if it did not think the process would yield a positive return. So a rational consumer can infer that firms spending a great deal on advertising are likely to have a higher-quality product than a competitor who does not advertise.

A wonderful example of this is Columbia Sportswear, a high-end maker and distributor of outerwear, sportswear, footwear, headgear, camping equipment, and ski apparel. For many years, Columbia ads featured the company's boss, Gert Boyle. She was better known as "Ma Boyle, One Tough Mother," thanks to a decades-long ad campaign for the company's outdoor apparel products. Columbia differentiated itself from its competitors, whose ads usually featured attractive young hikers and skiers, by chronicling the adventures of Boyle and her son, Tim, who gamely endured a variety of extreme conditions while bundled up in Columbia outerwear. The commercials reinforced the idea that Columbia products are worth a premium.

Advertising in Different Markets

Many firms engage in advertising, but advertising is not equally productive in all market structures. In our continuum from competitive markets to monopoly, markets that function under monopolistic competition invest the most in advertising.

ADVERTISING IN COMPETITIVE MARKETS As you know by now, competitive firms sell nearly identical products at an identical price. For this

TABLE 12.2

Advertising and Demand

Company / Product	Advertising slogan	How it increases demand
Convention and Visitors Authority / Las Vegas 	"What Happens Here, Stays Here."	The slogan attempts to convince travelers that they will have a better vacation in Las Vegas than anywhere else.
Red Bull / energy drink 	"Red Bull Gives You Wings."	The tagline promises energy and concentration to get things done and meet deadlines.
Frito-Lay / potato chips 	"Betcha Can't Eat Just One."	The message that one potato chip is not enough to satisfy your craving appeals to chip buyers who choose better taste over lower-priced generics.
Apple / personal electronic devices	"Think Different."	The slogan subtly hints that competitors' products are all pretty much the same—and boring.
Twitter / social media service	"It's What's Happening."	The suggestion is that not using the service means being out of touch with the world.
Visa / credit card 	"It's Everywhere You Want to Be."	Widespread acceptance and usability are two of the major reasons for carrying a credit card.
Skittles / candy 	"Taste the Rainbow."	The emphasis is on taste and a variety of flavors.

FIGURE 12.5

Advertising and the Demand Curve

A successful advertising campaign increases demand. Advertising also makes the demand curve more inelastic, or vertical, by informing consumers about differences they care about. After advertising, consumers desire the good more intensely, which makes the demand curve for the firm's product somewhat more vertical.

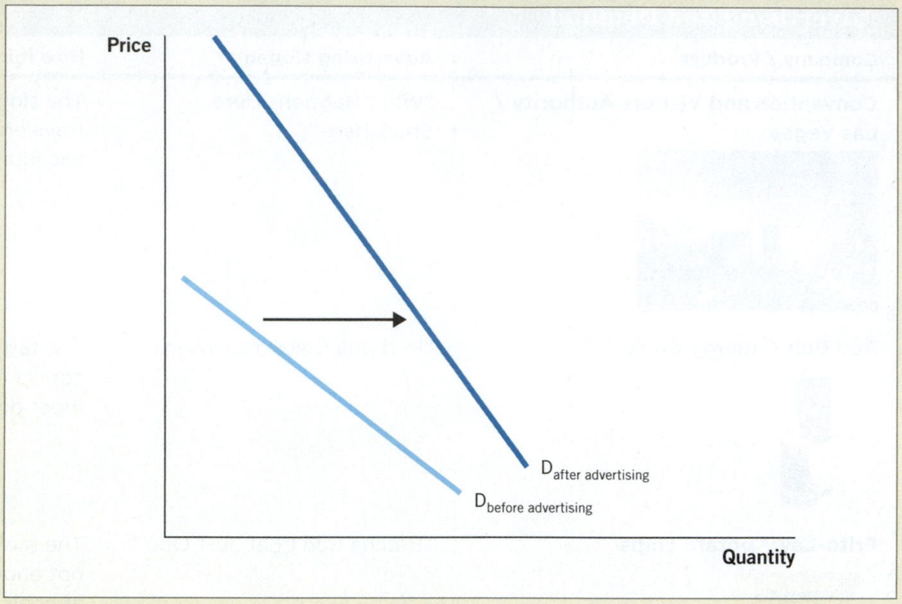

reason, advertising raises a firm's costs without directly influencing its sales. Advertising for an undifferentiated good functions like a public good for the industry as a whole: the benefits flow to every firm in the market through increased market demand for the product. Each firm sells essentially the same good, so consumers can find the product at many competing locations at the same price. An individual firm that advertises in this market is at a competitive disadvantage because it will have higher costs that it cannot pass on to the consumer.

This does not mean that we never see advertising in competitive markets. Although individual firms do not benefit from advertising, competitive industries as a whole can. For example, you have probably heard the slogan "Beef. It's What's for Dinner." The campaign, which began in 1992, is recognized by over 80% of Americans and has been widely credited with increasing the demand for beef products. The campaign was funded by the National Cattlemen's Beef Association, an organization that puts millions of dollars a year into advertising. In fact, industrywide marketing campaigns such as "It's Not Just for Breakfast Anymore" by the Florida Orange Juice Growers Association or "Got Milk?" by the National Milk Processor Board generally indicate that competitive firms have joined forces to advertise in an effort to increase demand. Other examples include "The Incredible, Edible Egg" and "Pork. The Other White Meat."

ADVERTISING UNDER MONOPOLISTIC COMPETITION Advertising is widespread under monopolistic competition because firms have differentiated products. Let's look at the advertising behavior of pizza companies. Television commercials by national chains such as Domino's, Pizza Hut, Papa

ECONOMICS *in the* MEDIA

Advertising

MAD MEN

Mad Men, which ran for seven seasons on AMC, is a show about the golden age of the advertising industry. The main character, Don Draper, is a marketing whiz. In season 6, he makes a pitch for a series of ads to sell ketchup. Gesturing at huge color photos of food that is just a condiment away from perfection, Draper explains the campaign's concept. "What's missing? One thing. Pass the Heinz." Draper understands that the goal of an ad campaign is to increase demand for a good or service and also to make the demand for whatever is being sold more inelastic. This gives the seller more pricing power and allows them to charge a higher markup.

Draper's "Pass the Heinz" pitch is rejected, because the client can't wrap his head around the idea of ads that don't show the product. Fast-forward 50 years, though, and in 2017, Heinz began running the ads, faithfully copied from Draper's presentation (with full credit given). The idea was brilliant—just ahead of its time.

There's just one thing missing.

John's, and Little Caesars are widespread, as are flyers and advertisements for local pizza places. Because each pizza is slightly different, each firm's advertising increases the demand for its product and changes the slope of the demand curve. In short, the gains from advertising go directly to the firm spending the money. These benefits generate a strong incentive to advertise to gain new customers or to keep customers from switching to other products. Because each firm feels the same way, advertising becomes the norm among monopolistically competitive firms.

Incentives

SNAPSHOT

Advertising and the Super Bowl

Super Bowl commercials are watched at least as closely as the football game itself. Fans love these usually creative and comedic ads. But economists pay close attention for different reasons. Who's advertising and what does it say about those industries? Are the ads money well spent, or do they increase business costs without making a noticeable difference in profits? Here we examine advertising from 1967 to 2019.

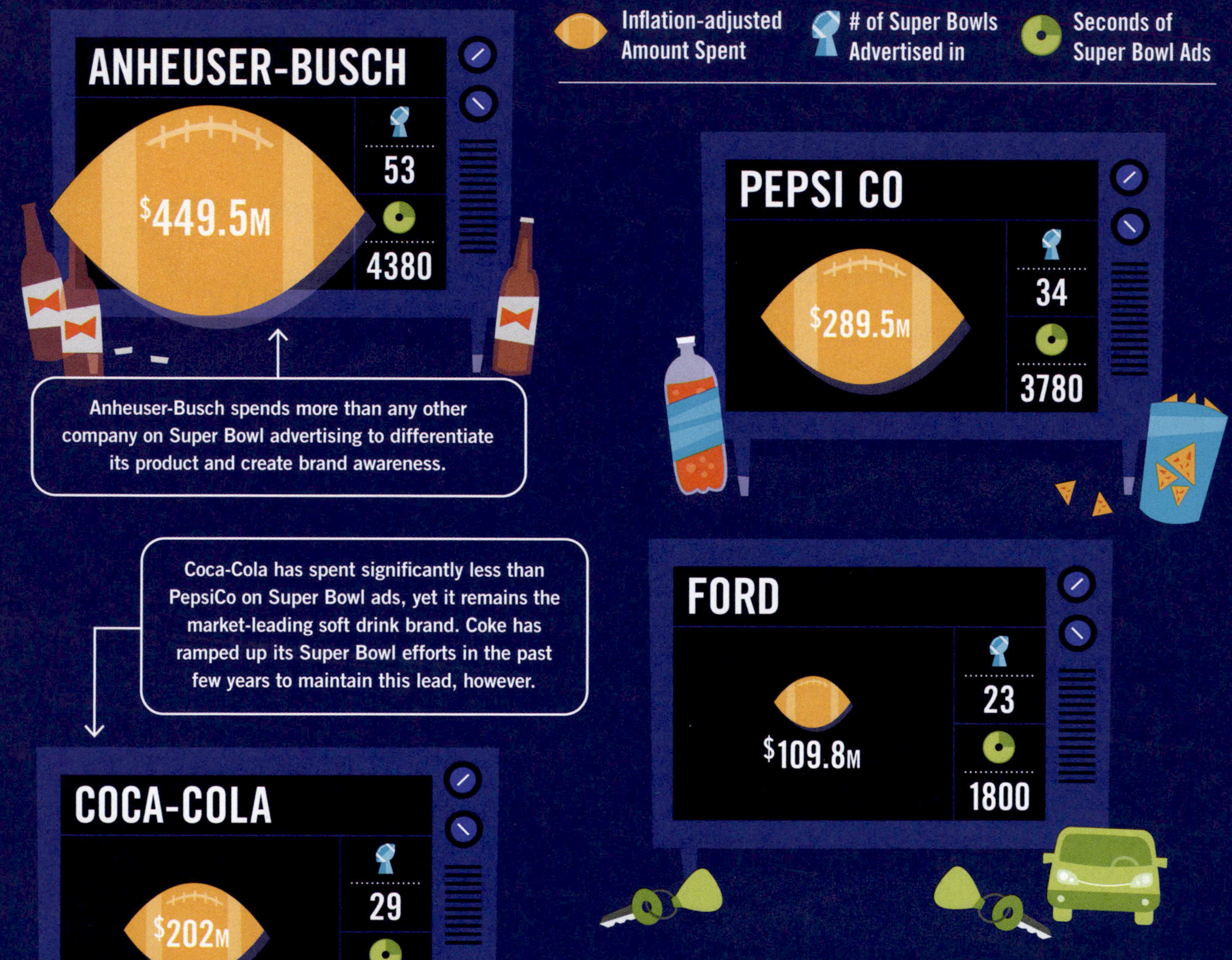
Inflation-adjusted Amount Spent
# of Super Bowls Advertised in
Seconds of Super Bowl Ads
ANHEUSER-BUSCH
$449.5M
53
4380
Anheuser-Busch spends more than any other company on Super Bowl advertising to differentiate its product and create brand awareness.
PEPSI CO
$289.5M
34
3780
Coca-Cola has spent significantly less than PepsiCo on Super Bowl ads, yet it remains the market-leading soft drink brand. Coke has ramped up its Super Bowl efforts in the past few years to maintain this lead, however.
FORD
$109.8M
23
1800

COCA-COLA
$202M
29
2242

Some of these companies, especially Coca-Cola and Pepsi, are considered oligopolists rather than monopolistic competitors. We'll discuss oligopoly in the next chapter.

REVIEW QUESTIONS

- Draw what happens to a brand's demand curve when it successfully achieves product differentiation through advertising.
- Describe the risks and rewards of advertising from the perspective of both the brand and the consumer.

ECONOMICS IN THE REAL WORLD

WHAT HAPPENED TO SEARS?

Sears, JCPenney, Kohl's, and the Gap are all famous brick-and-mortar retailers. Depending on how old you are, at some point in your life you probably spent a lot of time in one of these stores. Kohl's and the Gap struggled for a time but appear to be back on course for growth and viability. JCPenney and Sears, on the other hand, are all but done for. The last year Sears made a profit was 2010.*

A few generations ago, a Sears credit card was as important as one from American Express. Sears is also historically important because it was the Sears catalog, first mailed in 1893, that allowed non-city dwellers access to products previously available only in cities.

So what has happened to Sears? Online giant Amazon and bad management have had major impacts since the mid-2000s. But Sears started losing business in the early 1990s. What happened then was the rapid rise of Walmart, which gave consumers significantly lower prices because of its sophisticated inventory control. By then, Sears had diversified into many areas, which caused it to lose focus on its main retail business. The rise of Walmart meant that Sears had to become more efficient (lower its markup) to survive, but because of the way Sears had expanded, its cost structure was higher than Walmart's.

What economics lesson can we extract from the Sears saga? A business must never take its success for granted, and you never know where your most fierce competitor will emerge from. Ever hear of Bentonville, Arkansas? That's where Walmart started (and is still headquartered).

*Hiroko Tabuchi and Rachel Abrams, "4 Different Turnaround Tales at Retailers Sears, Kohl's, Gap and J.C. Penney," *New York Times*, Feb. 26, 2015, https://www.nytimes.com/2015/02/27/business/4-different-turnaround-tales-at-retailers-sears-kohls-gap-and-jc-penney.html.

ADVERTISING AS A MONOPOLIST The monopolist sells a unique product without close substitutes. The fact that consumers have few, if any, good alternatives when deciding to buy the good makes the monopolist less likely to advertise than a monopolistic competitor. When consumer choice is limited, the firm does not have to advertise to get business. In addition, the competitive aspect is missing, so there is no need to advertise to prevent consumers from switching to rival products. However, that does not mean that the monopolist never advertises.

The monopolist may wish to advertise to inform the consumer about its product and stimulate demand. This strategy can be beneficial as long as the gains from advertising are enough to cover the cost of advertising. For example, De Beers, the giant diamond cartel, controls most of the world's supply of rough-cut diamonds. The company does not need to advertise to fend off competitors, but it advertises nevertheless because it is interested in creating more demand for diamonds. De Beers created the famous "A Diamond Is Forever" campaign.

The Negative Effects of Advertising

We have seen the benefits of advertising, but there are also drawbacks. Two of the most significant drawbacks are that advertising raises costs and can be deceitful.

ADVERTISING AND COSTS Advertising costs are reflected in the firm's average total cost curve. Figure 12.6 shows the paradox of advertising for most firms. When a firm advertises, it hopes to increase demand for the product and sell more units—say, from point 1 at Q_1 to point 2 at the higher quantity Q_2. If the firm can sell enough additional units, it will enjoy economies of scale, and the average total cost will fall from ATC_1 to ATC_2. This return on the advertising investment looks like a good business decision.

However, the reality of advertising is much more complex. Under monopolistic competition, each firm is competing with many other firms selling somewhat different products. Rival firms will respond with advertising of their own. This dynamic makes advertising the norm in monopolistic competition. Each firm engages in competitive advertising to win new customers and keep the old ones. As a result, the impact on each individual firm's demand largely cancels out. This result is evident in the movement from point 1 to point 3 in Figure 12.6. Costs rise from ATC_1 to ATC_3 on the higher LRATC curve, but the quantity demanded may remain at Q_1. The net result is that advertising creates higher costs but no change in quantity produced and a decrease in profit. In this case, we can think of advertising as causing a negative *business-stealing externality* whereby no individual firm can easily gain market share but feels compelled to advertise to protect its customer base.

We have seen that advertising raises costs for the producer. It also raises prices for consumers. In fact, consumers who consistently favor a particular brand of a product have more inelastic demand than those who are willing to switch from one product to another. Therefore, brand loyalty often means higher prices. Let's look at an example.

FIGURE 12.6

Advertising Increases Cost

By advertising, the firm hopes to increase demand (or quantity) from point 1 to point 2. In this scenario, the increase in demand from Q_1 to Q_2 is large enough to create economies of scale even though advertising causes the long-run average total cost curve (LRATC) to rise. Because monopolistically competitive firms each advertise, the advertising efforts often cancel one another out. As a result, long-run average total costs rise without demand increasing much, so the firm may move from point 1 to point 3 instead.

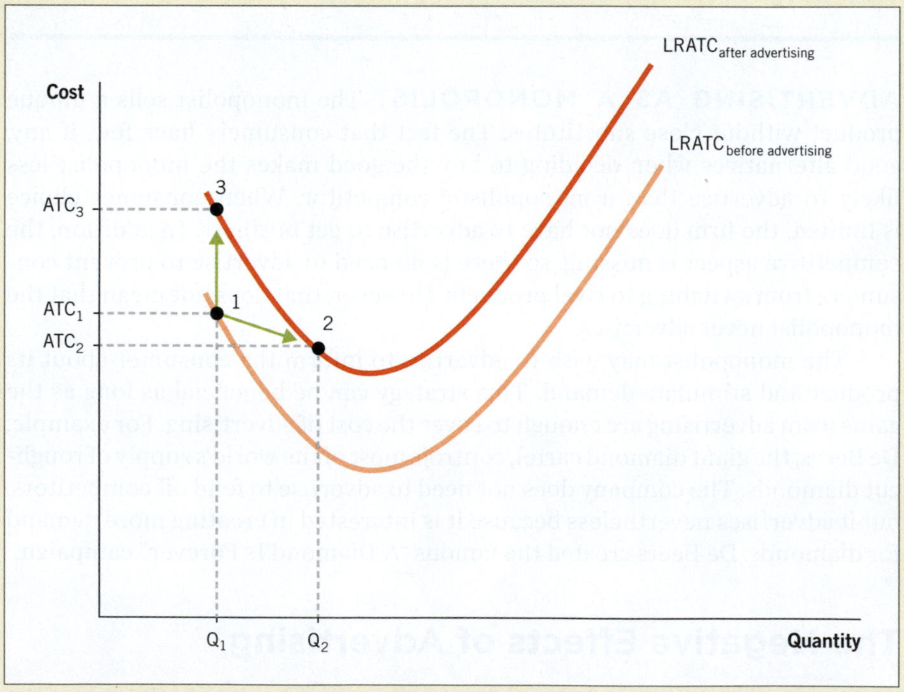

ECONOMICS *in the* MEDIA

Advertising

LITTLE CAESARS—THE BEST THING SINCE SLICED BREAD

Even Sliced Bread's workers are eating Little Caesars.

This 2020 Super Bowl commercial for Little Caesars pizza is a riff on the saying "It's the best thing since sliced bread!" The ad imagines Sliced Bread as a company and shows its panicked response when demand for the firm's only product suddenly declines, as hungry consumers are caught up in a wave of enthusiasm for home-delivered Little Caesars.

Once an enterprising competitor has convinced both the public and media that it has "the new best thing," it is hard for a legacy firm like Sliced Bread to recover market share without any new product of its own to offer. We usually focus on how advertising increases demand and makes it more inelastic. But in a mature market, a successful ad campaign for one product takes away from the demand for substitute products. This dynamic is what drives rival firms to compete intensely through advertising.

The CEO of Sliced Bread is none other than Rainn Wilson, who plays Dwight Schrute on *The Office*. At the end of the commercial, Sliced Bread goes out of business and Rainn Wilson ends up delivering pizza—Little Caesars, no less. Ouch.

Pearl ear studs are a nice gift, but they are even better when they come in a . . .

. . . blue box.

Suppose you buy all your jewelry at Tiffany's. One day, you enter the store to pick up pearl ear studs. You can get a small pair of pearl studs at Tiffany's for $300. But it turns out you can get studs of the same size, quality, and origin (freshwater) at Pearl World for $43, and you can find them online at Amazon for $19. There are no identifying marks on the jewelry that would enable you, or a seasoned jeweler, to tell the ear studs apart! Why would you buy them at Tiffany's when you can purchase them for far less elsewhere? The answer, it turns out, is that buying ear studs is a lot like consuming many other goods: name recognition matters. So do perception and brand loyalty. Many jewelry buyers also take cues from the storefront, how the staff dress, and how the jewelry is packaged. Spending $300 total is a lot of money for the privilege of getting Tiffany's blue box. Consumers believe that Tiffany's jewelry is better, when all the store is doing is charging more markup.

TRUTH IN ADVERTISING Finally, many advertising campaigns are not just informative—they are designed to produce a psychological response. When an ad moves you to buy or act in a particular way, it becomes manipulative. Because advertising can be such a powerful way to reach customers, there is a temptation to lie about a product. To prevent firms from spreading misinformation about their products, the Federal Trade Commission (FTC) regulates advertising and promotes economic efficiency. At the FTC, the Division of Advertising Practices protects consumers by enforcing truth-in-advertising laws. While the commission does not have enough resources to track down every violation, it does pay particular attention to claims involving food, nonprescription drugs, dietary supplements, alcohol, and tobacco. Unsubstantiated claims are particularly prevalent on the Internet, and they tend to target vulnerable populations seeking quick fixes to a variety of medical conditions.

Of course, even with regulatory oversight, consumers must still be vigilant. At best, the FTC can remove products from the market and levy fines against companies that make unsubstantiated claims. However, the damage is often already done. The Latin phrase *caveat emptor*, or "buyer beware," sums up the dangers of false information.

Sometimes the way a product is advertised is not illegal but is still borderline unethical. Firms often engage in price deception, or tricks to make you think a price is lower than it really is. Gas stations deploy this technique by quoting prices ending in a 9/10 of a cent fraction, to slightly understate how much you are paying. But a more egregious example of price deception comes from Mars, which sells Snickers, far and away the most popular snack-sized candy bar sold in the United States. For a time, Mars sold Snickers and 2xSnickers. One would think that "two times" Snickers would be two Snickers in one longer package, right? That's the deception: the bars in 2xSnickers are smaller!

2xSnickers should really be called 1.5xSnickers.

PRACTICE WHAT YOU KNOW

Advertising: Brands versus Generics

Why do some frozen pizzas cost more than others when brands that offer similar quality are only a few feet away in the frozen foods aisle? To answer that question, consider the following ones:

QUESTION: What would graphs showing price and output look like for DiGiorno and for a generic pizza? What is the markup for DiGiorno?

ANSWER: Here is the graph for DiGiorno.

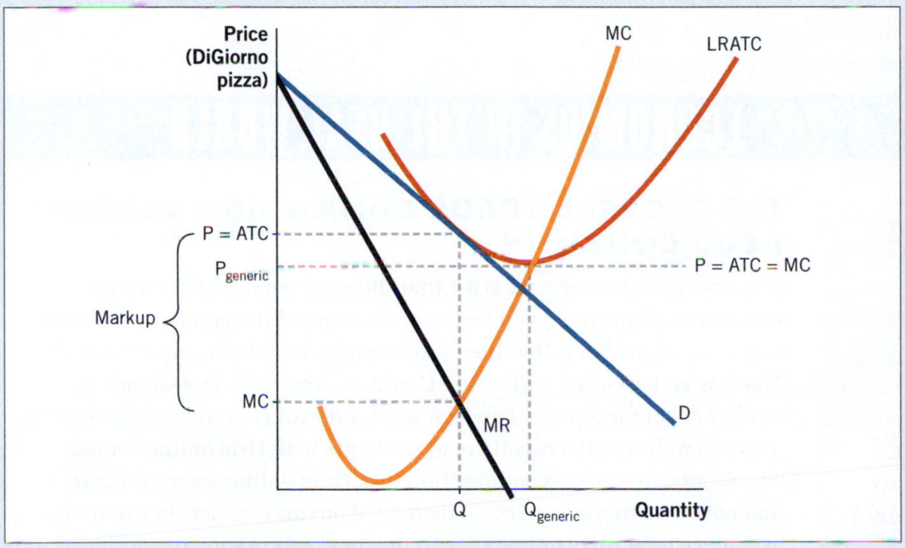

DiGiorno or generic?

And here is the graph for the generic pizza.

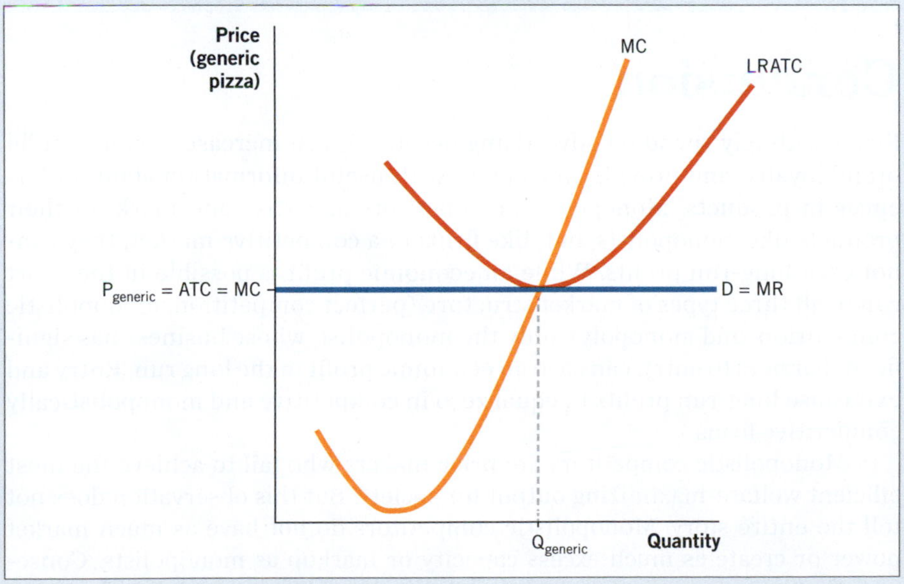

(CONTINUED)

QUESTION: Which company has a stronger incentive to maintain strict quality control in the production process, DiGiorno or a generic brand? Why?

ANSWER: DiGiorno has a catchy slogan: "It's Not Delivery. It's DiGiorno!" This statement tries to position the product as being just as good as a freshly delivered pizza. Some customers who buy frozen pizzas will opt for DiGiorno over comparable generics because they are familiar with the company's advertising claim about its quality. Therefore, DiGiorno has a stronger incentive to make sure the product delivers as advertised. Because generic, or store-name, brands are purchased mostly on the basis of price, the customer generally does not have high expectations about the quality.

ECONOMICS IN THE REAL WORLD

The FTC found 1-800 Contacts guilty of manipulative advertising.

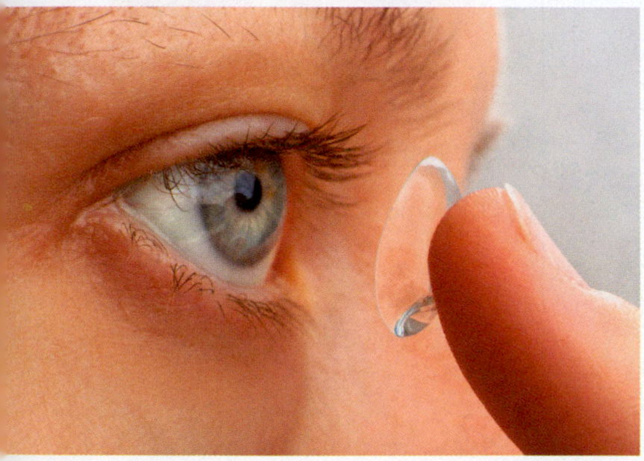

THE FEDERAL TRADE COMMISSION VERSUS 1-800 CONTACTS

When we search online, we trust that the most pertinent results are shown first. How would you feel—and how would it change your buying behavior—if you knew that the search results were being manipulated? That's what happened with 1-800 Contacts, America's largest online retailer of contact lenses. The firm was found guilty of unlawfully orchestrating a web of anticompetitive agreements with rival online contact lens sellers, to suppress competition in certain online search forums that advertise to consumers. So instead of buying contacts in a monopolistically competitive online space, consumers were shown search results with much higher prices.

Conclusion

Firms willingly spend on advertising because it can increase demand, build brand loyalty, and provide consumers with useful information about differences in products. Monopolistic competitors advertise and mark up their products like monopolists, but, like firms in a competitive market, they cannot earn long-run profits. While an economic profit is possible in the short run in all three types of market structure (perfect competition, monopolistic competition, and monopoly), only the monopolist, whose business has significant barriers to entry, can earn an economic profit in the long run. Entry and exit cause long-run profits to equal zero in competitive and monopolistically competitive firms.

Monopolistic competitors are price makers who fail to achieve the most efficient welfare-maximizing output for society. But this observation does not tell the entire story. Monopolistic competitors do not have as much market power or create as much excess capacity or markup as monopolists. Consequently, the monopolistic competitor lacks the ability to exploit consumers.

· ECONOMICS *for* LIFE ·

Product Differentiation: Would You Buy a Franchise?

- Restaurant failures are very high and running a franchise can lower your risk.
- Franchises provide brand familiarity.
- However, rights to franchise can come with very high fees. The five restaurants with the highest combined franchise and start-up costs are:

  Golden Corral, $6.8M

  Buffalo Wild Wings, $3.2M

  Culver's, $2.8M

  KFC, $2.5M

  Denny's, $2.4M

Franchises are valuable in markets where product differentiation matters. McDonald's, Panera Bread, and KFC all have a different take on serving fast food. But what does it mean to own a franchise?

Franchises are sold to individual owners, who operate subject to the terms of their agreement with the parent company. For instance, purchasing a McDonald's franchise and opening a new store can cost over $2 million. McDonald's also requires the individual restaurant owner to charge certain prices and offer menu items selected by the parent corporation. As a result, customers who prefer a certain type and quality of food know that the dining experience at each McDonald's will be similar. Most franchises also come with noncompete clauses that guarantee that another franchise will not open nearby. This guarantee gives the franchise owner the exclusive right to sell a differentiated product in a given area.

Suppose you want to start a restaurant. Why would you, or anyone else, be willing to pay over $2 million just for the right to sell food? For that amount, you could open your own restaurant with a custom menu and interior, create your own marketing plan, and locate anywhere you like. For example, Golden Corral and Buffalo Wild Wings are two restaurants with high start-up costs exceeding $3 million. Golden Corral is the largest buffet-style restaurant in the country, and Buffalo Wild Wings is one of the top locations to watch sporting events. You might think it would make more sense to avoid the franchising costs by opening your own buffet or setting up a bank of big-screen TVs. However, failures in the restaurant industry are high. With a franchise, the customer knows what to expect. Translation: high franchise fees enable firms to charge a higher markup because consumer demand is more inelastic.

Franchise owners are assured of visibility and a ready supply of customers. Purchasing a franchise means more potential customers will notice your restaurant, and that drives up revenues. Is that worth $2 million or more? Yes, in some cases. Suppose you'll do $1 million in annual sales as part of a franchise, but only $0.5 million on your own. That half-million difference over 20 years means $10 million more in revenue, a healthy chunk of which will turn into profits. This is the magic of franchising.

How much would you pay for a KFC franchise?

The result is not perfect, but widespread monopolistic competition generally serves consumers and society well.

In the next chapter, we continue our exploration of market structure with *oligopoly,* which produces results that are much closer to monopoly than monopolistic competition.

ANSWERING *the* BIG QUESTIONS

What is monopolistic competition?

- Monopolistic competition is a market structure characterized by low barriers to entry and many firms selling differentiated products.
- Differentiation of products takes three forms: differentiation by style or type, location, and quality.

What are the differences among monopolistic competition, competitive markets, and monopoly?

- Monopolistic competitors, like monopolists, are price makers with downward-sloping demand curves. Whenever the demand curve is downward sloping, the firm is able to mark up the price above marginal cost. The results are excess capacity and an inefficient level of output.
- In the long run, barriers to entry enable a monopoly to earn an economic profit. This is not the case for monopolistic competition or competitive markets.

Why is advertising prevalent in monopolistic competition?

- Advertising performs useful functions under monopolistic competition: it conveys information about the price of the goods offered for sale, the location of products, and new products. It also signals differences in quality. However, advertising also encourages brand loyalty, which makes it harder for other businesses to successfully enter the market. Advertising can be manipulative and misleading.

CHAPTER PROBLEMS

Concepts You Should Know

excess capacity (p. 375)
markup (p. 375)
monopolistic competition (p. 368)
product differentiation (p. 368)

Questions for Review

1. Why is product differentiation necessary for monopolistic competition? What are three types of product differentiation?
2. How is monopolistic competition like competitive markets? How is monopolistic competition like monopoly?
3. Why do monopolistically competitive firms produce less than those operating at the most efficient scale of production?
4. Draw a graph that shows a monopolistic competitor making an economic profit in the short run and a graph that shows a monopolistic competitor making no economic profit in the long run.
5. Monopolistic competition produces a result that is inefficient. Does this outcome mean that monopolistically competitive markets should be regulated? Discuss.
6. Draw a typical demand curve for competitive markets, monopolistic competition, and monopoly. Which of these demand curves is the most inelastic? Why?
7. How does advertising benefit society? In what ways can advertising be harmful?
8. When you buy a generic product instead of its name-brand counterpart, is the good you purchase really inferior, or is it the same good, simply repackaged by the name-brand manufacturer under another label?

Study Problems (*✷ solved at the end of the section*)

✷ 1. At your high school reunion, a friend describes his plan to take a break from his florist shop and sail around the world. He says that if he continues to make the same economic profit for the next five years, he will be able to afford the trip. Do you think your friend will be able to achieve his dream in five years? What do you expect to happen to his firm's profits in the long run?

2. Which of the following could be considered a monopolistic competitor?
   - **a.** a local corn farmer
   - **b.** Pacific Gas & Electric Company
   - **c.** a pizza delivery business
   - **d.** a grocery store
   - **e.** Vera Wang, fashion designer

3. Which of the following are the same under monopolistic competition and in a competitive market in the long run?
   - **a.** the markup the firm charges
   - **b.** the price the firm charges to consumers
   - **c.** the firm's excess capacity
   - **d.** the average total cost of production
   - **e.** the amount of advertising
   - **f.** the firm's profit
   - **g.** the efficiency of the market structure

4. In competitive markets, price is equal to marginal cost in the long run. Explain why this statement is not true for monopolistic competition.

5. Econoburgers, a fast-food restaurant in a crowded local market, has reached a long-run equilibrium.
   - **a.** Draw a diagram showing demand, marginal revenue, average total cost, and marginal cost curves for Econoburgers.
   - **b.** How much profit is Econoburgers making?
   - **c.** Suppose that the government decides to regulate burger production to make it mor efficient. Explain what would happen to t' price of Econoburgers and the firm's out

✱ **6.** Consider two different companies. The first manufactures cardboard, and the second sells books. Which firm is more likely to advertise?

7. In the diagram that follows, identify the demand curve that is consistent with a monopolistic competitor making zero long-run economic profit. Explain why you have chosen that demand curve and why the other two demand curves are not consistent with monopolistic competition.

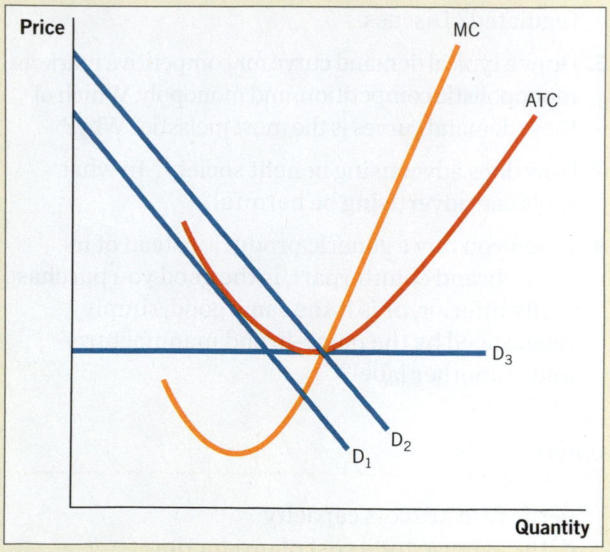

8. Titleist has an advertising slogan: "#1 Ball in Golf." Consumers can also buy generic golf balls. The manufacturers of generic golf balls do not engage in any advertising. Assume that the average total cost of producing Titleist and generic golf balls is the same.

a. Create a graph showing the price and the markup for Titleist.
b. In a separate graph, show the price and the output for the generic firms.
c. Who has a stronger incentive to maintain strict quality control in the production process—Titleist or the generic firms? Why?

9. Taste of India is a small restaurant in a small town. The owner of Taste of India marks up his dishes by 300%. Indian Cuisine is a small restaurant in a large city. The owner of Indian Cuisine marks up her dishes by 200%. Explain why the markup is higher in the small town.

✱ **10.** Read the following online article: http://20somethingfinance.com/why-eyeglasses-are-so-expensive-how-you-can-pay-less. Using your understanding of monopolistic competition and markup, explain why retail customers pay so much more for eyeglasses than online customers do. You can also watch this video from *Adam Ruins Everything* for an interesting explanation: www.youtube.com/watch?v=CAeHuDcy_bY.

✱ **11.** Consider a monopolistically competitive firm. From the point of view of the remaining firms, as firms leave the industry we can think of this as a shift to the

a. left for each individual firm's supply curve.
b. left in each individual firm's MC curve.
c. right in each individual firm's ATC curve.
d. right in each individual firm's demand curve.

Solved Problems

…he florist business is monopolistically competi-
… This means firms are free to enter and exit at
… Firms will enter because your friend's
…ing an economic profit. As new florist
… added competition will drive
…ing your friend's profits to fall.
…means he will not be able to
… He will earn only enough
…ts, or what is known as
… That is not to say
…n to sail around the world, but it won't happen as fast as he would like because other firms will enter the market and limit his profits going forward.

6. The cardboard firm manufactures a product that is a component used mostly by other firms that need to package final products for sale. As a result, any efforts at advertising will only raise costs without increasing the demand for cardboard. This situation contrasts with that of the bookseller, who advertises to attract consumers to the store. More traffic means more purchases of books and other items sold in the store. The bookstore has some market power and markup. In this case, it pays to advertise. A cardboard manufacturing firm sells exactly the same product as other cardboard producers, so it has no market power, and any advertising expenses will only make its cost higher than its rivals'.

10. There are many retailers (LensCrafters, Pearle, Sears, Target), but the brands they sell all come from Italian eyeglass manufacturer Luxottica. Luxottica prevents these major retailers from discounting the frames and will pull their brands if they do. However, if you don't care about the brand of eyeglasses you wear, you can find a pair online for well under $100. Online retailers aren't selling a brand, so they attract customers with much more elastic demand compared with customers who want their frames to be fashionable. This scenario fits perfectly with the idea of markup. Firms with brand-loyal customers have much higher markup than firms with customers who do not care about the brand they purchase.

11. The correct answer is d: each individual firm's demand curve shifts to the right. The reason is that as firms exit, each remaining firm picks up additional customers.

CHAPTER

Oligopoly and Strategic Behavior

Cell Phone Companies Are Competitive.

Cell phone use today is everywhere. More than 97% of Americans own a cell phone, and more than 85%, a smartphone. And one estimate of usage shows the average smartphone user taps it 2,617 times a day!* But for all this usage, chances are that you receive service from one of three major cell phone carriers in the United States: AT&T, Verizon, or T-Mobile. Together, these firms control 95% of all cellular service. In some respects, this market is very competitive. For example, cell phone companies advertise intensely, and they offer a variety of phones with voice and data plans. Also, there are differences in network coverage and in the number of applications users can access. But despite outward appearances, the cell phone companies do not do business in a competitive or even a monopolistically competitive market. One important reason for this is the expense of building and maintaining a cellular network. The largest cell phone companies have invested billions of dollars in infrastructure in order to attract customers based on cell phone network quality and speed and the plans and services the companies provide. Therefore, the cost of entry is very high. As we learned in Chapter 10, barriers to entry are a key feature of monopolies.

*"Mobile Fact Sheet," Pew Research Center, April 7, 2021, https://www.pewresearch.org/internet/fact-sheet/mobile; Michael Winnick, "Putting a Finger on Our Phone Obsession," *dscout* (blog), June 16, 2016, https://blog.dscout.com/people-nerds/mobile-touches.

Gamers delight, 5G networks will make your cell phones even more powerful! Whatever this customer is seeing in her 3D display has apparently made quite an impression.

The cell phone industry has features of both competition and monopoly: competition is fierce, but smaller firms and potential entrants into the market find it difficult to enter and compete. This mixture of characteristics represents another form of market structure—*oligopoly*. In this chapter, we examine oligopoly by comparing it with other market structures already familiar to you. We then look at some of the strategic behaviors firms in an oligopoly employ, an examination that leads us into the fascinating topic of game theory.

· BIG QUESTIONS ·

- What is oligopoly?
- How does game theory explain strategic behavior?
- How do government policies affect oligopoly behavior?
- What are network externalities?

What Is Oligopoly?

Oligopoly is a form of market structure that exists when a small number of firms sell a differentiated product in a market with high barriers to entry.

Oligopoly is a form of market structure that exists when a small number of firms sell a product in a market with significant barriers to entry. An oligopolist is like a monopolistic competitor in that it often sells a differentiated product. But like pure monopolists, oligopolists enjoy significant barriers to entry. Table 13.1 compares the differences and similarities between the four market structures.

We have seen that firms in monopolistically competitive markets usually have a limited amount of market power. As a result, buyers often find low prices (but not as low as competitive markets) and wide availability. In contrast, an oligopolist sells in a market with significant barriers to entry and fewer rivals. Thus, the oligopolist has more market power than a firm operating under

...ligopoly to Other Market Structures

Monopolistic competition	Oligopoly	Monopoly
...any sellers	A few sellers	One seller
...entiated product	Differentiated product (most of the time)	Unique product without close substitutes
...y entry and exit	Barriers to entry	Significant barriers to entry

TABLE 13.2

Highly Concentrated Industries in the United States

Industry	Concentration ratio of the four largest firms (%)	Top firms
Search engines	98.5	Google, Yahoo, Microsoft
Wireless telecommunications	94.7	Verizon, AT&T, T-Mobile, Sprint
Satellite TV providers	94.5	DirecTV, Dish Network
Soda production	93.7	Coca-Cola, PepsiCo, Keurig Dr Pepper
Sanitary paper products	92.7	Kimberly-Clark, Procter & Gamble, Georgia-Pacific
Tire manufacturing (domestic)	91.3	Michelin, Goodyear, Bridgestone, Continental
Major household appliances	90.0	Whirlpool, Electrolux, General Electric, LG
Automobile manufacturing (domestic)	87.0	General Motors, Toyota, Ford, Fiat-Chrysler
Music streaming services	77.0	Spotify, Apple Music, Amazon, Tencent

Source: Andrea Alegria, Agata Kaczanowska, and Lauren Setar, "Highly Concentrated: Companies That Dominate Their Industries," IBISWorld, February 2012, www.ibisworld.com; and author's adjustments.

monopolistic competition. However, because an oligopolistic market has more than one seller, no single oligopolist has as much market power as a monopolist.

Our study of oligopoly begins with a look at how economists measure market power in an industry. We then work through a simplified model of oligopoly to explore the choices that oligopolists make.

Measuring the Concentration of Industries

In markets with only a few sellers, industry output is highly concentrated among a few large firms. Economists use *concentration ratios* as a measure of the oligopoly power present in an industry. The most common measure, known as the four-firm concentration ratio, expresses the sales of the four largest firms in an industry as a percentage of that industry's total sales. Table 13.2 lists the four-firm concentration ratios for highly concentrated industries in the United States. This ratio is determined by taking the output of the four largest firms in an industry and dividing that output by the total production in the entire industry.

In highly concentrated industries like search engines, wireless telecommunications, and satellite TV providers, the market share held by the four largest firms approaches 100%. At the bottom of our list of most concentrated industries is domestic automobile manufacturing. General Motors, Fiat Chrysler, Ford, and Toyota (which has seven manufacturing plants in the United States) dominate the domestic automobile industry (in case you are wondering, the company Tesla is highly valued but has about 3% market share). These large firms have significant market power.

However, when evaluating market power in an industry, it is important to be aware of international activity. In several industries, including automobile and tire manufacturing, intense global competition keeps the market power of U.S. companies in check. For instance, domestic manufacturers that produce automobiles also

Competition from foreign car companies keeps the market power of the U.S.-based automobile companies in check.

must compete globally against cars produced elsewhere. This means that vehicles produced by Honda, Nissan, Volkswagen, Kia, and Volvo, to name just a few companies, limit the market power of domestic producers. As a result, the concentration ratio is a rough gauge of oligopoly power—not an absolute measure.

Collusion and Cartels in a Simple Duopoly Example

In this section, we explore the two conflicting tendencies found in oligopoly: oligopolists would like to act like monopolists, but they often end up competing like monopolistic competitors. To help us understand oligopoly behavior, we start with a simplified example: an industry consisting of only two firms, known as a *duopoly*. Duopolies (such as Boeing and Airbus in the wide-body jet market) are rare in national and international markets, but not that uncommon in small, local markets. For example, in many small communities, the number of cell phone carriers is limited. Imagine a small town where only two providers have cell phone towers. In this case, the cell towers are a sunk cost (see Chapter 9); both towers were built to service all of the customers in the town, so each carrier has substantial excess capacity when the customers are divided between the two carriers. Also, because there is extra capacity on each network, the marginal cost of adding additional customers is zero.

Table 13.3 shows the community's demand for cell phones. Because the prices and quantities listed in the first two columns are negatively related, the data are consistent with a downward-sloping demand curve.

Column 3 calculates the total revenue from columns 1 and 2. With Table 13.3 as our guide, we will examine the output in this market under three scenarios: competition, monopoly, and duopoly.

TABLE 13.3

The Demand Schedule for Cell Phones

Here we assume that 1 customer = 1 cell phone = 1 purchase of cell phone service.

(1) Price/month (P)	(2) Number of customers (Q)	(3) Total revenue (TR) (P) × (Q)
$180	0	$0
165	100	16,500
150	200	30,000
135	300	40,500
120	400	48,000
105	500	52,500
90	600	54,000
75	700	52,500
60	800	48,000
45	900	40,500
30	1,000	30,000
15	1,100	16,500
0	1,200	0

Duopoly sits between the two extremes. Competition still exists, but it is not as extensive as you would see in competitive markets, which ruthlessly drive the price down to cost. Nor does the result always mirror that of monopoly, where competitive pressures are completely absent. In an oligopoly, a small number of firms feel competitive pressures and also enjoy some of the advantages of monopoly.

COMPETITIVE OUTCOME Recall that competitive markets drive prices down to the point at which marginal revenue is equal to the marginal cost. So if the market is highly competitive and the marginal cost is zero, we would expect the final price of cell phone service to be zero and the quantity supplied to be 1,200 customers—the number of people who live in the small town. At this point, anyone who desires cell phone service would be able to receive it without cost. Because efficiency exists when the output is maximized, and because everyone who lives in the community would have cell phone service, the result would be socially efficient. However, it is unrealistic to expect this outcome. Cell phone companies provide a good that is nonrival and also excludable; in other words, they sell a club good (see Chapter 7). Because these firms are in business to make money, they will not provide something for nothing.

Marginal thinking

MONOPOLY OUTCOME At the other extreme of the market structure continuum, a monopolist faces no competition, and price decisions do not depend on the activity of other firms. A monopolist can search for the price that brings it the most profit. Looking at Table 13.3, we see that total revenue peaks at $54,000. At this point, the price is $90 per month, and 600 customers sign up for cell phone service. Compared with a competitive market, the monopoly price is higher and the quantity sold is lower. The result is a loss of efficiency.

DUOPOLY OUTCOME In a duopoly, the two firms can decide to cooperate—even though this practice is illegal in the United States, as we will discuss shortly. If the duopolists cooperate, we say that they collude. **Collusion** is an agreement between rival firms that specifies the price each firm charges and the quantity it produces. The firms that collude can act like a single monopolist to maximize their profits. In this case, the monopolist would maximize its profit by charging $90 and serving 600 customers. If the duopolists divide the market equally, they will each have 300 customers who pay $90, for a total of $27,000 in revenue each.

Collusion is an agreement among rival firms that specifies the price each firm charges and the quantity it produces.

When two or more firms act in unison, economists refer to them as a **cartel**. Many countries prohibit cartels. In the United States, **antitrust laws** prohibit collusion. However, even if collusion were legal, it would probably fail more often than not. Imagine that two theoretical cell phone companies, AT-Phone and Horizon, have formed a cartel and agreed that each will serve 300 customers at a price of $90 per month per customer. But AT-Phone and Horizon each have an incentive to earn more revenue by lowering their price while the rival company keeps the agreement. Suppose AT-Phone lowers its price to $75. Looking at Table 13.3, we see that at this price the total market demand rises to 700 customers—and AT-phone will capture the entire market, by selling at the lowest price. So AT-Phone will serve 700 customers, and its revenue will be 700 × $75, or $52,500. This is an improvement of $25,500 over what AT-Phone made when the market price was $90 and the customers were equally divided.

A **cartel** is a group of two or more firms that act in unison.

Antitrust laws attempt to prevent oligopolies from behaving like monopolies.

Incentives

TABLE 13.4

Outcomes under Competition, Duopoly, and Monopoly

	Competitive markets	Duopoly	Monopoly
Price	$0	$0–90	$90
Output	1,200	600–1,200	600
Socially efficient?	Yes	Only when the price is $0 and output is 1,200	No
Explanation	Because the marginal cost of providing cell phone service is zero, the price is eventually driven to zero. Since firms are in business to make a profit, it is unrealistic to expect this result.	Because firms are mutually interdependent, each adopts a strategy based on the actions of its rival. The two firms may decide to collude and charge $90, or competitive pressures may lead them to charge a much lower price.	The monopolist is free to choose the profit-maximizing output. In the cell phone example, it maximizes its total revenue. As a result, the monopolist charges $90 and serves 600 customers.

How would Horizon react? At the very least, unless it wants to earn $0, it had better match AT-Phone's lower price. Horizon would then attract 350 customers, half the market at a price of $75, and now AT-Phone and Horizon would each bring in revenue of 350 × $75, or $26,250, leaving each firm making $750 less than when they served only 600 customers total. From what we know about competitive markets, we might expect the competition between the two firms to cause a price war in which price eventually falls to zero. Duopolists are unlikely to participate in an all-out price war because both firms would no longer be making any profit, but we cannot know to what extent competitive pressures will determine each firm's decision.

Table 13.4 summarizes the different results under competition, duopoly, and monopoly using our cell phone example. From this example, we see that a market with a small number of sellers is characterized by **mutual interdependence**, which is a market situation in which the actions of one firm have an impact on the price and output of its competitors. As a result, a firm's market share is determined by the products it offers, the prices it charges, and the actions of its rivals.

Mutual interdependence is a market situation where the actions of one firm have an impact on the price and output of its competitors.

Oligopolists want to emulate the monopoly outcome, but the push to compete with their rivals often makes it difficult to maintain a cartel. Yet the idea that cartels are unstable is not guaranteed. When a stable cartel is not achieved, firms in oligopoly fall short of fully maximizing profits. But they also do not compete to the same degree as firms in competitive markets. Therefore, when a market is an oligopoly, output is likely to be higher than under a monopoly and lower than within a competitive market. As you would expect, the amount of output affects the prices. The higher output (compared with monopoly) makes oligopoly prices generally lower than monopoly prices, and the lower output (compared with a competitive market) makes oligopoly prices higher than those found in competitive markets.

Price leadership occurs when a dominant firm in an industry sets the price that maximizes its profits and the smaller firms in the industry follow by setting their prices to match the price leader.

In many industries, smaller firms may take a cue from the decisions made by the price leader. **Price leadership** occurs when a single firm, known as the price leader, produces a large share of the total output in the industry. The price leader sets the price and output level that maximizes its own profits. Smaller firms then set their prices to match the price leader. Because the impact on price is small to begin with, it makes sense that smaller rivals tend to follow the price leader.

Price leadership is not illegal because it does not involve collusion. Rather, it relies on an understanding that an effort to resist changes implemented by the price leader will lead to both increased price competition and lower profits for every firm in the industry. Because the firms act in accordance with one another, this practice is commonly known as *tacit collusion*.

One well-known example of price leadership is pricing patterns in the airline industry. On almost any route with multiple carrier options, a price search for flights will reveal almost identical prices on basic economy-class flights. This similarity of prices happens even though the firms do not collude to set a profit-maximizing price. Rather, when one firm sets a fare, the other carriers feel compelled to match it. Price leadership works best when the largest firm in an industry raises or lowers its price and smaller rivals follow suit.

ECONOMICS IN THE REAL WORLD

OPEC: AN INTERNATIONAL CARTEL

What would oil prices be like if OPEC didn't exist?

The best-known cartel is the Organization of the Petroleum Exporting Countries, or OPEC, a group of nations responsible for most of the world's output of crude oil. It was founded in 1960, and in 2016 OPEC added more nations to form OPEC+. The members collude to limit worldwide oil supply to keep prices high, an act that would be illegal under U.S. antitrust law but is legal under international law. OPEC+ controls almost 90% of the world's known oil reserves and accounts for almost 55% of the world's crude production, giving the cartel's 23 member nations significant collective market power.

For much of its existence, OPEC has acted effectively to manipulate the price of oil by manipulating supply, being careful to keep the price below the cost of alternative energy sources. There have, however, been threats to the consortium's unity, in the form of embargoes (government prohibitions on the trade of oil), oil gluts, and production disputes. In recent years, the shale oil boom in the United States and Canada has been a particular threat to OPEC+, driving the price of oil well below what it was just a few years ago. Member nations are divided over how to respond. Reduce output? Or flood the market to push the price down further and try to drive the North American firms out of business? If the OPEC+ nations cannot agree on a strategy, an all-out global oil price war is a distinct possibility.

Oligopoly with More Than Two Firms

We have seen how firms behave in a duopoly. What happens when more firms enter the market? The addition of a third firm complicates efforts to maintain a cartel and increases the possibility of a more competitive result.

We can see this interaction in the cell phone market. The three major companies are not all equal. If AT&T and Verizon were the only two providers, the market might have very little competition. However, T-Mobile plays a crucial role in changing the market dynamic. Even though T-Mobile has significantly less market share than either of its bigger rivals, it still has developed an extensive cellular network in order to compete. Because T-Mobile has a smaller subscriber base and significant excess capacity, it aggressively competes on price. As a result, in many (but not all) respects, the entire cell phone industry functions competitively.

To see why, consider what the addition of a third firm will do to the market. When the third firm enters the market, there are two effects to consider—price and output. For example, if the third firm builds a cell tower, it will increase the overall capacity to provide cell phone service. As we observed in the duopoly example, if the total number of cell phone contracts (the supply) increases, all the firms must charge a lower price. This is the **price effect**, and it reflects how a change in price affects the firm's revenue. But because the marginal cost of providing cell phone service is essentially zero, the price each firm charges is substantially higher than the marginal cost of adding a new customer to the network. When the firm sells an additional unit, it generates additional revenues for the firm. This **output effect** occurs when a change in price affects the number of customers in a market.

The **price effect** reflects how a change in price affects the firm's revenue.

The **output effect** occurs when a change in price affects the number of customers in a market.

The price effect and output effect make it difficult to maintain a cartel when there are more than two firms. Generally, as the number of firms grows, each individual firm becomes less concerned about its impact on the overall price, because any price above marginal cost creates a profit. Therefore, individual firms are more willing to lower prices because doing so creates a large output effect for the individual firm and only a small price effect in the market.

Of course, not all firms are the same size. Therefore, smaller and larger firms in an oligopolistic market react differently to the price and output effects. Increased output at smaller firms will have a negligible impact on overall prices because small firms represent only a tiny fraction of the market supply. But the same is not true for firms with a large market share. Decisions at these firms will have a substantial impact on price and output because the overall amount supplied in the market will change appreciably. In other words, in an oligopoly, the decisions of one firm directly affect other firms.

PRACTICE WHAT YOU KNOW

Oligopoly: Can You Recognize the Oligopolist?

QUESTION: Which firm is the oligopolist?

a. Firm A is in retail. It is one of the largest and most popular clothing stores in the country. It also competes with many rivals and faces intense price competition.

b. Firm B is in the auto rental business. It is not the biggest of the several major auto rental firms in the United States, but significant barriers to entry enable it to serve customers across the nation more conveniently and at a lower price than local rivals.

c. Firm C is a restaurant in a small, isolated community. It is the only local eatery. People drive from miles away to eat there.

(CONTINUED)

ANSWER: Firm A sells clothing, a product with many competing brands and outlets. The competition is intense, which means that the firm has little market power. As a result, firm A is a player in a competitive market. It is not an oligopolist. Firm B faces competition from other large national car rental companies, but barriers to entry at many airports prevent smaller firms from securing space inside the terminal. This means that car rental companies are oligopolists. Firm C is a monopolist. It is the only place to eat out in the isolated community, and no other restaurant is nearby. It is not an oligopolist.

CHALLENGE QUESTION: Is the airline industry (a number of major airlines but many smaller rivals) a good example of oligopoly, or of monopolistic competition?

ANSWER: If you simply look at the number of airlines operating in the United States, you find dozens—more than enough, on a ground-level view—to make cartels and other monopoly-like behaviors seem unlikely. But if you look again, this time from 30,000 feet, you see that four major carriers (American, Delta, Southwest, and United) account for 80% of all domestic departures. In addition, many small airports are only served by one or two carriers, making price collusion relatively easy on many routes. Finally, significant start-up costs make the cost of entry into the market relatively high. That's not to say that airlines face no competition—one of the four largest U.S. carriers, Southwest, used to be a small regional airline but was so successful at building its brand and keeping costs low that it was able to expand across the country. Still, with the high barriers to entry (it is hard to secure gates at airports), consolidation among the largest carriers, and differentiated routes, each carrier enjoys pricing power. This makes the airline industry a better example of oligopoly than of monopolistic competition.

How Does Game Theory Explain Strategic Behavior?

Decision-making under oligopoly can be complex. **Game theory** is a branch of mathematics that economists use to analyze the strategic behavior of decision-makers who have to consider the behavior of others around them. In particular, game theory can help us determine what level of cooperation is most likely to occur. A game consists of a set of players, a set of strategies available to those players, and a specification of the payoffs for each combination of strategies. The game is usually represented by a payoff matrix that shows the players, strategies, and payoffs. It is presumed that each player acts simultaneously or without knowing the actions of the other.

Game theory is a branch of mathematics that economists use to analyze the strategic behavior of decision-makers.

In this section, we will learn about the prisoner's dilemma, an example from game theory that helps us understand how dominant strategies often frame short-run decisions. (In its simplest form, the prisoner's dilemma is a game played just once, not repeatedly over time.) We will use the idea of the dominant strategy to explain why oligopolists often choose to advertise. Finally, we will come full circle and argue that the dominant strategy in a game may be overcome in the long run, through repeated interactions.

Strategic Behavior and the Dominant Strategy

We have seen that in oligopoly there is mutual interdependence: a rival's business choices affect the earnings the other rivals can expect to make. To learn more about the decisions firms make, we will explore a fundamental problem in game theory known as the *prisoner's dilemma*. The dilemma takes its name from a famous scenario devised by pioneer game theorist Al Tucker soon after World War II.

The scenario goes like this: Two prisoners are being interrogated separately about a crime they both participated in, and each is offered a plea bargain to cooperate with the authorities by testifying against the other. If both suspects refuse to cooperate with the authorities, neither can be convicted of a more serious crime, though they will both have to spend some time in jail. But the police have offered full immunity if one cooperates and the other does not. This means that each suspect has an incentive to betray the other. The problem is that if they both confess, they will spend more time in jail than if they had both stayed quiet. When decision-makers face incentives that make it difficult to achieve mutually beneficial outcomes, we say they are in a **prisoner's dilemma**. This situation makes the payoff for cooperating with the authorities more attractive than the result of keeping quiet.

The **prisoner's dilemma** occurs when decision-makers face incentives that make it difficult to achieve mutually beneficial outcomes.

We can understand the outcomes of the prisoner's dilemma by looking at the payoff matrix in Figure 13.1. Starting with the white box in the upper left corner, we see that if both suspects testify against each other, they each get 10 years in jail. If one suspect testifies while his partner remains quiet—the upper right and lower left boxes—he goes free and his partner gets 25 years

FIGURE 13.1

The Prisoner's Dilemma

The two suspects know that if they both keep quiet, they will spend only 1 year in jail. The prisoner's dilemma occurs because the decision to testify results in no jail time for the one who testifies if the other does not testify. However, this outcome means that both are likely to testify and get 10 years.

		Tony Montana	
		Testify	Keep quiet
Manny Ribera	Testify	10 years in jail 10 years in jail	25 years in jail goes free
	Keep quiet	goes free 25 years in jail	1 year in jail 1 year in jail

in jail. If both keep quiet—the result in the lower right corner—they each get off with 1 year in jail. This result is better than the outcome in which both prisoners testify.

Incentives

Because each suspect is interrogated separately, the decision about what to tell the police cannot be made cooperatively; thus, each prisoner faces a dilemma. The interrogation process makes the situation a noncooperative "game" and changes the incentives each party faces.

Under these circumstances, what will our suspects choose? Let's begin with the outcomes for Tony Montana. Suppose he testifies. If Manny Ribera also testifies, Tony will get 10 years in jail (the upper left box). If Manny keeps quiet, Tony will go free (the lower left box). Now suppose that Tony decides to keep quiet. If Manny testifies, Tony can expect 25 years in jail (the upper right box). If Manny keeps quiet, Tony will get 1 year in jail (the lower right box). No matter what choice Manny makes, Tony is always better off choosing to testify. If his partner testifies and he testifies, he gets 10 years in jail as opposed to 25 if he keeps quiet. If his partner keeps quiet and he testifies, Tony goes free as opposed to spending a year in jail if he also keeps quiet. The same analysis applies to the outcomes for Manny.

When a player always prefers one strategy, regardless of what his opponent chooses, we say it is a **dominant strategy**. We can see a dominant strategy at work in the case of our two suspects. They know that if they both keep quiet, they will spend one year in jail. The dilemma occurs because both suspects are more likely to testify and get 10 years in jail. The choice to testify is obvious for two reasons. First, neither suspect can monitor the actions of the other after they are separated. Second, once each suspect understands that his partner will save jail time if he testifies, he realizes that the incentives are not in favor of keeping quiet.

A **dominant strategy** exists when a player will always prefer one strategy, regardless of what his or her opponent chooses.

The dominant strategy in our example is also a Nash equilibrium, named for mathematician John Nash. A **Nash equilibrium** occurs when all economic decision-makers have no incentive to change their current decision. If each suspect reasons that the other will testify, the best response is also to testify. Each suspect may wish that he and his partner could coordinate their actions and agree to keep quiet. However, without the possibility of coordination, neither has an incentive to withhold testimony. So they both think strategically and decide to testify.

A **Nash equilibrium** occurs when all economic decision-makers opt to keep the status quo.

Incentives

Duopoly and the Prisoner's Dilemma

The prisoner's dilemma example suggests that cooperation can be difficult to achieve. What this means for oligopoly is that it is not natural or easy for firms to collude. To get a better sense of the incentives that oligopolists face, let's revisit the situation of AT-Phone and Horizon, each trying to decide whether to charge $90 or $75 for cell phone plans. Figure 13.2 puts some of the information from Table 13.3 into a payoff matrix and highlights the revenue AT-Phone and Horizon could earn, depending on the price each firm chooses.

We see that when AT-Phone sets a high price ($90), Horizon can earn either $27,000, by setting a high price, or $52,500, by setting a low price. When AT-Phone sets a low price ($75), Horizon can earn either $0 with a high price

ECONOMICS *in the* MEDIA

Kami no Tou (2020)

Kami no Tou (*Tower of God* in English) is a Japanese animated series about a fictional world where people compete in mysterious challenges in order to move up through the levels of a fantastical tower—the Tower of God. Upon reaching the top, a person is granted any wish they care to name. That's an incredibly powerful incentive to succeed, no?

One of the challenges, the Crown Game, is played in three-person teams. Each team tries to gain possession of the crown. One person must wear the crown and sit on the throne, while the two teammates protect the crown wearer against attacks from the other teams. The defending team wins if they can hold off all attacking parties for three minutes. The attacking teams win if they dethrone or de-crown the crown wearer.

Tower of God requires an understanding of game theory. The dominant strategy in the Crown Game is to obtain the crown as soon as possible and defend it, otherwise your team must compete to take the crown while fighting off other teams who are still attacking you! Since a "wish of your choice" is an incredibly valuable prize, this means that it is in everyone's best interest to fight for the crown at any cost, making this the Nash equilibrium in the game.

Can you keep the crown?

or $26,250 with a low price. Either way, Horizon is better off setting the low price. The same reasoning holds for AT-Phone: choosing the low price instead of the high one means getting either $52,500 instead of $27,000 or else $26,250 instead of $0, depending on what Horizon does. So the low price is the dominant strategy for both firms. This produces a Nash equilibrium, where both firms make $26,250. This is the prisoner's dilemma: each firm has an incentive to lower its price to generate more revenue than if they had colluded and kept prices high, but acting on this incentive causes them both to earn less revenue than if they had kept prices high.

Incentives

Unfortunately for the two firms, it's not just a matter of settling for $26,250 instead of $27,000, because the Nash equilibrium is only for the given payoff matrix. Once the possibility of dropping the price to $60 floats into view, there's a new payoff matrix in which $75 is the high price and $60 is the low price. Lather, rinse, repeat with the price war "shampoo," and pretty soon both firms are practically giving cell phone service away for free. At that point, they're really, really wishing they'd figured out how to operate as a cartel and both earn $27,000 instead.

FIGURE 13.2

		AT-Phone: High price: $90	AT-Phone: Low price: $75
Horizon	High price: $90	$27,000 revenue (AT-Phone); $27,000 revenue (Horizon)	$52,500 revenue (AT-Phone); $0 revenue (Horizon)
Horizon	Low price: $75	$0 revenue (AT-Phone); $52,500 revenue (Horizon)	$26,250 revenue (AT-Phone); $26,250 revenue (Horizon)

The Prisoner's Dilemma in Duopoly

Each company has a dominant strategy to serve more customers by lowering its price. But when both firms pursue that strategy, they end up in a Nash equilibrium where both firms are worse off than if they'd both chosen differently. They earn just $26,250, when $27,000 was seemingly within reach.

Advertising and Game Theory

We have seen that oligopolists function like monopolistic competitors in that they sell differentiated products. We know that advertising is commonplace in markets with a differentiated product. In the case of an oligopoly, mutual interdependence means that advertising can create a contest between firms trying to gain customers. The result may be skyrocketing advertising budgets and little, or no, net gain of customers. Therefore, oligopolists have an incentive to scale back their advertising, but only if their rivals also agree to scale back. Like all cooperative action among competitors, this is easier said than done.

Incentives

Figure 13.3 highlights the advertising choices of Coca-Cola and PepsiCo, two fierce rivals in the soft-drink industry. Together, Coca-Cola and PepsiCo account for 72% of the soft-drink market, with Coca-Cola being the slightly larger of the two firms. Both companies are known for their advertising campaigns, which cost hundreds of millions of dollars. To determine if they gain anything by spending so much on advertising, let's look at the dominant strategy. In the absence of cooperation, each firm will choose to advertise, because the payoffs under advertising ($100 million or $150 million) exceed those of not advertising ($75 million or $125 million). When each firm chooses to advertise, it generates a profit of $100 million. This is a second-best outcome compared with the $125 million profit each could earn if neither firm advertises. The dilemma is that each firm needs to advertise to market its product and retain its customer base, but most advertising expenditures end up canceling each other out and costing the companies millions of dollars.

ECONOMICS *in the* MEDIA

Prisoner's Dilemma

WHY DO SUPERHEROES FIGHT?

If you were a superhero, would you rather fight or talk it out?

The movie *Captain America: Civil War* (2016) features a common comic trope: two groups of heroes end up fighting each other. After a superhero mishap results in the deaths of hundreds of people, the public demands that the government regulate the conduct of those with superpowers. Iron Man agrees with having the Avengers put under government control, while Captain America does not. The two heroes reach a stalemate, and they start to recruit members of the hero fraternity to their respective sides. Eventually Iron Man tries to bring Captain America in, and an epic battle ensues.

It's all very dramatic—but what is going on here? These are heroes, after all. Why would they fight each other, when there are so many villains to worry about? Many of the heroes are indeed concerned that fighting each other sends a bad message. And, of course, any battle where the fighters have superpowers is liable to result in a lot of civilian casualties. Nevertheless, the two sides lurch pell-mell into a messy (but highly watchable) confrontation.

While this seems like an outrageous outcome, fit only for the comics, there is a perfectly good economic explanation for this faceoff between two of Marvel's great protagonists: it's a prisoner's dilemma. In the payoff matrix, the dominant strategy is to fight. While we might like to see the two sides sit down and hash out their differences, each of them gets a bigger payoff for digging in their heels. The largest joint payoff (the combined benefit to both sides) occurs when both sides talk things out, but if one side decides to fight while the other side opts for peaceful talk, the "fight" side can get everything it wants, without compromising. These are the payoffs in the upper right and lower left boxes. Because the dominant strategy is to fight, the parties end up in the lower right box, even though the joint payoff is lowest there. Now it's time for civilians to head indoors and stay there, because things are about to get ugly.

		Captain America	
		Talk it out	Fight for what you believe
Iron Man	Talk it out	Captain America: 4; Iron Man: 4	Captain America: 6; Iron Man: 1
	Fight for what you believe	Captain America: 1; Iron Man: 6	Captain America: 2; Iron Man: 2

Why is there an Avengers Civil War? Or for that matter, why is it Batman versus Superman? The answer isn't that the comic characters are irrational, or are being blackmailed, or even that someone is controlling their minds. The answer is that they are in a prisoner's dilemma.

FIGURE 13.3

		Coca-Cola: Advertises	Coca-Cola: Does not advertise
PepsiCo	Advertises	$100 million profit (Coca-Cola) $100 million profit (PepsiCo)	$75 million profit (Coca-Cola) $150 million profit (PepsiCo)
	Does not advertise	$150 million profit (Coca-Cola) $75 million profit (PepsiCo)	$125 million profit (Coca-Cola) $125 million profit (PepsiCo)

The Prisoner's Dilemma and Advertising

The two companies each have a dominant strategy to advertise. We can see this strategy by observing that Coca-Cola and PepsiCo each make $25 million more profit by choosing to advertise. As a result, they both end up in the upper left box earning $100 million profit when they could have each made $125 million profit in the lower right box if they had agreed not to advertise.

Escaping the Prisoner's Dilemma in the Long Run

We have seen how game theory can be a useful tool for understanding strategic decision-making in noncooperative environments. However, the dominant strategy does not consider the possible long-run benefits of cooperation.

Game theorist Robert Axelrod decided to examine the choices participants make in a long-run setting. He ran a sophisticated computer simulation in which he invited scholars to submit strategies for securing points in a prisoner's dilemma tournament over many rounds. All the submissions were collected and paired, and the results were scored. After each simulation, Axelrod eliminated the weakest strategy and reran the tournament with the remaining strategies. This evolutionary approach continued until the best strategy remained. Among all strategies, including those that were solely cooperative or noncooperative, tit-for-tat dominated. **Tit-for-tat** is a long-run strategy that promotes cooperation among participants by mimicking the opponent's most recent decision with repayment in kind. As the name implies, a tit-for-tat strategy is one in which you do whatever your opponent does. If your opponent breaks the agreement, you break the agreement, too. If the opponent behaves properly, then you behave properly, too.

Tit-for-tat
is a long-run strategy that promotes cooperation among participants by mimicking the opponent's most recent decision with repayment in kind.

Because the joint payoffs for cooperation are high in a prisoner's dilemma, tit-for-tat begins with the players cooperating. In subsequent rounds, the tit-for-tat strategy mimics whatever the other player did in the previous round.

Incentives

SNAPSHOT

Airlines in the Prisoner's Dilemma

American Airlines and Delta Airlines once found themselves in a classic prisoner's dilemma. It all started when Delta wanted to expand its share of the lucrative Dallas-to-Chicago route, where American was the dominant carrier. Delta offered a substantial fare cut on that route to attract new travelers. American threatened a price war by offering its own fare cut on the Delta-dominated Dallas-to-Atlanta route.

Both airlines had a dominant strategy to cut their fare on the targeted route. Why? If one airline cut its fares and the other did not, the airline that did would earn a large profit ($100,000) while the other suffered a large loss (-$200,000). This was each airline's best possible outcome.

Even if the rival cut its fare too, lowering the price was still the right move—the dominant strategy—for each airline. Why? Because if an airline failed to match the fare of its rival, it would make less profit than before.

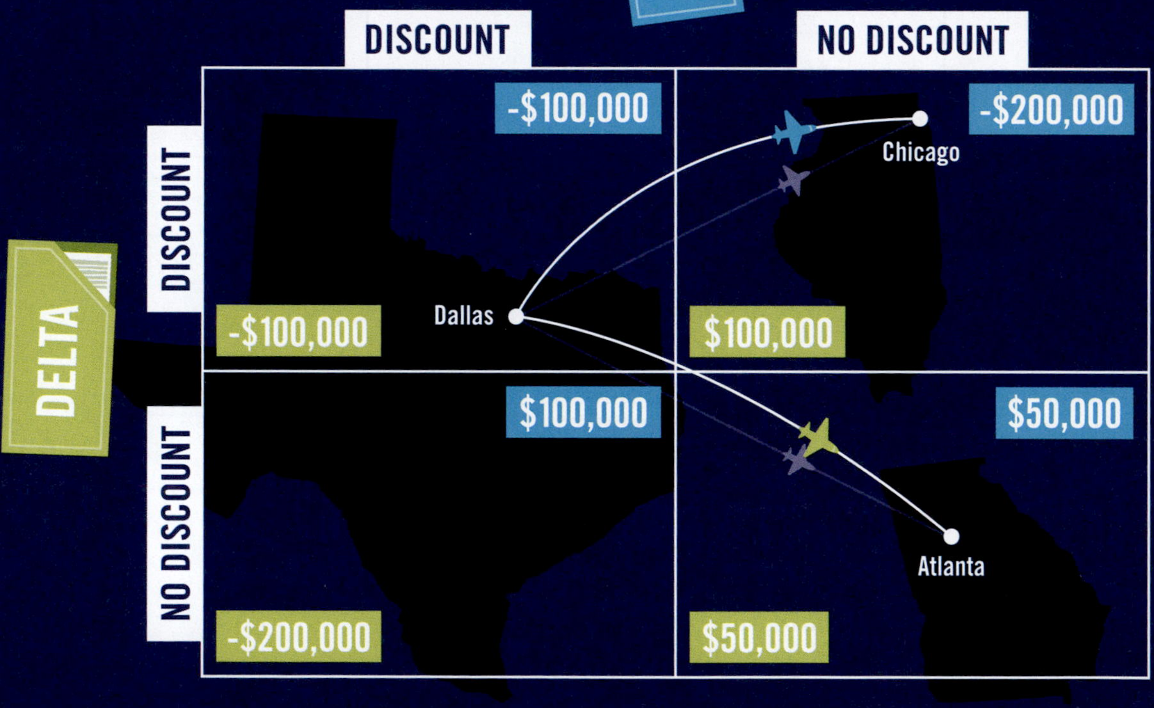

The hallmark of a prisoner's dilemma is when two rivals follow their dominant strategy and the result is not the best result for both. It would have been better if no fare discounts were ever considered.

What happened? Fortunately for both airlines, they posted their planned fare cuts on a computer system that allowed them to see what their rival was doing. They each saw the price war starting, backed down, and escaped the prisoner's dilemma!

REVIEW QUESTIONS

- Which expected outcome in the matrix reflects the outcome of this American/Delta pricing war?
- Explain how the ability to communicate can allow two parties to escape a prisoner's dilemma.

The genius behind tit-for-tat is that it changes the incentives and encourages cooperation. Turning back to our example in Figure 13.3, suppose that Coca-Cola and PepsiCo want to save on advertising expenses. The companies expect to have repeated interactions, so they both know from past experience that any effort to start a new advertising campaign will be immediately countered by the other firm. Because the companies react to each other's moves in kind, any effort to exploit the dominant strategy of advertising will ultimately fail. This dynamic can alter the incentives the firms face in the long run and lead to mutually beneficial behavior.

Tit-for-tat makes it less desirable to advertise by eliminating the long-run benefits. Advertising is still a dominant strategy in the short run because the payoffs with advertising ($100 million or $150 million) exceed those of not advertising ($75 million or $125 million). In the short run, the firm that advertises could earn $25 million extra, but in every subsequent round—if the rival responds in kind—the firm should expect profits of $100 million because its rival will also be advertising. As a result, there is a large long-run opportunity cost for not cooperating. If one firm stops advertising and the other follows suit, they will each find themselves making $125 million in the long run. Why hasn't this outcome happened in the real world? Because Coke and Pepsi don't trust each other enough to earn the dividend that comes from an advertising truce.

Opportunity cost

The prisoner's dilemma nicely captures why cooperation is so difficult in the short run. But most interactions in life occur over the long run. For example, scam artists and sketchy companies take advantage of short-run opportunities that cannot last because relationships in the long run—with businesses and with people—involve mutual trust. Cooperation is the default because you know that the other side is invested in the relationship. Under these circumstances, the tit-for-tat strategy works well.

ECONOMICS in the MEDIA

The Long-Run Benefits of Cooperation

THE EVOLUTION OF TRUST

Designer Nicky Case (a member of Forbes' "30 under 30" list for Games development) created an interactive simulation (https://ncase.me/trust/) based on Robert Axelrod's groundbreaking 1984 book, *The Evolution of Cooperation.* When you play the simulation, you encounter a variety of strategies that you might deploy in the repeated prisoner's dilemma.

In the repeated version of the game, it's important that neither player knows when the last round is. Why? If the players knew, then in the last round they would both definitely cheat, since there'd be no later rounds to worry about. But then by backward induction, each player should cheat in the second-last round, as well, since there will be no effect on the other player's choice in the last round. This logic continues until both players simply decide to cheat in the first round. That's a pretty depressing outcome, but it's not what Axelrod found in the long run with an unknown stopping point. Instead, he found that tit-for-tat did better than all other approaches. To observe Axelrod's result, Case has you play against five different strategies to show which are the most effective at creating cooperative outcomes. The entire simulation takes about thirty minutes to play—give it a try!

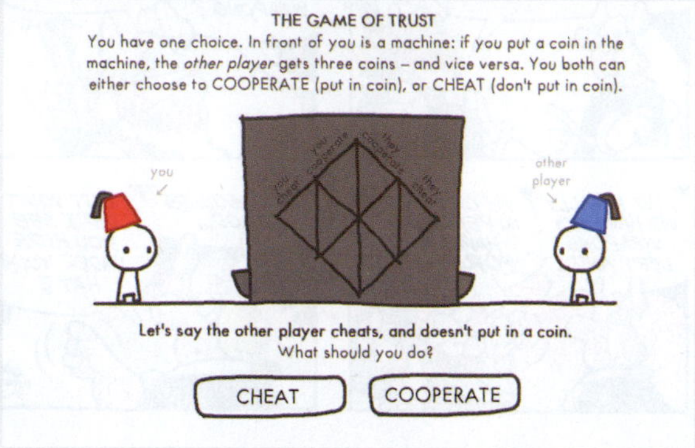

Should your strategy be "copycat," "all cheat," "all cooperate," "grudger," or "detective"? Find out by trying the simulation!

Sequential Games

Backward induction in game theory is the process of deducing backward from the end of a scenario to infer a sequence of optimal actions.

Not all games involve simultaneous decisions. Sometimes one player must move first and then the other player responds to the first move. In this case it is possible for the first player to utilize **backward induction** to get the best possible result. Backward induction in game theory is the process of deducing backward from the end of a scenario to infer a sequence of optimal actions.

To help visualize this situation, look at Figure 13.4. The payoff matrix summarizes the payoffs that Iggy and Azalea face in a noncooperative game. Neither Iggy nor Azalea has a dominant strategy, so it is impossible to predict what the final outcome will be.

A **decision tree** illustrates all of the possible outcomes in a sequential game.

However, if we let one player go first, the game has a predictable conclusion. To see this process at work, look at Figure 13.5. This type of diagram is known as a **decision tree**; it illustrates all of the possible outcomes in a sequential game. Let's imagine that Azalea goes first and Iggy chooses second.

In a sequential game, the first player can restrict the set of outcomes to one of the branches at the top of the decision tree. When Azalea chooses Agree, Iggy works off the lower left set of branches and must choose between making $20,000 if she agrees or $75,000 if she disagrees. Of course, Iggy chooses to

		Iggy	
		Agree	Disagree
Azalea	Agree	$20,000 $60,000	$75,000 $50,000
	Disagree	$50,000 $35,000	$25,000 $75,000

FIGURE 13.4

To Cooperate or Not

Iggy and Azalea do not have dominant strategies, so the outcome of this game cannot be determined.

disagree. In this case, the final outcome is $50,000 for Azalea and $75,000 for Iggy. If Azalea instead chose Disagree to start, Iggy would be faced with the payoffs on the lower right side of the decision tree. Here, Iggy would get $50,000 if she agrees and $25,000 if she disagrees, so this time she agrees. Now the final outcome is $35,000 for Azalea and $50,000 for Iggy.

Because Azalea has full information about all of the payoffs in the matrix, she knows what Iggy will choose at the end of each set of branches. This

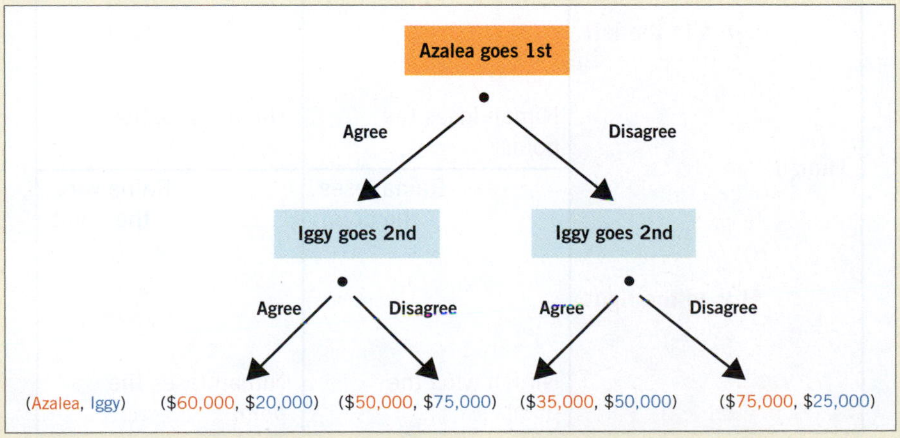

FIGURE 13.5

Decision Tree for a Sequential Game

Azalea will agree, knowing that Iggy will disagree. This game guarantees Azalea $50,000 and Iggy $75,000.

knowledge allows her to use backward induction to earn $50,000 for herself by selecting Agree with the full knowledge that Iggy will choose Disagree.

There are many examples of sequential games in life. Chess and checkers are two popular board games that utilize backward induction. Likewise, many business decisions are also sequential in nature, and once a particular path is taken, it becomes easier to predict how future decisions will unfold. For instance, when a firm decides to launch a new advertising campaign, it is easier for the firm to predict how a rival will react by examining the remaining choices along a decision tree.

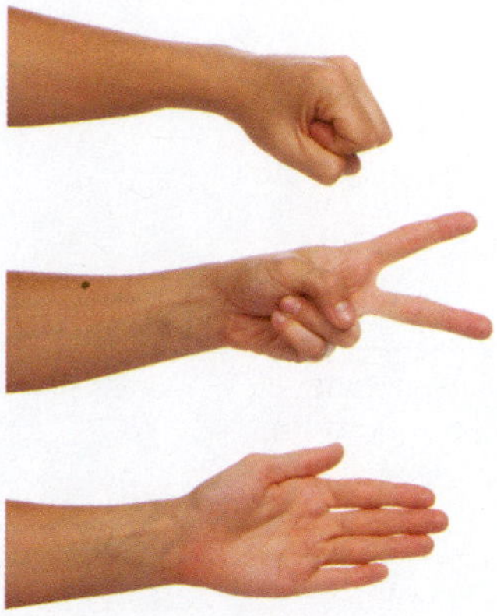

Rock-paper-scissors is a game without a dominant strategy.

A Caution about Game Theory

Game theory is a decision-making tool, but not all games have dominant strategies that make player decisions easy to predict. Perhaps the best example is the game known as rock-paper-scissors. This simple game has no dominant strategy: paper beats rock (because the paper will cover the rock) and rock beats scissors (because the rock will break the scissors), but scissors beats paper (because the scissors will cut the paper). The preferred choice is strictly a function of what the other player selects. Many situations in life and business are more like rock-paper-scissors than the prisoner's dilemma. Winning at business in the long run often occurs because you are one step ahead of the competition, not because you deploy a strategy that attempts to take advantage of a short-run opportunity.

Consider two sisters who enjoy playing racquetball together. They are of equal ability, so each point comes down to whether a player guesses correctly about where the other player will hit the ball. Take a look at Figure 13.6. The

FIGURE 13.6

No Dominant Strategy Exists

Neither Raina nor Nimah has a dominant strategy that guarantees winning the point. The four outcomes are equally likely on successive points, and there is no way to predict how the next point will be played. As a result, there is no Nash equilibrium here.

		Raina	
		Guesses to the left	Guesses to the right
Nimah	Hits to the left	Raina wins the point Nimah loses the point	Raina loses the point Nimah wins the point
	Hits to the right	Raina loses the point Nimah wins the point	Raina wins the point Nimah loses the point

ECONOMICS in the MEDIA

Sequential Games

WHY DID RACHEL LET ELEANOR WIN A GAME OF MAHJONG?

In *Crazy Rich Asians* (2018), the lead character, Rachel, is an economics professor who teaches game theory at NYU, where her boyfriend, Nick, teaches history. After they've dated seriously for a year, Nick invites Rachel to Singapore to meet his crazy-rich family. Things do not go well. Nick's mother, Eleanor, wants to protect Nick from ending up with someone who, Eleanor thinks, is not right for Nick. The upshot is that Rachel and Eleanor end up in a prisoner's dilemma, making suboptimal decisions.

Simplifying the action of the movie a bit, let's consider the situation Eleanor and Rachel face. Rachel wants to keep Nick for herself because she earns either 2 or 5 "happiness points" playing that strategy, whereas giving Nick up brings her only 1 or 4 points. Eleanor's reasons for wanting to keep Nick for herself are exactly the same. As a result, there is a Nash equilibrium at (2, 2) in the upper left box.

The plot takes a remarkable turn when Rachel recognizes that she and Eleanor are stuck, and that if they remain at odds, neither of them will ever win. Ever the economist, Rachel decides to break the prisoner's dilemma by initiating a sequential game where she moves first, deliberately leaving herself vulnerable if Eleanor continues to play the dominant strategy.

An inspired scene where the two play mahjong sets the stage. As the game unfolds, Rachel lets Eleanor know that Nick has proposed to her earlier but Rachel did not accept. She goes on to explain that she knows Nick would never really be happy if he had to leave his family to be with her. Rachel then lays down a tile that Eleanor picks up in order to win the mahjong game. After Rachel finishes explaining her decision, she stands up and reveals all her tiles. The tile she gave Eleanor would have won Rachel the game. Rachel has communicated to Eleanor that she could have accepted Nick's proposal, but she respects Eleanor in her role as family matriarch enough to sacrifice for Nick's good. Rachel's strategic gesture, proving that she was willing to bend for the sake of family, breaks the cycle of mistrust and prompts Eleanor to bless the marriage.

We see the result of Rachel's actions in the following decision tree and payoff matrix.

By saying no to Nick's proposal, Rachel has made Eleanor's choice simpler: she will gain either 5 or 4.

		Eleanor: Reject Rachel	Eleanor: Accept Rachel
Rachel	Accept proposal	Eleanor 2, Rachel 2	Eleanor 1, Rachel 5
	Reject proposal	Eleanor 5, Rachel 1	Eleanor 4, Rachel 4

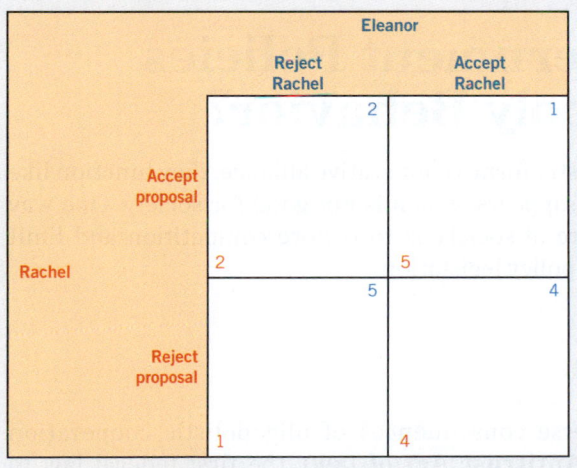

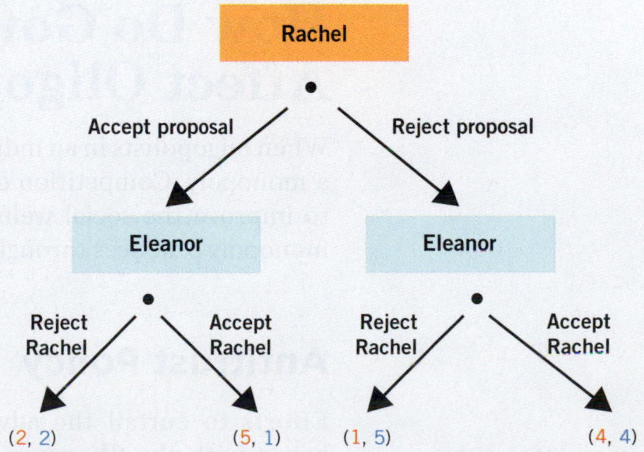

(CONTINUED)

She can still choose the 5 outcome, but Rachel has given her a very powerful reason to accept the (4, 4) outcome. Rachel makes one last statement before leaving: "So, I just wanted you to know that one day, when he marries another lucky girl who is enough for you . . . that it was because of me . . . a poor, raised-by-a-single-mother, low-class, immigrant nobody." Soon after, Eleanor understands that Rachel guaranteed her at least a 4, when Rachel could have chosen to say yes, and Eleanor would have earned no more than 2. This prompts Eleanor to reject the short-run dominant strategy and choose Rachel as her daughter-in-law. From that point forward, they are entering a long-run cooperative equilibrium, and (4, 4) maximizes their joint welfare by maximizing the sum of all payouts!

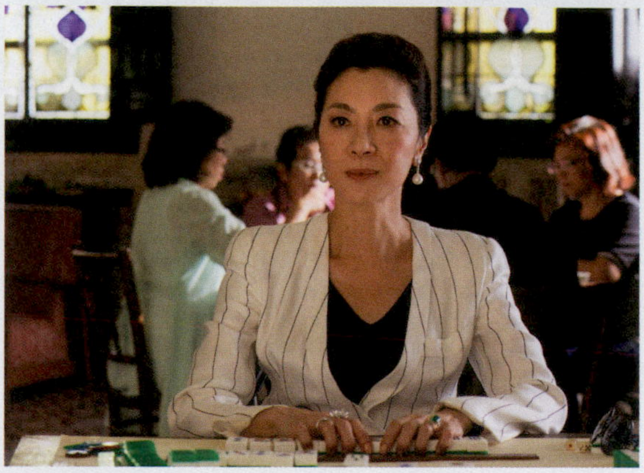
Good luck beating a game theorist at mahjong!

success of Nimah and Raina depends on how well each one guesses where the other one will hit the ball.

In this competition, neither Raina nor Nimah has a dominant strategy that guarantees success. Sometimes Nimah wins when hitting to the right; at other times she loses the point. Sometimes Raina wins when she guesses to the left; at other times she loses. Each player guesses correctly only half the time. Because we cannot say what each player will do from one point to another, there is no Nash equilibrium. Any of the four outcomes are equally likely on successive points, and there is no way to predict how the next point will be played. In other words, we cannot expect every game to include a prisoner's dilemma and produce a Nash equilibrium. Game theory, like real life, has many different possible outcomes.

How Do Government Policies Affect Oligopoly Behavior?

When oligopolists in an industry form a cooperative alliance, they function like a monopoly. Competition disappears, which is not good for society. One way to improve the social welfare of society is to restore competition and limit monopoly practices through policy legislation.

Antitrust Policy

The **Sherman Antitrust Act** (1890) was the first federal law limiting cartels and monopolies.

Efforts to curtail the adverse consequences of oligopolistic cooperation began with the **Sherman Antitrust Act** of 1890, the first federal law to place limits on cartels and monopolies. The Sherman Act was created in response to the increase in concentration ratios in many leading U.S. industries, including steel, railroads, mining, textiles, and oil. Prior to passage of the Sherman Act, firms were free to pursue contracts that created mutually beneficial outcomes. Once the act took effect, however, certain cooperative actions became criminal. Section 2 of the Sherman Act reads, "Every person who shall monopolize, or attempt to monopolize, or combine or conspire with any other person or persons, to monopolize any part of the trade or commerce among the several States, or with foreign nations, shall be deemed guilty of a felony."

The **Clayton Act** of 1914 targets corporate behaviors that reduce competition. Large corporations had been vilified during the presidential election of 1912, and the Sherman Act was seen as largely ineffective in curbing monopoly power. To strengthen antitrust policy, the Clayton Act added to the list of activities deemed socially detrimental, including:

The **Clayton Act** (1914) targets corporate behaviors that reduce competition.

1. *price discrimination* if it lessens competition or creates monopoly
2. *exclusive dealings* that restrict a buyer's ability to deal with competitors
3. *tying arrangements* that require the buyer to purchase an additional product in order to purchase the first
4. *mergers and acquisitions* that lessen competition, or situations in which a person serves as a director on more than one board in the same industry

As the Clayton Act makes clear, there are many ways to reduce competition.

PRACTICE WHAT YOU KNOW

Dominant Strategy: Dine-In or Take-Out?

Should a barbeque joint in a small rural town offer dine-in service, or just take-out?

QUESTION: Bad to the Bone and Meats and More are the only two barbeque joints in a small town. Post-pandemic, they face the same choice as most other restaurants: offer dine-in meals, or stick to take-out service. If neither place offers dine-in, variable costs are low and each firm earns $2,000 a month. If both places offer dine-in service, variable costs shoot up, causing each firm to lose $1,000 a month. Finally, if just one establishment opens up for dine-in, that one earns a profit of $5,000, while the other, take-out-only one loses $5,000. What is the dominant strategy for Bad to the Bone? Is there a Nash equilibrium?

ANSWER: With take-out only, Bad to the Bone will either lose $5,000 or make $2,000, depending on what Meats and More does. With dine-in service, Bad to the Bone will either lose $1,000 or make $5,000, again depending on its rival's actions. Suppose that Meats and More decides to offer dine-in. In that case, Bad to the Bone's best response is to offer dine-in, as well, because -$1,000 > -$5,000. Now imagine that Meats and More goes with take-out only. Dine-in remains Bad to the Bone's best response, because $5,000 > $2,000. So regardless of what Meats and More does, Bad to the Bone's best response—and therefore its dominant strategy—is to offer dine-in service.

(CONTINUED)

Meats and More has the same dominant strategy and the same payoffs. Therefore, each company will offer dine-in service and lose $1,000. Neither firm has a reason to switch to the take-out-only strategy, because that would involve immediately starting to lose $5,000. The Nash equilibrium is for both places to offer dine-in service.

		Bad to the Bone	
		Offers dine-in	Sticks to take-out
Meats and More	Offers dine-in	Loses $1,000 Loses $1,000	Loses $5,000 Makes $5,000
	Sticks to take-out	Makes $5,000 Loses $5,000	Makes $2,000 Makes $2,000

Over the past hundred years, lawmakers have continued to refine antitrust policy. Additional legislation along with court interpretations of existing antitrust law have made it difficult to determine whether a company has violated the law. The U.S. Justice Department is charged with oversight, but it often lacks the resources to fully investigate every case. Antitrust law is complex, and cases are hard to prosecute, but these laws are essential to maintaining a competitive business environment. Without effective restraints on excessive market power, firms would organize into cartels more often or would find other ways to restrict competition. Table 13.5 briefly describes some of the most influential antitrust cases in history.

Predatory Pricing

Predatory pricing occurs when firms deliberately set their prices below average variable costs with the intent of driving rivals out of the market.

While firms have a strong incentive to cooperate in order to keep prices high, they also want to keep potential rivals out of the market. **Predatory pricing** is the practice of setting prices deliberately below average variable costs with the intent of driving rivals out of the market. The firm suffers a short-run loss in order to prevent rivals from entering the market or to drive rival firms out of business in the long run. Once the rivals are gone, the firm should be able to act like a monopolist.

TABLE 13.5

Influential Antitrust Cases in History

Defendant	Year	Description
Standard Oil	1911	Standard Oil was founded in 1870. By 1897, the company had driven the price of oil down to 6 cents a gallon, which put many of its competitors out of business. Subsequently, Standard Oil became the largest company in the world. In 1906, the U.S. government filed suit against Standard Oil for violating the Sherman Antitrust Act. Three years later, the company was found guilty and forced to break up into 34 independent companies.
AT&T	1982	In 1974, the U.S. Attorney General filed suit against AT&T for violating antitrust laws. It took seven years before a settlement was reached to split the company into seven new companies, each serving a different region of the United States. However, five of the seven have since merged to become AT&T Incorporated, which is now one of the largest companies in the world.
Microsoft	2001	When Internet Explorer was introduced in 1995, Microsoft insisted that it was a feature rather than a new Windows product. The U.S. Department of Justice did not agree and filed suit against Microsoft for illegally discouraging competition to protect its software monopoly. The government argued that Microsoft leveraged its power from the operating systems market into the browser market by strong-arming personal computer manufacturers like Dell into favoring Internet Explorer over Netscape. After court decisions and appeals, a settlement ordered Microsoft to share application programming interfaces with third-party companies. Today, Internet Explorer has largely been replaced by Chrome and Firefox.
Google	2015	The European Union began investigating whether Google used its dominant market share as a search engine to gain an unfair advantage over competitors. After a lengthy investigation, the EU fined Google $2.8 billion in 2017 for diverting traffic away from search results that favored its rivals and toward results that favored Google's own products. As of 2019, Google remains the search engine of choice in 92% of all searches in Europe, and competitors continue to press for additional sanctions.
The NCAA	2021	By long-standing NCAA policy, college athletes were "amateurs," eligible for scholarships but not entitled to any other form of compensation, even while schools raked in money not just through ticket sales but through things like the sale of jerseys with former players' names on them. The Supreme Court ruled unanimously that the NCAA's policy was a violation of antitrust law. Now, student athletes can be given paid internships, computers, and other education-related benefits and can also use their name, image, or likeness for compensation from third parties like businesses. Even so, they cannot earn salaries for their work as athletes.

Because Walmart keeps its prices low, there is no evidence that it engages in predatory pricing.

Predatory pricing is illegal, but it is difficult to prosecute. Neither the court system nor economists have a simple rule that helps to determine when a firm steps over the line. Predatory pricing can look and feel like spirited competition. Moreover, the concern is not the competitive aspect or lower prices, but the effect on the market when all rivals fail. To prove that predatory pricing has occurred, the courts need evidence that the firm's prices increased significantly after its rivals failed.

Walmart is often cited as a firm that engages in predatory pricing because its low prices effectively drive many smaller companies out of business. However, there is no evidence that Walmart has ever systematically raised prices after a rival failed. Therefore, its price strategy does not meet the legal standard for predatory pricing. Similarly, Microsoft came under intense scrutiny in the 1990s for giving away its browser, Internet Explorer, in order to undercut Netscape, which also ended up giving away its browser. Microsoft understood that the key to its long-term success was the dominance of the Windows platform. Bundling Internet Explorer with Microsoft Office enabled the company not only to gain over 80% of the browser market but also to keep its leadership with the Windows operating system. Eventually, Microsoft was prosecuted by the government—but not for predatory pricing, which could not be proved because Microsoft never significantly raised the price of Internet Explorer. Instead, the government prosecuted Microsoft for tying the purchase of Internet Explorer to the Windows operating system in order to restrict competition. The Microsoft case lasted over four years, and it ended in a settlement that placed restrictions on the firm's business practices.

PRACTICE WHAT YOU KNOW

Predatory Pricing: Price Wars

Predatory pricing? Check out the competing signs in the photo!

You've undoubtedly encountered a price war at some point. It could be two gas stations, clothing outlets, or restaurants charging prices that seem unbelievably low.

QUESTION: Is a price war between two adjacent pizza restaurants evidence of predatory pricing?

ANSWER: One essential element for proving predatory pricing is evidence of the intent to raise prices after others are driven out of business. That is a problem in this example. Suppose one of the pizza places closes. The remaining firm could then raise its price substantially. But barriers to entry in the restaurant industry are low in most metropolitan areas, so any efforts to maintain high prices for long will fail. Customers will vote with their feet and wallets by choosing another pizza place a little farther away that offers a better value. Or a new competitor will sense that the victor is vulnerable because of the high prices and will open a new pizza parlor nearby. Either way, the market is monopolistically competitive, so any market power created by driving out one rival will be fleeting.

The aggressive price war is not evidence of predatory pricing. Instead, it is probably just promotional pricing to protect market share. Firms often price some items below their variable costs to attract customers. These firms hope to make up the difference and then some with high profit margins on other items, such as beverages and side dishes.

What Are Network Externalities?

We end this chapter by considering a special kind of externality that often occurs in oligopoly. A **network externality** occurs when the number of customers who purchase or use a good influences the demand. When a network externality exists, firms with many customers often find it easier to attract new customers and to keep their regular customers from switching to other rivals. In the early days of social networking, for example, MySpace had many more users than Facebook. How did Facebook gain over 2.2 billion users when it had to play catch-up? Facebook built a better social network, and MySpace was slow to respond to the threat. By the time MySpace did respond, it was too late: Facebook was on its way. Now the tables are turned, as Facebook is the dominant social networking platform with over 2.5 billion active users. Moreover, among most demographics, the sheer size of Facebook makes it a better place to do social networking than Google+, Twitter, WhatsApp, WeChat, Instagram, or LinkedIn. However, even though Facebook now enjoys significant network externalities, it must be mindful to keep innovating or else it might end up forgotten like MySpace.

A **network externality** occurs when the number of customers who purchase or use a product influences the quantity demanded.

Most network externalities involve the introduction of new technologies. For instance, some technologies need to reach a critical mass before consumers can effectively use them. Consider that today everyone seems to have a cell phone. However, when cell phones were introduced in the United States in 1983, coverage was quite limited. The first users could not surf the

Internet, roam, text, or use many of the applications we enjoy today. Moreover, the phones were large and bulky. How did we get from that situation in 1983 to today? As additional people bought cell phones, networks expanded and manufacturers and telephone companies responded by building more cell towers and offering better phones. The expansion of networks brought more users, and the new adopters benefited from the steadily expanding customer base.

Other technologies have gone through similar transformations. The Internet, fax machines, and apps all depend on the number of users. If you were the only person on the Internet or the only person with the ability to send and receive a fax, your technical capacity would have little value. In a world with ever-changing technology, first adopters pave the way for the next generation of users.

Switching costs are the costs incurred when a consumer changes from one supplier to another.

In addition to the advantages of forming a larger network, customers may face significant switching costs if they leave. **Switching costs** are the costs incurred when a consumer changes from one supplier to another. For instance, the transition from listening to music on CDs to using digital music files involved a substantial switching cost for many users. Today, there are switching costs among the many digital music options, as streaming companies like Spotify and AppleMusic try to lock you in with subscriptions that do not end until you cancel them. When consumers face switching costs, the demand for the existing product becomes more inelastic. As a result, oligopolists not only leverage the number of customers they maintain in their network, but also try to make

PRACTICE WHAT YOU KNOW

Does Netflix benefit from network externalities?

Examples of Network Externalities

QUESTION: In which two of these examples are network externalities important?

a. college alumni

b. Netflix

c. a local bakery that sells fresh bread

ANSWERS:

a. Colleges and universities with more alumni are able to raise funds more easily than smaller schools, so the size of the alumni network matters. The number of alumni also matters when graduates look for jobs, because alumni are often inclined to hire individuals who went to the same school. For example, Penn State University has the nation's largest alumni base. This means that each PSU graduate benefits from network externalities.

b. Netflix's size enables it to offer a vast array of on-demand movies and TV shows. If it were smaller, Netflix would be unable to make as many obscure titles available. This means that Netflix customers benefit from network externalities by having more titles to choose from.

c. The local bakery is a small company. If it attracts more customers, each one will have to compete harder to get fresh bread. Because the bakery's supply of bread is limited, additional customers create congestion, and network externalities do not exist.

ECONOMICS *for* LIFE

How Oligopolies Shape Our Lives as Consumers

- The rate at which new businesses are created has been steadily falling since the 1970s.
- Vertical integration allows a firm to exert enormous control over the prices consumers pay.
- Heavily consolidated industries can lose the incentive to innovate.

Oligopolies are big business, and they shape our lives in many ways. HBO's John Oliver has a really informative and funny take on corporate consolidation on his show *Last Week Tonight* (available to stream on YouTube). Oliver points out many of the features of oligopoly that are potentially problematic for consumers, but he also gives some screen time to Jim Cramer, a well-known pro-business personality. Watching this video will make you think about how consolidation plays a key role in a wide range of industries—everything from air travel to eyewear to beer.

Here are some ways corporate consolidation is shaping our lives:

- The rate at which new businesses are created has been steadily falling since the 1970s, and one reason for that is that big businesses are becoming more consolidated.
- Some brands you might think are indie, like Burt's Bees, Tom's of Maine, and Goose Island Beer, are actually run by large corporations.
- Airline industry consolidation has allowed firms to raise $4.2 billion in ancillary fees for additional baggage, seat assignments, and priority check-in.
- In the eyewear industry, most of the name-brand frames (e.g., Prada, Dolce & Gabbana, Burberry, and Ralph Lauren) are manufactured by the same firm, Luxottica, which also owns most of the eyewear retailers (Pearle, Lens Crafters, Sunglass Hut, and Target Optical). This level of vertical integration allows Luxottica to exert enormous control over the prices consumers pay.
- Heavily consolidated industries can lose the incentive to innovate.

Who do you trust to tell you the truth? Jim Cramer or John Oliver?

Users of the first-generation cell phone, the Motorola DynaTAC 8000X, created a positive network externality for future users.

switching to another network more difficult. For instance, firms promote customer loyalty through frequent flier benefits, hotel reward points, and credit card reward programs to create higher switching costs.

An excellent example of the costs of switching are the costs associated with cell phone services. Contract termination fees apply to many cell phone agreements if the contract is broken. This tactic creates high switching costs for many cell phone customers. To reduce switching costs, the Federal Communications Commission in 2003 began requiring that phone companies allow customers to take their cell phone numbers with them when they change to a different provider. This change in the law has reduced the costs of switching from one provider to another and has made the cell phone market more competitive.

Oligopolists are keenly aware of the power of network externalities. As new markets develop, the first firm into an industry often gains a large customer base. When there are positive network externalities, the customer base enables the firm to grow quickly. In addition, consumers are often more comfortable purchasing from an established firm. These two factors favor the formation of large firms and make it difficult for smaller competitors to gain customers. As a result, the presence of significant positive network externalities causes small firms to be driven out of business or forces them to merge with larger competitors.

Conclusion

Incentives

Firms in oligopoly markets can compete or collude to create monopoly conditions. The result is often hard to predict. In many cases, the presence of a dominant short-run strategy causes firms to compete on price and advertising even though doing so yields a lower economic profit. In contrast, the potential success of a tit-for-tat strategy suggests that oligopolistic firms are capable of cooperating to jointly maximize their long-run profits. Whether oligopoly mirrors the result found in monopolistic competition or monopoly matters a great deal because society's welfare is higher when more competition is present. Because oligopoly is not a market structure with a predictable outcome, each oligopolistic industry must be assessed on a case-by-case basis by examining data and utilizing game theory. For these reasons, the study of oligopoly is one of the most fascinating parts of the theory of the firm.

· ANSWERING *the* BIG QUESTIONS ·

What is oligopoly?

- Oligopoly is a type of market structure that exists when a small number of firms sell a differentiated product in a market with significant barriers to entry. An oligopolist is like a monopolistic competitor in that it sells differentiated products. It is like a monopolist in that it enjoys significant barriers to entry. The small number of sellers in oligopoly leads to mutual interdependence.
- Oligopolists have a tendency to collude and to form cartels in the hope of achieving monopoly-like profits.
- Oligopolistic markets are socially inefficient because price and marginal cost are not equal. The result under oligopoly falls somewhere between the competitive market and monopoly outcomes.

How does game theory explain strategic behavior?

- Game theory helps to determine when cooperation among oligopolists is most likely to occur. In many cases, cooperation fails to occur because decision-makers have dominant strategies that lead them to be uncooperative. As a result, firms compete with price or advertising when they could potentially earn more profit by curtailing these activities.
- Games become more complicated when they are played multiple times, so short-run dominant strategies often disappear. Whenever repeated interaction occurs, decision-makers fare better under tit-for-tat, an approach that maximizes the long-run profit.

How do government policies affect oligopoly behavior?

- Antitrust law is complex, and cases are hard to prosecute. Nevertheless, these laws are essential in providing oligopolistic firms an incentive to compete rather than collude.
- Antitrust policy limits price discrimination, exclusive dealings, tying arrangements, mergers and acquisitions that limit competition, and predatory pricing.

What are network externalities?

- A network externality occurs when the number of customers who purchase or use a good influences the quantity demanded. The presence of significant positive network externalities can cause small firms to go out of business.

CHAPTER PROBLEMS

Concepts You Should Know

Questions for Review

1. Compare the price and output under oligopoly with that of monopoly and monopolistic competition.

2. How does the addition of another firm affect the ability of the firms in an oligopolistic industry to form an effective cartel?

3. What is predatory pricing?

4. How is game theory relevant to oligopoly? Does it help to explain monopoly? Give reasons for your response.

5. What does the prisoner's dilemma indicate about the longevity of collusive agreements?

6. What is a Nash equilibrium? How does it differ from a dominant strategy?

7. What practices do antitrust laws prohibit?

8. What are network externalities? Explain why network externalities matter to an oligopolist.

Study Problems (*✱ solved at the end of this section*)

1. Some places limit the number of hours that alcohol can be sold on Sunday. Is it possible that this sales restriction could help liquor stores? Use game theory to construct your answer. (**Hint:** Even without restrictions on the hours of operation, individual stores could still limit Sunday sales if they wanted to.)

2. Which of the following markets are oligopolistic?

a. passenger airlines
b. cereal
c. fast food
d. wheat
e. high-end skateboards
f. the college bookstore on your campus

✱ **3.** Imagine that your roommate's alarm goes off at 4:30 every morning, and she hits snooze every 10 minutes until 6:00, when you both need to get up. She insists that this maddening procedure is the only way she is able to wake up. How would you respond? Is there a nonviolent way you can convince her to change her morning wake-up routine? (**Hint:** Think about a tit-for-tat strategy.)

4. After teaching a class on game theory, your instructor announces that if every student skips the last question on the next exam, everyone will receive full credit for that question. However, if one or more students answer the last question, all responses will be graded and those who skip the question will get a zero on that question. Will the entire class skip the last question? Explain your response.

5. For which of the following are network externalities important?

a. gas stations
b. American Association of Retired Persons (AARP)
c. eHarmony, an Internet dating site

6. Your economics instructor is at it again (see question 4). This time, you have to do a two-student project. Assume that you and your partner are both interested in maximizing your grade, but you are both very busy and would be happier if you could get a good grade with less work.

		Your partner: Work hard	Your partner: Work less hard
You	Work hard	Grade = A, but your partner had to work 10 hours. Happiness = 7/10. Grade = A, but you had to work 10 hours. Happiness = 7/10.	Grade = A, and your partner only worked 5 hours. Happiness = 9/10. Grade = A, but you had to work 15 hours. Happiness = 4/10.
	Work less hard	Grade = A, but your partner had to work 15 hours. Happiness = 4/10. Grade = A, and you only worked 5 hours. Happiness = 9/10.	Grade = B, but your partner only worked 5 hours. Happiness = 6/10. Grade = B, but you only worked 5 hours. Happiness = 6/10.

a. What is your dominant strategy? Explain.
b. What is your partner's dominant strategy? Explain.
c. What is the Nash equilibrium in this situation? Explain.
d. If you and your partner are required to work together on a number of projects throughout the semester, how might this requirement change the outcome you predicted in parts (a), (b), and (c)?

7. Suppose that the marginal cost of mining gold is constant at $300 per ounce and the demand schedule is as follows:

Price (per oz.)	Quantity (oz.)
$1,000	1,000
900	2,000
800	3,000
700	4,000
600	5,000
500	6,000
400	7,000
300	8,000

a. If the number of suppliers is large, what would be the price and quantity?
b. If there is only one supplier, what would be the price and quantity?
c. If there are only two suppliers and they form a cartel, what would be the price and quantity?
d. Suppose that one of the two cartel members in part (c) decides to increase its production by 1,000 ounces while the other member keeps its production constant. What will happen to the revenues of both firms?

* **8.** Trade agreements encourage countries to curtail tariffs (taxes on imports) so that goods may flow across international boundaries without restrictions. Using the following payoff matrix, determine the best policies for China and the United States.

		China: Low tariffs	China: High tariffs
United States	Low tariffs	China gains $50 billion U.S. gains $50 billion	China gains $100 billion U.S. gains $10 billion
	High tariffs	China gains $10 billion U.S. gains $100 billion	China gains $25 billion U.S. gains $25 billion

a. What is the dominant strategy for the United States?
b. What is the dominant strategy for China?
c. What is the Nash equilibrium for these two countries?
d. Suppose that the United States and China enter into a trade agreement that simultaneously lowers trade barriers in both countries. Is this agreement a good idea? Explain your response.

9. A small town has only one pizza place, The Pizza Factory. A small competitor, Perfect Pies, is thinking about entering the market. The profits of these two firms depend on whether Perfect Pies enters the market and whether The Pizza Factory—as a price leader—decides to set a high price or a low price. Use the payoff matrix below to answer the questions that follow.

		Perfect Pies	
		Enter	**Stay out**
The Pizza Factory	**High price**	Perfect Pies makes $10,000 The Pizza Factory makes $20,000	Perfect Pies makes $0 The Pizza Factory makes $50,000
	Low price	Perfect Pies loses $10,000 The Pizza Factory makes $10,000	Perfect Pies makes $0 The Pizza Factory makes $25,000

a. What is the dominant strategy of The Pizza Factory?
b. Does Perfect Pies have a dominant strategy?
c. What is the Nash equilibrium in this situation?
d. The combined profit for both firms is highest when The Pizza Factory sets a high price and Perfect Pies stays out of the market. If Perfect Pies enters the market, how will this entry affect the profits of The Pizza Factory? Would The Pizza Factory be willing to pay Perfect Pies not to enter the market? Explain.

10. Two brands of coffee makers, Keurig and Tassimo, are vying for the convenience market. Keurig is the market-share leader and has the largest variety of cups used to make coffees and teas. Tassimo makes a smaller machine that brews faster, but it lacks the variety of coffees and teas sold by Keurig. To complicate matters, Keurig and Tassimo users cannot easily switch from one manufacturer to the other, because the cups that each manufacturer uses are a different size. Which manufacturer is likely to dominate the market in the long run?

✷ **11.** The TV show *The Big Bang Theory* popularized an interesting way of resolving disputes that goes beyond the familiar rock-paper-scissors game. Watch the video at this link: https://rpsls.net/#hnp7x. Is there a dominant strategy in rock-paper-scissors-lizard-Spock?

12. Most large banks charge the same or nearly the same interest rate. When market conditions require an adjustment, one of the major banks announces a change in its rate and other banks quickly follow suit. What model of oligopoly behavior explains why this happens?

✷ **13.** Suppose that Muber is currently the only firm providing rideshares, but a second firm, Wyft, is considering entering the market. Prior to learning what Wyft will do, Muber must decide whether to make a costly investment to improve its own product. The decision tree for this game is diagrammed below, with the payoffs assumed to be the ones shown.

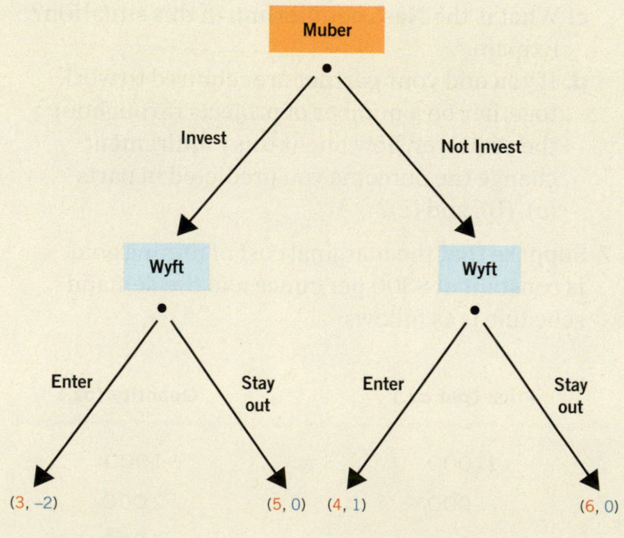

What is the equilibrium outcome of this game?

✷ **14.** The owner of a small restaurant has one person who is responsible for keeping things clean throughout the day. Should the owner be more concerned that the restrooms are always clean, or the kitchen? Is there a dominant strategy?

Solved Problems

3. If your roommate does not wake up immediately, a tit-for-tat response would be for you to get up. Once up, you should turn on the lights, get dressed, and make enough noise that your roommate cannot easily sleep. If you use this approach, it won't take long for your roommate to realize that she should set the alarm for a more reasonable time and *not* hit the snooze button. When your roommate no longer relies on the snooze button to wake up, you can return to your normal sleeping pattern and stay in bed for as long as you wish.

8. a. The dominant strategy for the United States is to impose high tariffs, because it always earns more from that strategy than if it imposes low tariffs, no matter what policy China pursues.

b. The dominant strategy for China is to impose high tariffs, because it always earns more from that strategy than if it imposes low tariffs, no matter what policy the United States pursues.

c. The Nash equilibrium for both countries is to levy high tariffs. Each country will earn $25 billion.

d. China and the United States would each benefit from cooperatively lowering trade barriers. In that case, each country would earn $50 billion.

11. There is not a dominant strategy in this variation of rock-paper-scissors, but the guys can't bring themselves to answer with paper, even though it disproves Spock, because they respect him so much.

13. Muber will invest, and Wyft will stay out. How do we know this? Muber will use backward induction to solve this sequential problem. If Muber decides to invest, it restricts Wyft's outcomes to either −2 (if it enters) or 0 (if it stays out). Wyft prefers 0 to −2, so it stays out. Now consider what happens if Muber does not invest. In this case, Wyft makes 1 (if it enters) or 0 (if it stays out). Wyft prefers 1 to 0, so it enters. Since Muber knows what Wyft will choose in both cases, Muber must examine how well it does based on Wyft's choices. When Muber invests, Wyft stays out and Muber earns 5. If Muber decides to not invest, Wyft enters and Muber earns 4. Muber prefers 5 to 4, so Muber will choose to invest.

14. Dirty restrooms cost businesses lost sales, customer referrals, and repeat business. This is especially important for restaurants. So the owner will direct the employee to clean the restrooms more often than the kitchen. Cleaning the restrooms is the dominant strategy, because customers routinely use the restrooms but rarely see the kitchen.

PART IV

Labor Markets and EARNINGS

CHAPTER

14

The Demand and Supply of Resources

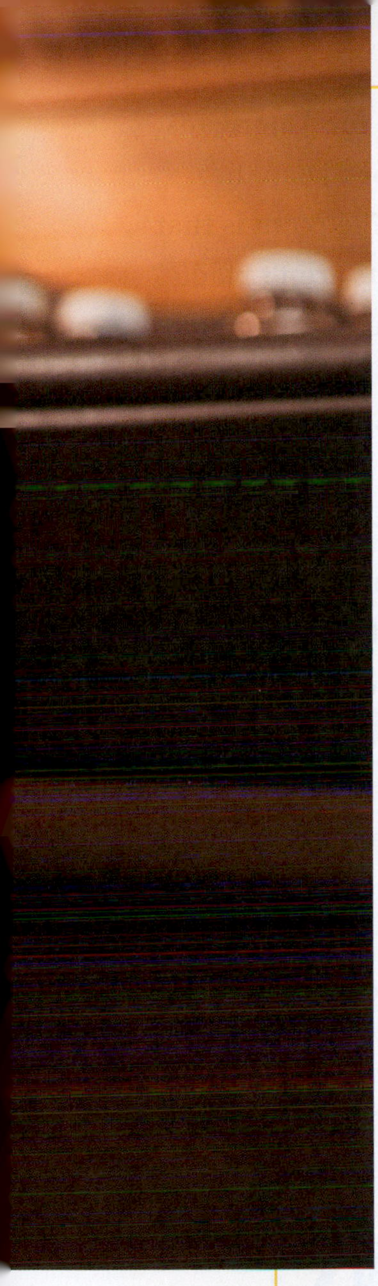

Is Outsourcing Bad for the Economy?

When U.S. jobs are outsourced (sent to other countries), workers in the United States lose their jobs. People commonly think that outsourcing is bad for the U.S. economy, but the situation is not that simple. Outsourced jobs are relocated from high-labor-cost areas to low-labor-cost areas. Often, a U.S. job lost to outsourcing creates more than one job in another country. In addition, outsourcing lowers the cost of manufacturing goods and providing services. Those lower costs translate into lower prices for U.S. consumers and streamlined production processes for U.S. businesses. The improved efficiency helps U.S. firms compete in the global economy. In this chapter, we examine the demand and supply of resources throughout the economy. The outsourcing of jobs is a very visible result of these resource flows and an essential part of the market economy.

Consider Allen Edmonds, an American shoe company that has selectively shifted some of their production to the Dominican Republic. Quality footwear is stylish and hip, but consumers don't have unlimited budgets. To keep prices in the right range for the target market, Allen Edmonds decided to trim production costs by offshoring some of the early production stages. That enabled them to keep final assembly stateside. This move

These wingtips are assembled in the USA, but the uppers are probably stitched together overseas. If you want to buy American, how "American" must your shoes be?

has made their shoes a little more affordable for Americans who appreciate fine footwear, and it has helped keep the doors open at the main plant in Wisconsin. The point is that outsourcing is not a binary outcome. Products aren't made 100% in the United States or 100% elsewhere. The components are generally sourced from around the globe, and designed, manufactured, and assembled wherever these are most cost-effective.

In earlier chapters, we saw that profit-maximizing firms must decide how much to produce. For production to be successful, firms must combine the right amounts of labor and capital to maximize output while simultaneously holding down costs. Because labor often constitutes the largest share of the costs of production, we begin by looking at the labor market. We use supply and demand to illustrate the role of the labor market in the U.S. economy. We then extend the lessons learned about labor into the markets for land and capital. In Chapter 15, we expand our understanding of the labor market by examining income inequality, unemployment, discrimination, and poverty.

· BIG QUESTIONS ·

- What are the factors of production?
- Where does the demand for labor come from?
- Where does the supply of labor come from?
- What are the determinants of demand and supply in the labor market?
- What role do land and capital play in production?

What Are the Factors of Production?

Wages and salaries account for two-thirds of all the income generated by the U.S. economy. The remaining one-third of income goes to the owners of land and capital. Together, labor, land, and capital make up the *factors of production*, or the *inputs* used in producing goods and services. (For a review of these terms, see Chapter 8.)

For instance, let's imagine that Sophia wants to open a Mexican restaurant named Agaves. Sophia will need a dining room staff, cooks, dishwashers, and managers to coordinate everyone else; these are the labor inputs. She also will need a physical location; this is the land input. Finally, she will need a building in which to operate, along with ovens and other kitchen equipment, seating and tableware, and a cash register; these are the capital inputs.

Of course, Sophia's restaurant won't need any inputs if there is no demand for the food she plans to sell. The demand for each of the factors of production that go into her restaurant (land, labor, and capital) is said to be a *derived demand* because the factors are inputs the firm uses to supply a good in another market—in this case, the market for Mexican cuisine. Let's say Sophia secures the land, builds a building, and hires employees to produce the food she will serve. She is willing to spend a lot of money up front to build and staff the restaurant because she expects there to be demand for the food her restaurant will prepare and serve.

Derived demand—the demand for an input used in the production process—is not limited to the demand for a certain type of cuisine. For example,

A lack of customers is an ominous sign for restaurant workers.

Derived demand is the demand for an input used in the production process.

PRACTICE WHAT YOU KNOW

Derived Demand: Tip Income

Your friend waits tables 60 hours a week at a small restaurant. He is discouraged because he works hard but can't seem to make enough money to cover his bills. He complains that the restaurant does not have enough business and that is why he has to work so many hours just to make ends meet.

QUESTION: As an economist, what advice would you give him?

ANSWER: Because labor is a derived demand, he should apply for a job at a more popular restaurant. Working at a place with more customers will help him earn more tip income.

Want more tip income? Follow the crowd.

Why do economists generally earn more than elementary school teachers?

consumer demand for iPads causes Apple to demand the resources needed to make them. The switches, glass, memory, battery, and other parts have little value alone, but when assembled into an iPad, they become a device that many people find very useful. Therefore, when economists speak of derived demand, they are differentiating between the demand for a product or service and the demand for the resources used to make or produce that product or service.

Where Does the Demand for Labor Come From?

As a student, you are probably hoping that one day your education will translate into tangible skills that employers will seek. As you choose a major, you might be thinking about potential earnings in different occupations. Have you ever wondered why there is so much variability in levels of salary and wages? For instance, economists generally earn more than elementary school teachers but less than engineers. Workers on night shifts earn more than those who do the same job during the day. And professional athletes and successful actors make much more for jobs that are not as essential as the work performed by janitors, construction workers, and nurses. In one respect, the explanation is surprisingly obvious: demand helps to regulate the labor market in much the same way that it helps to determine the prices of goods and services sold in the marketplace.

To understand why some people get paid more than others, we need to explore each worker's output at the margin, or the *marginal product of labor*. In fact, the value that each worker creates for a firm is highly correlated with the demand for labor. Then, to develop a more complete understanding of how the labor market works, we will examine the factors that influence labor demand.

The Marginal Product of Labor

To gain a concrete appreciation for how labor demand is determined, let's look at the restaurant business—a highly competitive market. In Chapter 8, we saw that a firm determines how many workers to hire by comparing the output of labor with the wages the firm must pay. We will apply this analysis of production to the labor market in the restaurant business. Table 14.1 should look familiar to you; it highlights the key determinants of the labor hiring process.

The **marginal product of labor** is the change in output associated with adding one additional worker.

Let's work our way through the table. Column 1 lists the number of laborers, and column 2 reports the daily numbers of meals that can be produced with differing numbers of workers. Column 3 shows the **marginal product of labor**, or the change Δ (Greek delta) in output associated with adding one additional worker. For instance, when the firm moves from three employees to four, output expands from 120 meals to 140 meals. The increase of 20 meals is the marginal product of labor for the fourth worker. Note that the values in column 3 decline as additional workers are added. Recall from Chapter 8 that each successive worker adds less value, a phenomenon known as *diminishing marginal product*.

TABLE 14.1

Deciding How Many Laborers to Hire

(1) Labor (number of workers)	(2) Output (daily meals produced)	(3) Marginal product of labor	(4) Value of the marginal product of labor	(5) Wage (daily)	(6) Marginal profit
		Δ Output	Price ($10) × marginal product of labor		Value of the marginal product of labor − wage
0	0				
1	50	50	$500	$100	$400
2	90	40	400	100	300
3	120	30	300	100	200
4	140	20	200	100	100
5	150	10	100	100	0
6	150	0	0	100	−100

It is useful to know the marginal product of labor, which tells us how much each additional worker adds to the firm's output. Combining the marginal product of labor with the price the firm charges gives us a tool we can use to explain how many workers the firm will hire. Suppose that Sophia's Mexican restaurant Agaves charges $10 for each meal. When the firm multiplies the marginal product of labor in column 3 by the price it charges, $10 per meal, we see the value of the marginal product in column 4. The **value of the marginal product (VMP)** the *marginal benefit of an input*, calculated as the marginal product multiplied by the unit price of the output. The firm compares the *marginal benefit* in column 4 with the *marginal cost* of achieving that gain—the wage that must be paid—in column 5. This process reduces the hiring decision to a simple cost-benefit analysis in which the wage (column 5) is subtracted from the value of the marginal product (column 4) to determine each worker's marginal profit (column 6).

The **value of the marginal product (VMP)** is the marginal benefit of an input, calculated as the marginal product multiplied by the unit price of the output.

You can see from the green numbers that the marginal profit is positive for the first four workers. You might be tempted to argue that the firm should quit hiring once it has four workers because the marginal profit is zero for the fifth worker, shown in black. However, this argument is not valid because the firm can hire part-time workers. If the firm hires four full-time workers plus a fifth part-time worker, the fifth worker's VMP is greater than the wage the firm pays. Because the marginal profit is negative for the sixth worker, shown in red, the firm would not hire the sixth worker.

Marginal thinking

Figure 14.1 plots the value of the marginal product (VMP) from Table 14.1. Look at the curve: What do you see? Does it remind you of a demand curve? The VMP is the firm's willingness to pay for each laborer. In other words, it is the firm's labor demand curve.

The VMP curve slopes downward due to diminishing marginal product—which we see in column 3 of Table 14.1. As long as the value of the marginal product is higher than the market wage, shown in column 5 as $100 a day, the firm will hire more workers. For example, when the firm hires the first worker, the VMP is $500. This amount easily exceeds the market wage of hiring an extra

FIGURE 14.1

The Value of the Marginal Product

The value of the marginal product (VMP) is the firm's labor demand curve. When the value of the marginal product is higher than the market wage, the firm will hire more workers. However, because labor is subject to diminishing marginal product, eventually the value created by hiring additional labor falls below the market wage.

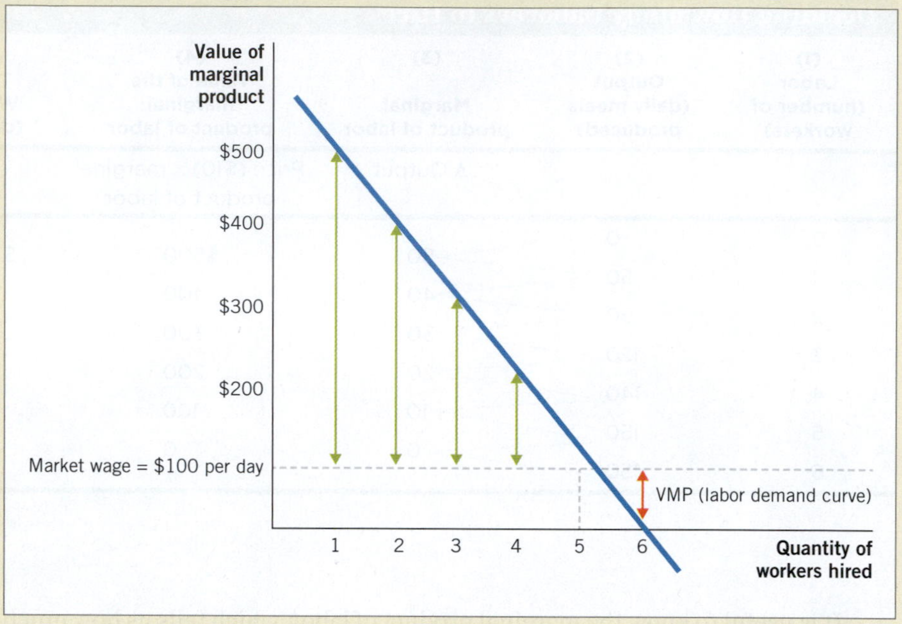

worker and creates a marginal profit of $400. Figure 14.1 illustrates the additional profit from the first worker with the longest green arrow under the labor demand curve and above the market wage. The second, third, and fourth workers generate additional profit of $300, $200, and $100, respectively, represented by the progressively shorter green arrows. As the value of the marginal product declines, there will be a point at which hiring additional workers will cause profits to fall. Because labor is subject to diminishing marginal product, the value created by hiring additional labor eventually falls below the market wage.

Changes in the Demand for Labor

We know that customers desire good food and that restaurants like Agaves hire workers to satisfy their customers. Figure 14.2 illustrates the relationship between the demand for restaurant meals and the demand for restaurant workers. Notice that the demand for labor is downward sloping; at high wages, Agaves will use fewer workers; at lower wages, it will hire more workers. We illustrate the law of demand with the blue arrow that moves along the original demand curve (D_1). Recall from Chapter 3 that a change in price results in a change in the quantity demanded. In addition, the demand for workers depends on, or is derived from, the number of customers who place orders. So changes in the restaurant business as a whole can shift the original demand curve and influence the number of workers the restaurant hires. For example, if the number of customers increases, the demand for workers will increase, or shift to the right to D_2. Likewise, if the number of customers decreases, the demand for workers will decrease, or shift to the left to D_3.

FIGURE 14.2

The Labor Demand Curve

When the wages of workers change, the quantity of workers demanded, shown by the blue arrow moving along the demand curve D_1, also changes. Changes that shift the entire labor demand curve, shown by the gray horizontal arrows, include changes in demand for the product that the firm produces and changes in cost.

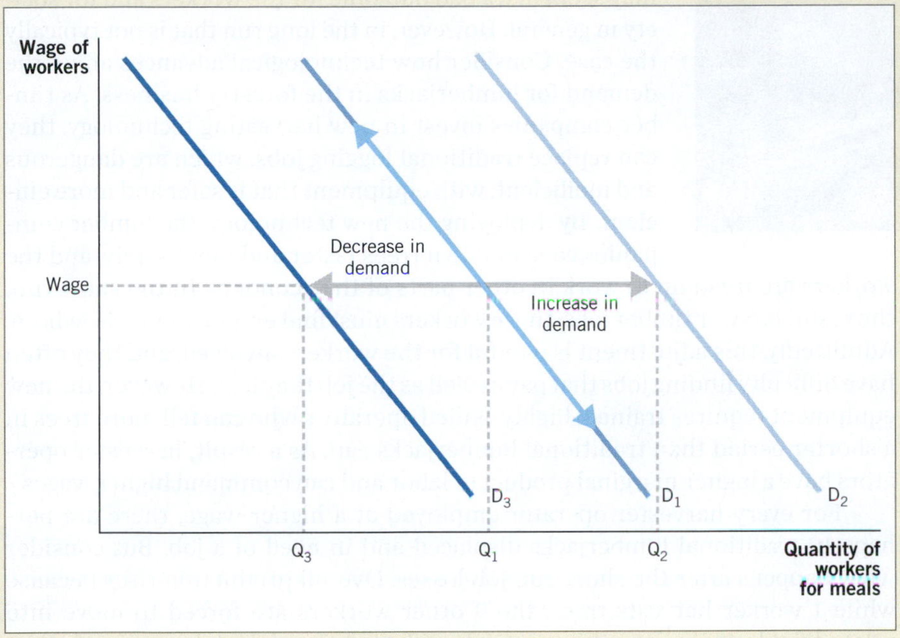

Two primary factors shift labor demand: (1) a change in demand for the product the firm produces and (2) a change in the cost of producing that product.

CHANGES IN DEMAND FOR THE PRODUCT THE FIRM PRODUCES

Because a firm is primarily interested in making a profit, it hires workers only when the value of the marginal product of labor is higher than the cost of hiring labor. Consider Agaves. If a rival Mexican restaurant closes down, many of its customers will likely switch to Agaves. Then Agaves will need to prepare more meals, which will cause the entire demand curve for cooks, table clearers, and waitstaff to shift outward to D_2 in Figure 14.2.

Marginal thinking

CHANGES IN COST A change in the cost of production can sometimes be positive, such as when a new technology makes production less expensive. It can also be negative, such as when an increase in the cost of a needed raw material makes production more expensive.

In terms of a positive change for the firm, technology can act as a substitute for workers or can make existing workers more efficient. For example, microwave ovens enable restaurants to prepare the same number of meals with fewer workers compared to earlier technology. The same is true with the growing trend of using conveyor belts and automated systems to help prepare meals or even serve them. Therefore, changes in technology can lower a firm's demand for workers.

Touch screens at McDonald's automate order taking.

One John Deere 1270G harvester can replace 10 lumberjacks.

In the short run, substituting technology for workers may seem like a bad outcome for the workers and for society in general. However, in the long run that is not typically the case. Consider how technological advances affect the demand for lumberjacks in the forestry business. As timber companies invest in new harvesting technology, they can replace traditional logging jobs, which are dangerous and inefficient, with equipment that is safer and more efficient. By deploying the new technology, the lumber companies can cut down trees faster and more safely, and the workers are freed up to work in other parts of the economy. In the short run, the result is fewer timber jobs; those workers must find employment elsewhere. Admittedly, this adjustment is painful for the workers involved, and they often have difficulty finding jobs that pay as well as the job they lost. However, the new equipment requires trained, highly skilled operators who can fell more trees in a shorter period than traditional lumberjacks can. As a result, harvester operators have a higher marginal product of labor and can command higher wages.

For every harvester operator employed at a higher wage, there are perhaps 10 traditional lumberjacks displaced and in need of a job. But consider what happens after the short-run job losses. Overall production rises because while 1 worker harvests trees, the 9 other workers are forced to move into related fields or do something entirely different. It might take some of these displaced workers many years to find new work, but when they eventually do, society benefits in the long run. What once required 10 workers to produce now takes only 1, and the 9 other workers are able to work in other jobs and grow the economy in different ways.

PRACTICE WHAT YOU KNOW

How many flower barrettes could you make in an hour?

Value of the Marginal Product of Labor: Flower Barrettes

In *The Big Bang Theory*, Penny starts a business making flower barrettes. Sheldon wonders if she can make a profit.

QUESTION: Penny can make five flower barrettes each hour. She works 8 hours each day. Penny is paid $75.00 a day. The firm can sell the barrettes for $1.99 each. What is Penny's value of the marginal product of labor? What is the barrette firm's marginal profit from hiring her?

ANSWER: In 8 hours, Penny can make 40 barrettes. Because each barrette sells for $1.99, her value of the marginal product of labor, or VMP_{labor}, is $40 \times \$1.99$, or $79.60. Her VMP_{labor} is greater than the daily wage she receives, so the marginal profit from hiring her is $\$79.60 - \$75.00$, or $4.60.

CHALLENGE QUESTION: Suppose that the market price of barrettes begins to drop. At what price would Penny's job be in jeopardy?

ANSWER: Penny's VMP_{labor} is her output times the price the firm charges. Penny's wage is $75 a day, so with her making 40 barrettes per day, the VMP_{labor} pencils out to $\$75/40 = \$1.875$ per barrette. That's a scant 11.5 cents less than the current selling price. A small price drop will cause Penny to lose her job.

ECONOMICS *in the* MEDIA

Changes in the Demand for Labor

WALL•E

In this classic animated sci-fi film from 2008, a future megacorporation called Buy N Large has caused so much overconsumption that Earth's resources are entirely used up. Humans escape their ruined home planet on spaceships where automation has rendered human labor superfluous. The humans become obese and ride around in hovering chairs while staring at computer screens all day long. The people in *Wall-E* drink "cupcakes-in-a-cup," they never exercise, and if they happen to fall off their hovering chairs, they can no longer walk and must wait for a robot to help them up.

Getting replaced by automation and robots would be a drag, but the future doesn't have to look like *Wall-E*.

This dystopian future occurs because automation and robots have left people with nothing to do, economically speaking. Yikes! But what will happen if, instead, automation and robotics *augment* our productivity? In that alternative future, we will have less work to do, but we will be able to devote our leisure time to travel and other hobbies and passions. There is no doubt that the age of robots is nearing. You can be replaced, or you can find a way to work with, or alongside, robots to increase the value of the marginal product of your labor. The time to think about this is now, before you enter a field where automation is likely to replace you entirely.

To summarize, if labor becomes more productive, the VMP curve (demand for labor) shifts to the right, driving up both wages and employment, which is exactly what occurs with the demand for harvester operators. There is the potential for substitution as well, causing the demand for traditional labor to fall. This is what has happened to traditional lumberjack jobs, leading to a decrease in those workers' wages.

Where Does the Supply of Labor Come From?

In this section, we examine the connection between the wage rate and the number of workers who are willing to supply their services to employers. Because workers also value leisure, the supply curve is not always directly related to the wage rate. Indeed, at high wage levels, some workers may desire to cut back the number of hours they work. Other factors that influence the labor supply include other employment opportunities, the changing composition of the workforce, migration, and immigration; we explore these factors as well.

The Labor-Leisure Trade-Off

Trade-offs

People work because they need to earn a living. While it is certainly true that many workers enjoy their jobs, this does not mean they would work for nothing. In other words, while many people experience satisfaction in their work, most of us have other interests, obligations, and goals. As a result, the supply of labor depends both on the wage that is offered and on how individuals want to use their time. We call this relationship the *labor-leisure trade-off*.

In our society today, most individuals must work to meet their basic needs. However, once those needs are met, a worker might be more inclined to use his or her time in leisure. Would higher wages induce an employee to give up leisure and work more hours? The answer is both yes and no!

The **substitution effect** occurs when laborers work more hours at higher wages, substituting labor for leisure.

Opportunity cost

At higher wage rates, workers may be willing to work more hours, or substitute labor for leisure. This effect is known as the **substitution effect**. One way to think about the substitution effect is to note that higher wages make leisure time more expensive, because the opportunity cost of enjoying more leisure means giving up more income. For instance, suppose Emeril is a short-order cook at Agaves. He works 40 hours at \$10 per hour and can also work 4 hours overtime at the same wage. If Emeril decides to work the overtime, he ends up working 44 hours and earns \$440. In that case, he substitutes more labor for less leisure.

The **income effect** occurs when laborers work fewer hours at higher wages, using their additional income to demand more leisure.

But at higher wage rates, some workers may work fewer hours, or substitute leisure for labor. This effect is known as the **income effect**. Leisure is a normal good (see Chapter 3), so as income rises, some workers may use their additional income to demand more leisure. As a consequence, at high income levels the income effect may outweigh the substitution effect and cause the supply curve to bend backward. For example, suppose Rachael chooses to work overtime for \$10 per hour. Her total pay (like Emeril's) will be \$10 × 44, or \$440. If her wage rises to \$11, she may continue to work the overtime at a higher wage. However, if she does not work overtime, she will earn as much as she earned before the wage increase (\$11 × 40 = \$440), and she might choose to discontinue the overtime altogether or work fewer overtime hours. The income effect is at work when Rachael's wage goes up and she chooses to work fewer hours.

Figure 14.3 shows what can happen to the labor supply curve when the supply of labor responds directly to wage increases. When the wage rises progressively from W_1 to W_2 to W_3, the number of hours worked increases from Q_1 to Q_2 to Q_3, along the curve labeled S_{normal}. However, at high wage rates the number of hours worked is large. As a result, workers might experience diminishing marginal utility from the additional income and thus might value increased leisure time more than increased income. In this situation, workers might choose to work less, and the normal supply curve bends backward between W_2 and W_3 because as the wage goes up, the hours worked go down.

A **backward-bending labor supply curve** occurs when workers value additional leisure more than additional income.

The **backward-bending labor supply curve** occurs when workers value additional leisure more than additional income. The labor supply curve bends backward when the income effect is large enough to offset the substitution effect that typically causes individuals to work more when the wage rate is higher. Because most workers in the real world do not reach wage level W_2 (that is, a wage at which they might begin to value leisure more than labor), we will draw the supply curve as upward sloping throughout the chapter. Nevertheless, it is important to recognize that the direct relationship we normally observe does not always hold.

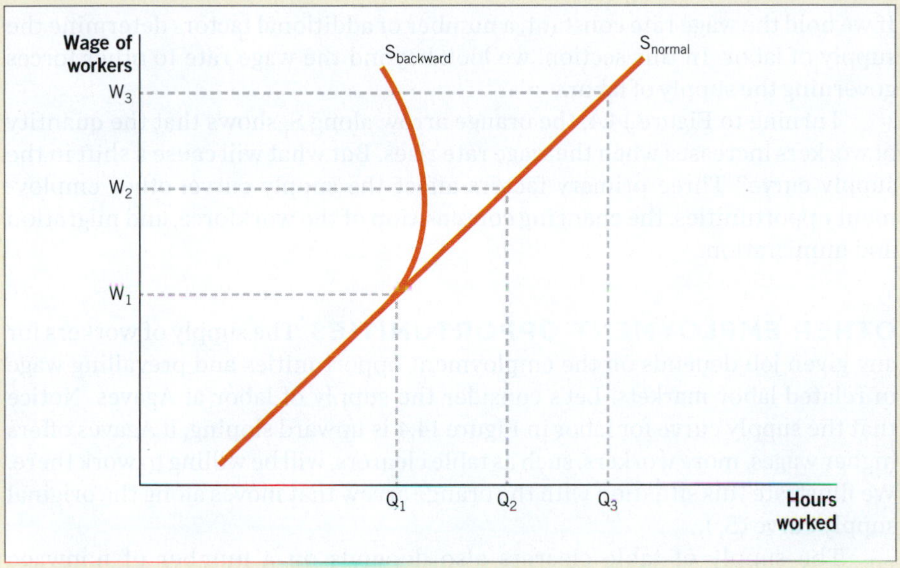

FIGURE 14.3

The Labor Supply Curve

At high wage levels (in this figure, above W_2), the income effect may become larger than the substitution effect and cause the labor supply curve to bend backward. The backward-bending supply curve occurs when additional leisure time becomes more valuable than additional income.

ECONOMICS IN THE REAL WORLD

THE LABOR-LEISURE TRADE-OFF

The statistician Nathan Yau created a simulation called "A Day in the Life of Americans," available at his site flowingdata.com, using data from the American Time Use Survey. As the clock on the upper left ticks along, you see 1,000 dots representing the ways Americans' days typically unfold. Watching the entire simulation will deepen your appreciation for what Americans typically do with their time, and all the trade-offs that take place during a workday.

Trade-offs

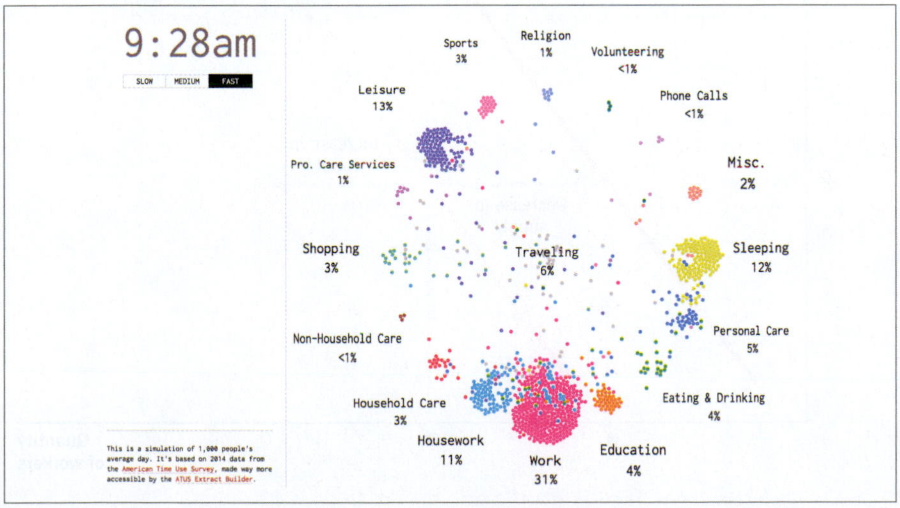

What do you do with your time when you are not working?

Changes in the Supply of Labor

If we hold the wage rate constant, a number of additional factors determine the supply of labor. In this section, we look beyond the wage rate to other forces governing the supply of labor.

Turning to Figure 14.4, the orange arrow along S_1 shows that the quantity of workers increases when the wage rate rises. But what will cause a shift in the supply curve? Three primary factors affect the supply curve: other employment opportunities, the changing composition of the workforce, and migration and immigration.

OTHER EMPLOYMENT OPPORTUNITIES The supply of workers for any given job depends on the employment opportunities and prevailing wage in related labor markets. Let's consider the supply of labor at Agaves. Notice that the supply curve for labor in Figure 14.4 is upward sloping; if Agaves offers higher wages, more workers, such as table clearers, will be willing to work there. We illustrate this situation with the orange arrow that moves along the original supply curve (S_1).

The supply of table clearers also depends on a number of nonwage factors. Because table clearers are generally young and largely unskilled, the number of laborers willing to work is influenced by the prevailing wages in similar jobs. For instance, if the wages of stockers at local grocery stores increase, some of the table clearers at Agaves will decide to stock shelves at local grocery stores instead. The supply of table clearers will decrease and cause a leftward shift to S_3. If the wages of stockers were to fall below the

FIGURE 14.4

The Labor Supply Curve

A change in the quantity supplied occurs when wages change, causing a movement along the supply curve S_1, shown by the orange arrow. Changes in the supply of labor (the quantity of workers), shown by the gray horizontal arrows, can occur due to other employment opportunities, the changing composition of the workforce, immigration, and migration.

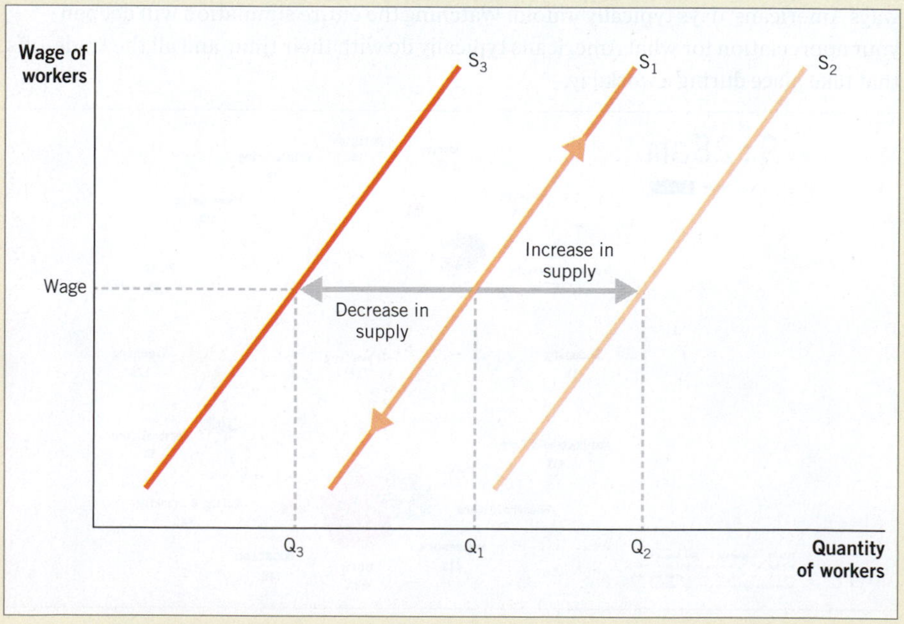

wages of table clearers, the supply of table clearers would increase, or shift to the right to S_2. These shifts reflect the fact that when jobs requiring comparable skills have different wage rates, the number of workers willing to supply labor for the lower-wage job will shrink and the number willing to supply labor for the better-paid job will grow.

THE CHANGING COMPOSITION OF THE WORKFORCE Over the last 35 years, the female/male labor force participation ratio has increased significantly in most developed countries. A ratio of 100% indicates that females and males participated equally. According to the World Bank, the United States saw its female/male ratio rise from 66% to 83%, Switzerland from 67% to 86%, and New Zealand from 65% to 87%. Overall, there are many more women employed in the workforce today than there were a generation ago, and the supply of workers in many occupations has expanded significantly as a result.

IMMIGRATION AND MIGRATION Demographic factors, including immigration and migration, also play a crucial role in the supply of labor. For example, immigration—both legal and illegal—increases the available supply of workers by a significant amount each year.

In 2019, over half a million people from foreign countries entered the United States through legal channels and gained permission to seek employment. There are over 40 million legal immigrants in the United States. In addition, illegal immigrants account for close to 10 million workers in the United States, many of whom enter the country to work as hotel maids, janitors, and fruit pickers. Often when states suggest or pass a tough immigration law, businesses in food and beverage, agriculture, and construction protest because they need inexpensive labor to remain competitive, and U.S. citizens are reluctant to work these jobs. Many states have wrestled with the issue, but policies that address illegal immigration remain controversial, and the solutions are difficult. The states need the cheap labor but don't want to pay additional costs, such as medical care and the cost of schooling the illegal immigrants' children.

For the purposes of this discussion, we consider migration to be the process of moving from one place to another within the United States. Although the U.S. population grows at an annual rate of approximately 1%, there are significant regional differences. Indeed, large population influxes lead to marked regional changes in the demand for labor and the supply of people looking for work. In 2019, the 10 fastest-growing states were in the South or West, with some states adding as much as 6% to their population in a single year. From 2010 to 2019, Nevada, Utah, North Carolina, Idaho, and Texas all added at least 20% to their populations.

It is worth noting that statewide data can hide significant localized changes. For example, population data from 2019 indicate that a number of counties experienced 40% or more population growth between 2010 and 2019. The biggest population gain near a major metropolitan area was in Hays County, Texas, a suburb of Austin that grew by nearly 50%. Most of the fastest-growing counties are, like Hays, relatively distant suburbs of major metropolitan areas. These are areas where new homes are available at comparatively reasonable prices.

ECONOMICS IN THE REAL WORLD

Can't find reliable workers? No problem. Get a robot to do the job.

SUPPLY OF LABOR

Where Have All the Workers Gone (and Who Is Going to Replace Them)?

In recent years, there has been strong growth in the fast-food industry, including fast-casual dining. At the same time, younger workers are far less likely to participate in the workforce than they used to be. This is a problem for an industry that has historically relied on abundant cheap labor to produce inexpensive food.

One solution to this labor-shortage problem is automation. In 2018, Caliburger introduced Flippy, the first hamburger-flipping robot. Flippy costs $60,000, and there is also a $12,000 recurring annual fee for cleaning and maintenance, but Caliburger is confident that the investment is worth the high fixed cost. Caliburger is banking on decreased wait times, better consistency in food preparation, and less food waste. Plus, Flippy doesn't need vacations or health insurance. Lately, the burger chain White Castle has also begun using Flippy. Meanwhile, robots are starting to replace baristas at drink counters, too, making boba milk teas and specialty coffees in locations where entry-level wages are high.

What Are the Determinants of Demand and Supply in the Labor Market?

In earlier chapters, we saw how markets reconcile the forces of demand and supply through pricing. Now that we have considered the forces governing demand and supply in the labor market, we are ready to see how the equilibrium

PRACTICE WHAT YOU KNOW

If you got a big raise, would you travel the world?

The Labor Supply Curve: What Would You Do with a Big Raise?

QUESTION: Your friend is concerned about his uncle, who just received a big raise. Your friend doesn't understand why his uncle wants to take time off from his job to travel. Can you help him understand why his uncle might want to cut back on his hours?

ANSWER: Ordinarily, we think of the labor supply curve as upward sloping, in which case higher wages translate into more hours worked and less leisure time. However, when the wage rate becomes high enough, some workers choose to substitute leisure for labor because they feel that enjoying free time is more valuable than earning more money. In this case, the labor supply curve bends backward, and the worker spends fewer hours working as his wage rises. Your friend's uncle is reflecting this tendency.

wage is established. We can then examine the labor market in greater detail and identify what causes shortages and surpluses of labor, why outsourcing occurs, and what happens when there is a single buyer of labor. The goal of this section is to provide a rich set of examples that help you become comfortable using demand and supply curves to understand how the labor market operates.

How Does the Market for Labor Reach Equilibrium?

We can think about wages as the price at which workers are willing to "rent" their time to employers. Turning to Figure 14.5, we see that at wages above equilibrium (W_E), the supply of workers willing to rent their time exceeds the demand for that time. The result is a surplus of available workers. The surplus, in turn, places downward pressure on wages. As wages drop, fewer workers are willing to rent their time to employers. When wages drop to the equilibrium wage, the surplus of workers is eliminated. At that point, the number of workers willing to work in that profession at that wage is exactly equal to the number of job openings that exist at that wage.

A similar process guides the labor market toward equilibrium from low wages. At wages below the equilibrium, the demand for labor exceeds the

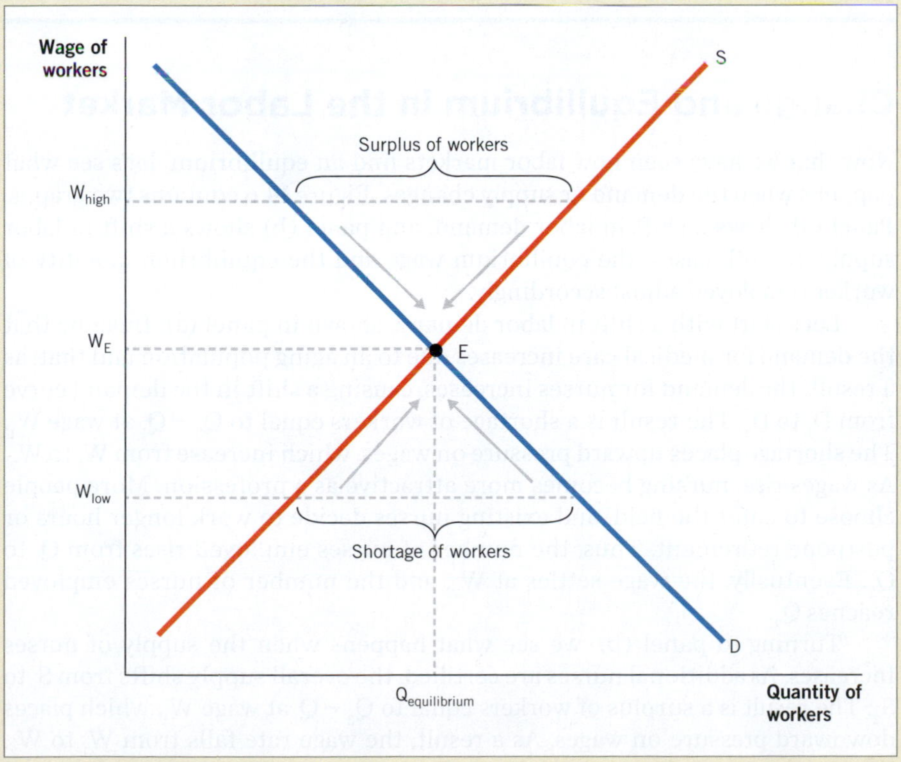

FIGURE 14.5

Equilibrium in the Labor Market

At high wages (W_{high}), a surplus of workers exists. The wage rate is driven down until the supply of workers and the demand for workers reach equilibrium. At low wages (W_{low}), a shortage occurs. The shortage forces the wage rate up until the equilibrium wage is reached and the shortage disappears.

available supply. The shortage forces firms to offer higher wages to attract workers. As a result, wages rise until the shortage is eliminated at the equilibrium wage.

ECONOMICS IN THE REAL WORLD

WHERE ARE THE MEDICAL PROVIDERS?

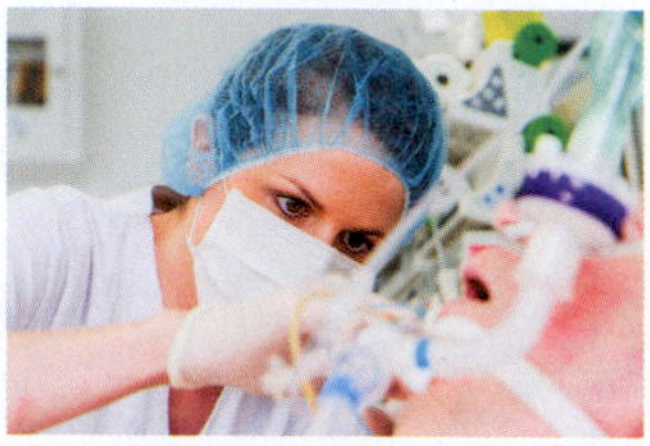

Entering an occupation with a shortage of workers will result in higher pay.

The United States is experiencing a shortage of medical providers, and the demand for workers in the medical field is expected to rise dramatically throughout the 2020s, as the ranks of the elderly swell with aging baby boomers. According to the Bureau of Labor Statistics, six of the ten fastest-growing occupations in the United States are in the medical field: nurse practitioners, home health and personal care aides, physical therapy assistants, occupational therapy assistants, medical and health services managers, and physician assistants.

Because the training for these jobs takes two or more years to complete, the labor market for care providers won't return to equilibrium immediately. The provider shortage will persist for a number of years, until the quantity of providers supplied to the market increases. The median pay of nurse practitioners, medical and health services managers, and physician assistants already exceeds $100,000. Given the ongoing shortage, you might want to consider a career in health care. Not only will you find immediate employment once trained, you'll also experience rising wages while the shortage lasts. Remember that when a market is out of balance, forces kick in to restore it to equilibrium.

Change and Equilibrium in the Labor Market

Now that we have seen how labor markets find an equilibrium, let's see what happens when the demand or supply changes. Figure 14.6 contains two graphs. Panel (a) shows a shift in labor demand, and panel (b) shows a shift in labor supply. In both cases, the equilibrium wage and the equilibrium quantity of workers employed adjust accordingly.

Let's start with a shift in labor demand, shown in panel (a). Imagine that the demand for medical care increases due to an aging population and that, as a result, the demand for nurses increases, causing a shift in the demand curve from D_1 to D_2. The result is a shortage of workers equal to $Q_3 - Q_1$ at wage W_1. The shortage places upward pressure on wages, which increase from W_1 to W_2. As wages rise, nursing becomes more attractive as a profession. More people choose to enter the field, and existing nurses decide to work longer hours or postpone retirement. Thus, the number of nurses employed rises from Q_1 to Q_2. Eventually, the wage settles at W_2, and the number of nurses employed reaches Q_2.

Turning to panel (b), we see what happens when the supply of nurses increases. As additional nurses are certified, the overall supply shifts from S_1 to S_2. The result is a surplus of workers equal to $Q_3 - Q_1$ at wage W_1, which places downward pressure on wages. As a result, the wage rate falls from W_1 to W_2. Eventually, the market wage settles at W_2, the new equilibrium point is E_2, and the number of nurses employed reaches Q_2.

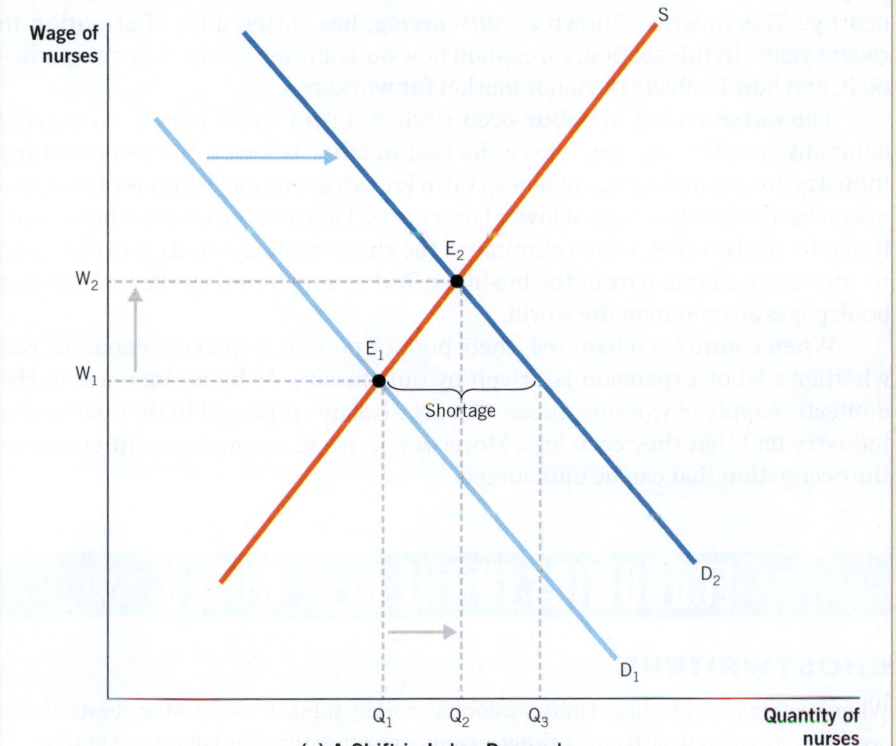

(a) A Shift in Labor Demand

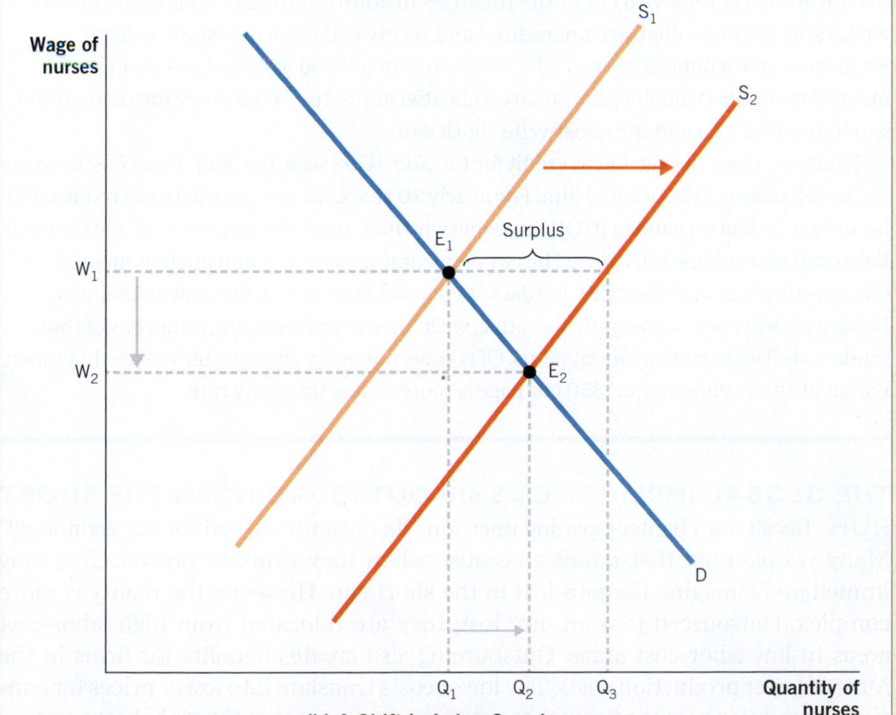

(b) A Shift in Labor Supply

FIGURE 14.6

Shifting the Labor Market Equilibrium

In panel (a), the demand for nurses increases, creating a shortage of workers equal to $Q_3 - Q_1$, which leads to a higher equilibrium wage (W_2) and a higher quantity of nurses employed (Q_2) than before. In panel (b), the supply of nurses increases. The result is a surplus of workers equal to $Q_3 - Q_1$, causing the equilibrium wage to fall (to W_2) and the number of nurses employed to rise (to Q_2).

Outsourcing

Why would a firm hire someone from outside if it has a qualified employee nearby? This practice, known as *outsourcing*, has gotten a lot of attention in recent years. In this section, we explain how outsourcing works, why companies do it, and how it affects the labor market for workers.

Outsourcing of labor occurs when a firm shifts jobs to an outside company, usually overseas, where the cost of labor is lower.

The **outsourcing of labor** occurs when a firm shifts jobs to an outside company, usually overseas, where the cost of labor is lower. In the publishing industry, for example, page make-up (also known as composition) is often done overseas to take advantage of lower labor costs. This outsourcing has been facilitated by the Internet, which eliminates the shipping delays and costs that used to constitute a large part of the business. Today, a qualified worker can lay out book pages anywhere in the world.

When countries outsource, their pool of potential workers expands. But whether a labor expansion is driven by outsourcing or by an increase in the domestic supply of workers, those who are already employed in that particular industry find that they earn less. Moreover, a rise in unemployment occurs in the occupation that can be outsourced.

ECONOMICS IN THE REAL WORLD

GHOSTWRITERS

When we think of outsourced jobs, we don't generally think of books. Many bestsellers, however, are written partly or entirely by someone other than the advertised author. Co-authors may receive a cut of the royalties in addition to cash fees, while ghostwriters, as they're called, are uncredited and receive all their payment up front. Suppose you're a famous person who has a story to tell and a publisher's deadline to meet. Your time is valuable, so you hire a ghostwriter to turn your story into something worth reading. You and the ghostwriter both win.

Star Wars fans know George Lucas as the author of *A New Hope*, the first novel based on the movies. But it was Alan Dean Foster who actually wrote the book.

Everyone gives George Lucas credit for the *Star Wars* saga, but Alan Dean Foster wrote the novelization of the original film. For nearly 20 years, he was contractually required to lie and say he had no hand in it! Other people who have used ghostwriters include Gwyneth Paltrow (two cookbooks), Prince Harry (an upcoming memoir), and businesspeople like one-time General Electric CEO Jack Welch and Starbucks CEO Howard Schultz. Being a ghostwriter can be quite lucrative, with top writers receiving hundreds of thousands of dollars to remain anonymous. Of course, not every ghostwriter makes that much. For an ordinary ghostwriter, $50 per page is more or less the going rate.

THE GLOBAL IMPLICATIONS OF OUTSOURCING IN THE SHORT RUN Recall our chapter-opening question, "Is outsourcing bad for the economy?" Many people hold that opinion because when they think of outsourcing, they immediately imagine the jobs lost in the short run. However, the reality is more complex. Outsourced jobs are not lost; they are relocated from high-labor-cost areas to low-labor-cost areas. Outsourcing also creates benefits for firms in the form of lower production costs. The lower costs translate into lower prices for consumers and also help the firms that outsource to compete in the global economy.

Outsourcing need not cost the United States jobs. Consider what happens when foreign countries outsource their production to the United States. For example, the German auto manufacturer Mercedes-Benz currently has many of its cars built in Alabama. If you were an assembly-line worker in Germany who had spent a lifetime making cars for Mercedes, you would likely be upset if your job was outsourced to North America. You would feel just like the American technician who loses a job to someone in India or the software writer who is replaced by a worker in China. Outsourcing always produces a job winner and a job loser. In the case of foreign outsourcing to the United States, employment in this country rises. In fact, the Mercedes-Benz plant in Alabama employs more than 3,000 workers. Those jobs were transferred to the United States because the company felt that it would be more profitable to hire American workers and make the vehicles in the United States rather than construct them in Germany and ship them across the Atlantic.

The Mercedes-Benz plant near Tuscaloosa, Alabama, illustrates that outsourcing is more than just a one-way street.

Figure 14.7 shows how outsourcing by foreign firms helps to increase U.S. labor demand. In panel (a), we see the job loss and lower wages that occur in Germany when jobs are outsourced to the United States. As the demand for labor in Germany falls from D_1 to D_2, wages drop to W_2 and employment declines to Q_2. Panel (b) illustrates the corresponding increase in demand for U.S. labor in Alabama. As demand shifts from D_1 to D_2, wages rise to W_2 and employment rises to Q_2.

Because each nation will experience outsourcing flows out of and into the country, it is impossible to say anything definitive about the overall impact of outsourcing on labor in the short run. However, it is highly unlikely that workers who lose high-paying jobs toward the end of their working lives will be able to find other jobs that pay equally well.

THE GLOBAL IMPLICATIONS OF OUTSOURCING IN THE LONG RUN Although we see mixed results for outsourcing in the short run, we can say that in the long run outsourcing benefits domestic consumers and producers. In fact, outsourcing is a key component in international trade. Throughout this book, we have seen that trade creates value. When companies and even countries specialize, they become more efficient. The efficiency gains, or cost savings, help producers to expand production. In the absence of trade barriers, lower costs benefit consumers in domestic and international markets through lower prices, and the outsourcing of jobs provides the income for foreign workers to purchase domestic imports. Therefore, the mutually interdependent nature of international trade enhances overall social welfare.

Trade creates value

FIGURE 14.7

Shifting the Labor Market Equilibrium

Outsourcing creates more demand in one market at the expense of the other. In panel (a), the demand for German labor declines from D_1 to D_2, leading to lower wages and less employment. Panel (b) shows the increase in the demand for labor from D_1 to D_2 in Alabama. The results are higher wages and more employment.

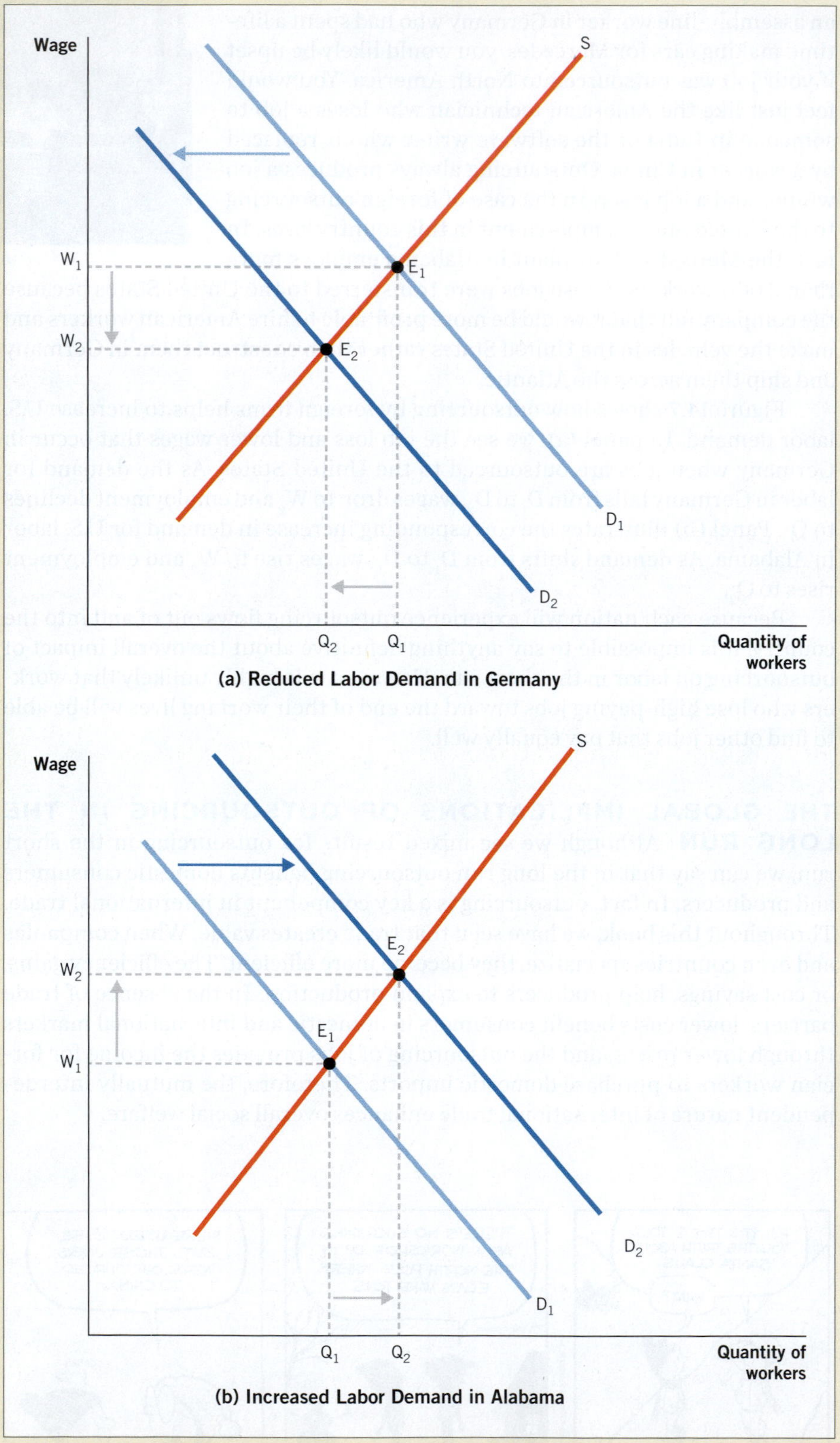

Monopsony

In looking at supply, demand, and equilibrium in the labor market, we have assumed that the market for labor is competitive. But that is not always the case. Sometimes the labor market has only a few buyers or sellers who are able to capture market power. One extreme form of market power is **monopsony**, which occurs when only a single buyer exists. Like a monopolist, a monopsonist has a great deal of market power. As a consequence, the output in the labor market will favor a monopsonist whenever one is present.

Monopsony is a situation in which there is only one buyer.

In Chapter 10, we examined how a monopolist behaves. Compared with a firm in a competitive market, the monopolist charges a higher price for the product it sells. Likewise, a monopsonist in the labor market can leverage its market power. Because it is the only firm hiring, it can pay its workers less. Isolated college towns are a good example. Workers who wish to live in such college towns often find that almost all the available jobs are through the college. Because it is the chief provider of jobs, the college has a monopsony in the labor market. It can use its market power to hire many local workers at low wages.

WHY DO SOME WORKERS MAKE MORE THAN OTHERS? While most workers generally spend 35 to 40 hours a week at work, the amount they earn varies dramatically. Table 14.2 presents a number of simple questions that answer the larger question, "Why do some workers make more than others?"

TABLE 14.2

Why Some Workers Make More than Others

Question	Answer
Why do economists generally earn more than elementary school teachers?	Supply is the key. There are fewer qualified economists than certified elementary school teachers. Therefore, the equilibrium wage in economics is higher than it is in elementary education. It's also important to note that demand factors may be part of the explanation. The value of the marginal product of labor of economists is generally higher than that of most elementary school teachers because many economists work in industry, which pays higher wages than the public sector.
Why do people who work the night shift earn more than those who do the same job during the day?	Again, supply is the key. Fewer people are willing to work at night, so the wage necessary to attract labor to perform the job must be higher. (That is, night shift workers earn what is called a *compensating differential*, which we discuss in Chapter 15.)
Why do professional athletes and successful actors make so much when what they do is not essential?	Demand and supply both play important roles here. The paying public is willing, even eager, to spend a large amount of income on entertainment. Thus, demand for entertainment is high. On the supply end of the equation, the number of individuals who capture the imagination of the paying public is small, and they are therefore paid handsomely. Since the value of the marginal product that they create is incredibly high, and the supply of workers with these skills is quite small, accomplished athletes and actors earn huge incomes.
Why do janitors, construction workers, and nurses—whose jobs are essential—have salaries that are a tiny fraction of celebrities' salaries?	Demand again. The value of the marginal product of labor created in these essential jobs is low, so their employers are unable to pay high wages.

PRACTICE WHAT YOU KNOW

Labor is always subject to changes in demand.

Changes in Labor Demand

QUESTION: A company builds a new facility that doubles its workspace and equipment. How is labor affected?

ANSWER: The company has probably experienced additional demand for the product it sells. Therefore, it needs additional employees to staff the facility, causing a positive shift in the demand curve. When the demand for labor rises, wages increase and so does the number of people employed.

QUESTION: A company decides to outsource 100 jobs from a facility in Indiana to Indonesia. How is labor affected in the short run?

ANSWER: This situation leads to two changes. First, a decrease in demand for labor in Indiana results in lower wages there and fewer workers hired. Second, an increase in demand for labor in Indonesia results in higher wages there and more workers hired.

The table shows how demand and supply determine wages in a variety of settings. Workers with a high-value marginal product of labor invariably earn more than those with a lower-value marginal product of labor. It is important to note that working an "essential" job does not guarantee a high income. Instead, the highest incomes are reserved for jobs with a high demand for workers and a low supply of them. In other words, our preconceived notions of fairness take a backseat to the underlying market forces that govern pay. In the next chapter, we consider many additional factors that determine wages, including wage discrimination.

What Role Do Land and Capital Play in Production?

In addition to labor, firms need land and capital to produce goods and services. In this section, we complete our analysis of the resource market by considering how land and capital enter into the production process. Returning to the restaurant Agaves, we know that the business hires labor to make meals. But to do their jobs, the workers need equipment, tables, chairs, cash registers, and a kitchen. Without a physical location and a host of capital resources, labor would be irrelevant.

The Market for Land

Like the demand for labor, the demand for land is determined by the value of the marginal product it generates. However, unlike the supply of labor, the supply of land is ordinarily fixed. We can think of it as nonresponsive to prices, or perfectly inelastic.

In Figure 14.8, the vertical supply curve reflects the inelastic supply. The price of land is determined by the intersection of supply and demand. Notice the label on the vertical axis, which reflects the price of land as the rental price necessary to use it, not the price necessary to purchase it. When evaluating a firm's economic situation, we do not count the entire purchase price of the land it needs. To do so would dramatically overstate the cost of land in the production process because the land is not used up, but only occupied for a certain period. For example, consider a car that you buy. You drive it for a year and put 15,000 miles on it. Counting the entire purchase price of the car would overstate the true operating cost for one year of service. The true cost of operating the vehicle includes wear and tear along with operating expenses, such as gasoline, maintenance, and service visits. A similar process is at work with land. Firms that own land consider the rent they could have earned if they had rented the land out for the year. This method nicely captures the opportunity cost of using the land.

Opportunity cost

Because the supply of land is usually fixed, changes in demand determine the rental price. When demand is low—say, at D_1—the rental price received, P_1, is also low. When demand is high—say, at D_2—the rental price of land is high, at P_2. Apartment rentals near college campuses provide a good example of the conditions under which the demand for land is high. Because students and faculty want to live near campus, the demand for land is often much higher there than even a few blocks away. Like labor, the demand for land is derived from

FIGURE 14.8

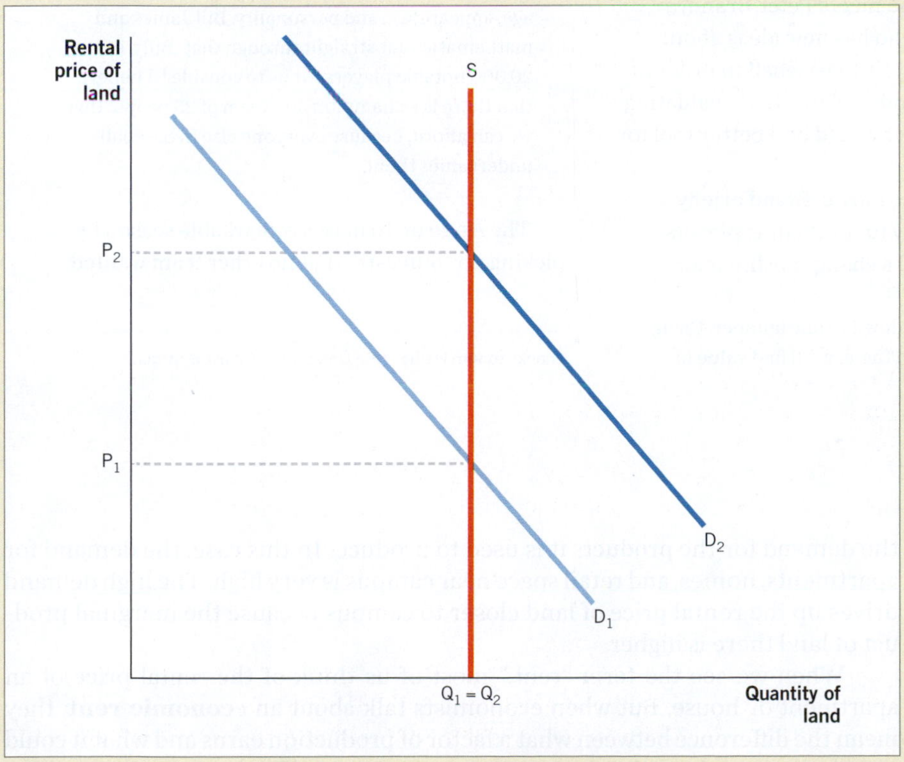

Supply and Demand in the Market for Land

Because the supply of land is fixed, the price it commands depends on demand. If demand increases from D_1 to D_2, the price will rise from P_1 to P_2. Note that "price" here reflects the rental price of the land, not the purchase price.

ECONOMICS in the MEDIA

Value of the Marginal Product of Labor

MONEYBALL

Moneyball (2011), a film based on Michael Lewis's 2003 book of the same name, details the struggles of the Oakland Athletics, a major-league baseball team. The franchise attempts to overcome some seemingly impossible obstacles with the help of its general manager, Billy Beane, by applying innovative statistical analysis, known as sabermetrics, pioneered by statistician Bill James.

Traditional baseball scouts use experience, intuition, and subjective criteria to evaluate potential players. However, Beane, formerly a heavily recruited high school player who failed to have a successful professional career, knows firsthand that this method of scouting does not guarantee success. The Oakland A's lack the financial ability to pay as much as other teams. While trying to negotiate a trade with the Cleveland Indians, Beane meets Peter Brand, a young Yale economist who has new ideas about applying statistical analysis to baseball in order to build a better team. Brand explains that evaluating a player's marginal product would be a better tool for recruitment.

In the key scene in the movie, Brand briefly explains his methodology for evaluating players and how the A's can build a championship team:

> It's about getting things down to one number. Using the stats the way we read them, we'll find value in players that no one else can see. People are overlooked for a variety of biased reasons and perceived flaws: age, appearance, and personality. Bill James and mathematics cut straight through that. Billy, of the 20,000 notable players for us to consider, I believe that there is a championship team of 25 people that we can afford, because everyone else in baseball undervalues them.

Can a young economist's algorithm save the Oakland A's?

The A's go on to have a remarkable season by picking up "outcasts" that no other team wanted.

Thanks to Kim Holder (the University of West Georgia).

the demand for the products it is used to produce. In this case, the demand for apartments, homes, and retail space near campus is very high. The high demand drives up the rental price of land closer to campus because the marginal product of land there is higher.

Marginal thinking

Economic rent is the difference between what a factor of production earns and what it could earn in the next-best alternative.

When we see the term "rent," most of us think of the rental price of an apartment or house. But when economists talk about an **economic rent**, they mean the difference between what a factor of production earns and what it could earn in the next-best alternative. Economic rent is different from *rent seeking*. Recall from Chapter 10 that rent seeking occurs when firms compete to seek a

A satellite photo shows manufactured islands in Dubai, United Arab Emirates—an exception to our assumption that the amount of land is fixed.

monopoly position. In contrast, economic rent refers to investors' ability to beat their opportunity cost. For instance, in the case of housing near college campuses, a small studio apartment generally commands a much higher rent than a similar apartment located 10 miles away. Why? The rent near campus must be high enough to compensate the property owners for using their land for an apartment instead of in other ways that might also be profitable in the area—for example, for a single residence, a business, or a parking lot. Once you move 10 miles farther out, the number of people interested in using the land for these purposes declines.

More generally, in areas where many people would like to live or work, rental prices are often very high. Take San Francisco, where the average rental unit cost a staggering $3,500 a month before COVID-19 hit. That eye-popping amount makes most apartment rental prices in the United States seem downright inexpensive. During and after the pandemic, many workers relocated away from urban areas. As a result, San Francisco's rents have dropped over 10% on average, to $3,100. That's still quite a bit pricier than Peoria or Scranton, though. The ability to earn a substantial economic rent comes back to opportunity costs: because there are so many other potential uses of property in densely populated areas, rents are correspondingly higher.

Opportunity cost

The Market for Capital

Capital, or the equipment and materials needed to produce goods, is a necessary factor of production. The demand for capital is determined by the value of the marginal product it creates. Like the demand for land and labor, the demand for capital is a derived demand: a firm requires capital only if the product it produces is in demand. The demand for capital is also downward sloping, reflecting the fact that the value of the marginal product associated with its use declines as the amount used rises.

When to Use More Labor, Land, or Capital

Firms must evaluate whether hiring additional labor, utilizing more land, or deploying more capital will constitute the best use of their resources. To do this, they compare the value of the marginal product per dollar spent across the three factors of production.

Let's consider an example. Suppose that a company pays its employees $15 per hour, the rental rate of land is $5,000 per acre per year, and the rental rate of capital is $1,000 per year. The company's manager determines that the value of the marginal product of labor is $450, the value of the marginal product of an acre of land is $125,000, and the value of the marginal product of capital is $40,000. Is the firm using the right mix of resources? Table 14.3 compares the ratios of the value of the marginal product (VMP) of each factor of production with the cost of attaining that value (this calculation gives us the "bang per buck" for each resource, or the relative benefit of using each resource).

Looking at these results, we see that the highest bang per buck (column 4) is the value $40 created by dividing the VMP of capital by the rental price of capital. When we compare this value with the bang per buck for labor and land, we see that the firm is getting more benefit per dollar spent on capital than from labor ($30) or land ($25). Therefore, the firm would benefit from using capital more intensively. As it does so, the VMP of capital in column 2 will fall due to diminishing returns, and the bang per buck for capital will drop from $40 in column 4 to a number that is more in line with bang per buck for labor and land. Conversely, the firm is using land ($25) too intensively, and it would benefit from using less. Doing so will raise the VMP it produces and increase its bang per buck for land. By using less land and more capital and by tweaking the use of labor as well, the firm will eventually bring the value created by all three factors to a point at which the bang per buck spent is equal for each of the factors. At that point, the firm will be utilizing its resources efficiently.

Marginal thinking

Why does all this matter? Because the world is always changing: wages rise and fall, as do property values and the cost of acquiring capital. A firm must constantly adjust the mix of land, labor, and capital it uses to get the largest return. Moreover, the markets for land, labor, and capital are connected. The amount of labor that a firm uses depends not only on the marginal product of labor, but also on the marginal product of land and capital. Therefore, a change in the supply of one factor will alter the returns of all factors. For instance, if wages fall, firms will be inclined to hire more labor. But if they hire more labor, they will use less capital. Capital itself is not any more, or less, productive. Rather, lower wages reduce the demand for capital. In this situation, the demand curve for capital would shift to the left, lowering the rental price of capital as well as the quantity of capital deployed.

TABLE 14.3

Determining the Bang per Buck for Each Resource

(1) Factor of production	(2) Value of the marginal product	(3) Wage or rental price	(4) Bang per buck
Labor	$450	$15	$450 ÷ 15 = $30
Land	125,000	5,000	125,000 ÷ 5,000 = 25
Capital	40,000	1,000	40,000 ÷ 1,000 = 40

SNAPSHOT

Outsourcing

Outsourcing, though painful for those whose jobs are outsourced, is simply the application of a fundamental economic principle—keep costs as low as possible. Labor is usually the most expensive input for a business, so all managers must seek to pay the lowest wage that still ensures an effective workforce. Firms seek the right balance of costs and relevant skills when outsourcing jobs. Here is a look at three representative jobs in the United States, Mexico, China, and India, with salaries measured as a percentage of the typical U.S. salary.

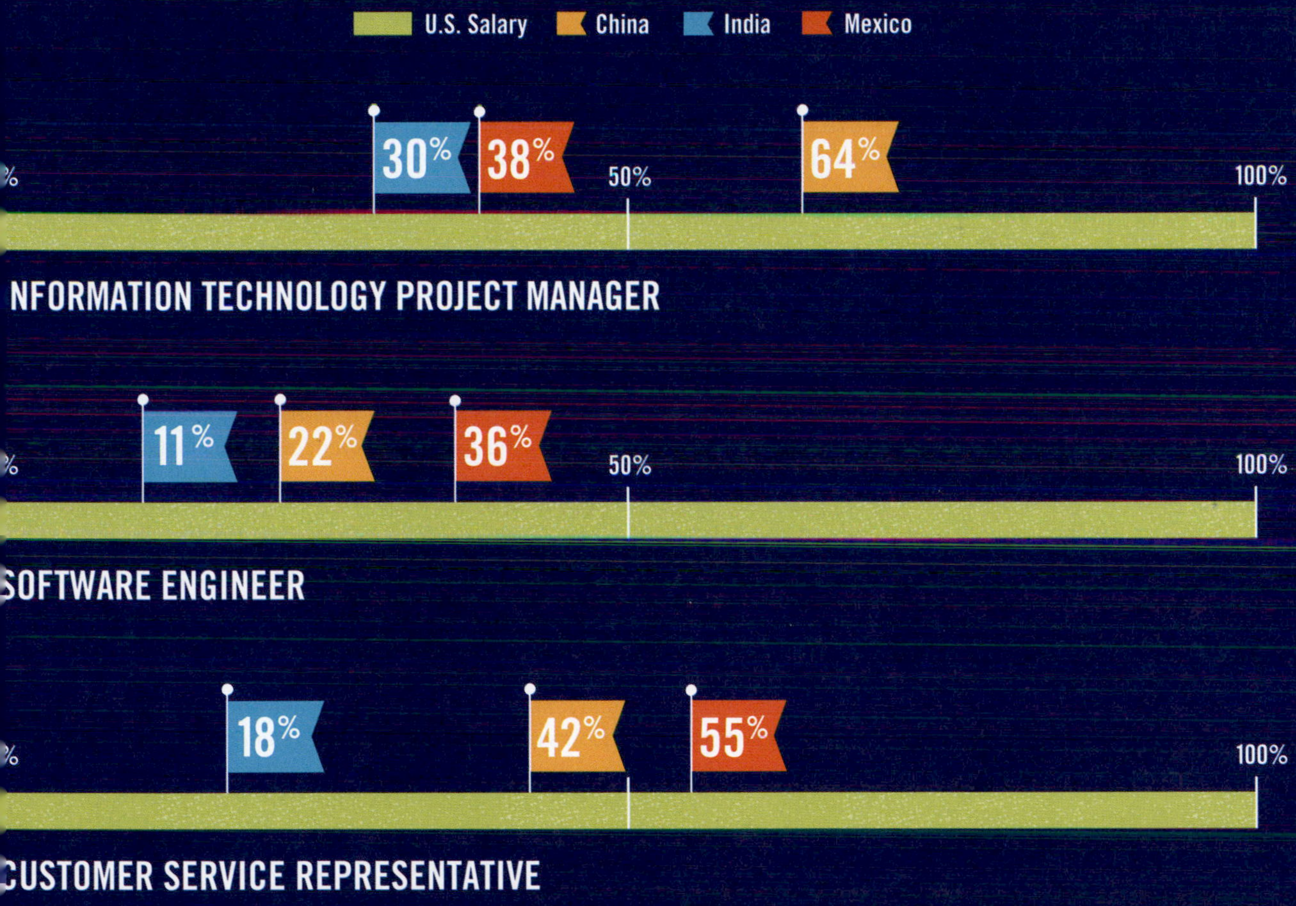

The communications and transportation revolutions, along with the increasing skill level of foreign labor, have created conditions for the outsourcing of millions of U.S. jobs to China, India, and Latin America.

Outsourcing is about comparative advantage. Firms hire foreign workers who hold a comparative advantage and can produce a good or service more cheaply and at a lower opportunity cost than domestic workers.

REVIEW QUESTIONS

- Software engineering jobs are outsourced from the United States to India. Use supply and demand curves to sketch the effects on the U.S. and Indian labor forces.
- Outsourcing is controversial. Explain why by citing effects to the economy both in the short run and long run.

ECONOMICS IN THE REAL WORLD

Tesla factory in California. Where are the workers?

SKILLED WORK WITHOUT THE WORKER

While the many robots in auto factories typically perform only one function, at the Tesla electric automobile factory in Fremont, California, a robot might perform up to four tasks. And it does it all without a coffee break—three shifts a day, 365 days a year. This is the future. A new wave of robots, far more adept than those now commonly used by automakers and other heavy manufacturers, are replacing workers around the world in both manufacturing and distribution. Factories like Tesla's are a striking counterpoint to those used by Apple and other consumer electronics giants, which until recently employed hundreds of thousands of low-skilled workers but must now update their production methods, or risk falling behind their rivals.

The falling costs and growing sophistication of robots have touched off a renewed debate among economists and technologists over how quickly jobs will be lost. The advent of low-cost automation foretells changes similar to those of the revolution in agricultural technology over the last century, which decreased farming employment in the United States from 40% of the workforce to about 2% today.

Robot manufacturers say that in many applications, robots are already more cost-effective than humans. In one example, a robotic manufacturing system initially cost $250,000 and replaced two machine operators, each earning $50,000 a year. Over the 15-year life of the system, the machines yielded $3.5 million in labor savings.

Some jobs are still outside the range of automation: construction jobs that require workers to move in unpredictable settings and perform different tasks that are not repetitive; assembly work that requires tactile feedback like placing fiberglass panels inside airplanes, boats, or cars; and assembly jobs where only a limited quantity of the product is made or where there are many versions of each product, which would require expensive reprogramming of robots. Moreover, Tesla may rely on automation in its Fremont plant, but it is still the area's biggest employer, with over 10,000 workers compared to 3,200 for the local school district in the number 2 spot—so there are still plenty of jobs that automation can't reach—yet.

But that list is growing shorter. Older robots cannot do such work because computer vision systems were costly and limited to carefully controlled environments where the lighting was just right. But thanks to an inexpensive stereo camera and software that lets the system see shapes with the same ease as humans, new types of robot can quickly discern the irregular dimensions of randomly placed objects.

"We're on the cusp of completely changing manufacturing and distribution," says Gary Bradski, a machine-vision scientist. "I think it's not as singular an event, but it will ultimately have as big an impact as the Internet."

Source: Adapted from "Skilled Work, Without the Worker" by John Markoff, *New York Times*, August 18, 2012, https://www.nytimes.com/2012/08/19/business/new-wave-of-adept-robots-is-changing-global-industry.html. Data updated in 2021.

Conclusion

Throughout this chapter, we learned that the compensation for factor inputs depends on the interaction between demand and supply. Resource demand is derived from the demand for the final product a firm produces, and resource

PRACTICE WHAT YOU KNOW

Bang for the Buck: When to Use More Capital or More Labor

How are all those dishes going to get clean?

Suppose Agaves is considering the purchase of a new industrial dishwasher. The unit cleans faster and uses less labor and less water, but it costs $10,000. Should the restaurant make the capital expenditure, or would it be better off saving the money and incurring higher operating costs? To help decide what Agaves should do, consider this information: the dishwasher has a usable life of five years before it will need to be replaced. It will save the restaurant $300 a year in water and 10 hours of labor each week. Human dishwashers are currently paid $8 per hour.

QUESTION: Should Agaves purchase the new dishwasher?

ANSWER: This is the kind of question every business wrestles with on a regular basis. And the way to answer it is very straightforward. A firm should invest in new capital when the value of the marginal product it creates per dollar spent is greater than the value of the marginal product per dollar spent on the next-best alternative. In other words, a firm should invest in new capital when the bang per buck exceeds that of labor and other investments. Let's compare the total cost of purchasing the dishwasher with the total savings. The total cost of the dishwasher is $10,000, but the savings are larger.

Item	Amount saved	Total for five years
Water	$300/year	$1,500
Labor	10 hours per week × $8/hour = $80/week × 52 weeks = $4,160/year	20,800
Total		22,300

The total savings over five years is $22,300. This makes the investment in the dishwasher the best choice!

supply depends on the other opportunities and compensation levels that exist in the market. As a result, the equilibrium prices and outputs in the markets for land, labor, and capital reflect, in large part, the forces of demand and supply.

In the next chapter, we examine income and poverty. As you will discover, there are many factors beyond the demand for and supply of workers that explain why some workers make more than others. For instance, wages also depend on the amount of human capital required for a job, as well as location, lifestyle choices, union membership, and the riskiness of the profession. Understanding these elements will deepen your understanding of why workers earn what they do.

It is true that outsourcing destroys some jobs in high-labor-cost areas, but it also creates jobs in low-labor-cost areas. As a result, it lowers the cost of manufacturing goods and providing services. This improved efficiency helps firms

· ECONOMICS *for* LIFE ·

Will Your Future Job Be Automated?

- The best way to ensure that your future job is not automated is to be valuable to your organization.
- Developing new skills and knowledge is integral to maintaining and increasing the value of the marginal product of your labor.
- When you are highly valued, it will be difficult to replace you.
- Low-skill occupations tend to be the most at risk.

When you select an academic major and learn a set of skills, you hope they will enable you to find stable employment. Finding stable employment becomes more challenging in an environment where labor is easily automated. So as you seek employment, you need to consider the long-term likelihood that your job could be replaced. To help you think about your future career, let's consider jobs that are likely to be automated and jobs that are more likely to still be done by humans.

Researchers estimate that nearly half of all U.S. jobs may be at risk in the coming decades, with lower-paid occupations among the most vulnerable. In 2017 Bloomberg.com created a tool within an article to "Find Out If Your Job Will Be Automated." It projected which jobs are at increased risk of being replaced, which included nearly 50% of all U.S. jobs. Type your current job or potential future occupation into the search bar (as shown in the figure) to see where the researchers peg the probability of your job being automated.

Source: Mark Whitehouse and Mira Rojanasakul, "Find Out If Your Job Will Be Automated," Bloomberg.com, July 7, 2017, https://www.bloomberg.com/graphics/2017-job-risk/.

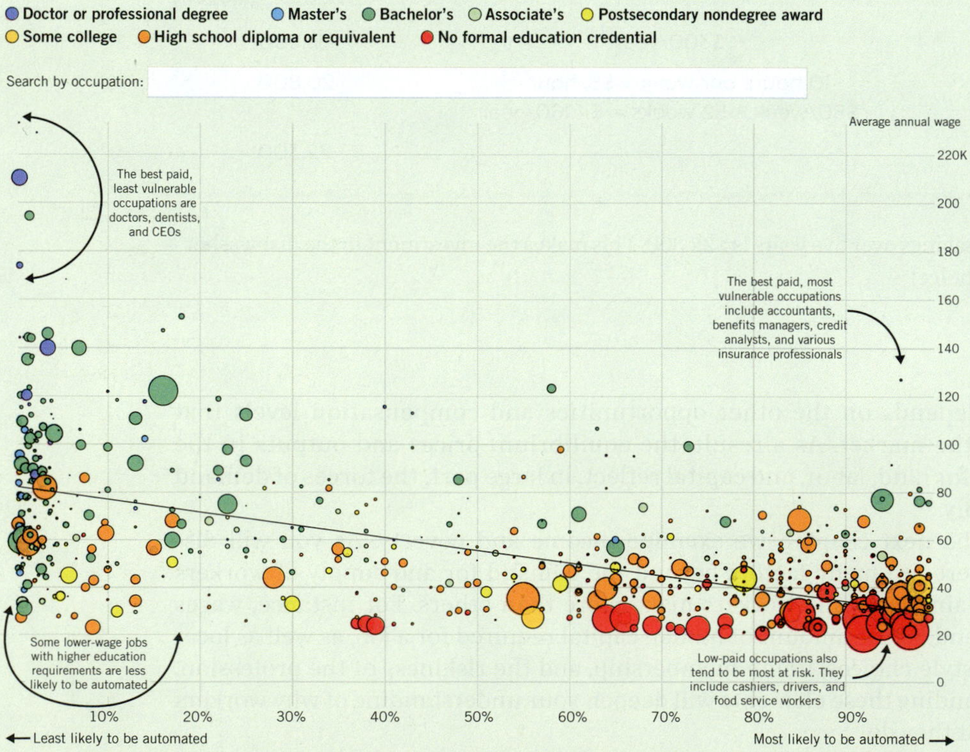

Might your job be automated? Follow the link in the feature above and enter your job in the search bar to find out.

that outsource by enabling them to better compete in the global economy. Outsourcing is one of the many ways firms adapt when labor costs rise. Firms also utilize more capital and deploy more technology when labor costs increase. And, workers must create a high value of the marginal product of labor to keep automation and robotics from making them superfluous as workers. ✷

- ANSWERING *the* BIG QUESTIONS -

What are the factors of production?

- Labor, land, and capital are the factors of production, or the inputs used in producing goods and services.

Where does the demand for labor come from?

- The demand for each factor of production is a derived demand that stems from a firm's desire to supply a good in another market. Labor demand is contingent on the value of the marginal product that is produced, and the value of the marginal product is equivalent to the firm's labor demand curve.

Where does the supply of labor come from?

- The supply of labor comes from the wage rate that is offered. Each worker faces the labor-leisure trade-off. At high wage levels, the income effect may become larger than the substitution effect and cause the labor supply curve to bend backward. Changes in the supply of labor can result from other employment opportunities, the changing composition of the workforce, immigration, and migration.

What are the determinants of demand and supply in the labor market?

- Labor markets bring the forces of demand and supply together in a wage signal that conveys information to both sides of the market. At wages above the equilibrium, the supply of workers exceeds the demand for labor. The result is a surplus of available workers that places downward pressure on wages until they reach the equilibrium wage, at which point the surplus is eliminated. At wages below the equilibrium, the demand for labor exceeds the available supply of workers, and a shortage develops. The shortage forces firms to offer higher wages to attract workers. Wages rise until they reach the equilibrium wage, at which point the shortage is eliminated.
- There is no definitive result for outsourcing of labor in the short run. In the long run, outsourcing moves jobs to workers who are more productive and enhances overall social welfare.

What role do land and capital play in production?

- Land and capital (as well as labor) are the factors of production across which firms compare the value of the marginal product per dollar spent. Firms seek to equalize the revenue per dollar spent on each input, thereby maximizing their efficiency.

CHAPTER PROBLEMS

Concepts You Should Know

backward-bending labor supply curve (p. 444)
derived demand (p. 437)
economic rent (p. 458)
income effect (p. 444)
marginal product of labor (p. 438)
monopsony (p. 455)
outsourcing of labor (p. 452)
substitution effect (p. 444)
value of the marginal product (VMP) (p. 439)

Questions for Review

1. Why is the demand for factor inputs a derived demand?
2. What rule does a firm use when deciding to hire an additional worker?
3. What are the two shifters of labor demand? What are the four shifters of labor supply?
4. What can cause the labor supply curve to bend backward?
5. If wages are below the equilibrium level, what would cause them to rise?
6. What would happen to movie stars' wages if all major film studios merged into a single firm, creating a monopsony for film actors?
7. If workers became more productive (that is, produced more output in the same amount of time), what would happen to the demand for labor, the wages of labor, and the number of workers employed?
8. How is economic rent different from rent seeking?
9. How does outsourcing affect wages and employment in the short run and in the long run?

Study Problems (*✱ solved at the end of this section*)

1. Maria is a hostess at a local restaurant. When she earned $8 per hour, she worked 35 hours per week. When her wage increased to $10 per hour, she decided to work 40 hours per week. However, when her wage increased again to $12 per hour, she decided to cut back to 37 hours per week. Draw Maria's supply curve. How would you explain her actions to someone who is unfamiliar with economics?
2. Would a burrito stand hire an additional worker for $15.00 an hour if that worker could produce an extra 30 burritos and each burrito made added $1.60 in revenues?

✱ 3. Pam's Pretzels has a production function shown in the following table. It costs Pam's Pretzels $80 per day per worker. Each pretzel sells for $3.

Quantity of labor	Quantity of pretzels
0	0
1	100
2	180
3	240
4	280
5	310
6	330
7	340
8	320

a. Compute the marginal product and the value of the marginal product that each worker creates.
b. How many workers should Pam's Pretzels hire?

4. Jimi owns a music school that specializes in teaching guitar. Jimi has a limited supply of rooms for his instructors to use for lessons. As a result, each successive instructor adds less to Jimi's output of lessons. The following table lists Jimi's production function. Guitar lessons cost $25 per hour.

Quantity of labor	Quantity of lessons (hours)
0	0
1	10
2	17
3	23
4	28
5	32
6	35
7	37
8	38

   a. Construct Jimi's labor demand schedule at each of the following daily wage rates for instructors: $75, $100, $125, $150, $175, $200.
   b. Suppose that the market price of guitar lessons increases to $35 per hour. What does Jimi's new labor demand schedule look like at the daily wage rates listed in part (a)?

5. In an effort to create a healthcare safety net, the government requires employers to provide healthcare coverage to all employees. What impact will this increased coverage have in the following labor markets in the short run?
   a. the demand for doctors
   b. the demand for medical equipment
   c. the supply of hospital beds

6. A million-dollar lottery winner decides to quit working. How can you explain this behavior using economics?

7. Illustrate each of the following changes with a labor supply and demand diagram. (Use a separate diagram for each part.) Diagram the new equilibrium point, and note how the wage and quantity of workers employed changes.
   a. There is a sudden migration out of an area.
   b. Laborers are willing to work more hours.
   c. Fewer workers are willing to work the night shift.
   d. The demand for California wines suddenly increases.

* 8. A football team is trying to decide which of two running backs (A or B) to sign to a one-year contract.

Predicted statistics	Player A	Player B
Touchdowns	7	10
Yards gained	1,200	1,000
Fumbles	4	5

The team has done a statistical analysis to determine the value of each touchdown, yard gained, and fumble to the team's revenue. Each touchdown is worth an extra $250,000, each yard gained is worth $1,500, and each fumble costs $75,000. Player A costs $3.0 million and player B costs $2.5 million. Based on their predicted statistics in the table above, which player should the team sign?

9. Farmers in Utopia experience perfect weather throughout the entire growing season, and as a result their crop is double its normal size. Draw a labor supply and demand diagram and use the diagram to explain how this bumper crop will affect each of the following.
   a. the price of the crop
   b. the marginal product of workers who harvest the crop
   c. the demand for the workers who harvest the crop

10. What will happen to the equilibrium wage of crop harvesters in Dystopia if the price of the crop falls by 50% and the marginal product of the workers increases by 25%?

11. Suppose that the current wage rate is $20 per hour, the rental rate of land is $10,000 per acre, and the rental rate of capital is $2,500. The manager of a firm determines that the value of the marginal product of labor is $400, the value of the marginal product of an acre of land is $200,000, and the value of the marginal product of capital is $4,000. Is the firm maximizing profit? Explain your response.

* 12. What country made the shirt you are wearing? Go ahead and check the tag and write down your answer. Even though we can't predict the exact country your shirt is from, there is a surprising answer in the Solved Problems section, which you should check out.

13. Why are most iPhones manufactured and assembled in China and then shipped to the United States, even though Apple was founded in California and most of Apple's workforce still reside in this country?

* 14. We saw that a backward-bending supply curve of labor can cause individual workers to work less at high wage levels. But one doesn't generally see market supply curves bend backward. Can you explain why we don't generally see that but see it here?

15. Use labor supply and demand curves to illustrate what will happen to the wages of each of the following as the United States ages.

a. teachers
b. dog walkers

Solved Problems

3. a.

Quantity of labor	Quantity of pretzels	Marginal product	Value of the marginal product
0	0	0	$0
1	100	100	300
2	180	80	240
3	240	60	180
4	280	40	120
5	310	30	90
6	330	20	60
7	340	10	30
8	320	−20	−60

b. The VMP of the fifth worker is $90 and each worker costs $80, so Pam should hire five workers. Hiring the sixth worker would cause her to lose $20.

8.

Predicted statistics	Player A	VMP of Player A	Player B	VMP of Player B
Touchdowns	7	$1,750,000	10	$2,500,000
Yards gained	1,200	1,800,000	1,000	1,500,000
Fumbles	4	−300,000	5	−375,000
Total value		3,250,000		3,625,000

Player A has a predicted VMP of $3.25 million and a cost of $3.0 million. Player B has a predicted VMP of $3.625 million and a cost of $2.5 million. Since player B's predicted VMP exceeds his salary by $1.125 million and player A's predicted VMP exceeds his salary by only $0.25 million, the team should sign player B.

12. Forget the country of origin on your tag—that is just where the final product was assembled. Your shirt is actually a product of a global supply chain that includes cotton seeds engineered in the United States, cotton grown in India, sewing machines manufactured in Germany, a collar lining from Brazil, and inexpensive labor from the place on your tag (where all the pieces were sewn together). The tag chronicles the end of your shirt's journey, so it gets the credit; but behind the scenes it takes a planet to make every shirt, and that is the surprising answer to the question.

14. In general, rising prices draw more suppliers. This is also true for wages in a particular market: as wages rise, more workers will choose that occupation, thereby ensuring that the market supply of labor increases. For the labor market as a whole, however, the supply of workers is more or less fixed (barring unrestricted immigration), and so there is a cap on the number of worker-hours per month that the market can supply. If wages continue to rise, the supply of labor becomes completely inelastic and the supply curve becomes vertical. This makes it possible for the income effect to begin to overtake the substitution effect if wages rise still further, as workers enjoy the same pay while working fewer hours.

CHAPTER

15

Income, Inequality, and Poverty

Do You Think Workers Are Paid Fairly?

If you wish to earn a sizable income, it is not enough to be good at something; that "something" needs to be an occupation that society values highly. What matters are your skills, what you produce, and the supply of workers in your chosen profession. How hard you work often has little to do with how much you get paid.

Just think about schoolteachers. Most put in long hours, including evenings spent grading papers and prepping for the next day's classes to help impact and influence their students' lives. The pay they earn can be pretty low relative to the time they spend on the job. One study noted that teachers are paid 20% less than other college graduates with similar education levels, and this gap has been widening since the 1990s.* Now compare this job in terms of an emerging work category also dependent upon influencing others, a social media influencer. Influencers with 100,000 or more followers can make between $40,000 and $100,000 a year, though their influence is typically more focused on trends and fads. Is this fair?

In this chapter, we continue our exploration of labor by examining income and inequality in labor markets.

*Economic Policy Institute, September 17, 2020, https://www.epi.org/publication/teacher-pay-penalty-dips-but-persists-in-2019-public-school-teachers-earn-about-20-less-in-weekly-wages-than-nonteacher-college-graduates/.

Nicki Dingraudo is both a teacher *and* a social media influencer. As *The Sprinkle Topped Teacher* on Instagram, she supplements her teaching income by providing other teachers with unique tools that make course preparation easier, which she promotes using social media.

Examining those at the upper and lower ends of the income ladder helps us explain the many forces that determine income, including the characteristics of successful wage earners and the roadblocks the poor encounter when they try to escape poverty. In addition, we explore the incidence of poverty, poverty trends, and measurement issues. Examining the poverty statistics, and understanding the causes of poverty, allows society to craft economic policies that more effectively help those in need.

· BIG QUESTIONS ·

- What factors determine wages?
- What is wage discrimination, and what are important factors that cause income inequality?
- How do we measure income inequality?
- How do economists analyze poverty?

What Factors Determine Wages?

The reasons why some workers get paid more than others are complex. We learned in Chapter 14 that the forces of supply and demand explain a large part of wage inequality. However, numerous additional factors contribute to differences in earnings. Various nonmonetary factors cause some occupations to pay higher or lower wages than supply and demand would seem to dictate. In some markets, a "winner-take-all" structure can lead to a small number of workers capturing a large majority of the total earnings.

Are you being paid enough to risk a fall?

The Nonmonetary Determinants of Wages

Some jobs have characteristics that make them more desirable or less desirable. Also, no two workers are exactly alike. Differences in jobs and worker ability affect the supply and demand of labor. In this section, we examine the nonmonetary determinants of wages, including compensating differentials, education and human capital, the life-cycle wage pattern, location and lifestyle, unions, and efficiency wages.

COMPENSATING DIFFERENTIALS Some jobs are more unpleasant, risky, stressful, inconvenient, or monotonous than others. If the characteristics of a job make it unattractive, firms must offer more to attract workers. For instance, roofing, logging, and deep-sea fishing are some of the most dangerous occupations in the world. Workers who do these jobs must be compensated with higher wages to offset the higher risk of injury. A **compensating differential** is the difference in wages offered to offset the desirability or undesirability of a job. If a job's characteristics make it unattractive, the compensating wage differential must be positive. The pay must make the job "worth it."

A **compensating differential** is the difference in wages offered to offset the desirability or undesirability of a job.

In contrast, some jobs are highly desirable. For example, restaurant critics sample a lot of great food, radio DJs spend the day playing their favorite music, and video game testers try beta versions before they are released. Some jobs are simply more fun, exciting, prestigious, or stimulating than others. In these cases, the compensating differential is negative and the firm offers lower wages. Video game testing is so desirable that, according to one online career guide to the industry, pay can start as low as $8 an hour for a temporary position.*

Incentives

EDUCATION AND HUMAN CAPITAL Many complex jobs require substantial education, training, and industry experience. Qualifying to receive the specialized education required for certain occupations—for example, getting into medical school—is often very difficult. Relatively few students are able to pursue these degrees. In addition, such specialized education is expensive, in terms of both tuition and forgone income.

Opportunity cost

The set of skills that workers acquire on the job and through education are collectively known as **human capital**. Unlike other forms of capital, investments in human capital accrue to the employee. As a result, workers who have high human capital can market their skills among competing firms. Engineers, doctors, and members of other professions that require extensive education and training can command high wages in part because the human capital needed to do those jobs is high. In contrast, low-skilled workers such as ushers, baggers, and sales associates earn less because the human capital required to do those jobs is quite low; it is easy to find replacements.

Human capital is the set of skills workers acquire on the job and through education.

Table 15.1 shows the relationship between education and pay. Increased human capital (education) qualifies a worker for jobs paying higher wages. Workers who earn advanced degrees have a higher marginal product of labor because their extra schooling has presumably given them additional skills for the job. But they also have invested heavily in education. Higher wages are a compensating differential that rewards additional education.

THE LIFE-CYCLE WAGE PATTERN Certain kinds of human capital are acquired on the job, over time. Workers who are just starting out have limited experience. As these workers age, they receive training and accumulate experience, making them more productive and able to earn higher wages. However, for older workers the gains from increased experience are eventually offset by diminishing returns. Consequently, wages typically peak when workers are in their early 60s and then slowly fall thereafter. This pattern, known as the **life-cycle wage pattern**, refers to the predictable effect age has on earnings over a person's working life.

The **life-cycle wage pattern** refers to the predictable effect age has on earnings over the course of a person's working life. Wages peak for people in their early 60s and then slowly fall thereafter.

*Game Industry Career Guide, accessed December 2021, https://www.gameindustrycareerguide.com/video-game-tester-salary/.

TABLE 15.1

The Relationship between Education and Pay

Education level	Median usual weekly earnings ($)
Advanced degree (doctoral, professional, master's)	$1,641
Bachelor's degree	$1,314
Associate's degree or some college	$915
High school diploma	$793
Less than a high school diploma	$620
All workers	$1,048

Source: U.S. Bureau of Labor Statistics, Current Population Survey, 2021.

Note: Data are for persons age 25 and over. Earnings are for full-time wage and salary workers.

ECONOMICS IN THE REAL WORLD

WHAT DOES A DEGREE SIGNAL?

An alternative perspective on the value of education is that earning a degree, particularly from a big-name institution, serves as a signal of a potential employee's potential. Students who have done well in college send a signal: they are able to learn quickly and perform well under stress. Further, prospective employers might assume that a student who gets into an elite college is sending another a signal—of the student's intelligence and willingness to work hard.

But does this signal work? It is possible to test the importance of signaling by looking at the returns to earning a college degree, controlling for institutional quality. At many elite institutions, the four-year price tag has reached extraordinary levels. For example, attending the University of Chicago, the most expensive institution in the country, cost $81,531 in 2019–2020.* What type of return do graduates of such highly selective (and expensive) institutions make on their sizable investments? And are those returns the result of a rigorous education or a result of the institution's reputation? It is difficult to answer this question because the students who attend more selective institutions are more likely to have higher earnings potential regardless of where they attend college. These students enter college as high achievers, a trait that carries forward into the workplace no matter where they attend school.

Is it the amount of education you obtain or other traits that determine your financial success?

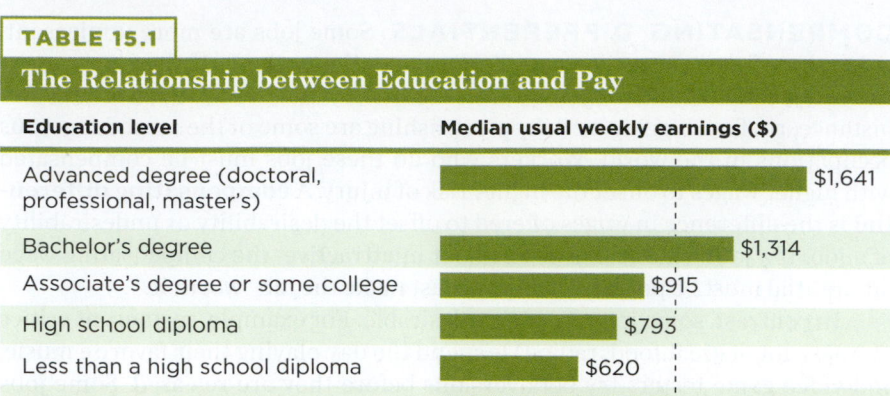

Economists Stacy Berg Dale and Alan Krueger examined the financial outcomes for over 6,000 students who were accepted or rejected by a comparable set of colleges.† They found that 20 years after graduation, students who had been

*Jessica Learish, "The 50 Most Expensive Colleges in America, Ranked," CBSNews.com, updated May 4, 2021, https://www.cbsnews.com/pictures/the-50-most-expensive-colleges-in-america/.

†Stacy Berg Dale and Alan B. Krueger, "Estimating the Payoff to Attending a More Selective College: An Application of Selection on Observables and Unobservables," *Quarterly Journal of Economics* 117, no. 4 (2002), http://www.jstor.org/stable/4132484.

accepted at more selective colleges but decided to attend a less selective college earned the same amount as their counterparts from more selective colleges. This finding indicates that actually attending a prestigious school is less important for future career success than the qualities that enable students to get *accepted* at a prestigious school.

Although Table 15.1 shows that additional education pays, the reason is not simply an increase in human capital. There is also a signal that employers can interpret about other, less observable qualities. For instance, Harvard graduates presumably learn a great deal in their time at school, but they were also highly motivated and likely to be successful even before they went to college. Part of the increase in income that is attributable to completing college depends on a set of other traits that the student already possessed, independent of the school or the degree.

How much more would you pay to live near here?

LOCATION AND LIFESTYLE For most people, sipping margaritas in Key West, Florida, sounds more appealing than living in Eureka, Nevada, along the most isolated stretch of road in the continental United States. Likewise, being able to see a show, visit a museum, or go to a Yankees game in New York City constitutes a different lifestyle from what you'd experience in Dodge City, Kansas. People find some places more desirable than others. So how does location affect wages? Where the climate is more pleasant, all other things being equal, people are willing to accept lower wages because the nonmonetary benefits of enjoying the weather act as a compensating differential. Similarly, jobs in places where the cost of living is significantly higher than elsewhere pay higher wages as a cost-of-living adjustment. The higher wage helps employees afford a quality of life similar to what they would enjoy if they worked in less expensive areas.

Choice of lifestyle is also a major factor in determining wage differences. Some workers are not particularly concerned with maximizing their income; instead, they care more about working for a cause. This is true for many employees of nonprofits or religious organizations or even for people who take care of loved ones. Others follow a dream of being a musician, writer, or actor. And still others are guided by a passion such as skiing or surfing. Indeed, many workers view their pay as less important than doing something they are passionate about.

UNIONS A **union** is a group of workers who bargain *collectively* for better wages and benefits by having a small committee of workers and union officials who represent all workers in negotiations with management. The union's leverage is the threat of a work stoppage, known as a **strike**, if an agreement is not reached. Unions are able to secure increased wages by creating significant market power over the supply of labor available to a firm. In effect, unions can raise wages because they represent labor, and labor is an indispensable input in the production process. Collective bargaining can be an effective negotiating tool when the threat of a walkout is credible.

A **union** is a group of workers who bargain collectively for better wages and benefits.

A **strike** is a work stoppage designed to aid a union's bargaining position.

U.S. law prohibits some unions from going on strike, including those representing many transit workers, some public school teachers, law enforcement officers, and workers in other essential services. If workers in one of these

Does going on strike result in higher wages?

industries reach an impasse in wage and benefit negotiations, the employee union is required to submit to the decision of an impartial third party, a process known as *binding arbitration*. The television show *Judge Judy* is an example of binding arbitration in action: two parties with a grievance agree in advance of the show to accept the verdict of Judith Sheindlin, who will hear their cases and make a decision on TV. The case stays out of the courts. Similarly, many Internet service providers require subscribers to settle any complaints through arbitration and not by means of a lawsuit.

The impact of unions in the United States has changed since the early days of unionization in the late 1800s. Early studies of the union wage premium found wages to be as much as 30% higher for unionized workers. At the height of unionization approximately 60 years ago, one in three jobs was a unionized position. Today, only about one in eight workers belongs to a union, and most empirical studies find the union wage premium to be between 10% and 20%. One factor driving the demise of unions in the United Sates has been the decline of the manufacturing sector. Another factor has been the relocation of many businesses from states where unions are strong to states where they have less clout.

EFFICIENCY WAGES In terms of paying wages, one approach stands out as unique. Ordinarily, we think of wages being determined in the labor market at the intersection of supply and demand. When the labor market is in equilibrium, the wage guarantees that every qualified worker can find employment. In other words, the equilibrium wage is the minimum market-clearing price in the market for labor. However, some firms willingly pay **efficiency wages**, which are *higher* than the equilibrium wage.

Efficiency wages are wages higher than equilibrium wages, offered to increase worker productivity.

Why would a business do that? Surprisingly, many economists see efficiency wages as a way to increase profits. For starters, they feel that above-equilibrium wages should (1) attract more high-quality job applicants, (2) encourage good employees, whom the firm has spent money training, to stick around instead of taking a job someplace else, and (3) give every worker a greater incentive to work hard and not get fired. Firms using these wages maintain they will lead to increased **productivity**, the effectiveness of effort as measured in terms of the rate of output per unit of input.

Productivity is the effectiveness of effort as measured in terms of the rate of output per unit of input.

Further, these firms reason that well-paid workers are more likely to be loyal workers, who feel good about their firm and take pride in doing their jobs well. Workers who feel loyalty toward the firm outperform workers, even highly competent ones, who are just punching the clock for a check. This makes the firm yet more profitable. If the gains in overall labor productivity are higher than the increased cost associated with efficiency wages, the result is greater profit for the firm. This positive result means that despite seemingly contradicting the logic of the market, efficiency wages can often make good economic sense. For any company playing the long game, efficiency wages can be a small price to pay to establish a loyal, highly productive workforce.

Want your workers to work harder? Pay them more than your competitors do!

Do efficiency wages work? Or is a firm better off paying equilibrium wages and being content with less-committed workers and higher turnover? Economists Natalia Emanuel and

TABLE 15.2

The Key Nonmonetary Determinants of Wage Differences

Determinant	Impact on wages	In pictures
Compensating differentials	Some workers are eager to have jobs that are more fun, exciting, prestigious, or stimulating than others. As a result, they are willing to accept lower wages. Conversely, jobs that are unpleasant or risky require higher wages.	
Human capital	Many jobs require substantial education, training, and experience. As a result, workers who acquire additional amounts of human capital can command higher wages.	
Location and lifestyle	When the location is desirable, the compensating wage will be lower. Similarly, when employment is for a highly valued cause, wage is less important. In both situations, the compensating wage will be lower.	
Unions	Because firms cannot do without labor, unions can threaten a strike to negotiate higher wages.	
Efficiency wages	The firm pays above-equilibrium wages to help reduce slacking, decrease turnover, and increase productivity.	

Emma Harrington have studied the question empirically. In their research, they examined wages and productivity among warehouse workers at an unnamed Fortune 500 online retailer. The workers received a pay increase from $16 to $18. They found that for every $1 increase in wages, employees moved 6% more boxes per hour and employee turnover dropped by 19%. The cost savings from not having to hire and train new employees, combined with improved productivity, more than paid for itself, boosting the company's bottom line in addition to improving employees' lives.*

Incentives

We have seen that wages are influenced by factors that include compensating differentials, human capital, the life-cycle wage pattern, location and lifestyle, union membership, and the presence of efficiency wages. Table 15.2 summarizes these nonmonetary determinants of income differences.

Winner-Take-All

In 1930, baseball legend Babe Ruth demanded and received a salary of $80,000 from the New York Yankees. This would be approximately $1 million in today's dollars. Babe Ruth earned a lot more than the other baseball players of his era. When told that President Herbert Hoover earned less than he was asking for,

*Emma Harrington and Natalia Emanuel, "The Payoffs of Higher Pay: Elasticities of Productivity and Labor Supply with Respect to Wages," Working Paper, updated December 28, 2020, https://scholar.harvard.edu/eharrington/publications/payoffs-higher-pay-elasticities-productivity-and-labor-supply-respect-wages.

PRACTICE WHAT YOU KNOW

Forbes magazine named Cisco Systems the 2021 best company to work for—not surprising, considering that it places a focus on employee well-being.

Efficiency Wages: Which Company Pays an Efficiency Wage?

You are considering two job offers. Company A is well known and respected and offers a year-end bonus based on your productivity relative to other workers. This could substantially boost your income, but the company's base wage is relatively low. Company B is not as well known, but its wages are higher than the norm in your field. This company does not offer a year-end bonus.

QUESTION: Which company, A or B, is the efficiency wage employer?

ANSWER: Efficiency wages are a mechanism that some companies use to reduce turnover, encourage teamwork, and create loyalty. Company A's bonus plan will reward the best producers, but the average and less-than-average workers will become frustrated and leave. Company A is not paying efficiency wages; it is simply using incentives tied to productivity. Company B is the efficiency wage employer because it pays every worker somewhat higher wages to reduce turnover.

CHALLENGE QUESTION: Target, Wegmans, and Costco offered their associates hazard pay during the COVID-19 outbreak, in addition to their regular wages. Was this an efficiency wage?

Incentives

ANSWER: The hazard pay is a compensating differential (higher pay for an increased chance of contracting the virus while working). But it could also be viewed as an efficiency wage—an incentive to reduce turnover and boost productivity, and perhaps a morale-booster for workers who were feeling unappreciated. During the lockdown, firms paying higher wages were at a competitive advantage in retaining workers or finding more productive workers from a larger-than-normal applicant pool.

Ruth famously said, "I had a better year than he did." In fact, the annual salary of the president of the United States ($400,000 a year) is far less than that of top professional athletes, movie stars, college presidents, and many corporate CEOs.

Why does the most important job in the world pay less than jobs with far less value to society? Part of the answer involves compensating differentials. Being president of the United States means being the most powerful person in the world, so paid compensation is only a small part of the benefit of holding that office, relative to the power and exclusivity of the position. The other part of the answer has to do with the way labor markets function. Pay at the top of most professions is subject to a form of competition known as **winner-take-all**. This term does not refer to whether a person wins or loses, but rather to situations where extremely small differences in ability among different people lead to sizable differences in compensation. This compensation structure has been common in professional sports and in the entertainment industry for many years, but it also exists in the legal profession, medicine, journalism, investment banking, fashion design, and corporate management.

Winner-take-all occurs when extremely small differences in ability lead to sizable differences in compensation.

Incentives

In a winner-take-all market, being a little bit better than one's rivals can be worth a tremendous amount. For example, in 2021, baseball star Fernando Tatis Jr. earned $25 million playing for his team, the San Diego Padres. As good as Tatis is, he is not six times better than an average major-league baseball player, who makes $4 million. Nor is he a thousand times better than a typical minor-league player, who earns just a few thousand dollars a month while waiting and hoping for the call-up to the majors. Most minor-leaguers run almost as fast, and play their positions almost as well, as their major-league counterparts who make hundreds of times more money.

Fernando Tatis Jr. has 25 million reasons a year to practice, but not all professional baseball players are as fortunate.

What Is Wage Discrimination, and What Are Important Factors That Cause Income Inequality?

When workers with the same ability as others are not paid the same because of their race, ethnic origin, sex, age, religion, or some other group characteristic, we say they are experiencing **wage discrimination**. Because of its importance for individuals and for policymakers, economists study the topic of wage discrimination by trying to understand its effects in the past and to help address wage discrimination today. In this section, we explore some of their observations.

Wage discrimination occurs when workers with the same ability as others are not paid the same because of their race, ethnic origin, sex, age, religion, or some other group characteristic.

Looking at the Data

Table 15.3 presents median weekly earnings in the United States by sex, race or ethnic group, and age. Looking at the data, we see large earnings differences across many groups in U.S. society. In particular, female workers earn 19% less than their male counterparts. In 2009, President Obama signed the Lilly Ledbetter Fair Pay Act, which gives victims of wage discrimination more time to file a complaint with the government. The act is named after a former Goodyear employee who sued the company in 2007. The courts determined that she was paid 15% to 40% less than her male counterparts. The fact that a major U.S. corporation was violating the Equal Pay Act of 1963 almost 50 years after its passage was a poignant reminder that wage discrimination still occurs in our society.

For every $1 men make, women make, on average, 81 cents.

The problem can be insidious. When executives at the software company Salesforce challenged their CEO to conduct a pay equity audit of the company, he readily agreed. He was confident that his male and female workers were being paid equally. When the results came back, he later wrote, "they were tough to swallow. Salesforce did have a pay gap; glaring differences were scattered throughout every division, department, and geographical region. The virus, in other words, was everywhere."* Today, Salesforce conducts an annual equity audit.

*Monica Langley and Mark Benioff, "How Salesforce Closed the Pay Gap between Men and Women," (book excerpt), *Wired*, October 15, 2018, https://www.wired.com/story/how-salesforce-closed-pay-gap-between-men-women/.

TABLE 15.3

Median Weekly Earnings by Group

Group	Median earnings in 2020	Percentage difference within each group
Males	$1,094	–
Females	$899	−18%
White	$1,024	–
Black	$799	−21%
Asian	$1,281	+27%
Hispanic	$779	−23%
Early-career workers (25–34)	$922	−20%
Mid-career workers (35–54)	$1,122	–
Late-career workers (55–64)	$1,113	−1%

Source: U.S. Bureau of Labor Statistics, 2021, https://www.bls.gov/news.release/pdf/wkyeng.pdf.

ECONOMICS IN THE REAL WORLD

THE EFFECTS OF BEAUTY ON EARNINGS

According to research that spans the labor market from the law profession to college teaching and in countries as different as the United States and China, beauty matters. How much? You might be surprised. As related by economist Daniel S. Hamermesh in his book *Beauty Pays*, beautiful people make as much as 10% more than people with average looks, while those whose looks are considered significantly below average may make as much as 25% below normal. Talent and hard work do matter, of course, but there is a significant "beauty premium."

The influence of beauty on wages can be viewed in two ways. First, beauty can be seen as a marketable trait that has value in many professions. Actors, fashion models, restaurant servers, and litigators all rely on their appearance to make a living, so it is

Zendaya, Priyanka Chopra, Lenny Kravitz—three of the decade's most beautiful people.

not surprising that beauty is correlated with wages in those professions. If beautiful people are more productive in certain jobs because of their beauty, then attractiveness is simply a measure of the value of the marginal product they generate. In other words, being beautiful is a form of human capital the worker possesses.

However, a second interpretation finds evidence of bias. If employers prefer "beautiful" people as employees, even in professions where appearance has nothing to do with productivity, then part of the earnings increase associated with beauty might reflect that preference. In addition, the success of workers who are more beautiful could also reflect the preferences of customers who prefer to buy products and services from attractive people.

Because it is impossible to determine whether the beauty premium is a result of increased productivity or of bias, we have to acknowledge the possibility that the truth, in many situations, could be a little bit of both.

While most economists acknowledge that bias plays a role in wage discrimination, they believe that broader factors related to human capital play major roles, too. For example, women and men often hold different types of jobs, and certain jobs pay more than others. Higher wages in jobs such as road work and construction reflect in part a compensating differential for exposure to extreme temperatures, bad weather, and other dangers, and men are more likely to work in these jobs. Additionally, more women than men take time off from work to raise a family, meaning that women ultimately have fewer years of work experience, put in fewer paid work hours per year, are less likely to work a full-time schedule, and leave the labor force for longer periods. In contrast, men normally take less, if any, time off to raise children. When COVID-19 forced schoolchildren into remote-learning situations, mothers were much more likely than fathers to take time off from work so they could stay home and supervise.* In the long term, these differences tend to lead to lower levels of human capital and overall lower wages for women.

Economist Claudia Goldin's careful examination of the gender wage gap data suggests that the gap stems not from gender bias, but from work design. She found that people who work the longest and least flexible hours make the highest salaries per unit of time—and those people tend to be men, because women are more likely to be juggling caregiving responsibilities.† This research suggests that one way to help close the gap would be for employers to be more flexible about work hours and to pay part-time workers a pro-rated share of what full-time workers earn. This added flexibility should also help all workers juggle careers, family, and other interests. The work of economists Francine Blau and Lawrence Kahn explains some of the important causes of the gender pay gap. Their research finds that 62% of the pay gap is attributable to the first six causes listed in Figure 15.1. Unmeasured factors—including gender bias—account for the other 38% of the gap.‡

*Emma Charlton, "COVID-19 Lockdown Hits Working Mothers Harder than Fathers," World Economic Forum, June 4, 2020, https://www.weforum.org/agenda/2020/06/covid19-lockdown-working-mothers-gender-gap/; Douglas Clement, "Jobs or Kids: Parenting during the Pandemic," Federal Reserve Bank of Minneapolis, July 8, 2020, https://www.minneapolisfed.org/article/2020/jobs-or-kids-parenting-during-the-pandemic.

†Claudia Goldin, "Hours Flexibility and the Gender Gap in Pay," Scholar.harvard.edu, April 2015, https://scholar.harvard.edu/files/goldin/files/goldin_equalpay-cap.pdf.

‡Francine D. Blau and Lawrence M. Kahn, "The Gender Wage Gap: Extent, Trends, and Explanations," 2017, *Journal of Economic Literature, 55*(3): 789–865.

FIGURE 15.1

What Do We Know about What Causes the Gender Pay Gap?

Studies show that a large portion of the gender pay gap comes from factors that cannot be measured.

Source: Journal of Economic Literature, 2017.

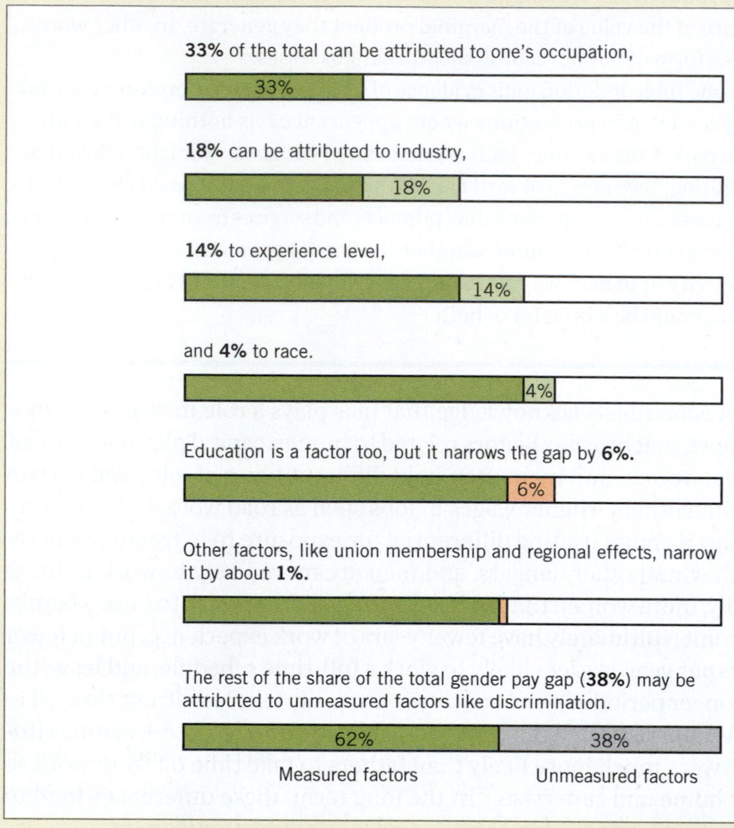

33% of the total can be attributed to one's occupation,
33%
18% can be attributed to industry,
18%
14% to experience level,
14%
and **4%** to race.
4%
Education is a factor too, but it narrows the gap by **6%.**
6%
Other factors, like union membership and regional effects, narrow it by about **1%.**
The rest of the share of the total gender pay gap (**38%**) may be attributed to unmeasured factors like discrimination.
62%
38%
Measured factors
Unmeasured factors

ECONOMICS IN THE REAL WORLD

WAGE INEQUALITY: WHAT UBER CAN TEACH US ABOUT THE GENDER PAY GAP

Uber pays drivers based on an algorithm that is gender-blind. Driver pay is determined by a pay structure tied to output (rides completed) and a surge multiplier (for peak demand times). Researchers studied data from over 1 million Uber drivers and found that men earned 6% more per hour than women. Perplexed, they dug deeper into the data to find the causes of the gender pay gap. What they found was that the gender gap could be explained by three factors: experience (men, on average, have worked for Uber longer), working hours (men tend to work later at night and more often in less-safe areas), and driving speed (men drive faster, on average, than women). One of the researchers, Rebecca Diamond, sums up the findings nicely:

> Uber shows that even when you strip away all of this stuff, you definitely don't go to a gender gap of zero, and you still have this important experience component, where you work more and you learn about how to do the job better, and you get better at doing the job. So you can't say it's all going to be perfect in this new gig economy. [But it's] not because of discrimination, or problems in how we compensate workers. It really is about working more hours and gaining knowledge on the job, and differences in gender preferences.

Do male Uber drivers earn more than females? Read more to find out.

	All	Men	Women
Weekly earnings	$376.38	$397.68	$268.18
Hourly earnings	$21.07	$21.28	$20.04
Hours per week	17.06	17.98	12.82
Trips per week	29.83	31.52	21.83
Six-month attrition rate	68.1%	65.0%	76.5%
Number of drivers	1,873,474	1,361,289	512,185
Number driver/weeks	24,832,168	20,210,399	4,621,760
Number of Uber trips	740,627,707	646,965,269	93,662,438

Source: Cody Cook et al., "The Gender Earnings Gap in the Gig Economy: Evidence from over a Million Rideshare Drivers," *Review of Economic Studies* 88, no. 5, October 2021, https://doi.org/10.1093/restud/rdaa081.

Other factors are thought of as *structural* factors that characterize social and economic arrangements on a large scale. These may be considered macroeconomic factors, but they have very real implications at the micro level. Some structural factors that foster inequality come down to differences of social or economic status or privilege. Four in particular are inequities in education, the role of wealth, the role of corruption, and occupational crowding.

INEQUITIES IN EDUCATION Differences in education aren't just about the degrees people choose to earn. There are also systemic inequities. These days, few countries put up formal barriers to education based on gender, ethnicity, or religion. But other sources of inequity exist in most nations, including the United States. For instance, the low quality of some inner-city schools can limit the educational attainment of students, many of whom are minorities. Economists expect the wage disparities among groups to decrease as these educational differences (and the resulting differences in human capital) become less pronounced.

THE ROLE OF WEALTH How much does a privileged background matter? According to controlled studies, children born into wealthy households earn about 10% more than children born into low-income households. Wealth gives a child from an affluent home access to better education, private tutoring, a healthier diet, and many other intangible benefits that provide a head start in life. These early advantages often lead to higher levels of human capital that translate into higher wages. Differences in wealth also reinforce systemic inequities in education, because wealthier communities have more money to spend on teacher salaries, computers, facilities like theaters and athletic fields, and extracurricular activities like science camps.

ECONOMICS IN THE REAL WORLD

RACE AND REAL ESTATE

Here is a disturbing tale about race-based discrimination. In September of 2021, *USA Today* reported on how an Ohio family put their home on the market and quickly got a good offer, above $500,000. But the property appraisal came back over $40,000 short of what it needed to be for the buyer's mortgage loan to go through. When the sellers pointed out to the bank that the appraisal report contained false information, the bank wouldn't budge.

The sellers, an African American family, had a pretty good idea what the problem was. When they needed another appraisal for a second interested buyer, the sellers "whitewashed" their home by replacing all the family photos with photos borrowed from a white neighbor. Then they asked the neighbor to pose as the homeowner when the new appraiser showed up. Sure enough, the second appraisal came in more than $90,000 above the first one.

Sadly, this was not an isolated incident. One study found that appraisals undervalue homes in Black neighborhoods by an average of almost $50,000. Some of this is no doubt due to biases of individual appraisers. However, the U.S. real estate market has a long history of being systematically unfair to Black homeowners and home buyers. "Redlining" was the once-common practice of labeling entire Black or immigrant neighborhoods as too risky for banks to invest in. That practice is illegal now, but systemic bias against Black home buyers lives on. One recent study of the mortgage lending industry found that its computer algorithms were as much as 80% more likely to reject a Black loan applicant compared with a comparably qualified white one. Basically, the algorithms look race-neutral, but they pick up on subtle differences between Black and white households.*

*Emmanuel Martinez and Lauren Kirchner, "The Secret Bias Hidden in Mortgage-Approval Algorithms," The Markup, August 25, 2021, https://themarkup.org/denied/2021/08/25/the-secret-bias-hidden-in-mortgage-approval-algorithms.

THE ROLE OF CORRUPTION One principle of the rule of law is that public officials must perform their duties without favoritism, and without using their position for personal gain. However, the rule of law is stronger in some societies than in others. Many countries suffer from widespread corruption. Consider Colombia, a country sometimes best known for its drug trade, corrupt political parties, and large underground economy. All told, these factors are estimated to drain away at least 1% of Colombia's potential economic output, and possibly several percentage points higher.† This may not seem like a lot, but on the scale of a country it has huge implications.

Corruption can play a large role in income inequality. In societies where corruption is common, working hard or being innovative is not enough; getting ahead often requires bribing officials to obtain business permits or to ward off competitors. Moreover, when investors cannot be sure their assets are safe from government seizure or criminal activity, they are less likely to develop a business. Under political systems that are subject to bribery and other forms of corruption, dishonest people benefit at the expense of the poor. Corruption drives out legitimate business opportunities and magnifies income inequality.

†Universidad Externado de Colombia, "10 Facts You Did Not Know about Corruption in Colombia," August 17, 2018, https://dernegocios.uexternado.edu.co/negociacion/10-cosas-que-no-sabias-sobre-la-corrupcion-en-colombia/; Steven Grattan, "Colombia's Rampant Corruption a Hot Topic in Presidential Vote," Reuters, June 15, 2018, https://www.reuters.com/article/us-colombia-election-corruption/colombias-rampant-corruption-a-hot-topic-in-presidential-vote-idUSKBN1JB252.

OCCUPATIONAL CROWDING Another factor deserving particular attention is **occupational crowding**—the phenomenon of relegating a group of workers to a narrow range of jobs in the economy. To understand how occupational crowding works, imagine a community named Utopia with only two types of jobs: a small number in engineering and a large number in secretarial services. Furthermore, men and women are equally proficient at both occupations, and everyone in the community is happy to work either job. Under these assumptions, we would expect the wages for engineers and secretaries to be the same.

Was your kindergarten teacher male or female?

Occupational crowding is the phenomenon of relegating a group of workers to a narrow range of jobs in the economy.

Now imagine that not everyone in Utopia has the same opportunities. Suppose we roll back the clock to a time when women in Utopia are not allowed to work as engineers. Women who want to work can only find employment as secretaries. As a result of this occupational crowding, workers who have limited opportunities (women, in this example) find themselves competing with one another, as well as with the men who cannot get engineering jobs, for secretarial positions. As a result, wages fall in secretarial jobs and rise in engineering. Because only men can work in engineering, they are paid more than their similarly qualified female counterparts, who are crowded into secretarial positions and earn less. Furthermore, because women who want to work can only receive a low wage as a secretary, many effectively decide to stay at home and produce nonmarket services, such as child-rearing. These services have a higher value to the women who make this choice than the wages they could earn as secretaries. Of course, women today are not restricted to secretarial jobs, so how do women fare in the most common jobs? Figure 15.2 compares men's and women's wages by common job categories in the United States.

Why do occupational crowding and wage differentials continue? Rigidity in changing occupations, social customs (including ones driven by prejudice), and personal preferences are all part of the explanation. However, many economists see a change coming. Because more women than men attend colleges and universities, women are now primarily responsible for expanding the supply of workers in most fields. As the supply of workers expands, the net effect will likely be lower wages in traditionally male-dominated jobs. At the same time, traditionally female-dominated jobs will see rising wages as women leave those jobs for better opportunities. The net result is that the wage gap will narrow over time.

A CAUTIOUSLY OPTIMISTIC OUTLOOK Because few employers will admit to bias, researchers can only infer the amount of bias-driven discrimination after first correcting for observable differences. The unobservable differences that remain are presumed to reflect bias. While the number is hotly debated, most economists estimate that bias accounts for less than 5% of observed wage differences. They also see many signs of improvement.

Though it is still real, the gender gap is shrinking. In 1960 women in the workforce earned, on average, 60 cents for every dollar men earned. Today women earn 82 cents for every dollar men earn, and the gap continues to close by about half a cent each year. In addition, women are no longer clustered in less rigorous academic programs than men, so women are more prepared to get jobs that pay better. In 2021, for example, more women than men in the United States received doctoral degrees. The number of women at every level of

FIGURE 15.2

The Gender Pay Gap

The following graph shows a selection of the occupations with the largest and smallest gender earnings gap, as reported by the U.S. Department of Labor. For more data on this topic, visit https://www.dol.gov/agencies/wb/data/earnings.

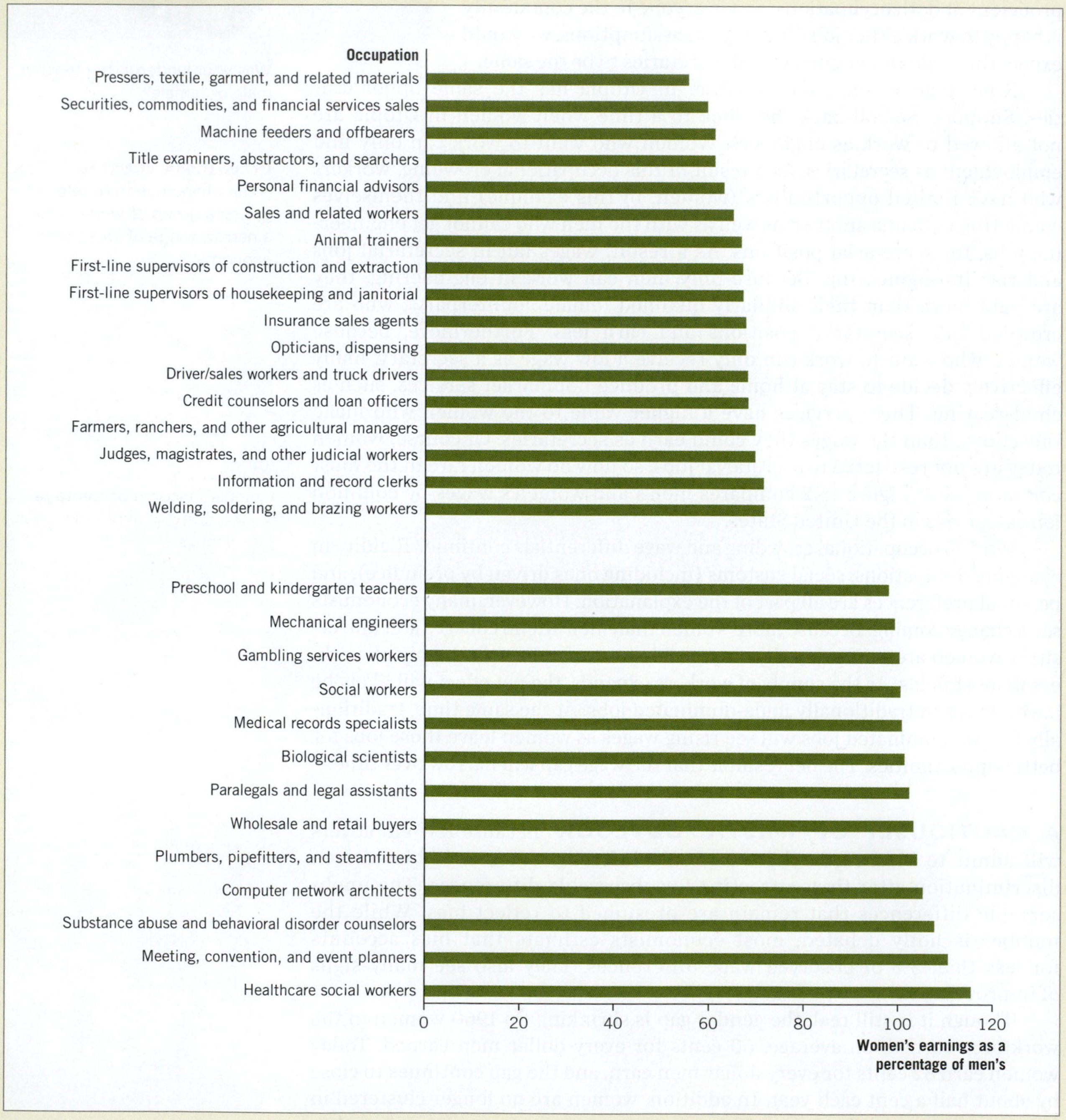

academia has been rising for decades. There are now three women for every two men enrolled in postsecondary education. Over time, this education advantage may offset some of the other factors that have kept men's wages higher than women's.

How Do We Measure Income Inequality?

How do we measure income inequality in a country? To answer this question, we begin by looking at income inequality in the United States. Economists study the distribution of household income in the United States by quintiles, or five groups of equal size, ranging from the poorest fifth (20%) of households to the top fifth. Figure 15.3 shows the data from 2019.

According to the U.S. Bureau of the Census, the poorest 20% of households makes just 3.1% of all income earned in the United States. The next quintile, the second fifth, earns 8.3% of income. In other words, fully 40% of U.S. households (the bottom two quintiles) account for only 11.4% of earned income. The middle quintile earns 14.1%, the second-highest quintile, 22.7%, and the top quintile, 51.9%. Being a pie chart, Figure 15.3 vividly shows the wide disparity between the percentage of total U.S. income earned by the poorest households (3.1%) and by the richest households (51.9%). If we divide the percentage of income earned by households in the top fifth (51.9%) by the percentage of income earned by households in the bottom fifth (3.1%), we get an **income inequality ratio** of about 17. Looking at the numbers this way, we can say that households in the top fifth have approximately 17 times the income of those in the bottom fifth. Viewing that number in isolation makes the amount of income inequality in the United States seem large. However, we have not yet adjusted the data to reflect

The **income inequality ratio** is calculated by dividing the top quintile's income percentage by the bottom quintile's income percentage.

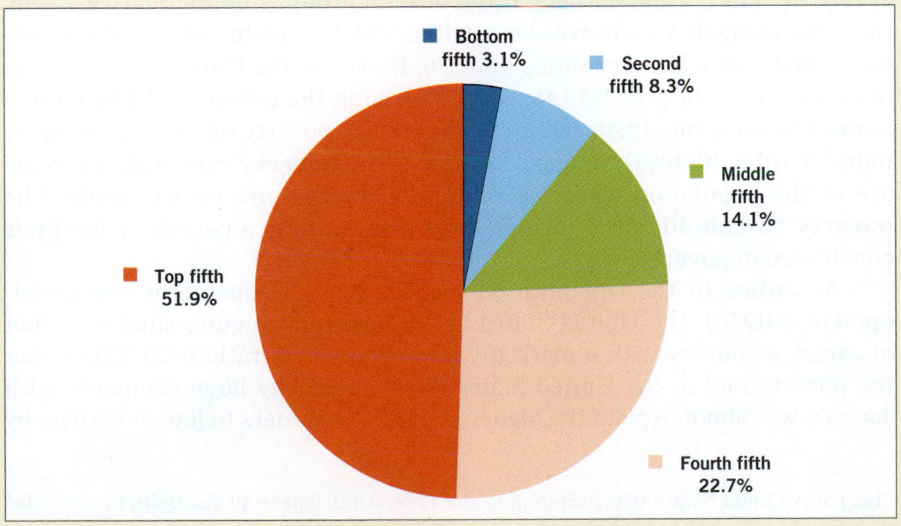

FIGURE 15.3

The Distribution of Income in the United States by Quintile

The top fifth of income earners makes 51.9% of all income, an amount greater than the combined incomes of the four remaining quintiles. Income declines across the quintiles, falling to 3.1% in the lowest fifth.

Source: Statista, 2019 data.

TABLE 15.4

Income Inequality Ratios (after Controlling for Taxes and Subsidies) in Selected Countries

Country	Inequality ratio (richest 20% ÷ poorest 20%)
Iceland	3.5
Canada	4.9
Japan	6.2
United Kingdom	6.5
United States	8.4
Mexico	8.6
Chile	10.3
Costa Rica	14.5

Source: OECD data, https://data.oecd.org/inequality/income-inequality.htm.

disposable income. When taxes and subsidies are included, the U.S. income inequality ratio drops to 8.4.*

To provide some perspective, Table 15.4 compares the income inequalities in selected countries using disposable income. As you can see, the U.S. income inequality ratio of 8.4 after controlling for taxes and subsidies is high compared with that of other highly developed nations.

UNDERSTANDING OBSERVED INEQUALITY Translating income inequality into a number, as we've done with the income quintiles, can mask the true nature of income inequality. In this section, we step back and consider what the income inequality ratio can tell us and what it cannot tell us.

Because the income inequality ratio measures the success of top earners against that of bottom earners, if the bottom group is doing relatively well, then the inequality ratio will be smaller, which explains why many highly developed countries have ratios under 6. However, the United States has an inequality ratio of over 8 (8.4). What is driving the difference? The United States has many highly successful workers and a poverty rate similar to those found in other highly developed countries. The **poverty rate** is the percentage of the population whose income is below the poverty threshold. The **poverty threshold** is the income level below which a person or family is considered impoverished.

The **poverty rate** is the percentage of the population whose income is below the poverty threshold.

The **poverty threshold** is the income level below which a person or family is considered impoverished.

According to the Organization for Economic Cooperation and Development (OECD), the United States has a poverty rate quite similar to that of Japan, a country with a markedly lower inequality ratio (6.2). Given that the poverty rate in the United States is not unusually large compared with Japan's, we cannot explain the higher ratio of top earners to lowest earners by

*Tax Policy Center, "T20-0039: Average Effective Federal Tax Rates—All Tax Units, by Expanded Cash Income Percentile, 2020," TPC, Urban Institute & Brookings Institution, February 26, 2020, https://www.taxpolicycenter.org/model-estimates/baseline-share-federal-taxes-february-2020/t20-0039-average-effective-federal-tax.

pointing to the percentage of poor people. Rather, it is the relative success of the top income earners in the United States that causes the markedly higher inequality ratio. In other words, there are more high-income earners in the United States than in Japan.

High levels of income inequality also occur when the poorest are *really* poor. For example, there are many successful people in Mexico, Chile, and Costa Rica. The problem in these countries is that the success of some people is benchmarked against the extreme poverty of many others. Therefore, high inequality ratios can be a telltale sign of a serious poverty problem. Suppose that the poorest quintile of the population in Chile has an average disposable income of $6,100, while those in the top quintile have a disposable income of $60,800. The income inequality ratio is $60,800/$6,100 = 10.0. By comparison, consider Canada. If the poorest quintile of the population in Canada has an average disposable income of $12,500, while those in the top quintile earn an average of $60,800, the income inequality ratio there is $60,800/$12,500 = 4.9. In both countries, the top quintile is doing equally well, but the widespread poverty in Chile produces an alarming income inequality ratio. In this example, the inequality ratio signals a significant poverty problem.

In sum: A high income inequality ratio can occur if people at the bottom earn very little or if the income of high-income earners is much greater than the income of others. The key point to remember is that even though income inequality ratios give us some idea about the degree of inequality in a society, a single number cannot fully reflect the sources of the underlying differences in income.

THE GINI INDEX An alternative way of representing income inequality across countries is to use the **Gini index**, which represents the income distribution of a nation's residents. Its value fluctuates between 0 (no income inequality) and 100 (extreme income inequality). If every individual's income is equal in a society, the Gini index (or Gini coefficient) is 0. A nation where one individual gets all the income, while everyone else gets nothing, would have a Gini index of 100 (Figure 15.4).

The **Gini index** is a measurement of the income distribution of a country's residents.

The **Lorenz curve** is a visual way of representing the Gini index. A perfectly equal distribution of income is represented by the green 45-degree line in Figure 15.5. As the income distribution becomes more unequal, the Lorenz curve, represented by the orange line in Figure 15.5, shifts downward and to the right. The Gini index is calculated by taking the area between the two curves, shaded and labeled A, and dividing that amount by the total of area A plus area B. Area A represents the amount of income *inequality* in society, while area B represents the amount of income *equality* in society. Calculating the Gini index gives us a number between 0 and 1. Economists multiply this number by 100 to represent the score as a whole number between 0 and 100.

The **Lorenz curve** is a visual representation of the Gini index.

The Lorenz curve is especially helpful for seeing how income inequality has changed over time. Income inequality has become greater in the United States over the last 50 years. The blue line in Figure 15.6 shows the Lorenz curve in 1970. The red line shows the Lorenz curve in 2019. Notice that the red Lorenz curve from 2019 shifted down and to the right, away from the perfect income equality line, indicating more income inequality in 2019 compared to 1970. The Gini index in 1970 was 34; by 2019, it had climbed to 40.

FIGURE 15.4

World Bank Gini Index from 2014 to 2019

Countries color-coded in green have the lowest Gini index, while those in shades of red have the highest Gini index.

Source: World Bank, https://data.worldbank.org/indicator.

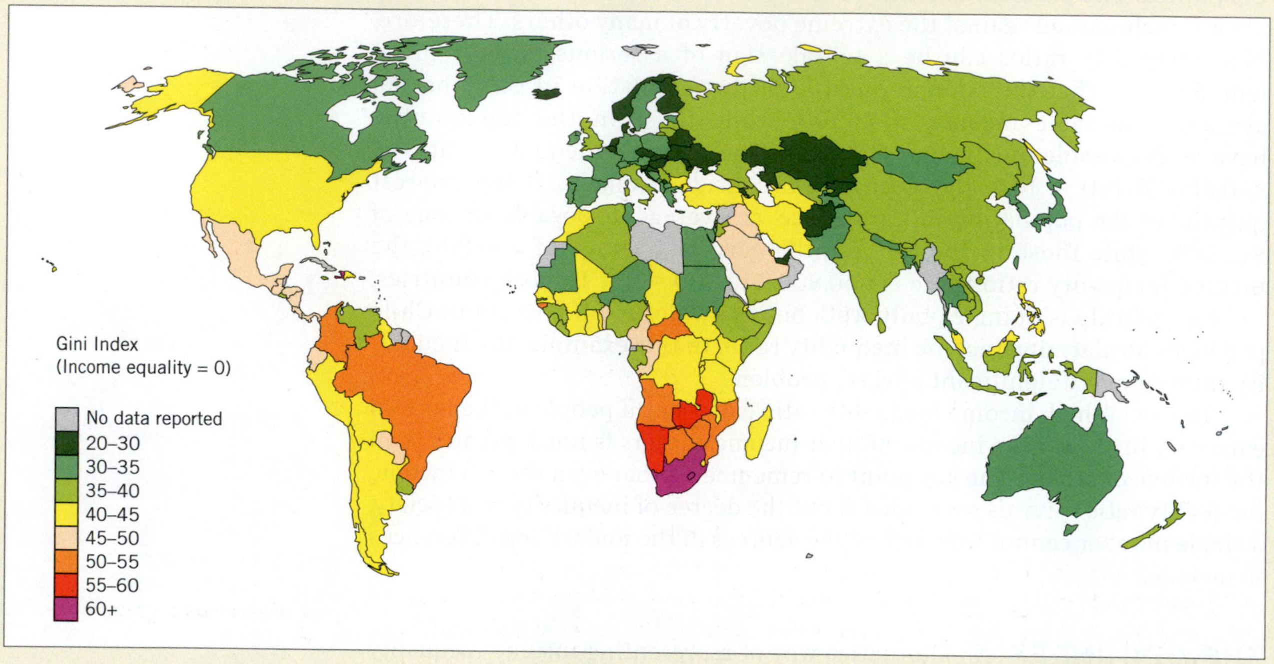

FIGURE 15.5

The Gini Index and the Lorenz Curve

The green curve indicates complete income equality. As income inequality increases, the orange curve shifts down and to the right.

Source: M. Tracy Hunter, https://commons.wikimedia.org/wiki/File:2014_Gini_Index_World_Map,_income_inequality_distribution_by_country_per_World_Bank.svg.

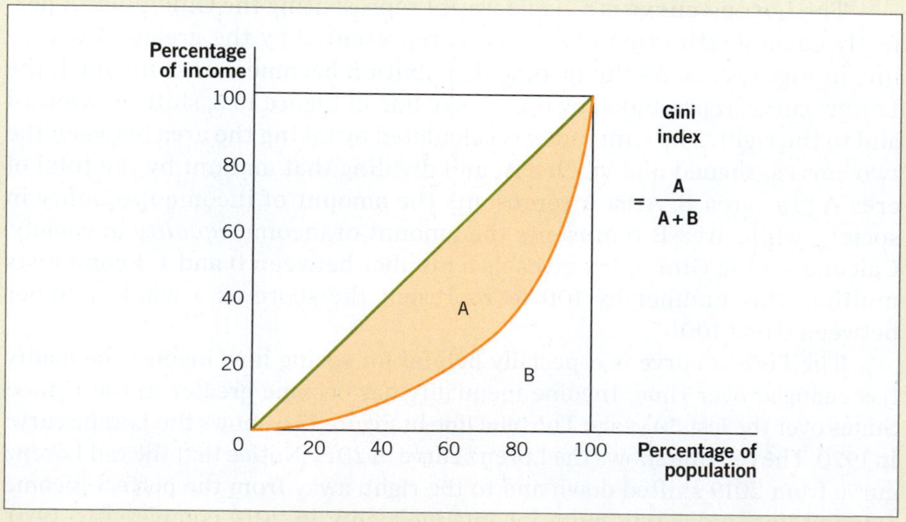

FIGURE 15.6

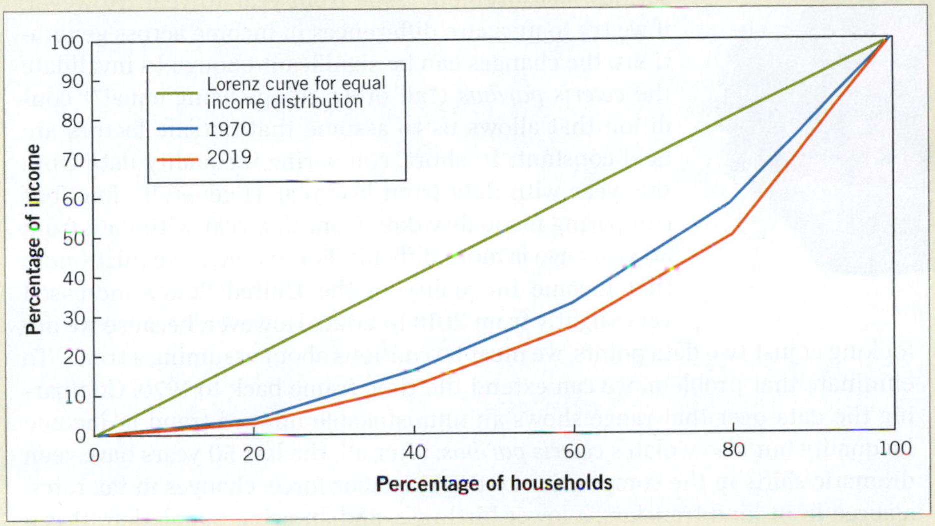

Lorenz Curves for the United States, 1970 and 2019

The Gini index in the United States was 34 in 1970. By 2019, it had climbed to 40, indicating an increase in income inequality.

DIFFICULTIES IN MEASURING INCOME INEQUALITY The Gini index and the Lorenz curve leave out some potentially important information. For example, they do not account for **in-kind transfers**—that is, goods and services that are given to the poor instead of cash. Examples of in-kind services are government-subsidized housing and the Subsidized Nutrition Assistance Program (SNAP) that provides food-purchasing assistance for low- and no-income people living in the United States. In addition, the data do not account for unreported or illegally obtained income. Because less developed countries generally have larger **underground economies** than developed countries do, their income data are even less reliable.

In-kind transfers are transfers (mostly to the poor) in the form of goods or services instead of cash.

Underground economies are composed of markets in which goods or services are traded illegally.

Many economists also note that income data alone do not capture the value created from goods and services produced in the household. For example, if you mow your own lawn or grow your own vegetables, those activities have a positive value not expressed in your income data. In less developed countries, many households engage in very few market transactions and produce a large portion of their own goods and services. If we do not count these, our comparison of data with other countries will overstate the amount of inequality present in the less developed countries. Finally, the number of workers per household and the median age of each worker differ from country to country. When households contain more workers or those workers are, on average, older and therefore more experienced, comparing inequality across countries is more likely to be misleading.

A NEW STUDY CLAIMS IF STAY-AT-HOME MOMS WERE PAID...
FOR WHAT ALL THEIR WORK WAS WORTH, THEY'D MAKE $130,000 A YEAR!
GEE, MAYBE I SHOULD CONSIDER STAYING AT HOME, TOO!
www.comics.com
© 2005 by NEA, Inc.

Growing your own vegetables is an activity not counted in official income data.

Individually, none of these shortcomings poses a serious measurement issue from year to year. However, if we try to measure differences in income across generations, the changes can be significant enough to invalidate the *ceteris paribus* ("all other things being equal") condition that allows us to assume that outside factors are held constant. In short, comparing inequality data from this year with data from last year is generally fine, but comparing inequality data from this year with data from 50 years ago is more difficult. For instance, we might note that income inequality in the United States increased very slightly from 2018 to 2020. However, because we are looking at just two data points, we must be cautious about assuming a trend. To eliminate that problem, we can extend the time frame back to 1970. Comparing the data over that range shows an unmistakable upward trend in income inequality but also violates *ceteris paribus*; after all, the last 50 years have seen dramatic shifts in the composition of the U.S. labor force, changes in tax rates, a surge in in-kind transfers, a lower birthrate, and an aging population. It is a complex task to determine the impact of these changes on income inequality. Economist Anne Case and Nobel Prize winner Angus Deaton write of the Gini coefficient: "By collapsing the whole rainbow of the income distribution into a single statistical point of white light, it necessarily conceals much of great interest."*

Finally, the standard calculations and models we have discussed assume that the income distribution is a direct reflection of a society's well-being. However, we must be very careful not to infer too much about how well people are living based on their income alone. Indeed, income analysis does not offer a complete picture of human welfare. In Chapter 16, we will see that income is only one factor determining human happiness and well-being. People also value leisure time, nonwage benefits, a sense of community, safety from crime, and social networks, among other things.

Income Mobility

Income mobility is the ability of workers to move up or down the economic ladder over time.

When workers have a realistic chance of moving up the economic ladder, each person has an incentive to work harder and invest in human capital. **Income mobility** is the ability of workers to move up or down the economic ladder over time. As Figure 15.7 shows, income mobility in the United States is low compared to peer countries. Strikingly, income mobility is almost twice as high in Canada as in the United States.

Why does this matter? In other countries with more income mobility, the expected number of generations it would take the offspring from a household in the bottom quintile to reach the mean income in society is anywhere from two to four. In the United States, that number is five. In other words, people with low incomes in the United States are more likely to continue to have low incomes as they age, compared with people in many other countries.

*Angus Deaton and Anne Case, "Rebottling the Gini: Why This Headline Measure of Inequality Misses Everything That Matters," *Prospect*, updated March 2020, https://www.prospectmagazine.co.uk/economics-and-finance/rebottling-the-gini-why-this-headline-measure-of-inequality-misses-everything-that-matters.

SNAPSHOT

Income Inequality around the World

"The rich get richer, and the poor get poorer" is a simple yet profound way to think about income inequality. As top earners make more and bottom earners make less, the inequality rate increases. It's a combination of these factors, not just extreme wealth or extreme poverty, that leads to huge gaps between those at the very top and those at the very bottom.

$$\text{Inequality Ratio} = \frac{\text{Income Earned by Top 20\%}}{\text{Income Earned by Bottom 20\%}}$$

- Income Earned by Top 20%
- Income Earned by Bottom 20%
- Inequality Ratio
- Poverty Rate

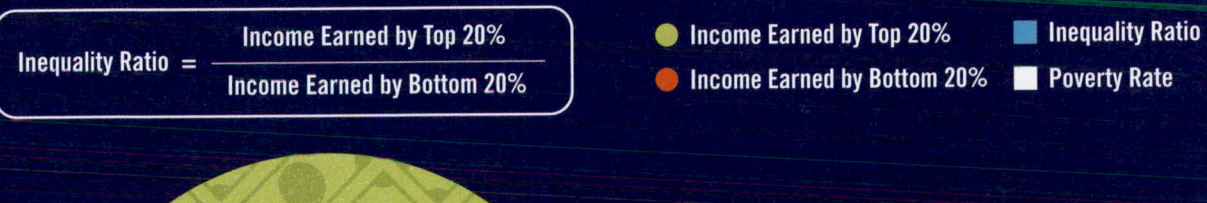

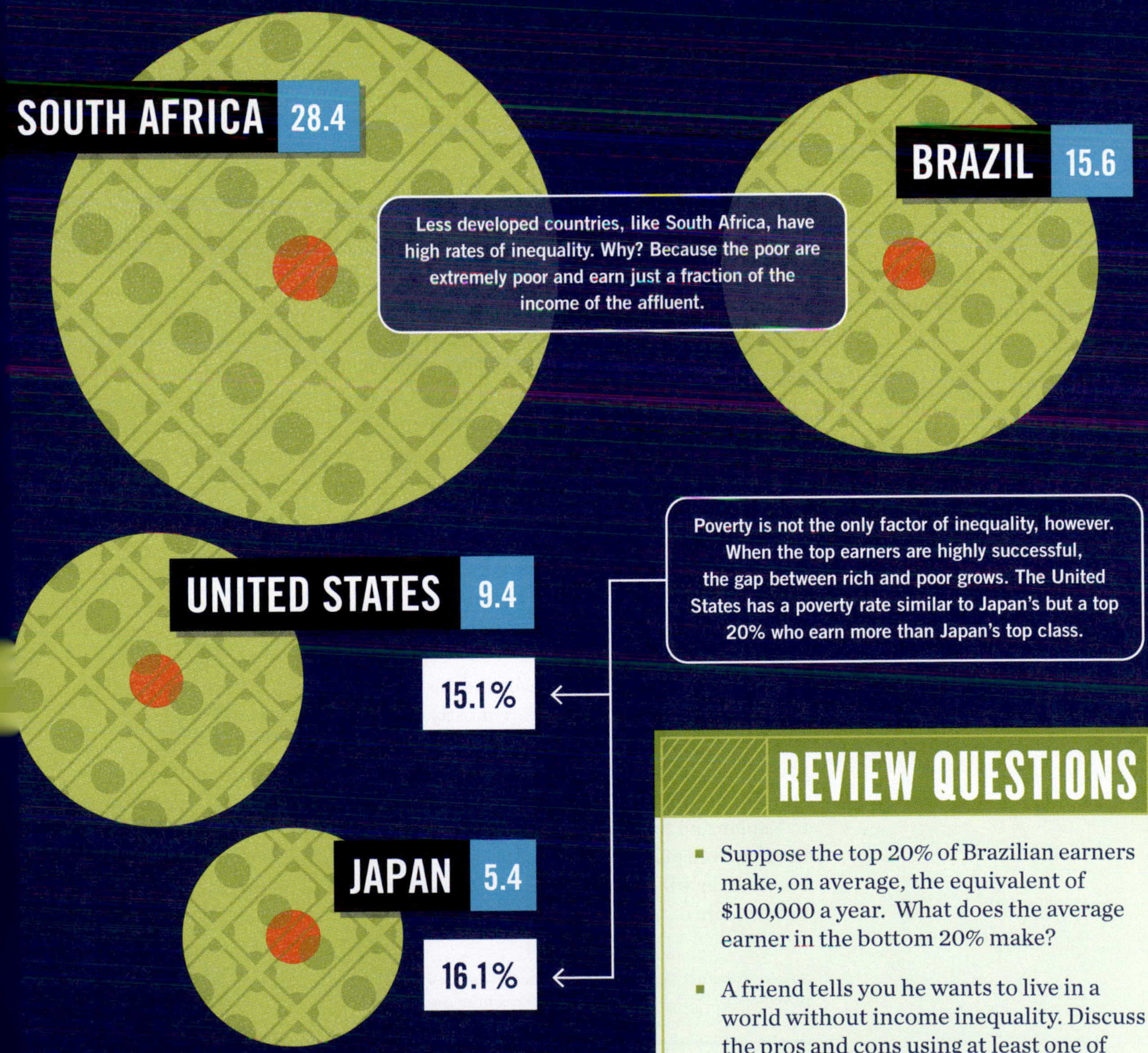

SOUTH AFRICA 28.4
Less developed countries, like South Africa, have high rates of inequality. Why? Because the poor are extremely poor and earn just a fraction of the income of the affluent.
BRAZIL 15.6
Poverty is not the only factor of inequality, however. When the top earners are highly successful, the gap between rich and poor grows. The United States has a poverty rate similar to Japan's but a top 20% who earn more than Japan's top class.
UNITED STATES 9.4
15.1%
JAPAN 5.4
16.1%

Sources: United Nations Development Programme, Human Development Reports 2018; CIA World Factbook

REVIEW QUESTIONS

- Suppose the top 20% of Brazilian earners make, on average, the equivalent of $100,000 a year. What does the average earner in the bottom 20% make?
- A friend tells you he wants to live in a world without income inequality. Discuss the pros and cons using at least one of the five foundations of economics from Chapter 1.

FIGURE 15.7

Income Mobility in the United States Compared with Other Countries

How likely is a child from a low-income family to reach the top income quintile as an adult? Less likely in the United States than in the United Kingdom, Denmark, or Canada.

Sources: Brookings; DB Global Research.

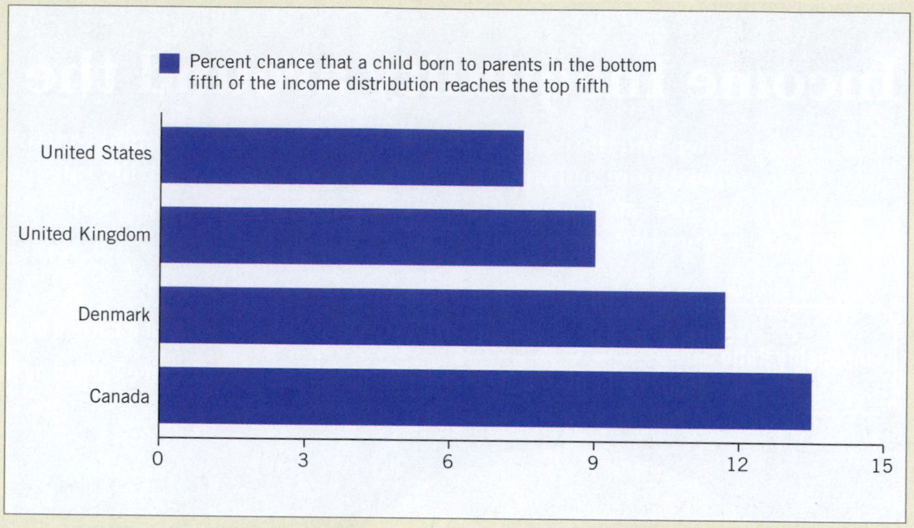

ECONOMICS IN THE REAL WORLD

WHAT ABOUT TAXING "WEALTH"?

Are taxes fair? Do the proverbial One Percent pay enough? Economists disagree! Some think that the rich naturally get richer and richer, essentially because money attracts more money. For example, economists Thomas Piketty and Emmanuel Saez have published an influential study making the case that fast growing investments give wealthy dynasties huge advantages over everyone else. These economists support a tax on wealth, meaning a tax on things you own, as opposed to a tax on income you earn. Currently, the only wealth tax most Americans are familiar with is the property tax paid by homeowners. Piketty and Saez would like to see a wealth tax that targets the 75,000 richest households in America. They would pay taxes not just on their big houses but on their investment holdings—stocks, bonds, and so on. Currently, financial assets are only taxed when they're sold.

Economists like Steve Kaplan and Joshua Rauh have a different take. They argue that the extremely rich are mostly creating their wealth. Modern technology is a big driver of this phenomenon. "You can scale your business using technology, and you can use people in India and China and all over the world," says Kaplan. "You couldn't do that as effectively 30 years ago." According to Kaplan and Rauh, a wealth tax will discourage entrepreneurs and people in finance from pursuing the successes the rest of us benefit from. They also think a wealth tax will be hard to administer and will lead to highly creative forms of tax avoidance.

Source: Howard R. Gold, "Never Mind the 1 Percent. Let's Talk About the 0.01 Percent," *Chicago Booth Review*, November 29, 2017, https://www.chicagobooth.edu/review/never-mind-1-percent-lets-talk-about-001-percent.

ECONOMICS *in the* MEDIA

Income Mobility

THE SIMPSONS: EXAMINING ALL OF HOMER'S JOBS

The long-running cartoon series *The Simpsons* features Homer Simpson as a lazy doofus who has somehow managed to work an amazing variety of jobs over the years. In 2017, the website *Vox* did an economic analysis of all the jobs Homer ever held over the course of 600 episodes, from 1989 to 2016. The 100-plus jobs ranged from convenience store clerk, bodyguard, and ordained minister to more exotic gigs such as a moonshine taste tester and a cannonball performance artist (for both of which Homer's practically bomb-proof stomach was an asset). Sometimes Homer caught a break and temporarily ended up in a high-paying position. Other times, his pay was even lower than what he earned in his regular job as a safety inspector ($37,500 in today's money per Homer's paycheck in Season 7) at the local nuclear power plant.

Having identified a hundred or so of Homer's jobs and assigned each a salary, *Vox*'s team then tracked the fluctuations in Homer's average earnings over time. They found that he stays stuck in the lower-middle-class income quintile; he has stagnated like much of the middle class during the time of the show's run. In many ways that is not surprising, since Homer lacks a college education and is not a very motivated worker. After three decades, he remains right where he started: a reminder of why income mobility (or in this case the lack of it) matters so much. When people are able to move across the income quintiles easily, long-term poverty is less likely.

Source: Zachary Crockett, "What Homer Simpson's 100+ jobs Tell Us about America's Middle Class," Vox.com, updated September 15, 2016, https://www.vox.com/2016/9/6/12752476/the-simpsons-homer-middle-class.

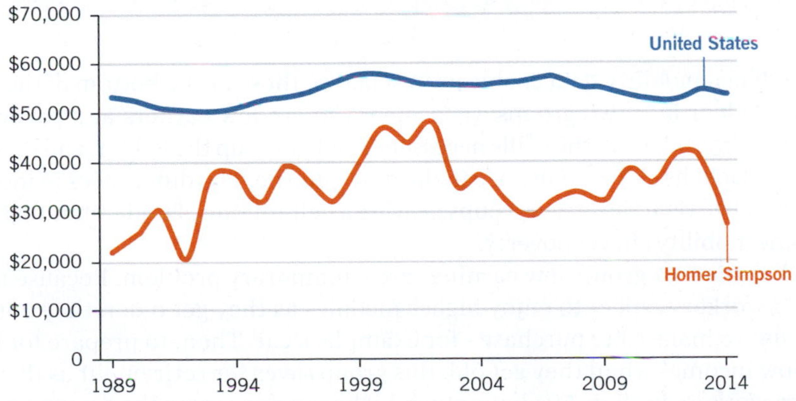

Homer Simpson's fictional pay places him in the lower-middle class.

PRACTICE WHAT YOU KNOW

The good life: so near, yet so far.

Income Inequality: The Beginning and End of Inequality

Consider two communities, Alpha and Omega. Alpha has 10 residents, 5 who earn $90,000 and 5 who earn $30,000. Omega also has 10 residents, 5 who earn $250,000 and 5 who earn $50,000.

QUESTION: What is the income inequality ratio in each community?

ANSWER: To answer this question, we must use quintile analysis. Because there are 10 residents in Alpha, the top 2 earners represent the top quintile and the lowest 2 earners represent the bottom quintile. Therefore, the degree of income inequality in Alpha using quintiles analysis is $90,000 ÷ $30,000, or 3. In Omega, the top 2 earners represent the top quintile and the lowest 2 earners represent the bottom quintile. Therefore, the degree of income inequality in Omega is $250,000 ÷ $50,000, or 5.

QUESTION: Which community has the more unequal distribution of income, and why?

ANSWER: Omega has the more unequal distribution of income because the quintile analysis yields an income inequality ratio of 5, versus 3 for Alpha.

QUESTION: Can you think of a reason why someone might prefer to live in Omega?

ANSWER: Each rich citizen of Omega earns more than each rich citizen of Alpha, and each poor citizen of Omega earns more than each poor citizen of Alpha. Admittedly, there is more income inequality in Omega, but there is also more income across the entire income distribution. Thus, one might prefer Omega if the absolute amount of income is what matters more, or one might prefer Alpha if relative equality is what matters more.

Official mobility data enable us to separate those at the bottom of the economic ladder into two groups: (1) people who are low earners at a particular point in time but have the skills necessary to advance up the ladder, and (2) people who lack the skills to advance to the next quintile. The differences in income mobility between these two groups provide a helpful way of understanding how income mobility affects poverty.

For the first group, low earnings are a temporary problem. Because most young workers expect to enjoy higher incomes as they get older, they borrow in order to make a big purchase—for example, a car. Then, to prepare for having low incomes when they get old, this group saves for retirement as they get older; workers in their 50s have much higher savings rates than young workers and retirees. On reaching retirement, earnings fall; but if the worker has saved enough, retirement need not be a period of low consumption. This is one aspect of the life-cycle wage pattern: changes in borrowing and saving patterns over one's life smooth out the consumption pattern. In other words, for many people, a low income at a point in time does not necessarily reflect a low standard of living.

The second group, which we now turn our attention to, is in an entirely different situation. They do not escape the lowest quintile but instead spend their entire lives near or below the poverty threshold.

How Do Economists Analyze Poverty?

Poverty remains an ongoing challenge in the United States. According to the Census Bureau, close to 11% of all households are below the poverty threshold. To help us understand the issues, we begin with poverty statistics. Then, once we understand the scope of the problem, we examine possible policy solutions.

Those below the poverty threshold are unable to make ends meet.

The Poverty Rate

For the last 50 years, the U.S. Bureau of the Census has been tracking the poverty rate, or the percentage of the population whose income is below the poverty threshold. To keep up with inflation, the poverty threshold is adjusted each year for changes in the overall level of prices in the economy. However, an individual family's threshold is calculated to include only the money that represents income earned by family members in the household. It does not include in-kind transfers, nor are the data adjusted for cost-of-living differences in the family's specific geographical area. For these reasons, poverty thresholds are a crude yardstick. Figure 15.8 shows the poverty rate for households in the United States from 1960 to 2020.

In 1964, Congress passed the Equal Opportunity Act and a number of other measures designed to fight poverty. Despite those initiatives, the rate of poverty today is comparable to what it was 50 years ago. This result is surprising, because the U.S. economy's output has roughly doubled in that time. One would have hoped that the economy's progress could be enjoyed at the bottom of the economic ladder as well as at the top. Unfortunately, the stagnant poverty rate suggests that the gains from economic growth over that period have accrued to

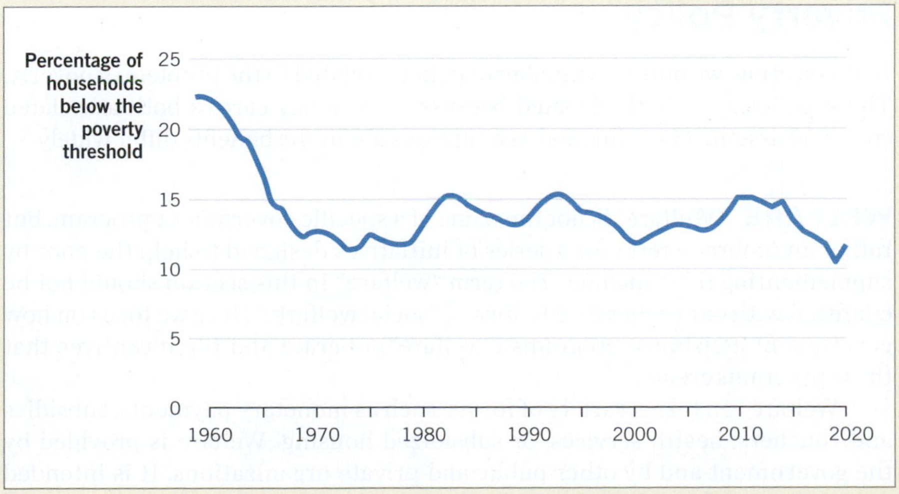

FIGURE 15.8

Poverty Rate for U.S. Households, 1960–2020

Poverty rates for households fluctuated from 1960 through 2020.

Source: U.S. Bureau of the Census.

TABLE 15.5

The Poverty Rate for Various Groups, 2019

Group	Poverty rate (percentage)
Age	
Children (under 18)	14
Adults (18–64)	9
Elderly (65 or older)	9
Race/Ethnicity	
White	9
Asian	7
Hispanic	16
Black	19
Type of household	
Married couple	4
Male head only	12
Female head only	23

Source: U.S. Bureau of the Census, 2019.

households in the middle and upper quintiles, rather than to the poor. Poverty has remained persistent, in part because many low-income workers lack the necessary skills to earn a living wage and, at the same time, investments by firms in automation and technology have reduced the demand for these workers.

Table 15.5 illustrates that children, female heads of household, and certain minorities disproportionately feel the incidence of poverty. When we combine at-risk groups—for example, Black or Hispanic women who are heads of household—the poverty rate can exceed 40%.

Poverty Policy

Trade-offs

In this section, we outline a number of policies related to the problem of poverty. These policies are hotly debated because each policy carries both associated costs and assumed benefits, and assumptions about the benefits differ widely.

WELFARE "Welfare" is not the name of a specific government program, but rather an umbrella term for a series of initiatives designed to help the poor by supplementing their income. The term "welfare" in this section should not be confused with our earlier discussions of "social welfare." Here we focus on how government assistance programs ("welfare") operate and the incentives that these programs create.

Welfare can take a variety of forms, such as monetary payments, subsidies and vouchers, health services, or subsidized housing. Welfare is provided by the government and by other public and private organizations. It is intended to help the unemployed, those with illnesses or disabilities that prevent them from working, the elderly, veterans, and households with dependent children.

An individual's eligibility for welfare is often limited to a set amount of time and is valid only as long as the recipient's income remains below the eligibility cutoff. Examples of welfare programs include Temporary Assistance for Needy Families (TANF), which provides financial support to families with dependent children; the Supplemental Security Income (SSI) program, which provides financial support to those who are unable to work; and the Subsidized Nutrition Assistance Program (SNAP), which gives financial assistance to those who need help to purchase basic foods.

IN-KIND TRANSFERS In addition to financial assistance, the poor can receive direct assistance in the form of goods and services. The government provides health care to the poor through Medicaid. **Medicaid** is a joint federal and state program that helps low-income individuals and households pay for the costs associated with long-term medical care. Communities or cities often provide organized assistance like shelters, and local community food banks, religious organizations, and private charities like Habitat for Humanity and Toys for Tots all provide in-kind benefits to the poor.

Medicaid is a joint federal and state program that helps low-income individuals and households pay for the costs associated with long-term medical care.

The idea behind in-kind transfers is that recipients might use cash transfers to buy "temptation goods," such as alcohol, cigarettes, or other nonessentials. In-kind transfers can be targeted at essential services. However, not everyone agrees that in-kind transfers are a good idea. Skeptics view them as paternalistic, inefficient, and disrespectful. They argue that cash payments allow recipients to make the choices that best fit their needs. Defenders of cash transfers also point to recent studies by organizations like the World Bank, which find that recipients spend relatively little on temptation goods.*

THE EARNED INCOME TAX CREDIT (EITC) The Earned Income Tax Credit (EITC) is a tax credit designed to encourage low-income workers to work more. At very low income levels, EITC offers an incentive to work by supplementing earned income with a tax credit of approximately $6,000 a year. The amount is determined, in part, by the number of dependent children in the household and the location. Once a family reaches an income level above its earnings threshold, EITC is phased out, and workers gradually lose the tax credit. Under many welfare and in-kind transfer programs, the qualifying income is a specific cutoff point; an individual or household is either eligible or not. In contrast, EITC is gradually reduced, which means that workers do not face a sizable disincentive to work as the program is phased out.

EITC, which was established in 1975, helps over 25 million families, making it the largest poverty-fighting tool in the United States. The government estimates that EITC payments are sufficient to lift more than 5 million households out of poverty each year. In addition, EITC creates stronger work incentives than those found under traditional antipoverty programs that critics argue discourage recipients from working.

Incentives

THE MINIMUM WAGE The minimum wage is often viewed as an antipoverty measure. However, we learned in Chapter 6 that the minimum wage

*David K. Evans and Anna Popova, "Cash Transfers and Temptation Goods: A Review of Global Evidence," World Bank Policy Research Working Paper, May 2014, https://documents1.worldbank.org/curated/en/617631468001808739/pdf/WPS6886.pdf.

ECONOMICS *in the* MEDIA

Poverty

THE HUNGER GAMES

Where would you rather live, the Capitol district or District 12?

The *Hunger Games* series of dystopian-themed books written by Suzanne Collins (and later made into feature films) chronicles the life of Katniss Everdeen, a teenager living in the post-apocalyptic country of Panem, which has been divided into twelve districts. Life in each district is unique, with vast differences in wealth, resources, and production. The wealthy Capitol district governs the economy by heavily regulating all aspects of life in the other poverty-stricken districts. One of the methods of control is the annual Hunger Games, where a boy and a girl are chosen from each district to battle to the death. The survivor earns extra food and a life of luxury.

Katniss Everdeen lives in District 12, an area with striking similarities to the coal mining Appalachian region of the United States. In District 12, inhabitants work in the mines. They struggle to make ends meet, often go hungry, and have a permeating sense of desolation because there is no escape.

The rising income inequality we see in the United States is not as extreme as we find in *The Hunger Games*, but it does remind us that we need to pay attention to income inequality in our society. When an income distribution becomes too unequal, the result is often political and social instability. *The Hunger Games* challenges us to think about economic freedom, the role of institutions in creating growth, the extent to which governments should regulate economic activity, and how policy decisions made today will shape the future world.

Trade-offs

creates trade-offs. Firms often respond to higher minimum wages by hiring fewer workers and utilizing more capital-intensive production processes, such as self-checkout lanes and robotic production. Because the minimum wage does not guarantee employment, the most it offers to a low-skill worker is a slightly larger paycheck. At the same time, a higher minimum wage can make low-skill jobs harder to find. In other cases, the minimum wage is set below the equilibrium wage in an area and does workers no good at all.

Problems with Traditional Aid

Incentives

While trying to be well meaning, many welfare programs can create unintended work disincentives, especially when we examine the combined effects of welfare and in-kind transfer programs.

As an example, consider a family of five with a combined income of $30,000 a year. Suppose that the family qualifies for public assistance that amounts to another $10,000 in benefits. The family's combined income from employment and benefits thus rises to $40,000. What happens if another family member gets a part-time job and income from wages rises from $30,000 to $40,000? Under the current law, an income of $40,000 disqualifies the family from receiving most of the financial assistance it had been getting. As a result, the family's benefits fall from $10,000 to $2,000 per year. Now the family nets $42,000 total. The person who secured part-time employment may feel that working isn't worth it, because even though the family earned an additional $10,000, they lost $8,000 in welfare benefits. Because the family is able to raise its net income by only $2,000, it has effectively returned $8,000. The loss of those benefits as they are phased out feels like an 80% tax, which creates a large disincentive to work.

This is a basic dilemma that poverty-reducing programs face: those that provide substantial benefits can discourage participation in the workforce because a recipient who starts to work, in many cases, no longer qualifies for the benefits and loses them.

While few people dispute that welfare programs are well intentioned, many economists are concerned about the programs' unintended consequences. A society that establishes a generous welfare package for the poor will find that it faces a Samaritan's dilemma. A **Samaritan's dilemma** occurs when an act of charity creates disincentives for recipients to take care of themselves. President Bill Clinton's 1996 vow "to end welfare as we know it" and for welfare to be "a second chance, not a way of life" attempted to address this dilemma by providing benefits for only a limited period of time. Clinton changed the payout structure for federal assistance and encouraged states to require employment searches as a condition for receiving aid. In addition, the TANF program imposed a five-year maximum for the time during which a recipient can receive benefits. This strategy changed welfare from an entitlement under the law into a temporary safety net, thereby reducing the Samaritan's dilemma.

A **Samaritan's dilemma** occurs when an act of charity creates disincentives for recipients to take care of themselves.

Incentives

ECONOMICS IN THE REAL WORLD

MUHAMMAD YUNUS AND THE GRAMEEN BANK

In 2006, Yunus received the Nobel Peace Prize.

In 2006, economist Muhammad Yunus received the Nobel Peace Prize for his work helping poor families in Bangladesh. What did Yunus do to win that honor? He founded the Grameen Bank, which was instrumental in creating a new type of loan that has loaned more than $10 billion to poor people in Bangladesh in an effort to eliminate extreme poverty.

The Grameen Bank gives out very small loans, known as *microcredit,* to poor Bangladeshis who are unable to qualify for conventional loans from traditional lenders. The loans are provided without collateral, and repayment is based on an honor system. By conventional standards that sounds preposterous, but it works! The Grameen Bank reports a 97% repayment rate, and according to one survey, over 50% of the families of Grameen borrowers have moved above the poverty line.

It all started with just a few thousand dollars. In 1974, Yunus, who was trained as an economist in the United States, returned to Bangladesh and lent $27 to each of 42 villagers who made bamboo furniture. The loans, which were all paid back, enabled the villagers to cut out middlemen and purchase their own raw materials. A few years later, Yunus won government approval to open the Grameen Bank, named for the Bengali word for "rural."

Since then, the microcredit banner has been picked up by other organizations. Unfortunately, the movement has suffered growing pains. Some of the new lenders are out not to help the poor but to make a profit. Government regulators are stretched thin. Based on empirical studies, some economists question how much microcredit really improves economic conditions. On top of all that, in poor communities hit hard by the COVID-19 outbreak, loan repayment has dropped sharply, threatening many lenders with insolvency.

Conclusion

Income and work have long been a subject of discussion and contention. We find that some jobs pay much more than others, and working hard and performing well at one's job does not guarantee good pay. People and jobs differ in many dimensions, and wages usually respond accordingly, though wages are affected by compensating differentials, location, education and human capital, union membership, and efficiency wages, all of which create significant income inequality.

This chapter is ultimately about trade-offs and incentives—two of our five foundations of economics. The debate about how society should handle income, poverty, and inequality is complex, and passions run deep. Depending on your perspective, you can point to data showing that society is improving (the narrowing wage gap between females and males) or worsening (increased levels of income inequality). In economics there are always trade-offs. Policies designed

PRACTICE WHAT YOU KNOW

Welfare is an economic means of lending a helping hand.

Samaritan's Dilemma: Does Welfare Cause Unemployment?

The state you live in is considering two different welfare programs. The first plan guarantees $8,000 for each person. The second plan does not guarantee any payments, but it doubles any income earned up to $12,000.

QUESTION: Which program creates the lesser amount of unemployment?

ANSWER: Think about incentives. Under the first plan, recipients' benefits are not tied to work. The $8,000 is guaranteed. However, the second plan will pay more if recipients do work. This policy acts as a positive incentive to get a job. For instance, someone who works 20 hours a week and earns $10 per hour would make $200 per week, or about $10,000 a year. Under the second plan, that person would receive an additional $10,000 from the government. Therefore, we can say that the second program reduces the amount of unemployment.

Incentives

· ECONOMICS *for* LIFE ·

It's Expensive to Be Poor

- The poor pay more for staples than the rich do, since they can't afford to buy in bulk.
- The poor pay more for auto insurance.
- The poor pay more to maintain checking accounts and credit cards.
- The poor are more likely to rent than own their housing, and this is more costly in the long run.

"Anyone who has ever struggled with poverty knows how extremely expensive it is to be poor."—James Baldwin

Imagine what it's like to earn $25,000 a year versus $250,000. A person earning $25,000 annually makes about $12.50 an hour—an amount near the minimum wage. A person making $250,000, on the other hand, is in the top five percent of all earners. Suppose these two people with different income levels are trying to do the same things: buy toilet paper and other staples, purchase car insurance, use a checking account and credit cards, and find a place to live.

The person making $25,000 annually is likely to be living paycheck to paycheck. When they buy staples, they rarely have enough extra cash to buy things like toilet paper in bulk, so they end up paying a lot more for those items in smaller units and also spending a lot more time in the process. A study by the Consumer Federation of America (CFA) found that the five major car insurers charge low-income drivers almost $700 a year more for minimum coverage than they do drivers with higher incomes. People living paycheck to paycheck don't have a lot in their checking accounts, so they often pay monthly fees imposed by financial institutions for insufficient deposits. Likewise, people who can't pay off their credit card each month end up paying hefty fees in interest. In addition, most poor people rent a place to live rather than own one. This is costly in two ways: they don't receive the mortgage interest deduction on their taxes, and they're not building up equity.

Conversely, our quarter-million per year rich person is able to buy many household items in bulk, receiving a significant discount in the process. Because of the socioeconomic group they are in, they get much lower quotes on auto insurance. They have enough in the bank to avoid monthly minimums, and they pay off their credit card bills every month—not only avoiding high interest charges but also profiting from promotions that provide air travel points, cash back, and other goodies. The wealthy also are far more likely to own the home they live in. (For Americans who can afford it, home ownership is often their single biggest financial investment.)

to reduce income inequality may cause highly productive workers to work less. Poverty initiatives may have unintended consequences as well. Unfortunately, good intentions alone won't close the wage gap or decrease income inequality, but the judicious use of incentives just might. ✷

ANSWERING *the* BIG QUESTIONS

What factors determine wages?

- Supply and demand play a key role in determining wages, along with a number of nonmonetary determinants of earnings, such as compensating differentials, education and human capital, the life-cycle wage pattern, location and lifestyle, union membership, efficiency wages, and the winner-take-all phenomenon.

What is wage discrimination, and what are important factors that cause income inequality?

- Income inequality is sometimes the result of bias on the part of employers or managers. However, other important factors are sociological and structural. Economic studies estimate that bias-driven wage discrimination accounts for less than 5% of wage differences.
- Sociological factors include differences in men's and women's preferred work patterns. Structural factors include inequalities in education and wealth, corruption, and occupational crowding.

How do we measure income inequality?

- The income inequality ratio is sometimes used to measure a nation's level of inequality. Another measure of inequality is the Gini index.
- Income mobility is the ability of workers to move up or down the economic ladder over time. Where income mobility is low, poverty is harder to escape from.

How do economists analyze poverty?

- Economists determine the poverty rate by establishing a poverty threshold.
- The poverty rate in the United States is now slightly higher than it was 50 years ago, despite many efforts (welfare, in-kind transfers, and EITC) to reduce it.
- Efforts to reduce poverty are subject to the Samaritan's dilemma because they can create disincentives for recipients to support themselves.

CHAPTER PROBLEMS

Concepts You Should Know

compensating differential (p. 473)
efficiency wages (p. 476)
Gini index (p. 489)
human capital (p. 473)
income mobility (p. 492)
income inequality ratio (p. 487)
in-kind transfers (p. 491)
life-cycle wage pattern (p. 473)
Lorenz curve (p. 489)
Medicaid (p. 499)
occupational crowding (p. 485)
poverty rate (p. 488)
poverty threshold (p. 488)
productivity (p. 476)
Samaritan's dilemma (p. 501)
strike (p. 475)
underground economies (p. 491)
union (p. 475)
wage discrimination (p. 479)
winner-take-all (p. 478)

Questions for Review

1. Why do garbage collectors sometimes make more than furniture movers?

2. What are efficiency wages? Why are some employers willing to pay them?

3. Why is it difficult to determine the amount of wage discrimination in the workplace?

4. Discuss some of the reasons why full-time working women make, on average, 81% as much as full-time working men.

5. How does the degree of income inequality in the United States compare with that in similarly developed countries? How does U.S. income inequality compare with that in less developed nations?

6. Why do high rates of income mobility mitigate income inequality?

7. Which antipoverty program (welfare, in-kind transfers, or EITC) creates the strongest incentive for recipients to work? Why?

Study Problems (*✱ solved at the end of this section*)

1. Suppose that society restricted the economic opportunities of right-handed persons to jobs in construction, while left-handed persons can work any job.

a. Would wages in construction be higher or lower than wages for other jobs?

b. Would left-handed workers make more or less than right-handed workers?

c. Now suppose that right-handers are allowed to work any job they like. What effect would this change have on the wages of right-handers and left-handers over time?

2. Internships are considered a vital stepping-stone to full-time employment after college, but not all internship positions are paid. Why do some students take unpaid internships when they could be working summer jobs and earning an income? Include a discussion of human capital in your answer.

3. Consider two communities. In Middletown, two families earn $40,000 each, six families earn $50,000 each, and two earn $60,000 each. In Polarity, four families earn $10,000 each, two earn $50,000 each, and four earn $90,000 each. Which community has the more unequal distribution of income as measured by the income inequality ratio? Explain your response.

4. The United States has attracted many highly productive immigrants who work in fields such as education, health, and technology. How do these immigrants affect income inequality in the United States? Is this type of immigration good or bad for the United States, and why? What impact is this type of immigration having on the countries that are losing some of their best workers?

✱ **5.** Suppose that a wealthy friend asks for your advice on how to reduce income inequality. Your friend wants to know if it would be better to give $100 million to poor people who will never attend college or to offer $100 million in financial aid to students who could not otherwise afford to attend college. What advice would you give, and why?

6. What effect would doubling the minimum wage have on income inequality? Explain your answer.

* **7.** Suppose that a company has 10 employees. It agrees to pay each worker on the basis of productivity. The individual workers' outputs are 10, 14, 15, 16, 18, 19, 21, 23, 25, and 30 units. However, some of the workers complain that they are earning less than the other workers, so they appeal to management to help reduce the income inequality. As a result, the company decides to pay each worker the same salary. But the next time the company measures each worker's output, they find that 6, 7, 7, 8, 10, 10, 11, 11, 12, and 12 units are produced. Why did this happen? Would you recommend that the company continue the new compensation system? Explain your response.

8. The government is considering three possible welfare programs:

a. Give each low-income household $10,000.
b. Give each low-income household $20,000 minus the recipient's income.
c. Match the income of each low-income household, where the maximum it can receive in benefits is capped at $10,000.

Which program will do the most to help the poor? Describe the work incentives under each program.

9. A number of very famous people (Tiger Woods, Brad Pitt, Mark Zuckerberg, Oprah Winfrey, Bill Gates) all dropped out of college. Why would anyone drop out of college when college graduates typically make significantly more than college dropouts?

* **10.** Tracy Chapman's song "Fast Car" reminds us how difficult it is to escape poverty. Identify the reasons in the song that keep Tracy trapped in poverty. (To listen to the song, visit https://www.youtube.com/watch?v=AIOAlaACuv4.)

11. Suppose that next summer you get two job offers, one as a lifeguard and the other as a garbage collector. Each job pays $15 an hour, and you are required to work 30 hours a week.

a. Which job are you more likely to take?
b. If no one wants to work as a garbage collector and everyone wants to be a lifeguard, what will happen to the wages in both jobs?

* **12.** Which of the following explanations (compensating differentials, discrimination, human capital, occupational crowding, winner-take-all) describes each of the following situations?

a. A person who is perceived as unattractive earns less than a person seen as attractive.
b. Alexa is more educated and better trained than Felix.
c. A Nobel-prize winning economist earns significantly more than other economists.
d. More women work as elementary school teachers than men.

13. In one society, 25% of the people earn $30,000 per year, 50% earn $60,000, and 25% earn $90,000. Draw the Lorenz curve and calculate the Gini index.

14. In the following figure, which country has the greatest level of equality? Which has the most inequality? Which country has the most desirable Lorenz curve? (**Hint:** Pause and think before you answer the last question.)

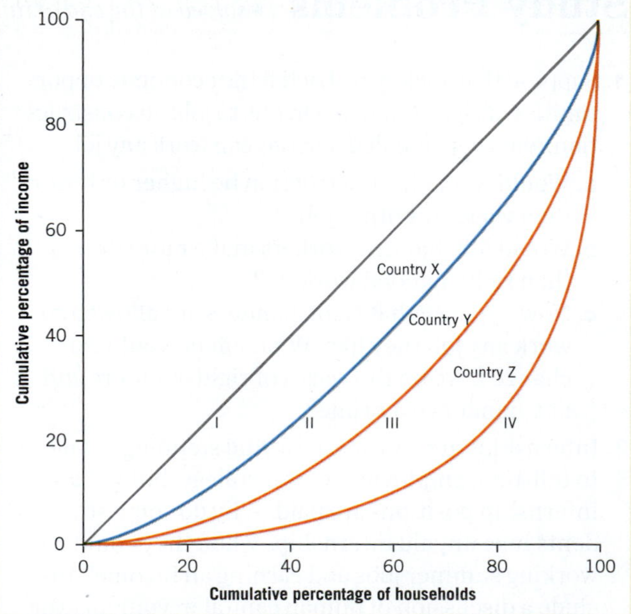

Solved Problems

5. The return on your wealthy friend's investment will be higher if the money is given to students with the aptitude, but not the income, to go to college. After all, college students earn substantially more than high school graduates do. Therefore, an investment in additional education will raise the marginal revenue product of the poor students' labor. With the higher earning power a college degree provides, more people will be lifted out of poverty, thereby reducing the amount of income inequality in the future.

7. Begin by calculating the average output when each worker's wage is based on the amount he or she produces: 10 + 14 + 15 + 16 + 18 + 19 + 21 + 23 + 25 + 30 = 191, and 191 (÷10 = 19.1). Then compute the average output when the company decides to pay each worker the same wage: 6 + 7 + 7 + 8 + 10 + 10 + 11 + 11 + 12 + 12 + 94, and 94 (÷10 = 9.4). The output has dropped by approximately one-half! Why? The company forgot about incentives. In this case, an attempt to create equal pay caused a disincentive problem (because hard work is not rewarded), and the workers all reduced their work effort. The new compensation system should be scrapped.

10. Tracy's condition is difficult because she lives in the country and the jobs are in the city—which is why she wants a "fast car" to drive away in. She also comes from a broken family; her mother left her father because he had a drinking problem. The lack of nearby job opportunities and the necessity of caring for her father prevents Tracy from taking advantage of economic opportunities elsewhere.

12. **a.** discrimination
b. human capital
c. winner-take-all
d. occupational crowding

PART V

Special Topics in MICROECONOMICS

CHAPTER 16

Consumer Choice

The More Money You Have, the Happier You'll Be? Not So Fast.

As a college student, you would probably be delighted if someone surprised you with a gift of $100. But to a successful stockbroker, $100 is mere pocket change. The more dollars you have, the less you value each additional one. And there can come a point where more money is actually undesirable. Consider Jack Whittaker, who won a $315 million Powerball jackpot in 2002, which at the time was the biggest single-winner jackpot in American lottery history. He later divorced and went completely broke, was arrested for DUI, and was robbed on two separate occasions while carrying over $100,000. (Who carries *that much* money?) Worst of all, he lost his granddaughter to a drug overdose, which he blamed on the lottery win as well. Whittaker told an interviewer in 2007: "My wife said she wished that she had torn the ticket up. Well, I wish that we tore the ticket up too." Too much money can make you very unhappy!

Some lottery winners do just fine, of course. But it's so common for winners to deal badly with the sudden wealth, and all the attention from "friends" who suddenly emerge from the woodwork, that there's a name for this phenomenon: the lottery curse. The root problem is that winners suddenly face a whole ton of choices they hadn't faced

"Are we ready to ruin another life? The (un)lucky number is . . . !" Let's hope winners of these payoffs escape the lottery curse.

before and aren't well-equipped to make. In this chapter, we use our understanding of income constraints, price, and personal satisfaction to determine which economic choices yield the greatest benefits.

· BIG QUESTIONS ·

- How do economists model consumer satisfaction?
- How do consumers optimize their purchasing decisions?
- What is the diamond-water paradox?

How Do Economists Model Consumer Satisfaction?

Trade-offs

The coronavirus pandemic has forced policymakers to confront tough choices. In particular, how do they balance the need to keep the economy going against people's need to be safe? Economists typically feel the ideal solution to this problem achieves the highest *utility* summed across all people—what is often called "the greatest good for the greatest number." In this chapter, we show how economists put numbers to happiness and calamity. That may seem coldhearted, but the goal is to benefit society by using scarce resources to do the most good. In doing so, economists are often forced to consider the opportunity costs of taking one path and forgoing another. When economists make these choices, they use particular economic tools. While these tools help public health officials in deciding when to reopen schools, permit public gatherings, and so on, they are also tools for making smarter personal decisions.

To better understand the decisions that consumers make, economists attempt to measure the satisfaction that consumers get when they make purchases. **Utility** is defined as a measure of the level of satisfaction that a consumer enjoys from the consumption of goods and services. Utility theory seeks to measure contentment, or satisfaction. To understand why people buy the goods and services they do, we need to recognize that some products produce more utility than others and that everyone receives different levels of satisfaction from the same good or service. In other words, utility varies from individual to individual. To quantify this idea of relative satisfaction, economists measure utility with a unit they refer to as a **util**.

Utility is a measure of the level of satisfaction that a consumer enjoys from the consumption of goods and services.

A **util** is a personal unit of satisfaction used to measure the enjoyment from consumption of a good or service.

There is tremendous value in modeling decisions this way. When we understand utility, we can predict what people are likely to purchase. We model consumer behavior in a manner similar to the way we model how a firm makes decisions or how the labor market works. We expect the firm to maximize profits, the laborer to accept the best offer, and the consumer to find the combination of goods that gives the most utility. For example, a brownie lover may get 25 utils from her favorite snack, but someone who is less susceptible to the pleasures of chewy, gooey chocolate may rate the same brownie at 10 utils. However, these are not completely accurate measurements of relative utility. Who can say whether one person's 25 utils represents more actual satisfaction than another person's 10? Even if you and a friend agree that you each receive 10 utils from eating brownies, you cannot say that you both experience the same amount of satisfaction; each of you has a unique personal scale. However, the level of enjoyment one receives can be internally consistent. For example, if you rate a brownie at 25 utils and a slice of apple pie at 15 utils, we know that you like brownies more than apple pie.

Utility, or what most of us think of as satisfaction, is a balance between economic and personal factors. Even though there is an inherent problem with equating money and satisfaction, this has not stopped researchers from exploring the connection.

In the next section, we explore the connection between total utility and marginal utility. This connection will help us understand why more money does not necessarily bring more satisfaction.

Do you prefer a slice of apple pie . . .

. . . or a fudge brownie?

ECONOMICS IN THE REAL WORLD

HAPPINESS INDEX

Since 2006, the Organisation for Economic Co-operation and Development (OECD) has published the Better Life Index—popularly called the "happiness index"—which compiles social and economic data for 40 highly developed countries. The OECD measures well-being across these countries, based on 11 topics it has identified as essential in the areas of material living conditions and quality of life.

Which countries are happiest? The OECD doesn't rank them, and the results depend on the relative importance assigned to the different measurements. Australia rates highly in most categories. What makes Australians so happy? It's not their income, which averages only $33,000 per year in U.S. dollars. However, Australians live to an average age of 83 (three years longer than typical in developed countries), experience low amounts of pollution, display a high degree of civic engagement, and enjoy a very high life satisfaction rating.

In contrast, the OECD identifies the United States as having nearly the highest income (second only to tiny Luxembourg), but it scores substantially lower in work-life balance than many of the other top countries do. Just as with individuals, with nations it's hard to make comparisons. Are Australians happier than Americans, or vice versa? Without knowing how much importance people attach to longevity compared to income, it's hard to say. Still, when one country outscores another in virtually every category, we can be pretty sure there's a corresponding difference in happiness levels. Thus, it seems clear that Americans and Australians are better off overall than the citizens of Mexico, where safety concerns, poor education, and low levels of income combine to produce a very low rating.

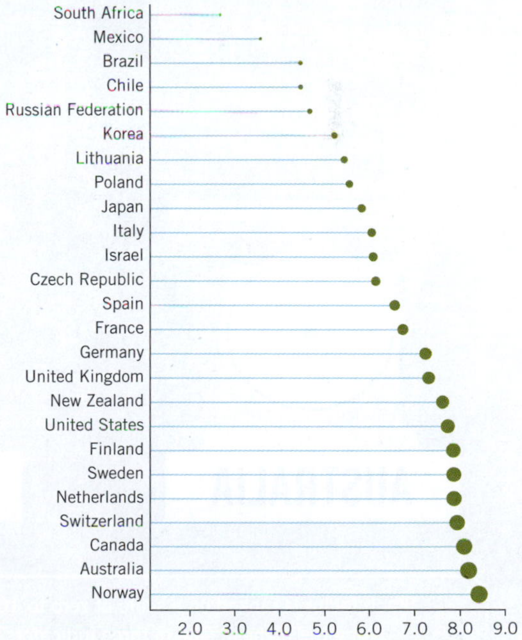

The Better Life Index informs us about the most satisfying places to live.

SNAPSHOT

The OECD Better Life Index

The OECD Better Life Index attempts to measure 11 key factors of material well-being in each of its 34 member countries. The goal of the index is to provide member governments with a snapshot of how their citizens are living, thus providing a road map for future policy priorities. Some factors are objectively measured, such as average household income. Others are more subjective, such as "life satisfaction," and are measured from survey responses. Below is a look at the results in three countries.

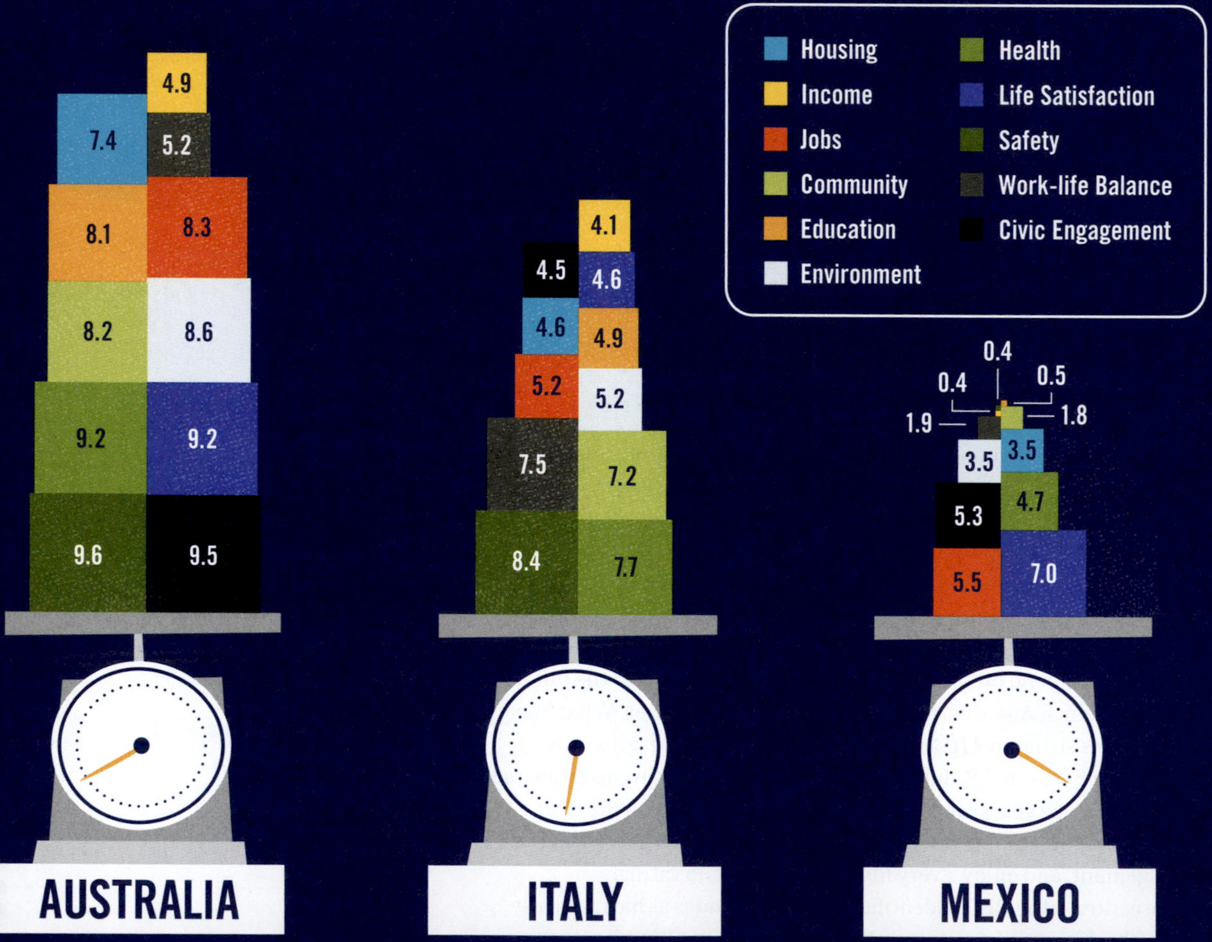

10.0

Each factor is ranked on a scale of zero to 10, with 10 being the highest. One to three indicators go into each measurement. For instance, "Jobs" is measured through the unemployment rate, job security, and personal earnings.

What do these numbers say about a nation's quality of life? It depends on which factors you think are most important. At www.oecdbetterlifeindex.org you can weight the different categories, create an index, and see how nations compare.

REVIEW QUESTIONS

- Mexico has five glaring challenges to the well-being of its citizens. What are they?
- Visit the OECD website and create your own index. Are any of the 11 factors trade-offs?

Total Utility and Marginal Utility

Thinking about the choices that consumers make can help us understand how to increase total utility. Consider a person who really likes brownies. In this case, the **marginal utility** is the additional satisfaction enjoyed from consuming one more brownie. In the table on the left-hand side of Figure 16.1, we see that the first brownie eaten brings 25 total utils. Eating additional brownies increases total utility until it reaches 75 utils after eating five brownies.

The graph in panel (a) of Figure 16.1 reveals that while the total utility (the green curve) rises until it reaches 75, the rate of increase (that is, the increase

Marginal thinking

Marginal utility is the additional satisfaction derived from consuming one more unit of a good or service.

FIGURE 16.1

Total Utility and Marginal Utility

The relationship between total utility and marginal utility can be seen by observing the dashed line that connects panels (a) and (b). Because the marginal utility becomes negative after five brownies are consumed, the total utility eventually falls after a certain number of brownies are eaten. To the left of the dashed line, the marginal utility is positive in panel (b) and the total utility is rising in panel (a). Conversely, to the right of the dashed line, the marginal utility is negative and the total utility is falling.

Number of brownies eaten	Total utility (utils)	Marginal utility (utils per brownie)
0	0	
1	25	25
2	45	20
3	60	15
4	70	10
5	75	5
6	75	0
7	70	−5
8	60	−10
9	45	−15
10	25	−20

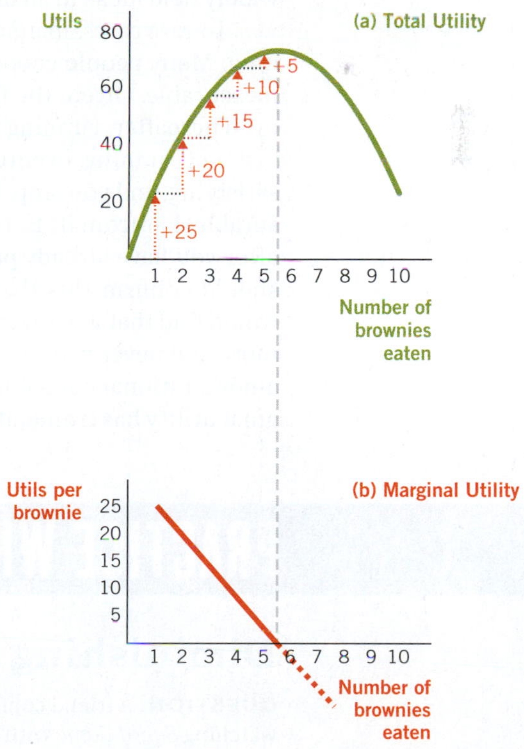

Running is fun for only so long.

in marginal utility) falls from 25 utils for the first brownie down to 5 additional utils for the fifth. The marginal utility values from the table are plotted in panel (b), which shows that marginal utility declines steadily as consumption rises.

The relationship between total utility and marginal utility is evident when we observe the dashed line that connects panels (a) and (b). Because the marginal utility becomes negative after five brownies are consumed, the total utility eventually falls. To the left of the dashed line, the marginal utility is positive in panel (b) and the total utility is rising in panel (a). Conversely, to the right of the dashed line, the marginal utility is negative, and the total utility is falling.

When marginal utility becomes negative, the consumer is tired of eating brownies. At that point, the brownies are no longer adding to the consumer's utility, and he or she will stop eating them.

Diminishing Marginal Utility

Diminishing marginal utility occurs when marginal utility declines as consumption increases.

As you can see in panel (b) of Figure 16.1, the satisfaction that a consumer derives from consuming a good or service declines with each additional unit consumed. Consider what happens when you participate in a favorite activity for an hour and then decide to do something else. **Diminishing marginal utility** occurs when marginal utility declines as consumption increases. The concept of diminishing marginal utility is so universal that it is one of the most widely held ideas in all of economics.

In rare cases, marginal utility can rise—but only temporarily. Consider running. Many people choose to run for recreation because it is both healthy and pleasurable. Often, the first mile is difficult as the runner's body gets warmed up. Thereafter, running is easier—for a while. No matter how good you are at distance running, eventually the extra miles become more exhausting and less satisfying, and you stop. This does not mean that running is not healthy or pleasurable. Far from it! But it does mean that forcing yourself to do more running after you have already pushed your limit yields less utility. Your own intuition should confirm this theory. If increasing marginal utility were possible, you would find that with every passing second you would enjoy what you were doing more and never want to stop. Because economists do not observe this behavior among rational consumers, we can be highly confident that diminishing marginal utility has tremendous explanatory power.

PRACTICE WHAT YOU KNOW

Diminishing Marginal Utility

QUESTION: A friend confides to you that a third friend has gradually lost interest in watching *Squid Game* with her and has begun saying she's too busy. How would you advise your friend to handle the situation?

ANSWER: Tell your friend about diminishing marginal utility. After a while, the dramatic premise that at first makes a show like *Squid Game* so watchable no longer

(CONTINUED)

seems fresh and new. Then suggest to your friend that they mix it up and do something different together. If that doesn't work, it may not be *Squid Game* that is the problem—it may be that your friend's friend has grown tired of her.

CHALLENGE QUESTION: How could you tell whether the marginal utility someone derived from a TV show had not just gone down to zero but gone negative?

ANSWER: A person whose marginal utility had gone negative would not just show a lack of interest in the show but would be willing to pay a price to avoid watching it. "If you agree to watch something else, I'll do the dishes!"

Relax. You can choose not to watch *Squid Game*.

Table 16.1 highlights how diminishing marginal utility can serve to explain a number of interesting real-world situations. Do not skip this table! It is very useful in helping you understand the concept of diminishing marginal utility.

TABLE 16.1

Examples of Diminishing Marginal Utility

	Example	Explanation using diminishing marginal utility
	Discounts on two-day passes to amusement parks	The excitement on the first day is palpable. You run to rides, don't mind waiting in line, and experience the thrill for the first time. By the second day, the enthusiasm has worn off and the lower price entices you to return.
	Discounts on season tickets	Over the course of any season, people anticipate some games and concerts more highly than other games and concerts. To encourage patrons to buy the entire season package, venues must discount the total price.
	All-you-can-eat buffet	All-you-can-eat buffets offer the promise of unlimited food, but the average diner has a limited capacity. Eating more eventually leads to negative marginal utility. Restaurants assume that diminishing utility will limit how much their customers eat.
	Unlimited minutes with phone plans	Phone companies rely on the diminishing marginal utility of conversation. Phone companies offer "unlimited" plans because they know that consumers will not stay on their phones indefinitely.
	Pokémon GO	Remember the summer of 2016 when Pokémon GO first appeared? Everyone was playing, and capturing digital monsters was so much fun. But you soon tired of the grind . . . and most people quit—that's diminishing marginal utility.
	Nathan's Famous Hot Dog Eating Contest	Many people enjoy eating a hot dog or two or three, but Nathan's Eating Contest is very difficult to watch. The idea of eating so many hot dogs makes a lot of people queasy.

How Do Consumers Optimize Their Purchasing Decisions?

Maximizing utility requires that consumers get the most satisfaction out of every dollar they spend, or what is commonly called "getting the biggest bang for the buck." When a consumer gets the most bang for the buck, we say that the consumer has *optimized* his or her purchasing decisions. However, optimization is easier said than done. Over the course of the year, each of us will make thousands of purchases of different amounts. Our budgets are generally not unlimited, and we try to spend in a way that enables us to meet both our short-run and our long-run needs. The combination of goods and services that maximizes the satisfaction, or utility, we get from our income or budget is the **consumer optimum**.

The **consumer optimum** is the combination of goods and services that maximizes the consumer's utility for a given income or budget.

Finding the consumer optimum can be tricky, though. Take our eating habits, for instance. Home-cooked meals were once the norm, but today, households rely increasingly on ready-to-eat foods. This trend has persisted even as ready-to-eat has gotten more expensive, compared with home cooking. Does that mean we prefer food out of the microwave over food made from scratch? Not really, says a study led by economist Rachel Griffith. The explanation is that cooking takes time. If the person who would do the cooking is a wage earner—a situation that was once rare but now is completely normal—that person's time is economically valuable. With the time cost factored in, a home-cooked meal is more expensive than a pre-made one.

Or is it? A steady diet of high-fat, high-sodium ready-to-eat food takes a long-term toll on one's health. If that cost to health is added to the information mix, heat-and-serve meals don't look like such a bargain, after all. What does this tell us? When time becomes more valuable, people naturally respond by purchasing time-saving alternatives, even when those alternatives have unintended health consequences. The long-run consequences are often missed by people seeking to maximize their utility in the short-run. Keep this in mind as we move forward in the chapter.

In this section, we examine the decision process that leads to the consumer optimum. We start with two goods and then generalize those findings across a consumer's entire income or budget.

Consumer Purchasing Decisions

Opportunity cost

Let's begin by imagining a world with only two goods: Pepsi and pizza. This example will help us focus on the opportunity cost of purchasing Pepsi instead of pizza, or pizza instead of Pepsi.

Pepsi is available for $1 per can, and each pizza slice costs $2. Suppose you have $10 to spend. How much of each good should you buy in order to maximize your satisfaction? Before we can answer that question, we need a rule for making decisions. To reach your consumer optimum, you must allocate your available money by choosing goods that give you the most utility per dollar spent. By getting the biggest bang for your buck, you will end up optimizing your choices. This relationship, shown below in terms of marginal utility (MU), helps quantify the decision. So if you get more for your money by purchasing Pepsi rather than pizza, then you should buy Pepsi—and vice versa.

$$\frac{MU_{Pepsi}}{Price_{Pepsi}} \quad \textbf{Which is larger?} \quad \frac{MU_{pizza}}{Price_{pizza}}$$

If we divide the marginal utility of a good by its price, we get the utility per dollar spent. Because you wish to optimize your utility, a direct comparison of the marginal utility per dollar spent on Pepsi versus pizza gives you a road map to your consumer satisfaction. Table 16.2 shows the marginal utility for each can of Pepsi (column 2) and the marginal utility for each slice of pizza (column 5).

To decide what to consume first, look at column 3, which lists the marginal utility per dollar spent for Pepsi, and column 6, which lists the marginal utility per dollar spent for pizza. Now it's time to make your first spending decision—whether to drink a Pepsi or eat a slice of pizza. Because the marginal utility per dollar spent for the first slice of pizza (10) is higher than the marginal utility for the first can of Pepsi (9), you order a slice of pizza, which costs $2. You have $8 left.

After eating the first slice of pizza, you can choose between having a second slice of pizza, which brings 8 utils per dollar spent, and having the first can of Pepsi, which brings 9 utils per dollar spent. This time you order a Pepsi, which costs $1. You have $7 left.

Now you can choose between having a second slice of pizza, representing 8 utils per dollar spent, and having a second can of Pepsi, also 8 utils per dollar spent. Because both choices yield the same amount of utility per dollar spent and you have enough money to afford both, we'll assume you would probably purchase both at the same time. Your purchase costs another $3, which leaves you with $4.

Your next choice is between the third slice of pizza at 6 utils per dollar spent and the third can of Pepsi at 7 utils per dollar spent. Pepsi is the better value, so you buy that. You are left with $3 for your final choice: between the third slice of pizza at 6 utils per dollar spent and the fourth can of Pepsi at 6 utils per dollar spent. Since you have exactly $3 left and the items are of equal utility, you buy both, and you have no money left.

TABLE 16.2

The Consumer Optimum with Pepsi and Pizza

(1) Pepsi consumed (cans)	(2) Marginal utility (MU Pepsi)	(3) MU Pepsi / Price Pepsi (Pepsi $1/can)	(4) Pizza consumed (slices)	(5) Marginal utility (MU pizza)	(6) MU pizza / Price pizza (pizza $2/slice)
1	9	9/1 = 9	1	20	20/2 = 10
2	8	8/1 = 8	2	16	16/2 = 8
3	7	7/1 = 7	3	12	12/2 = 6
4	6	6/1 = 6	4	8	8/2 = 4
5	5	5/1 = 5	5	4	4/2 = 2
6	4	4/1 = 4	6	0	0/2 = 0
7	3	3/1 = 3	7	−4	−4/2 = −2
8	2	2/1 = 2	8	−8	−8/2 = −4
9	1	1/1 = 1	9	−12	−12/2 = −6
10	0	0/1 = 0	10	−16	−16/2 = −8

Let's see how well you have done. Looking at column 2 in Table 16.2, we calculate that the four Pepsis you consumed yielded a total utility of 9 + 8 + 7 + 6 = 30 utils. Looking at column 5, we see that three slices of pizza yielded a total utility of 20 + 16 + 12 = 48. Adding the two together (30 + 48) gives 78 total utils of satisfaction. This is the most utility you can afford with $10. To see why, look at Table 16.3, which reports the maximum utility for every affordable combination of Pepsi and pizza.

The optimum combination of Pepsi and pizza is highlighted in red. This is the result we found by comparing the marginal utilities per dollar spent in Table 16.2. Notice that Table 16.3 confirms that this process results in the highest total utility. All other affordable combinations of Pepsi and pizza produce less utility. Table 16.3 also illustrates diminishing marginal utility. If you select either pizza or Pepsi exclusively, you will have a much lower total utility: 60 utils with pizza and 45 utils with Pepsi. In addition, the preferred outcome of four Pepsis and three pizza slices corresponds to a modest amount of each good; this outcome avoids the utility reduction associated with excessive consumption of either good.

By thinking at the margin about which good provides the highest marginal utility, you also maximize your total utility. Of course, most people rarely think this way. But as consumers we make marginal choices all the time. Instead of adding up utils, we think "that isn't worth it" or "that's a steal." Consumer choice is not so much a conscious calculation as an instinct to seek the most satisfaction. Next we extend our analysis by generalizing the two-good example.

Marginal Thinking with More Than Two Goods

The idea of measuring utility makes our instinctive sense more explicit and enables us to solve simple optimization problems. For instance, when you travel without the aid of GPS, you instinctively make choices about which route to take to save time. The decision to turn left or right when you come to a stop sign is a decision at the margin: one route will be better than the other. If you consistently make the best choices about which way to turn, you will arrive at your destination sooner. This is why economists focus on marginal thinking.

Marginal thinking

In reality, life is more complex than the simple two-good model implies. When you have $10 to spend, you may choose among many goods. Because you buy many items at all kinds of prices over the course of a year, you must juggle

TABLE 16.3

The Maximum Utility from Different Combinations of Pepsi and Pizza

Affordable combination of pizza and Pepsi	Total utility
5 pizza slices (20 + 16 + 12 + 8 + 4)	60 utils
2 Pepsis (9 + 8) and 4 pizza slices (20 + 16 + 12 + 8)	73 utils
4 Pepsis (9 + 8 + 7 + 6) and 3 pizza slices (20 + 16 + 12)	**78 utils**
6 Pepsis (9 + 8 + 7 + 6 + 5 + 4) and 2 pizza slices (20 + 16)	75 utils
8 Pepsis (9 + 8 + 7 + 6 + 5 + 4 + 3 + 2) and 1 pizza slice (20)	64 utils
10 Pepsis (9 + 8 + 7 + 6 + 5 + 4 + 3 + 2 + 1 + 0)	45 utils

hundreds (or thousands) of purchases so that you enjoy roughly the same utility per dollar spent. Consumer optimum captures this idea by comparing the utility gained with the price paid for every item a consumer buys. In other words, a consumer's income or budget is balanced so that the ratio of the marginal utility (MU) per dollar spent on every item, from good A to good Z, is equal. In mathematical terms:

$$\frac{MU_A}{Price_A} = \frac{MU_B}{Price_B} = \ldots = \frac{MU_Z}{Price_Z}$$

Left or right? One way will get you to your destination sooner.

It should be noted that, because goods aren't infinitely divisible (we can't buy a fraction of a soda can), we can't always make the fractions come out exactly equal. Still, we maximize utility by buying the goods with the higher fractions, and in the end the marginal utilities per dollar spent for each good end up approximately equal.

In the next section, we explore the relationship between changes in price and changes in the consumer optimum.

Price Changes and the Consumer Optimum

Recall our example of pizza and Pepsi: you reached an optimum when you purchased four Pepsis and three slices of pizza. At that point, the marginal utility per dollar spent for Pepsi and pizza was equal:

$$\frac{MU_{pizza}\ (12\ utils)}{\$2} = \frac{MU_{Pepsi}\ (6\ utils)}{\$1}$$

In the earlier example, the prices of a slice of pizza ($2) and a can of Pepsi ($1) were held constant. But suppose that the price of a slice of pizza drops to $1.50. This new price causes the ratio of $MU_{pizza} \div Price_{pizza}$ to change from $12 \div 2$, or 6 utils per dollar, to $12 \div 1.5$, or 8 utils per dollar. The lower price for pizza increases the quantity of slices the consumer will buy:

$$\frac{MU_{pizza}\ (12\ utils)}{\$1.50} > \frac{MU_{Pepsi}\ (6\ utils)}{\$1}$$

As a result, we can say that lower prices increase the marginal utility per dollar spent and cause consumers to buy more of a good. Higher prices have the opposite effect by lowering the marginal utility per dollar spent. If that conclusion sounds an awful lot like the law of demand, it is! We have just restated the law of demand in terms of marginal utility.

Marginal thinking

We know that according to the law of demand (see Chapter 3), the quantity demanded falls when the price rises, and the quantity demanded rises when the price falls—all other things being equal. If we think of consumer desire for a particular product as demand, it makes sense to find a connection between the prices consumers pay, the quantity they buy, and the marginal utility they receive.

A lower price has two effects. First, because the marginal utility per dollar spent is now higher, consumers substitute the product that has become relatively less expensive—this is the **substitution effect**. Second, at the same

The **substitution effect** occurs when consumers substitute a product that has become relatively less expensive as the result of a price change.

The **real-income effect** occurs when there is a change in purchasing power as a result of a change in the price of a good.

time, a lower price can also change the purchasing power of income—this is the **real-income effect**. (For a basic discussion of the trends behind these effects, see Chapter 3.)

Let's go back to our Pepsi and pizza example to separate these two effects. A lower price for a slice of pizza makes it more affordable. If slices are $2 each, a consumer with a budget of $10 can afford five slices. If the price drops to $1.50 per slice, the consumer can afford six slices and still have $1 left over.

When the price of a slice of pizza is $2, your optimum is three slices of pizza and four Pepsis. If we drop the price of a slice of pizza to $1.50, you save 50 cents per slice. Because you are purchasing three slices, you save $1.50—which is enough to buy another slice. Looking back at column 5 in Table 16.2, we see that the fourth slice of pizza yields an additional 8 utils. Alternatively, you could use the $1.50 you saved on pizza to buy a fifth can of Pepsi—which has a marginal utility of 5—and still have 50 cents left over.

The lower price of pizza may cause you to substitute pizza for Pepsi because pizza has become relatively less expensive. This is the substitution effect at work. In addition, you have more purchasing power through the money you save from the lower-priced pizza. This is the real-income effect.

The real-income effect matters only when prices change enough to cause a measurable effect on the purchasing power of the consumer's income or budget. For example, suppose that a 10% price reduction in peanut butter cups occurs. Will there be a substitution effect, a real-income effect, or both? The key to answering this question is to consider how much money is saved. Most candy bars cost less than a dollar, so a 10% reduction in price would be less than 10 cents. The lower price will motivate some consumers to switch to peanut butter cups—a substitution effect that can be observed through increased purchases of peanut butter cups. However, the real-income effect is negligible. The consumer has saved less than 10 cents. The money saved could be used to purchase other goods; but very few goods cost so little, and the enhanced purchasing power is effectively zero. Thus, the answer to the question is that there will be a modest substitution effect and essentially no real-income effect.

ECONOMICS IN THE REAL WORLD

WOULD YOU PAY $149 FOR A DRINK AT STARBUCKS?

Your favorite Starbucks creation typically costs about $5. Now suppose you do what the guy on the left did, and spend over $100 on extra shots, add-ins, and flavors, all in a punchbowl-sized "cup." Would you enjoy the drink more? Maybe. But 20 times more? Not a chance. How do we know this? The law of diminishing marginal utility tells us that additional units of the same good will eventually bring less marginal utility.

In addition, substantial income and substitution effects are at work when you consider what $149 could buy instead of coffee. For many people, $149 is enough to purchase weeks' worth of groceries. It is hard to imagine that a single Starbucks drink could provide more utility than you would experience from the variety of food you would eat over the course of a few weeks. If you are interested in learning more about the curious obsession some people have with purchasing a super-expensive Starbucks creation, check out this link: http://www.caffeineinformer.com/what-is-the-most-expensive-starbucks-drink.

A $149 cup of Starbucks coffee, and yes, that's the actual size. What's the most *you* would pay for your favorite drink?

What Is the Diamond-Water Paradox?

Now that you understand the connection between prices and utility, we can tackle one of the most interesting puzzles in economics—the **diamond-water paradox**. First described by Adam Smith in 1776, the diamond-water paradox explains why water, which is essential to life, is inexpensive, while diamonds, which do not sustain life, are expensive. Many people of Smith's era found the paradox perplexing. Today, we can use consumer choice theory to answer the question.

The **diamond-water paradox** explains why water, which is essential to life, is inexpensive, while diamonds, which do not sustain life, are expensive.

Essentially, the diamond-water paradox unfairly compares the amount of marginal utility a person receives from a small quantity of something rare (the diamond) with the marginal utility received from consuming a small amount of additional water after already consuming a large amount.

We know that marginal utility is captured in the law of demand and therefore by the price of a good. For example, when the price of diamonds increases, the quantity demanded declines. We learned in Chapter 5 that in graphical terms, the consumer surplus is the area under the demand curve and above the price, or the gains from trade that a consumer enjoys. Therefore, if the price of diamonds rises, consumers will enjoy less surplus when buying them.

PRACTICE WHAT YOU KNOW

Consumer Optimum

QUESTION: Suppose your favorite magazine, *The Economist*, costs $6 per issue and *People* magazine costs $4 per issue. If you receive 20 utils when you read *People*, how many additional utils would you need to get from reading *The Economist* to prompt you to pony up the extra $2 to purchase it instead of *People* magazine?

ANSWER: To answer the question, you first need to equate the marginal utility (MU) per dollar spent for both magazines and solve for the missing variable, the utility from *The Economist*:

$$\frac{MU_{The\ Economist}\ (X\ utils)}{\$6} = \frac{MU_{People}\ (20\ utils)}{\$4}$$

$$\frac{X}{\$6} = \frac{20}{\$4}$$

$$X = \frac{\$120}{\$4}$$

$$X = 30$$

When the $MU_{The\ Economist}$ is equal to 30 utils, you are indifferent between purchasing either of the two magazines (that is, each magazine would bring you equal satisfaction). Because the question asks how many *additional* utils are needed to justify purchasing *The Economist*, you should subtract the utils from *People*, or 20, to get the difference, which is 30 – 20, or 10 utils.

FIGURE 16.2

The Diamond-Water Paradox

The diamond-water paradox exists because people fail to recognize that demand and supply are equally important in determining the value a good creates in society. The demand for water is large, while the demand for diamonds is small. If we look at the amount of consumer surplus, we observe that the blue area (TU_w, which represents the consumer surplus for water) is much larger than the dotted area (TU_d, which represents the consumer surplus for diamonds) because water is essential for life. As a result, water creates significantly more total utility (TU) than diamonds. However, because water is abundant in most places, the price, P_{water}, is low. In contrast, diamonds are rare and the price, $P_{diamond}$, is high.

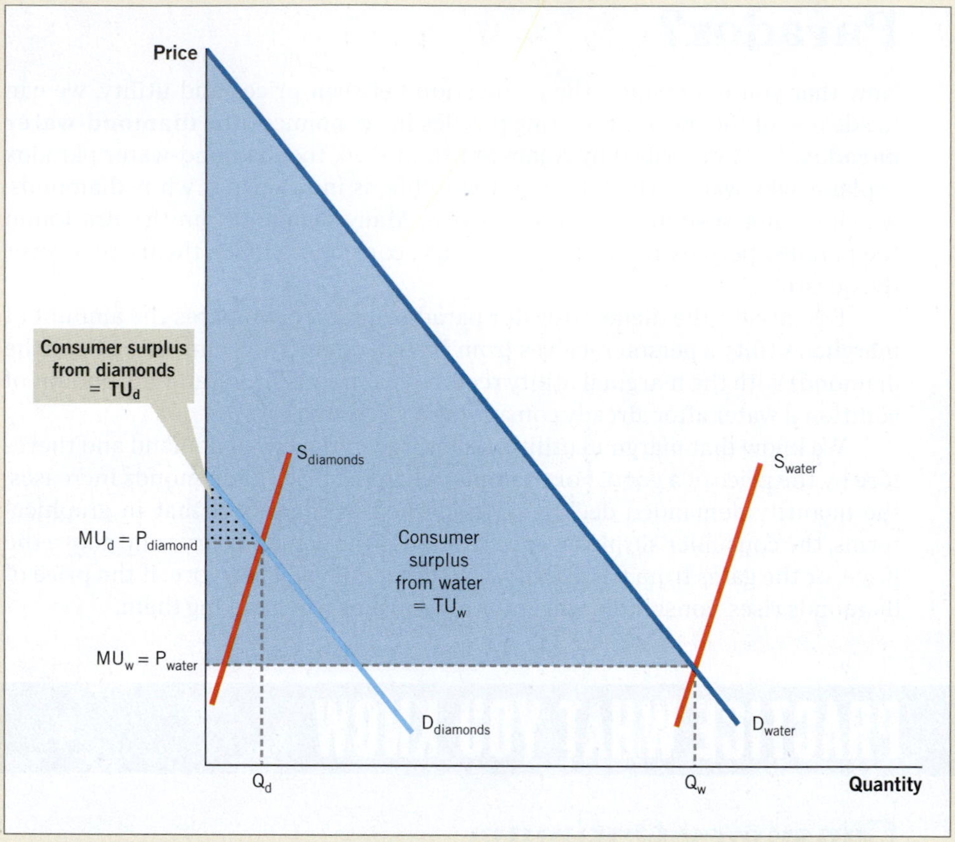

Figure 16.2 contrasts the demand and supply equilibrium in both the market for water and the market for diamonds. Notice that the consumer surplus is the area highlighted in blue for water and the triangular area highlighted with dots for diamonds. The blue area of total utility for water (TU_w) is much larger than the dotted area of total utility for diamonds (TU_d) because water is essential for life. Therefore, water creates significantly more total utility than diamonds do. However, in most places in the United States, water is very plentiful, so people take additional units of it for granted. In fact, it is so plentiful that if someone were to offer you a gallon of water right now, you would probably hesitate to take it. But what if someone offered you a gallon-size bucket of diamonds? You bet you would take that! Therefore, it should not surprise you that something quite plentiful, water, would yield less marginal utility than something rare, diamonds ($MU_w < MU_d$). However, if water were as rare as diamonds, there is no doubt that the price of water would exceed the price of diamonds.

Let's consider how we use water. We bathe in it, cook with it, and drink it. Each of those uses has high value, so the marginal utility of water is high. But we also use it to water our lawns and fill our fish tanks. Those uses are not nearly as essential, so the marginal utility of water for these uses is much lower. The reason we use water in both essential and nonessential ways is that its price is relatively low, so low-value uses, like filling fish tanks, yield enough utility to justify the cost. Because water is abundant in most places, the price (P_{water}) is

ECONOMICS in the MEDIA

How to Buy Happiness

The relationship between money and happiness has been studied scientifically. Economists Daniel Kahneman and Angus Deaton looked at how people's self-reported emotional well-being tracked with their incomes. In a 2010 paper, the two researchers estimated that the well-being people experience levels off at around $100,000 in yearly income (in today's dollars). A 2021 study, by another economist, suggests that well-being tops out at a higher income, but the basic finding stands: beyond a certain point, more money doesn't translate into more happiness—not for the average wealthy person, anyway. Most of us find this hard to accept. We want more money because we think it will make us better off. As columnist Arthur Brooks puts it, "When it comes to money and happiness, there is a glitch in our psychological code."

Now, this does not mean that money doesn't matter to happiness at all. On the contrary, when a raise at work makes the difference between worrying about the rent and knowing you have it covered, that's an obvious improvement in emotional well-being. But once all our material needs are all comfortably met, we must get a little more creative if we want added income to bring extra happiness. For anyone in that fortunate position, Brooks has three suggestions. First, *buy experiences*. Go on vacations with friends and family, and build memories. Second, *buy time*. Pay someone to take care of your yard, and then use your free time to be with loved ones. (Don't spent that time on Twitter!) Finally, *support worthy causes*. You will get a happiness boost you can't get any other way. The common element in all three recommendations is other people. "The joys of money are nothing," Brooks says, "without other people."

In 2020, *Show Me the Monet*, Banksy's playful take on a famous Impressionist painting, sold at auction for a whopping $9.8 million. In the 2005 work, Banksy added abandoned shopping carts and an orange traffic cone to Claude Monet's classic image of water lilies in his garden at Giverny. We have just one question for the buyer, though: do you understand how to buy happiness?

Source: Adapted from Arthur C. Brooks, "How to Buy Happiness," *Atlantic*, April 15, 2021, https://www.theatlantic.com/family/archive/2021/04/money-income-buy-happiness/618601/.

low. In contrast, diamonds are rare, and their price ($P_{diamond}$) is high. The cost of obtaining a diamond means that a consumer must get a great deal of marginal utility from the purchase of a diamond to justify the expense, which explains why diamonds are given as gifts for extremely special occasions.

Conclusion

Does having more money make people more satisfied? The answer is no. More money enables people to buy more goods, but because of diminishing marginal utility, the increases in satisfaction from being able to buy more goods or

ECONOMICS *for* LIFE

Worth It

- You really need or want it (inelastic demand).
- No acceptable substitute good is available at a lower price.
- It is a good bang for the buck (MU/P is high).
- You can afford it without spending beyond your means.

Buzzfeed's *Worth It* is sometimes the number 1 show on YouTube. The show features Steven Lim and Andrew Ilnyckyj. The premise is simple: the hosts try an inexpensive, a moderately-priced, and a very expensive version of the same good. They then debate the merits of each version and explain why it is either "worth it" or not.

Life works the same way. We make thousands of decisions over the course of each year to either make a purchase, not purchase, or find a substitute product instead. *Worth It* is really about the hunt for the consumer optimum, where the extra value we get from buying one more unit of a good is the same across all the items we purchase. Whether something is "worth it" also applies to how we spend our time and energy. In a world of scarcity, we must use our limited resources wisely, or else we end up with fewer utils (less enjoyment).

Would you buy a $47 taco and eat it in one bite?

higher-quality goods become progressively smaller with rising income. So we could say that having more money makes people somewhat more satisfied. But it seems appropriate to add that the relationship between quality of life and money is not direct. More money sometimes leads to more utility, and at other times more money means more problems.

As we have seen in this chapter, price plays a key role in determining utility. Because consumers face a budget and wish to maximize their utility, the prices they pay determine their marginal utility per dollar spent. Comparing the marginal utility per dollar spent across many goods helps us understand individuals' consumption patterns. Diminishing marginal utility also helps to describe consumer choice. Because marginal utility declines with additional consumption, consumers do not exclusively purchase their favorite products. Instead, they diversify their choices in order to gain more utility. In addition, changes in prices have two different effects: one on real income and a separate substitution effect that together determine the composition of the bundle of goods purchased.

In the next chapter, we question how much individuals use consumer choice theory to make their decisions. The approach known as behavioral economics argues that decision-makers are not entirely rational about the choices they make.

Finally, in the appendix that follows, we refine consumer theory by discussing indifference curves. Please read the appendix to get a glimpse into how economists model consumer choice in greater detail. ✷

ANSWERING *the* BIG QUESTIONS

How do economists model consumer satisfaction?

- Economists model consumer satisfaction by examining utility, which is a measure of the level of satisfaction that a consumer enjoys from the consumption of goods and services.
- Utility diminishes with additional consumption. This property limits the amount of any particular good or service that a person will consume.

How do consumers optimize their purchasing decisions?

- Consumers optimize their purchasing decisions by finding the combination of goods and services that maximizes the level of satisfaction from a given income or budget. The consumer optimum occurs when a consumer maximizes the utility from his or her income or budget, so that the marginal utility per dollar spent on every item purchased is equal to that of every other item purchased.
- Changes in price have two distinct effects on consumer behavior. If the price falls, the marginal utility per dollar spent will be higher. As a result, consumers will substitute the product that has become relatively less expensive. This is the substitution effect. If the lower price also results in substantial savings, it causes an increase in purchasing power, known as the real-income effect.

What is the diamond-water paradox?

- The diamond-water paradox explains why water, which is essential to life, is inexpensive, while diamonds, which do not sustain life, are expensive. Many people of Adam Smith's era, in the eighteenth century, found the paradox perplexing. We can solve the diamond-water paradox by recognizing that the price of water is low because its supply is abundant, and the price of diamonds is high because their supply is small. If water were as rare as diamonds, there is no doubt that the price of water would exceed the price of diamonds.

CHAPTER PROBLEMS

Concepts You Should Know

consumer optimum (p. 518)
diamond-water paradox (p. 523)
diminishing marginal utility (p. 516)
marginal utility (p. 515)
real-income effect (p. 522)
substitution effect (p. 521)
util (p. 512)
utility (p. 512)

Questions for Review

1. After watching a movie, you and your friend both indicate that you liked it. Does this mean that each of you received the same amount of utility? Explain your response.
2. What is the relationship between total utility and marginal utility?
3. How is diminishing marginal utility reflected in the law of demand?
4. What does it mean when we say that the marginal utility per dollar spent is equal for two goods?

Study Problems *(✱ solved at the end of the section)*

1. A local pizza restaurant charges full price for the first pizza but offers 50% off on a second pizza. Using marginal utility, explain the restaurant's pricing strategy.
2. Suppose that the price of trail mix is $4 per pound and the price of cashews is $6 per pound. If you get 30 utils from the last pound of cashews you consume, how many utils would you have to get from the last pound of trail mix to be in consumer equilibrium?
3. Fill in the missing information in the table below:

Number of cookies	Total utility of cookies	Marginal utility of cookies	Number of pretzels	Total utility of pretzels	Marginal utility of pretzels
0	0	—	0	0	—
1	—	25	1	10	—
2	—	15	2	18	—
3	—	10	3	24	6
4	—	5	4	—	4
5	55	—	5	—	2
6	50	—	6	—	0

4. Use the table in problem 3. Suppose that you have a budget of $8 and that cookies and pretzels cost $1 each. What is the consumer optimum?
5. Use the table in problem 3. What is the consumer optimum if the price of cookies rises from $1 to $1.50 and the price of pretzels remains at $1?
6. You are considering either dining at Cici's, an all-you-can-eat pizza chain, or buying pizza by the slice at a local pizzeria for $2 per slice. At which restaurant are you likely to obtain the most marginal utility from the last slice you eat? Explain your response.
7. In consumer equilibrium, a person buys four cups of coffee at $2 per cup and two muffins at $2 per muffin each day. If the price of a cup of coffee rises to $3, what would you expect to happen to the amount of coffee and muffins this person consumes?
8. How do dollar stores survive when *none* of the items sold brings a high amount of total utility to consumers?

✱ 9. Imagine that the total utility from consuming five tacos is 10, 16, 19, 20, and 17 utils, respectively. When does marginal utility begin to diminish?

10. You and your friends are considering vacationing in either Cabo San Lucas or Cancun for spring break. When you first researched the cost of your hotel and flights, the total price was $1,000 to each destination. However, a sale has lowered the total cost of going to Cancun to $800. Does this change create a substitution effect, a real-income effect, or both? Explain.

✷ **11.** Everyone wears underwear, but comparatively few people wear ties. Why are ties so much more expensive than underwear if the demand for underwear is so much greater than the demand for ties?

12. Do you agree with Henry David Thoreau's quote, "Happiness is like a butterfly; the more you chase it, the more it will elude you, but if you turn your attention to other things, it will come and sit softly on your shoulder"? Explain your answer using diminishing marginal utility. Now consider this quote by Bengali Nobel laureate Rabindranath Tagore: "Ours is a society in which . . . [t]here is a continual screwing up of the ideal level of convenience and comfort, the increase in which is proportionately less than the energy it consumes." What do you think is happening to marginal utility?

✷ **13.** A health study found that patients who experience severe pain may feel better if they curse as a coping mechanism. Based on what you have learned about economics, would you expect to see a difference in pain relief between people who normally use profanity and those who do not normally use profanity?

14. Suppose that Gina's marginal utility from drinking milk is 5 utils per ounce, and her marginal utility from eating cereal is 10 utils per ounce. If the price of milk is 50 cents per ounce and the price of cereal is 80 cents per ounce, is Gina maximizing her utility? If so, explain how you know. If not, explain how she should change her spending to increase her utility.

15. Refer to the following Marginal Utility (MU) table:

$Q_{mangoes}$	$MU_{mangoes}$	$Q_{pineapples}$	$MU_{pineapples}$
1	20	1	24
2	15	2	18
3	10	3	12
4	5	4	6

You have a budget of $10. Pineapples cost $2, and mangoes cost $1. How many of each should you buy to maximize total utility?

Solved Problems

9. The key to answering this question is to realize that the data are expressed in total utils. The first taco brings the consumer 10 utils. Consuming the second taco yields 16 − 10, or 6 additional utils. Since there are fewer extra utils from the second taco (6) than the utils from the first taco (10), diminishing marginal utility begins after the first taco.

11. Recall that demand is only half of the market. The other half is supply. Far fewer ties are produced than items of underwear. The supply of ties also plays a role in determining the price. In addition, ties are a fashion statement, which makes ties a luxury good. Underwear is a necessity. As a result, ties are a lot like diamonds: there is a small overall market, and prices are high. Underwear is a lot like water: there is a very large overall market, and prices are low. The fact that ties generally cost more does not mean that ties are more valuable to society. Rather, people get more marginal utility from purchasing the "perfect" tie as opposed to finding the "perfect" underwear.

13. The researchers found that patients who infrequently cursed in their daily lives experienced more pain relief when they were in severe pain. Those who regularly cursed in their daily lives experienced almost no pain relief from cursing. This result is not surprising when you recall the law of diminishing marginal utility. For additional information, see https://doi.org/10.1016/j.jpain.2011.09.004.

APPENDIX

16A

Indifference Curve Analysis

A topographic map and indifference curve analysis share many of the same properties.

There is much more to economic analysis than the simple supply and demand model can capture. Chapter 16 considered how consumers can get the biggest bang for their buck, or the greatest utility out of their purchases. Here we explore the question in more detail, using the tool of indifference curve analysis. The purpose of this appendix is to get you thinking at a deeper level about the connections between price changes and consumption decisions.

Indifference Curves

Indifference curves are a tool that economists use to describe the trade-offs that exist when consumers make decisions.

An **indifference curve** represents the various combinations of two goods that yield the same level of satisfaction, or utility. The simplest way to think about indifference curves is to envision a topographical map on which each line represents a specific elevation. When you look at a topographical map, you see ridges, mountains, valleys, and the subtle flow of the land. An indifference curve conveys the same complex information about personal satisfaction. Indifference curves visually rise to a peak called the **maximization point**, or the point at which utility is maximized. The only limitation of this analysis is that this book is a two-dimensional space used to illustrate a three-dimensional concept. Let's set this concern aside and focus on achieving the maximization point, where total utility is highest.

An **indifference curve** represents the various combinations of two goods that yield the same level of personal satisfaction, or utility.

A **maximization point** is the point at which a certain combination of two goods yields the greatest possible utility.

Returning to our example of pizza and Pepsi, recall that you had $10 to spend and only two items to purchase: Pepsi at $1 per can and pizza at $2 per slice. Like all consumers, you will optimize your utility by maximizing the marginal utility per dollar spent, so you select four Pepsis and three slices of pizza. But what happens if your budget is unlimited? If you're free to spend as much you like, how much pizza and Pepsi would you want?

Economic "Goods" and "Bads"

To answer the question we just posed, we'll start with another question: Are Pepsi and pizza always economic "goods"? This may seem like a strange question, but think about your own consumption habits. Do you keep eating something after you feel full? Do you continue to eat even if your stomach aches? At some point, we all stop eating and drinking. In this sense, economic goods, like Pepsi and pizza, are "good" only up to a point. Once we are full, however, the utility from attaining another unit of the good becomes negative—a "bad."

Each indifference curve represents lines of equal satisfaction. For simplicity, Figure 16A.1 shows the indifference curve as circles around the point of maximum satisfaction. The closer the indifference curve is to the maximization point, the higher the consumer's level of satisfaction.

FIGURE 16A.1

Indifference Curves

The maximization point indicates where a consumer attains the most utility. In quadrant I, both Pepsi and pizza are "goods" (because their consumption involves the reactions of either tasting great or getting full), so attaining more of each will cause utility to rise toward the maximization point. In quadrants II, III, and IV, either pizza or Pepsi is a "bad" or both are (because at those levels of consumption they make the consumer feel either too full or sick). Because the consumer must pay to acquire pizza and Pepsi, and because at least one of the items is reducing the consumer's utility in quadrants II, III, and IV, the most affordable path to the highest utility—that is, the maximization point—is quadrant I. (Notice that the labels are qualitative and reflect decreasing utility with additional consumption.)

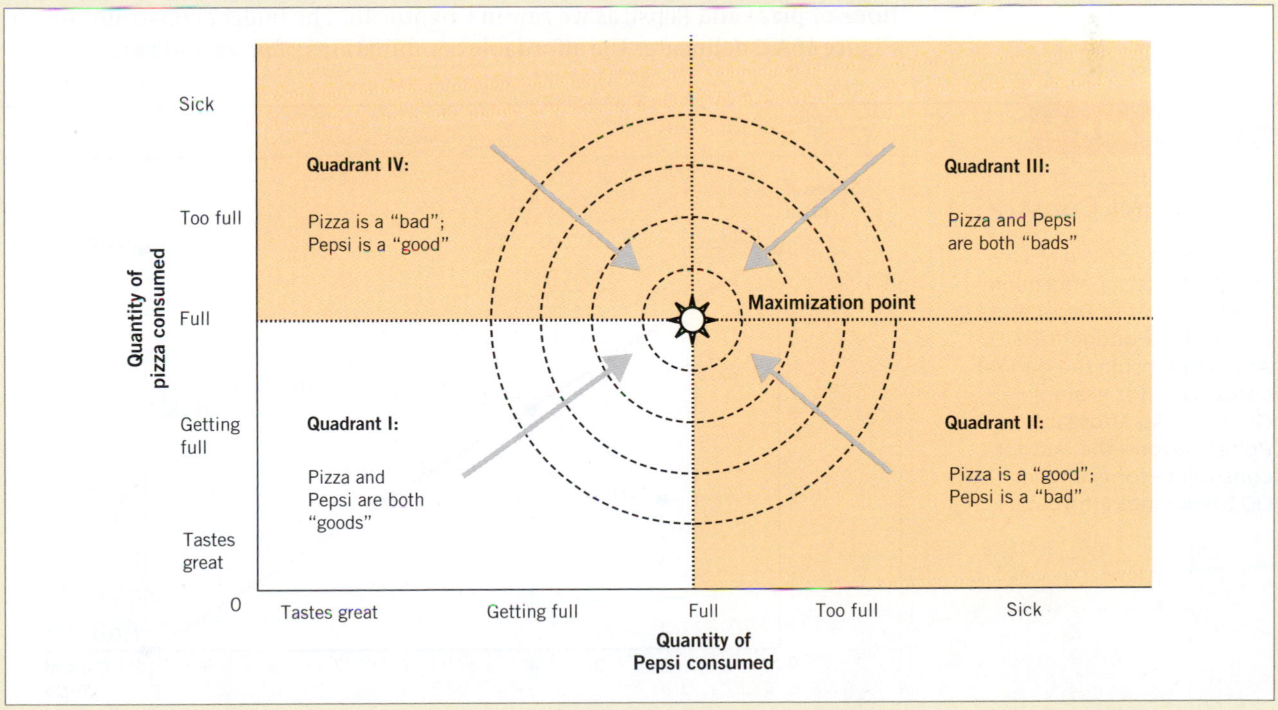

Indifference curves are best seen as approaching the maximization point from all directions (like climbing up a mountain on four different sides). In any hike, some paths are better than others. Figure 16A.1 illustrates four separate ways to reach the maximization point. However, only one of the paths makes any sense. In quadrants II, III, and IV, either pizza or Pepsi is a "bad" or both are "bads" (because at those levels of consumption one or both of them make the consumer feel too full or sick). Because the consumer must pay to acquire pizza and Pepsi, and because at least one of them is reducing the consumer's utility, the consumer's satisfaction will increase by purchasing less of the "bad." In other words, why would anyone willingly pay to feel worse? Quadrants II, III, and IV are highlighted in orange because people are unlikely to choose an option that makes them feel too full or sick. That leaves quadrant I as the preferred path to the highest utility. In quadrant I, increasing amounts of pizza and Pepsi produce more utility. (Notice that the labels in Figure 16A.1 are qualitative and reflect decreasing utility with additional consumption.)

The Budget Constraint

The **budget constraint** is the set of consumption bundles that represent the maximum amount the consumer can afford.

Figure 16A.1 illustrates the choices facing a consumer with an unlimited budget and no opportunity costs. However, in real life we need to account for a person's budget and the cost of acquiring each good. The amount a person has to spend is the **budget constraint**, or the set of consumption bundles that represent the maximum amount the consumer can afford. If you have $10 to spend on pizza ($2 per slice) and Pepsi ($1 per can), you could choose to purchase 10 cans of Pepsi and forgo the pizza. Alternatively, you could purchase 5 slices of pizza and do without the Pepsi. Or you could choose a number of different combinations of pizza and Pepsi, as we saw in Chapter 16. The budget constraint line in Figure 16A.2 delineates the affordable combinations of pizza and Pepsi.

FIGURE 16A.2

The Budget Constraint

The budget constraint line shows the set of affordable combinations of Pepsi and pizza with a budget of $10. Any point inside the budget constraint—for example (2,2)—is also affordable. Points beyond the budget constraint—for example (10,5)—are not affordable.

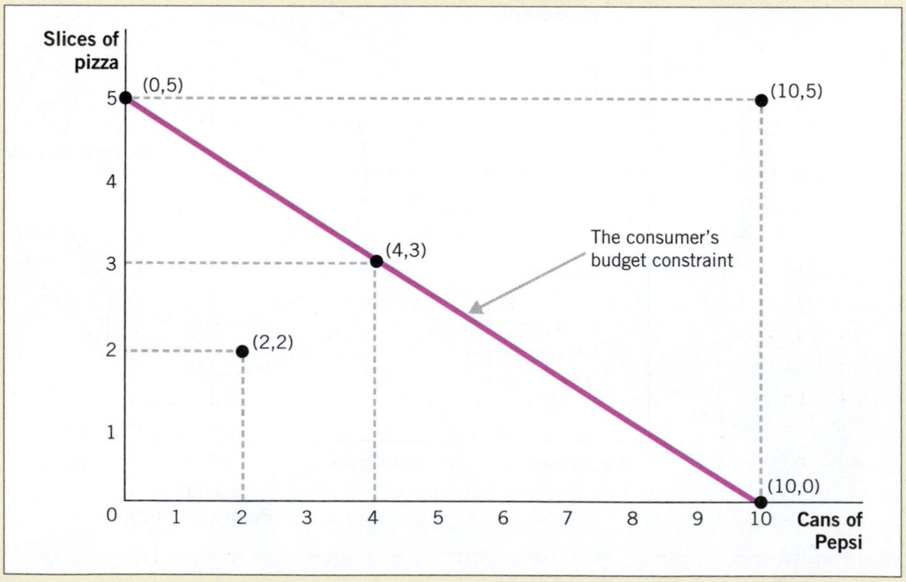

There are many different affordable combinations of the two goods. Let's take the pairs along the budget constraint line first. If you spend your entire $10 on Pepsi, the combination of coordinates would be the point (10,0), which represents 10 cans of Pepsi and 0 slices of pizza. If you spend your entire budget on pizza, the coordinates would be (0,5). These two points are the extreme outcomes. By connecting these two points with a line—the budget constraint—we can see the many combinations that would fully exhaust $10. As a consumer, your goal is to pick the combination that maximizes your satisfaction, subject to your budget constraint. One possibility would be to spend the $10 on four cans of Pepsi and three slices of pizza (4,3), which happens to be the point of utility maximization we discovered in this chapter (see Table 16.3).

What about the points located below and above the budget constraint? For example, looking again at Figure 16A.2, at the point (2,2) you would be spending $6—that is, $2 on Pepsi and $4 on pizza. You would still have $4 to spend on more of either good. Because both goods are desirable, spending the leftover money in your budget will increase your level of satisfaction. So the combination (2,2) represents a failure to maximize utility. On the other side of the budget constraint line, we find the point (10,5). This combination, which would cost you $20 to attain, represents a combination of items you cannot afford. From this example, you can see that the budget constraint is a limiting set of choices, or a constraint imposed by scarcity.

In the next section, we examine indifference curves in greater detail. Once we fully understand the properties that characterize indifference curves, we can join them with the budget constraint to better describe how consumers make choices.

Properties of Indifference Curves

It is useful to keep in mind several assumptions about indifference curves. The properties described in this section help ensure that our model is logically consistent.

Indifference Curves Are Typically Bowed Inward

A rational consumer will operate only in quadrant I in Figure 16A.1. Within that quadrant, the higher indifference curves (those nearer the utility maximization point) are bowed inward (convex) and are preferred to the lower ones (nearer the origin). Our model eliminates any outcome in quadrants II through IV by requiring that goods be "good," not "bad." Because quadrants II through IV result in less utility and greater expenditures, no rational consumer would ever willingly operate in these regions.

Figure 16A.3 shows an indifference curve that reflects the trade-off between two goods. Because the indifference curve bows inward, the **marginal rate of substitution (MRS)**, or the rate at which a consumer is willing to trade one good for another along the indifference curve, varies. The MRS is reflected in the slope of the indifference curve in the figure. Points A and B are both on the same indifference curve, so the consumer finds the combinations (1,5) and (2,3) to be equally attractive. Between points A and B, the consumer must receive two slices of pizza to compensate for the loss of a can of Pepsi. We can see this in the

The **marginal rate of substitution (MRS)** is the rate at which a consumer is willing to trade one good for another along an indifference curve.

Trade-offs

FIGURE 16A.3

The Marginal Rate of Substitution

The marginal rate of substitution (MRS) along an indifference curve varies, as reflected in the slope of the indifference curve. Because Pepsi and pizza are both subject to diminishing marginal utility, it takes more of the plentiful good to keep the consumer indifferent when giving up another good that is in short supply.

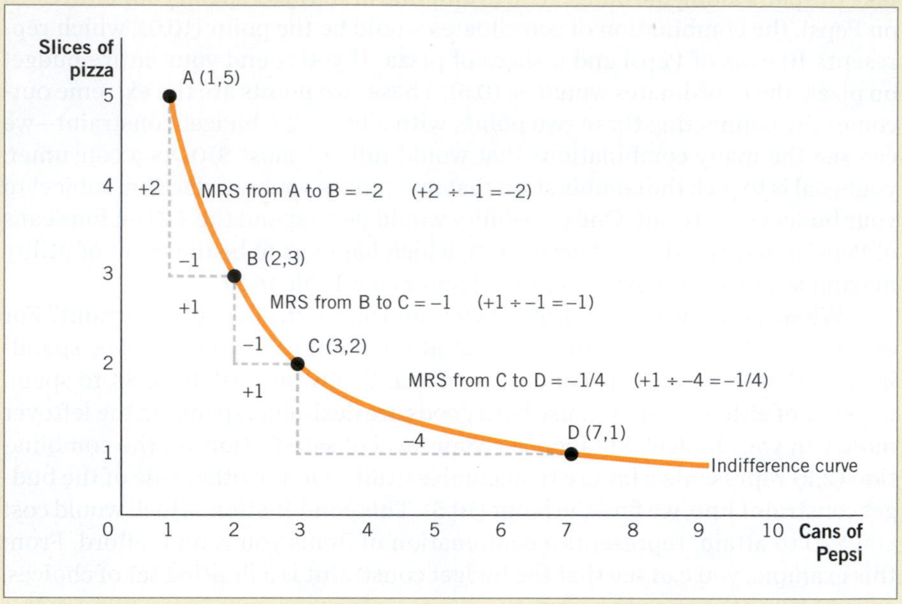

figure by observing that the consumer chooses only two cans of Pepsi and three slices of pizza at (2,3). Because the marginal utility from consuming Pepsi is high when the amount consumed is low, giving up an additional Pepsi requires that the consumer receive back two slices of pizza to reach the point (1,5). Therefore, the marginal rate of substitution (MRS) is –2 (because +2 ÷ –1 = –2).

However, if we examine the same indifference curve between points C and D, we see that the consumer is also indifferent between the combinations (3,2) and (7,1). However, this time the consumer is willing to give up four cans of Pepsi to get one more slice of pizza, so the MRS is –4 (because +1 ÷ –4 = –1/4). Why is there such a big difference between (3,2) and (7,1) compared with (2,3) and (1,5)? At (7,1), the consumer has a lot of Pepsi and very little pizza to enjoy it with. As a result, the marginal utility of the second slice of pizza is so high that it is worth four Pepsis! We can see the change in the marginal rate of substitution visually, because the slope between points A and B is steeper than it is between points C and D.

Marginal thinking

What explains why Pepsi is more valuable between points A and B? The consumer starts with only two cans. Pizza is more valuable between points C and D because the consumer starts with only two slices of pizza. Because Pepsi and pizza are both subject to diminishing marginal utility, it takes more of the plentiful good to keep the consumer indifferent when giving up another good that is in short supply.

Indifference Curves Cannot Be Thick

Another property of indifference curves is that they cannot be thick. If they could be thick, then it would be possible to draw two points inside an indifference curve where one of the two points was preferred to the other. Therefore, a

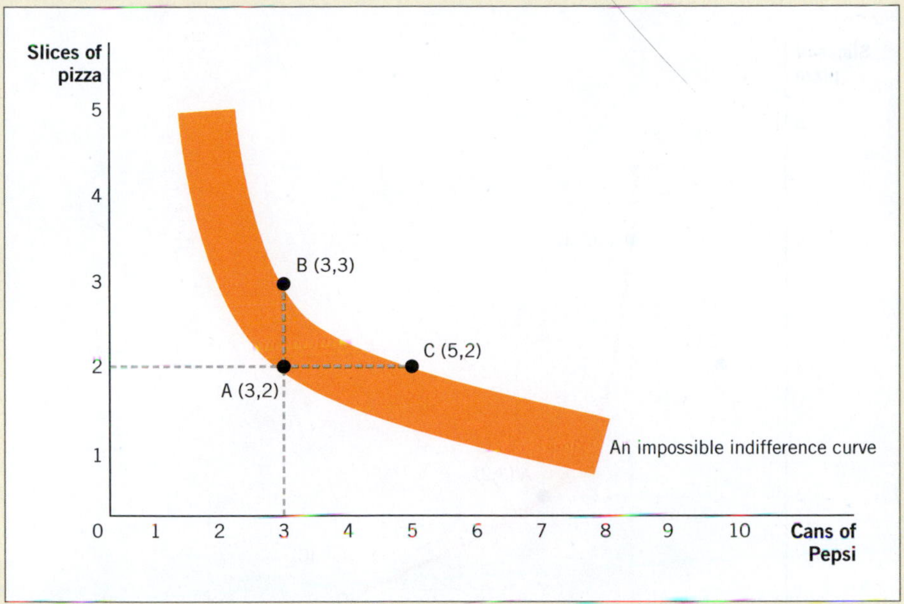

FIGURE 16A.4

Indifference Curves Cannot Be Thick

If indifference curves could be thick, it would be possible to draw two points inside the curve in a way that indicates that one of the two points is preferred to the other. Point B has one extra slice of pizza and point C has two extra cans of Pepsi compared with point A. Therefore, the consumer cannot be indifferent between these three points, and the indifference curve cannot be thick.

consumer could be indifferent between those points. In Figure 16A.4, points A, B, and C are all located on the same (impossible) indifference curve. However, points B and C are both strictly preferred to point A. Why? Because point B has one extra slice of pizza compared with point A, and point C has two extra cans of Pepsi compared with point A. Because more pizza and Pepsi adds to the consumer's utility, the consumer cannot be indifferent between these three points.

Indifference Curves Cannot Intersect

Indifference curves, by their very nature, cannot intersect. To understand why, let's look at a hypothetical case. Figure 16A.5 shows two indifference curves crossing at point A. Points A and B are both located along the light orange curve (IC_1), so we know that those two points bring the consumer the same utility. Points A and C are both located along the darker orange curve (IC_2), so those two points also yield the same utility for the consumer. Therefore, the utility at point A equals the utility at point B, and the utility at point A also equals the utility at point C. This means that the utility at point B should also equal the utility at point C, but that cannot be true. Point B is located at (1,3), and point C is located at (2,4). Because (2,4) strictly dominates (1,3), point C is preferred to point B. Therefore, we can say that indifference curves cannot intersect without violating the assumption that consumers are rational utility maximizers.

We have seen that indifference curves have three properties: they are bowed inward toward the origin (convex); they cannot be thick; and they cannot intersect. These properties guarantee that they take the general levels shown in quadrant I of Figure 16A.1.

FIGURE 16A.5

Indifference Curves Cannot Intersect

The utility at point B should equal the utility at point C, but that cannot be true even though the utility at point B is equal to the utility at point A (along IC_1) and the utility at point C is equal to the utility at point A (along IC_2). Point B is located at (1,3) and point C is located at (2,4). Because (2,4) strictly dominates (1,3), point C is preferred to point B. Indifference curves cannot intersect.

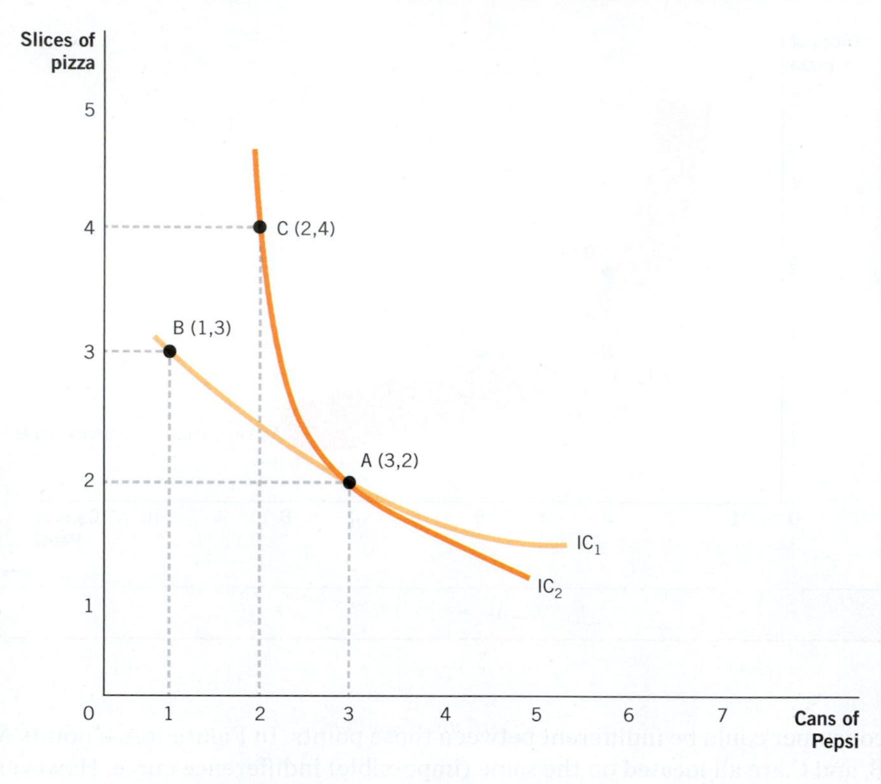

Extreme Preferences: Perfect Substitutes and Perfect Complements

As we have just seen, indifference curves typically are convex and bow inward toward the origin. However, there are two exceptions: *perfect substitutes* and *perfect complements*. These are found on either side of the standard-shaped, convex indifference curve.

Perfect substitutes exist when the consumer is completely indifferent between two goods, resulting in a straight-line indifference curve with a constant marginal rate of substitution.

Perfect complements exist when the consumer is interested in consuming two goods in fixed proportions, resulting in a right-angle indifference curve.

Perfect substitutes exist when a consumer is completely indifferent between two goods. Suppose that you cannot taste any difference between Aquafina and Evian bottled water. You would be indifferent between drinking one additional bottle of Aquafina or one additional bottle of Evian. Turning to panel (a) of Figure 16A.6, you can see that the indifference curves (IC_1, IC_2, IC_3, IC_4) for these two goods are straight, parallel lines with a marginal rate of substitution, or slope, of −1 everywhere along the curve. However, it's important to note that the slope of an indifference curve of perfect substitutes need not always be −1; it can be any constant rate. Because perfect substitutes have a marginal rate of substitution with a constant rate, they are drawn as straight lines.

Perfect complements exist when a consumer is interested in consuming two goods in fixed proportions. Shoes are an excellent example. We buy shoes in pairs because the left or right shoe is not valuable by itself; we need both shoes

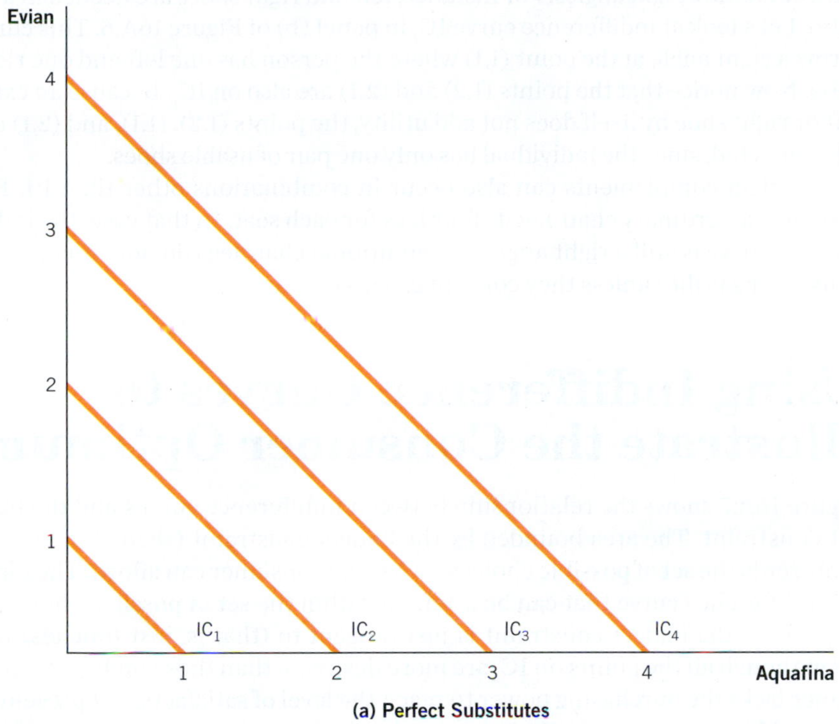

(a) Perfect Substitutes

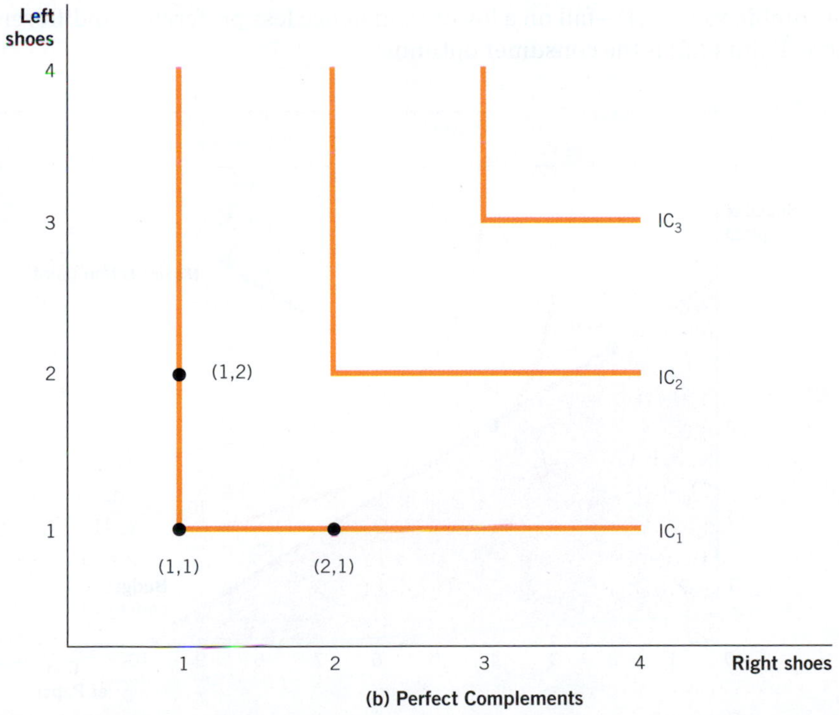

(b) Perfect Complements

FIGURE 16A.6

Perfect Substitutes and Perfect Complements

(a) Because perfect substitutes have a marginal rate of substitution that is constant, they are drawn as straight lines. In this case, the MRS, or slope, is –1 everywhere along the lines, or curves. (b) Perfect complements are drawn as right angles. A typical indifference curve that reflects the trade-off between two goods that are not perfect substitutes or perfect complements has a marginal rate of substitution that falls between these two extremes.

to be able to walk comfortably. This explains why shoes are not sold individually. An extra left or right shoe has no marginal value to the consumer, so the indifference curves are right angles. For instance, left and right shoes are needed in a 1:1 ratio. Let's look at indifference curve IC_1 in panel (b) of Figure 16A.6. This curve forms a right angle at the point (1,1) where the person has one left and one right shoe. Now notice that the points (1,2) and (2,1) are also on IC_1. Because an extra left or right shoe by itself does not add utility, the points (1,2), (1,1), and (2,1) are all connected, since the individual has only one pair of usable shoes.

Perfect complements can also occur in combinations other than 1:1. For instance, an ordinary chair needs four legs for each seat. In that case, the indifference curve is still a right angle, but additional chair legs do not enhance the consumer's utility unless they come in groups of four.

Using Indifference Curves to Illustrate the Consumer Optimum

Figure 16A.7 shows the relationship between indifference curves and the budget constraint. The area bounded by the budget constraint (shaded in purple) represents the set of possible choices—what the consumer can afford. The highest indifference curve that can be attained within the set of possible choices is IC_3, where the budget constraint is just tangent to (that is, just touches) IC_3. Even though all the points on IC_4 are more desirable than those on IC_3, the consumer lacks the purchasing power to reach the level of satisfaction represented by IC_4. Moreover, the point (4,3) is now clearly the preferred choice among the set of possible decisions. Other choices that are also affordable—for example, the combination (2,4)—fall on a lower (and hence less preferable) indifference curve. Point (4,3) is the consumer optimum.

FIGURE 16A.7

Consumer Optimum

Progressively higher indifference curves bring the consumer closer to the maximization point. Because the budget constraint limits what the consumer can afford, the tangency of the budget constraint with the highest indifference curve represents the highest level of affordable satisfaction—that is, the consumer optimum. In this case, the point (4,3) represents the consumer's preferred combination of Pepsi and pizza.

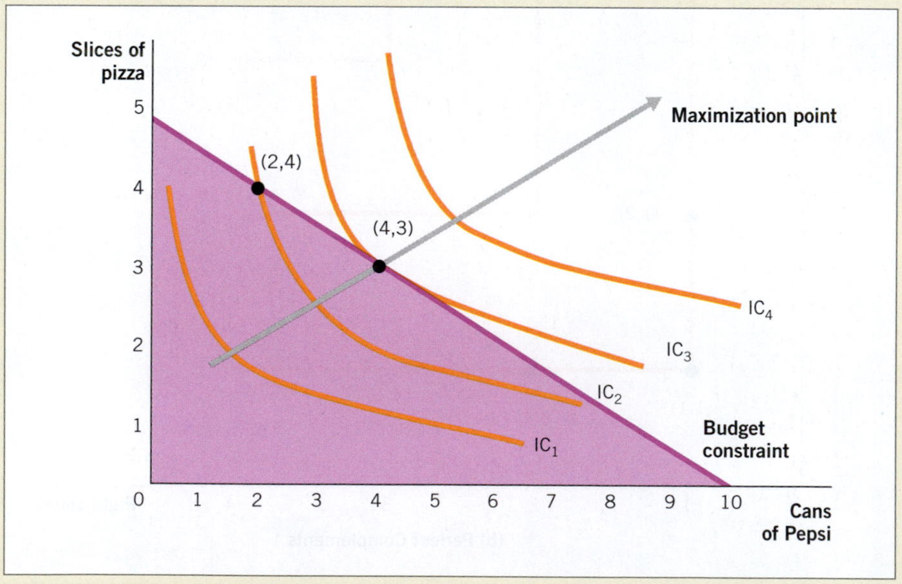

Progressively higher indifference curves bring the consumer closer to the maximization point. Because the budget constraint limits what the consumer can afford, the tangency of the budget constraint with the highest indifference curve represents the highest affordable level of satisfaction—that is, the consumer optimum.

Using Indifference Curves to Illustrate the Real-Income and Substitution Effects

The power of indifference curve analysis is its ability to display how price changes affect consumption choices. Part of the intuition behind the analysis involves understanding when the substitution effect is likely to dominate the real-income effect, and vice versa.

In our example, you have only $10, so a price increase on Pepsi from $1 to $2 per can would represent a financial burden, significantly lowering your real purchasing power. However, we can easily think of cases in which a change in the price of Pepsi wouldn't matter. Suppose yours is a typical American household with a median annual income of $60,000. While out shopping, you observe that a local Toyota car dealer is offering 10% off new cars and a nearby grocery store is selling Pepsi at a 10% discount. Because of the substitution effect, more people will buy Toyotas instead of Hondas, and more people will buy Pepsi instead of Coca-Cola. However, the real-income effects will be quite different. Saving 10% on the price of a new car could easily amount to a savings of $3,000 or more. In contrast, saving 10% on a 2-liter bottle of Pepsi will save only a couple of dimes. In the case of the new car, there is a substantial real-income effect, while the amount you save on the Pepsi is almost immaterial.

As we have just seen, changes in prices can have two distinct effects. The first is a substitution effect, under which changes in price will cause the consumer to substitute toward a good that becomes relatively less expensive. In our Pepsi/pizza example, suppose that the price of Pepsi rises to $2 per can. This price increase reduces your marginal utility per dollar of consuming Pepsi. As a result, you would probably buy fewer Pepsis and use the remaining money to purchase more pizza. In effect, you would substitute the relatively less expensive good (pizza) for the relatively more expensive good (Pepsi).

However, this is not the only effect at work. The change in the product price will also alter the purchasing power of your money, or income. And a change in purchasing power generates a real-income effect. In this case, your $10 will not go as far as it used to. In Figure 16A.8, we can see that the inward rotation of the budget constraint along the *x* axis from BC_1 to BC_2 is a result of the rise in the price of Pepsi. At $2 per can, you can no longer afford to buy 10 cans; the most you can purchase is 5. Therefore, the budget constraint moves inward along the *x* axis to 5 units while remaining constant along the *y* axis (because the price of pizza did not change). As a result, the combination (4,3) is no longer affordable. The higher price of Pepsi produces a new consumer optimum at (2,3) along IC_2. The end result is predictable: a rise in the price of Pepsi causes you to purchase less Pepsi and yields a lower level of satisfaction at IC_2 than your former point on IC_3 did, which is no longer possible.

FIGURE 16A.8

How a Change in Price Rotates the Budget Constraint

The inward rotation of the budget constraint along the *x* axis from BC_1 to BC_2 is a result of the rise in the price of Pepsi. At the price of \$2 a can, you can no longer afford to buy 10 cans; the most you can purchase is five. Therefore, the budget constraint moves inward along the *x* axis to 5 units (causing utility to fall from IC_3 to IC_2) while remaining constant along the *y* axis (because the price of pizza slices did not change).

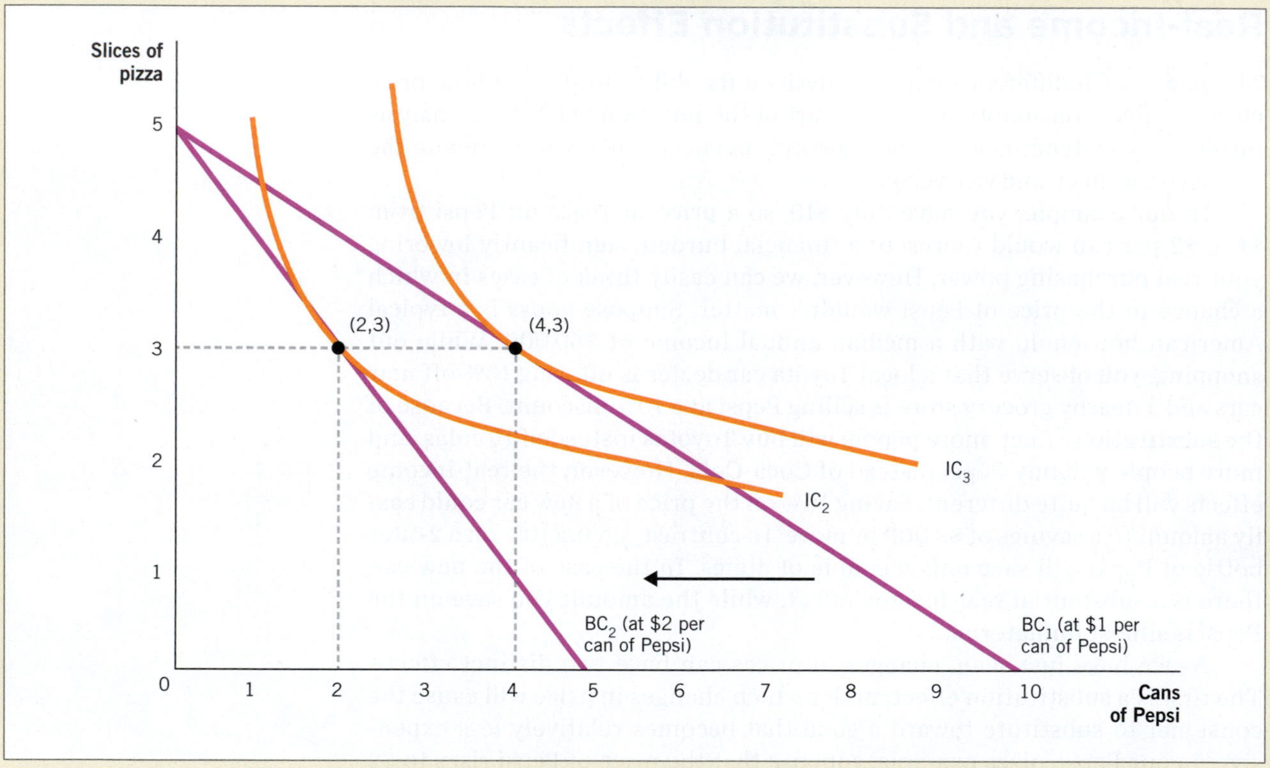

Separating the Substitution Effect from the Real-Income Effect

In this section, we separate the substitution effect from the real-income effect, and we see how the two effects can either reinforce each other or tend to cancel each other out (see Figure 16A.9).

With Pepsi at its new \$2-per-can price, you're ready to buy your revised optimum quantities, 2 cans of Pepsi and 3 slices of pizza. Then you learn that Pepsi has briefly gone on sale, at its old price of \$1 per can. How will you respond? Since at the old Pepsi price, your optimum was at (4,3), we know you'll end up back there again. But let's break your move from (2,3) to (4,3) into two steps.

Step 1. You were about to content yourself with 2 Pepsis and 3 pizza slices. Since that purchase now comes to \$8 instead of \$10, you just caught a break. But notice: theoretically you could be equally happy *for even less* than \$8. Simply slide along curve IC_2 to the consumption point that is cheapest, given the sale on Pepsi. That would be point A, where you're buying about 2½ cans of Pepsi and 2½ slices of pizza, for a total price of right around $7.50. We can even draw a new budget constraint through this point—call it BC "two point five"—based on the new prices, where we pretend that you have only $7.50 to spend. With that budget, Point A is your consumer optimum. You're just as happy as you would have been at (2,3), but you've saved money by substituting Pepsi for pizza, because Pepsi is cheaper compared with pizza than it was before. This is the substitution effect. (You would also, by the way, be substituting Pepsi for pizza if instead the price of pizza had gone up. What matters for the substitution effect is how *relative* prices change.)

Step 2. Okay, so you can't actually buy fractional Pepsis and pizza slices. It doesn't matter, though, because you're not actually on a $7.50 budget. You're on a $10 budget, and therefore able to buy both more pizza and more Pepsi. So, we shift the $7.50 line out to make it a $10 constraint, keeping the slope the same to reflect the current pizza-to-Pepsi price ratio. This is the real-income effect,

FIGURE 16A.9

Separating the Substitution Effect from the Real-Income Effect

Breaking down the movement from IC_2 to IC_3 into the substitution effect and the real-income effect allows us to see how each impacts the consumer's choice. The substitution effect increases the amount of Pepsi consumed and decreases the consumption of pizza, as indicated by the blue arrows and the leveling out of the budget constraint, from BC_2 to $BC_{2.5}$. The real-income effect increases the amounts of both Pepsi and pizza, as indicated by the green arrows and the shift of the budget constraint, from $BC_{2.5}$ to BC_3.

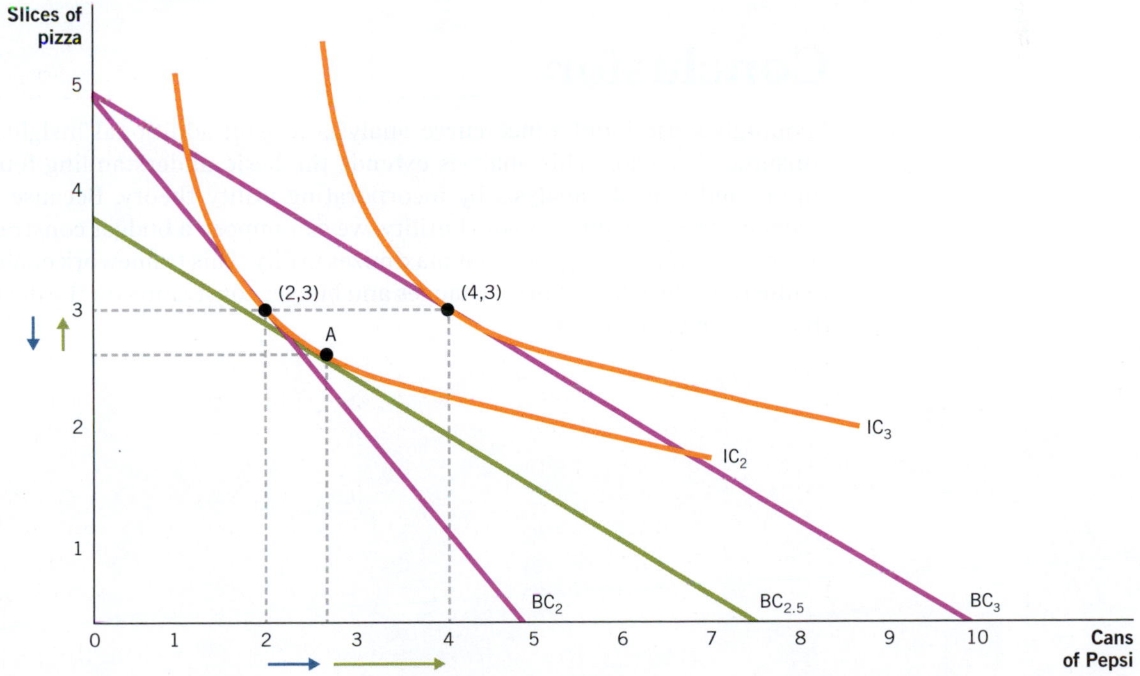

which is based on purchasing power. Again, you seek your consumer optimum, where the \$10 budget constraint, BC_3 (formerly known as BC_1), grazes curve IC_3, and that's point (4,3). Enjoy your meal!

The substitution and real-income effects influenced the consumption quantities of pizza and Pepsi in different ways. With pizza the effects canceled out: you bought less pizza because of the substitution effect (the blue arrow pointing down) but more pizza because of the real-income effect (the green arrow pointing up). That's how you started and ended at 3 slices. With Pepsi, on the other hand, the two effects reinforced each other: you bought more Pepsi because of the substitution effect, going from 2 cans to $2\frac{1}{2}$ (the blue arrow pointing right), and yet more because of the real-income effect, going from $2\frac{1}{2}$ cans to 4 (the green arrow pointing right). More generally, whenever the price of a good decreases, the result will be an increase in the amount consumed, because the real-income and substitution effects point in the same direction. By contrast, because the real-income effect and substitution effect move in opposite directions with respect to the good whose price has not changed, the result is ambiguous for that good (pizza), and any change in consumption depends on which effect—the substitution effect or the real-income effect—is greater. Here, they happened to be equal.

In our example, when the price of Pepsi drops back to \$1 per can, it produces a large real-income effect. Prior to the price drop, you were spending \$4 out of your \$10 budget on Pepsi, so Pepsi expenditures represented 40% of your budget. Because Pepsi is a big component of your budget, a halving of its price causes a sizable real-income effect. This is not always the case, however. For example, if the price of a candy bar were to halve, the typical household would barely notice this change. In cases like that, the real-income effect is negligible and the substitution effect tends to dominate.

Conclusion

Economists use indifference curve analysis to gain additional insights into consumer behavior. This analysis extends the basic understanding found in supply and demand analysis by incorporating utility theory. Because indifference curves are lines of equal utility, we can impose a budget constraint to describe the bundle of goods that maximizes utility. This framework enables us to illustrate the effect of price changes and budget constraints on the decisions that consumers make. ✷

APPENDIX PROBLEMS

Concepts You Should Know

budget constraint (p. 532)
indifference curve (p. 530)
marginal rate of substitution (MRS) (p. 533)
maximization point (p. 530)
perfect complements (p. 536)
perfect substitutes (p. 536)

Questions for Review

1. If your budget increases, what generally happens to the amount of utility you experience?
2. If your budget increases, is it possible for your utility to fall? Explain your response.
3. What is the difference between an economic "good" and an economic "bad"?
4. Describe what happens to your budget constraint if the price of one item in your budget decreases. Show the result on a graph.
5. A friend mentions to you that the campus coffee shop offers a 10% discount each Thursday morning before 10 a.m. Is this discount more likely to cause a significant substitution effect or a significant real-income effect? Explain.

Study Problems (*✱ solved at the end of the section)*

1. Ji-yoon has $20. Fish sandwiches cost $5, and a cup of espresso costs $4. Draw Ji-yoon's budget constraint. If espresso goes on sale for $2 a cup, what does her new budget constraint look like?
2. When you head home for dinner, your mother always sets the table with one spoon, two forks, and one knife. Draw her indifference curves for forks and knives.
3. ✱ Marco's indifference curves for movies and bowling look like the figure to the right.

   Each game of bowling costs $4, and each movie costs $8. If Marco has $24 to spend, how many times will he go bowling? How many times will he go to the movies?

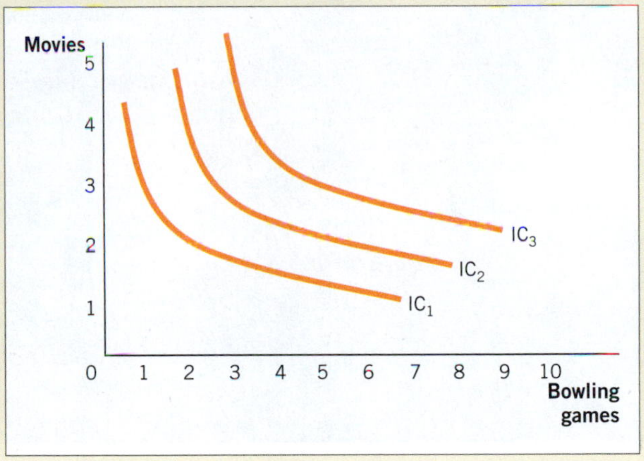

Solved Problem

3. Because Marco has $24 to spend, he can afford $24 ÷ $4, or six games of bowling. If he spends his money instead on movies, he can afford $24 ÷ $8, or three movies. Because Marco's budget constraint (BC) is just tangent to IC_1 at the point (2,2), Marco will go to two movies and bowl two games.

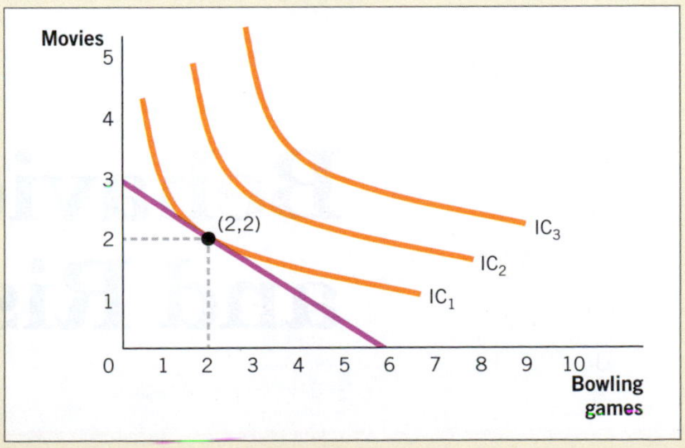

CHAPTER

17

Behavioral Economics and Risk Taking

People Don't Always Make Rational Decisions.

In this textbook, we have proceeded as if every person were *Homo economicus,* a rationally self-interested decision-maker. This idealized individual is acutely aware of opportunities in the environment and strives to maximize the benefits received from each course of action while minimizing the costs. What does *Homo economicus* look like? If you are a fan of *Star Trek,* you'll recall Spock, the Vulcan with perfect logic. He eschewed human emotion and didn't face many of the complications it creates for making decisions. Spock is *Star Trek*'s *Homo economicus.*

Kirk, by contrast, famously goes with his gut when the chips are down. In *Star Trek Into Darkness,* he saves a planet's inhabitants by making a snap decision to ignore the Prime Directive (not for the first time) and letting them see the *Enterprise*. Kirk's seat-of-his-pants style of decision-making often serves him and his shipmates, and various and sundry aliens, well. Remember, though: this is fiction! In the real world, the story is more complicated. Sometimes our instincts do steer us in the right direction. More commonly, however, they lead us astray in various subtle ways. In this chapter, we'll see how that happens. To fold the broadest possible set of human behavior into economic analysis, we must turn to the field of *behavioral*

Yet again, Spock has his mind blown by Kirk trusting his gut and getting away with it. "Why does he *do* that?" Spock is thinking. Answer: He's Kirk. This is how he rolls.

economics, which enables us to capture a wider range of human motivations than the rational-agent model alone affords.

· BIG QUESTIONS ·

- How do economists explain irrational behavior?
- What is the role of risk in decision-making?

How Do Economists Explain Irrational Behavior?

Like economics, psychology endeavors to understand the choices people make. One key difference is that psychologists do not assume that people always behave in a fully rational way. As a result, psychologists have a much broader toolbox at their disposal to describe human behavior. **Behavioral economics** is the field of economics that draws on insights from experimental psychology to explore how people make economic decisions.

Behavioral economics is the field of economics that draws on insights from experimental psychology to explore how people make economic decisions.

Until relatively recently, economists have ignored many human behaviors that do not fit their models. For example, because traditional economic theory assumed that people make optimal decisions, economic theorists did not try to explain why people might make an impulse purchase. Behavioral economists, however, understand that many behaviors contradict standard assumptions about rationality. They employ the idea of **bounded rationality**, which proposes that although decision-makers want a good outcome, either they are not capable of performing the problem-solving that traditional economic theory assumes or they are not inclined to do so.

Bounded rationality (also called limited reasoning) proposes that although decision-makers want a good outcome, either they are not capable of performing the problem solving that traditional economic theory assumes or they are not inclined to do so.

Bounded rationality, or limited reasoning, can be explained in three ways. First, the information the individual uses to make the decision may be limited or incomplete. Second, the human brain has a limited capacity to process information. Third, there is often a limited amount of time in which to make a decision. These limitations prevent the decision-maker from reaching the results predicted under perfect rationality.

For example, suppose you're about to get married and find yourself at Kleinfeld Bridal with your bridesmaids. You enter the store to begin your search for the perfect wedding dress. You find a dress you like, but its price is higher than you were planning to spend. Do you make the purchase or not? The decision to buy depends on whether you believe that the value is high enough to justify the price. But there is a problem: you have a limited amount of information. In a fully rational world, you would check out alternatives in other stores and on the Internet and then make the decision to purchase the dress only after you were satisfied it was the best possible choice. Full rationality also assumes that your brain is able to recall the features of every dress. However, a dress you tried on at one location often blurs into another dress you tried on elsewhere. Wedding dresses are selected under a binding deadline. This deadline means that you, the bride, must reach a decision quickly. Collectively, these three reasons often prevent a bride from achieving the result that economists' rational models predict. In reality, you walk into a store, see something you love, and make the purchase using partial information. Whenever people end up making decisions without perfect information, the decisions reflect bounded rationality.

We will continue our discussion of behavioral economics by examining various behaviors that do not fit assumptions about fully rational behavior. These include misperceptions of probabilities, inconsistencies in decision-making, and judgments about fairness when making decisions. The goal in this section is to help you recognize and understand many of the behaviors that lead to contradictions between what economic models predict and what people actually do.

Will you say yes to the dress?

Misperceptions of Probabilities

Economic models that assume rationality in decision-making do not account for the way people perceive the probability of events. Low-probability events are often overanticipated, and high-probability events are often underanticipated. To understand why, we consider several familiar examples, including games of chance, difficulties in assessing probabilities, and seeing patterns where none exist.

GAMES OF CHANCE Playing games of chance—for example, a lottery or a slot machine—is generally a losing proposition. Yet even with great odds against winning, millions of people spend money to play games of chance. How can we explain this behavior?

For some people, the remote chance of winning a lottery offers hope that they will be able to purchase something they need but cannot afford or even to escape from poverty. In many cases, people have incomplete information about the probabilities and prize structures. Most lottery players do not calculate the exact odds of winning. Lottery agencies typically highlight winners, as if the game has a positive expected value, which gets people excited about playing. Imagine how sobering it would be if every headline trumpeting the newest lottery millionaire was followed by all the names of people who lost. In fact, almost all games of chance have *negative expected values* for the participants, meaning that players are not likely to succeed at the game.

Players often operate under the irrational belief that they have control over the outcome. They are sure that playing certain numbers or patterns (for example, birthdays, anniversaries, or other lucky numbers) will bring success. Many players also feel they must stick with their favorite numbers to avoid regret;

Many games of chance return only about 50 cents for every dollar played.

everyone has heard stories about players who changed from their lucky pattern only to watch it win.

In contrast, some gaming behaviors are rational. For example, the film *21* depicts how skilled blackjack players, working in tandem, can beat the casinos by betting strategically and paying close attention to the cards on the table. In fact, some individuals are able to win at blackjack by counting the cards that have been dealt. Anytime the expected value of a gamble is positive, there is an incentive to play. For instance, if a friend wants to wager \$10.00 on the flip of a coin and promises you \$25.00 if you guess right, the expected value is half of \$25.00, or \$12.50. (There are only 2 possible outcomes, heads or tails, so your chances of winning are 1 in 2, or $\frac{1}{2}$. So $\frac{1}{2} \times \$25.00 = \$12.50$.) Because \$12.50 is greater than the \$10.00 you are wagering, we say that the gamble has a *positive expected value*. When the expected value of a gamble is positive, we actually expect that the more you play, the more likely it is that your earnings will be larger than your losses.

Incentives

Gambles can also make sense when you have very little to lose or no other options. And some people find the thrill of gambling enjoyable as entertainment, whether they win or lose. However, most gambling behaviors do not have rational motivations. Gambling often creates addictions that lead players to make poor financial decisions.

THE DIFFICULTIES IN ASSESSING PROBABILITIES In our discussion of games of chance, we saw that people who gamble do not usually evaluate probabilities in a rational way. But this irrational decision-making also happens with many other behaviors besides gambling. For example, on a per-mile basis, traveling by airplane is approximately 10 times safer than traveling by automobile. However, millions of people who refuse to fly because they are afraid of a crash do not hesitate to get into a car. Driving seems to create a false sense of control over one's surroundings.

The long-running television game show *Let's Make a Deal* provides a well-known example of the difficulties in assessing probabilities accurately. At the end of the show, the host would ask a contestant to choose one of three curtains. Behind each curtain was one of three possible prizes: a car, a nice but less expensive item, or a worthless joke item. Contestants could have maximized their chances of winning the car if they had used probability theory to make a selection. However, contestants rarely chose in a rational way.

If you were a contestant, would you make a rational choice?

Suppose you are a contestant on a game show like *Let's Make a Deal*. You pick curtain number 3. The host, who knows what is behind the curtains, opens a different one—say, curtain number 1, which has a pen filled with chickens (the joke prize). He then offers you the opportunity to switch your choice to curtain number 2. According to probability theory, what is the right thing to do? Most contestants would stay with their original choice because they figure that now they have a 50/50 chance of winning the car. But the probability of winning with your original

ECONOMICS *in the* MEDIA

Misperceptions of Probabilities

THE BIG BANG THEORY: THE SEPTUM DEVIATION

At the start of the episode, Leonard returns from a visit with his doctor, who explained to Leonard why he snores and gets sinus infections.

SHELDON: Hey, how did it go?

LEONARD: Oh, not fun. The doctor shoved a camera up into my sinuses.

AMY: Did they figure out what's wrong?

LEONARD: Yeah. It's a deviated septum. The surgery to correct it is simple. He's gonna do it next week.

Alarmed, Sheldon tries to convince Leonard that the risk of death from elective surgery is higher than most people realize. However, Sheldon seems fixated on a series of extremely unlikely possibilities.

SHELDON: I've been crunching the numbers, and so far, I've gotten your probability of death all the way to a sphincter-tightening one in 300 . . . What about epilepsy?

LEONARD: I don't have epilepsy.

SHELDON: You don't, but the surgeon might, hmm? And your carotid artery is just one shaky scalpel away from becoming the dancing fountain at Disneyland.

LEONARD: Sheldon, do you realize that driving is riskier than surgery?

Is Sheldon overthinking the risks of Leonard's minor surgery?

SHELDON: I do. I have the drive to the hospital right here. That is if you make it to the car without falling down the stairs.

LEONARD: Buddy, I, I get that you're worried about me and I, I appreciate that, but I'm not going to die.

SHELDON: You don't know that.

LEONARD: Well, I do know that it won't be from an asteroid strike.

SHELDON: You know who else said that? Every cocky *T. Rex* currently swimming around in the gas tank of your car.

choice remains 1/3, because the chance that you guessed correctly the first time is unchanged. Equally, the chance that one of the other curtains contains the car is still 2/3. But with curtain number 1 revealed as the joke prize, that 2/3 probability now belongs entirely to curtain number 2. Therefore, the contestant should take the switch, because it upgrades the chance of winning the car from 1/3 to 2/3. Few contestants make the switch, though. Almost all contestants think that each of the two remaining unopened curtains has an equal probability of holding the car, so they decide not to switch for fear of regretting their decision. Not switching indicates a failure to understand the opportunity costs involved in the decision.

Opportunity cost

The difficulty in recognizing the true underlying probabilities, combined with an irrational fear of regret, leads to many poor decisions. Understanding these tendencies helps economists to evaluate why some decisions are difficult to get right.

SEEING PATTERNS WHERE NONE EXIST Two fallacies, or false ways of thinking, help explain how some people make decisions: the *gambler's fallacy* and the *hot hand fallacy*.

The **gambler's fallacy** is the belief that recent outcomes are unlikely to be repeated and that outcomes that have not occurred recently are due to happen soon.

The **gambler's fallacy** is the belief that recent outcomes are unlikely to be repeated and that outcomes that have not occurred recently are due to happen soon. For example, studies examining state lotteries find that bets on recent winning numbers decline. Because the selection of winning numbers is made randomly, just like flipping coins, the probability that a certain number will be a winner in one week is not related to whether the number came up in the previous week. In other words, someone who uses the gambler's fallacy believes that if many "heads" have occurred in a row, then "tails" is more likely to occur next.

The **hot hand fallacy** is the belief that random sequences exhibit a positive correlation (relationship).

The **hot hand fallacy** is the belief that random sequences exhibit a positive correlation (relationship). The classic study in this area examined perceptions about the game of basketball. Most sports enthusiasts believe that a player who has scored several baskets in a row—one with a "hot hand"—is more likely to score a basket with his or her next shot than at another time. However, the study found no positive correlation between success in one shot and success in the next shot.

ECONOMICS IN THE REAL WORLD

HOW BEHAVIORAL ECONOMICS HELPS TO EXPLAIN STOCK PRICE VOLATILITY

Let's examine some of the traps that people fall into when they invest in the stock market. In a fully rational world, the gambler's fallacy and the hot hand fallacy would not exist. In the real world, however, people are prone to seeing patterns in data even when there are none. Investors, for example, often believe that the rise and fall of the stock market is driven by specific events and by underlying metrics such as profitability, market share, and return on investment. But, in fact, investors often react with a herd mentality by rushing into stocks that appear to be doing well—reflecting the hot hand fallacy—and selling off stocks when a downward trend seems to be occurring. Similarly, there are times when investors believe that the stock market has run up or down too rapidly and they expect its direction to change soon—reflecting the gambler's fallacy.

Ulrike Malmendier, *Homo economicus* mythbuster.

Ulrike Malmendier studies behavioral economics and is a leading expert on how biases affect corporate decisions, stock prices, and markets in general. "Biases don't only affect decision-making by small investors and consumers; they also affect top business leaders," Malmendier says. She likes to quote Warren Buffett, who once remarked, "I'd be a bum on the street with a tin cup if the markets were efficient."

In her work on hubris, she found that executives who won prestigious awards, such as "CEO of the Year," tended to underperform their noncelebrity peers in the years just after the prestigious award was bestowed, proving that overconfidence could be detrimental to profits. One likely way this plays out is that award-winning CEOs think they have a hot hand and therefore take risks they shouldn't.*

In addition, some segments of the market are driven by investor psychology instead of metrics that measure valuation. Research has also shown that mood matters: believe it or not, there is a small correlation between the weather and how the stock market trades on a particular day. The market is more likely to move higher when it is sunny on Wall Street than when it is cloudy! The very fact that the weather in Lower Manhattan could have anything to do with how the overall stock market performs is strong evidence that some market participants are not rational.

*Ed Andrews, "Faculty Rock Stars," *Berkeley Haas*, Summer 2014, https://web.archive.org/web/20171019123619/http://www.haas.berkeley.edu/groups/pubs/berkeleyhaas/summer2014/faculty-rock-stars-ulrike-malmendier.html.

PRACTICE WHAT YOU KNOW

Gambler's Fallacy or Hot Hand Fallacy? Patterns on Exams

Do you ever wonder what it means when the same answer comes up many times in a row?

Your instructor is normally conscientious and makes sure that exam answers are randomly distributed. However, you notice that the first five answers on the multiple-choice section are all C. Unsure what this pattern means, you consider the next question. You do not know the answer and are forced to guess. You decide to avoid C because you figure that C cannot happen six times in a row.

QUESTION: Which is at work: the gambler's fallacy or the hot hand fallacy?

ANSWER: According to the gambler's fallacy, recent events are less likely to be repeated again in the near future. So it is the gambler's fallacy at work here in your decision to avoid marking another C. If you had acted on the hot hand fallacy, you would have believed that random sequences exhibit a positive correlation and therefore would have marked the next answer as C.

CHALLENGE QUESTION: Suppose that instead of all C's, the first five answers are B, A, C, D, B. Again, you are forced to guess. You avoid B because it's the one answer that was already used twice. Is this reasonable?

ANSWER: It's the same gambler's fallacy again, just in subtler form. If the answers are random, it doesn't matter what the first five answers were. They have *nothing to do* with the sixth answer.

Inconsistencies in Decision-Making

Trade-offs

If people were entirely rational, they would always be consistent. So the way a question is asked should not alter our responses, but research has shown that it does. Likewise, rational decision-making requires the ability to take the long-run trade-offs into account: if the returns are large enough, people should be willing to sacrifice current enjoyment for future benefits. Yet many of us make shortsighted decisions. In this section, we examine a variety of decision-making mistakes, including framing effects, priming effects, status quo bias, intertemporal decision-making, and the endowment effect.

The **framing effect** occurs when people change their answer depending on how the question is asked (or change their decision depending on how alternatives are presented).

FRAMING EFFECTS AND PRIMING EFFECTS We have seen a number of ways in which economic models do not entirely account for the behavior of real people. One common mistake that people make involves the **framing effect**, which occurs when an answer is influenced by the way a question is asked or a decision is influenced by the way alternatives are presented. Consider an employer-sponsored retirement plan. Companies can either (1) ask employees if they want to join or (2) use an automatic enrollment system and ask employees to let them know if they do not wish to participate. Studies have shown that workers who are asked if they want to join tend to participate at a much lower rate than those who are automatically enrolled and must say they want to opt out. Surely, a rational economic decision-maker would determine whether to participate by evaluating the plan itself, not by responding to the way the employer presents the option to participate. However, people are rarely that rational!

The **priming effect** occurs when the order of the questions influences the answers.

Another decision-making pitfall, known as the **priming effect**, occurs when the order of the questions influences the answers. For example, consider two groups of college students. The first group is asked "How happy are you?" followed by "How many dates have you had in the last year?" The second group is asked "How many dates have you had in the last year?" followed by "How happy are you?" The questions are the same, but they are presented in reverse order. In the second group, students who had gone out on more dates reported being much happier than similar students in the first group! In other words, because they were reminded of the number of dates first, those who had more dates believed they were happier.

Status quo bias exists when decision-makers want to keep things the way they are.

STATUS QUO BIAS When people want to keep things the way they are, they may exhibit what is known as the **status quo bias**. This bias leads decision-makers to try to protect what they have, even when an objective evaluation of their circumstances suggests that a change would be beneficial.

The status quo bias causes people to behave conservatively. The cost of this behavior is missed opportunities that could potentially enhance welfare. For example, an individual with status quo bias would maintain a savings account with a low interest rate instead of actively shopping for better rates elsewhere. This person would lose the potential benefits from higher returns on savings.

Status quo bias also explains why new products and ideas have trouble gaining traction: many potential customers prefer to leave things the way they are, even if something new might make more sense. Consider the $1 coin. It is far more durable than the $1 bill. It is also easier to tell the $1 coin apart from

ECONOMICS in the MEDIA

Framing

INSIDE OUT

Pixar's *Inside Out* (2015) is a sweet fable about how five human emotions impact everyday decisions. The film shows that humans do not behave rationally but instead are guided by mental shortcuts and influenced by emotional biases. Moreover, our different emotions provide different ways of framing the same situation. If there's an opportunity to go out in the rain, Joy will ask if we want to go jump around in puddles, while Sadness will ask if we want to stand outside while our boots fill with water. Fear will wonder if it is safe and suggest we stay inside—that's the status quo bias.

Our lives are a whirlwind of emotions that make fully rational decisions impossible most of the time.

Joy, the default emotion in the movie, influences us in ways that are usually good, but not always. Joy helps us face challenges and makes life worth living. Joy also derives utility from small acts of kindness and gives us the pluck to smile when life gets tough. But too much optimism is itself a kind of bias. When we are happy, we don't believe that bad things will happen to us, like traffic accidents—so we may drive too fast. (Joy rides, anyone?) Riley, the teenage girl who is the film's main character, needed more than simply Joy in her life. Riley also needed Sadness to help her cope with her cross-country move. Our emotions are complex, and each plays a crucial role in helping us navigate life. So it shouldn't be surprising to anyone trying to explain human behavior that our emotional states will influence our choices and how rationally or irrationally we make them.

the other coins and bills in your wallet, and if people used the coin, the government would save about $5 billion in production costs over the next 30 years. That sounds like a slam-dunk policy change, but it is not. Americans like their dollar bills and rarely use the $1 coins in circulation even though they repeatedly use nickels, dimes, and quarters to make change, to feed parking meters, and to buy from vending machines. Introducing more of the $1 coin and eliminating the $1 bill would be rational, but the status quo bias has prevented the change from happening.

Are you on Team Dollar Bill or Team Dollar Coin?

ECONOMICS IN THE REAL WORLD

ARE YOU AN ORGAN DONOR?

More than 25,000 organ transplants take place every year in the United States, with the vast majority coming from deceased donors. Demand greatly exceeds supply. Over 100,000 people are currently on organ donation waiting lists. Most Americans are

In the United States, you must opt in to become an organ donor.

aware of the need, and 90% of all Americans say they support donation. But only 30% know the essential steps to take to become a donor.

There are two main donor systems: the "opt-in" system and the "opt-out" system. In an opt-in system, individuals must give explicit consent to be a donor. In an opt-out system, anyone who has not explicitly refused is considered a donor.

In the United States, donors are required to opt in. Because opting in generally produces fewer donors than opting out, many states have sought to raise donation awareness by allowing consent to be noted on individual driver's licenses.

In Europe, many countries have opt-out systems, where consent is presumed. The difference is crucial. After all, in places with opt-in systems, many people who would be willing to donate organs never actually take the time to complete the necessary steps to opt in. In countries like France and Poland, where people must opt out, over 90% of citizens do not explicitly opt out, which means they give consent. This strategy yields organ donation rates that are significantly higher than those of opt-in programs.

According to traditional economic analysis, opting in or opting out should not matter—the results should be the same. The fact that we find strong evidence to the contrary is a compelling illustration of the status quo bias.

Intertemporal decision-making involves planning to do something over a period of time, which requires valuing the present and the future consistently.

INTERTEMPORAL DECISION-MAKING Intertemporal decisions occur across time. **Intertemporal decision-making**—that is, planning to do something over a period of time—requires the ability to value the present and the future consistently. For instance, many people, despite their best intentions, do not end up saving enough for retirement. The temptation to spend money today ends up overwhelming the willpower to save for tomorrow. In a perfectly rational world, a person would not need outside assistance to save enough for retirement. In the real world, however, workers depend on 401(k) plans and other work-sponsored retirement programs to deduct funds from their paycheck so that they don't spend that portion of their income on other things. It may seem odd that people would need an outside agency to help them do something that is in their own long-term interest, but as long as their intertemporal decisions are likely to be inconsistent, the additional commitment helps them to achieve their long-run objectives.

The ability to resist temptation is illustrated by a classic research experiment conducted at a preschool at Stanford University in 1972. One at a time, individual children were led into a room devoid of distractions and were offered a marshmallow. The researchers explained to each child that he or she could eat the marshmallow right away or wait for 15 minutes and be rewarded with a second marshmallow. Very few of the 600 children in the study ate the marshmallow immediately. Most tried to fight the temptation. Of those who tried to wait, approximately one-third held out long enough to earn the second marshmallow. That finding is interesting by itself, but what happened next is truly amazing. Many of the parents of the children in the original study noticed that the children who had delayed gratification seemed to perform better as they progressed through school. Researchers have tracked the participants over the course of 40 years and found that the delayed-gratification group had higher SAT scores, more savings, and larger retirement accounts.

Can you resist eating one marshmallow now in order to get a second one later?

The Endowment Effect

What belongs to us, and what we give away, always seems very precious, because once we own something, we value it more. Think of Gollum in *The Lord of the Rings*, obsessed with recovering a ring he has lost. That's the **endowment effect**, and it explains why the loss of value associated with selling an item, or giving it up, is typically greater than the financial or emotional gain associated with obtaining the item in the first place. The endowment effect lies outside traditional economic theory, which assumes that humans consistently make rational decisions.

The **endowment effect** is the principle that once we own something, we value it more.

There's extensive evidence that physically handling an object can increase our perceived ownership of it. The so-called IKEA effect is a prime example. IKEA has mazelike showrooms that encourage customers to touch and try out every item in sight. But the responsibility of assembly for anything you buy lies with you. There are obvious cost savings for the company. But the real genius of this sales model is that by letting you touch items in the showroom, and then requiring you to assemble your table or bed frame at home, IKEA encourages you to value their product more than if you had just bought it as a finished piece.

Judgments about Fairness

The pursuit of fairness is another common behavior that is important in economic decisions but that standard economic theory cannot explain. For example, fairness is one of the key drivers in determining tax rate structure for income taxes. Proponents of fairness believe in progressive taxation, whereby the rich pay a higher tax rate on their income than those in lower income brackets do. Likewise, some people object to the high pay of chief executive officers or the high profits of some corporations because they believe there should be an upper limit to what constitutes fair compensation.

Dear customer: Build it yourself and you will cherish it. Love, IKEA.

SNAPSHOT

Opt-Out Is Optimal

Some of the most successful applications of behavioral economics are "opt-out" programs, which automatically enroll eligible people unless they explicitly choose not to participate. The incentives and freedom of choice are exactly the same as in "opt-in" programs, where members must choose to participate, but enrollments are significantly higher under opt-out. Here's a look at three remarkable results.

Participation Rate

You can never start saving soon enough, and sending part of your paycheck into a 401(k) retirement account is a great way to do it. Opt-out programs are far more successful than opt-in programs at encouraging young workers to participate.

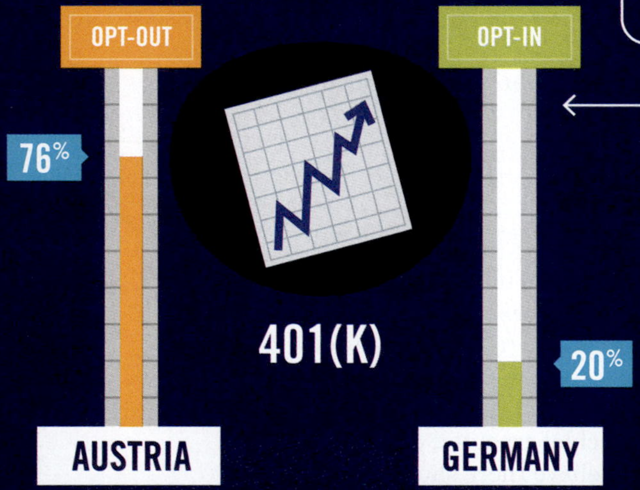

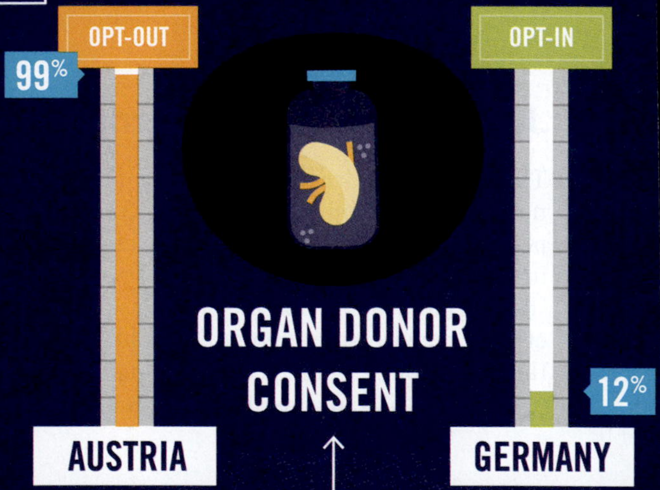

Tragically, thousands of people die each year waiting for an organ transplant. Opt-out organ donor consent programs lead to higher participation and more saved lives.

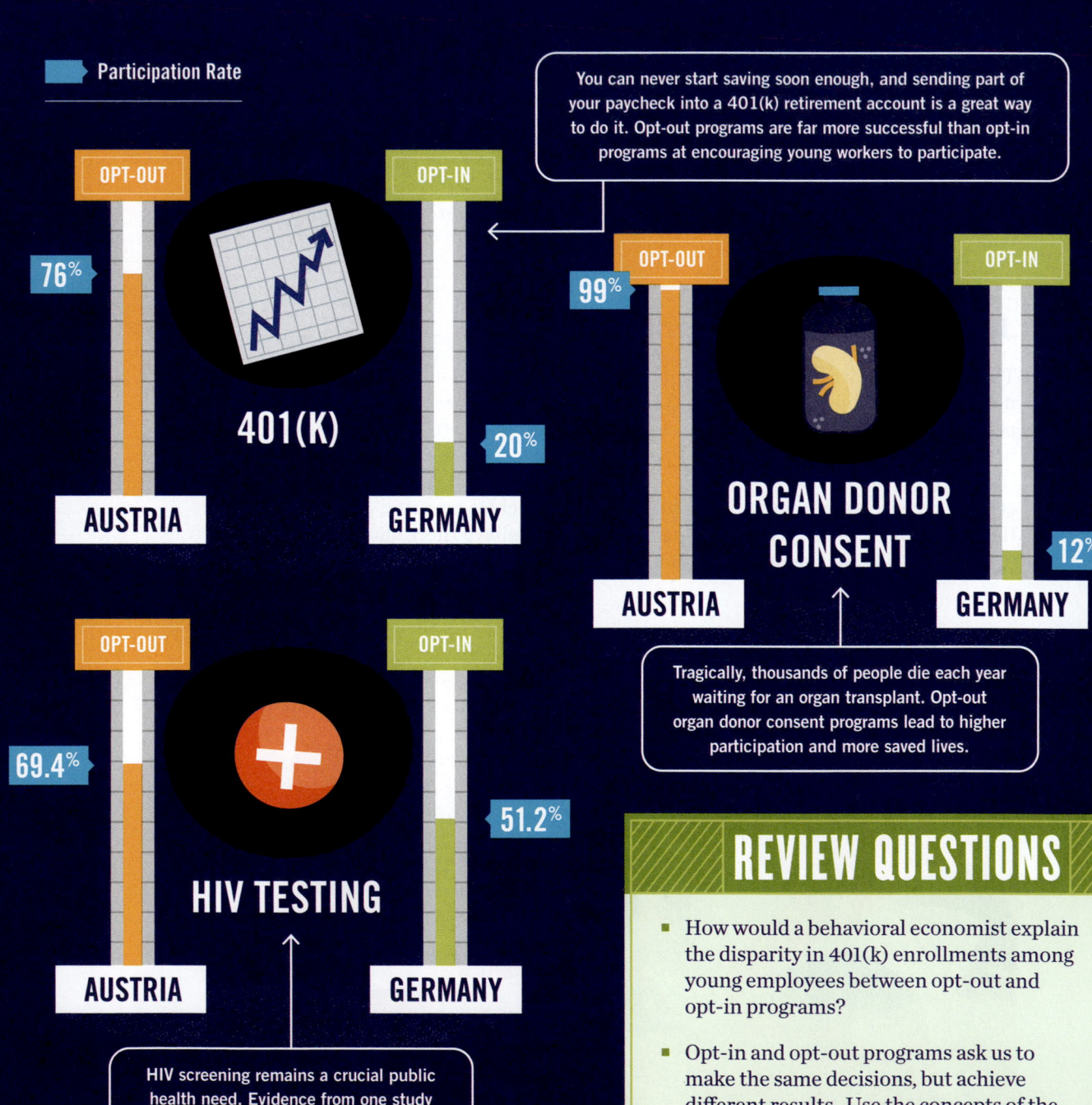

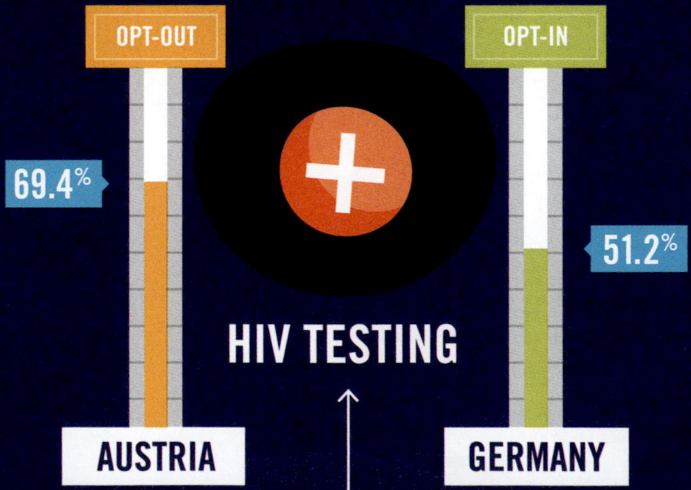

HIV screening remains a crucial public health need. Evidence from one study indicates that opt-out consent at emergency rooms leads to substantially more individuals agreeing to be tested.

REVIEW QUESTIONS

- How would a behavioral economist explain the disparity in 401(k) enrollments among young employees between opt-out and opt-in programs?
- Opt-in and opt-out programs ask us to make the same decisions, but achieve different results. Use the concepts of the framing effect and nonrational behavior to explain why.

FIGURE 17.1

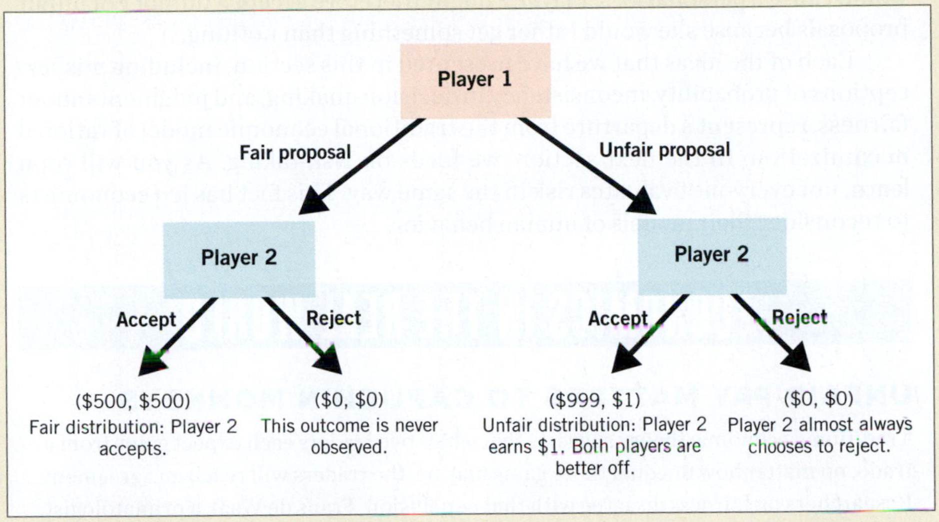

The Decision Tree for the Ultimatum Game

The decision tree for the ultimatum game has four branches. If player 1 makes a fair proposal, player 2 will accept the distribution and both players will earn $500. However, if player 1 makes an unfair proposal, player 2 may reject the distribution even though this rejection means receiving nothing.

While fairness is not normally modeled in economics, behavioral economists have developed experiments to determine the role of fairness in personal decisions. The **ultimatum game** is an economic experiment in which two players decide how to divide a sum of money. The game shows how fairness enters into the rational decision-making process. In the game, player 1 is given a sum of money and is asked to propose a way of splitting it with player 2. Player 2 can either accept or reject the proposal. If player 2 accepts, the sum is split according to the proposal. However, if player 2 rejects the proposal, neither player gets anything. The game is played only once, so the first player does not have to worry about reciprocity.

The **ultimatum game** is an economic experiment in which two players decide how to divide a sum of money.

Consider an ultimatum game that asks player 1 to share $1,000 with player 2. Player 1 must decide how fair to make the proposal. The decision tree in Figure 17.1 highlights four possible outcomes to two very different proposals—a fair proposal and an unfair proposal.

Traditional economic theory presumes that both players are fully rational and wish to maximize their income. Player 1 should therefore maximize his gains by offering the minimum, $1, to player 2. The reasoning is that player 2 values $1 more than nothing and so will accept the proposal, leaving player 1 with $999. But real people are not always economic maximizers because they generally believe that fairness matters. Most of the time, player 2 would find such an unfair division infuriating and reject it.

Player 1 knows that player 2 will definitely accept an offer of $500; this division of the money is exactly equal and therefore fair. Thus, the probability of a 50/50 agreement is 100%. In contrast, the probability of player 2 accepting an offer of $1 is close to 0%. Offering increasing amounts from $1 to $500 will continue to raise the probability of an acceptance until it reaches 100% at $500.

Player 2's role is simpler: her only decision is whether to accept or reject the proposal. Player 2 desires a fair distribution but has no direct control over the division. To punish player 1 for being unfair, player 2 must reject the proposal altogether. The trade-off of penalizing player 1 for unfairness is a complete

Trade-offs

loss of any prize. So while player 2 may not like any given proposal, rejecting it would cause a personal loss. Player 2 might therefore accept a number of unfair proposals because she would rather get something than nothing.

Each of the ideas that we have presented in this section, including misperceptions of probability, inconsistency in decision-making, and judgments about fairness, represent a departure from the traditional economic model of rational maximization. In the next section, we focus on risk-taking. As you will soon learn, not everyone evaluates risk in the same way. This fact has led economists to reconsider their models of human behavior.

ECONOMICS IN THE REAL WORLD

UNFAIR PAY MATTERS TO CAPUCHIN MONKEYS

Sour grapes? A capuchin monkey throws away cucumber to protest unfairness.

Traditional economic theory suggests that when two traders each expect gains from a trade, no matter how unequal those gains may be, the traders will reach an agreement. Researchers on fairness disagree with that conclusion. Frans de Waal, a primatologist, uses capuchin monkeys to argue that fairness matters throughout the animal kingdom. His short TED talk, which is equal parts *America's Funniest Home Videos* and Econ 101, is available on YouTube. It shows how a capuchin monkey given cucumbers as a reward is beside itself when it realizes its companion is receiving grapes. If you're thinking, "Okay, but they're just monkeys," consider how you'd react if you were invited to a party and were served cantaloupe while everyone else got lobster salad. Would you say, "Hey, free cantaloupe"? Or would you find a way to express your displeasure?

What Is the Role of Risk in Decision-Making?

In this section, we examine the role that risk plays in decision-making. The standard economic model of consumer choice assumes that people are consistent in their risk-taking preferences. However, people's risk tolerances actually vary widely and are subject to change. Thus, risk-taking behavior is not nearly as simple or predictable as economists once believed. We begin with a phenomenon known as *preference reversal*. We then consider how negative surprises can cause people to take more risk, which is explained by *prospect theory*.

Preference Reversals

Risk-averse people prefer a sure thing over a gamble with a higher expected value.

Risk-neutral people choose the highest expected value regardless of the risk.

Risk-takers prefer gambles with lower expected values, and potentially higher winnings, over a sure thing.

As you know, trying to predict human behavior is not easy. Maurice Allais, the recipient of the 1988 Nobel Prize in Economics, noticed that people's tolerance for risk appeared to change in different situations. This observation did not agree with the standard economic model, which assumes that an individual's risk tolerance is constant and places the individual into one of three distinct groups: **risk-averse people**, who prefer a sure thing over a gamble with a higher expected value; **risk-neutral people**, who choose the highest expected value regardless of the risk; and **risk-takers**, who prefer gambles with lower expected values, and potentially higher winnings, over a sure thing.

ECONOMICS in the MEDIA

Preference Reversals

"MINE"

Taylor's dream illustrates one version of a preference reversal.

The music video for Taylor Swift's 2010 hit begins with Swift walking into a coffee shop. When she sits down, she notices a couple arguing at a nearby table. This reminds Swift about her parents arguing when she was very young. Just then, the waiter drops by to take Swift's order. She looks up and dreams of what life would be like with him. We see them running together in the waves at the beach, then unpacking boxes as they move in together. Later, the two argue, resulting in Swift running away from their house and crying, just like she did when she was young and saw her parents arguing. Her boyfriend follows her, and they reconcile. They get married and have two sons. The video ends with Swift reemerging from her dream and ordering her food at the coffee shop.

In the song's refrain, Swift sings, "You made a rebel of a careless man's careful daughter." Think about that line, keeping in mind that a "rebel" is a risk-taker. Does that remind you of a concept from this chapter? It should—this is a preference reversal. The entire song is about someone (Swift) who is normally risk-averse but falls for this guy so hard that she lets her guard down and acts differently. Instead of running away when it comes time to fall in love, she stays in the relationship. In other words, the song is about finding someone who makes you believe in love so much that you are willing to take a chance for the first time in your life.

Allais developed a means of assessing risk behavior by presenting the set of choices (known as the Allais paradox) depicted in Table 17.1. Individuals were asked to choose their preferred options between gambles A and B and then again between gambles C and D.

TABLE 17.1

The Allais Paradox

Choose gamble A or B	
Gamble A	**Gamble B**
No gamble—receive $1 million in cash 100% of the time	A lottery ticket that pays $5 million 10% of the time, $1 million 89% of the time, and nothing 1% of the time
Choose gamble C or D	
Gamble C	**Gamble D**
A lottery ticket that pays $5 million 10% of the time and nothing 90% of the time	A lottery ticket that pays $1 million 11% of the time and nothing 89% of the time

Economic science predicts that people will choose consistently according to their risk preference. As a result, economists understood that risk-averse individuals would choose the pair A and D. Likewise, the pair B and C makes sense if the participants are risk-neutral and wish to maximize the expected value of the gambles. Let's see why.

1. *Risk-Averse People:* People who select gamble A over gamble B take the sure thing. If they are asked to choose between C and D, we would expect them to try to maximize their chances of winning something by selecting D, because it has the higher probability of winning.
2. *Risk-Neutral People:* Gamble B has a higher expected value than gamble A. We know that gamble A always pays $1 million because it occurs 100% of the time. Calculating gamble B's expected value is more complicated. The expected value is computed by multiplying each outcome by its respective probability. For gamble B, this means that the expected value is ($5 million $\times$ 0.10) + ($1 million $\times$ 0.89), which equals $1.39 million. So a risk-neutral player will select gamble B. Likewise, gamble C has a higher expected value than gamble D. Gamble C has an expected value of ($5 million $\times$ 0.10), or $0.5 million. Gamble D's expected value is ($1 million $\times$ 0.11), or $0.11 million. Therefore, a risk-neutral player who thinks at the margin will choose gambles B and C in order to maximize potential winnings from the game.

Marginal thinking

3. *Risk-Takers:* Because risk-takers prefer risk, they would choose gambles B and C even if they were not already the gambles with the highest expected values.

While we would expect people to be consistent in their choices, Allais found that approximately 30% of his research population selected gambles A and C, which are contrasting pairs. Gamble A is the sure thing; however, gamble C, even though it has the higher expected value, carries more risk. This scenario illustrates a *preference reversal*. A **preference reversal** occurs when risk tolerance is not consistent. Allais argued that a person's risk tolerance depends on his or her financial circumstances. Someone who chooses gamble A over gamble B prefers the certainty of a large financial prize—the guarantee of $1 million over the uncertainty of the larger prize. Choosing gamble A could be seen as similar to purchasing insurance: you pay a fee, known as a *premium*, to protect your winnings. In this case, you forfeit the chance to win $5 million. In contrast, gambles C and D offer small chances of success, and therefore the choice is more like playing the lottery.

A **preference reversal** occurs when risk tolerance is not consistent.

People who play games of chance are more likely to participate in games with large prizes—for example, Powerball—because the winnings will measurably improve their financial status. Allais showed that people care about how much they might win and also how much they stand to lose. This distinction causes people to choose gambles A and C. By establishing that many people behave this way, Allais reshaped the traditional economic view of risk-taking behavior.

It turns out that preference reversals are more common than economists once believed. For example, almost 80% of all income tax filers expect to get a refund because they overpaid in the previous year. This behavior is odd, since there is an opportunity cost of waiting to get money back from the government when it didn't need to be paid in the first place. Employees could have asked their employers to withhold less and enjoyed their money sooner. Individuals who

· ECONOMICS *in the* MEDIA ·

Risk-Taking Behavior

JACKASS FOREVER

The final installment of the *Jackass* franchise reunites the *Jackass* crew for one more epic adventure after a 10-year hiatus. The film is loaded with new, gloriously dumb pranks and hijinks—not that you should try these at home! The premise of the series is simple: the crew dare each other into attempting increasingly risky stunts. It's not a question of whether someone will get hurt, but how badly.

The *Jackass* films are cover-your-eyes humor at its finest. As viewers, we may imagine trying the stunts ourselves, but we remain comfortably seated, beverage in hand. This is because most of us are risk-averse or risk-neutral. We buy insurance to protect ourselves against loss. The *Jackass* crew, on the other hand, are thrill seekers, who live for the adrenaline rush. Risk-takers like them head to Vegas to "win," even though the odds are stacked against them. You can't explain human behavior fully without understanding the incentives that drive some people to take on risk and cause others to avoid it.

Some people never learned that what goes up must come down.

choose to wait to receive their money later are said to have a time preference that is weakly positive. In most circumstances, people have strongly positive time preferences: they prefer to have what they want sooner rather than later. So what do these taxpayers do when they learn the amount of their refund? In many cases, they pay their tax preparers an additional fee to have their refunds sent to their bank accounts electronically so they can receive the money sooner! Traditional economic analysis is unable to explain this behavior; but armed with Allais's insights, we now see this behavior as a preference reversal.

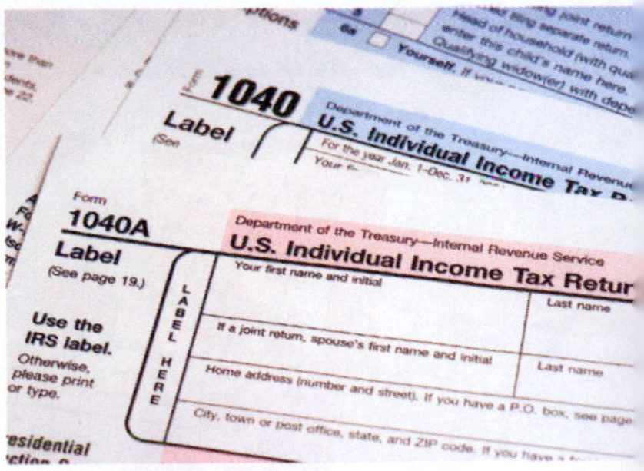

Withholding too much in the previous year and then paying your accountant to file for a rapid refund is a good example of a preference reversal.

Prospect Theory

The game in the television show *Deal or No Deal* provides an opportunity for economists to examine the risk choices that contestants make in a high-stakes setting. *Deal or No Deal* created particular excitement among researchers who study game shows, because its game involves no skill whatsoever. Taking skill out of the equation makes it easier to analyze players' strategy choices. Other TV game shows, such as *Jeopardy!*, require skill to win prizes. Highly skilled players may have different risk tolerances than their less skilled counterparts. As a result, part of the beauty of studying the *Deal or No Deal* game is that the outcome is a pure exercise in probability theory.

For those who are unfamiliar with *Deal or No Deal,* here is how the game works. Each of 26 models holds a briefcase containing a sum of money, varying from 1 cent to $1 million. The contestant picks one briefcase as her own and then begins to open the other 25 briefcases one at a time, slowly revealing a little more about what her own case might contain. Suspense builds, and the contestant's chance of a big payoff grows as small sums are eliminated and the $1 million case and other valuable cases remain unopened. As cases are eliminated, a "banker" periodically calls the host to offer the contestant a "deal" in exchange for quitting the game.

Opportunity cost

At the start of the game, the expected value (EV) of the chosen briefcase is determined as follows:

$$EV_{briefcase} = \$0.01 \times (1/26) + \$1 \times (1/26) + \$5 \times (1/26) + \ldots + \$1M \times (1/26)$$

This value computes to about $131,000. As the game progresses and more and more cases are opened, the "banker's" settlement offers are based on whether the expected value of the briefcase has increased or decreased since the last offer.

Deciding when to take the "deal" makes the game compelling.

Some contestants on the show behaved as the traditional model of risk behavior predicts: they maximized the expected value of the briefcase while remaining risk-neutral. Because contestants who are risk neutral don't make for exciting television, the "banker" would typically offer a "deal" that was far less than the expected value of the remaining cases throughout the early part of the game. This move encouraged contestants to play longer, so that the excitement and tension would have a chance to build.

But not all contestants did what the traditional model expected them to do. For example, some contestants took more risks if they suffered setbacks

PRACTICE WHAT YOU KNOW

How do you handle risky decisions?

Risk Aversion: Risk-Taking Behavior

QUESTION: You have a choice between selecting heads or tails. If your guess is correct, you earn $2,000. But you earn nothing if you are incorrect. Alternatively, you can simply take $750 without the gamble. You decide to take the $750. Is your choice evidence of risk aversion or risk-taking?

ANSWER: The expected value of a 50/50 outcome worth $2,000 is $1,000. Therefore, the decision to take the sure thing, which is $250 less, is evidence of risk aversion.

QUESTION: You have a choice between (a) predicting the roll of a six-sided die, with a $3,000 prize for a correct answer, or (b) taking a sure $750. You decide to roll the die. Is your choice evidence of risk aversion or risk-taking?

ANSWER: The expected value of the roll of the die is $1/6 \times \$3{,}000$, or $500. Therefore, the $750 sure thing has an expected value that is $250 more. By rolling the die, you are taking the option with the lower expected value and also more risk. Therefore, you are a risk-taker.

early in the game, such as opening the $1 million briefcase. This behavior is consistent with *prospect theory* from psychology. **Prospect theory**, developed by Daniel Kahneman and Amos Tversky, suggests that people weigh decisions according to subjective utilities of gains and losses. The theory implies that people evaluate the risks that lead to gains separately from the risks that lead to losses. This concept is useful because it explains why some investors try to make up for losses by taking more chances rather than by maximizing the utility they receive from money under a rigid calculation of expected value.

Prospect theory suggests that individuals weigh the utilities and risks of gains and losses differently.

ECONOMICS IN THE REAL WORLD

DOES HOARDING MAKE SENSE?

If others are pointlessly hoarding toilet paper, what should you do? Answer: hoard, too.

During the COVID-19 lockdown, it was understandable that people would hoard masks and disinfectant. After all, the demand for those commodities had just spiked. It made sense to worry that in the short term there wasn't going to be enough of them to go around. But what possessed people to start hoarding toilet paper?

Prior to the pandemic, we mostly took Adam Smith's invisible hand for granted. Local store shelves were stocked, and if we did our shopping at Amazon, Alexa could have the stuff we ordered delivered the next day. Once the pandemic was upon us, though, our expectations were upended. No one was sure how long the shelter-at-home orders would last. Would the lockdown get so bad that stores had to close for a time? Would delivery drivers have to stop working? It was all very unsettling.

Economists have learned to lean on insights from psychology to understand how people are likely to behave when they're in the grip of fear and uncertainty. These emotions can impair our brain's executive functioning, causing us to lose self-control and start thinking and acting impulsively. When we are driven by impulse, we're no longer logically weighing the marginal costs and marginal benefits of our actions. We're liable to observe what others are doing and just follow suit. This is known as the bandwagon effect. Adding to that is the phenomenon of loss aversion, where we feel stronger regret by missing out on something, compared to the pleasure we would feel from gaining a similar amount.

So at the height of the COVID-19 anxiety, for a lot of us the sight of someone else loading up a cart with toilet paper triggered a reflex: "I'd better do the same!" It didn't matter that the other person was shopping for a big family and we were just shopping for ourselves. And because of loss aversion, many people grabbed toilet paper whenever they found it, knowing they would later kick themselves if they ran out after not taking the opportunity to stock up.

The thing is, this might have started out as monkey-see, monkey-do behavior, but once the hoarding ball got rolling, it became perfectly logical to join in the hoarding. After all, there was now going to be a very real shortage of a good that everybody uses. This didn't just happen with toilet paper. The same thing happened with dried beans, canned meat, and other goods. Of course, this made the shortages worse, causing even more people to hoard, creating a vicious cycle in which rationality reinforced irrationality.

· ECONOMICS *for* LIFE ·

Bounded Rationality: How to Guard Yourself against Crime

- Raise the probability the criminal will be seen (trim bushes around your property, install motion-sensing lights).
- Raise the costs of entering (deadbolts, security doors, and security bars on windows).
- Raise the probability the criminal will be caught (alarm systems, barking dog).

A rational thief would look for an easier target.

Suppose that a recent crime wave has hit your community and you are concerned about your family's security. Determined to make your house safe, you consider many options: an alarm system, bars on your windows, deadbolts for your doors, better lighting around your house, and a guard dog. Which of these solutions will protect you from a criminal at the lowest cost? All of them provide a measure of protection—but there's another solution that provides deterrence at an extremely low cost.

The level of security you need depends, in part, on how rational you expect the burglar to be. A fully rational burglar would stake out a place, test for an alarm system before breaking in, and choose a home that is an easy target. In other words, the burglar would gather full information. But what if the burglar is not fully rational?

Because criminals look for the easiest target to rob, they will find a house that is easy to break into without detection. If you trim away the shrubs and install floodlights, criminals will realize they can be seen approaching your home. A few hundred dollars spent on better lighting will dramatically lower your chances of being robbed. However, if you believe in bounded rationality, there is an even better answer: a criminal may not know what is inside your house, so a couple of prominently displayed "Beware of dog!" signs would discourage the burglar for less than $10! In other words, the would-be thief has incomplete information and only a limited amount of time to select a target. A quick scan of your house would identify the "Beware of dog!" signs and cause him to move on.

This is an example of bounded rationality because only limited, and in this case unreliable, information is all that is easily available regarding possible alternatives and their consequences. Knowing that burglars face this constraint can be a key to keeping them away. Of course, you could also buy a sign making it clear you were armed. On the one hand, yes, you'll deter some burglars. On the other hand, you may end up attracting *armed* burglars who are after your (possibly nonexistent) gun collection. Now who's the person with the bounded rationality?

Conclusion

Behavioral economics challenges the traditional economic model and invites a deeper understanding of human behavior. Armed with the insights from behavioral economics, we can answer questions that span a wider range of behaviors. We have seen behavioral economics at work in the examples in this chapter, which include the "opt-in" or "opt-out" debate, the economics of risk-taking, the effects of question design, and the status quo bias. These ideas do not fit squarely into traditional economic analysis. You have learned enough at this point to question the assumptions we have made throughout this book. In the next chapter, we apply all of the tools we have acquired to examine one of the most important sectors of the economy—health care and health insurance. ✱

· ANSWERING *the* BIG QUESTIONS ·

How do economists explain irrational behavior?

- Economists use a number of concepts from behavioral economics to explain how people make choices that display irrational behavior. These concepts include bounded rationality, misperceptions of probabilities, framing effects and priming effects, the status quo bias, intertemporal decision-making, the endowment effect, judgments about fairness, preference reversals, and prospect theory.
- Folding the behavioral approach into the standard model makes economists' predictions about human behavior much more robust.

What is the role of risk in decision-making?

- Risk influences decision-making because people can be risk-averse, risk-neutral, or risk-takers.
- In the traditional economic model, risk tolerances are assumed to be constant. If an individual is a risk-taker by nature, he or she will take risks in any circumstance. Likewise, if an individual does not like to take chances, he or she will avoid risk.
- Maurice Allais proved that many people have inconsistent risk preferences, or what are known as preference reversals. Moreover, he showed that simply because some people's preferences are not constant does not necessarily mean that their decisions are irrational.
- Prospect theory suggests that individuals weigh the utilities and risks of gains and losses differently and are therefore willing to take on additional risk to try to recover losses caused by negative shocks.

CHAPTER PROBLEMS

Concepts You Should Know

behavioral economics (p. 546)
bounded rationality (p. 546)
endowment effect (p. 555)
framing effect (p. 552)
gambler's fallacy (p. 550)
hot hand fallacy (p. 550)
intertemporal decision-making (p. 554)
preference reversal (p. 560)
priming effect (p. 552)
prospect theory (p. 563)
risk-averse people (p. 558)
risk-neutral people (p. 558)
risk-takers (p. 558)
status quo bias (p. 552)
ultimatum game (p. 557)

Questions for Review

1. What is bounded rationality? How is this concept relevant to economic modeling?
2. What are the hot hand fallacy and the gambler's fallacy? Give an example of each.
3. How does the status quo bias reduce the potential utility that consumers enjoy?
4. Economists use the ultimatum game to test judgments of fairness. What result does economic theory predict?
5. What is prospect theory? Have you ever suffered a setback early in a process (for example, seeking a job or applying for college) that caused you to alter your behavior later on?

Study Problems (*∗ solved at the end of the section*)

∗ 1. You have a choice between two jobs. The first job pays $50,000 annually. The second job has a base pay of $40,000 with a 30% chance that you will receive an annual bonus of $25,000. You decide to take the $50,000 job. On the basis of this decision, can we tell if you are risk-averse or a risk-taker? Explain your response.

2. Suppose that Danny Ocean decides to play roulette, one of the most popular casino games. Roulette is attractive to gamblers because the house's advantage is small (less than 5%). If Danny Ocean plays roulette and wins big, is this evidence that Danny is risk-averse or a risk-taker? Explain.

3. Many voters go to the polls every four years to cast their ballot for president. The common refrain from those who vote is that their vote "counts" and that voting is important. A skeptical economist points out that with over 100 million ballots cast, the probability that any individual's vote will be decisive is close to 0%. What idea, discussed in this chapter, explains why so many people actually vote?

4. Your instructor is very conscientious and always makes sure that exam answers are randomly distributed. However, you notice that the first five answers on the true/false section are all "true." Unsure what this pattern means, you consider the sixth question. However, you do not know the answer. What answer would you give if you believed in the gambler's fallacy? What answer would you give if you believed in the hot hand fallacy?

∗ 5. Suppose that a university wishes to maximize the response rate for teaching evaluations. The administration develops an easy-to-use online evaluation system that each student can complete at the end of the semester. However, very few students bother to complete the survey. The registrar's office suggests that the online teaching evaluations be linked to course scheduling. When students access the course scheduling system, they are redirected to the teaching evaluations. Under this plan, each student can opt out and go directly to the course scheduling system. Do you think this plan will work to raise the response rate on teaching evaluations? What would traditional economic theory predict? What would a behavioral economist predict?

6. Raul likes his hamburgers with American cheese, lettuce, and ketchup. Whenever he places an order for a burger, he automatically orders these three toppings. What type of behavior is Raul exhibiting? What does traditional economic theory say about Raul's preferences? What would a behavioral economist say?

7. Many people give to charity and leave tips. What prediction does traditional economic theory make about each of these activities? (**Hint:** Think of the person's narrow self-interest.) What concept from behavioral economics explains this behavior?

8. Given a choice of an extra $1,000 or a gamble with the same expected value, a person prefers the $1,000. But given a choice of a loss of $1,000 or a gamble with the same expected value, the same person prefers the gamble. How would a behavioral economist describe this decision?

* 9. A researcher asks you the following question: "Would you rather have a 10% chance of mortality or a 90% chance of survival?" What concept from behavioral economics is illustrated here? What is the difference between the two choices, if any? Which choice do you think most people make?

* 10. How might the concept of diminishing marginal utility, from Chapter 16, be used to compare and contrast the preferences of the risk-averse and the risk-neutral person?

* 11. Under what circumstances would it make economic sense to be a risk-taker?

12. Two people are playing an ultimatum game with $100. Player 1 can make an offer to player 2, who can either accept or reject it. If player 2 accepts, then they split the money according to player 1's offer. If player 2 rejects, neither of them gets any money. Player 1 offers $2 to player 2. What does *traditional economic theory* say player 2 will do?

Solved Problems

1. The first job pays $50,000 annually, so it has an expected value of $50,000. The second job has a base pay of $40,000 with a 30% chance that you will receive an annual bonus of $25,000. To determine the expected value of the second job, the calculation looks like this: $40,000 + (0.3 × $25,000) = $40,000 + $7,500 = $47,500. Since you decided to take the job with higher expected value, we cannot tell if you are a risk-taker or risk-averse.

5. Because students who access the course scheduling system are redirected to the teaching evaluations, they are forced to opt out if they do not wish to evaluate the instructors. As a result, a behavioral economist would predict that the new system will raise the teaching evaluation response rate. Traditional economic theory would predict that the response rate will not change simply based on whether or not students opt in or opt out.

9. According to traditional economics, how the question is framed should not matter. But behavioral economics correctly predicts that it does: when asked to choose which of the two outcomes they prefer, a significant majority chooses "a 90% chance of survival," even though this statement is equivalent to "a 10% chance of mortality."

10. Let's use Table 17.1 to think about the answer. A person whose marginal utility of money is constant—or decreases only modestly as the amount of money increases—will choose gambles B and C, the gambles with the highest expected monetary value and therefore the highest expected utility. This is the risk-neutral person. The risk-averse person, who chooses gamble A over gamble B, is giving up a 10% chance of getting lots more than $1M in order eliminate a 1% chance of getting nothing. Apparently, this person's marginal utility of money diminishes very sharply after $1M.

11. Again, let's use Table 17.1 to formulate an answer, and this time imagine a choice between gamble A and gamble C. Someone who prefers a 10% chance of $5M (and otherwise nothing) over a guarantee of $1M would qualify as a risk-taker, because their expected payoff is only $500,000. This kind of preference would make sense for someone in the middle of a very expensive life crisis, where $1M would not be enough to make a difference but $5M would make a big difference.

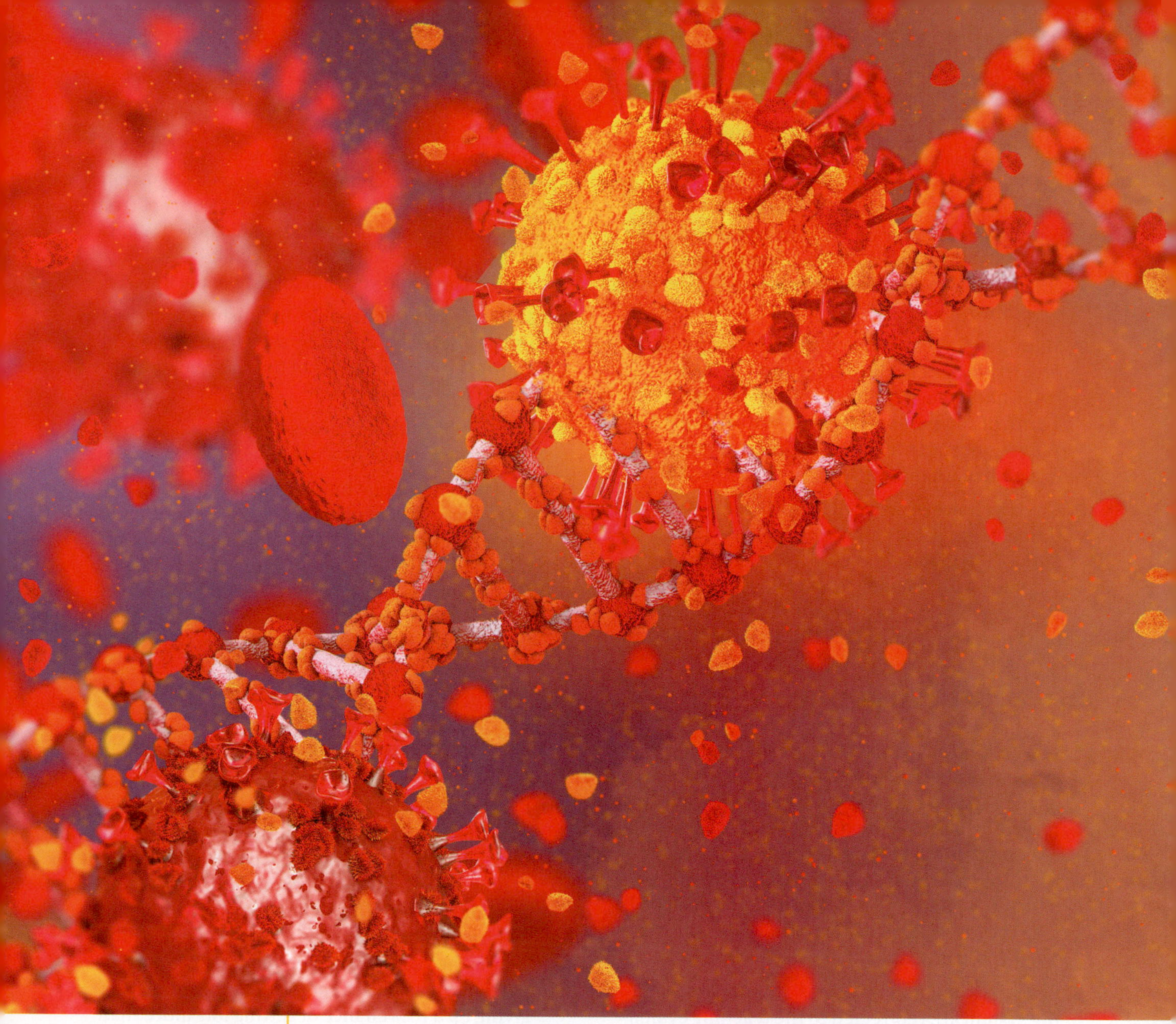

CHAPTER

18

Health Insurance and Health Care

There's No Such Thing as a Free Lunch.

We have come a long way in our exploration of microeconomics. In this chapter, we apply our economic toolkit to one particular industry: health care. The debate over healthcare spending is at the core of the healthcare crisis in the United States. The goal of this chapter is not to sway your opinion but to provide a simple set of tools to focus your thinking about how medical care can best serve individuals and society as a whole.

When you are young, health care is often the last thing on your mind—until you need it. Imagine you wake up in the morning feeling feverish. It might just be the flu, but you're worried it's COVID-19. What do you do? If you're a student at a four-year school, you can walk down to your campus health center and get checked out. Your student health insurance will cover the cost. If you're a part-time DoorDash driver, on the other hand, the cost of a clinic visit will come out of your own pocket. Now what?

Many people believe that the best way to handle all such scenarios would be universal health care: just cover everyone with government-funded national health insurance. As a step in that direction, the Affordable Care Act passed under President Obama (the federal healthcare law often called "Obamacare") mandated expanded coverage. It's the reason you could stay on your parents' plan until your 26th birthday.

But what about the costs? Proponents of universal health care argue that it would make health care less expensive on

COVID-19 is scary enough with good medical insurance. Without good insurance, the bill after your recovery might shock you!

a per-person basis. Conservative policymakers, however, push back and argue that mandatory coverage is inefficient and intrusive, and that universal coverage would be a budget-buster for the government. Even Obamacare is controversial—in particular, the mandate to obtain coverage—and neither side of the aisle is satisfied with the political compromises that led to the legislation. So for now, the United States is stuck with a patchwork system of health care and coverage that is neither market based nor government run, and certainly not anywhere near efficient.

Trade-offs

That means we can all benefit from taking a closer look at ways to improve health insurance and health care, and what trade-offs would make sense. In this chapter, we describe how the health-care industry works and how the government and the market can each make the delivery of health care more efficient. We consider how health care is delivered, who pays, and what makes the provision of medical care unlike the delivery of services in any other sector of the economy. Then we use supply and demand analysis to look at how the medical market functions. One important aspect of medical care is the role that information plays in the incentive structure for patients and providers. Finally, we examine a number of case studies to pull all this information together, so you can decide for yourself where you stand on one of the most important issues of the twenty-first century.

· BIG QUESTIONS ·

- What are the important issues in the healthcare industry?
- How does asymmetric information affect healthcare delivery?
- How do demand and supply contribute to high medical costs?
- How do incentives influence the quality of health care?

What Are the Important Issues in the Healthcare Industry?

Health care is big business. If you add the education and automobile sectors together, they represent about 10% of national economic output. But health care alone accounts for more than 17% of the nation's economic output. That's 1 out of every 6 dollars spent annually in the United States—roughly $3.8 trillion, or over $10,000 for every citizen. No matter how you slice it, that is a lot of money.

In this section, we examine the key issues in health care: how much is spent on it, where the money goes, and who the key players in the industry are. The goal is to give you a sense of how the sector functions. Then we turn our attention to supply and demand. First, though, we take a brief look at how health care has changed over the past hundred or so years.

The History of U.S. Health Care

At the start of the twentieth century, life expectancy in the United States was slightly less than 50 years. Now life expectancy is close to 80 years—a longevity gain that would have been unthinkable a few generations ago. Let's go back in time to examine the way medical care was delivered and see some of the advances that have improved the human condition.

Early in the twentieth century, infectious diseases were the most common cause of death in the United States.* Typhoid, diphtheria, gangrene, gastritis, smallpox, and tuberculosis were major killers. Moreover, the state of medical knowledge was so dismal that a cure was often far worse than the condition it was supposed to treat. For instance, tobacco was recommended for

*"Achievements in Public Health, 1900–1999: Control of Infectious Diseases," *Morbidity and Mortality Weekly Report*, Centers for Disease Control and Prevention, accessed January 2022, https://www.cdc.gov/mmwr/preview/mmwrhtml/mm4829a1.htm.

Cutting-edge medical equipment: then . . .

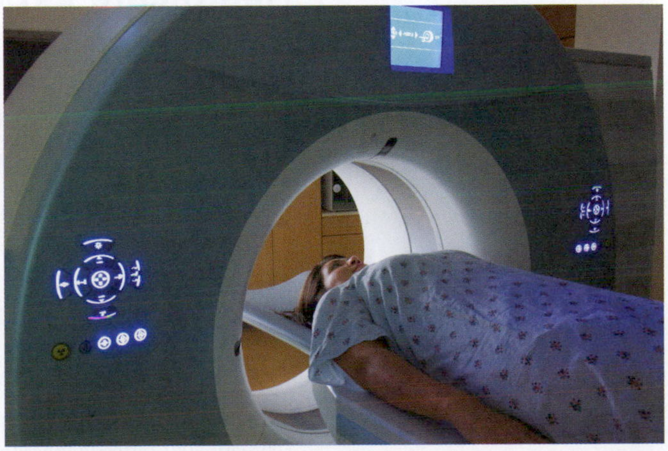

. . . and now.

the treatment of bronchitis and asthma, and leeches were used to fight laryngitis. Throughout the first half of the twentieth century, a trip to the doctor was painful, and it rarely produced positive results.

Since 1950, advances in cellular biology and discoveries in biochemistry have led to a better understanding of diseases and more precise diagnostic tests. Antibiotics have made death from bacterial infections extremely rare. Smallpox has been eradicated. New threats occasionally appear, like HIV, Ebola, and COVID-19, but given time, the medical community has been consistently able to develop effective vaccines and treatments. In addition, discoveries in biomedical engineering have led to the widespread use of imaging techniques such as ultrasound, computerized axial tomography (CAT scans), and nuclear magnetic resonance imaging (MRI). Finally, pharmaceutical companies have developed "miracle" drugs for fighting many conditions, including high blood pressure, leukemia, and bad cholesterol, thereby limiting the need for more invasive treatments.

Trade-offs

Each of these amazing medical advances costs money—sometimes, lots of money. As a society, we have made a trade-off: in exchange for a dramatically longer life expectancy, we now devote much more of our personal and government budgets to health care.

The coronavirus pandemic also accelerated changes in the delivery of medical care. In 2019, telemedicine was largely invisible. Seemingly overnight, in 2020, telemedicine became the entry point for diagnosis. In 2019, nursing homes and assisted living facilities were the norm. Since COVID-19, more families have wanted their loved ones living at home, sometimes with the help of home care aides. Problems with mental health substantially increased; for example, in October 2020 an estimated 37% of adults in New York State were reporting poor mental health, three times the normal number, with slightly higher percentages for African Americans, Hispanics, and 18-to-34-year-olds.* COVID-19 also showed how unprepared we were for a pandemic. Our medical infrastructure might be rethought to deliver essential equipment and supplies more nimbly, and production of some key pharmaceuticals may be brought back stateside, to avoid supply chain issues in foreign countries.

Healthcare Expenditures

We have noted that healthcare expenditures in the United States are more than 17% of economic output. As you can see in Table 18.1, this total is quite a bit higher than similar expenditures in Canada and Mexico. Canada spends about 10% of its economic output on health care, and Mexico spends slightly more than 5%.

The United States spends significantly more on health care than our neighbors to the north and south, but life expectancy in the United States is lower than in Canada. How does Canada achieve a higher life expectancy while spending less money? And why doesn't Mexico, which spends only about

*NYS Health Foundation, "Mental Health Impact of the Coronavirus Pandemic in New York State," February 2021, https://nyshealthfoundation.org/wp-content/uploads/2021/02/mental-health-impact-coronavirus-pandemic-new-york-state.pdf.

TABLE 18.1

Selected Healthcare Facts

Country	Total expenditure on health (percentage of economic output)	Per capita expenditure on health (in U.S. dollars)	Life expectancy at birth, total population (in years)
Mexico	5.4	989	75.4
Canada	10.4	4,826	81.9
U.S.	17.2	10,209	78.6

Source: OECD Health Division, Health Data 2018: Frequently Requested Data.

one-tenth of what we do on health care per capita (see Table 18.1), trail farther behind the United States than it does? To answer those questions, consider the usual assumption of *ceteris paribus*, or other things being constant. We all agree that increased healthcare expenditures are making people healthier, probably happier (because they feel better), and more productive—this is true for most countries. However, longevity is also a function of environmental factors, genetics, and lifestyle choices—variables that are not constant across countries. The question we should be asking is not how much money we are spending, but whether we are getting our money's worth. In other words, in this context economists are most concerned with the impediments to the efficient delivery of medical care.

Why does health care take up so much of our budget? There are a number of reasons. Health insurance plays a contributing role. When private insurance covers most treatment costs, many patients agree to tests or medical visits they wouldn't be willing to pay for out of pocket. Also, doctors are more willing to order tests that might not be necessary if they know the patient isn't paying directly. Medicare and Medicaid, the two government-sponsored forms of health insurance, add to the overall demand for medical services by providing medical coverage to the elderly (Medicare) and poor (Medicaid). And we know that anytime there is more demand for services, the market price rises in response, as long as supply remains constant.

Another reason for high healthcare costs is the number of uninsured people in the United States—approximately 30 million in 2019. When uninsured people need immediate medical treatment, they often seek care from emergency rooms and clinics, which raises costs in two ways. First, emergency care is extraordinarily expensive—much more so than routine care. Second, waiting until one has an acute condition that requires immediate attention often requires more treatment than would occur with preventive care or an early diagnosis. For example, an insured person who develops a cough with fever is likely to see a physician. If the patient has bronchitis, a few days of medicine and rest will be all it takes to feel better. However, an uninsured person who develops bronchitis is less likely to seek medical help and risks the possibility of a worsening condition, such as pneumonia, which can be difficult and costly to treat.

Demand for Medicare is quite inelastic, so when competition is absent (which is usually the case), hospitals and other providers can charge what they want, and patients will have to pay. In addition, many people are not proactive about their health. Many health problems could be dramatically reduced and costs contained if people curbed habits such as cigarette use, excessive alcohol

FIGURE 18.1

Health Production Function

The marginal product of medical care, indicated by the slope of the health production function, is higher at point A than at point B. For example, we would prefer to spend money on COVID-19 vaccinations to avoid the illness rather than spend it on ventilators for those who contract the virus and become critically ill. The vaccine, which keeps people from getting sick in the first place, has a much higher marginal product.

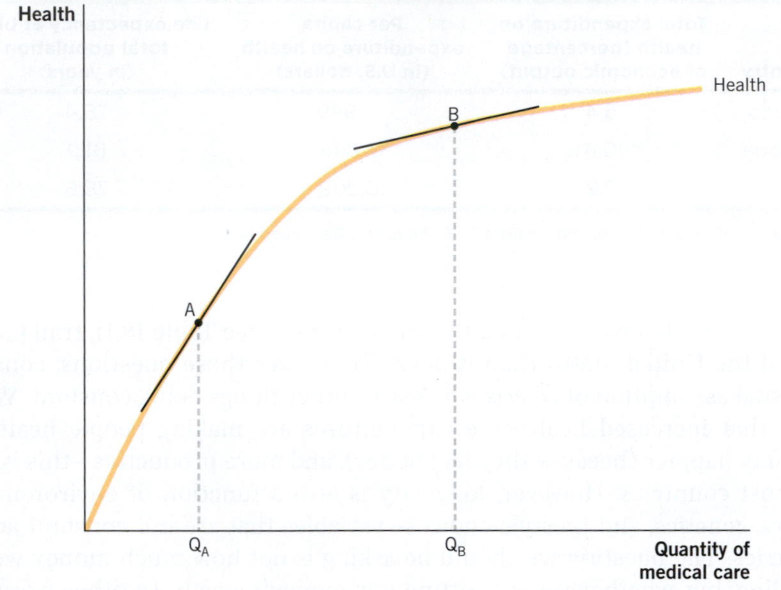

consumption, and overeating and if they exercised more. Finally, heroic end-of-life efforts are extraordinarily expensive. These efforts may extend life for a few months, days, or hours, and they come at a steep price; spending on the last year of care in a life is estimated to take up 8.5% of all medical spending in the United States.*

Diminishing Returns

In the United States, it has become the norm to spare no expense in the effort to extend life for even a few days. However, providing more medical care is subject to diminishing returns, as we can see in Figure 18.1. The orange curve shows a society's aggregate health production function, a measure of health reflecting the population's longevity, general health, and quality of life. This function initially rises rapidly when small amounts of health care are provided, but the benefits of additional care are progressively smaller. To understand why, compare points A and B. At point A, only a small amount of medical care is provided (Q_A), but this care has a large impact on health. The slope at point A represents the marginal product of medical care. However, by the time we reach point B at a higher amount of care provided (Q_B), the marginal product of medical care (the slope) is much flatter, indicating that diminishing returns have set in.

Marginal thinking

*Eric French et al., "End-of-Life Medical Expenses," November 19, 2018, Federal Reserve Bank of Richmond, https://www.richmondfed.org/-/media/richmondfedorg/publications/research/working_papers/2018/pdf/wp18-18.pdf.

Higher medical care expenditures, beyond some point, are unlikely to measurably improve longevity and quality of life because many other factors—for example, disease, genetics, and lifestyle—also play a key role in determining health, quality of life, and longevity. As we move out along the medical production function, extending life becomes progressively more difficult, so it is not surprising that medical costs rise appreciably. Given this pattern, society must answer two questions. First, what is the optimal mix of expenditures on medical care? Second, could society get more from each dollar spent by reallocating dollars away from heroic efforts to extend life and toward prevention and medical research instead?

Figure 18.2 shows where the typical health dollar goes. Hospital care, physicians, and clinics account for a little more than half of all medical expenses. After that, prescription drugs, dental care, home health care, and nursing homes each represent smaller parts of healthcare expenditures. Here we note a paradox. On the one hand, medical care has become much more efficient as medical records are increasingly computerized and many procedures that required days of hospitalization a generation ago can now take place on an outpatient basis. Thus, reducing medical costs through efficiency gains is ongoing. Yet, on the other hand, costs continue to rise. What is going on? In the next section, we examine the incentives that patients, providers, and insurance companies face when making medical decisions and how the incentive structure contributes to escalating costs.

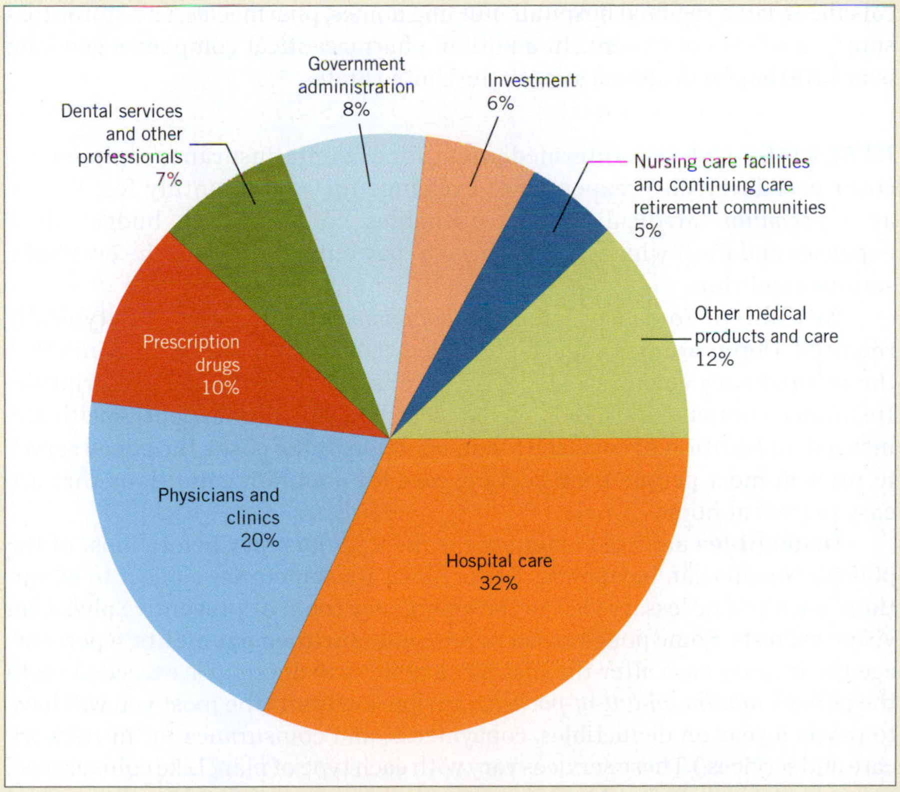

FIGURE 18.2

The Nation's Health Dollar

In a typical year, hospital care, physicians, and clinics make up over half of all healthcare expenditures, which totaled $3.5 trillion in 2018.

Source: Centers for Medicare and Medicaid Services, Office of the Actuary, National Health Statistics Group. See "National Health Expenditure Data," cms.gov.

Who's Who in Health Care, and How Does Insurance Work?

Healthcare consumption is different from that of most other goods and services. Like the others, healthcare services have consumers and producers; but because of intermediaries, such as insurance companies, the two rarely connect directly on payments. This situation generates a unique set of incentives and leads to distortions in the standard supply and demand analysis. It is important to understand how medical care is delivered and paid for, as well as the incentives that patients, medical providers, and insurers face when making decisions.

Incentives

CONSUMERS The two biggest consumers of medical care are patients and the government. Patients demand medical care to prevent and treat illness. The federal government runs Medicare, a program that provides medical assistance to the elderly, and partially funds Medicaid, a state-run program that provides medical assistance to the poor. Medicare and Medicaid are social insurance programs that each serve over 40 million enrollees. The two programs account for approximately one-third of all medical spending in the United States and represent about one-fourth of all U.S. government expenditures.

PRODUCERS The medical care industry employs millions of workers, including doctors, nurses, psychologists, technicians, and many more. There are also over 500,000 medical facilities in this country, including small medical offices, large regional hospitals, nursing homes, pharmacies, and stores that supply medical equipment. In addition, pharmaceutical companies generate over $300 billion in annual sales in the United States.

INTERMEDIARIES Intermediaries—for example, insurance companies—cover certain medical expenses in exchange for a set monthly fee, known as a *premium*. Medical insurance enables consumers to budget their expenses and limit what they will have to pay out of pocket in the event of a serious condition.

Copayments are fixed amounts the insured must pay when receiving a medical service or filling a prescription.

In addition to the premium, a *copayment* or deductible is typically required. **Copayments** (sometimes called "copays") are fixed amounts that the insured pays when receiving a medical service or filling a prescription. Insurance companies use copayments in part to share expenses with the insured. In addition to covering a small portion of the costs, the copay serves to prevent most people from seeking care for common conditions that are easy to treat at home.

Deductibles are fixed amounts the insured must pay before most of the policy's benefits can be applied.

Coinsurance payments are a percentage of costs the insured must pay after exceeding the insurance policy's deductible up to the policy's contribution limit.

Deductibles are fixed amounts the insured must pay before most of the policy's benefits can be applied. Deductibles are sometimes subject to exceptions, such as a necessary visit to the emergency room or preventive physician visits and tests. Some policies also require **coinsurance payments**, a percentage the insured pays after the insurance policy's deductible is exceeded up to the policy's *maximum-out-of-pocket* contribution limit (the most you will have to pay in a year on deductibles, copayments, and coinsurance for in-network care and services.) These services vary with each type of plan. Like coinsurance, copayments and deductibles work to encourage consumers to use medical services judiciously.

Insurance companies use the premiums, copayments, deductibles, and coinsurance they receive from their customers to pay medical suppliers. For example, you may not need an appendectomy this year, but a predictable number of insured customers will. Using statistical techniques, an insurance company with millions of customers can accurately predict how many of its customers will visit the doctor and require hospitalization and other services. This statistical analysis enables the company to estimate its costs in advance and set premiums that generate a profit for the company.

Many people receive medical care through *health maintenance organizations,* or HMOs—another example of an intermediary. HMOs provide managed care for their patients by assigning them a primary care physician (PCP) who oversees their medical care. The HMO then monitors the primary care provider to ensure that unnecessary care is not prescribed. HMOs earn revenue from premiums, copayments, deductibles, and coinsurance. Many insurance plans allow the insured to make choices. *Preferred provider organizations,* or PPOs, are a type of health insurance arrangement that gives plan participants relative freedom to choose the doctors and hospitals they want to visit.

Another kind of insurance company sells insurance against medical malpractice, or negligent treatment on the part of doctors. The doctor pays a set fee to the insurer, which in turn pays for the legal damages that arise if the doctor faces a malpractice claim. By analyzing statistics about the number of malpractice cases for each type of medical procedure performed each year, insurers can estimate the probability that a particular physician will face a malpractice claim; the insurers then incorporate that risk into the premium they charge to doctors.

PHARMACEUTICAL COMPANIES Pharmaceutical companies are another major player in the healthcare industry as they develop the drugs used to treat a wide variety of conditions. Global pharmaceutical sales are almost $1 trillion. The United States accounts for about 30% of this $1 trillion—that's a lot of prescriptions! Pharmaceutical companies spend billions of dollars developing and testing potential drugs. One drug can take years or decades to develop. Once a drug is developed, it must receive approval by the U. S. Food and Drug Administration (FDA) before it can be sold. The development cost, time required, and risk that a drug may turn out to be problematic or ineffective combine to make the development of new drugs an expensive proposition.

Medical Costs

To understand why medical costs are so high, we must look at the incentives that drive the decisions of the major players. Consumers want every treatment to be covered, providers want a steady stream of business and don't want to be sued for malpractice, and the insurance companies and pharmaceutical companies want to make profits. These market dynamics showcase the inherent conflict that exists between consumers, producers, and intermediaries, and it helps explain the difficulty of providing medical care at a reasonable cost.

Because patient copayments are only a tiny fraction of the total cost of care, the effective marginal cost of seeking medical treatment is quite low. As a result, consumers increase the quantity of medical care they demand. Some physicians prescribe more care than is medically necessary in order to earn

PRACTICE WHAT YOU KNOW

"I work out . . ."

Physical Fitness

QUESTION: You go in for a physical, and your doctor suggests that you get more exercise. So you decide to start working out. The increased physical activity has a big payoff and soon you feel much better, so you decide to double your efforts and get in even better shape. However, you notice that the gains from doubling your workout effort do not make you feel much better. What economic concept explains this effect?

ANSWER: More of a good thing isn't always better. Physical activity extends longevity and increases quality of life up to a point. However, working out is subject to *diminishing returns*. In other words, a small amount of physical activity has a big payoff, but lifting more weights or running more miles, after a certain point, does not increase your overall health—it simply maintains your health.

more income and to avoid malpractice lawsuits. Meanwhile, insurance companies, which are caught in the middle between patients and medical providers, do their best to contain costs, but they find that controlling the behavior of patients and providers is difficult. Consequently, escalating costs result from a system with poorly designed incentive mechanisms. In the case of Medicare and Medicaid, the government attempts to control costs by setting caps on the reimbursements paid to providers for medical treatments. An unintended consequence of government price setting is that it forces physicians and medical centers to raise prices for other procedures not covered by Medicare and Medicaid.

Incentives

How Does Asymmetric Information Affect Healthcare Delivery?

We have seen that incentives play an important role in the delivery of medical care. Another important element is the information and lack of information available to participants. Imbalances in information, known as **asymmetric information**, occur whenever one party knows more than the other. Asymmetric information has two forms: *adverse selection* and the *principal-agent problem.*

Asymmetric information is an imbalance in information that occurs when one party knows more than the other.

Adverse Selection

Most of us know very little about medicine. We know when we don't feel well and that we want to feel better, so we seek medical attention. Because we know very little about the service we are buying, we are poor judges of quality. For example, how can you know if your doctor is qualified or better than another doctor? **Adverse selection** exists when one party has information about some aspect of product quality that the other party does not have. As a result, the party with the limited information should be concerned that the other party will misrepresent information to gain an advantage.

Adverse selection exists when one party has information about some aspect of product quality that the other party does not have.

When one side knows more than the other, the only way to avoid an adverse outcome is to gather better information. Suppose that you are new in town and need medical care. You haven't had a chance to meet anyone and find out whom to see or where to go for care. Fortunately, there is a way to avoid the worst doctors: websites like RateMDs.com provide patient feedback on the quality of care they have received. Armed with knowledge from sources like these, you can request to be treated by doctors whom you know to be competent and have strong reputations. Conducting this research helps new residents avoid below-average care. More generally, it is important for patients to take charge of their own health care and learn all they can about a condition and its treatment so they are prepared to ask questions and make better decisions about treatment options. When patients are better informed, adverse selection is minimized.

Adverse selection also applies when buyers are more likely to seek insurance if they are more likely to need it. Consider a life insurance company. The company wants to avoid selling an inexpensive policy to someone who is likely to die prematurely, so before selling a policy to that applicant, the insurance company has to gather additional information about the person. It can require a medical exam and delay eligibility for full benefits until it can determine that the applicant has no preexisting health conditions. The process of gathering information about the applicant is crucial to minimizing the risk associated with adverse selection. In fact, the process is similar for automobile insurance, in which drivers with poor records pay substantially higher premiums and safe drivers pay substantially lower ones.

The Principal-Agent Problem

Patients generally trust doctors to make good treatment decisions. A **principal-agent problem** arises when a principal entrusts an agent to complete a task and the agent does not do so in a satisfactory way. Some nonmedical examples will be familiar to you. Parents (the principal) hire a babysitter (the agent) to watch their children, but the babysitter might talk on the phone instead. A company manager (the agent) might try to maximize his own salary instead of working to increase value for the shareholders (the principal). Finally, a politician (the agent) might be more likely to grant favors to interest groups than to focus on the needs of his or her constituents (the principal).

A **principal-agent problem** arises when a principal entrusts an agent to complete a task and the agent does not do so in a satisfactory way.

In a medical setting, the principal-agent problem occurs whenever patients cannot directly observe how medical providers and insurers are managing their patients' interests. The lack of oversight on the part of patients gives their agents, the physicians and insurance companies, some freedom to pursue other objectives that do not directly benefit patients. In the case of medicine, doctors and hospitals may order more tests, procedures, or visits to specialists than are medically necessary. The physician or the hospital may be more concerned about making profits or avoiding medical malpractice lawsuits

ECONOMICS in the MEDIA

Moral Hazard

"KING-SIZE HOMER"

In this episode of *The Simpsons*, a new corporate fitness policy is intended to help the power plant workers become healthier. Morning exercises are instituted, and the employees are whipped into shape. But Homer hates working out, so he decides to gain a lot of weight in order to claim disability and work at home. To qualify, he must weigh at least 300 pounds. To get to that weight, he must go on an eating binge. Of course, his behavior is not what the designers of the fitness policy had in mind.

This amusing episode is a good example of moral hazard, and it showcases how well-intentioned policies can often be abused.

Moral hazard makes Homer decide to gain weight.

than ensuring the patient's health and well-being. At the same time, insurance companies may want to save on treatment costs in order to maximize profit. In both cases, the patient's desire for the best medical care conflicts with the objectives of the agents who deliver their care.

Behavioral Dynamics in Healthcare Delivery

Moral hazard is the lack of incentive to guard against risk where one is protected from its consequences.

Health care is also subject to the problem of **moral hazard**, which is the lack of incentive to guard against risk where one is protected from its consequences. Moral hazard does not necessarily refer to behavior that is "immoral" or "unethical." But it does imply that some people will change their behavior when their risk exposure is reduced and an "it's insured" mentality sets in. This mentality can lead to inefficient outcomes, such as visiting the doctor more often than necessary.

In the example mentioned, there is a moral hazard problem that can be lessened by restructuring the incentives. For the patient, a higher copayment will discourage unnecessary visits to the doctor.

Incentives

To solve a moral hazard problem in medical care, it is necessary to fix the incentive structure. Many health insurance companies address moral hazard by encouraging preventive care, which lowers medical costs. They also impose payment limits on treatments for preventable conditions, such as gum disease and tooth decay.

PRACTICE WHAT YOU KNOW

Asymmetric Information

QUESTION: You decide to use an online dating site, but you are not entirely sure if the posted picture of someone is accurate. Is adverse selection, the principal-agent problem, moral hazard, or some combination of these at work?

ANSWER: Adverse selection is at work. The person you are interested in knows more about herself than you do. They can, and probably would, post a flattering picture of themselves. When you finally meet the person, you are likely to be disappointed.

QUESTION: You hire a friend to feed your cat and change the litter twice a day while you are on spring break. However, your friend only visits your apartment every other day, and your cat shows its disapproval by using your bedspread as a litter box. Why is this an example of the principal-agent problem?

ANSWER: Because you have arranged for your friend to act on your behalf, but he cares less about your cat than you do and therefore wasn't conscientious about looking after it.

CHALLENGE QUESTION: How are adverse selection and moral hazard also involved in the cat-sitting fiasco?

ANSWER: Adverse selection is involved because you relied on a friend in a one-time arrangement. If you used a professional pet-sitter, you would have more information about his or her performance—first through references and after that through your own experiences. Moral hazard is involved because your friend won't have to sleep in that bed the cat peed on. Because your friend was protected from the consequences of his negligence, he wasn't as worried as you would have been about making sure the cat stuck to the litter box.

How Do Demand and Supply Contribute to High Medical Costs?

Now that we have a basic understanding of how the healthcare industry functions and who the key players are, we can examine the way demand and supply operate in the market for health care. On the demand side, we consider what makes healthcare demand stubbornly inelastic. Health care, when you need it, is not about the price—it is about getting the care you need. When you consider this fact and the presence of third-party payments, or payments made by insurance companies, you can begin to understand why medical expenses have risen so rapidly. On the supply side, medical licensing requirements and expensive technology help explain why the supply of medical services is limited, as does the increasing complexity of technology involved. The combination of strongly inelastic demand and limited supply pushes up prices for medical services.

Healthcare Demand

Health care is usually a necessity, and it doesn't have many good alternatives. These two facts explain why the demand for health care is typically inelastic. For example, going without a heart transplant when you need one isn't an option. In fact, a 2002 RAND Corporation study found that health care has an average price elasticity coefficient of −0.17. This means that a 1% increase in the price of health care will lead to a 0.17% reduction in healthcare expenditures. Recall that as an elasticity coefficient approaches zero, demand becomes more inelastic. So we can say that the demand for medical care is quite inelastic. (For a refresher on elasticity, see Chapter 4.). Breaking down medical care into subcategories reveals that consumers have more elastic demand for pharmaceuticals (−0.44), specialist visits (−0.32), MRIs (−0.29) and mental health/substance abuse care (−0.26), and more inelastic demand for ambulance transport (−0.07), emergency room treatment (−0.04), and kidney dialysis (essentially zero).* But even the most elastic demand, for pharmaceuticals, lies between $E_D = -1$ and $E_D = 0$ and so would be considered relatively inelastic.

There are some situations, however, in which healthcare expenditures can be reduced. For example, otherwise healthy people with minor colds and other viruses can use home remedies, such as drinking fluids and resting, rather than make an expensive visit to the doctor. So the price elasticity of demand depends on the severity of the medical need and the sense of urgency involved in treatment. Urgent needs have the most inelastic demand. As the time horizon expands from the short run to the long run, the demand for health care becomes progressively more elastic. Nonemergency long-term treatments have the greatest price elasticity. For instance, a significant portion of the adult population postpones routine dental visits, despite the obvious benefits. Later, when a tooth goes bad, some people choose extractions, which are less expensive (though less attractive) than root canals and crowns.

In recent years, demand for health care has grown. As people live longer, demand rises for expensive medical goods and services, including hearing aids, replacement joints, and assisted living and nursing home facilities. In an aging population, the incidence of certain illnesses and conditions—for example, cancer and Alzheimer's disease—rises. In addition, new technologies have made it possible to treat medical conditions for which there previously was no treatment. While these medical advances have improved the quality of life for many consumers, they drive up demand for more advanced medical procedures, equipment, and specialty drugs.

People who are risk averse (see Chapter 17) generally choose to purchase health insurance because it protects them against the possibility of extreme financial hardship in the case of severe illness or other medical problems. But insurance may distort their idea of costs and cause them to change their behavior, which creates a moral hazard problem. For example, if an insurance policy does not require the patient to pay anything, or requires very little, to see the doctor, the patient may wind up seeing the doctor more often than necessary.

---

*Ringel, Jeanne S., Susan D. Hosek, Ben A. Vollaard, and Sergej Mahnovski, *The Elasticity of Demand for Health Care: A Review of the Literature and Its Application to the Military Health System*, Santa Monica, CA: RAND Corporation, 2002. https://www.rand.org/pubs/monograph_reports/MR1355.html; Ellis RP, Martins B, Zhu W. *Health care demand elasticities by type of service*, J Health Econ, 2017 Sep; 55:232-243. doi: 10.1016/j.jhealeco.2017.07.007.

ECONOMICS in the MEDIA

Health Insurance

SUPERSTORE

The sitcom *Superstore* features Amy Dubanowski (America Ferrera) and her fellow employees at Cloud 9, a big-box establishment where you can buy everything from toothpaste to a sofa. In the episode "Health Fund," the employees try to create a fund to pay for medical expenses within their group. While they only mention the word *insurance* with respect to the poor coverage they get through their employer, what they are trying to create is really a group insurance plan. They are attempting to pool their risk by all chipping in up front and then covering actual expenses as they arise.

Within a few hours, however, the plan is over-extended by tens of thousands of dollars, due to an immediate flood of participant claims. At this point the simple plan becomes increasingly complex, as Amy and Jonah (Ben Feldman) try to separate people into high- and low-risk groups with differentiated premiums. They also confront traditional insurance problems, like adverse selection, where the high-risk people are the ones most eager to get coverage. There is also evidence of moral hazard, where people change their behavior—or at least their interest in seeing a doctor—due to insurance coverage. Further complex adjustments to the plan lead an exasperated employee to declare, "Guys, we're making it too difficult. We just gotta simplify. Cover everything, exclude no one, and make it affordable."

Do you think America Ferrera and Ben Feldman have better health insurance than the characters they play on *Superstore*?

Credit: Thanks to Clair Smith, of St. John Fisher College, for this idea.

Consider how this situation affects two patients. Ana does not have insurance and therefore must pay the full cost of medical care out of pocket. Bashir has an insurance policy that requires a small copayment for medical care. Figure 18.3 illustrates the difference between how Ana (point A) and Bashir (point B) might react. Let's suppose they both get sick five times during the year. Because Ana pays the full cost of seeking treatment ($100 per physician office visit), she will go to the doctor's office only three times. She ends up paying $300. Bashir pays $10 per visit, so he will go to the doctor's office five times for a total cost to him of $50. The insurance company picks up the rest of the cost for Bashir, or $90 per visit.

The overall impact of a $10 copayment on healthcare costs is large. In the Ana/Bashir scenario, since each visit costs $100, total healthcare costs for the office visits are $300 when a patient is uninsured, but $500 with healthcare coverage—a $200 increase in total healthcare costs. Because in our example

FIGURE 18.3

Price and the Quantity Demanded of Medical Care Services

Without insurance, the consumer bears the entire cost of an office visit, or $100. At this amount, the consumer (Ana) might think twice about whether the medical care is truly necessary. As a result of these costs, Ana makes three office visits per year, represented by point A. However, when a consumer has insurance and pays only a $10 copayment per visit, the marginal price drops and the quantity demanded increases. This insured consumer, Bashir, makes five office visits per year, represented by point B.

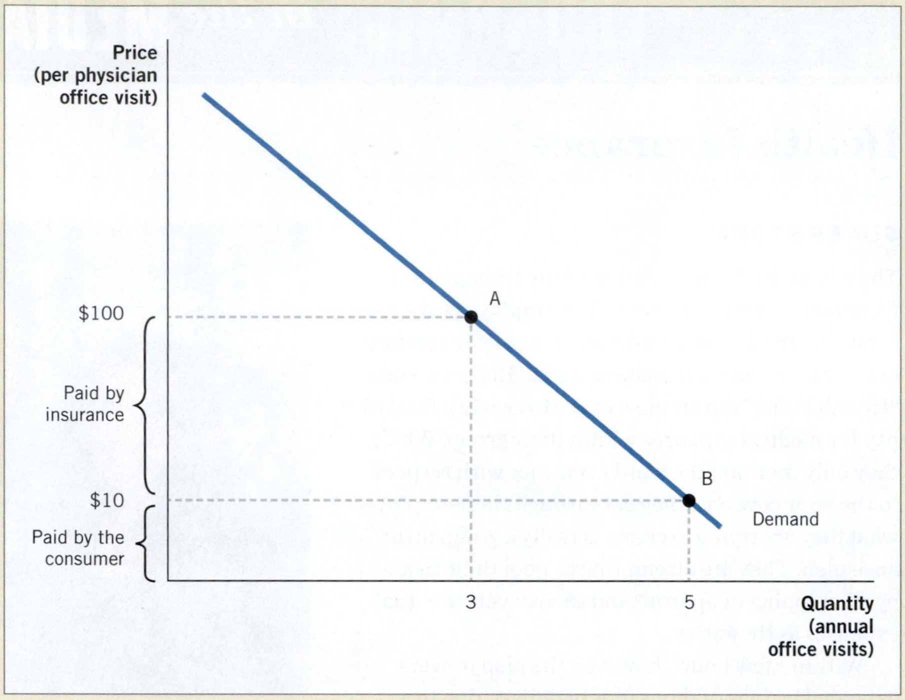

the insurance companies are paying 90% of the cost, the consumer has little reason not to seek medical attention, even for minor problems that will respond to home treatment. The two extra visits per year illustrate a change in consumer behavior as a result of the lower copayment, helping to explain why overall costs are higher.

Healthcare Supply

While consumers worry about the price, or premium, they pay for health insurance, producers are concerned about profits. As much as we might like to think that medical providers care only about our health, we must acknowledge that they are providing a service for which they expect to be paid. Therefore, it is more accurate to think of healthcare providers in the same way we think of any other producers: when the price rises, they are willing to supply additional health care. Producers of medical care such as physicians and hospitals also enjoy significant market power. In this section, we consider how licensing requirements limit the supply of certain healthcare providers and thereby impact the market.

Becoming a skilled medical provider is a lengthy process that requires extensive training, education, and certification. Physicians must secure licenses from a medical board before they can practice, and nurses must become registered. Thus, restrictions associated with entering the medical profession limit the supply of workers. This point is captured in Figure 18.4, which illustrates how barriers to entry limit the number of physicians and nurses, and the associated effect on their wages.

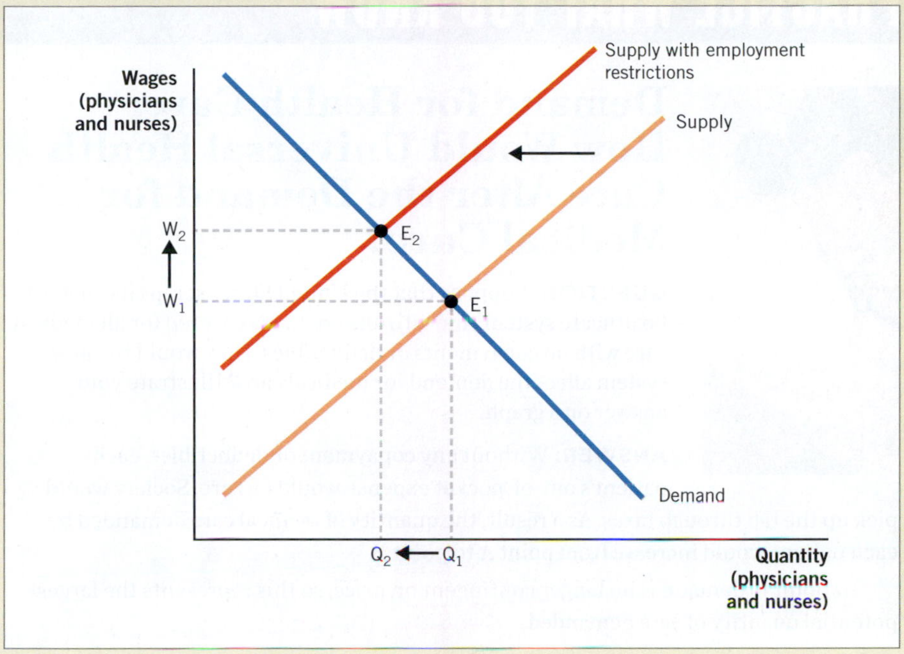

FIGURE 18.4

Barriers to Entry Limit the Supply of Certain Medical Workers

Restrictions associated with entering the medical profession limit the supply of certain workers. These restrictions cause a decrease in the quantity supplied of physicians and nurses from Q_1 to Q_2 and an increase in wages from W_1 to W_2.

Barriers to entry in the medical profession restrict the supply of physicians and nurses. The subsequent decrease in the quantity supplied of these medical workers (from Q_1 to Q_2) causes their wages to increase (from W_1 to W_2). In addition, many medical facilities do not face direct competition. For example, many small communities have only one hospital. In these cases, familiarity, the need for immediate care, and convenience make the nearest hospital the default option for most patients. Because economies of scale are important in the provision of medical care, even large metropolitan areas tend to have only a few large hospitals rather than many smaller competitors. As the population base expands, larger hospitals can afford to offer a wider set of services than smaller hospitals do. For instance, the need for pediatric care units, oncology centers, organ transplant centers, and a host of other services require that the hospital develop a particular expertise. The availability of specialized care is, of course, a good thing. However, as hospitals become larger and more highly specialized, competitive pressures subside and they are able to charge higher fees.

The market power of suppliers is held in check to some extent by insurance companies and by the Medicare and Medicaid programs. Also, some services are not reimbursed by insurance. And the insurance companies push back against certain other medical charges by limiting the amount they reimburse, as do Medicare and Medicaid for certain treatments. In addition, elective medical services, such as Lasik eye surgery, are typically not reimbursed by insurance plans. As a result, consumer demand is quite elastic for some services. While high medical care costs continue to be a significant policy concern, one researcher, Melinda Buntin, a professor in the Vanderbilt University School

PRACTICE WHAT YOU KNOW

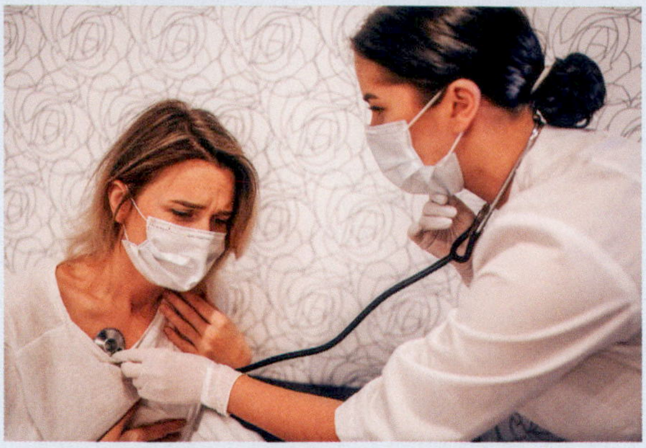

An increase in the quantity of medical care demanded for services might mean that "hurry up and wait" becomes a common experience for most patients.

Demand for Health Care: How Would Universal Health Care Alter the Demand for Medical Care?

QUESTION: Suppose that the United States scraps its current healthcare system, and citizens are 100% covered for all medical care with no copayments or deductibles. How would the new system affect the demand for medical care? Illustrate your answer on a graph.

ANSWER: Without any copayment or deductibles, each patient's out-of-pocket expense would be zero. Society would pick up the tab through taxes. As a result, the quantity of medical care demanded by each patient would increase from point A to point B.

At point B, demand is no longer contingent on price, so this represents the largest potential quantity of care demanded.

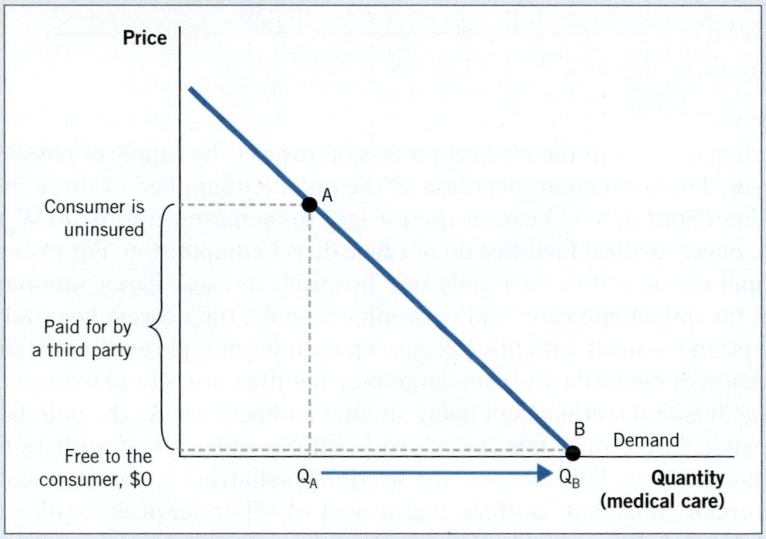

of Health Policy, has found that Medicare spending did not rise as fast as the overall economy and inflation from 2010 to 2016. If this trend holds, healthcare spending as a percentage of GDP will slowly decline over time.*

*Melinda J. B. Buntin, "How to Reduce Health Care Costs: Understanding the Cost of Health Care in America," Testimony for Senate Committee, June 27, 2018, https://www.help.senate.gov/imo/media/doc/Buntin.pdf.

How Do Incentives Influence the Quality of Health Care?

In this section, we apply what we've learned about health care. First, we look at the universal healthcare debate by comparing the healthcare systems in the United States and Canada. Then we examine the shortage of human organs available for transplant. By considering these two issues, we can see how incentives influence the quality of health care patients receive.

Incentives

Single-Payer versus Private Health Care

Rationing is a fact of life because we live in a world of scarcity. The simplest way of thinking about the health-care issue is to understand how different rationing mechanisms are used in medical care. In the United States, the primary rationing mechanism is the consumer's ability to pay. One consequence of using prices to ration medical care is that close to 35 million U.S. citizens forgo some medical care because they lack insurance or the means to pay for care on their own. In Canada, no citizen lacks the means to pay because medical care is paid for by taxes. This does not mean that medical care there is unlimited, however. In Canada, rationing occurs through wait times, fewer doctors, and limited availability of certain drugs.

Which country has better health care, the United States or Canada?

As in almost all things economic, there is a trade-off. No medical system creates the perfect set of incentives. In the United States, a large majority of citizens have the means to pay for medical care, have access to some of the best medical facilities in the world, and face relatively short wait times. However, under the current U.S. system, access to the best facilities is limited, and longer wait times exist for the poorest members of society. The Affordable Care Act has reduced some of the disparities between the rich and the poor, but a system of private health care makes those differences impossible to eliminate.

Trade-offs

In Canada, each citizen is treated equally, but access to immediate medical treatment is more restricted. We saw in Table 18.1 that Canada spends far less than the United States per capita ($4,826 versus $10,209). How does Canada provide medical care to every citizen at approximately half the price of the U.S. system? There are several ways. First, the government sets the rates paid to medical providers. Second, physicians are not permitted to have private practices. Third, hospitals receive grants from the government to cover the costs of providing care. This system, in which there is only a *single payer*, makes the government the single buyer, or monopsonist, of most medical care. (See Chapter 14 for a discussion of monopsony.) In other words, in a **single-payer system**, the government covers the cost of providing most health care, and citizens pay their share through taxes.

In a **single-payer system**, the government covers the cost of providing most health care, and citizens pay their share through taxes.

The Canadian government uses its leverage as a monopsonist to set compensation levels for physicians below the competitive market wage rate. Under Canada's Health Act, government funding is required for medically necessary care, but only if that care is delivered in hospitals or by certified physicians. This means that the Canadian government funds about 70% of all medical expenses, with the remaining 30% of costs being generated by prescription

DATA SNAPSHOT

Health: United States vs. Canada

Is the healthcare dollar being spent as efficiently as possible to maintain the health of Americans? To answer this question, it's helpful to compare our situation to other countries, such as Canada. The United States and Canada have very different healthcare systems. Canada's is primarily a publicly funded, single-payer system with the government paying 70% of all health-related expenses. The United States' is primarily a privately funded, multi-payer system with the government paying approximately 48% of all health-related expenses.

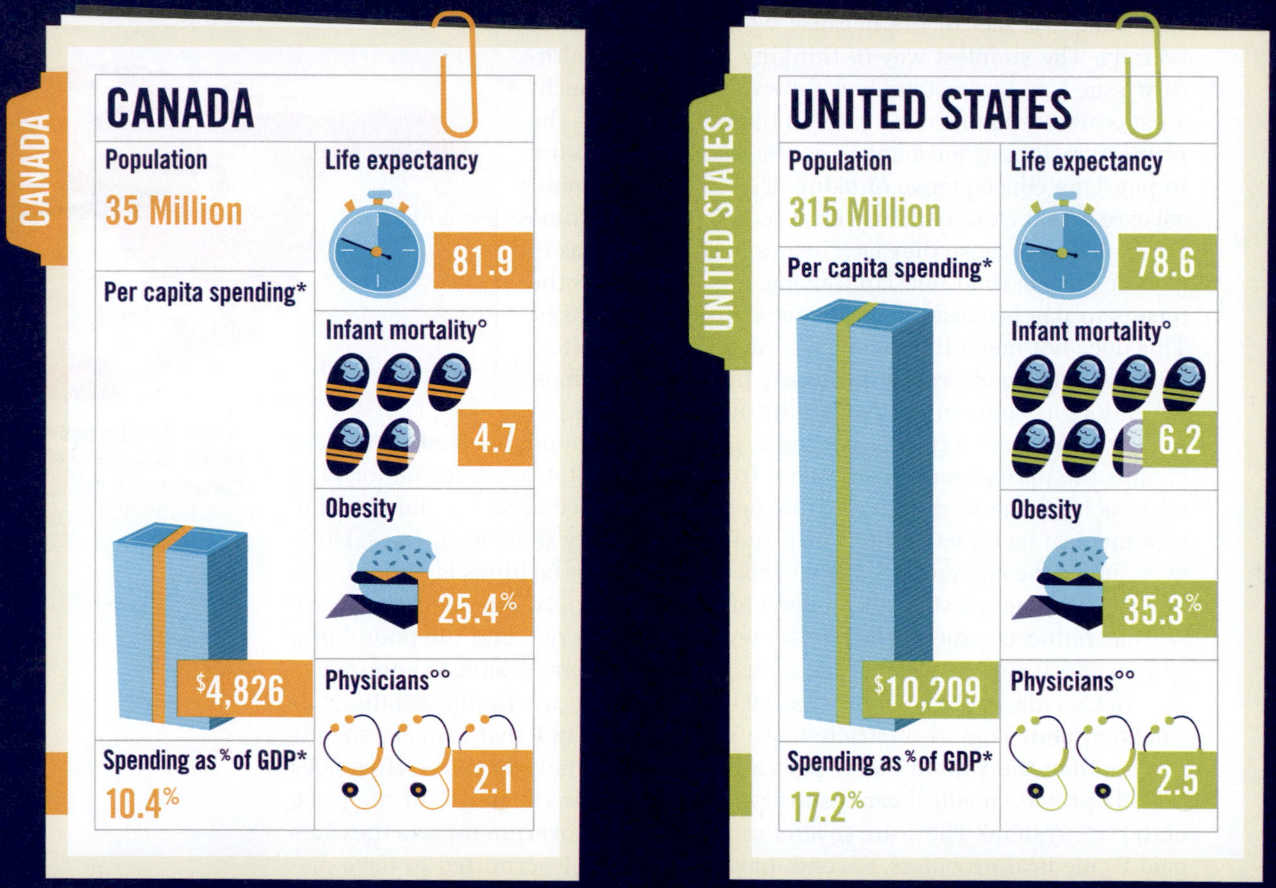

** Total expenditure, public and private   ° Per 1,000 live births   °° Per 1,000 people*

Sources: OECD, World Health Organization, CIA World Factbook.

Both countries achieve similar health outcomes, but health care is a clear example of trade-offs. The Canadian system cuts costs, while patients in the United States benefit from shorter wait times for care and the best medical facilities in the world.

REVIEW QUESTIONS

- How do you think the obesity level in the United States contributes to healthcare costs?
- What are the benefits and costs of a private versus a public healthcare system?

medications, long-term care, physical therapy, and dental care. In these areas, private insurance operates in much the same way it does in the United States.

However, there is a difference between access and availability. Because Canada keeps tight control over medical costs, people with conditions that are not life-threatening often face extended waits. One report notes that in 2020, "Canadians could expect to wait 5.4 weeks for a computed tomography (CT) scan, 11.1 weeks for a magnetic resonance imaging (MRI) scan, and 3.5 weeks for an ultrasound."* However, services that are not regulated—for example, veterinarian visits—provide access to medical care without waiting. Dogs in Canada have no trouble getting MRIs and chemotherapy quickly—unlike their human counterparts, who have to wait—but of course the pet owner has to pay the full expense.

ECONOMICS IN THE REAL WORLD

HEALTHCARE EFFICIENCY

The Bloomberg Health Efficiency Index tracks medical costs and value-for-the-dollar for over 50 economically developed nations. The Efficiency Index was created in 2015 to rank countries whose citizens have average life spans of at least 70 years, GDP per capita exceeding $5,000, and a minimum population of 5 million. The findings show that Americans aren't getting their money's worth. Only Switzerland spent more than the United States—but Switzerland's investment in medical care delivered an extra 4.2 years of extra life. A sampling of nations is shown in Table 18.2.

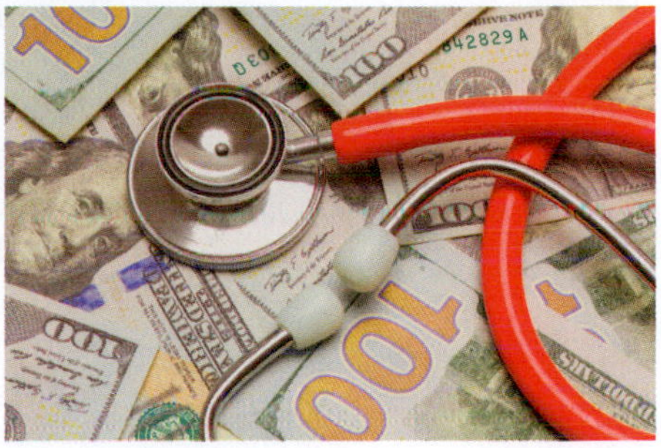

Creating a more efficient health-care delivery system is one of the United States' greatest challenges of the 21st century.

*Bacchus Barua and Mackenzie Moir, "Waiting Your Turn: Wait Times for Health Care in Canada, 2020 Report," Fraser Institute, December 10, 2020, https://www.fraserinstitute.org/studies/waiting-your-turn-wait-times-for-health-care-in-canada-2020.

TABLE 18.2

Healthcare Efficiency in Select Countries, 2020

Rank	Economy	Efficiency score	Life expectancy	Relative cost %	Absolute cost in USD
1	Singapore	67.8	83.2	4.4	2,619
2	Hong Kong	64.9	84.9	6.2	2,849
6	Ireland	45.2	82.3	7.2	4,977
8	New Zealand	41.7	81.9	9.2	3,937
10	Japan	40.2	84.2	10.9	4,169
12	China	38.0	76.7	5.2	441
27	Canada	22.5	82.0	10.6	4,755
50	Mexico	4.6	75.0	5.5	495
53	Russia	2.8	72.7	5.3	586
55	United States	−4.9	78.5	17.1	10,246
56	Brazil	−8.4	75.7	9.5	929

Source: https://www.bloomberg.com/news/articles/2020-12-18/asia-trounces-u-s-in-health-efficiency-index-amid-pandemic.

The Human Organ Shortage

Many altruistic people donate blood each year to help save the lives of tens of thousands of other people. Their generosity makes transplants and other surgeries possible. Unfortunately, the same level of generosity does not apply to organ donations. The quantity of replacement organs demanded exceeds the quantity of replacement organs supplied each year, resulting in thousands of deaths. Many of these deaths would be preventable if people were allowed to sell organs. However, the National Organ Transplant Act of 1984 makes it illegal to do so in the United States. Restrictions do not cover the entire body: people can sell platelets, sperm, and ova (the female reproductive cell). In those markets, prices determine who donates. With blood, kidneys, livers, and lungs, the donors are not paid. This discrepancy has created two unintended consequences. First, many people die unnecessarily: in the United States, more than 6,000 patients on transplant waiting lists die each year. Second, the demand for human organs has created a billion-dollar-a-year illegal market.

Let's consider the market for kidneys. Figure 18.5 illustrates how the supply of and demand for human kidneys works. Almost everyone has two kidneys, and a person's life can continue almost normally with only one healthy kidney. Of course, there are risks associated with donation, including complications from the surgery and during recovery, as well as no longer having a backup kidney. However, since there are roughly 300 million "spare" kidneys in the United States (because the population is 300 million), there is a large pool of potential donors who are good matches for recipients awaiting a transplant.

FIGURE 18.5

The Supply and Demand for Human Kidneys

Restrictions on selling kidneys limit the supply of organs as shown by $\text{Supply}_{\text{restricted}}$ and cause the shortage noted between Q_D and Q_S. An illegal market develops with a whopping price of $125,000.

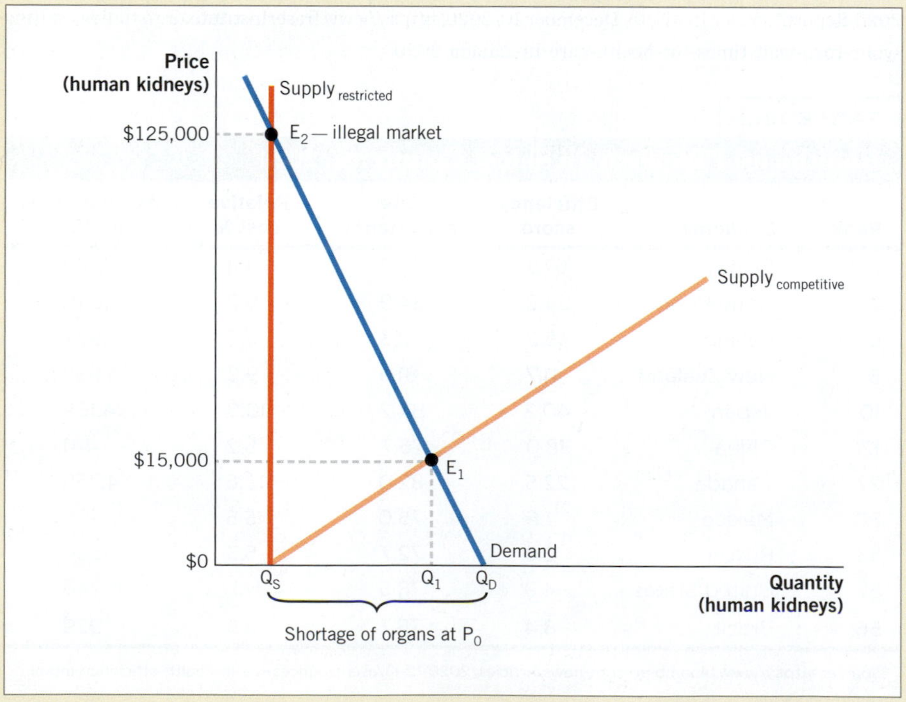

Because kidneys cannot be legally bought and sold, the supply curve shown in Figure 18.5 does not respond to price. As a result, the curve becomes a vertical line at point Q_S (quantity supplied). Notice that the quantity supplied is not zero because many people donate kidneys to friends and family members in need. Others participate in exchange programs under which they donate a kidney to someone they don't know in exchange for someone else agreeing to donate a kidney to their friend or family member. (Exchange programs help to provide better matches so that the recipient is less likely to reject the kidney transplant.*) Moreover, a few altruistic persons donate their kidneys to complete strangers. Nevertheless, the quantity supplied still falls short of the quantity demanded, because $Q_D > Q_S$ at a price of $0.

Trade creates value

Markets would normally reconcile a shortage by increasing prices. In Figure 18.5, an equilibrium market price of $15,000 is shown ($E_1$). Economists have estimated that this would be the market price if the sale of kidneys were legal in the United States. Because such sales are illegal, the nation faces the shortage illustrated in Figure 18.5. Over 4,000 people die each year in this country waiting for a kidney transplant. Many others have a low quality of life while waiting to receive a kidney. Because patients waiting for human organs eventually die without a transplant, an illegal market for kidney transplants has developed outside the United States. However, the price—which sometimes can cost over $100,000 for the organ alone†—requires doctors, hospitals, staff, and patients to circumvent the law. As a consequence, the illegal-market price (at E_2) is much higher than it would be if a competitive market for human kidneys existed.

In its simplest form, the issue is essentially this: why should the affluent, who can afford to pay for organ transplants, continue to live, while the poor, who also need organ transplants, die? That hardly seems fair. Unfortunately, altruism alone has not provided enough organs to meet demand, leading to a shortage of many vital organs. Because we continue to experience shortages of human organs, the supply must be rationed. Whether the rationing takes place through markets, waiting in line, or via some other mechanism is a matter of efficiency. As a result, using markets, in some form, may be one way to prevent avoidable deaths. However, the ethical considerations are significant. For example, if organs can be bought and sold, what would prevent the use of coercion to force people to sell their organs?

Of course, the ethical dilemma becomes moot if viable artificial organs can be created. And in fact, in this regard medical science is making progress toward someday solving the organ shortage. In the meantime, if you are uncomfortable with markets determining the price, remember that relying solely on altruism is not enough. If we really want to increase the supply of organs, we need to try incentives and harness behavioral economics. Some proposals along this line include allowing people to receive tax deductions, college scholarships, or guaranteed health care in exchange for donating an organ. A behavioral solution (see Chapter 17) would require people to opt out of organ donations in the event of their death—instead of the current practice in which people often opt-in to this decision when they update their driver's license. All these suggestions would reduce the ethical dilemma while still harnessing the power of economics to save lives.

Incentives

*Alvin E. Roth, Tayfun Sönmez, M. Utku Ünver, "Kidney Exchange," *The Quarterly Journal of Economics* 119, no. 2 (May 2004): 457–88.

†Edecio Martinez, "Black Market Kidneys, $160,000 a Pop," CBSNews.com, accessed January 2022, https://www.cbsnews.com/news/black-market-kidneys-160000-a-pop/.

· ECONOMICS *in the* MEDIA ·

The Illegal Human Organ Market

LAW & ORDER: SPECIAL VICTIMS UNIT

In one episode of *Law & Order: Special Victims Unit,* the officers try to track down a sleazy kidney dealer. What makes the episode compelling is the tension between doing what the law requires—stopping an illegal kidney transplant mid-surgery—and subsequently wrestling with watching the patient suffer as a result. In addition, the officers interview the dealer, the physician, patients on kidney waiting lists, and an administrator of the national kidney wait list. Their opinions, which run a wide gamut, allow the viewer to experience all of the emotions and arguments for and against the purchase of kidneys.

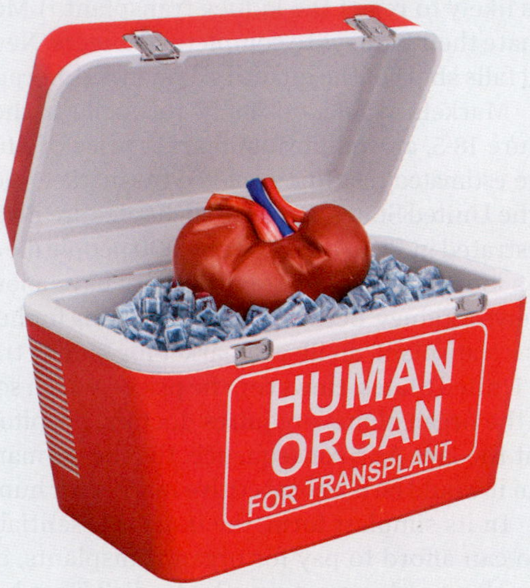

The SVU team explores the issues of dealing in illegal kidneys.

Each character tugs on viewers' emotions in a different way. The sleazy dealer proudly proclaims that he is making his customers happy and that the officers wouldn't be so judgmental if one of their own family members needed a kidney. The physician who does the transplant explains he is not driven by making money but by saving lives. The patients all know where they can get an illegal kidney, but most accept their fate within the current system. The administrator of the wait list argues that they have enough trouble getting people to volunteer as it is, asking: "What would happen if donors learned that we had made an exception and approved the transplant of an illegally purchased kidney?" By the end of the episode, we see that the economic and ethical dimensions of the issue are not clear-cut.

ECONOMICS IN THE REAL WORLD

With a little help from one another, we can all access the bountiful harvest.

THE MEDICAL HEALTH CARE PIE IS DISPROPORTIONATELY CONSUMED

Per capita, America spends more than any other nation on health care. Unfortunately, the benefits of all that spending are distributed very unevenly. For one thing, there's inequity based on wealth and income. If you're financially well off, or if you have health insurance through your employer, you'll get good care. But if you are poor and uninsured, that's a different story.

The other big source of healthcare inequity relates to race and ethnicity. A 2003 report by the National Academies' Institute of Medicine found that racial and ethnic minorities tended to receive a lower quality of health care than nonminorities, even after factors such as patients' insurance status and income were adjusted for. The problem hasn't gone away. In the time of COVID-19, this has been all the more concerning, because minorities have had higher risks of infection and death than whites. Partly, this is because minorities are disproportionately represented in high-risk occupations (everything from nursing to hospitality to assembly-line work), and partly it is because higher rates among minorities of preexisting conditions, such as diabetes and hypertension, have made COVID-19 more deadly. Most minorities are about 2.5 times as likely as whites to come down with COVID-19. And once sick, minority patients are significantly more likely to die.

So what should we do? Changing the makeup of the healthcare system in ways we have been exploring in the chapter is one way, of course. However, because poverty and minority status are correlated, many economists see focusing on separate non-health policies targeted at low-income families as a way to help minorities. For example, low-wage workers often struggle to afford decent housing. Even when they're able to pay the rent, there may not be money left over for routine doctor visits or emergency clinic visits. Policies or incentives that increase the supply of affordable housing are a clear solution here, though these vary greatly. Frequently mentioned ideas include the construction of new low-income housing, the repair of existing low-income housing, changes in zoning laws, and policies that extend debt forgiveness and block evictions in order to reduce the share of income the poor have to pay for shelter.

Another area cited for improvement relates to how low-income households often lack the access to educational tools that middle-class households take for granted: books, computers, and high-speed Internet. Children who lag educationally eventually lag in health outcomes. Any enhanced educational opportunities for low-income households are typically seen as a priority, to help disadvantaged students keep pace with their classmates.

Sources: Institute of Medicine, *Unequal Treatment: Confronting Racial and Ethnic Disparities in Health Care* (Washington, DC: National Academies Press, 2003); Rand Corporation, "Children at Risk: Consequences for School Readiness and Beyond," 2005, https://www.rand.org/content/dam/rand/pubs/research_briefs/2005/RAND_RB9144.pdf; Economic Policy Institute, "Education Inequalities at the School Starting Gate," 2017, https://www.epi.org/publication/education-inequalities-at-the-school-starting-gate/; Center on Society and Health, Virginia Commonwealth University, "Education: It Matters More to Health than Ever Before," 2015, https://societyhealth.vcu.edu/work/the-projects/education-it-matters-more-to-health-than-ever-before.html.

Conclusion

When people speak about health care, they often debate the merits of universal health care versus private medical care, as if the issue involves just those two factors. This obscures the important economic considerations at work on the micro level. The reality is that the healthcare debate exists on many margins and requires complex trade-offs. The way the various participants deal with different healthcare issues affects how well our nation's overall healthcare system functions. Supply and demand works just fine in explaining the incentives that participants face when considering healthcare options; what complicates the analysis is the impact of third parties on the incentives patients face.

Health care straddles the boundary between microeconomic analysis, which focuses on individual behavior, and macroeconomics, in which society's overarching concern is how to best spend so large an amount of money. Moreover, health decisions are an unavoidable part of our individual lives. Medical expenditures account for one out of every six dollars spent in the United States. Therefore, micro forces that lead to fundamental changes to the healthcare system will have a large impact—a macro effect—on our economy.

· ECONOMICS *for* LIFE ·

Obamacare: A Primer

Formally called the Affordable Care Act (ACA), Obamacare is a federal law, signed by President Barack Obama in 2010, that provided fundamental reform of the U.S. healthcare and health insurance system. To help you understand the Affordable Care Act, we have created this primer.

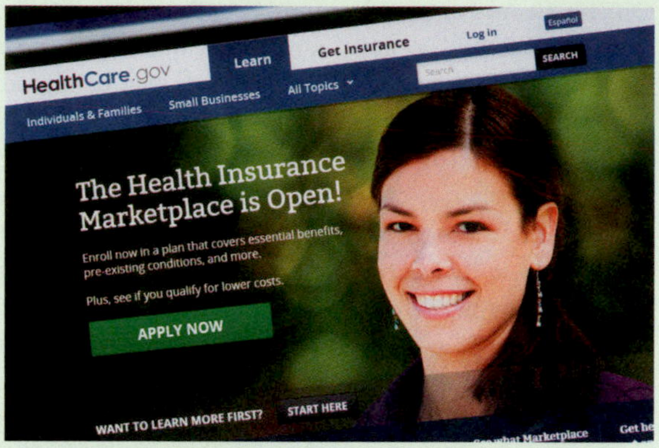

Learn about the Affordable Care Act.

1. The ACA does not create health insurance. The legislation regulates the health insurance industry and is designed to increase the quality, affordability, and availability of private insurance.
2. Young adults can stay on their parents' plan until age 26. Before the ACA was passed, it was common for young adults to fall off their parents' plans and, due to low income, forgo health care. Under the ACA, most young adults qualify for federal subsidies or Medicaid through the Health Insurance Marketplace.
3. The ACA created new health insurance exchanges to promote increased enrollment, deliver subsidies, and help spread risk to ensure that the costs associated with expensive medical treatments are shared more broadly across large groups of people, rather than spread across just a few beneficiaries. If you don't have coverage, you can use the Health Insurance Marketplace (healthcare.gov) to buy a private insurance plan. The cost of your marketplace health insurance works on a sliding scale. Those who make less pay less. Poorer Americans are eligible for premium tax credits through the marketplace. These tax credits subsidize the cost of insurance premiums.
4. All new plans sold on or off the marketplace must include a wide range of new benefits. These include wellness visits and preventive tests and treatments at no additional out-of-pocket cost. Preventive care is much cheaper than addressing serious medical issues too late, so this provision of the ACA is intended to lower overall costs.
5. The ACA does away with discrimination based on preexisting conditions and gender, so these factors no longer affect the cost of insurance on or off the marketplace. You can't be denied health coverage based on health status. You can't be dropped from coverage when you are sick. These changes spread risk more evenly and encourage people to get medical care sooner.

ANSWERING *the* BIG QUESTIONS

What are the important issues in the healthcare industry?

- The healthcare debate is about efficiency and cost containment. Increases in longevity and quality of life are subject to diminishing returns and require choices with difficult trade-offs.
- The widespread use of insurance alters the incentives consumers and producers face when making healthcare decisions. Consumers pay premiums up front and much smaller deductibles and copayments when seeking medical care. Producers receive the bulk of their revenue from intermediaries such as insurance companies. The result is a system in which consumers demand more medical care because they are insured and many providers have an incentive to order additional tests or procedures that may not be absolutely necessary.

How does asymmetric information affect healthcare delivery?

- Asymmetric information (adverse selection, the principal-agent problem, and moral hazard) affects incentives in healthcare delivery. Insurance companies try to structure their plans to encourage patients to seek care only when it is needed and also to seek preventive care. The companies can achieve these goals by making many preventive care visits free and establishing deductibles and copayments that are high enough to discourage unnecessary trips to the doctor or a demand for additional procedures.
- Inelastic demand for many medical services, combined with third-party payments that significantly lower out-of-pocket expenses to consumers, gives rise to a serious moral hazard problem in which patients demand more medical care than is medically advisable. To solve a moral hazard problem, it is necessary to fix the incentive structure. Moral hazard explains why many insurance companies encourage preventive care: it lowers medical costs. It also explains why insurance companies impose payment limits on preventable conditions.

How do demand and supply contribute to high medical costs?

- Inelastic demand and third-party payments help explain why medical expenses have risen so rapidly. The combination of third-party payments and inelastic demand for medical care increases the quantity of medical care demanded; both factors also result in increased expenditures. As we learned previously, more demand means higher prices, all else equal.
- In addition, licensing requirements limit the supply of key healthcare providers. Licensing requirements provide a supply-side explanation for increased medical expenditures. In addition, hospital charges are rarely subject to competitive pressures. In many small communities, there is only one local hospital, clinic, or specialist nearby. Providers therefore have market power, which they can use in setting prices.

How do incentives influence the quality of health care?

- A single-payer system makes the government the single buyer, or monopsonist, of most medical care. The government uses its leverage as a monopsonist to set compensation levels for providers below the competitive market wage rate.
- Single-payer systems ration medical services through increased wait times, whereas private healthcare systems ration medical care through prices.
- The demand for many replacement organs exceeds the supply made available each year. However, because of the National Organ Transplant Act of 1984, it is illegal to sell most organs in the United States. This restriction results in thousands of deaths annually, many of which would be preventable if people were allowed to sell organs in legal markets.

CHAPTER PROBLEMS

Concepts You Should Know

adverse selection (p. 579)
asymmetric information (p. 578)
coinsurance payments (p. 576)
copayments (p. 576)
deductibles (p. 576)
moral hazard (p. 580)
principal-agent problem (p. 579)
single-payer system (p. 587)

Questions for Review

1. What is asymmetric information? How is it relevant to medical care?
2. Give one example each of adverse selection, moral hazard, and the principal-agent problem.
3. For each of the examples you gave in question 2, discuss a solution that lessens the asymmetric information problem.
4. Describe why the marginal product of medical care declines as medical expenditures rise.
5. What are two primary reasons healthcare demand has increased dramatically over the last 20 years?
6. What is a supply-related reason for high medical care costs?
7. What are the two primary ways in which health care is rationed?

Study Problems (*✱solved at the end of the section*)

1. Suppose that a medical specialist charges $300 per consultation. If your insurance charges you a $25 copay, what is the marginal cost of your consultation? Suppose that a second patient has a different policy that requires a 25% coinsurance payment, but no copay. What is the second patient's marginal cost of the consultation? Which patient is more likely to see the specialist?

✱ 2. Newer automobiles have many safety features, including antilock brakes, side airbags, traction control, and rear backup sensors, to help prevent accidents. Do these safety features lead the drivers of newer vehicles to drive more safely? In your answer, consider how an increased number of safety features affects the problem of moral hazard.

3. A customer wants a new life insurance policy. Even though the customer's medical records indicate a good health history, the insurance company requires a physical exam before coverage can be extended. Why would the insurance company insist on a physical exam?

4. Indicate whether the following medical services have elastic or inelastic demand.
   a. an annual physical for someone between the ages of 20 and 35
   b. an MRI used to detect cancer
   c. the removal of a noncancerous mole on your back
   d. seeing a physician when your child has a temperature of 104°F

5. Most people have two working kidneys, but humans need only one working kidney to survive. If the sale of kidneys were legalized, what would happen to the price and the number of kidneys sold in the market? Would a shortage of kidneys continue to exist? Explain your response.

✱ 6. An isolated community has one hospital. The next closest hospital is 2 hours away. Given what you have learned about monopoly, what prices would you expect the hospital to charge? How much care would you expect it to provide? Compare the prices and amount of care provided to those of a comparably sized hospital in a major metropolitan area where competition is prevalent.

7. One insurance plan costs $100 a month and has a $50 copayment for all services. Another insurance plan costs $50 a month and requires patients to pay a 15% coinsurance. A consumer is trying to decide which plan to purchase. Which plan would the consumer select with an anticipated $200 per month in medical bills? What about $600 per month in medical bills? Set up an equation to determine the monthly amount of medical expenses at which the consumer would be indifferent between the two plans.

8. For each of the following situations, determine whether adverse selection, moral hazard, or the principal-agent problem is at work.

    a. You decide to buy a scalped ticket before a concert, but you are not entirely sure the ticket is legitimate.

    b. A contractor takes a long time to finish the construction work he promised after you gave him his final payment.

    c. You hire a neighborhood teenager to mow your grass once a week over the summer while you are traveling. The teenager mows your grass every three weeks instead.

✱ 9. "To economists, human life is not of infinite value." Explain this statement and its economic implications for end-of-life care.

10. What characteristics make the market for health care different from other markets?

11. Suppose you recently broke your arm, and as part of your recovery process, you are considering how many times to go to physical therapy. The marginal cost (MC) of a visit to the physical therapist is constant and equal to $300. That is what you have to pay per visit, assuming you don't have insurance.

    a. How many times should you visit the physical therapist?

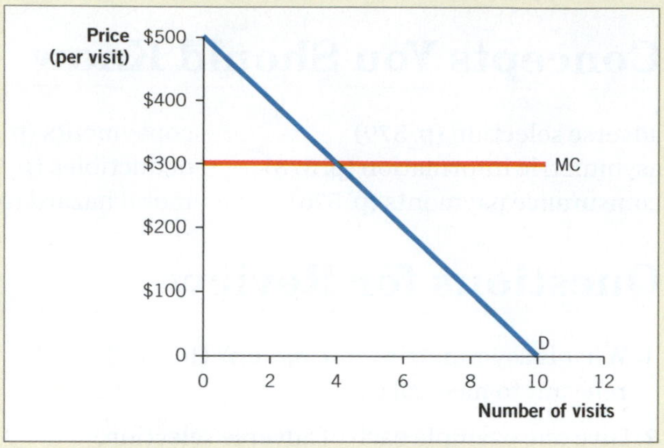

    b. If you have full health coverage (with no copay or deductible) how many times will you visit the physical therapist?

    c. What is the deadweight loss that arises due to full health coverage? (**Hint:** Deadweight loss is the difference between the willingness to pay and the additional cost of production that arises when the consumer has no copay or deductible.)

✱ 12. We learned that when caps are placed on how much a physician can be paid for a service under Medicare, doctors charge more for other services. Can you think of anything else a physician might decide to do if they feel that what Medicare pays is insufficient to cover their costs?

Solved Problems

2. When drivers feel safer, they drive faster—not more safely. The higher speed offsets the safety gain from safety features that help prevent accidents or make them survivable. Drivers of vehicles who feel especially safe are more likely to take on hazardous conditions and become involved in accidents. In other words, they alter their behavior when driving a safer car. The change in behavior is evidence of a moral hazard problem.

6. Because the demand for medical care is quite inelastic, an isolated hospital with significant monopoly power will charge more and offer fewer services. In contrast, a comparably sized hospital in a major metropolitan area where competition is prevalent is forced to charge the market price and offer more services to attract consumers.

9. Human life is not of infinite value because we live in a world of trade-offs. An "infinite value" implies that the value is so high that all medical paths are worth pursuing. However, one must be mindful of the marginal cost of care versus the amount of additional life that end-of-life care buys. This consideration is especially important at the end of life when extraordinary medical efforts might mean only a few extra days of low-quality life. The law of diminishing returns applies, and the application of this economic principle suggests that resources should be redirected from end-of-life care to preventive care with larger returns.

12. Medicare is a government program, but physicians are not required to participate. Therefore, another option is not to participate, which is exactly what some doctors decide to do. These doctors have decided that as long as they're able to keep their appointment books reasonably full with non-Medicare patients, the opportunity cost of taking Medicare patients is too high.

TS6 HC
DCC KD

PART VI

Macroeconomic BASICS

CHAPTER

19

Introduction to Macroeconomics and Gross Domestic Product

Service Industries Play an Increasingly Important Role in the Global Economy.

Amazon is one of the biggest and fastest-growing companies in the world. The coronavirus pandemic that began in 2019 and escalated in 2020 actually helped the online retailer, as sales rose by 40% in the midst of the crisis. At this point, the company accounts for half of all online sales revenue in the country. Its nearest competitor, eBay, accounts for less than 7%. Amazon's success has made founder Jeff Bezos the world's richest person, with a net worth somewhere north of $150 billion.

There's no doubt Amazon plays a major role in the global economy, but what does the company actually contribute? It doesn't grow crops, mine minerals, or manufacture goods. What exactly does Amazon do that's economically so significant?

Amazon provides a service: it helps people buy goods produced by others. This service is an important contributor to our U.S. economy, as shown by the fact that most of us have bought something from Amazon at some point.

The service Amazon provides is an intangible but important form of output, and this service provides income to many people throughout the economy. Over the past several

Amazon only sold books in the 1990s. Now it's one of the biggest Internet retailers in the world, offering everything from power tools to tropical fruit to movie passes, thanks to high-tech process management. Firms like Amazon are a big reason why the U.S. economy still produces more than one-fifth of all the output in the world, despite the strong growth in China and elsewhere.

decades, the entire U.S. economy has evolved from an economy that primarily manufactured goods to one that provides services like retail, healthcare, financial, and food services. In this chapter, we discuss how economists measure overall production in an economy, production that includes both goods and services. The primary measure is called gross domestic product, or GDP.

· BIG QUESTIONS ·

- How is macroeconomics different from microeconomics?
- What does GDP tell us about the economy?
- How is GDP computed?
- What are some shortcomings of GDP data?

How Is Macroeconomics Different from Microeconomics?

Macroeconomics is the study of the economy of an entire nation or society. This is different from microeconomics, which considers the behavior of individual people, firms, and industries. In microeconomics, you study what people buy, what jobs they take, and how they distribute their income between consumption and savings; you also examine the decisions of firms and how they compete with other firms. In macroeconomics, you consider the causes and consequences of changes in the *national* output of goods and services, overall *national* employment levels, and the *overall* price level in an economy.

Here's a more specific example. In microeconomics, you study the markets for particular goods like salmon (an example from Chapter 3). You study the behavior of people who consume salmon and firms that sell salmon—demanders and suppliers. Then you bring them together to see how the equilibrium price depends on the behavior of both demanders and suppliers.

Macroeconomics is the study of the broader economy. It looks at the big picture created by all markets in the economy—the markets for salmon, coffee, computers, cars, haircuts, and health care, to name just a few. In macroeconomics, we examine *total* output in an economy rather than just from a single firm or industry. We look at *total* employment across the economy rather than employment at a single firm. We consider *all* prices in the economy rather than the price of just one product, such as salmon. To illustrate these differences,

A pink slip for one person is a microeconomic issue . . .

. . . but widespread unemployment is a macroeconomic issue.

Table 19.1 compares a selection of topics from the different perspectives of microeconomics and macroeconomics.

What Does GDP Tell Us about the Economy?

Economists measure the total output of an economy as a gauge of its overall health. An economy producing more and more valuable output is a healthy economy. If output falls for a certain period, there is something wrong in the economy. The same is true for individuals. If you have a fever for a few days, your output goes down—you don't go to the gym, you study less, and you might call in sick for work. Similarly, we measure national economic output because it gives us a good sense of the overall health of the economy, much like a thermometer that measures your body temperature can give you an indication of your overall health. In this section, we introduce and explain our measure of an economy's output.

TABLE 19.1

Comparing the Perspectives of Microeconomics and Macroeconomics

Topic	Microeconomics	Macroeconomics
Income	The income of a person or the revenue of a firm	The income of an entire nation or a national economy
Output	The production of a single worker, firm, or industry	The production of an entire economy
Employment	The job status and decisions of an individual or firm	The job status of a national population, particularly the number of people who are unemployed
Prices	The price of a single good	The combined prices of all goods in an economy

Adding up dollar sales is a way of measuring both production and income.

Production Equals Income

This chapter is about the measurement of a nation's output, but it's also about the measurement of a nation's income. There's a good reason to cover output and income together: they are essentially the same thing. Nations and individuals that produce large amounts of highly valued output are relatively wealthy. Nations and individuals that don't produce much highly valued output are relatively poor. This is no coincidence.

Let's say you open a coffee shop in your college town. You buy or rent the supplies and equipment you need to produce coffee—everything from coffee beans and espresso machines to electricity. You hire the workers you need to keep the business running. Using these resources, you produce output such as cappuccinos, espressos, and draft coffee. On the first day, you sell 600 coffee drinks at an average price of $4 each, for a total of $2,400. This dollar figure is a measure of your firm's production, or output, on that day, and it is also a measure of the income received by you and your resource suppliers. If you sell even more coffee on the second day, the income generated increases. If you sell less, the income goes down.

Gross domestic product (GDP) is the market value of all final goods and services produced within a country during a specific period.

The same holds true for nations. **Gross domestic product (GDP)** is the market value of all final goods and services produced within a nation during a specific period of time—typically, a year. GDP is the primary measure of a nation's output and income. Recall our discussion in Chapter 1 about how the circular flow diagram illustrates the relationship between spending and income in a macroeconomy. Households spend to buy goods and services and the spending becomes income to supplier households, in payment for their work and other resources.

GDP is the sum of all the output from coffee shops, doctor's offices, software firms, fast-food restaurants, and all the other firms that produce goods and services within a nation's borders. GDP is computed as the total amount spent to buy those goods and services. All that spending becomes income to the firms' owners and the resource suppliers. This dual function of GDP is part of the reason we focus on GDP as a barometer of the economy. When GDP goes up, national output and income are both higher. When GDP falls, the economy is producing less than before, and total national income is falling.

Three Uses of GDP Data

Before analyzing the components of GDP, let's see why GDP is such an important indicator. In this section, we briefly explain the three primary uses of GDP data: to measure living standards, to measure economic growth, and to measure business cycles so we can determine whether an economy is experiencing recession or expansion.

MEASURING LIVING STANDARDS Imagine two very different nations. In the first, people work long hours in physically taxing labor, and yet their pay enables them to purchase only life's barest necessities—meager amounts of clothing, shelter, and even food. In this nation, very few individuals can afford to see a doctor, and even high school education is only for the relatively wealthy. In the second nation, virtually no one starves, people tend to work in climate-controlled environments, and almost everyone graduates from high school, with many going on to earn college degrees. The first nation experiences life similar to that in the United States two centuries ago; the second describes life in the United States today. Everyone agrees that living standards are higher in the United States today, because most people can afford more of what they generally desire: goods, services, and leisure.

We can see these differences in living standards in GDP data. Indeed, GDP in the modern United States is much higher than it was in the nineteenth century. Both output and income are higher, which indicates that living standards are also higher. While not perfect, GDP offers us a way of estimating living standards across both time and place.

Let's look at the nations with the highest GDPs in the world. Table 19.2 lists the world's largest economies by GDP in 2019. Column 3 shows GDP for the top 11 economies, giving a picture of each nation's overall output and income. Total world GDP in 2019 was $88 trillion, which means the United States ($21.4 trillion) alone produced 24% of all final goods and services in the world. The most significant recent movement is by China, which now stands in second place but was only seventh in 1999.

Although total GDP is important, it is not the best indicator of living standards for a typical person. Table 19.2 reveals that in 2019, China produced nearly three times as much GDP as Japan, yet China's population is about 10 times the population of Japan. If we divide each nation's GDP by its population, we find that in Japan there was over $40,000 GDP (or income) for every person, and in China only about $10,000 per person.

When we want to gauge living standards for an average person, we compute **per capita GDP**, which is GDP per person. That is, we divide the country's total GDP by its population. Per capita GDP is listed in the last column of Table 19.2.

Per capita GDP is GDP per person.

TABLE 19.2

World's Largest Economies by GDP, 2019

Rank	Country	2019 GDP (billions of dollars)	Per capita GDP (U.S. dollars)
1	United States	$21,428	$65,280
2	China	14,343	10,261
3	Japan	5,082	40,246
4	Germany	3,846	46,258
5	India	2,875	2,104
6	United Kingdom	2,827	42,300
7	France	2,716	40,493
8	Italy	2,001	33,187
9	Brazil	1,840	8,717
10	Canada	1,736	46,195
11	Russian Federation	1,700	11,585

Source: World Bank.

FIGURE 19.1

U.S. Real Per Capita GDP, 1970–2021

The positive slope in this graph indicates increased living standards in the United States since 1970. It shows that the average person earns significantly more income today, even after adjusting for inflation and economic downturns. Over this period, real GDP per person increased by an average of 1.7% per year.

Source: U.S. Bureau of Economic Analysis; U.S. Census Bureau.

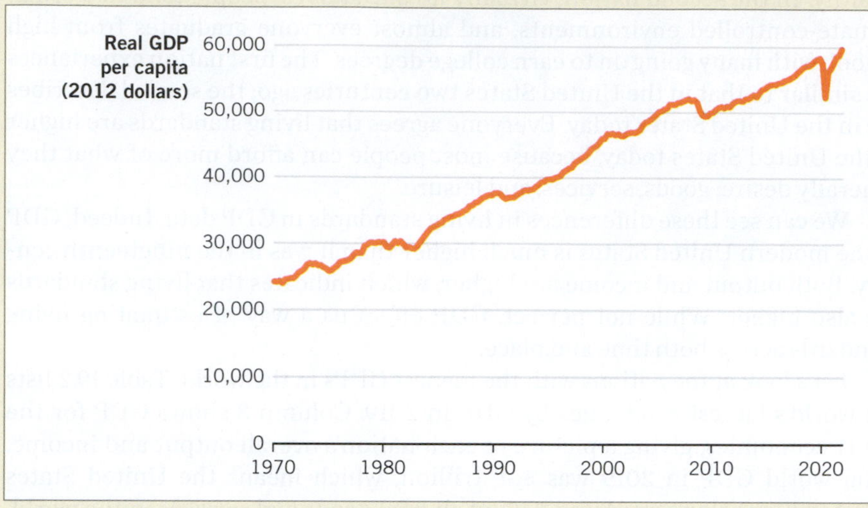

MEASURING ECONOMIC GROWTH We also use GDP data to measure economic growth. You can think of *economic growth* as changes in living standards over time. When economies grow, living standards rise, and this outcome is evident in GDP data.

Figure 19.1 shows the change in real per capita GDP in the United States from 1970 to 2020. The overall positive slope of the curve indicates that U.S. living standards rose over the course of 50 years, even though growth was not positive every year. The data show that income for the average person in 2020 was more than double what it was in 1970 (even after adjusting for inflation). So the typical person can now afford about twice as much in education, food, vacations, air-conditioning, housing, and cars as the average person in 1970.

You might notice that in this section we have added the word "real" to our discussion of GDP. Figure 19.1 plots *real* per capita GDP. Because we are now looking at data over several years, we have to adjust the GDP data for price changes that occur over time. Prices of goods and services almost always rise through time because of inflation. **Inflation** is the growth in the overall level of prices in an economy. Because GDP is calculated using market values (prices) of goods and services, inflation causes GDP to go up even if there is no change in the quantity of goods and services produced. Therefore, when we look at GDP data over time, we have to adjust it for the effects of inflation. **Real GDP** is GDP adjusted for price changes. We discuss how to compute real GDP later in this chapter. For now, just note that any time we evaluate GDP figures across different time periods, we must use real GDP to account for inflation.

Inflation
is the growth in the overall level of prices in an economy.

Real GDP
is GDP adjusted for changes in prices.

Economic growth
is measured as the percentage change in real per capita GDP.

Economic growth is measured as the percentage change in real per capita GDP. Notice that this measure starts with GDP data but then adjusts for both population growth and inflation. Given this definition, you should view Figure 19.1 as a picture of economic growth in the United States. But despite what you see in the U.S. GDP data, you should not presume that economic growth is automatic or even typical. Figure 19.2 shows the long-run experience of six other nations with six distinct experiences from 1950 to 2018. In Poland, Turkey, and Mexico, real per capita GDP levels rose significantly, more than tripling

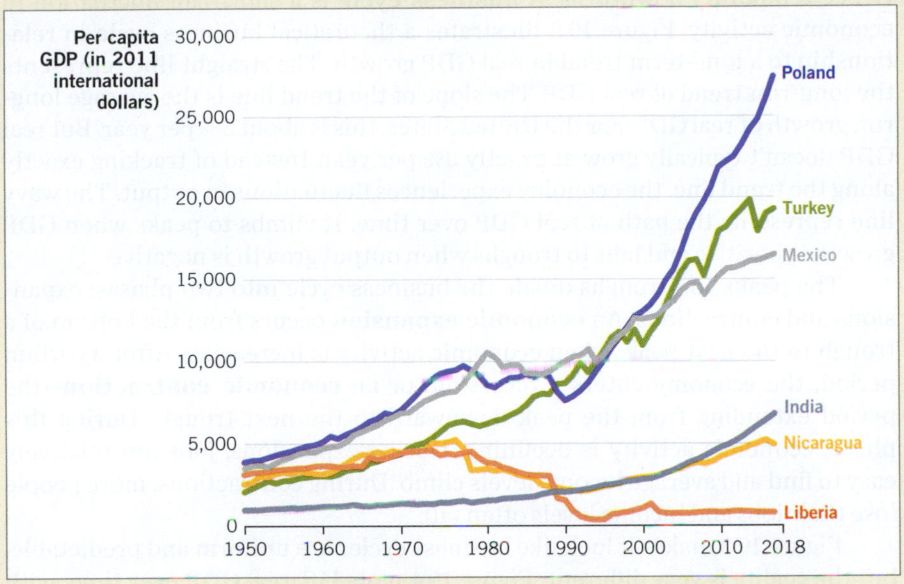

FIGURE 19.2

Real Per Capita GDP in Six Nations, 1950–2018

Growth in real per capita GDP in six nations shows that growth is not guaranteed. The levels for Poland, Turkey, and Mexico more than tripled since 1950. And while India and Nicaragua began to grow more recently, Liberia has lost ground.

Source: The Maddison Project, 2020 release, https://www.rug.nl/ggdc/historicaldevelopment/maddison/releases.

between 1950 and 2018. India's remained very low for many years but began growing steadily in the last two decades. Nicaragua has not improved since the mid-1970s, and sadly, per capita real GDP is now lower in Liberia than it was in 1950.

Economic growth is a primary topic in macroeconomics. In Chapters 24 and 25, we consider the factors that lead to the type of growth that the United States, Poland, Turkey, Mexico, and, more recently, India have enjoyed. We also consider why economies like those of Nicaragua and Liberia struggle to grow. Because real per capita GDP measures living standards, these issues are critical to real people's lives around the globe.

MEASURING BUSINESS CYCLES We have seen that GDP data are used to measure living standards and economic growth. GDP is also used to determine whether an economy is expanding or contracting in the short run. In recent years, this use of GDP has received a lot of media attention because of concerns about recessions. A **recession** is a short-term economic downturn that typically lasts about six to eighteen months. Even the mere threat of recession strikes fear in people's hearts because income levels fall and many individuals lose their jobs or cannot find work during recessions. The U.S. recession that began in December 2007 and lasted until June 2009 has been dubbed the **Great Recession** because of its length and depth. The Great Recession was felt across almost all of the globe. Our most recent recession began in March 2020 and was brought on by the COVID-19 outbreak. Economic shutdowns and quarantines around the globe fueled a significant economic decline, officially declared a period of recession later in June.*

A **recession** is a short-term economic downturn.

The **Great Recession** was the U.S. recession that lasted from December 2007 to June 2009.

*National Bureau of Economic Research, "Determination of the February 2020 Peak in US Economic Activity," *NBER News*, June 8, 2020, https://www.nber.org/cycles/june2020.html.

A **business cycle** is a short-run fluctuation in economic activity.

Even if an economy is expanding in the long run, it is normal for it to experience temporary downturns. A **business cycle** is a short-run fluctuation in economic activity. Figure 19.3 illustrates a theoretical business cycle in relationship to a long-term trend in real GDP growth. The straight line represents the long-run trend of real GDP. The slope of the trend line is the average long-run growth of real GDP. For the United States, this is about 3% per year. But real GDP doesn't typically grow at exactly 3% per year. Instead of tracking exactly along the trend line, the economy experiences fluctuations in output. The wavy line represents the path of real GDP over time. It climbs to peaks when GDP growth is positive and falls to troughs when output growth is negative.

An **economic expansion** is a phase of the business cycle during which economic activity is increasing.

An **economic contraction** is a phase of the business cycle during which economic activity is decreasing.

The peaks and troughs divide the business cycle into two phases: expansions and contractions. An **economic expansion** occurs from the bottom of a trough to the next peak, when economic activity is increasing. After a certain period, the economy enters a recession, or an **economic contraction**—the period extending from the peak downward to the next trough. During this phase, economic activity is declining. During expansions, jobs are relatively easy to find and average income levels climb. During contractions, more people lose their jobs and income levels often fall.

Figure 19.3 makes it look like business cycles are uniform and predictable, but the reality is very different. Figure 19.4 plots U.S. real GDP over time, with contractionary periods—the recessions—shaded. GDP declined during these recessionary periods, but not in a consistent, predictable pattern. The coronavirus pandemic that caused the most recent recession was completely unexpected. It was what Chapter 2 calls an exogenous factor.

Many people think recessions are more common today, and/or more severe, than they have been in the past. In reality, the opposite is true. Figure 19.5 shows how U.S. recessions have gotten steadily rarer and shorter in the last 150 years. The graph shows thirty-year intervals, and each bar represents the number of months (out of 360) spent in recession for each interval. The decline is consistent and striking. During the first time window, from 1871 to 1900, about half of the months were spent in recession! But in the most recent thirty-year window, 1991 to 2020, less than 10% of the months experienced recession.

FIGURE 19.3

The Business Cycle

The long-run trend of GDP shows consistent growth. The business cycle reflects the fluctuations an economy typically exhibits. Economic activity increases during the expansion period of the business cycle but declines during the contraction phase. In real life, the cycle is not nearly as smooth and easy to spot as pictured here.

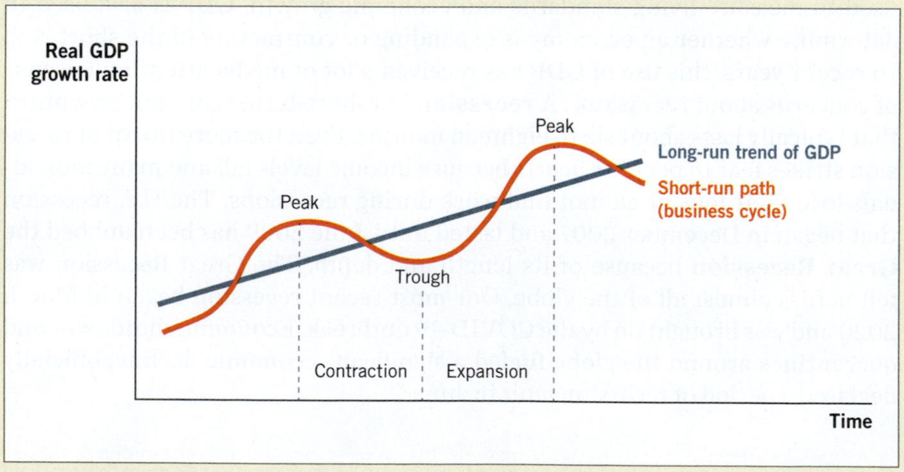

FIGURE 19.4

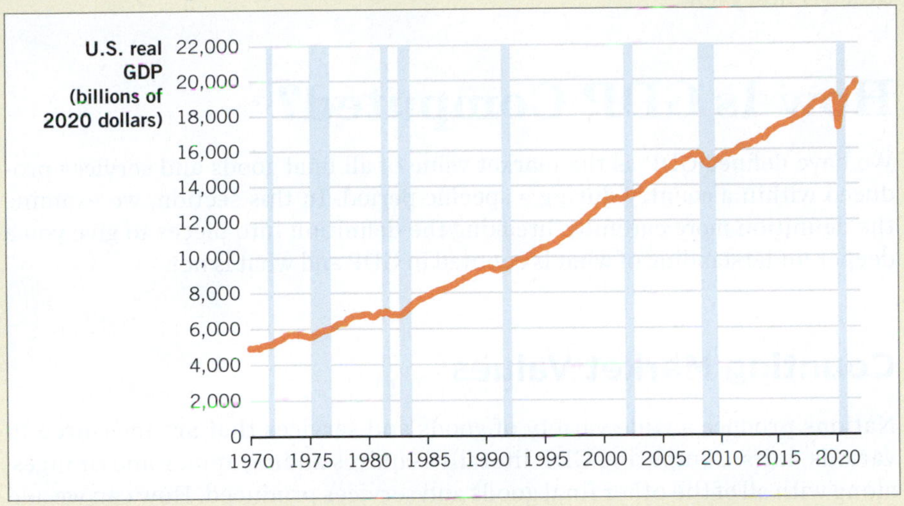

U.S. Real GDP and Recessions, 1970–2021

Over time, U.S. real GDP fluctuates. The shaded areas indicate periods of recession, when real GDP declines. The coronavirus recession began in March 2020 and was ongoing when this data was compiled.

Source: U.S. Bureau of Economic Analysis.

FIGURE 19.5

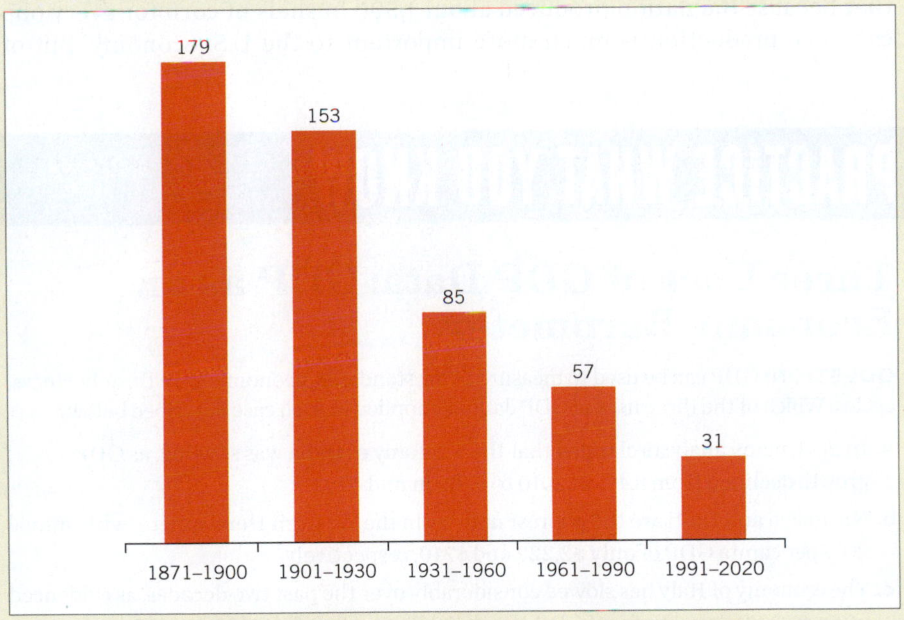

Number of Months U.S. Economy in Recession

Since 1870, each successive thirty-year period has brought the U.S. fewer months of recession than the period before it.

Source: National Bureau of Economic Research.

There are at least two reasons why people today overestimate the occurrence of recession. One reason is that the effects of recessions sometimes linger long after the recession itself is officially over. Most of us are vividly aware of the coronavirus recession. Perhaps one of your parents, or a friend's, lost their job. But most economists see this recession as an exceptional event. Another reason is that bad news tends to attract media attention. Whenever something happens that spells potential trouble for the economy, the media take note and people react. The bottom line is that recessions, tough as they may be to go through, are getting rarer all the time, and this good-news trend has been the pattern for over a century now.

How Is GDP Computed?

We have defined GDP as the market value of all final goods and services produced within a country during a specific period. In this section, we examine the definition more carefully, breaking the definition into pieces to give you a deeper understanding of what is counted in GDP and what is not.

Counting Market Values

Nations produce a wide variety of goods and services that are measured in various units. Computing GDP literally requires adding apples and oranges, along with all of the other final goods and services produced. How can we add everything from cars to corn to haircuts to gasoline to prescription drugs in a way that makes sense? Certainly, we can't just add quantities. For example, in 2014, the United States produced about 8 million motor vehicles and about 12 billion bushels of corn. Looking only at quantities, one might conclude that because the nation produced about 1,500 bushels of corn for every one car, corn production is much more important to the U.S. economy. But of

PRACTICE WHAT YOU KNOW

What does GDP data tell us about Haiti?

Three Uses of GDP Data: GDP as an Economic Barometer

QUESTION: GDP can be used to measure living standards, economic growth, or business cycles. Which of the three uses of GDP data was applied in each case described below?

a. In 2011, many analysts claimed that the economy of India was slowing, as GDP growth declined from 8.4% in 2010 to 6.9% in mid-2011.

b. Nicaragua and Haiti are the poorest nations in the Western Hemisphere, with annual 2017 per capita GDP of only \$2,222 and \$740, respectively.

c. The economy of Italy has slowed considerably over the past two decades, as evidenced by an average growth of real GDP of only 0.15% per year from 1996 to 2016.

ANSWERS:

a. This case reflects the use of GDP data to identify and measure business cycles and indicates a potential recession. The statement describes a short-run window of data.

b. This statement uses data to show living standards. The numbers indicate that average Nicaraguans and Haitians have to live on very small amounts of income each year.

c. This observation considers growth rates over 20 years, which means that GDP was applied to look at long-run economic growth.

FIGURE 19.6

Using Market Values to Compute GDP

GDP reflects market values added together for many types of goods. In this simple example, the contribution to GDP from corn production is $60 billion, and the contribution from car production is $240 billion.

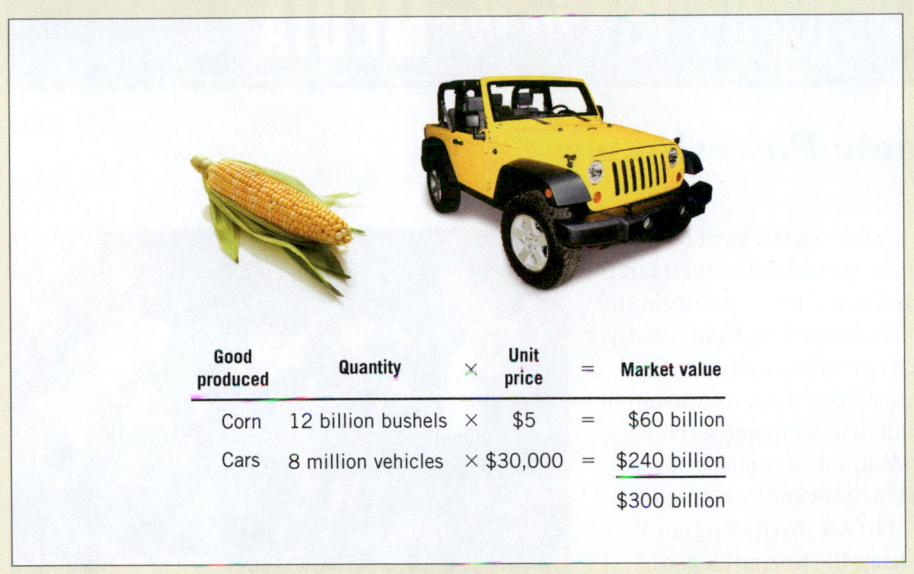

Good produced	Quantity	×	Unit price	=	Market value
Corn	12 billion bushels	×	$5	=	$60 billion
Cars	8 million vehicles	×	$30,000	=	$240 billion
					$300 billion

course this conclusion is wrong; a bushel of corn is not worth nearly as much as a car.

To add corn and cars and the other goods and services in GDP, economists use market values. That is, we include not only the quantity data but also the price of the good or service. Figure 19.6 offers an example with fairly realistic data. If corn production is 12 billion bushels and these bushels sell for $5 each, the contribution of corn to GDP is $60 billion. If car production is 8 million vehicles and cars sell for $30,000 each, the contribution of cars to GDP is $240 billion. If these were the only goods produced in a given year, GDP would be $60 billion + $240 billion = $300 billion.

As we have said, GDP reflects market values, and these values include both price and quantity information. Remember that we use GDP data to evaluate the health of an economy. A nation's economic health depends on the total quantities of goods and services produced, as represented in the Quantity column of Figure 19.6. Market values allow us to add together many types of goods. However, market values rely on prices, which can rise when inflation occurs. What if the prices of both cars and corn rise but the quantities produced remain unchanged? In that case, GDP rises even though the production level stays the same. This is why we compute real GDP by adjusting for inflation (we discuss how to adjust for inflation later in this chapter).

Including Goods and Services

Physical goods are easy to visualize, but less than half of U.S. GDP comes from goods; the majority comes from services. **Services** are outputs that provide benefits without producing a tangible product. Consider a service like a visit to your doctor for a physical. The doctor examines you and offers some medical advice, but you leave with no tangible output.

Services
are outputs that provide benefits without producing a tangible product.

ECONOMICS in the MEDIA

BTS: Economic Powerhouse

Over the past few years, the Korean boy band BTS has taken the world by storm. Maybe you know their 2021 hits "Butter" and "Permission to Dance." According to Stacey Vanek Smith of the *Indicator from Planet Money*, BTS is responsible, directly or indirectly, for about 0.5% of South Korea's entire GDP.* That's one band, all by itself, generating $8 billion in economic activity.

How is this possible? Well, a single online concert pulled in over $70 million in ticket and merchandise sales. But the popularity of BTS is also leading music fans around the world to learn the Korean language, travel to Korea, watch Korean movies, and buy Korean clothing. The band's fans, officially known as ARMY, are infatuated with Korean culture and all its trappings.

What makes BTS different from other bands? *The Indicator* suggests that the bond between BTS and its fans stems from the band members' transparency about their personal lives, and especially about their struggles. Whatever the case, when a band has an economic impact as big as BTS does, they probably don't need permission to dance.

Are you ready to join the ARMY?

**The Indicator from Planet Money*, "BTS: The Band That Moves The Economy," National Public Radio, July 28, 2021, https://www.npr.org/2021/07/28/1021968141/bts-the-band-that-moves-the-economy.

When considering the proportion of goods and services in U.S. GDP, it is important to note that the composition of U.S. GDP has evolved over time. In the past, the dominant U.S. industries produced manufactured goods, such as autos, steel, and household goods. Today, a majority of U.S. GDP is service output, such as medical, financial, transportation, education, and technology services. Figure 19.7 shows services as a share of U.S. GDP since 1950. As you can see, service output now accounts for about two-thirds of all U.S. output.

Most economists are not concerned about this move toward a service-dominated economy, but others lament this shift. These others remember that manufacturing industries were a source of prosperity for the U.S. economy in the past and then assume they are necessary for future growth. This is not a partisan issue; politicians from both major parties generally focus on manufacturing jobs and output. However, this argument does not give due credit to progressive economic growth.

A century ago, the significant economic growth in the United States came from manufacturing output. But two centuries ago, U.S. economic growth came from agricultural output. Economies evolve. The fact that innovations in manufacturing spurred past growth does not mean that future growth should not occur through services.

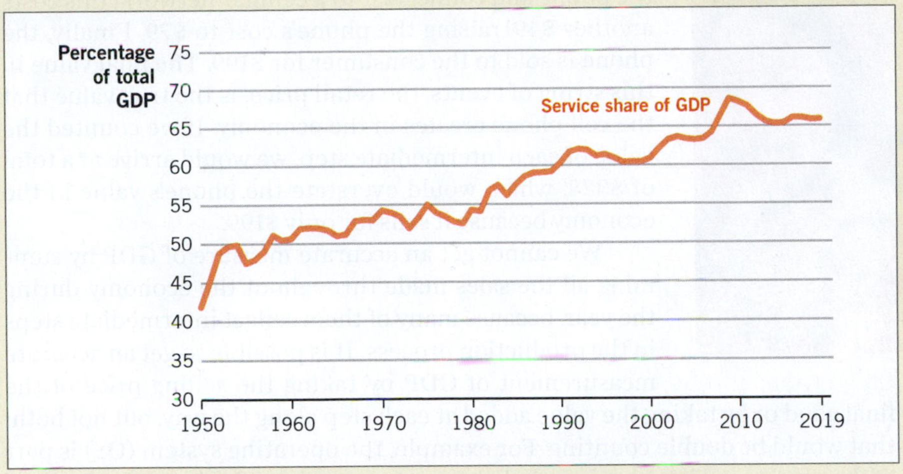

FIGURE 19.7

Services as a Share of U.S. GDP, 1950–2019

A century ago, the U.S. economy produced mostly manufactured goods. This trend has shifted in recent decades, and now services account for about two-thirds of U.S. output.

Source: U.S. Bureau of Economic Analysis.

Including Only Final Goods and Services

As we have said, GDP is the sum of spending on goods and services. However, not *all* spending is included. To see why, consider all the spending involved in building a single good—a cell phone. Table 19.3 outlines intermediate steps required to produce a cell phone that sells for $199. In the process of producing this phone, the manufacturer uses many intermediate goods.

Intermediate goods are goods that firms repackage or bundle with other goods for sale at a later stage. For example, the cell phone's outer case and keyboard are intermediate goods because the phone manufacturer combines them with other intermediate goods, such as the operating system, to produce the cell phone, which is the final good. **Final goods** are goods that are sold to final users. The sale of the cell phone is included as part of GDP, but the value of the intermediate goods is not.

Intermediate goods are goods that firms repackage or bundle with other goods for sale at a later stage.

Final goods are goods sold to final users.

What happens if we count the value added during each intermediate step in making a cell phone? We start with the outer case and keyboard, which costs $5 to produce. Once the case and keyboard have been purchased, the component hardware, which costs $10, must be installed, bringing the value of the phone to $15. The operating system software, which costs $15, is then installed,

TABLE 19.3

Intermediate Steps in Cell Phone Production

Steps	Value added during step	Prices of completed steps
1. Assemble outer case and keyboard	$5	$5
2. Prepare internal hardware	10	15
3. Install operating system	15	30
4. Connect to network	49	79
5. Transact retail sale	120	199
Total	$199	$328

This Intel processor is an intermediate good, buried inside your computer.

raising the cost to $30. Next, a service provider purchases the phone and connects it to a cellular network; this costs another $49, raising the phone's cost to $79. Finally, the phone is sold to the consumer for $199. The final value in this string of events, the retail price, is the true value that the cell phone creates in the economy. If we counted the value of each intermediate step, we would arrive at a total of $328, which would overstate the phone's value in the economy because it sells for only $199.

We cannot get an accurate measure of GDP by summing all the sales made throughout the economy during the year, because many of them reflect intermediate steps in the production process. It is possible to get an accurate measurement of GDP by taking the selling price of the final good or by taking the value added at each step along the way, but not both; that would be double counting. For example, the operating system (OS) is part of the phone, and its value is included as part of the phone in the final sale. If we counted the sale of the OS to the phone manufacturer and then again as a part of the phone, we would be double counting and thus overstating GDP.

Within a Country

The word "domestic" in the phrase "gross domestic product" is important. GDP includes only goods and services produced domestically, or within a nation's physical borders. The output of foreign-owned firms that is produced inside the United States is included in U.S. GDP, but the output of U.S. firms that is produced overseas is included in the GDP of the overseas nation. For example, Nike is a U.S. firm that produces shoes in Thailand. Thus, all the shoes produced in Thailand count as GDP for Thailand. By the same token, cars that Mercedes-Benz produces at a plant in Alabama count as GDP for the United States.

Gross national product (GNP) is the output produced by workers and resources owned by residents of the nation.

Gross national product (GNP), an alternative measure of national output, is the output produced by workers and resources owned by residents of the nation. Thus, shoes produced by Nike in Thailand would count as part of U.S. GNP, since the owners of Nike are citizens (and residents) of the United States. Many nations prefer GDP to GNP, because much of their domestic output is produced by foreign-owned firms (like Nike shoes produced in Thailand), and they like to see this output count for them. For these nations, GDP is larger than GNP. These countries prefer GDP because it measures the production that takes place within their borders. Thus, GDP has become the standard measure of international output. As national economies have become more globalized with more production taking place outside the home country, GDP is now used more often than GNP to measure a nation's overall production.

Nike shoes produced in Thailand count as GDP for Thailand but as GNP for the United States.

From a Particular Time Period

GDP only counts goods and services produced during a given time period. Goods or services produced in earlier years do not count in the current year's GDP. For instance, when a new car is produced, it adds to GDP in the year it is produced. However, a used car that is resold does not count in current GDP, because it was already counted in GDP for the year when it was first produced. If we counted the used car when it was resold, we would be counting that car as part of GDP twice (double counting).

In addition, sales of financial assets such as stocks and bonds do not count toward GDP. After all, these kinds of sales, which we will discuss in Chapter 23, do not create anything new; they simply transfer ownership from one person to another. In this way, they are like used goods. However, brokerage fees do count as payment for the brokerage service, and they are included in GDP.

We have now examined the GDP definition in greater detail. In the next section, we consider the way GDP is actually measured by adding together different types of expenditures.

Ice cream cones count as nondurable consumption goods.

Looking at GDP as Different Types of Expenditures

In this section, we look more closely at the different categories of goods and services included in GDP. The Bureau of Economic Analysis (BEA) is the U.S. government agency that tallies GDP data in a process called *national income accounting*. The BEA breaks GDP into four major categories: consumption (C), investment (I), government purchases (G), and net exports (NX). Using this framework, it is possible to express GDP as the following equation:

$$GDP = C + I + G + NX \qquad \textbf{(EQUATION 19.1)}$$

Table 19.4 details the composition of U.S. GDP in 2021. For that year, total GDP was $22,997.5 billion, or about $23 trillion. To get a sense of what that

TABLE 19.4

Composition of U.S. GDP, 2021

Category	Individual expenditures (billions of dollars)	Total expenditures per category (billions of dollars)	Percentage of GDP
Consumption (C)		**$15,746.9**	68.5%
Durable goods	$2,026.6		
Nondurable goods	3,456.2		
Services	10,264.1		
Investment (I)		**4,113.4**	17.9%
Fixed Investment	4,139.4		
Change in business inventories	−25.9		
Government purchases (G)		**4,053.0**	17.6%
Federal	1,565.0		
State and local	2,488.0		
Net Exports (NX)		**−915.90**	−4.0%
Exports	2,479.9		
Imports	3,395.8		
Total GDP		**$22,997.5**	100.0%

Source: Bureau of Economic Analysis.

Refrigerators count as durable consumption goods.

amount represents, imagine laying 23 trillion one-dollar bills from end to end. That would be enough to cover every U.S. highway, street, and county road more than twice!

Looking at Table 19.4, you can see that consumption is by far the largest component of GDP, followed by investment and then by government purchases. Note that the value of net exports is negative. This negative value occurs because the United States imports more goods than it exports. Let's take a closer look at each of these four components of GDP.

Consumption
is the purchase of final goods and services by households, excluding new housing.

CONSUMPTION **Consumption** (C) is the purchase of final goods and services by households, with the exception of new housing. Most people spend a large majority of their income on consumption goods and services. Consumption goods include everything from groceries to automobiles. You can see in Table 19.4 that services are a very big portion of consumption spending. They include things such as haircuts, doctor's visits, and help from a real estate agent.

Consumption goods can be divided into two categories: nondurable and durable. *Nondurable* consumption goods are consumed over a short period, and *durable* consumption goods are consumed over a long period. This distinction is important when the economy swings back and forth between good times and bad times. Sales of durable goods—for example, automobiles, appliances, and computers—are subject to significant cyclical fluctuations that correspond to the health of the economy. Because durable goods are generally designed to last for many years, consumers tend to purchase more of these goods when the economy is strong. In contrast, when the economy is weak, they put off purchases of durables and make what they already have last longer—for example, working with an old computer for another year rather than replacing it with a new model right away. However, nondurables don't last very long, so consumers often purchase them regardless of economic conditions.

Investment
is private spending on the tools, plant, and equipment used to produce future output.

INVESTMENT When you hear the word "investment," you likely think of savings or stocks and bonds. But in macroeconomics, **investment** (I) refers to private spending on the tools, plant, and equipment used to produce future output. Investment is something as simple as the purchase of a shovel, a tractor, or a personal computer to help a small business produce goods and services for its customers. But investment also includes more complex endeavors, such as the construction of large factories. For example, when Pfizer builds a new factory to manufacture a new drug, it is making an investment. When Walmart builds a new warehouse, that expense is investment. And when a new house is built, that also counts as investment. This way of accounting for house purchases may seem odd, since most of us think of a home purchase as an act of consumption; but in the national income accounts, such a purchase counts as an investment.

When firms buy tools to aid in production, they are making an investment.

Investment also includes all purchases by businesses that add to their inventories. For example, in preparation for the Christmas buying season, an electronics retailer orders more TVs, cameras, and computers. GDP rises when business inventories increase. GDP is calculated this way because we want to measure output in the period it is produced. Investment in inventory is just one more way that firms spend today to increase output in the future.

Investment spending makes up only about one-sixth of all GDP, but don't underestimate its importance. Most economists agree that investment spending leads to greater future GDP. Tools, including both physical machinery and software, industrial plants to extract raw materials and manufacture goods, and infrastructure such as railways and power grids all help an economy produce more in the future. We will talk more about investment in later chapters.

GOVERNMENT SPENDING National, state, and local governments purchase many goods and services. These purchases are included in GDP as **government spending** (G), which includes spending by all levels of government on final goods and services. For example, every government employee receives a salary, which is considered part of GDP. Similarly, governments spend money purchasing buildings, equipment, and supplies from private-sector firms. Governments also spend on public works projects, including national defense, highway construction, schools, and post offices. *Transfer payments* the government makes to households, such as welfare payments, social security, and unemployment insurance, do not count as GDP, since they are not direct purchases of new goods and services.

Government spending includes spending by all levels of government on final goods and services.

NET EXPORTS The United States produces some goods and services that are exported to other countries, and it imports some goods and services produced elsewhere. But only exports add to GDP because they are produced domestically. Imports are tracked, but they do not add to GDP, because our goal is to measure domestic production accurately. As it turns out, imports enter into GDP calculations twice: once positively and once negatively, and the net result is zero. Let's start with net exports. **Net exports** (NX) are total exports minus total imports. We can write the calculation of net exports in equation form as

Net exports are total exports minus total imports.

$$\text{net exports (NX)} = \text{exports} - \text{imports}$$

(EQUATION 19.2)

When spending on imports is larger than spending on exports, net exports are negative. Net exports are typically negative for the United States.

Notice that imports enter the GDP calculations as a negative value: GDP = C + I + G + (exports − imports). From this equation you might conclude that imports are harmful to an economy, because they seem to reduce GDP. But imports are then used for one of the other GDP categories (C, I, or G), and so they enter positively there. In this way, imports are accounted for without increasing or decreasing GDP. For example, let's say we import $10 million worth of bananas from Guatemala. These bananas increase consumption by $10 million, but they also increase imports by $10 million, and so net exports falls by $10 million. The net result is that GDP is unaffected, as C rises by the same amount that NX falls.

However, adding the different components together (C, I, G, and NX) in the process of national income accounting really is just that—accounting. The primary goal of the national income accounts is to keep a record of how people are buying the goods and services produced in a nation. More imports coming in means more goods and services for people in that nation. All else equal, imports do not make us worse off.

Real GDP: Adjusting GDP for Price Changes

According to the Bureau of Economic Analysis, in 2012, the U.S. economy produced GDP of $16.2 trillion. Just nine years later, in 2021, it produced over $23 trillion. That's a 42% increase in just nine years. Is that really possible? Think

FIGURE 19.8

U.S. Nominal and Real GDP, 2012–2021

Nominal GDP typically rises faster than real GDP because nominal GDP reflects both growth in real production and growth in prices (inflation). From 2012 to 2021, nominal GDP in the United States rose by 42%, but the increase in real GDP during the same period was 20%. The difference is price level growth, or inflation.

Source: U.S. Bureau of Economic Analysis.

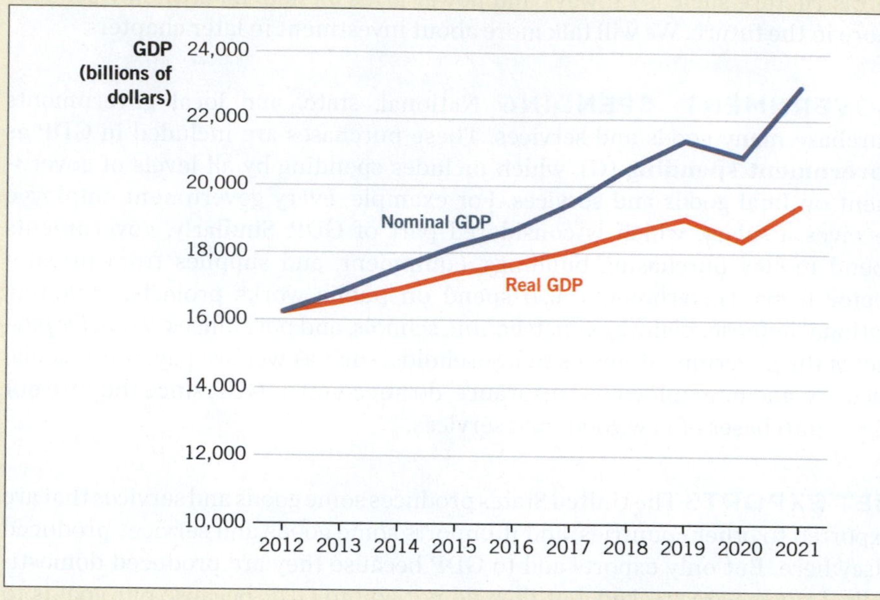

about this question in long-run historical terms. Is it possible that the nation's economy grew to $16 trillion over more than two centuries, but then just nine years later surpassed $23 trillion? If we look more closely, we'll see that some of this recent increase in GDP data is actually due to inflation.

The raw GDP data, based on market values, is computed on the basis of the prices of goods and services current at the time GDP is calculated. Economists refer to these prices as the *current prices*. The GDP calculated from current prices is called **nominal GDP**. Figure 19.8 compares U.S. nominal and real GDP from 2012 to 2021. Notice that nominal GDP rises much faster than real GDP. While nominal GDP rose by 42%, real GDP increased by 20%. The difference between these percentages reflects price level growth, or inflation.

Nominal GDP is GDP measured in current prices and not adjusted for inflation.

Computing nominal GDP is straightforward: we add the market values (actual prices) of all final goods and services. But to compute real GDP, we also need a measure of overall prices, known as a price level. A **price level** is an index of the average prices of goods and services throughout the economy. It goes up when prices generally rise, and it falls when prices across the economy fall. Chapter 21 explores prices and the calculation of price levels. For now, just take the price data as given, and think of the price level as an indicator of changes in the general level of all prices across the economy.

A **price level** is an index of the average prices of goods and services throughout the economy.

The price level in GDP data, the **GDP deflator**, includes the prices of the final goods and services counted in GDP. The GDP deflator "deflates" all the price inflation out of nominal GDP so that we can see real GDP. Let's look at some actual data. Table 19.5 shows U.S. nominal GDP and price level data from 2009 to 2021. Focus on the years 2012 and 2013 and notice that the price level was set at 100 in 2012 and rose to 102 in 2013. These numbers indicate that, on average, prices across the economy rose by 2% between 2012 and 2013.

The **GDP deflator** is a measure of the price level used to calculate real GDP.

TABLE 19.5

U.S. Nominal GDP and Price Level, 2009–2021

Year	Nominal GDP (billions of dollars)	Price Level (GDP deflator)
2009	$14,478.1	95
2010	15,049.0	96
2011	15,599.7	98
2012	16,254.0	100
2013	16,843.2	102
2014	17,550.7	104
2015	18,206.0	105
2016	18,695.1	106
2017	19,479.6	108
2018	20,527.2	110
2019	21,372.6	112
2020	20,893.7	114
2021	22,997.5	118

Source: Bureau of Economic Analysis.

To compute real GDP, we use the current prices of goods and services and then adjust them to prices from an agreed-upon common time period, or *base period*. We do this in two steps:

1. Divide nominal GDP by the price level.
2. Multiply the result by the price level (100) from the base period.

Putting these two steps together, we compute real GDP for any time period (t) as

$$\text{real GDP}_t = \underbrace{\frac{\text{nominal GDP}_t}{\text{price level}_t}}_{\textbf{Step 1}} \underbrace{\times\ 100}_{\textbf{Step 2}}$$

(EQUATION 19.3)

For example, nominal GDP in 2021 was \$22,998 billion, and the price level was 118. To convert nominal GDP to real GDP, we divide by 118 and then multiply by 100:

$$= \frac{\$22{,}998}{118} \times 100 = \$19{,}490 \text{ billion}$$

Table 19.6 illustrates both steps of this conversion. The figure \$19,490 billion is the U.S. real GDP in 2021, adjusted for inflation. Economists and the financial media use other terms for real GDP; sometimes they might say "GDP in 2012 prices" or "GDP in constant 2012 dollars." Whenever you consider changes in GDP over time, you should look for these terms to ensure that the data are not biased by price changes.

TABLE 19.6

Converting Nominal GDP into Real GDP

Data for 2021:
Nominal GDP = $22,998 billion
Price level (GDP deflator) = 118

General steps	Our example
Step 1: Filter out current prices.	$22,998 ÷ 118 = $194.90
Step 2: Input base-period prices.	$194.90 × 100 = $19,490

Growth Rates

For many macroeconomic applications, it is useful to calculate growth rates. For example, let's say you read that the GDP in Thailand in 2019 was $544 billion. This figure may not mean much to you, or you may take it as bad news, since $544 billion is a small fraction of U.S. GDP. But maybe you also read that Thailand's GDP grew by 7.4% in 2019 (it did!). In that case, you'd have a more positive (and more accurate) impression. In general, growth rates convey additional helpful information.

Growth rates are calculated as percentage changes in a variable. For example, the growth of U.S. nominal GDP in 2021 is computed as

(EQUATION 19.4)

$$\text{nominal GDP growth in 2021} = \frac{\text{GDP}_{2021} - \text{GDP}_{2020}}{\text{GDP}_{2020}} \times 100$$

Unless noted otherwise, the data come from the end of the period. Therefore, the nominal GDP growth computed by Equation 19.4 tells us the percentage change in U.S. GDP from the end of 2020 to the end of 2021, or over the course of 2021. Using actual data, the calculation is

$$\text{nominal GDP growth in 2021} = \text{\% change in nominal GDP}$$

$$= \frac{22{,}998 - 20{,}894}{20{,}894} \times 100 = 10.1\%$$

We can also compute the growth rate of the price level (GDP deflator) for 2021:

$$\text{price level growth rate} = \text{\% change in price level}$$

$$= \frac{118 - 114}{114} \times 100 = 3.5\%$$

This means that throughout the U.S. economy in 2021, inflation was 3.5%.

Armed with these two computations, we can derive one more useful formula for evaluating GDP data. Recall that nominal GDP, which is from raw GDP data, includes information on both the price level and real GDP. When either of these factors changes, nominal GDP is affected. In fact, the growth rate of nominal GDP is approximately equal to the sum of the growth rates of these two factors:

$$\text{growth of nominal GDP} \approx \text{growth of real GDP} + \text{growth of price level} \qquad \textbf{(EQUATION 19.5)}$$

Since growth rates are calculated as percentage changes, we can rewrite Equation 19.5 as

$$\text{\% change in nominal GDP} \approx \text{\% change in real GDP} + \text{\% change in price level} \qquad \textbf{(EQUATION 19.6)}$$

Equation 19.6 gives us a simple way of separating GDP growth into its respective parts. For example, since we know that nominal GDP grew by 10.1% in 2021 and the price level grew by 3.5%, the remaining nominal GDP growth of 6.6% (10.1% − 3.5%) is attributable to growth in real GDP.

What Are Some Shortcomings of GDP Data?

We began this chapter with a claim that GDP is the single best measure of economic activity. Along the way, we have learned that nominal GDP fails to account for changes in prices, and so real GDP is a better measure of economic activity. We also talked about how real GDP per capita accounts for population differences. You will be relieved to learn that by now we have finished introducing new variations of GDP! However, there are some problems with relying on GDP data as a measure of a nation's well-being. In this section, we highlight four shortcomings that limit the effectiveness of GDP as a measure of the health of an economy. We also look at the relationship between GDP and happiness. At the end of this section, we consider why economists continue to rely on GDP.

Nonmarket Goods

Many goods and services are produced but not sold in a market. These are then not counted in GDP data even though they create value for society. For instance, work done at home, such as an individual caring for their children, washing their dishes, mowing their lawn, or washing their car, are services produced but not counted in GDP. When the nonmarket segment of an economy is large, the result can be a dramatic undercounting of the annual output being produced. In less-developed societies where many households live off the land and produce goods for their own consumption, GDP—the measure of market activity—is a less reliable measure of economic output.

ECONOMICS in the MEDIA

"GDP, OMG!"

THE INDICATOR FROM PLANET MONEY

NPR produces two of the best economics podcast series available; they are called *Planet Money* and *The Indicator from Planet Money*. These podcasts are certainly written by knowledgeable economists and are also quite entertaining. They are pitched to popular audiences but are still educational, especially on basic economics. If you are looking for an easy and fun way to learn economics along with your class material this semester, this is the podcast for you.

In July 2018, one *Indicator* episode was on the measurement of GDP. The hosts used the opportunity to consider the very strong growth of the second quarter of 2018. In less than 10 minutes, they asked and answered five questions about GDP.

First, they asked: "What is GDP?" In answering this question, they gave examples of each type of GDP expenditure. For consumption, they referenced coffee from Starbucks; for investment, they cited purchases of new equipment by Ford, to help produce pickup trucks; for government spending, they pointed to firefighting equipment and tanks for the military; and for exports, they talked about smartphones and financial services.

Their second question was about the 4.1% growth in the second quarter of 2018: "Is that a lot faster than normal?" The answer is "Yes!" In fact, normal growth is less than 3%, so the middle of 2018 was a particularly strong period for GDP growth.

The third question got to the cause of the strong growth: "What made the economy grow so fast in the second quarter?" The answer is that consumption and exports were particularly high. The tax cuts of the previous year seem to have had an effect on consumer spending in 2018.

Fourth, they asked: "What were the lowlights?" Here they pointed to the cause of the export surge and they postulated that it was due to impending tariffs that threatened to interrupt trade flows in the future. They also noted that business investment didn't grow as much as previously.

Finally, they asked: "Is 4.1% growth sustainable?" Their answer was reasonable and based on a consensus of most economists, which is that 4.1% growth is great but unfortunately not likely to last.

Underground Economy

The underground, or shadow, economy encompasses transactions that are not reported to the government and therefore are not taxed. These transactions are often settled in cash. Some of these exchanges are for illegal goods and services, such as narcotics and illegal gambling. However, many underground transactions are for legal goods and services, but these activities are not reported in

PRACTICE WHAT YOU KNOW

Computing Real and Nominal GDP Growth: GDP Growth in Mexico

How much is Mexico's economy growing?

The following table presents GDP data for Mexico. Use the data from the table to answer the following questions.

Year	Nominal GDP growth rate	Price-level growth rate
2013	3.1%	1.8%
2014	7.0	4.7
2015	5.7	3.1
2016	6.9	4.6

Source: World Bank.

QUESTION: What was the rate of growth of real GDP in Mexico in 2016?

ANSWER: Using Equation 19.6,

$$\%\text{ change in real GDP} + \%\text{ change in price level} \approx \%\text{ change in nominal GDP}$$

Rewriting the equation, we can solve for real GDP growth as

$$\%\text{ change in real GDP} \approx \%\text{ change in nominal GDP} - \%\text{ change in price level}$$

For 2016, we have

$$\%\text{ change in real GDP} \approx 6.9 - 4.6 \approx 2.3\%$$

QUESTION: How would you compute real GDP growth in Mexico in 2013?

ANSWER: Using the 2013 data in the same equation, we get

$$\%\text{ change in real GDP} \approx 3.1 - 1.8 \approx 1.3\%$$

This means that 2016 was a much better year than 2013 for the Mexican economy.

CHALLENGE QUESTION: If a citizen of Mexico buys $50,000 worth of stock in Apple Inc. (a U.S. company), and pays a 10% trading fee to a U.S. stockbroker, how much is added to U.S. GDP?

ANSWER: $5,000. Only the fee for the broker adds to GDP, since it is a service. The $50,000 stock purchase does not count toward production, since it is just a change of ownership.

order to avoid taxes. Legal activities that go unreported include tips for waiting tables and tending bar, lawn services, and even home renovations. Because underground transactions are not reported, they are not easily measured and so they are not included in U.S. GDP calculations. However, as we explain in Economics in the Real World (p. 626), many European nations now

Not counted in GDP: washing your own car.

include illegal underground activities when calculating their GDP.

How big is the underground economy? No one is exactly sure. Economist Friedrich Schneider has estimated that for wealthy developed economies it is roughly 15% of GDP and that in transitioning economies the percentage rises to between 21% and 30% of GDP. However, in the world's most underdeveloped economies, like those of Nigeria or Armenia, the underground economy can be as much as 40% of GDP.

The United States is widely believed to have one of the smallest shadow economies in the world, with less than 10% of GDP unaccounted for in the official measurement. Why is the underground economy so small in the United States? The simple answer is that in the United States and in many other developed economies, most citizens can earn more by legitimately participating in the economy than by engaging in illegal activities. In short, a strong economy that generates jobs and opportunities for advancement helps to reduce the size of the underground economy. In addition, corruption is much less common. This means that participants in the economy rarely face demands for bribes or kickbacks from authorities or organized crime. This is not the case in many developing nations. For example, Somalia, which ranks last on Transparency International's corruption index, has widespread piracy and virtually no formal economy.

ECONOMICS IN THE REAL WORLD

SEX, DRUGS, AND GDP IN EUROPE

In September 2014, the GDP for the European Union (EU)* increased by 3.53% overnight. That is a full year's worth of very solid growth. But it didn't make Europeans any wealthier, because it was actually just the result of a new way of defining and calculating GDP. Eurostat (the economic statistics office of the European Commission) redefined GDP to include many transactions that were previously uncounted and are actually illegal across much of Europe.

The new GDP definition includes illegal drug deals, prostitution, and even sales of stolen goods. Specifically, it includes illegal transactions as long as both parties agree to the transaction.

Ostensibly, Eurostat is trying to capture part of the shadow economy that is typically not measured in GDP. Unfortunately, the process becomes even more complicated when the legality of goods and services varies across nations. For example, Figure 19.9 shows how cannabis laws vary across Europe. Cannabis is essentially legal in some nations (the Netherlands) but strictly illegal in others (France, for example).

Normalizing the accounting standards across nations makes sense. But illegal activities are difficult to measure. In addition, if the illegal activities are a relatively stable portion of GDP, then there is really no bias when they are not included. In fact, the new estimates, in an attempt to provide a more complete measure, may actually introduce more error into GDP measurement due to the difficulty of estimating illegal trade.

*The EU is a group of 27 European nations that have pledged economic cooperation.

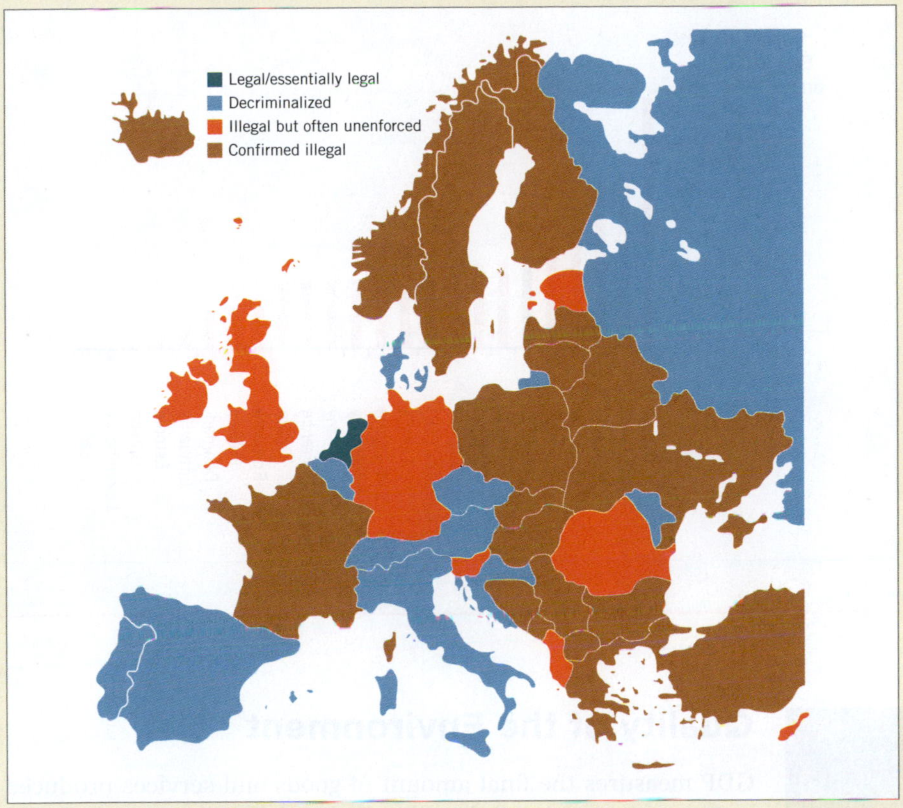

FIGURE 19.9

Legality of Cannabis in the European Union

The legality of cannabis varies drastically across the European Union. For example, cannabis is essentially legal in the Netherlands but strictly illegal in France. Previously, only legal transactions were counted as part of GDP in the European Union. However, the new standards adopted in 2014 include illegal transactions in European nations, so long as both parties agree to the transaction. Therefore, illegal trades in France are now counted as part of GDP so that French GDP and Dutch GDP both include transactions for the same goods and services.

Source: Wikimedia Commons.

So why the change in definition? One possibility is that many European nations are dealing with high deficit- (and debt-) to-GDP ratios, and some of these new measurements (in a backhanded way) help lower these ratios. The European Commission has explicit rules regarding these budget measures: a nation's deficit in a given fiscal year is not to exceed 3% of its GDP, and the national debt is not to exceed 60% of GDP. When nations exceed these bounds, the governing council is directed to use coercive measures called excessive deficit procedures (EDPs). The council has been lax in enforcing EDPs in recent years. However, increasing GDP by simply redefining how it is measured automatically lowers deficit and debt ratios and helps nations that have higher government debt levels.

Figure 19.10 shows the effect of the new GDP definition on each nation's GDP level in 2013 (along with the overall EU and Euroarea). Note that we look at 2013, the year before the law change, to isolate the effects of a definitional change in the accounting of GDP. The countries are ordered according to their GDP gains from the new GDP measurements. (ESA 2010 stands for European System Accounts.)

As you can see, GDP for Cyprus jumped 9.8% due to the accounting change, shrinking the country's debt-to-GDP ratio by a full half of a percentage point in 2013—from 5.4% to 4.9%. Clearly, the new accounting rule exaggerates debt reduction in Cyprus as the country tries to move closer to the EU goal of 3%.

In short, while new GDP accounting rules in Europe may normalize national income accounting across the Eurozone, they are particularly helpful to nations that have high government debt levels.

FIGURE 19.10

Increase in GDP Due to Accounting Change

This data shows how the GDP of each European nation changed as a result of the new GDP accounting rules (ESA). The overall average for the EU was a 3.53% increase in GDP, but the GDP of Cyprus jumped 9.8%. Note that we look at 2013, the year before the law change, to isolate the effects of a definitional change in the accounting of GDP.

Source: Eurostat.

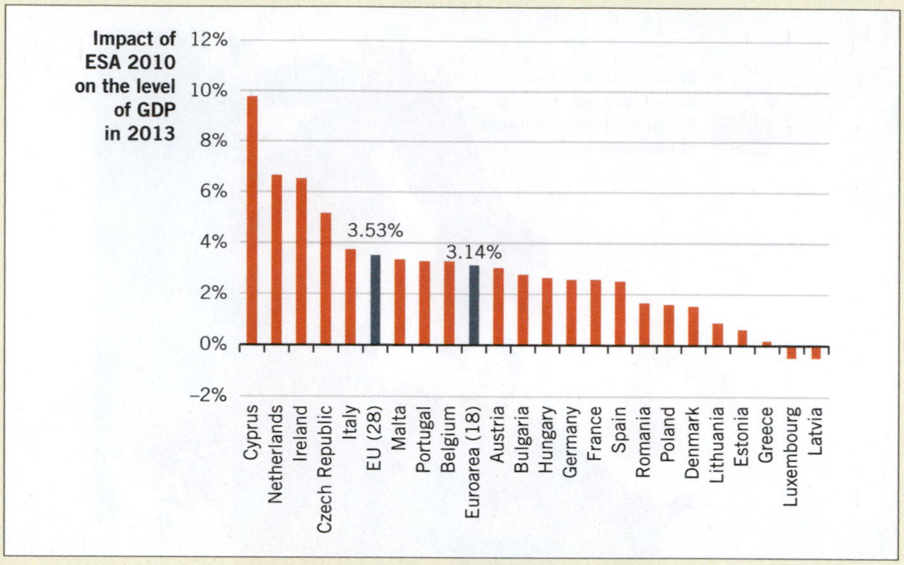

Not counted in GDP: a clean environment.

Quality of the Environment

GDP measures the final amount of goods and services produced in a given period, but it does not distinguish how those goods and services are produced. In particular, it does not account for negative environmental side effects that sometimes occur in production. Imagine two economies, both with the same real GDP per capita. One economy relies on clean energy for its production, and the other has weak environmental standards. Citizens in both countries enjoy the same standard of living, but their well-being is not the same. The lax environmental standards in the second economy lead to air and water pollution as well as health problems for its citizens. Since there is more to quality of life than the goods and services we buy, using GDP to infer that both places are equally desirable is unsound.

Leisure Time

Because GDP only counts market activity, it fails to capture how long workers labor to produce goods and services. For most developed nations, according to the OECD (Organization for Economic Cooperation and Development), the average workweek is 37 hours. However, there are wide variations from country to country. At the high end, laborers in Colombia average around 48 hours per week. In contrast, laborers in the Netherlands average fewer than 30 hours per week. The United States is near the middle of the pack, with an average workweek of 39 hours. This means that comparisons of GDP across countries are problematic because they do not account for the extra

· ECONOMICS *in the* MEDIA ·

The Underground Economy

BREAKING BAD

"Money up front!" Walter demands.

Over five tensely plotted seasons, *Breaking Bad* tells the story of Walter White (played by Bryan Cranston), a high school chemistry teacher who becomes a drug kingpin after being diagnosed with terminal lung cancer. By making and selling methamphetamine, he plans to build a fortune that will leave his family financially secure after he dies. As the show progresses, White's priorities shift and we see the outcome of his decisions.

Early on, Walter bluffs his way into a meeting with a feared drug lord named Tuco (Raymond Cruz) and persuades him (with the help of explosives!) to buy two pounds of crystal meth per week, at $35,000 per pound. As Walter's partner, Jesse Pinkman (Aaron Paul), later explains, sourcing the chemicals needed for that level of production is going to be a huge challenge. But if the two of them can manage it, they stand to make a lot of money.

Let's think about how this is accounted for in economics. The purchases of those chemicals will be legal and will therefore count toward GDP. So will the purchase of equipment, such as scales to weigh out portions for packaging. But from there on, the market activity goes underground. The sale to Tuco (a sale of goods) is $70,000 per week to a single customer. Then there's Tuco's revenue from selling the drug on the street (a high-markup resale of the same goods), the cut Tuco pays for labor and the associated risk (a sale of services), and the under-the-table money Walter and Jesse later pay their shady lawyer and his gun-toting fixer (more services). All of those transactions are left off the books as far as official GDP is concerned.

One of the ironies of measuring GDP is that even though the many transactions are not part of GDP, the work of the people involved in fighting the war on drugs (police, FBI investigators) is included in GDP. So are the sales of drug paraphernalia passed over the counter, with a wink and a nod, as if they were intended for legal purposes such as tobacco consumption.

time available to workers in countries with substantially fewer hours worked. A comparison between the United States and Greece, which also averages 39 hours per workweek, would be valid; but a comparison of U.S. GDP with that of the Netherlands or Colombia is misleading.

GDP and Happiness

Throughout this chapter, we have presented real per capita GDP as a measure of living standards. But let's be careful; economists do not generally claim that money can buy happiness. However, it is a fact that, *ceteris paribus*, greater

-DATA SNAPSHOT-

Looking at GDP in the United States

Gross domestic product (GDP) is the single most important indicator of macroeconomic performance. It gives us a snapshot of the overall health of the economy because it measures both output and income. These graphics illustrate the four pieces of GDP—consumption, investment, government spending, and net exports—and how these pieces changed from 1970 to 2018. On the bottom left, you can also see how real GDP has more than tripled since 1970.

(In billions of 2021 dollars)	1970	2021
TOTAL GDP	**$6,105**	**$22,912**
Consumption	$3,661	$16,132
Investment	$678	$4,302
Government	$1,859	$3,996
Net Exports	-$94	-$1,518

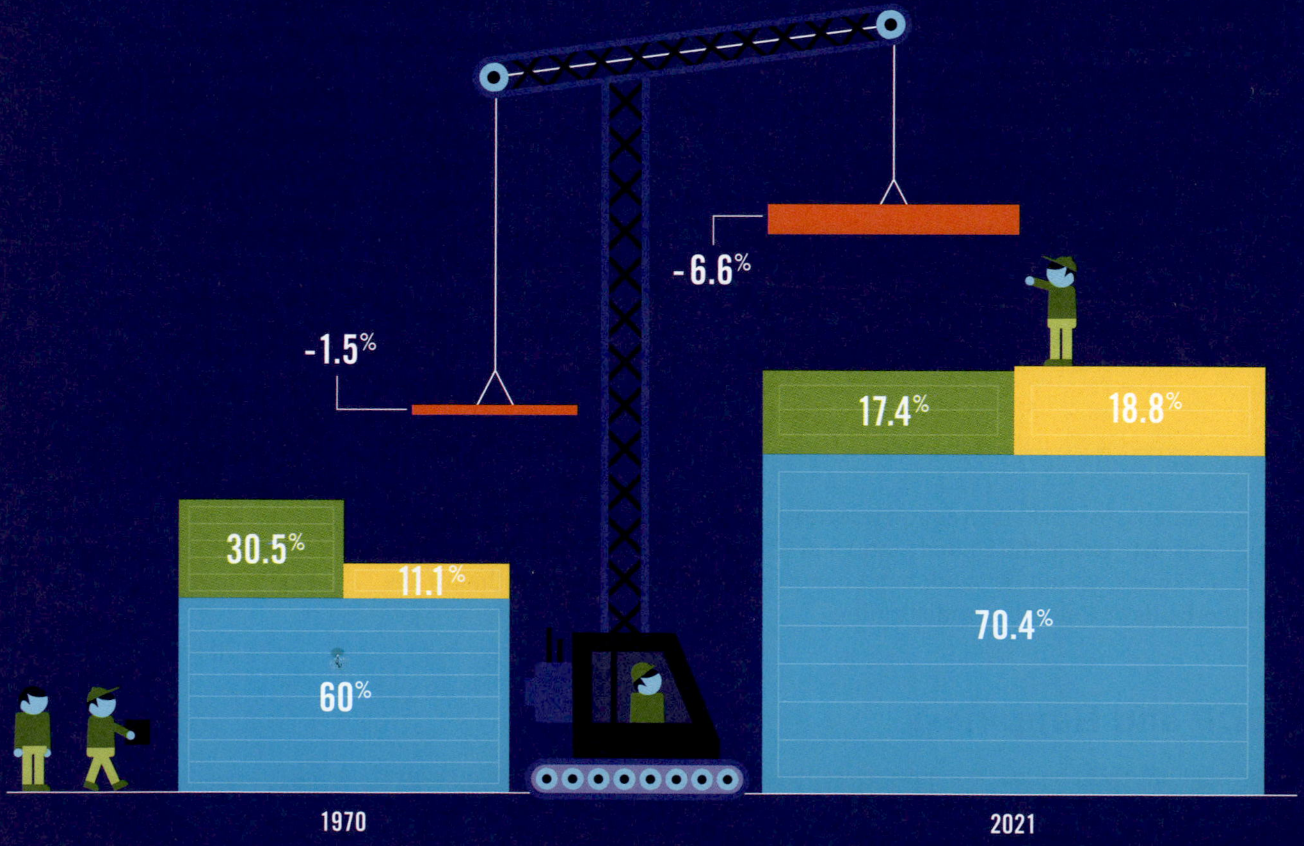

Percentage Breakdowns, 1970 vs. 2021

By measuring the components of each piece of GDP, we can see how the makeup of the U.S. economy has changed over time.

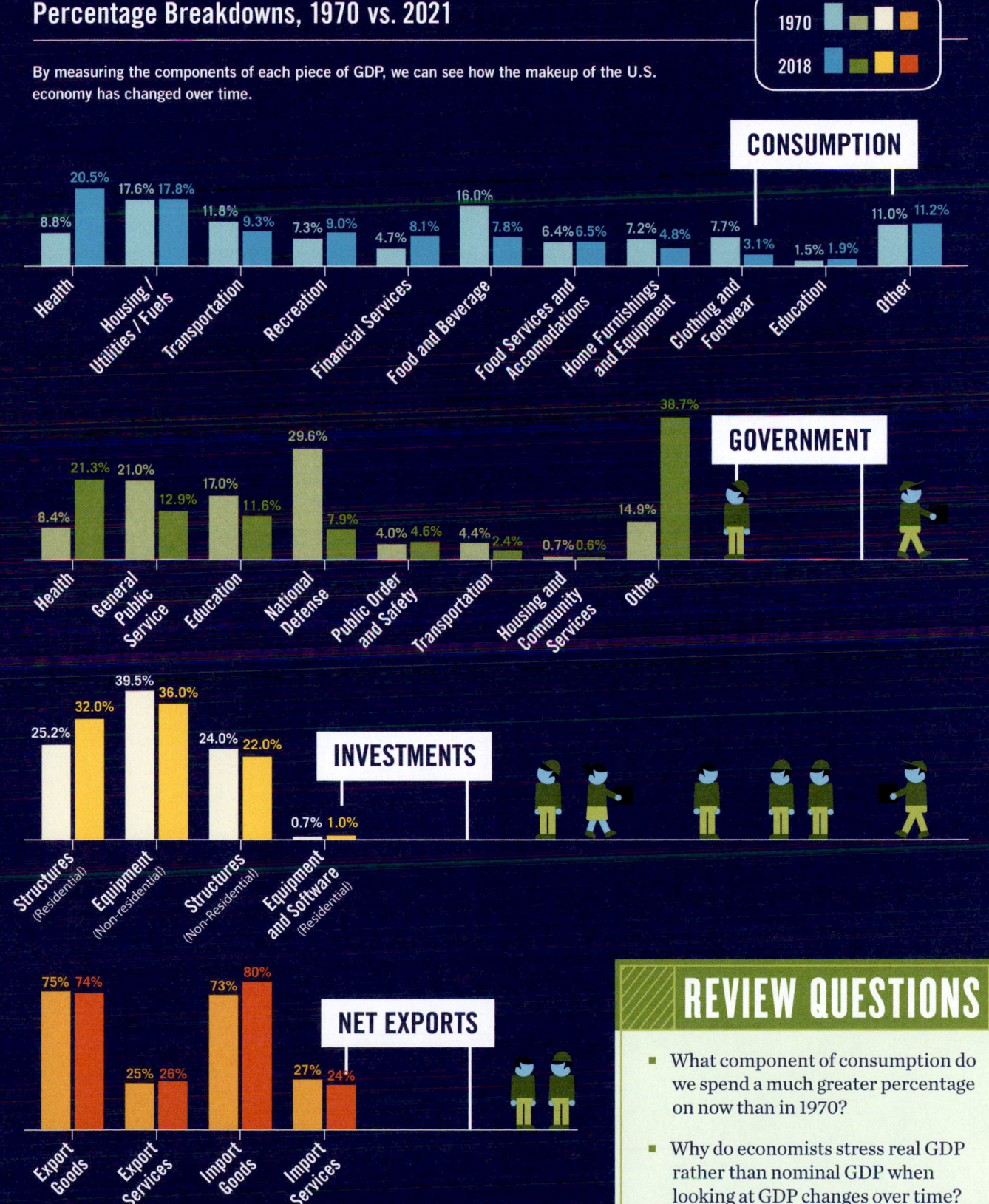

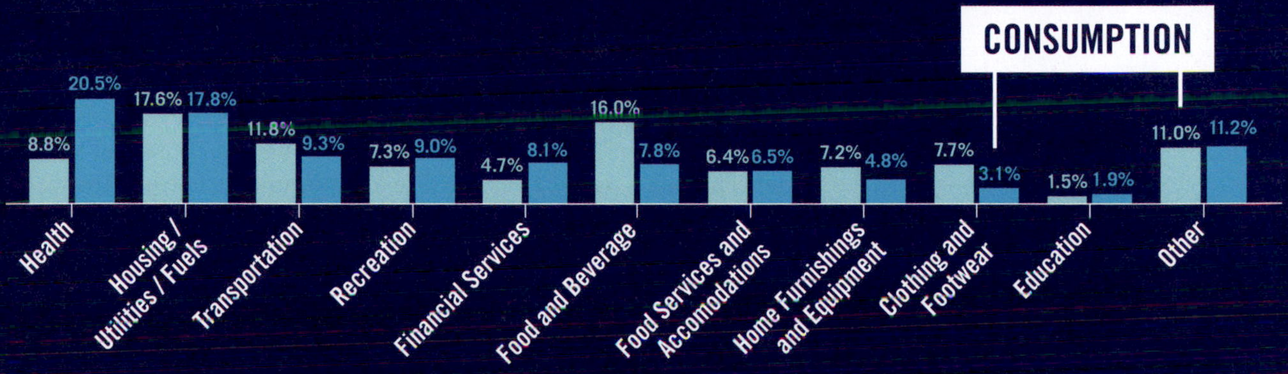

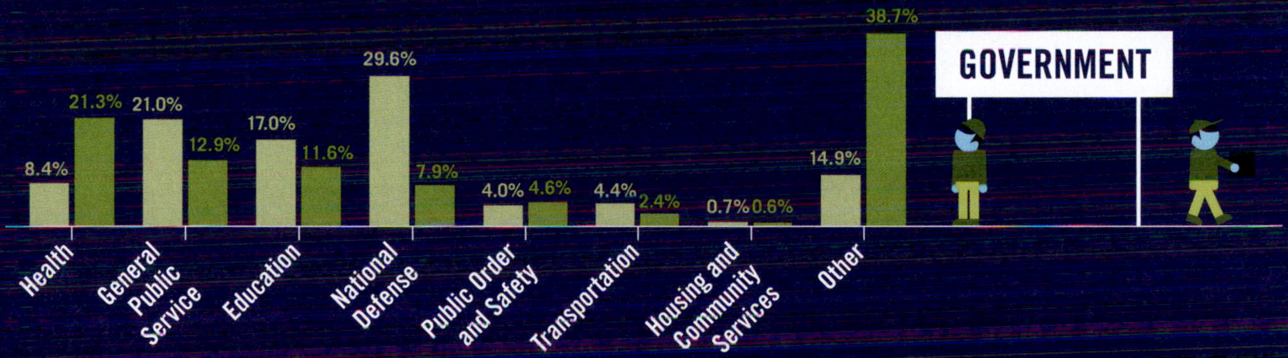

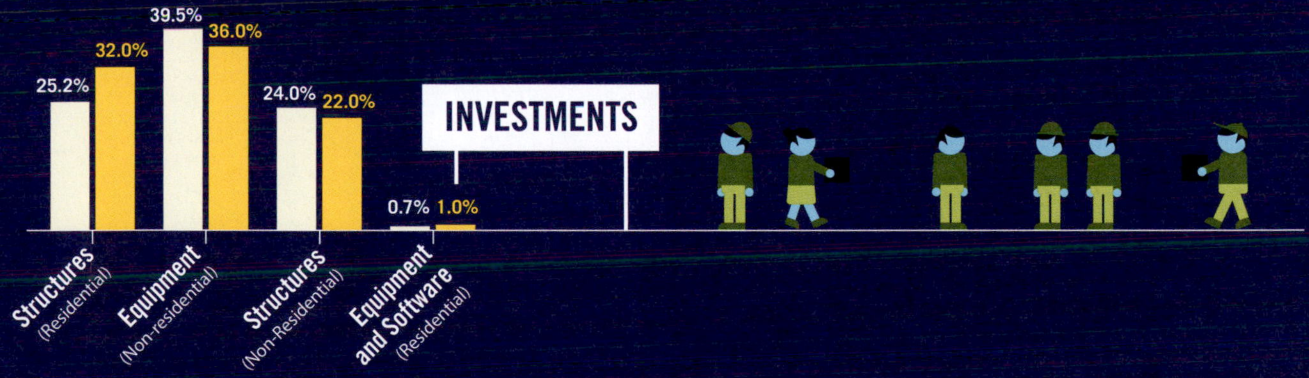

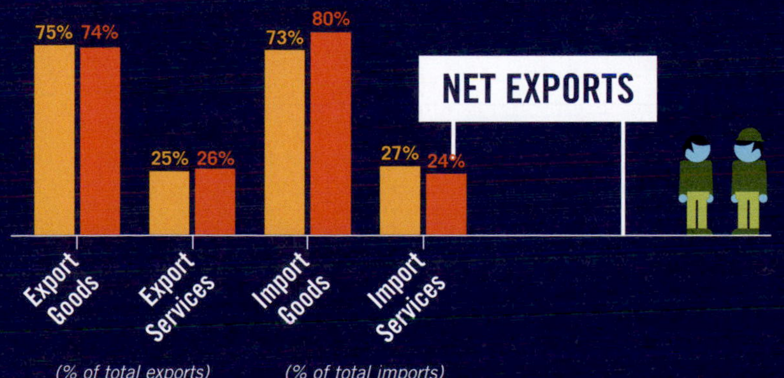

REVIEW QUESTIONS

- What component of consumption do we spend a much greater percentage on now than in 1970?
- Why do economists stress real GDP rather than nominal GDP when looking at GDP changes over time?

wealth does make it easier to afford conveniences, experiences, and even health and well-being that contribute to life satisfaction or happiness. Per capita GDP is positively correlated with many human welfare outcomes that nearly everybody finds desirable: higher life expectancy, higher levels of education, and reduced infant mortality. This probably doesn't surprise you; income allows people to buy better health care, medicines, and education, among other purchases.

Recent research done by economists Betsey Stevenson and Justin Wolfers seems to support these assumptions. Their research has found a consistently positive relationship between self-reported life satisfaction and income. In their research, Stevenson and Wolfers asked questions similar to those found on other surveys used to study happiness and life satisfaction:

"Here is a ladder representing the 'ladder of life.' Let's suppose that the top of the ladder represents the best possible life for you, and the bottom, the worst possible life for you. On which step of the ladder do you feel you personally stand at the present time [0–10 steps]?"

You can imagine how the data will look: people and nations with relatively low life satisfaction will give answers in the 3–4 range, while people and nations with relatively high life satisfaction will give answers in the 6–8 range.

Here are two key results from Stevenson and Wolfers' research:

1. WEALTHIER INDIVIDUALS REPORT GREATER LIFE SATISFACTION THAN POORER PEOPLE IN THE SAME COUNTRY.

Figure 19.11 shows how life satisfaction varies across varying income levels in the 10 most populous countries. The vertical axis measures the life satisfaction variable, and the horizontal axis measures income on a log scale. Clearly, life satisfaction climbs with income: all the lines have a positive and similar slope. Even though Brazilians are especially happy for their given income levels,

FIGURE 19.11

Life Satisfaction and Income by Country

This shows a positive relationship between self-reported life satisfaction (happiness) and household income in ten nations. Wealthier people inside each nation express greater happiness than poorer people in the same nation.

Source: Betsey Stevenson and Justin Wolfers, "Subjective Well-Being and Income: Is There Any Evidence of Satiation?" NBER Working Paper 18992, April 2013, https://doi.org//10.3386/w18992.

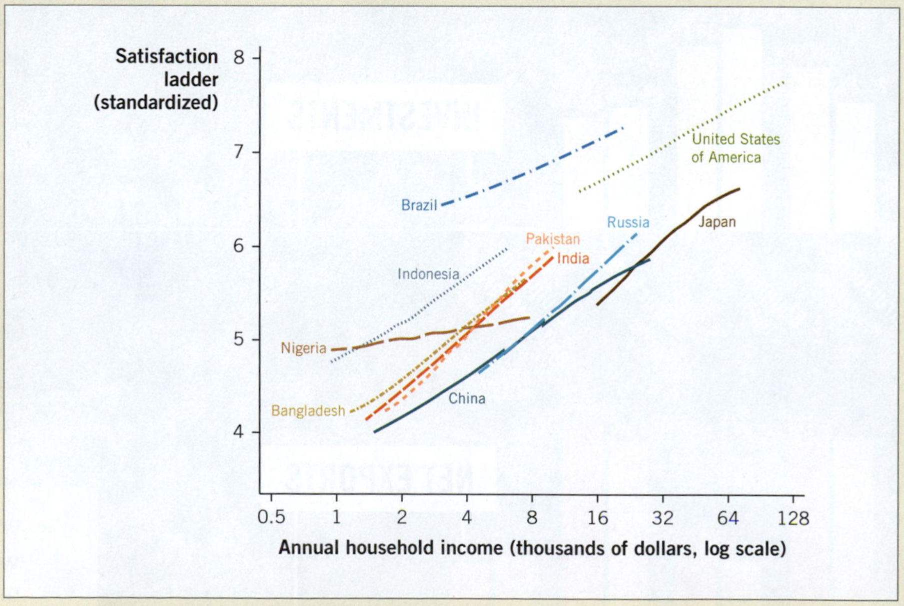

the general relationship for Brazilians is similar to that for Indians, Russians, and Japanese.

In addition, Stevenson and Wolfers point out the importance of paying attention to percentage changes in that variable, rather than absolute changes. For example, an income change from $400 to $500 is a 25% change, but a change from $40,000 to $50,000 is also a 25% change.

Why do percentage changes matter in this study? Basic economics assumes a diminishing utility of income, which means that increases in life satisfaction (utility) per dollar should decline as income increases. This study demonstrates that percentage changes do matter: the data indicate that a doubling of income leads to about a 0.35 unit increase on the life satisfaction ladder.

Not counted in GDP: extra time to relax.

2. WEALTHIER NATIONS REPORT GREATER LIFE SATISFACTION THAN POORER NATIONS. Figure 19.12 plots the cross-country data. Each dot represents an individual nation, and the dots together tell a consistent story. First, this shows a clear positive relationship between life satisfaction and income around the globe. Second, there really is a lot of variation in happiness, even at a given income level. For example, compare Mexico and Bulgaria.

In conclusion, survey data from around the globe and across time indicate that increases in income lead to higher life satisfaction, or happiness. Money may not be able to buy happiness, but there is significant evidence that more income presents more opportunities to "pursue happiness."

FIGURE 19.12

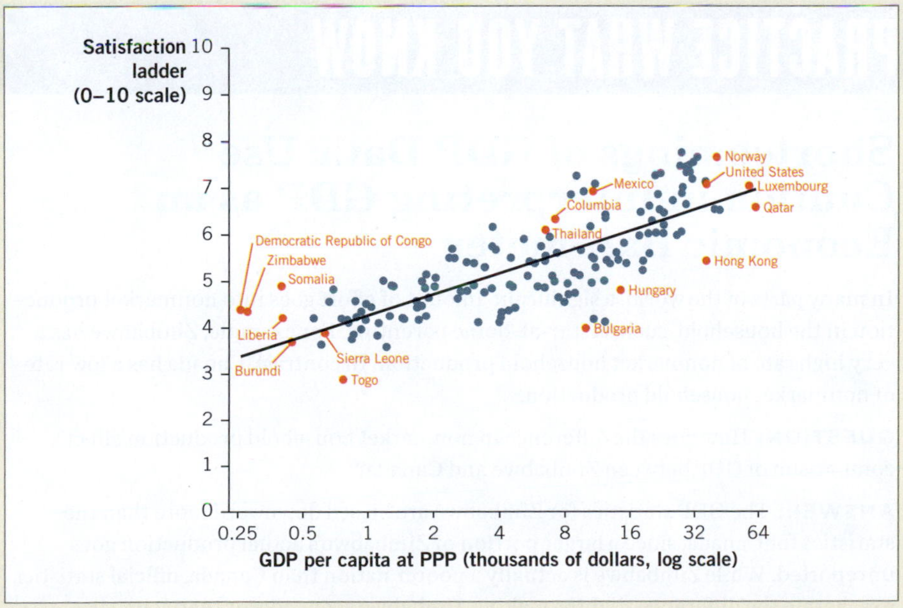

Life Satisfaction and Income around the Globe

Individuals in nations with higher income levels (GDP per capita) report greater happiness on the life satisfaction ladder.

Source: Betsey Stevenson and Justin Wolfers, "Subjective Well-Being and Income: Is There Any Evidence of Satiation?" NBER Working Paper 18992, April 2013, https://doi.org//10.3386/w18992.

Why Do Economists Continue to Rely on GDP Data?

In addition to the production of goods and services, there are many other measurements that economists might use to determine a country's standard of living: life expectancy, educational levels, access to health care, crime rates, and so on. One problem with including these additional factors in GDP is that they are difficult to measure and rank. Moreover, the combined statistic that we would generate would be even more challenging to understand. Therefore, we limit GDP to measuring economic production, knowing that it is not a perfect measure of well-being. In addition, GDP is actually correlated with many of the variables we care about, like a cleaner environment, better access to high-quality health care, more education, more leisure time, and lower crime rates.

Conclusion

We began this chapter describing a changing U.S. economy, one increasing the production of services instead of goods. However, the tool we use to measure both is GDP, and GDP is a measure that works well. In the short run, it helps us recognize business cycles, including the ups of an expansion and the downs of a recession. GDP also serves as a reasonably good indicator of living standards around the globe and over time. Nations with better living conditions are also nations with higher GDP. Thus, even though it has some shortcomings, GDP is a sound indicator of the overall health of an economy.

In the next chapter, we look at another macroeconomic indicator—the unemployment rate. The unemployment rate and other job indicators give us an additional dimension on which to consider the health of an economy. ✷

PRACTICE WHAT YOU KNOW

Some nations have more stay-at-home parents than others. How does this affect GDP comparisons?

Shortcomings of GDP Data: Use Caution in Interpreting GDP as an Economic Barometer

In many parts of the world, a significant amount of effort goes into nonmarket production in the household, such as stay-at-home parenting. For example, Zimbabwe has a very high rate of nonmarket household production. In contrast, Canada has a low rate of nonmarket household production.

QUESTION: How does the difference in nonmarket household production affect a comparison of GDP between Zimbabwe and Canada?

ANSWER: The GDP statistics for Zimbabwe are biased downward more than the statistics for Canada, since a larger portion of Zimbabwe's actual production goes unreported. While Zimbabwe is actually a poorer nation than Canada, official statistics exaggerate the difference slightly, making Zimbabwe seem poorer than it is.

· ECONOMICS *for* LIFE ·

Economic Growth Statistics: Deciphering Data Reports

- Always check that long-run values are adjusted for inflation.
- Three percent is a nice benchmark for overall real GDP growth.
- Two percent is a nice benchmark for per capita GDP growth.
- Context dictates "per capita" versus total income usage.

Economic reports in the media are often misleading.

The media constantly bring us news of the latest economic developments. In addition to monthly reports on unemployment and inflation, there are monthly releases and revisions of GDP data for the United States and other nations. These updates often get a lot of attention. Unfortunately, media reports are not as careful with their economics terminology as we would like. Because they're not worded carefully, the reports can be misleading.

After learning about historical experiences with economic growth, you might find new interest in the economic growth reports that appear almost every month in the mainstream media. However, you must carefully evaluate the data they present. Now that you have perspective on growth statistics, you can determine for yourself whether economic news is positive or negative. For example, an article from the *New York Times* offers the following synopsis of economic growth in China for the previous quarter:

> China's economic output was 6.1 percent higher in the first quarter than a year earlier . . . China's annual growth rate appeared slow in the first quarter after the 6.8 percent rate in the fourth quarter of 2008, partly because it was being compared with the economy's formidable output in the first quarter of last year.*

China's economy grew at over 6%, and yet this rate is described as "slow." By now, you know that 6% is an incredibly fast rate of growth.

Good economists are very careful with language, and certain terms have very specific meanings. For example, we know that "economic growth" always refers to changes in real *per capita* GDP, not simply GDP or real GDP. But economic reports in mainstream media outlets often blur this distinction. That is exactly the case with the report in the *New York Times* article just cited.

Even though the report's author uses the term "annual growth rate," additional research reveals that he is talking about real GDP growth, but not adjusting the data for population changes. This mistake is fairly common, so you should watch for it when you read economic growth reports. It turns out that the population growth rate in China was about 0.6% in 2009. This means that the growth rate of real per capita GDP in China was actually about 5.5%, which is still very impressive.

*Keith Bradsher, "China's Economic Growth Slows in First Quarter," *New York Times*, April 16, 2009.

ANSWERING *the* BIG QUESTIONS

How is macroeconomics different from microeconomics?

- Microeconomics is the study of individuals and firms, but macroeconomics considers the entire economy.
- Many of the topics in both areas of study are the same; these topics include income, employment, and output. But the macro perspective is much broader than the micro perspective.

What does GDP tell us about the economy?

- GDP measures both output and income in a macroeconomy.
- It is a gauge of productivity and the overall level of wealth in an economy.
- We use GDP data to measure living standards, economic growth, and business cycle conditions.

How is GDP computed?

- GDP is the total market value of all final goods and services produced in an economy in a specific time period, usually a year.
- Economists typically compute GDP by adding four types of expenditures in the economy: consumption (C), investment (I), government spending (G), and net exports (NX). Net exports are total exports minus total imports.
- For many applications, it is also necessary to compute real GDP, adjusting GDP for changes in prices (inflation).

What are some shortcomings of GDP data?

- GDP data do not include the production of nonmarket goods, the underground economy, production effects on the environment, or the value placed on leisure time.

CHAPTER PROBLEMS

Concepts You Should Know

business cycle (p. 610)
consumption (p. 618)
economic contraction (p. 610)
economic expansion (p. 610)
economic growth (p. 608)
final goods (p. 615)
GDP deflator (p. 620)
government spending (p. 619)
Great Recession (p. 609)
gross domestic product (GDP) (p. 606)
gross national product (GNP) (p. 616)
inflation (p. 608)
intermediate goods (p. 615)
investment (p. 618)
net exports (p. 619)
nominal GDP (p. 620)
per capita GDP (p. 607)
price level (p. 620)
real GDP (p. 608)
recession (p. 609)
services (p. 613)

Questions for Review

1. Explain the relationship between output and income for both an individual and an entire economy.
2. What is the largest component (C, I, G, or NX) of GDP? Give an example of each component.
3. A farmer sells cotton to a clothing company for $100,000, and the clothing company turns the cotton into T-shirts that it sells to a store for a total of $200,000. How much did GDP increase as a result of these transactions?
4. A friend of yours is reading a financial blog and comes to you for some advice about GDP. She wants to know whether she should pay attention to nominal GDP or real GDP. Which one do you recommend, and why?
5. Is a larger GDP always better than a smaller GDP? Explain your answer with an example.
6. If Max receives an unemployment check, would we include that transfer payment from the government in this year's GDP? Why or why not?
7. Phil owns an old set of golf clubs that he purchased for $1,000 seven years ago. He decides to post them on Craigslist and quickly sells the clubs for $450. How does this sale affect GDP?
8. Real GDP for 2015 is less than nominal GDP for that year. But real GDP for 2000 is more than nominal GDP for that year. Why?
9. What are the four shortcomings with using GDP as a measure of well-being?
10. Economists Betsey Stevenson and Justin Wolfers have researched the relationship between GDP and happiness.
    a. Briefly summarize their two main findings (one or two sentences each).
    b. What two types of evidence (two different empirical tests) did Stevenson and Wolfers use to support their findings?

Study Problems (*✱solved at the end of the section*)

1. A friend who knows of your interest in economics comes up to you after reading the latest GDP data and excitedly exclaims, "Did you see that nominal GDP rose from $22 trillion to $22.5 trillion?" What should you tell your friend about this news?
2. In the following situations, explain what is counted (or is not counted) in this year's GDP.
    a. You bought the latest PlayStation model at GameStop last year and resold it on eBay this year.

b. You purchase a new copy of *Investing for Dummies* at Barnes & Noble.

c. You purchase a historic home using the services of a real estate agent.

d. You detail your car so it is spotless inside and out.

e. You purchase a new hard drive for your old laptop.

f. Your physical therapist receives $300 for physical therapy services but reports only $100.

g. Apple buys 150,000 motherboards for use in making new computers.

h. Toyota produces 10,000 new Camrys that remain unsold at the end of the year.

3. To which component of GDP expenditure (C, I, G, or NX) does each of the following belong?

a. Swiss chocolates imported from Europe

b. a driver's license you receive from the Department of Motor Vehicles

c. a candle you buy at a local store

d. a new house

4. A mechanic builds an engine and then sells it to a customized body shop for $7,000. The body shop installs the engine in a car and sells the car to a dealer for $30,000. The dealer then sells the finished vehicle for $45,000. A consumer drives off with the car. By how much does GDP increase? What is the value added at each step of the production process? How does the total value added compare with the amount by which GDP increased?

5. In this chapter, we used nominal GDP data from Table 19.5 to compute 2021 GDP in 2012 dollars. Using the same steps, use the data from Table 19.5 to compute 2020 GDP in 2012 dollars.

6. Many goods and services are illegally sold or legally sold but not reported to the government. How would increased efforts to count those goods and services affect GDP data?

7. Leisure time is not included in GDP, but what would happen if it was included? Would high-work countries like South Korea fare better in international comparisons of well-being, or worse?

* **8.** Fill in the missing data in the following table.

Year	Nominal GDP (thousands of $)	Real GDP (thousands of $)	GDP Deflator
2018	$100	_____	100.0
2019	_____	$110	108.0
2020	130	117	_____
2021	150	_____	120.0
2022	_____	136	125.0

* **9.** Consider an economy that only produces two goods: strawberries and cream. Use the following table to compute nominal GDP, real GDP, and the GDP deflator for each year. (Year 2015 is the base year.)

Year	Price of strawberries (per pint)	Quantity of strawberries (pints)	Price of cream (per pint)	Quantity of cream (pints)
2020	$3.00	100	$2.00	200
2021	4.00	125	2.50	400
2022	5.00	150	3.00	500

* **10.** The following table presents GDP data for an imaginary economy.

a. Fill in the blanks.

Year	Nominal GDP (in billions)	GDP Deflator (2010 = base year)	Real GDP (billions of 2010 dollars)
1980	$500	20	_____
1990	1,000	25	_____
2000	3,000	_____	$6,000
2010	_____	80	7,500
2020	_____	100	9,000

b. Compute both nominal and real GDP growth from the end of 1980 to the end of 1990. Note that your result is not an annual growth rate; it is the total growth over the entire decade.

11. Determine whether the following are final or intermediate goods:

a. a gallon of milk purchased by you at the supermarket
b. a gallon of milk purchased by Starbucks for their cappuccinos
c. a computer bought by you to surf the Net
d. a computer bought by your college for use in the library
e. a tractor bought by your local county government to mow grass
f. a tractor bought by farmer Glenn to plow his cornfields
g. corn seed used by farmer Glenn to grow corn

12. GDP per capita is a helpful indicator of living standards across nations. But there are shortcomings in GDP calculations. In the following examples, determine in which direction, if any, measured GDP will incorrectly estimate the living standards of that country.

a. In India, a greater portion of workers produce nonmarket output. All else equal, this can cause India's measured GDP to ________ its living standards.
b. In China, the air pollution is much greater. All else equal, this can cause China's measured GDP to ________ its living standards.
c. In Greece, many transactions occur in the underground economy—more than in the United States, for example. All else equal, this can cause Greece's measured GDP to ________ its living standards.
d. In France, the average work week is shorter than that in the U.S. All else equal, this can cause France's measured GDP to ________ its living standards.

13. The GDP data in the following table are all end-of-year data for Spain.

a. Fill in the blanks in the table.

	GDP (in millions of current Euros)	GDP (in millions of constant 2010 Euros)	GDP Deflator
2014	$266,227	______	100.8
2015	275,418	$273,372	______
2016	______	281,610	101.6

b. What was the rate of real GDP growth for Spain in 2016?
c. What was the rate of inflation in Spain in 2016?

Solved Problems

8.

Year	Nominal GDP (thousands of $)	Real GDP (thousands of $)	GDP Deflator
2018	$100	$100	100.0
2019	118.8	110	108.0
2020	130	117	111.1
2021	150	125	120.0
2022	170	136	125.0

To solve for the missing data, use the following equation (and 2018 as the base year):

$$\text{real GDP}_{\text{year}} = \frac{\text{nominal GDP}_{\text{year}}}{\text{price level}_{\text{year}}} \times \text{base year price level}$$

For 2018: $\text{real GDP}_{2018} = (\$100 \div 100.0) \times 100.0 = \underline{\$100}$

For 2019: $\$110{,}000 = (\text{nominal GDP}_{2019} \div 108.0) \times 100.0$

$\text{nominal GDP}_{2019} = (\$110 \div 100.0) \times 108.0 = \underline{\$118.8}$

For 2020: $\$117{,}000 = (\$130{,}000 \div \text{GDP deflator}_{2020}) \times 100.0$

$\text{GDP deflator}_{2020} = (\$130 \div \$117) \times 100.0$

$\text{GDP deflator}_{2020} = \underline{111.1}$

For 2021: $\text{real GDP}_{2021} = (\$150{,}000 \div 120.0) \times 100.0$

$\text{real GDP}_{2021} = \underline{\$125}$

For 2022: $\$136{,}000 = (\text{nominal GDP}_{2022} \div 125.0) \times 100.0$

$\text{nominal GDP}_{2022} = (\$136{,}000 \div 100.0) \times 125.0$

$\text{nominal GDP}_{2022} = \underline{\$170{,}000}$

9.

Year	Nominal GDP	Real GDP	GDP Deflator
2020	$700	$700	100.0
2021	1,500	1,175	127.7
2022	2,250	1,450	155.2

First, let's calculate nominal GDP for each of the three years by adding up the market values of the strawberries and cream produced during that year.

For 2020: $\text{nominal GDP}_{2020} = (\$3.00 \times 100) + (\$2.00 \times 200) = \$700$

For 2021: $\text{nominal GDP}_{2021} = (\$4.00 \times 125) + (\$2.50 \times 400) = \$1{,}500$

For 2022: $\text{nominal GDP}_{2022} = (\$5.00 \times 150) + (\$3.00 \times 500) = \$2{,}250$

Now, let's calculate real GDP in 2020 dollars by multiplying the quantities produced in each year by the 2020 prices.

For 2020: $\text{real GDP}_{2020} = (\$3.00 \times 100) + (\$2.00 \times 200) = \$700$

For 2021: $\text{real GDP}_{2021} = (\$3.00 \times 125) + (\$2.00 \times 400) = \$1{,}175$

For 2022: $\text{real GDP}_{2022} = (\$3.00 \times 150) + (\$2.00 \times 500) = \$1{,}450$

Finally, using the nominal GDP and real GDP numbers we calculated above, let's calculate the GDP deflator by using the following formula:

$$\text{GDP deflator}_{\text{year}} = \frac{\text{nominal GDP}_{\text{year}}}{\text{real GDP}_{\text{year}}} \times 100.0$$

GDP $\text{deflator}_{2020} = 100.0$. Since 2020 is given as the base year, the GDP deflator must be 100.0.

For 2021: GDP $\text{deflator}_{2021} = (\$1{,}500 \div \$1{,}175) \times 100 = 127.7$

For 2022: GDP $\text{deflator}_{2022} = (\$2{,}250 \div \$1{,}450) \times 100 = 155.2$

10. a. Recall Equation 19.3:

$$\text{real GDP}_t = \frac{\text{nominal GDP}_t}{\text{price level}_t} \times 100$$

Year	Nominal GDP (in billions)	GDP Deflator (2010 = base year)	Real GDP (billions of 2010 dollars)
1980	$500	20	$2,500
1990	1,000	25	4,000
2000	3,000	50	6,000
2010	6,000	80	7,500
2020	9,000	100	9,000

Since we know that the GDP deflator is used as the price level, for 1980 we use Equation 19.3 to solve for real GDP:

$$\text{real GDP}_{1980} = (\$500/20) \times 100 = \$2{,}500$$

For 1990, we use Equation 19.3 to solve for real GDP:

$$\text{real GDP}_{1990} = (\$1{,}000/25) \times 100 = \$4{,}000$$

For 2000, we use Equation 19.3 to solve for the GDP deflator:

$$\$6{,}000 = (\$3{,}000/\text{price level}_t) \times 100 = 50$$

For 2010, we use Equation 19.3 to solve for nominal GDP:

$$\$7{,}500 = (\text{nominal GDP}_t/80) \times 100 = \$6000$$

For 2020, we know that nominal GDP is equal to real GDP because this is the base year.

b. nominal GDP growth = (nominal GDP in 1990 – nominal GDP in 1980)/ nominal GDP in 1980 = ($1,000 – $500)/$500 = 1.0 = 100%

real GDP growth = (real GDP in 1990 − real GDP in 1980)/ real GDP in 1980 = ($4,000 − $2,500)/$2,500 = $1,500/$2,500 = 3/5 = 60%

CHAPTER

20 Unemployment

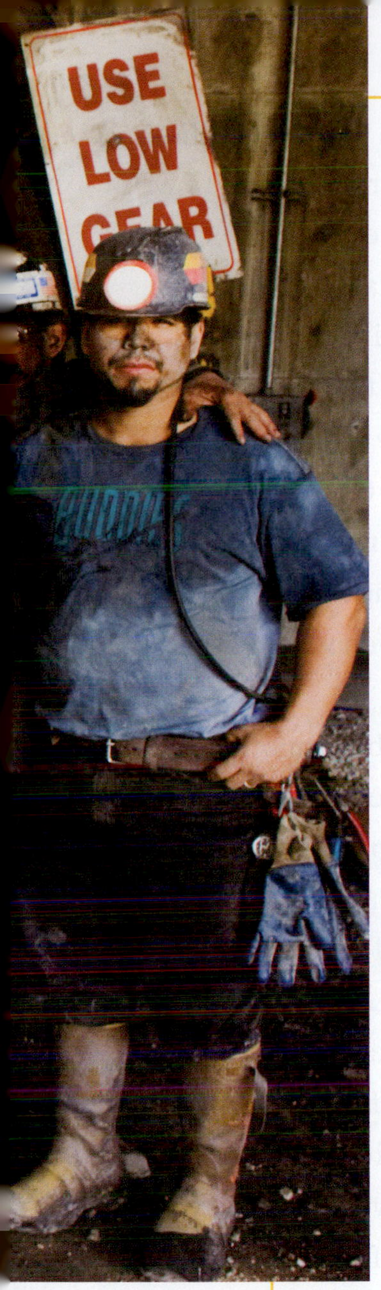

Even Dynamic, Growing Economies Grapple with Unemployment.

The world economy is changing. Some industries are bursting with new job opportunities. Others are shrinking. In the United States, the coal industry continues its century-long decline. In 1923, there were 863,000 coal miners in the United States. By 2020, the number was less than 43,000.

The decline in U.S. coal has multiple causes. New exploration and extraction techniques make oil and natural gas cheap alternatives for fueling factories and electric power plants. Wind and solar energy are now major players in the energy market, especially in the western U.S. Meanwhile, the costs of complying with tightening environmental regulations make it harder for coal plants to operate profitably. Year after year, thousands of laid-off miners have had to look for jobs elsewhere. Miners who are too old to learn a new trade retire early. Young people who might have gone into mining are turning elsewhere.

But while this is painful for the mining industry, it is normal for specific industries to rise and fall even when the overall economy is progressing. On the whole, the U.S. economy is much better off than it was in 1923: real GDP is now approximately 20 times larger, and total employment

These Colorado coal miners do a very tough job. But they know, as well as anyone, that their industry is on a downward slide. Most economists forecast that the decline of the last 100 years will continue, even when the overall U.S. economy is expanding.

has grown from about 30 million jobs to more than 150 million. Furthermore, coal is not alone. It is normal for industries to rise and fall over time as economies grow and evolve. The U.S. apparel industry has gone through changes that parallel coal's. These days, automation technology is disrupting even white-collar professions like medicine and law. This textbook, in fact, illustrates the point: books like this were once typeset by hand in the United States, but now they are typeset digitally, and very often overseas. The fact is, industrial churn is normal in a dynamic, growing economy. This churn is one reason why we always have some unemployed workers, even when the economy is growing.

Of course, not all unemployment is caused by economic progress. Much unemployment is caused by economic declines, such as the Great Recession described in Chapter 19 and the shutdowns of the COVID-19 pandemic. Both normal "churn" unemployment and cyclical, recession-caused unemployment are examined in this chapter.

After GDP, the unemployment rate is the second most important indicator of economic health. In this chapter, we examine the causes of unemployment and explain how it is measured. By looking at some historical data in context, we will begin to understand when unemployment is a matter of concern.

· BIG QUESTIONS ·

- What are the major reasons for unemployment?
- What can we learn from the employment data?

What Are the Major Reasons for Unemployment?

Perhaps you know someone who has lost their job. Losing a job is particularly difficult when you are unable to transition easily to another one. After all, many of us depend on our jobs just to survive. Being willing and able to work, but unable to find a job—there are few greater frustrations. **Unemployment** occurs when a worker who is not currently employed is searching for a job without success.

Unemployment occurs when a worker who is not currently employed is searching for a job without success.

People leave their jobs for many reasons. Some do so voluntarily: they may return to school, take another job, or decide to leave the workforce to care for their children. Others lose a job they wish to keep: an employee might be fired for poor performance, let go because a company is downsizing, or laid off because the overall economy is struggling. When macroeconomists consider unemployment, they explicitly look at workers who seek employment but are unable to secure it. We use the unemployment rate to monitor the level of unemployment in an economy. The **unemployment rate** (u) is the percentage of the labor force that is unemployed. Figure 20.1 plots the U.S. unemployment rate from 1970 to 2021. This graph is one way of quickly illustrating national economic frustration—as the unemployment rate climbs, people are more likely to be disappointed in their pursuit of a job. The shaded regions are periods of recession; notice how the unemployment rate soared during the coronavirus recession in early 2020.

The **unemployment rate** is the percentage of the labor force that is unemployed.

Economists distinguish three types of unemployment: structural, frictional, and cyclical. You can think of each type as deriving from a different source. As it turns out, structural and frictional unemployment occur even when the economy is healthy and growing. For this reason, they are often called *natural unemployment*. We consider these first.

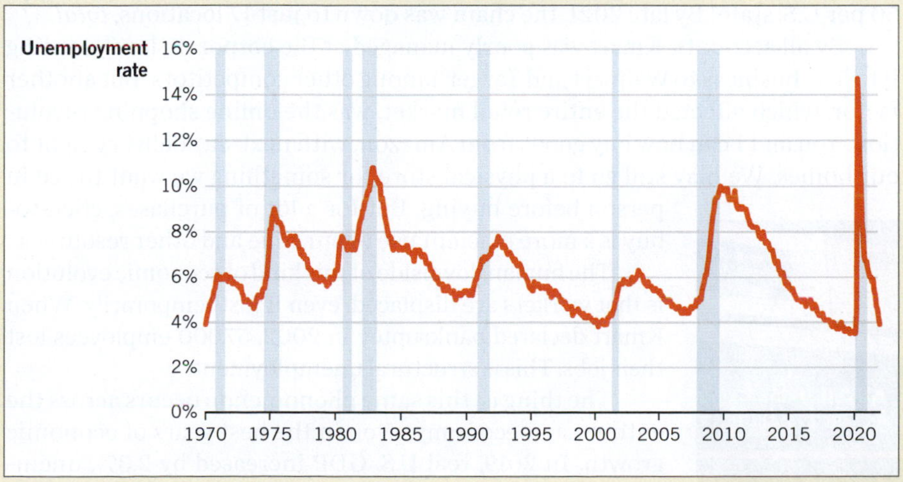

FIGURE 20.1

U.S. Unemployment Rate, 1970–2021

The unemployment rate is an important indicator of the economy's health. Since 1970, the average unemployment rate in the United States has been about 6%. In April 2020, the unemployment rate spiked up to 14.7%, the highest level since the Great Depression.

Source: U.S. Bureau of Labor Statistics.

Structural Unemployment

Unemployment is a burden on households and on the whole economy: resources are wasted when idle workers sit on the sidelines. However, a dynamic growing economy is one that adapts and changes. No one would consider it an improvement to return to the economy of early America, where 90% of Americans toiled at manual farmwork and earned subsistence wages that just barely covered the cost of food and shelter. The transformation to our modern economy has brought new jobs but also requires different skills. This makes some jobs obsolete, which inevitably leads to some unemployment, even if just temporarily. And herein lies the dilemma: dynamic growing economies are also evolving economies. If we want an economy that adapts to changes in consumer demands and technology, we must accept some unemployment, at least temporarily, as a by-product of the growth.

Consider that in the past we produced no computers, cell phones, or polio vaccines, and the invention of these products led to great job creation. Improving technologies in these fields enabled us to produce more and better output with fewer resources or fewer employees. Over time, we also produced less of some other things—such as black and white televisions, cassette tapes, and typewriters. These structural changes left some workers unemployed.

CREATIVE DESTRUCTION As new industries are created, some old ones are destroyed. The economist Joseph Schumpeter coined the term *creative destruction* to describe this process of economic evolution. **Creative destruction** occurs when the introduction of new products and technologies leads to the end of other industries and jobs. As some jobs become obsolete, the result is **structural unemployment**, which is caused by changes in the industrial makeup (structure) of the economy. Although structural unemployment can cause transitional problems, it is often a sign of a healthy, growing economy.

Creative destruction occurs when the introduction of new products and technologies leads to the end of other industries and jobs.

Structural unemployment is unemployment caused by changes in the industrial makeup (structure) of the economy.

Consider the fate of big-box department stores like Kmart, Sears, and JCPenney. These stores thrived in the twentieth century, but in the 1990s things began to go sour for them. Kmart alone had 2,486 locations in 1994. That's 50 per U.S. state! By late 2021, the chain was down to just 17 locations, *total*.

By all accounts, Kmart was poorly managed at the corporate level, causing it to lose business to Walmart and Target, among other competitors. But another factor, which affected the entire retail market, was the online shopping revolution. You and I can now buy goods from Amazon, with next-day delivery right to our homes. We may still go to a physical store for something we want to see in person before buying. But for a lot of purchases, click-to-buy is a more efficient use of our time and other resources.

Say goodbye to this Kmart in California. It closed in 2021.

The human downside of this kind of economic evolution is that workers are displaced, even if just temporarily. When Kmart declared bankruptcy in 2002, 57,000 employees lost their jobs. This is structural unemployment.

The thing is, this same phenomenon occurs across the entire macroeconomy, even in the best years of economic growth. In 2019, real U.S. GDP increased by 2.3%, unemployment rates were at historical lows, and 12.1 million new jobs were created overall. Yet even then, there were 68 million job separations (workers who quit or were laid off). In a dynamic economy, job turnover is normal.

AN EVOLVING ECONOMY Our evolving economy has led to drastic changes in the type of work Americans do, especially over the long run. Figure 20.2 shows how jobs in the United States have evolved over the past two centuries. In 1800, over 90% of Americans worked in agriculture, either as farmers or as farm laborers. A century later, in 1900, only about half of U.S. workers were employed in farming. The rest were split between manufacturing jobs and service-related jobs. In 1900, manufacturing jobs may have been in railroad or steel production, while service jobs included teaching and accounting. Today, five out of six American workers are employed in service-related jobs. Since 1979, U.S. manufacturing employment has fallen from almost 20 million jobs to less than 13 million. Over the same period, employment in service industries has risen from 65 million jobs to nearly 130 million. While we have long had teachers and accountants, there are many new service jobs in fields such as engineering, finance, transportation, health, and government.

The trends presented in Figure 20.2 illustrate creative destruction: the structure of the economy evolves, and this leads to different types of jobs. This long view presents the most positive angle on this process. After all, most of us would prefer working at modern jobs rather than toiling with simple farm tools in a field all day. But along the way, as jobs shift, some temporary structural unemployment inevitably occurs.

FIGURE 20.2

The Evolution of Jobs in the United States

Over the past two centuries, jobs in the United States have evolved from being primarily agricultural to industrial (manufacturing) and then to service.

Source: Federal Reserve Bank of Dallas.

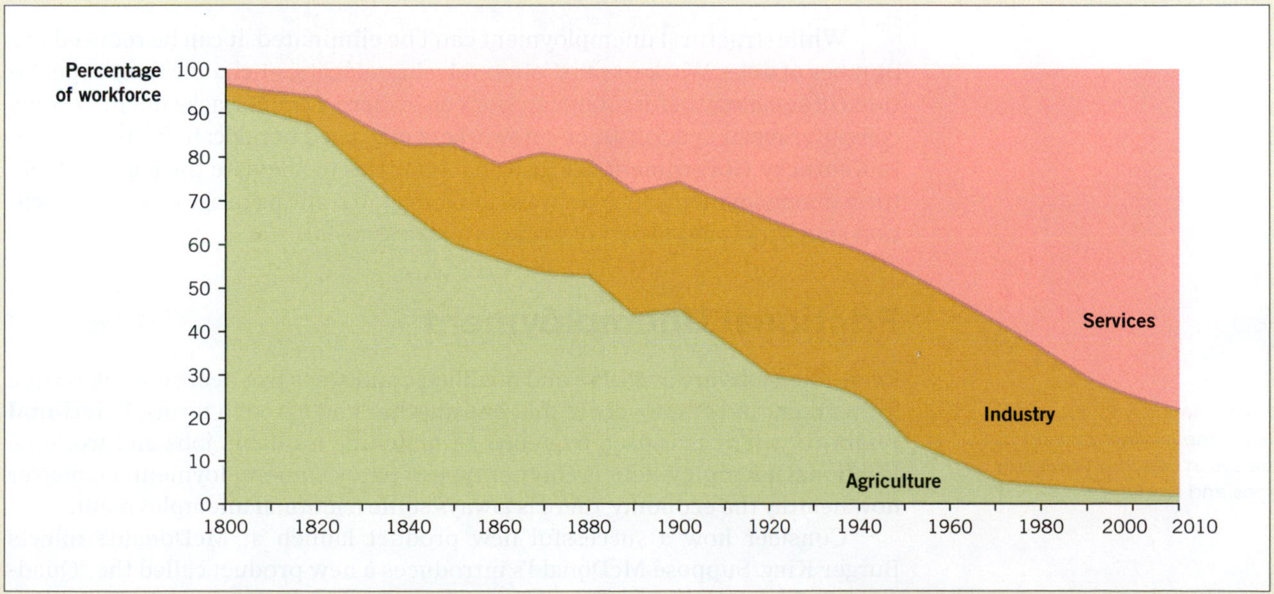

ECONOMICS IN THE REAL WORLD

MOST AMERICANS DON'T WANT FARMWORK

Why don't Americans want a career picking grapes?

In September 2010, Garance Burke of the Associated Press (AP) wrote an article about the frustration of U.S. farmers trying to find American workers to harvest fruit and vegetables. Even though the unemployment rate at the time was very high, Americans did not apply for available farm jobs. Burke noted that the few Americans who do take such jobs usually don't stay in the fields for long. The AP analysis showed that from January to June 2010, California farmers advertised 1,160 jobs available to U.S. citizens and legal residents, yet only 36 people were hired. One farmer named Steve Fortin noted problems with American workers: "we saw absentee problems, and we had people asking for time off after they had just started. Some were actually planting the plants upside down."

Comedian Stephen Colbert partnered with the United Farm Workers (UFW) union in a "Take Our Jobs" campaign, aimed at getting farm jobs filled with American workers. Colbert even spent a day picking beans in a field, concluding that farmwork is "really, really hard."

Ironically, during the 2007–2009 recession, many migrant farm jobs were available but unemployed Americans refused to apply for them. This trend continued during the COVID-19 recession when agricultural jobs remained plentiful.* This lack of interest contrasts with worker attitudes during the Great Depression more than 80 years earlier, when displaced farmers from the Great Plains flooded California looking for work. So when some people today claim that immigrants are taking jobs away from U.S. citizens, we can say that in the heart of the nation's biggest farming state, this is certainly not true. In addition, when we look at the long-run trend in U.S. jobs, which shows a movement away from agricultural work and into service-sector jobs, we shouldn't be too alarmed.

*Jenny Shaffstall, "Five Facts About the Ag Labor Shortage," Farm Journal, July 27, 2021, https://www.agweb.com/news/business/taxes-and-finance/five-facts-about-ag-labor-shortage.

While structural unemployment can't be eliminated, it can be reduced in a number of ways. Workers must often retrain, relocate, or change their expectations in some way before they can work elsewhere. Lumberjacks might become computer repair specialists, or autoworkers may need to relocate from Michigan to Kentucky. Government can also enact policies to alleviate the pain of structural unemployment, such as by establishing job training programs and relocation subsidies (paying part of workers' moving costs).

Frictional Unemployment

Frictional unemployment is unemployment caused by delays in matching available jobs and workers.

Even when jobs are available and qualified employees live nearby, it takes time for workers and employers to find one another and agree to terms. **Frictional unemployment** is caused by delays in matching available jobs and workers. Frictional unemployment is another type of natural unemployment: no matter how healthy the economy, there is always some frictional unemployment.

Consider how a successful new product launch at McDonald's affects Burger King. Suppose McDonald's introduces a new product called the "Quadstack," which is really just four Quarter Pounders stacked on top of one another. Now imagine that customers can't get enough of the new sandwich. Because

ECONOMICS *in the* MEDIA

Structural Unemployment

THE OFFICE

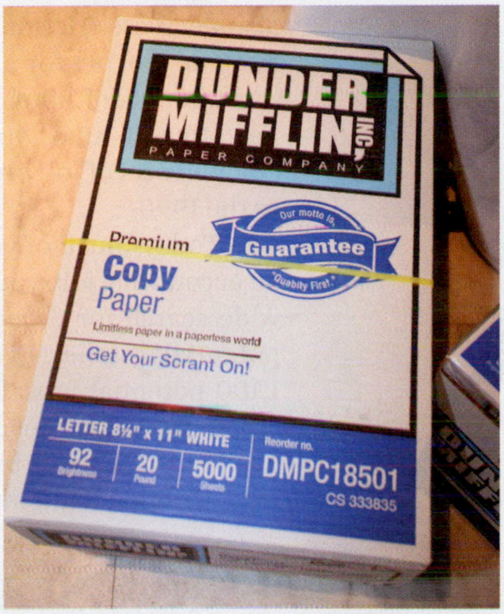

Is technical progress always good news?

In the TV show *The Office*, Angela, Kevin, and Oscar are accountants at the Scranton branch office of Dunder Mifflin, a paper company. In one episode, a representative from the corporate office (which oversees all branches) unveils a new accounting system. Ryan, from corporate, explains to Angela, Kevin, and Oscar that the new system automates most of the billing process, so that when a customer places an order, it gets emailed to the warehouse and a copy goes directly to the customer's in-box.

Angela then asks, "How do we bill them?" and Ryan responds, "You don't. The invoicing, account reconciliation, and all the follow-up claims just go right to your BlackBerry." At this point, Oscar asks, "So what do the accountants do?" Ryan responds, "Well, unless there is a real problem client, nothing."

Angela and Oscar immediately understand that their jobs are becoming obsolete. But Kevin still doesn't understand. So after Ryan has left the room, Kevin crows, "This is the greatest thing that has ever happened to us!" Angela responds, "No, it's not." Kevin still doesn't get it, jumping in with, "Are you kidding me?" Oscar then delivers the bad news: "It was already a stretch that they needed three of us. Now they don't even need one."

In this story, Angela, Oscar, and Kevin are seeing the effects of structural unemployment, as technological advances are making their jobs redundant. This is true in the short run because less labor is needed to complete the billing process. However, the structural unemployment that is about to occur is a by-product of a dynamic and growing economy, and most economists would assume that with possibly some additional retraining the three accountants will find work elsewhere.

of the spike in business, McDonald's needs to hire more employees. At the same time, Burger King loses customers to McDonald's and decides to lay off some workers. Of course, the laid-off Burger King workers will take some time searching for new jobs. And McDonald's will take time deciding how many new workers it needs and which applicants to hire. Because some workers are unemployed during this transition, frictional unemployment results.

Searching for a job has never been easier.

Frictional unemployment occurs even in the healthiest economy. Because we live in a world of imperfect information, there are incentives for employees to keep searching for the perfect job and for employers to search longer for the best employees. For example, as you approach graduation from college, you will take time to search for a job and determine which offer to accept. Similarly, employers rarely hire the first applicant they see, even though it is costly to leave a position vacant. Even if there is a perfect job available for every worker, it takes time to match workers and jobs. These time lags create friction in the labor market, and the result is frictional unemployment.

Even though frictional unemployment is natural, its level can rise or fall over time. Let's look at two factors that affect frictional unemployment: information availability and government policies.

INFORMATION AVAILABILITY Any factors that shorten job searches also decrease frictional unemployment. The Internet is a dramatic example: imagine looking for a job without it. You'd read newspaper ads, make dozens or hundreds of phone calls, and make several in-person visits to employers. Yet after all that, you'd still have a great deal of uncertainty about your complete set of job prospects. This was the reality for job searchers as recently as the 1990s.

Today, much of your job search is conducted online. If you are looking for an accounting job, you might search for a job at Indeed.com. In 2020 a nationwide search for accounting job opportunities for CPAs yielded over 25,000 potential matches. Even narrowing this search to, say, the state of Virginia nets 1,100 potential jobs. The point is that the vast pool of information available through the Internet enables workers and companies to find one another more quickly and to make better matches with substantially lower costs. The result is lower frictional unemployment.

GOVERNMENT POLICIES Any factors that lengthen the job search process increase frictional unemployment. These factors include government policies, such as unemployment compensation, and regulations related to the hiring and firing of employees.

Unemployment insurance also known as federal jobless benefits, is a government program that reduces the hardship of joblessness by guaranteeing that unemployed workers receive a percentage of their former income while unemployed.

Unemployment Insurance and Incentives To reduce the hardship of joblessness, government-provided **unemployment insurance**, also known as *federal jobless benefits*, guarantees that unemployed workers receive a percentage of their former income while unemployed. Governments provide unemployment insurance for many reasons. The benefit cushions the economic consequences of being laid off, and it provides workers time to search for new employment. In addition, unemployment insurance can help contain macroeconomic problems before they spread to other industries. Consider what happens if the auto industry is struggling and workers are laid off: the unemployed autoworkers are no longer able to pay for goods and services they used to buy, and the reduction in their overall spending hurts other industries. For example, if unemployed workers can't pay their mortgages, lenders will suffer and the downturn will spread to the financial industry. Viewed in this way, unemployment insurance serves to reduce the severity of the overall economic contraction.

However, unemployment insurance creates unintended consequences. For one thing, receiving the cushion of unemployment benefits makes some less inclined to search for and take a job. These workers spend more time unemployed when they have insurance; without unemployment insurance, they have a greater incentive to seek immediate employment. When COVID-19 concerns forced a partial shutdown of the U.S. economy in 2020, the federal government stepped in. It supplemented state unemployment benefits with an additional $600 per week from April to July of 2020, and smaller amounts for several months after that. Given the exceptional circumstances, most economists applauded the move. Yes, the extra benefits would incentivize some workers to stay unemployed longer. But giving households help with making ends meet kept the economy from crashing completely due to a collapse in consumer spending.

Incentives

Regulations on Hiring and Firing Government regulations on hiring and firing also contribute to frictional unemployment. Regulations on hiring include restrictions on who can and must be interviewed, paperwork that employers must complete for new hires, and additional tax documents that must be filed for new employees. Regulations on firing include mandatory severance pay, written justification, and government fines. While these regulations may be instituted to help workers by giving them greater job security, they have unintended consequences. When it is difficult to hire employees, firms take longer to do so, which increases frictional unemployment. When it is difficult to fire employees, firms take greater care in hiring them. Again, the longer search time increases frictional unemployment.

ECONOMICS IN THE REAL WORLD

EMPLOYMENT, SPANISH STYLE

Compared with most other nations, the United States has relatively few labor market regulations. However, many European nations have especially stringent regulations. Consider Spain, where mandated severance pay is particularly generous. Until 2012, any Spanish firm that wished to fire a worker was required to pay that worker for 45 days for every year the worker had been employed with the company. Thus, if a firm wanted to fire a 10-year employee, it had to pay that person for 450 days after his or her employment ended. (In 2012, the required severance pay was reduced to 20 days of pay for every year of employment.) This regulation makes it very difficult for young workers to break into the labor force. In fact, unemployment rates for workers aged 24 and younger were over 30% in 2018! These regulations also incentivize firms to search longer for the right workers to fill open positions, thereby increasing frictional unemployment. Another regulation seen in Spain is mandated annual increases in wages and benefits. That is, firms are required by law to give pay and benefits raises every year. Think about this regulation as if you were the manager of a Spanish business firm: before you ever hire and retain a worker for more than a year, you will want to make sure that this individual is worthy of the current pay plus raises. Like mandatory severance pay, this regulation increases the time firms spend searching for just the right match, again increasing frictional unemployment. Figure 20.3 plots the unemployment rates for Spain and the United States from 2000 to 2018. Notice how much higher the Spanish unemployment rate is. Even in 2017, when the Spanish economy was growing briskly, the unemployment rate remained above 15%. Much of this unemployment is due to frictional unemployment caused by labor market regulations. These regulations were put in place to help workers, but economics tells us that incentives affect behavior, and these regulations change firms' hiring incentives.

Incentives

FIGURE 20.3

Unemployment Rate in the United States and Spain, 2000–2018

From 2000 to 2018, the unemployment rate in Spain was much higher than the unemployment rate in the United States. This difference is largely a result of Spanish labor market regulations, many of which were put in place to help workers. But the reality is that these regulations increase frictional unemployment.

Source: Federal Reserve Bank of St. Louis, FRED database.

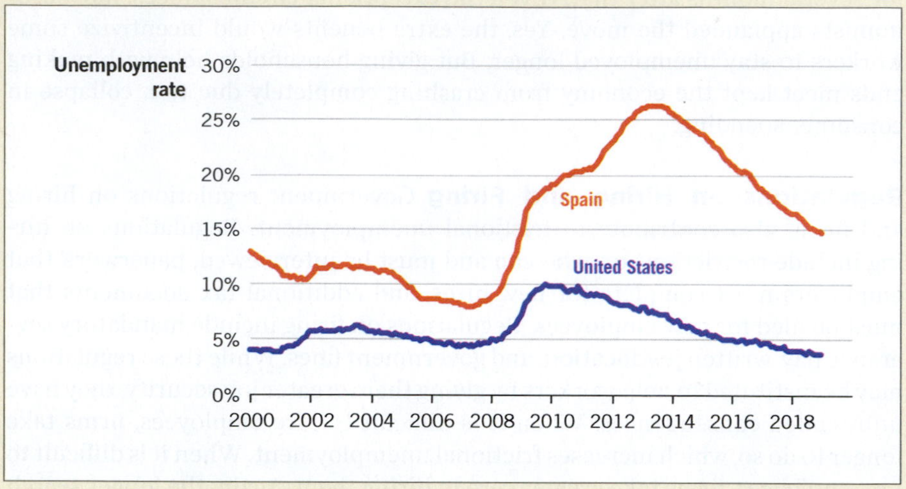

Cyclical Unemployment

Cyclical unemployment is unemployment caused by economic downturns.

The third type of unemployment, **cyclical unemployment**, is caused by recessions, or economic downturns. This type of unemployment generates the greatest concern among economists and policymakers. It is the most serious type of unemployment because it means that jobs are not available for many people who want to work. And while both structural and frictional unemployment are consistent with a growing, evolving economy, the root cause of cyclical unemployment is an unhealthy economy. Referring back to Figure 20.1, notice the spikes in unemployment during recessions. Those spikes are cyclical unemployment. Unlike structural unemployment and frictional unemployment, cyclical unemployment is not considered a natural type of unemployment.

The coronavirus-induced spike in the 2020 unemployment rate was considered cyclical unemployment. When the rate climbed to 14.7% in April, this was a symptom of the recession (a downturn in the business cycle). As business closures and social distancing persisted through 2020, the unemployment rate remained high.

During the coronavirus pandemic, passing out unemployment benefit application dorms became an "all hands on deck" situation for city workers in some municipalities. Here is the scene in Hialeah, Florida.

The Natural Rate of Unemployment

We have seen that there are three types of unemployment: structural, frictional, and cyclical. Figure 20.4 illustrates the relationship between these types of unemployment during both recessionary and healthy economic conditions. Notice that structural and frictional unemployment are always present, even when the economy is healthy and growing. During these healthy periods, cyclical unemployment disappears. During recessionary periods, cyclical unemployment emerges. It is also possible for structural and frictional unemployment to increase in economic

FIGURE 20.4

Three Types of Unemployment

Even during healthy economic periods, both structural and frictional unemployment are present. During recessions, cyclical unemployment appears. At the same time, structural and frictional unemployment may grow. As a result, the natural rate of unemployment increases.

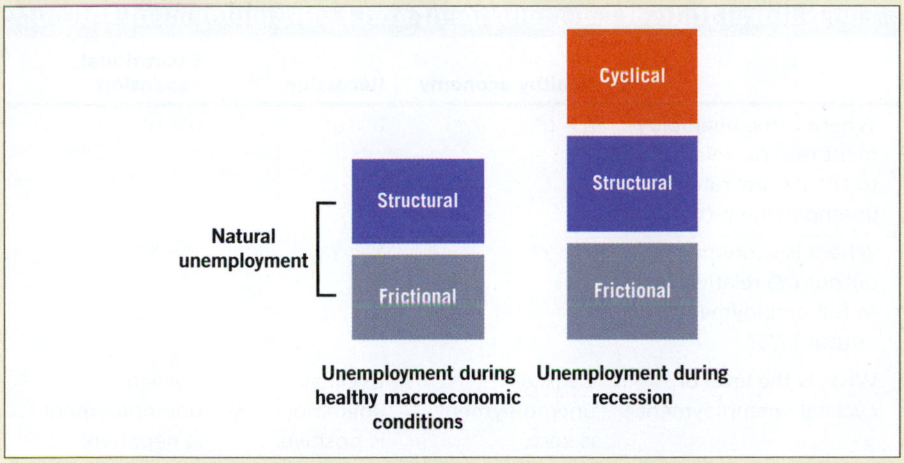

slowdowns. Structural unemployment might increase if the slowdown leads to changes in the structure of the economy: some jobs or industries may shrink permanently. Frictional unemployment might increase if government policies or other factors increase the job search time for unemployed workers.

Due to natural unemployment from structural and frictional factors, zero unemployment is not a realistic goal. If policymakers consistently strive for zero unemployment, they may take actions that harm the economy. For example, in the 1970s, policymakers tried to push unemployment down past natural levels by putting more and more money into the economy. This strategy led to other complications like inflation, but it failed to reduce unemployment.

Given that some unemployment is natural, it is helpful to identify the normal or expected level. The **natural rate of unemployment** (u^*) is the typical unemployment rate that occurs when the economy is growing normally. Maintaining this natural rate is a more appropriate goal for policymakers. Economists never know the exact numerical value of the natural rate, in part because it changes over time. Currently, most economists feel that the natural rate of unemployment in the United States is between 4% and 5%.

The **natural rate of unemployment** is the typical unemployment rate that occurs when the economy is growing normally.

As Table 20.1 summarizes, the actual unemployment rate at any particular time can equal, exceed, or fall below the economy's natural rate of unemployment. Let's think about each of these scenarios in turn. When the economy is healthy, the unemployment rate is equal to its natural rate (no cyclical unemployment exists). When the unemployment rate is equal to the natural rate, the output level produced in the economy is called **full-employment output** (Y^*). Recall from Chapter 19 that we measure economic output with real GDP (for the rest of the book, our shorthand notation is this: real GDP $= Y$). When the economy is in recession, cyclical unemployment materializes and the unemployment rate rises above the natural rate ($u > u^*$). At that point, we say the economy is producing at less than full-employment output levels ($Y < Y^*$).

Full-employment output, also called potential output or potential GDP, is the economy's output level when the unemployment rate is equal to the natural rate.

It is possible for the actual unemployment rate to fall below the natural rate ($u < u^*$). This can happen temporarily when the economy is expanding beyond its long-run capabilities. What conditions might bring about a lower-than-natural unemployment rate? Demand for output might be so high that firms keep their

TABLE 20.1

The Natural Rate of Unemployment and Full-Employment Output

	Healthy economy	Recession	Exceptional expansion
Where is the unemployment rate (u) relative to the natural rate of unemployment (u*)?	$u = u^*$	$u > u^*$	$u < u^*$
Where is economic output (Y) relative to full-employment output (Y*)?	$Y = Y^*$	$Y < Y^*$	$Y > Y^*$
What is the level of cyclical unemployment?	Cyclical unemployment is zero.	Cyclical unemployment is positive.	Cyclical unemployment is negative.

factories open for an extra shift and pay their workers overtime. When output is at greater-than-full-employment output ($Y > Y^*$) and the unemployment rate is less than the natural rate ($u < u^*$), resources are being employed at levels that are not sustainable in the long run. To visualize this situation, consider your own productivity as deadlines approach. Perhaps you have several exams in one week, so you decide to set aside most other activities and study 15 hours a day. Studying this much may yield good results, and you may be able to do it for a little while, but most of us cannot sustain such an effort over a long period.

Economists also refer to full-employment output (Y^*) as *potential output* or *potential GDP*. Unless additional changes are made, the economy cannot sustain an output greater than Y^* in the long run.

What Can We Learn from the Employment Data?

Who exactly counts as "unemployed"? For example, many college students don't have jobs, but that doesn't mean they are officially unemployed. Before examining historical unemployment rates in detail, we need to clarify how unemployment is measured in official employment statistics. In this section, we also look at some challenges of measuring unemployment.

The Unemployment Rate

Earlier in this chapter, we defined the unemployment rate (u) as the percentage of the labor force that is unemployed. We measure the unemployment rate as follows:

(EQUATION 20.1)

$$\text{unemployment rate} = u = \frac{\text{number unemployed}}{\text{labor force}} \times 100$$

PRACTICE WHAT YOU KNOW

Three Types of Unemployment: Which Type Is It?

QUESTION: In each of the following situations, decide whether the unemployment that occurs is a result of cyclical, frictional, or structural changes. Explain your responses.

a. Workers in a high-end restaurant are laid off when the establishment experiences a decline in demand during a recession.

c. Two hundred automobile workers lose their jobs as a result of a permanent reduction in the demand for automobiles.

c. A new college graduate takes three months to find his first job.

How long will you search for work?

ANSWERS:

a. *Cyclical changes.* Short-run fluctuations in the demand for workers often result from the ebb and flow of the business cycle. When the economy picks up, the laid-off workers may be rehired.

b. *Structural changes.* Since the changes described here are long-run in nature, these workers cannot expect their old jobs to return. Therefore, they must engage in retraining to reenter the labor force. Because they will be unable to find work until the retraining process is complete, the lost jobs represent a fundamental shift in the demand for labor.

c. *Frictional changes.* The recent college graduate has skills that the economy values, but finding an employer still takes time. This short-run job search process is a perfectly natural part of finding a job.

CHALLENGE QUESTION: A recently laid-off paralegal sees on the evening news that the unemployment rate stands at 3.8%. What category of economic change is *unlikely* to be the cause of the paralegal's unemployed status?

ANSWER: The paralegal's job loss is unlikely to be due to cyclical changes, because these occur during economic slowdowns. With the unemployment rate slightly below the natural level of 4% to 5%, the economy is clearly not in a slowdown.

Let's look at this definition more closely. To be officially unemployed, a person must be part of the labor force. A member of the **labor force** is defined as someone who is already employed or actively seeking work. If a jobless person has not sought a job in four weeks, that person is not counted in the labor force. In addition, only *work-eligible* people are counted. People who are institutionalized, children under the age of 16, and military workers are not considered in the official work-eligible population. Thus, some of the large groups of people not in the labor force are retirees, stay-at-home parents, people in jail, military personnel, children under age 16, and many full-time students. Together, these groups account for just under 25% of the U.S. population. Thus, only three in four Americans are work-eligible.

The **labor force** includes people who are already employed or actively seeking work and are part of the work-eligible population.

FIGURE 20.5

Unemployment in the United States, December 2021

To compute the unemployment rate, we divide the work-eligible population between those who are in the labor force and those who are not. To be counted in the labor force, a person must either have a job or be actively seeking work. The unemployment rate is the percentage of the labor force that is unemployed.

Source: U.S. Bureau of Labor Statistics.

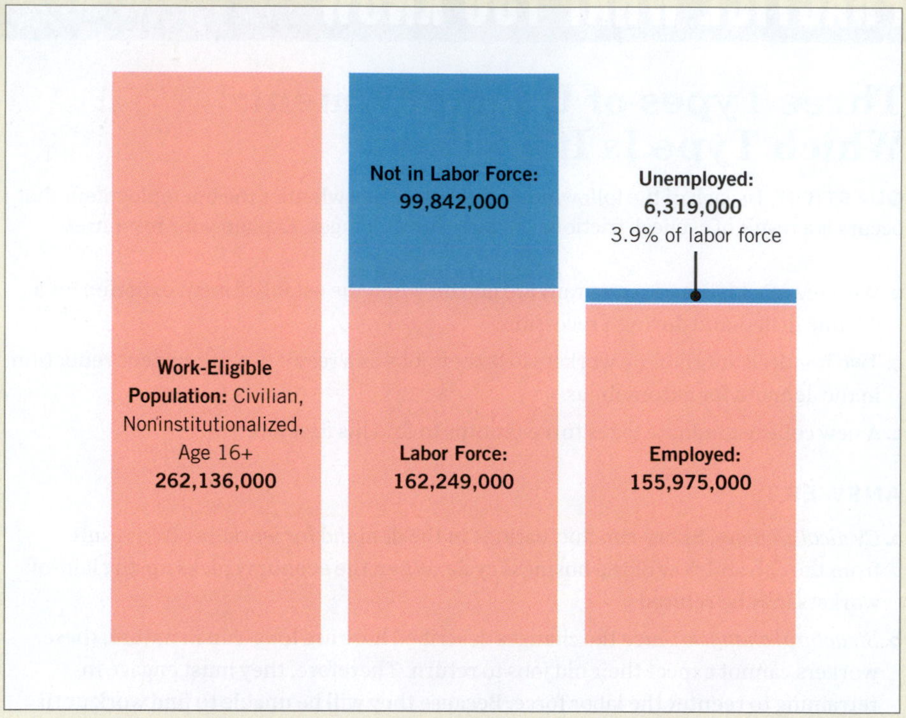

Figure 20.5 provides a breakdown of the work-eligible population (262,136,000) at the very end of 2021. Approximately two-thirds of this population was in the labor force (162,249,000), and of this number, 6,319,000 were unemployed. Plugging these numbers into Equation 20.1 yields

$$u = \frac{6{,}319{,}000}{162{,}249{,}000} = 3.9\%$$

HISTORICAL UNEMPLOYMENT RATES We now turn to historical data. One of our goals is to give you a good sense of normal conditions. It's also helpful to examine periods when particularly high unemployment rates prevailed. In Chapter 26, we discuss possible reasons for these difficult periods.

Figure 20.6 shows the U.S. unemployment rate from 1970 to 2021, with the blue vertical bars representing periods of recession. Notice how the U.S. unemployment rate consistently spikes during recessions, and how long it takes for unemployment to return to the natural level of 4% to 5% after each recession. But no matter how lengthy or significant an economic expansion (the nonshaded regions), some unemployment always remains. This unemployment exists because structural and frictional unemployment are always positive. For example, in November 2018, real GDP for the United States was expanding, and the unemployment rate (as Figure 20.6 shows) was 3.7%. That was the lowest U.S. unemployment rate since 1970—but still above zero.

FIGURE 20.6

U.S. Unemployment Rate and Recessions, 1970–2021

The U.S. unemployment rate consistently spikes during recessions, which are indicated here by the blue-shaded bars. During recessions, cyclical unemployment rises. During nonrecessionary periods, the unemployment rate drops to (and below) the natural rate of 4% to 5%, with only structural and frictional unemployment remaining.

Source: U.S. Bureau of Labor Statistics.

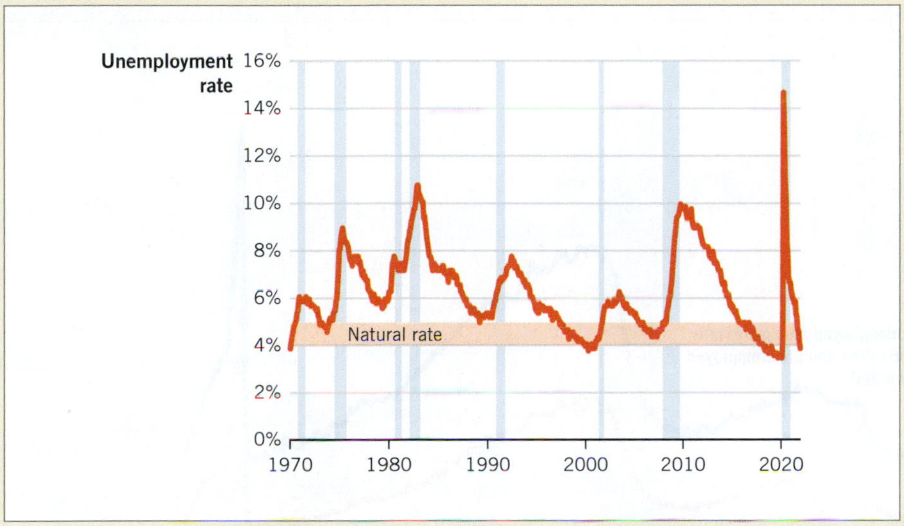

SHORTCOMINGS OF THE UNEMPLOYMENT RATE The unemployment rate, released monthly, is a timely and consistent indicator of the health of the macroeconomy. However, it is not a perfect economic indicator. We now consider two shortcomings in unemployment data.

One shortcoming of the unemployment rate is related to exclusions in the data. People who are unemployed for a long time may just stop looking for work—not because they don't want a job, but because they quit looking. When they stop searching, they fall out of the labor force and no longer count as unemployed; in other words, they are excluded from the statistics. **Marginally attached workers** are defined as those who are not working, have looked for a job in the past 12 months and are willing to work, but have not sought employment in the past four weeks.

Marginally attached workers are not working, have looked for a job in the past 12 months, and are willing to work, but have not sought employment in the past four weeks.

Another group not properly accounted for is composed of **underemployed workers**, defined as workers who have part-time jobs but who would like to have full-time jobs. These workers are not counted as unemployed. Yet both of these groups grow during economic downturns. Figure 20.7 shows the official U.S. unemployment rate (the Bureau of Labor Statistics uses the label "U-3" for the standard unemployment rate) for the period 2000–2021 versus an alternative measure that includes marginally attached and underemployed workers (this measure is called "U-6"). Not only is the alternative measure much higher than the unemployment rate, but the difference expands significantly during and after recessions (the blue vertical bars).

Underemployed workers have part-time jobs but would prefer to work full-time.

FIGURE 20.7

A Broader Measure of U.S. Labor Market Problems, 2000–2021

The orange line includes workers who are unemployed given the standard definitions (U-3). The blue line represents a broader measure of labor market problems (U-6) and includes marginally attached and underemployed workers. The gap between this broader measure and the official unemployment rate grows when the economy enters a recession.

Source: U.S. Bureau of Labor Statistics.

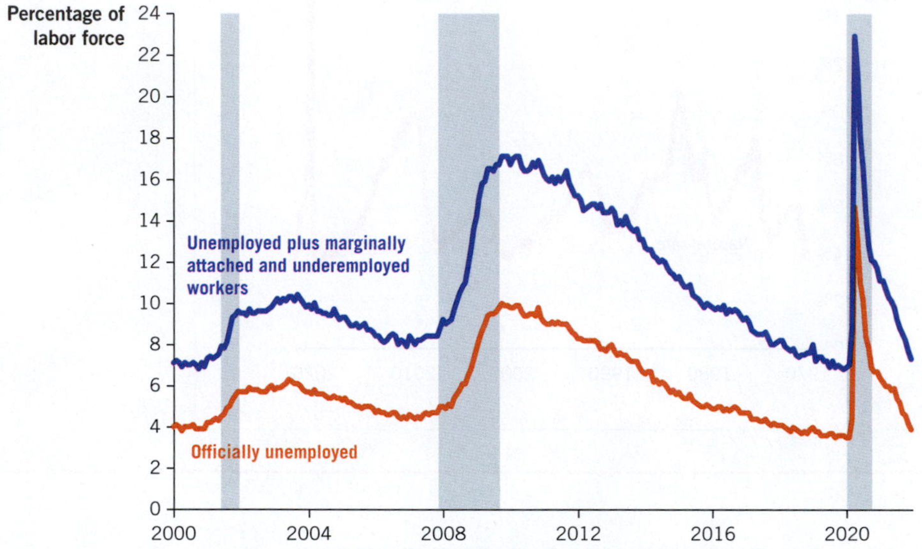

A second shortcoming of the official measurement of unemployment is that it does not specify who is unemployed or how long they have been out of work. Are people unemployed for short spells, or is their joblessness long-term? If most unemployment is short-term, we might not be as concerned with a higher unemployment rate, because it indicates that unemployment is temporary rather than a long-term problem for workers. To help fill in this part of the unemployment picture, the Bureau of Labor Statistics keeps an alternative measure of unemployment that tracks how long workers have been unemployed.

Table 20.2 shows the duration of unemployment in the United States in January 2010 and January 2019. The year 2010 came just after a long recessionary period in the U.S. economy. At that time, more than 56.7% of total unemployment was long-term (15 weeks or more), with 39.8% of those unemployed out of work 27 weeks or longer. In contrast, consider 2019, nearly a decade after the recession finished. By 2019, 68.9% of unemployment was short-term, and only 31.1% long-term. So when unemployment rates rise, the duration of unemployment often increases too.

TABLE 20.2

Duration of Unemployment in the United States, 2010 and 2019

	Percentage of total unemployed	
Duration	**2010**	**2019**
Short-term	44.4%	68.9%
Less than 5 weeks	21.5	38.5
5–14 weeks	22.8	30.4
Long-term	56.7	31.1
15–26 weeks	15.9	12.7
27 weeks or longer	39.8	18.4

Source: Bureau of Economic Analysis.

Other Labor Market Indicators

Macroeconomists use several other indicators to get a more complete picture of the labor market. These include the labor force participation rate and statistics on gender and race.

LABOR FORCE PARTICIPATION The size of the labor force is itself an important macroeconomic statistic. To see why, consider two hypothetical island economies, each with an overall population of one million people. These two islands, called 2K and 2K21, are identical except in the size of their labor forces. Recall that the labor force includes all people who are employed or actively searching for work. On the first island, 2K, the labor force is 670,000, or about two-thirds of the total population. On the second island, 2K21, the labor force is just 615,000 workers, even though 2K21's overall population is the same as 2K's. This means that island 2K has 55,000 more workers to produce goods and services for a population that is exactly the same size as 2K21's. We can measure the difference between these two islands with the **labor force participation rate (LFPR)**, which is the portion of the work-eligible population that is in the labor force:

The **labor force participation rate** is the percentage of the work-eligible population that is in the labor force.

$$\text{labor force participation rate} = \frac{\text{labor force}}{\text{work-eligible population}} \times 100$$

On island 2K, the labor force participation rate is 67%; but on 2K21, the rate is just 61.5%.

As it turns out, these are the labor force participation rates for the U.S. economy in the years 2000 and 2021. Figure 20.8 shows the evolution of the labor force participation rate in the United States from 1995 to 2021. You can see that it peaks at 67.3% in 2000 but eventually settles at around 63%, before briefly plunging as low as 60.2% at the start of the coronavirus recession. All else equal, this means that in 2021 there were fewer people working relative to the overall U.S. population than in any of the previous years shown, including 2000. Economists aren't sure about all of the reasons for this decline in the LFPR, but it isn't good news for the economy, as it means that fewer people are working to produce the nation's output. A low labor force participation rate implies untapped

FIGURE 20.8

U.S. Labor Force Participation Rate, 1995–2021

The labor force participation rate in the United States peaked at 67.3% in 2000 but has fallen significantly since then. While labor force participation seems to have leveled off around 63% for most of the last decade, it fell to just 60.2% in the early part of the coronavirus recession.

Source: U.S. Bureau of Labor Statistics.

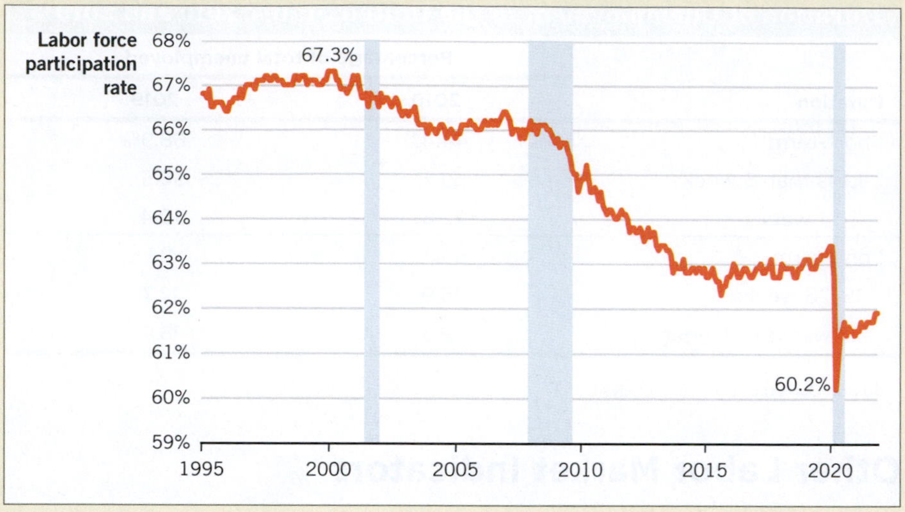

production potential: there are people that could be working but for various reasons are not.

The labor force participation rate in the United States is likely to fall even further over the coming decades, due to the aging of the labor force. The term "baby boom" refers to the period after World War II when U.S. birthrates temporarily rose dramatically. The U.S. Census Bureau pegs this period at 1946–1964. There is now a bubble in the U.S. population known as the "baby boomers." (This might include your parents.) But as the oldest baby boomers are now retiring, the labor force participation rate will naturally fall, all else equal. This means fewer workers contributing to GDP. At the same time, federal expenses allocated toward retirees—for example, Social Security and Medicare—will rise. As you can see in Figure 20.8, these demographic changes are coming at a time when the U.S. labor force participation rate is already declining.

GENDER AND RACE LABOR FORCE STATISTICS Figure 20.9 shows U.S. labor force participation rates for male and female workers, starting in 1950. As you can see, the composition of the labor force today is markedly different from that of two generations ago. Not only are more women working (from 33% in 1950 to 58% in 2021), but male labor force participation has fallen dramatically (from over 86% in 1950 to just 69% in 2021). Men still remain more likely to participate in the labor force than women, but the participation gap has significantly narrowed.

Men are more likely to stay at home today than they were two generations ago.

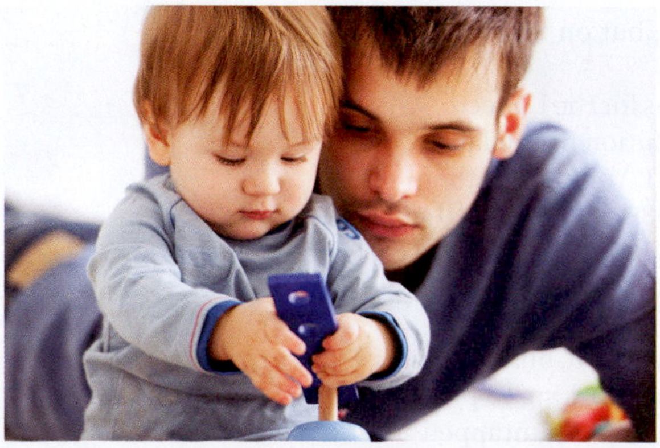

How do we explain the fact that fewer males are working? A number of reasons account for the decline. Men are living longer, acquiring more education, and spending more time helping to raise families. Because men who are retired, in school, or staying at home to care for children are not counted as part of the labor force, the labor force participation rate for males is lower.

FIGURE 20.9

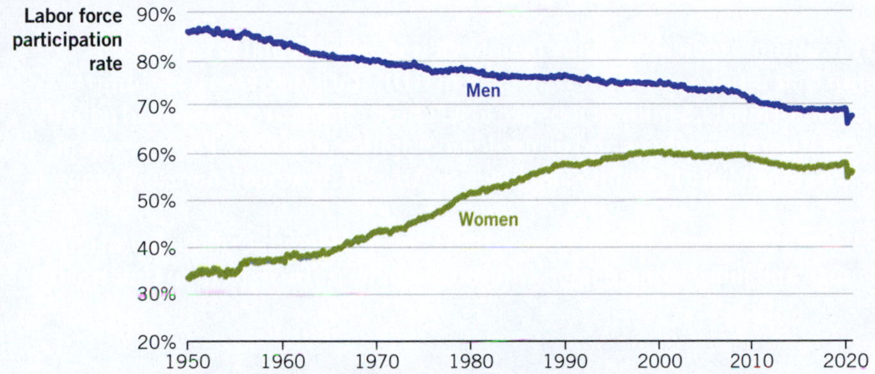

Trends in U.S. Labor Force Participation, 1950–2020

Over the past 70 years, the composition of the U.S. labor force has shifted drastically. While more women have entered the labor force, the percentage of men in the labor force has dropped from almost 90% to under 70%.

Source: U.S. Bureau of Labor Statistics.

TABLE 20.3

U.S. Unemployment and Labor Force Participation Rates by Gender and Race, February 2022

Group	Unemployment rate	Labor force participation rate
Overall	3.8%	62.3%
Overall (age 16+)		
Black males	6.8	65.7
Black females	6.4	59.2
White males	3.3	68.5
White females	3.4	56.0
Teenagers (age 16–19)		
Black males	17.5	27.2
Black females	18.0	24.8
White males	10.2	39.2
White females	8.5	38.7

Source: U.S. Bureau of Labor Statistics.

Unemployment rates also vary widely across age and race. Table 20.3 breaks down these statistics by age, race, and gender. Looking first at unemployment rates, in February 2022, the overall unemployment rate was 3.8%. But the rate ranges from a low of 3.3% for white males to a high of 18% for black teenage females. Notice also that labor force participation rates are very low among teenagers, with white teenagers at about 39% but black females at 25%.

-DATA SNAPSHOT-

Unemployment and the Labor Force

The unemployment rate is a primary economic indicator. Many people view it as particularly important because it measures a level of hardship that is not necessarily conveyed in GDP statistics. Every 1% jump in the U.S. unemployment rate means an additional 1.5 million jobs are lost. These effects are not spread equally over society, and there can be great variation across races and other demographic categories. For an example of a demographic comparison, rates are shown here for white and black or African American men and women.

The labor force participation rate tells a vivid story about the United States over the course of the twentieth and early twenty-first centuries. As more and more women have entered, men have also exited, so that the two rates have converged.

Unemployment Rate by Demographic, 1972–2021

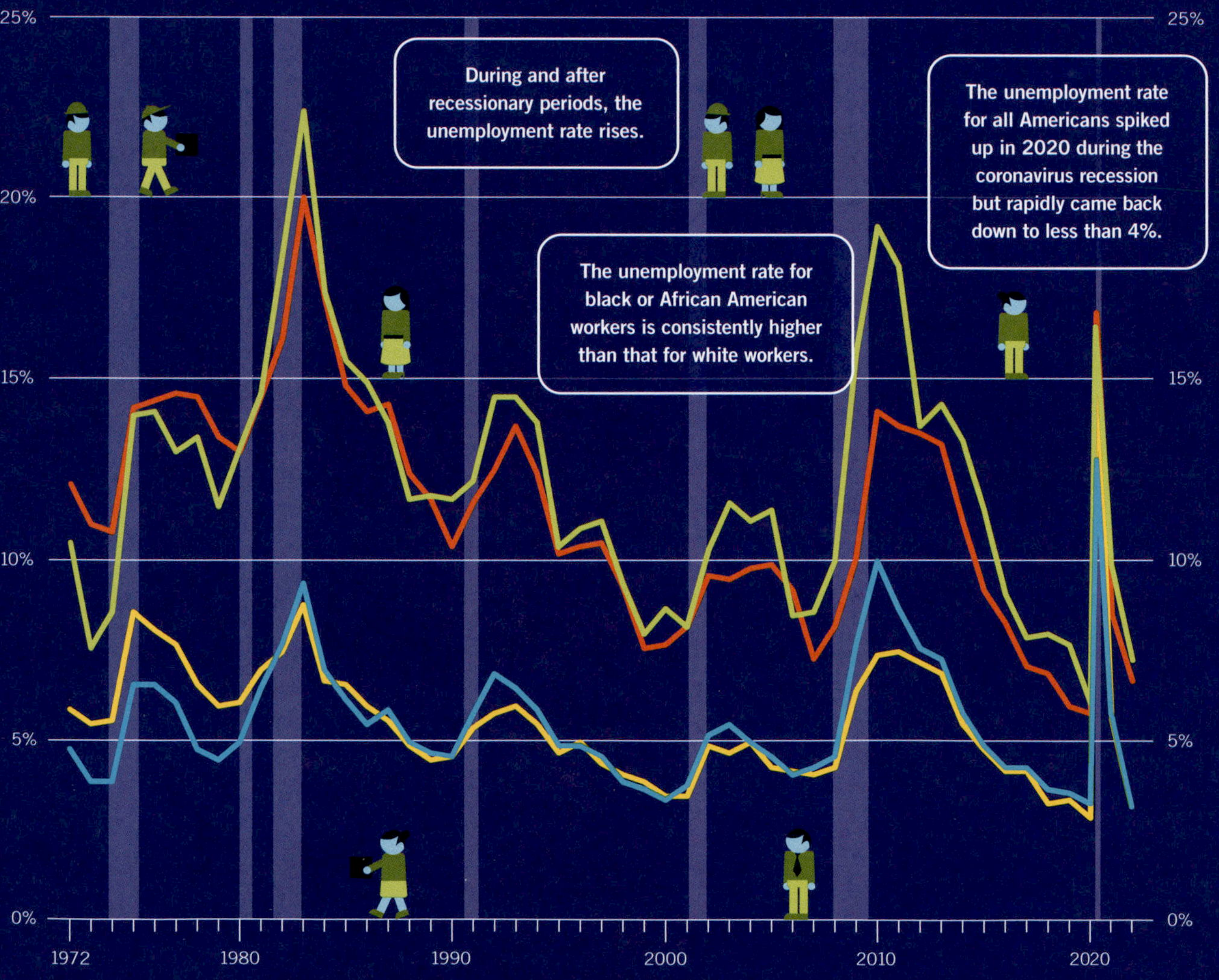

25%
20%
15%
10%
5%
0%
1972
1980
1990
2000
2010
2020
During and after recessionary periods, the unemployment rate rises.
The unemployment rate for black or African American workers is consistently higher than that for white workers.
The unemployment rate for all Americans spiked up in 2020 during the coronavirus recession but rapidly came back down to less than 4%.

REVIEW QUESTIONS

- In the Great Recession of the late 2007–2009, roughly how many percentage points did the unemployment rate of black or African American men rise?
- How do you explain the labor force participation rate changes between men and women?

Labor Force Participation Rate by Demographic, 1972–2021

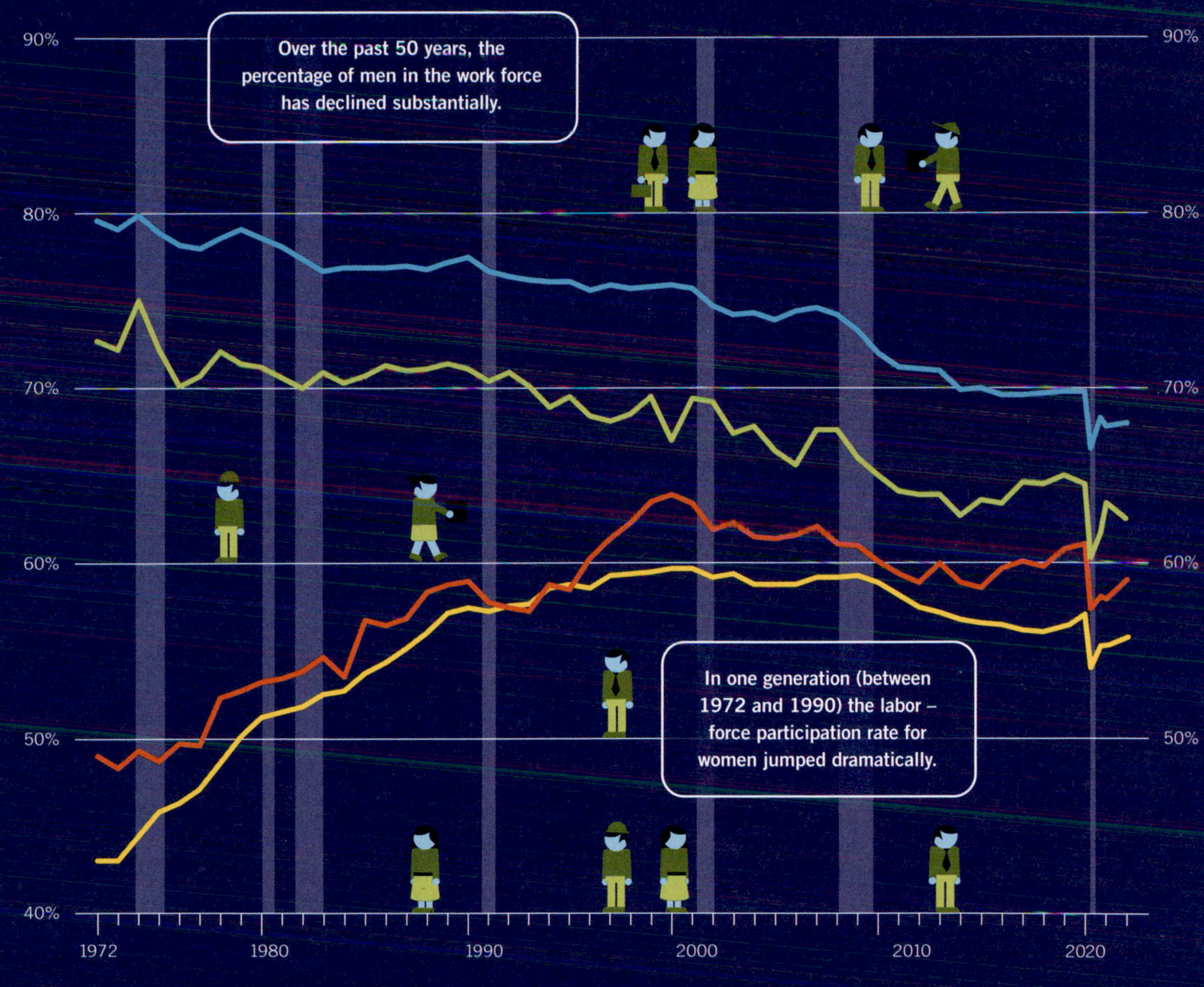

Source: Bureau of Labor Statistics.

PRACTICE WHAT YOU KNOW

By the summer of 2020, Covid had put millions of Americans out of work.

Unemployment and Labor Force Participation Rates: Can You Compute the Rates?

The following data are from April 2020 in the United States. Note that this was the worst month of the COVID-19 recession.

Work-eligible population = 259,896,000
Labor force = 156,478,000
Employed = 133,370,000

QUESTION: Using the data, how would you compute the number of unemployed workers, the unemployment rate, and the labor force participation rate for the U.S. in April 2020?

ANSWER: The unemployment rate is the total number of unemployed as a percentage of the labor force. First, determine the number of unemployed as the total labor force minus the number of employed:

$$\text{unemployed} = \text{labor force} - \text{employed} = 23{,}108{,}000$$

Use this information to determine the unemployment rate, which is the number of unemployed divided by the labor force:

$$\text{unemployed} \div \text{labor force} = 14.8\%$$

Take a moment to consider just how large that unemployment rate was, in the midst of the economic shutdown in April 2020. Just two months earlier, the unemployment rate was below 4%!

Finally, the labor force participation rate is the labor force as a percentage of the work-eligible population:

$$\begin{aligned}\text{labor force participation rate} &= \text{labor force} \div \text{working-eligible population} \\ &= 156{,}478{,}000 \div 259{,}896{,}000 \\ &= 60.2\%\end{aligned}$$

Conclusion

This chapter began with the observation that many industries decline as an economy changes and grows, and that these changes inevitably lead to some unemployment. But we have also seen that cyclical unemployment is a reliable indicator of macroeconomic problems. Whenever the unemployment rate is above the natural rate, there is certainly room for improvement. And this also means that policymakers shouldn't aim for zero unemployment—mainly

ECONOMICS *for* LIFE

Finish Your Degree!

- Getting your bachelor's degree greatly reduces your chance of unemployment.
- Getting a professional degree typically leads to big jumps in earnings.

College students often fret over which major will increase their chances of getting a good job. Your major certainly matters for getting the job you want, and it may also affect your future income. But the figure below shows just how important it is to finish your degree, no matter what your major may be.

The chart plots unemployment rates by level of educational attainment. The data shown here are from 2021, but you can find current data by visiting the Bureau of Labor Statistics (BLS) at www.bls.gov. Notice how the unemployment rate drops as the level of educational attainment increases. Your choice of major certainly affects your future earnings, but this table shows unemployment rates across all majors. In particular, look at the big drop in the unemployment rate for those who complete a bachelor's degree or higher. The unemployment rate is about half that of those who earn only a high school diploma. The most important major, it turns out, is the one that holds your interest long enough to guarantee that you graduate!

Want to give yourself the best chance of getting a job?

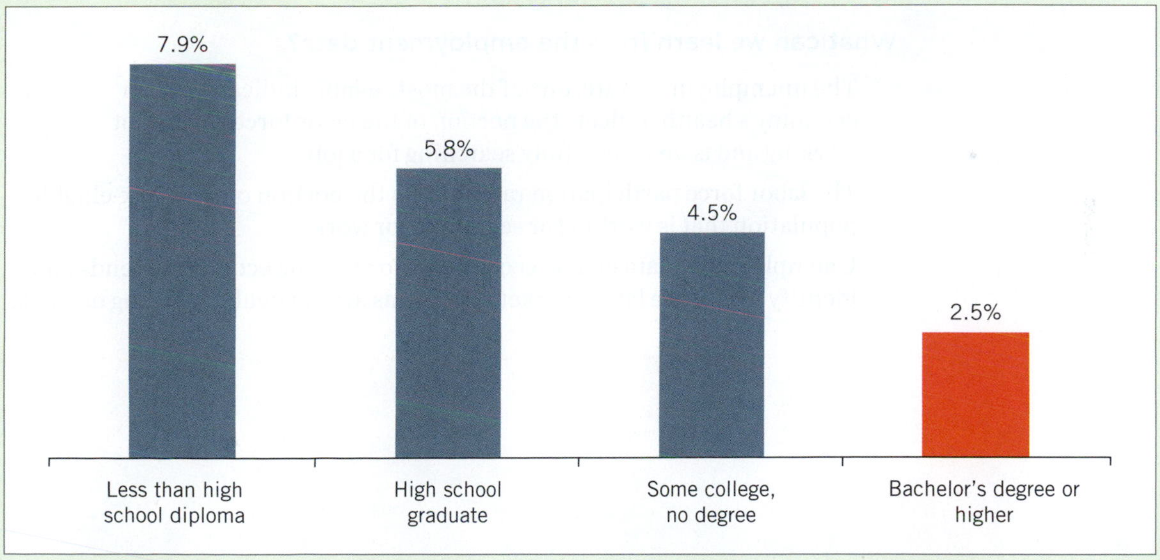

U.S. unemployment rate by educational attainment, 2021.

because some unemployment is natural. People pay attention to the unemployment rate because it can affect them personally, but economists monitor the unemployment rate as an important macroeconomic indicator. In addition to real GDP, we use the unemployment rate to assess the position of the economy relative to the business cycle. Because employment data are released more frequently than GDP data, they offer a timely snapshot of current conditions. For this reason, the first Friday of every month, when the employment data are released, tends to be a nervous day, especially during turbulent economic times.

In the next chapter, we will look more closely at a third important macroeconomic indicator—inflation. ✷

ANSWERING *the* BIG QUESTIONS

What are the major reasons for unemployment?

- There are three types of unemployment: structural unemployment, frictional unemployment, and cyclical unemployment.
- Structural unemployment is caused by changes in the structure of the economy that make some jobs obsolete.
- Frictional unemployment is affected by information availability and government policies.
- Cyclical unemployment is caused by recessionary conditions that eliminate jobs during a downturn in the business cycle.

What can we learn from the employment data?

- The unemployment rate, one of the most reliable indicators of an economy's health, reflects the portion of the labor force that is not working and is unsuccessfully searching for a job.
- The labor force participation rate reflects the portion of the work-eligible population that is working or searching for work.
- Unemployment data enable economists to examine economic trends and identify where the labor market conditions are particularly strong or weak.

CHAPTER PROBLEMS

Concepts You Should Know

creative destruction (p. 646)
cyclical unemployment (p. 652)
frictional unemployment (p. 648)
full-employment output (p. 653)
labor force (p. 655)
labor force participation rate (p. 659)
marginally attached workers (p. 657)
natural rate of unemployment (p. 653)
structural unemployment (p. 646)
underemployed workers (p. 657)
unemployment (p. 645)
unemployment insurance (p. 650)
unemployment rate (p. 645)

Questions for Review

1. Until the late 1960s, most economists assumed that less unemployment was always preferable to more unemployment. Define and explain the two types of unemployment that are consistent with a dynamic, growing economy.

2. Is there any unemployment when an economy has "full employment"? If so, what type(s)?

3. The news media almost always bemoans the current state of the U.S. economy. How does the most recent unemployment rate relate to the long-run average?

4. What type of unemployment is affected when online job search engines reduce the time necessary for job searches? Does this outcome affect the natural rate of unemployment? If so, how?

5. What groups does the Bureau of Labor Statistics count in the labor force? Explain why the official unemployment rate tends to underestimate the level of labor market problems.

6. Does the duration of unemployment matter? Explain your answer.

7. What does an increase in the natural rate of unemployment imply about each of the three types of unemployment?

8. What can cause an increase in frictional unemployment? Give at least one example. What can cause an increase in structural unemployment? Give at least one example.

Study Problems (*∗solved at the end of the section*)

1. In his song "Allentown," Billy Joel sings about the demise of the steel and coal industries in Pennsylvania. Why do you think the loss of manufacturing jobs was so difficult on the workers in areas like Allentown and parts of the Midwest where manufacturing was once the largest employer? What type of unemployment is the song about?

2. In January 2019, the U.S. economy added 302,000 new jobs. Yet the unemployment rate rose from 3.9% to 4.0%. How is this possible?

3. A country with a civilian (work-eligible) population of 90,000 (all over age 16) has 70,000 employed and 10,000 unemployed persons. Of the unemployed, 5,000 are frictionally unemployed and another 3,000 are structurally unemployed. On the basis of these data, answer the following questions.

a. What is the size of the labor force?
b. What is the unemployment rate?
c. What is the natural rate of unemployment for this country?
d. Is this economy in recession or expansion? Explain.

4. Visit www.bls.gov and search through the tables on unemployment to answer the following questions.

a. What is the current national unemployment rate for the United States?
b. What is the current unemployment rate among people of your age, sex, and race?

5. Consider a country with 300 million residents, a labor force of 150 million, and 10 million unemployed. Answer the following questions.

a. What is the labor force participation rate?
b. What is the unemployment rate?
c. If 5 million of the unemployed become discouraged and stop looking for work, what is the new unemployment rate?
d. Suppose instead that 30 million jobs are created, attracting 20 million new people into the labor force. What would be the new rates for labor force participation and unemployment?

* **6.** Consider the following hypothetical data from the peaceable nation of Hooland, where there is no military, the entire population is over the age of 16, and no one is institutionalized for any reason. Then answer the questions.

Classification	Number of people
Total population	200 million
Employed	141 million
Full-time students	10 million
Homemakers	25 million
Retired persons	15 million
Seeking work but without a job	9 million

a. What is the unemployment rate in Hooland?
b. What is the labor force participation rate in Hooland?

For questions c through f: assume that 15 million Hoolandian homemakers begin seeking jobs, and that 10 million find jobs.

c. Now what is the rate of unemployment in Hooland?
d. How does this change affect cyclical unemployment in Hooland?
e. What will happen to per capita GDP?
f. Is the economy of Hooland better off after the homemakers enter the labor force? Explain your response.

* **7.** In each of the following situations, determine whether or not the person would be considered unemployed.

a. A 15-year-old offers to pet-sit, but no one hires her.
b. A college graduate spends the summer after graduation touring Europe before starting a job search.
c. A part-time teacher works only two days a week, even though he would like a full-time job.
d. An automobile worker becomes discouraged about the prospects for future employment and decides to stop looking for work.

* **8.** The table below presents real data from the U.S. labor market in January 2021. Fill in any numbers that are missing.

Civilian, noninstitutionalized, 16+ population	
Labor force	
Employed	150,031,000
Unemployed	
Labor force participation rate	61.4%
Unemployment rate	6.3%

9. The table below shows employment data for the imaginary country of Karakara in 2018.

Classification	2018
Total population	100
Employed	57
Full-time students	14
Homemakers	16
Retired persons	10
Seeking work, but without a job	3

a. How many people are in the 2018 labor force for Karakara?
b. What is the 2018 unemployment rate?

Following a number of very prosperous years, Karakara entered a recession in 2019. As a result, many companies went out of business and 12 people lost their jobs.

c. Assuming everyone who lost their job immediately began to look for a new job, what was the unemployment rate and the labor force participation rate in 2019?

d. Did cyclical unemployment go up, down, or stay the same in 2019?

Classification	2020
Total population	100
Employed	48
Full-time students	18
Homemakers	20
Retired persons	12
Seeking work, but without a job	2

The economy began to recover in 2020. The second table shows the employment data in 2020. As you can see, some of the people who lost their jobs during the recession had trouble finding new jobs, and decided to go back to school, or to become homemakers.

e. What is the economic term used to describe the people who gave up looking for a job?

f. What was the unemployment rate and the labor force participation rate in 2020?

g. Imagine that, as the recovery continues, some of the people who gave up looking for work in 2020 decided to reenter the workforce. In particular, suppose that in 2021, 10 people decided to reenter the labor force, and three of them find jobs. What is the new unemployment rate and the labor force participation rate? Write your answer, in percentage terms, in the table below.

New unemployment rate	________
Labor force participation rate	________

Solved Problems

6. a. The unemployment rate in Hooland is 6%. To calculate the unemployment rate, use:

unemployment rate = u = (number of unemployed ÷ labor force) × 100

- The number of unemployed: 9 million
- Labor force can be calculated in two ways:
  - Employed plus unemployed:

    141 million + 9 million = 150 million

  - Total population minus those not in labor force (students, homemakers, retirees):

    200 million − (10 million + 25 million + 15 million) = 150 million

Note: Because the total population is only composed of noninstitutionalized civilians over the age of 16, we can use this number (200 million) as the relevant population.

unemployment rate = u = (number of unemployed ÷ labor force) × 100 = (9 ÷ 150) × 100 = 6%

b. The labor force participation rate in Hooland is 75%. To calculate the labor force participation rate, use:

labor force participation rate = (labor force ÷ population) × 100

- Labor force (calculated above): 150 million
- Population: 200 million

labor force participation rate = (labor force ÷ population) × 100 = (150 ÷ 200) × 100 = 75%

c. Now the rate of unemployment in Hooland is 8.5%. To calculate the new unemployment rate, use the same equation as above. However, the figures have changed with new entrants to the labor force:

- The new number of unemployed:

  9 million + 5 million = 14 million

- The new number of employed:

$$141 \text{ million} + 10 \text{ million} = 151 \text{ million}$$

- The new labor force can be calculated in three ways:
  - Previous labor force plus new entrants:

$$150 \text{ million} + 15 \text{ million} = 165 \text{ million}$$

  - Employed plus unemployed:

$$151 \text{ million} + 14 \text{ million} = 165 \text{ million}$$

  - Total population minus those not in labor force (students, homemakers, retirees):

$$200 \text{ million} - (10 \text{ million} + 10 \text{ million} + 15 \text{ million}) = 165 \text{ million}$$

$$\text{unemployment rate} = u = (\text{number of unemployed} \div \text{labor force}) \times 100 = (14 \div 165) \times 100 = 8.5\%$$

Note: Even though the number of employed increased, because the size of the labor force increased by more, the unemployment rate has increased.

d. The change does not affect cyclical unemployment, which is generally associated with economic downturns. Instead, the entrance of new workers into the labor force represents a change in the labor force participation rate. In general, the entry of new workers to the labor force is associated with good economic times. Because most of the homemakers were able to find jobs, we can conclude that the economy of Hooland is growing.

e. With an increase in the number of employed workers, total output in the economy will increase. However, the size of the population has not changed. Thus, per capita GDP will increase as a result of the change.

f. Hooland has a stronger economy with more working homemakers. Even though the unemployment rate has increased as a result of many homemakers entering the labor force, the increase in unemployment is not the result of economic downturn; rather, it is a sign of a growing economy. Hooland has a stronger economy with higher GDP per capita and a greater labor force participation rate as a result of this change.

7. a. No. The relevant population used to measure unemployment and the labor force comprises work-eligible individuals 16 years of age or older. This 15-year-old is not part of the relevant population, so she is not considered unemployed.

b. No. To be counted in the unemployment statistics, an individual must have made efforts to get a job in the past four weeks. This college graduate is not actively seeking work during the summer, so he is not counted as an unemployed individual.

c. No. This part-time teacher is underemployed because he would prefer a full-time position, but under the unemployment rate measurements he is considered to be employed.

d. No. The automobile worker is a marginally attached worker if he has searched for work in the past year but stopped looking for work over four weeks ago. However, since he is not actively looking for work now, he is no longer considered part of the labor force.

8. First, determine the number in the labor force. We know that the labor force is composed of the employed and the unemployed. We also know that the unemployment rate is 5.7% of the labor force, so

$$100\% = 5.7\% + \text{portion of the labor force that is employed}$$

This means that the portion employed is 94.3%. If 94.3% of the labor force is employed, and the number employed is 148,201,000, then we can determine the size of the labor force as

$$\frac{148{,}201{,}000}{\text{labor force}} = 0.943$$

Therefore,

labor force = 157,159,067 (rounding to the nearest whole number)

Next, we find the size of the civilian, noninstitutional, 16+ population (pop). We know that

$$\text{labor force participation rate} = \frac{\text{labor force}}{\text{pop}}$$

and we already know the labor force participation rate and the labor force. Therefore,

$$62.9\% = \frac{157{,}159{,}067}{\text{pop}}$$

$$\text{pop} = \frac{157{,}159{,}067}{0.629}$$

$$\text{population} = \underline{249{,}855{,}432}$$

Finally, we can now solve for the number unemployed because we know the total size of the labor force and the number employed:

$$\text{labor force} = \text{employed} + \text{unemployed}$$

$$157{,}159{,}067 = 148{,}201{,}000 + \text{unemployed}$$

$$\text{unemployed} = \underline{8{,}958{,}067}$$

CHAPTER

21

The Price Level and Inflation

High Inflation Can Be Catastrophic for an Economy.

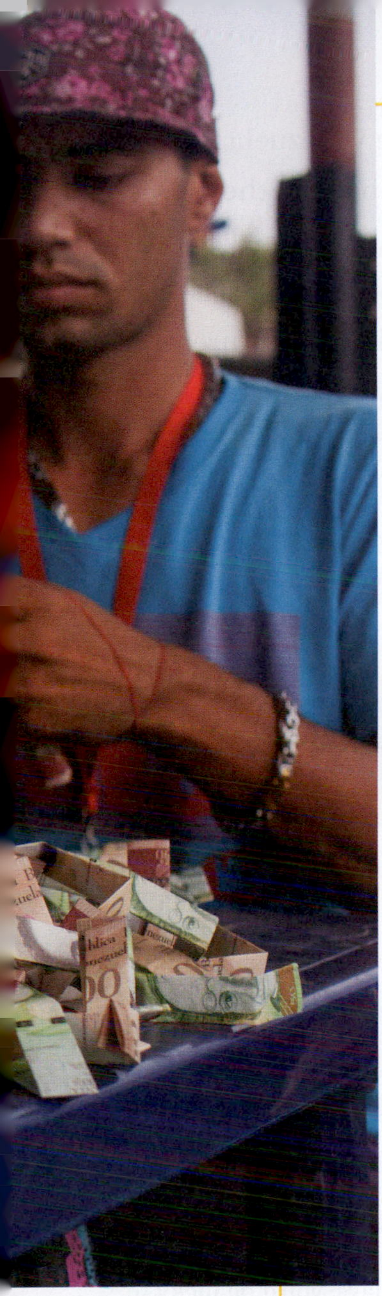

In 2018, the cost of a dozen eggs in Venezuela climbed to 8 million bolivars, up from 140 bolivars just four years earlier. But egg prices weren't the only problem—overall prices rose at a rate of 1 million percent in 2018. The Venezuela inflation disaster began in 2014, when the price of oil plunged on the world market. Oil represents about three-fourths of the value of all Venezuelan exports. When oil's price fell, the Venezuelan government desperately needed funds, and so it started printing bolivars—lots and lots of bolivars. Over the ensuing years, trying to stay ahead of inflation and expectations, it accelerated the growth of the supply of bolivars, and this led to more and more inflation. For Venezuelan citizens, it was a disaster. More than half the population earns the minimum wage. But this minimum wage, also set by the government, was just 180 million bolivars per month in 2018. This meant that an average citizen would have had to work a day and a half just to buy a dozen eggs.

In most of the world, the situation is nowhere like in Venezuela. In 2021, overall inflation in the United States rose above 5% for only the second time in the last thirty years. While this may seem high, as recently as the early 1980s, the annual overall U.S. inflation rate was close to 15%. And 15% is

When the price level rises at 1 million percent per year, paper currency becomes almost worthless. In Venezuela, people have found other creative uses for their bolivars.

At the end of 2021, the U.S. government reported a 12.5% increase over the previous 12 months in the price of meat/poultry/fish and eggs, a pricing category it monitors that is made up of these food staples.

low compared with rates seen in a country like Venezuela. Still, no one in the United States wants to go back to the days of 15% inflation, and most economists are concerned about rising rates. Inflation certainly has been a problem in the past, and there is no guarantee that we are safe from it in the future.

High inflation can cause the destruction of wealth across an entire economy, and equally important, unpredictable inflation can wreak havoc within an economy—as we will see in the pages ahead.

· BIG QUESTIONS ·

- How is inflation measured?
- What problems does inflation bring?
- What is the cause of inflation?

How Is Inflation Measured?

You might notice price changes on a shopping trip or when you see a reference to prices in an old book or movie. For example, in the 1960 movie *Psycho*, a hotel room for one night was priced at just $10. Nowadays, you'd be lucky to get a room for ten times that amount. In Chapter 19, we defined inflation as the growth in the overall level of prices in an economy. When overall prices rise, this affects our budget; it limits how much we can buy with our income. On the other hand, if overall prices fall, our income goes further and we can buy more goods.

Imagine an annual inflation rate of 100%. At this rate, prices double every year. How would this affect your life? Would it change what you buy? Would it change your savings plans? Would it change the salary you negotiate with your employer? Yes, it would change your life on a daily basis. Now imagine that prices double *every day*. This was the situation in Zimbabwe in 2008, when the inflation rate reached almost 80 billion percent per month! This is an example of what economists call *hyperinflation*, an extremely high rate of inflation, and it completely stymies economic activity. In Zimbabwe, for example, average citizens could barely afford necessities like bread and eggs.

Figure 21.1 shows inflation in the United States from 1970 to 2021. Over this long time range, the average inflation rate was 4%. Beginning in the early 1980s, inflation rates in the U.S. came down and averaged about 2% for many years. In 2021, the inflation rate climbed above 7%, to its highest level since 1982. Looking again at Figure 21.1, you can see a brief spell of deflation in 2009. **Deflation** occurs when overall prices fall; it is negative inflation. The 2009 deflation was driven largely by falling energy prices at the beginning of a recession.

Zimbabweans show off devalued currency at a 2008 political rally. How is it possible to have 1 billion dollars and not be able to afford dinner?

Measuring inflation is straightforward but requires precision. Inflation is *not* defined as an increase in any one particular price—it is an increase in the overall price level. Prices don't all move together; some prices fall even when most others rise. In addition, some prices affect consumers more than others. A 10% increase in housing prices is significantly more painful than a 10% increase in hot dog prices. So before we can measure inflation, we have to agree on what prices to monitor and how much weight we'll give to each price. In the United States, the Bureau of Labor Statistics (BLS) measures and reports inflation data. In this section, we describe how the BLS estimates the overall price level. (Remember from Chapter 19 that the price level is an index of the average prices of goods and services throughout an economy.) The BLS's goals are to (1) determine the prices of all the goods and services a typical consumer buys and (2) identify how much of a typical consumer's budget is spent on these particular items.

Deflation occurs when overall prices fall.

The Consumer Price Index (CPI)

We start with the most common price level used to compute inflation. The **consumer price index (CPI)** is the measure of the price level based on the consumption patterns of a typical consumer. When you read or hear about inflation

The **consumer price index (CPI)** is a measure of the price level based on the consumption patterns of a typical consumer.

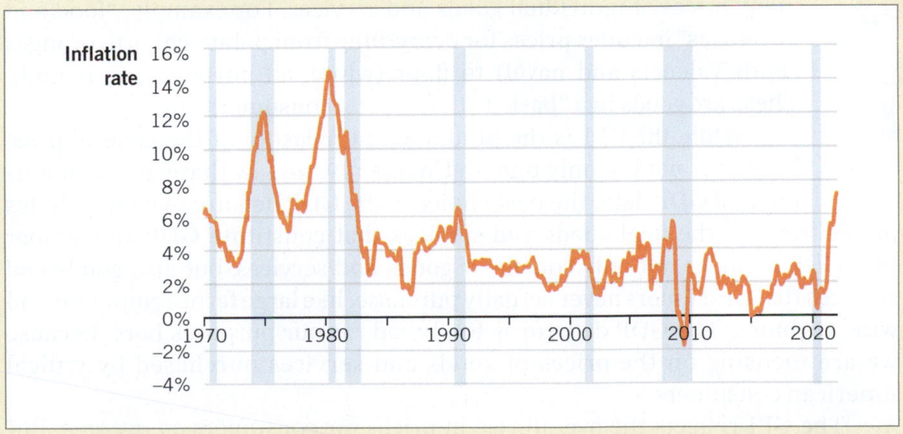

FIGURE 21.1

Inflation in the United States, 1970–2021

From 1970 to 2021, inflation rates in the United States averaged 4%. This number is high because of excessive inflation in the 1970s. The inflation rate peaked at over 14% in 1980. In the past twenty-five years, inflation has averaged only about 2.15%, but the surge to over 7% in 2021 worried many economists.

Source: U.S. Bureau of Labor Statistics.

FIGURE 21.2

The Pieces of the Consumer Price Index, December 2021

The weights assigned to the different categories of expenditures are based on the spending patterns of a typical American. For example, 17% of a typical American's spending is on transportation; this includes car payments and fuel, among other expenses.

Source: U.S. Bureau of Labor Statistics.

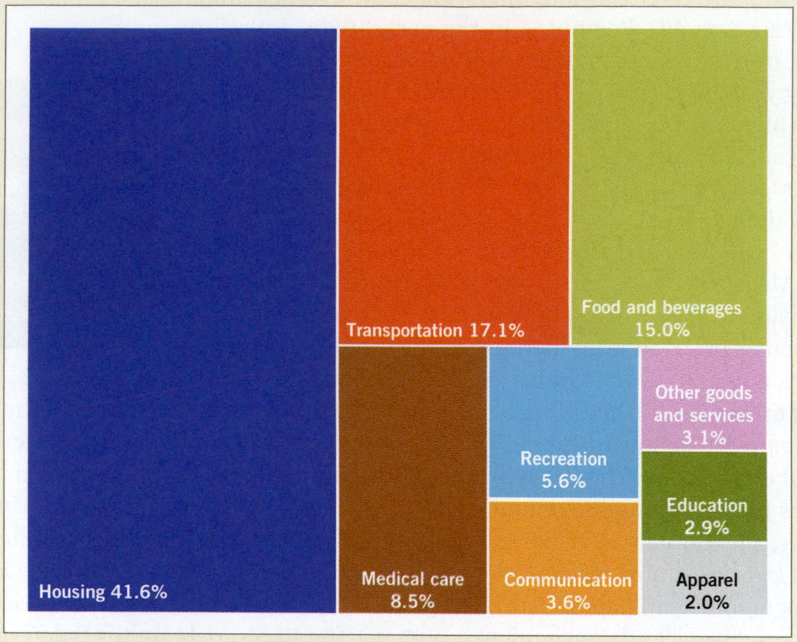

The CPI is based on prices from a typical "basket" of all consumer goods and services.

in the media, the report almost certainly focuses on this measure. The CPI is essentially the price of a typical "basket" of goods and services purchased by a representative consumer in the United States. What's in that basket? In addition to groceries, there is clothing, transportation, housing, medical care, education, and many other goods and services. The idea is to include everything that a typical consumer buys. Tracking these prices gives us a realistic measure of a typical consumer's cost of living.

Figure 21.2 displays how the CPI was allocated among major spending categories in December 2021. Each of these categories includes many prices of individual goods and services. For example, "food and beverages" includes prices for everything from potato chips to oranges (both Valencia and navel) to flour (white, all purpose, per pound). These are goods in a "basket" that typical consumers buy.

While the CPI is the predominant measure of the general price level, it is not the only one. In Chapter 19, we saw that when computing real GDP data, the best choice is the GDP deflator, which includes prices from all the final goods and services that constitute GDP. Remember that GDP includes not only consumer goods and services, but also goods and services that consumers never actually purchase, like large farm equipment and wind turbines. The GDP deflator is too broad for our purposes here, because we are focusing on the prices of goods and services purchased by typical American consumers.

The CPI reflects the overall rise in prices for consumers *on average*. But of course, none of us is exactly typical in our spending. College students allocate significantly more than average to spending on education; senior citizens spend more than average on medical care; a fashionista spends more than average on clothing; and those with lengthy commutes spend more than average on transportation.

COMPUTING THE CPI Each month, the BLS conducts surveys by sending employees into stores in 38 geographical locations to gather and input price information on over 8,000 goods and services. The BLS collects prices on everything from apples in Chicago to electricity in Scranton, Pennsylvania, to gasoline in San Diego, California. In addition to inputting price information, the BLS surveyors estimate how each good and service affects a typical consumer's budget. Once they do this, they attach a weight to the price of each good or service in the consumer's "basket." For example, Figure 21.2 indicates that the typical consumer spends 17% of his or her budget on transportation. Therefore, transportation prices receive 17% of the total weight in the typical consumer's basket of goods and services. Once the BLS has compiled the prices and budget allocation weights, it can construct the CPI.

To illustrate how this works, let's build a price index using just three goods. Imagine that when you go to the movies you notice you are spending more for that outing than you did last year. You decide to construct a price index to see exactly how the price increases are affecting your budget. You decide to name your index the EPI (entertainment price index). For the sake of this example, assume that a typical night at the movie theater includes two movie tickets, one box of popcorn, and two medium Cokes. This is the basket of goods (the popcorn and Cokes) and service (movie) included in your EPI.

The first four columns in Figure 21.3 show your EPI data for the first year, 2022. The second column shows the respective quantities of goods and service

FIGURE 21.3

		2022		2023	
Good	Quantity	Unit price	Total cost	Unit price	Total cost
 Popcorn	1	$6	$6	$8	$8
 Coke	2	$5	$10	$5	$10
 Movie ticket	2	$12	$24	$13	$26
Basket price			**$40**		**$44**
Index (EPI)		$\frac{\$40}{\$40} \times 100 = 100$		$\frac{\$44}{\$40} \times 100 = 110$	

Calculating a Simple Price Index

In calculating this entertainment price index (EPI), we use the same steps that the Bureau of Labor Statistics goes through when calculating the CPI. First, we determine the typical basket of goods. Then we calculate the total price of the basket in a base year, 2022 in this example, and set that base year at 100 (creating an index). For subsequent years, we add up the new prices for the same basket of goods, then divide by the basket price in the base year, and then multiply by 100 to determine the new index number.

in your basket, and the third column displays the unit prices of these goods and service. The price of popcorn is $6 per box, the Cokes are $5 each, and the movie tickets are $12 each. The fourth column shows how much you pay in total for each good or service; this number is price multiplied by quantity. For example, in 2022, the price of a ticket was $12, so you paid a total of $24 for two tickets. Adding up, we get the total price for your basket of goods and service in 2022, which was $40. This is how much you spent for all goods and service in your EPI in 2022.

Let's now move to 2023. First, note that your consumption pattern hasn't changed; you still buy the same basket of goods and service. But some of the prices did change in 2023. Popcorn is now priced at $8 per box, and the movie ticket costs $13. Note that not all prices have changed; the cost of a Coke remains the same.

To see how the new 2023 prices affect your spending, we compute the total cost required to consume the same goods and service in the same quantities. The last column shows the costs of each component in your basket. The sum of these is now $44.

The final step is to create an index. You need an index because in the real world, adding a lot of prices together yields a huge number that would be difficult to work with. So we create an index that is equal to 100 at a fixed point in time—your base year. In our example, we can use 2022 for the base year. To convert to your index, we divide the basket price in each year by the basket price value from the base year and multiply by 100:

(EQUATION 21.1)

$$\text{price index} = \frac{\text{basket price}}{\text{basket price in base year}} \times 100$$

Using this formula, you can confirm that the EPI for 2022 is 100 and that the EPI for 2023 is 110 (see the last line of Figure 21.3).

When the Bureau of Labor Statistics computes the CPI for the United States, it follows the same basic steps:

1. Define the basket of goods and services and their appropriate weights.
2. Determine the prices of goods across periods.
3. Convert to the index number for each period.

ECONOMICS IN THE REAL WORLD

SLEUTHING FOR PRICES

Tracking the prices in the CPI requires a great deal of effort and precision. The Bureau of Labor Statistics (BLS) is the U.S. government agency that is responsible for estimating the consumer price index. As of 2015, the BLS employed 428 "economic assistants." Their job is to fan out around the nation and determine the actual prices of goods and services—every month. This is no easy task because the items in the market basket are constantly changing. In September 2013, Emily Wax-Thibodeaux of the *Washington Post* followed one of these economic assistants on a typical day's work. The BLS employee, Caren Gaffney, drove around the state of Virginia for more than eight hours tracking prices on gasoline, sugar, and beer.

Paper towels are one example of a typical consumer item.

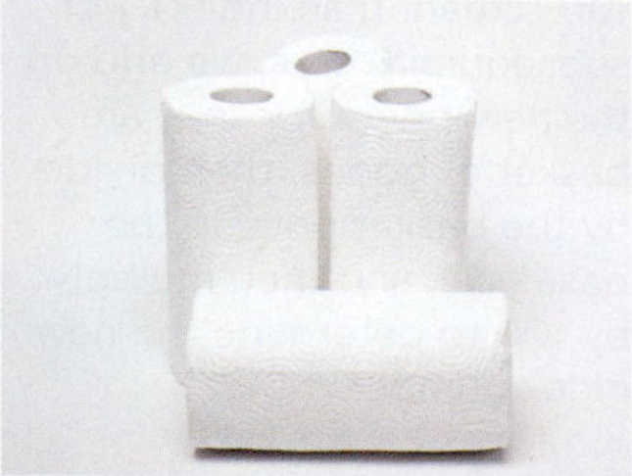

The priced items were very specific. For the gas price alone, Gaffney needed to determine the octane grade, whether the quoted prices depended on the day of the week, and whether the customer paid with cash or credit. The BLS tracks 200 different price categories, and each category includes the prices of several hundred goods and services. For example, the BLS tracks the prices of four types of margarine (sticks, soft, vegetable blend sticks, and vegetable blend soft). Paper towels may seem like a pretty standard item, but it turns out there are 31 different varieties of some brands.

In macroeconomics, we generally watch a single overall number (the CPI or the GDP deflator) that indicates how much prices have changed. But it's important to remember that thousands of prices are tracked each month by government workers like Caren Gaffney.

Source: Emily Wax-Thibodeaux, "The Government's Human Price Scanners," *Washington Post*, November 11, 2013, https://www.washingtonpost.com/politics/the-governments-human-price-scanners/2013/11/11/a4225dc2-4576-11e3-bf0c-cebf37c6f484_story.html.

Measuring Inflation Rates

Once the CPI is computed, economists use it to measure inflation rates. The inflation rate (i) is a growth rate and is calculated as the percentage change in the price level (P) during a period of time. Using the CPI as the price level, the inflation rate during period 2 is

$$\text{inflation rate (i)} = \frac{P_2 - P_1}{P_1} \times 100 \qquad \textbf{(EQUATION 21.2)}$$

In our entertainment price index example, the CPI rose from 100 to 110 in one year. So the inflation rate for that year was 10%, computed as

$$\text{inflation rate (i)} = \frac{110 - 100}{100} \times 100 = 10\%$$

The BLS releases CPI estimates every month. Normally, inflation rates are measured over the course of a year, showing how much the price level grows in 12 months. Figure 21.4 shows the historical relationship between the U.S. inflation rate and the CPI. Panel (a) plots the U.S. CPI from 1970 to 2021. The base period for the CPI is set for 1982–1984, so it goes through 100 in 1983. The CPI was just 38 in 1970 and rose to 280 by 2021. This means that the typical basket of consumer goods and services cost more than seven times as much in 2021 compared to 1970.

Panel (b) of Figure 21.4 plots inflation rates based on the CPI data in panel (a). The inflation graph reveals a number of historical observations that are important to our study of macroeconomics. For example, when you look at the graph, you might wonder what was going on in the 1970s. While some economists have recently been concerned to see inflation higher than 7% in 2021, inflation has been relatively low and stable since the 1970s, averaging less than 3%. From 1970 to 1981, by contrast, the inflation rate averaged 8%, including the twelve months from April 1979 to March 1980, when it was over 14.5%. We'll explain the reasons for these historically high rates in Chapter 31. For now, in comparing the two graphs in Figure 21.4, notice that the CPI increased more rapidly from 1979 to 1980 than in any other period shown.

FIGURE 21.4

The CPI and Inflation, 1970–2021

Panel (a) shows the CPI from 1970 to 2021. The index of prices for a typical consumer's basket of goods was at 38 in 1970 but rose to 280 by 2021. Panel (b) shows the U.S. inflation rate, computed as the growth rate of the CPI. A rapidly rising CPI, like we see in panel (a) during the 1970s, is reflected in the high inflation rate.

Source: U.S. Bureau of Labor Statistics.

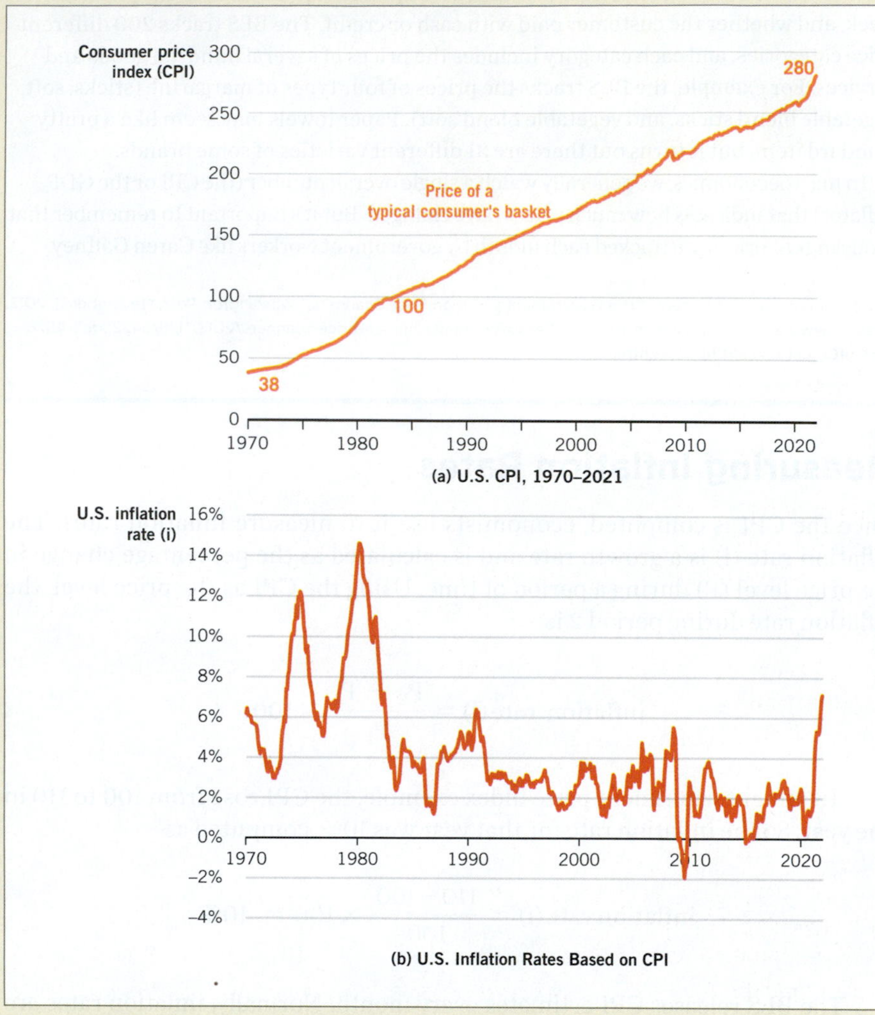

ECONOMICS IN THE REAL WORLD

PRICES DON'T ALL MOVE TOGETHER

While it's clear that prices generally rise, not all prices go up. When the CPI rises, it indicates that the price of the overall consumer basket rises. However, some individual prices stay the same or even fall. For example, consumer electronic prices almost always fall. When flat-panel plasma TVs were introduced in the late 1990s, a 40-inch model cost more than $7,000. Twenty years later, 60-inch flat-panel TVs are available for less than $500. This is the result of technological advancements: as time passes, it often takes fewer resources to produce the same item or something better.

The 1984 Macintosh price was $2,495 . . .

. . . but this 2021 Apple iMac costs just $1,299.

Computers are another example. In 1984, Apple introduced the Macintosh computer at a price of $2,495. The CPU for the Macintosh ran at 7.83 MHz, and the 9-inch monitor was black and white. Today, you can buy an Apple iMac for as little as $1,299. The 2021 iteration has a brand-new Apple-designed 3.2 GHz processor, an 11.5 mm–thin monitor, and a 1080p FaceTime camera, and it even comes in your choice of colors! The new computer is better by any measure, yet it costs less than the early model. These kinds of changes in quality make it difficult to measure the CPI, but it is clear that many prices actually fall over time.

Using the CPI to Compare Dollar Values over Time

Prices convey a lot of information, but prices from different periods can be quite confusing. For example, in 1924, a consumer could buy a fully constructed, 1,600-square-foot home through a physical catalog distributed by Sears at a price of just $1,969. But how does that price compare with today's prices? In addition to measuring inflation rates, we can use the CPI to answer these types of questions.

To compare the prices of goods over time, we convert all prices to today's prices, or "prices in today's dollars." Here is the formula:

$$\text{price in today's dollars} = \text{price in earlier time} \times \frac{\text{price level today}}{\text{price level in earlier time}} \qquad \textbf{(EQUATION 21.3)}$$

Following this formula, we can compute the 2021 price of the 1924 Sears home. The CPI in 2021 was 280, and the CPI in 1924 was 17, so the computation is

$$\text{price in } 2021 = \$1{,}969 \times \frac{280}{17} = \$32{,}431$$

In fact, the 1924 Sears price would be pretty low even today.

SNAPSHOT

The Pieces of the CPI

The price level we often use to measure inflation is the Consumer Price Index (CPI), which is driven by the prices paid by a typical American consumer. The data below shows the various categories in which U.S. citizens spend their income.

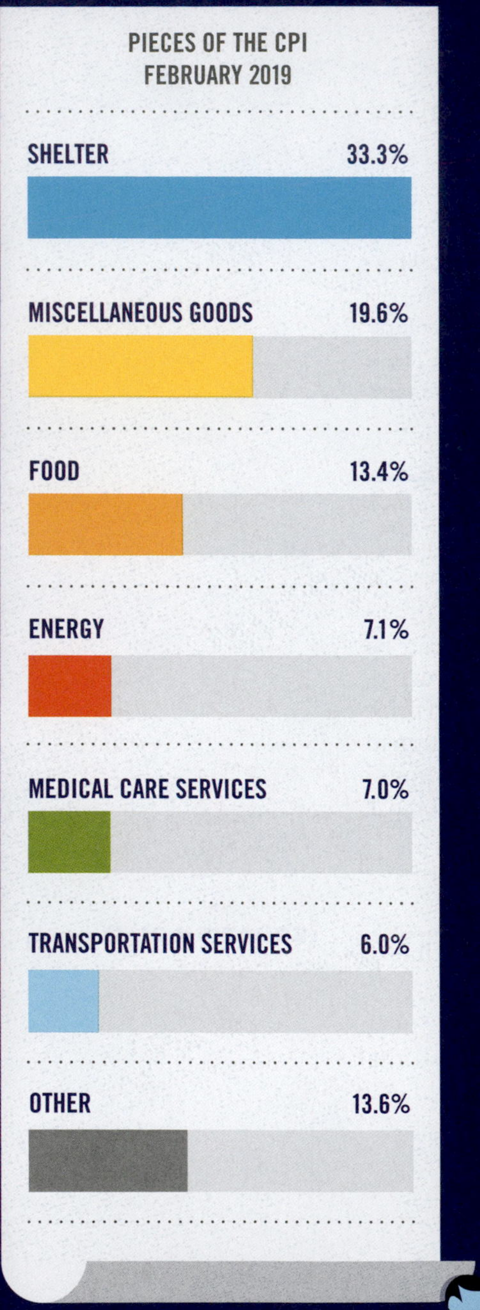

SHELTER	33.3%
Owner's payments	24.1%
Rent	7.9%
Other	1.3%

MISCELLANEOUS GOODS	19.6%
New Vehicles	3.7%
Apparel	3.0%
Used cars and trucks	2.4%
Medical care commodities	1.7%
Alcoholic beverages	1.0%
Tobacco and smoking products	0.7%
Other	7.1%

FOOD	13.4%
Food at home	7.3%
Food away from home	6.1%

ENERGY	7.1%
Gasoline	3.5%
Electricity	2.6%
Other	1.1%

MEDICAL CARE SERVICES	7.0%
Hospital services	2.3%
Physician's services	1.7%
Other	2.9%

TRANSPORTATION SERVICES	6.0%
Motor vehicle insurance	2.4%
Motor vehicle maintenance and repair	1.1%
Airline fares	0.7%
Other	1.8%

OTHER	13.6%

REVIEW QUESTIONS

- What portion of a monthly budget does a typical U.S. consumer spend on new vehicles?
- Explain how these numbers are used in CPI calculations.

Source: Bureau of Labor Statistics

TABLE 21.1

Converting Past Prices into Modern Dollar Values

	Product	Year	Price	Conversion	2021 dollars	2021 actual price
	Coca-Cola (12 oz.)	1942	$0.05	$\$0.05 \times (280 \div 16)$	$0.88	$0.89
	Hershey's chocolate bar (1.55 oz.)	1921	0.05	$\$0.05 \times (280 \div 18)$	0.78	0.98
	McDonald's hamburger	1955	0.15	$\$0.15 \times (280 \div 27)$	1.56	1.00
	Nabisco's Oreo cookies (1 lb.)	1922	0.32	$\$0.32 \times (280 \div 17)$	5.27	3.79

Table 21.1 takes past prices from some iconic foods and converts them to 2021 dollars. For example, the price of a 1-pound bag of Oreo cookies was 32 cents in 1922. Using Equation 21.3, we multiply $0.32 by the 2021 price level (280) and divide by the 1922 price level (17) to determine the old price in 2021 dollars. It turns out that, once converted, the old price is $5.27, which is much higher than the 2021 actual price of $3.79. The price in 2021 dollars corrects for the overall amount of inflation since 1922, helps make sense of historical prices, and dispels the notion that everything was less expensive in the past. This observation is nominally true but not especially interesting. Adjusting for inflation provides a real comparison, which is what good economists always look for.

ECONOMICS IN THE REAL WORLD

WHICH MOVIES ARE MOST POPULAR?

Is *Avatar* really the most successful movie of all time?

After a successful new movie comes out, the film industry totals up box office receipts and other revenue to see how well the movie has done. But the list is biased toward recent movies, because the data are in nominal terms and not adjusted for inflation.

For example, *Avatar* is ranked as the highest-grossing film of all time, because it earned more dollars (nominal revenue) than any other film, ever. *Titanic* held the top spot from 1998 to 2009, and before that *Star Wars* was number one from 1977 to 1997. Table 21.2 lists the top ten movies of all time, ranked by total nominal receipts. This list may not surprise you—there are several recent movies, like *Avengers: Endgame*. But doesn't it seem odd that *Furious 7* would be the ninth-most-popular movie ever made? It turns out this is only true in nominal terms, the tally of receipts *not* adjusted for inflation.

Table 21.3 presents the top ten movies of all time after adjusting for inflation. This list is more meaningful since the receipts of older movies are now comparable to the newer data. After adjustments for inflation, *Avatar* falls to number four. The most impressive

TABLE 21.2

Top Movies of All Time, Ranked by Nominal Receipts

	Rank	Movie	Receipts (millions)	Receipts adjusted for inflation, 2021 (millions)
	1	*Avatar* (2009)	$2,847	$3,623
	2	*Avengers: Endgame* (2019)	2,798	2,987
	3	*Titanic* (1997)	2,202	3,745
	4	*Star Wars: Ep. VII - The Force Awakens* (2015)	2,070	2,384
	5	*Avengers: Infinity War* (2018)	2,048	2,227
	6	*Jurassic World* (2015)	1,671	1,924
	7	*The Lion King* (1994)	1,668	1,781
	8	*The Avengers* (2012)	1,519	1,806
	9	*Furious 7* (2015)	1,515	1,745
	10	*Frozen II* (2019)	1,450	1,548

Source: https://www.boxofficemojo.com/alltime/world/.

result on the list has to come from *Gone with the Wind*. Not only is the 1939 movie ranked number one, but the total revenue is almost double that from *Bambi*, which comes in at the second-place position. Of course, these rankings are always subject to change. In 2019, *Avengers: Endgame* raked in over $1 billion worldwide in its first weekend (!) and proceeded to land on both top ten lists in short order.

TABLE 21.3

Top Movies of All Time, Ranked by Real Receipts

	Rank	Movie	Receipts (millions)	Receipts adjusted for inflation, 2021 (millions)
	1	*Gone with the Wind* (1939)	$402	$7,903
	2	*Bambi* (1942)	447	4,480
	3	*Titanic* (1997)	2,202	3,745
	4	*Avatar* (2009)	2,847	3,623
	5	*Snow White and the Seven Dwarfs* (1937)	185	3,506
	6	*Star Wars: Ep. IV - A New Hope* (1977)	775	3,493
	7	*Avengers: Endgame* (2019)	2,798	2,987
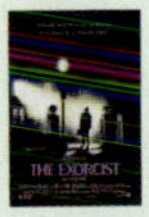	8	*The Exorcist* (1973)	441	2,714
	9	*Jaws* (1975)	471	2,392
	10	*Star Wars: Ep. VII - The Force Awakens* (2015)	2,070	2,384

Source: https://www.boxofficemojo.com/alltime/world/.

The Accuracy of the CPI

We have seen that computing the CPI is not simple. Yet to understand what is happening in the macroeconomy, it is important that the CPI be accurate. For example, sometimes a rapid fall in inflation signals a recession, as it did in 1982 and 2008. Like real GDP and the unemployment rate, inflation is an indicator of national economic conditions.

Wage contracts for over 200,000 UPS employees are adjusted for inflation in reference to the CPI.

But there is another reason the CPI needs to be accurate: when employers adjust wages for inflation, they generally use the CPI. For example, when the United Auto Workers (UAW) union signs a wage agreement with General Motors, the agreement specifies wages for autoworkers several years in advance. Since future inflation is unknown and the UAW wants to protect its workers from excess inflation, the agreement stipulates that wages will be tied to the CPI. Therefore, when the CPI rises, the wages of UAW workers rise; when the CPI falls, the wages of UAW workers fall. So if the CPI overstates inflation, the miscalculation can cost companies millions of dollars. If the CPI understates inflation, this hurts workers, since their wages will not rise as much as they should.

How accurate is the CPI? If consumers always bought the same goods and services from the same suppliers, it would be extremely accurate, and economists could easily track prices over time. But this is not realistic. As time goes by, consumers buy different goods and services from different stores at different locations, and the quality of goods and services changes over time. So the typical basket keeps changing, and this makes it difficult to measure its price. The most common concern is that the CPI overstates true inflation. There are three reasons for this concern: the substitution of different goods and services; changes in quality; and the availability of new goods, services, and locations.

SUBSTITUTION When the price of a good rises, consumers instinctively look to substitute less expensive alternatives. This makes CPI calculations difficult because the typical consumer basket changes. Earlier, when we calculated an entertainment price index, we assumed that you always bought the same quantities of all goods and services, even when the price of popcorn rose and the price of Coke remained the same. However, it is more realistic to assume that if the price of popcorn rises, then some people will choose a less expensive snack. In other words, they find a substitute for popcorn. But when consumers substitute less expensive goods, that change alters the weights of all the goods and services in the typical consumption basket. Without acknowledging the substitution of less expensive items, the CPI would exaggerate the effects of the price increase, leading to upward bias (the reported CPI would be too high). Since 1999, the BLS has used a formula that accounts for both the price increase and the shift in goods and services consumption.

CHANGES IN QUALITY Over time, the quality of goods and services generally improves. For example, the movie theater you frequent may soon begin to offer all movies in 3D. Because this technology is more expensive than the older technology, the price of a ticket might rise from \$10 to \$12. The increase will seem like inflation, since ticket prices will go up. And yet, consumers get "more" movie for their buck, because the quality will have improved. If the CPI did not account for quality changes, it would have an upward bias in the true cost of living. But the BLS uses an adjustment method to account for quality changes.

NEW GOODS, SERVICES, AND LOCATIONS In a dynamic, growing economy, new goods and services are introduced and new buying options

ECONOMICS *in the* MEDIA

Equating Dollar Values through Time

AUSTIN POWERS: INTERNATIONAL MAN OF MYSTERY

The Austin Powers series is a hilarious spoof of the James Bond films. In *Austin Powers: International Man of Mystery*, we're introduced to British secret agent Austin Powers, who was cryofrozen at the end of the 1960s. Thirty years later, Austin Powers is thawed to help capture his nemesis, Dr. Evil, who was cryofrozen at the same time as Austin and has now stolen a nuclear weapon to hold the world hostage.

Being frozen for 30 years causes Dr. Evil to underestimate how much he should ask for in ransom money: "Gentlemen, it's come to my attention that a breakaway Russian republic called Kreplachistan will be transferring a nuclear warhead to the United Nations in a few days. Here's the plan. We get the warhead, and we hold the world ransom . . . FOR ONE MILLION DOLLARS!"

There is an uncomfortable pause.

Dr. Evil's Number Two speaks up: "Don't you think we should ask for more than a million dollars? A million dollars isn't that much money these days. Virtucon alone makes over nine billion dollars a year."

Dr. Evil responds (pleasantly surprised): "Oh, really? Okay then, we hold the world ransom for . . . ONE HUNDRED BILLION DOLLARS!"

"ONE HUNDRED BILLION DOLLARS!"

Austin Powers: International Man of Mystery takes place in 1997, and Dr. Evil was frozen in 1967. How much did the price level rise over those 30 years? The CPI was 33.4 in 1967 and 160.5 in 1997. Dividing 160.5 by 33.4 yields a ratio of 4.8. So if Dr. Evil thought that $1 million was a lot of money in 1967, an equivalent amount in 1997 would be $4.8 million. Dr. Evil does not let that stop him from asking for more!

FIGURE 21.5

The Chained CPI versus the Traditional CPI

The chained CPI reduces the upward bias of the traditional CPI by updating the consumer's basket of goods and services every month. This single correction accounts for price reductions that typically occur during the first few years after a new product has been introduced.

Source: U.S. Bureau of Labor Statistics.

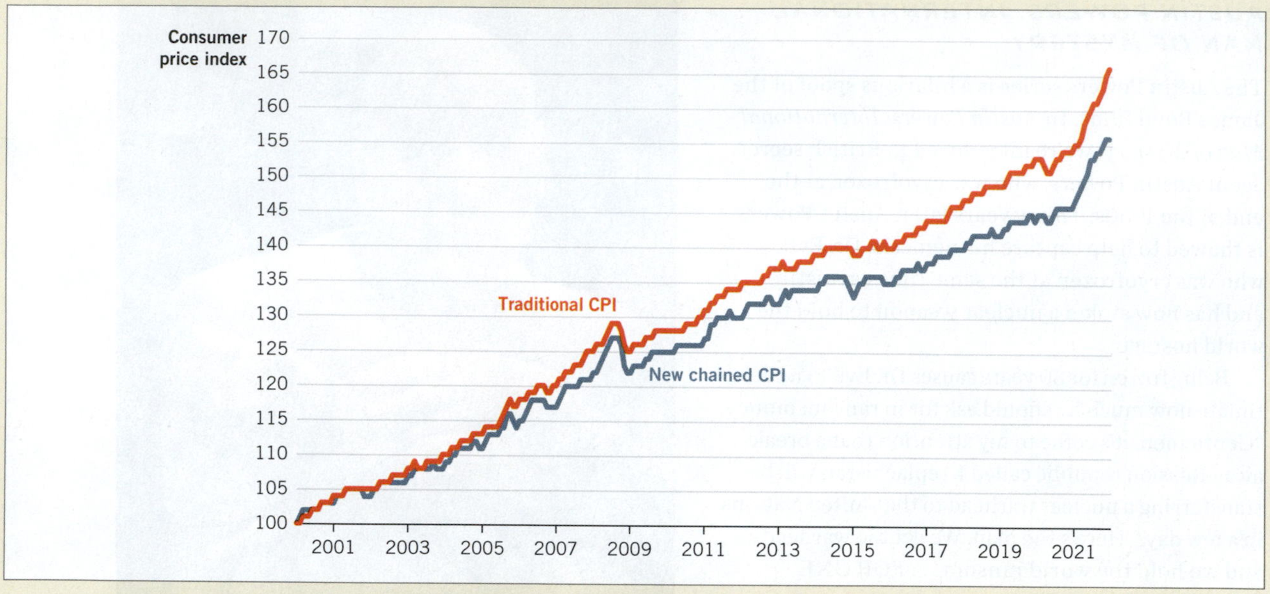

become available. For example, tablet computers, flash drives, and even cell phones weren't in the typical consumer's basket 25 years ago. In addition, Amazon and eBay weren't options for consumers to make purchases before the 1990s.

Traditionally, the BLS updated the CPI basket of goods and services only after long time delays. This strategy biased the CPI in an upward direction for two reasons. First, the prices of new products typically drop in the first few years after their introduction. If the CPI basket doesn't include the latest prices, this price drop is lost. Second, new retail outlets such as Internet stores typically offer lower prices than traditional retail stores. If the BLS continued to check prices only at traditional retail stores, it would overstate the price consumers actually pay for goods and services.

The **chained CPI** is a measure of the CPI in which the typical consumer's "basket" of goods and services considered is updated monthly.

In an effort to measure this upward bias, the BLS began computing a chained CPI in 2000. The **chained CPI** is a measure of the CPI in which the typical consumer's basket of goods and services is updated monthly. While it's more difficult to measure and takes longer to estimate, the chained CPI is a better indicator of inflation for the typical consumer. Figure 21.5 shows the two CPI measures together. The vertical distance between the two lines indicates the upward bias of the traditional CPI, which updates the basket of goods and services less often. Notice that the distance grows over time.

PRACTICE WHAT YOU KNOW

Using the CPI to Equate Prices over Time: How Cheap Were the First Super Bowl Tickets?

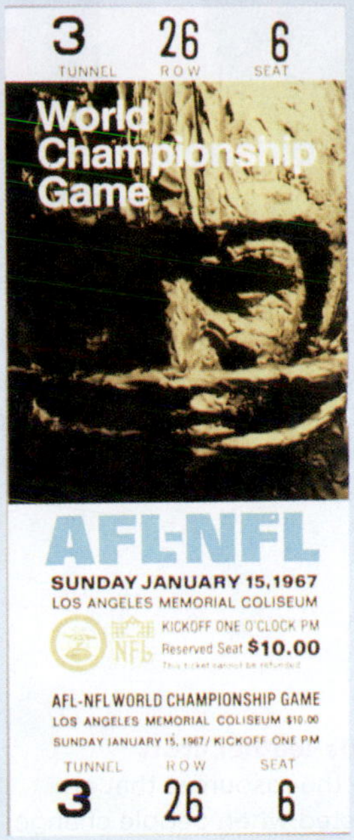

A 1967 Super Bowl ticket.

Ticket prices to America's premier sporting event, the Super Bowl, were much lower when it was first played in 1967. In fact, you could have bought a ticket for as little as $6. This seems very low by today's prices. In 2021, many seats sold for more than $5,000 each.

QUESTION: If the CPI from 1967 was 33 and the CPI for 2021 was 280, how would you convert the price of a $6 ticket in 1967 to 2021 dollars?

ANSWER: For this question, we need to use Equation 21.3:

$$\text{price in today's dollars} = \text{price in earlier time} \times \frac{\text{price level today}}{\text{price level in earlier time}}$$

The 1967 price was $6, so we substitute this price and the two price levels from above to get

$$\text{price in 2021 dollars} = \$6 \times \frac{280}{33} = \$51$$

It turns out that the old Super Bowl tickets were indeed cheap—you'd be lucky to get a hot dog and a soda at a modern Super Bowl for $51.

CHALLENGE QUESTION: NFL players are now paid, on average, more than $2 million per year. What salary from 1967 would be equivalent to $2 million in 2021?

ANSWER: To answer this, you have to turn the equation around and solve for the dollar value from an earlier time:

$$\text{equivalent 1967 salary} = \text{salary in 2021} \times (\text{price level in 1967} / \text{price level in 2021})$$

$$= \$2 \text{ million} \times \frac{33}{280}$$

Solving this way, you get: $235,714. As it turns out, the average NFL salary in the late 1960s was only about $25,000, so today's players are making almost 10 times more income, even in real terms!

What Problems Does Inflation Bring?

Many people believe inflation is most harmful because it reduces the purchasing power of their income. For example, consider that prices were much lower in the 1970s; therefore, it's easy to think that an annual salary of $10,000 at that

When inflation reaches the levels witnessed in Venezuela in 2018, shoe-leather costs are significant.

time could buy a lot more than it can today. Well, this would be true if all else were equal. But salaries are prices, too (prices for labor), and inflation causes them to rise as well. Remember: inflation is an overall rise in prices throughout the economy.

But this does not mean that inflation is harmless. Indeed, inflation does impose many costs on an economy. In this section, we discuss these costs. They include shoe-leather costs, money illusion, menu costs, uncertainty over future price levels, wealth redistribution, price confusion, and tax distortions.

Shoe-Leather Costs

Inflation is costly for society when it causes people to do things they wouldn't do in an environment of price stability. The higher the rate of inflation, the more likely people are to change their normal patterns of spending and money-holding. This is because inflation is essentially a tax on holding money. As prices of goods and services rise with inflation, the value of dollars in people's wallets falls. This problem is not currently severe in the United States because inflation rates are very low. But in hyperinflation, the value of dollars falls daily.

Shoe-leather costs are the resources that are wasted when people change their behavior to avoid holding money.

To avoid the "tax" on holding money, people hold less money, which means more trips to the bank to make withdrawals. **Shoe-leather costs** are the resources that are wasted when people change their behavior to avoid holding money. In times past, these costs referred to the actual expense of replacing shoes that might get worn out as a result of making many trips to the bank. Today, these include fuel costs and the time used for multiple trips to a bank or ATM.

Money Illusion

The second problem from inflation is among the least understood. Even when people know inflation has occurred, they do not always react rationally. So although wages and prices might rise because of inflation, people frequently respond as if the prices are higher in real terms. For example, if the price of a movie goes up by 10% but wages and other prices also rise by 10%, nothing changes in real terms. But many people mistakenly conclude that movies have become more expensive. If they treat a price increase from inflation as a change in relative price, they may go see fewer movies or make other decisions based on the new price. Economists call this *money illusion*. **Money illusion** occurs when people interpret nominal changes in wages or prices as real changes.

Money illusion occurs when people interpret nominal changes in wages or prices as real changes.

Money illusion is an easy trap to fall into. Let's see if we can trick you into it. Consider the cost-of-living data presented in Table 21.4. The index scores show relative living costs for an average person living in various U.S. cities. The index is set so that 100 is the cost of living in an average U.S. city.

For this example, let's focus on two particular cities: Washington, DC and Atlanta. The index score for Washington is 102; for Atlanta, it is 94. These index scores imply that a salary of $94,000 for a person living in Atlanta is equivalent to a salary of $102,000 for a person living in Washington, even though the difference is $8,000.

TABLE 21.4

The Cost of Living in Selected U.S. Cities

City	Cost-of-living index number
San Diego, CA	116
San Francisco, CA	115
Boston, MA	109
Los Angeles, CA	106
Denver, CO	104
Washington, DC	102
U.S. City Average	100
Philadelphia, PA	99
Chicago, IL	97
Atlanta, GA	94
Dallas, TX	91
St. Louis, MO	89
Tampa, FL	89

Source: U.S. Bureau of Labor Statistics, 2020.

Now imagine that you are living in Atlanta and earning $94,000, but your firm offers to relocate you to Washington at a pay rate of $100,000. Doesn't that seem like a pretty large raise? You might be excited to call your parents and tell them you'll be making "six figures." But, in fact, it is a pay cut in real terms, since you can buy less with $100,000 in Washington than you can with $94,000 in Atlanta. Money illusion makes it feel like a raise.

The key distinction in this situation is between real wages and nominal wages. The concept of a nominal wage is analogous to nominal GDP. A worker's **nominal wage** is his or her wage expressed in current dollars, like $50 per hour or $100,000 per year. The **real wage** is the nominal wage adjusted for changes in the price level. The real wage is more informative because it describes what the worker earns in terms of purchasing power. So while a salary of $100,000 a year may sound high, if the CPI doubles, that salary does not go far.

A worker's **nominal wage** is his or her wage expressed in current dollars.

The **real wage** is the nominal wage adjusted for changes in the price level.

Significant macroeconomic problems arise if workers fall victim to money illusion when they interpret the value of their wages, because the illusion causes them to focus on their nominal wage instead of their real wage. For example, when prices fall, any given nominal wage is worth more in real terms. In Chapter 26, we'll see that macroeconomic adjustments can depend on whether workers are willing to let wages fall when other prices fall. Money illusion causes these adjustments to take longer than they should, and this delay tends to lengthen economic downturns.

Menu Costs

The act of physically changing prices is also costly. **Menu costs** are the costs of changing prices. While some businesses can change prices easily—for example, gas pumps and signs at gas stations are designed for this purpose—businesses

Menu costs are the costs of changing prices.

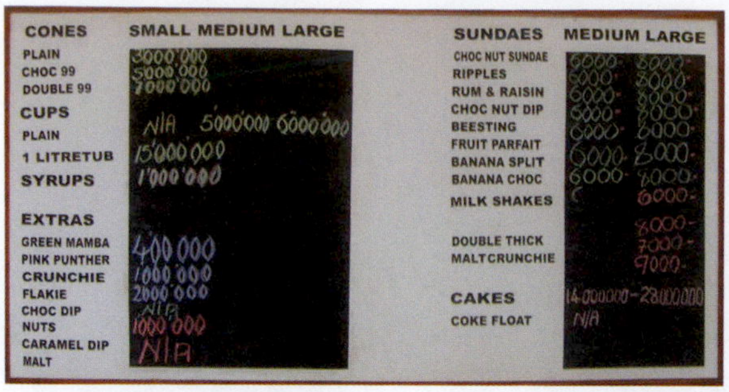

Chalk menus are one way to limit menu costs. This menu is from an ice cream parlor in Zimbabwe during its 2008 hyperinflation. Notice that the price of a small chocolate cone is 5 million Zimbabwean dollars.

such as restaurants can find it expensive to print new menus when their prices change.

Other costs considered in this category are not directly related to menus. For example, changing prices can make regular customers angry enough to take their business elsewhere. Think about your favorite lunch spot. Perhaps you regularly buy a bagel and lemonade for $5 at Bodo's Bagels. What if the price for this combination suddenly increases to $6? You might be annoyed enough to go somewhere else next time.

Menu costs discourage firms from adjusting prices quickly. When some prices are slow to respond, the effects of macroeconomic disturbances are magnified.

Future Price Level Uncertainty

Imagine you decide to open a new coffee shop in your college town. You want to produce espressos, café mochas, and cappuccinos. Of course, you hope to sell these for a profit. But before you can sell a single cup of coffee, you have to spend funds on your resources. You have to buy (that is, invest in) capital goods like an espresso bar, tables, chairs, and a cash register. You also have to hire workers and promise to pay them. All firms, large and small, face this situation. Before any revenue arrives from the sales of output, firms have to spend on resources. This also applies to the overall macroeconomy: to increase GDP in the future, firms must invest today. The funds required to make these investments are typically borrowed from others.

Output
is the product the firm creates.

The timeline of production shown in Figure 21.6 illustrates how this process works. At the end, the firm sells its output. **Output** is the product the firm creates. The key point is that in a normal production process, funds are spent today and then repaid in the future—after the output sells. But for this sequence of events to occur, businesses must make promises to deliver payments in the future: these include payments to workers and lenders. Thus, two types of long-term agreements form the foundation for production: wage and loan contracts. Both of these involve the delivery of dollars in future periods.

FIGURE 21.6

The Timeline of Production

The way output is typically produced begins with preparation that includes purchases of equipment, labor, and other resources. Actual output and revenue from the sale of output come later. Thus, a firm can only begin production with promises of future payments to resource suppliers.

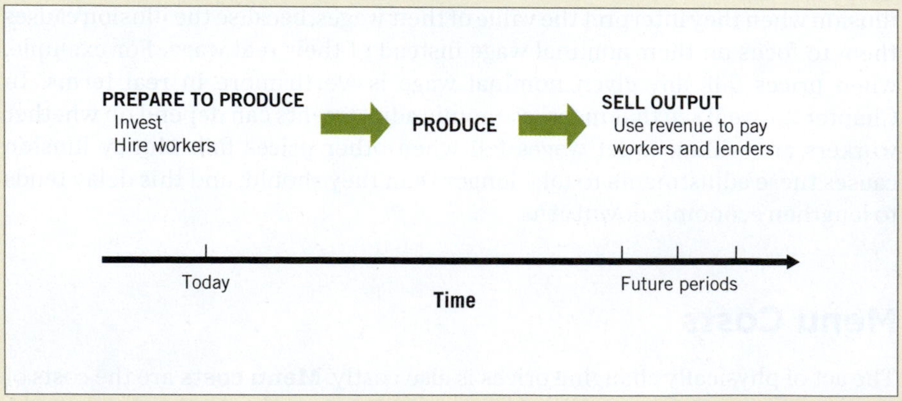

But inflation affects the real value of these future dollars. When inflation confuses workers and lenders, these essential long-term agreements seem risky and lenders are less likely to agree to them. Chapter 22 focuses on the market for loans in an economy, and we cover this topic at a deeper level there. For now, we note that inflation can cripple loan markets because people don't know future price levels. When firms cannot borrow money or hire long-term workers, future production is limited. Thus, inflation risk can lead to lower economic output, which is GDP.

Wealth Redistribution

Inflation can also redistribute wealth between borrowers and lenders. Returning to our coffee shop example, imagine that you borrow $50,000 to start your business. You borrow this sum from a bank with the promise of paying back $60,000 in five years. Now if inflation unexpectedly rises during those five years, the inflation devalues your future payment to the bank. As a result, you are better off, but the bank is worse off. Thus, surprise inflation redistributes wealth from lenders to borrowers.

If both you and the bank fully expect the inflation to occur, the bank requires more in return for the loan, so the inflation is less of a problem. In the United States, until very recently, inflation has been low and steady since the early 1980s. Therefore, surprises have been rare. But nations with high inflation rates also have a high variability of inflation, which makes it difficult to predict the future. This is one more reason why high inflation increases the risk of making the loans that are an important source of funding for business ventures.

You might assume that deflation, or falling prices, brings only positive side effects for the economy. After all, wouldn't it be great if the prices of the goods and services you purchase began falling? But unexpected deflation redistributes wealth in the other direction—from borrowers to lenders. Consider again the $50,000 loan with promised repayment of $60,000 in five years. Now, if prices fall unexpectedly over the course of the five years, the real value of the $60,000 loan repayment increases. This helps the lender but harms the borrower. Steady deflation discourages borrowing and, therefore, discourages consumption. This is not helpful to the economy as a whole.

Price Confusion

Market prices are signals to consumers and firms—signals that help allocate resources in a market economy. For example, if demand increases, prices rise and firms have an incentive to increase the quantity of output they supply. All else equal, firms take rising prices as a signal to increase output and falling prices as a signal to decrease output. But prices also rise from inflation. If firms cannot determine which price changes are due to inflation, resources may be misdirected in the economy.

Figure 21.7 illustrates the dilemma firms face in this context. Initially, it may appear that output prices are rising as a result of an increase in demand. But if the cause is inflation, prices throughout the economy rise and the optimal output for the firm should remain at the original output level. If firms always

FIGURE 21.7

"Why Did My Price Change?"

Price changes send information, or signals, to businesses. However, higher prices can be the result of either a real increase in demand or inflation. If upward pressure on prices is the result of greater demand, the profit-maximizing firm should increase its output. But if the price increase is the result of inflation, the firm should not change its level of output.

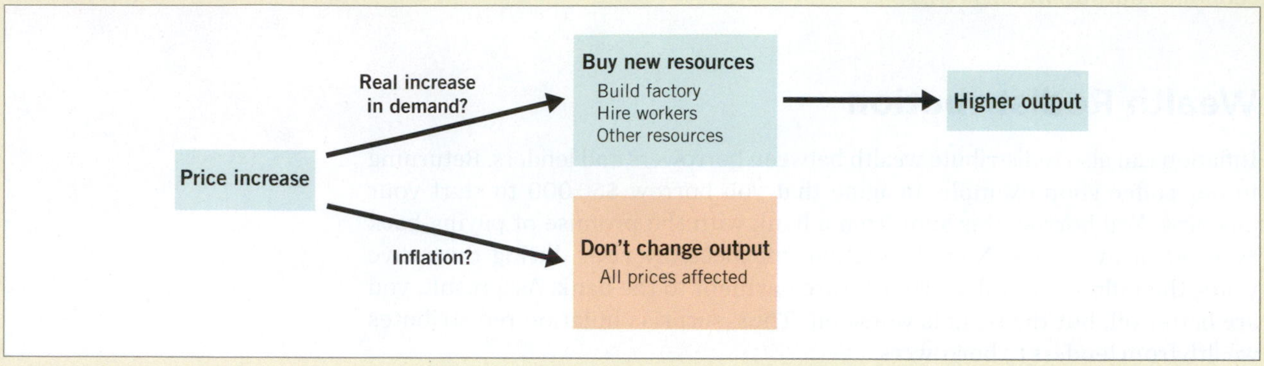

react to price increases by increasing their output, they run the risk of over-building. This can be painful later.

The housing market in the United States provides a good example of price confusion. In 2005, housing prices were high and rising. We can look back now and recognize a price bubble that did not reflect real long-run increases in demand. However, high prices at the time spurred many builders to develop more properties. When housing prices later fell, many of those builders declared bankruptcy. The crash in housing prices was one of the contributing factors to the Great Recession, which began at the end of 2007.

Tax Distortions

Even if inflation causes all prices to rise uniformly, there are still distortionary effects. These will occur because tax laws do not typically account for inflation. One area in which particularly distortionary effects occur is capital gains taxes.

Capital gains taxes are taxes on the gains realized by selling an asset for more than its purchase price.

Capital gains taxes are taxes on the gains realized by selling an asset for more than its purchase price. For example, if someone bought a piece of land as an investment in 1990 for $130,000 and then sold it in 2020 for $260,000, they made a $130,000 capital gain on the sale of the land, and this capital gain is taxed. However, it turns out that the CPI rose by exactly the same amount between 1990 and 2020: the CPI was 130 in 1990 and climbed to 260 by 2020. Therefore, the value of the land just kept pace with inflation. In real terms, the value of the land did not climb. But the seller would still be required to pay a significant tax on the sale. As it turns out, the amount of their tax was determined by inflation and not by the tax laws; if there had been no inflation, the seller would have owed no tax.

Capital gains are realized on more than just real estate sales. Capital gains also arise with the sales of stocks, bonds, and other financial securities. As we

TABLE 21.5

The Costs of Inflation

Cost of inflation	Description
Shoe-leather costs	Time and resources are spent to guard against the effects of inflation.
Money illusion	Consumers misinterpret nominal changes as real changes.
Menu costs	Firms incur extra costs to change their output prices.
Future price level uncertainty	Long-term agreements may not be signed if lenders, firms, and workers are unsure about future price levels.
Wealth redistribution	Surprise inflation redistributes wealth from lenders to borrowers.
Price confusion	Inflation makes it difficult to read price signals, and this confusion can lead to a misallocation of resources.
Tax distortions	Inflation makes capital gains appear larger and thus increases tax burdens.

will discuss in Chapter 23, these securities are a crucial ingredient to a growing and expanding economy. But inflation combined with a capital gains tax means that most people will be less likely to make these kinds of purchases. One possible solution is to rewrite the tax laws to take account of inflation's effects.

In this section, we have detailed several economic costs that arise from inflation. Table 21.5 summarizes these costs.

PRACTICE WHAT YOU KNOW

Problems with Inflation: How Big Is Your Raise in Real Terms?

Your boss calls you into his office and tells you he has good news. Because of your stellar performance and hard work, you have earned a 3% raise for next year. But when you think about your future pay, you should also know how much inflation has eroded your current pay. For example, if the inflation rate is 3% per year, then you need a 3% raise just to keep pace with inflation. Note that you can see inflation rates for yourself by visiting the Bureau of Labor Statistics web site (www.bls.gov). Once there, look up inflation rates based on the CPI.

QUESTION: In what situation would a 3% raise signify a lower real wage?

ANSWER: If the inflation rate is greater than 3%, then a 3% raise would actually be a decline in your real wage.

QUESTION: What inflation problem must you overcome to correctly see the value of your raise?

ANSWER: Money illusion. You must evaluate the real, rather than the nominal, value of your pay.

The printing press: the cause of inflation.

What Is the Cause of Inflation?

Because inflation brings serious macroeconomic costs, you might assume there is significant debate about its cause. But that assumption would be incorrect. Economists recognize that the primary cause of price increases across the entire economy is due to increases in the quantity of money in the economy relative to the quantity of goods and services. Economist Milton Friedman famously said, "Inflation is always and everywhere a monetary phenomenon." What he meant is that inflation is consistently caused by increases in a nation's money supply relative to the quantity of real goods and services in the economy.

Figure 21.8 shows average inflation rates and the money supply growth rates across 138 nations for the years 1996–2016. It is difficult to distinguish all 138 nations, because almost all of the data points are clumped together in the region where average inflation was less than 10%. This scatterplot makes it clear that inflation and money growth are certainly tied together. A few nations with very high average inflation rates are easy to pick out. For example, in this sample, the average inflation rate in Angola was 52% per year, and that inflation stemmed from a monetary growth rate of about 66%.

In Chapter 31, we will address this question more formally; we will use a macroeconomic model to show how monetary expansion translates into inflation. But the intuition is straightforward: when the supply of money in an economy grows *relative to the quantity of goods and services*, then it takes more money to buy any particular good or service. Money then becomes less valuable relative to goods and services—and this relationship constitutes inflation. The principle holds true regardless of the type of money used. For example, when Spanish

FIGURE 21.8

Inflation and Money Growth Rates in 138 countries, 1996–2016

The relationship between inflation rates and money growth rates is clear over long periods of time. This relationship applies to nations with low inflation rates and to nations with high inflation rates.

Source: World Bank.

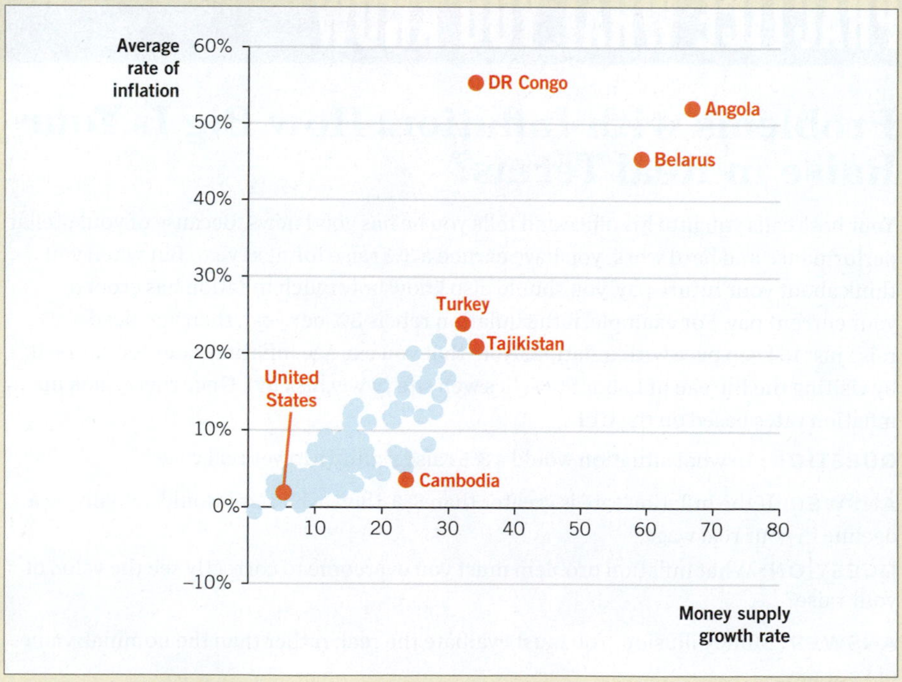

conquistadors brought gold back to Europe from Latin America in the sixteenth century, the supply of money (gold) in Europe increased, and this led to inflation.

The Equation of Exchange

The data presented in the last section show that more money in an economy generally leads to higher prices. Theoretically, this relationship makes sense. For example, if you have a given level of real GDP in an economy and the money supply doubles, you have twice as many dollars chasing the same quantity of final goods and services. Eventually, it will take about twice as many dollars to buy any particular good or service—which means prices double.

We can summarize that long-run relationship between the price level and the quantity of money with a simple relationship known as the **equation of exchange**. The equation of exchange specifies the long-run relationship between the money supply, the price level, real GDP, and the velocity of money. The actual equation is

The **equation of exchange** specifies the long-run relationship between the money supply, the price level, real GDP, and the velocity of money.

$$M \times V = P \times Y$$

The right side of the equation is nominal GDP, or real GDP (Y) times the price level (P). The left side includes the quantity of money in the economy (M) and the velocity of money (V). The **velocity of money** is the number of times a unit of money exchanges hands in a given year. The equation of exchange represents the fact that GDP in a given year is purchased with money, but that money can (and does) turn over more than once in a given year. We'll define money (M) very carefully in Chapter 30, but for now you should know that money includes more than paper currency and coins. Money includes whatever we use in exchange for goods and services. This makes the money supply difficult to measure. The promotional discount coupons that come in the mail serve as money. So do "miles" accumulated through airline travel, and reward points awarded for using a credit card. The latest money innovation is cryptocurrency.

The **velocity of money** is the number of times a unit of money exchanges hands in a given year.

Nevertheless, the equation of exchange is a helpful theoretical tool. The equation of exchange gives a direct relationship between prices and the size of the money supply, especially if velocity doesn't change much. To see this relationship, consider another version of the equation of exchange, this time in growth rates:

$$\%\Delta M + \%\Delta V \approx \%\Delta P + \%\Delta Y$$

This equation uses mathematical symbols that may be new to you. First, that Δ is the Greek letter delta, and it means "change in." So $\%\Delta V$ means "percent change in velocity" and $\%\Delta P$ means "percent change in price level." Also $\approx$ means "is approximately equal to," so the value on one side of the equation is very close but not the same as the other.

This form of the equation is a helpful approximation because we often think in terms of growth rates. Let's consider four cases, all of which are summarized in Table 21.6.

First, consider a case where velocity and real GDP are constant, that is, $\%\Delta V = 0$ and $\%\Delta Y = 0$. In this case, it is clear that the growth rate of the money supply ($\%\Delta M$) will translate exactly to the growth rate of the price level ($\%\Delta P$), which is the definition of inflation. If money grows by 2%, inflation will also be 2%.

TABLE 21.6

Four Scenarios for the Equation of Exchange

	%ΔM	+	%ΔV	=	%ΔP	+	%ΔY
	Money growth		Velocity growth		Inflation		Real GDP growth
Case 1	2	+	0	=	2	+	0
Case 2	2	+	0	=	0	+	2
Case 3	4	+	0	=	2	+	2
Case 4	9	+	−5	=	2	+	2

As shown in case 1 in Table 21.6, the quantity of goods and services does not change but the money supply grows. As a result, you have 2% more money to use to purchase the same quantity of goods and services, so prices rise by 2%.

Now consider a more realistic case in which real GDP is growing. Let's continue the assumptions that the money supply grows at 2% and velocity does not change. In this case, if real GDP grows at 2% in a given year, then there is no change in the price level (%ΔP = 0). In this scenario, presented as case 2 in Table 21.6, the money supply grows at exactly the same rate as real GDP, so there is no effect on the price level.

Consider a third, even more realistic case. A typical year brings both real GDP growth and some inflation. In this case, if velocity is constant, the money supply is growing at a greater rate than real GDP growth. Case 3 in Table 21.6 presents such a scenario: real GDP grows at 2% and inflation is also 2%. In this case, with constant velocity, the growth rate of the money supply must be 4%.

Finally, let's consider a case where velocity changes (case 4 in Table 21.6). Changes in velocity occur when those who hold money (for example, individuals and banks) decide to change their spending habits. If people and banks decide to spend their dollars at faster rates, velocity rises. When people and banks decide to hold on to money longer, velocity falls. Let's consider this latter possibility, since it is related to changes in the macroeconomy during the severe recession from 2007 to 2009. What if velocity falls by 5% (%ΔV = −5)? Let's assume that real GDP rises by 2% and that the money supply grows by 9%. Our equation implies that despite the large money supply increase, inflation (%ΔP) is just 2%. Inflation is low because people and banks have decided to hold on to their money longer. The equation of exchange helps us see that changes in all four of these variables—money, velocity, the price level, and real GDP—must be accounted for.

ECONOMICS IN THE REAL WORLD

THE COVID-ERA INFLATION SPIKE

In 2021, the inflation rate in the United States climbed above 6% for the first time in decades (see Figure 21.1). While that is still pretty tame by global standards, it's higher than what most American economists like to see. The U.S. government's stated goal is to keep inflation down around 2% on average. Inflation that goes higher, and stays there for an extended time, risks stirring up the problems we have discussed in this chapter.

You might reasonably wonder how inflation got so high, especially given our discussion of the equation of exchange. In particular, we just discussed how inflation is caused by growth in the quantity of money in the economy, relative to the quantity of goods and services. Therefore, if we know what causes inflation, how did it get so high?

Economists have different opinions on why this happened. One reason is that it is simply becoming difficult to control the quantity of money in the economy. We discuss this more fully in Chapter 30, but for now, note that the combined actions of individuals and banks also affect the quantity of money in circulation in the economy. For example, since 2008, banks have been holding onto more and more money, not lending it but instead setting it aside on "reserve." If banks decide to start lending out this money, it leads to more money in the economy and then inflation. Another reason is that those in the government trying to control inflation never know exactly what will change behavior. A case in point occurred in 2021. As the government was taking actions to support the pandemic economy, including sending checks to most Americans, Americans spent this money at a faster rate than government economists anticipated. In particular, while unable to go out to spend it on restaurants, travel, and other services, they bought far more goods than expected. With more cash on hand, Americans continued to spend even as prices rose, as sellers saw opportunities to raise prices and because many goods became hard to get because of this demand.* Only in 2022 did parts of the government start taking actions to control this, changing some policies that it was advocating for in 2021. The bottom line is that inflation is harder to control today than it was in the past.

*Jeanna Smialek, "Inflation Has Arrived. Here's What You Need to Know." *New York Times*, January 10, 2022, https://www.nytimes.com/article/inflation-definition.html?searchResultPosition=2; Gabriel T. Rubin, "Why Do Prices Keep Going Up and What's the Cause of Inflation?" *Wall Street Journal*, December 10, 2021, https://www.wsj.com/articles/what-is-inflation-cause-stock-market-11637623703?page=1; Josh Zumbrun, "Inflation, Supply Chain, Omicron Expected to Take a Bigger Toll on Global Growth," *Wall Street Journal*, January 25, 2022, https://www.wsj.com/articles/inflation-supply-chain-omicron-expected-to-take-a-bigger-toll-on-global-growth-11643119381?page=1.

The Reasons Why Governments Inflate the Money Supply

In this chapter, we discussed several problems that stem from inflation: shoe-leather costs, money illusion, menu costs, future price level uncertainty, wealth redistribution, price confusion, and tax distortions. And yet we know what causes inflation. Thus, it is reasonable to wonder why inflation is often still a macroeconomic problem. We point to two reasons: large government debts and short-term gains.

First, large government debts often spur governments to choose to increase the money supply rapidly. When a government owes large sums and also controls the supply of money, there is a natural urge to print more money to pay off debts. After World War I, the German government owed billions of dollars to other nations and to its workers, so it resorted to printing more money—and this action led to inflation rates of almost 30 thousand percent in late 1923.

Second, surprise increases in the money supply can temporarily stimulate an economy toward more rapid growth rates. We'll look at this issue very closely in Chapter 31, but the short-term economic boost is a constant temptation for short-sighted governments. The problems from inflation are often long-term and difficult to overcome. Unfortunately, to realize any benefits from inflation, the government must keep surprising people in the economy. As a result of these attempts to stay ahead of expectations, inflation can spiral out of control.

Conclusion

This chapter began with the story of Venezuela, where hyperinflation has added to the serious woes of that economy. And while inflation rates have been low in the United States for several years now, at times in the past they have been very high—such as during the 1970s. In addition, inflation rates in some other nations remain high.

Inflation, along with the unemployment rate and changes in real GDP, is an important indicator of overall macroeconomic conditions. Now that we have covered these three, we move next to savings and the determination of interest rates. ✷

ECONOMICS for LIFE

Inflation Devalues Dollars: Preparing Your Future for Inflation

- Remember that things will likely cost more in the future when you retire due to inflation.
- To keep up, or grow, your savings has to earn an annual return that is at least the same rate or more.
- Money saved in a mattress will always lose value because of inflation! You need to think about investing it somewhere.

How many nest eggs will you need to put aside to keep pace with inflation?

In this chapter, we talked about how inflation devalues the money you currently hold and the money you've been promised in the future. One problem you may encounter is how to prepare for retirement in the face of inflation. Perhaps you are not worried about this, since the inflation rate in the United States over the past 50 years has averaged 4%, and more recently the average has been only 2%. But even these low rates mean that dollars will be worth significantly less 40 years from now.

One way to think about the effect of inflation on future dollars is to ask what amount of future dollars it will take to match the real value of $1.00 today. The graph below answers this question based on a retirement date of 40 years in the future. The different inflation rates are specified at the bottom.

Thus, if the inflation rate averages 4% over the next four decades, you'll need $4.80 just to buy the same goods and services you can buy today for $1.00.

What does this mean for your overall retirement plans? Let's say you decide you could live on $50,000 per year if you retired today. If the inflation rate is 4% between now and your retirement date, you would need enough savings to supply yourself with 50,000 × $4.80, or $240,000 per year, just to keep pace with inflation.

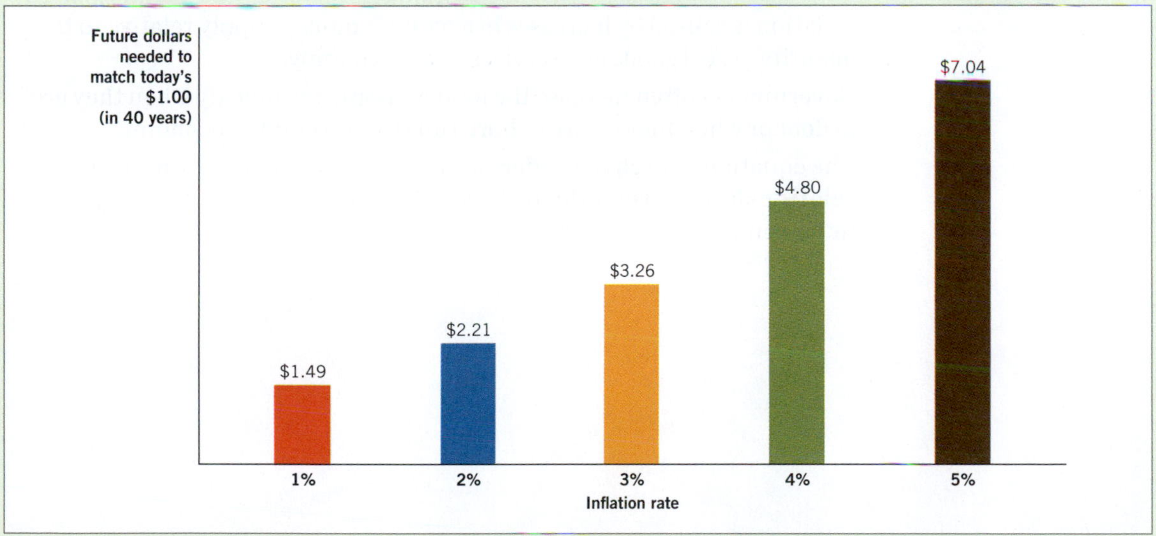

ANSWERING *the* BIG QUESTIONS

How is inflation measured?

- The inflation rate is calculated as the percentage change in the overall level of prices.
- Economists use the consumer price index (CPI) to determine the general level of prices in the economy.
- Determining which prices to include in the CPI can be challenging for several reasons: consumers change what they buy over time; the quality of goods and services changes; and new goods, services, and sales locations are introduced.

What problems does inflation bring?

- Inflation imposes shoe-leather costs: it causes people to waste resources as they seek to avoid holding money.
- Inflation can cause people to make decisions based on nominal rather than real monetary values, a problem known as money illusion.
- Inflation adds menu costs, as sellers need to physically change prices.
- Inflation introduces uncertainty about future price levels. Because uncertainty makes it difficult for consumers and producers to plan, it impedes economic progress.
- Unexpected inflation redistributes wealth from lenders to borrowers.
- Inflation creates price confusion: that is, it makes it difficult for producers to read price signals correctly. The result may be a misallocation of resources.
- Inflation distorts people's tax obligations.

What is the cause of inflation?

- Inflation is caused by increases in a nation's money supply relative to the quantity of real goods and services in the economy.
- Governments often increase the money supply too quickly when they are in debt or when they desire a short-run stimulus for the economy.
- The equation of exchange offers a simple summary of the long-run relationship between the inflation rate and quantity of money in an economy.

·CHAPTER PROBLEMS·

Concepts You Should Know

capital gains taxes (p. 694)
chained CPI (p. 688)
consumer price index (CPI) (p. 675)
deflation (p. 675)
equation of exchange (p. 697)
menu costs (p. 691)
money illusion (p. 690)
nominal wage (p. 691)
output (p. 692)
real wage (p. 691)
shoe-leather costs (p. 690)
velocity of money (p. 697)

Questions for Review

1. The price of a typical laptop computer has fallen from $2,000 in 1985 to $800 today. At the same time, the consumer price index has risen from 100 to 280. Adjusting for inflation, how much did the price of laptops change? Does this answer seem right to you, or is it missing something? Explain your response.

2. What three issues are at the center of the debate regarding the accuracy of the CPI? Give an example of each issue.

3. If the prices of homes go up by 5% and the prices of concert tickets rise by 10%, which will have the larger impact on the CPI? Why?

4. If a country is experiencing a relatively high rate of inflation, what impact will this have on the country's long-term rate of economic growth?

5. In a sentence or two, evaluate the accuracy of the following statement, including a clear and precise statement of historical comparison: Inflation in the United States last year was 0%. This is close to the historical level.

6. Wage agreements and loan contracts are two types of multiperiod agreements that are important for economic growth. Suppose you sign a two-year job contract with Wells Fargo stipulating that you will receive an annual salary of $93,500 plus an additional 2% above that in the second year, to account for expected inflation.

a. If the inflation rate turns out to be 3% rather than 2%, who will be hurt? Why?
b. If the inflation rate turns out to be 1% rather than 2%, who will be hurt? Why?

Suppose that you also take out a $1,000 loan at the Cavalier Credit Union. The loan agreement stipulates that you must pay it back with 4% interest in one year, and again, the inflation rate is expected to be 2%.

c. If the inflation rate turns out to be 3% rather than 2%, who will be hurt? Why?
d. If the inflation rate turns out to be 3% rather than 2%, who will be helped? Why?

7. What are the seven problems caused by inflation? Briefly explain each one.

8. Here is a list of potential problems that inflation might cause. Use the space on the left to name each of these with the terms used in this chapter.

a. ________ Lenders and workers are reluctant to help firms produce output because the real value of future dollar payoffs is unclear.
b. ________ Workers make decisions on the basis of nominal rather than real wage changes.
c. ________ Unexpected inflation reduces the real value of loan repayments.
d. ________ Firms cannot distinguish whether there is a change in the relative price of their good or a change in the overall price level.
e. ________ Restaurants need to spend resources to alter the prices on their menus.
f. ________ Individuals own stock shares for many years and then sell them and are required to pay taxes on the nominal capital gain.
g. ________ People leave work early to shop before inflation changes prices.

9. Inflation causes a lot of problems for the macroeconomy.
   a. What is the key misconception people have about inflation, and why does this problem generally not accompany inflation?
   b. In this chapter, we discussed the problem of price confusion and the problem of future price uncertainty. Explain the difference between these two problems.
   c. Wealth redistribution is another problem caused by inflation. What is this problem, and how is it related to the future price uncertainty?

10. People often confuse real and nominal variables in macroeconomics.
   a. Give a hypothetical example where nominal wages rise but real wages do not, using specific numbers to illustrate changes in all relevant macroeconomic variables.
   b. Give a hypothetical example of a situation where real wages rise but nominal wages fall, using specific numbers to illustrate changes in all relevant macroeconomic variables.

11. Explain the difference(s) between the CPI and the GDP deflator.

Study Problems *(* solved at the end of the section)*

1. In 1991, the Barenaked Ladies released their hit song "If I Had a Million Dollars." How much money would the group need in 2021 to have the same amount of real purchasing power they had in 1991? Note that the consumer price index in 1991 was 136.2, and in 2021 it was 280.

2. Visit the Bureau of Labor Statistics web site for the CPI (www.bls.gov/cpi), and find the latest news release. Table 1 in that release presents CPI data for all items and also for many individual categories.
   a. How much has the entire index changed (in percentage terms) in the past year?
   b. Now identify and list the five individual categories that have increased the most in the past year.

3. While rooting through the attic, you discover a box of old tax forms. You find that your grandmother made $75 working part-time during December 1964, when the CPI was 31.3. How much would you need to have earned in January of this year to have at least as much real income as your grandmother did in 1964? To determine the CPI for January of this year, you can visit the Bureau of Labor Statistics web site (www.bls.gov).

* 4. Suppose that the residents of Greenland play golf incessantly. In fact, golf is the only thing they spend their money on. They buy golf balls, clubs, and tees. In 2021, they bought 1,000 golf balls for $2.00 each, 100 clubs for $50.00 each, and 500 tees for $0.10 each. In 2022, they bought 1,000 golf balls for $2.50 each, 100 clubs for $75.00 each, and 500 tees for $0.12 each.
   a. What was the CPI for each year?
   b. What was the inflation rate in 2022?

* 5. If healthcare costs make up 10% of total expenditures and they rise by 15% while the other components in the consumer price index remain constant, by how much will the price index rise?

* 6. The equation of exchange is helpful for determining the effect of money supply changes on the price level. Use the equation of exchange to answer each of the following questions.
   a. Real GDP grows at 3% and inflation is equal to 2%, but there is no change in velocity. What can you conclude about the change in the money supply?
   b. Real GDP falls by 3% and there is no inflation, but the money supply grew by 5%. What is the implied change in velocity?
   c. Real GDP increases by 3%, velocity does not change, and the money supply grows by 10%. What is the implied rate of inflation?
   d. The money supply grows at 6%, velocity is constant, and inflation is 3%. What can you conclude about the rate of real GDP growth?

7. Let's say you graduate from college and accept a job in 2021. You decide to compare your starting salary with your grandfather's and mother's starting salaries. The salaries you compare are:

- You: $80,000 per year beginning in 2021
- Your mother: $50,000 per year beginning in 1983
- Your grandfather: $20,000 per year beginning in 1965

To compare these salaries, you decide to use the CPI, using 1983 as the base year.

a. Why is the CPI a good price index to use for this comparison?

b. Fill in the missing data point in the following table:

Year	CPI
1965	30
1983	____
2015	238
2021	280

c. Convert both your mother's salary and your grandfather's salary to 2021 dollars. Enter your answers in the table below.

Grandfather's 1965 salary in 2021 dollars	________
Mother's 1983 salary in 2021 dollars	________

✷ **8.** In the following chart, which of these prices would be included in the CPI? Which would be included in the GDP deflator? Which would be included in both or neither? Mark the correct option for each price.

Price of	CPI	GDP Deflator	Both	Neither
Toothpaste	☐	☐	☐	☐
Industrial coolant	☐	☐	☐	☐
Milk you bought in a grocery store	☐	☐	☐	☐
Milk bought by Starbucks from a food distributor	☐	☐	☐	☐
An Intel computer chip bought by Dell to put into a laptop computer	☐	☐	☐	☐
Bus fare for a trip to a shopping mall	☐	☐	☐	☐
A doctor's appointment, to get a physical	☐	☐	☐	☐

9. In the United States, average income levels vary across racial lines. In particular, Asians tend to earn more than whites, and both groups earn more than Hispanics and blacks. However, in 2016, economist Jeff Guo looked closely at the data and noted that much of the difference between Asians and other groups could be attributed to the fact that Asians tend to live in more expensive urban areas. In real terms, their wages are not so different from those of other groups.

a. In 2016, Asian American households earned an average annual income of $82,270, but if the average price level across the United States was 100, the price level where Asian Americans tended to live was 109. Calculate a comparable real income for Asian Americans.

b. Black Americans earned an average of $44,170 per year in 2016 but tended to live in areas with lower average prices than all races combined. The average price level where Black Americans lived was 98.374. Assume that the average price level across the United States was 100, and then compute a real earnings figure that is comparable to average incomes across the United States.

c. Hispanic Americans had an average annual income of $45,320 in 2016, but when adjusted for the price levels in their area, this number falls to $43,890. Given these two figures, what was the implied price level in the areas where Hispanic Americans lived?

Solved Problems

4. a. We'll use the quantities from the first year to designate the weights. To build a price index, we first need to choose which year we will use as the base year. Let 2021 be the base year. Next we define our basket as the goods consumed in 2022: 1,000 golf balls, 100 clubs, and 500 tees. In 2021, this basket cost as follows:

$$(1{,}000 \times \$2) + (100 \times \$50) + (500 \times \$0.10) = \$7{,}050$$

In 2022, this basket cost as follows:

$$(1{,}000 \times \$2.50) + (100 \times \$75) + (500 \times \$0.12) = \$10{,}060$$

Dividing the cost of the basket in each year by the cost of the basket in the base year and multiplying by 100 gives us the CPI for each year. For 2021, the CPI is calculated as

$$(\$7{,}050 \div \$7{,}050) \times 100 = 100$$

For 2022, the CPI is calculated as

$$(\$10{,}060 \div \$7{,}050) \times 100 = 142.7$$

b. The inflation rate is defined as $[(CPI_2 - CPI_1) \div CPI_1] \times 100$. Plugging the values from part (a) into the formula, we get an inflation rate of 42.7%:

$$[(142.7 - 100) \div 100] \times 100 = 42.7$$

5. The CPI will rise by 1.5%. Suppose the CPI in the first year is 100. If healthcare costs are 10% of total expenditures, then they account for 10 of the 100 points, with the other 90 points falling in other categories. If healthcare costs rise by 15% in the second year, then those 10 points become 11.5 points. Since the prices of the other categories have not changed, the CPI now stands at 101.5, since $11.5 + 90 = 101.5$.

Using our formula for calculating the inflation rate, the rise in healthcare costs has raised the overall price level by 1.5%:

$$[(101.5 - 100) \div 100] \times 100 = 1.5$$

6. Using the equation of exchange in rates of growth, we know that

$$\%\Delta M + \%\Delta V \approx \%\Delta P + \%\Delta Y$$

a. $\%\Delta M + 0 \approx 2\% + 3\%$
Thus, $\%\Delta M \approx 5\%$.

b. $5\% + \%\Delta V \approx 0 + -3\%$
Thus, $\%\Delta V \approx -8\%$.

c. $10\% + 0 \approx \%\Delta P + 3\%$
Thus, $\%\Delta P \approx 7\%$.

d. $6\% + 0 \approx 3\% + \%\Delta Y$
Thus, $\%\Delta Y \approx 3\%$.

8.

		GDP		
Price of	**CPI**	**Deflator**	**Both**	**Neither**
Toothpaste	□	□	■	□
Industrial coolant	□	■	□	□
Milk you bought in a grocery store	□	□	■	□
Milk bought by Starbucks from a food distributor	□	□	□	■
An Intel computer chip bought by Dell to put into a laptop computer	□	□	□	■
Bus fare for a trip to a shopping mall	□	□	■	□
A doctor's appointment, to get a physical	□	□	■	□

CHAPTER

22

Savings, Interest Rates, and the Market for Loanable Funds

The Market for Loanable Funds Is a Bridge between Savers and Borrowers.

Firms that want to grow have to invest in resources, and these firms generally need someone to lend them funds. Without an efficient and safe market for loans, firms cannot borrow in order to buy what they need to increase their production output. If they don't increase their output, they won't contribute to GDP growth.

Meanwhile, households need to save—for a rainy day, for kids' college tuition, for retirement. Tucking cash under a mattress is one way to go. But a better way is to deposit funds in a bank or other financial institution. After all, why not put one's savings someplace where they're not only safe but will earn more by being loaned out at interest?

Banks take care of the arrangements, allowing savers to become lenders without going to extra trouble. The banks earn a profit by taking a cut. They are the middlemen in the loanable funds market, the bridge between savers and borrowers. When this bridge is safe and functioning well, savers can earn a predictable return on their funds and borrowers can consistently find funds to build, expand, and produce GDP.

In this chapter, we discuss many of the same topics you might study in a course on banking or financial institutions,

The Brooklyn Bridge connects Manhattan, home to many of the United States' biggest financial institutions, and Brooklyn, home to many high-tech firms. When those firms need funds for investment, they often look across the river to the financial firms at the other end of the bridge.

but our emphasis is different. We are interested in studying how financial institutions and markets affect the macroeconomy. When we are finished, you will understand why interest rates rise and fall, and you will also appreciate the necessity of the loanable funds market in the larger macroeconomy.

Just about anything you read or hear about interest rates in the popular media leaves you with the impression that the government sets interest rates. This isn't exactly true. For sure, the government can influence many rates. But almost all interest rates in the U.S. economy are determined privately—by the market forces of supply and demand. In fact, you can understand why interest rates rise and fall by applying supply and demand analysis to the market for loans. That's what we do in this chapter. Along the way, we also consider the many factors that influence savers and borrowers.

· BIG QUESTIONS ·

- What is the loanable funds market?
- What factors shift the supply of loanable funds?
- What factors shift the demand for loanable funds?
- How do we apply the loanable funds market model?

What Is the Loanable Funds Market?

Imagine you are an entrepreneur who decides to start a company that will produce and sell college apparel. If you succeed, you'll contribute to national GDP. But you don't really think of it this way; you just hope you've discovered a great business opportunity. Before you sell your first shirt, hat, or sweatpants, however, you have to spend money on the resources you'll use in the production process. For example, if you plan on silk-screening your college logo onto hooded sweatshirts, you have to buy sweatshirts, ink, and a screen-printing press.

Since you have no revenue yet, you need to borrow cash in order to make these investments. For that, you need to go to a financial market. Financial markets are where firms and governments obtain funds, or *financing*, for their operations. These funds come primarily from household savings across the economy.

In economics, we analyze financial markets in the context of a **loanable funds market**. This is the market where savers supply funds for loans to borrowers. This market is not a single physical location but includes places like stock exchanges, investment banks, mutual fund firms, and commercial banks. In this section, we explain the particular characteristics of the loanable funds market and the significant role it plays in the overall economy.

The **loanable funds market** is the market where savers supply funds for loans to borrowers.

Figure 22.1 illustrates the role of the loanable funds market. Savings flow in and become loans for borrowers. We could call it the market for savings or the market for loans. The term "loanable funds" captures the information in both.

On the left side of the figure, the suppliers of funds—those who save—include households and foreign entities. Households are private individuals and families. Foreign entities include foreign governments, firms, and private citizens that choose to save in the United States. For most of the applications we discuss, we focus on households as the primary suppliers of loanable funds. If you have a checking or savings account at a bank, you are a supplier of loanable funds. You deposit funds into your bank account, but these funds don't just sit in a vault; banks loan out the majority of these funds. Household savings in retirement accounts, stocks, bonds, and mutual funds are other big sources of loanable funds.

The demanders, or borrowers, of loanable funds include firms and governments. In this chapter, we focus on firms as the primary borrowers of loanable funds. To reinforce the significance of this market, think about why borrowing takes place: firms borrow to invest, to buy tools and equipment, and to build factories. Firms looking to produce output in the future must borrow to pay their expenses today.

Figure 22.2 shows the production timeline we introduced in Chapter 21. At the end of the timeline is output, or GDP. When output is sold, it produces revenue for the firms, and the revenue serves to pay bills. But future GDP

FIGURE 22.1

The Role of the Loanable Funds Market

The market for loanable funds is where savers bring funds and make them available to borrowers. Households (private individuals and families) are the primary suppliers of loanable funds. Firms are the primary demanders, or borrowers, of loanable funds. When this market is functioning well, firms get the funds necessary for production and savers are paid for lending.

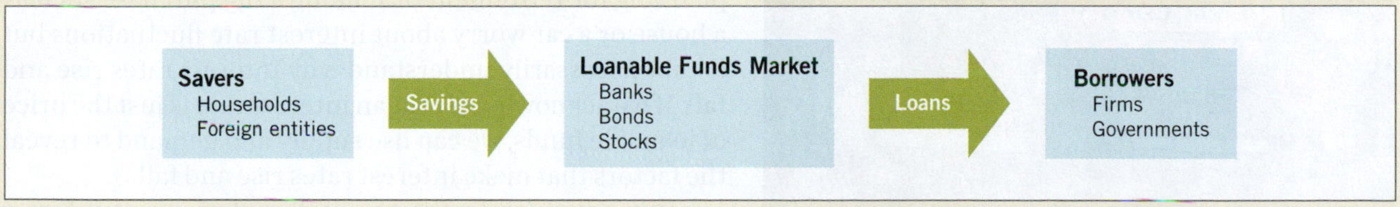

FIGURE 22.2

The Timeline of Production

The production timeline illustrates that GDP depends critically on the loanable funds market. At the end of the production timeline we see output, or GDP. But before a firm can produce output, it must purchase resources. Since these purchases occur before the revenue comes in, firms must borrow at the beginning of the timeline.

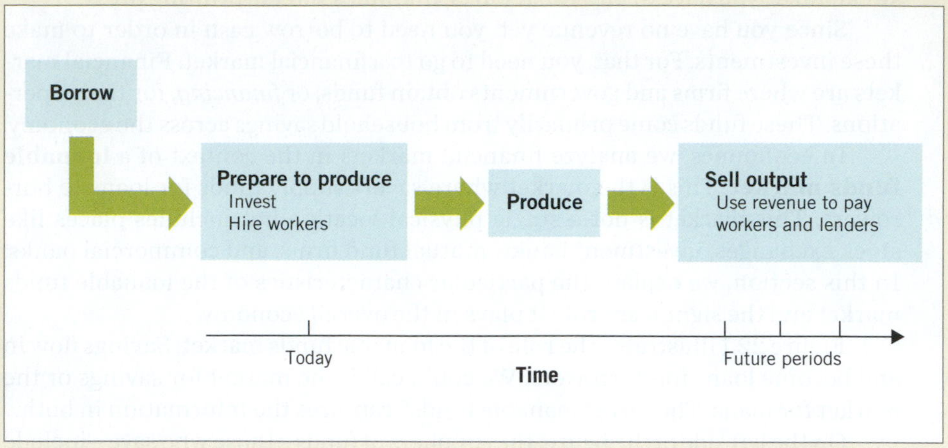

depends on spending today for necessary resources. This spending comes before any revenue is gained from the sale of output. Therefore, firms must borrow in order to generate future GDP—that's how important the loanable funds market is to the entire economy. Without a well-functioning loanable funds market, future GDP dries up.

Borrowing fuels investment, which creates future output. But notice that *every dollar borrowed requires a dollar saved.* Without savings, we cannot sustain future production. If you want to borrow to buy the resources you need to produce college apparel, someone else has to save. Working backward, the chain of crucial relationships looks like this: output (GDP) requires investment; investment requires borrowing; borrowing requires savings. And all the links in this chain require a loanable funds market that efficiently channels funds from savers to borrowers.

An **interest rate** is a price of loanable funds, quoted as a percentage of the original loan amount.

We study this crucial market from the perspective of prices, quantities, supply, and demand—like any other market. The demanders (or consumers) are borrowers who want to invest; the suppliers are savers. Figure 22.3 presents a picture of supply (savings) and demand (investment) for loanable funds, along with a summary of the distinctions of the loanable funds market. The price in this market is the interest rate; the good is loanable funds. These loanable funds are the dollars' worth of savings that are transformed into dollars of investment.

Before you can sell college apparel, you have to buy equipment and other supplies.

This demand and supply approach helps to clarify the role of interest rates. An **interest rate** is a price of loanable funds. It is like the price of toothpaste or computers or hoodies; it is simply quoted differently—as a percentage of the original loan amount. People who are thinking about planning for retirement or making a big purchase such as a house or a car worry about interest rate fluctuations but do not necessarily understand why interest rates rise and fall. If we acknowledge that an interest rate is just the price of loanable funds, we can use supply and demand to reveal the factors that make interest rates rise and fall.

We now turn to the two different views of interest rates: the saver's view and the borrower's view.

FIGURE 22.3

The Loanable Funds Market

Savings (S) is channeled into investment (D) in the loanable funds market. In this market, loanable funds are the goods bought and sold. The price is an interest rate. This price, like any other market-determined price, is determined by the interaction between supply and demand.

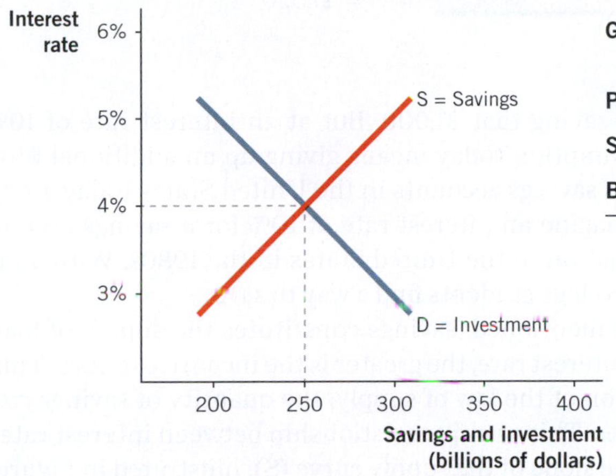

Good	Loanable funds: savings available for a loan
Price	Interest rate
Seller/Suppliers	Savers
Buyers/Demanders	Borrowers

Interest Rates as a Reward for Saving

If you are a saver, the interest rate is the return you get for supplying funds. For example, let's say your parents gave you some cash when you left for college this term. After buying textbooks, groceries, and other supplies, you have $1,000 left, which you consider saving. You go to a bank near campus and inquire about opening a new account. In this transaction, the bank is the buyer, and it offers a certain price for the use of your savings. When it does offer a price, it is not in dollars. The bank quotes a price in an interest rate, or as a percentage of how much you save. But the interest rate communicates the same information. So if you are saving $1,000, the bank might tell you, "We'll pay you 2% if you save that money for a year." Because 2% of $1,000 is $20, this is equivalent to saying, "We'll pay you $20 if you save that money for a year."

If you save $1,000 for one year with an interest rate of 2%, your total amount of savings is $1,020 at the end of the year, which is computed as

$$\$1{,}000 + (2\% \text{ of } \$1{,}000) = \$1{,}000 + \$20 = \$1{,}020$$

For savers, the interest rate is a reward. Every dollar saved today returns more in the saver's account in the future. The higher the interest rate, the greater the return will be in the future. Table 22.1 illustrates how interest rates affect $1,000 worth of savings. An interest rate of 2% yields $1,020 one year later; an interest rate of 10% yields $1,100.

Think of the interest rate as the opportunity cost of consumption. With a 4% interest rate and a $1,000 purchase today, you are giving up the $40 you

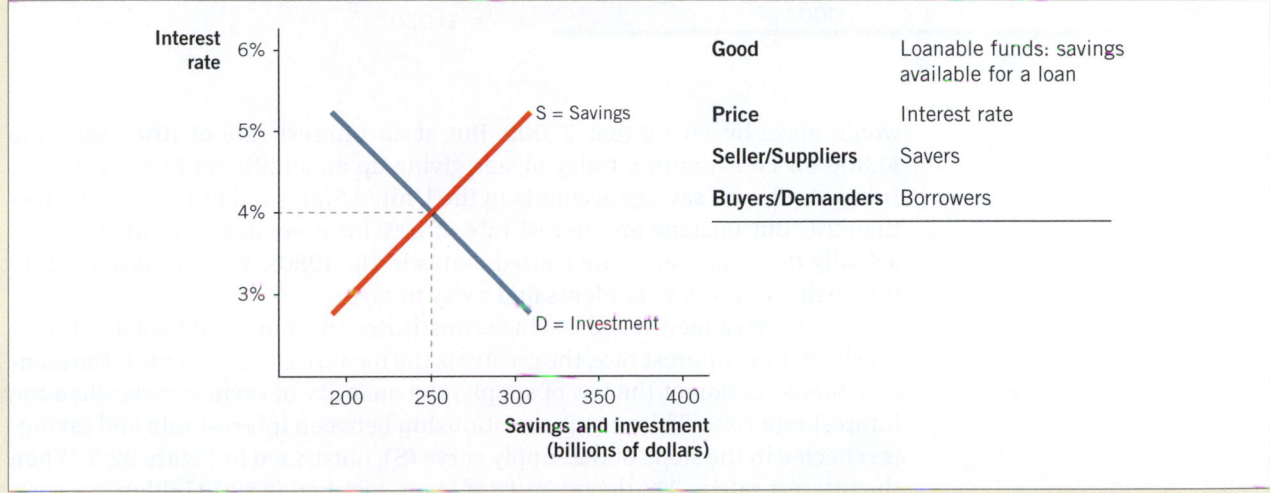

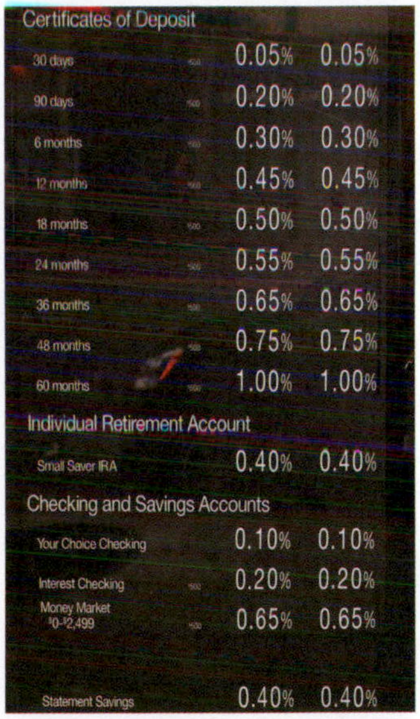

Banks are willing to pay you for your savings. The price they pay is the interest rate.

Opportunity cost

TABLE 22.1

Higher Interest Rates and Greater Future Returns

Interest rate	Value of $1,000 after one year
2%	$1,020
4	1,040
6	1,060
10	1,100

If you save $1,000 for one year at an interest rate of 2%, this leads to $1,020 next year, computed as

$1,000 + (2% of $1,000)
= $1,000 + (0.02 × $1,000)
= $1,000 + $20
= $1,020

would make by saving that $1,000. But at an interest rate of 10%, using the $1,000 for consumption today means giving up an additional $100 next year. Interest rates on savings accounts in the United States today are typically less than 2%. But imagine an interest rate of 10% for a savings account. This was actually the situation in the United States in the 1980s. With an interest rate that high, even college students find a way to save.

Incentives

As we have mentioned, savings constitutes the supply of loanable funds. The higher the interest rate, the greater is the incentive to save. This is the loanable funds version of the law of supply: the quantity of savings rises when the interest rate rises. This positive relationship between interest rate and savings is reflected in the slope of the supply curve (S), illustrated in Figure 22.3. When the interest rate is 3%, the quantity of loans supplied is $200 billion per year; at 4% the quantity supplied increases to $250 billion; and at 5% it increases to $300 billion.

Interest Rates as a Cost of Borrowing

We now turn to the demand, or borrowing, side of the loanable funds market. For this we shift to the firm's perspective and return to your plan to produce college apparel. Recall that you need to buy the sweatshirts, paint, and a screen-printing press to produce hoodies and other products with a college logo. Assume you need $100,000 to start your business. If you borrow $100,000 for one year at an interest rate of 4%, you'll need to repay $104,000 in one year. It makes sense to do this only if your *expected return* is greater than 4%, or $4,000, on this investment. The **expected return** on a capital investment is the anticipated rate of return based on the probabilities of all possible outcomes. This is a firm's best guess of the future percentage return on an investment.

The **expected return** on a capital investment is the anticipated rate of return based on the probabilities of all possible outcomes.

For borrowers, the interest rate is the cost of borrowing. Firms borrow only if the expected return on their investment is greater than the cost of the loan. For example, at an interest rate of 6%, a firm would borrow only if it expected to make more than a 6% return with its use of the funds. Let's state this as a rule:

Profit-maximizing firms borrow to fund an investment if and only if the expected return on the investment is greater than the interest rate on the loan.

The lower the interest rate, the more likely a business will succeed in earning enough to exceed the interest it will owe at the end of the year. For example, if your firm can borrow at an interest rate of just 3%, you'll need to make a return greater than 3%. There are probably several investments available today that would pay more than a 5% return; but there are even more that would yield returns greater than 3% and more still that would pay greater than 1%. If we apply our rule from above, we'll see a larger quantity of loans demanded as the interest rate drops. This gives us the negative relationship between the interest rate and quantity demanded of loans, reflected in the slope of the demand curve for loanable funds.

The graph of the loanable funds market in Figure 22.3 illustrates the demand curve (D) for loanable funds across the entire U.S. economy. At an interest rate of 5%, the quantity of loans demanded by all business firms in the economy is $200 billion. This indicates that firms believe that only $200 billion worth of investment will pay returns greater than 5%. At an interest rate of 4%, firms estimate that another $50 billion worth of total loans will earn between 4% and 5%, and the quantity of loans demanded rises to $250 billion. Lower interest rates lead to a greater quantity demanded of loanable funds.

How Inflation Affects Interest Rates

If you save $1,000 for a year at an interest rate of 2%, your reward for saving is $20. But inflation affects the real value of this reward. For example, imagine that the inflation rate is exactly 2% during the year you save. This means that next year it will take $1,020 to buy the same quantity of goods and services you are able to buy this year for $1,000. In this case, your interest rate of 2% and the inflation rate of 2% cancel each other out. You break even, and that's not much of a reward.

When making decisions about saving and borrowing, people care more about the real interest rate than the nominal interest rate. The **real interest rate** is the interest rate corrected for inflation; it is the rate of return in terms of real purchasing power. In contrast, the **nominal interest rate** is the interest rate before it is corrected for inflation; it is the *stated* interest rate. In our example, the interest rate of 2% is the nominal interest rate. But with 2% inflation, the real return on your savings disappears, and the real interest rate is zero—or 0%. In general, we can approximate the real interest rate by subtracting the inflation rate from the nominal interest rate in an equation known as the **Fisher equation**:

The **real interest rate** is the interest rate corrected for inflation. It is the rate of return in terms of real purchasing power.

The **nominal interest rate** is the interest rate before it is corrected for inflation. It is the stated interest rate.

The **Fisher equation** states that the real interest rate equals the nominal interest rate minus the inflation rate.

$$\text{real interest rate} = \text{nominal interest rate} - \text{inflation rate}$$

(EQUATION 22.1)

For example, if the inflation rate this year is 2%, a nominal interest rate of 6% on your savings would yield a 4% real interest rate. The Fisher equation is named after Irving Fisher, the economist who formulated the relationship between inflation and interest rates.

Savers and borrowers care about the real rate of interest on a loan because this is the rate that describes how their funds' real purchasing power changes over the course of the loan. Because the interest rate is a result of supply and demand in the market for loanable funds, higher inflation rates lead to higher nominal interest rates to compensate lenders for the loss of purchasing power. We can rewrite the Fisher equation to see how inflation generally increases nominal interest rates:

$$\text{nominal interest rate} = \text{real interest rate} + \text{inflation rate}$$

(EQUATION 22.2)

For a given real interest rate, the higher the rate of inflation, the higher the nominal interest rate. Table 22.2 shows how the nominal interest rate rises with inflation rates for a given level of the real interest rate. If the real interest rate is

TABLE 22.2

How Inflation Affects Nominal Interest Rates

Inflation rate		Real interest rate		Nominal interest rate
0%	+	4%	=	4%
2	+	4	=	6
4	+	4	=	8

4% and there is no inflation, then the nominal interest rate is also 4%. But if the inflation rate rises to 2%, the nominal interest rate increases to 6%. If the inflation rate rises further to 4%, then the nominal interest rate rises to 8%.

We can picture the Fisher equation by looking at real and nominal interest rates over time. Figure 22.4 plots the real and nominal interest rates in the United States from 1970 to 2020. The difference between them is the inflation rate. Notice that this gap was particularly high during the inflationary 1970s but that it narrowed considerably as inflation rates fell in the 1980s. For several years after 2008, the nominal interest rate in the United States was essentially zero. Because inflation rates were around 2%, the real interest rate was negative.

Unless otherwise stated, in this text we use the nominal interest rate. The nominal interest rate is the stated interest rate—the rate you read about in the news and have to pay attention to when conducting your own financial transactions. When inflation is low and steady, as it was from 1995 to 2020, the difference between real and nominal interest rates doesn't fluctuate much. However, borrowers and savers do care greatly about the real interest rate, especially during periods of high inflation, when the real rate of interest paid or earned is significantly different from the nominal rate.

In the next two sections, we consider the factors that cause shifts in the supply of and demand for loanable funds.

FIGURE 22.4

Real and Nominal Interest Rates, 1970–2020

The difference between the real interest rate and the nominal interest rate is the rate of inflation. The experience of the 1970s illustrates that the nominal interest rate is historically high when inflation is also high.

Sources: Federal Reserve Bank of St. Louis FRED database; Bureau of Labor Statistics.

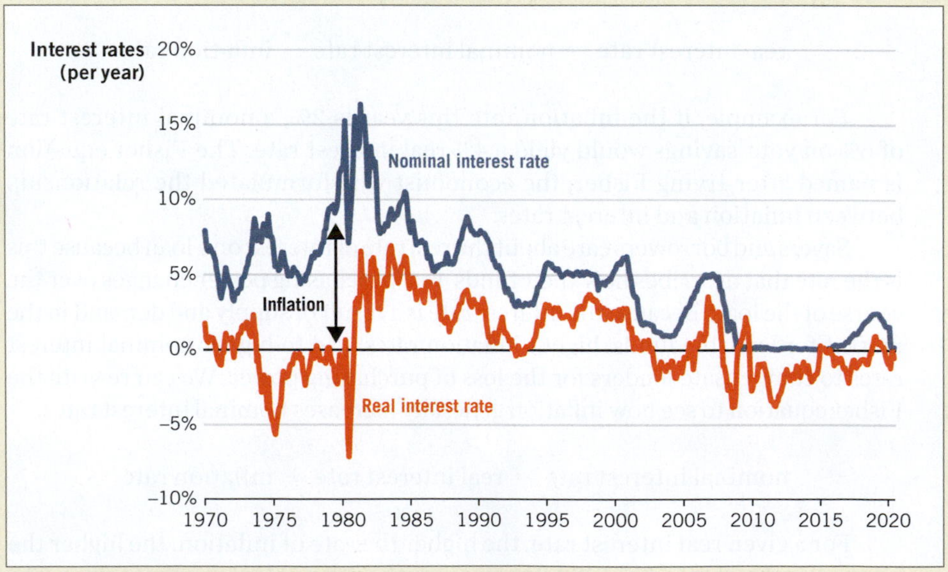

PRACTICE WHAT YOU KNOW

Interest Rates and Quantity Supplied and Demanded: U.S. Interest Rates Have Fallen

In 1981, many interest rates in the United States were 15%, but the inflation rate was 10%. In 2015, many interest rates were less than 1%, and the inflation rate was 2%.

QUESTION: What were the real interest rates in 1981 and 2015?

ANSWER: Using equation 22.1, we compute the real interest rate as

$$\text{real interest rate} = \text{nominal interest rate} - \text{inflation rate}$$

For 1981, the real interest rate was: 15% − 10% = 5%.
For 2015, the real interest rate was: 1% − 2% = −1%.

QUESTION: All else equal, how does the drop in interest rates between 1981 and 2015 affect the quantity of loanable funds supplied?

ANSWER: The quantity supplied decreases along the supply curve. Lower interest rates reduce the incentive to save.

CHALLENGE QUESTION: Which would you prefer, a 5% real interest rate, or a −1% real interest rate?

ANSWER: It depends on whether you plan to be a borrower or a lender. If you are borrowing to open a firm, or to buy a house or a car, you like the low rate. But if you are saving for the future by depositing funds at the bank (and thus lending to the bank), you like the high rate.

What Factors Shift the Supply of Loanable Funds?

Recall that the supply of loanable funds comes from savings. If you have either a savings or a checking account, you are a participant in this market. We turn now to three factors that shift the supply curve for loanable funds: income and wealth, time preferences, and consumption smoothing. When these factors change, the supply curve shifts.

Income and Wealth

Imagine that a distant relative dies and you inherit $20,000. What will you do with this unexpected wealth? You might celebrate with a fancy meal and a shopping spree. But most of us would also save some. All else equal, people prefer more savings. Thus, increases in either income or wealth generally produce increases in savings. If income and wealth decline, people save less. These changes shift the loanable funds supply curve.

As wealth increases in India, many of the funds its citizens save find their way into the U.S. loanable funds market.

The relationship between income and savings is true across the globe. As nations gain wealth, they save more, and not always in their own nation. Over the past twenty years, the increase in foreign savings has often made its way into the U.S. loanable funds market. For example, a businessman in Mumbai, India, may find himself with extra savings. He likely puts some into an Indian bank and some into Indian stocks and bonds. But there's a good chance he also channels some of his savings into the United States. Historically, U.S. financial markets have offered relatively greater returns than markets in other countries. In addition, the U.S. financial markets are often considered less risky than other global markets because of the size and relative robustness of the U.S. economy. Therefore, as global economies have grown, there has been an increase in foreign savings in the United States.

The increase in foreign savings came at a good time for the United States because domestic savings began falling in the 1980s. Without the influx of foreign funds, U.S. firms would have had difficulty funding investment. Of course, there is no guarantee that foreign savings will continue to flow into the United States at the same rates. But as long as some foreign funds still enter the U.S. financial markets, their presence allows more opportunities for domestic firms to borrow for investment than if firms relied solely on domestic savers.

Time Preferences

The term **time preferences** refers to the fact that people prefer to receive goods and services sooner rather than later.

Do you care when a friend repays your loan?

Imagine that your parents promised you a cash reward for getting a good grade in economics. Does it matter to you if they pay immediately or wait until you graduate? Of course it matters! You want the money as soon as you earn it. This is not unusual. People always prefer to receive funds sooner rather than later, and the same applies to goods and services. The term **time preferences** refers to the fact that people prefer to receive goods and services sooner rather than later. Because people have time preferences, someone must pay them to save. While time preferences are generally stable over time, if the rate of time preference in a society changes, the supply of loanable funds shifts.

While we all prefer sooner to later, some people have greater time preferences than others. Think of those with the strongest time preferences as being the least patient: they *strongly* prefer now to later. Someone with weaker time preferences has more patience. All else equal, people with stronger time preferences save less than people with weaker time preferences.

There are other ways time preferences are observed. For example, people with very strong time preferences may not go to college, since the returns to getting a college education are not typically realized until years later. Time

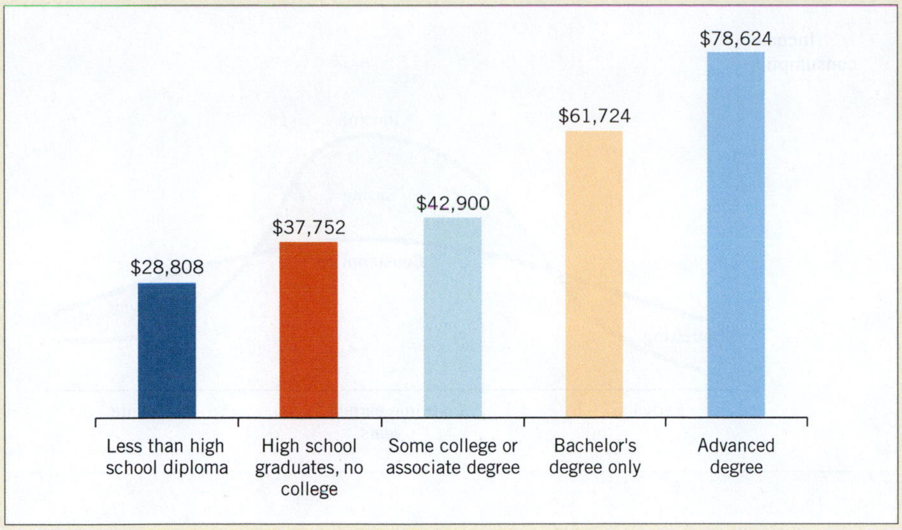

FIGURE 22.5

Median Annual Salary and Educational Attainment, 2018

It takes patience, or relatively low time preferences, to stay in school. But annual earnings based on years of schooling shows that education pays off for most graduates.

Source: Bureau of Labor Statistics.

spent in college is time that could have been spent earning income. The fact that you are a college student demonstrates that you are more patient than some others who choose instead to work for more income now.

You'll be happy to know there is a definite payoff to getting a college education. College graduates earn significantly more than high school graduates. Figure 22.5 shows median annual salary in the United States by educational attainment. Some college dropouts—for example, Mark Zuckerberg (creator of Facebook)—earn millions of dollars a year. But Figure 22.5 shows that the median worker with a bachelor's degree earns almost $20,000 more a year than those who don't graduate from college. Patience pays off!

Opportunity cost

Consumption Smoothing

Over the course of a typical lifetime, income varies drastically. Early in life, income levels are relatively low, but income generally rises through midlife. As people near retirement, their income levels fall again. Figure 22.6 illustrates a typical economic life cycle. Income (the green line) is highest in the middle "prime earning years" and lower at both the beginning and end of an individual's work life.

But no one wants to *consume* according to this pattern over the course of a lifetime; most people prefer to consume more evenly over the course of their life. When we are young, we often borrow and spend more than we are earning. We may borrow for a college education or to buy our first home. When we retire, our income levels fall, but we don't want our spending to fall by the same amount. So we generally smooth our consumption over the course of our life. The blue line in Figure 22.6 represents a normal consumption pattern, which is smoother than the income pattern. This **consumption smoothing** is accomplished with the help of the loanable funds market.

Consumption smoothing occurs when people borrow and save to smooth consumption over their lifetime.

Early in life, we borrow so we can spend more than we earn. In Figure 22.6, borrowing is the pink area between income and consumption in early life.

FIGURE 22.6

Savings over a Typical Life Cycle

For most people, income is relatively low in early life, rises in their prime earning years, and falls in later life. But people generally prefer to smooth their consumption over the course of their life. This means they borrow early in life for items like education and their first home; save during midlife when their income is highest; and finally, draw down savings when they retire.

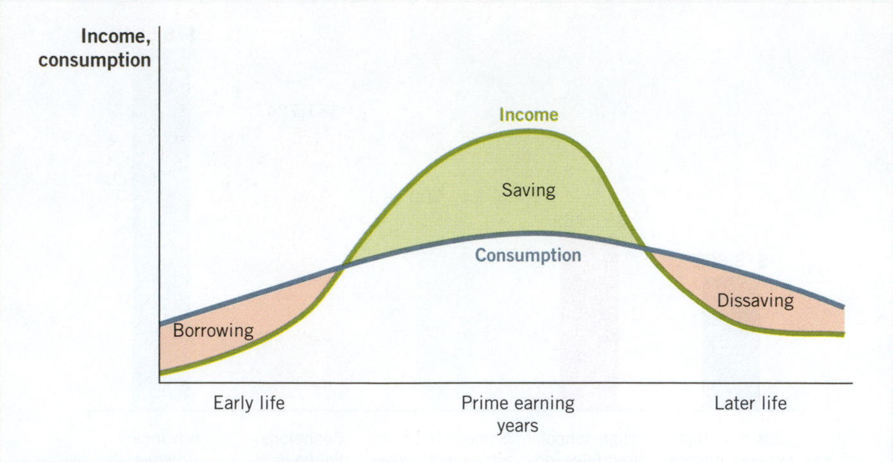

Midlife, or the prime earning years, is the time to repay loans and save for retirement. During this period of the life cycle, the income line exceeds the consumption line, and people save—that is the green area. Later in life, when people retire and their income falls, they often live on their savings. Economists call this **dissaving**. Dissaving occurs when people withdraw funds from their previously accumulated savings. Figure 22.6 shows dissavings as the pink area between income and consumption in later life.

Dissaving occurs when people withdraw funds from their previously accumulated savings.

We can use the concept of consumption smoothing to clarify a situation currently affecting the U.S. economy. If we have a steady flow of people moving into each life stage, the amount of savings in the economy is stable and there is a steady supply in the market for loanable funds. But if a significant portion of the population leaves the prime earning years at the same time, overall savings will fall. As it turns out, this is the current situation in the United States, because the baby boomers are now retiring from the labor force. The oldest members of this group reached retirement age in 2011. Over the next ten to fifteen years, U.S. workers will enter retirement in record numbers. This means an exit from the prime earning years and, consequently, much less in savings. Furthermore, similar issues are facing other nations, including Japan, Germany, and Italy. We'll come back to this issue later in this chapter.

Figure 22.7 illustrates the effect on the supply of loanable funds when there are changes in income and wealth, time preferences, or consumption smoothing. The initial supply of loanable funds is represented by S_1. The supply of loanable funds increases to S_2 if there is a change that leads to an increase in savings at all levels of the interest rate. For example, an increase in foreign income and wealth increases the supply of savings. Similarly, if people's time preferences fall—if they become more patient—the supply of loanable funds increases. Finally, if a relatively large portion of the population moves into midlife, when savings is highest, this also increases savings from S_1 to S_2.

At other times, however, the supply of loanable funds might decrease. For example, if income and wealth decline, people save less across all interest rates. This is illustrated as a shift from S_1 to S_3 in Figure 22.7. If time preferences

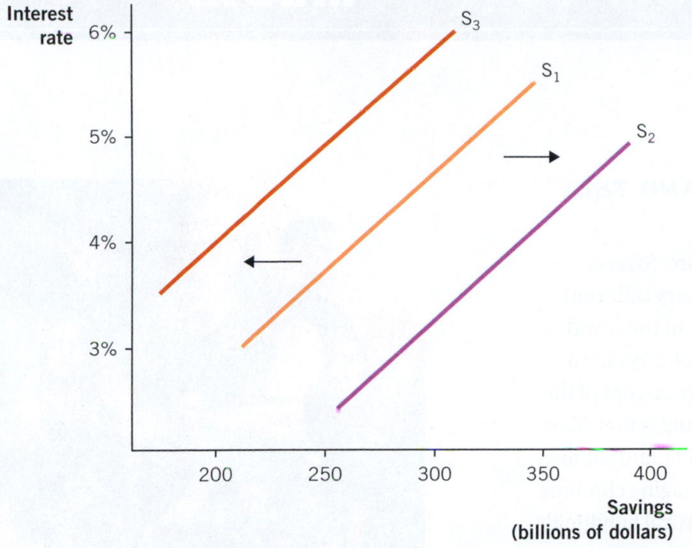

FIGURE 22.7

Shifts in the Supply of Loanable Funds

The supply of loanable funds shifts to the right when there are decreases in time preferences, increases in income and wealth, and more people in midlife, when savings is highest. The supply of loanable funds shifts to the left when there are increases in time preferences, decreases in income and wealth, and fewer people in midlife, when savings is highest.

increase, people become more impatient, which reduces the supply of loanable funds. Finally, if a relatively large population group moves out of the prime earning years and into retirement, the supply of loanable funds decreases. This last example describes what is happening in the United States right now.

Table 22.3 summarizes our discussion of the factors that either increase or decrease the supply of loanable funds.

TABLE 22.3

Factors That Shift the Supply of Loanable Funds

Factor	Direction of effect	Explanation
Income and wealth	• *Increases* in income and wealth *increase* the supply of loanable funds. • *Decreases* in income and wealth *decrease* the supply of loanable funds.	Savings is more affordable when people have greater income and wealth.
Time preferences	• *Increases* in time preferences *decrease* the supply of loanable funds. • *Decreases* in time preferences *increase* the supply of loanable funds.	Lower time preferences indicate that people are more patient and more likely to save for the future.
Consumption smoothing	• If *more* people are in midlife and their prime earning years, savings is *higher*. • If *fewer* people are in midlife, savings is *lower*.	Income varies over the life cycle, but people generally like to smooth their consumption.

· ECONOMICS *in the* MEDIA ·

Time Preferences

FREE SOLO AND THE FAST AND THE FURIOUS

What do Alex Honnold and Dominic Toretto have in common? At first glance, they seem very different.

Alex is perhaps the best rock climber in the world. The 2018 film *Free Solo* documents his solitary climb up Yosemite's El Capitan. What makes the ascent of the 2,900-foot vertical rock face so astonishing is that Alex used no safety ropes or other climbing aids, and yet managed the feat in just under four hours. Imagine climbing as fast as possible, relying entirely on natural handholds and footholds, when any slip would likely cost you your life. For Alex, this is not just an enjoyable pastime but a passion he dropped out of college to pursue.

Dominic Toretto is the fictional character at the center of the *Fast and Furious* movie franchise. Originally an auto mechanic, Dom (played by Vin Diesel) becomes the leader of a group of street racers. These are no ordinary speed freaks. Over the course of the film series, they defeat a Mexican drug lord, rob a bank in Brazil, and destroy a Russian nuclear submarine. They do all this while racing cars in and out of traffic, and into and out of buildings, and performing bizarre vehicle maneuvers while flying through the air. Explosions and gunfire are commonplace, but Dom always manages to walk away.

Alex Honnold does his best work by himself, in silence, on the face of a rock in some of the most beautiful natural locations in the world. Dominic Toretto works with a team (his "family") and is happiest when he has the pedal floored and the roar of a supercar engine in his ears. Both, however, exhibit very strong time preferences. Both have abandoned stable lives and predictable futures to flirt with death on a daily basis. They are trading the modest joys of a conventional existence, and likely much longer lives, for the thrill of mortal danger while they are young. They strongly prefer their adventures sooner rather than later.

"I live my life a quarter mile at a time," says Dom Toretto.

ECONOMICS IN THE REAL WORLD

WHY DID AMERICAN SAVINGS SPIKE SO HIGH IN 2020?

The **savings rate** is personal saving as a fraction of disposable (after-tax) income.

Historically, Americans have been notoriously low savers. From 1990 through 2019, the personal savings rate in the U.S. averaged just 6.4%. The **savings rate** is personal saving as a fraction of disposable (after-tax) income. So during the three decades after 1990, American workers set aside just $6.40 in savings out of every $100 in income.

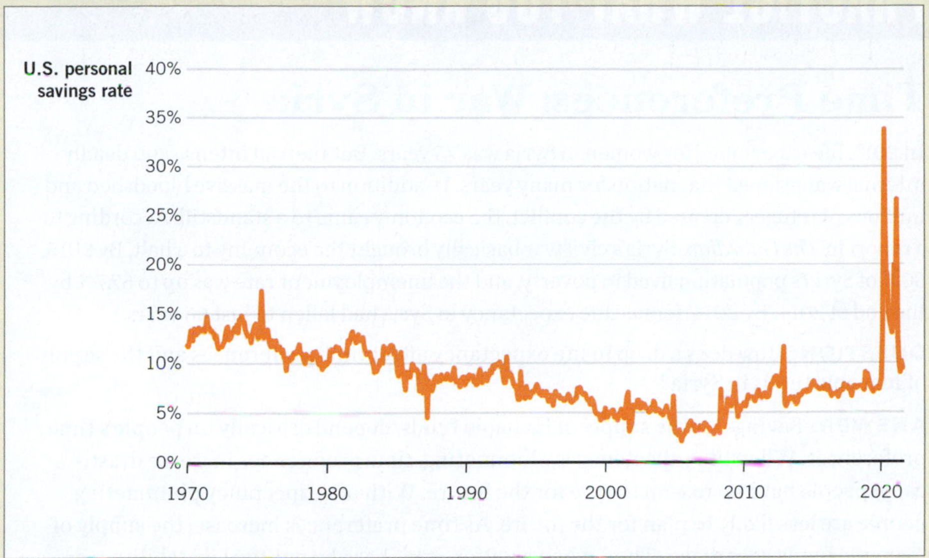

FIGURE 22.8

Savings Rate in the United States, 1990–2021

In the United States, the savings rate (savings as a portion of disposable income) had been quite low in the three decades leading up to the COVID-19 pandemic. When the pandemic hit, store closings and uncertainties combined to reduce spending, so savings rates soared. Savings rates declined some as the economy started to reopen, but overall rates remained relatively high.

Source: U.S. Bureau of Economic Analysis.

For comparison, in 2016 the savings rate was 9.6% in Germany, 15.8% in Sweden, and a whopping 17.8% in Switzerland.*

In 2020, however, Americans suddenly started saving much, much more. Figure 22.8 shows the U.S. personal savings rate from 1990 to 2021. Notice the giant spikes in 2020 and 2021. In April of 2020, the rate shot up to 33.8%!

Where did these spikes come from? The causes, as described by researchers at the Federal Reserve Bank of Kansas City,† have to do with how both consumers and government policymakers responded to COVID-19. Recall that in April 2020, the economy was largely shut down. Consumers began saving much more of their take-home pay, both because many retail stores were closed and because consumers were nervous about the future. On top of that, government programs funneled money to households, through stimulus checks and unemployment benefits. So incomes rose and consumption fell. That combination produced a massive increase in savings rates, though most of the increase in savings was concentrated among those with higher incomes. It will be interesting to see whether savings return to their earlier (much lower) levels over the next few years.

*"Household Savings Rates around the World," howmuch.net, April 12, 2016, https://howmuch.net/articles/saving-rates-around-the-world.

†Rick Babson, "Study Shows Surge in Savings during the Pandemic," Federal Reserve Bank of Kansas City, April 29, 2021, https://www.kansascityfed.org/ten/2021-spring-ten-magazine/study-shows-surge-in-savings-during-the-pandemic.

What Factors Shift the Demand for Loanable Funds?

To look at the demand side, we shift perspective to those who borrow in the loanable funds market. As we have seen, the demand for loanable funds derives from the desire to invest or purchase capital goods that aid in future

PRACTICE WHAT YOU KNOW

One of the difficult side effects of war is a collapse of loanable funds markets.

Time Preferences: War in Syria

In 2010, life expectancy for women in Syria was 75 years. But then an intense and deadly internal war gripped that nation for many years. In addition to the massive bloodshed and millions of refugees created by the conflict, the economy came to a standstill. According to a report in *The Guardian*, Syria's civil war basically brought the economy to a halt. By 2015, 80% of Syria's population lived in poverty, and the unemployment rate was up to 57.7% by the end of 2014. By 2014, female life expectancy in Syria had fallen to just 66 years.*

QUESTION: How does a drop in life expectancy affect time preferences and the supply of loanable funds in Syria?

ANSWER: Savings, or the supply of loanable funds, depend critically on people's time preferences. When life expectancy is plummeting, time preferences increase drastically: people have no reason to save for the future. With life expectancy plummeting, people are less likely to plan for the future. As time preferences increase, the supply of loanable funds goes down. Thus, when a nation is hit hard by political instability, war, or even a pandemic, one side effect is lower savings, which means a reduced supply of loanable funds—which in turn leads to lower economic output in the future.

Thankfully, by 2017, life expectancy in Syria began to tick up again, rising to 69 years for women. Let's hope this trend continues.

*Associated Press, "Syria's War: 80% in Poverty, Life Expectancy Cut by 20 Years, $200bn Lost," *Guardian*, March 12, 2015, http://www.theguardian.com/world/2015/mar/12/syrias-war-80-in-poverty-life-expectancy-cut-by-20-years-200bn-lost.

production. We know that the interest rate matters, and this relationship is reflected in the slope of the demand curve. We now turn to factors that cause shifts in the demand for loanable funds. We focus on three: the productivity of capital, investor confidence, and government borrowing.

Productivity of Capital

Consider a firm trying to decide whether to borrow for an investment. Perhaps your own firm is trying to decide whether to borrow to buy a new silk-screening machine, the S-1000, for your college clothing business. This machine is capital, and its purchase counts as an investment. To determine whether you should take a loan, recall our rule: a firm should borrow to fund an investment only if the expected return is greater than the interest rate on the loan. Therefore, if the interest rate on the loan is 4%, you will borrow to buy the S-1000 only if you expect to earn more than a 4% return from it.

Let's say that after crunching the numbers on expected costs and sales from the S-1000, you estimate a return of just 2% from an investment in the S-1000. You decide not to buy the new machine.

But then something changes. That something is the availability of the brand-new S-2000. The S-2000 is an improved machine that prints T-shirts at double the rate of the S-1000. Given this new machine, which is slightly more expensive, you calculate an expected return of 5%, so you decide to take the loan and buy the machine. Thus, your demand for loanable funds increases as a direct result of the availability of the new machine, which is twice as productive as the earlier machine.

What are the implications for the macroeconomy? Remember that firms borrow to finance capital purchases. Therefore, the level of demand for loans depends on the productivity of capital. Changes in capital productivity shift the demand for loanable funds. If capital is more productive, the demand for loans increases; if capital is less productive, the demand for loans decreases.

Productivity can change for a number of reasons. Consider the impact of the Internet. A connection to the Internet provides quick access to data and networking capabilities that people only dreamed about thirty-five years ago. The Internet also increases the productivity of computers, which are a major capital expense. Over the past twenty-five years, an increase in expected returns associated with the Internet made investment in computer equipment (capital) more attractive. This means that investment in capital yields greater returns, which in turn increases the demand for loans. When capital is more productive, firms are more likely to borrow to finance purchases of this type of capital.

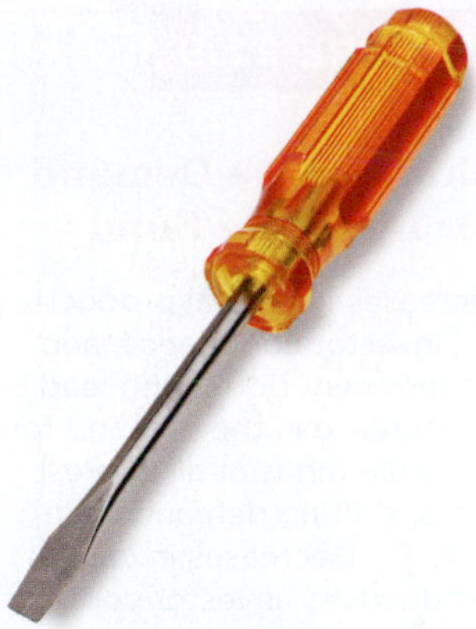

This manual screwdriver depicts capital . . .

. . . and this electric version of a screwdriver represents an increase in capital productivity.

Investor Confidence

The demand for loanable funds also depends on the beliefs or expectations of the investors at business firms. If a firm believes its sales will increase in the future, it invests more today to build for future sales. If, instead, it believes its future sales will fall, it invests less today. **Investor confidence** is a measure of what firms expect for future economic activity. If confidence is high, they are more likely to borrow for investment at any interest rate. Economist John Maynard Keynes referred to an investor's drive to action as "animal spirits," meaning that investment demand may not even be based on rational decisions or real factors in the economy.

Investor confidence is a measure of what firms expect for future economic activity.

Figure 22.9 illustrates shifts in the demand for loanable funds. If capital productivity increases, demand for investment increases from D_1 to D_2—that is, demand is higher across all interest rates. Similarly, if investor confidence rises, demand for loanable funds increases from D_1 to D_2. In contrast, if capital productivity or investor confidence falls, the demand for loanable funds falls from D_1 to D_3.

Government Borrowing

Governments are big enough borrowers that they can shift the demand for loanable funds all by themselves. We cover this in greater detail in Chapter 28 when we discuss government budgets. For now, just note that increases in government borrowing are reflected as increases in the demand for loanable funds and this shifts the demand curve to the right, while decreases in government borrowing lead to leftward shifts in demand.

FIGURE 22.9

Shifts in the Demand for Loanable Funds

Increases in capital productivity, investor confidence, and government borrowing lead to an increase in the demand for loanable funds at all interest rates, shifting demand from D_1 to D_2. Decreases in capital productivity, investor confidence, and government borrowing decrease the demand for loanable funds from D_1 to D_3.

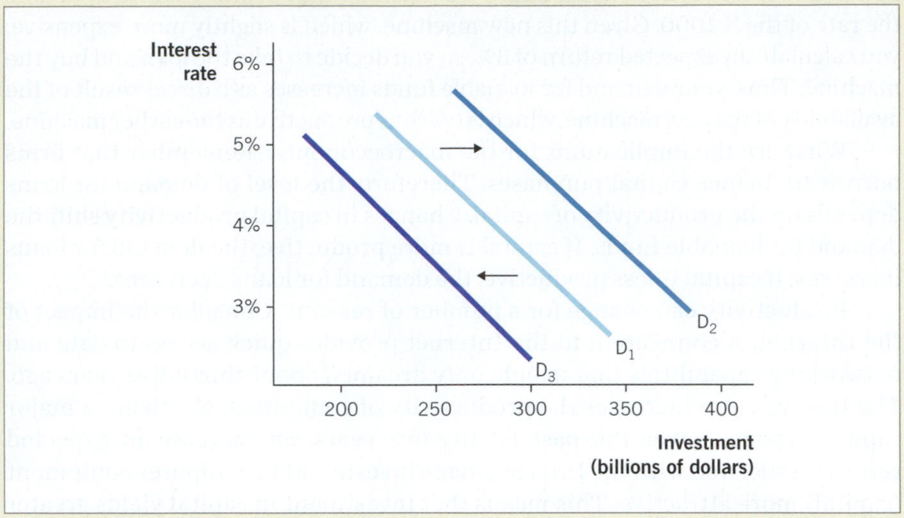

PRACTICE WHAT YOU KNOW

How dangerous is this sponge?

Demand for Loanable Funds: SpongeBob and Loanable Funds

QUESTION: Which one of the following changes would shift the demand for loanable funds, and how?

a. Research shows that watching the cartoon *SpongeBob SquarePants* can shorten a child's attention span. Now assume that an entire generation of children grows up watching this cartoon, resulting in adults who are less patient (their time preferences have increased).

b. A technological advance leads to greater capital productivity.

c. The interest rate falls.

ANSWER:

a. This factor would not affect the demand for loanable funds, but it would affect the supply of loanable funds. Less patience means that time preferences increase and the supply of loanable funds declines.

b. This technological advance would increase the demand for loanable funds.

c. The falling interest rate would lead to a movement along the demand curve, rather than a shift in the demand curve for loanable funds. A decrease in the interest rate could be caused by a decrease in the supply of loanable funds.

How Do We Apply the Loanable Funds Market Model?

We are now ready to use the loanable funds market model to study applications we see in the real world. First, we consider the implications of equilibrium in the loanable funds market. After that, we examine past and future views of the U.S. loanable funds market.

Equilibrium

Equilibrium in the loanable funds market occurs at the interest rate where the plans of savers match the plans of borrowers—that is, where quantity supplied equals quantity demanded. In Figure 22.10, this occurs at an interest rate of 4%, where savers are willing to save $250 billion and borrowers desire $250 billion in loans (in other words, they seek to invest $250 billion). At interest rates above 4%, the quantity of loanable funds supplied exceeds the quantity demanded, and this imbalance leads to downward pressure on the interest rate. At interest rates below 4%, the quantity demanded exceeds the quantity supplied, and this imbalance leads to upward pressure on the interest rate.

The loanable funds market, like other markets, naturally tends to move toward equilibrium, where supply is equal to demand. This equilibrium condition reinforces a key relationship between savings and investment. Equilibrium occurs when

$$savings = investment$$

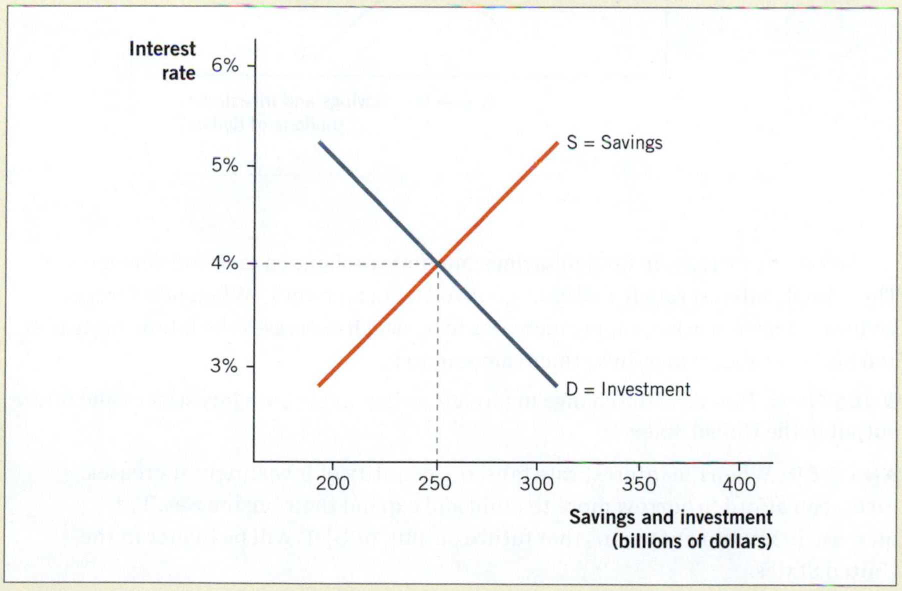

FIGURE 22.10

Equilibrium in the Market for Loanable Funds

Equilibrium in the loanable funds market occurs where supply equals demand, at an interest rate of 4% and a quantity of $250 billion. Because investment is limited by savings, exactly $250 billion is saved and $250 billion is invested.

PRACTICE WHAT YOU KNOW

How does foreign economic growth affect the U.S. loanable funds market?

Working with the Loanable Funds Model: Foreign Savings in the United States

Recently, the economies of China and India have begun to grow very rapidly. This increases their citizens' income and wealth. In turn, these citizens increase their savings in their country and also in the United States.

QUESTION: When foreign savings enter the U.S. loanable funds market, which curve is affected—supply or demand? How is this curve affected?

ANSWER: The supply of loanable funds increases as savings increase.

QUESTION: How would you graph the U.S. loanable funds market both before and after the increase in foreign savings?

ANSWER:

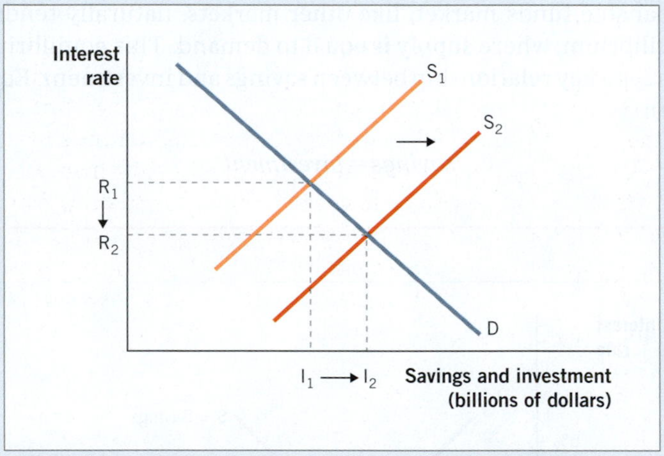

Before the increase in foreign savings, supply is designated as S_1 and demand as D. These imply interest rate R_1 and savings/investment amount I_1. When new foreign savings enter the market, supply increases to S_2, which decreases the interest rate to R_2 and increases the savings/investment amount to I_2.

QUESTION: How does the change in foreign savings affect both investment and future output in the United States?

ANSWER: When the interest rate falls, the quantity of investment increases. Firms can afford to borrow more to build and expand their businesses. This increase in investment means that future output, or GDP, will be higher in the United States.

In Figure 22.10, households and foreign entities have decided to save a combined total of $250 billion at an interest rate of 4%. Subsequently, firms borrow this $250 billion for investment. Thus, dollars that are saved make their way into the loanable funds market and are then channeled to firms for investment purposes.

Equilibrium also helps to clarify an important principle we'll return to often in this text. Investment requires saving because

Every dollar borrowed requires a dollar saved.

If an economy is to grow over time, someone has to invest in capital that helps to produce more in the future. But investment requires savings. Without savings, the economy cannot grow.

Equilibrium is a helpful starting point for understanding how the loanable funds market functions. But in the real world, financial market conditions change frequently. We can account for these changes in our model by using shifts in the supply and demand curves. Let's consider two examples: a shift in demand and a shift in the supply of loanable funds.

A Decrease in the Demand for Loanable Funds

When the overall economy slows, firms often reduce investment, since they expect reduced sales in future periods; this move reflects a decline in investor confidence. This happened recently in the United States during the coronavirus recession that began in March 2020. Panel (a) of Figure 22.11 shows how a decline in investor confidence affects the loanable funds market. When investment demand declines (shown in the figure as a shift from D_{2019} to D_{2020}), the loanable funds model predicts lower interest rates (a drop from R_1 to R_2) and a lower equilibrium level of investment (a drop from I_1 to I_2). Panel (b) of Figure 22.11 shows that investment fell during all three recessions that occurred between 2000 and 2020. At the onset of the coronavirus recession in the second quarter of 2020, real investment fell 14.5%.

A Decrease in the Supply of Loanable Funds

Let's now return to the potential effects of the baby boomers' retirement over the next ten to fifteen years. As we saw in the discussion of consumption smoothing, this will likely lead to a decrease in the supply of loanable funds in the United States. Figure 22.12 illustrates this kind of change. The curve labeled S_{2020} represents the supply of loanable funds in 2020. But as the baby boomers retire, supply may shift back to $S_{2030?}$ one decade later.

All else equal, this shift means lower investment (in the figure, a drop from I_1 to I_2) and lower GDP growth going forward. However, many other factors may change over the next few years to increase savings in the United States. For example, as other nations grow, foreigners may continue to increase their savings in the United States. Or perhaps the savings rate in the United States will remain at a higher level. These increases could offset the effects of the baby boomers' retirement and keep interest rates low for U.S. firms.

FIGURE 22.11

A Decline in Investment Demand

(a) When decision-makers at firms lose confidence in the future direction of the economy, investment demand declines and lower investment results. (b) In the United States, real investment declined during all three recessions that occurred before 2020.

Source: Panel (b): U.S. Bureau of Economic Analysis.

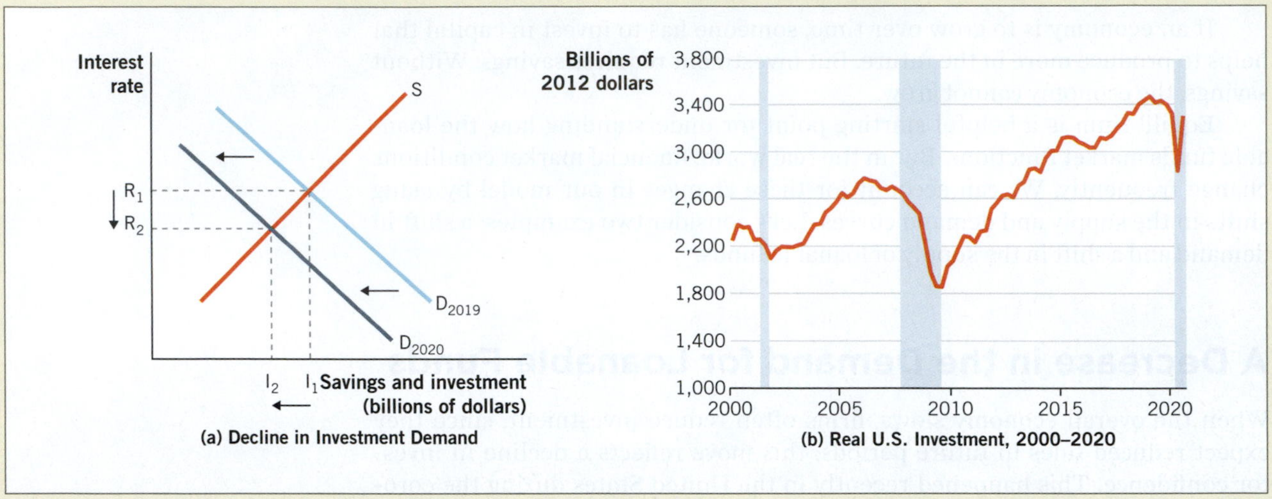

FIGURE 22.12

The Possible Future of the U.S. Loanable Funds Market

As baby boomers retire and draw down their savings, supply in the loanable funds market will decrease. Then if there are not increases in saving from other sources, interest rates will rise, leading to lower levels of investment.

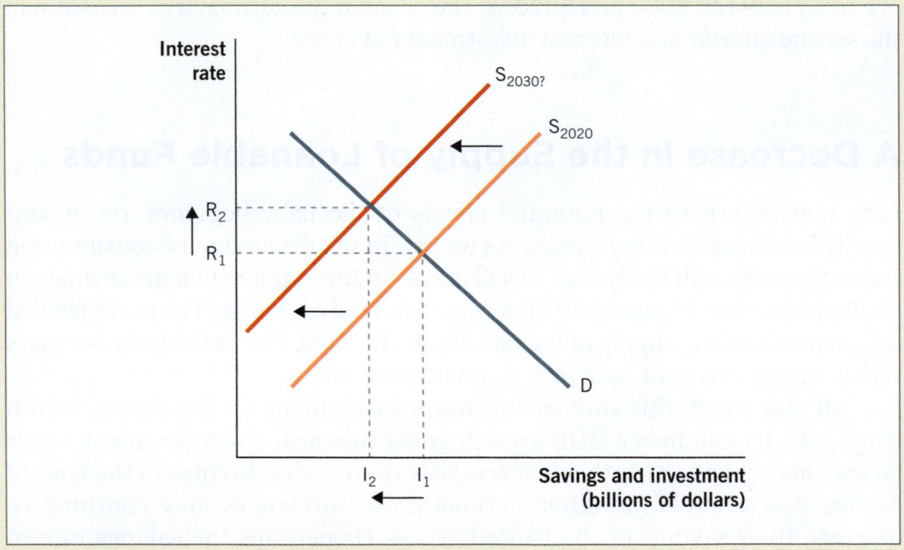

· ECONOMICS *for* LIFE ·

Compound Interest: When Should You Start Saving for Retirement?

- Lower time preferences translate to more savings.
- Small savings early in life lead to big gains later.

When you graduate from college, get a job, and start earning a steady income, you'll have several choices to make. Should you buy or lease a car? Should you buy or rent a home? Should you donate money or time to charity? Regardless of your decisions on issues such as these, you should always make room in your budget for savings.

We know that everyone has positive time preferences, so all else equal, you probably would rather consume now than later. But all else is not equal. That is, a little less consumption now will lead to a lot more consumption later, even under assumptions of very reasonable interest rates. The return to savings is like an exponential function: the longer you save, the greater the return to your savings, even at a constant interest rate. The reason is based on compound interest, which implies that the interest you earn becomes savings—which also bears interest. Let's see how this works.

Consider two people who choose alternate paths. Dirk understands the power of compound interest and chooses to start saving $100 per month when he is 25 years old. Lee has stronger time preferences and decides to wait until age 45 to start saving $100 per month. If both Dirk and Lee work until they are 65 years old, Dirk saves for 40 years and Lee saves for 20.

You might guess that Dirk will end up with twice as much in his retirement account, since he saves twice as long. But you'd be wrong. It turns out that Lee's retirement savings will increase to $53,988. That's not too bad, considering he will have saved just $100 per month over 20 years, or 240 months—the interest payments certainly helped. But what about Dirk? His retirement savings will be worth $281,767! That's more than five times the size of Lee's, and Dirk only made twice as many payments.

Compound interest produces more interest income.

What did we assume to get these returns? We assumed a 7% interest rate, which is the long-run historical real rate of return on a diversified stock portfolio. But any interest rate would illustrate the key point here: compound interest increases the value of your savings exponentially. So even with very strong time preferences, it makes sense to start saving early.

The graph illustrates the returns to saving $100 per month at an average annual return of 7% until retirement. The only difference is when you start saving. Notice that as you move along the horizontal axis, for each additional five years' worth of savings, the amount by which total savings grows will increase.

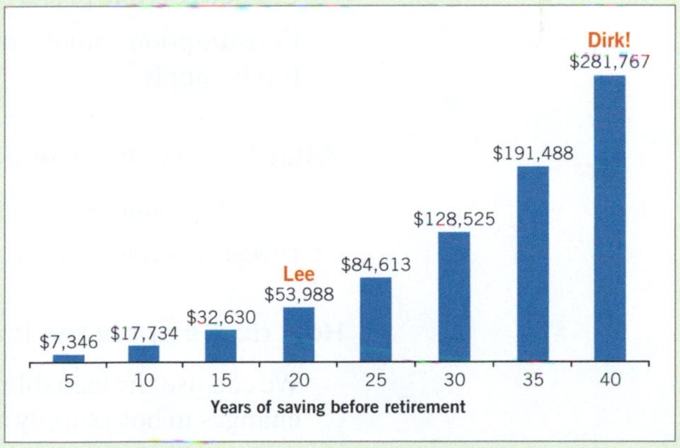

Conclusion

We began this chapter talking about the market in which firms that want to borrow money for investment spending meet up with households that are saving money and are willing to lend it out. The interest rates at which borrowing and lending occur are set in this market through the interaction of supply and demand. The discussion in this chapter has provided the foundation we need to discuss interest rates and financial markets further.

In macroeconomics, few topics are more important than investment. And investment is the result of equilibrium in the market for loanable funds. Savers supply the funds that support loans; borrowers are investors who demand the loans. Equilibrium determines the quantity of investment and the interest rate in an economy.

In the next chapter, we extend our analysis of the market for loanable funds by looking at other methods for borrowing and lending. These include stocks, bonds, and other financial securities. ✷

ANSWERING *the* BIG QUESTIONS

What is the loanable funds market?

- The loanable funds market connects savers with borrowers.
- Savers are suppliers of loanable funds, and they earn interest as a reward for saving.
- Borrowers are demanders of loanable funds, and they pay interest as the cost of borrowing.

What factors shift the supply of loanable funds?

- Changes in income and wealth shift the supply of loanable funds.
- Changes in time preferences also affect the supply of loanable funds.
- Consumption smoothing is another factor that shifts the loanable funds supply.

What factors shift the demand for loanable funds?

- Capital productivity affects the demand for loanable funds.
- Investor confidence also affects the demand for loanable funds.

How do we apply the loanable funds market model?

- We can use the loanable funds market model to examine real-world changes in both supply and demand for loanable funds.
- The loanable funds model also clarifies the important conclusion that every dollar borrowed requires a dollar saved.

CHAPTER PROBLEMS

Concepts You Should Know

consumption smoothing (p. 719)
dissaving (p. 720)
expected return (p. 714)
Fisher equation (p. 715)
interest rate (p. 712)
investor confidence (p. 725)
loanable funds market (p. 711)
nominal interest rate (p. 715)
real interest rate (p. 715)
savings rate (p. 722)
time preferences (p. 718)

Questions for Review

1. Explain the importance of the loanable funds market to basic GDP in a macroeconomy.
2. All else equal, what does a lower interest rate mean for firms? What does a lower interest rate mean for savers?
3. Consider two alternatives to prepare for retirement: (1) saving in a bank where your funds earn interest and (2) buying fine art that rises in value over time. Each grows your retirement account over time.
   a. If the rates of return on fine art purchases fall, how would you expect the allocation of retirement funds to change across the macroeconomy?
   b. If the national savings rate is based only on the first option (saving in a bank), then what happens to the national savings rate when the allocation of retirement funds shifts as you describe in your response to part (a)?
   c. In addition to art, people often purchase real estate, stocks, and/or bonds as part of their savings, even though these assets are also not counted in the official data on personal savings. Discuss how these purchases affect the official data on a nation's savings rate.
4. List the factors that affect the supply side of the loanable funds market. Which factors shift the curve?
5. List the factors that affect the demand side of the loanable funds market. Which factors shift the curve?
6. Why does inflation have a positive effect on the nominal interest rate?
7. Many people believe that a high interest rate is bad for the economy. Of course, all else equal, a higher interest rate means greater borrowing costs for firms. But a high interest rate is also helpful to some people in the economy.
   a. What group of people benefits from a higher interest rate? Explain how they benefit.
   b. A high interest rate can also indicate that something positive is happening in the economy. Describe how positive factors can lead to an increase in the demand for loanable funds and then an increase in the interest rate.

Study Problems *(* solved at the end of the section)*

1. Assume that the residents of a nation become more patient (experience a reduction in their time preferences).
   a. What will happen to the interest rate in that nation? What will happen to the equilibrium level of investment in that nation? Explain your answers.
   b. In the long run, how will the lower time preferences affect the levels of capital and income growth in that nation?
2. Many interest rates in the United States have fallen over the past couple of decades. Which of the following factors could have been the cause?
   a. increase in the demand for loanable funds
   b. decrease in the demand for loanable funds
   c. increase in the supply of loanable funds
   d. decrease in the supply of loanable funds

3. Use the Fisher equation to fill in the blanks in the following table:

Inflation rate	Real interest rate	Nominal interest rate
______	2%	7%
______	0	7
2%	______	6
9	______	6
2	2	______
10	2	______

✱ 4. Consider two hypothetical nations: Wahooland and Wildcat Island. Initially, these nations are identical in every way. In particular, they are the same with regard to population size and age, income and wealth, and time preferences. They also have the same interest rate, savings, and investment.

a. Suddenly, in the year 2015, the interest rate in Wahooland rises. After some investigating, economists determine that nothing has happened to the supply of loanable funds. Therefore, what are the possible reasons for this rise in the interest rate in Wahooland?

b. Given your answer to part (a), what can you say about the level of investment in Wahooland relative to that in Wildcat Island in 2015? What can you say about future income levels in Wahooland versus Wildcat Island?

c. Often, we think of a lower interest rate as always being preferable to a higher interest rate. What has this question taught us about that idea?

✱ 5. Some people have proposed an increase in the retirement age for U.S. citizens. Consider the effects of this proposed new policy.

a. How would this change affect supply and demand in the market for loanable funds?

b. How would this change affect the equilibrium interest rate and investment?

c. In the long run, how would this change affect real GDP in the United States?

6. The Ragged Mountain Running Shop (RMRS) sells running shoes and apparel in Charlottesville, Virginia. The owners of RMRS are considering the possibility of opening new retail locations. After careful market analysis, they estimate the expected returns at five new potential locations. These estimates are listed in the following table, along with the amount RMRS would need to borrow in order to open each location:

Crozet	6%	$100,000
Downtown Charlottesville	4	100,000
Harrisonburg	11	80,000
Waynesboro	2	60,000
West End of Richmond	8	200,000

a. RMRS approaches the Virginia National Bank (VNB) with hopes of borrowing to expand into other locations. Which locations will RMRS open if VNB offers them a loan at an interest rate of 7%? What if VNB offers loans at a lower interest rate of 5%?

b. What is the total dollar amount of loans that RMRS takes at an interest rate of 7%? At an interest rate of 5%?

c. Use the information in the table to graph the demand curve for investment for RMRS.

7. Suppose that several new technological innovations result in greater capital productivity in the U.S. economy. We know that these innovations have several macroeconomic effects. Let's concentrate on the changes in the loanable funds market and assume no other changes occur.

a. On a sheet of paper, draw the loanable funds market in initial equilibrium. Be sure to label all curves and axes correctly.

b. On your graph, illustrate how the technological innovations affect the loanable funds market.

c. Assuming no other changes in the loanable funds market, state how these technological innovations affect the interest rate, the equilibrium level of investment, and future GDP.

8. Assume that the market for loanable funds in the United States is in equilibrium, with a 3% nominal interest rate and $500 billion worth of loans. Now assume that time preferences increase over a generation, due to shorter attention spans and greater impatience.
   a. Does this change shift the supply of loanable funds, the demand for loanable funds, or both?
   b. How does this change affect the interest rate and the equilibrium quantity of loans?

Solved Problems

4. a. If supply does not change, the rise in the interest rate must be due to a change in demand. If the rate went up, then demand must have increased. An increase in the demand for loanable funds occurs from an increase in the productivity of capital and/or an increase in investor confidence.
   b. Investment will be higher in Wahooland than in Wildcat Island. Future GDP will be higher in Wahooland, and this means that income will be higher.
   c. A higher interest rate can be caused by very productive capital. Thus, an innovative nation that tends to have new productive ideas and then high capital productivity might also have a higher interest rate. A higher interest rate can indicate very high returns to capital investment, which is certainly not bad for an economy.

5. a. The key is to examine how the policy change would affect savings through people's preferences for consumption smoothing. If U.S. workers start working longer, this would delay the dissaving period in their life and increase their savings. So supply would increase (shift outward). Demand would not change.
   b. The equilibrium interest rate would fall, and investment would increase.
   c. Real GDP would be greater, all else equal, due to the increase in investment. Basically, the new savings would become investment in capital. Thus, in the future there would be more tools for production in the United States, and output would be higher.

CHAPTER

23

Financial Markets and Securities

Foreign Loans Lead to Investment in an Economy and Can Pave the Way for Future Growth.

Many people are concerned that foreign nations own significant amounts of U.S. assets. China, in particular, owns many prominent real estate landmarks and more U.S. government debt than any other foreign nation. People worry that since we owe China and other nations money, these nations can control us. And to be sure, owners do have their say. When Chinese investors bought One Chase Manhattan Plaza in New York's financial district, they renamed it 28 Liberty Street—because 8 means good fortune in Chinese culture, and 28 should be twice as lucky.

But think of the situation in terms of loanable funds. From this perspective, the Chinese are lenders who are sending their savings into the United States. These Chinese savings help us build factories and buildings and keep our interest rates lower, helping both our government and private firms in the United States. These exchanges help both Chinese and U.S. citizens.

The financial vehicles we discuss in this chapter are necessary for economic growth and development. These include stocks, bonds, home mortgages, and other financial instruments. Even though we are covering financial topics, macroeconomics is the common thread that weaves through them; each helps you gain a more detailed understanding of

The Waldorf-Astoria in Manhattan is one of the most storied hotel properties in the United States. Built in 1931, it reigned until 1963 as the tallest hotel building in the world. As of 2014, however, it belongs to China's Anbang Insurance Group.

the factors that affect the overall economy. We can both minimize the negative effects of recessions and experience economic growth only when financial markets function efficiently. When there are problems in financial markets, economic growth is impossible.

· BIG QUESTIONS ·

- How do financial markets help the economy?
- What are the key financial tools for the macroeconomy?

How Do Financial Markets Help the Economy?

In financial markets, borrowers and lenders come together. The buyers (or borrowers) in financial markets are firms and governments in search of funds to undertake their daily operations. The sellers (or lenders) are savers looking for opportunities to earn a return on their savings. In Chapter 22, we introduced the loanable funds market as a way of thinking about financial markets through the lens of supply and demand. In this chapter, we present an institutional view of financial markets. That is, we consider what types of firms operate in the middle of financial markets and what types of tools they use to facilitate the exchanges between savers and borrowers.

The major players in the middle of financial markets are called financial intermediaries. **Financial intermediaries** are firms that help to channel funds from savers to borrowers. Banks are one example of a financial intermediary. **Banks** are private firms that accept deposits and extend loans. Banks and other financial intermediaries are important for the macroeconomy because they are at the center of financial markets: they help connect borrowers with savers.

Financial intermediaries are firms that help to channel funds from savers to borrowers.

Banks are private firms that accept deposits and extend loans.

Direct and Indirect Financing

When firms seek funding to pay for resources for production, they go to the loanable funds market. There are two different paths through the loanable funds market: indirect finance and direct finance. **Indirect finance** occurs when savers lend funds to financial intermediaries, which then loan these funds to borrowers. In this case, savers are indirectly financing the investments of firms.

Direct finance occurs when borrowers go directly to savers for funds. If you want a loan to start or expand a small business, you might go to a bank. But

Indirect finance occurs when savers deposit funds into banks, which then loan these funds to borrowers.

Direct finance occurs when borrowers go directly to savers for funds.

large established firms can skip financial intermediaries and go directly to these savers when they need funds.

Figure 23.1 shows the two alternate routes through the loanable funds market. The top half illustrates indirect finance, in which banks and other financial intermediaries facilitate the exchanges between lenders (that is, savers) and borrowers. If you have a savings or checking account at a bank, you participate in the loanable funds market as a lender. Banks package together the savings of many depositors like you to extend loans. The bottom half of Figure 23.1 illustrates direct finance, in which borrowers bypass financial intermediaries and go directly to savers for funds.

To undertake direct finance, firms need a contract that specifies the terms and conditions of the loan. These contracts usually take the form of a security. A **security** is a tradable contract that entitles its owner to certain rights. For example, a **bond** is a security that represents a debt to be paid. If you own a bond, it means someone owes you money—it is a formal IOU. Bonds are a tool of direct finance because they enable borrowers to go directly to savers for funds. If a firm sells a bond to an individual, it is borrowing funds that will be repaid at a later date. For example, in 2018 the Target Corporation had $13 billion in bonds outstanding. This means the Target Corporation owed $13 billion to the owners of those bonds.

A **security** is a tradable contract that entitles its owner to certain rights.

A **bond** is a security that represents a debt to be paid.

The Importance of Financial Markets

Financial markets play a vital role in the macroeconomy. Macroeconomic growth is based on the production of GDP across the economy. This production comes from individual firms, such as cupcake shops, department stores, computer

FIGURE 23.1

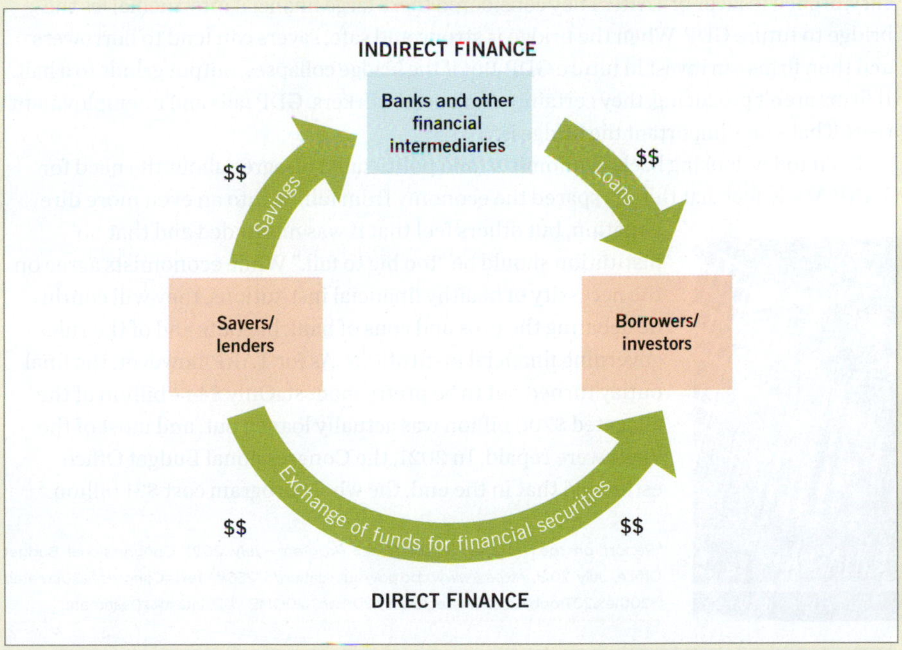

Direct versus Indirect Finance

Funds make their way through the loanable funds market through two distinct paths. Indirect finance occurs when savers and borrowers utilize banks or other financial intermediaries. Alternatively, direct finance occurs when borrowers go directly to savers for their funds.

producers, and airplane manufacturers. But these firms need funding to build and buy the resources they use to produce their goods and services. These funds come from financial markets.

Consider what happens when financial markets break down. In 2007, several U.S. financial institutions began faltering. In September 2008, Lehman Brothers, a financial intermediary with over $600 billion in assets, went bankrupt. Other financial intermediaries all over the world became less inclined to extend loans. Because firms found it more difficult to borrow, economic contraction was inevitable. This contraction was the Great Recession that lasted through mid-2009.

ECONOMICS IN THE REAL WORLD

SHOULD WE BAIL OUT BIG BANKS?

In September 2008, Lehman Brothers, one of the largest financial firms, went bankrupt as many of the real estate loans they were holding went sour. After the Lehman Brothers bankruptcy (which followed the earlier collapse of Bear Stearns), it appeared there might be a domino effect that would lead to the collapse of many large banks. To avoid this potential disaster, the U.S. government implemented the Troubled Asset Relief Program—which came to be known as TARP—in October 2008. TARP allocated $700 billion to keep banks from failing. The money was used to aid banks that had made bad loans.

TARP was very controversial from the beginning. On the one hand, the government was clearly bailing out big banks after many had made poor business decisions, and people from all walks of life questioned why the government would use taxpayer funds to help banks that seemed to contribute to the recession, especially since most people in the general population were still struggling financially.

Others, including both Presidents Bush and Obama and their secretaries of the treasury, argued in favor of TARP. They considered these large financial intermediaries the bridge to future GDP. When the bridge is strong and safe, savers can lend to borrowers and then firms can invest in future GDP. But if the bridge collapses, output grinds to a halt. If firms aren't producing, they certainly don't need workers. GDP falls and unemployment rises. That's how important the bridge is.

Even today, looking back, economists (and politicians) disagree about the need for TARP. Many feel that this act spared the economy from falling into an even more dire situation, but others feel that it was misguided and that no institution should be "too big to fail." While economists agree on the necessity of healthy financial institutions, they will continue debating the pros and cons of bank bailouts and of the rules governing financial institutions. As for TARP, however, the final outlay turned out to be pretty modest. Only $444 billion of the allocated $700 billion was actually loaned out, and most of the loans were repaid. In 2021, the Congressional Budget Office estimated that in the end, the whole program cost $31 billion.*

Do America's wealthiest banks really need taxpayer-funded bailouts?

*_Report on the Troubled Asset Relief Program—July 2021,_ Congressional Budget Office, July 2021, https://www.cbo.gov/publication/57256#:~:text=Congress%20created%20the%20Troubled%20Asset,lower%20than%20OMB's%20latest%20estimate.

PRACTICE WHAT YOU KNOW

Direct versus Indirect Finance: Which Is It?

These are some of the resources necessary to produce Lemon Bliss cupcakes.

Your friend Krista wants to open a cupcake shop. She needs to buy many resources before she can sell cupcakes and earn revenue. She is uncertain as to whether she should use direct or indirect financing.

QUESTION: For each of the following alternatives, is the financing considered direct or indirect?

a. Krista borrows money from a friend.

b. Krista takes a loan from her small local bank.

c. Krista arranges a loan from a large national bank.

d. Krista issues bonds and sells them to people in her neighborhood.

ANSWERS:

a. This is direct finance: Krista, the borrower, goes directly to a saver without the aid of a financial intermediary.

b. This is indirect finance: the bank makes the loan to Krista from the funds of various savers.

c. This is also indirect finance; the size of the bank does not matter.

d. This is direct finance: Krista goes directly to savers. It doesn't matter if the bonds are sold to people she happens to know.

CHALLENGE QUESTION: Suppose Krista decides to apply for a loan at a local bank. What factors will the bank consider when responding to Krista's application?

ANSWER: The bank will consider how much Krista is asking for, and for how long (the time period before she pays the money back). The bank will also consider the risk that Krista will not be able to repay the loan. Finally, the bank will think about the opportunity cost; that is, the loans the bank could make to others instead, if it turns Krista down. All these factors will go into deciding whether Krista gets the loan and what interest she will pay if she does.

What Are the Key Financial Tools for the Macroeconomy?

In this section, we explore tools used in financial markets to help fund investment. We focus on tools that matter for the macroeconomy, including bonds, stocks, Treasury securities, home mortgages, and private-sector securities created by the process of securitization. We start with bonds.

Bonds

Firms issue several types of securities to raise funds, but we can view them all as variations of a basic corporate bond.

Let's say your friend Kara wants to open a new website design business. But first she needs a loan to buy computers and software. Initially, Kara goes to a bank for a loan, but it turns her away because her company is new and viewed as very risky. So Kara comes to you and asks for a one-year loan. You know Kara well, so you agree to loan her some money with the understanding that she will repay the funds plus interest exactly one year later.

To formalize your agreement, you decide to draw up an IOU contract like the one presented in Figure 23.2. When you "buy" this contract from Kara, you are lending her funds with the promise that she'll pay you $10,000 in one year. The contract is essentially the same as a corporate or government bond, and it serves the same purpose. This is an example of direct finance, with the borrower going directly to a saver who lends them money.

Like any bond, your contract contains three important pieces of information: the name of the borrower, the repayment date, and the amount due at repayment. In this example, the name of the borrower is Kara Alexis; the repayment date is February 20, 2024. The date on which the loan repayment is due is the **maturity date**. Finally, every bond contract also specifies the **face value**, or **par value**, of the bond. This is the bond's value at maturity—the amount due at repayment. For notation purposes, we'll call the face value p_m because it is the price, or value, of the bond at maturity.

The **maturity date** of a bond is the date on which the loan repayment is due.

A bond's **face value**, or **par value**, is the bond's value at maturity—the amount due at repayment.

Perhaps you noticed that Figure 23.2 shows the bond's face value, but not the amount of the initial loan. In fact, you and Kara must come to an agreement about how much you will loan her. But with a bond agreement, the face value is typically set at a round number like $10,000. When you and Kara settle on the initial loan amount, you are agreeing to the dollar price of the bond (p). The price of the bond is the original dollar amount of the loan. For example, if you agree on a price of $8,000 for Kara's bond, that is the amount you loan her. From your perspective, you loan her $8,000 today for the promise that she'll pay you $10,000 in one year. From Kara's perspective, she now has $8,000 she can use to buy computers and software for her website design business, and she can begin producing GDP. But one year from now she has to repay you $10,000.

FIGURE 23.2

A Basic Bond Security

A simple IOU contract between two friends is like a bond. It specifies three things: (1) the name of the borrower (here, Kara Alexis); (2) the repayment date (February 20, 2024); (3) the amount due at repayment ($10,000).

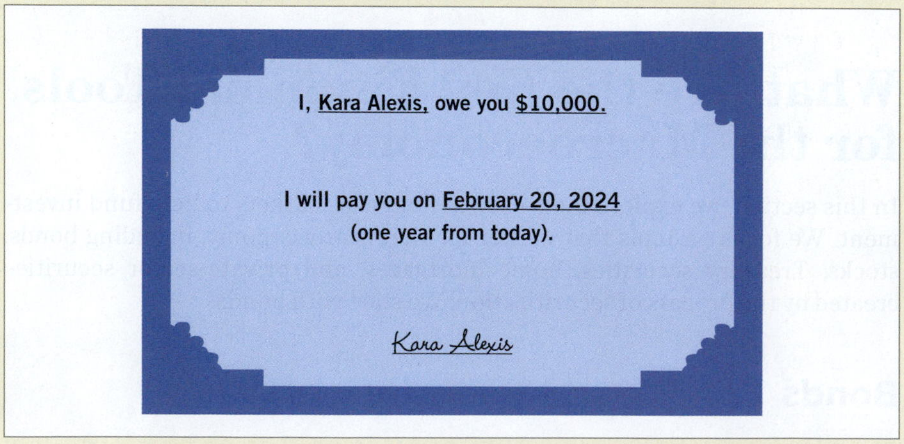
I, Kara Alexis, owe you $10,000.
I will pay you on February 20, 2024
(one year from today).
Kara Alexis

That's how a basic bond security works. Many bonds also include *coupons* that specify periodic interest payments to the bond owner. That distinction is not important for our purposes, so we focus on bonds that entail a single payment when the bond matures.

We now build on this foundation by discussing how interest rates relate to bond prices and how default risk affects the price of a bond.

THE BOND DOLLAR PRICE AND INTEREST RATE In the previous discussion, we described Kara's bond in dollar prices. But loan prices are generally quoted in interest rates. Therefore, we need to consider how the bond's dollar price (p) is related to its interest rate (r). To determine the interest rate on this bond, we have to find the rate of return on the dollars that are loaned. For example, you "buy" Kara's bond for \$8,000, and one year later the bond is worth \$10,000. In percentage terms, the value of the bond increases by 25%. Thus, the rate of return, or interest rate, is computed as a growth rate, where the price of the bond is growing from its initial value (p_0):

$$\text{interest rate} = R = \frac{\text{face value} - \text{initial price}}{\text{initial price}} = \frac{p_m - p_0}{p_0}$$

(EQUATION 23.1)

If the price of the bond is \$8,000, the interest rate is computed as

$$R = \frac{p_m - p_0}{p_0} = \frac{\$10{,}000 - \$8{,}000}{\$8{,}000} = 25\%$$

We used growth rates when we discussed GDP growth and inflation. Here, the interest rate is computed as a growth rate; it is the growth rate of the original funds invested.

With bonds, the face value is fixed—it is printed on the front of the bond. Thus, *the dollar price of a bond determines the bond's interest rate.* If you know the dollar price of a given bond, you can determine the interest rate. Table 23.1 shows several alternative prices for a \$10,000 one-year bond. Notice that the lower the price, the higher the interest rate, because it takes fewer dollars for the lender to earn \$10,000 one year later.

Each price implies a different interest rate. For example, if Kara sells you the \$10,000 bond for only \$7,500, the interest rate rises to 33%. This is much better for you, since you buy the bond for \$7,500 and are repaid that amount plus \$2,500 in interest only one year later. But this is worse for Kara because she is getting just \$7,500 this year, with the same promise to repay you \$10,000 next year.

TABLE 23.1

Dollar Price and Interest Rate for a \$10,000 One-Year Bond

Dollar price (p_0)	Interest rate (R)
\$9,000	11%
8,000	25
7,500	33
5,000	100

Notice that as the price of the bond drops, the interest rate on the bond rises. If the bond price drops to $5,000, the interest rate climbs to 100%. This relationship holds by definition: *the dollar price and interest rate of a bond have an inverse relationship*.

In Chapter 22, we saw that the interest rate on a loan is the cost of borrowing and the reward for saving. Higher interest rates (lower dollar prices) hurt borrowers and help lenders. As a lender, you want to buy bonds for the lowest price possible because you want the highest possible interest rate on your savings. The borrower wants to sell bonds for the highest price possible so that she can pay the lowest possible interest rate.

A primary factor in determining the interest rate on bonds is the borrower's default risk, a topic to which we now turn.

DEFAULT RISK Some financial transactions are very complex and potentially lead to many different outcomes. But bonds are fairly straightforward. If the bond owner holds the bond until maturity, there are only two possible outcomes: the borrower pays the maturity value of the bond, or the borrower defaults on the loan. These possibilities are illustrated in Figure 23.3. For the bond owner, then, the risk of default is the primary concern. **Default risk** is the risk that the borrower will not pay the face value of a bond on the maturity date.

Default risk is the risk that the borrower will not pay the face value of a bond on the maturity date.

All else equal, the greater the default risk, the lower the price of a bond. Consider the bond Kara is selling to finance her start-up website design company. If you really trust Kara and believe her business will succeed, you might buy her $10,000 bond for $9,500. At this price, she promises to pay you about 5.25% interest for the use of your funds for a year. However, if you are skeptical about either Kara's integrity or the prospects for her business success, you may be willing to pay only $8,000 for the bond. At this price, she will pay 25%

FIGURE 23.3

Two Possible Outcomes with a Bond

With a bond, both the maturity date and the face value are certain. Thus, there are only two possible outcomes if a bond owner holds the bond until maturity: either the borrower will pay the face value, or she will default. Because these are the only two possible outcomes, default risk is the primary concern of a bond owner.

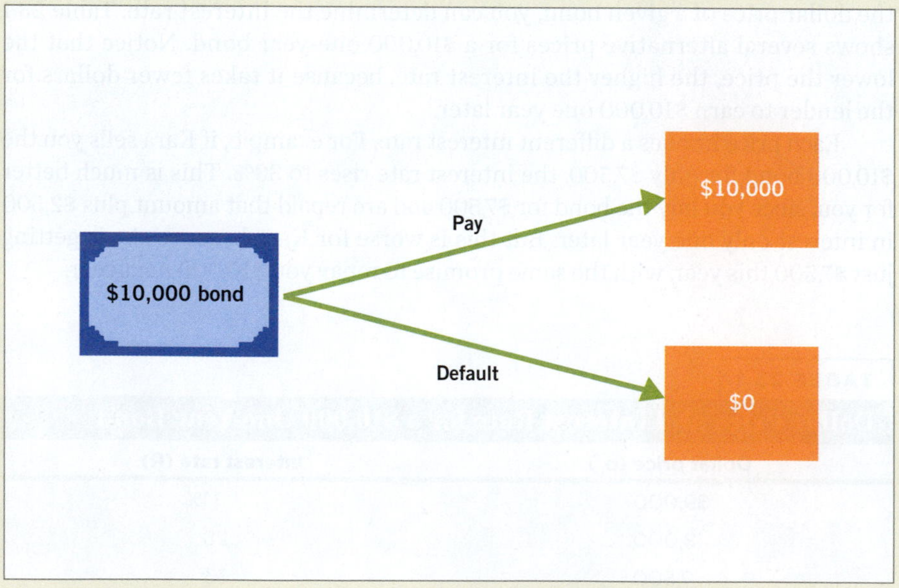

interest for the loan instead. This scenario illustrates an important bond price principle: a *bond's interest rate rises with default risk*.

Consider bonds offered by the Target Corporation. Target is a large company with many capital investments. As mentioned earlier, the Target Corporation had $13 billion in bonds outstanding in 2018. Clearly, there is a significant market for Target bonds. Consider the hypothetical supply and demand for one-year $100,000 Target bonds illustrated in Figure 23.4. Initially, with the demand curve at D_1 and supply at S, the equilibrium price is $98,000.

Now let's assume that something negative happens to the future prospects of Target's business. Perhaps Walmart attracts customers away from Target. This news reduces the probability that Target will pay off its bonds as they mature; in other words, it increases Target's default risk. As such, the demand for Target bonds declines from D_1 to D_2. As demand declines, the market price of Target bonds falls from $98,000 to $97,000, which means the interest rate rises (because the dollar price and interest rate on a bond always move in opposite directions). As a result, we can generalize to say that increases in default risk (1) cause a drop in the price that firms can charge for their bonds and (2) cause an increase in their bonds' interest rate.

BOND RATINGS Default risk is important to bondholders, and it helps to determine the price of the bond. But typical individuals have difficulty judging the default risk of any one company, let alone the thousands of firms that sell bonds in a developed economy. To address this problem, private rating agencies evaluate and then grade the default risk of borrowing entities. They give a grade that reflects the likelihood of default. Three ratings agencies are particularly prominent in the United States: Moody's, Standard and Poor's, and Fitch. The ratings systems are similar for all three firms, so we'll choose Standard and Poor's (S&P) for explanatory purposes.

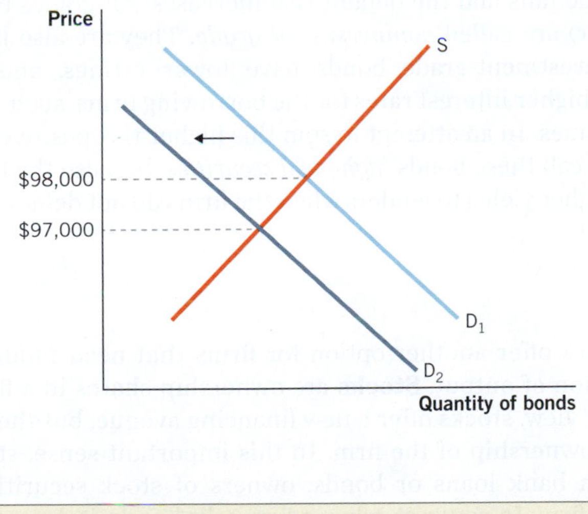

FIGURE 23.4

How Increased Default Risk Affects the Market for $100,000 Target Bonds

The initial price in the market for Target bonds is $98,000. But an increase in default risk reduces the demand for Target bonds, resulting in a lower price and a higher interest rate. This outcome drives up the borrowing costs for Target.

TABLE 23.2

Sample Bond Ratings

S&P*	Grade	Examples
AAA	Prime	Apple, Germany, Harvard University, Johnson & Johnson, Microsoft, University of Virginia
AA	High	Amazon, Berkshire Hathaway, Exxon, Nestlé, Nike, Procter & Gamble, Samsung, Toyota, United States, Walmart
A	Upper medium	Anheuser-Busch, Boeing, BP, China, Coca-Cola, Duke University, Ford, GE, IBM, Intel, J.P. Morgan, Louis Vuitton, L'Oreal, Lowe's, Pepsi, Royal Dutch Shell, Siemens, Spain, Target, UnitedHealth Group, Visa, Walt Disney
BBB	Lower medium	American Express, AT&T, Best Buy, eBay, FedEx, General Motors, Goldman Sachs, Heineken, HP, India, Kellogg's, Kraft, McDonald's, McKesson, Mexico, Starbucks, Verizon, Volkswagen
BB	Noninvestment or speculative	American Airlines, Brazil, Marriott, MGM, T-Mobile, Twitter, United Airlines
B	Highly speculative	Argentina, Egypt, Greece, J.C. Penney, Netflix, Office Depot, Staples, Tesla, Turkey, U.S. Steel
CCC	Extremely speculative	Bombardier, P. F. Chang's
CC	In or near default	Neiman Marcus, PetSmart, Sears

*As of 2018.

The most stable firms, those most likely to pay their debts, are given a rating of AAA. In the recent past, firms like Johnson & Johnson and Microsoft have achieved AAA ratings. A high rating is desirable for firms because it directly translates into higher prices and lower interest rates on the firm's bonds. Moreover, the firm's operating costs are directly affected by its bond rating, because the interest rate is the cost of a key resource for its production. If Microsoft's bond rating falls from AAA to AA, this change increases the company's cost in the same way that its costs would rise if its employees negotiated higher wages or if another key resource became more expensive.

Table 23.2 shows selected bond ratings from 2018. As we move down the table, the grade falls and the default risk increases. All grades below medium (BB and lower) are called *noninvestment grade*. They are also known as *junk bonds*. Noninvestment-grade bonds have lower ratings, and these lower ratings mean higher interest rates for the borrowing firms, such as Twitter and American Airlines. In an attempt to spin this higher risk positively, bond salesmen prefer to call these bonds *high-yield securities*, because the higher interest rates mean higher yields to lenders when the firms do not default.

Stocks

Stocks
are ownership shares in a firm.

Stock securities offer another option for firms that need funding to finance their production of output. **Stocks** are ownership shares in a firm. From the firm's point of view, stocks offer a new financing avenue, but they also involve ceding some ownership of the firm. In this important sense, stocks are very different from bank loans or bonds: owners of stock securities are actual owners of the firm. In contrast, when a firm sells bonds, it does not cede direct control of the firm to new owners.

Why would a firm sell stocks instead of bonds? One reason is that bond financing leaves the firm with a lot of bills that must eventually be paid. For example, when IBM sells $10 million worth of 10-year bonds, the company takes on the obligation to pay $10 million in 10 years. If the firm cannot pay this debt, the owners may need to declare bankruptcy and lose the firm altogether. With stocks, however, the owners can sell shares of the firm to others and move forward without the burden of debt.

From the lender's perspective, stock ownership is also different from bond ownership. Because stock owners (shareholders) are owners of the firm, they have some influence on the firm's operations. In fact, a shareholder who owns more than 50% of the shares of the firm is the majority shareholder and controls more than 50% of the ownership votes. A majority shareholder can determine the direction of the company, an influence not available to bondholders.

You can own part of Spotify! To see its current share price, type its ticker symbol (SPOT) into a search engine.

In the United States, the overall size of the U.S. bond market is about the same as that of the stock market. In 2021, the total value of bonds traded in U.S. markets was $51.5 trillion, while the value of all stocks traded in U.S. markets was $49 trillion.*

Secondary Markets

Most people who purchase stocks and bonds use brokers, who buy the stocks and bonds in secondary markets. **Secondary markets** are markets in which securities are traded after their first sale. Secondary markets are like used-car markets, but the "used" assets are securities. There's nothing wrong with a used security; it just means the buyer is not purchasing the security directly from the firm whose name is on it. You probably recognize the names of some important secondary stock markets. They include the New York Stock Exchange (NYSE) and NASDAQ (the National Association of Securities Dealers Automated Quotations).

Secondary markets are markets in which securities are traded after their first sale.

The existence of a secondary market for a given security increases the demand for that security. Consider the difference between a Target Corporation bond and the hypothetical bond you bought from Kara Alexis to help fund her website design company. Whoever buys the Target bond can sell it with a quick call to a broker or with the click of a mouse. The ease of resale is valuable and therefore worth a higher price. But when you buy Kara's bond, you have to hold on to it until you can personally locate another buyer. This sort of complication greatly limits the demand for bonds that cannot be resold in secondary markets, which lowers the price (that is, raises the interest rate).

The NYSE is the largest secondary stock market in the world.

Figure 23.5 illustrates the impact secondary markets have on security prices. If a secondary market exists for a security, then the demand for the security increases (from D_1 to D_2); in turn, the increased demand causes the price of the security to rise (from p_1 to p_2), all else being equal. For the firm, the existence of a secondary market is helpful because it lowers the interest rate the firm pays on its bonds and therefore its cost of borrowing.

*Securities Industry and Financial Markets Association (SIFMA), "US Fixed Income Securities Statistics," December 17, 2021, https://www.sifma.org/resources/research/us-fixed-income-securities-statistics/; Siblis Research, "Total Market Value of U.S. Stock Market," accessed January 20, 2022, https://siblisresearch.com/data/us-stock-market-value/.

FIGURE 23.5

The Effect of Secondary Markets on Security Prices

The existence of secondary markets increases the demand for securities. When demand increases, the price rises (and the interest rate falls). Secondary markets allow firms to borrow at lower interest rates.

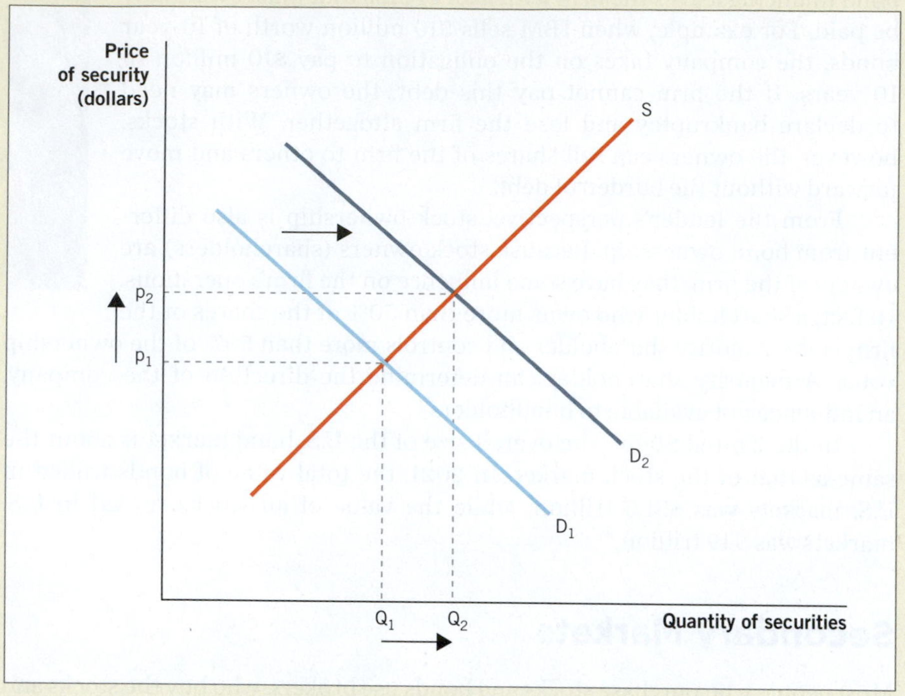

Secondary markets are a valuable institution of market economies because they lower the cost of borrowing. This is true of secondary markets for any asset, not just stocks and bonds. For example, let's say you are considering buying a particular house. Your real estate agent tells you the price is very reasonable, but there is one unusual stipulation: you can never sell the house after you buy it. Of course, this is not a realistic stipulation, but think about how it would affect your willingness to buy the home. The purchase would be more risky, and no buyer would pay as much for that house as for one that could be resold. Secondary markets, by offering future sale opportunities for securities, increase the demand for them.

ECONOMICS IN THE REAL WORLD

STOCK MARKET INDICES: DOW JONES VERSUS S&P

Media reports about the stock market tend to focus on stock price indices like the Dow Jones Industrial Average and the Standard and Poor's 500 (S&P 500). Just as the consumer price index (CPI) tracks general consumer prices, these stock market indices track overall stock prices. The CPI, recall, is a weighted average of all consumer prices, where the weights are determined by the portion of the typical consumer budget spent on any given item. An increase in the CPI indicates a corresponding rise in the general level of consumer prices. Similarly, the rise and fall of stock indices indicate a corresponding rise and fall in the general level of stock prices.

One of the most widely followed stock indexes is the Dow Jones Industrial Average (the Dow). When the Dow was first published in 1896, it tracked 12 companies. Today,

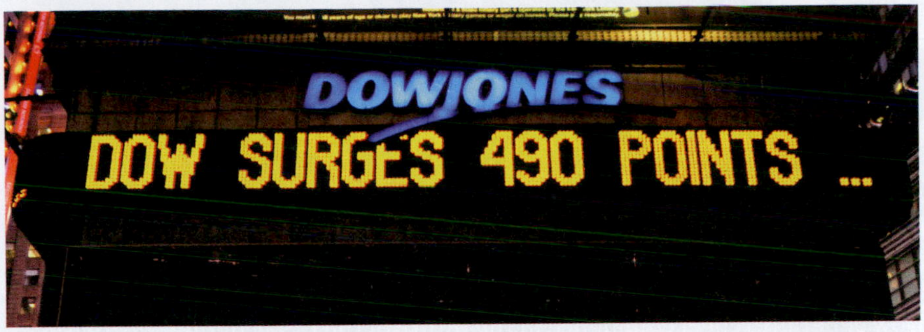

Is it good news when the Dow Jones Industrial Average goes up?

it tracks 30 companies selected by the editors of the *Wall Street Journal*. The editors maintain the index so that it represents companies in all the important sectors of the economy. To stay up to date, the Dow must occasionally change the companies in its index. For example, when the technology sector came to the forefront in the late 1990s, Intel and Microsoft were added. In 2015, Apple replaced AT&T. Most recently, General Electric, which had been part of the Dow virtually from the beginning, was replaced in 2018 by the parent company that owns Walgreens drug stores.

One of the advantages of the Dow is that it provides historical data all the way back to May 26, 1896. At that time, the calculation was very simple: an investor added the price of all 12 stocks and divided the sum by 12 to compute a simple average. Today, the Dow incorporates 30 stock prices in the average, but it is essentially computed in the same way. This means the Dow tracks only the price of the stock, not the overall value of a company or the relative values of the companies in the stock market.

The S&P 500 index weights the stock prices by the *market value* of the companies it tracks. The market value is the total number of stock shares multiplied by the price per share. Under a market value–weighted index, the stock prices of large companies have a greater impact. For instance, Apple (with a market value of over $2.5 trillion at the start of 2022) weighs much more heavily than Nike (with a market value of just over $225 billion at the same time). Moreover, there is another difference between the S&P 500 and the Dow Jones index: while the Dow tracks only 30 companies, the S&P 500 tracks 500 companies, thus providing a much broader representation of the stock market.

In many respects, the Dow is an artifact of simpler times, when computing a broadly based index was time intensive. Today, spreadsheets can crunch all the stock price data in milliseconds. Nevertheless, the Dow has been a very reliable measure of market performance, and it also provides a continuous record of historical information that cannot be replaced by more recent indices.

Treasury Securities

So far in our discussion, we have considered firms as the major type of borrowing entity in an economy. But governments are significant borrowers, too. According to the U.S. Treasury Department, the U.S. federal government has more than $30 trillion worth of debt—that's about $90,000 per person. All this borrowing takes place through bond sales. **Treasury securities** are the bonds sold by the U.S. government to pay for the national debt.

Treasury securities are the bonds sold by the U.S. government to pay for the national debt.

Treasury securities are sold through auctions to large financial firms. The auction price determines the interest rate. After a Treasury security is sold the

DATA SNAPSHOT

The Dow Jones Industrial Average

The Dow Jones Industrial Average is perhaps the most closely watched financial market indicator. The Dow tracks average stock prices of 30 firms that represent major industries in the U.S. economy; these include Coca-Cola, Walmart, Disney, Microsoft, Apple, Visa, and Boeing. Since the Dow represents a broad array of industries, movements indicate changes in private investors' expectations about the future direction of the macroeconomy. Increases in the Dow generally reflect confidence in the future of the U.S. economy; decreases mean people are pessimistic. While other economic indicators take months to measure, the Dow is an instantaneous indicator of how private investors view future economic conditions.

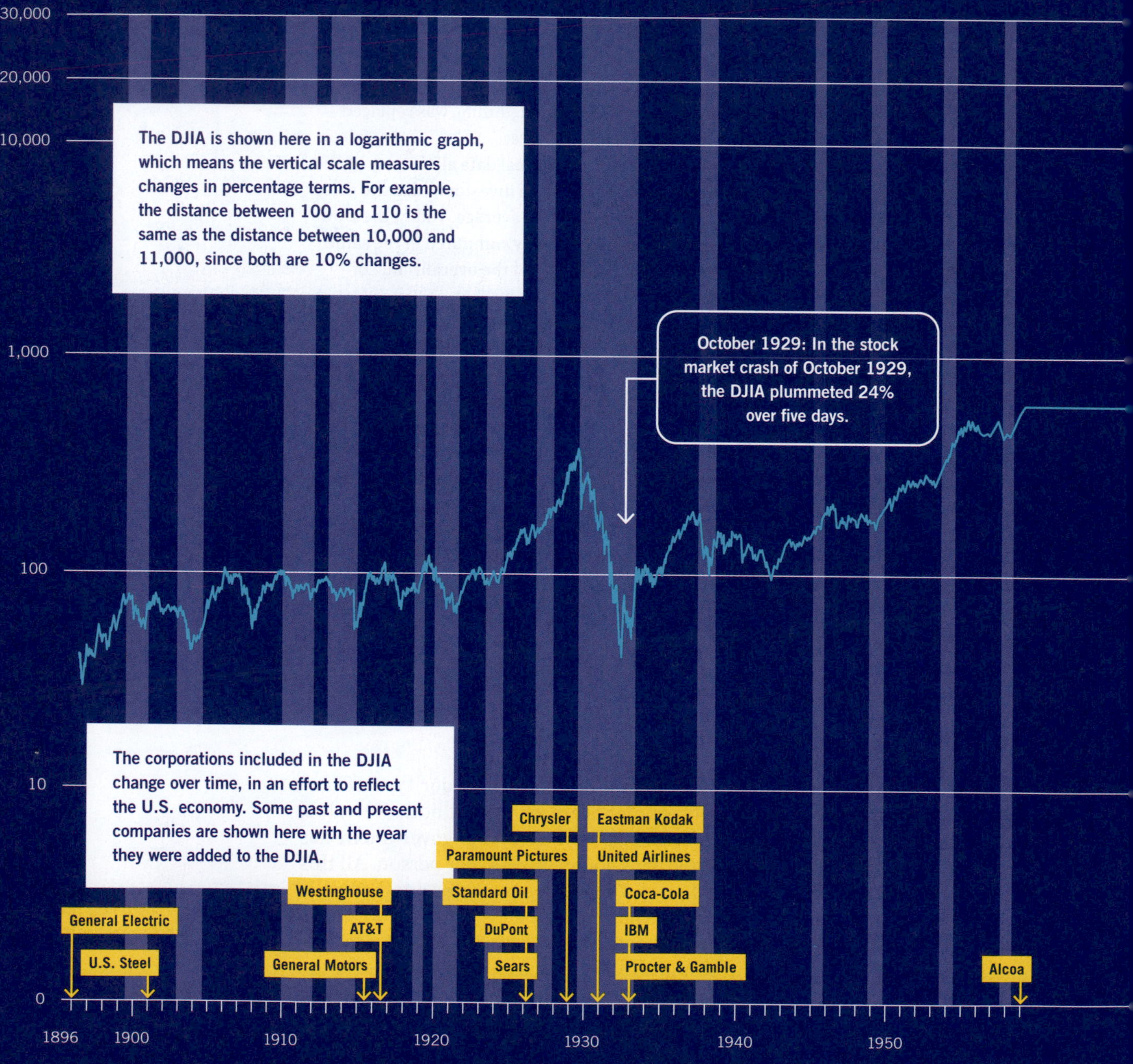

30,000
20,000
10,000
1,000
100
10
0
The DJIA is shown here in a logarithmic graph, which means the vertical scale measures changes in percentage terms. For example, the distance between 100 and 110 is the same as the distance between 10,000 and 11,000, since both are 10% changes.
October 1929: In the stock market crash of October 1929, the DJIA plummeted 24% over five days.
The corporations included in the DJIA change over time, in an effort to reflect the U.S. economy. Some past and present companies are shown here with the year they were added to the DJIA.
General Electric
U.S. Steel
Westinghouse
AT&T
General Motors
Chrysler
Paramount Pictures
Standard Oil
DuPont
Sears
Eastman Kodak
United Airlines
Coca-Cola
IBM
Procter & Gamble
Alcoa
1896
1900
1910
1920
1930
1940
1950

REVIEW QUESTIONS

- Approximately how long did it take the Dow to rise from 1,000 to 10,000? From 10,000 to 25,000?
- Why do movements in overall stock prices indicate something about the entire macroeconomy?

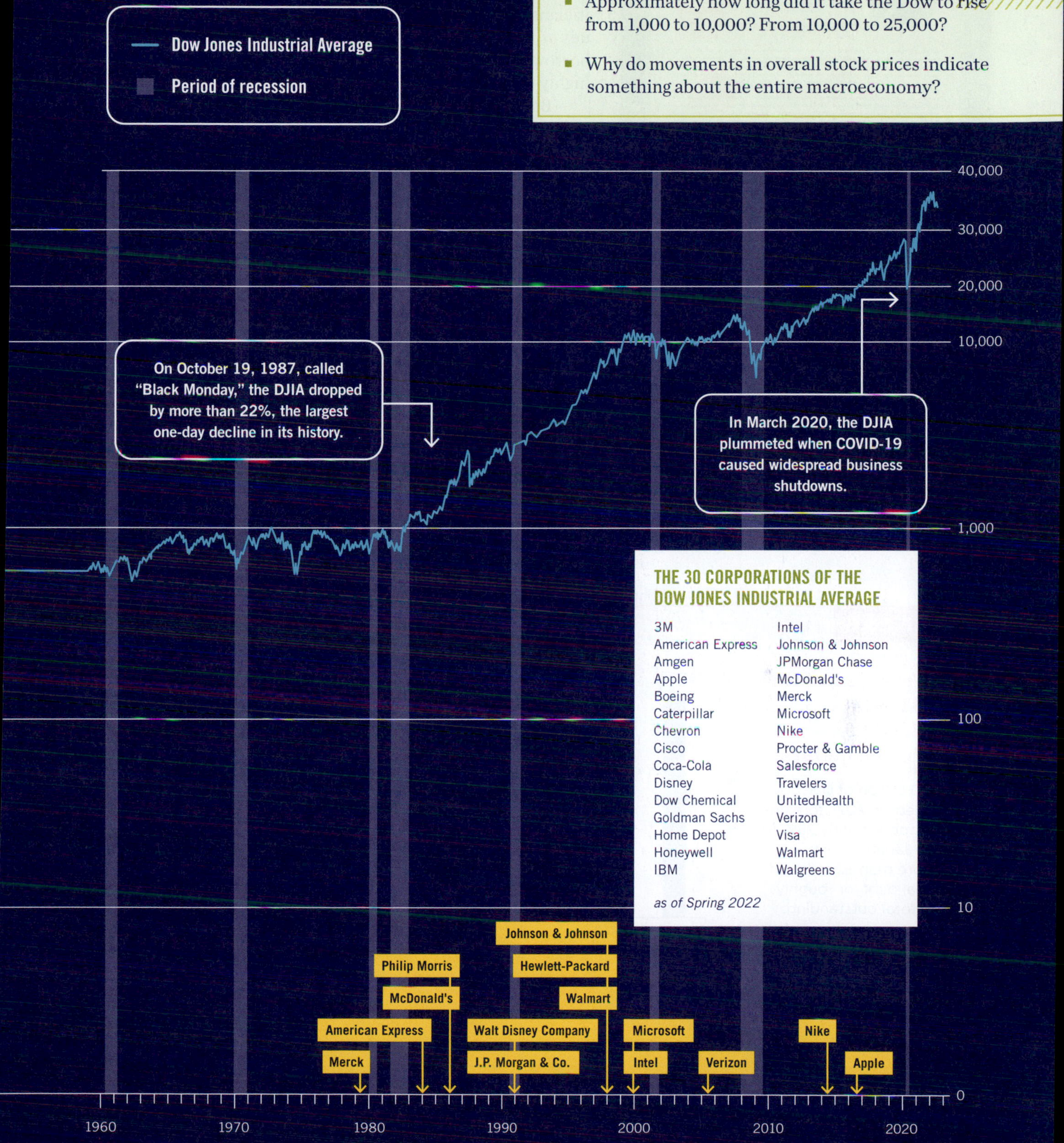

THE 30 CORPORATIONS OF THE DOW JONES INDUSTRIAL AVERAGE

3M	Intel
American Express	Johnson & Johnson
Amgen	JPMorgan Chase
Apple	McDonald's
Boeing	Merck
Caterpillar	Microsoft
Chevron	Nike
Cisco	Procter & Gamble
Coca-Cola	Salesforce
Disney	Travelers
Dow Chemical	UnitedHealth
Goldman Sachs	Verizon
Home Depot	Visa
Honeywell	Walmart
IBM	Walgreens

as of Spring 2022

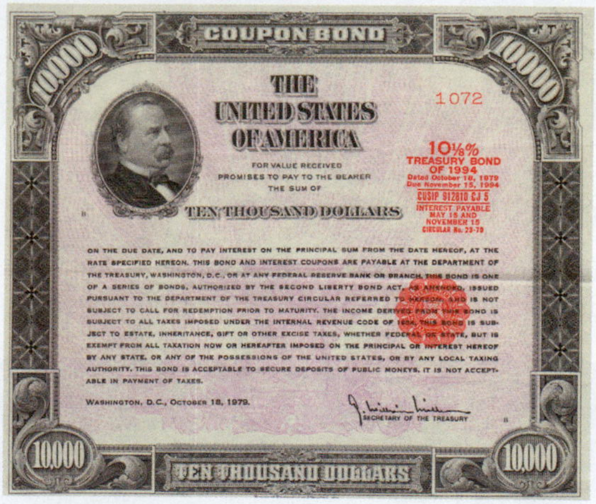

U.S. Treasury securities are used to pay for government spending when tax revenue falls short.

first time, anyone can buy it in the large and active secondary market for U.S. Treasury securities.

U.S. Treasury securities are generally considered less risky than any other bond, because borrowers don't expect the U.S. government to default on its debts. Even when politicians threaten actions that could lead to default, the values of U.S. securities have stayed historically steady because borrowers on the whole have felt that a U.S. loan default is highly unlikely.

Because Treasury bonds are safe, firms and governments from all over the world buy U.S. Treasury securities as a way to limit risk. In 2021, approximately $7.6 trillion (about 25%) of U.S. federal debt was held by foreigners. Figure 23.6 shows the breakdown of foreign ownership of U.S. Treasury securities.

As we noted at the start of the chapter, a common concern is that nations like China will exert undue influence on the U.S. government if we owe them money. But in 2021, China owned only about 3% of the total U.S. debt. As we also noted in the chapter opener, people concerned about foreign ownership of U.S. national debt generally don't consider that foreign savings help keep interest rates lower in the United States. This means that U.S. firms and governments can undertake their activities at lower costs. In turn, lower interest rates mean more investment and greater future GDP. That is a clear benefit of foreign investment in the United States.

Treasury securities play many roles in the macroeconomy. For example, they are used when the government alters the supply of money in the economy, which we discuss in Chapter 30. In addition, if the government decides to increase spending without raising taxes, it must pay for the additional spending by borrowing—by selling bonds. We will explore this role of Treasury securities in Chapter 28.

FIGURE 23.6

Major Foreign Holders of U.S. Treasury Securities, 2021 (in billions of dollars)

Of the $30 trillion of U.S. government debt in 2021, foreigners held approximately 25%. China and Japan together owned more than $2 trillion of our national debt, or roughly 8% of the total outstanding.

Source: U.S. Treasury Department.

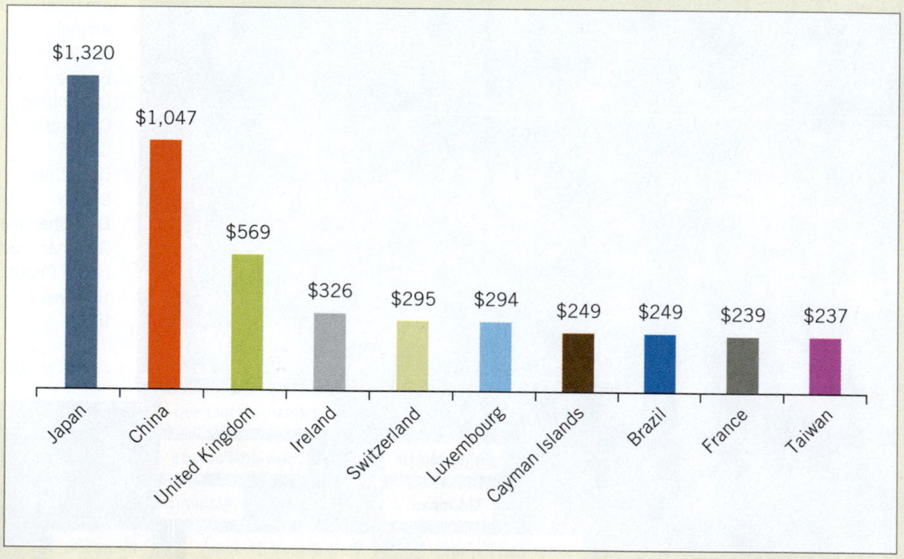

FIGURE 23.7

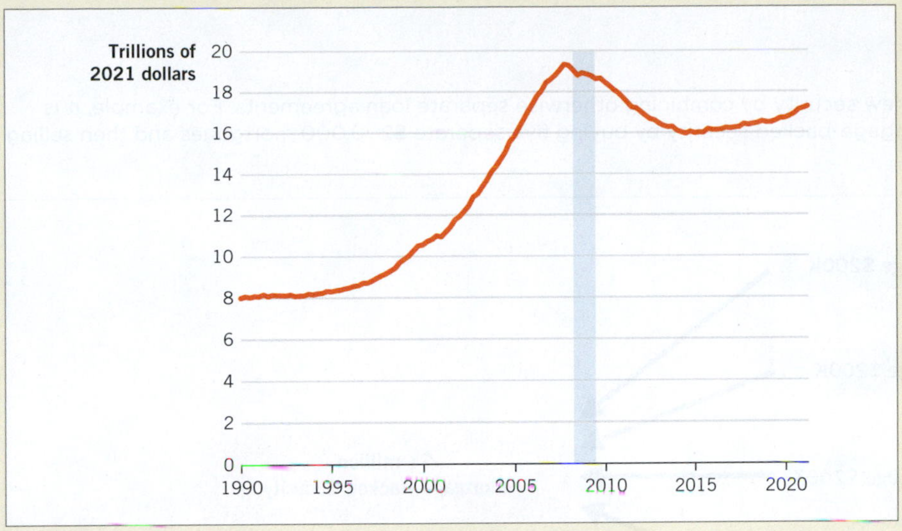

Total Size of U.S. Mortgage Market, 1990–2021

The home mortgage market in the United States expanded greatly, leading up to the recession in 2008. In 1990, there was $8 trillion worth of home mortgages in the United States. The market expanded to over $19 trillion before contracting in the aftermath of the Great Recession.

Source: Federal Reserve.

Home Mortgages

Another important borrowing tool in the United States is the home mortgage loan, which individuals use to pay for homes. The most common mortgage loan lasts 30 years from inception and is paid off with 360 monthly payments. These mortgages are really just variations on the basic bond security we have described in this chapter. When a family wants to buy a home, they take on a mortgage loan, which is a contract that states their willingness to repay the loan over several years—just like a firm signing a bond contract.

The macroeconomic significance of home mortgages has grown over time as more and more people own homes. Figure 23.7 shows the growth in the U.S. mortgage market from 1990 to 2021. The graph plots the total size of the market in real (2021) dollars. The period of the Great Recession is shaded (December 2007 to June 2009). The U.S. home mortgage market expanded greatly in the years leading up to the recession. In 1990, there was about $8 trillion in U.S. mortgages. By 2007, the market had expanded to over $19 trillion. As of late 2021, the U.S. mortgage market has still not returned to the levels we saw in 2007. However, low interest rates during the coronavirus pandemic are driving new borrowing and putting the mortgage market back into growth mode.

Securitization

Since the 1980s, bonds, stocks, and other financial securities, including home mortgages, have been bundled together to create new financial assets in a process called securitization. **Securitization** is the creation of a new security by combining otherwise separate loan agreements. These agreements are then bought and sold like any other agreement on secondary markets.

Securitization is the creation of a new security by combining otherwise separate loan agreements.

For example, consider two common personal loans: home mortgages and student loans. The United States has secondary markets in which home mortgages and student loans are bought and sold daily. Figure 23.8 illustrates how

FIGURE 23.8

Securitization

Securitization is the creation of a new security by combining otherwise separate loan agreements. For example, it is possible to create a $1 million mortgage-backed security by buying five separate $200,000 mortgages and then selling them together as a bundle.

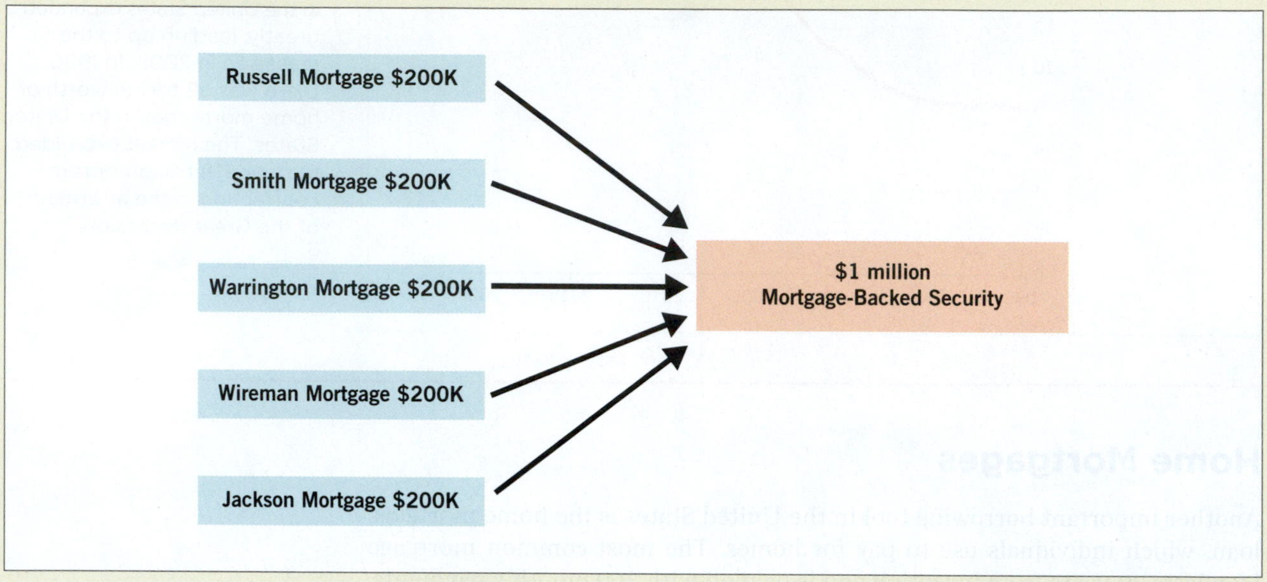

mortgage-backed securities are created. Each mortgage-backed security (MBS) is a combination, or bundle, of mortgages. The new security is then available for resale in secondary markets.

Most economists believe that these tools are important because opportunities for firms and individuals expand when credit is available. More credit leads to lower borrowing costs, which certainly help borrowers. When interest rates are lower, investment opportunities expand for everything from factories to roads to homes to education. And as we noted earlier, secondary markets reduce borrowing costs. In a few years, you may take out a mortgage to buy a home. There is a chance your mortgage will be bundled together with others into a big security that can be bought and sold. The mere existence of this market means you'll pay a lower interest rate on your mortgage loan. For these reasons, there are incentives to create new markets for all varieties of loan agreements.

Incentives

Indeed, securitization lowers interest rates for borrowers. It also offers new opportunities for lenders. For example, people from all over the globe can now buy securities tied to the U.S. mortgage market. But lenders need to correctly evaluate the risk associated with these newly created securities. When the U.S. home mortgage market began collapsing in 2007, the negative reverberations were felt not only in the United States but worldwide. For example, because Icelandic banks owned a large number of securities tied to the U.S. home mortgage market, both the economy and government of Iceland collapsed during 2008–2009.

PRACTICE WHAT YOU KNOW

The Effects of Foreign Investment: What If We Limit Foreign Ownership of Our National Debt?

Keeping Chinese money out of the market for U.S. Treasury bonds will drive their price down and the interest rate up.

Imagine that a new law significantly limits foreign ownership of U.S. Treasury bonds.

QUESTION: How would you graph the market for Treasury bonds showing how the new law will affect demand?

ANSWER: Demand will decline because the new law limits foreign demand.

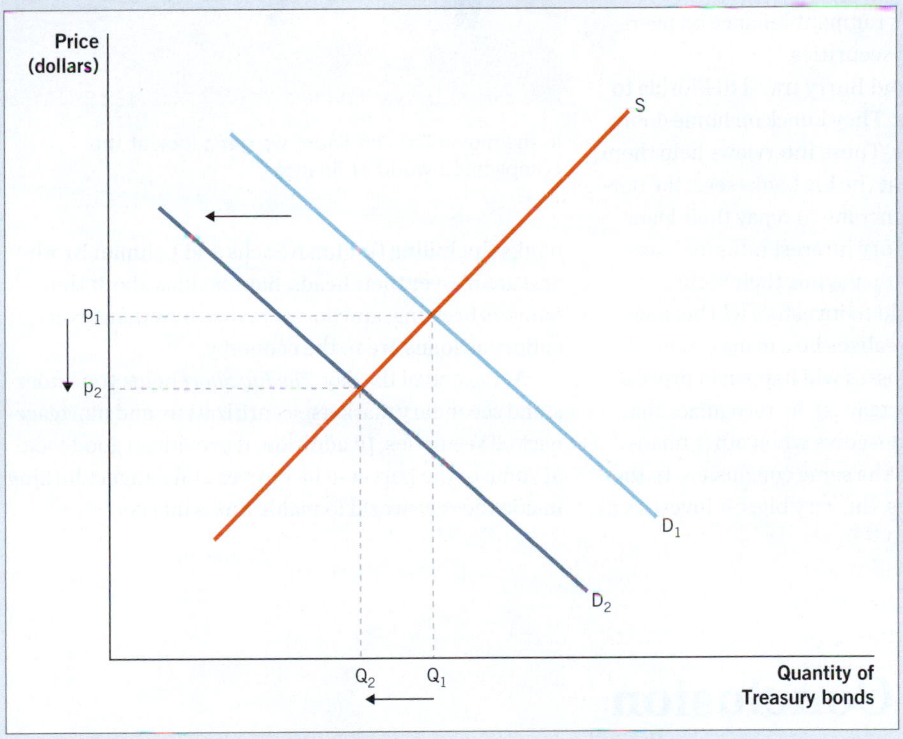

QUESTION: What will happen to the price of Treasury bonds?

ANSWER: The price of Treasury bonds will decline. When demand falls, the new equilibrium price will be lower.

QUESTION: What will happen to the interest rate on Treasury bonds?

ANSWER: The interest rate on Treasury bonds will increase, because dollar price and the interest rate move in opposite directions. A lower price means the government will sell each bond for fewer dollars, so it will be paying higher interest to the bond owner.

In the end, restrictions on foreign investment will lead to higher domestic interest rates.

ECONOMICS *in the* MEDIA

Direct Finance

THE BIG SHORT

The Big Short (2015) is based on the book with the same title by Michael Lewis. The movie is essentially a documentary that doesn't feel like a documentary, as the actors carefully explain the details of the financial collapse that led to the Great Recession in 2007.

The movie introduces Mark Baum (played by Steve Carrell) and Michael Burry (played by Christian Bale), who were among the few people who recognized the dangers in the economy's rampant reliance on overvalued mortgage-backed securities.

In the movie, Baum and Burry travel to Florida to interview real borrowers. They knock on home doors and visit local businesses. These interviews help them see what almost nobody at the big banks sees: the borrowers will not have the income to repay their loans when their low introductory interest rates increase. When these borrowers stop paying, their securitized mortgages being sold to investors will become worthless. When Baum realizes he can make a lot of money by betting these losses will happen (a process called "shorting" the mortgages), he recognizes that the economy will take a nosedive when other financial insiders finally reach the same conclusion. In the meantime, he determines, the very biggest investment banks (including Goldman Sachs and Lehman Brothers) are in over their heads, have no idea about the dangers brewing, and do not realize how dangerous subprime loans are to the economy.

In the movie *The Big Short*, we get a look at the complicated world of finance.

At the end of the day, *The Big Short* helps you understand secondary markets, securitization, and mortgage-backed securities. In addition, it provides a good look at some of the perverse incentives and dangers lurking inside the real-world loanable funds market.

Conclusion

We began this chapter with the idea that borrowing from foreign countries—that is, foreign ownership of a nation's debt—is often helpful to a nation's economy. Funds flowing into the U.S. loanable funds market help lead to economic expansion, no matter where they originate. One of the themes throughout this chapter has been the importance of saving and lending to the macroeconomy. With indirect finance, banks and financial intermediaries help channel funds from savers to borrowers. With direct finance, firms sell securities such as stocks and bonds directly to savers. These securities enable savers to earn returns on their savings while also giving firms access to funds for investment.

In the chapters that follow, we'll see that these financial institutions play a major role in the macroeconomy.✷

· ECONOMICS *for* LIFE ·

Long-Run Returns for Stocks versus Bonds

- Stocks earn significantly more than bonds over time.
- Stock returns are much riskier than bond returns.

Which should you choose: stocks or bonds?

In this chapter, we focused on the importance of stocks and bonds for financing the activities of firms and governments. You may be wondering which of these instruments would best serve your own personal savings plan.

Let's begin by looking at the historical returns for stocks versus bonds. The bar graph below shows that from 1970 to 2020, the nominal return for long-term Treasury bonds was 6.9%. But over the same period, stocks yielded 10.8%.

Perhaps this doesn't seem like a huge difference. But think of it this way: Imagine that your grandparents decided to set aside $100 for you in 1970. If they bought bonds for you, over 50 years their savings would have grown to $2,802 in 2020 dollars. If they instead chose a diversified group of stocks, their savings would have grown to $16,893 in 2020 dollars (inflation averaged about 4% over this period, but that would affect the real returns on bonds and stocks similarly). These alternatives are plotted in the graph below.

To be sure, stocks are riskier. Just look at how the value of your savings would have fluctuated over the years. With stocks, the value of your savings would have sometimes climbed or fallen by more than $1,000 a year. With bonds, the fluctuations would have been much smaller. Therefore, if you are extremely averse to risk, you might choose bonds. But in the long run, taking more risk with stocks has historically been more lucrative. Your grandparents would probably advise you to choose stocks while you are young and then shift toward the safety of bonds as you age and move closer to cashing in.

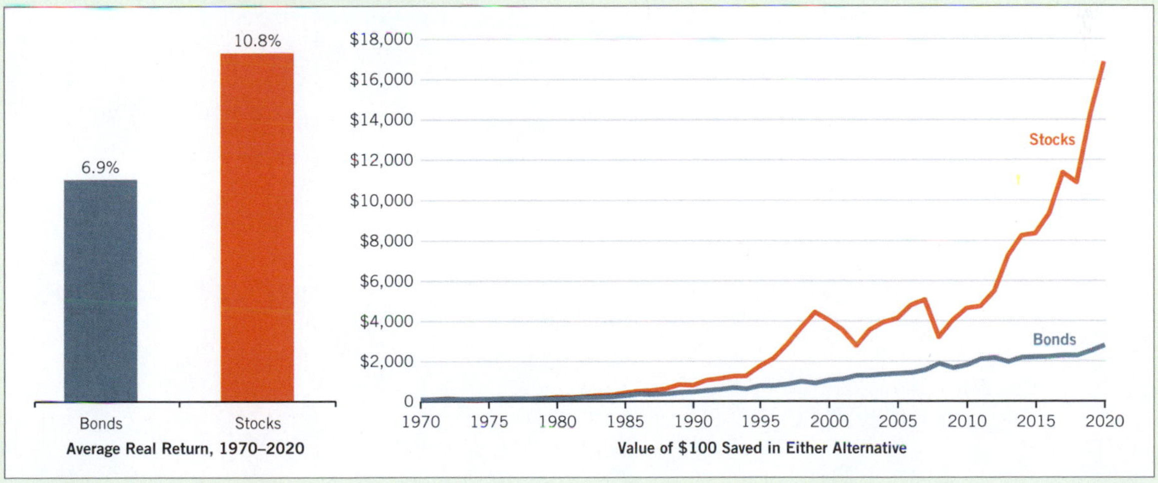

ANSWERING *the* BIG QUESTIONS

How do financial markets help the economy?

- Financial markets help channel funds to investment opportunities throughout the economy.
- Direct finance occurs when savers lend directly to borrowers; indirect finance occurs when savers and borrowers go through financial intermediaries.

What are the key financial tools for the macroeconomy?

- Bonds serve as a basic instrument of direct finance: they provide a tool with which firms and governments can finance their activities.
- Stocks are an additional source of funds for firms. They give the security holder an ownership share in the firm.
- Secondary markets make securities more valuable and offer more avenues for funds to flow to investors.
- Treasury securities are the bonds sold by the U.S. government to finance the national debt. They play a prominent role in macroeconomic policy.
- Home mortgages are the contracts that people sign to borrow for the purchase of a home. Because the mortgage market is so large, the entire macroeconomy is affected by its condition.

CHAPTER PROBLEMS

Concepts You Should Know

banks (p. 738)
bond (p. 739)
default risk (p. 744)
direct finance (p. 738)
face value (p. 742)
financial intermediaries (p. 738)
indirect finance (p. 738)
maturity date (p. 742)
par value (p. 742)
secondary markets (p. 747)
securitization (p. 753)
security (p. 739)
stocks (p. 746)
Treasury securities (p. 749)

Questions for Review

1. What is the difference between direct and indirect finance? Discuss the reasons why a firm (a borrower) might choose each method. Discuss the reasons why a saver might choose each method.
2. What is securitization? Discuss how securitization benefits borrowers.
3. One principle we learned in this chapter is that the dollar price and the interest rate on a bond move in opposite directions. Why is this always the case?
4. What is the primary use of U.S. Treasury securities? Why are the interest rates on Treasury securities so low? If people worried about the United States defaulting on the national debt, what would you expect to happen to interest rates on U.S. Treasury securities? Why?
5. Why might a firm prefer to finance its investments with bonds rather than stocks? Alternatively, why might a firm prefer stocks to bonds?
6. What is a mortgage-backed security (MBS)? Why is it difficult for ratings agencies to determine the risk of an MBS? Describe how the existence of MBSs helps homebuyers in the United States. Describe how MBS markets spread financial troubles around the world when U.S. home prices dropped in 2008.
7. What is a U.S. Treasury bond? Why are Treasury bonds such a popular asset in world markets?

Study Problems (* *solved at the end of the section*)

1. Toyota bonds are rated AA, and Ford bonds are rated BB. Suppose the price of a $1,000 one-year Toyota bond is $970.
   a. What is the rate of return on the one-year Toyota bond?
   b. The price of a $1,000 one-year Ford bond must be:
      i. less than $970
      ii. greater than $970
      iii. $970
      iv. There is insufficient information to answer this question.
   c. The rate of return on a $1,000 one-year Ford bond must be:
      i. less than the return on the Toyota bond
      ii. greater than the return on the Toyota bond
      iii. the same as the return on the Toyota bond
      iv. There is insufficient information to answer this question.

* 2. In 2008, when the U.S. automobile industry was struggling, the price of Ford Motor Company bonds rose. In this question, you need to calculate how the price increase also affected the interest rate.
   a. What was the interest rate on a one-year Ford bond with a face value of $5,000 and a price of $4,750?
   b. What was the new interest rate on a one-year Ford bond with a face value of $5,000 and a price of $4,950?

* 3. Let's say you own a firm that produces and sells Ping-Pong tables. The name of your company is iPong because your tables have a plug-in jack for all Apple products. To finance a new factory, you decide to sell bonds. Your bonds are rated BBB.
   a. Draw supply and demand curves for your iPong bonds. (The quantity of bonds is measured along

the *x* axis and the price along the *y* axis.) Label the supply curve S, the demand curve D, and the equilibrium price p.

b. How will the demand for iPong bonds be affected if a new secondary market agrees to buy and sell iPong bonds? Illustrate the new demand curve in the graph from part (a), and label it D_{SM}. What are the effects on the price and interest rate on iPong bonds?

4. This question involves the hypothetical iPong firm from question 3.

a. How will demand be affected if a ratings agency upgrades your bond rating to AA?

b. How will the ratings upgrade affect the price of your bond?

c. How will the ratings upgrade affect your cost of borrowing?

5. Use supply and demand curves to illustrate how default risk affects both the price and the interest rate of a bond.

6. In this chapter, we discussed Target Corporation bonds to illustrate the effect of default risk on the price of a bond. In particular, when the default risk rises, the demand for a bond falls and then the equilibrium price falls. In our example, the price of a $100,000 Target bond fell from $98,000 to $97,000.

a. What is the interest rate on a one-year $100,000 bond that sells for $98,000?

b. What is the interest rate on a one-year $100,000 bond that sells for $97,000?

* **7.** The following table presents partial information for several different bonds that each mature in one year. Use the information given along with Equation 23.1 to fill in the blank cells in the table.

Bond	Face value p_m	Initial price p_0	Interest rate R
A	$10,000	$9,000.00	______
B	10,000	______	10%
C	______	98,039.22	2

8. The data in the following table are for two different bonds that both mature in exactly one year.

Borrower	S&P rating	Face value	Price
Maddie's Pasta	AA	$10,000	$9,500
Tricia's Smoothies	A	10,000	______

a. What is the annual rate of return (R) for the Maddie bond?

b. Assume that inflation is exactly 2% for the next year. Use the Fisher equation (from Chapter 22) to calculate the real interest rate on the Maddie bond.

c. What is the par value of the Maddie bond?

d. Will the price of the Tricia bond be greater or less than the price of the Maddie bond? Explain your reasoning.

e. Will the interest rate (R) on the Tricia bond be greater or less than the interest rate on the Maddie bond? Explain your reasoning.

9. A $10,000 one-year AAA University of Virginia (UVA) bond sold for $9,850.

a. What is the implied interest rate on this bond?

b. Given that Duke University bonds are rated AA, what can you say about the price of a $10,000 one-year Duke University bond in the context of this question? Explain your reasoning.

c. In 2016, the nominal interest rate on short-term U.S. Treasury securities was 3.0% and the real interest rate was 0.9%. Use this information to determine the rate of inflation in 2016, using the Fisher equation from Chapter 22.

Solved Problems

2. a. Use the formula

$$R = \frac{p_m - p_0}{p_0}$$

Then compute: $R = (\$5{,}000 - \$4{,}750) \div \$4{,}750 = \$250 \div \$4{,}750 = 5.26\%$

b. $R = (\$5{,}000 - \$4{,}950) \div \$4{,}950 = \$50 \div \$4{,}950 = 1.01\%$

Therefore, when the price of the bond rose by $200, the interest rate decreased from 5.26% to just 1.01%.

3. a.

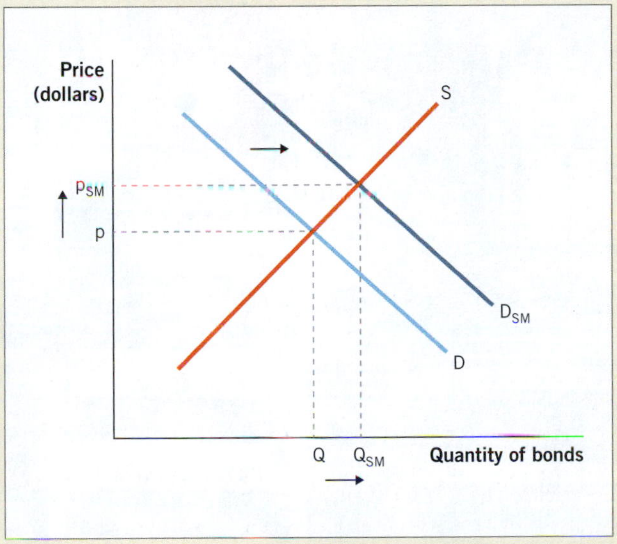

b. If a secondary market is available to sell bonds, the demand for the bonds will increase because the bonds will become more attractive to buyers. When a secondary market exists, you can always resell any bond you own. If there is no secondary market, you are stuck with it once you have it.

In the graph, demand increases and price rises. The result is lower interest rates for your iPong firm.

7. a. For bond A, we are given both the initial price (p_0) and the face value (p_m). We can insert these values into Equation 23.1 and then solve for the interest rate:

$$R = \frac{p_m - p_0}{p_0} = \frac{\$10{,}000 - \$9{,}000}{\$9{,}000} = \frac{\$1{,}000}{\$9{,}000} = \frac{1}{9} = 11.1\%$$

b. For bond B, we are given the face value (p_m) and the interest rate (r), which we can insert into Equation 23.1 to solve for the initial price (p_0):

$$10\% = 0.10 = \frac{\$10{,}000 - p_0}{p_0}$$

$$0.10p_0 = \$10{,}000 - p_0$$

$$0.10p_0 + p_0 = \$10{,}000$$

$$p_0 = \frac{\$10{,}000}{1.10} = \$9{,}090.91$$

c. For bond C, we are given the initial price (p_0) and the interest rate R, which we can plug into Equation 23.1 and solve for the price at maturity (p_m):

$$2\% = 0.02 = \frac{p_m - \$98{,}039.22}{\$98{,}039.22}$$

$$0.02 \times \$98{,}039.22 = p_m - \$98{,}039.22$$

$$\$1{,}960.78 = p_m - \$98{,}039.22$$

$$p_m = \$100{,}000$$

S-3
S-2

PART VII

The Long and Short of MACROECONOMICS

CHAPTER

24

Economic Growth and the Wealth of Nations

There's More to Prosperity Than Natural Resources.

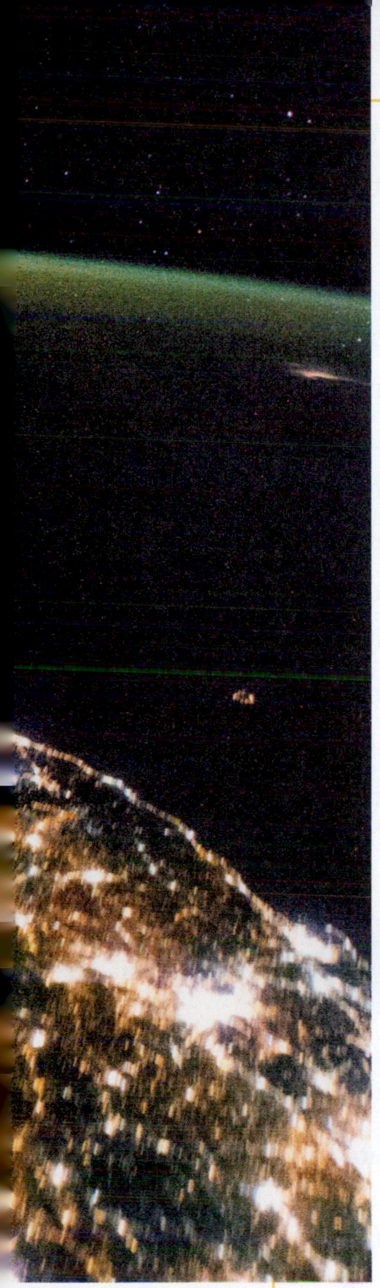

Many people believe that natural resources, such as trees, oil, and farmland, are the primary sources of economic growth. They believe that nations like the United States and Australia are prosperous because these nations have vast natural resources to use in the production of goods and services. A variation on this idea emphasizes geography: nations with the best shipping locations and the mildest climates have more prosperous economies. But what about the two Koreas? North Korea and South Korea have the same labor force and natural resources—the geography is virtually identical and the people on both sides of the border come from the same families. In 1960, their income levels were very similar and very low, each with less than $1,700 in per capita GDP. Today, however, the two economies are as different as night and day. South Korea's economic output is now about $40,000 per person, while North Korea is essentially stuck at the 1960 level. South Korea is one of the world's leading industrial nations, a major exporter of electronics, automobiles, and other goods to the tune of over $500 billion per year. Meanwhile, North Korea, with a population about half the size, exports less than $1 billion in goods. Nearly all those goods are purchased by China, without whose support the North Korean regime would

The two Koreas at night, in an image based on satellite photography: South Korea, bursting with light, and North Korea, mired in economic darkness. North Korea's self-imposed political and economic isolation has earned it the nickname "The Hermit Kingdom."

have collapsed a long time ago. Over the course of this chapter and the next, we explore what economics has to say about differences in economic growth across nations like North and South Korea.

Striving for economic growth is not only about accumulating more wealth. Yes, economic growth brings smartphones and Jet Skis, but it's much more important than that. Economic growth offers the potential for more women and infants to survive childbirth, more people to have access to clean water and better sanitation, and more people to live healthier, longer, and more educated lives.

In this chapter, we begin by looking at the implications of economic growth for human welfare. We then consider the impact of an economy's resources and technology on economic growth. Finally, we discuss the key elements an economy needs in order to grow.

· BIG QUESTIONS ·

- Why does economic growth matter?
- How do resources and technology contribute to economic growth?
- What institutions foster economic growth?
- How are some economists testing new ideas?

Why Does Economic Growth Matter?

In 1900, life expectancy in the United States was 47 years. About 140 of every 1,000 children died before their first birthday. Only about one-third of American homes had running water; and income, in 2021 dollars, was less than $5,500 per person. Most people lived less than a mile from their job and almost nobody owned an automobile. Yes, this is a description of life in the United States in 1900, but it is also a description of life in low-income countries today. What happened in the United States in the meantime? The answer is: economic growth.

In this section, we examine how economic growth affects the lives of people around the world. We also examine the historical data on economic growth and explain some mathematics of growth rates.

Some Ugly Facts

Before looking at data on growth, we need to recall how economists measure economic growth. In Chapter 19, we defined **economic growth** as the percentage change in real per capita GDP. We know that real per capita GDP measures the average level of income in a nation. For most people, life is not all about the pursuit of more income. However, economic growth does alleviate human misery and lengthen lives. Wealthier societies provide better living standards, which include better nutrition, educational opportunities, health care, freedom, and even sources of entertainment.

Economic growth is measured as the percentage change in real per capita GDP.

Let's look around the world and compare life in low-income countries with life in high-income countries. Table 24.1 presents human welfare indicators for some of the world's highest- and lowest-income nations in 2020. Among the low-income nations are Afghanistan, Ethiopia, North Korea, Liberia, Niger, Syria, and Yemen. The high-income nations include Australia, Denmark, Israel, Japan, Germany, South Korea, and the United States.

Consider the first group of indicators, which are related to mortality. In low-income countries, 47 out of every 1,000 babies die at birth or in the first year of life, while in high-income nations the number is only 4 out of every 1,000. This means that infants are about 12 times more likely to die in low-income nations. Those that survive one year in low-income nations are about 13 times more likely to die before their fifth birthday, as indicated by the under-5 mortality rates. Overall, life expectancy in low-income nations is 64 years, while in high-income nations it is 81 years. Just being born in a high-income nation adds 17 years to an individual's life.

TABLE 24.1

Living Conditions in Low- versus High-Income Nations, 2020

Life indicators	Low income	High income
GDP per capita (PPP)	$691	$44,003
Infant mortality rate (per 1,000 live births)	47	4
Under-5 mortality rate (per 1,000)	66	5
Life expectancy at birth (years)	64	81
Physicians (per 10,000)	3	37
Access to safely managed sanitation service (%)	18	87
Access to electricity (%)	40.9	100
Mobile cellular subscriptions (per 100 people)	60	128
Literacy rate, adult male (%)	69	99
Literacy rate, adult female (%)	54	99
Female/male secondary enrollment (ratio)	0.36	1.00

Source: World Bank, World Development Indicators, 2020.

Note: Low income is $1,045 or less and includes 27 nations. High income is $12,696 or more and includes 80 nations. See list of nations here: https://datahelpdesk.worldbank.org/knowledgebase/articles/906519-world-bank-country-and-lending-groups.

Clean water, even in a bag, saves lives.

The second group of indicators in Table 24.1 helps to explain the mortality data. High-income nations have over 10 times as many doctors per person: 37 physicians per 10,000 people versus 3 per 10,000. Well-managed sanitation is available to fewer than 1 in 5 people in low-income nations, while it is available to almost 9 in 10 people in high-income nations. Lack of access to basic services like electricity and phone communication also contributes to mortality differences.

The last group of indicators in Table 24.1 tells the sobering story about education. First, notice that literacy rates in low-income countries are significantly lower than literacy rates in high-income countries. But there is also a significant difference in literacy rates between men and women in low-income nations: 69% of men can read, but only 54% of women are literate. Furthermore, in low-income nations women have less access to secondary (high school) education than men; equal access implies an enrollment ratio of 1.00, but in low-income nations the ratio is only 0.36. So while educational opportunities are rarer for all people in low-income nations, women fare worse than men by far.

The data in Table 24.1 support the contention that per capita GDP matters—not for the sake of more income per se, but because it correlates with better human welfare conditions, which matter to everyone.

Learning from the Past

We can learn a lot about the roots of economic growth by considering the past. Historically, a common person's life focused on subsistence, simply trying to find enough food, shelter, and clothing to survive. As we saw in the previous section, even today many people still live on the margins of subsistence. What can history tell us about how high-income nations achieved economic development? The answer will help clarify possible policy alternatives going forward.

WE WERE ALL POOR ONCE When you look around the globe today, you see rich nations and poor nations. You can probably name many rich nations: the United States, Japan, Taiwan, and the Western European nations, among others. You might also know the very poor nations: much of Africa, parts of Latin America, and significant parts of Asia. But the world was not always this way. If we consider the longer history of humankind, only recently did the incomes of common people rise above subsistence level. The Europe of 1750, for instance, was not noticeably richer than Europe at the time of the birth of Jesus of Nazareth.

Consider the very long run. Angus Maddison, a noted economic historian, estimated GDP levels for many nations and for the whole world back to the year AD 1. This remarkable data set is now available at the Maddison Project web site. Figure 24.1 plots Maddison's estimates of real per capita GDP in 2010 U.S. dollars. Clearly, there was a historical break around 1800 that dramatically changed the path of average world living standards.

Maddison estimated the average level of income in the world in 1820 at about $1,100. This would be comparable to you having an annual income of

FIGURE 24.1

Long-Run World Real Per Capita GDP (in 2010 U.S. dollars)

Historical accounts often focus on monarchs and other wealthy people. But for the average person, living standards across the globe didn't change considerably from the time of Jesus to the time of Thomas Jefferson. The data plotted here show per capita GDP in 2010 U.S. dollars, which is adjusted for prices across both time and place.

Source: Angus Maddison, "Statistics on World Population, GDP and Per Capita GDP, 1-2008 AD." All figures converted to 2010 U.S. dollars.

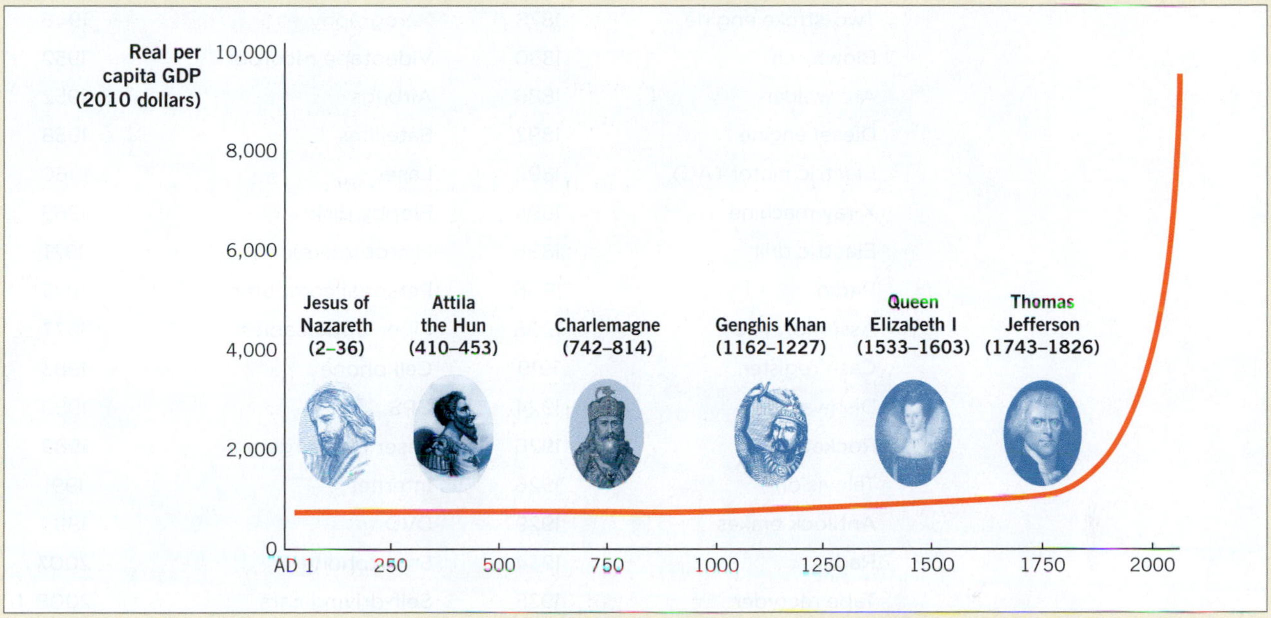

about $1,100. If you had to live on $1,100 for an entire year, it's clear your solitary focus would be on basic necessities like food, clothing, and shelter. Of course, there were certainly rich individuals over the course of history, but until relatively recently, the average person's life was essentially one of subsistence living. Consider Alice Toe, the Liberian girl profiled in the Economics in the Real World feature on page 772. This type of life, where even meals are uncertain, was the basic experience for the average person for nearly all of human history.

Of course, there were global variations in income before 1700. For example, average income in Western Europe in 1600 was about $1,400, while in Latin America it was less than $700. This means Western Europeans were twice as wealthy as Latin Americans in 1600. But average Europeans were still very poor!

The Industrial Revolution, during which many economies moved away from agriculture and toward manufacturing in the 1800s, is at the very center of the big increase in world income growth. Beginning with the Industrial Revolution, the rate of technical progress increased so rapidly, it was able to outpace population growth. The foundation for the Industrial Revolution was laid in the preceding decades, and these foundations included private property protection and several technological innovations. We don't claim that the Industrial Revolution was idyllic for those who lived through it, but the legal and other institutional innovations of that era paved the way for the unprecedented gains in human welfare that people have since experienced.

TABLE 24.2

Important Inventions since the U.S. Civil War

Typewriter	1867	Electron microscope	1939
Sheep shears	1868	Electric clothes dryer	1940
Telephone	1876	Nuclear reactor	1942
Phonograph	1877	Microwave oven	1945
Milking machine	1878	Computer	1946
Two-stroke engine	1878	Xerography	1946
Blowtorch	1880	Videotape recorder	1952
Arc welder	1886	Airbags	1952
Diesel engine	1892	Satellites	1958
Electric motor (AC)	1892	Laser	1960
X-ray machine	1895	Floppy disk	1965
Electric drill	1895	Microprocessor	1971
Radio	1906	Personal computer	1975
Assembly line	1908	Fiber-optic cables	1977
Cash register	1919	Cell phone	1983
Dishwasher	1924	GPS	1989
Rocket	1926	Laser eye surgery	1989
Television	1926	Internet	1991
Antilock brakes	1929	DVD	1995
Radar	1934	Smartphone	2007
Tape recorder	1935	Self-driving cars	2008
Jet engine	1939	Gene-editing technology	2013

Sources: Michael Cox and Richard Alm, *Myths of Rich and Poor* (New York: Basic Books, 1999), and miscellaneous other sources.

These data do not imply that life is always easy and predictably comfortable for everyone in the modern world. But opportunities for the average person alive today are very different from those for the average person in past centuries. Table 24.2 lists a sampling of some of the major innovations of the past century and a half. Try to imagine life without any of these, and you'll get a sense of the gains we've made since the Industrial Revolution.

SOME GOT RICH, OTHERS STAYED POOR Although wealth has increased over the past two centuries, it is not evenly distributed around the globe. Figure 24.2 shows real per capita GDP (in 2020 U.S. dollars) for various world regions. In 1820, the income of the average U.S. citizen was $3,160, or about $9 per day. Imagine trying to live on $9 per day in today's world—that is, $9 to buy all the food, clothing, shelter, education, transportation, and anything else you might need to purchase. That was life in the United States in 1820. But it also describes the plight of many people in the world today.

By 1920, some regions had broken the stranglehold of poverty. In 1920, real per capita GDP in Western Europe was $5,772; in the United States, it was $11,999.

FIGURE 24.2

Real Per Capita GDP over 200 Years (in 2020 U.S. dollars)

Two hundred years ago, all regions and nations were poor. The modern differences in wealth we see around the world today began to emerge before 1900. But the twentieth century saw unprecedented growth take hold in the United States and Western Europe. Unfortunately, some parts of the globe today are no better off than the United States and Western Europe were in 1800.

Source: Maddison Project Database (MPD) 2020.

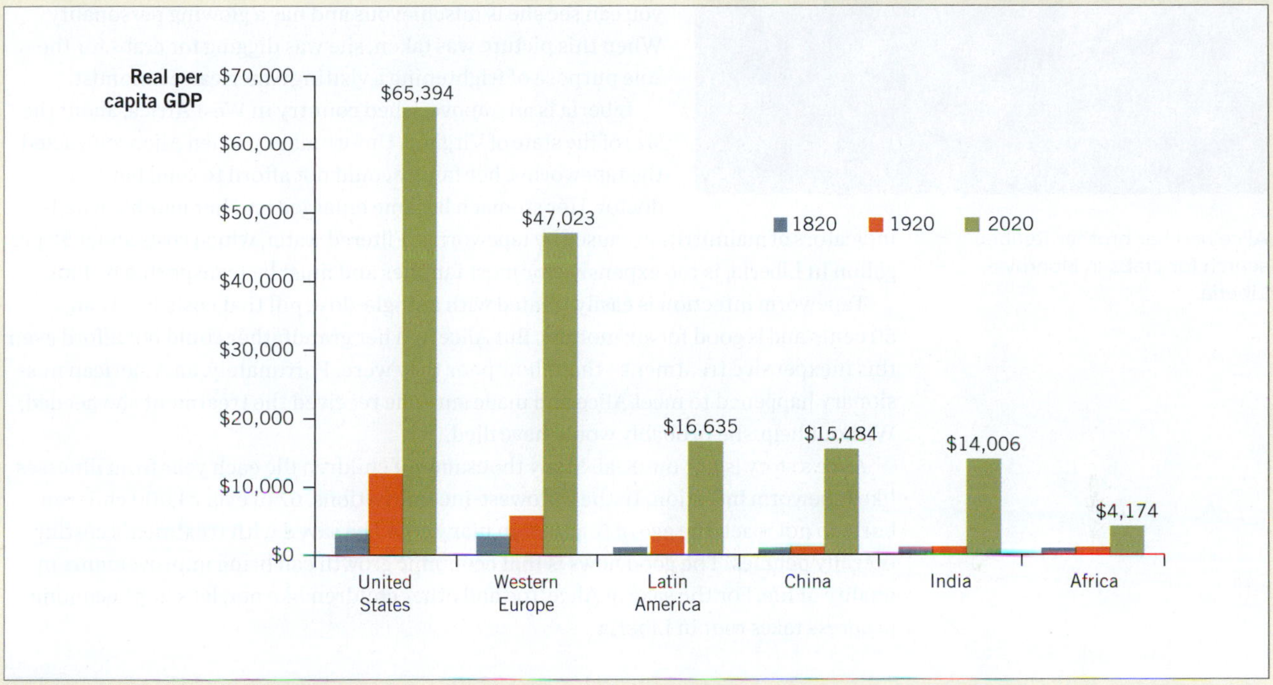

Prior to 1920, general income levels this high had never been experienced. But in China, India, and sub-Saharan Africa, the averages were still just over $1,000 in 1920. The twentieth century proved to be even more prosperous for some, as the income gap widened between the United States and Western Europe and the rest of the world. Unfortunately, real per capita income in sub-Saharan Africa today is just $4,174, or about the average level in the United States in 1858.

While many of the current disparities between nations began about 200 years ago, some nations have moved from poor to rich as recently as the past few decades. In 1950, for example, South Korea, with real per capita GDP (in 2021 dollars) of just $1,179, was poorer than Nicaragua, at $3,031. But by 2018, South Korea was one of the wealthiest countries in the world, with a per capita income of $44,823, while Nicaragua had grown to $5,852 in per capita income.*

*Maddison Project Database 2020, Groningen Growth and Development Centre, University of Groningen, accessed January 2022, https://www.rug.nl/ggdc/historicaldevelopment/maddison/releases/maddison-project-database-2020.

ECONOMICS IN THE REAL WORLD

Alice and her brother Reuben search for crabs in Monrovia, Liberia.

ONE CHILD WHO NEEDS ECONOMIC PROGRESS

This is a true story about a girl named Alice Toe, a young girl who was 3 years old when she contracted tapeworms by drinking water from her neighborhood well in Monrovia, Liberia. Alice is pictured at left with her brother Reuben. From the look on her face, you can see she is mischievous and has a glowing personality. When this picture was taken, she was digging for crabs for the sole purpose of frightening a visiting American economist.

Liberia is an impoverished country in West Africa, about the size of the state of Virginia. Unfortunately, when Alice contracted the tapeworms, her family could not afford to send her to a doctor. Her stomach became enlarged and her hair bleached—indicators of malnutrition caused by tapeworms. Filtered water, which costs about $3 per gallon in Liberia, is too expensive for most families and must be transported by foot.

Tapeworm infection is easily treated with a single-dose pill that costs less than 50 cents and is good for six months. But Alice and her grandfather could not afford even this inexpensive treatment—that's how poor they were. Fortunately, an American missionary happened to meet Alice and made sure she received the treatment she needed. Without help, she probably would have died.

Alice's story is not unusual. Many thousands of children die each year from illnesses like tapeworm infection. In the 27 lowest-income nations, 67 of every 1,000 children born do not reach the age of 5, although many could be saved with treatments costing literally pennies. The good news is that economic growth can bring improvements in quality of life. For the sake of Alice Toe and other children like her, let's hope economic progress takes root in Liberia.

Measuring Economic Growth

Overall, people today are much wealthier than they were 200 years ago. However, this prosperity did not occur overnight. Rather, income grew a little bit each year. There is a striking mathematical truth about growth: small differences in growth rates lead to large differences in wealth levels over time. In this section, we explain how economic growth rates are computed, and we consider the level of growth a nation needs for its population to experience significant improvements in living standards.

THE MATHEMATICS OF GROWTH RATES The big break out of poverty began during the nineteenth century. Table 24.3 shows data on world economic growth in different periods. From 1800 to 1900, average world GDP growth was only 0.64% per year. From 1900 to 1950, world economic growth increased to 1.04%. The difference between 0.64% and 1.04% might seem trivial. But when economic growth increases by 0.4% and is sustained for many years, it makes a big difference. In this section, we show how growth is calculated.

We have seen that economic growth is the annual growth rate of real per capita GDP. It is our measure of how an average person's income changes over

TABLE 24.3

World Economic Growth for Different Historical Eras

Years	Annual growth rate
AD 1–1800	0.02%
1800–1900	0.64
1900–1950	1.04
1950–2000	2.12

Source: Angus Maddison, "Statistics on World Population, GDP and Per Capita GDP, 1–2008 AD."

time, including an allowance for price changes. But the government reports overall GDP data in nominal terms. Therefore, to get an accurate growth rate, we need to account for both inflation and population growth. We can use the following equation to approximate economic growth, where %Δ indicates the percentage change in a variable:

$$\text{economic growth} \approx \%\Delta \text{ in nominal GDP} - \%\Delta \text{ price level} - \%\Delta \text{ population} \qquad \textbf{(EQUATION 24.1)}$$

Let's walk through the equation for economic growth using actual U.S. data as shown in Table 24.4. Starting with nominal GDP data for 2018 and 2019, we compute nominal GDP growth of 4.1%. But part of the increase in nominal GDP is due to inflation. In 2019, the price level, as measured by the GDP deflator, grew by 1.8%. We subtract this inflation rate from nominal GDP growth to get real GDP growth of 2.3%. This number applies to the entire nation, but population also increased by 0.5% in 2019. When we subtract population growth, we are left with 1.8% as the rate of economic growth for the United States in 2019. This growth rate was slightly lower than normal: since 1950, average economic growth in the United States has been about 2%.

A word of caution about terminology is in order. There's a big difference between nominal GDP growth, real GDP growth, and real per capita GDP growth. (In Table 24.4, these terms appear in orange.) But sloppy economic reporting sometimes confuses the terms. You may read something like "the U.S. economy grew by 2.3% in 2019," which refers to real GDP growth and is not calculated on a per capita basis. It would be an even bigger mistake to claim that

TABLE 24.4

Computing an Economic Growth Rate

U.S. GDP in 2018 (in millions)	$20,580,200	
U.S. GDP in 2019 (in millions)	$21,427,700	
Nominal GDP growth	4.1%	
– Price growth (inflation)	1.8%	
= Real GDP growth	2.3%	
– Population growth	0.5%	
≈ Real per capita GDP growth	1.8%	≈ Economic growth

Sources: GDP data, U.S. Bureau of Economic Analysis, https://www.bea.gov/data/gdp/gross-domestic-product; population data, U.S. Census Bureau, https://www.census.gov/newsroom/press-releases/2019/popest-nation.html.

U.S. economic growth in 2019 was 4.1%, a number not adjusted for either population growth or inflation. Such confusing wording is a common mistake in reports on international economic growth statistics.

GROWTH RATES AND INCOME LEVELS Before we consider policies that might aid economic growth, we need to look more closely at how growth rates affect income levels.

First, consider how significant it is when income doubles, or increases by 100%. If your income doubled today—all else being equal—you could afford twice as much of everything you are currently buying. Now imagine what would happen if income doubled for an entire country or even for all countries. In the United States, real per capita GDP doubled in the 40 years between 1980 and 2020. This means that the average person living in the United States now can afford twice as much food, clothing, transportation, education, and even government services as the average U.S. resident in 1980. That's quite a difference.

But increasing real income by 100% in a single year is not realistic. Let's use an annual growth rate closer to reality—say, 2%, which has historically been an average rate of economic growth for the United States. With 2% annual growth, how long does it take to double your income? For example, let's say you graduate and, given your expertise in economics, you get several job offers. One offer is for $50,000 per year with a guaranteed raise of 2% every year. How long would it take for your salary to reach $100,000?

The first answer that pops into your head might be 50 years (based on the idea that 2% growth for 50 years might add to 100% growth). But this answer would be wrong, because it ignores the fact that growth compounds over time. As your salary grows, 2% growth leads to larger and larger dollar increases. Because of this compounding effect, it actually would take only about 35 years to double your income at a 2% growth rate.

Table 24.5 illustrates the process of compounding over time by showing the increase from year to year. Income starts at $50,000 in year 1, and a 2% increase yields $1,000, so one year of growth results in an income of $51,000 in year 2. Subsequent 2% growth in the second year yields $1,020 of new income (2% of $51,000), so after two years your income is $52,020. Looking at year 3, the 2% increase yields $1,040.40. Each year, the dollar increase in income (the green numbers in the third column) gets larger, as 2% of a growing number continues to grow. This scenario corresponds with the experience of the U.S. economy.

TABLE 24.5

Compound Growth

	Income	2% increase in income	Income in next year
Year 1	$50,000.00	$1,000.00	$51,000.00
Year 2	51,000.00	1,020.00	52,020.00
Year 3	52,020.00	1,040.40	53,060.40
Year 4	53,060.40	1,061.21	54,121.61
Year 5	54,121.61	1,082.43	55,204.04
...			
Year 35	100,000		

TABLE 24.6

A Dollar of Income at Different Growth Rates

Annual growth rate	Years to double	Value after 70 years (approximate)
0%	Never	$1
1	70	2
2	35	4
3	23.3	8
4	17.5	16

Since 1970, real per capita GDP in the United States has more than doubled. Yet this jump occurred while U.S. economic growth rates averaged "only" about 2%.

THE RULE OF 70 In the previous example, we saw that when income grows at 2% per year, it doubles in approximately 35 years. A simple rule known as the **rule of 70** determines the length of time necessary for a sum of money to double at a particular growth rate. According to the rule of 70:

The **rule of 70** states that if the annual growth rate of a variable is *x*%, the size of that variable doubles approximately every 70 ÷ *x* years.

If the annual growth rate of a variable is x%, the size of that variable doubles approximately every 70 ÷ x years.

The rule of 70 is an approximation, but it works well with typical economic growth rates.

Table 24.6 illustrates the rule of 70 by showing how long it takes for a single dollar of income to double in value, given different growth rates. At a growth rate of 1%, each dollar of income doubles approximately every 70 ÷ 1 years. If growth increases to 2%, a dollar of income then doubles approximately every 70 ÷ 2 = 35 years. Consider the impact of a 4% growth rate. If this rate can be sustained, income doubles approximately every 70 ÷ 4 = 17.5 years. In 70 years, income doubles 4 times, ending up at approximately 16 times its starting value! China has been recently growing at almost 10% per year, and indeed its per capita income has been doubling about every seven years, which is remarkable and literally world changing.

The rule of 70 shows us that small and consistent growth rates, if sustained for a decade or two, can greatly improve living standards. Over the long course of history, growth rates were essentially zero. But the past two centuries have seen small, consistent growth rates, and the standard of living for many has increased dramatically.

We can look at actual growth rates of various countries over a long period to see the impact on income levels. Table 24.7 presents growth rates of several countries over the 66 years from 1950 to 2016. Let's start with Haiti and Turkey. In 1950, both nations had about $2,500 in annual income per person. But Turkey grew at 3% a year, and Haiti actually experienced negative net growth over these 66 years. As a result, the average income in Turkey is now 10 times that of Haiti.

Further down Table 24.7, you see other nations that grew at rates faster even than Turkey. In 1950, Japan's per capita income was just a little higher than Turkey's, at $3,023. Yet 3.9% annual growth for 66 years led to income of $37,465 per person by 2016 in Japan. South Korea, with a staggering 5.3% growth over the entire period, moved from being among the world's very poorest economies to being among the richest.

TABLE 24.7

Economic Growth, 1950–2016

	Average annual growth rate		Real per capita GDP in 1950	Real per capita GDP in 2016
less than 1% growth	−0.5%	Haiti	2,485	1,728
	−0.3	Afghanistan	2,392	1,929
	−0.3	Liberia	1,005	829
	0.3	Burundi	536	665
about 1% growth	1.1	Honduras	2,381	4,796
	1.1	Kenya	1,496	3,169
	1.2	Argentina	8,759	18,875
about 2% growth	1.9	United States	15,241	53,015
	2.1	Hungary	6,034	23,279
	2.1	Mexico	4,179	16,133
	2.1	Sweden	11,385	44,659
greater than 2% growth	3.0	Turkey	2,583	17,906
	3.1	Spain	4,098	30,110
	3.1	India	824	6,125
	3.1	Israel	4,192	31,701
	3.9	Japan	3,023	37,465
	4.6	Botswana	779	15,198
	4.6	China	637	12,569
	5.3	South Korea	1,178	36,103

Sources: Maddison Project Database, version 2018; Jutta Bolt, Robert Inklaar, Herman de Jong, and Jan Luiten van Zanden, "Rebasing 'Maddison': New Income Comparisons and the Shape of Long-Run Economic Development," Maddison Project Working Paper No. 10, January 2018, https://www.rug.nl/ggdc/historicaldevelopment/maddison/research.

Note: Real GDP per capita figures are rounded to the nearest dollar, and population figures are rounded to the nearest 1,000.

Perhaps the biggest recent growth story is China's. Only 20 years ago, it was among the world's poorer nations. Over the past 20 years, China has grown at over 8% a year. Even if its astonishing growth slows considerably, China will still likely move into the group of the wealthiest nations in the coming decades.

Clearly, economic growth experiences have varied widely across time and place. But relatively small and consistent growth rates are sufficient to move a nation out of poverty over the period of a few generations. And this movement out of poverty really matters for the people who live in these nations.

ECONOMICS IN THE REAL WORLD

HOW DOES 2% GROWTH AFFECT AVERAGE PEOPLE?

We have seen that annual economic growth in the United States averaged about 2% per year over the past 50 years. What does this economic growth mean for a typical person's everyday life? Another way of thinking about this is to consider what life was like when your grandparents were young. To illustrate, we've assembled some basic data in Table 24.8 to give you an idea of how the average person's life in the United States in 1960 compares to life today.

Average real income in the United States is four times the level of 1960, but what about other factors that affect our everyday lives? For one thing, Americans today live about 13% longer (78.7 years versus 69.7 years). But we also have access to almost twice as many doctors, live in houses more than twice as big, enjoy more education, and own more and better cars and household appliances. On average, we work 6.4 fewer hours per week and hold jobs that are physically less taxing (fewer jobs in agriculture and manufacturing). In 1960, there were no cell phones, and roughly three out of four homes had a single telephone. Today, there are more telephones than there are people in the United States. In addition, many modern amenities were not available in 1960. Can you imagine life without a computer, the Internet, streaming music, microwave ovens, and central air conditioning? Take a look at Table 24.8 to see a striking contrast.

In what ways is life different now from when your grandparents were young?

This entire Shanghai skyline was built in the past 30 years, vividly illustrating the effects of rapid economic growth.

TABLE 24.8

The United States: 1960 versus 2018

General Characteristics	1960	2018
Life expectancy	69.7 years	78.7 years
Physicians per 10,000 people	14.8	26
Years of school completed	10.5 (median)	13 (average)
Portion of income spent on food	27%	11%
Average workweek	40.9 hours	34.5 hours
Workforce in agriculture or manufacturing	37%	16%
Home ownership	61.9%	64.3%
New Home		
Size	1,200 square feet	2,645 square feet
Bedrooms	2	4
Bathrooms	1	3
Central air conditioning?	no	yes
Best-Selling Car		
Model	Chevrolet Impala	Toyota Camry
Price (2018 dollars)	$22,637	$23,645
Miles per gallon	13–16	29–41
Horsepower	135	203
Air conditioning?	optional	standard
Automatic transmission?	optional	standard
Airbags?	no	standard
Power locks and windows?	no	standard
TV		
Size	23 inches	65 inches
Display	black & white	high-definition color
Price (2018 dollars)	$1,594	$699

Sources: U.S. Census Bureau, *Statistical Abstract of the United States*; U.S. Bureau of Labor Statistics.

PRACTICE WHAT YOU KNOW

Computing Economic Growth in Brazil

From 2000 until 2014, economic growth in Brazil averaged 2.3 percent. But in the five years that followed, 2015–2019, real per capita GDP fell by an average of 1.27% per year. The data below are for 2019.

Nominal GDP growth rate	GDP deflator growth rate	Population growth rate
−2.04%	4.15%	0.75%

QUESTION: What was the rate of economic growth for Brazil in 2019?

ANSWER: First, recall Equation 24.1:

$$\text{economic growth} \approx \%\Delta \text{ nominal GDP} - \%\Delta \text{ price level} - \%\Delta \text{ population}$$

Now, for Brazil, we have

$$\text{economic growth} \approx -2.04 - 4.15 - 0.75 = -6.94\%$$

QUESTION: If the price level (as measured by the GDP deflator) continues to grow at 4.15% per year, approximately how long will it take for prices to double?

ANSWER: We use the rule of 70:

$$70 \div 4.15 \approx 16.9 \text{ years}$$

CHALLENGE QUESTION: Suppose that Brazil's per capita real GDP was $10,000 in 2000, and from that year onward, the country sustains an economic growth rate of exactly 2% for 70 years. What will Brazil's per capita GDP be in 2070?

ANSWER: By the rule of 70, real per capita GDP will double every $70/x$ years. In this case, $x=2$, so doubling occurs every 35 years. Over the course of 70 years, real per capita GDP then doubles twice. So the original level of $10,000 turns into $40,000 per person after 70 years.

Source: World Bank, World Development Indicators.

How much does inflation affect Brazil's growth data?

DATA SNAPSHOT

Economic Growth, 1950–2016

Economic growth, measured as the growth rate of per capita real GDP, is the key determinant of living standards in nations across time. The map shows the average annual growth rates of nations across the globe from 1950 to 2016. On the right, we give a snapshot of the differences in living conditions between wealthy nations and poor nations.

LESS THAN 1% GROWTH

With 0% growth, nations are no better off than they were in 1950.

Haiti	-0.55
Liberia	-0.29
Zimbabwe	0.43
Nicaragua	0.46
Venezuelaa	0.71

1% – 1.6% GROWTH

With 1% growth, living standards nearly doubled over 58 years.

South Africa	1.07
Argentina	1.17
New Zealand	1.38
El Salvador	1.41
Nigeria	1.54

1.7% – 2.5% GROWTH

With 2% growth, living standards almost quadrupled over 58 years.

Morocco	1.86
United States	1.91
Canada	1.94
Mexico	2.07
Brazil	2.40

GREATER THAN 2.5% GROWTH

With 3% growth, some of the poorest nations are now among the richest.

Israel	3.11
Japan	3.89
Botswana	4.60
China	4.62
South Korea	5.32

Incomplete Data

All dollar figures are 2016 U.S. dollars.

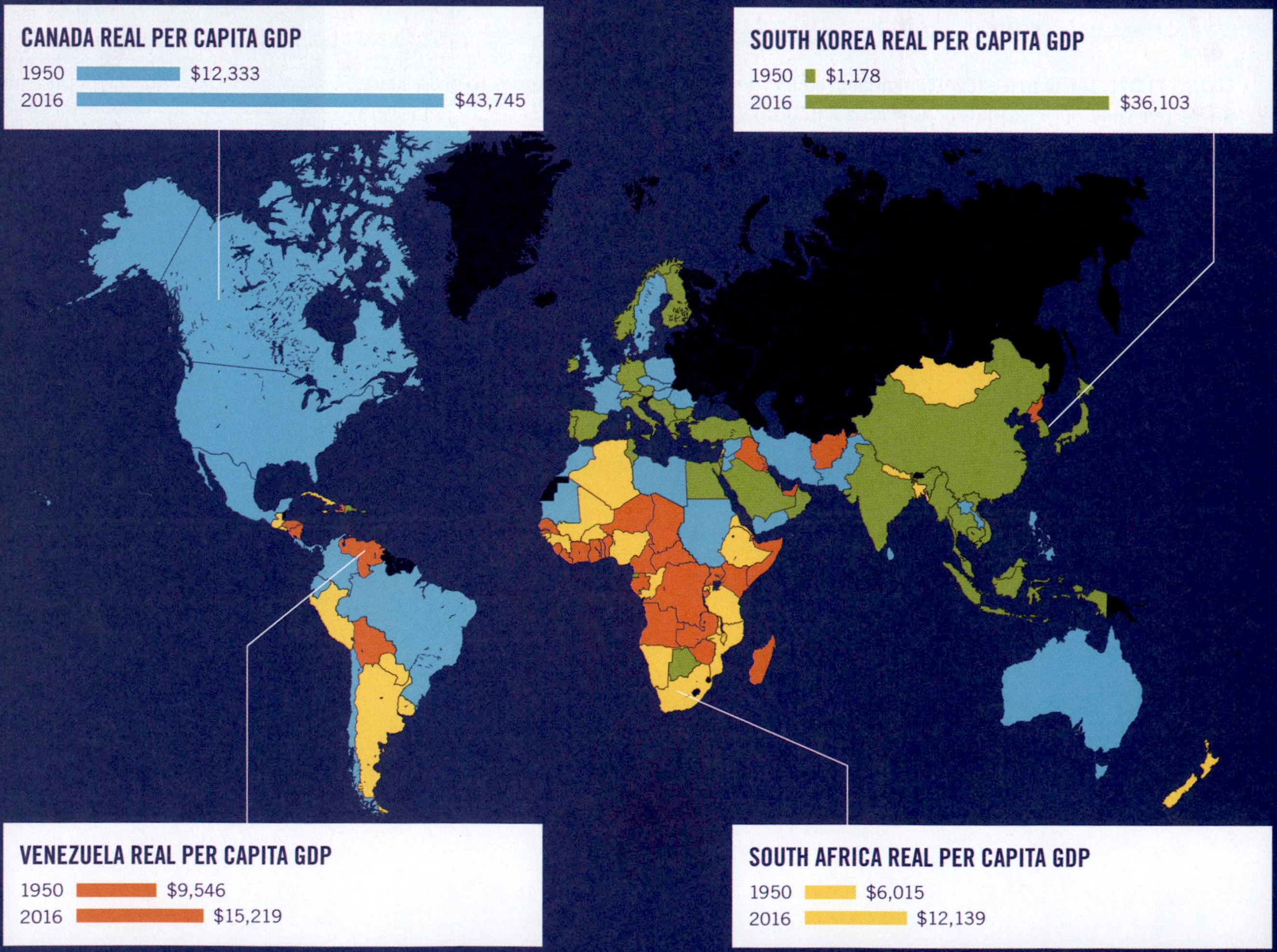

CANADA REAL PER CAPITA GDP
1950 $12,333
2016 $43,745
SOUTH KOREA REAL PER CAPITA GDP
1950 $1,178
2016 $36,103
VENEZUELA REAL PER CAPITA GDP
1950 $9,546
2016 $15,219
SOUTH AFRICA REAL PER CAPITA GDP
1950 $6,015
2016 $12,139

Human Welfare: Highest-Income versus Lowest-Income Nations

Poor nations include the 34 nations classified as "low income" by the World Bank. Rich nations include the 81 nations classified as "high income."

Poor Nation
Rich Nation

	Poor Nation	Rich Nation
GDP per Capita	$2,075	$47,305
Life Expectancy at Birth (Years)	63	80
Infant Mortality Rate (Per 1,000 Live Births)	49	5
Under-5 Mortality Rate (Per 1,000)	69	5
Physicians (Per 10,000 People)	3	30
Access to Electricity	39%	100%
Access to Improved Water Source	66%	100%
Access to Improved Sanitation	28%	99%
Female to Male Secondary Enrollment (Ratio)	0.83	0.99
Mobile Cell Phone Subscriptions (Per 100 People)	62	125
Literacy Rate, Adult Males	67%	99%
Literacy Rate, Adult Females	52%	99%

REVIEW QUESTIONS

- On average, how much longer do people live in rich versus poor nations?
- If a growth rate of 1.1% persists in South Africa, how long will it take for income to double? Hint: use the Rule of 70.

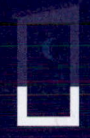

· ECONOMICS *in the* MEDIA ·

"The Magic Washing Machine"

Hans Rosling, a Swedish professor of international health and the cofounder of the Gapminder Foundation, was particularly good at data visualization, especially as applied to development economics. The web site Gapminder.org shows the uniquely stimulating graphics he helped pioneer.

Rosling was also a gifted public speaker and delivered many TED Talks. One of his best was on how washing machines revolutionize the lives of people around the world. In the video, Rosling recalls the day his mother got her first washing machine, which his parents had saved for years to buy. The grandmother was especially excited to see the new machine. She had spent many years heating water with firewood and then handwashing the laundry for their large family. It was a big day as the Roslings gathered around the new machine to "watch electricity do that work."

Hans Rosling showed how the washing machine revolutionized life for women around the globe.

As Hans Rosling notes, only a fraction of families in the world can afford washing machines. Well over half the world's population (and in most cultures, this job is almost exclusively done by women) must regularly wash clothes by hand. This time-intensive chore often requires a trip to a lake or river. It can consume most of a day, and it must be repeated over and over again.

But the washing machine is "magic," because it frees people to use their time in other activities. Rosling's mother told him, "Now Hans, we have loaded the laundry. The machine will make the work. And now we can go to the library. Because this is the magic: you load the laundry and what do you get out of the machine? You get books out of the machines, children's books." He added, "And mother got time to read for me. She loved this." There is so much economics in these simple statements. The mother's time was a very scarce resource. And time spent washing clothes had high opportunity costs: it kept her from reading with her son. But the new technology, the washing machine, allowed Hans's mother to both do laundry and read with her children.

Rosling concludes with this flurry of gratitude: "And what we said, my mother and me, 'Thank you industrialization. Thank you steel mill. Thank you power station. And thank you chemical processing industry that gave us time to read books!'" We can all hope for economic growth to spread around the world, so that more people can experience the magic of washing machines.

How Do Resources and Technology Contribute to Economic Growth?

At this point, you may wonder what can be done to provide the best opportunity for economic growth. We see economic growth in many, though certainly not all, nations. But even in those that have grown in the past, future growth is not assured. We now turn to major sources of economic growth.

Economists continue to debate the relative importance of the factors leading to economic growth. However, there is a general consensus on the significance of three factors for economic growth: *resources*, *technology*, and *institutions*. In this section, we examine the first two; later in the chapter, we look at institutions.

Resources

All else equal, the higher the quantity and quality of resources available, the more output a nation can produce. **Resources**, also known as **factors of production**, are the inputs used to produce goods and services. The discovery or cultivation of new resources is a source of economic growth. Economists divide resources into three major categories: natural resources, physical capital, and human capital.

Resources, also known as **factors of production**, are the inputs used to produce goods and services.

NATURAL RESOURCES Natural resources include physical land and the inputs occurring naturally in or on the land. Coal, iron ore, diamonds, and lumber are examples of natural resources. Less obvious examples are mountains, beaches, temperate weather patterns, and scenic views—resources that residents enjoy consuming and that sometimes lead to tourism as a major industry.

Natural resources are an important source of economic wealth for nations. For example, the United States has fertile farmland, forests, coal, iron ore, and oil; the United States supplied more than 12% of the world's oil in 2014.

Geography, or the physical location of a nation, is also a natural resource that can contribute to economic growth. Geographical location facilitates trade and affects other important variables, such as weather and disease control. The world map in Figure 24.3 shows global GDP per square kilometer. As you can see, locations on coasts or along rivers have developed more rapidly than areas inland. These coastal or waterway-based locations were more naturally suited to trade in the days before railroads, trucks, and airplanes.

Natural resources clearly help to increase economic development, but they are not enough to make a nation wealthy. Many poor nations are rich in natural resources. For example, Liberia has mahogany forests, iron ore deposits, rubber tree forests, diamonds, and a beautiful coastline along the Atlantic Ocean. Yet despite all these, Liberia is poor. In contrast, think about Hong Kong, which is now part of China. Hong Kong is very small and densely populated with few natural resources. Yet the citizens of Hong Kong are among the wealthiest in the world.

Diamonds may be a girl's best friend, but are they essential for economic growth?

PHYSICAL CAPITAL The second category of resources is physical capital, or just capital. Recall that capital comprises the tools and equipment used in the production of goods and services. Examples of capital are factories, tractors,

FIGURE 24.3

Global GDP Density

The world's wealthiest areas (shown in darker colors on this map) are often those located near natural shipping lanes along coasts and rivers, where trade naturally flowed. This pattern is evidence that geography matters in economic development.

Source: John Luke Gallup, Jeffrey D. Sachs, and Andrew D. Mellinger, "Geography and Economic Development," Working Paper No. 1, Center for International Development at Harvard University, March 1999.

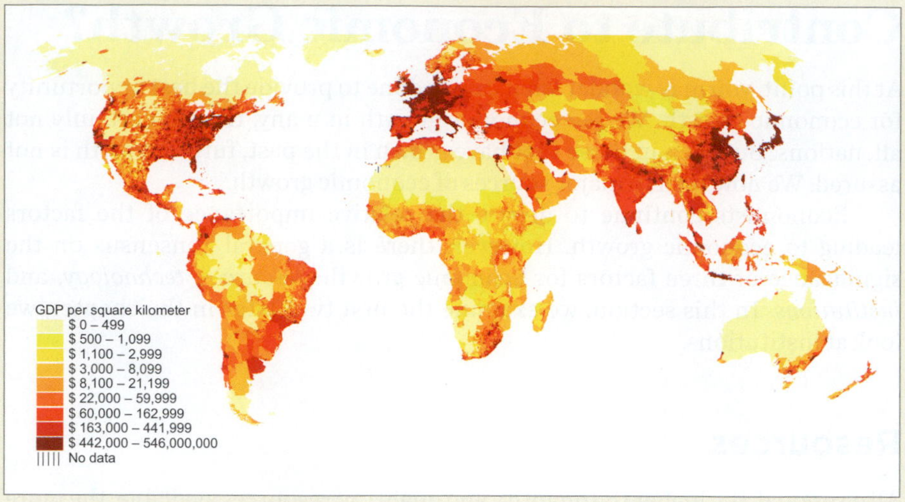

roads and bridges, computers, and shovels. The purpose of capital is to aid in the production of future output.

Consider the shipping container, a basic tool that has aided the movement of goods around the globe. A shipping container is a standard-size (20- or 40-foot-long) box used to move goods worldwide. In 1954, a typical cargo ship traveling from New York to Germany might have carried as many as 194,582 individual items. The transportation involved bags, barrels, cartons, and many other different means of packaging and storing goods. Loading and unloading the ship required armies of men working long hours for days on end. Not surprisingly, shipping goods from one country to another was expensive.

The standardized shipping container was first used in 1956. Suddenly, it was possible to move cargo around the globe without repacking every time the mode of transportation changed. Once a cargo ship enters the port, cranes lift the containers 200 feet in the air and unload about 40 large boxes each hour. Dozens of ships are unloaded at a time, and computers run most of the operation. A container full of iPads can be loaded onto the back of a truck in Shenzhen, China, transported to port, and loaded onto a ship that carries 3,000 containers. The ship can bring the iPads to the United States, where the containers are loaded onto a train and, later, a truck. This movement happens without anyone touching the contents. Clearly, the shipping container is a tool that has revolutionized world trade and improved lives.

This cargo ship, bearing hundreds of individual shipping containers, is arriving at the Port of Oakland, California, with goods from Asia.

As the quantity of physical capital per worker rises, so does output per worker: workers are more productive with more and better tools. Look around the world: the productive nations have impressive roads, bridges, buildings, and factories. In poor nations, paved roads are nonexistent or in disrepair, vehicles are of lower quality, and computers are a luxury. Even public electricity and sewage treatment facilities are rare in parts of many developing nations.

Because of the obvious correlation between tools and wealth, many of the early contributions to growth theory focused on the role of physical capital. As a result, much international aid was used to build roads and factories, in the hope that prosperity would follow automatically. But today, most economists understand that capital alone is not sufficient to produce economic growth. Factories, dams, and other large capital projects bring wealth only when they mesh well with the rest of the economy. A steel factory is of little use in a region better suited for growing corn. Without a good rail network or proper roads, a steel factory cannot get the tools it needs and cannot easily sell its products. Dams fall into disrepair within a few years if they are not maintained. Water pipes are a wonderful modern invention, but if they are not kept in good shape, human waste from toilets contaminates the water supply. The point is that simply building new capital in a nation does not ensure future sustained economic growth.

Education enhances human capital, but is it the key ingredient to economic growth?

HUMAN CAPITAL The output of a nation also depends on its workers. **Human capital** is the resource represented by the quantity, knowledge, and skills of the workers in an economy. It is possible to expand human capital by either increasing the number of workers available, educating the existing labor force, or both.

Human capital
is the resource represented by the quantity, knowledge, and skills of the workers in an economy.

We often think in terms of the sheer quantity of workers: all else being equal, a nation with more workers produces more output. But more output does not necessarily mean more economic growth. In fact, economic growth requires more output *per capita*. Adding more workers to an economy may increase total GDP without increasing per capita GDP. However, if more workers from a given population enter the labor force, GDP per capita can increase. For example, as we discussed in Chapter 20, women have entered the U.S. labor force in record numbers over the past 50 years as they have moved from homemaking services not counted in official GDP statistics to the official labor force. As more women join the official labor force, their formally measured output increases both GDP and per capita GDP.

There is another important dimension of human capital: the knowledge and skills of the workers themselves. In this context, it is possible to increase human capital through education and training. Training includes everything from basic literacy to college education and from software competencies to specific job training.

Not many people would doubt that a more educated labor force is more productive. And certainly, to boost per capita output, educating the labor force is more helpful than merely increasing the quantity of workers. But education alone is not enough to ensure economic progress. For many years, for example, India struggled with economic growth, even while its population was significantly more literate than those of other developing nations.

Technology

We know that the world would be much poorer without computers, automobiles, electric light bulbs, and other goods that have resulted from productive ideas. **Technology** is the knowledge available for use in production. Though

Technology
is the knowledge available for use in production.

A **technological advancement** introduces new techniques or methods so that firms can produce more valuable outputs per unit of input.

technology is often embodied in machines and productive techniques, it is really just knowledge. New technology enables us to produce more while using fewer of our limited resources. A **technological advancement** introduces new techniques or methods so that firms can produce more valuable outputs per unit of input. We can either produce more with the same resources or use fewer resources to produce the same quantity.

For example, the assembly line was an important idea. Henry Ford adopted and improved the assembly-line method in 1913 at the Ford Motor Company. In this new approach to the factory, workers focused on well-defined jobs such as screwing on individual parts. A conveyor belt moved the parts around the factory to workers' stations. The workers themselves, by staying put rather than moving around the production floor, experienced a lower rate of accidents and other mishaps.

Agriculture is a sector where technological advances are easy to spot. For example, we know that land resources are necessary to produce corn. But technological advances mean that over time it has become possible to grow and harvest more corn per acre of land. In fact, in the United States, the corn yield per acre is now six times what it was in 1930. In 1930, we produced about 25 bushels of corn per acre, but now the yield is consistently over 150 bushels per acre. Higher yields are a result of technology that has produced hybrid seeds, herbicides, fertilizers, and irrigation techniques.

Figure 24.4 presents another example. There are now significantly fewer milk cows in the United States than at any time since 1920. But total milk output

PRACTICE WHAT YOU KNOW

Resources: Growth Policy

The Akosombo Dam in Ghana was built with international aid funds.

Many policies have been advocated to help nations escape poverty, and the policies often focus on the importance of resources.

QUESTION: For each policy listed below, which resource is the primary focus: natural resources, physical capital, or human resources?

a. international loans for infrastructure like roads, bridges, and dams

b. mandated primary education

c. restrictions on the development of forested land

d. population controls

e. international aid for construction of a shoe factory

ANSWERS:

a. Infrastructure is physical capital.

b. Education involves human capital.

c. These restrictions focus on maintaining a certain level of natural resources.

d. Population controls often result from a shortsighted focus on physical capital per capita. The fewer people a nation has, the more tools there are per person.

e. The focus here is physical capital.

FIGURE 24.4

Fewer Cows but More Milk

U.S. dairy cow populations continue to decline, but the average cow now produces five times more milk than in 1924. This means that even with fewer cows, farmers produce 2.3 times more milk than they did in 1924.

Source: USDA.

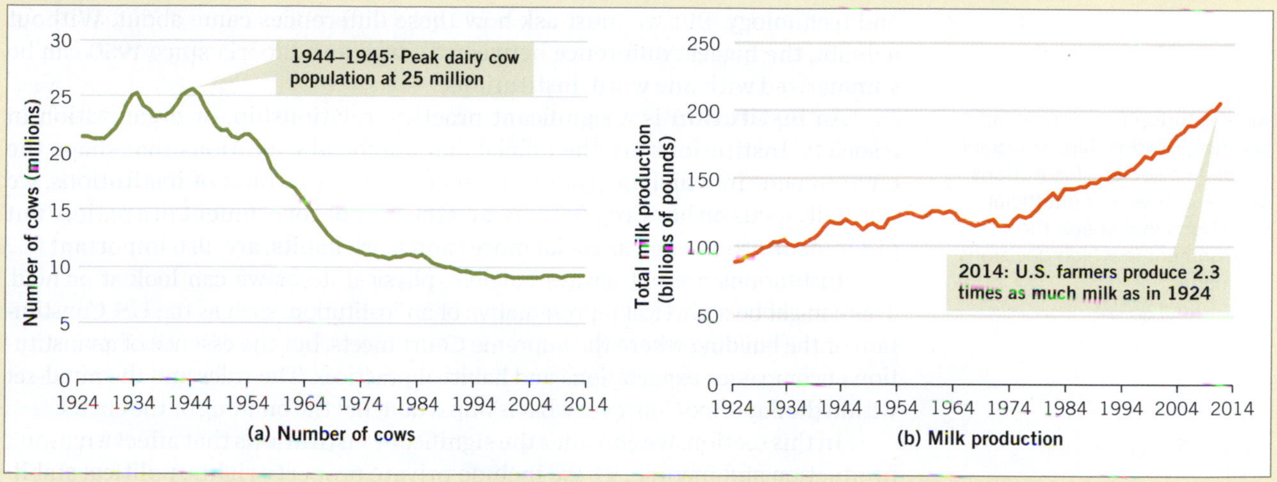

is at historic highs because dairy farmers can now get about five times as much milk out of each cow. While strategic breeding has played a large role in this increase, even simple technology has factored in this change. For example, farmers now line the cows' stalls with 6 to 8 inches of sand. The sand is comfortable to lie on, it offers uniform support, and it stays cooler in the summer. In the end, the cows produce more milk. This is one simple example of how new ideas or technological advancements enable us to produce more while using fewer resources.

Like capital, technology produces value only when it is combined with other inputs. Simply carrying plans for a shoe factory to Haiti would not generate much economic value. The mere knowledge of how to produce shoes, while important, is only one piece of the growth puzzle. An economy must have the physical capital to produce shoes, must have the human capital to staff the factory and assembly line, and must create favorable conditions and incentives for potential investors. Economic growth occurs when all these conditions come together. That is one reason why it is incorrect to identify technological innovations as the sole cause of differences in wealth across nations.

Moreover, technological innovations do not occur randomly across the globe. Some places produce large clusters of such innovations. Consider that information technology largely comes from MIT and Silicon Valley, movie and television ideas generally come from Hollywood, and new fashion designs regularly come from Paris, Milan, Tokyo, and New York. Technological innovations tend to breed more innovations. This conclusion leads us to reword an earlier question: Why do some regions innovate (and grow) more than others? A large part of the answer lies in our next topic, institutions.

What Institutions Foster Economic Growth?

In 1950, residents in the African nation of Liberia were wealthier than those on the Southeast Asian island of Taiwan. Today, however, per capita GDP in Taiwan is more than 20 times that of Liberia. Yes, much of this wealth gap stems from obvious current differences in physical capital, human capital, and technology. But we must ask how these differences came about. Without a doubt, the biggest difference between Taiwan and Liberia since 1950 can be summarized with one word: institutions.

An **institution** is a significant practice, relationship, or organization in a society. Institutions are the official and unofficial conditions that shape the environment in which decisions are made.

An **institution** is a significant practice, relationship, or organization in a society. Institutions are the official and unofficial conditions that shape the environment in which decisions are made. When we think of institutions, we normally focus on laws, regulations, and the type of government in a nation. But other institutions, such as social mores and work habits, are also important.

Institutions are not always tangible, physical items we can look at or hold. There might be a physical representative of an institution, such as the U.S. Constitution or the building where the Supreme Court meets, but the essence of an institution encompasses expectations and habitual practices. The rules and the mind-set within the Supreme Court are what is important, not the building or the chairs.

In this section, we consider the significant institutions that affect a nation's production and income. These include private property rights, political stability and the rule of law, competitive and open markets, efficient taxes, and stable money and prices. Many of these are examined in detail elsewhere in this book, so we cover them only briefly here.

Private Property Rights

Private property rights are the rights of individuals to own property, to use it in production, and to own the resulting output.

The single greatest incentive for voluntary production is ownership of what you produce. The existence of **private property rights** means individuals can own property—including houses, land, and other resources—and when they use their property in production, they own the resulting output.

Think about the differences in private property rights between Liberia and Taiwan. In Liberia, the system of ownership titles is not dependable. As a result, Liberians who wish to purchase land often must buy the land multiple times from different "owners," because there is no dependable record of true ownership. Taiwan, in contrast, has a well-defined system of law and property rights protection. Without such a system, people have very little incentive to improve the value of their assets.

In the past two decades, the government of China has relaxed its laws against private property ownership, a move that has spurred unprecedented growth. These market reforms began with a risky experiment in the rural community of Xiaogang. In 1978, the heads of 21 families in Xiaogang signed an agreement that became the genesis of private property rights in China. This remarkable document read:

> December 1978, Mr. Yan's Home. We divide the field (land) to every household. Every leader of the household should sign and stamp. If we are able to produce, every household should promise to finish any amount they are required to turn in to the government, no longer asking the government

for food or money. If this fails, even if we go to jail or have our heads shaved, we will not regret. Everyone else (the common people who are not officers and signees of this agreement) also promise to raise our children until they are eighteen years old. First signer: Hong Chang Yan.*

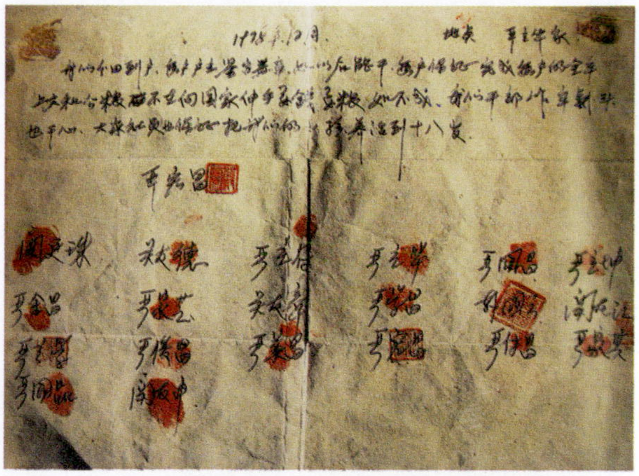

This little Chinese agreement between 21 poor rural families helped to bring private property rights to modern China.

The agreement stipulated each family would continue to produce the government quota for their agricultural output. But they would begin keeping anything they produced above this quota. They also agreed to stop taking food or money from the government. This agreement was dangerous in 1978—so dangerous, they stipulated they would raise one another's children if any of the signees were put in jail.

The Xiaogang agreement led to an agricultural boom that other communities copied. Seeing the success of this property rights experiment, Deng Xiaoping and other Chinese leaders subsequently instituted market reforms in agriculture in the 1980s and then in manufacturing in the 1990s. China's economy is growing rapidly today not because the Chinese found new resources or updated their technology. The Chinese are wealthier because they now recognize private property rights in many different industries.

Political Stability and the Rule of Law

Incentives

To understand the importance of political stability and the rule of law, consider again Liberia and Taiwan. Before 2006, Liberia endured 35 years of political unrest. Government officials assumed office through the use of violence, and national leaders consistently used their power to eradicate their opponents. In contrast, Taiwan's political climate has been relatively stable since 1949. If you were an entrepreneur deciding where to build a factory, would you want to invest millions of dollars in a country with constant violent unrest, or would you choose a peaceful country instead? Which nation would you predict is more likely to see new factories and technological innovation?

Political instability is a disincentive for investment. After all, investment makes sense only if there is a fairly certain payoff at the end. In an environment of political instability, there is no incentive to invest in either human or physical capital because there is no predictable future payoff.

Consistent and trustworthy enforcement of a nation's laws is crucial for economic growth. Corruption is one of the most common and dangerous impediments to economic growth. When government officials steal, elicit bribes, or hand out favors to friends, incentives for private investment are reduced. If individuals from all walks of life cannot count on a fair system and the opportunity to earn returns in their investments in human or physical capital, investment declines. And this decline reduces future growth.

Bullet casings litter the street in Monrovia, Liberia, in 2003.

The World Justice Project has collected data on the rule of law across the world. Figure 24.5 shows the nations broken down into four groups, based on income, with an average rule-of-law index for each. It is no surprise that nations scoring in the top group on this index are also the nations with the highest levels of per capita GDP. The most corrupt nations are also those with the lowest levels of income.

*Literal translation by Chuhan Wang.

FIGURE 24.5

The Rule of Law and Per Capita Income

Consistent and fair enforcement of a nation's laws pays off with economic growth, and data from the World Justice Project back this up. High-income nations are also nations that adhere most closely to the rule of law, and nations where the law is routinely ignored (where corruption is more rampant) also have lower incomes.

Source: World Justice Project, "Annual Report 2011." GDP figures are adjusted using PPP (constant 2005 international $), 2005–2009.

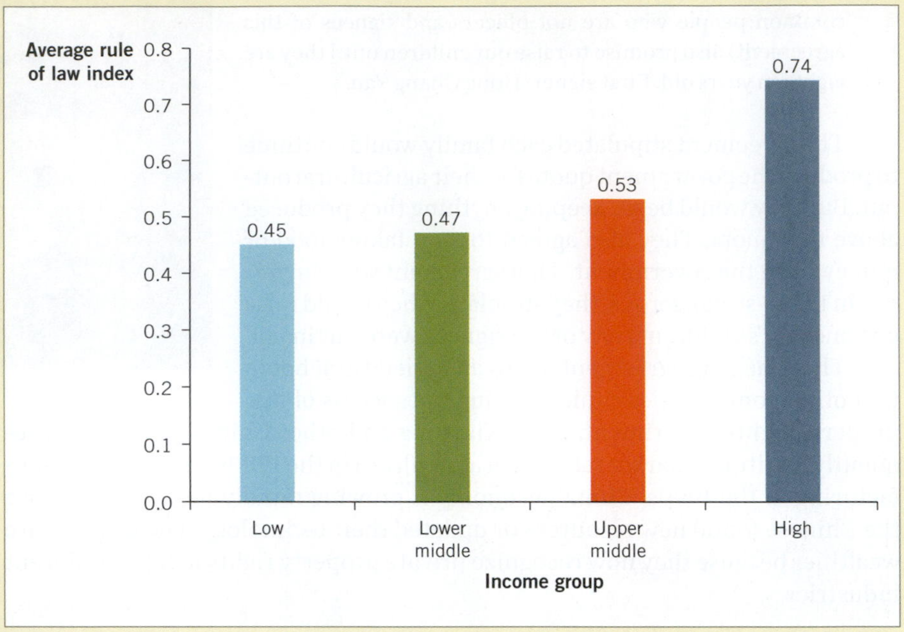

ECONOMICS IN THE REAL WORLD

WHAT CAN PARKING VIOLATIONS TEACH US ABOUT INTERNATIONAL INSTITUTIONS?

Would you get more parking tickets if you weren't compelled to pay for them?

Until 2002, diplomatic immunity protected United Nations diplomats in New York City from fines or arrest stemming from parking violations. This immunity gave economists Raymond Fisman and Edward Miguel the idea for a unique natural experiment: they studied how officials responded to the lack of legal consequences for violating the law. Parking violations under these conditions are an example of corruption because they represent the abuse of power for private gain. Therefore, by comparing the level of parking violations of diplomats from different societies, the economists created a way to compare corruption norms among different cultures.

Fisman and Miguel compared unpaid parking violations with existing survey-based indices on levels of corruption across nations. They found that diplomats from high-corruption nations accumulated significantly more unpaid parking violations than those from low-corruption nations. Among the worst offenders were diplomats from Kuwait, Egypt, Chad, Sudan, and Bulgaria. Among those with zero unpaid parking violations were diplomats from Australia, Canada, Denmark, Japan, and Norway.

This finding suggests that cultural or social norms related to corruption are quite persistent: even when stationed thousands of miles away, diplomats behave as if they are at home. Norms related to corruption are apparently deeply ingrained.

In 2002, enforcement authorities acquired the right to confiscate the diplomatic license plates of violators. And guess what? Unpaid violations dropped by almost 98%. This outcome illustrates the power of incentives in influencing human behavior.

Competitive and Open Markets

In this section, we take a quick look at three institutions essential for economic growth: competitive markets, international trade, and the flow of funds across borders. These market characteristics are covered in detail elsewhere in this book.

COMPETITIVE MARKETS In Chapter 3, we explored how competitive markets ensure consumers can buy goods at the lowest possible prices. When markets aren't competitive, people who want to participate face barriers to entry, which inhibit competition and innovation. Yet many nations monopolize key industries by preventing competition or by establishing government ownership of industries. These policies limit macroeconomic growth.

INTERNATIONAL TRADE Recall from Chapter 2 that trade creates value. In some cases, trade enables nations to consume goods and services they would not produce on their own. Specialization and trade make all nations better off because each can produce goods for which it enjoys a comparative advantage. Output increases when nations (1) produce the goods and services for which they have the lowest opportunity cost and (2) trade for the other goods and services they wish to consume.

Trade creates value

International trade barriers reduce the benefits available from specialization and trade. Chapter 32 is devoted to the study of international trade.

FLOW OF FUNDS ACROSS BORDERS In Chapter 22, we talked about the importance of savings for economic growth. For example, the inflow of foreign savings has helped to keep interest rates low in the United States even as domestic savings rates have fallen. If firms and individuals are to invest in physical or human capital, someone has to save. Opportunities for investment expand if there is access to savings from around the globe. That is, if foreigners can funnel their savings into your nation's economy, your nation's firms can use these funds to expand. However, many developing nations have restrictions on foreign ownership of land and physical capital within their borders. Restrictions on the flow of capital across borders handcuff domestic firms, which are then forced to seek funds solely from domestic savers.

Efficient Taxes

On the one hand, taxes must be high enough to support effective government. Political stability, the rule of law, and the protection of private property rights all require strong and consistent government. And taxes provide the revenue to pay for government services. On the other hand, if we tax activities fundamental to economic growth, there will be fewer of these activities. In market economies, output and income are strictly intertwined. If we tax income, we are taxing output, and that is GDP. So although taxes are necessary, they can also reduce incentives for production.

Incentives

Before the federal government instituted an income tax, government services were largely funded by taxes on imports. But international trade is also an essential institution for economic growth. So taxes on imports also impede growth.

Efficient taxes are taxes sufficient to fund the activities of government while impeding production and consumption decisions as little as possible. It is not easy to determine the efficient level of taxes or even to determine what activities should be taxed. We will discuss this issue further in Chapter 29, when we discuss fiscal policy.

Stable Money and Prices

High and variable inflation is a sure way to reduce incentives for investment and production. In Chapter 22, we saw that inflation increases uncertainty about future price levels. When people are unsure about future price levels, they are

ECONOMICS *in the* MEDIA

The Economics of *Black Panther*

For most of human history, possessing natural resources was thought to be the best way for a country to expand production. Wars were fought over ownership of land, waterways, and mineral deposits. However, merely acquiring those resources doesn't guarantee economic vitality. Other prerequisites for economic growth include technology and institutions like a stable government.

All of these things serendipitously come together for the country of Wakanda, whose origins are told in the opening minutes of the Marvel movie *Black Panther*. After the first Black Panther united warring tribes under his leadership, the people of Wakanda turned to developing their nation through technological advancements made possible by the mysterious properties of vibranium, a metal of meteoric origin found only in Wakanda. The country grew to be prosperous and technologically far more advanced than the nations around it. While those other countries suffered the evils of slavery and war, Wakanda enjoyed a benefit common to countries that grow: it remained at peace.

In one respect, though, Wakanda's story goes against the conventional wisdom of economic theory. In order to evade the sinister attentions of vibranium-seeking outsiders, Wakanda not only avoided trade with other nations but developed cloaking technology to keep the country's very existence concealed from the rest of the world. For real countries, at least, most economists advocate free trade with other nations as a way to stimulate economic growth, but when the nations who would be your trading partners are constantly at war, perhaps it pays to fly below the radar.

Wakanda's path to remarkable success was unconventional.

ECONOMICS *for* LIFE

Learning More and Helping Alleviate Global Poverty

- The best way to learn about global poverty is to travel to low-income nations.
- There are several books you can read to learn more about the economics of global poverty.

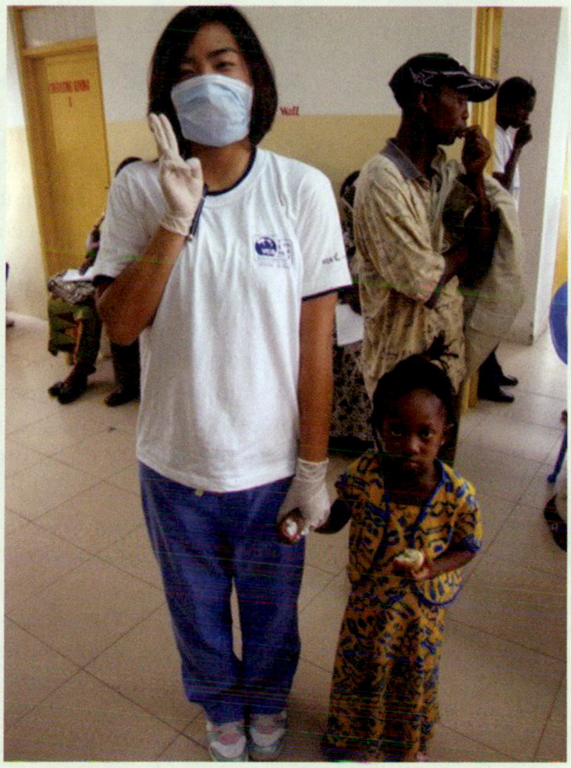

A University of Virginia student helps with eye surgeries in Tema, Ghana.

The information presented in this chapter reveals a picture of significant and persistent poverty across much of the globe. It is possible that this discussion and your classroom lectures have inspired you to learn more about global poverty or even to try to help those who are less fortunate around the globe. Toward those ends, we can give a little advice.

The surest way to learn about world economic reality is to travel to a developing nation. We suggest taking an alternative spring break or even studying abroad for an entire semester in a developing nation. These are costly ventures, but they will almost certainly change your perspective on life. If you get the chance to travel, be sure to speak directly to people on the streets and ask them to share their personal stories with you. Talk to small business owners, parents, and children. If possible, try to speak to people who have nothing to gain by sharing their story.

You may wish to give financially to help the less fortunate around the globe. There are many international aid charities, but unfortunately, not all are truly helpful or even completely honest. We recommend visiting the website for Givewell (www.givewell.org), which researches charitable organizations from around the world and recommends a few that have proved to be honest and effective.

If you want to study more about growth economics, you should start with two books. The first book is by economist William Easterly, titled *The Elusive Quest for Growth: Economists' Adventures and Misadventures in the Tropics*. In this book, Easterly weaves personal narrative and economic theory together in a unique way to help you understand how economic theories regarding growth have evolved through the years. He both explains past failures and argues compellingly for future policy proposals. The second book, by economists Daron Acemoglu and James Robinson, is called *Why Nations Fail: The Origins of Power, Prosperity, and Poverty*. This book presents the very best arguments for institutions as the primary source of economic growth. Even though this book is written by leading macroeconomists, it is enjoyable reading for mass audiences.

The 2019 Nobel Prize-winning economists Abhijit Banjeree, Esther Duflo, and Michael Kremer transformed the field with their work using randomized controlled trials.

more reluctant to sign contracts that deliver dollar payoffs in the future. Thus, unpredictable inflation diminishes future growth possibilities. In the United States, the Federal Reserve (the Fed) is charged with administering monetary policy. The Fed is designed to reduce incentives for politically motivated monetary policy, which typically leads to highly variable inflation rates. We cover the Fed in greater detail in Chapter 30.

How Are Some Economists Testing New Ideas?

Measuring short-term impacts of growth is a challenge in economics. The 2019 Nobel Prize in Economics went to the development economists Abhijit Banerjee, Esther Duflo, and Michael Kremer for major contributions in this area. Duflo is the second female winner in economics and the youngest winner ever. The Nobel was given for pioneering fieldwork using randomized controlled trials (RCTs) in developing nations. An RCT randomly groups people to compare and test how policies and incentives affect economic growth.

For example, intestinal hookworms are common in developing countries and often keep students out of school. Using an RCT, Kremer found that deworming programs had a much larger effect than anticipated. Kremer introduced deworming drugs into random school districts and saw improved health and less absenteeism. This included "spillover effects" to nearby communities, where deworming some individuals reduced the chance that others would become infected. The programs have since been expanded.

Using RCTs in India, Banerjee and Duflo found that plans involving "microcredit"—short-term business loans as small as $20, given for no collateral—were not as helpful in reducing poverty as some had thought (though particularly enthusiastic entrepreneurs showed positive results). Duflo and Kremer also studied incentives given to farmers in developing countries to encourage investment in fertilizer for larger crop yields. They found it was most effective to offer discounts to purchase fertilizer at harvest time for future use.

This trio changed the practice of development economics. Economists now fan out around the globe testing new ideas in RCTs.

Conclusion

In this chapter we considered the three sources of economic growth: resources, technology, and institutions. But we also cautioned against an overemphasis on resources and pointed to the necessity of growth-fostering institutions.

In the next chapter, we cover the theory that supports this modern economic analysis.✷

ANSWERING *the* BIG QUESTIONS

Why does economic growth matter?

- Economic growth affects human welfare in meaningful ways.
- Historical data show that sustained economic growth is a relatively modern phenomenon.
- Relatively small but consistent growth rates are an effective path out of poverty.

How do resources and technology contribute to economic growth?

- Natural resources, physical capital, and human capital all contribute to economic growth.
- Technological advancement, which leads to the production of more output per unit of input, also sustains economic growth.

What institutions foster economic growth?

- Private property rights secure ownership of what an individual produces, creating incentives for increased output.
- Political stability and the rule of law allow people to make production decisions without concern for corrupt government.
- Competitive and open markets allow everyone to benefit from global productivity.
- Efficient taxes are high enough to support effective government, but low enough to provide positive incentives for production.
- Stable money and prices allow people to make long-term production decisions with minimal risk.

How are some economists testing new ideas?

- Fieldwork using randomized controlled trials (RCTs) is changing development economics.
- An RCT randomly groups people to compare and test policies and incentives.

CHAPTER PROBLEMS

Concepts You Should Know

economic growth (p. 767)
factors of production (p. 783)
human capital (p. 785)
institution (p. 788)
private property rights (p. 788)
resources (p. 783)
rule of 70 (p. 775)
technological advancement (p. 786)
technology (p. 785)

Questions for Review

1. What are the three factors influencing economic growth?
2. What is human capital, and how is it different from the quantity of workers available for work? Name three ways to increase a nation's human capital. Is an increase in the size of the labor force also an increase in human capital? Explain your answer.
3. How is economic growth measured?
4. Describe the pattern of world economic growth over the past 2,000 years. Approximately when did economic growth really take off?
5. List five human welfare conditions positively affected by economic growth.
6. Many historical accounts credit the economic success of the United States to its abundance of natural resources.
   a. What is missing from this argument?
   b. Name five poor nations with significant natural resources.
7. The flow of funds across borders is a source of growth for economies. Use what you learned about loanable funds in Chapter 22 to describe how foreign funds might expand output in a nation.
8. In 2011, when the U.S. unemployment rate was over 9%, President Barack Obama said, "There are some structural issues with our economy where a lot of businesses have learned to become much more efficient with a lot fewer workers. You see it when you go to a bank and you use an ATM, you don't go to a bank teller, or you go to the airport and you're using a kiosk instead of checking in at the gate." Discuss the president's quote in terms of both short-run unemployment and long-run growth.
9. The difference between 1% growth and 2% growth seems insignificant. Explain why it really matters.
10. What do economists mean by the term "institutions"? Name five different laws that are institutions affecting production incentives. Name three social practices that affect production in a society.

Study Problems *(✷ solved at the end of the section)*

✷ 1. Real per capita GDP in China in 1959 was about $350, but it doubled to about $700 by 1978, when Deng Xiaoping started market reforms.
   a. What was the average annual economic growth rate in China over the 20 years from 1959 to 1978?
   b. Chinese real per capita GDP doubled again in only seven years, reaching $1,400 by 1986. What was the average annual economic growth rate between 1979 and 1986?

✷ 2. The table below presents long-run macroeconomic data for two hypothetical nations, A and B:

	A	B
Nominal GDP growth	12%	5%
Inflation	10	2
Nominal interest	4	4
Unemployment rate	12	5
Population growth	1.5	1

Assume both nations start with real GDP of $1,000 per citizen. Fill in the blanks in the following table, assuming the data on the previous page apply for every year considered.

	A	B
Economic growth rate	______	______
Years required for real per capita GDP to double	______	______
Real per capita GDP 140 years later	______	______

3. Let's revisit the data from Table 24.3, showing the following world economic growth rates for specific historical eras:

Years	Growth rate
AD 1–1800	0.02%
1800–1900	0.64
1900–1950	1.04
1950–2000	2.12

Approximately how many years will it take for average real per capita GDP to double at each of those growth rates?

4. Use the data in the table below to compute economic growth rates for the United States for 2008, 2009, and 2010. Note that all data are from the end of the year specified.

Date	Nominal GDP (billions of current $)	GDP deflator	Population growth rate
2007	$14,061.8	106.30	1.01%
2008	14,369.1	108.62	0.93
2009	14,119.0	109.61	0.87
2010	14,660.4	110.66	0.90

5. The rule of 70 applies in any growth rate application. Let's say you have $1,000 in savings and you have three alternatives:

- a savings account earning 1% interest per year
- a U.S. Treasury bond earning 3% interest per year
- a stock market mutual fund earning 8% interest per year

Approximately how long would it take to double your savings in each of the three accounts?

6. Assume you plan to retire in 40 years and are evaluating the three different accounts listed in question 5. How much would your $1,000 be worth in 40 years under each of the three alternatives?

* **7.** Economic growth is a very particular concept in economics. The term "economic growth" is not always used correctly in media reports.

a. Define economic growth.

b. Consider the following economy:

Year	Nominal GDP (trillions of dollars)	Price level
2014	$18	240
2015	20	250

Is it possible to calculate the economic growth rate in 2015 given the information above? If so, calculate the economic growth rate. If not, what other information would you need to calculate the economic growth rate?

8. The data below are for the United States in 2009 and 2010.

	Nominal GDP growth rate	GDP deflator growth rate	Money supply growth rate	Nominal interest rate	Real interest rate	Population growth rate	Unemployment rate
2009	−2.0%	0.8%	2.2%	3.0%	2.2%	0.7%	9.5%
2010	3.8	1.2	4.5	2.5	1.3	0.6	9.9

a. Use the approximation formula discussed in the chapter to calculate the approximate rate of economic growth (in percentage terms) for both 2009 and 2010.

b. Determine the approximate number of years it will take for living standards to double in the United States, if the economic growth rate from 2010 is sustained.

9. Understanding economic growth is a significant part of macroeconomics.

a. Define economic growth.

b. The table below shows economic data for the imaginary nation of Lexieland in 2019 and 2020.

Year	Nominal GDP (billions of dollars)	Price level	Population	Nominal interest rate
2019	50	200	50	2%
2020	60	216	55	3

If possible, using the data above, calculate Lexieland's approximate economic growth rate for the year 2020. If you do not have enough information, what other information would you need?

10. The long-run average rate of real GDP growth in the United States is about 3%.

a. The following are other (approximate) long-run annual averages for the United States:

Inflation rate: 4%	Population growth rate: 1%
Immigration rate: 0.5%	Unemployment rate: 6%
Labor force participation rate: 70%	Velocity of money: 2%
Nominal interest rate: 3%	

What is the long run average rate of per capita real GDP growth for the United States?

b. Currently, average annual income in the United States is about $60,000. If the U.S economy grows at the rate you just computed for the next 70 years, what will be the average income level in 70 years?

c. Average annual income in China is now about $9,000. If economic growth in China is 5% for the next 70 years, what will be its average income level in 70 years?

Solved Problems

1. a. The rule of 70 tells us we can divide 70 by the rate of growth to approximate the number of years it takes for a variable to double. Therefore, if we know the number of years a variable actually did take to double, we can rearrange the rule of 70 to approximate the average annual growth rate, x:

$$70 \div x = 20$$
$$70 \div 20 = x$$
$$= 3.5$$

Therefore, the Chinese economy grew at an approximate average of 3.5% per year over the 20-year period from 1959 to 1978.

b. Now, with real per capita GDP doubling in approximately seven years, the rule of 70 implies

$$70 \div 7 = 10$$

Therefore, China grew an average of 10% over the seven-year period from 1979 to 1986.

2. To determine economic growth rate, we use the approximations formula:

- Economic growth ≈ %Δ in nominal GDP – %Δ price level – %Δ population
- For nation A: 12% – 10% – 1.5% = 0.5%
- For nation B: 5% – 2% – 1% = 2%

To determine the approximate number of years required for real per capita GDP to double, we use the rule of 70:

- For nation A: 70 ÷ 0.5 = 140
- For nation B: 70 ÷ 2 = 35

To determine real per capita GDP 140 years later, we use the rule of 70 results. Nation A's level doubles in exactly 140 years, so it will be two times the original level of $1,000, or $2,000. Nation B's level doubles after 35 years and then doubles again after 35 more. So after 70 years, its level of real per capita GDP is four times the original level. It doubles again in 35 years, so after 105 years, it is eight times the original level. Then it doubles again in 35 more years, so after 140 years, its real per capita GDP is $16,000, which is 16 times the original level.

	A	B
Economic growth rate	0.5%	2%
Years required for real per capita GDP to double	140	35
Real per capita GDP 140 years later	$2,000	$16,000

7. a. Economic growth is measured as the percentage change in real per capita GDP.

b. It is not possible to calculate the economic growth rate from the data because we also need the growth rate of the population.

CHAPTER

25 Growth Theory

Buildings, Roads, Mosquito Nets, and Other Capital Are Not the Key to Economic Growth.

If we look around the world, it is easy to spot high-income nations and low-income nations. Rich, developed nations have impressive capital, including highways, factories, office buildings, and laboratories. Poor, underdeveloped nations have fewer modern factories and buildings, and their roads and other infrastructure are often in disrepair. Think of North and South Korea, as we saw in the last chapter, where one can literally see the difference from outer space. Clearly, wealth and physical capital go hand in hand, and it is tempting to conclude that physical capital is the *source* of wealth: if poor nations can just acquire more and better tools, they too, can be wealthy.

However, correlation does not prove causation. Physical capital does contribute to growth, but it is less important than you might think. Often, physical capital is the result of growth, rather than the cause of it. Institutions, not infrastructure, are the real key to economic vitality. In the last chapter we saw in concrete terms how institutions matter. This chapter now provides the theoretical backbone of growth analysis. We begin with a brief description of

Remember that satellite image of North and South Korea? This is the Ryugyong Hotel in North Korea's capital, Pyongyang. It's been under construction on and off for three decades and is still not done. Why the epic construction fail? Because the institutions of North Korea reward loyalty to the regime over engineering competence.

how economic theories develop. After that, we consider the evolution of growth theory, starting with the growth model created by the American economist Robert Solow. The Solow model formed the foundation for growth theory beginning in the 1950s. After discussing the theory and implications of the Solow model, we consider New Growth Theory and its implied policy prescriptions.

· BIG QUESTIONS ·

- How do macroeconomic theories evolve?
- What is the Solow growth model?
- How does technology affect growth?
- Why are institutions the key to economic growth?

How Do Macroeconomic Theories Evolve?

This chapter marks our first major step into macroeconomic theory, or modeling. In Chapter 2, we discussed the characteristics of good economic models: they are simple, flexible, and useful for making accurate predictions. In this chapter, we present a model of economic growth that simplifies from the real world yet also helps us make powerful predictions about economic growth. The stakes are high: growth theory and policy have significant impacts on human lives. Therefore, it's important to consistently reevaluate growth theory in light of real-world results.

Today, economists agree that economic growth is determined by a combination of resources, technology, and institutions. But this consensus is the result of an evolution in growth theory that started almost 60 years ago with the contributions of economist Robert Solow. Although the theory has changed significantly over the past two decades, Solow's growth model still forms the core of New Growth Theory.

In many academic disciplines, new theories are fodder for intellectual debates, with no direct effect on human lives. But in economics, theories are put to the test in the real world, often very soon after they are first articulated. Figure 25.1 illustrates the relationship between economic ideas and real-world events. At the top of the circle, we begin with observations of the real world,

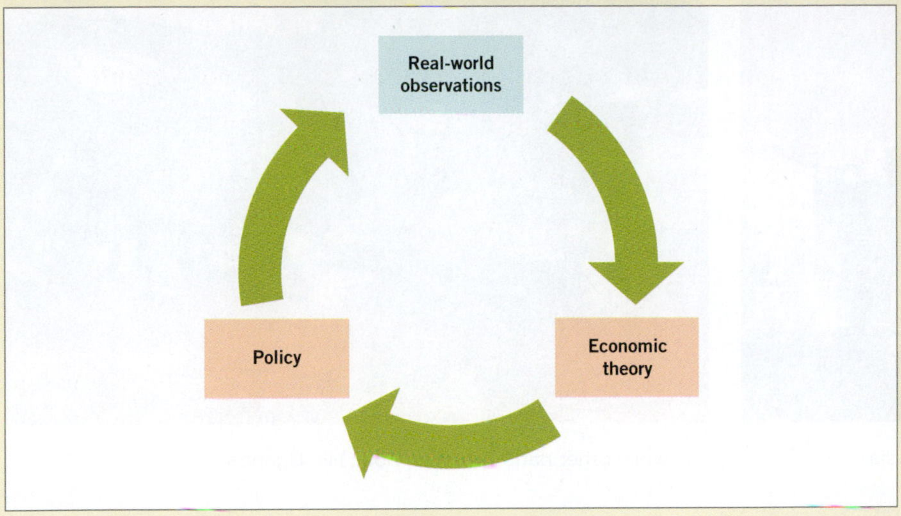

FIGURE 25.1

The Interplay between the Real World and Economic Theory

Observations of the real world shape economic theory. Economic theory then informs policy decisions designed to meet certain economic goals. Once these policies are implemented, they affect the real world. Further real-world observations contribute to additional advances in economic theory, and the cycle continues.

which inform a theory as it develops. Once an economic theory is developed, it can influence the policies used to pursue certain economic goals. These policies affect the daily lives and well-being of real people. Finally, as economists observe the effects of policy in the real world, they continue to revise economic theory.

Economic growth models affect the welfare of billions of people worldwide. The results can be beneficial. But if growth theory is wrong or incomplete, it can lead to faulty policy prescriptions that result in poverty. We revisit this point toward the end of the chapter.

The Evolution of Growth Theory

In 1776, Adam Smith published his renowned book *An Inquiry into the Nature and Causes of the Wealth of Nations.* This book was the first real economics textbook and, as the title indicates, it focused on what makes a nation wealthy. The central question, paraphrased from the title, is: Why do some nations prosper while others do not? More than two centuries later, we still grapple with the nature and causes of the wealth of nations.

Economists are not alone in their pursuit of answers to this question. As travel becomes easier and the world economy becomes more integrated, people are more aware of poverty around the globe. Many college students today ask the same questions as economists: Why are so many people poor, and what can be done about it?

This link between economic theory and human welfare is what drives many scholars to study the theory of economic growth. As the Nobel Prize–winning macroeconomist Robert Lucas wrote in 1988:

> Is there some action a government of India could take that would lead the Indian economy to grow like Indonesia's or Egypt's? If so, what exactly? If not, what is it about the "nature of India" that makes it so? The consequences for human welfare involved in questions like these are simply staggering: *Once one starts to think about them it is hard to think of anything else.*

Why are some nations rich, like Malaysia . . .

. . . while other nations remain poor, like Uganda?

Economic growth has not always been the primary focus of macroeconomics. After the Great Depression in the 1930s, macroeconomics focused on the study of business cycles, or short-run expansions and contractions. Growth theory began with the Solow model in the 1950s and still serves as the foundation for growth theory, both in method and in policy. Therefore, while growth theory has evolved, it is helpful to consider the Solow model as both a starting point and the basis of current theory.

What Is the Solow Growth Model?

If you travel around the globe and visit nations with different levels of income, you will notice significant differences in the physical tools available for use in production. Wealthy nations have more factories, better roads, more and better computers—that is, they have more physical capital. Simply viewing the difference in capital, it is easy to conclude that capital automatically yields economic growth.

This was the basic premise of early growth theory: there are rich nations and there are poor nations, and the rich nations are those with capital. Natural resources and human capital are important in the Solow growth model, but the focus is primarily on *physical capital*. So when we speak simply of capital, we mean physical capital; and where human capital is also part of the picture, we will call that labor.

We begin our tour of the Solow model by looking at a nation's production function, which describes how changes in capital affect real output.

A Nation's Production Function

A **production function** for a firm describes the relationship between the inputs the firm uses and the output it creates.

The Solow model starts with a *production function* for the entire economy. In microeconomic theory, a firm's **production function** describes the relationship between the inputs a firm uses and the output it creates. For example, at a single McDonald's restaurant, the daily output depends on both the number of employees and the capital tools employees have to work with. In equation form, the production function for a single firm is

$$q = f(\text{labor, capital})$$ **(EQUATION 25.1)**

where q is the firm's output. Equation 25.1 says that output *is a function of* the quantities of labor and capital that the firm uses. For McDonald's, the output is the number of meals produced.

In macroeconomics, we extend the production function to an entire nation or macroeconomy. The **aggregate production function** describes the relationship between all the inputs used in the macroeconomy and the economy's total output, where GDP is output. In its simplest form, the aggregate production function tells us that GDP is a function of three broad types of resources, or factors of production, which are the inputs used in producing goods and services. These inputs are capital, labor, and natural resources. We can state the aggregate production function in equation form as

The **aggregate production function** describes the relationship between all the inputs used in the macroeconomy and the economy's total output (GDP).

$$GDP = Y = F(\text{labor, capital, natural resources})$$ **(EQUATION 25.2)**

where Y is real output, or GDP.

We can think about the relationship between input and output in a very simple economy. Consider a situation in which there is only one person in the macroeconomy—for example, the character Chuck Noland (played by Tom Hanks) in the 2000 movie *Cast Away*, who finds himself stranded on an island in the South Pacific after his plane crashes. Chuck's individual, or microeconomic, decisions are also macroeconomic decisions, because he is the only person in the economy. The GDP of Chuck's island includes only what he produces with his resources. Let's say Chuck spends his days harvesting fruit on the island. In this case, GDP is equal to whatever fruit Chuck harvests. Table 25.1 shows Chuck's production function and some of the resources he has available.

Chuck's output is the fruit he harvests from around his island. His resources include his labor, the capital of a bamboo ladder, and the island's

In the film *Cast Away*, Chuck Noland's individual, or microeconomic, decisions are also macroeconomic decisions, because he is the only person in the economy.

TABLE 25.1

Chuck Noland's Production Function

	Production function	
	GDP = F(labor, capital, natural resources)	
GDP	**Resources**	**Example**
	Labor	Chuck's time and knowledge
Fruit	Capital	Bamboo ladder
	Natural resources	Fruit trees and bamboo

natural resources, such as bamboo and fruit trees. All else equal, the more Chuck has of any of these resources, the more GDP he can produce. Economic growth occurs when Chuck produces more fruit per week.

In many ways, the production function for a large macroeconomy is the same as for Chuck Noland's one-man economy. Consider the economy of India. In India, output depends on the resources available for production, and India has significant natural resources, such as iron ore, coal, timber, and farmland. In terms of human capital, India has a large labor force with about 500 million workers, and a literacy rate of almost 75%. Finally, India has built up a very large stock of capital—highways, factories, ports, machinery, etc. All of these resources enable the nation to produce an annual GDP of more than $2.6 trillion.

THE FOCUS ON CAPITAL RESOURCES While the Solow model recognizes contributions from both labor and capital, many economists and policymakers focused on capital. As we noted in the chapter opener, early growth theorists saw that capital resources in wealthy nations far exceed those available in developing nations. After all, there are more factories, highways, bridges, and dams in wealthy nations. It seemed logical to conclude that capital is the key to growth.

In addition, periods of investment growth in developed economies are also periods of economic expansion. Figure 25.2 plots U.S. economic growth rates

FIGURE 25.2

Real GDP and Investment Growth Rates, 1970–2017

Growth in real investment is positively correlated with growth in real GDP. The big question is whether this correlation implies causation.

Source: Bureau of Economic Analysis.

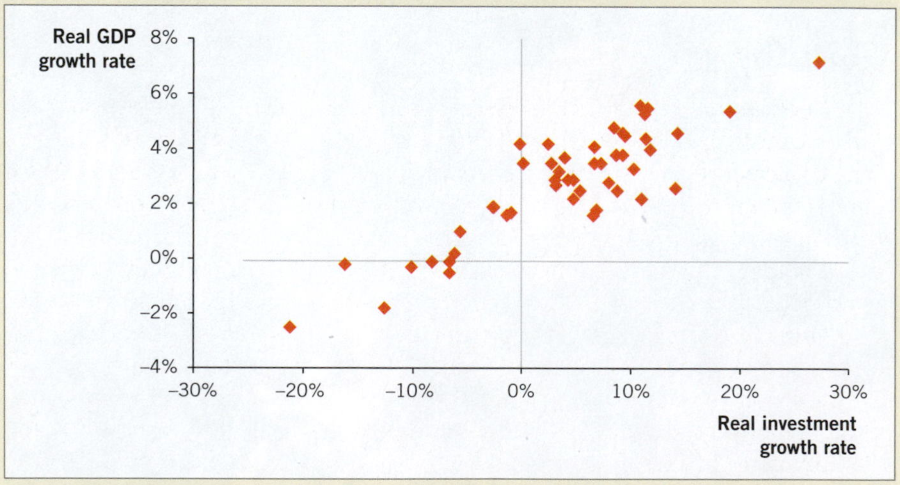

with investment growth rates from 1970 to 2017. The data show a clear positive correlation between real GDP growth and the rate of investment growth—another reason to believe that investment and capital are the primary sources of economic growth.

Earlier, we noted the interplay of theory and real-world observations. This is one example. Capital *appears* to cause economic growth, because there is such a strong correlation between capital and output. And, certainly, no one disputes that workers are more productive when they have more tools. For now, however, we continue our focus on capital. Later, we explore alternative growth sources omitted from this early work.

A ladder would help!

Diminishing Marginal Products

The castaway Chuck Noland would have been happy to find a new grove of mangoes on his island, and his newfound resources would have increased his GDP. Natural resources also help large, developed macroeconomies. For example, discoveries of natural gas in the United States have increased dramatically over the past two decades. This new energy resource enables the United States to produce more with cheaper resources. To quantify how helpful a resource may be, economists employ the concept of *marginal product*. The **marginal product** of an input is the change in output associated with one additional unit of an input. More resources increase output, so we say the marginal product of each resource is positive.

The **marginal product** of an input is the change in output divided by the change in input.

DIMINISHING MARGINAL PRODUCT IN A ONE-PERSON ECONOMY

To illustrate some important properties of production functions, let's take a closer look at the production function of Chuck Noland. Initially, Chuck produces GDP by climbing trees and picking fruit. With this method, he is able to gather 1 bushel of fruit in a week. He produces this weekly GDP without the aid of any capital. Now, let's say Chuck decides to take a week to build a bamboo ladder. Building the ladder is a costly investment, because it takes him away from producing fruit for a whole week. But then, after he has the ladder as capital, his weekly output grows to 4 bushels. This means the marginal product (MP) of his ladder is 3 bushels of fruit per week:

Marginal thinking

$$MP_{capital} = \text{change in output given the change in capital} = 3$$

Chuck is so happy with his ladder that he builds a second ladder (perhaps to leave one on each side of the island). Now his weekly output climbs to 6 bushels of fruit. Because he produces 4 bushels with one ladder and 6 bushels with two ladders, the marginal product of the second ladder is 2 bushels. Note that it is less than the marginal product of the first ladder. The marginal product of the second ladder is not as large because while the first ladder completely altered the way Chuck harvests fruit, the second ladder just makes his job a little easier.

Figure 25.3 shows the hypothetical relationship between Chuck's output and the number of ladders he uses. Looking first at the table on the right, note that the second column shows total output (bushels per week), which depends on the number of ladders. The third column shows the marginal product of each ladder. Notice that the marginal product declines as more ladders are added. This outcome reflects the principle of **diminishing marginal product**, which states that the marginal product of an input falls as the quantity of the input

Diminishing marginal product occurs when the marginal product of an input falls as the quantity of the input rises.

FIGURE 25.3

Chuck Noland's Production Function

The table shows how output (bushels per week) increases as the number of ladders increases; it describes the relationship between output and capital inputs. The graph is a picture of the production function. Output increases with capital, but each unit of capital yields less additional output. The shape of the production function, in which the slope is declining, illustrates the diminishing marginal product of capital.

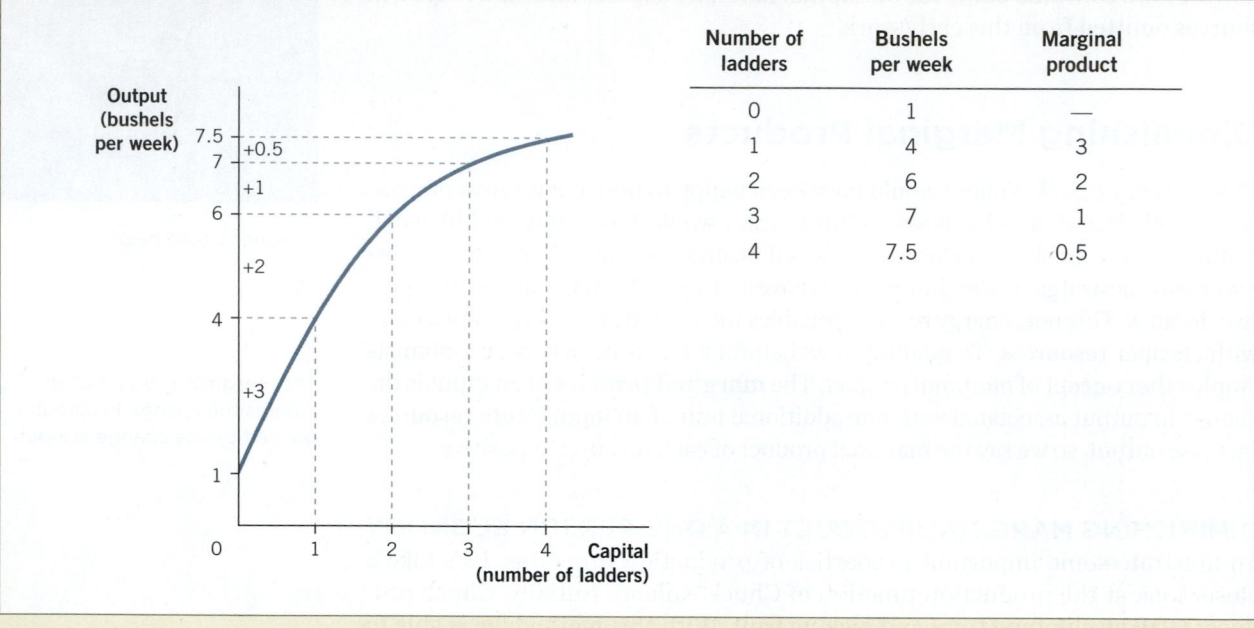

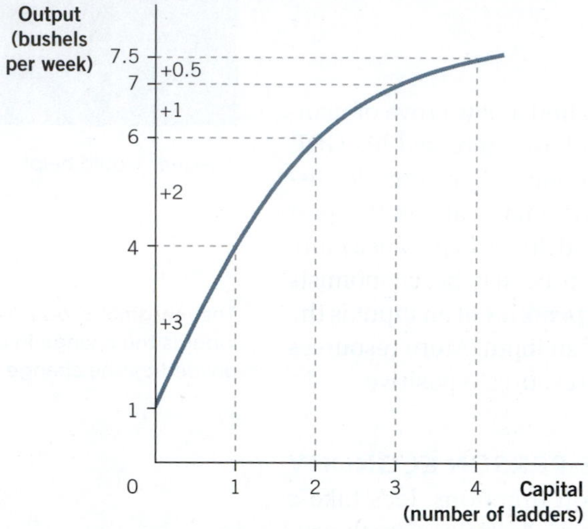

Number of ladders	Bushels per week	Marginal product
0	1	—
1	4	3
2	6	2
3	7	1
4	7.5	0.5

rises. Diminishing marginal product generally applies across all factors of production at both microeconomic and macroeconomic levels.

The left side of Figure 25.3 is a graph of Chuck's production function: it plots the points from the first two columns of the table on the right. With no ladders, the production function indicates 1 bushel of fruit; but then as ladders are added, output climbs along the curve. The slope of the curve flattens out because the marginal product of the added ladders diminishes.

This principle of diminishing marginal productivity is not special to our example of one man alone on an island. It is a phenomenon that holds for resources in a macroeconomy in general, and it is a cornerstone insight of the Solow growth model. Sometimes, the name of this principle is simplified to *diminishing returns*. The following discussion places this concept in the macroeconomic context of the U.S. interstate highway system.

HIGHWAYS AND THE PRODUCTION FUNCTION In the United States, we have a system of interstate highways built by the federal government. This interstate highway system is essentially a 50,000-mile capital good that we use to help produce GDP. The network of highways connects major cities of the United States. These highways increase GDP in the United States, because they help us transport goods and services across the nation. For example, a

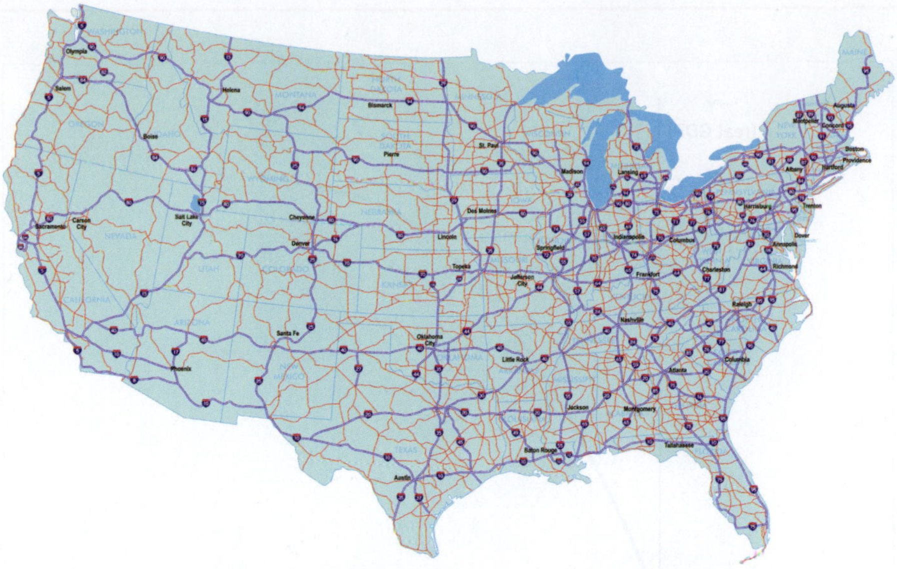

How much would GDP fall without our interstate highways?

couch manufactured in High Point, North Carolina, can be transported exclusively by interstate highway to Cleveland, Ohio, in less than 8 hours. Before the construction of the interstate system, the same trip between High Point and Cleveland would have taken twice as long, required more gasoline due to inefficient speeds, and caused much more wear and tear on the vehicles used.

If the interstate highway system were somehow to close down completely, GDP would fall immediately. But what would happen to GDP if the government created a second interstate highway system with 50,000 miles of additional roads crisscrossing the United States? That is, what would be the marginal product of an additional interstate highway system? The impact would be positive, but much smaller than that of the original network. This example illustrates diminishing returns: the marginal product of highways declines as more and more become available. The production relationship is just like that of Chuck Noland's ladders.

Figure 25.4 is a graph of the aggregate production function—the production function for the entire economy. On the vertical axis, we have output for the macroeconomy, which is real GDP (Y). To simplify, we assume no population growth and so economic growth is represented as movements up along the vertical axis. On the horizontal axis, capital resources (K) increase from left to right. Notice that the slope of the function is positive, which indicates positive marginal product. But the marginal product of capital also declines as more capital is added. For example, the difference in output from the increase in capital from K_1 to K_2 is larger than the change in output from a change in capital from K_3 to K_4. This outcome illustrates the declining marginal product of capital.

The aggregate production function has formed the basis for most discussions in growth theory since 1956. Economic growth is represented by upward movement along the vertical axis. Indeed, if we focus *only* on this simple formulation, economic growth happens only with investment in capital. Diminishing returns, or declining marginal productivity, is the key assumption of the Solow model. As we shall see, this single assumption leads to striking implications for the macroeconomy.

FIGURE 25.4

The Aggregate Production Function

The aggregate production function graphs the relationship between output (Y, or real GDP) and capital inputs (K). The shape of the production function illustrates two important features of production. First, the marginal production of resources is positive, as indicated by the positive slope. Second, the marginal product of additional resources declines as more resources are added. This result is evident in the declining slope of the function.

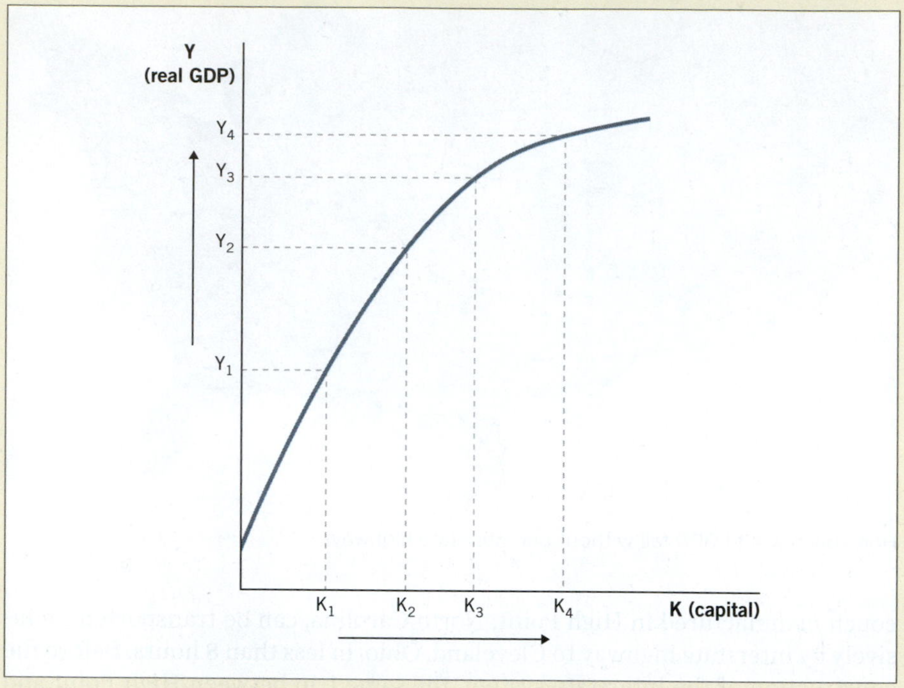

Implications of the Solow Model

We can use the basic framework of the production function with an emphasis on capital and diminishing returns to flesh out the two important implications of the Solow model: the conditions of a *steady state* and *convergence*.

Incentives

THE STEADY STATE How many ladders should Chuck Noland build? It takes a week to build each ladder, and each additional ladder adds less output than the one before. Therefore, at some point Chuck has no incentive to build additional ladders. Perhaps Chuck's incentive declines after he builds two ladders. Looking back at Figure 25.3, you can see that a third ladder yields only 1 more bushel of fruit. Let's assume that Chuck decides it is not worth a week of work (to build a ladder) for 1 more bushel of fruit. Therefore, he builds only two ladders, and his output remains at 6 bushels a week. At this point, economic growth for Chuck stops.

The Solow model implies the same outcome for large macroeconomies. Because the marginal product of capital decreases, at some point there is no reason to build (that is, invest in) more capital. Let's assume this occurs at K_3 in Figure 25.4. This means there is no incentive to build additional capital beyond K_3 because the benefits in terms of additional output no longer exceed the cost of building capital. Since there is no incentive to build capital past K_3, and since we are assuming that capital is the source of growth, the economy stops growing once it reaches K_3. In this example, K_3 is the economy's **steady state**, the condition of a macroeconomy when there is no new net investment.

The **steady state** is the condition of a macroeconomy when there is no new net investment.

An economy at the steady state is like an airplane at its cruising altitude.

Once an economy reaches the steady state, there is no change in either capital or real income. The steady state is a direct implication of diminishing returns: when the marginal return to capital declines, at some point there is no incentive to build more capital. The steady state is not a very encouraging situation. You can think of the steady state as the "stagnant state," because when the economy reaches its steady state, real GDP is no longer increasing and economic growth stops.

It is important to distinguish between *investment* and *net investment*. Over time, capital wears out: roads get potholes, tractors break down, and factories become obsolete. This is known as capital depreciation. **Depreciation** is a decline in the value of a resource over time. Depreciation is natural with capital, and it erodes the capital stock. Without new investment, capital declines over time, so some positive investment is needed to offset depreciation. But if investment is exactly enough to replace depreciated items, the capital stock will not increase—and this means no net investment. **Net investment** is investment minus depreciation. For the capital stock to increase, net investment must be positive.

Depreciation
is a fall in the value of a resource over time.

Net investment
is investment minus depreciation.

This distinction between investment and net investment is important when we consider the steady state. In the steady state, net investment equals zero. There may be positive investment, but this is investment to replace worn-out machines and tools. So when an economy reaches its steady state, the capital stock stays constant. For example, if three ladders represent a steady-state condition on Chuck Noland's island, he may repair his ladders periodically. Repairing the ladders to maintain a level of capital counts as investment, but not as positive net investment.

CONVERGENCE If nations with large stocks of capital reach their steady state and stop growing, nations with less capital can catch up by adding to their capital stock. This means that nations all over the globe could potentially converge to the same level of wealth. **Convergence** is the idea that per capita GDPs across nations equalize as nations approach the steady state. Here is the logic of the Solow model: Rich nations are rich because they have more capital. But as these nations approach their steady state, the returns to capital decline and the growth slows. When a nation reaches a steady state, its economic growth stops. But if a nation has not yet reached the steady state, adding capital still leads to growth. Therefore, investment in developing nations should yield

Convergence
is the idea that per capita GDPs across nations equalize as nations approach the steady state.

PRACTICE WHAT YOU KNOW

Hurricane Maria caused an estimated $90 billion in damage to Puerto Rico and the U.S. Virgin Islands.

Changes in Resources: Natural Disasters

In September 2017, Hurricane Maria slammed into Puerto Rico, killing many people and destroying significant capital, including roads, homes, factories, and bridges.

QUESTION: How would you use an aggregate production function to illustrate the way a major destruction of capital affects a macroeconomy in the short run?

ANSWER:

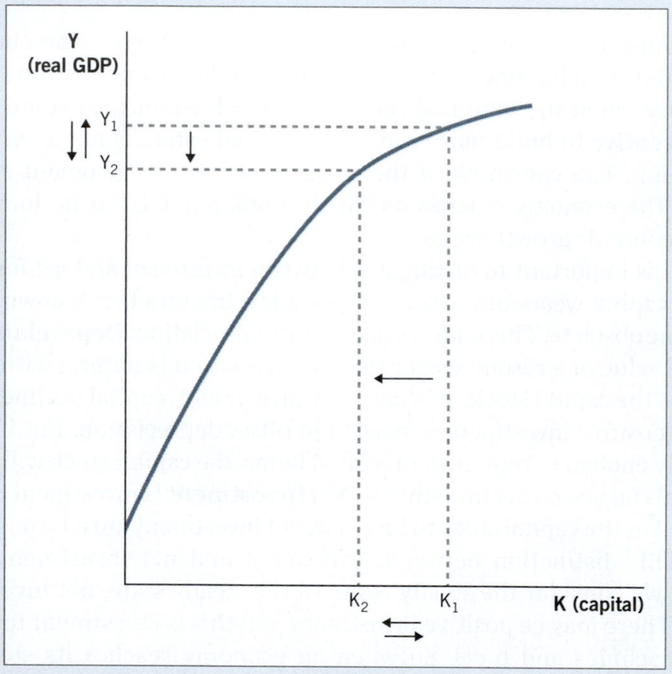

This is an unusual situation, in which the level of capital actually falls. Because capital (K) is on the horizontal axis of the production function, the decline in capital moves Puerto Rico back along its production function. Assuming the original level of capital is indicated as K_1, we can illustrate the effect of Maria as a change to a lower level, say K_2. This means less GDP for Puerto Rico (Y falls from Y_1 to Y_2) until the capital is rebuilt.

QUESTION: With no further changes, what happens to real GDP in the long run?

ANSWER: With no further changes, real GDP returns to the steady-state output level (K_1) in the long run. At the new level of capital after the storm (K_2), the marginal product of additional capital is relatively high, so there is a greater return to building new capital. But in the long run, because there was no shift in the production function, the level of capital returns to the steady-state level (K_1), which means output also returns to its steady-state level (Y_1).

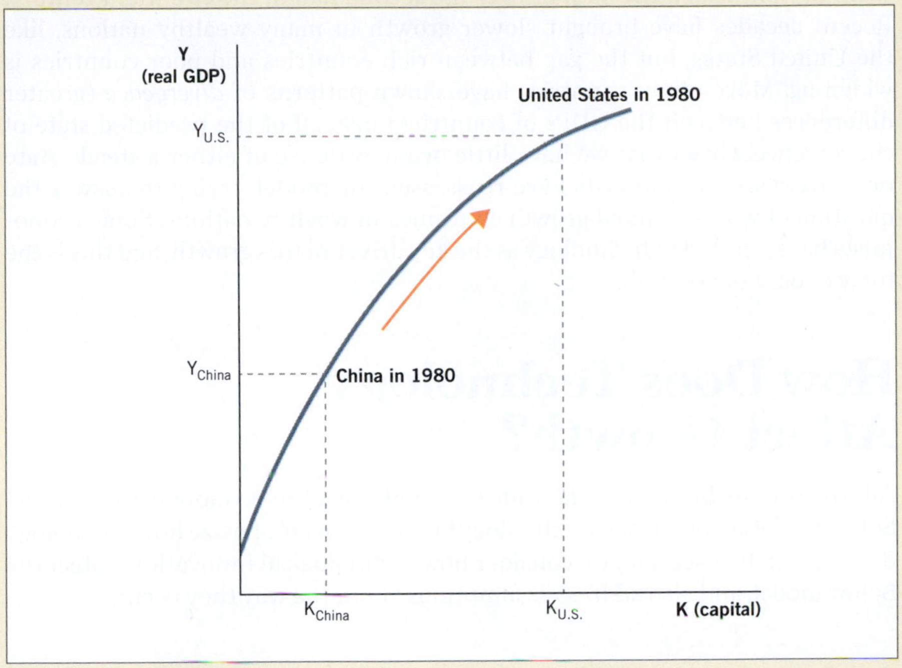

FIGURE 25.5

Convergence

In 1980, the United States had much more capital than China did; this was one reason why real GDP for the United States was much higher. But in the years since, China has increased its capital stock substantially and has grown much more rapidly than the United States. The Solow model implies that the United States is closer to its steady state and therefore grows more slowly than China.

relatively greater returns, and this outcome should lead to more capital in developing nations.

Consider the United States and China. In 1980, the United States was wealthy, but China was poor. Figure 25.5 shows both nations as they might have appeared on a production function in 1980. Yet since 1980, growth rates in China have exceeded growth rates in the United States. This blast of growth in China has been accompanied by rapid industrialization—that is, the creation of new capital. According to the Solow model, the new capital in China yields greater returns because the nation started with less capital.

If this basic model were completely realistic, new factories in poor nations would typically yield higher returns than those in rich nations. Investors seeking to build new factories would turn to nations like Haiti, Nicaragua, and North Korea—nations with relatively small capital stocks.

According to the Solow theory, developing nations should catch up because the older, developed economies have already made new discoveries and have documented mistakes to avoid in the development process. Developing nations can jump right into acquiring the best equipment, tools, and practices. For example, if they are building cars, they don't have to start with a Model T and a basic labor-intensive assembly line; they can immediately establish a modern plant resembling those of, say, Ford, Honda, and Volkswagen.

But reality has been much different from what the theory implies. First, although we have seen cases of rapid growth in poor nations, convergence has been rare. In addition to China, the nations of South Korea, Singapore, India, Chile, and others have done well. But they are exceptions. Very recently, it seems some growth is sprouting in African nations, but for the second half of the twentieth century, most poor nations continued to stagnate, rather than converge to the economic levels of wealthier nations. Second, growth did not seem to slow in wealthy nations over the second half of the twentieth century. Recent decades have brought slower growth in many wealthy nations, like the United States, but the gap between rich countries and poor countries is widening. More often, countries have shown patterns of *divergence* (greater differences between the GDPs of countries) instead of the predicted state of convergence. Given that we have little or no evidence of either a steady state or convergence, economists have reassessed the model, trying to answer the question of why sustained growth continues in wealthy nations. Some economists have pointed to technology as the key driver of this growth, and this is the topic of our next section.

How Does Technology Affect Growth?

Advances in technology, or new ideas, can also lead to economic growth. The Solow model acknowledges technology but does not emphasize how technology develops. In this section, we consider how technological innovations affect the Solow model, and also address assumptions about the way they occur.

Technology and the Production Function

In 1994, Intel introduced a revolutionary computer chip for personal computers—the Pentium chip. The original Pentium could perform 166 million operations per second and was more than three times faster than its predecessor chip. But by 2019, just 25 years later, Intel's new chip, the Core i9 10900X, could perform 1.5 *trillion* operations per second. The new chip costs less and uses less energy than the old chip and yet is about 9,000 times faster!

These Intel chips give us a good picture of what technology does. A computer chip is capital—it is a tool that helps us produce. Faster chips mean more output with the same amount of capital.

Now let's see how new technology affects the Solow growth model. First, consider the production function. Figure 25.6 shows two production functions: F_1 is the initial production function, when computers are running on Pentium chips. F_2 is the production function after faster chips arrive. Note the new production function is steeper than the old one. The slope is determined by the marginal product of capital, and the new computer chips make capital more

Older map technology took lots of time . . .

. . . but the new map technology is faster.

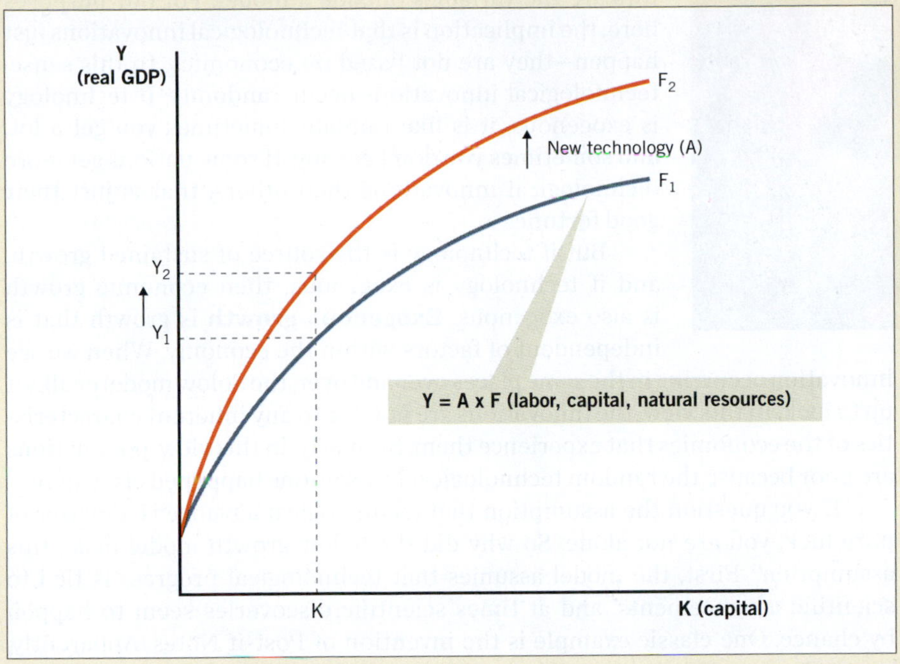

FIGURE 25.6

New Technology and the Production Function

New technology increases the slope of the production function as the marginal product of capital increases. The old production function is shown as F_1 and the new production function as F_2. After the technological innovation (represented by A), capital is more productive, and this outcome leads to new economic growth. If technology continues to advance, economic growth can be sustained.

productive at all levels. For any given level of capital, real GDP is higher. These are the kinds of technological changes that fuel sustained economic growth.

We can also use an equation to see how the production function is altered. The aggregate production function now includes an allowance for technological advancement:

$$Y = A \times F(\text{labor, capital, natural resources}) \qquad \text{(EQUATION 25.3)}$$

where A accounts for technological change. The addition of A to the basic model helps to explain continued economic growth. Without new technology, the economy eventually reaches a steady state, and growth stops. But new technology means output is higher for any given level of capital, because it makes resources more productive. New technology shifts real output, and therefore income, up to new levels.

Economists and policymakers of course see this shift as very important, and it has driven many political decisions. Before looking at policy implications that derive from the Solow model, let's first look more closely at how technological change occurs in the model.

Exogenous Technological Change

Why do people innovate? What drives them to create better ways of producing? If technology is the source of sustained growth, the answer to this question is critical.

In the Solow model, there is no real answer to the question of what causes technological innovation. The model assumes that technological change occurs

The discovery of the glue used for Post-it Notes was accidental. When the notes are used to paper a friend's car, the act is normally premeditated.

exogenously. Recall from Chapter 2 that exogenous factors are the variables outside a model. For our purposes here, the implication is that technological innovations just happen—they are not based on economics. In this sense, technological innovations occur randomly. If technology is exogenous, it is like rainfall: sometimes you get a lot, and sometimes you don't get any. If some nations get more technological innovations than others, that is just their good fortune.

But if technology is the source of sustained growth, and if technology is exogenous, then economic growth is also exogenous. **Exogenous growth** is growth that is independent of factors within the economy. When we see innovation occurring in the same places over and over, the Solow model chalks it up to luck. In this view, the innovations are not due to any inherent characteristics of the economies that experience them. Similarly, in this view, poor nations are poor because the random technological innovations happened elsewhere.

Exogenous growth is growth that is independent of factors within the economy.

If you question the assumption that technological advance is a matter of pure luck, you are not alone. So why did the Solow growth model make this assumption? First, the model assumes that technological progress is tied to scientific advancements, and at times scientific discoveries seem to happen by chance. One classic example is the invention of Post-it Notes. Apparently, researchers at 3M accidentally stumbled onto a formula for glue that made Post-it Notes possible. In this sense, the discovery was seemingly random luck.

Second, this model, like most economic models, is developed mathematically. The assumption of exogenous technological change made the theoretical growth models simpler to solve than an alternative model where technological change is dependent upon multiple factors in the economy.

As we will see in the final section of this chapter, economists in the 1980s developed other models (or techniques) to help incorporate technological change into the original model.

Policy Implications of the Solow Model

At the beginning of this chapter, we discussed how macroeconomic theory often translates directly into policy. We are now in a position to consider the policy prescriptions that emerge from the Solow growth model. Proponents of the Solow model emphasize the importance of capital and technology. Thus, for low-income nations to grow, they need the latest technology embedded in capital goods. High-income nations and individuals around the globe can help others grow by providing aid to purchase the latest capital.

As the Solow model grew in popularity in the 1950s, two specific types of aid were developed to implement this approach. First, actual capital goods were built with aid from developed nations. For example, in 1964, with funding from the United States, Great Britain, and the World Bank, the Akosombo Dam was built in the West African nation of Ghana to create hydroelectric power, and to form a lake useful for water transportation and a fishing industry.

Second, international aid was sent directly to developing nations to help them fund investment in infrastructure such as highways, bridges, and modern ports, as well as other types of capital. These aid payments were intended to

PRACTICE WHAT YOU KNOW

Technological Innovations: How Is the Production Function Affected?

This tractor was state-of-the-art technology in 1910.

When new technology is introduced, it makes capital more productive. For example, modern tractors are faster and more powerful than tractors used a century ago.

QUESTION: How does this type of change affect the production function?

ANSWER: The production function gets steeper at each point. For example, when the level of capital is K, the slope of production function F_2 is steeper than the slope of F_1. The reason is that capital is now more productive at every level. The first unit of capital adds more to output than before, and the 500th unit of capital adds more to output than before. The marginal product of capital, which is embedded in the slope of the production function, is now higher at all levels.

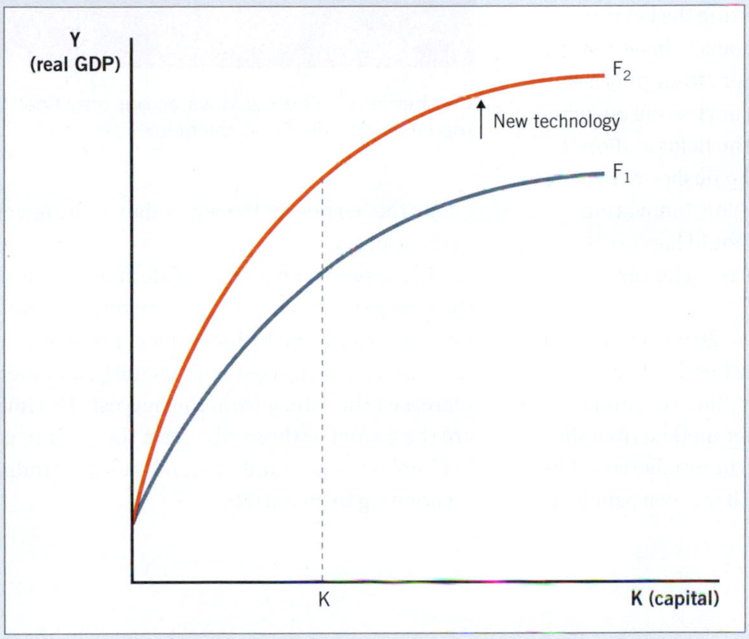

CHALLENGE QUESTION: What happens in the loanable funds market when new technology leads to more productive capital (see Chapter 22, if necessary)?

ANSWER: Productivity of capital shifts the demand for loanable funds. New technology would lead to an increase in demand for loans and, all else equal, interest rates would rise.

help poor nations build capital infrastructure that would pave the way to economic growth.

While there were of course some successes, economists and policymakers are largely discouraged by the results of these policy initiatives. For example, fifty-three years after the Akosombo Dam was completed, average income levels

ECONOMICS in the MEDIA

Technological Change

MODERN MARVELS

Cranberries don't grow in water, but they float to the top when farmers flood the fields.

Modern Marvels is a television series on the History Channel. It often showcases technological innovations that have revolutionized the way goods and services are produced. In Season 13, an episode titled "Harvesters 2" included a look at cranberry harvesting around the globe.

Cranberries are grown on low-lying vines. In the past, cranberry harvesting involved many workers carefully hand-harvesting the berries. But cranberries also have air pockets inside them, and these pockets enable farmers to employ a wet harvest. The big innovation in harvesting occurred when farmers began flooding the fields and then knocking the cranberries off the bushes with water-reel harvesters called beaters. This innovation meant that just a few workers could harvest 10 acres of cranberries in a single day, saving hundreds of hours of labor.

Incentives

The beaters make the harvest go quickly, but they also tend to damage some of the berries. Recently, Habelman Brothers, a cranberry farm in Tomah, Wisconsin, began using a gentler method than the water-reel so as not to damage the cranberries. Their harvesters use waterwheels with wooden panels to knock the berries off the vines, damaging fewer berries in the process.

These two innovations—water harvesting and the new, gentler waterwheel—are both examples of innovations caused by incentives. The first innovation cut harvesting costs significantly, and the second increased the return from the harvest. The innovators are the farmers—those who have the most to gain. Technology is not random; it is a result of individuals responding to incentives.

in Ghana have risen by just $1,200 per person, and this is not an isolated story. After billions of dollars in aid, nations such as Zimbabwe, Liberia, and Haiti are just as poor today as they were in 1960. In contrast, Taiwan, Chile, China, and India received almost no international aid and yet have grown rapidly.

The application of the Solow model to growth policy was often not successful. In fact, most of the twentieth century witnessed very few success stories and a series of failures. Consider the continent of Africa. Thirty-seven African nations achieved independence from 1956 to 1977, offering a unique opportunity to apply the Solow model. Yet by the late twentieth century, it was clear that these policies had failed across the continent, as many African nations were no better off than they were when they gained their independence decades earlier, even while much of the rest of the globe had experienced significant economic gains. Around the end of the twentieth century, these real-world policy results led to a reexamination of growth theory. Economist Dambisa Moyo wrote a book, *Dead Aid: Why Aid Is Not Working and How There Is a Better Way for Africa,* about this failure of international aid across Africa. She argued that foreign aid often led to corruption and nations becoming dependent on this aid. But she also points to policies that can yield growth in low-income nations. We discuss some of these in the next section.

Zambian economist Dambisa Moyo argues that international aid has inhibited growth in Africa.

Why Are Institutions the Key to Economic Growth?

Over the past thirty years, a resurgence in growth theory has been spurred by the belief that some economies grow faster *for reasons particular to those economies.* In some nations, and even in pockets within nations, technology advances more quickly than elsewhere. This resurgent growth theory has been dubbed **New Growth Theory**. It is an approach to long-run growth that focuses on technological change and the incentives fostering innovation inside an economy. The Solow model acknowledges the importance of new ideas and technology, but essentially assumes they spring up exogenously and therefore cannot be predicted. By contrast, New Growth Theory recognizes that economic growth generally appears to be endogenous. **Endogenous growth** is growth driven by factors inside an economy. For example, it is not random coincidence that assembly lines, sewing machines, air conditioning, personal computers, and the Internet were all developed in the United States. These advances spurred economic growth and improved people's lives. Why did they all occur in one nation? This is the focus of New Growth Theory.

New Growth Theory is an approach to long-run growth that focuses on technological change and the incentives fostering innovation inside an economy.

Endogenous growth is growth driven by factors inside an economy.

Economist Paul Romer was awarded the 2018 Nobel Prize in Economics in large part based on his work as a founder of New Growth Theory. A famous 1990 paper of his, "Endogenous Technological Change," helped to shift economic theory's focus toward ideas and innovations, and why they occur in some places but not others. Today, many economists stress the importance of institutions as a key factor contributing to endogenous economic growth. We introduced institutions in Chapter 24. In the next section, we examine how institutions can provide a foundation for economic growth.

Endogenous growth originates inside an economy, as it does inside an organism.

The Role of Institutions

Consider the city of Nogales, which straddles the U.S.-Mexico border. The northern half of the city is in Arizona, while the southern half is in the Mexican state of Sonora. But life in these two halves is drastically different: average income in the northern half is three times that in the southern half. The residents of the northern half are much better educated, the roads are much better, and infant mortality is much lower. These are two halves of the same city, so they have the same natural resources, virtually identical geographical locations, the same ethnicities and weather. Why, then, are they so different?

TABLE 25.2

Institutions That Foster Economic Growth	
1. Political stability and the rule of law	5. The flow of funds across borders
2. Private property rights	6. Efficient taxes
3. Competitive markets	7. Stable money and prices
4. International trade	

According to economist Daron Acemoglu, who wrote about the city in *Esquire* magazine in 2009:

> The key difference is that those on the north side of the border enjoy law and order and dependable government services—they can go about their daily activities and jobs without fear for their life or safety or property rights. On the other side, the inhabitants have *institutions* that perpetuate crime, graft, and insecurity. [emphasis added]

In other words, Acemoglu and many other economists feel that institutions are a key ingredient in the list of factors driving economic growth. Recall from Chapter 24 that institutions are significant practices, relationships, or organizations in society that frame the incentive structure within which individuals and business firms act. Institutions are the rules of the game, both formal and informal, framing the environment within which production takes place. They help determine the costs and benefits of production. Table 25.2 lists the institutions important for growth.

If we include institutions in the aggregate production function, we have

(EQUATION 25.4)

$$Y = A \times F(\text{labor, capital, natural resources, } \textbf{institutions})$$

Incentives

Institutions can lay the groundwork for natural endogenous growth. With these institutions in place, there are incentives for new technology to emerge and drive growth.

Figure 25.7 shows how institutions can affect the production function, causing it to rise from F_1 to F_2. Notice that the production function shifts up at all points, since institutions affect output across all levels of capital. Consider the shift toward private property rights that has occurred in China since the 1980s. As we discussed in Chapter 24, the shift toward private property rights changed incentives for producers, who now get to keep much of the income from their output. This change created the incentives for the exploding growth we now see in China.

Institutions Determine Incentives

Incentives

We need to consider how institutions affect production decisions. Let's begin with an individual firm's decision to produce. Imagine you are considering whether to open a new website design business. You decide you will start such a business only if you expect to at least break even—that is, your payoff must cover your costs. We can state this common condition as follows:

Voluntary investment and production occur only if *expected payoff* ≥ *costs.*

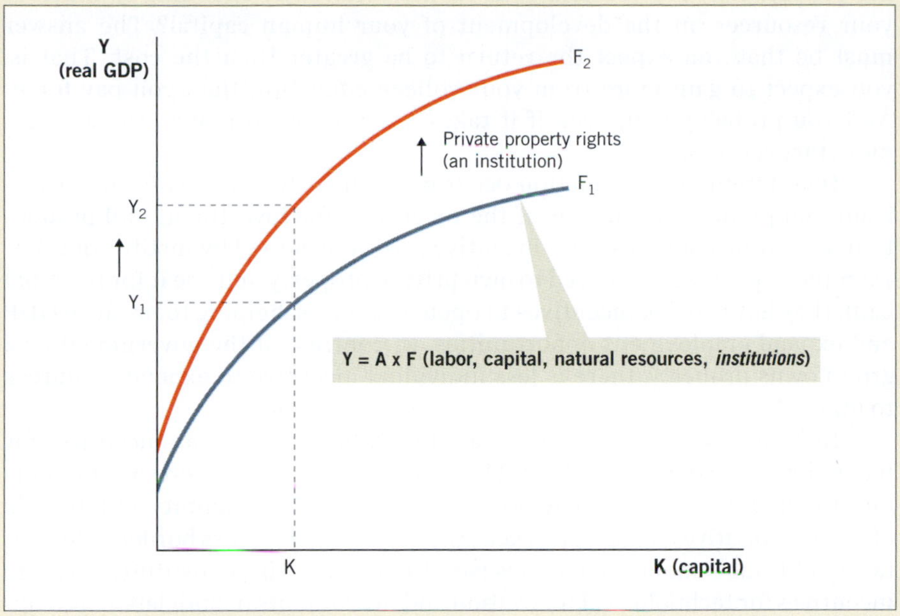

FIGURE 25.7

Efficient Institutions and the Production Function

The adoption of efficient institutions shifts a nation's production function upward. Efficient institutions (such as private property rights, shown here) make it possible for nations to produce more with any given level of resources, and they increase incentives for technological innovation.

The payoffs come later than the costs and are uncertain, which is why we call them *expected payoffs*.

No matter what your output—website design, college gear, cupcakes, or tractors—the payoffs come after production and after sales. The exact time lag depends on the type of output, but payoffs from output come sometime after expenditures on resources. Because of the delay and the resources required, firms need to believe that resource expenditures, including time, patience, and effort, will offer a real payoff in the future.

Institutions make a difference: this is how Shanghai, the financial capital of China, looked in 1990 . . .

. . . and this is how Shanghai looked, just 20 years later, in 2010. The difference: institutional changes based on economic incentives for production and growth.

Or consider your decision to invest in your human capital by attending college. Why are you and your family voluntarily spending so much of your resources on the development of your human capital? The answer must be that you expect the return to be greater than the cost. That is, you expect to gain more from your college education than you pay for it. And you probably will, even if it takes a few years to realize the greatest monetary returns.

Investment and production occur naturally if future payoffs are significant and predictable—that is, if the incentives for investment and production are strong enough. These incentives are determined by institutions. For example, if people are allowed to own private property and use it for personal gain, they have strong incentives to open a business, helping to produce GDP and expand employment opportunities. In contrast, if the government or a group owns property, there is less individual incentive to expend resources to innovate.

Institutions that foster growth are institutions that create incentives for technological change. In Chapter 24, we saw that the institutions most important for growth include private property rights, political stability and the rule of law, competitive and open markets, the flow of funds across borders, efficient taxes, and stable money and prices (see Table 25.2). These institutions create incentives for technological innovation and investments in both labor and capital. Figure 25.8 illustrates this relationship between institutions and economic growth. Institutions create incentives for production and investment. If the right incentives are in place, production and investment occur naturally, and the result is more labor, more capital, and technological advancement—all of which lead to economic growth.

FIGURE 25.8

Institutions, Incentives, and Endogenous Growth

The goal is economic growth, but it all starts with institutions. Institutions provide the incentives that motivate choices made by people in an economy. The right institutions provide incentives for people to invent new technology and to invest in human and physical capital. These actions lead to economic growth.

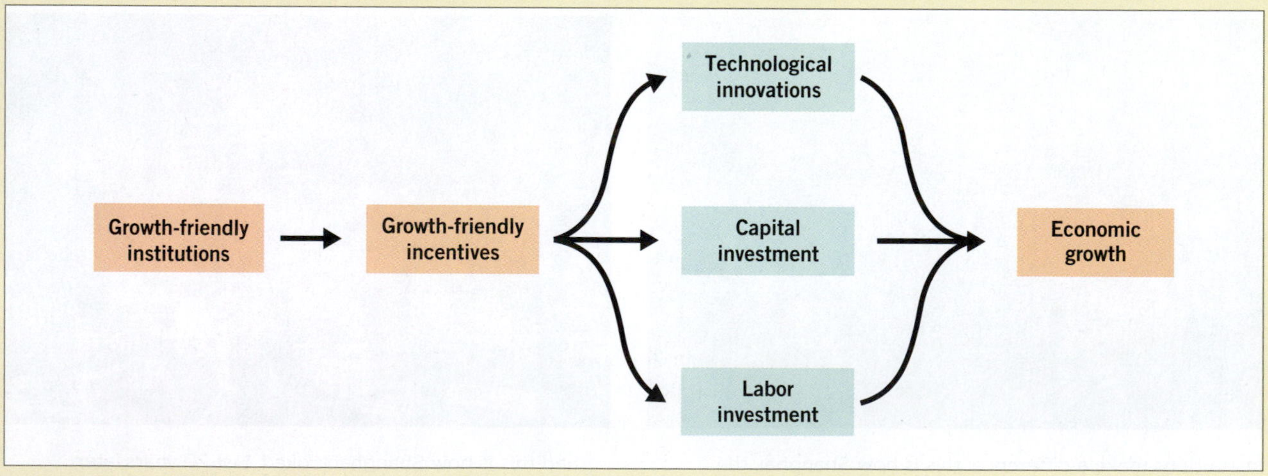

FIGURE 25.9

Institutions That Inhibit Endogenous Growth

People must work and invest today in order to get payoffs from output in the future. Inefficient institutions (such as political instability, corruption, inflation, and high tax rates) reduce the expected future payoffs and thus reduce the incentives for production. Growth-fostering institutions are those that maximize expected future payoffs for producers.

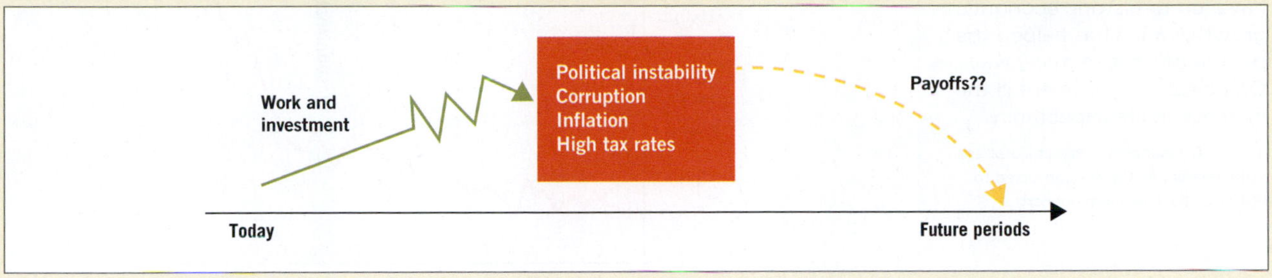

As Daron Acemoglu observed in Nogales, weak or malfunctioning institutions can also act to reduce expected payoffs, through corruption, political instability, high and variable inflation, and high tax rates. A key to sustained growth is to eliminate these barriers. Figure 25.9 illustrates how inefficient institutions impede growth. Because payoffs from productive actions come in the future, anything that reduces the likelihood of these payoffs reduces the incentive for investment today. Resources are not enough. Some nations grow faster due to their institutions. Others grow slowly because of theirs. Unless institutions are the same across nations, we should not expect convergence.

New Growth Theory acknowledges the core truths of the Solow model: resources and technology are sources of economic growth. But it also recognizes the importance of institutions for technological change. This emphasis on institutions matters for policy. For example, international aid, even aid invested in capital goods, cannot lead to growth when corruption and political instability are rampant in the recipient nation. Institutions are the key ingredient to long-run growth.

ECONOMICS IN THE REAL WORLD

CHILE: A MODERN GROWTH MIRACLE

Several nations, after struggling for centuries with little economic growth, have recently begun to grow at impressive rates. The best-known examples are China and India. Not as well known is the recent economic growth in Chile, a country that saw growth even under the rule of a harsh military dictator.

From 1985 to 2016, the growth of real per capita GDP in Chile averaged 3.7%. The rule of 70 (see Chapter 24) tells us that it takes approximately 19 years to double living standards at that rate. In fact, real GDP for Chile rose from just $7,000 per person to over $21,000 per person in the 31 years from 1985 to 2016. You can see this increase in the real per capita GDP shown in panel (a) of Figure 25.10. This is quite a change from Chile's past experience. Chile grew by less than 1% a year from 1900 to 1985.

FIGURE 25.10

Economic Growth and Life Expectancy in Chile

Institutional reforms in Chile have led to historic economic growth, which has helped the people of Chile in many ways. One clear improvement is the increase in life expectancy.

Source: (a) Maddison Project Database, 2018 version. All figures converted to 2010 dollars. (b) Gapminder.org.

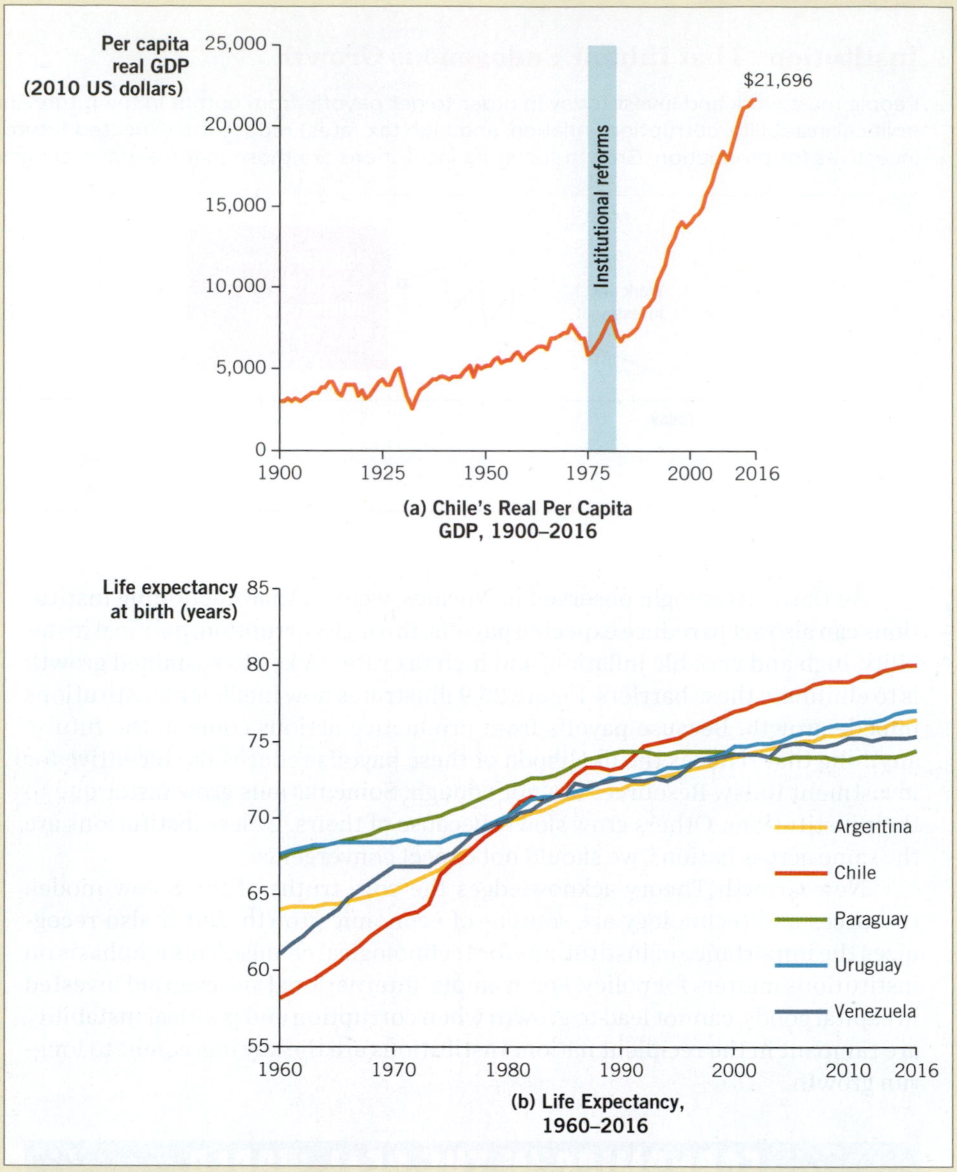

As we have seen, economic growth means many lives change for the better. One vivid indicator of these changes is life expectancy. Panel (b) of Figure 25.10 shows that life expectancy in Chile increased from 58 years in 1960 to 80 years by 2016. This increase of 22 years in average life span moved Chile ahead of many of its Latin American neighbors.

What is the cause of Chile's growth? In a word—institutions. In 1975, Chile began significant economic reforms. In addition to lowering trade barriers and instituting monetary and price stability (inflation was 665% in 1974), the government privatized many state-owned businesses and removed controls on wages and prices. These reforms were put in place during the regime of a particularly brutal dictator, Augusto Pinochet. While Pinochet inflicted much suffering on the Chilean people, the economic results of the institutional changes are still striking.

Chile's recent growth is as breathtaking as the view of Santiago, its capital city.

PRACTICE WHAT YOU KNOW

Solow Growth Theory versus New Growth Theory: What Policy Is Implied?

QUESTION: Below is a list of policy proposals advanced to help the economies of developing nations. Determine whether each proposal is more consistent with the Solow model, New Growth Theory, neither, or both.

a. unrestricted international aid to help build a power plant

b. aid for a power plant, dependent on democratic reforms

c. reductions in trade restrictions

This cargo ship brings goods from Asia to the United States. Which growth model would encourage this kind of international trade?

ANSWER:

a. This policy proposal is consistent with the Solow model: capital leads to growth.

b. This policy proposal is consistent with both Solow and New Growth Theory. The power plant is capital, but the aid is dependent on institutional reform.

c. This policy proposal is consistent with New Growth Theory. Open trade is an institutional reform that leads to greater competition and more options for citizens in developing nations.

· ECONOMICS *for* LIFE ·

Institutions of Growth: Applying for a Patent

- Patent laws create incentives for innovation.
- If you have a patentable idea, you can sell it to others.

Patricia Bath is a medical doctor who also invented the laserphaco probe, a device that uses lasers to remove cataracts. Patented by Dr. Bath in 1988, the probe revolutionized cataract surgery. Inventions like this are technological innovations that, as we have seen, are a source of economic growth.

Patent laws are an important institution that has helped to pave the way for many technological advancements. Patents create a 20-year monopoly for the inventor or owner of the patent. This monopoly is an incentive that encourages innovation. Patent laws are thus an institution that encourages new inventions that shift the economy's production function upward.

If you have an idea that you'd like to patent, you need to apply for your patent through the U.S. Patent Office. In addition to a detailed description of your patent, you'll need to create a drawing that specifies exactly how your idea is new and different. Finally, it is a good idea to hire a patent attorney to edit your patent application so you can reduce the chances that someone will copy your idea later.

Even if you don't have the resources to capitalize on your invention, you can always try to sell your patent to someone who can.

You may not be as successful as Patricia Bath, but you can be sure that patents are a legal way to make monopoly profit.

Patricia Bath is a doctor and inventor.

So, you see, patents are a socially beneficial arrangement, both for those who come up with new ideas and for those whose lives will be improved.

Conclusion

We opened this chapter with the misconception that physical capital is the essential ingredient for economic growth. We have seen that while capital is helpful, physical tools are not enough to ensure long-run growth. Without institutions that provide incentives to produce, sustained growth does not take root.

Many people think macroeconomics is all about business cycles and recessions. Our goal in this chapter has been to present the ideas behind long-run growth theory, rather than short-run cycles. In Chapter 26, we present a model that economists use to study short-run business cycles. ✷

- ANSWERING *the* BIG QUESTIONS -

How do macroeconomic theories evolve?

- Macroeconomic theories evolve in relationship to observations in the real world. Policies often follow from theory. Policies produce results, which in turn influence revisions of economic theory.

What is the Solow growth model?

- The Solow growth model is a model of economic growth based on a production function for the economy.
- The key feature of the production function is diminishing returns.
- The Solow growth model posits that diminishing returns lead economies toward a zero-growth steady state.
- The Solow growth model further posits that given steady states, economies tend to converge over time.

How does technology affect growth?

- Technology is a source of sustained economic growth.
- In the Solow model, technology is exogenous.

Why are institutions the key to economic growth?

- New Growth Theory emphasizes that institutions are the key source of economic growth.
- Institutions determine incentives for production.
- Efficient institutions can lead to endogenous growth.

CHAPTER PROBLEMS

Concepts You Should Know

aggregate production function (p. 805)
convergence (p. 811)
depreciation (p. 811)
diminishing marginal product (p. 807)
endogenous growth (p. 819)
exogenous growth (p. 816)
marginal product (p. 807)
net investment (p. 811)
New Growth Theory (p. 819)
production function (p. 804)
steady state (p. 810)

Questions for Review

1. Modern economic theory points to three sources of economic growth. What are these three sources? Give an example of each.
2. About 50 years ago, Robert Solow formulated a simple model of economic growth. What are the two key properties of the aggregate production function at the center of Solow's first contribution?
3. Explain why a nation cannot continue to grow forever by just adding more capital.
4. The Solow model assumes that technological changes are exogenous. What does the term "exogenous" mean? Why does the assumption of exogenous technological change matter for growth policy? What does this assumption imply about growth rates across nations over time?
5. China is a land of vast resources. In addition, technology is easily transportable across international borders. If we rule out these two sources of growth, to what can we attribute the economic growth in China since 1979?
6. The basic Solow growth model implies convergence. What is convergence? What key assumption about the marginal product of capital implies convergence?
7. How can an increase in educational opportunities increase growth? Use a graph to illustrate how educational opportunities affect a nation's production function.
8. Robert Solow formulated a model that still serves as the basis for growth theory.
   a. What is the steady state of an economy, and what key piece of the Solow model implies that the steady state is an inevitable outcome?
   b. Explain the concept of convergence in growth theory. What has been the general experience with regard to convergence across the globe in the years since the Solow papers were published?
9. New Growth Theory uses the basic Solow production function as a starting point, but the emphasis is much different.
   a. What is the key theoretical distinction between New Growth Theory and the Solow growth model?
   b. How does this one difference affect policy recommendations?
10. Explain why the lack of economic growth in North Korea is best understood in the context of New Growth Theory, rather than the Solow model.
11. Diminishing marginal productivity is a key assumption in growth theory, beginning with Solow's model. Name the two important implications of this assumption in the Solow model.

Study Problems *(✷ solved at the end of the section)*

1. The Solow model focuses on how resources affect output. In this chapter, we focused on capital.
   a. Name the other two major categories of resources.
   b. Draw an aggregate production function with a typical shape; label this function F.
   c. Draw a second production function that indicates a technological advancement; label this new function F_1.
2. Define human capital. Draw a graph that illustrates an increase in effective labor on a production function.

3. Suppose the people in the United States increase their savings rate. How will this change affect the rate of economic growth in the United States?

* **4.** TheThe Solow model is still at the core of New Growth Theory.

a. Draw an aggregate production function for a hypothetical nation. Draw the production function as we do in this chapter, with an emphasis on the capital resource. Label both axes and label your production function F_0.

b. Suppose several million new workers enter the nation. Show this change on your graph in part (a), carefully distinguishing the new situation from the old. If you have a new production function, label it F_1.

c. Now suppose the nation invests in new capital, increasing the total capital stock in the nation. Show this change on your graph in part (b), carefully distinguishing the new situation from the old.

* **5.** The following list describes policy proposals advanced to help the economies of developing nations. Determine whether each proposal is consistent with the Solow model, New Growth Theory, both, or neither.

a. microfinance (very small short-term loans for small businesses)

b. a system of private property rights

c. international governmental loans to build a shoe factory

d. international aid for a power plant based on objective corruption controls

e. unrestricted international aid to build roads

f. low tax rates

6. Robinson Crusoe is alone on an island. His GDP is the fish he produces using fishing poles (capital). The table below shows how his weekly fish output varies across different numbers of fishing poles.

Fishing poles	Fish per week	MPK
0	0	____
1	30	____
2	40	____
3	48	____

a. Fill in the blanks in the third column with the marginal product of capital for all units for which this is computable.

b. Assume Crusoe reaches a steady state at 2 fishing poles. Describe the investment, if any, that Crusoe undertakes once he has 2 fishing poles, assuming no technological changes. Be careful with your terminology here.

c. Suppose Crusoe, through new ideas, is able to increase his output by 2% per week. How many weeks will it take for Crusoe to increase his output from 40 fish per week to 80 fish per week?

7. The aggregate production function is at the very center of growth theory.

a. Plot an aggregate production function with its typical shape. Be sure to label both axes. Label this function F_0.

b. Suppose we discover massive new oil reserves under central Virginia. On the graph you drew in part (a), show how this oil discovery changes the production function. Label the new production function F_1.

Solved Problems

4. a. The key here is to label the graph correctly and have a declining slope.

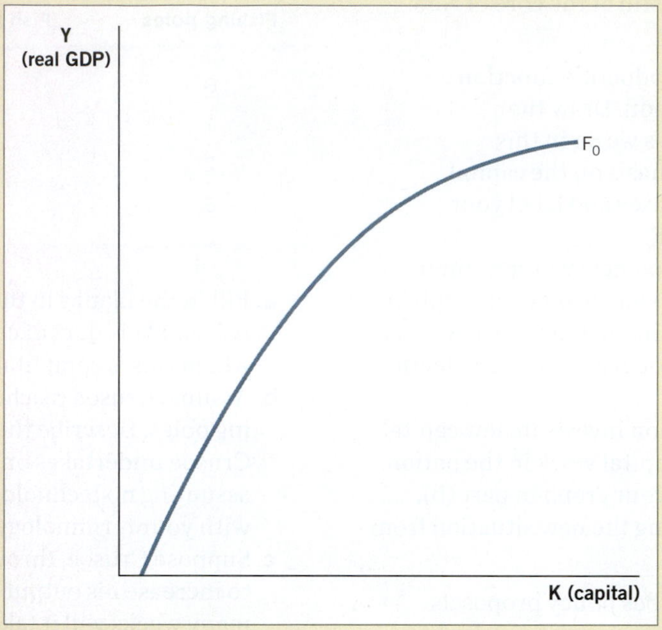

b. The key here is to shift the graph upward. More workers mean more total output because the nation now has more resources.

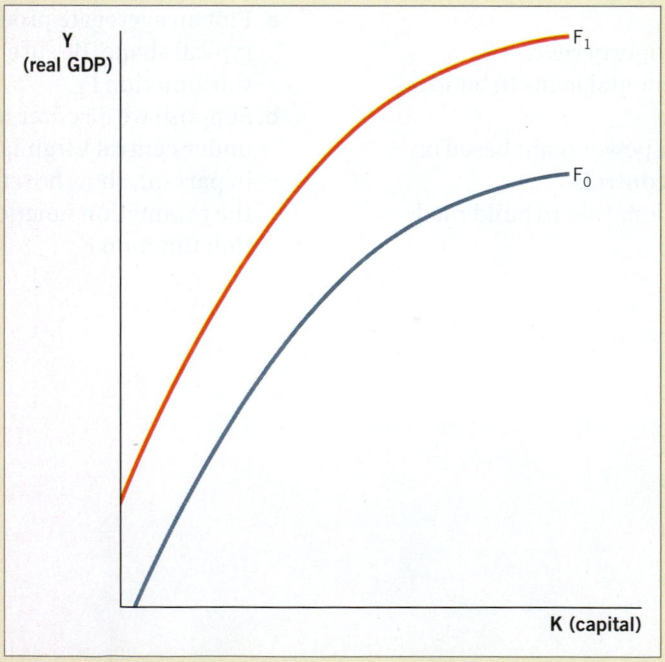

c. The key here is that there is a movement along a given production function, from K_0 to K_1.

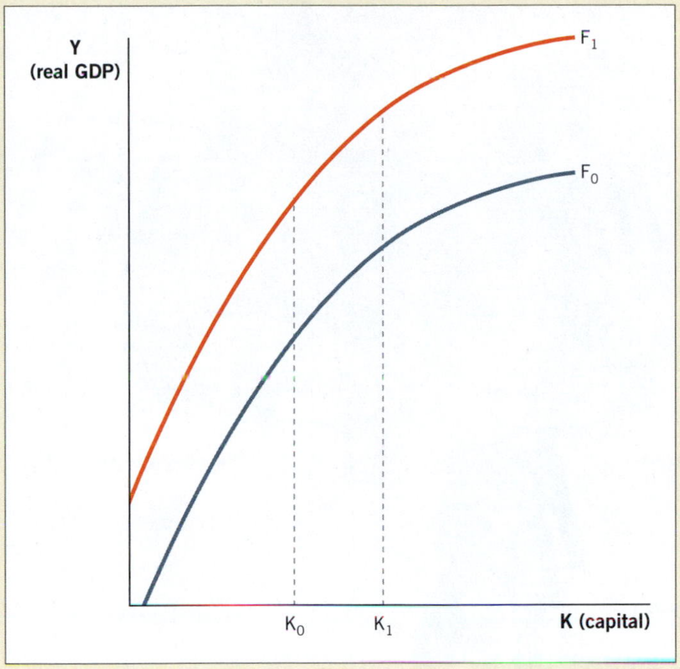

5. a. New Growth Theory or else neither (either answer is defensible): Microfinance loans might help small businesses, and it is possible that the introduction of microfinance could be considered an institutional change. However, if other political and economic institutions are not conducive to growth, microfinance will not be enough.

b. New Growth Theory: Private property rights are an institution shown to foster growth but would not have been relevant before institutions were incorporated into New Growth Theory.

c. Solow: Loans for capital development are a direct policy proposal from the Solow growth model.

d. Both: Here the focus is on capital *along with* institutional changes.

e. Solow: Here the emphasis is solely on capital.

f. New Growth Theory: Low tax rates are an institution focused on growth.

CHAPTER

26 The Aggregate Demand–Aggregate Supply Model

The Economy Does Not Follow a Predictable Cycle of Expansion and Contraction.

In March 2020, the global economy fell off a cliff, plunged into turmoil by the coronavirus pandemic. Prior to the outbreak, the American economy had been in its longest expansion on record, with the unemployment rate below 4%. Then output plummeted, and the unemployment rate rose to almost 15% by April. Oddly, some analysts had been warning in the months prior of an impending recession. While they didn't foresee a pandemic, they predicted a downturn simply because it had been so long since the last recession.

Many consider the pattern of economic ups and downs to be inevitable. The term "business cycle" is a popular way to describe the recession-expansion phenomenon, because so many people are convinced that the recession-expansion pattern occurs in a regular cycle. Yet, despite recent turmoil, recessions are relatively rare. While there have been 23 U.S. recessions since 1900, with the declaration of a recession in 2020 as a result of the coronavirus pandemic, there have still been only four since 1982. Complicating matters, no two recessions are exactly alike in cause or effect.

If your interest in macroeconomics stems from a desire to learn more about recessions and their causes, this is

The emergence of the coronavirus (COVID-19) and subsequent orders to stay at home led to a massive decrease in business activity in 2020. By mid-March, the normally bustling Oculus transit hub in New York City was almost empty.

the chapter for you. In this chapter we focus on short-run fluctuations in the macroeconomy and build a model that helps us understand why they happen. This model will also help us see how the three big macroeconomic variables discussed in earlier chapters, namely GDP, unemployment, and inflation, fit together.

· BIG QUESTIONS ·

- What is the aggregate demand–aggregate supply model?
- What is aggregate demand?
- What is aggregate supply?
- How does the aggregate demand–aggregate supply model help us understand the economy?

What Is the Aggregate Demand–Aggregate Supply Model?

In macroeconomics, there are two major paths of study. One direction explores long-run growth and development. The second direction examines short-run fluctuations, or business cycles. The two paths are complementary: both study GDP growth, employment, and the people, firms, and governments that impact the economy. But they are certainly distinct: growth economics focuses on theories and policies that affect economic progress over several decades, whereas business cycle theory typically focuses on time horizons of five years or less.

In Chapter 19, we presented the idea of a basic business cycle, in which real GDP increases for a while during the expansionary phase and then decreases during the contractionary, or recessionary, phase. The business cycle is most evident in real GDP growth and unemployment rates. During recessions, real GDP growth slows and the unemployment rate rises. During expansions, real GDP growth expands and the unemployment rate falls.

Panel (a) of Figure 26.1 shows real GDP growth rates by quarter for the United States from 1990 to 2021. The blue vertical bars indicate four recessions during this period. During each recession, real GDP growth slowed and even turned negative. The first year of the COVID-19 pandemic, 2020, saw a brief, startling plunge in GDP in the second quarter, followed by a dramatic bounce-back in the third. Panel (b) plots the unemployment rate over the same period. The unemployment

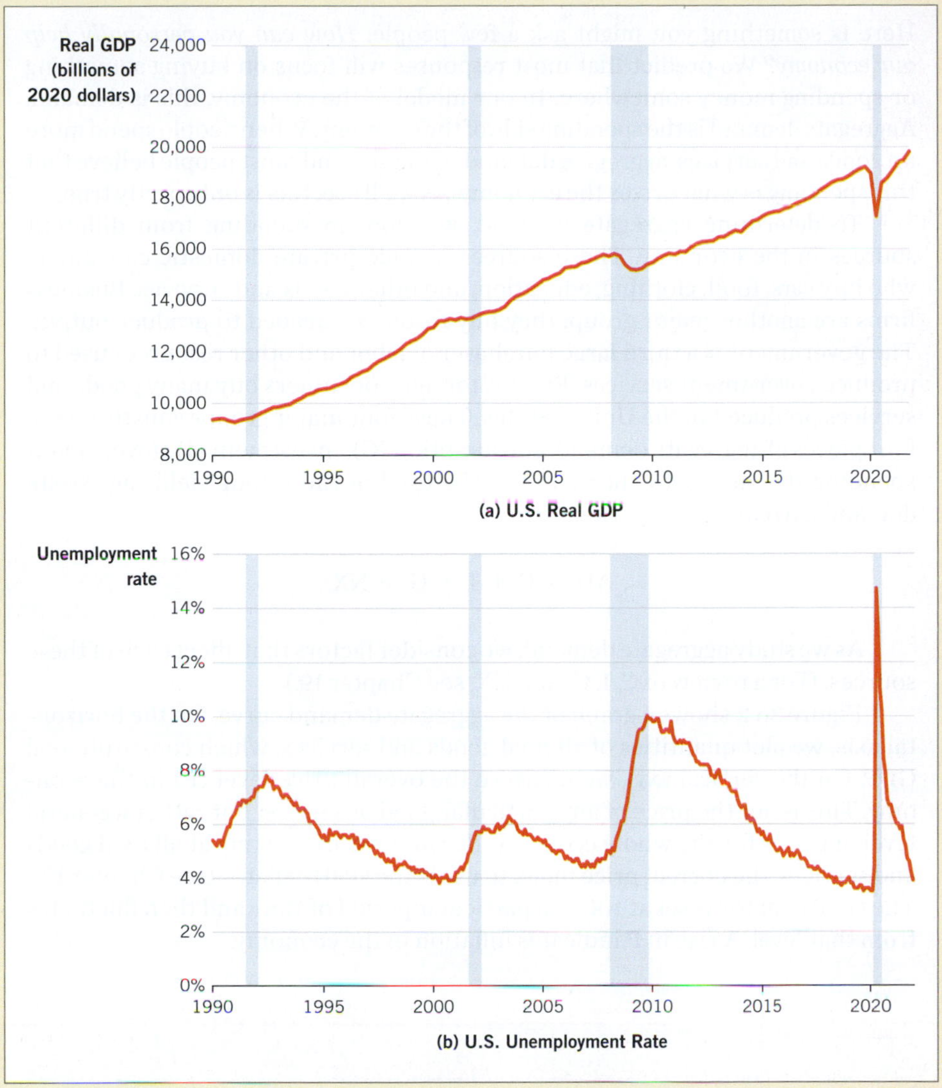

FIGURE 26.1

U.S. Real GDP Growth, Unemployment Rates, and Recessions, 1990–2021

Business cycles are readily observable in real GDP and unemployment rates. Panel (a) shows that real GDP plateaus or declines during recessions. Panel (b) shows how the unemployment rate spikes during recessions, then gradually falls as the economy expands.

Sources: (a) U.S. Bureau of Economic Analysis; (b) U.S. Bureau of Labor Statistics.

rate rose sharply during each of the recessions and then fell afterward. The highest unemployment rate during this period was 14.7% in April 2020.

The model we use to study business cycles is the aggregate demand–aggregate (AD–AS) supply model. At the core of the model are the familiar concepts of demand and supply. In earlier chapters, we looked at the demand and supply of a single good, like pizza or gasoline. Now we consider demand and supply of all final goods and services in an economy—the demand for and supply of GDP. **Aggregate demand** is the total demand for final goods and services in an economy. **Aggregate supply** is the total supply of final goods and services in an economy. The word "aggregate" means total.

Aggregate demand is the total demand for final goods and services in an economy.

Aggregate supply is the total supply of final goods and services in an economy.

We consider each side of the economy separately before bringing them together. The next section explains aggregate demand, and then we turn to aggregate supply.

What Is Aggregate Demand?

Here is something you might ask a few people: *How can you personally help our economy?* We predict that most responses will focus on buying something or spending money somewhere. In our model of the economy, this is demand. Aggregate demand is the spending side of the economy. When people spend more on goods and services, aggregate demand increases, and most people believe that this spending is what drives the economy. As we'll see, this is only partly true.

To determine aggregate demand, we sum up spending from different sources in the economy. These sources include private domestic consumers who buy cars, food, clothing, education, and other goods and services. Business firms are another major group; they buy resources needed to produce output. The government is a third large purchaser of labor and other resources used to produce government services. Finally, foreign consumers buy many goods and services produced in the United States. These four major groups constitute the four pieces of aggregate demand: consumption (C), investment (I), government spending (G), and net exports (NX). The total of these four yields aggregate demand (AD) in a given period:

(EQUATION 26.1)

$$AD = C + I + G + NX$$

As we study aggregate demand, we consider factors that affect each of these sources. (For a review of C, I, G, and NX, see Chapter 19.)

Figure 26.2 shows a graph of the aggregate demand curve. On the horizontal axis, we plot quantities of all final goods and services, which constitute real GDP. On the vertical axis, we measure the overall price level (P) in the economy. This is not the price of any particular good or service, but rather a general level of prices for the whole economy. Because we are looking at all final goods and services, the correct price index to use is the GDP deflator (see Chapter 19). The GDP deflator is set at 100 in a particular period of time and then fluctuates from that level. A rise in P indicates inflation in the economy.

FIGURE 26.2

The Aggregate Demand Curve

The aggregate demand curve shows the negative relationship between the quantity demanded of real GDP and the economy's price level (P).

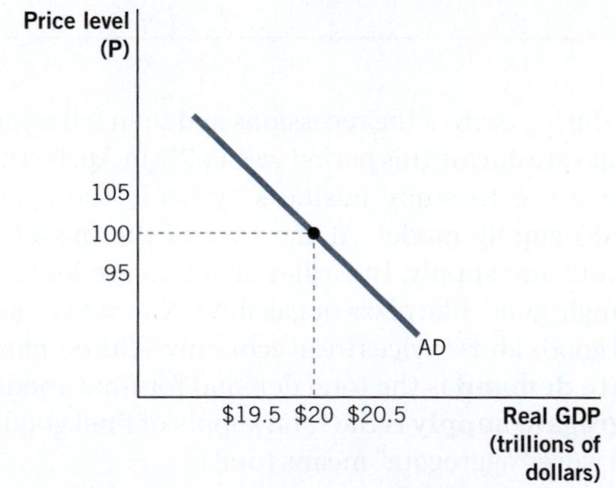

On the graph in Figure 26.2, we have labeled a particular point where the price level is 100 and the quantity of aggregate demand is $20 trillion. The negative slope of the aggregate demand curve means that increases in the price level lead to decreases in the quantity of aggregate demand. When the price level falls, the quantity of aggregate demand rises. But be careful here: aggregate demand does not slope downward for the same reason that individual demand curves slope downward. In the next section, we explain the reasons for the negative slope of the aggregate demand curve.

The Slope of the Aggregate Demand Curve

All else equal, increases in the price level lead to decreases in the quantity of aggregate demand. You might agree with this statement without closely evaluating it, because it sounds like the relationship between the quantity demanded of a single good and its price. But now we are evaluating the whole economy. Remember that the price level is the general price level of all final goods and services. Aggregate demand and aggregate supply don't just measure the quantity of pizzas demanded and supplied; they measure the production of all the firms in all the markets that constitute the economy. Therefore, substitutions from one market to another have no effect on the total amount of output, or real GDP. Substituting out of pizza and into chicken nuggets doesn't change GDP.

There are three reasons for this negative relationship between the quantity of aggregate demand and the price level: the wealth effect, the interest rate effect, and the international trade effect.

Wealth
is the net value of one's accumulated assets.

The **wealth effect** is the change in the quantity of aggregate demand that results from wealth changes due to price-level changes.

THE WEALTH EFFECT If you wake up tomorrow morning and all prices have suddenly doubled, you'll be poorer in real terms than you are today. Because your *wealth* has fallen, you'll likely consume less. **Wealth** is the net value of one's accumulated assets. Your wealth is the total net value of everything you own, including the money in your wallet and in your bank accounts. The **wealth effect** is the change in the quantity of aggregate demand that results from wealth changes due to price-level changes.

For example, if you and your friends have $60 to buy pizza, you can afford to buy four $15 pizzas. But if inflation causes the price of a pizza to rise to $20, you can afford only three pizzas. Similarly, a rise in prices all over the economy reduces real wealth in the economy, and then the quantity of aggregate demand falls. In contrast, if prices fall, real wealth increases, and then the quantity of aggregate demand also increases.

If you hold money as part of your wealth, the price level affects its real value.

THE INTEREST RATE EFFECT If the price level rises and real wealth falls, people also save less. Therefore, in addition to the wealth effect, an increase in the price level affects people's savings. Let's say you are on a budget that allows you to buy groceries and save a little each month. If the price level rises, you'll probably cut back on both areas. When you spend less on groceries, your actions are reflecting the wealth effect.

The **interest rate effect** occurs when a change in the price level leads to a change in interest rates and therefore in the quantity of aggregate demand.

The **international trade effect** occurs when a change in the price level leads to a change in the quantity of net exports demanded.

When you cut back on savings, your action leads to the interest rate effect. The **interest rate effect** occurs when a change in the price level leads to a change in interest rates and therefore in the quantity of aggregate demand. Remember that every dollar borrowed requires a dollar saved. Therefore, when savings decline, the quantity of investment declines, and this is part of aggregate demand.

Figure 26.3 shows the loanable funds market before and after a decrease in savings. Initially, the demand and supply of loanable funds are indicated by curves D and S_1, and the equilibrium interest rate is 3%. If the economy's price level rises, people save less, which shifts supply to S_2. The reduction in supply leads to a higher interest rate of 4%, at which point the quantity of investment falls from I_1 to I_2. Because investment is one piece of aggregate demand, a decrease in investment decreases overall aggregate demand. Thus, a change in the price level initiates a cascade of events with the result that firms invest less at higher interest rates because individuals are saving less.

Jeep Grand Cherokee: produced in Detroit, Michigan.

THE INTERNATIONAL TRADE EFFECT When we draw our aggregate demand curve, the price level and real GDP represent those from the domestic market—in this case the United States. In the context of the world economy, we must also consider U.S. prices *relative to* the prices from other countries. When the U.S. price level rises, all else equal, U.S. goods are relatively more expensive than goods from other countries, and the quantity demanded of U.S. goods falls. The **international trade effect** occurs when a change in the price level leads to a change in the quantity of net exports demanded.

FIGURE 26.3

The Interest Rate Effect in the Loanable Funds Market

If the economy's price level rises, people save less. The decline in savings from S_1 to S_2 leads to an increase in the interest rate from 3% to 4%. At this higher interest rate, the quantity of investment falls from I_1 to I_2 because investment is more costly. Because investment is a component of aggregate demand, a fall in equilibrium investment that occurs with a rise in price level causes the quantity of aggregate demand to fall.

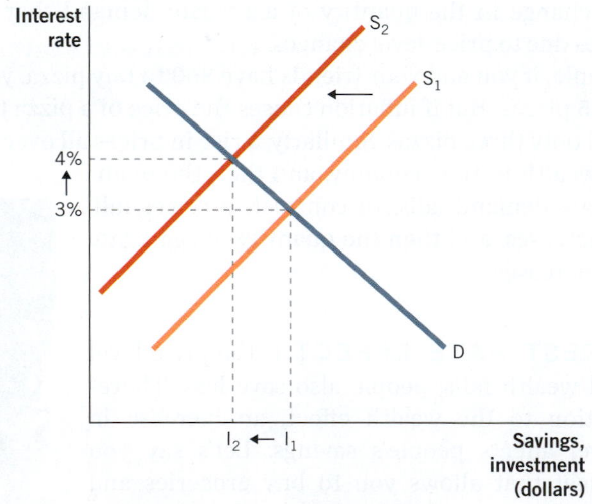

Consider two similar sport utility vehicles: a Jeep Grand Cherokee and a Toyota 4Runner. The Jeep is produced in the United States in Detroit, Michigan. The Toyota is produced in a suburb of Tahara, Aichi, Japan. When the prices of U.S. goods rise relative to the prices of Japanese goods, consumers are more likely to choose the Toyota, so U.S. exports fall and imports rise.

Toyota 4Runner: produced in Tahara, Aichi, Japan.

Figure 26.4 shows all three effects working together to affect the quantity of aggregate demand. Each begins with a change in the economy's price level. When the price level rises from 100 to 110, consumption (C) declines from the wealth effect, investment (I) declines via the interest rate effect, and net exports (NX) fall due to the international trade effect. In reality, the three effects do not influence aggregate demand equally. The international trade effect is relatively small because exports are a relatively small part of GDP. Because consumption is by far the largest component of GDP, the wealth effect is the most significant.

It is important to distinguish between *shifts in* the aggregate demand curve versus *movements along* the aggregate demand curve. In this section, we have identified three effects related to movements along the aggregate demand curve. These all originate with a change in the economy's price level. In contrast, shifts in the demand curve occur when people demand more, or fewer, goods and services at any given price level. These shifts can come from any of the components of aggregate demand: consumption, investment, government spending, or net exports. In the next section, we consider the factors that shift the aggregate demand curve.

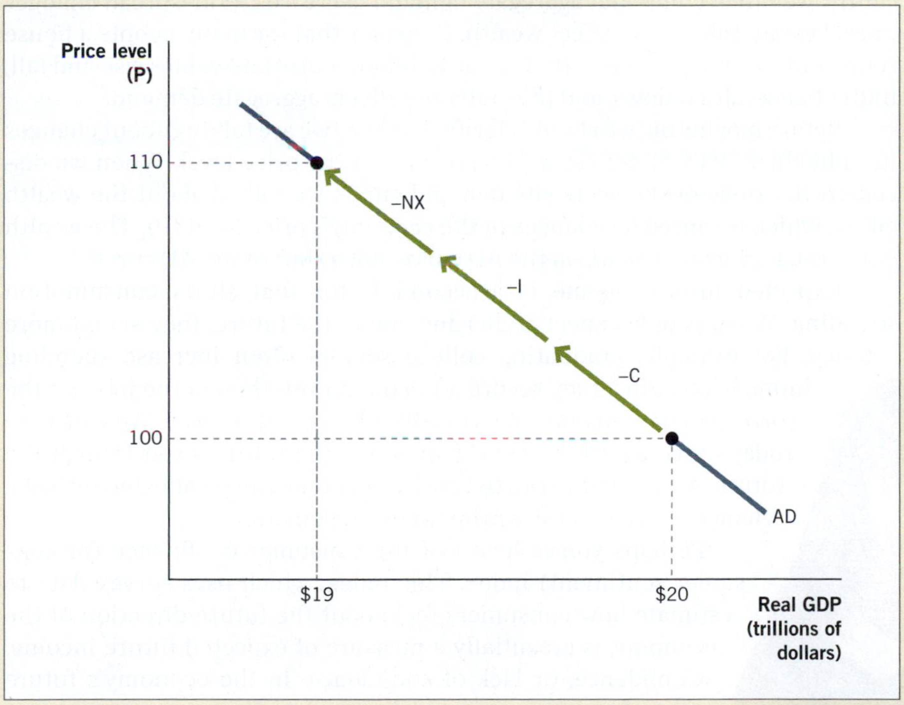

FIGURE 26.4

The Slope of the Aggregate Demand Curve

When the price level rises, the quantity of aggregate demand falls. This negative relationship is due to three different effects: (1) the wealth effect implies a lower quantity of consumption (C) demand because real wealth falls at higher price levels; (2) the interest rate effect implies a lower quantity of investment (I) demand due to higher interest rates; (3) the international trade effect implies a lower quantity of net export (NX) demand due to relatively higher domestic prices. Each effect focuses on a different component of aggregate demand.

Median home prices fell from $248,000 to $222,000 between 2007 and 2010. That roughly 10% drop led to a significant decrease in many people's wealth, as well as a decline in aggregate demand.

Shifts in Aggregate Demand

When people demand more goods and services at all price levels, aggregate demand increases and the AD curve shifts to the right. When people demand fewer goods and services at all price levels, aggregate demand decreases and the AD curve shifts to the left.

In thinking about the many factors that shift aggregate demand, it is helpful to categorize them into the different types of aggregate demand spending: consumption (C), investment (I), government spending (G), and net exports (NX). We begin with factors that cause changes in consumption spending.

SHIFTS IN CONSUMPTION Consumption spending accounts for about 70% of all spending in GDP. In this section, we cover three factors that shift consumption spending. The first is people's current wealth. Imagine for a moment that your wealth increased overnight. If your great-aunt died and left you $1 million, you'd increase your consumption spending: you'd eat out more often, upgrade your wardrobe, and maybe even shop for some bigger-ticket items. This observation also applies to entire nations. When national wealth increases, the consumption component of aggregate demand increases. When wealth falls, consumption declines.

For example, many people own stocks or mutual funds that are tied to the stock market. So when the stock market fluctuates, the wealth of a large portion of the population is affected. When overall stock values rise, wealth increases, which increases aggregate demand. However, if the stock market falls significantly, wealth declines and aggregate demand decreases. Widespread changes in real estate values also affect wealth. Consider that for many people a house represents a large portion of their wealth. When real estate values rise and fall, individual wealth follows, and this outcome affects aggregate demand.

Before moving on, we should clarify that here we are talking about changes in individuals' wealth *not* caused by changes in the price level. When we discussed the slope of the aggregate demand curve, we talked about the wealth effect, which is caused by changes in the economy's price level (P). The wealth effect causes a *movement along* the AD curve, not a shift of the AD curve.

Expected future income is a second factor that shifts consumption spending. When people expect higher income in the future, they spend more today. For example, graduating college seniors often increase spending immediately after they secure a job offer, even though the job and the corresponding income are typically a few months away. We consume today based on what we anticipate for the future, even though the future is uncertain. Still, the entire economy can be affected by just a change in the general sentiment of consumers.

How much income does your future hold?

Perhaps you've heard of the consumer confidence (or consumer sentiment) index. This index, which uses survey data to estimate how consumers feel about the future direction of the economy, is essentially a measure of expected future income. Confidence, or lack of confidence, in the economy's future changes consumer spending today. Consumer confidence can swing up and down with unpredictable events such as national elections or international turmoil. When these sentiments change, they change consumption spending and shift the aggregate demand curve.

Finally, taxes also affect consumption spending. When consumers pay lower taxes, they can afford to spend more. When taxes rise, consumers have less to spend. In Chapter 29, we cover the effect of taxes on consumption in greater detail. For now, we note that higher taxes lead to lower consumption and lower aggregate demand.

SHIFTS IN INVESTMENT In this section, we consider four factors that shift investment demand. Investment shifts when decision-makers at firms decide to increase or decrease spending on capital goods. One possibility is that business firm confidence changes. Keep in mind that in macroeconomics, business firms are the investors, when they spend on plant and equipment used in future production. When firms decide that the future of their industry or the overall economy is positive, they might decide to purchase tools to increase production and future profits. On the other hand, decreases in business firm confidence lead to decreases in investment and decreases in aggregate demand.

Interest rates also shift investment demand. An increase in interest rates makes investment more expensive for firms, decreasing aggregate demand. In contrast, lower interest rates decrease the cost of borrowing for firms and increase the investment component of aggregate demand. While we typically focus on investment effects from interest rate changes, consumption is also affected by changes in interest rates. At lower interest rates, the return to savings falls and so consumers are more likely to spend their income.

Increases in the quantity of money in an economy also increase aggregate demand through investment. All else equal, more money leads to lower interest rates in the economy. Lower interest rates then mean that firms can borrow more cheaply. As a result, investment demand expands. On the other hand, if the money supply decreases, interest rates rise and investment demand falls. This relationship between money and aggregate demand is sometimes more complicated than explained here. For this reason, Chapter 31 is devoted to the effects of money changes on the economy.

PRACTICE WHAT YOU KNOW

Aggregate Demand: Shifts in Aggregate Demand versus Movements along the Aggregate Demand Curve

One of the challenges in applying the aggregate demand–aggregate supply model is distinguishing shifts in aggregate demand from movements along the aggregate demand curve. Here we present four scenarios.

QUESTION: Does each scenario below cause a movement along the curve or a shift in the curve? Explain your response each time.

1. Consumers read positive economic news and then expect strong future economic growth.

(CONTINUED)

Textile workers in Nicaragua depend on the export economy as a source of jobs.

2. Due to an increase in the price level in the United States, consumers substitute out of clothes made in the United States and into clothes made in Nicaragua.
3. Several European economies go into recession.
4. A decrease in the price level leads to greater real wealth and more savings, which reduces the interest rate and increases investment.

ANSWERS:

1. This scenario involves an increase in expected future income, which increases aggregate demand and causes a positive (rightward) shift in the curve.
2. This scenario begins with a change in the price level, so we know it will involve a movement along the curve. Here the price level rises, so it is a movement back along the curve, signaling a decrease in the quantity of aggregate demand.
3. Foreign recession leads to lower foreign income and wealth, an outcome that decreases the demand for goods and services made in the United States. Less demand for U.S. products causes a decrease in aggregate demand in the United States, leading to a negative (leftward) shift in the aggregate demand curve.
4. Because this scenario involves a change in the price level, it will lead to a movement along the aggregate demand curve. In this case, the lower prices lead to the interest rate effect and an increase in the quantity of aggregate demand.

SHIFTS IN GOVERNMENT SPENDING Government spending is the third category of aggregate demand, and the piece that policymakers influence most directly. For example, when federal or state governments increase spending to build a new highway, aggregate demand increases. When government spending falls, aggregate demand decreases. Often, these changes are a result of policy decisions made in direct response to economic conditions. For example, if consumption and investment spending fall, the government may increase spending to counteract the decline in aggregate demand. Chapter 29 covers this topic more extensively.

SHIFTS IN NET EXPORTS The fourth and final piece of aggregate demand is net exports. This category of demand shifts in response to changes in foreign income and the value of the U.S. dollar.

When the income of people in foreign nations grows, their demand for U.S. goods increases. The result is an increase in U.S. net exports, which are the final component of aggregate demand. In contrast, if a foreign nation goes into recession, its demand for U.S. goods and services falls. One recent positive example is the growth of large emerging economies and their demand for U.S. goods. As Brazil, China, and India have grown wealthier, their demand for U.S. goods and services has increased.

Exchange rates are another factor that shifts aggregate demand by changing net exports. We cover exchange rates fully in Chapter 33. For now, think in terms of the value of the dollar in world markets. When the value of the dollar rises relative to the currency of other nations, Americans find that imports are

FIGURE 26.5

Factors That Shift the Aggregate Demand Curve

The aggregate demand curve shifts to the right with *increases* in real wealth, expected future income, business firm confidence, the quantity of money, government spending, and foreign income, or with a *decrease* in taxes, interest rates, and the value of the dollar. The aggregate demand curve shifts to the left with *decreases* in real wealth, expected future income, business firm confidence, the quantity of money, government spending, and foreign income, or with an *increase* in taxes, interest rates, and the value of the dollar.

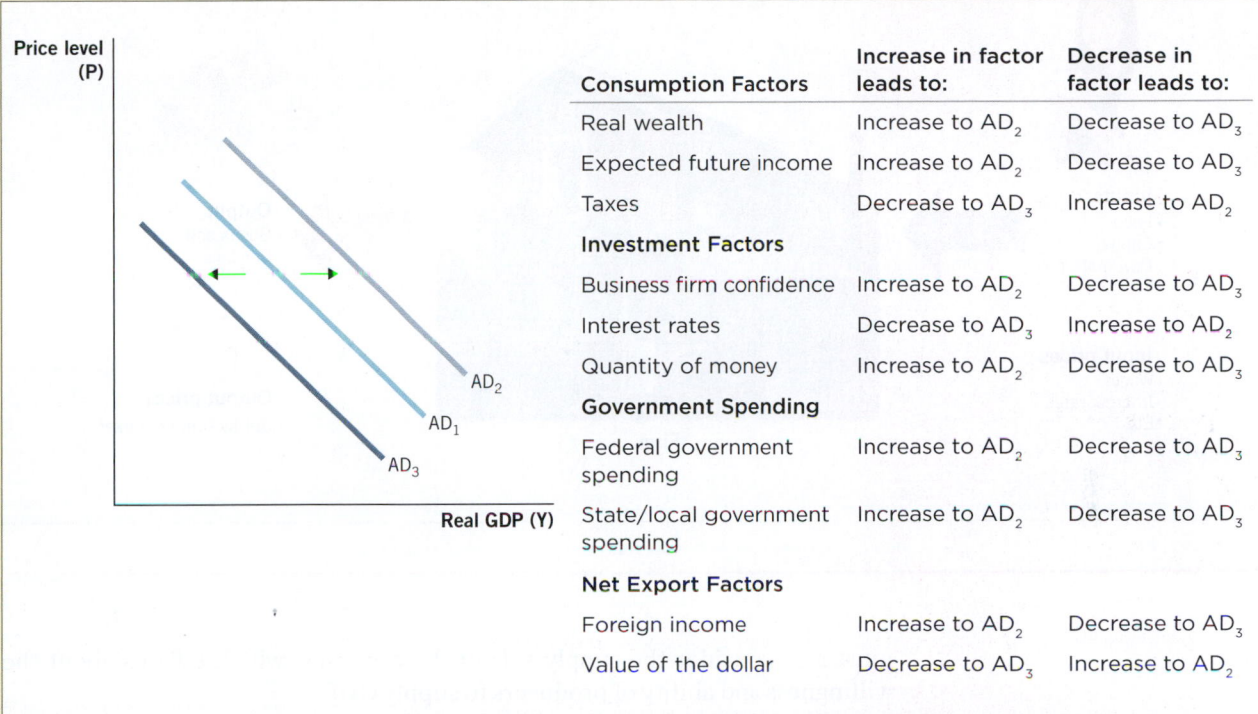

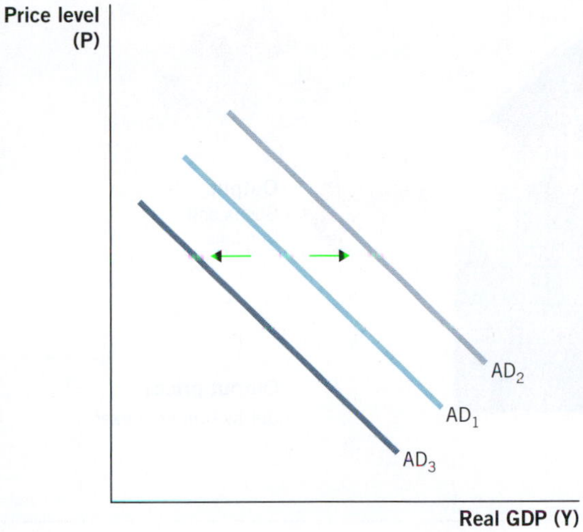

Consumption Factors	Increase in factor leads to:	Decrease in factor leads to:
Real wealth	Increase to AD_2	Decrease to AD_3
Expected future income	Increase to AD_2	Decrease to AD_3
Taxes	Decrease to AD_3	Increase to AD_2
Investment Factors		
Business firm confidence	Increase to AD_2	Decrease to AD_3
Interest rates	Decrease to AD_3	Increase to AD_2
Quantity of money	Increase to AD_2	Decrease to AD_3
Government Spending		
Federal government spending	Increase to AD_2	Decrease to AD_3
State/local government spending	Increase to AD_2	Decrease to AD_3
Net Export Factors		
Foreign income	Increase to AD_2	Decrease to AD_3
Value of the dollar	Decrease to AD_3	Increase to AD_2

less expensive. At the same time, it becomes more expensive for other nations to buy U.S. exports. These two factors combine to reduce net exports, so a stronger dollar leads to a decline in net exports, which reduces aggregate demand.

Figure 26.5 summarizes the effects of the four categories of factors that shift aggregate demand. On the graph, initial aggregate demand is shown as AD_1. Aggregate demand shifts to the right (to AD_2) with *increases* in consumption, investment, government spending, or net exports. In contrast, aggregate demand shifts to the left (to AD_3) with *decreases* in consumption, investment, government spending, or net exports.

What Is Aggregate Supply?

We have seen that aggregate demand embodies the spending desires of an economy. It tells us how many goods and services people want to buy at different price levels. But peoples' wants and desires alone do not determine GDP. We

FIGURE 26.6

The Function of the Firm

The firm uses inputs, or factors of production, to produce its output in a particular way. Input prices, such as wages for workers, affect the firm's costs. Output prices affect the firm's revenue.

must also consider the supply side of the economy, which tells us about the willingness and ability of producers to supply GDP.

Most of us relate easily to the demand side because we buy things all the time. To understand the supply side, we need to consider the perspective of those who produce and sell goods and services. For example, imagine you own a coffee shop where you produce drinks such as espressos, lattes, and iced coffee. Your inputs include workers, coffee beans, milk, water, and espresso machines. You buy inputs and combine them in a particular way to produce your output.

Figure 26.6 presents an overview of the basic function of the firm. In the middle is the firm, where inputs are turned into output. The input prices, such as wages and interest rates on loans, help determine the firm's costs. The output prices, such as the cost of an espresso, determine the firm's revenue.

In macroeconomics, the **long run** is a period of time sufficient for all prices to adjust.

In macroeconomics, the **short run** is the period of time in which some prices have not yet adjusted.

To understand aggregate supply, we need to consider how changes in the overall price level (P) affect the supply decisions of the firm. But the influence of the price level on aggregate supply depends on the time frame. The **long run** in macroeconomics is a period of time sufficient for all prices to adjust. The long run doesn't arrive after a set period of time; it arrives when all prices have adjusted. In the **short run**, some prices change but others take more time. In macroeconomics, the short run is the period of time in which some prices have not yet adjusted.

Long-Run Aggregate Supply

As we've discussed several times in this text, the long-run output of an economy depends on resources, technology, and institutions. The short run may bring fluctuations in real GDP, but in the long run the economy moves toward full-employment output (Y^*). The price level does not affect long-run aggregate supply. Think of it this way: in the long run, the number of paper dollars we exchange for our goods and services does not affect our ability to produce.

Figure 26.7 plots the economy's long-run aggregate supply curve (LRAS). Notice that since we plot LRAS with the economy's price level (P) on the vertical axis and real GDP (Y) on the horizontal axis, long-run aggregate supply is a vertical line at Y^*, which is full-employment output. In Chapter 20, we defined full-employment output as the output produced in the economy when unemployment (u) is at the natural rate (u^*). This is the output level sustainable for the long run in the economy. Because prices don't affect full-employment output, the LRAS curve is a vertical line at Y^*. If the price level is 100, the quantity of aggregate supply is equal to Y^*. If the price level rises to 110 or falls to 90, output in the long run is still Y^*.

SHIFTS IN LONG-RUN AGGREGATE SUPPLY The long-run aggregate supply curve shifts when there is a long-run change in a nation's ability to produce output, or a change in Y^*. The factors that shift long-run aggregate supply are the same factors that determine economic growth: resources, technology, and institutions.

For example, new technology leads to increases in long-run aggregate supply. Consider what happens if driverless cars enable people to travel more quickly and free up congestion on the roads. This new technology

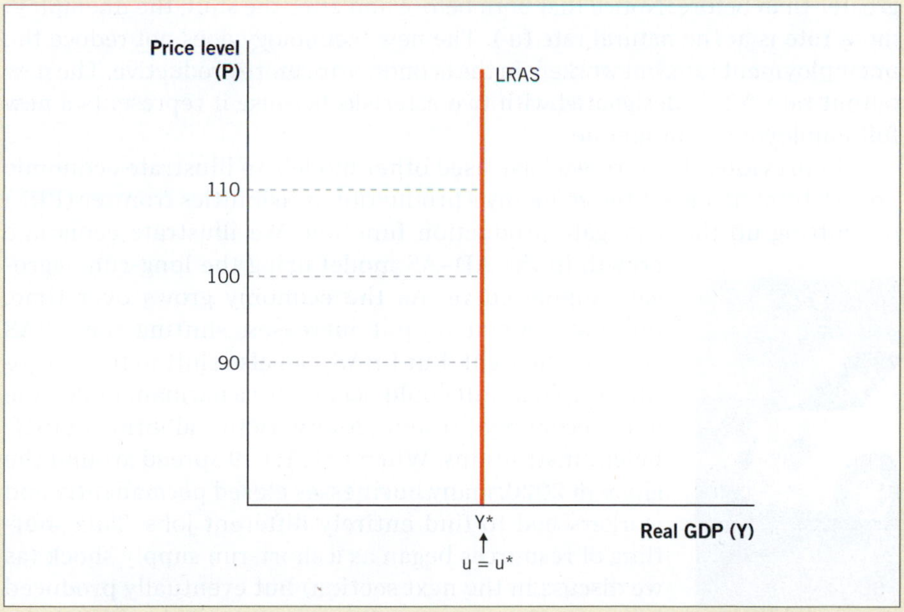

FIGURE 26.7

The Long-Run Aggregate Supply Curve

The LRAS curve is vertical at Y^* because in the long run the price level does not affect the quantity of aggregate supply. Y^* is full-employment output, where the unemployment rate (u) is equal to the natural rate (u^*).

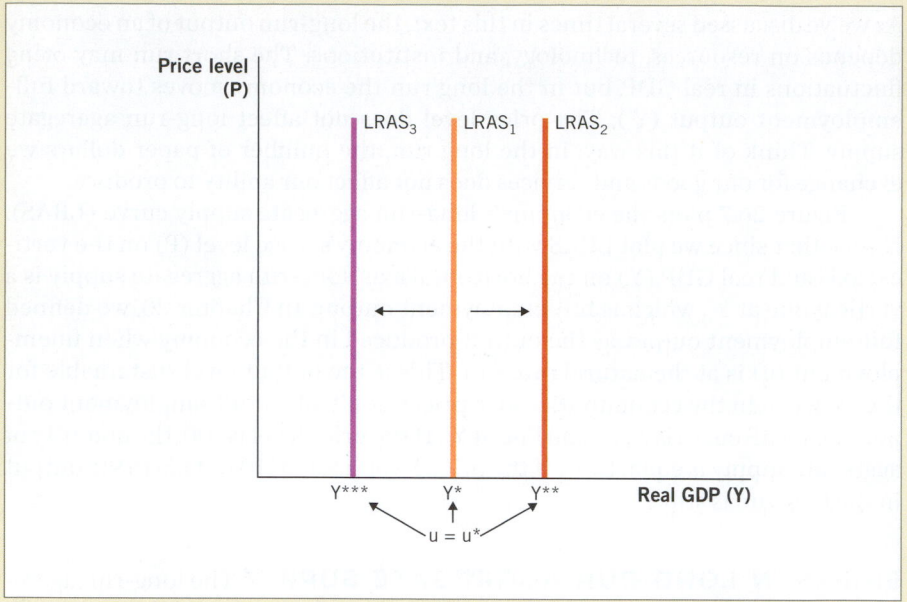

FIGURE 26.8

Shifts in Long-Run Aggregate Supply

Shifts in the long-run aggregate supply curve occur when there is a change in an economy's resources, technology, or institutions. A technological advance moves an economy from $LRAS_1$ to $LRAS_2$. This is a picture of economic growth. When the LRAS curve shifts to the right, this shift also indicates a change in the economy's full-employment output level from Y^* to Y^{**}. The unemployment rate does not change, but workers are more productive.

will lead to an increase in long-run aggregate supply because it increases productivity in the economy: we can produce more with our limited resources.

Figure 26.8 illustrates a shift in long-run aggregate supply. Initially, the LRAS curve is vertical at Y^*, which depends on resources, technology, and institutions. After the new driverless technology is introduced, $LRAS_1$ shifts to the right (to $LRAS_2$) because now the full-employment output in the economy is greater than before. Notice that both before and after the shift, the unemployment rate is at the natural rate (u^*). The new technology does not reduce the unemployment rate, but workers in the economy are more productive. The new output rate, Y^{**}, is designated with two asterisks because it represents a new full-employment output rate.

In previous chapters, we have used other models to illustrate economic growth by shifting out the economy's production possibilities frontier (PPF) or shifting up the aggregate production function. We illustrate economic growth in the AD–AS model using the long-run aggregate supply curve. As the economy grows over time, full-employment output increases, shifting the LRAS curve to the right. But $LRAS_1$ can also shift to the left (to $LRAS_3$). This shift could occur with a permanent decline in the economy's resources or with the adoption of inefficient institutions. When COVID-19 spread around the globe in 2020, many businesses closed permanently and workers had to find entirely different jobs. This shuffling of resources began as a short-run supply shock (as we discuss in the next section) but eventually produced long-run changes in resource usage. This shifted the LRAS leftward.

If driverless cars improve traffic conditions and allow people to enjoy work or leisure during their commute, the economy's LRAS curve shifts to the right.

ECONOMICS *in the* MEDIA

Aggregate Supply in *Charlie and the Chocolate Factory*

In *Charlie and the Chocolate Factory*, Willy Wonka is the owner of a mysterious chocolate factory that produces chocolates and candies beloved around the world. He stages a contest where five golden tickets are hidden in Wonka products, each good for a tour of the factory. One of the tickets finds its way into the hands of young Charlie Bucket. The story was a book first and made into a movie in 1971 (*Willie Wonka & the Chocolate Factory*), but the 2005 remake introduces a new twist: the contest causes so much demand for chocolate that people start buying more toothpaste to clean their teeth. Lots more. To keep up with the increased demand, toothpaste makers automate their production processes.

Even when things look bad for the Buckets, they stick together.

At first, this is bad news for the Bucket family. Charlie's father loses his job putting caps on toothpaste tubes, as he is replaced by a faster, more efficient robot that works for free. But while the father frets about this, Charlie's mom assures her husband that his luck will change. And it does, as by the end of the movie the father has a better job, servicing the robot that replaced him! This job obviously pays better, too, as the Buckets, who previously subsisted solely on cabbage soup, now enjoy turkey for dinner. Ultimately, new technology has created more productivity and a higher-paying job.

If we multiply this story across other jobs in other industries, we get what economists see happening in the real world when automation comes to the workplace: a shift in aggregate supply. Research has shown that robots do replace jobs and reduce wages for some workers, especially in areas where manufacturing is centered.* Other research projects that this trend will increase as COVID-19 drives companies to automate more jobs in which human contact is high. Still, in the long run, overall jobs and wages should grow, driven by this new technology. This will help the overall economy, but it will require retraining and additional education for a lot of workers, a transition that can be challenging and difficult for many.†

*Daron Acemoglu and Pascual Restropo, "Robots and Jobs: Evidence from US Labor Markets," *Journal of Political Economy*, 128, no. 6 (June 2020), https://doi.org/10.1086/705716.
†Susan Lund et al., "The Future of Work after COVID-19," McKinsey Global Institute, February 18, 2021, https://www.mckinsey.com/featured-insights/future-of-work/the-future-of-work-after-covid-19.

Short-Run Aggregate Supply

We just saw that the price level does not affect aggregate supply in the long run. However, in the short run there is a positive relationship between the price level and the quantity of aggregate supply. We consider three reasons for this relationship: inflexible input prices, menu costs, and money illusion.

First, consider input prices. One common input price is worker's wages, and these do not adjust quickly. For example, at your coffee shop, you pay the baristas a particular wage, and this wage is set for a period of time. In addition,

DATA SNAPSHOT

The Business Cycle

Since 1970, the U.S. economy has experienced seven recessions. These business cycle fluctuations are most visible in observations of real GDP growth and the unemployment rate. During recessions, real GDP typically falls and the unemployment rate climbs. During expansions, real GDP expands and the unemployment rate falls back toward the natural rate.

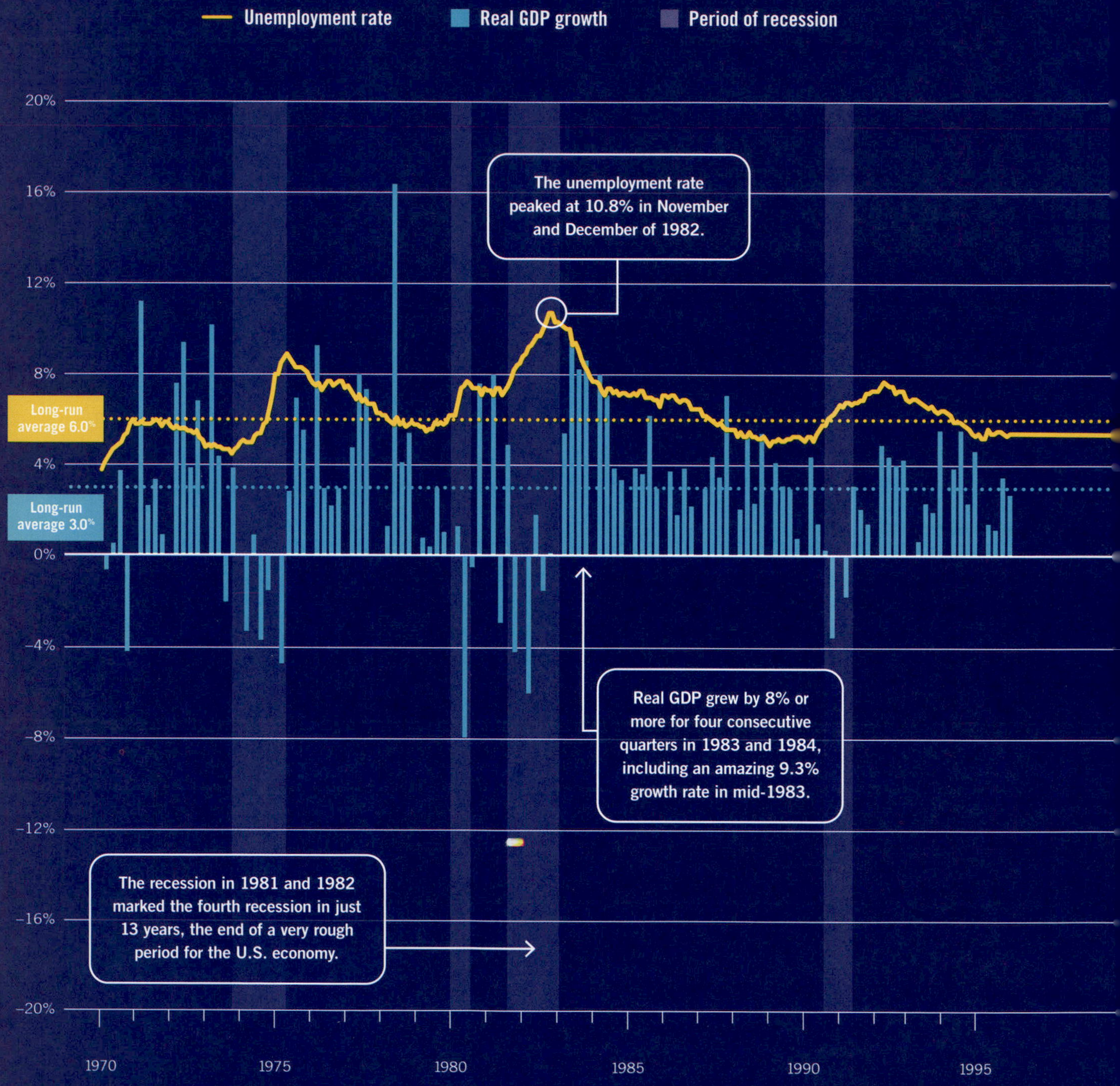

Unemployment rate
Real GDP growth
Period of recession
20%
16%
12%
8%
4%
0%
-4%
-8%
-12%
-16%
-20%
Long-run average 6.0%
Long-run average 3.0%
The unemployment rate peaked at 10.8% in November and December of 1982.
Real GDP grew by 8% or more for four consecutive quarters in 1983 and 1984, including an amazing 9.3% growth rate in mid-1983.
The recession in 1981 and 1982 marked the fourth recession in just 13 years, the end of a very rough period for the U.S. economy.
1970
1975
1980
1985
1990
1995

REVIEW QUESTIONS

- Looking at the year immediately following each recession, can you determine which economic recovery was most difficult? On what do you base your answer?
- If the unemployment rate is below the natural rate, what does this imply about aggregate demand?

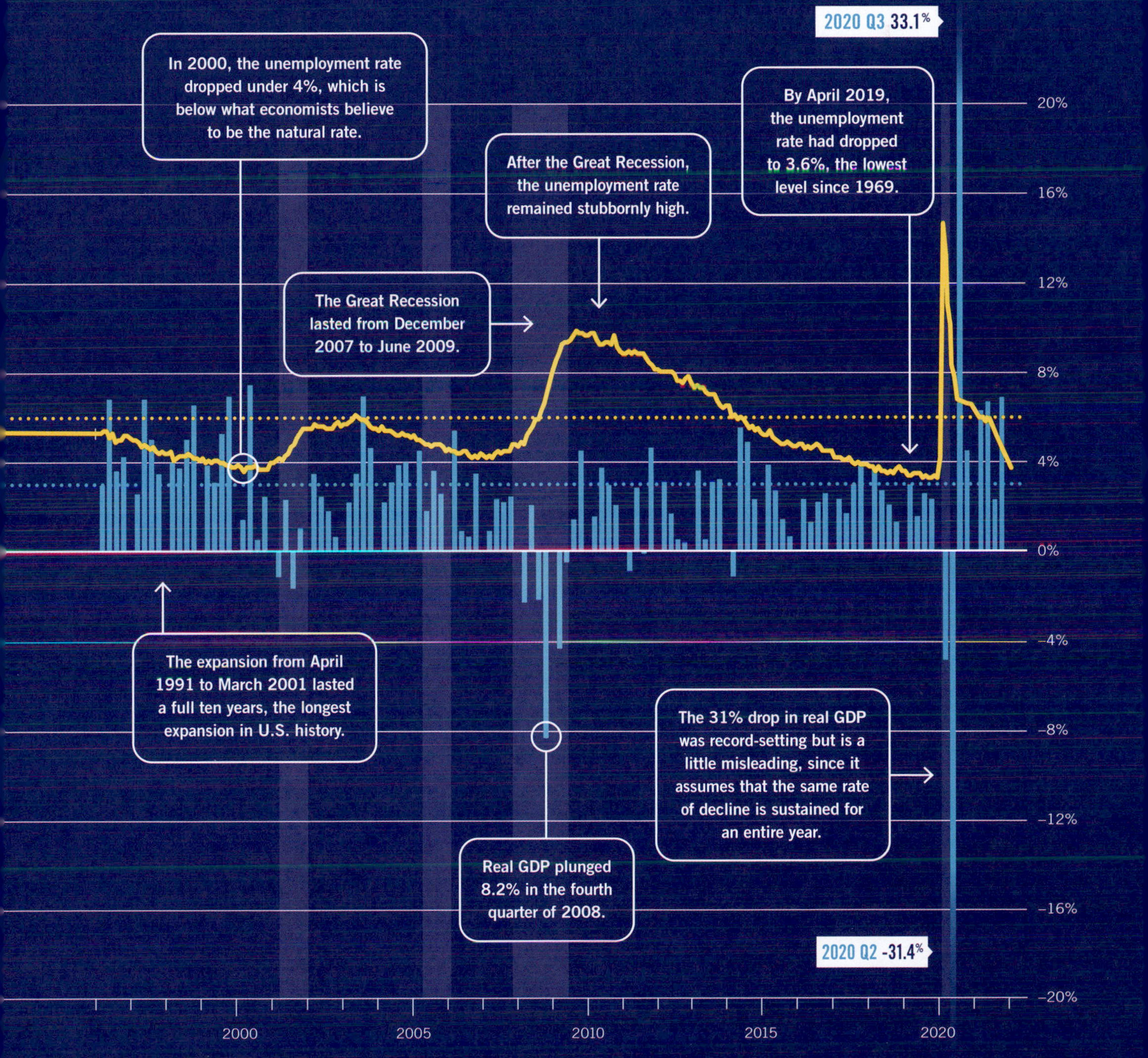
2020 Q3 33.1%
In 2000, the unemployment rate dropped under 4%, which is below what economists believe to be the natural rate.
By April 2019, the unemployment rate had dropped to 3.6%, the lowest level since 1969.
After the Great Recession, the unemployment rate remained stubbornly high.
The Great Recession lasted from December 2007 to June 2009.
The expansion from April 1991 to March 2001 lasted a full ten years, the longest expansion in U.S. history.
The 31% drop in real GDP was record-setting but is a little misleading, since it assumes that the same rate of decline is sustained for an entire year.
Real GDP plunged 8.2% in the fourth quarter of 2008.
2020 Q2 -31.4%
20%
16%
12%
8%
4%
0%
–4%
–8%
–12%
–16%
–20%
2000
2005
2010
2015
2020

interest rates for your business loans are normally fixed. Economists say these input prices are *sticky,* because they "stick" at a certain level and take time to change. In contrast, output prices (like the price of the coffee beverages) are more flexible. Whereas input prices are often set by written contract, output prices are generally easy to change. In a neighborhood coffee shop, prices are often written on a chalkboard, making them very easy to change from day to day.

The distinction between sticky input prices and flexible output prices is at the center of our discussion of aggregate supply, because it affects the way firms react when prices do move. Think about your coffee shop. You might negotiate one-year contracts with your workers. Your coffee bean suppliers fix their prices for a certain period as well. If inflation begins to push up all prices in the macroeconomy, you pull out your chalkboard eraser and raise the price of lattes, espressos, and mochas; these are output prices and they are flexible. But your input prices are sticky (the coffee beans still cost the same, and you have to pay your employees the same amount)—at least for a while. Therefore, your costs remain the same. And here is the link to aggregate supply: because your costs don't rise but your revenues do, it makes sense for you to increase output. When you and other firms raise output, GDP rises.

The dynamic between sticky input prices and flexible output prices explains the positive slope of the short-run aggregate supply curve. Figure 26.9 shows the short-run aggregate supply curve, labeled as SRAS. When the price level rises from 100 to 110, firms produce more in the short run because input prices are sticky, and real GDP rises from $20 trillion to $21 trillion. When the price level falls to 90, firms produce less in the short run because flexible output prices fall but sticky input prices stay relatively high. The result is a decrease in real GDP to $19 trillion.

FIGURE 26.9

The Short-Run Aggregate Supply Curve

The positive slope of the short-run aggregate supply curve indicates that increases in the economy's price level lead to an increase in the quantity of aggregate supply in the short run. For example, if the price level rises from 100 to 110, the quantity of aggregate supply rises from $20 trillion to $21 trillion in the short run. The reason is that some prices are sticky in the short run.

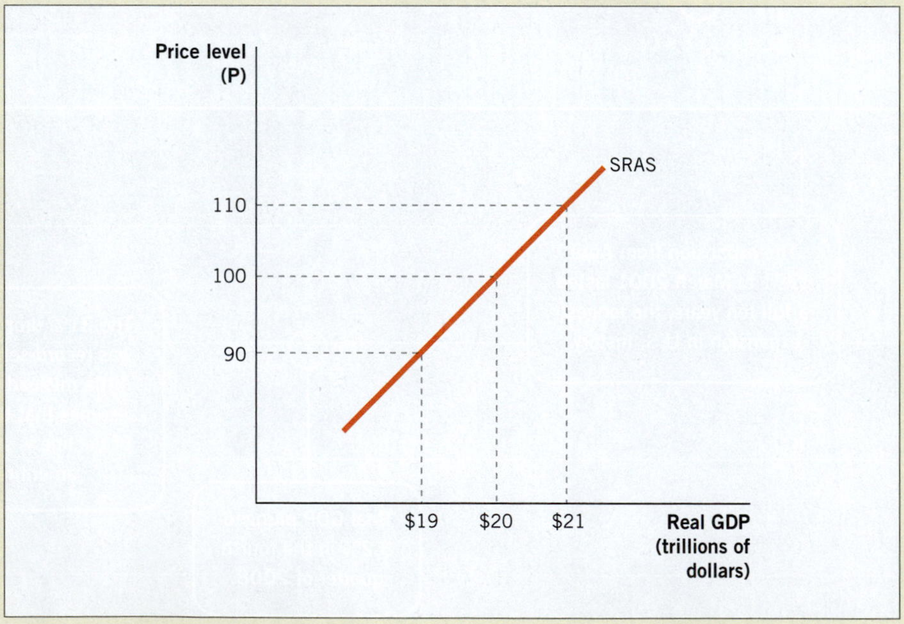

There are other reasons why aggregate supply might be positively related to the price level in the short run. Menu costs, which we introduced in Chapter 21, are another factor that affects short-run aggregate supply. If the general price level is rising but a firm decides not to adjust its prices because of menu costs, customers will want more of its output. If firms decide to increase output rather than print new menus, the quantity of aggregate supply increases. So again, output is positively related to the price level in the short run.

These output prices are very flexible—they can be changed with the push of a button.

We also talked about the problem of money illusion in Chapter 21. Recall that *money illusion* occurs when people interpret nominal values as real values. In terms of aggregate supply, if output prices are falling but workers are reluctant to accept nominal pay decreases, they reinforce the stickiness of input prices. If input prices don't fall with output prices, firms reduce output in response to general price-level changes.

Any type of price stickiness leads to a positively sloped aggregate supply curve in the short run. But keep in mind that since all prices can change in the long run, the long-run aggregate supply curve is vertical at the full-employment output level.

SHIFTS IN SHORT-RUN AGGREGATE SUPPLY When the long-run aggregate supply curve shifts, it signals a change that affects the economy in both the long run and the short run. Therefore, all long-run aggregate supply curve shifts (caused by changes in resources, technology, and institutions) also cause the short-run aggregate supply curve to shift. But, in addition, the short-run aggregate supply curve sometimes shifts on its own. Typically, these shifts are due to changes that directly affect firms' costs of production and form their incentives for supply.

The primary cause of shifts in short-run aggregate supply is changes in input or resource prices. Aggregate supply is the total quantity of GDP supplied by firms in the economy, as it relates to the overall price level. When input costs fall, production costs fall, and then firms produce more output at any given price level. This means short-run aggregate supply increases, or shifts to the right. The short-run aggregate supply curve exists because input prices and other prices are sticky and do not always adjust immediately when aggregate demand shifts. So when these prices do change, the short-run aggregate supply curve shifts. When input prices rise, short-run aggregate supply declines (the curve shifts to the left).

The coronavirus pandemic in 2020 was a negative supply shock that led to business closures.

Although input prices can change for many reasons, we will cover just two main ones. The first is a change in workers' wages. Where workers are unionized, the unions engage in collective bargaining that leads to wage agreements between the workers as a group and their employers. If workers underestimated inflation in the past, this will inform their negotiations for higher wages in the future. For instance, let's say workers sign wage contracts under the assumption that inflation will be about 2% in the next year. If the inflation rate turns out to be 5% instead, the union will push for a more aggressive raise next time. This will cause the short-run aggregate supply curve to shift to the left, as input prices climb.

Along these same lines, if you are going to sign a long-term wage contract by yourself, you'll probably also form some expectation about future prices. After all, the real value of your future income depends on prices in the future. All else equal, when workers and firms expect higher prices in the future, they negotiate higher wages. The result is higher labor costs, which reduce firms' profitability and make them less willing to produce at any price level. Therefore, higher expected future prices lead to a lower aggregate supply. The process works in reverse if workers and firms expect a lower price level. Subsequent negotiations produce a labor agreement with lower wages, which reduces labor costs. When labor costs fall, additional production is more profitable at any price level, and the short-run aggregate supply curve shifts to the right.

A second cause of short-run aggregate supply shifts is *supply shocks*. Sometimes, exogenous surprise events occur that change firms' production costs and shift aggregate supply. **Supply shocks** are surprise events that change firms' production costs. The spread of COVID-19 in the spring of 2020 is a vivid example. Recall how the effects of the virus spread rapidly around the globe. In the United States, many businesses shut down completely beginning in mid-March, and others drastically scaled back their output. These included restaurants, movie theaters, hotels, and airports. This sudden effect is best characterized as a shock to the supply side of the economy. It is as if we lost the use of many resources that we typically depend on to produce goods and services.

Supply shocks are surprise events that change a firm's production costs.

When supply shocks are temporary, they shift only the short-run aggregate supply curve. Supply shocks can be negative or positive. (Think about all those businesses reopening after the worst of the pandemic was over.) Negative supply shocks lead to higher input prices and higher production costs, shifting the short-run aggregate supply curve to the left; positive supply shocks reduce input prices and production costs, shifting the short-run aggregate supply curve to the right.

A price change in an important factor of production is another supply shock. For example, from July 2007 to July 2008, oil prices in the United States doubled from \$70 a barrel to over \$140 a barrel. You may recall this period because gas prices rose from about \$2 per gallon to more than \$4 per gallon in the summer of 2008. Figure 26.10 plots the price of oil from 2000 to 2020. Oil is an important input to many production processes, so when its price doubles, a macroeconomic supply shock occurs. More recently, the drop from over \$100 barrel to less than \$50 in late 2014 was a positive supply shock for the macroeconomy.

Figure 26.11 shows how changes in input prices shift the short-run aggregate supply curve. Short-run aggregate supply increases (the curve shifts to the right to $SRAS_2$) when resource prices fall. This could occur when negotiation leads to lower worker wages or when there is a positive supply shock. Short-run aggregate supply decreases (the curve shifts to the left to $SRAS_3$) when resource prices rise. This happens when workers negotiate higher wages or when negative supply shocks increase resource prices.

FIGURE 26.10

Price of Crude Oil

The increase in crude oil prices is an example of a negative supply shock because production costs for firms throughout the economy rise drastically.

Source: U.S. Energy Information Administration.

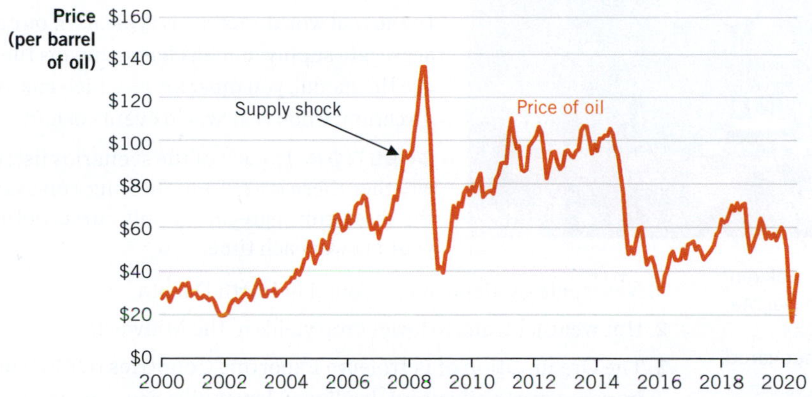

FIGURE 26.11

How Changes in Input Prices Shift the Short-Run Aggregate Supply Curve

The short-run aggregate supply curve shifts to the right (from $SRAS_1$ to $SRAS_2$) when resource prices fall. This could occur when negotiations lead to lower wages or when there is a positive supply shock. The curve shifts to the left (from $SRAS_1$ to $SRAS_3$) when resource prices rise. This happens when workers negotiate higher wages or when negative supply shocks increase resource prices.

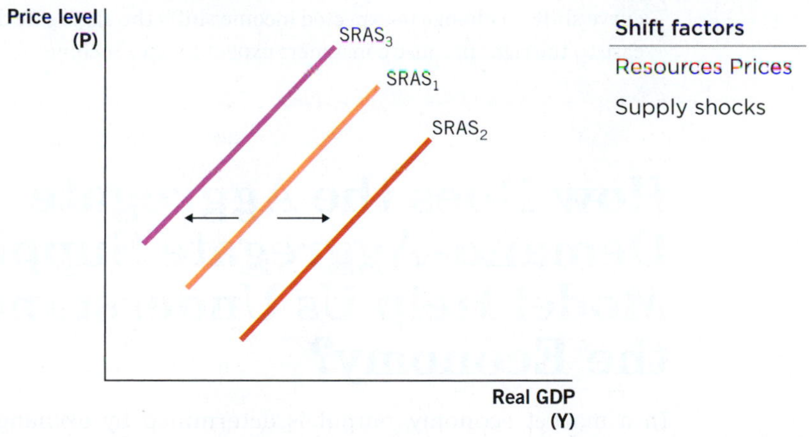

PRACTICE WHAT YOU KNOW

This oil rig sits atop the Bakken shale formation in North Dakota, where vast new shale gas resources have been discovered.

Long-Run Aggregate Supply and Short-Run Aggregate Supply: Which Curve Shifts?

In the real world, change is typical. In our aggregate demand–aggregate supply model, change means the curves shift. To use the model, you must know which curve shifts, and in which direction, when real-world events occur.

QUESTION: In each of the scenarios listed below, determine whether there is a shift in the long-run aggregate supply curve, the short-run aggregate supply curve, both, or neither. Explain your answer each time.

1. New shale gas deposits are found in North Dakota.
2. Hot weather leads to lower crop yields in the Midwest.
3. The Organization of Petroleum Exporting Countries (OPEC) meets and agrees to increase world oil output, leading to lower oil prices for six months.
4. U.S. consumers expect greater income in 2023.

ANSWERS:

1. This scenario leads to an increase in both long-run aggregate supply and short-run aggregate supply. The shale gas discovery represents new resources, which shifts the long-run aggregate supply curve to the right. In addition, every shift in the long-run aggregate supply curve affects the short-run aggregate supply curve.
2. The lower crop yields are temporary, so only the short-run aggregate supply curve shifts to the left. After the bad weather passes, the short-run aggregate supply curve shifts back to the right.
3. This scenario causes only the short-run aggregate supply curve to shift to the right because it is due to a temporary change in oil quantities.
4. Neither the short-run aggregate supply curve nor the long-run aggregate supply curve shifts. A change in expected income shifts the aggregate demand curve, in this case to the right because consumers expect greater income.

How Does the Aggregate Demand–Aggregate Supply Model Help Us Understand the Economy?

In a market economy, output is determined by exchanges between buyers and sellers, which are represented in our model by aggregate demand and aggregate supply. In this section, we bring aggregate demand and aggregate supply together and also consider how changes in the economy affect real

GDP, unemployment, and the price level. As we are about to see, the economy tends to move to the point at which aggregate demand and aggregate supply are equal.

Equilibrium in the Aggregate Demand–Aggregate Supply Model

Figure 26.12 plots the aggregate demand and the aggregate supply curves on the same axes. The point where they intersect, A, is the equilibrium point where the opposing forces of supply and demand are balanced. At point A, the price level is P^* and the output level is Y^*. Prices naturally adjust to move the economy toward this equilibrium point.

To understand why the economy tends toward equilibrium at price level P^*, consider other possible price levels. For example, at price level P_H, which is higher than P^*, aggregate supply is greater than aggregate demand. Here, firms produce more than consumers desire at current prices. Therefore, prices naturally begin to fall to eliminate a potential surplus of goods and services. As prices fall, the quantity of aggregate demand increases and the economy moves toward a new equilibrium at P^*.

In contrast, if the price level is P_L, which is lower than P^*, aggregate demand exceeds aggregate supply. At P_L, buyers desire more than producers are willing to supply. Because aggregate demand exceeds aggregate supply, prices rise and the price level moves toward P^*. The only price level where the plans of suppliers and demanders match is P^*. Market forces automatically push the economy to the price level where aggregate demand equals aggregate supply.

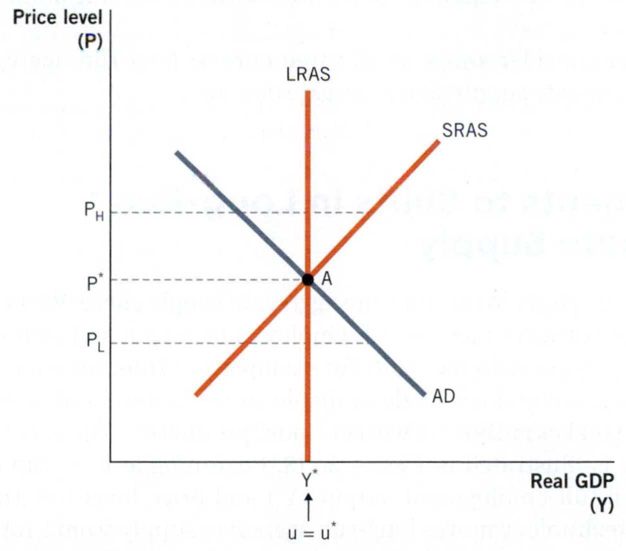

FIGURE 26.12

Equilibrium in the Aggregate Demand–Aggregate Supply Model

Forces in the economy naturally move it toward equilibrium at point A, where aggregate supply equals aggregate demand, $P = P^*$, $Y = Y^*$, and $u = u^*$. At P_H, aggregate supply exceeds aggregate demand, which puts downward pressure on prices and moves the economy toward equilibrium at P^*. At P_L, where aggregate demand exceeds aggregate supply, upward pressure on prices moves the economy toward equilibrium at P^*.

We can also describe this equilibrium in equation form. In equilibrium, both long-run and short-run aggregate supply are equal to aggregate demand:

(EQUATION 26.2)

$$\text{LRAS} = \text{SRAS} = \text{AD}$$

Aggregate supply is the real GDP produced, which we indicate as Y. Aggregate demand derives from four components: C, I, G, and NX. Therefore, we can rewrite equation 26.2 as:

(EQUATION 26.3)

$$Y = C + I + G + NX$$

Now we know what equilibrium looks like in our model. Equation 26.3 is our reference point for thinking about the economy at a particular point in time.

But the real world brings constant change: everything from technology to weather to wealth and expectations can change. Now that we've built our model of the macroeconomy, we can use it to examine how real-world changes affect the economy.

In what follows, both in this chapter and for the remainder of the book, we consider many real-world factors that lead to changes in the macroeconomy. When we consider a change, we follow a particular sequence of steps to the new equilibrium. Once we determine the new equilibrium, we can assess the effects of the change on real GDP, unemployment, and the price level. The five steps are as follows:

1. Begin with the model in long-run equilibrium.
2. Determine which curve(s) are affected by the change(s), and identify the direction(s) of the change(s).
3. Shift the curve(s) in the appropriate direction(s).
4. Determine the new short-run and/or long-run equilibrium points.
5. Compare the new equilibrium point(s) with the starting point.

Next we consider shifts in all three curves: long-run aggregate supply, short-run aggregate supply, and aggregate demand.

Adjustments to Shifts in Long-Run Aggregate Supply

Let's begin with shifts in the long-run aggregate supply curve. We have seen that technological advances increase full-employment output and shift the long-run aggregate supply curve to the right. For example, the Internet is a relatively new and important technology, made available to the general public in the 1990s. The Internet makes millions of workers more productive. The effect on the overall economy is illustrated in Figure 26.13. Beginning at long-run equilibrium point A, with full-employment output (Y^*) and price level 100, the introduction of new technology moves long-run aggregate supply from LRAS_1 to LRAS_2. Recall that changes in long-run aggregate supply also affect the short run, so the short-run aggregate supply shifts from SRAS_1 to SRAS_2. Assuming this technological change is the only change in the economy, we move to long-run

FIGURE 26.13

How Long-Run Aggregate Supply Shifts Affect the Economy

Beginning at long-run equilibrium point A, the price level is 100 and output is at full employment (Y^*). New technology shifts long-run aggregate supply from $LRAS_1$ to $LRAS_2$ because the economy can now produce more at any price level. The new long-run equilibrium is at point B, and there is now a new, higher full-employment rate of output (Y^{**}). Note that the unemployment rate (u) is equal to the natural rate (u^*) both before and after the shift.

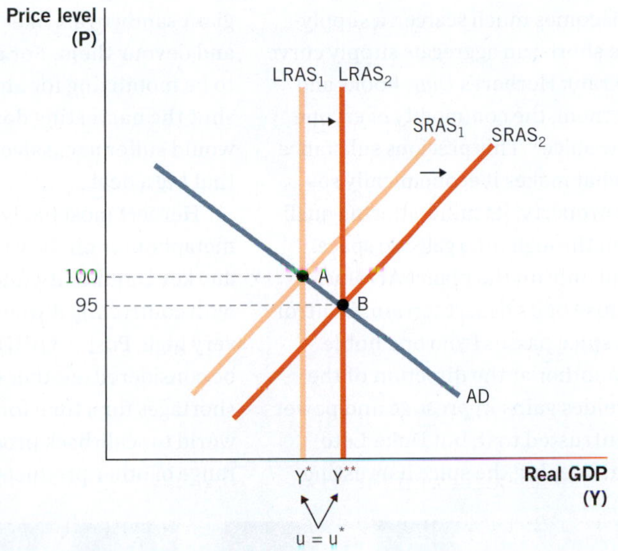

equilibrium at point B. Notice that at point B the economy has a new full-employment output level at Y^{**}.

All else equal, technological progress leads to more output and a lower price level, which drops from 100 to 95. Before the Internet, the unemployment rate was at the natural rate (u^*). After the new technology becomes available, employment remains at u^*; but better tools mean workers can produce more output (Y^{**} vs. Y^*). This also applies to other factors that shift long-run aggregate supply to the right, such as the discovery of new resources or the introduction of new institutions favorable to growth.

Adjustments to Shifts in Short-Run Aggregate Supply

Now let's consider a change in short-run aggregate supply. One possibility is a short-run supply disruption caused by an oil pipeline break, a negative supply shock. Because oil is a widely used input, the disruption temporarily raises

ECONOMICS *in the* MEDIA

"He Who Controls the Spice, Controls the Universe"—the Impact of a Precious Commodity in *Dune*

When a commodity essential for the functioning of an economy suddenly becomes much scarcer, a supply-shock occurs and the short-run aggregate supply curve shifts to the left. In Frank Herbert's *Dune* books and the movies based on them, the commodity everyone relies on is called "the spice." This precious substance has many uses, but what makes it economically so valuable is a curious property: its mind-altering qualities enable navigation through intergalactic space.

The spice is found only on the planet Arrakis, known as Dune because of its desert terrain. Control of the planet and its spice passes from one noble family, or house, to another at the direction of the emperor. House Atreides gains in prestige and power when the planet is entrusted to it, but Duke Leto Atreides worries that keeping the spice harvesting operations going will be a challenge. For one thing, giant sandworms like to catch workers by surprise and devour them. For another, a rival house seems to be mobilizing for an attack. If anything were to shut the harvesting down, the entire known universe would suffer a massive supply shock. The spice is that big a deal.

Herbert most likely thought of the spice as a metaphor for oil. However, the spice can symbolize any key commodity, and the power and risk associated with controlling it when supply is short and demand is very high. Post–COVID-19, semiconductor chips could be considered another example of "the spice." Chip shortages for a time forced manufacturers around the world to scale back production of cars, TVs, and a wide range of other products.

In *Dune*, whoever controls "the spice" can change the course of empires.

FIGURE 26.14

How Short-Run Aggregate Supply Shifts Affect the Economy

A temporary negative supply shock shifts short-run aggregate supply from $SRAS_1$ to $SRAS_2$. In the short run, the economy moves to equilibrium at point b (denoted with a lowercase letter to distinguish from long-run equilibrium). This equilibrium entails higher prices, lower real GDP, and higher unemployment. In the long run, the economy returns to equilibrium at point A.

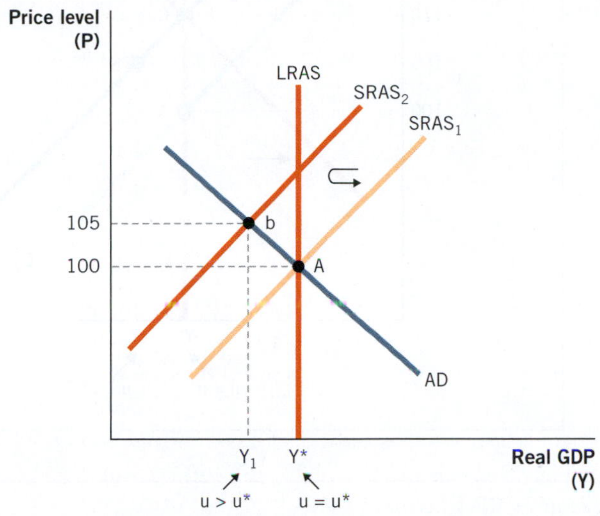

production costs. We show this supply shock in Figure 26.14 by shifting short-run aggregate supply to the left, from $SRAS_1$ to $SRAS_2$. The new equilibrium is at point b, with a higher price level (105) and lower level of output (Y_1). Because this is a short-run equilibrium, we use the lowercase b. The lower output means increased unemployment in the short run ($u > u^*$). Notice that nothing happens to long-run aggregate supply—in the long run, the pipeline is fixed and oil is produced at full-employment output level Y^* again.

Because the disruption is temporary, eventually the short-run aggregate supply curve shifts back to the right until it reaches $SRAS_1$ again. Short-run disruptions in aggregate supply do not alter long-run equilibrium in the economy; eventually, the price level, output, and unemployment rate return to their long-run equilibrium levels at point A. But in the short run, the negative shift brings higher unemployment and lower real GDP.

Adjustments to Shifts in Aggregate Demand

Aggregate demand shifts for many reasons. Shifts might even occur from changes in expectations of market participants rather than from real factors in the economy, and yet even these subjective factors affect the macroeconomy. For example, consider an unexpected change in consumer confidence: consumers wake up one morning with expectations of higher future

FIGURE 26.15

How Aggregate Demand Shifts Affect the Economy

An increase in aggregate demand moves the economy from the initial equilibrium at point A to a new short-run equilibrium at point b. The positive aggregate demand shift increases real GDP and decreases unemployment in the short run ($u < u^*$). In the short run, prices adjust—but only partially, because some prices are sticky. In the long run, when all prices adjust, the short-run aggregate supply curve shifts to $SRAS_2$, and the economy moves to long-run equilibrium at point C, where $Y = Y^*$ and $u = u^*$.

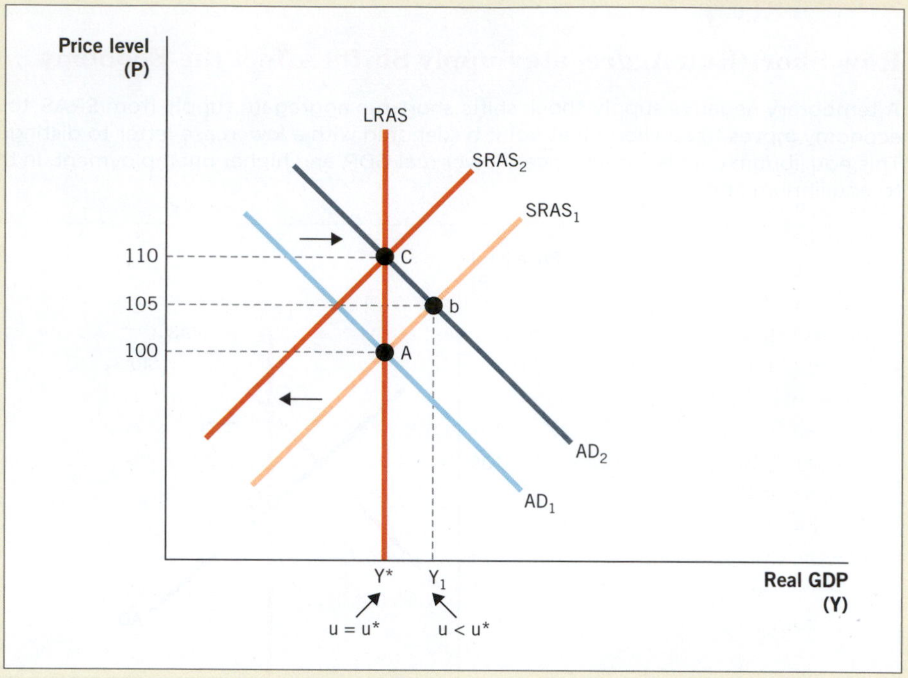

income. This then increases aggregate demand as consumers spend more. Can this kind of change have real effects on the economy? That is, will a change in consumer confidence affect unemployment and real GDP? Let's look at the model.

Figure 26.15 illustrates changes in the economy from an uptick in consumer confidence. We start in long-run equilibrium at point A, where the price level is 100, real GDP is at full-employment output Y^*, and unemployment is equal to the natural rate ($u = u^*$). More spending means aggregate demand shifts from AD_1 to AD_2, and the economy moves to short-run equilibrium at point b. The short-run equilibrium is relevant here, because in the short run some prices are sticky, so that even though there is upward pressure on prices, only some prices adjust and the price level rises to 105. But this short-run equilibrium is also associated with higher real GDP (Y_1) and an unemployment rate of u_1, which is less than the natural rate, u^*. Thus, changes in aggregate demand do affect the real economy (Y and u), at least in the short run.

Our initial results seem very positive—after all, unemployment falls and real GDP rises in the short run. But we need to complete the story by following it through to long-run equilibrium. Recall the difference between the long run and the short run: in the long run, all prices adjust. As all prices adjust, short-run aggregate supply shifts back from $SRAS_1$ to $SRAS_2$. The economy then moves to long-run equilibrium at point C. Notice that at C we are back to the original output level (Y^*) and unemployment level (u^*), but prices are higher ($P = 110$). The model is telling us that demand changes have no real effects (on Y and u) in the long run as only the price level (a nominal variable) is affected.

ECONOMICS IN THE REAL WORLD

THE DROUGHT OF 2012 LED TO MANY HIGHER PRICES

The summer of 2012 was one of the hottest on record for the United States. High temperatures led to extremely low yields in both corn and soybean crops. In fact, in 2012, each acre of corn planted in the United States yielded just 123 bushels, down from 147 bushels the year before and much lower than the 158 bushels in 2013.

Corn is one of those individual goods that also serves as an input to many other types of output, so when the price of corn rises, it takes many other prices with it. For example, corn is an important feed source for cattle. The 2012 jump in corn prices contributed to increases of more than 30% in beef and pork prices over the next few years. Corn is an ingredient in many other consumer products, as well: cereal, soda, cake mixes, candy bars, and even makeup. Thus, when corn prices rise, the prices of all these products also go up, all else equal.

The record temperatures are a classic example of a supply shock, and the result is exactly what the aggregate demand–aggregate supply model predicts: the short-run aggregate supply curve shifts to the left, leading to higher prices throughout the economy.

These Iowa fields were supposed to be much greener in July 2012.

TABLE 26.1

Summary of Results from Aggregate Demand Shifts

	Increase in aggregate demand		Decrease in aggregate demand	
	Short run	**Long run**	**Short run**	**Long run**
Real GDP	Y rises	Y returns to original level	Y falls	Y returns to original level
Unemployment	u falls	u returns to original level	u rises	u returns to original level
Price level	P rises	P rises even further	P falls	P falls even further

What are the consequences of this move to long-run equilibrium, and how does it compare with the short-run equilibrium? At point b, real GDP is up and unemployment is down. But not everyone is happy. For example, workers with sticky wages must pay more for their final goods and services, but without a wage increase in the short run.

But since all prices can adjust eventually, the economy moves to point C in the long run. Let's consider this whole episode from the view of your small business, the coffee shop. In the short run, output prices (written in chalk, remember) can move up with other macroeconomic prices. But input prices take time to adjust. In the long run, you will renegotiate wages and all other long-term contracts. Thus, if there is a 10% increase in prices throughout the economy, both input and output prices can eventually rise by 10%. The price of a $4 latte rises to $4.40, and the barista wage of $10 per hour rises to $11 per hour. When input prices rise to match output price changes, the short-run aggregate supply curve shifts to $SRAS_2$. In the long run, after all prices have adjusted, the price level does not affect the quantity of output supplied. This is why output returns to Y^*, the full-employment level.

Table 26.1 summarizes the economic effects of aggregate demand changes in both the short run and the long run. The last two columns summarize the effects of decreases in aggregate demand. These decreases in aggregate demand are a particular source of debate among macroeconomists. We'll examine the historical effects of changes in aggregate demand in Chapter 27.

PRACTICE WHAT YOU KNOW

The Indonesian town of Palu was devastated by a tsunami in 2018.

Using the Aggregate Demand–Aggregate Supply Model: A Tsunami Hits Indonesia

In 2018, a magnitude 7.5 earthquake triggered a tsunami that came ashore at the town of Palu in Indonesia. Nearly 5,000 people were killed and the lives of hundreds of thousands were disrupted. Most of the port city was destroyed, and in some places there was so much water, houses just sank into the ground. Infrastructures such as roads and power lines were destroyed.

QUESTION: How would you use the aggregate demand–aggregate supply model to illustrate the effect of this disaster on the Indonesian economy?

(CONTINUED)

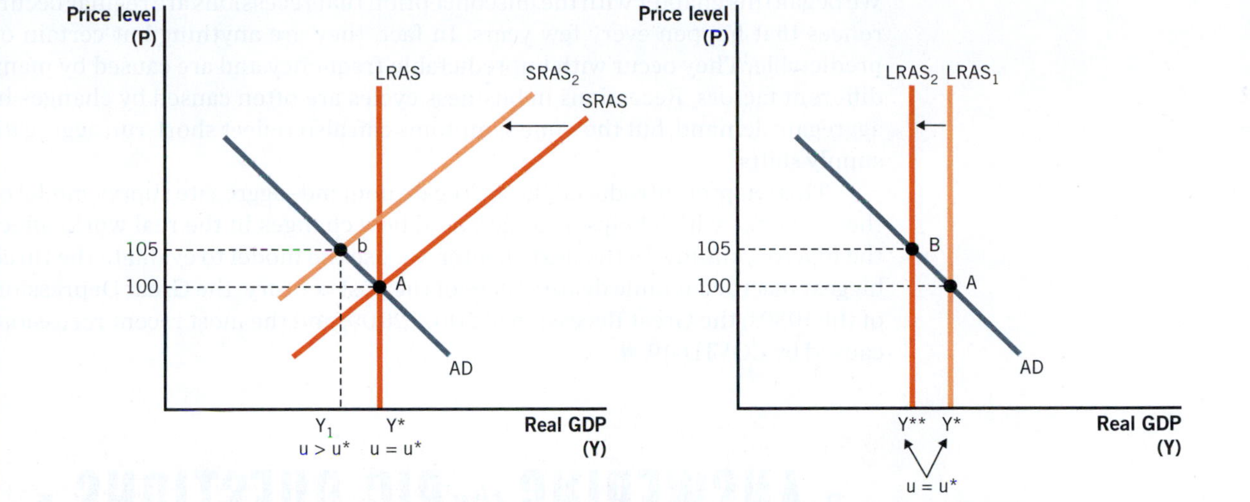

(a) Short-Run Effects

(b) Long-Run Effects

ANSWER: The Palu tsunami was a natural disaster, so it's hoped that its effects will be temporary and will only impact the short-run aggregate supply. Keep in mind that if a disaster is severe enough to destroy resources, the long-run aggregate supply will also decline. As an extreme example, think about the destruction of the ancient Roman city of Pompeii in AD 79 when Mt. Vesuvius erupted. Over 2,000 people were killed, and the city was buried for nearly 2,000 years. Since all of the city's inputs were completely destroyed, economic output would have fallen in the long run as well as in the short run.

Let's consider the short-run effects of the Palu tsunami. The SRAS curve shifts to the left in panel (a). Output falls and employment is interrupted, causing u to rise above u*. Some jobs are temporarily lost while things get cleaned up. Price levels also rise. This is illustrated by the shift from the long-run equilibrium point A to the short-run equilibrium point b.

If there is a long-run impact on output, the result is different. In panel (b), the LRAS curve shifts to the left due to the destruction of resources, resulting in a new long-run equilibrium B. Notice that the unemployment rate (u) is equal to the natural rate (u*) both before and after the shift. Jobs remain because there's plenty of work to do in the aftermath of a natural disaster. However, in the long run Indonesia has fewer resources after the tsunami than it had before, and this outcome limits the nation's economic growth.

QUESTION: How does the Indonesian disaster affect the U.S. economy?

ANSWER: Real foreign income falls in Indonesia, which leads to a decline in aggregate demand for U.S. goods and services. The U.S. aggregate demand curve shifts to the left.

Conclusion

We began this chapter with the misconception that recessions are regular occurrences that happen every few years. In fact, they are anything but certain or predictable. They occur with unpredictable frequency and are caused by many different factors. Recessions in business cycles are often caused by changes in aggregate demand, but the same symptoms can also reflect short-run aggregate supply shifts.

This chapter introduced the aggregate demand–aggregate supply model of the economy, which helps us understand how changes in the real world affect the macroeconomy. In the next chapter, we use the model to evaluate the three biggest macroeconomic disturbances of the past century: the Great Depression of the 1930s; the Great Recession of 2007–2009; and the most recent recession, caused by COVID-19. ✳

▪ ANSWERING *the* BIG QUESTIONS ▪

What is the aggregate demand–aggregate supply model?

- The aggregate demand–aggregate supply model is a model that economists use to study business cycles (short-run fluctuations in the economy).

What is aggregate demand?

- Aggregate demand represents the spending side of the economy. It is the total demand for final goods and services in an economy. It includes consumption, investment, government spending, and net exports.
- The slope of the aggregate demand curve is negative due to the wealth effect, the interest rate effect, and the international trade effect.
- The aggregate demand curve shifts when there are changes in consumption factors (real wealth, expected future income, taxes), investment factors (firm confidence, interest rates, the quantity of money), government spending (at the federal, state, and local levels), or net export factors (foreign income and the value of the U.S. dollar).

What is aggregate supply?

- Aggregate supply represents the producing side of the economy. It is the total supply of final goods and services in an economy.
- The long-run aggregate supply curve is relevant when all prices are flexible. This curve is vertical at full-employment output and is not influenced by the price level.
- In the short run, when some prices are sticky, the short-run aggregate supply curve is relevant. This curve indicates a positive relationship between the price level and real output supplied.

How does the aggregate demand–aggregate supply model help us understand the economy?

- We can use the aggregate demand–aggregate supply model to see how changes in either aggregate demand or aggregate supply (or both) affect real GDP, unemployment, and the price level.

CHAPTER PROBLEMS

Concepts You Should Know

aggregate demand (p. 835)
aggregate supply (p. 835)
interest rate effect (p. 838)
international trade effect (p. 838)
long run (p. 844)
short run (p. 844)
supply shocks (p. 852)
wealth (p. 837)
wealth effect (p. 837)

Questions for Review

1. What are three reasons the aggregate demand curve slopes downward? Name at least three factors that shift the aggregate demand curve.
2. What are three reasons the short-run aggregate supply curve slopes upward? Name at least three factors that shift the short-run aggregate supply curve.
3. How are the factors that shift the long-run aggregate supply curve different from those that shift the short-run aggregate supply curve?
4. Why is the long-run aggregate supply curve vertical?
5. How does strong economic growth in China affect aggregate demand in the United States?
6. Suppose the economy is in a recession caused by lower aggregate demand. If no policy action is taken, what will happen to the price level, output, and employment in the long run?
7. Consider two economies, both in recession. In the first economy, all workers have long-term contracts that guarantee high nominal wages for the next five years. In the second economy, all workers have annual contracts indexed to changes in the price level. Which economy will return to the natural rate of output first? Explain your response.
8. The interest rate effect can be viewed as a chain of reactions in the economy.
   a. Below is the chain of reactions with some of the steps filled in. Fill in the missing steps in the chain and be sure to indicate the direction of change (using an up or down arrow).
   b. What component (or piece) of aggregate demand is primarily affected by the wealth effect?

Study Problems (* solved at the end of the section)

1. Describe whether the following changes cause the short-run aggregate supply to increase, decrease, or neither.
   a. The price level increases.
   b. Input prices decrease.
   c. Firms and workers expect the price level to fall.
   d. The price level decreases.
   e. New policies increase the cost of meeting government regulations.
   f. The number of workers in the labor force increases.
2. Describe whether the following changes cause the long-run aggregate supply to increase, decrease, or neither.
   a. The price level increases.
   b. The stock of capital in the economy increases.
   c. Natural resources increase.
   d. The price level decreases.
   e. Firms and workers expect the price level to rise.
   f. The number of workers in the labor force increases.

3. On the following graph, illustrate the short-run and long-run effects of an increase in aggregate demand. Describe what happens to the price level, output, and employment.

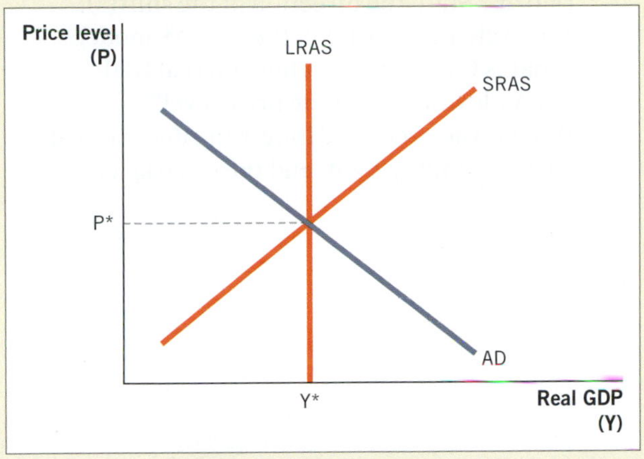

4. How does a lower price level in the United States affect the purchases of imported goods? Explain, using aggregate demand.

✱ 5. Describe whether the following changes cause aggregate demand to increase, decrease, or neither.

a. The price level increases.
b. Investment decreases.
c. Imports decrease and exports increase.
d. The price level decreases.
e. Consumption increases.
f. Government purchases decrease.

✱ 6. Suppose a sudden increase in aggregate demand moves the economy from its long-run equilibrium.

a. Illustrate this change using the aggregate demand–aggregate supply model.
b. What are the effects of this change in the short run and the long run?

7. In the summer of 2008, global oil prices spiked to extremely high levels before coming down again at the end of that year. This temporary event had global effects because oil is an important resource in the production of many goods and services. Focusing only on the U.S. economy, determine how this kind of event affects the price level, unemployment rate, and real GDP in both the short run and the long run. Assume the economy was in long-run equilibrium before this change, and consider only this stated change.

✱ 8. You work for Dr. Zhang, the autocratic dictator of Zhouland. After taking an economics course, you decide that devaluing your currency (Zhoullars) is the way to increase GDP. Following your advice, Dr. Zhang orders massive increases in the supply of Zhoullars, which reduces the value of Zhoullars in world markets. Use the AD–AS model to determine the effects on real GDP, unemployment, and the price level in Zhouland in both the short run and the long run. Assume the economy was in long-run equilibrium before this change, and consider only this stated change.

✱ 9. Recently, the value of the U.S. dollar has been rising in world markets.

a. Determine how the rising value of the dollar affects the U.S. price level, real GDP, and the unemployment rate in both the short run and the long run. For this part, assume these changes are unexpected by market participants.

You can use graphs to derive your answers, but place your answers in the boxes below (using an up arrow, a down arrow, or a dash if the level is consistent). Assume the economy starts in long-run equilibrium, assume no other changes, and make all comparisons to the initial long-run equilibrium.

Short run			Long run		
P	Y	u	P	Y	u

b. Under certain circumstances, it takes longer for the economy to adjust to long-run equilibrium following unanticipated changes. Do those circumstances apply here? Explain why or why not.

c. If instead these changes in the value of the dollar are completely anticipated in advance, how will the results differ in the short run?

10. Let's say that in 2022 the United States experiences abnormally good weather. This weather is particularly beneficial for agricultural crop production. Determine how the run of good weather affects the U.S. real GDP, price level, and unemployment rate in both the short run and the long run.

You can use graphs to derive your answers, but place your answers in the boxes below. Assume the economy starts in long-run equilibrium, assume no other changes, and make all comparisons to the initial long-run equilibrium.

Short run			Long run		
P	Y	u	P	Y	u

11. In 2018, the U.S. government passed a tax reform bill that reduced taxes for the prior year (2017) and then also for subsequent years.

a. Which curve(s) is (are) affected by the tax reform? State the direction of the shift(s).

b. Illustrate the shift(s) in the AD–AS model.

c. What is the short-run effect on real GDP, unemployment, and the price level?

d. What is the predicted long-run effect on real GDP, unemployment, and the price level?

Solved Problems

5. a. Neither. A change in the price level (P) leads to a movement along the AD curve. When the price level rises, the quantity of aggregate demand declines along the curve.

b. Investment (I) is one component of aggregate demand, so a decrease in investment decreases aggregate demand.

c. Net exports (NX) is a component of aggregate demand. An increase in exports and a decrease in imports imply that net exports rise, so aggregate demand increases.

d. Aggregate demand neither increases nor decreases with a change in the price level (P). A change in the price level leads to movement along the AD curve. When the price level decreases, the quantity of aggregate demand increases along the curve.

e. Consumption (C) is a component of aggregate demand, so an increase in consumption means an increase in aggregate demand.

f. Government purchases (G) are a component of aggregate demand, so a decrease in government purchases causes a decrease in aggregate demand.

6. a. Aggregate demand increases from AD_1 to AD_2. In the short run, equilibrium will be at point b. In the long run, equilibrium will move to point C.

b. In the short run, real GDP rises, the unemployment rate falls, and the price level rises. In the long run, real GDP goes back to the full-employment level, the unemployment rate returns to the natural rate, and the price level rises further.

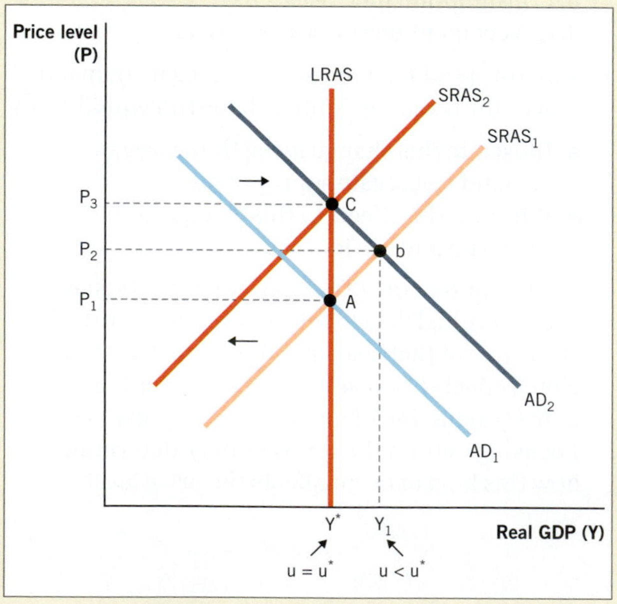

8. The reduction in the value of the Zhoullar means an increase or rightward shift in the aggregate demand curve. This change creates the same scenario pictured in the solution to problem 6; refer again to that figure.

In the short run, there is greater real GDP, lower unemployment, and a higher price level. This short-run equilibrium is pictured as point b in the figure.

In the long run, the only change is an increase in the price level (P), as indicated by the new long-run equilibrium at point C in the figure. Note that this explanation is consistent with the discussion of inflation in Chapter 22. That is, the cause of inflation is monetary expansion. When Dr. Zhang commanded that the number of Zhoullars should increase, he guaranteed that inflation would eventually arrive.

9. a. When the value of the U.S. dollar rises relative to other currencies, it means U.S. exports are relatively more expensive and imports from other nations are relatively less expensive. Therefore, net export demand falls and AD declines. The fall in AD leads to a new short-run equilibrium with a lower price level, lower real GDP, and higher unemployment. In the long run, the price level falls further, but real GDP and the unemployment rate return to their initial levels.

Short run			**Long run**		
P	Y	u	P	Y	u
↓	↓	↑	↓	—	—

b. It takes longer for the economy to adjust when prices are falling (rather than rising). That situation does apply here because prices need to fall to restore the economy back to long-run equilibrium.

c. If the results are completely anticipated, then the economy goes immediately to the long-run equilibrium. That is, even in the short run, prices fall, but real GDP and the unemployment rate remain at their long-run equilibrium levels.

CHAPTER 27

Recessions, Expansions, and the Debate over How to Manage Them

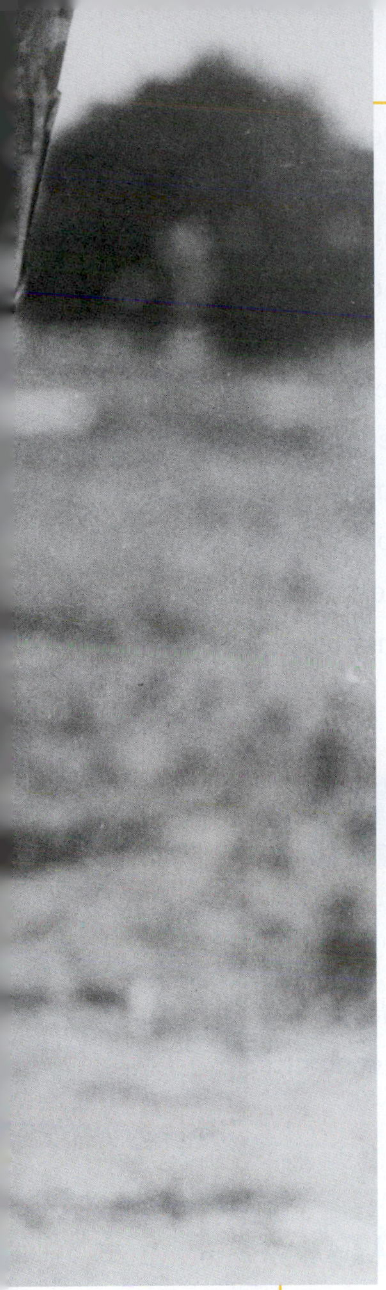

The Great Depression Was Unlike Any Recession We've Experienced Since.

The Great Depression of the 1930s gave birth to macroeconomics as a subdiscipline of economics. Previously, economists generally focused on microeconomics: they emphasized the interaction of supply and demand in individual markets. But the depth and duration of the Great Depression forced economists to pay more attention to overall economic aggregates. In the midst of the Depression, photographer Dorothea Lange documented the plight of migrant farm workers in California, thousands of whom were living in open-air camps and nearly starving. Driving north on Highway 101, Lange spotted Florence Owens, a mother tending to five of her children while her husband and the two oldest boys hiked into town to try to get the family's broken-down car fixed. Published in the *San Francisco News*, Lange's photos of Owens and her children quickly became iconic images of Americans beaten down by the hardships of the time but determined to persevere.

Although according to official statistics, the economy had started to turn the corner, people like Owens and her family still had several lean years ahead of them. The same was true elsewhere in the world, because the Great Depression was a sobering shock to the entire global economy, after the rapid industrial growth of the decade before.

Just outside Nipomo, CA, Florence Owens shelters with her children under a roadside lean-to. She and her husband were migrant workers, roaming the southwestern United States in search of work harvesting peas, lettuce, and cotton.

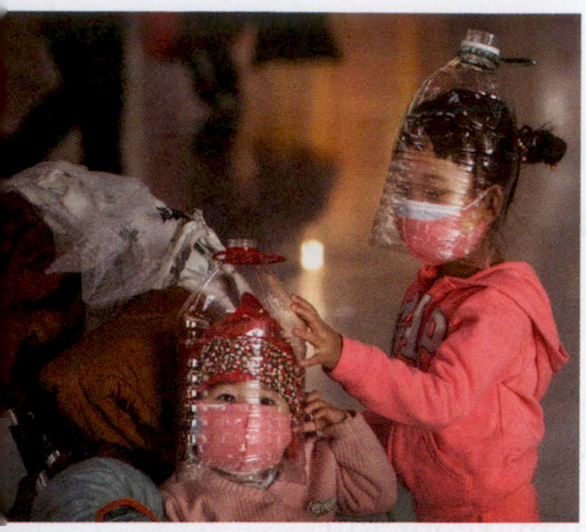

In the early days of the COVID-19 pandemic, people did what they could to try to protect their children.

Fortunately, we've not seen anything so severe since the Great Depression. However, recessions do still occur. In this chapter, we use our aggregate demand–aggregate supply (AD–AS) model to examine some causes of GDP stagnation and high unemployment. We also look closely at three major contractions in U.S. history: the Great Depression of the 1930s, the Great Recession from 2007 to 2009, and the coronavirus-caused recession that began in 2020. We then consider some of the major debates about the macroeconomy. All of this sets us up for coverage of government policy responses to business cycles: fiscal policy (Chapters 28 and 29) and monetary policy (Chapters 30 and 31).

· BIG QUESTIONS ·

- Why do recessions occur?
- What happened during three major recessions?
- What are the big disagreements in macroeconomics?

Why Do Recessions Occur?

Recessions are short-term economic downturns typically characterized by declines in real GDP growth and increases in the unemployment rate. We can use our AD–AS model to examine some different causes of recessions. In this section, we first consider a decline in aggregate demand and then turn to a decline in aggregate supply.

Declines in Aggregate Demand

Aggregate demand changes in response to many different factors. In Chapter 26 we divided these into four groups: consumption factors, investment factors, government spending, and net export factors. When aggregate demand declines, the economy moves to a new equilibrium, with lower real GDP and higher unemployment. For example, if business firm confidence declines, meaning that firms are less optimistic about future economic conditions, they

FIGURE 27.1

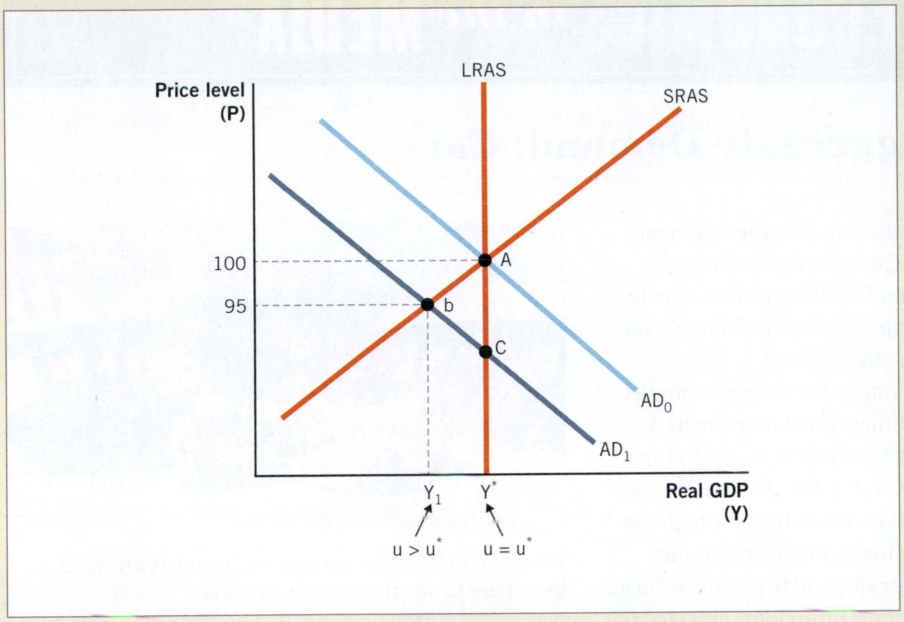

A Demand-Induced Recession

Negative shifts in aggregate demand can move the economy into a recessionary period. In this figure, the economy is initially in long-run equilibrium at point A before a negative shift in aggregate demand, from AD_0 to AD_1. The new equilibrium at point b brings lower real GDP (Y^* falls to Y_1) and higher unemployment ($u > u^*$). This is a classic demand-induced recession.

scale back their investment activity, which decreases aggregate demand. We illustrate a decline in AD in Figure 27.1. The economy is initially in long-run equilibrium at point A, with full-employment output (Y^*), unemployment at its natural rate (u^*), and the price level at 100. When aggregate demand declines from AD_0 to AD_1, the economy moves to a new, short-run equilibrium at point b. (Recall that long-run equilibria are denoted with upper-case letters, and short-run with lower case.) The short-run equilibrium is characterized by lower real GDP and a higher unemployment rate—standard recession conditions.

As we discussed in Chapter 26, if prices adjust downward in the long run, eventually the economy moves to a new long-run equilibrium at point C, with full-employment output (Y^*) restored and unemployment back to the natural rate (u^*). But the short run is painful. Laid-off workers suffer from lost income, and the retail locations and factories where they worked may be shuttered, no longer generating corporate tax revenue (and instead becoming targets for vandals). To minimize these effects, elected representatives and policymakers often look for ways to help move the economy back to full employment by shifting aggregate demand back to its initial level (AD_0). Economists generally feel that periods of high unemployment are the times when demand-stimulating governmental policies are most effective. Policy options include government spending increases, tax cuts, and expansionary monetary policy. (These are each discussed in the next four chapters.)

Many, if not all, recessions can be characterized by a fall in aggregate demand. Even when a decline in aggregate demand is not the initial cause, it often compounds problems, as people spend less due to drops in consumer or business firm confidence.

ECONOMICS *in the* MEDIA

A Drop in Aggregate Demand: *Cars*

In the Pixar movie *Cars*, the main character is a race car named Lightning McQueen, who becomes lost traveling between races and finds himself in a dusty town called Radiator Springs. It lies on old Route 66, away from the new interstate highway.

Radiator Springs was once a bustling community, but it has fallen on hard times. What happened? A little over halfway through the movie, we learn that the town used to be a travel stop for folks on their way across the country. However, when the new highway was built, it bypassed the town. Travelers passing through the area no longer stopped to patronize local businesses. Basically, the new interstate subjected the town to a sudden drop in aggregate demand.

The fictional fate of Radiator Springs mirrors the fate many real towns suffered because of the Federal Aid Highway Act of 1956, which earmarked $25 billion dollars for the construction of the Interstate Highway System. However, while the new highways bypassed many towns, they ran through others and provided those towns with an economic boost. Further, the new highway system promoted commerce across state lines. Today, most of us rely on the system even when we're not driving, because we buy goods transported on it. In the big picture, the story of the Interstate Highway System is not about lost demand, but about investment driving growth.

Welcome to Radiator Springs, McQueen. Wish you'd been here to see the place in its prime.

Declines in Aggregate Supply

Recession conditions, with high unemployment and lower real GDP, can also be caused by declines in aggregate supply, either short run or long run. First, consider a short-run decline. Recall that this happens when input prices rise. For example, in the summer of 2008, the price of oil rose to more than $100 per barrel; this pushed the price of gasoline above $4 per gallon across the United States (as a comparison, the highest pandemic price has been about $85 a barrel, in October 2021). Because oil and gasoline are important inputs for many production processes, these price jumps constituted a supply shock that caused the short-run aggregate supply curve to shift back. This is illustrated in Figure 27.2. Initially, the economy is in long-run equilibrium at point A, at full-employment output (Y^*), and with the natural rate of unemployment (u^*). But the supply shock (the oil and gas price increases) shifts short-run aggregate supply from $SRAS_0$ to $SRAS_1$. This shift moves the economy to a new short-run equilibrium (at point b) characterized by lower real GDP and higher unemployment. If the oil price spike is temporary, short-run aggregate supply eventually returns to its initial level ($SRAS_0$), and the economy returns to long-run equilibrium at A.

FIGURE 27.2

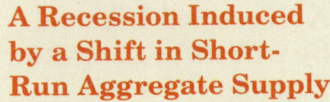

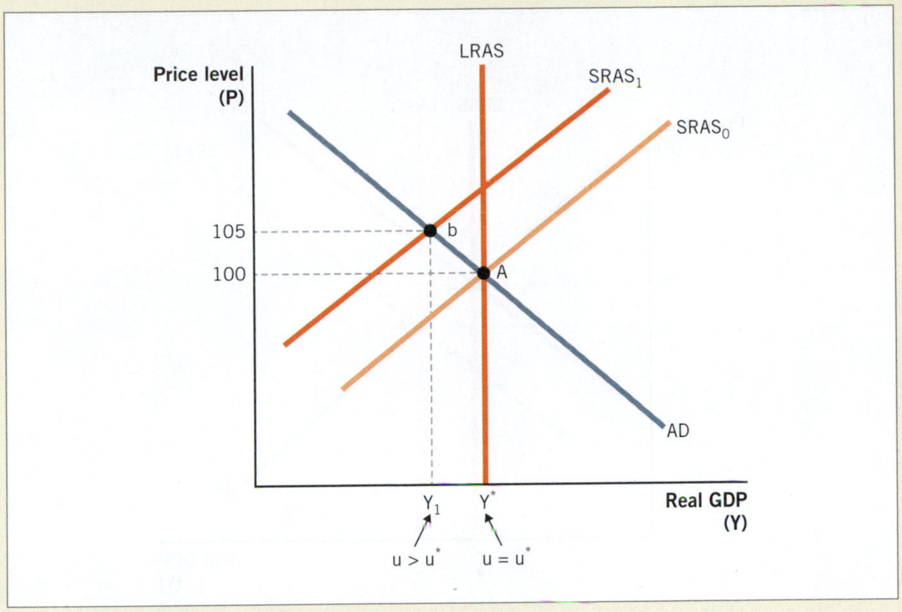

A Recession Induced by a Shift in Short-Run Aggregate Supply

Shifts in short-run aggregate supply can also bring recessionary conditions. In this figure, the economy is in long-run equilibrium at point A before short-run aggregate supply shifts back (to the left, from $SRAS_0$ to $SRAS_1$), perhaps due to a negative supply shock. The shift then moves the economy to a new short-run equilibrium at point b, where real GDP is lower ($Y_1 < Y^*$) and unemployment is higher ($u > u^*$).

Typically, this scenario is relatively harmless, so long as the supply shock doesn't last too long. Sometimes, however, the scenario can trigger a chain of events that lead to a longer recession. This is exactly what happened in 2020, when the coronavirus spread around the globe and led to widespread economic shutdowns. As the pandemic wore on, what began as a decline in short-run aggregate supply affected long-run resource availability and caused long-run aggregate supply to decline as well. We discuss this later in the chapter.

Now let's consider a decline in long-run aggregate supply. This is caused by negative changes in resources, technology, and institutions. An extreme example is a war fought on home soil; it destroys both labor and capital resources, as soldiers die and buildings or other tools are ruined. But whether the cause is war, natural disaster, or something else, a reduction in resources means full-employment output declines and the long-run aggregate supply curve shifts to the left. This is illustrated in Figure 27.3. The reduction of resources moves the economy from long-run equilibrium at point A to a new long-run equilibrium at point B, assuming no other changes take place in the economy. At the new equilibrium, the economy is at a new full-employment level of GDP (Y^{**}). While the unemployment rate is technically at the new natural rate of u^{**}, this rate is often higher than the old unemployment rate, since jobs are shifting around in the economy, and this leads to more structural and frictional unemployment. While it's fortunately rare, this type of downturn is particularly painful, because there may not be a policy fix to move the economy back to its initial output level. All new economic growth takes place from the new baseline of Y^{**}, rather than the initial level of real GDP (Y^*).

As we move on, remember that no two recessions are exactly alike. We've just considered shifts in aggregate demand, short-run aggregate supply, and long-run aggregate supply. In the textbook and on the chalkboard, it is easy to shift curves and see immediate results. In real life, it is not always clear what

FIGURE 27.3

A Recession Induced by a Shift in Long-Run Aggregate Supply

Negative shifts in long-run aggregate supply are less common, but they can also induce recessionary conditions. If long-run aggregate supply declines from $LRAS_0$ to $LRAS_1$ (taking short-run aggregate supply along with it), the economy moves to a new long-run equilibrium at point B, with lower real GDP ($Y^{**} < Y^*$) and higher unemployment ($u^{**} > u^*$). This case is particularly difficult, because the new equilibrium (B) is a long-run equilibrium, and so there is no inherent tendency for the economy to return to the earlier long-run equilibrium. All new growth occurs from Y^{**}.

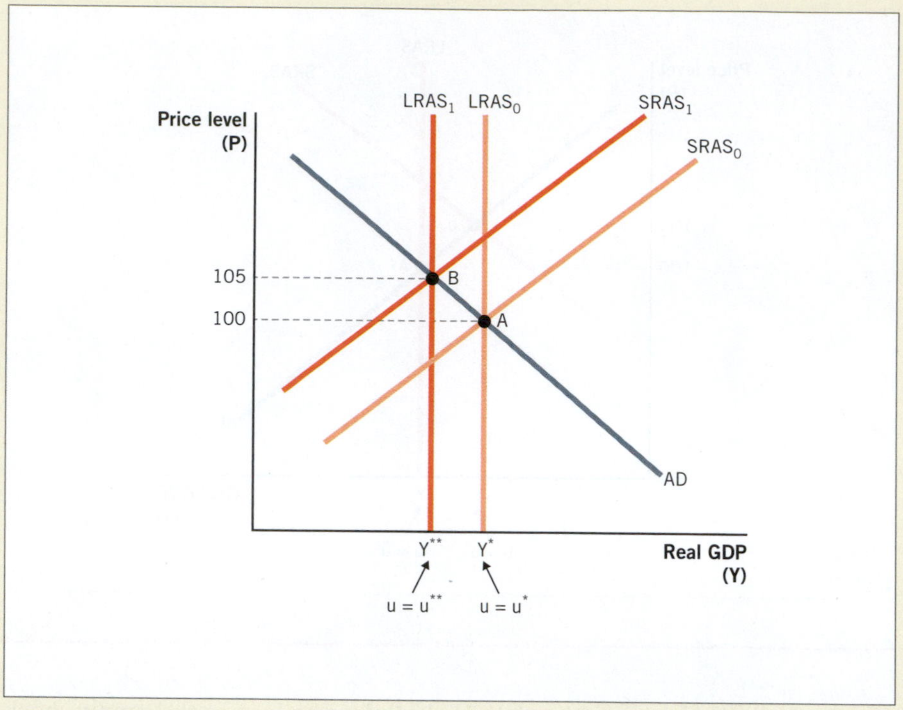

In this 1937 photo, the "Stalked by Stork" announcement on the man's sandwich board tells passers-by that he is an expectant father.

is happening, especially during an actual recession. In the next section, we consider the three worst U.S. recessions in the past century.

What Happened during Three Major Recessions?

In this section, we look at three major economic contractions in U.S. history: the Great Depression of the 1930s, the Great Recession (2007–2009), and the coronavirus recession of 2020. With each one, we begin with historical perspective and then move to analysis within our aggregate demand–aggregate supply model. This demonstrates the helpfulness of the model and prepares us to think about future recessions.

The Great Depression

Going into 1929, the United States was full of optimism. World War I was a distant memory, the country's industrial sector was expanding—it was the "Roaring Twenties." All that changed with the Great Depression, the single biggest economic contraction the United States has experienced.

THE MAGNITUDE OF THE GREAT DEPRESSION To convey the historic magnitude of the Great Depression, Figure 27.4 plots U.S. real GDP all the way from 1870 to 2019. We can quickly pick out the single worst

FIGURE 27.4

Real U.S. GDP, 1870–2019

When we look at U.S. real GDP growth over the long run, the Great Depression is the decline in the 1930s. This drop greatly changed how economists thought about the economy. To normalize across percentage changes, the plotted data appear as the logarithm of real GDP.

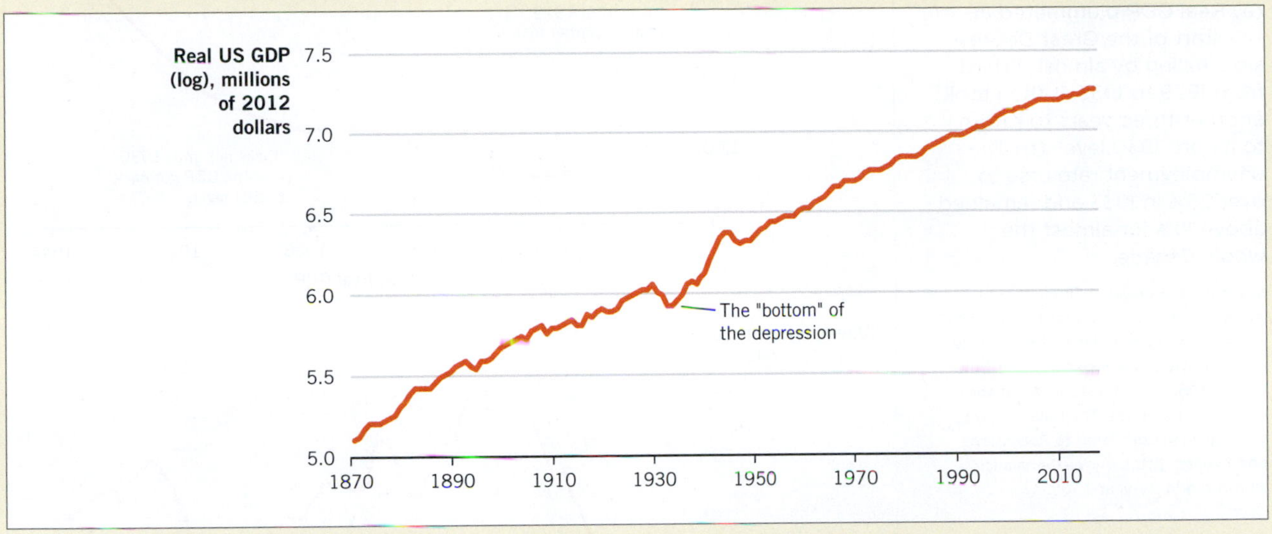

economic incident over that long haul—it's the massive drop around 1930. There have been other contractions in the U.S. economy since 1870, but none even comes close to the Great Depression in severity. Real GDP fell from \$1,253 billion in 1929 to \$923 billion in 1933 (both in 2020 dollars). Imagine a recession so severe that four years later the economy is producing almost 30% less.

During the Great Depression, shantytowns dubbed "Hoovervilles," after President Hoover, sprang up outside major U.S. cities.

Panel (a) of Figure 27.5 moves in for a closer look, showing real GDP during the Depression years, 1929 to 1944. Real GDP fell by nearly a third from 1929 to 1933, and then took another three years just to recover to its pre-recession level. Panel (b) plots the unemployment rate over the same time frame. In 1930, the unemployment rate was only 2.2%, but just three years later it had climbed to over 25%! In other words, by 1933 one in four workers was without a job. Particularly alarming was the length of the Depression: the unemployment rate remained above 15% for almost the entire decade of the 1930s. In the 90 years since the Great Depression ended, the U.S. unemployment rate has never again topped 15%.

USING OUR MODEL TO EXPLAIN THE GREAT DEPRESSION

The Great Depression was actually two separate recessions: August 1929 to March 1933 and May 1937 to June 1938. (There's no technical distinction between a recession and a depression—the latter is really just a severe recession.)

FIGURE 27.5

Real GDP and Unemployment during the Great Depression

(a) Real GDP plummeted at the start of the Great Depression, falling by almost a third from 1929 to 1933. It then took another three years to return to its pre-1930 level. (b) The unemployment rate rose to over 25% in 1933 and remained above 15% for almost the whole decade.

Sources: (a) Bureau of Economic Analysis; "U.S. GDP by Year, Compared to Recessions and Events," The Balance, https://www.thebalance.com/us-gdp-by-year-3305543; (b) Historical Statistics of the United States; The Balance, "U.S. GDP by Year, Compared to Recessions and Events," https://www.thebalance.com/us-gdp-by-year-3305543.

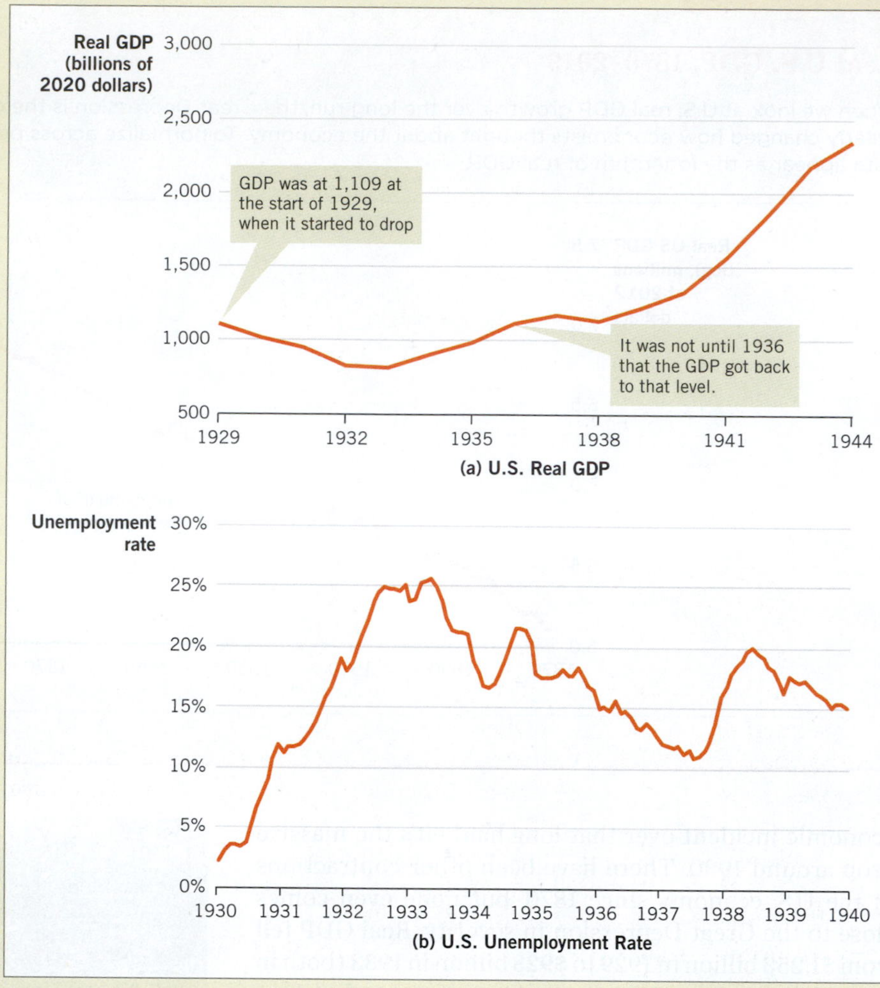

But here's something striking: even though real GDP finished the 1930s higher than it started, prices declined over the same period. At the end of the 1930s, the price level (measured by the GDP deflator) was still 20% lower than in 1929. The decline in prices tells us that the primary cause of the Great Depression was a drop in aggregate demand.

Figure 27.6 illustrates what happened. In 1929, the economy was in equilibrium at point A, with aggregate demand AD_{1929}. Then a significant decline in aggregate demand took place over several years, as indicated by a shift to AD_{1930+}. As we have seen, lower aggregate demand leads to lower real GDP (shown in the figure as Y_1), higher unemployment rates (25%), and a lower price level (shown here as a decline from 100 to 80). These outcomes match the symptoms of the Great Depression.

There were multiple causes of this aggregate demand decline. First, there was a decline in real wealth. The stock market crashed, beginning on October 24, 1929 (now known as "Black Thursday"). Between 1929 and 1932, stock prices (as measured by the Dow Jones Industrial Average) fell by almost 90%.

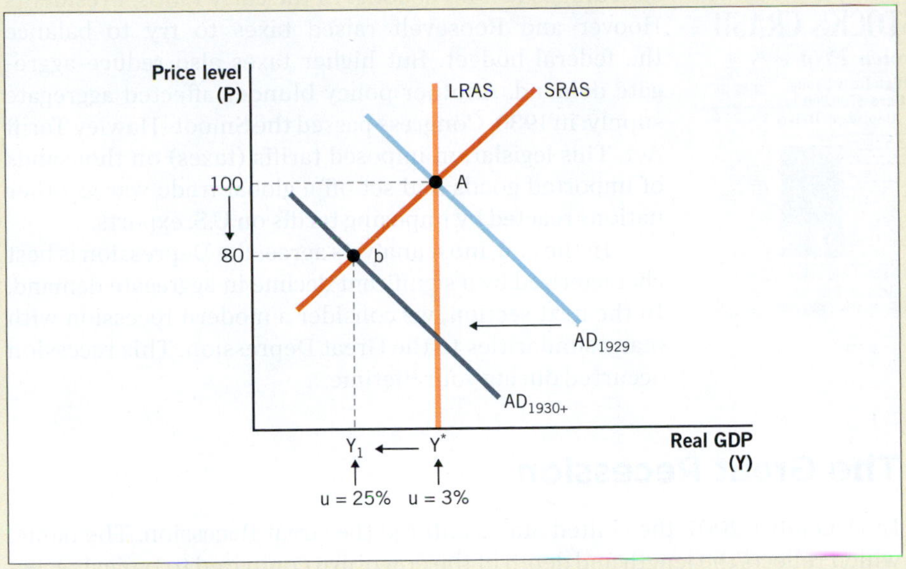

FIGURE 27.6

The Decline in Aggregate Demand during the Great Depression

A significant decline in aggregate demand after 1929 can help to explain all three symptoms of the Great Depression: a decline in real GDP (from Y^* to Y_1), an increase in the unemployment rate (from 3% to 25%), and a decrease in the price level (from 100 to 80).

But the Depression wasn't caused by the stock market crash alone. A second factor was a significant change in people's expectations, in reaction to the crash. In particular, expected future income declined—and we know that this factor decreases aggregate demand. When people expect to earn less in the future, they start spending less in the present.

The third and final cause, however, was the most important. Unfortunately, it turns out that much of the decline in aggregate demand was due to misguided macroeconomic policy. **Macroeconomic policy** encompasses governmental acts that influence the direction of the overall economy. Economists distinguish two different types of macroeconomic policy: fiscal policy and monetary policy. **Fiscal policy** comprises the use of the government's budget tools—government spending and taxes—to influence the macroeconomy. **Monetary policy** involves adjusting the money supply to influence the economy. We're not yet ready to talk in detail about macroeconomic policies (those are the topics of the next section of this book), but we can consider the policy blunders in the context of our aggregate demand–aggregate supply model.

Macroeconomic policy encompasses governmental acts that influence the macroeconomy.

Fiscal policy comprises the use of the government's budget tools—government spending and taxes—to influence the macroeconomy.

Monetary policy involves adjusting the money supply to influence the macroeconomy.

First, consider monetary policy. The government actually reduced the quantity of money in the economy in 1928 and 1929, in hopes of controlling stock prices that policymakers thought were too high. We know that reductions in the money supply lead to lower aggregate demand. Then, when financial panic spread, many people withdrew deposits from banks. As a result, more than 9,000 banks failed in the United States between 1929 and 1933. And while the government had the ability to lend to these ailing banks, it failed to do so. This led to even more shrinking of the money supply. In fact, between 1929 and 1933, the quantity of money circulating through the U.S. economy declined by a third. Economists today agree that these policy failures led to a significant decline in aggregate demand and were a significant contributor to the economic contraction in the beginning years of the Great Depression.

Was the stock market crash the only cause of the Great Depression?

There were other reasons why the Great Depression dragged on for so long. In the early 1930s, Presidents Hoover and Roosevelt raised taxes to try to balance the federal budget. But higher taxes also reduce aggregate demand. Another policy blunder affected aggregate supply: in 1930, Congress passed the Smoot–Hawley Tariff Act. This legislation imposed tariffs (taxes) on thousands of imported goods and set off a global trade war as other nations reacted by imposing tariffs on U.S. exports.

In the end, most analysts agree: the Depression is best characterized by a significant decline in aggregate demand. In the next section, we consider a modern recession with many similarities to the Great Depression. This recession occurred during your lifetime.

The Great Recession

In December 2007, the United States entered the Great Recession. The name, which reflects the length and depth of the downturn compared to typical recessions, also reminds us that some of the causes resemble those of the Great Depression (like significant problems in the financial markets). The title stuck when the effects of the recession refused to subside for several years after the recession was officially over.

THE DEPTH AND DURATION OF THE GREAT RECESSION

Officially, the Great Recession lasted 18 months, until June 2009, making it the longest of all recessions since World War II. Even so, this statistic understates how severely the U.S. economy was affected. For several years after the recession was technically over, unemployment remained high and real GDP grew slowly. Figure 27.7 shows U.S. real GDP in panel (a) and the unemployment rate in panel (b), both for the years 2005 to 2015. Notice how real GDP didn't return to its pre-recession level for almost four years. During a typical recession, real GDP falls slightly and then bounces back after about a year and a half. Even worse, the unemployment rate took nearly seven years to drop back below 6%.

Why was the Great Recession so severe? We'll use our aggregate demand and aggregate supply model to answer this question.

USING OUR MODEL TO EXPLAIN THE GREAT RECESSION

At first, most economists and policymakers assumed that the Great Recession was caused exclusively by lower aggregate demand. But while aggregate demand did indeed fall, hindsight reveals issues with aggregate supply, too.

Two main factors contributed to a large decrease in aggregate demand. The first was a fall in real wealth, due to a severe drop in housing prices beginning in 2007. Figure 27.8 shows home prices from 2000 to 2020. Notice the drop that began in 2007 and continued until 2011. People's homes are often the largest component of their wealth, so when real estate values fall, people's wealth drops. On top of that, U.S. stock shares lost a third of their value during 2008. For millions of people, this meant a massive loss of retirement savings. Both events contributed to large declines in real wealth, leading to lower aggregate demand.

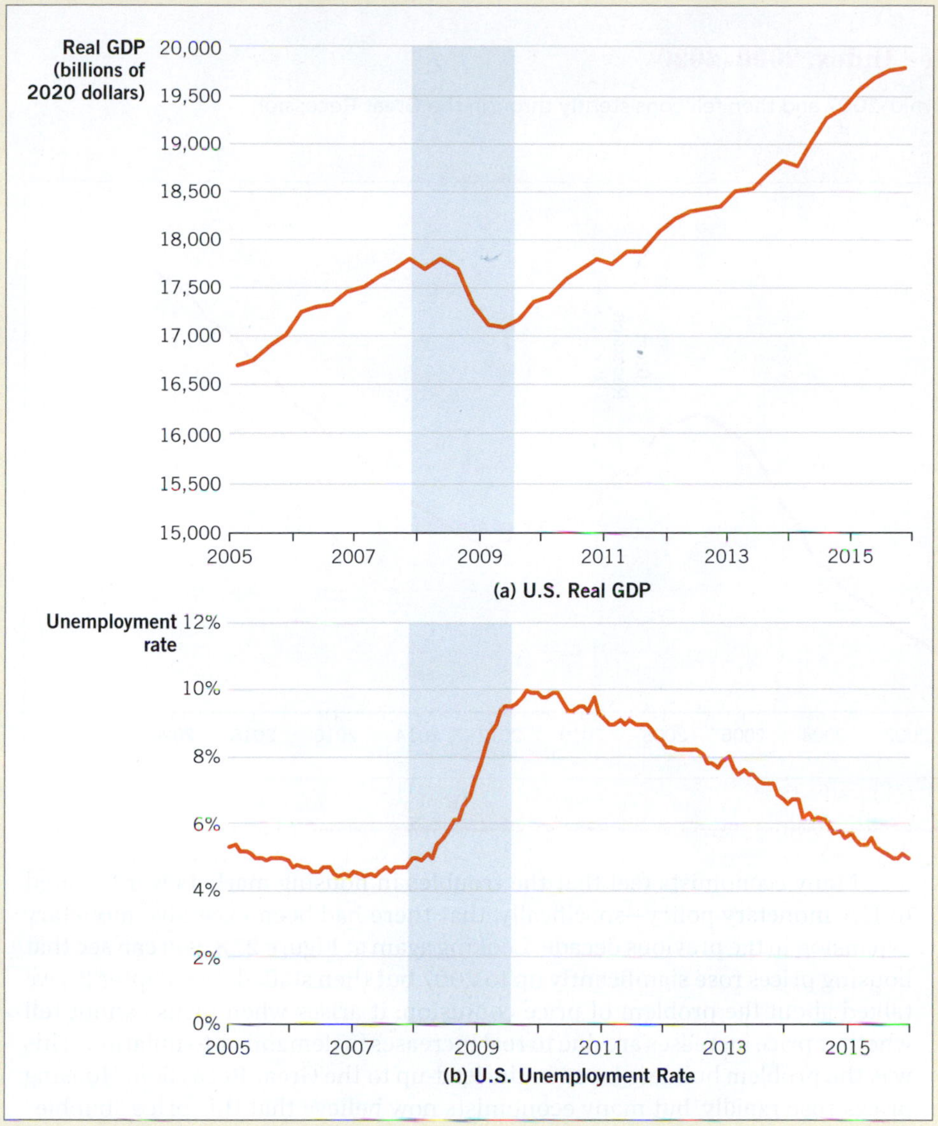

FIGURE 27.7

Real GDP and Unemployment during the Great Recession

(a) Real GDP began falling at the end of 2007. The biggest quarterly drop in real GDP over this period came in the fourth quarter of 2008, when the decrease was 8.4% (on an annualized basis). (b) Even after the Great Recession officially ended in mid-2009, the unemployment rate continued rising, peaking at 10% before starting to come down. It didn't drop back under 5% until 2016.

Sources: (a) Bureau of Economic Analysis; (b) Bureau of Labor Statistics.

The second big reason why aggregate demand fell was a decline in expected future income. Beginning in 2007, consumers realized that the economy was slowing down. Their expectations of future income went down. A popular measure of consumer confidence, the Consumer Sentiment Index (calculated at the University of Michigan), plummeted from 97 to 57 between 2007 and 2008.

Together, these two factors—a decline in wealth and a decline in expected future income—led to a decline in aggregate demand. But the length of the recession and the slow recovery indicate that there were also problems with long-run aggregate supply. We will briefly look at three key supply issues: poor resource allocation in the years leading up to the recession, particularly in the home-building industry; instability in the financial markets; and regulations passed to stabilize those markets.

FIGURE 27.8

U.S. House Purchase Price Index, 2000–2020

U.S. house prices began falling in mid-2007 and then fell consistently through the Great Recession.

Source: Federal Housing Finance Agency.

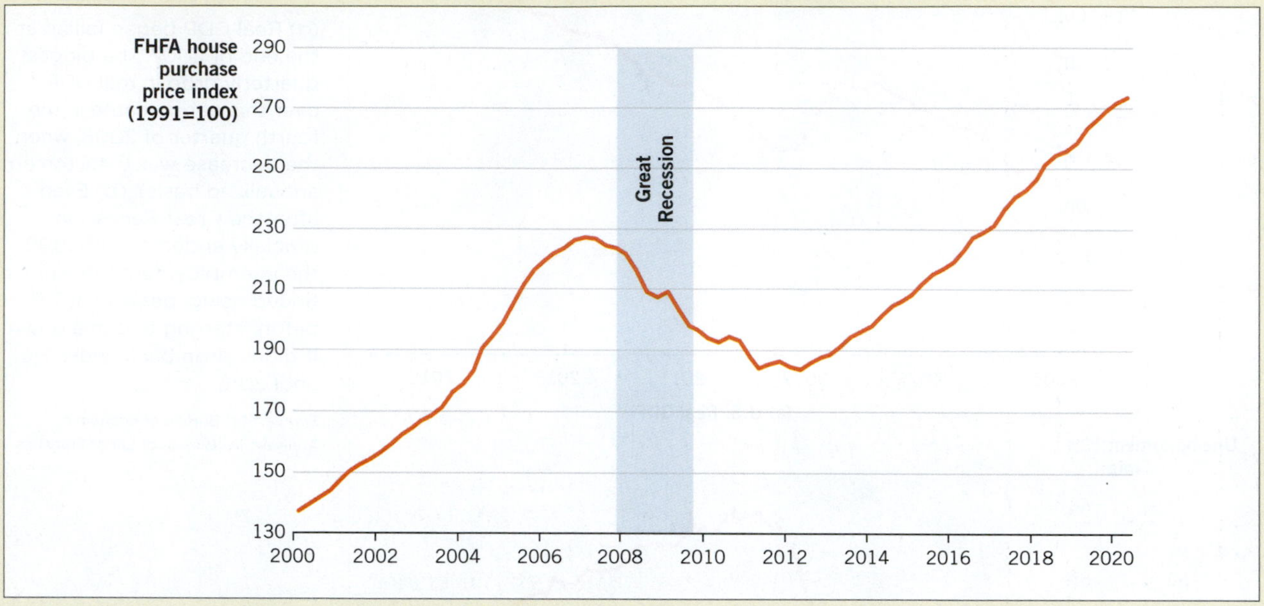

Many economists feel that the troubles in housing markets were related to U.S. monetary policy—specifically, that there had been excessive monetary expansion in the previous decade. Looking again at Figure 27.8, you can see that housing prices rose significantly up to 2007 but then stalled. In Chapter 21, we talked about the problem of price confusion: it arises when firms cannot tell whether price increases are due to real increases in demand or to inflation. This was the problem builders faced in the lead-up to the Great Recession. Housing prices rose rapidly, but many economists now believe that this price "bubble" was a result of monetary expansion. In 2008, the bubble burst.

During this time, very large business firms, including financial institutions like Lehman Brothers, Bank of America, and Goldman Sachs, accumulated significant assets in the housing market, in particular in the market for securitized home mortgages. Recall from Chapter 23 that home mortgages were securitized into mortgage-backed securities and that significant quantities of these were held by most of the largest financial institutions. When real estate values fell, so did the values of those securities. Now the firms holding those securities had a cash flow problem on their hands. Because of the financial firms' interdependence, the problem quickly spread throughout the United States and then to the rest of the world. A financial crisis signals a breakdown in the loanable funds market. When the loanable funds market doesn't function properly, firms can't get funding to produce output, and aggregate supply falls.

The **Dodd-Frank Act** is the primary regulatory response to the financial turmoil that contributed to the Great Recession.

Finally, new financial regulations enacted during the crisis changed the financial industry's operating environment. The **Dodd-Frank Act**, signed in

July 2010, was the primary regulatory response to the financial turmoil that contributed to the Great Recession. This act imposed new regulations on financial institutions and established several new oversight bodies, with the goal of reducing risk in financial markets. But while the new regulations may have done that, they also affected banks' day-to-day operations. The new constraints represented a permanent change in how financial institutions operate and contributed to the reduction in long-run aggregate supply.

Consider an analogy in which financial markets are a bridge between savers and borrowers in an economy. Funds flowing between savers and borrowers are the "traffic" flowing across the bridge. If the economy is to grow, firms must be able to borrow, and so the bridge must be safe and efficient. Financial crises are like accidents on the bridge that disrupt the flow of traffic and temporarily slow the economy. New financial regulations are like speed bumps or stricter speed limits, imposed to reduce the number of accidents and keep the traffic flowing. So while the new regulations can reduce instability in financial markets, we also acknowledge that fewer risky loans might also reduce growth in expansionary periods. In our model, we illustrate the permanent effects of the financial crisis and changes in institutions as a decline in long-run aggregate supply.

Figure 27.9 shows a decline in both aggregate demand and aggregate supply from 2007 to 2008. Aggregate demand shifted from AD_{2007} to AD_{2008}, and long-run aggregate supply shifted from $LRAS_{2007}$ to $LRAS_{2008}$. (Short-run aggregate supply is not pictured here; it shifts with the long-run curve.) In 2007, the economy was in equilibrium at point A; at that time, the unemployment rate (not pictured in Figure 27.9) was below 5%, and real GDP (Y*) was growing at a 3.6% rate in the second quarter of 2007.

Then conditions worsened as housing prices fell and financial market turmoil ensued, leading to lower real wealth and then to lower consumer confidence. The declines in aggregate demand and long-run aggregate supply moved the economy to a new equilibrium at point B. During this time, the unemployment rate climbed to 10%, and by the last quarter of 2008, real GDP

FIGURE 27.9

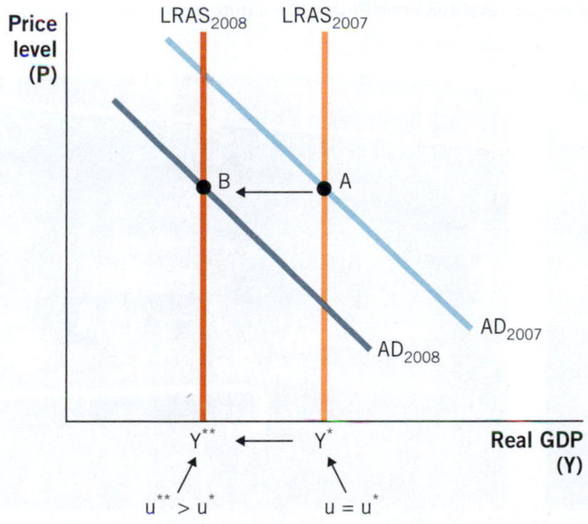

The Decline in Both Long-Run Aggregate Supply and Aggregate Demand, 2007–2008

Financial-market turmoil and lower consumer confidence led to decreases in both long-run aggregate supply and aggregate demand. The result was a new, lower level of real GDP and a higher rate of unemployment ($u^{**} > u^*$).

was declining by 8.9% (on an annual basis). The unemployment rate rose significantly beginning in 2008 and then continued for several years. This was due in part to an increase in cyclical unemployment, but it was also due to an increase in structural unemployment as the economy adjusted to new types of output in the wake of a decline in long-run aggregate supply.

ECONOMICS IN THE REAL WORLD

COMPARING THE GREAT RECESSION AND THE GREAT DEPRESSION

You lived through the Great Recession. Perhaps it affected you personally. Certainly, many people experienced hardships as a result of the economic downturn. However, very few of us were forced to move into shanties on the street.

The Great Depression was different. Living through it scarred an entire generation of Americans. Perhaps your great-grandparents were part of this generation. Now might be a good time to talk to them (if possible) and ask how their life changed during the 1930s.

Many American families lost their homes and jobs during the Depression. The best alternative for many, in some parts of the country, was sharecropping: living on a farm and harvesting the crops on behalf of the owners. For some other families, the best available living arrangement was in shantytowns dubbed Hoovervilles, after President Herbert Hoover (who served from 1929 to 1933). Although both homelessness and unemployment are still issues in the United States, the problems' extent is far smaller today—and was far smaller during the Great Recession—than it was during the Great Depression.

Consider that during the Great Recession years, 2007 to 2009, the number of Starbucks locations in the United States grew from 10,684 to 11,128.* Thus, a chain of coffee shops that sell basic drinks for about $4 each actually expanded during the Great Recession. Yes, the coffee is very good, but that could never have happened during the Great Depression. As a comparison, the Great Depression saw the rise of "penny restaurants," which would sell for 1 cent items that typically cost 15–40 cents elsewhere. Penny restaurants appeared all over the country and were often supported by local charitable groups or wealthy individuals. That should give you an idea how severe the Great Depression was, compared to the Great Recession.

*"Starbucks Company Statistics," Statistic Brain Research Institute, September 2012, statisticbrain.com.

Unemployed workers gather together in New York City, December 1937. They have a Christmas tree near their shanty.

Stores like this one would not have survived the Great Depression.

The Coronavirus Recession

In early 2020, the U.S. economy was experiencing its longest expansion on record: real GDP had grown for more than a decade, and the unemployment rate was just 3.5%, its lowest level since 1969. In the language of macroeconomics, the U.S. economy was at or near its full-employment level. Elsewhere, conditions were similarly favorable: the unemployment rate was 7.3% in Europe, 4.4% in China, and just 2.5% in Japan.

When major cities across the United States started seeing infection outbreaks, retail outlets shut their doors and hoped the crisis would pass quickly.

However, a worldwide catastrophe was unfolding. On January 1, 2020, Chinese government health inspectors at a market in Wuhan city took germ samples and cleansed parts of the market, hoping to contain an outbreak of a new type of coronavirus. Unfortunately, their efforts fell short. By January 23, when Wuhan's 11 million residents went into lockdown, the virus had already escaped and begun its spread across the globe.

The first coronavirus infection in the United States was diagnosed on January 20, 2020. The economy went into recession seven weeks later, right around March 10, as people began social distancing, travel was widely banned, and many U.S. states started restricting large gatherings. Major League Baseball and the NBA postponed their seasons. College athletic events, including the March Madness basketball tournament, were canceled. Restaurants, movie theaters, airports, and retail stores closed their doors. Universities sent students home and shifted to online instruction. We can't usually pinpoint the exact beginning of a recession, but here we can. You likely recall this period vividly, as daily life instantly changed for almost everyone.

THE MAGNITUDE OF THE CORONAVIRUS RECESSION Figure 27.10 shows U.S. real GDP and the unemployment rate from the year 2000 to the end of 2021. In both panels, the COVID-19 recession stands out dramatically. Looking at panel (a), you can see the "cliff" in the second quarter of 2020, where the U.S economy plunged into recession. Real GDP fell 9% in that quarter alone. This translates to a 31.7% annual drop—the hypothetical rate of decrease if the quarterly drop lasted a whole year. Panel (b) shows the effect on the unemployment rate. In April of 2020, the rate climbed to 14.7%, its highest point since the Great Depression.

However, the COVID-19 recession stands out in the data not only because it came on so quickly but also because of the rapid recovery. By early 2021, real GDP was back to its pre-recession level, and by the end of 2021, the unemployment rate had dropped back below 4%.

USING OUR MODEL TO EXPLAIN THE CORONAVIRUS RECESSION The coronavirus recession was different from the other two recessions we consider in this chapter. Most importantly, the main driver of this downturn was a global pandemic. Remember our definition of a supply shock: a surprise (exogenous) event that changes production costs. A pandemic is a classic short-run supply shock that shifts the short-run aggregate supply curve to the left. The COVID-19 pandemic was far worse than other recent pandemics (like SARS in 2003* and the H1N1 swine flu in 2009†), but it affected the economy in the same

Even during the most restrictive lockdowns, food shopping was a permitted essential activity.

*James W. LeDuc and M. Anita Barry, "SARS, the First Pandemic of the 21st Century," *Emerging Infectious Diseases* 10, no. 11 (November 2004), http://doi.org/10.3201/eid1011.040797_02.

†"2009 H1N1 Pandemic (H1N1pdm09 virus)," Centers for Disease Control and Prevention, U.S. Department of Health & Human Services, last modified June 11, 2019, https://www.cdc.gov/flu/pandemic-resources/2009-h1n1-pandemic.html.

FIGURE 27.10

U.S. Real GDP and Unemployment, 2000–2021

(a) Real GDP plummeted in the second quarter of 2020, at the fastest rate since the Great Depression. However, GDP returned to its pre-COVID level by early 2021, and by 2022, it was back to its pre-COVID trend. (b) The unemployment rate skyrocketed to 14.7% in April 2020, the highest level since the Great Depression, but by the end of 2021, the unemployment rate had dropped back below 4%.

Sources: (a) Bureau of Economic Analysis; (b) Bureau of Labor Statistics.

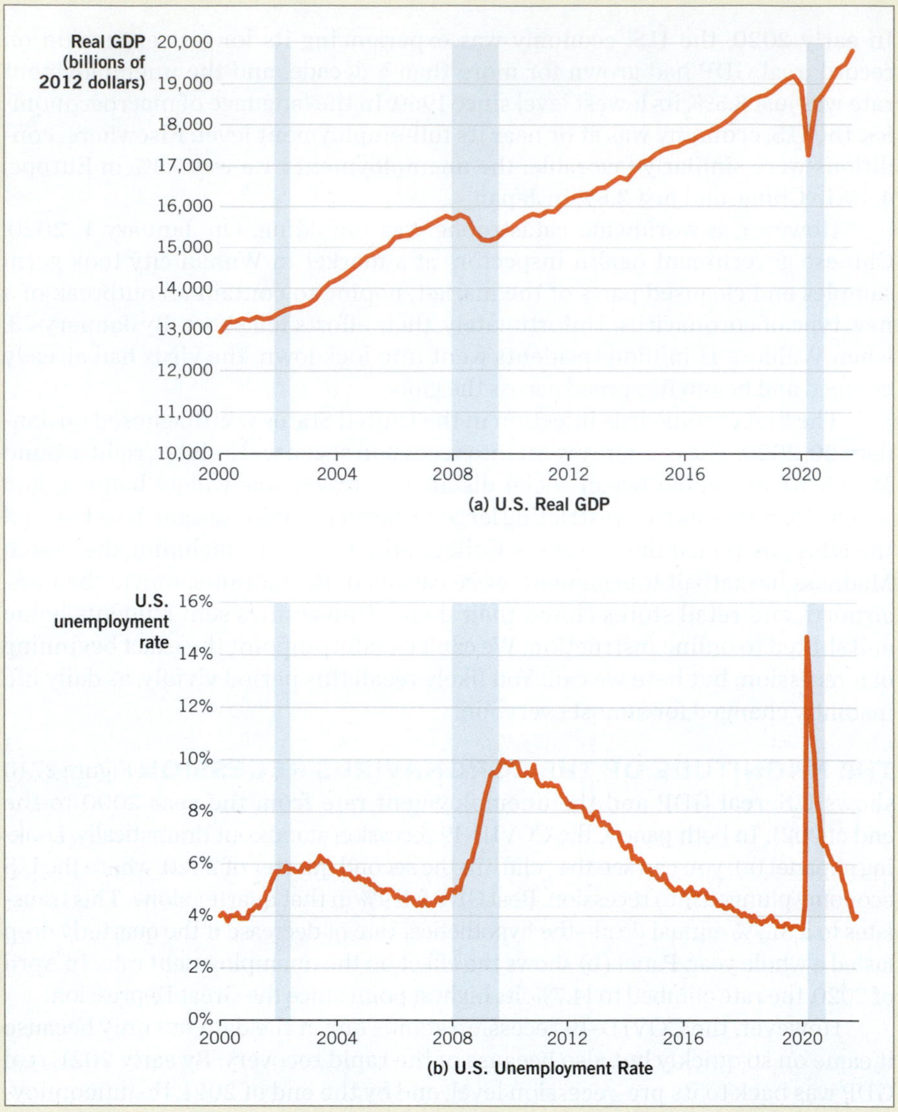

basic way—just much more severely. While the primary and largest cause of the 2020 recession was on the supply side, aggregate demand also fell. Real wealth fell, and extreme uncertainty reduced expected future income, both of which led to a decrease in AD.

Figure 27.11 illustrates these changes in the U.S. economy. At the end of 2019, the economy was in long-run equilibrium at point A, with short-run aggregate supply $SRAS_{2019}$, long-run aggregate supply LRAS, and aggregate demand AD_{2019}. The unemployment rate was below 4%, and real GDP increased by 2% in 2019.

By the following March, however, much of the U.S. economy was shutting down. You can see this in the model: short-run aggregate supply declined to $SRAS_{2020}$, and aggregate demand decreased to AD_{2020}. The reduction in SRAS followed increased production costs, due to factors like social distancing,

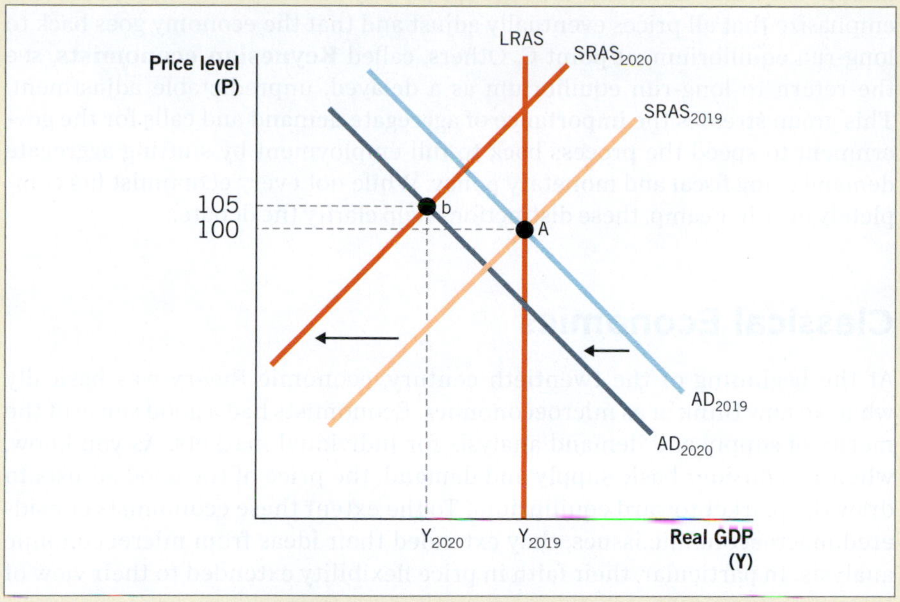

FIGURE 27.11

The Coronavirus Recession in the AD–AS Model

At the end of 2019, the U.S. economy had experienced a historically long expansionary period. In the figure, it was in equilibrium at Y_{2019} and P = 100. When the pandemic hit, short-run aggregate supply shifted from $SRAS_{2019}$ to $SRAS_{2020}$. Aggregate demand shifted too, from AD_{2019} to AD_{2020}, but the SRAS shift dominated, pushing the price level up.

international shipping interruptions, and general health risks from the virus itself. Think of what restaurants in your area had to do to stay open. Many found a way to provide outdoor seating, but the tents and awnings cost money, and so did the extra time it took servers to bring food out to tables. Even then, restaurants couldn't accommodate as many patrons as before, and they had difficulty hiring workers who were fearful of being exposed to the virus. That is what aggregate supply shifting left looked like: a lot of firms had to spend more to produce less.

After the shifts in SRAS and AD, the new short-run equilibrium was at point b with higher prices, lower real GDP, and higher unemployment. In the long run, as infection rates fell and behavior returned to normal (or close to it), SRAS and AD shifted back to the right, and the economy returned to long-run equilibrium. You can see this in the GDP data in Figure 27.10. The big plunge is the original leftward shift in SRAS, and then, quarter after quarter, the economy moves back toward its pre-COVID state.

What Are the Big Disagreements in Macroeconomics?

We now consider the major debates in macroeconomics by building on our discussion of the Great Depression. Most economists agree with the basic implications of the aggregate demand–aggregate supply model. However, economists disagree about the role of government and the economy's ability to self-correct. In this section, we try to clarify some of the issues on which this debate turns.

Perhaps the most contentious issue among macroeconomists involves the economy's adjustment to long-run equilibrium. Consider again the short-run

Classical economists stress the importance of aggregate supply and generally believe that the economy can adjust back to full-employment equilibrium on its own.

Keynesian economists stress the importance of aggregate demand and generally believe that the economy needs help returning to full-employment equilibrium.

equilibrium, b, in Figure 27.1. Some economists believe that adjustment can and should occur naturally. This group, broadly called **classical economists**, emphasize that all prices eventually adjust and that the economy goes back to long-run equilibrium, at point C. Others, called **Keynesian economists**, see the return to long-run equilibrium as a delayed, unpredictable adjustment. This group stresses the importance of aggregate demand and calls for the government to speed the process back to full employment by shifting aggregate demand using fiscal and monetary policy. While not every economist fits completely in either camp, these distinctions help clarify the debate.

Classical Economics

At the beginning of the twentieth century, economic theory was basically what we now think of as microeconomics. Economists had a good sense of the merits of supply and demand analysis for individual markets. As you know, when we consider basic supply and demand, the price of the good adjusts to draw the market toward equilibrium. To the extent these economists considered macroeconomic issues, they extended their ideas from microeconomic analysis. In particular, their faith in price flexibility extended to their view of the macroeconomy.

Thus, flexible prices form the foundation of the classical view of the macroeconomy. Consider the implications: if prices are completely flexible, the economy is essentially self-correcting. No matter what factors change in the economy, no matter which curves shift, with fully flexible prices the economy automatically maintains full employment (illustrated by the vertical long-run aggregate supply curve). Figure 27.12 illustrates the strictly classical view. Initially, the economy is in long-run equilibrium at point A. If aggregate demand

FIGURE 27.12

The Classical View of the Macroeconomy

In the classical view, prices adjust quickly in both directions. Therefore, shifts in aggregate demand do not lead to changes in output or employment because the output level stays at full employment. When prices are completely flexible, aggregate demand becomes less relevant, and changes in long-run aggregate supply are considered the primary source of economic prosperity.

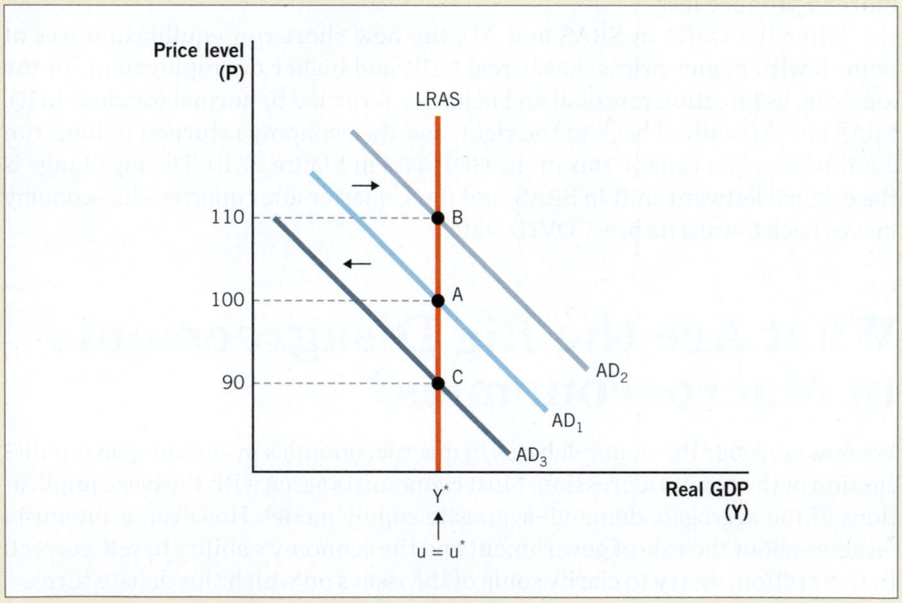

increases from AD_1 to AD_2, price flexibility means the economy moves to a new equilibrium at point B. At point B, real GDP is at full-employment output (Y^*), and the unemployment rate is at the natural rate ($u = u^*$). In short, increases in aggregate demand are not dangerous when prices quickly adjust.

The results are similar when aggregate demand declines. If aggregate demand falls from AD_1 to AD_3, price flexibility implies that the economy moves to long-run equilibrium at point C. (This outcome is very different from the story we told about the Great Depression, illustrated in Figure 27.8.) If prices are completely flexible, the economy quickly settles back at full-employment output and the natural rate of unemployment. Classical economists probably slept well at night, without worries about long-term economic contractions.

Because they believed that economy self-corrects back to full employment, classical economists were essentially laissez-faire in their policy recommendations. They had faith that market adjustments would take place quickly, so they saw no significant role for a governmental macroeconomic policy focusing on short-run fixes when the economy is underperforming or overperforming.

Today, some economists still lean toward this classical view. They don't worry much about aggregate demand shifts. These economists focus on economic policies designed to promote long-run growth; their main focus is on shifting long-run aggregate supply. Given this perspective, they see savings as a crucial positive factor in the economy: savings translate into investment, which increases capital and shifts the long-run aggregate supply curve to the right.

Keynesian Economics

Although the classical economists dominated economics early in the twentieth century, the experience of the Great Depression presented a challenge to the accepted wisdom. The Great Depression set the stage for a new approach to macroeconomics. John Maynard Keynes, a British economist, formulated this new doctrine. In 1936, Keynes published *The General Theory of Employment, Interest, and Money*. This book vaulted him into the forefront of macroeconomic debates because it offered a theory about why recessions might last a while. Indeed, the title of the book—*The General Theory*—implies that Keynes believed that an economy out of long-run equilibrium is not unusual. Proponents of this view came to be known as Keynesian economists.

Keynesian economists emphasize that after a decline in aggregate demand, some prices, particularly wages, are very slow to adjust downward to move the economy back to full employment. In short, wages and certain other prices are "sticky." As a result, high real wages prevent the labor market from reaching equilibrium and restoring full employment. Here we have an explanation for how prolonged recessions can happen. Keynes advocated governmental intervention to move the economy back to full employment. He argued that the government should try to shift the aggregate demand curve back to its initial level. According to Keynes, it is foolish to wait for long-run adjustments because, as he famously said, "In the long run we are all dead."

To the extent that wages and other prices are indeed sticky, demand declines spell serious trouble for the economy, because there is no natural adjustment back to full employment. So Keynesian economists focus on the demand side of the economy as the source of instability. Look back at Figure 27.11, which shows the decline in aggregate demand between 1929 and 1930+. This large decline was due to a fall in wealth, lower consumer confidence, and bad policy that led to a monetary contraction. If prices don't adjust downward, the short-run equilibrium at b becomes a long-run equilibrium.

Why would wages and other prices be sticky? One explanation is the presence of long-term wage contracts, especially when negotiated through collective bargaining agreements by unions. Certainly, a larger percentage of the labor force was unionized in the 1930s, and this no doubt contributed to wage rigidity. But money illusion may also have played a role (see Chapter 21). Imagine yourself as an employee in the midst of the Great Depression: times are tough, and now your employer is asks you to accept lower wages. This is a tough pill to swallow, even if, with falling consumer prices, you're not looking at a *real* wage decrease. You, or some of your coworkers, might refuse a wage cut. Employees who refuse a pay cut might lose their jobs. This begins a troubling cycle, as workers without jobs drastically cut their spending, and this leads to a reduction in economic activity. Recall the circular flow diagram we discussed in Chapter 1. The welfare of businesses and workers are intertwined.

Keynes recommended that the British and U.S. governments take action to increase aggregate demand. Keynes felt that, with additional government spending, governments could play a role in stopping the global economy's decline. Government spending can increase aggregate demand. Keynes recommended fiscal policy in the form of spending on social programs and additional infrastructure (we discuss this further in Chapter 29). During the Great Depression, a host of programs put into place as part of Franklin Delano Roosevelt's New Deal were designed to create immediate jobs and spending in the economy. If aggregate demand is too low because individuals and firms are reluctant to spend, Keynes argued, the government might fill the void by increasing the government-spending piece of aggregate demand.

The Keynesian view of the economy offered an explanation for the Great Depression (see the appendix to this chapter for more details on this view). In fact, after the nation emerged from the Great Depression, Keynesian theory became dominant in the field of economics.

Table 27.1 summarizes the major differences between classical and Keynesian economists.

TABLE 27.1

Classical versus Keynesian Economics

	Classical economics	Keynesian economics
Key time period	Long run	Short run
Price flexibility	Prices are flexible	Prices are sticky
Savings	Crucial to growth	A drain on demand
Key side of market	Supply	Demand
Market tendency	Stability, full employment	Instability, cyclical unemployment
Government intervention	Not necessary	Essential

PRACTICE WHAT YOU KNOW

The Big Debates: Guess Which View

QUESTION: Consider the four statements below. Which type of economist, Keynesian or classical, would likely make each statement? Explain your choice each time.

a. "If you want to help the economy, you should increase your spending."

b. "If you want to help the economy, you should increase your savings."

c. "Governmental policy should focus on counteracting short-run fluctuations in the economy."

d. "Governmental policy should not intervene in the business cycle because the economy can correct itself."

ANSWER:

a. *Keynesian.* The Keynesian approach focuses on spending, or aggregate demand, as the fundamental factor in the economy.

b. *Classical.* The classical approach focuses on long-run aggregate supply as the primary source of economic prosperity. In this view, increases in savings are necessary for increased investment, which shifts long-run aggregate supply to the right.

c. *Keynesian.* The Keynesian approach emphasizes inherent instability in the macroeconomy and the resulting need for governmental action to counteract the business cycle.

d. *Classical.* The classical approach emphasizes price flexibility, which means the economy can correct itself and naturally move back to full-employment output levels.

Which type of economist would recommend this shopping trip?

Conclusion

We began this chapter with a look at the severity of the Great Depression. While every recession brings hardship, we have seen that no other modern recession was nearly so severe as the Great Depression. We've now also considered two different views of the macro economy: the classical view and the Keynesian view. The views of most economists probably fall on a continuum between these two views, some emphasizing price adjustments and the importance of supply and others emphasizing price stickiness and the importance of demand. But most also see a role for governmental policy, especially during downturns when resources are idle.

Going forward, we can use the aggregate demand–aggregate supply model as a tool for analyzing governmental policy. This includes monetary policy, which adjusts the money supply, and fiscal policy, which adjusts taxes and spending. Over the next four chapters, we evaluate these policy alternatives and use the aggregate demand–aggregate supply model to understand how governmental policy affects the economy. ✷

ECONOMICS *in the* MEDIA

The Big Disagreements in Macroeconomics

"FEAR THE BOOM AND THE BUST"

It's Keynes versus Hayek in a YouTube video that has almost 10 million hits. It is a highly original rap video that imagines what two giants of economics, F. A. Hayek and John Maynard Keynes, would have to say to defend their ideas. F. A. Hayek represents the classical economists. Here are some of the best lines:

We've been going back and forth for a century.

[KEYNES] I want to steer markets,

[HAYEK] I want them set free.

There's a boom and bust cycle and good reason to fear it.

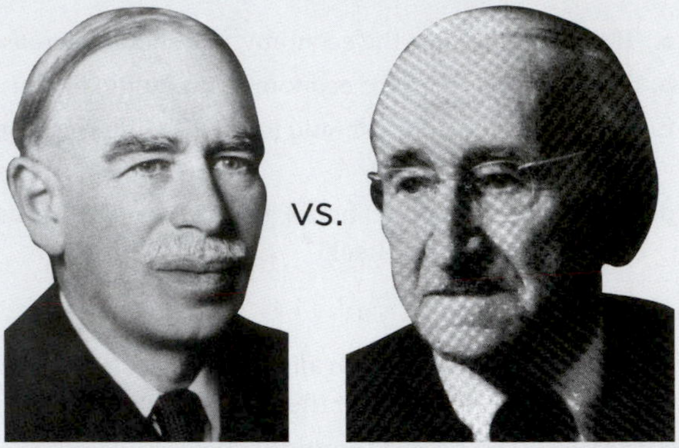

Keynes (left), sometimes referred to as "the father of macroeconomics," and Hayek, his dogged critic. Check out their "battle" on YouTube!

F. A. Hayek was one of the twentieth century's most significant defenders of free markets. In 1943, he wrote *The Road to Serfdom,* a book that cautions against central planning. Hayek characterizes markets as having the ability to organize spontaneously, to the benefit of an economy. *The Road to Serfdom* appeared in print just a few years after John Maynard Keynes published his *General Theory* in 1936. How could these two giants of economics see the world so differently?

The Austrian-born Hayek, who received the 1974 Nobel Prize in Economics, lived long enough to observe that economics had come full circle. His Nobel acceptance speech was titled "The Pretense of Knowledge." In the talk, he criticized the economics profession for being too quick to adopt Keynesian ideas. Keynes had argued that the economy moves slowly to long-run equilibrium. Hayek countered that efforts to stimulate demand presume that economists know what they are doing; he argued that just because we can build elaborate macroeconomic models does not mean the models can anticipate every change in the economy. Hayek pointed to the high inflation rates and high unemployment rates of the 1970s as evidence that the Keynesian model was incomplete. Accordingly, he concluded, it would be best to put our faith in the one thing all economists generally agree on: eventually the economy will naturally return to full-employment output levels.

"Fear the Boom and the Bust" presents the views of Hayek and Keynes to make you think. While you might not "get" the many references in the rap just yet, watch it anyway (and tell your friends to watch it). The subject it treats is an important, ongoing debate, and one of the goals of your study of economics is to acquire the information you need to decide for yourself what approach is best for the economy. The video's producers, EconStories, released a sequel a year later. You can view all their work at their YouTube channel: www.youtube.com/user/econstories.

· ANSWERING *the* BIG QUESTIONS ·

Why do recessions occur?

- Shifts in aggregate demand.
- Shifts in aggregate supply.

What happened during three major recessions?

- The Great Recession was characterized by shifts in both long-run aggregate supply and aggregate demand.
- The Great Recession was deeper and longer than typical U.S. recessions.
- The Great Depression was significantly worse than the Great Recession.
- The coronavirus recession began with a decline in short-run aggregate supply (SRAS), but then long-run aggregate supply (LRAS) and aggregate demand (AD) also declined.

What are the big disagreements in macroeconomics?

- The big debates in macroeconomics focus on the flexibility of prices and the emphasis on aggregate supply or aggregate demand. The two key schools of thought are classical economics and Keynesian economics.
- If prices are assumed to be flexible, the implication is a generally stable macroeconomy without significant need for government help.
- If prices are assumed to be sticky, the implication is an inherently unstable economy in need of government assistance.

CHAPTER PROBLEMS

Concepts You Should Know

classical economists (p. 888)
Dodd-Frank Act (p. 882)
fiscal policy (p. 879)
Keynesian economists (p. 888)
macroeconomic policy (p. 879)
monetary policy (p. 879)

Questions for Review

1. What were the cause(s) of the long-run aggregate supply shift during the Great Recession? What were the cause(s) of the aggregate demand shift during the Great Recession?
2. What specific numerical evidence would you give to explain why the Great Depression was so much worse than the Great Recession?
3. What is the key side (supply or demand) of the economy for Keynesian economists? What assumption about prices leads them to this emphasis? What is the key side of the economy (supply or demand) for classical economists? What assumption about prices leads them to this emphasis?
4. In Chapter 26, we covered three factors that shift long-run aggregate supply. What are those factors? Which of those factors changed during the period of the Great Recession, and how did they change?
5. In Chapter 26, we covered a list of factors that shift aggregate demand. Which of those factors changed during the Great Depression, and how did they change?
6. Consider the following statements about the macroeconomy. For each, indicate whether the statement best distinguishes the strict Keynesian view, strict classical view, or neither of these views.
   a. All prices are completely flexible.
   b. The primary focus is on aggregate supply.
   c. Spending is the key determinant of output.
   d. Capital is the key source of economic growth.
   e. Saving can be detrimental to the economy.
   f. The macroeconomy generally takes care of itself.
   g. Every dollar borrowed requires a dollar saved.
   h. The macroeconomy is inherently unstable.
   i. Full employment is at the natural rate of unemployment.
   j. Some prices don't adjust downward.
7. Name two reasons why prices might be sticky in the downward direction.

Study Problems (*✷ solved at the end of the section*)

✷ 1. Explain whether each of the following statements is more likely to come from a classical economist or a Keynesian economist:
   a. "The recent decline in consumer confidence will likely spell disaster for the economy."
   b. "Business managers making investment decisions play a crucial role in the short-run economy."
   c. "Consumer spending is down, but that is good news because it means savings is up."
   d. "In the long run we are all dead."
   e. "There is no reason to believe that most prices will take more than several months to adjust in either direction."

2. For this problem, we want to practice working with the aggregate demand–aggregate supply model.
   a. Set up an aggregate demand–aggregate supply model in long-run equilibrium, with both short-run and long-run aggregate supply curves and an aggregate demand curve. Label the equilibrium price level as P^* and the equilibrium level of real GDP as Y^*. Draw this model twice.
   b. Using the first set of curves you drew in part (a), now assume that aggregate demand and aggregate supply (both short-run and long-run) decline. If all curves shift by the same amount, what is the resulting change in real GDP and the

price level? What is the implied change in the unemployment rate?

c. Now, using the second set of curves from part (a), let aggregate demand decline by a large amount while the aggregate supply curves decline by a relatively small amount. What are the resulting short-run changes in real GDP and the price level? What is the implied short-run change in the unemployment rate?

d. Parts (b) and (c) describe the two different conditions of the Great Recession and the Great Depression. Which part refers to the Great Recession? Which part refers to the Great Depression?

3. Assume that the economy is in long-run equilibrium, with real GDP at the full-employment output level (Y^*) and the unemployment rate equal to the natural rate (u^*).

a. Now assume there is a drop in business firm confidence, that is, decision-makers at firms lose confidence in the future direction of the economy. Illustrate this change using the AD–AS model.

b. What happens to real GDP and unemployment in the short run?

c. What policy or policies would a Keynesian economist recommend to remedy this situation?

d. How would a classical economist respond to this situation?

Solved Problem

1. a. *Keynesian.* The key here is that Keynesian economists emphasize the role of aggregate demand, which depends on consumer confidence.

b. *Keynesian.* The key here is the emphasis on the short run. Investment is a component of aggregate demand and can have an impact on spending in the short run.

c. *Classical.* The key here is the classical emphasis on savings, which can lead to greater levels of lending in the loanable funds market—an outcome that increases capital in the long run.

d. *Keynesian.* In fact, this is a direct quote from John Maynard Keynes himself. The key here is that the quote de-emphasizes the long run in favor of the short run.

e. *Classical.* The key here is the emphasis on price flexibility.

APPENDIX

27A The Aggregate Expenditures Model

We have used the aggregate demand–aggregate supply (AD–AS) model to explain different reasons why the economy expands and contracts. In addition, we used the AD–AS model to explain the differences between classical economists and Keynesian economists. We observed that Keynesian economists focus on aggregate demand and sticky prices. In this appendix, we develop another model of the economy, the **aggregate expenditures (AE) model**, which extends the Keynesian perspective.

The **aggregate expenditures (AE) model** is a short-run model of economic fluctuations. It holds that prices are completely sticky (inflexible) and that aggregate demand (aggregate expenditures) determines the economy's level of output and income.

The AE model holds that prices are completely sticky and that aggregate demand therefore determines the economy's level of output and income. In fact, *aggregate expenditures* is another name for aggregate demand.

You may be wondering why some economists are willing to make the assumption that prices do not change. After all, we have seen that all prices adjust in the long run. We can therefore view the AE model strictly as a short-run model of the economy, where prices are inflexible. This model is particularly helpful in understanding economic downturns because, as we have seen, prices can be particularly inflexible in the downward direction.

The Components of Aggregate Expenditures

The four components of aggregate demand are consumption (C), investment (I), government spending (G), and net exports (NX). Aggregate expenditures is another way of describing aggregate demand. Let's consider each component.

Consumption

Recall that consumption expenditures constitute about 71% of all GDP spending. Because this component of aggregate expenditures is so large, it is the key to understanding the AE model. We start with a microeconomic example.

Let's say that your friend Kaitlyn has a job that pays her $3,000 a month after taxes. This $3,000 is Kaitlyn's monthly **disposable income** (Y_d), or income after taxes (Y – T). Kaitlyn is disciplined about saving a part of her income, using 80%, or $2,400 per month, for consumption. She saves the

Disposable income is income after taxes (Y – T).

remaining 20%, or $600, of her disposable income. Last year was a productive year for Kaitlyn, and she is excited because her boss rewarded her with a raise that works out to $200 more disposable income every month. After the raise, Kaitlyn decides to continue saving 20% of her new disposable income, which leaves 80% for consumption.

We are talking about Kaitlyn's propensity to spend her income on consumption as opposed to saving. The **marginal propensity to consume (MPC)** is the portion of additional income spent on consumption. Kaitlyn's MPC is 80%, or 0.8. The **marginal propensity to save (MPS)** is the portion of additional income saved. Kaitlyn's MPS is 20%, or 0.2. MPC and MPS sum to 1 because income is either spent or saved:

The **marginal propensity to consume (MPC)** is the portion of additional income spent on consumption.

The **marginal propensity to save (MPS)** is the portion of additional income saved.

$$MPC + MPS = 1 \quad \text{(EQUATION 27A.1)}$$

This equation applies to individuals like Kaitlyn but also to entire economies. The MPC for a national economy is the average portion of additional income that people in the economy spend on consumption.

We can look at data from the United States over time to see how consumption spending rises with disposable income. Figure 27A.1 shows data on consumption and disposable income for the United States for the years 1965–2014. You can see the positive relationship in the slope: as disposable income rises, so does consumption.

FIGURE 27A.1

U.S. Real Consumption and Disposable Income, 1965–2014

As real disposable income rises, consumption also increases. This is one way of viewing the consumption function for an entire economy.

Source: Bureau of Economic Analysis.

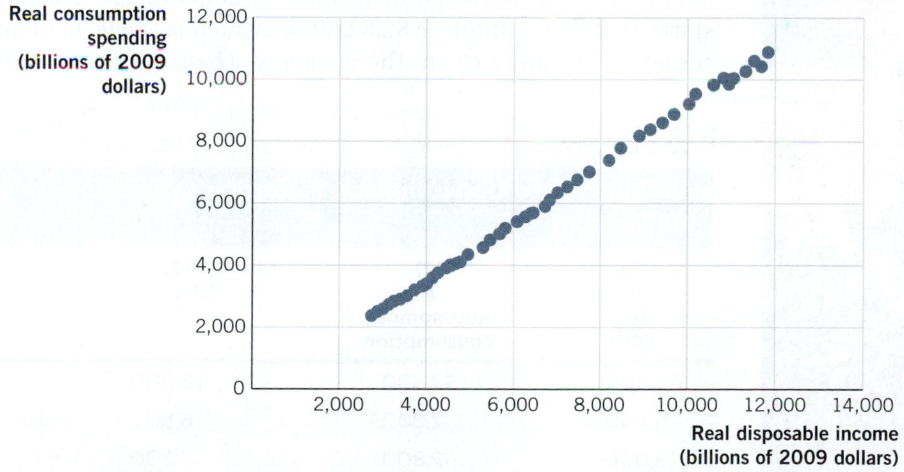

It is helpful to specify the relationship between national consumption spending and disposable income in equation form. This equation is called the **aggregate consumption function**:

(EQUATION 27A.2)

$$C = A + MPC \times (Y - T)$$

The **aggregate consumption function** is an equation that specifies the relationship between national income and national consumption.

Autonomous consumption spending is spending on consumption independent of the level of income.

This equation says that consumption rises with disposable income (Y − T). Whenever disposable income increases by $1, consumption rises by MPC, the marginal propensity to consume. The letter A in the equation represents **autonomous consumption spending**, which is spending on consumption independent of the level of income. (The word "autonomous" means "independent.") Viewed this way, Equation 27A.2 implies that even when income is zero, some consumption must take place (A), and for every dollar rise in disposable income, consumption rises by MPC.

For the remainder of this appendix, we make a simplifying assumption with regard to disposable income. We assume that taxes do not change, so all changes in income (Y) are the same changes in disposable income (Y − T). This assumption does not affect the major implications of the analysis, but it does make the model much simpler. With this assumption, the aggregate consumption function becomes

(EQUATION 27A.3)

$$C = A + MPC \times Y$$

Consider the consumption function presented in Table 27A.1 (all dollar values are in billions of dollars). In this example, autonomous consumption is equal to $2,800 billion, and the marginal propensity to consume is 0.6. The first column shows real GDP, or real income levels, ranging from $10,000 billion to $14,000 billion. Column 2 is autonomous consumption spending, which does not change with income level (by definition). Column 3 shows the MPC of 0.6 times the value of Y from column 1. Column 4 is the sum of columns 2 and 3: total consumption C = A + MPC × Y.

Figure 27A.2 plots this hypothetical consumption function with real income (Y) on the horizontal axis and consumption spending (C) on the vertical axis (both measured in trillions of dollars). The consumption function starts at $2,800 billion, or $2.8 trillion, which is the level of autonomous consumption spending (A) in the economy. Then, for every dollar of additional

A person's marginal propensity to consume is determined by the portion of disposable income changes they spend (versus save).

TABLE 27A.1

An Aggregate Consumption Function (all dollars in billions; MPC = 0.6)

(1) Y Real GDP	(2) A Autonomous consumption	(3) MPC × Y	(4) C A + MPC × Y
$10,000	$2,800	$6,000	$8,800
11,000	2,800	6,600	9,400
12,000	2,800	7,200	10,000
13,000	2,800	7,800	10,600
14,000	2,800	8,400	11,200

FIGURE 27A.2

Aggregate Consumption Function

The aggregate consumption function shows how consumption is affected by changes in real GDP, which is real income. The equation for this function is $C = \$2.8 + 0.6 \times Y$, which implies that autonomous consumption is \$2.8 trillion and that the marginal propensity to consume (MPC) is 0.6.

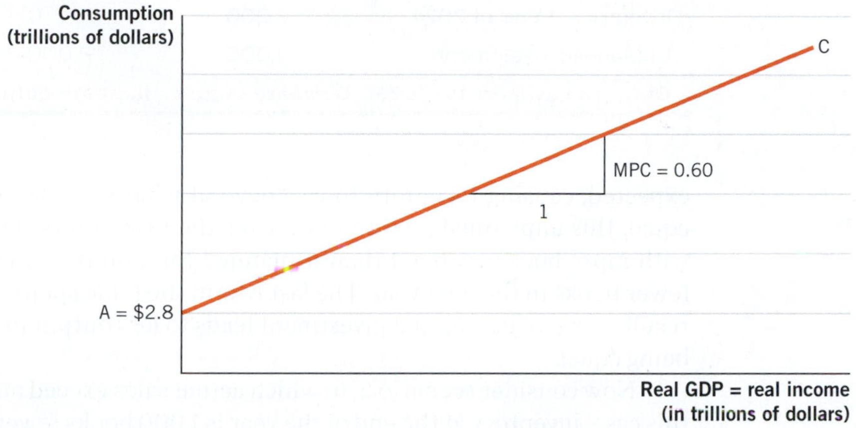

income, consumption rises by \$0.60, so the slope of the consumption function is 0.6. This slope is the marginal propensity to consume.

Investment

Recall that investment is private spending by firms on tools, plant, equipment, and inventory to produce future output. Inventories play a critical role in the AE model. Inventory investment is not perfectly predictable because firms typically don't know the exact number of goods and services they will sell in a given period.

For example, consider a book publisher who is trying to plan for sales of a popular book in 2024. Imagine that the publisher begins the year with an inventory of 1,000 books on hand and anticipates selling 20,000 books in 2024. The publisher would like to have the same level of inventory (1,000 copies) at the end of 2024. Based on these expectations and the current inventory, the publisher prints 20,000 books in 2024.

Now consider the three scenarios displayed in Table 27A.2. In scenario 1, actual sales are 19,000, which is less than the firm anticipated. In scenario 2, actual sales are 21,000, which is more than the firm anticipated. In scenario 3, actual sales are 20,000, exactly equal to anticipated sales.

Consider scenario 1. Here, sales are less than anticipated, and so inventory at the end of 2024 is more than the firm expected. This unplanned inventory is positive **unplanned investment**, which occurs when a firm sells less than

(Positive) **unplanned investment** occurs when expected sales exceed actual sales, leading to an increase in inventory.

TABLE 27A.2

Planned and Unplanned Inventory

	Scenario 1 Sales = 19,000 books	Scenario 2 Sales = 21,000 books	Scenario 3 Sales = 20,000 books
Inventory at end of 2023	1,000	1,000	1,000
Production	20,000	20,000	20,000
Actual sales in 2024	**19,000**	**21,000**	**20,000**
Inventory at end of 2024	2,000	0	1,000
Unplanned investment	1,000	-1,000	0
Output adjustment for 2025	**Decrease output**	**Increase output**	**No change**

expected, causing inventory to rise beyond what was planned. All else being equal, this unplanned investment means the firm enters the next year (2025) with more books on hand than it planned for, and it will react by producing fewer books in the next year. The last row in the table spells out this important result: positive unplanned investment leads to less output in the future, all else being equal.

Now consider scenario 2, in which actual sales exceed anticipated sales. In this case, inventory at the end of the year is 1,000 books fewer than anticipated. This is an unanticipated decrease in investment, or **negative unplanned investment**. In this case, when people buy more books than the publisher expects, inventories decrease. All else being equal, the publisher will increase production of books in the next year.

Negative unplanned investment occurs when actual sales exceed anticipated sales, leading to a decrease in inventory.

The only scenario that does not require future adjustments is scenario 3. In this case, actual sales equal expected sales, and there are no unexpected changes in inventory: actual investment equals planned investment.

Increases in inventory count as investment.

This example explains why firms across the economy adjust production each year, even when prices are fixed. When spending on output is greater than anticipated, inventories fall, which leads to output increases in subsequent periods. In contrast, if spending is less than anticipated, inventories pile up and then firms produce less in the future. Equilibrium occurs when spending plans match production plans.

An Economy without Government Spending or Net Exports

Before we consider the other components of AE, it is helpful to consider an economy without government spending or net exports. In this case, AE is equal to consumption (C) plus planned investment (PI):

$$AE = C + PI \qquad \text{(EQUATION 27A.4)}$$

Let's return to our numerical example. Table 27A.3 is a continuation of the example presented in Table 27A.1 but adds planned investment expenditures. Column 4 indicates $2,000 billion in planned investment expenditures. Note that planned investment expenditures are autonomous with respect to income levels—that is, they don't change with the level of real GDP (Y). In Chapter 26, we identified three factors that do affect the level of investment demand: business firm confidence, interest rates, and the quantity of money in the economy. This list does not include real income, and so we assume planned investment expenditures are autonomous with respect to real income (Y). We add consumption (column 3) and autonomous planned investment (column 4) to derive aggregate expenditures in column 5.

Figure 27A.3 graphs the AE line. The lower line, labeled C, is the consumption function, which begins at a level of A. Recall that A is the level of autonomous consumption spending, or the amount consumers spend in a hypothetical case where income (Y) is zero. Consumption increases with Y, and the slope is equal to the marginal propensity to consume (MPC).

To get aggregate expenditures (AE), we add planned investment (PI) and consumption. Because planned investment spending is autonomous, adding PI to C simply shifts up AE by the same amount at all levels.

TABLE 27A.3

Aggregate Expenditures with No Government Spending or Net Exports (all dollars in billions, MPC = 0.6)

(1) Y Real GDP	(2) A Autonomous consumption	(3) C A + MPC × Y	(4) PI Autonomous planned investment	(5) AE C + PI
$10,000	$2,800	$8,800	$2,000	$10,800
11,000	2,800	9,400	2,000	11,400
12,000	2,800	10,000	2,000	12,000
13,000	2,800	10,600	2,000	12,600
14,000	2,800	11,200	2,000	13,200

FIGURE 27A.3

Summing Consumption and Planned Investment to Get Aggregate Expenditures

Aggregate expenditures (AE) are the sum of all planned spending: consumption (C) and planned investment (PI). The lower line is consumption expenditures, which depend on the level of income (Y) in the economy. Consumption rises with income at a rate equal to the marginal propensity to consume (MPC). To get AE, we add planned investment (PI), which is assumed to be autonomous (unrelated to income). As a result, the AE line is parallel to the C line. The distance between the two lines is planned investment expenditures.

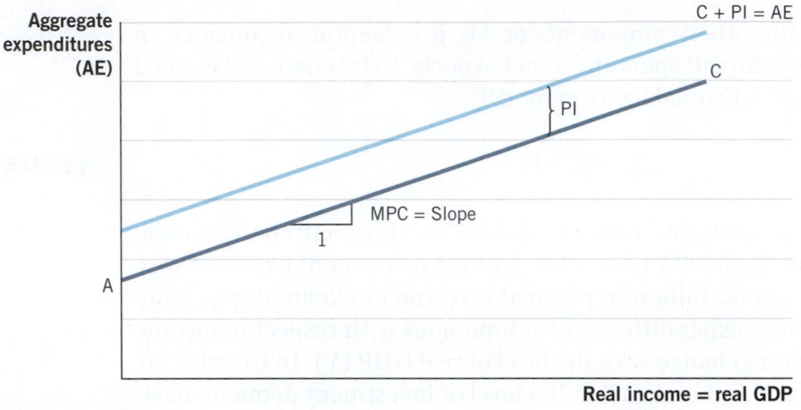

Equilibrium without Government Spending or Net Exports

Before we examine equilibrium in a general sense, let's consider a numerical example. Table 27A.4 continues our running example but adds column 6 to help us determine equilibrium.

In the AE model, equilibrium occurs when there is no reason for firms to adjust output decisions in the future. As we explained earlier, this point occurs

TABLE 27A.4

Equilibrium with No Government Spending or Net Exports (all dollars in billions; MPC = 0.6)

(1) Y Real GDP	(2) A Autonomous consumption	(3) C A + MPC × Y	(4) PI Autonomous planned investment	(5) AE C + PI	(6) AE − Y
$10,000	$2,800	$8,800	$2,000	$10,800	$800
11,000	2,800	9,400	2,000	11,400	400
12,000	**2,800**	**10,000**	**2,000**	**12,000**	**0**
13,000	2,800	10,600	2,000	12,600	−400
14,000	2,800	11,200	2,000	13,200	−800

when actual sales equal anticipated sales, so unplanned inventory investment equals zero. In the language of the AE model, equilibrium occurs when actual spending (Y) is equal to anticipated spending (AE), or when AE = Y.

In our example, equilibrium occurs where real GDP equals $12,000 billion, where there is no difference between AE and Y (indicated in column 6 of Table 27A.4). At real GDP levels below $12,000, aggregate expenditures are greater than actual output (Y). As a result, inventories decrease, and so firms increase output toward $12,000 billion in future periods. On the other hand, at real GDP levels above $12,000 billion, real output exceeds aggregate expenditures. In this case, inventories increase unexpectedly, and firms react in future periods by reducing output toward $12,000 billion. In our example, the only equilibrium point occurs at $12,000 billion.

This is an important result: the equilibrium level of output in the economy is determined by the level of aggregate expenditures. For example, if aggregate expenditures are equal to $11,000 billion, output in the economy will adjust until equilibrium is reached at $11,000 billion. In fact, any point where AE = Y is a possible equilibrium. Panel (a) of Figure 27A.4 plots three possible equilibrium points for a macroeconomy. These always occur where actual real GDP is equal to aggregate expenditures. Panel (b) of Figure 27A.4 presents a line that includes all possible equilibrium points. Notice that this line splits the quadrant into two equal halves and so is at a 45-degree angle. This 45-degree line is a critical piece of the AE model because it shows us all possible equilibrium outcomes.

FIGURE 27A.4

Equilibrium Points in the AE Model

Panel (a) shows three points that are possible equilibrium points in the AE model. For example, when AE is $12 trillion and Y is $12 trillion, then actual spending equals planned spending. In this case, there is no unplanned inventory change and the economy is in equilibrium. Panel (b) plots a line through all possible equilibrium points—that is, all points where AE = Y. This line is called the 45-degree line because it emanates from the origin at 45 degrees.

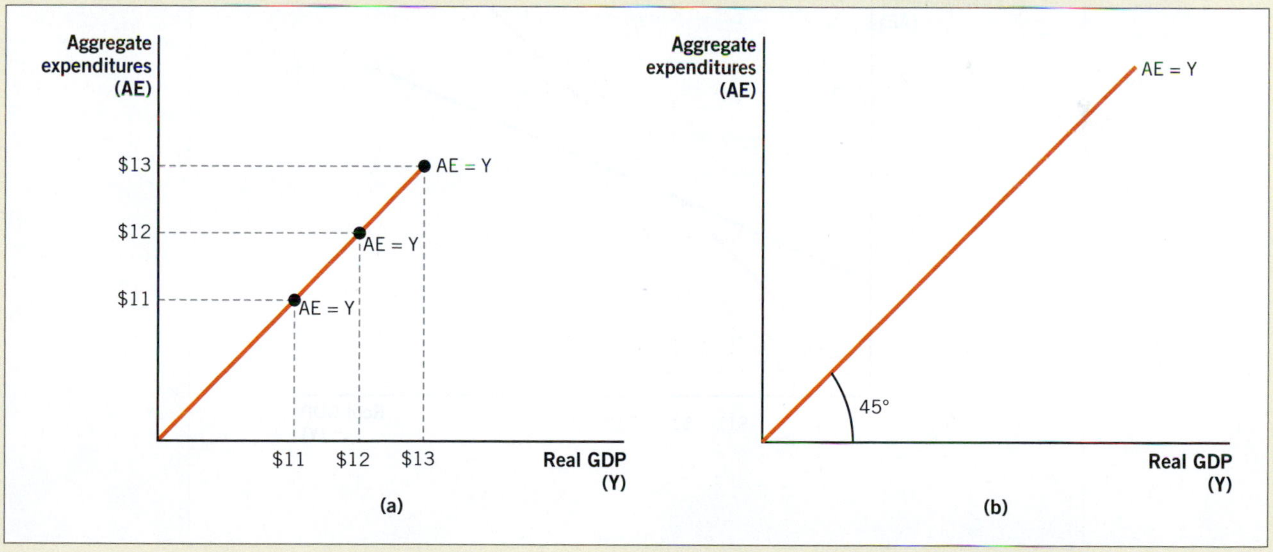

Let's put the 45-degree line together with aggregate expenditures (AE = C + PI) to determine which equilibrium will result. Figure 27A.5 plots the two lines we need for the AE model. The orange line is the 45-degree line that plots potential equilibrium points for the economy. The blue line is the actual level of AE for the economy, composed of expenditures on consumption and planned investment. Equilibrium occurs where planned AE is equal to actual (real) GDP. In this case, given the total level of AE, equilibrium occurs at $12 trillion. To see why this is the case, let's consider the adjustments that occur when actual (real) GDP is not equal to planned AE.

At a GDP of $11 trillion, planned spending (AE) is above actual output because the AE line (blue) is above the 45-degree equilibrium line (orange). In this case, spending is high relative to actual output, which leads to unplanned decreases in inventories. Thus, in the future, firms increase output to adjust to the higher level of planned spending, pushing output toward equilibrium at $12 trillion. This analysis applies to all points where the AE line is above the 45-degree line. That is, at all levels of output less than $12 trillion, firms increase future output and move toward $12 trillion of GDP.

FIGURE 27A.5

Equilibrium with No Government Spending or Net Exports

Equilibrium occurs at $12 trillion because that is the only point at which aggregate expenditures (AE) in the economy are exactly equal to what is produced (Y). At output levels below $12 trillion, such as $11 trillion, AE (planned spending, the blue line) is above Y (the orange line), which means spending is above production, which leads to unplanned decreases in inventory. Firms will react by increasing output toward $12 trillion in future periods. At output levels above $12 trillion, such as $13 trillion, AE is below Y, which means spending is above production, and this leads to unplanned increases in inventory. In this case, firms react by decreasing output toward $12 trillion in future periods.

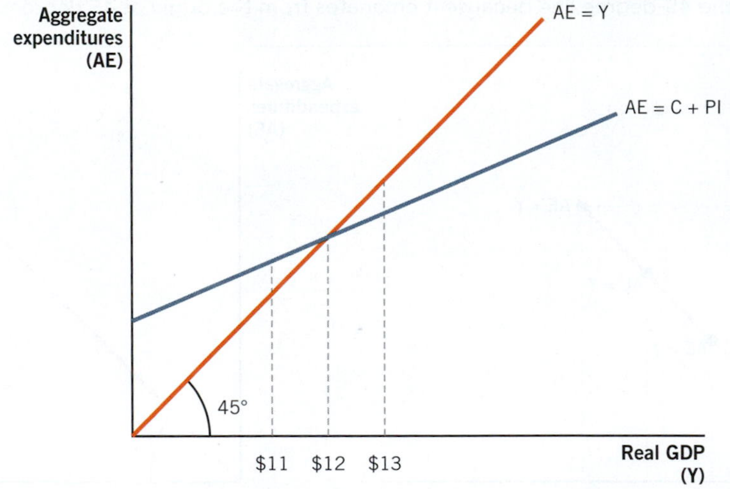

What happens if, instead, firms produce real GDP of $13 trillion? In this case, AE (the blue line) is below actual output (the orange line). This means spending is low relative to output, which leads to unplanned increases in inventories. Firms adjust in the future by reducing real output (Y) down toward equilibrium at $12 trillion.

In this example, output settles to equilibrium at $12 trillion. This is the only output level where firms' plans match the spending patterns of consumers and business firms.

Aggregate Expenditures with Government Spending and Net Exports

More realistically, aggregate expenditures also include government expenditures and net exports:

$$AE = C + PI + G + NX \quad \text{(EQUATION 27A.5)}$$

We can now add both government spending (G) and net exports (NX) to see how they affect the macroeconomic equilibrium. Figure 27A.6 shows the aggregate expenditures curve when we include consumption, planned investment, government, and net exports.

FIGURE 27A.6

Aggregate Expenditures with All Four Components

Aggregate expenditures (AE) are the total amount of spending in the economy from all four sources: consumption (C), planned investment (PI), government (G), and net exports (NX). Consumption spending depends on the level of income in the economy (Y) and increases at the rate of the marginal propensity to consume (MPC). The other components are assumed to be independent of the level of income, so the AE line shifts up in a parallel fashion when they are added.

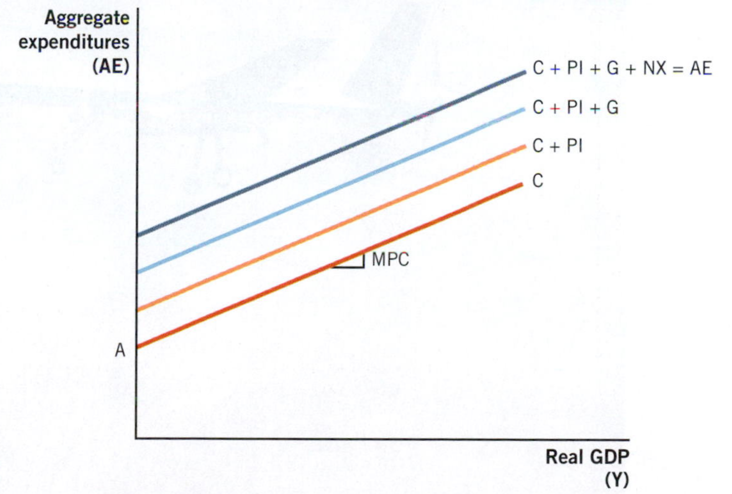

TABLE 27A.5

Equilibrium with All Components of Aggregate Expenditures (all dollars in billions; MPC = 0.6)

(1) Y Real GDP	(2) A Autonomous consumption	(3) C A + MPC × Y	(4) PI Planned investment	(5) G Government spending	(6) NX Net exports	(7) AE C + PI + G + NX	(8) AE − Y
$16,000	$2,800	$12,400	$2,000	$2,000	$400	$16,800	$800
17,000	2,800	13,000	2,000	2,000	400	17,400	400
18,000	**2,800**	**13,600**	**2,000**	**2,000**	**400**	**18,000**	**0**
19,000	2,800	14,200	2,000	2,000	400	18,600	−400
20,000	2,800	14,800	2,000	2,000	400	19,200	−800

Consider the economy presented in Table 27A.5. Looking at the components of aggregate expenditures, we see that autonomous consumption expenditures are $2,800 billion and the MPC is 0.6. Therefore, when income in the economy (Y) is equal to $17,000 billion, total consumption is $2,800 billion + 0.6 ($17,000) billion = $13,000 billion. This number appears in column 3. To get total AE, we also add planned investment ($2,000 billion), government spending ($2,000 billion), and net exports ($400 billion). These four components of aggregate expenditures sum to $17,400 billion. But $17,400 billion is greater than actual GDP, which is $17,000 billion. Inventories decrease by $400 billion, and so in future periods, firms increase output. The only output level that leads to equilibrium is $18,000 billion.

Government purchases, like this military drone, also contribute to aggregate expenditures.

PRACTICE WHAT YOU KNOW

Spending and Equilibrium in a Small Economy

Consider a small economy with autonomous consumption of $700 billion, an MPC of 0.5, planned investment of $150 billion, government spending of $100 billion, and net exports of $50 billion.

QUESTION: Determine AE in this economy when real GDP (Y) is equal to $1,500 billion, $2,000 billion, and $2,500 billion.

ANSWER: We can answer this question by filling in the values in the table below and then summing to get AE in the last column. Note that all dollars are in billions.

(1) Y Real GDP	(2) A Autonomous consumption	(3) C A + MPC × Y	(4) PI Planned investment	(5) G Government spending	(6) NX Net exports	(7) AE C + PI + G + NX
$1,500	$700	$1,450	$150	$100	$50	**$1,750**
2,000	700	1,700	150	100	50	**2,000**
2,500	700	1,950	150	100	50	**2,250**

QUESTION: What is the equilibrium level of real GDP in this economy?

ANSWER: The equilibrium level of real GDP is $2,000 billion because this is the only output level for which AE (the value in the last column) is equal to Y (the value in the first column).

What Are the Implications of the AE Model?

In this section, we examine what the AE model implies about economic outcomes and potential government policy responses to those outcomes.

Spending Determines Equilibrium Output and Income in the Economy

One key implication of the AE model is that planned aggregate spending dictates the equilibrium level of GDP in an economy. That is, spending determines income completely. Consider the three different levels of aggregate expenditures plotted in Figure 27A.7. When spending is equal to AE_0, the equilibrium level of income in the economy is Y_0. If planned spending increases to AE_1, equilibrium income rises to Y_1. In the AE model, spending increases always lead to increases in real GDP. These increases can result from any of the four sources: consumption, planned investment, government spending, or net exports. No matter which component increases, the result is the same.

In the AE model, spending drives the economy. The more people spend, the more income is created for others.

FIGURE 27A.7

Equilibrium Points in the AE Model

The total level of spending in the economy (AE) determines equilibrium output (Y) in the AE model. When AE = AE_0, the level of output is Y_0. If AE shifts up to AE_1, real GDP rises to Y_1. If, instead, AE shifts down to AE_2, real GDP falls to Y_2.

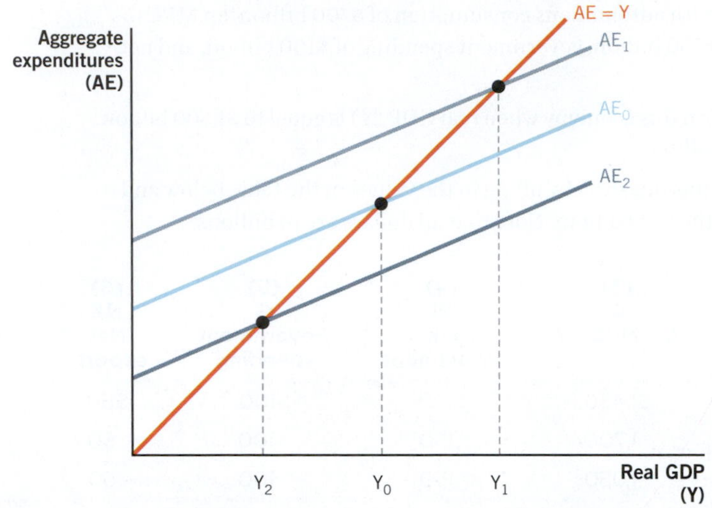

Consider the numerical example we presented earlier in Table 27A.5. In that example, equilibrium output in the economy occurs at real GDP equal to $18 trillion, which comes from consumption spending of $13.6 trillion, planned investment spending of $2 trillion, government spending of $2 trillion, and net exports of $0.4 trillion. Now consider what happens if spending on one of these components increases.

Let's say planned investment rises by $0.4 trillion. Perhaps business firm confidence rises and business decision-makers decide to invest in new factories for future production. Table 27A.6 shows the effect on equilibrium output in the

TABLE 27A.6

New Equilibrium with Higher Planned Investment Spending (all dollars in billions; MPC = 0.6)

(1) Y Real GDP	(2) A Autonomous consumption	(3) C A + MPC × Y	(4) PI Planned investment	(5) G Government spending	(6) NX Net exports	(7) AE C + PI + G + NX	(8) AE − Y
$16,000	$2,800	$12,400	$2,400	$2,000	$400	$17,200	$1,200
17,000	2,800	13,000	2,400	2,000	400	17,800	800
18,000	2,800	13,600	2,400	2,000	400	18,400	400
19,000	**2,800**	**14,200**	**2,400**	**2,000**	**400**	**19,000**	**0**
20,000	2,800	14,800	2,400	2,000	400	19,600	−400

TABLE 27A.7

New Equilibrium with Lower Planned Investment Spending (all dollars in billions; MPC = 0.6)

(1) Y Real GDP	(2) A Autonomous consumption	(3) C A + MPC × Y	(4) PI Planned investment	(5) G Government spending	(6) NX Net exports	(7) AE C + PI + G + NX	(8) AE − Y
$16,000	$2,800	$12,400	$1,600	$2,000	$400	$16,400	$400
17,000	**2,800**	**13,000**	**1,600**	**2,000**	**400**	**17,000**	**0**
18,000	2,800	13,600	1,600	2,000	400	17,600	−400
19,000	2,800	14,200	1,600	2,000	400	18,200	−800
20,000	2,800	14,800	1,600	2,000	400	18,800	−1,200

economy. When planned investment rises from $2 trillion to $2.4 trillion, equilibrium real GDP in the economy rises from $18 trillion to $19 trillion. The shift from AE_0 to AE_1 in Figure 27A.7 illustrates how an increase in spending leads to a higher level of real GDP in the economy. Anything that shifts AE upward—whether an increase in C, PI, G, NX, or a combination of these—will lead to an increase in real GDP. In short, spending determines real GDP.

Now consider the opposite scenario. Spending can also decline, and when it does, equilibrium GDP decreases. For example, suppose business firms become pessimistic about the future direction of the economy and decide to decrease investment spending by $0.4 trillion to $1.6 trillion. Table 27A.7 shows the new equilibrium. In this case, the equilibrium level of real GDP falls to $17 trillion.

This result holds no matter what the source of the decreased spending: C, PI, G, NX, or a combination of these components. This is why Keynesians favor government spending in an economic downturn: when G increases, real GDP rises.

Equilibrium Can Occur Away from Full Employment

A second important implication of the AE model is that equilibrium output can occur when the economy is not producing full-employment output. In fact, the primary benefit of the AE model is how clearly it can explain the idea of an extended recession when spending is low in an economy. In the AD–AS model we discussed in Chapter 26 and this appendix, there is an inherent tendency for the economy to adjust toward full-employment output, where the unemployment rate is equal to the natural rate of unemployment. But in the AE model, the equilibrium is completely determined by spending, regardless of whether or not the economy is at full employment.

This result implies that the economy can get stuck in a recession, with high unemployment and low real GDP, if spending drops. Notice that the tables and graphs in this appendix have not specified where full-employment output occurs. Equilibrium is determined by the level of spending in the economy, and this equilibrium may occur at less than full-employment output. For example, in Table 27A.5, equilibrium occurs at $18 trillion. But if full-employment output is $19 trillion, the unemployment rate might be 8% when output is at $18 trillion. This means that the economy is in a recession and there is no natural tendency for the economy to move up to $19 trillion.

The Spending Multiplier

In the example that accompanies Table 27A.6, we looked at the effects of an increase in planned investment spending from $2 trillion to $2.4 trillion. Let's think about how this spending increase leads to more income in the economy.

First, firms decide to increase planned investment by $0.4 trillion, or $400 billion. This means firms spend $0.4 trillion more on factories, tools, inventory, and other equipment, which they buy from other firms. As a result, the income of these other firms and their employees rises by $400 billion. But that is just the first step, because this new income also generates additional spending in the economy.

If the MPC is 0.6, then $400 billion in new income leads to $240 billion more in consumption spending (0.6 [$400 billion = $240 billion]). So the initial spending increase of $400 billion can generate spending of $640 billion ($400 billion + $240 billion). But the process doesn't stop there. Now there is another $240 billion of income to others in the economy, and they spend 60% of this income, which is $144 billion. And the process continues.

Table 27A.8 follows this spending example out for several rounds. In the end, if we add up all the new spending, we find a total increase in spending of $1,000 billion, or $1 trillion. Thus, any initial change in spending leads to a multiplied effect on real GDP.

The **spending multiplier** (m^s) is a number that tells us the total impact on spending from an initial change of a given amount. The total impact on spending is the spending multiplier times the change in spending.

To determine the total effect of a spending change on the economy, we use a formula for the **spending multiplier** (m^s), a number that tells us the total impact in spending from an initial change of a given amount. The formula for the spending multiplier is

(EQUATION 27A.6)

$$m^s = \frac{1}{1 - \text{MPC}}$$

TABLE 27A.8

Spending Increase Multiplying through the Economy (all dollars in billions; MPC = 0.6)

Round	Spending increase*
1	$400
2	240
3	144
4	86.4
.	.
.	.
.	.
Total	$1,000

*This table assumes an initial increase in spending of $400 billion.

In our example, the MPC is 0.6. We can use this number to solve for the spending multiplier:

$$m^s = \frac{1}{1 - \text{MPC}} = \frac{1}{1 - 0.6} = \frac{1}{0.4} = 2.5$$

Thus, an MPC of 0.6 implies that any $1 change in AE eventually leads to a $2.50 change in real GDP. Spending changes are very powerful. But be careful: this statement is true of both increases and decreases. Decreases in AE can lead to large decreases in real GDP. The AE model makes it easier to understand the Keynesian view of the macroeconomy. Spending (aggregate demand or aggregate expenditures) is the key. Therefore, Keynesians often advocate for an increase in government spending. According to the AE model, the new spending in G increases income immediately and then also through the multiplier effect.

Conclusion

The AE model matches the way many people believe the economy works: spending drives the key economic results. Increases in spending lead to more income and lower unemployment. Decreases in spending lead to less income and higher unemployment. It doesn't matter why spending fluctuates—those spending changes have real effects on the macroeconomy.

The AE model implies that the economy is very unstable, driven by consumer and business firm expectations and behavior. The results can be good, but they can also be very bad.

Even though the AE model is helpful in clarifying the Keynesian viewpoint, the same results can be demonstrated with the basic AD–AS model. As such, going forward in this text, we will rely on the AD–AS model to study the macroeconomy. ✷

APPENDIX PROBLEMS

Concepts You Should Know

aggregate consumption function (p. 898)
aggregate expenditures (AE) model (p. 896)
autonomous consumption spending (p. 898)
disposable income (p. 896)
marginal propensity to consume (MPC) (p. 897)
marginal propensity to save (MPS) (p. 897)
negative unplanned investment (p. 900)
spending multiplier (p. 910)
unplanned investment (p. 899)

Questions for Review

1. The slope of both the consumption function and the aggregate expenditures (AE) line is equal to the marginal propensity to consume (MPC).

a. Explain why the slope of the consumption function is equal to the MPC.

b. Explain why the slope of the AE line is equal to the MPC.

2. The AE model implies that a $1 change in government spending eventually leads to more than a $1 change in equilibrium real GDP. Explain how this multiplier process works.

3. Why is it that, in the AE model, all adjustments to equilibrium occur as changes in output? In other words, why does real GDP always change to move the economy to equilibrium?

Study Problem (✱ *solved at the end of the section*)

✱ **1.** Assume that the following values apply to the Spanish economy:

- Autonomous consumption (A) is $200 billion.
- The marginal propensity to consume (MPC) is 0.8.
- Planned investment expenditure is $50 billion across all income levels.
- Government spending is $100 billion across all income levels.
- Net exports are $50 billion across all income levels.

a. Fill in the missing values in the following table. (All dollars are in billions.)

Y Real GDP	A Autonomous consumption	C A + MPC × Y	PI Planned investment	G Government spending	NX Net exports	AE C + PI + G + NX	AE − Y
$1,000	____	____	____	____	____	____	____
1,500	____	____	____	____	____	____	____
2,000	____	____	____	____	____	____	____
2,500	____	____	____	____	____	____	____
3,000	____	____	____	____	____	____	____

b. What is the equilibrium GDP level for Spain as implied by the AE model in this example? How is this equilibrium determined?

c. At the current equilibrium GDP level, the unemployment rate in Spain is relatively high. Therefore, the government of Spain proposes to double the level of government spending (increase G to $200 billion). What is the new equilibrium level of real GDP?

d. What spending multiplier is implied by the MPC of 0.8?

Solved Problem

1. a. All dollars are in billions.

Y Real GDP	A Autonomous consumption	C A + MPC × Y	PI Planned investment	G Government spending	NX Net exports	AE C + PI + G + NX	AE − Y
$1,000	$200	$1,000	$50	$100	$50	$1,200	$200
1,500	200	1,400	50	100	50	1,600	100
2,000	200	1,800	50	100	50	2,000	0
2,500	200	2,200	50	100	50	2,400	−100
3,000	200	2,600	50	100	50	2,800	−200

b. The equilibrium output level will be at $2,000 billion because this is the only level of real GDP where AE = Y.

c. If G doubles to $200 billion, the new equilibrium output level is $2,500 billion because this is where the new AE = Y.

d. The spending multiplier is

$$m^s = \frac{1}{1 - MPC} = \frac{1}{1 - 0.8} = \frac{1}{0.2} = 5$$

PART VIII

Fiscal POLICY

CHAPTER

28

Federal Budgets: The Tools of Fiscal Policy

Federal Governments Typically Spend More Than They Bring In.

You don't have to look far to read about government budget problems. Does *any* government have enough money to pay its bills? Government debt seems to be mounting all over the globe. The U.S. federal budget has seen record deficits in recent years, with spending vastly surpassing revenue. These deficits existed even before the massive increases in government spending during the COVID-19 era. Government spending to fund responses to the pandemic fueled deficits of over $3 trillion in 2020 and another $2.75 trillion in 2021. (More on that later.)

Given the current budget environment, one might assume that governments never balance their budgets. Actually, the United States had a balanced budget as recently as 2001. If deficits are not inevitable, why are they so rampant? That is a question we'll be trying to answer over the course of the next two chapters.

In this chapter, we examine both sides of the government budget (outlays and revenues) and then bring them together to discuss deficits and the national debt. The primary goal of the chapter is to equip you with the knowledge you need to critically examine fiscal policy options. We frame the recent government budget struggles in context to give you a better sense of the magnitude of these problems, both historically and globally.

Any new plans for spending or taxes must be approved by both the Senate and the House of Representatives before the president signs them into law. As a result, passing a budget typically requires a fair amount of arm-twisting and favor-trading.

Of all the chapters in this text, this and the following chapter on fiscal policy are among the most important for your post-college life. Even though you probably won't end up working directly on government budgets, if you vote or otherwise participate in the political process, you'll need to consider what tax and spending plans make the most sense to you.

We first consider the spending side of the government budget. We then move to the revenue side, where we look closely at taxes. Finally, we bring these two sides together to examine budget deficits and government debt.

· BIG QUESTIONS ·

- How does the government spend?
- How does the government tax?
- What are budget deficits?

How Does the Government Spend?

A government's budget is a plan for both raising and spending funds for governmental activities. It is similar to a budget you may create for your own personal finances. The budget for the U.S government is a result of back-and-forth negotiations between the president and both houses of Congress. Typically, the White House Office of Management and Budget (OMB) prepares the initial version, as directed by the president with input from the Council of Economic Advisers. Congress then hashes out a final version that will eventually need the president's signature.

There are two sides to a budget: the sources of funds (income, or revenue) and the uses of funds (spending, or outlays). We start with the spending side. If we were looking at your personal budget, the spending categories might include tuition, books, food, and housing. For a federal (national) government, the budget includes items like national defense, education, highways, health care, and retirement benefits.

The current chair of the president's Council of Economic Advisers is Cecilia Rouse.

Government Outlays

When you look at U.S. federal government spending over many years (Figure 28.1 starts at 1970), you can see two periods where spending surged. The first surge, from 2008 to 2011, was to help the economy get through the Great Recession and shake off its lingering aftereffects. The second surge, which appears as a spike starting in 2020, was spending to offset the economic consequences of COVID-19. Over the next two chapters, we will unpack the major components of government spending. We'll address the surges that occur during recessions, and we'll also consider the government spending that occurs year in, year out, no matter what the economic conditions.

When you think of government spending, the first items that come to mind are probably goods and services like military equipment, schools, roads, bridges, and wages for government workers. These are part of the government spending component (G) in gross domestic product. But as we examine the total government budget, we also include **transfer payments**, which are payments made to groups or individuals when no good or service is received in return. With transfer payments, the government transfers funds from one group in the country to another. Transfer payments include income assistance (welfare) and Social Security payments to retired or disabled persons. Transfer payments constitute a large and growing share of U.S. federal outlays.

Transfer payments are payments made to groups or individuals when no good or service is received in return.

Government budgets combine spending and transfer payments into a broad category called **government outlays**. Table 28.1 shows the breakdown of U.S. government outlays for 2019. We divide outlays into three groups: mandatory outlays, discretionary spending, and interest payments. By far the largest portion of the federal budget is dedicated to **mandatory outlays**, which go to ongoing government programs like Social Security and Medicare. These programs are mandatory because existing laws mandate government funding for them. Mandatory outlays are not generally altered during the annual budgeting process; they require changes to existing laws. Sometimes mandatory outlays

Government outlays are the part of the government budget that includes both spending and transfer payments.

Mandatory outlays sometimes called *entitlement programs*, comprise government spending determined by ongoing government programs like Social Security and Medicare.

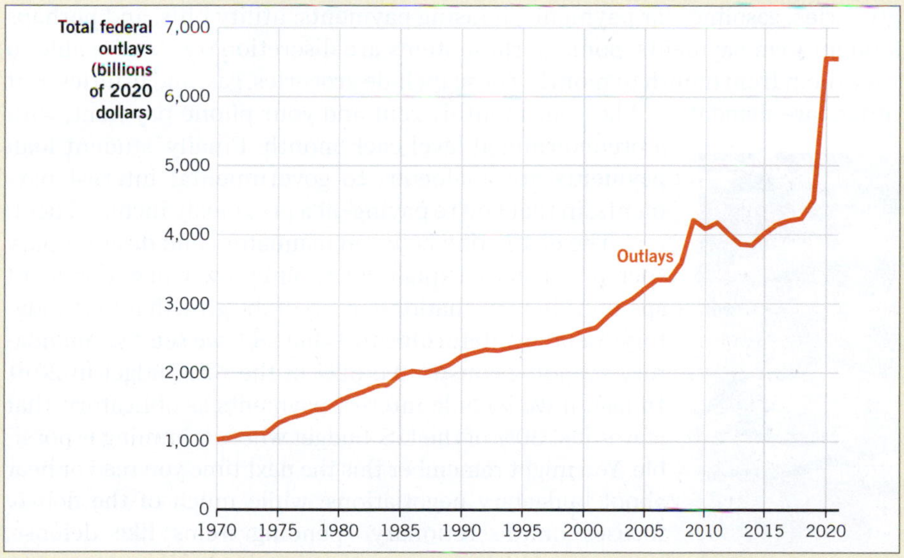

FIGURE 28.1

U.S. Government Outlays, 1970–2021

Total outlays represent the spending side of the national government's budget. This graph shows spending from 1970 to 2021. The two big spending increases from the last two recessions are clearly visible—the Great Recession that began in 2007 and the coronavirus recession that began in 2020.

Source: U.S. Office of Management and Budget.

TABLE 28.1

2019 U.S. Government Outlays

Category	2019 outlays (billions of dollars)	Percentage of total	
Social Security	$1,038.5	23.4%	Mandatory 62%
Medicare	775.3	17.4	
Income assistance	712.5	16.0	
Other plus receipts	208.2	4.7	
Defense	676.4	15.2	Discretionary 30%
Nondefense discretionary	660	14.8	
Interest	375.6	8.4	Interest 8%
Total	**$4,446.6**		

Source: Congressional Budget Office, www.cbo.gov/publication/53651.

Note: Due to rounding, these percentages do not add up to 100.

are called *entitlement programs,* because citizens who meet certain requirements are entitled to the benefits under current laws. We talk more about these in the next section.

Discretionary outlays comprise spending that is adjustable during the annual budget process.

Discretionary outlays are subject to adjustment during the annual budget process. Examples of discretionary spending include monies for bridges and roads, payments to government workers, and defense spending. When you think of prominent government spending items, you likely first think of discretionary items. But in fact, discretionary spending accounts for less than one-third of the U.S. government budget, which is now predominantly mandatory spending.

The final category in Table 28.1 is interest payments. These are payments made to current owners of U.S. Treasury bonds. For all practical purposes, these interest payments are also mandatory because they are not easy to alter, given a certain level of debt.

To understand these three broad categories better, imagine applying them to your own budget after you graduate from college. You'll need to plan for groceries, gasoline, car payments, housing payments, utility bills, and perhaps student loan payments. Some of these items are discretionary—you're able to vary them from month to month. These include groceries, gas, and utilities. But others are mandatory, like your monthly rent and your phone payment, with a predetermined level each month. Finally, student loan payments are analogous to governmental interest payments, in that you're paying off a previously incurred debt.

Discretionary government spending includes purchases of military equipment.

The distinction between mandatory and discretionary spending helps to explain the recent growth of government spending in many nations: much of the growth is in mandatory spending. Returning to Table 28.1, we see that mandatory spending constituted 62% of the U.S. budget in 2019. In fact, if we include interest payments as obligatory, that leaves just 30% of the U.S. budget where trimming is possible. You might remember this the next time you read or hear about budgetary negotiations: while much of the debate focuses on discretionary spending items like defense, bridges and highways, or educational subsidies, the majority of the budget actually goes to mandatory categories.

FIGURE 28.2

Historical Federal Outlay Shares, 1970–2017

The percentage of the budget allocated to mandatory spending programs has almost doubled since 1970. In contrast, discretionary spending is an ever-shrinking percentage of the federal budget.

Source: Congressional Budget Office.

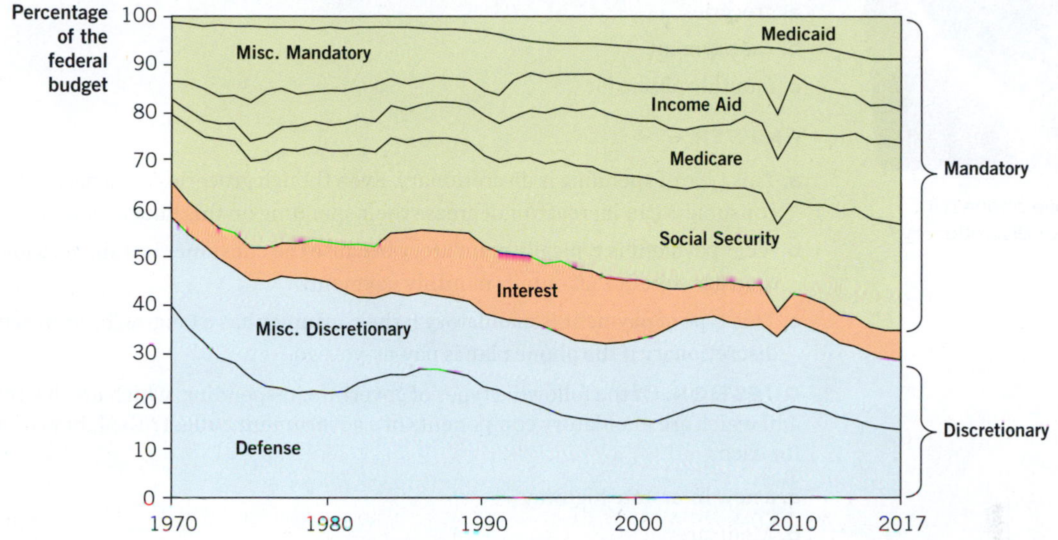

It wasn't always this way. Figure 28.2 plots U.S. budget categories as portions of total outlays for 1970–2017. The green-shaded categories represent mandatory spending. In 1970, mandatory spending was only about one-third of the federal budget. The cause of the growth in mandatory spending over the last 50 years is both political and demographic: new mandatory programs have been added, and an aging population has led to wider eligibility for many programs, like Social Security and Medicare. Miscellaneous mandatory spending programs include unemployment compensation, income assistance (welfare), and food stamps. Medicare was added in 1966 and then expanded in 2006. By 2017, Social Security and Medicare alone accounted for 42% of the U.S. federal budget, up from just 16% in 1970.

Congress authorized prescription drug coverage as part of Medicare in 2003.

Social Security and Medicare

In this section, we look more closely at Social Security and Medicare so we can try to understand why so many resources are devoted to these programs.

PRACTICE WHAT YOU KNOW

Is your mobile phone bill mandatory or discretionary?

Mandatory versus Discretionary Spending

QUESTION: Of the following types of private spending, which are discretionary and which are mandatory components of a consumer's budget? Explain your response for each.

a. groceries

b. car payment

c. monthly phone fee

ANSWER:

a. This type of spending is discretionary. Even though groceries are a necessity, consumers can increase or decrease their spending on this budget component.

b. A car payment is typically mandatory because the consumer has signed a long-term loan agreement that entails monthly payments.

c. This type of payment is mandatory if the consumer has a long-term contract but discretionary if the phone plan is pay-as-you-go.

QUESTION: Of the following types of government spending, which are discretionary and which are mandatory components of a government budget? Explain your response for each.

a. a new interstate highway

b. Medicare

c. international aid

ANSWER:

a. This type of spending is discretionary because the government can choose not to fund a new interstate highway.

b. This spending is mandatory because the government is obligated via previously enacted laws to pay Medicare expenses when recipients qualify.

c. This type of spending is discretionary. Each year, the government can choose how much to spend on aid to foreign governments.

Social Security is a U.S. government-administered retirement funding program.

In 1935, as part of the New Deal and in the midst of the Great Depression, the U.S. Congress and President Franklin Roosevelt created the Social Security program. **Social Security** is a government-administered retirement funding program. The program requires workers to contribute a portion of their earnings into the Social Security Trust Fund, with the promise that they'll receive these back (along with a modest growth rate) upon retirement. The goal of the program is to guarantee that no U.S. worker retires without retirement income.

To understand our current federal budget situation, it helps to consider the financial evolution of the Social Security program over time. At the beginning of the program, there were very few retirees receiving Social Security payouts, and at the same time many workers paying in. As a result, payments into the Trust Fund piled up, even with a low Social Security tax rate of just 2%. However, as time went on, more and more workers naturally retired and became eligible for payouts. At this point, as more workers retire and draw benefits from the program, the Trust Fund balance declines. To keep the Trust Fund from running out of funds, Social Security tax rates have had to increase. The total Social Security tax rate is now up to 12.4%.

Medicare is a mandated federal program that funds health care for people aged 65 and older. This program was established in 1965 with the goal of providing medical insurance for all retired workers. Like Social Security, the law requires current workers to pay Medicare taxes with the promise of receiving insurance upon retirement. In 2003, Medicare was extended into reimbursements for prescription drugs for retirees as well. The total Medicare tax rate is currently 2.9%.

Medicare
is a mandated U.S. federal program that funds health care for people age 65 and older.

Both Medicare and Social Security outlays are concentrated on the elderly population and so are greatly affected as population demographics shift. Given that these programs now account for more than 40% of all federal outlays, we should look more closely at demographic changes before digging further into the dynamics of the federal budget.

DEMOGRAPHICS Entitlement programs have come to dominate the federal budget, with Social Security and Medicare taking up ever-expanding shares. There are three underlying, and related, natural demographic reasons. First, people are living longer today than ever before, drawing postretirement benefits for a longer period of time. In 1930, life expectancy after age 60 was less than 14 years, limiting the length of time retirees collected Social Security benefits. Today, Americans live an average of 23 years after age 60. This is a big change from the assumptions on which the system was built.

Second, there are now far more workers retired and drawing benefits than before. To be eligible for Social Security and Medicare payments, workers pay taxes while they work. In the early years, very few were eligible for payouts, but millions were paying in. Both programs naturally generated substantial tax revenue with very few outlays for many years. But with so many workers now retired, the math has changed.

Third, in addition to a normal flow of retirees, the baby boomers (people born between 1946 and 1964) are now retiring. This is a disproportionately large population cohort. Thus, workers are retiring in record numbers, and this will continue for another 10-plus years. Figure 28.3 breaks down the U.S. population by age, as of July 2021, with horizontal bars showing the size of the population in different age groups. This is called a population pyramid, because it would resemble an actual pyramid for a population with steady growth driven by a high population of very young children that gradually declines with age. But factors such as the baby boom and a recent decline in birthrates since 2007 have produced this funny-shaped "pyramid" that is smaller at the bottom than in the middle. In 1960, there were more than 5 workers for every single Social Security beneficiary—so, 5 people paying in for every one person drawing out of the trust fund. With that ratio, it wasn't very hard to accumulate a large trust fund. However, as of 2021, we are down to just 2.7 workers paying into the system for every one beneficiary, and this ratio is projected to fall to 2.3 by 2035.*

Franklin Delano Roosevelt signed the original Social Security Act in 1935.

*Social Security Administration, "Fact Sheet: Social Security," accessed February 8, 2022, https://www.ssa.gov/news/press/factsheets/basicfact-alt.pdf.

FIGURE 28.3

U.S. Population by Age, 2021

This type of illustration of national population separated into age groups is often called a population pyramid, since with steady birthrates it would resemble an actual pyramid. But the U.S. population has evolved to be more top-heavy, with the baby boom (ages 55–73 in the graph) and then the recent decline in birthrates (seen in the shorter lines at the bottom) as major factors. All of this affects the federal budget, since over two-thirds of the budget is now allocated to programs for the elderly (Social Security and Medicare).

Source: U.S. Census Bureau, U.S. Population, July 2021.

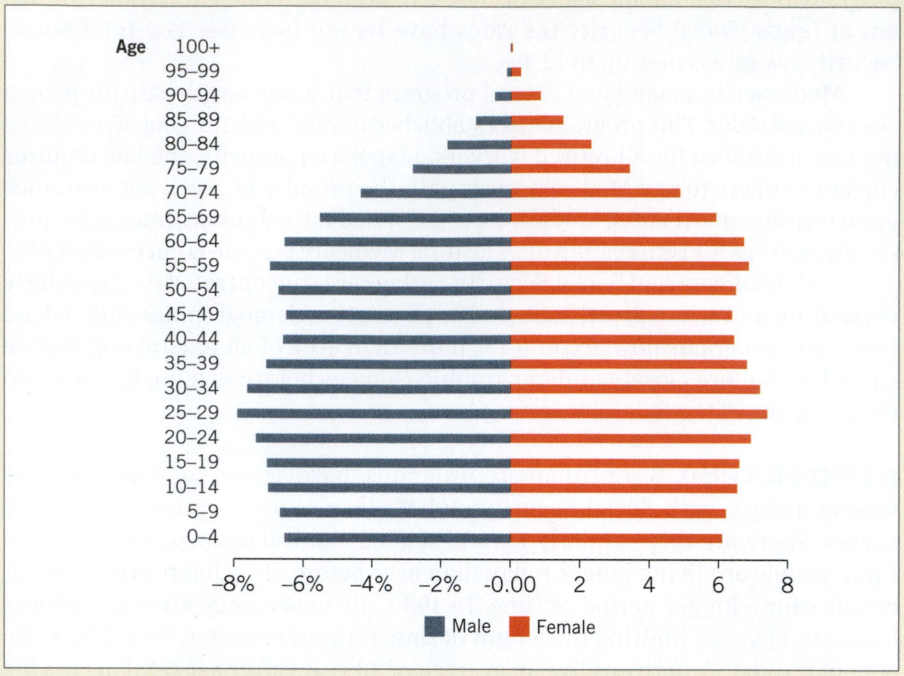

In the end, this matters greatly for the U.S. government budget, because so many workers are now exiting the labor force, and the younger population cohorts are relatively small. This shift requires ever-expanding outlays for the mandatory programs. Any substantive discussion about the national debt and deficits must focus on these programs.

ECONOMICS IN THE REAL WORLD

ARE THERE SIMPLE FIXES TO THE SOCIAL SECURITY AND MEDICARE FUNDING PROBLEMS?

If current Social Security and Medicare spending trends persist, the U.S. government budget will be severely strained in the not-too-distant future. But it may be possible to alter the spending trajectory, or perhaps even totally resolve the budget issues. Proposed solutions include the following:

1. *Increase the retirement age from 67 to 70.* The logic here begins with the recognition that people are living longer and healthier lives than when these programs were first implemented. If people work three years longer, they will spend three more years contributing to the Trust Fund and three fewer years drawing from it.
2. *Adjust the benefits computation using the consumer price index.* Benefit payments to retirees are adjusted for inflation on the basis of average wage levels when they retire. This policy is in place to ensure that workers' benefits keep up with standard-of-living changes during their working years. Currently, these payments are adjusted on the basis of an average wage index, which has historically increased

faster than the CPI. If, instead, the CPI were used to adjust benefits payments, the payments would grow more slowly and yet still adjust for inflation.

3. *Means-test for benefits.* As it stands now, retirees receive benefits from Medicare and Social Security regardless of their income level. Some analysts have suggested a decrease in benefits paid to wealthier recipients, who can more readily pay for their own retirement and medical care.

These proposed solutions might help to shore up the federal budget. But each would require a change in existing law—and the benefits are not clear-cut across the board. To be sure, raising the retirement age to 70 would definitely mean more revenue for the Trust Fund, and billions of dollars in savings. However, the payoff of indexing benefits to the CPI instead of the average wage index is less certain, since the CPI has actually risen faster than average wages in recent years. As for means-testing benefits, that would change worker incentives going forward, in effect punishing retirees who save on their own and can therefore afford more in retirement. The result? The average person won't save as much for retirement and will be that much more dependent on Uncle Sam. Finally, some people see means-testing as unfair. Medicare and Social Security are mandatory programs all workers must pay into (through taxes) during their time in the labor force. Means-testing implies that some workers won't receive the benefits from a program they were required to pay into.

These changes might reduce the benefits paid out in the short run and, in so doing, reduce pressure on the federal budget. But means-testing might also lead to greater problems in the long run, due to the saving disincentive.

Incentives

Spending and Current Fiscal Issues

Before turning to the revenue side of the budget, we should take a close look at the recent history of U.S. government outlays. Figure 28.4 shows real federal government outlays from 1990 to 2021. The first half of the graph shows

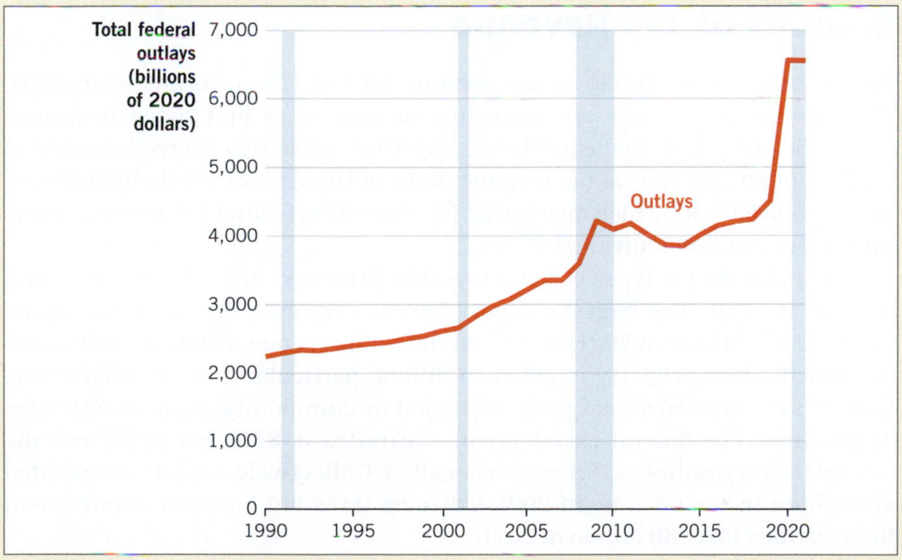

FIGURE 28.4

U.S. Government Outlays, 1990–2021

The rate of growth of U.S. government outlays has increased significantly in recent years. It is easy to spot the large spending increases during and after the Great Recession, and in response to the coronavirus recession.

Source: U.S. Office of Management and Budget.

relatively stable government spending, prior to our two most recent recessions. But in 2008, government outlays entered a turbulent period. We are really looking at three successive phases:

1. *1990 to 2008: Relative economic stability that required very little fiscal policy response.* In this period, the economy generally expanded, aside from two short recessions (in 1990 and 2001).
2. *2008 to 2020: The Great Recession followed by the longest economic expansion in U.S. history.* The increase in outlays from 2008 to 2011 was a direct policy response to the Great Recession. Government spending increased significantly at the beginning of this era. This was followed by more than ten years of economic expansion, from mid-2009 to early 2020.
3. *2020 and onward: The coronavirus recession caused by the global pandemic.* The U.S. government responded to the coronavirus recession with massive government spending increases. (We cover these more fully in Chapter 29.) This is the spike you see in Figure 28.4.

How Does the Government Tax?

Governments raise revenues in many ways. Fees assessed for government services—for example, admission fees to national parks—contribute small amounts. But almost all government revenue is raised through taxes.

No one enjoys paying taxes, but the government can't provide Social Security, Medicare, national defense, highways, and public education unless it brings in the tax revenue to pay for all those services. Yes, the government can borrow to cover the budget deficits it runs. But the government can't fund its operations entirely through borrowing. In this section, we detail the principal types of taxes the U.S. government collects.

Sources of Tax Revenue

Figure 28.5 shows sources of tax revenue for the U.S. government in 2021. The two largest sources are individual income taxes and social insurance (Social Security and Medicare) taxes. Together, these two sources accounted for 83% of all U.S. federal tax revenue. Both of these taxes are deducted from workers' paychecks, which means that for every $1 in federal tax revenue, $0.83 came from taxes on individual wages.

All other major types of taxes together produced just 17% of the federal revenue in 2021. The largest category here is corporate income taxes, which yielded $372 billion in 2021, or 9.2% of the total revenue. Estate and gift taxes are levied when property is gifted to others, particularly as an inheritance. Excise taxes are taxes on a particular good or commodity, such as cigarettes or gasoline. The federal excise tax on cigarettes is $1.01 per pack, and the federal tax on gasoline is 18.4 cents per gallon. Collectively, excise taxes yielded $75 billion in tax revenue in 2021. Customs taxes are taxes on imports, and these yielded just $80 billion in 2021.

Because income and social insurance taxes play such an outsize role, we will now discuss them in greater detail.

FIGURE 28.5

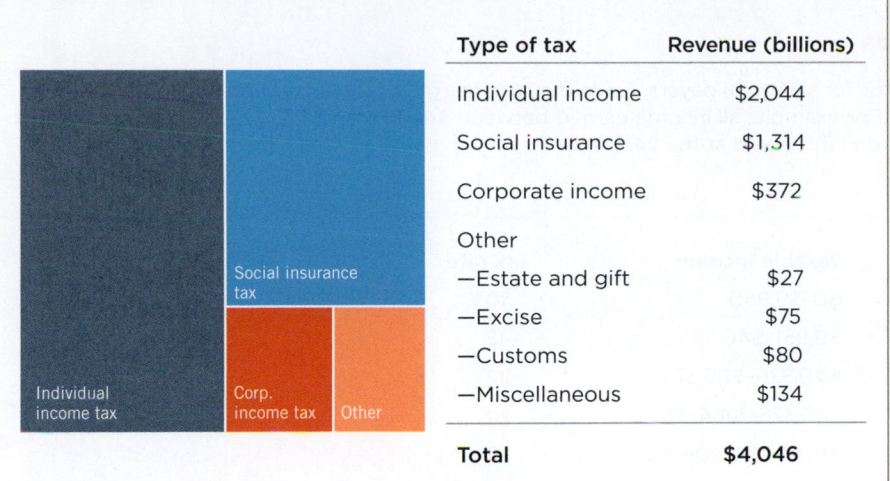

Type of tax	Revenue (billions)
Individual income	$2,044
Social insurance	$1,314
Corporate income	$372
Other	
—Estate and gift	$27
—Excise	$75
—Customs	$80
—Miscellaneous	$134
Total	**$4,046**

U.S. Federal Tax Revenue Sources, 2021

The major sources of tax revenue for the U.S. government are the two taxes on income: the individual income tax and the social insurance (Social Security and Medicare) tax. Together, these two categories accounted for 83% of all tax revenue in 2021. Total tax revenue in 2021 was $4.05 trillion.

Source: Congressional Budget Office, Historical Budget Data.

Taxes on Workers' Wages

After you graduate from college and secure a full-time job, you'll likely earn much larger paychecks than before. But those paychecks might be smaller than you expect based on your salary alone. Remember, the government pays for activities with tax revenue predominantly raised from taxes on income. Let's look more closely at the major taxes on income: the social insurance tax and the individual income tax.

SOCIAL INSURANCE TAX Earlier, we discussed government outlays for Social Security and Medicare, which together account for more than 40% of total U.S. federal spending. The money spent comes from taxes on workers' paychecks; the benefits received by each retiree depend on taxes paid in during his or her working years. Currently, the tax for these two programs amounts to 15.3% of a worker's pay. This is typically split in half, with 7.65% paid by the employee and 7.65% paid by the employer. People who are self-employed pay the full 15.3% (the Social Security portion of this tax is applicable to the first $142,800 an individual earns). These dollars go into the Social Security and Medicare trust funds that provide income and health care assistance to retirees.

INCOME TAX U.S. federal income taxes are set according to a scale that increases with income levels. In a **progressive income tax system**, people with higher incomes pay a larger percentage of their income in taxes than people with lower incomes do. Figure 28.6 shows 2021 federal income tax rates for single individuals. Notice, the tax rate climbs with income level. That is what is meant when the U.S. income tax system is described as "progressive"; it doesn't mean "a scheme favored by political liberals," even if liberals happen to approve.

In a **progressive income tax system**, people with higher incomes pay a larger portion of their income in taxes than people with lower incomes do.

The **marginal tax rate** is the tax rate paid on an individual's next dollar of income.

The tax rates specified in Figure 28.6 are marginal tax rates. A **marginal tax rate** is the tax rate paid on an individual's "next dollar" of income. Consider

FIGURE 28.6

2021 U.S. Federal Tax Rates

These tax rates are marginal tax rates for single taxpayers. Since they are marginal rates, they apply only to income dollars within the specified ranges. For example, all income earned between $40,526 and $86,375 is taxed at 22%; but if someone earns $86,376, that last dollar is taxed at the 24% rate.

Source: Internal Revenue Service.

Taxable Income	Tax rate
$0–$9,950	10%
$9,951–$40,525	12
$40,526–$86,375	22
$86,376–$164,925	24
$164,926–$209,425	32
$209,426–$523,600	35
Over $523,600	37

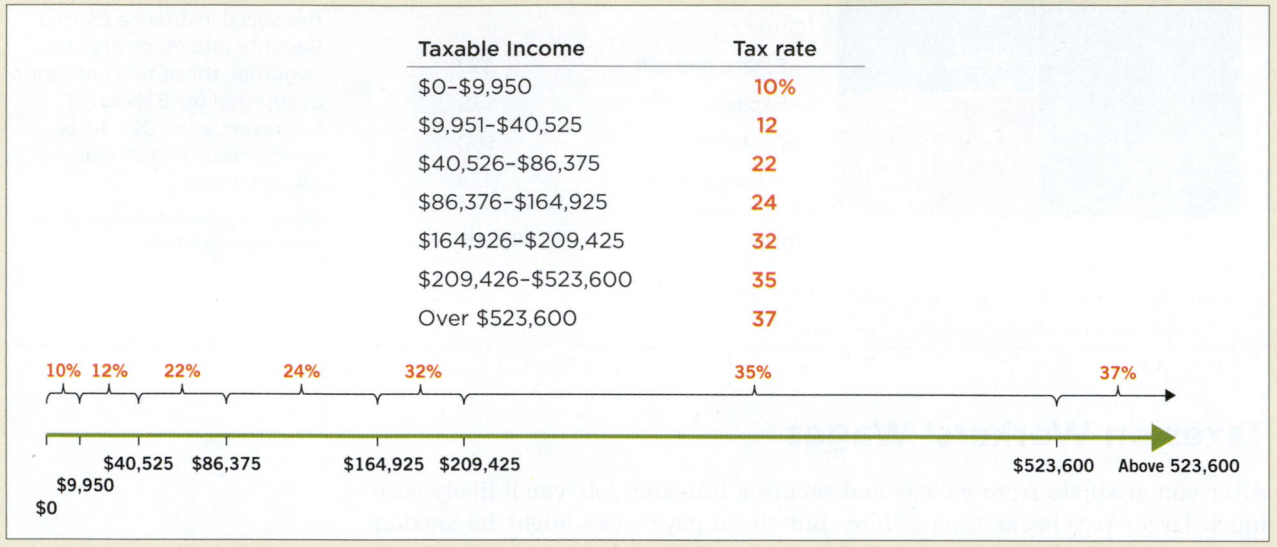

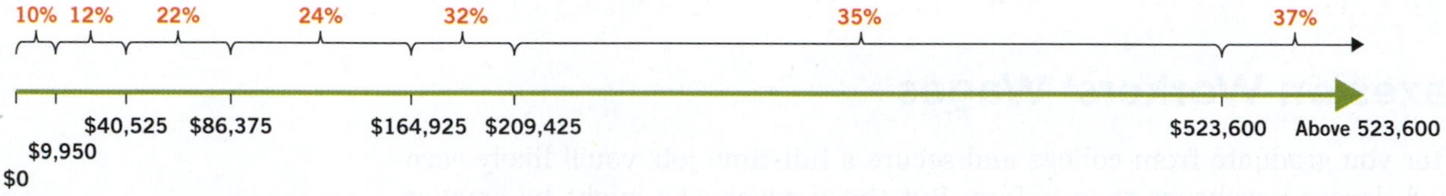

Marginal thinking

a worker in 2021 with a salary of $72,550. Assume this worker takes the standard tax deduction of $12,550, so taxable income is exactly $60,000. The tax schedule in Figure 28.6 puts someone with $60,000 of taxable income in the 22% tax bracket. This doesn't mean that the worker pays 22% of the entire $60,000 in taxes. What it means is that income *above $40,525* is taxed at 22 cents on the dollar. The same worker will pay 10% on every dollar of income up to $9,950, and 12% on the income between $9,950 and $40,525.

When we consider fiscal policy in Chapter 29, it will be critical to understand how income taxes are computed. Let's use the rates from Figure 28.6 to compute a tax bill based on a taxable income of $60,000. Note again that three different tax rates apply: 10% on income up to $9,950; 12% on income from $9,951 to $40,525; and 22% on income from $40,526 to $60,000. The total tax bill then comes to

$$
\begin{aligned}
0.10 \times \$9{,}950 &= \$995.00 \\
+0.12 \times (\$40{,}525 - \$9{,}950) &= \$3{,}669.00 \\
+0.22 \times (60{,}000 - \$40{,}525) &= \$4{,}284.50 \\
\hline
\textbf{Total} &= \textbf{\$8,948.50}
\end{aligned}
$$

Therefore, $60,000 in taxable income will accrue a federal income tax bill of $8,948.50, which is 14.9% of the taxable income ($60,000). This 14.9%

is the taxpayer's average tax rate. An **average tax rate** is the total tax paid divided by taxable income. Notice that the average tax rate is below the marginal tax rate (22%). This is generally the case in a progressive tax system, because the marginal tax rate applies to the last few dollars taxed, rather than all income.

The **average tax rate** is the total tax paid divided by the amount of taxable income.

Historical Income Tax Rates

Although income taxes seem like a fact of life, the U.S. income tax is only about 110 years old. Prior to 1913, there was no income tax in the United States; most tax revenues were generated by taxes on imports (tariffs). But import taxes were declining, so the government introduced income taxes as another source of revenue. The original income tax in the United States was similar to the current tax system, in that the rates were progressive. But it was very different in terms of the actual tax rates: the highest marginal rate in 1913 was just 6%, and that rate applied only to income greater than $500,000—over $11 million in today's dollars. Very few people were earning that kind of income in 1913. (Not many people earn that kind of income now, for that matter.)

Once income taxes were in place, marginal tax rates rose quickly. By 1918, in fact, the top marginal rate was up to 77%. This rate applied only to income over $2 million, but it meant that every dollar earned beyond $2 million netted only 23 cents to the income earner, after taxes. Figure 28.7 plots the top marginal income tax rates in the United States from 1913 to 2021. Note that while this figure shows only the top rate, it is a good indicator of the general level of rates over time.

We can point to many important dates in the evolution of U.S. income tax rates. During the 1930s, in the midst of the Great Depression, with income levels plunging, income tax revenues naturally fell. Presidents Hoover and

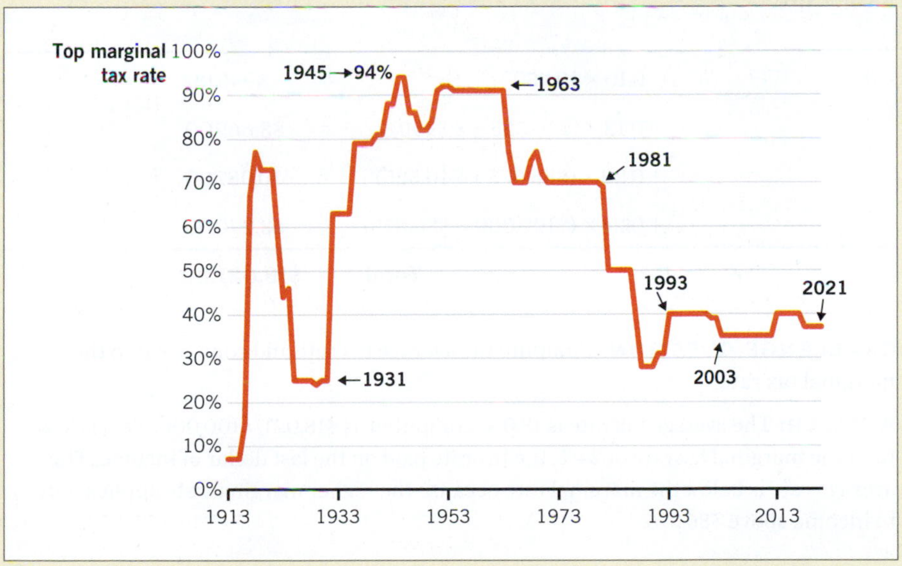

FIGURE 28.7

Historical Top U.S. Marginal Tax Rates, 1913–2021

Marginal rates are a good indicator of overall tax rates since 1913. There are several key historical dates. For example, after 1931, marginal tax rates increased significantly. Major downward revisions occurred in 1963 and in the 1980s.

Source: Internal Revenue Service.

Roosevelt, attempting to balance the federal budget, pressed Congress to increase top marginal rates to 80%. As you might expect, this did not help an already struggling economy. Later, in 1963, with top marginal rates at their historically highest level (over 90%), President Kennedy pushed for tax rate reductions that dropped the top rate to 70%. In the 1980s, President Reagan led the push to lower marginal tax rates even further; by the end of that decade, the top marginal rate was just 28%. In 1993, President Clinton proposed higher rates, and the top rate rose to 39.6%. President George W. Bush pushed through a temporary decrease in this top rate in 2003, and the lower rate of 35% persisted for 10 years, before the top rate returned to 39.6% in 2013. Finally, in December 2017, the top marginal tax rate fell to 37% as part of the Tax Cuts and Jobs Act of 2017, which we discuss later in this chapter. Over the course of a century, there was a great deal of fluctuation in marginal tax rates. Going forward, it is not likely that top rates will ever return to the levels witnessed prior to 1980.

PRACTICE WHAT YOU KNOW

Figuring out your income tax bill involves some basic math.

Government Revenue: Federal Taxes

Assume that your taxable income is $100,000. Use the 2021 marginal tax rates from Figure 28.6 to determine your taxes.

QUESTION: How would you compute your federal income tax?

ANSWER: Looking at Figure 28.6, keep in mind that the different rates apply only to the income in the specified bands. For example, the first tax rate of 10% applies only to income up to $9,950. Income between $9,951 and $40,525 is taxed at 12%. Use this pattern to determine the tax paid on all income up to $100,000. Multiply these rates by the income in the respective brackets, and sum these to get the total income tax:

$0.10 \times \$9{,}950$	=	$995.00
$+0.12 \times (\$40{,}525 - \$9{,}950)$	=	$3,669.00
$+0.22 \times (\$86{,}375 - \$40{,}525)$	=	$10,087.00
$+0.24 \times (\$100{,}000 - \$86{,}375)$	=	$3,270.00
Total	=	**$18,021.00**

CHALLENGE QUESTION: Compute the average tax rate and compare it to the marginal tax rate.

ANSWER: The average tax rate is 18.0%, computed as $18,021/$100,000. This is less than the marginal tax rate of 24%, the tax rate paid on the last dollar of income. The average rate is below the marginal rate because the higher marginal rate applies only to income above $86,375.

How Are Taxes Distributed across Income Levels in the United States?

In a progressive income tax system, tax rates rise with income. This means that high-income taxpayers pay more than low-income ones, not only in absolute terms (which would be true even with a flat tax) but as a percentage of income, and so they end up paying the lion's share of total taxes. This is certainly true in the United States. Figure 28.8 plots total U.S. federal tax shares paid by different income groups (by household) in the United States from 1980 to 2018. These are the shares of all federal taxes paid, including income taxes, Social Security and Medicare taxes, excise taxes, and corporate taxes. The top line represents the share of taxes paid by the wealthiest 20% of all households. You can see that this share has been rising over time and recently has been hovering around 70% of all federal taxes paid. In contrast, the 20% of U.S. households with the lowest incomes paid zero net federal taxes in 2018. (In this group, the positive taxes paid by some households were offset by tax credits paid to other households.) In fact, in 2018, the top 1% (not pictured) of all households paid about the same amount of total federal taxes as the entire bottom 80% combined (30%).

FIGURE 28.8

Percentage of Total Federal Income and Social Insurance Taxes Paid by Various Income Groups, 1980–2018

In 2018, the middle-income group in the United States (labeled as "Middle 20%") paid less than 10% of all income and social insurance taxes paid. The wealthiest 20% (the top line) of income earners paid almost 70% of all income and social insurance taxes in 2018.

Source: Tax Policy Center.

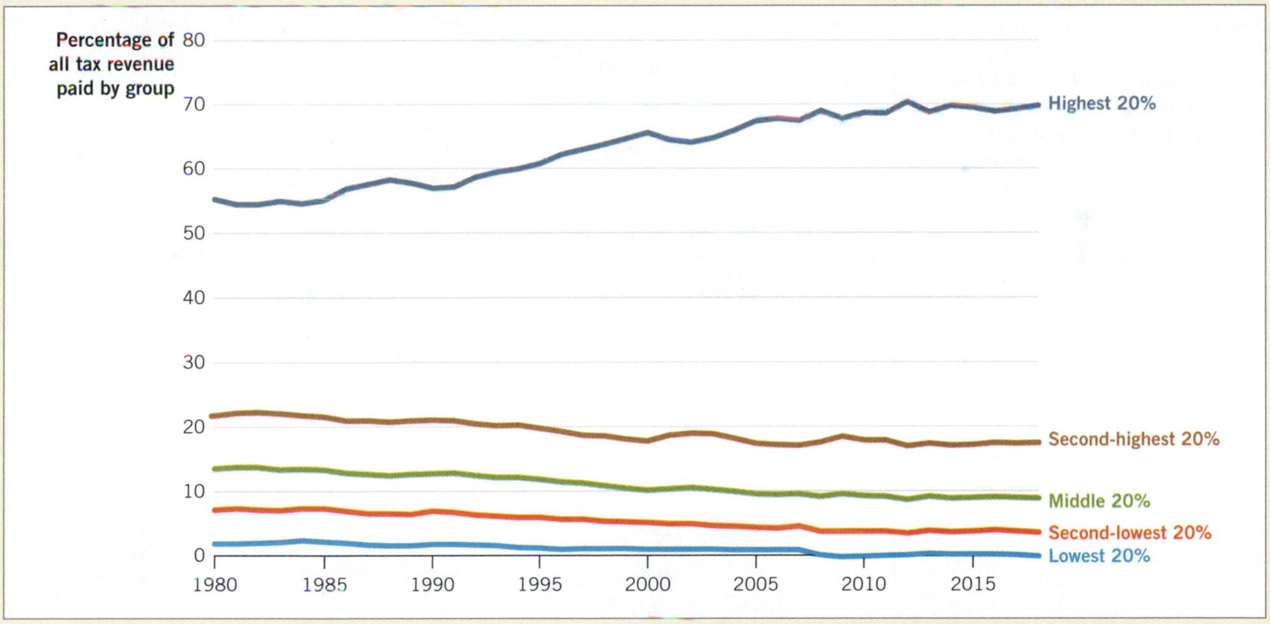

What Are Budget Deficits?

We are now ready to bring both sides of the budget together. Doing so enables us to examine the differences between spending and revenue. In this section, we define budget deficits and debt and also consider these in historical context.

Deficits

A **budget deficit** occurs when government outlays exceed revenue in a given time period, usually a year.

A **budget surplus** occurs when government revenue exceeds outlays in a given time period, usually a year.

A **budget deficit** occurs when government outlays exceed revenue in a given time period, usually a year. Panel (a) of Figure 28.9 plots U.S. budget outlays and revenues from 1970 to 2021, in billions of 2020 dollars. Outlays are displayed in orange and revenues in blue. You can see that outlays generally exceed revenue. The biggest difference came in 2020, when outlays were $6.55 trillion and revenue was just $3.42 trillion. The difference, $3.13 trillion, was the deficit for 2020.

It is also possible for the government to have a **budget surplus**, which occurs when revenue exceeds outlays. The most recent U.S. federal surpluses

FIGURE 28.9

U.S. Federal Budget Data, 1970–2021

(a) Real outlays are shown in orange, and revenue in blue, for the U.S. national government from 1970 to 2021. When outlays exceed revenue, the budget is in deficit for that year. (b) In the plot of the real budget balance, negative values indicate a deficit. The coronavirus recession, which began in 2020, and the government's response to it helped to create the 2020 deficit of $3.13 trillion, more than double the previous largest deficit (from 2009) in U.S. history.

Source: U.S. Office of Management and Budget.

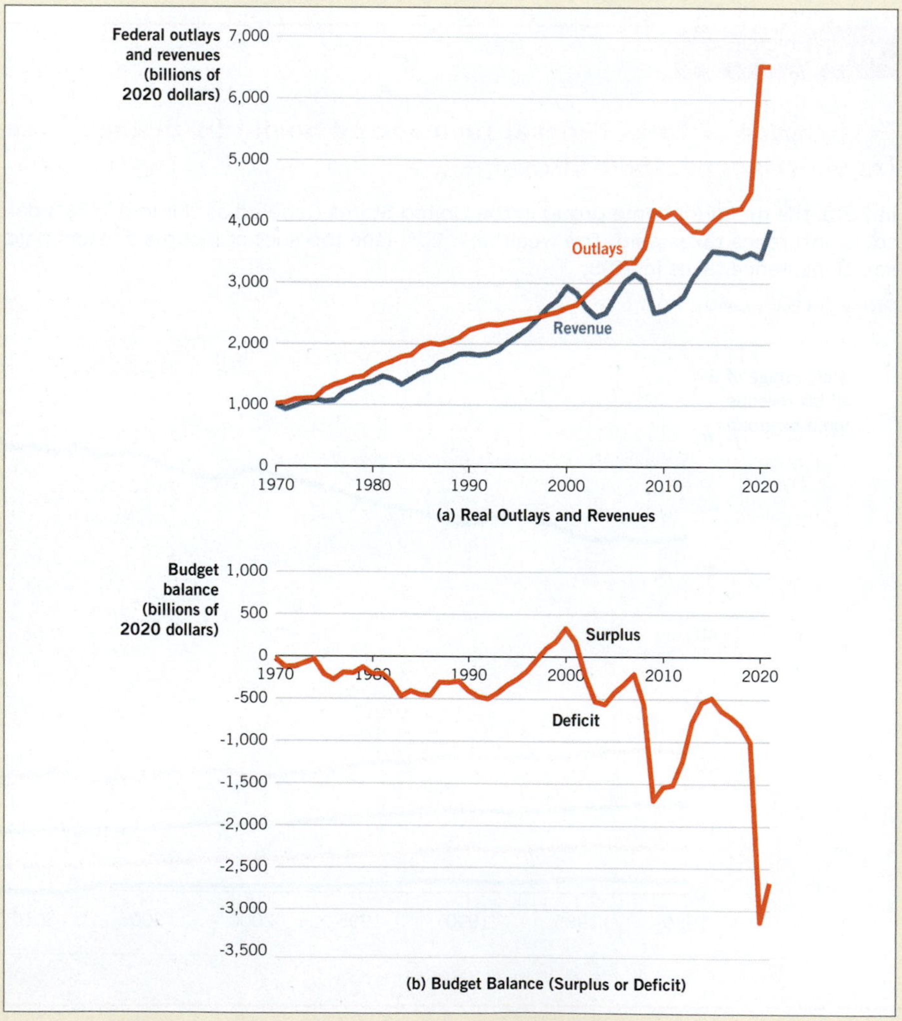

came in the four years from 1998 to 2001. Panel (b) of Figure 28.9 graphs the budget balance from 1970 to 2021. When the budget is in deficit, the balance is negative; when the budget is in surplus, the balance is positive.

The 2020 deficit of $3.13 trillion is the largest in U.S. history—larger in real dollar terms than the deficits generated during World War II in the 1940s. But dollar values for government budget figures, even in real dollars, are misleading over the long run, because the population and the size of the economy change. To control for both population and economic growth, economists often look at the budget deficit as a percentage of GDP. Dividing budget data by GDP scales it to the size of the economy. Figure 28.10 shows the U.S. federal outlays and revenue, both as a fraction of GDP, from 1970 to 2021. Over the entire period, outlays averaged 20.4% of GDP and revenues averaged 17.0% of GDP. These averages are shown as dashed lines in the figure. You can view these long-run averages as a benchmark for future budgets. Both outlays and revenues currently lie outside their long-run averages.

The blue vertical bars in Figure 28.10 indicate economic recessions. When a recession hits, tax revenue, which is largely tied to income, declines. In addition, for reasons we cover in the next chapter, government outlays often increase during recessions. Together these two results cause deficits to increase during recessions.

When the budget is in deficit, the government must borrow funds to pay for the difference between outlays and revenue. In Chapter 23, we introduced U.S. Treasury bonds as important financial assets in the loanable funds market. Now we can understand how those bonds originate: when tax revenues fall short of outlays, the government sells Treasury bonds to cover the difference. The aftereffects of COVID-19 and the government's response to it were still playing out in the summer of 2022.

FIGURE 28.10

U.S. Federal Outlays and Revenue as a Percentage of GDP, 1970–2021

The deficit-to-GDP ratio is a helpful gauge of the magnitude of deficits over time because it accounts for changes in population and economic growth. Here we illustrate outlays (orange) and revenue (blue) as a percentage of GDP. The deficit is the vertical distance between the lines. Dashed lines indicate long-run averages. These show us that recent spending has been above the long-run average and recent revenue has been below the long-run average. The blue bars indicate recessionary periods. As you can see, deficits grow during recessions.

Source: U.S. Office of Management and Budget.

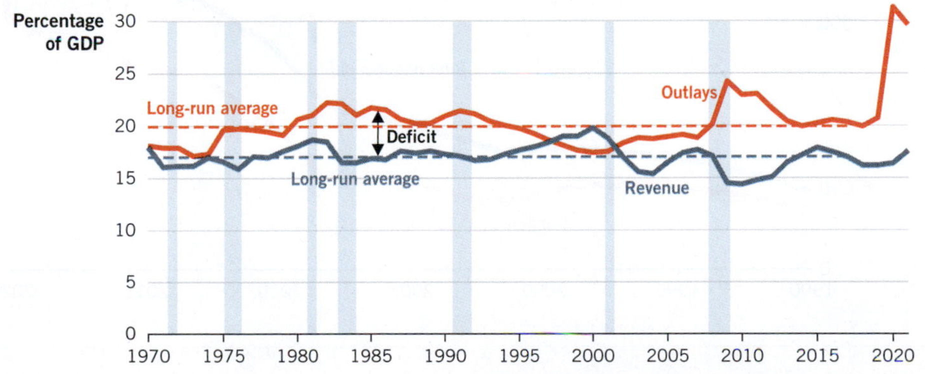

Deficits versus Debt

In your personal budget, it might happen that your spending (outlays) in a given month exceeds your income. In other words, you find you have a deficit. You might rely on funds from parents or grandparents to make up the difference, but this money counts either as income (if it's a gift) or as a loan (if you have to repay it). Often, you will have to borrow, perhaps by using a credit card. A loan, whether it is from a friend, relative, or credit card company, is a debt that must be paid.

A **debt** is the total of all accumulated and unpaid budget deficits.

It's easy to confuse the terms "deficit" and "debt." A deficit is a shortfall in revenue for a particular year's budget. A **debt** is the total of all accumulated and unpaid budget deficits. Consider your tuition bill over the course of your time in college. If you borrow $5,000 to help pay for your first year of college, that is your first-year deficit. If you borrow another $5,000 for your second year, you have a $5,000 deficit for each year, and your debt grows to $10,000. This is the same way that national debt grows. Any year in which there is a budget deficit leads to a larger national debt.

Figure 28.11 shows the U.S. national debt (in real terms) from 1990 to 2021. Notice that we distinguish total national debt and debt held by the public. The

FIGURE 28.11

U.S. National Debt, 1990–2021 (in billions of 2012 dollars)

The total amount of U.S. federal government debt (shown in blue) has grown to almost $25 trillion in recent years, even exceeding annual GDP in the United States. But much of this debt is owned by agencies of the government itself (the government owes money to itself). Therefore, many economists focus instead on the debt held by the general public (anyone besides the U.S. government). This amount (shown in orange) is $19 trillion and constitutes 78% of U.S. GDP. If you are curious about the current size of the U.S. national debt, you can visit the web site www.usdebtclock.org.

Source: U.S. Treasury, *Treasury Bulletin*.

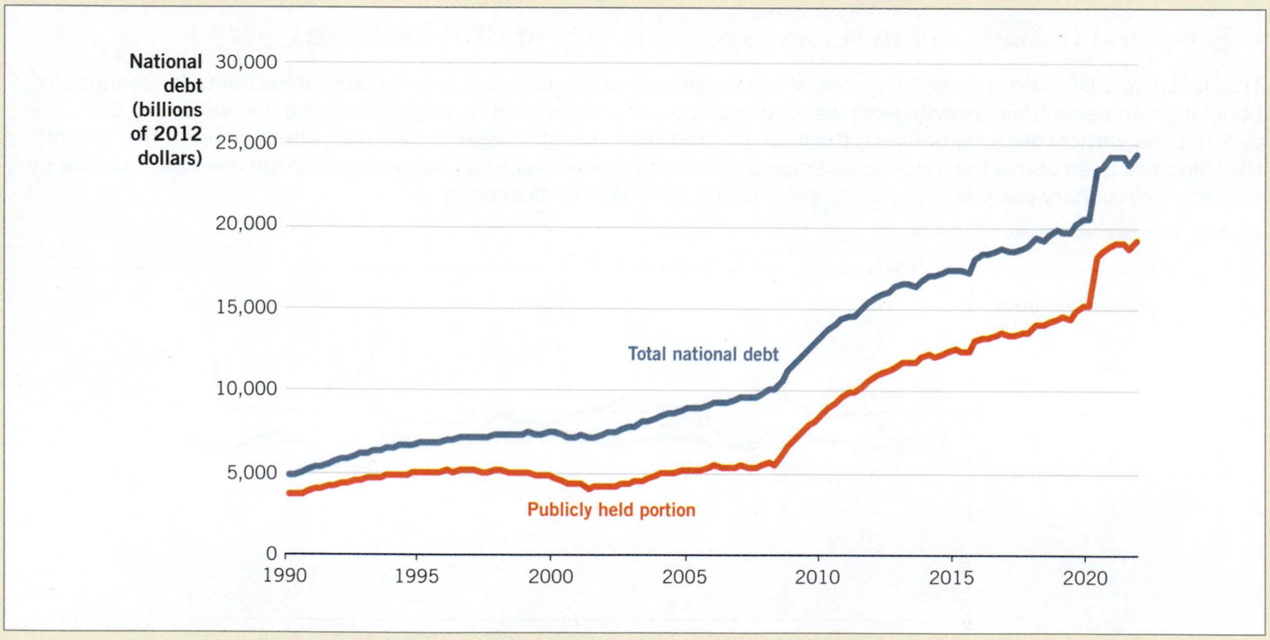

difference between these is debt owned internally by one of the many branches of the U.S. government. Sometimes, a given federal agency purchases Treasury bonds. For example, as part of its mandate to control the money supply, the Federal Reserve typically holds billions of dollars' worth of Treasury securities. Thus, it is helpful to distinguish total government debt that is not also owned by the government itself, and this is the publicly held portion. Figure 28.11 indicates that both measures have risen in recent years, a result of the large budget deficits.

While the U.S. national debt is historically large, relative to the size of the economy it is still smaller than that of many other nations, including many wealthy ones. Figure 28.12 shows publicly held debt-to-GDP ratios for several nations in 2020. The United States comes in at 128%, but Japan's ratio is over 260%.

FIGURE 28.12

International Debt-to-GDP Ratios, December 2020

While the U.S. debt-to-GDP ratio has grown to over 100% in recent years, this amount is still smaller than that of some other developed nations.

Source: Trading Economics, https://tradingeconomics.com/country-list/government-debt-to-gdp.

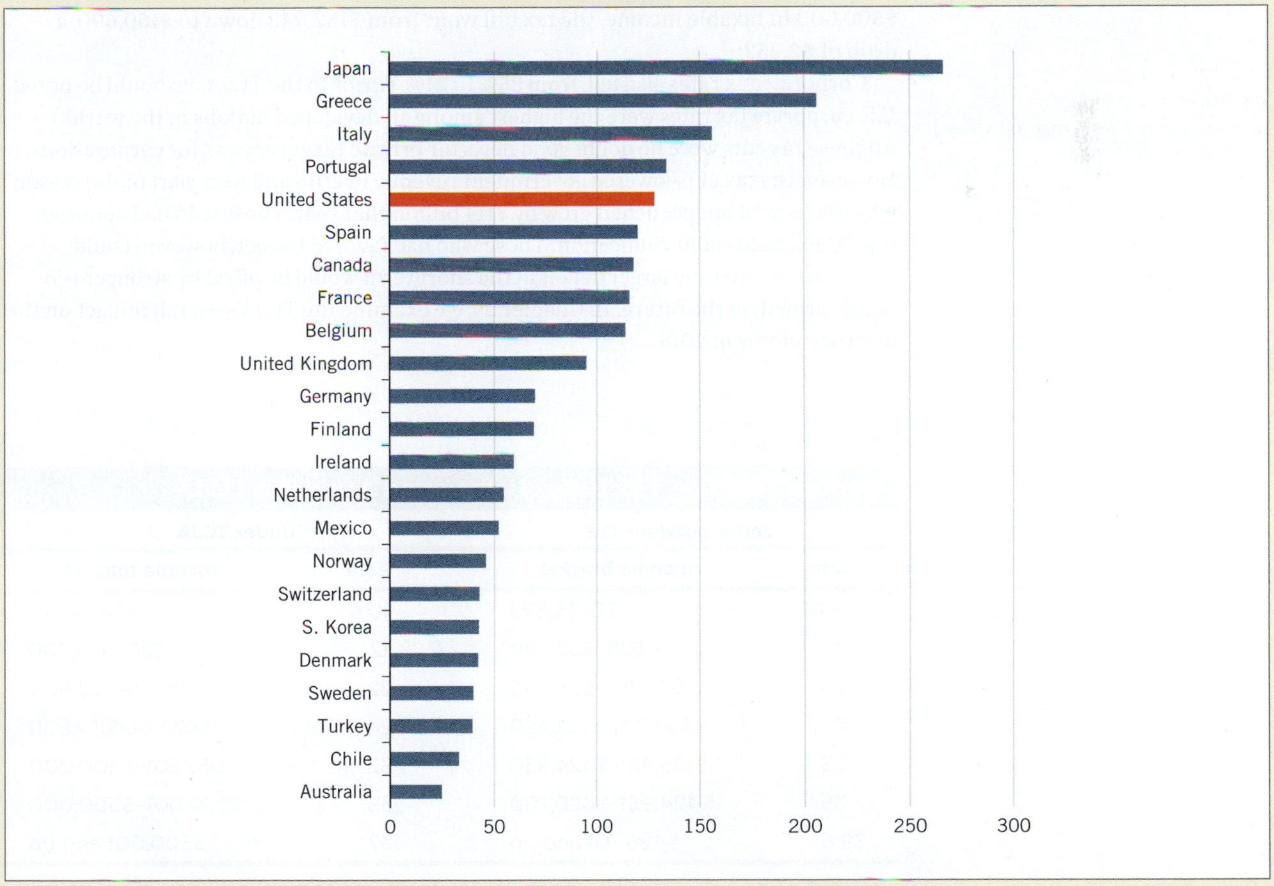

ECONOMICS IN THE REAL WORLD

THE TAX CUTS AND JOBS ACT OF 2017

In December of 2017, the U.S. Congress passed, and the president signed into law, the Tax Cuts and Jobs Act of 2017 (TCJA). The two major changes it made to federal tax law were a reduction in personal income tax rates for most taxpayers and a rate reduction for the tax on corporate profits. Many members of Congress voted against the bill, objecting that the federal deficit would rise and that a fiscal policy stimulus should be reserved for a time when the economy is struggling. (At the time the bill passed, the unemployment rate was 4.1%, real GDP was growing at 2.3% per year, and the federal budget deficit was over $1 trillion.) The act's defenders countered that there was no reason to delay a policy change that would give the economy a long-lasting shot in the arm.

Table 28.2 shows the 2018 tax rate structure for individual taxpayers before and after TCJA. As you can see, rates went down for almost all U.S. taxpayers. The rate for an earner's first $9,525 stayed at 10%, but after that, rates fell from 15%, 25%, and 28% to 12%, 22%, and 24%, respectively, all the way up to an annual income of $157,500. Meanwhile, for the highest-income earners, the marginal tax rate fell from 39.6% to 37%. The result was that at the lower end of the income scale, someone earning $30,000 in taxable income paid $3,410 in taxes, rather than $4,024 (without the TCJA), a tax break of $614. At the other end, for someone with $500,000 in taxable income, the tax bill went from $152,943 down to $150,690, a drop of $2,253.

Corporate tax rates also fell, from 35% to 21%. (Prior to the TCJA, it should be noted, U.S. corporate tax rates were the highest among all developed nations in the world.) All these tax cuts were no doubt good news for private taxpayers and for corporations. However, the tax cuts lowered government revenue in 2018 and were part of the reason why the federal budget deficit grew by $114 billion that year. Those who had opposed the TCJA could claim vindication. Those who had favored the act, however, could still maintain that the larger deficit in the short term would be offset by stronger economic growth in the future. In Chapter 29, we examine the TCJA's overall impact on the macroeconomy in 2018.

TABLE 28.2

Federal Income Tax Rates Before and After the TCJA

Under previous law		Under TCJA	
Rate	**Income bracket**	**Rate**	**Income bracket**
10%	$0–$9,525	10%	$0–$9,525
15	$9,526–$38,700	12	$9,526–$38,700
25	$38,701–$93,700	22	$38,701–$82,500
28	$93,701–$195,450	24	$82,501–$157,500
33	$195,451–$424,950	32	$157,501–$200,000
35	$424,951–$426,700	35	$200,001–$500,000
39.6	$426,701 and up	37	$500,001 and up

The TCJA passed both houses of Congress before the president signed it into law in December 2017.

Foreign Ownership of U.S. Federal Debt

As we saw in Chapter 23, many people are concerned about foreign ownership of U.S. debt. The concern stems from a fear that foreigners who own U.S. debt can control the country politically and economically. However, according to the U.S. Treasury, as of 2018, about 70% of U.S. national debt was held domestically, and just 30% internationally. China, Japan, Brazil, and the United Kingdom are the major foreign holders of U.S. debt.

Figure 28.13 shows foreign and domestic ownership of total real U.S. debt from 1990 to 2018. During this period, total national debt grew from $6 trillion to over $26 trillion (in 2019 dollars). However, domestic investors and U.S. government agencies were the purchasers of most of the new debt. The portion of U.S. government debt that is foreign owned is less than 30%.

While this foreign ownership of U.S. government debt is troubling for many Americans, it is important to recognize the benefits of foreign funds to the U.S. loanable funds market. As we discussed in Chapter 23, foreign lending increases the supply of loanable funds in the United States, helping to reduce interest rates. Lower interest rates mean that firms and governments in the United States can borrow at lower cost and thereby increase investment and hire more workers, and ultimately increase future production. Furthermore, the increase in foreign ownership is a natural by-product of emerging foreign economies—as they get wealthier, they buy more U.S. Treasury bonds.

FIGURE 28.13

Foreign and Domestic Ownership of U.S. Government Debt, 1990–2020

Most U.S. government debt is owned by Americans or by the U.S. government itself. The rest of this debt is held by people outside of the United States. This graph shows total national debt and internationally owned debt. The percentage owned internationally has grown in recent decades but is still less than one-third of the total.

Source: U.S. Treasury, *Treasury Bulletin*. Last two quarters are estimates based on July 2020 government projections.

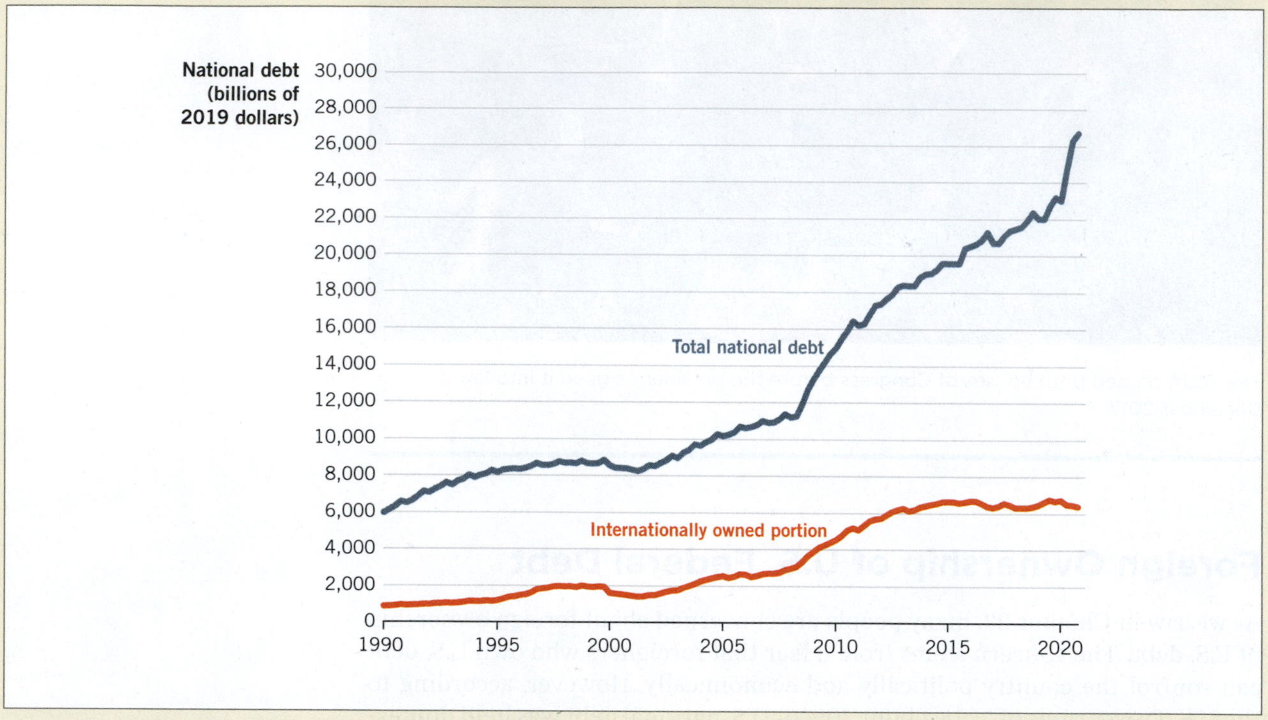

PRACTICE WHAT YOU KNOW

Federal Budgets: The U.S. Debt Crisis

The U.S. national debt grew substantially in the first decade of this century. The table below shows the data on the national debt from both 2001 and 2020.

Year	Total U.S. debt (billions of $)	Nominal GDP (billions of $)
2001	$5,807	$10,582
2020	26,945	20,894

(CONTINUED)

QUESTION: Using the data, compute the U.S. debt-to-GDP ratio in both 2001 and 2020.

ANSWER: For the year 2001, we compute the debt-to-GDP ratio as

$$\$5{,}807 \div \$10{,}582 = 0.55$$

For the year 2020, we compute the debt-to-GDP ratio as

$$\$26{,}945 \div \$20{,}894 = 1.29$$

QUESTION: What are the major reasons why the national debt increased so much between 2001 and 2020?

ANSWER: First, on the outlay side, U.S. government spending increased due to higher costs for Social Security and Medicare, and governmental responses to both the Great Recession and the COVID-19 recession.

Second, on the revenue side, tax receipts declined sharply during and after both recessions.

This running national debt clock is posted near Times Square in New York City.

Conclusion

We started this chapter with the observation that governments rarely balance their budgets. We then looked more closely at government outlays and revenues. This chapter lays the groundwork for us to examine fiscal policy in Chapter 29. Much of the debt and deficits we observed are a direct result of government budgetary maneuvers to affect the macroeconomy. Going forward, we now understand the institutions of fiscal policy. In Chapter 29, we'll learn about the economic theories that support fiscal policy. ✷

ECONOMICS *for* LIFE

Budgeting for Your Take-Home Pay

- Be sure to budget for your take-home pay rather than your total salary.
- In addition to state and local taxes, you also need to consider the cost of retirement and health benefits.

When you put together your budget, be sure to account for all the deductions from your paycheck.

Many college students have not yet held full-time jobs. So you are probably still planning for that day when you graduate and get your first big paycheck. We certainly don't want to discourage you, but we do offer a few words of caution for when you are budgeting your major expenses.

Let's say you graduate and obtain a good job in the city of your choice. You agree to a salary of $60,000 per year. This is a good starting salary (perhaps due to the economics courses you took!), so you start thinking about your personal budget. Consider a few of the biggest questions: How much can you afford for your monthly housing payment? How large a car payment can you afford? How much can you spend on groceries or dining out? How much should you save each month?

It's smart to think about these questions ahead of time. But when you plan, be sure to recognize that your take-home pay will be far less than $60,000. It is tempting to make a monthly budget based on the $5,000 per month your nominal salary implies. In the table shown here, we estimate the actual size of your paycheck.

First, we subtract federal income tax. Based on 2021 tax rates and assuming a standard deduction of $12,550, we determine that your annual tax bill is $6,187.50. Next we subtract 7.65% (of $60,000) for Social Security and Medicare. After that, we subtract 5% each for state income taxes (this is about average), benefits (like health insurance, dental, and optical), and retirement contributions.

After these deductions, you are left with just $3,351.88 per month! Your take-home pay is right around 33% less than your salary.

Therefore, when you are making major spending decisions about things such as housing and car payments, be sure to budget based on this much smaller figure. If you budget based on your salary alone, you won't be able to save, and you may even become dependent on credit cards.

	Monthly	**Yearly**
Salary	$5,000	$60,000
Federal income tax	515.62	6,187.50
Social Security/Medicare tax	382.50	4,590
State income tax	250	3,000
Benefits	250	3,000
Retirement	250	3,000
Take-home pay	3,351.88	40,222.50

- ANSWERING *the* BIG QUESTIONS -

How does the government spend?

- Government spending has grown sharply since 2000, and it is now about $6.5 trillion per year.
- Mandatory spending programs now constitute over 60% of government spending at the U.S. national level. These mandatory programs include Social Security, Medicare, and welfare programs.
- Interest on the national debt is about 8% of federal spending. Defense spending is 15% of federal spending. The remainder of the discretionary budget goes to discretionary government spending like highways, bridges, and the salaries of many government employees.

How does the government tax?

- The U.S. government raises about 83% of its revenues through taxes on paychecks: the income tax and the tax for Social Security and Medicare. The income tax yields about $2 trillion in revenue per year. It is a progressive tax, so wealthier Americans pay more in taxes than the poor do.

What are budget deficits?

- If total government outlays exceed revenue in a given year, the budget is in deficit.
- Deficits add to the national debt, which is the accumulated deficit over time.

CHAPTER PROBLEMS

Concepts You Should Know

average tax rate (p. 929)
budget deficit (p. 932)
budget surplus (p. 932)
debt (p. 934)
discretionary outlays (p. 920)
government outlays (p. 919)
mandatory outlays (p. 919)
marginal tax rate (p. 927)
Medicare (p. 923)
progressive income tax system (p. 927)
Social Security (p. 922)
transfer payments (p. 919)

Questions for Review

1. Since the 1960s, Social Security and Medicare have grown as portions of U.S. government spending.
   a. What major categories of government spending have shrunk during the same period?
   b. Has the U.S. budget become more or less flexible as a result of the growth in the mandatory programs? Explain your response.
2. Explain the difference between a budget deficit and the national debt.
3. Going back to 1965, there have been a few years in which the U.S. government budget was in surplus. What years were these? Why do you think those surpluses disappeared when they did? Figure 28.10 might be helpful in answering this question.
4. This question refers to Figure 28.10, which shows the U.S. outlays and revenue as portions of GDP.
   a. List four periods when the U.S. budget deficit was relatively large.
   b. What historical events were taking place in the United States during these four periods that may have led to these large deficits? Be specific.
5. Explain why mandatory outlays are predicted to grow (as a portion of the total budget) over the next two decades.
6. Explain the difference between average tax rates and marginal tax rates. Is it possible for a person's average tax rate to equal his or her marginal tax rate? If so, how?
7. Determine whether each of the following statements is true or false.
   a. About half of the current U.S. federal budget is allocated to national defense.
   b. About half of the current U.S. federal budget is allocated to mandatory (entitlement) programs.
   c. About 10% of our current federal budget is allocated to foreign aid.
   d. There was a recent proposal to increase defense spending by $30 billion (true!). If successful, the move will lead to the highest share of the national budget spent on defense since 1970.
   e. More than 75% of current federal revenue derives from taxes on wages (income and social insurance taxes).
   f. In the 1980s, President Reagan helped to reduce marginal tax rates from the highest level in U.S. history.
   g. Discretionary spending as a total portion of the federal budget is likely to increase as baby boomers retire.

Study Problems (✱ *solved at the end of the section*)

1. Use the marginal income tax rates in Figure 28.6 to compute the following:
   a. tax due on taxable income of $100,000, $200,000, and $500,000
   b. average tax rate on taxable income of $100,000, $200,000, and $500,000

2. Greece, Ireland, Portugal, and Spain all went through national budget difficulties a while back. Use the following data to answer questions regarding the sovereign debts of these nations. (All data come from the OECD and are in billions of current U.S. dollars.)

	2000		2010	
	Debt	GDP	Debt	GDP
Greece	$138	$127	$455	$308
Ireland	34	98	124	206
Portugal	62	118	203	231
Spain	292	586	734	1,420

   a. Compute the debt-to-GDP ratio for all four nations in both 2000 and 2010.
   b. Compute the average yearly budget deficit for each of the nations over this period.
   c. In your judgment, which of the four nations was in the worst fiscal shape in 2010? Use your earlier computations to justify your answer.

3. There are three different ways to report budget deficit data: nominal deficits, real deficits, and deficit-to-GDP ratios. Which of the three is most informative? Why?

✱ 4. Greece experienced significant national budget turmoil after the turn of the present century. In 2010, it was discovered that the government had been concealing the true size of the national debt for several years. The data in the following table reveal just how much the nation's officially reported national debt grew between 2000 and 2010. The data are in billions of U.S. dollars. Use the data to answer the questions that follow.

2000		2010	
Debt	GDP	Debt	GDP
$138	$127	$455	$308

   a. What was the average annual increase in the Greek debt over the 10-year span?
   b. What was the average annual budget deficit for Greece over this period?

✱ 5. Use the table in problem 4 to compute the debt-to-GDP ratio for Greece in both 2000 and 2010.

Solved Problems

4. **a.** The debt grew from $138 billion to $455 billion over 10 years, which was an increase of $317 billion, or an average of $31.7 billion per year.
   b. Given that the debt increased by $31.7 billion per year, this number was also the figure for the average annual deficit over this period.

5. For 2000: $138 \div 127 = 1.09$
   For 2010: $455 \div 308 = 1.48$

CHAPTER

29

Fiscal Policy

The Government Uses Fiscal Policy to Boost the Economy.

Unlike other recessions, the coronavirus recession began on a date we can pinpoint: March 11, 2020. That was the day many sectors of the U.S. economy shut down and people began social distancing in earnest. The federal government instituted border closures and other travel restrictions. Restaurants started doing take-out business only. Theme parks closed. Colleges sent their students home. In sports, the NBA and PGA suspended play mid-season, and the NCAA's "March Madness" basketball tournament was canceled. Most types of business were allowed to stay open, but since masks, hand sanitizer, and COVID-19 test kits were scarce, many closed anyway, out of concern for the safety of their staff and customers. The stock market responded to all this turmoil with a massive one-day drop quickly dubbed "Black Thursday."

It was immediately clear that the many people and businesses suffering from the shutdowns would need help. Over the next two months, Congress passed, and the president signed, spending packages adding up to more than $2.5 trillion. Included were tax rebates and unemployment compensation for individuals, and various kinds of assistance for businesses and state and local governments. Billions of dollars were earmarked for hard-hit industries like airlines and hospitals.

We can't yet say how it all worked out. But we do know that the economy, after plunging in the second quarter of 2020,

The federal government is often frustratingly slow to get things done—even basic, necessary jobs like budgeting. By the time President Biden signed the Consolidated Appropriations Act for 2022, the fiscal year was already halfway over.

actually rebounded somewhat in the third quarter—even in the midst of the pandemic. Economists attribute the rebound largely to the fiscal policy measures enacted in March and April of that year.

In this chapter, we consider how economists expect fiscal policy to affect the economy. We begin by discussing traditional demand-side fiscal policy in the aggregate demand–aggregate supply model. We then consider the potential shortcomings of this approach to fiscal policy. Finally, we consider fiscal policy focused on aggregate supply, which can be more effective when economic problems lie primarily on the supply side of the economy. That is what happened during the coronavirus pandemic.

· BIG QUESTIONS ·

- What is fiscal policy?
- What are the shortcomings of fiscal policy?
- What is supply-side fiscal policy?

What Is Fiscal Policy?

When the economy falters, people often look to government to help push the economy forward again. In fact, the government uses many different tools to try to affect the economy. Economists sort these into two types of policy: *monetary policy* and *fiscal policy*. Monetary policy is the use of the money supply to influence the economy. We will study monetary policy in Chapter 31. **Fiscal policy**, the subject of this chapter, involves the use of government budget tools, spending, and taxes to influence the macroeconomy. In the United States, tax and spending changes are legislated and approved by both Congress and the president.

Fiscal policy involves the use of government's budget tools, government spending, and taxes to influence the macroeconomy.

In this section, we first describe how the government can use fiscal policy to try to stimulate the economy; then we discuss how fiscal policy might be used to slow down rapid growth. Along the way, we consider how fiscal policy affects government budget deficits and debt. Finally, we examine the multiplier process, which describes the ways in which the effects of fiscal policy ripple through the economy.

Expansionary Fiscal Policy

Fiscal policy is typically focused on the spending or demand side of the economy. Private spending generally falls during recessions, so people look to the government to spend more and also to cut taxes to encourage private spending. **Expansionary fiscal policy** occurs when the government increases spending or decreases taxes to stimulate the economy toward expansion. In this section, we use the aggregate demand–aggregate supply model to examine the effects of expansionary fiscal policy.

Expansionary fiscal policy occurs when the government increases spending or decreases taxes to stimulate the economy toward expansion.

In Chapter 26, we introduced the aggregate demand–aggregate supply model. In that model, we showed that recession can occur as a result of a drop in aggregate demand. In theory, the economy can move itself back to full employment in the long run when all prices adjust. Consider the example presented in Figure 29.1. Initially, the economy is in long-run equilibrium at point A, with $P = 100$, $Y = Y^*$ (full employment), and $u = u^*$ (the natural unemployment rate). If aggregate demand declines from AD_1 to AD_2, the economy moves to short-run equilibrium at point b, with output at Y_1, which is less than full-employment output, and an unemployment rate greater than the natural rate.

At equilibrium point b, government officials can wait for the economy to adjust back to full-employment equilibrium at point C. This adjustment occurs when all prices adjust downward and short-run aggregate supply (SRAS) shifts downward to $SRAS_2$. But prices can take a while to adjust. In addition, recessions are difficult times for many people, and they expect the government to take action to ease their plight. Thus, government officials often choose to use fiscal policy to try to shift aggregate demand back to its original level. If their policy works, the economy returns to full-employment equilibrium at point A.

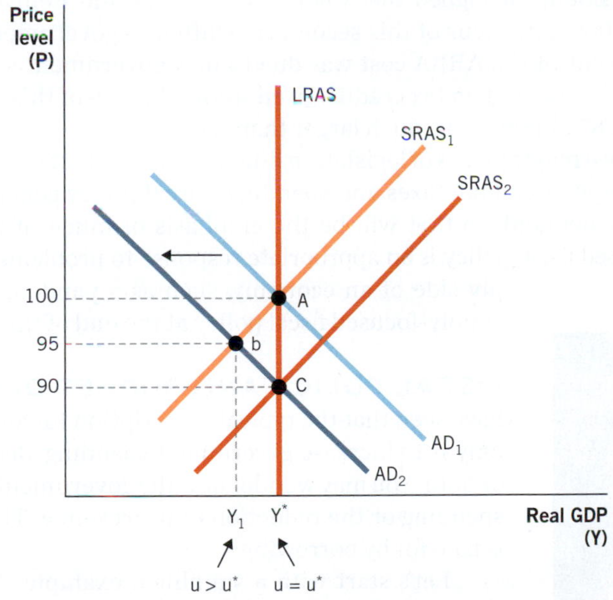

FIGURE 29.1

Expansionary Fiscal Policy

A decrease in aggregate demand from AD_1 to AD_2 moves the economy from point A to equilibrium at point b, with less than full-employment output (Y_1) and unemployment (u) greater than the natural rate (u*). In the long run, all prices adjust (short-run aggregate supply adjusts to $SRAS_2$), moving the economy back to full-employment equilibrium at point C. The goal of expansionary fiscal policy is to shift aggregate demand back to AD_1 so that the economy returns to full employment without waiting for long-run adjustments.

Fiscal policy can make use of government spending, taxes, or a combination of the two. Recall that aggregate demand has four pieces: consumption (C), investment (I), government spending (G), and net exports (NX). Therefore, increases in G directly increase aggregate demand. When private spending (consumption, investment, and net exports) is low, the government can increase demand directly by increasing G. Fiscal policy can also focus on consumption (C) by decreasing taxes. Decreases in taxes can increase aggregate demand because people have more of their income left to spend after paying their taxes. When people keep more of their paycheck, they can afford more consumption.

Recent history in the United States offers two prominent examples of expansionary fiscal policy. In the next section, we review these examples to clarify how fiscal policy uses both government spending and taxes.

FISCAL POLICY DURING THE GREAT RECESSION In the fall of 2007, the U.S. unemployment rate climbed from 4.6% to 5%. It was clear that economic conditions were worsening in the United States, and so the government took action. Political leaders decided that fiscal policy could help.

The government enacted two significant fiscal policy initiatives. The first, signed in February 2008 by President George W. Bush, was the Economic Stimulus Act of 2008. The cornerstone of this act was a tax rebate for Americans. They had already paid their taxes for 2007, and the stimulus act included a partial rebate of those previously paid taxes. The government mailed rebate checks to taxpayers: a typical four-person family received a check for $1,800 ($600 per adult and $300 per child). The overall cost of this action to government was $168 billion; it refunded about 1 of every 7 dollars paid in individual income taxes for 2007. The expectation was that American taxpayers would spend rather than save most of this $168 billion, thereby increasing aggregate demand and stimulating the economy.

However, after the first fiscal stimulus was passed, economic conditions worsened. In February 2009, less than one month after Barack Obama took office as president, he signed the American Recovery and Reinvestment Act (ARRA) of 2009. The focus of this second act shifted to government spending. Seventy percent of the ARRA cost was due to new government spending; the remaining 30% focused on tax credits. In addition, the size of this second fiscal stimulus—$787 billion—was much larger than the first.

These two major pieces of legislation illustrate the tools of fiscal policy that targets aggregate demand: taxes and spending. Fiscal policy generally focuses on aggregate demand, so that will be the emphasis of much of this chapter. Supply-focused fiscal policy is an appropriate response to problems on the supply side of an economy, such as a pandemic. We cover supply-focused fiscal policy at the end of this chapter.

President Obama signed the American Recovery and Reinvestment Act of 2009.

FISCAL POLICY AND BUDGET DEFICITS We have seen that the typical prescription for an ailing economy is to increase government spending, decrease taxes, or both. You may wonder how the government pays for the spending or the reduction in tax revenue. The difference is paid for by borrowing.

Let's start with a simplified example. Assume that the government is currently balancing the national budget so that outlays equal tax revenue. Then the economy slips into recession, and the government decides to increase government spending by $100 billion.

President Trump signed the CARES Act at the end of March 2020 . . .

. . . and one year later, President Biden signed the American Rescue Plan Act of 2021.

Without a corresponding increase in tax revenue, the government must pay for this spending by borrowing; it must sell $100 billion worth of Treasury bonds. As a result, the federal budget deficit increases.

But that's only part of the story. In reality, the budget deficit rises by more than $100 billion, because tax revenue falls. Recall from Chapter 28 that 80% of U.S. tax revenue derives from taxes on paychecks (income and social insurance taxes). In a recession, with income down and unemployment up, government tax revenue falls even if tax rates don't change.

We see both phenomena when we look at historical U.S. government outlays and revenue. Figure 29.2 shows U.S. federal outlays and tax revenue from

FIGURE 29.2

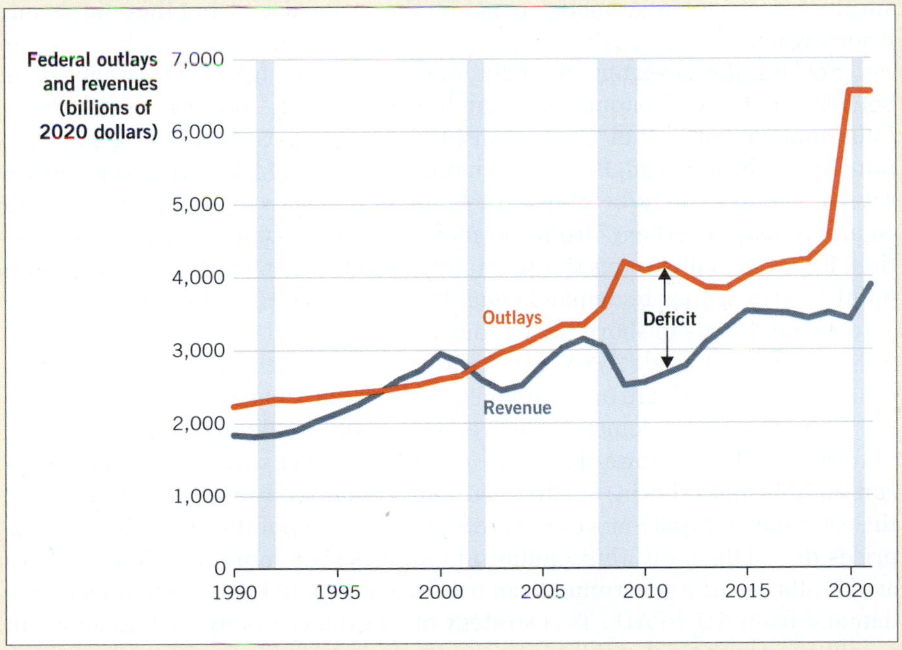

Real U.S. Outlays and Revenue, 1990–2021

The use of expansionary fiscal policy to counteract economic downturns leads to greater budget deficits. During recessionary periods, outlays increase and tax revenue falls. In 2001, these strategies erased the budget surplus; in 1990, 2008, and 2020, these strategies expanded the size of the deficit.

Source: Office of Management and Budget.

1990 to 2021, with recessionary periods indicated by vertical blue bars. There have been four recessions since 1990. In each, revenue fell and outlays rose, leading to larger deficits. The 2020 federal budget deficit topped $3 trillion, mostly due to fiscal policy in the coronavirus recession.

The bottom line is clear: expansionary fiscal policy inevitably leads to increases in budget deficits and the national debt during economic downturns. This policy prescription may seem odd. After all, if you personally fell on rough economic times, you might (reasonably) react differently. For example, if your employer were to cut you back from full-time to part-time employment, would it seem like a good idea to go on a spending binge? You might feel better while you were shopping, but it wouldn't help your financial situation much. From a macroeconomic perspective, however, expansionary fiscal policy might work for the overall economy, because spending by one person becomes income to another, which can snowball into income increases throughout the economy. We discuss this "multiplier" aspect of fiscal policy later in this chapter.

Contractionary Fiscal Policy

Contractionary fiscal policy occurs when the government decreases spending or increases taxes to slow economic expansion.

We have seen that expansionary fiscal policy is often used to try to increase aggregate demand during economic downturns. But there are also times when contractionary fiscal policy is used to reduce aggregate demand. **Contractionary fiscal policy** occurs when the government decreases spending or increases taxes to slow economic expansion.

There are two reasons why a government might want to reduce aggregate demand. First, as we discussed earlier, expansionary fiscal policy creates deficits during recessions. An increase in taxes or a decrease in spending during an economic expansion can work to reduce the budget deficit and pay off some government debt. For example, the U.S. government ran budget surpluses from 1998 to 2001, at the end of an extended period of economic expansion. These surpluses were not large enough to pay off the national debt, but they did shrink it somewhat.

Second, the government might want to reduce aggregate demand if it believes that the economy is expanding beyond its long-run capabilities. Full-employment output (Y^*) is considered the highest level of output sustainable in the long run. But if the unemployment rate falls below the natural rate (u^*), output may be above Y^*. Some economists then worry that the economy may "overheat" from too much spending, which can lead to inflation. Figure 29.3 illustrates this possibility, beginning at short-run equilibrium point a, with aggregate demand equal to AD_1. Notice that this level of aggregate demand leads to short-run equilibrium where real GDP is higher than its full-employment level ($Y_1 > Y^*$). In addition, at point a, the unemployment rate is below the natural rate ($u < u^*$), which is not sustainable in the long run.

When aggregate demand is high enough to drive unemployment below the natural rate, there is upward pressure on the price level, which is at 105 at short-run equilibrium point a. Further, without a reduction in aggregate demand, the economy naturally moves toward equilibrium at point C in the long run as prices fully adjust. But this equilibrium implies even more inflation. Thus, to avoid inflation, the government can use fiscal policy to try to reduce aggregate demand from AD_1 to AD_2. This strategy moves the economy back to long-run equilibrium with price stability at point B.

FIGURE 29.3

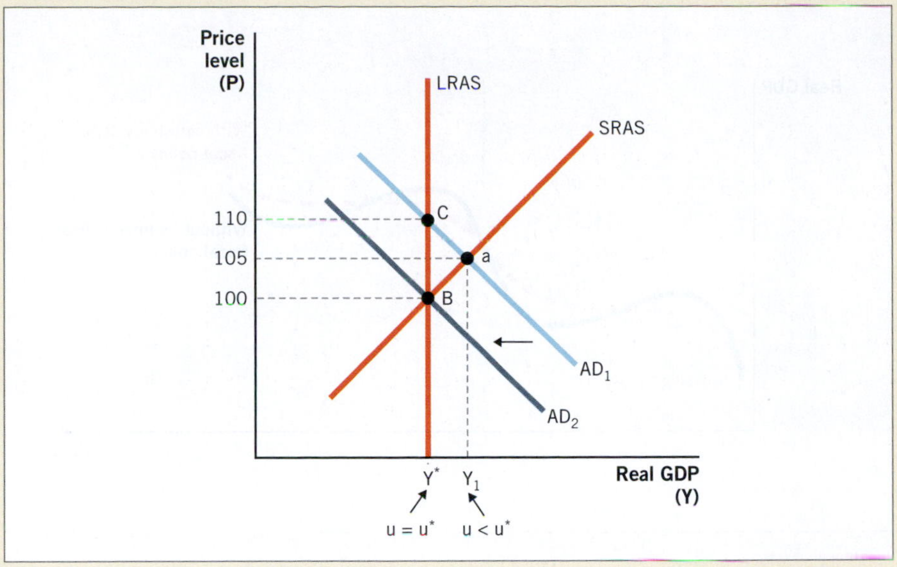

Contractionary Fiscal Policy

When policymakers believe that the economy is producing beyond its long-run capacity ($Y_1 > Y^*$), fiscal policy can be used to reduce aggregate demand. Contractionary fiscal policy moves the economy from short-run equilibrium at point a to equilibrium at point B, thus avoiding the inflationary outcome at point C.

Together, contractionary and expansionary fiscal policy can serve to counteract the ups and downs of business cycles. We examine this combination more closely in the next section.

COUNTERCYCLICAL FISCAL POLICY All else being equal, people generally prefer smoothness and predictability in their financial affairs. In Chapter 22, we talked about this characteristic in reference to consumption smoothing; in Chapter 23, we considered how people are risk averse. Along these lines, an economy that grows at a consistent rate is preferable to an economy that grows in an erratic fashion.

Fiscal policy that seeks to counteract business cycle fluctuations is known as **countercyclical fiscal policy**. It consists of using expansionary policy during economic downturns and contractionary policy during economic expansions. Figure 29.4 illustrates the goals of countercyclical fiscal policy. The natural path of the economy (without countercyclical fiscal policy) includes business cycles during which income and employment fluctuate. The goal of countercyclical fiscal policy is to reduce those fluctuations.

Countercyclical fiscal policy is fiscal policy that seeks to counteract business cycle fluctuations.

You might recall from Chapter 27 that Keynesian economists focus on aggregate demand (total spending) in the economy. Keynesian economics provides the theoretical foundation for countercyclical fiscal policy. In fact, Keynes's ideas provided a theoretical foundation for the New Deal government spending programs implemented in the United States in 1933 and 1935. And these ideas are behind the demand-focused fiscal policies in all recessions since.

Table 29.1 summarizes the tools of countercyclical fiscal policy, including the timing and effects of the policy on aggregate demand as well as its effects on the government budget deficit. In practice, while politicians are quick to reach for expansionary tools during economic downturns, they are much less quick to reach for contractionary tools in boom times. Expansionary policy is popular; contractionary policy isn't.

FIGURE 29.4

Countercyclical Fiscal Policy and the Business Cycle

The goal of countercyclical fiscal policy is to smooth out the fluctuations in the business cycle.

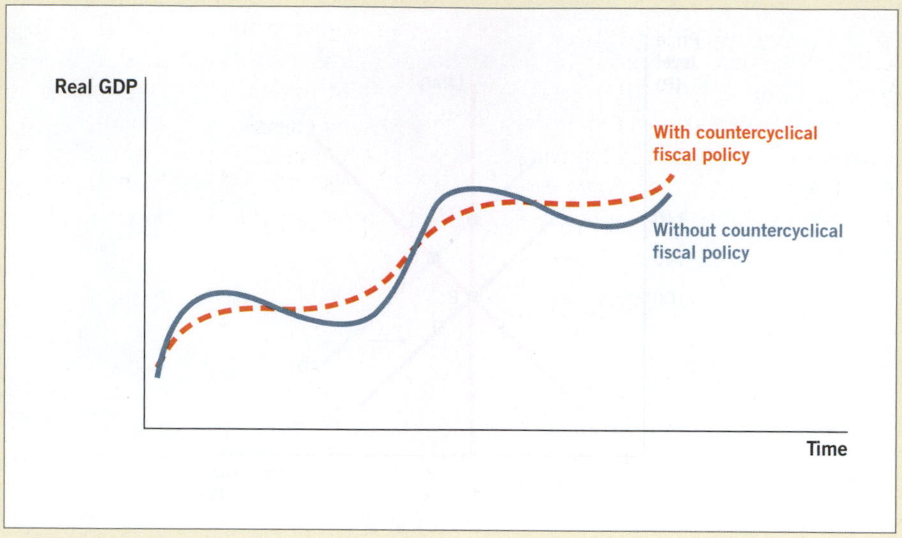

Multipliers

The tools of fiscal policy are possibly more powerful than our discussion thus far implies, because the initial effect can snowball over time. When fiscal policy shifts aggregate demand, some effects are felt immediately. But a large share of the impact occurs later, as spending effects ripple throughout the economy. To see this process clearly, we need to build on two concepts we learned in previous chapters. One should be familiar; the other is new.

TABLE 29.1

Countercyclical Fiscal Policy Tools

Fiscal policy action	Timing	Objective: How it affects aggregate demand (AD)	By-product: How it affects the budget deficit
Expansionary			
↑ Government spending (G)	When the economy is contracting	G is one component of AD, so increases in G directly increase AD.	Increases budget deficit
↓ Taxes (T)	When the economy is contracting	Decreasing T leaves more funds in the hands of consumers, who then spend more on consumption (C). When C rises, AD rises.	Increases budget deficit
Contractionary			
↓ Government spending (G)	When the economy is expanding	Decreases in G directly decrease AD.	Decreases budget deficit
↑ Taxes (T)	When the economy is expanding	Increasing T leaves fewer funds in the hands of consumers, who then spend less on consumption (C). When C falls, AD falls.	Decreases budget deficit

First, the familiar concept: recall from Chapter 19 that spending by one person becomes income to others. This is true not only for private spending but also for government spending. For example, if the government uses fiscal policy to increase spending on new roads, the dollars spent on those roads become income to the suppliers of the resources used in the production of the roads.

Now the new concept: increases in income generally lead to increases in consumption. When a person's income rises, he or she might save some of this new income but might be just as likely to spend part of it, too. The **marginal propensity to consume (MPC)** is the portion of additional income spent on consumption:

The **marginal propensity to consume (MPC)** is the portion of additional income spent on consumption.

$$MPC = \frac{\text{change in consumption}}{\text{change in income}}$$

(EQUATION 29.1)

For example, say you earn \$400 in new income, and you decide to spend \$300 and save \$100. Your marginal propensity to consume is then $\$300 \div \$400 = 0.75$. In other words, you spend 75% of your new income. The MPC isn't constant across all people, but it is a fraction between 0 and 1:

$$0 \leq MPC \leq 1$$

Let's consider a simple example of how spending changes affect the economy. For this example, let's say that the government decides to increase spending by \$100 billion and spends all of the funds on salaries for government workers. This government spending becomes new income for the government workers. Now let's assume that the MPC of these workers is 0.75, so these workers spend 75 cents of each dollar of their new income. In total, the government workers spend \$75 billion and save \$25 billion. The new spending becomes \$75 billion worth of income to others in the economy. We add this to the initial \$100 billion in government spending to get \$175 billion in new income. Furthermore, if the recipients of the \$75 billion income also turn around and spend 75% of it, they create another \$56.25 billion in new income for others in the economy, for a total of \$231.25 billion.

It's clear that the initial \$100 billion in government spending can create more than \$100 billion in income; this effect occurs through the "multiplying" we just described. The effect continues on, round after round, as new income earners spend a portion of their new income.

The multiplier effect is significant when we focus on aggregate demand in the economy. Each time people earn new income, they spend part of it. After all the dust settles, the total effect is a multiple of the original fiscal policy spending. Figure 29.5 illustrates this multiplier process for our current example. The table in the figure shows how spending becomes income and then how part of the new income is spent. The first round represents the government's initial spending of \$100 billion. The following rounds represent the new income generated by consumption spending. Because the MPC is 0.75 in this example, each round generates 75% of the income produced in the preceding round.

In the graph, we show aggregate demand. Each time spending increases, aggregate demand increases (shifts rightward). The initial aggregate demand is labeled AD_1. Each round of spending shifts aggregate demand to the right by less and less, until aggregate demand settles at AD_N, where N represents the completion of the multiplier process.

Your decision to spend or save has macroeconomic consequences.

FIGURE 29.5

The Spending Multiplier Process

Assume that MPC = 0.75 and the government increases spending by $100 billion. In the table, you can see how the spending multiplies throughout the economy; each round is 75% of the prior round. In the end, the total spending increase is four times the initial change in government spending. The graph illustrates the shifting aggregate demand curve as the spending multiplies throughout the economy

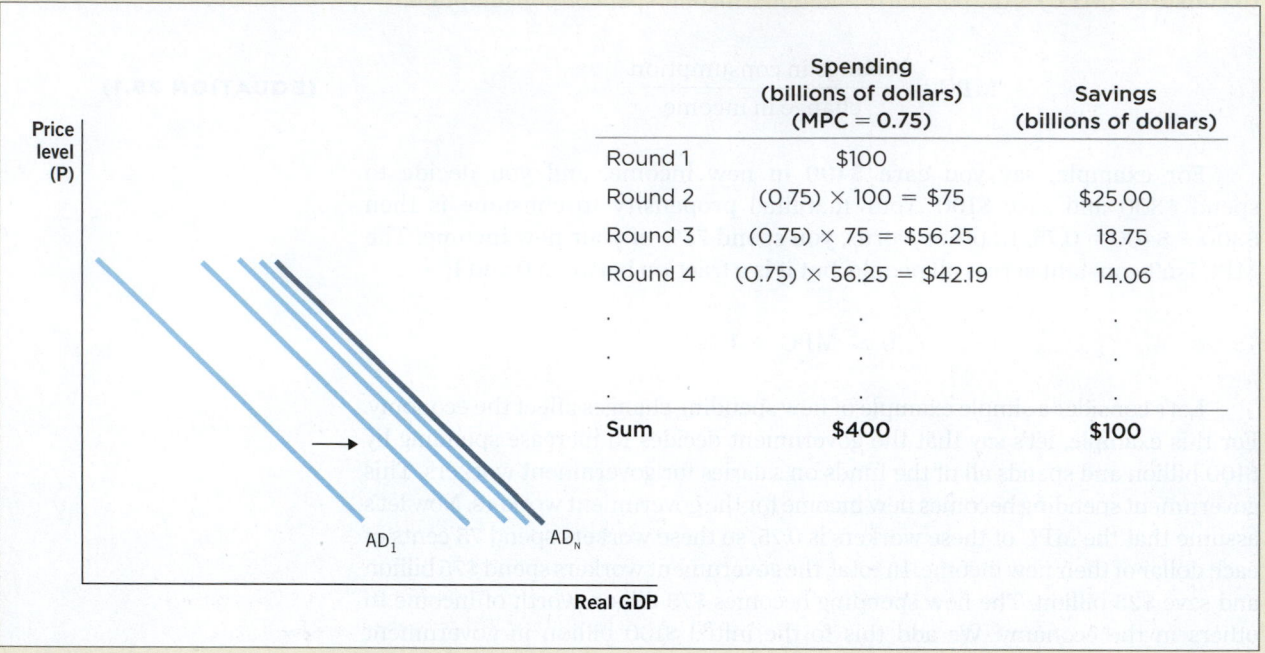

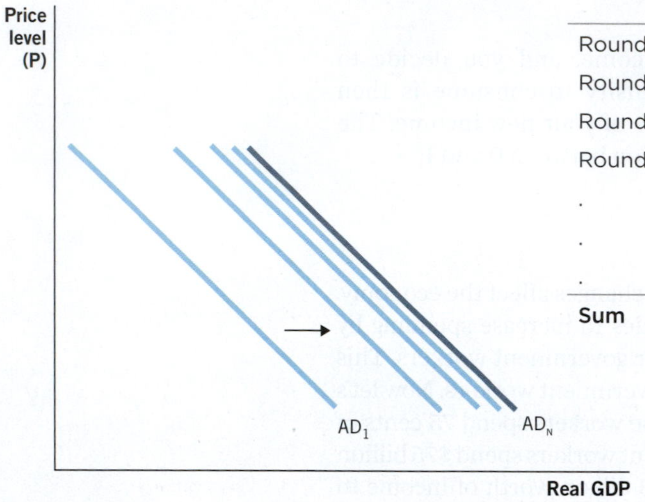

	Spending (billions of dollars) (MPC = 0.75)	Savings (billions of dollars)
Round 1	$100	
Round 2	(0.75) × 100 = $75	$25.00
Round 3	(0.75) × 75 = $56.25	18.75
Round 4	(0.75) × 56.25 = $42.19	14.06
.	.	.
.	.	.
.	.	.
Sum	$400	$100

The **spending multiplier** is a formula to determine the equation's effect on spending from an initial change of a given amount.

To determine the total effect on spending from any initial government expenditures, we use the *spending multiplier*. The **spending multiplier** (m^s) tells us the total impact on spending from an initial change of a given amount. The multiplier depends on the marginal propensity to consume: the greater the marginal propensity to consume, the greater the spending multiplier. The formula for the spending multiplier is

(EQUATION 29.2)

$$m^s = \frac{1}{(1 - \text{MPC})}$$

Because the MPC is a fraction between 0 and 1, in principle the multiplier must come out larger than 1. For example, if the marginal propensity to consume is 0.75, the multiplier is determined as:

$$m^s = \frac{1}{(1 - \text{MPC})} = \frac{1}{1 - 0.75} = \frac{1}{0.25} = 4$$

Sometimes, the spending multiplier is called the *Keynesian multiplier* or *fiscal multiplier*.

ECONOMICS *in the* MEDIA

Spending Multiplier

PAY IT FORWARD

In this movie, a drama from 2000, a young boy named Trevor (played by Haley Joel Osment) comes up with an idea that he thinks can change the world. Instead of paying people back for good deeds, Trevor suggests a new approach called "pay it forward." The idea is for him to help three people in some way. According to Trevor, "it has to be really big, something they can't do by themselves."

Then each of those three people helps three more. You can see how this idea leads to a multiplication of people helping other people.

Trevor's scheme is both similar to and different from the spending multiplier at the center of Keynesian fiscal policy. It is similar in that one person's "spending" leads to "spending" by others.

But we have seen that the spending multiplier is driven by the marginal propensity to consume, which is a fraction between 0 and 1, because people generally save part of any new income they earn. So the spending multiplication process slows down and eventually dies out.

Trevor explains his good-deed pyramid scheme.

However, the multiplier in *Pay it Forward* exceeds 1 because each person helps three people. In fact, Trevor's multiplier will be infinity because each good deed leads to three more. So the good deeds can continue to expand to more and more good deeds.

Note that the multiplier concept applies to all spending, no matter whether the spending is public or private. In addition, there is a multiplier associated with tax changes. A reduction in the tax rate leaves more income for consumers to spend. This spending multiplies throughout the economy in much the same way as government spending multiplies.

The multiplier process also works in reverse. If the government reduces spending or increases taxes, people have less income to spend, shifting the aggregate demand curve to the left. In terms of the aggregate demand curve in Figure 29.5, the initial decline in government spending leads to subsequent declines as the effects reverberate through the economy.

In theory, then, the spending multiplier implies that the tools of fiscal policy are very powerful. Not only can the government change its spending and taxing, but multiples of this spending then ripple throughout the economy over several periods. In reality, however, government spending multipliers are not very large. The largest multipliers occur with temporary deficit-financed increases in government spending, but even these rarely go above 1.5. Even

The multiplier effects of fiscal policy on an economy are similar to the rippling effects of a stone thrown into the water.

PRACTICE WHAT YOU KNOW

Eating out requires a mask, and stimulus spending.

Expansionary Fiscal Policy: Small Business Stimulus Spending

In early 2020, with the U.S. economy on the verge of what was expected to be a significant recession, President Trump promoted fiscal stimulus spending to encourage companies to keep their workers employed. Ultimately, Congress passed a series of measures to get money into the hands of small-business owners. Both Congress and the president expected that this stimulus plan would keep income flowing to households, thereby allowing them to spend money on necessities. Let's examine a simplified version of how economists might try to determine the effect of government spending projects on the macroeconomy.

QUESTION: Assume that the marginal propensity to consume (MPC) is equal to 0.5. What is the value of the government spending multiplier in this case?

ANSWER: Equation 29.2 gives us the formula for the spending multiplier:

$$m^s = \frac{1}{(1 - \text{MPC})} = \frac{1}{(1 - 0.5)} = \frac{1}{0.5} = 2$$

QUESTION: Given the size of the multiplier, what would be the change in income (GDP) from stimulus spending of \$800 billion?

ANSWER: The total impact would be: 2 × \$800 billion = \$1.6 trillion.

Valerie Ramey studies the short- and long-term macroeconomic effects of fiscal policy decisions.

more surprisingly, Valerie Ramey, an economist at the University of California, San Diego, estimates that multipliers are typically less than one—not something you'd expect based on how we derived the multiplier from the MPC.* This implies that government spending increases don't always translate into more overall spending. In the next section, we cover this more fully, as we discuss shortcomings of fiscal policy.

What Are the Shortcomings of Fiscal Policy?

At this point, you may wonder why fiscal policy doesn't always work perfectly in the real world. If fiscal policy is as simple as tweaking government spending and taxes and letting the multiplier go to work, why do recessions still happen? The first answer is that the real world isn't so simple. Millions of people make

*Valerie A. Ramey and Sarah Zubairy, "Government Spending Multipliers in Good Times and in Bad: Evidence from U.S. Historical Data," *Journal of Political Economy*, April 2019, https://econweb.ucsd.edu/~vramey/research/RZUS.pdf.

individual decisions that collectively affect the entire economy. While economists try to forecast variables and outcomes (how much will people spend versus save?), they can never be certain of the answers to these questions ahead of time. Even the most informed and educated guesses are still guesses and not guarantees.

But there are also more specific shortcomings of fiscal policy. In this section, we consider three issues that arise in the application of fiscal policy: time lags, crowding-out, and savings shifts.

Time Lags

Economic policy is intended to smooth out the economic variations that accompany a business cycle. So timing is important. But there are three time lags that accompany policy decisions: recognition lag, implementation lag, and impact lag.

1. *Recognition lag.* In the real world, it is difficult to determine when the economy is turning up or down. GDP data are released quarterly, and the final estimate for each quarter is not known until three months after the period in question. In addition, it often takes a while for unemployment rates to reflect macroeconomic conditions. Moreover, growth is not constant: one bad quarter does not always signal a recession, and one good quarter is not always the beginning of an expansion. All these factors make it hard to recognize turns in the business cycle.
2. *Implementation lag.* It also takes time to implement fiscal policy. In most nations, one or more governing bodies must approve tax and spending legislation. In the United States, such legislation must pass both houses of Congress and receive presidential approval before becoming law. For this reason, fiscal policy takes much longer to implement than monetary policy. For example, as we discussed earlier in this chapter, the Economic Stimulus Act of 2008 entailed sending tax rebate checks to U.S. taxpayers. The act passed in early February, yet most checks did not go out until about six months later, even though the recipients were known ahead of time.
3. *Impact lag.* Finally, it takes time for the complete effects of fiscal or monetary policy to materialize. The multiplier makes fiscal policy powerful, but it takes time to ripple through the economy.

If lags cause the effects of fiscal policy to be delayed for a year or 18 months, there is a risk that the policy can actually magnify the business cycle. That is, if the effects of expansionary fiscal policy hit when the economy is already expanding, the result may be excessive aggregate demand and inflation. And if contractionary fiscal policy is implemented and followed by time lags, the effects could lead to even deeper recessions.

How would you like it if your medications worked with an 18-month lag?

ECONOMICS IN THE REAL WORLD

RECOGNIZING LAGS

How long does it take to get a check in the mail? It can take a while even when the check is electronic.

Hindsight is 20/20. But in reality, it is very difficult to determine how the economy is performing at any particular point in time. One exception to this was the coronavirus pandemic in 2020. When the government mandated that businesses close and people shelter in place, everyone could see that the economic consequences would be severe. Very quickly, the number of people filing for unemployment insurance hit record numbers. Millions of people who were working one week found themselves without a job the next. As a result, Congress and the president went into action to pass a fiscal policy stimulus.

The normal lags that policymakers have to deal with were shortened to almost nothing due to the rapidity of the economy-wide shutdown. No one needed to wait for the official statistics on GDP to come out to know there was trouble. Thus, the recognition lag was rendered moot. There was still an implementation lag to deal with. Although Congress passed a stimulus package, and the president signed it almost immediately, it still took time to get the checks printed and distributed to people who needed them. Even the federal government can't send nearly 128 million checks to bank accounts or through the mail instantaneously. The implementation lag was also fairly short, but it still existed. The money sent to households was welcome, but it will take time to understand any impact it had.

AUTOMATIC STABILIZERS One possibility for alleviating lag problems are programs that automatically adjust government spending and taxes when economic conditions change. **Automatic stabilizers** are government programs that automatically implement countercyclical fiscal policy in response to economic conditions. Given that the prescription is to increase spending and decrease taxes during downturns and to decrease spending and increase taxes during expansions, there are several government programs that accomplish these goals automatically:

Automatic stabilizers are government programs that automatically implement countercyclical fiscal policy in response to economic conditions.

- *Progressive income tax rates* guarantee that individual tax bills fall when incomes fall (during recessions) and rise when incomes rise (during expansions).
- *Taxes on corporate profits* lower total tax bills when profits are lower (during contractions) and raise tax bills when profits are higher (typically during expansions).
- *Unemployment compensation* increases government spending automatically when the number of unemployed people rises and decreases government spending when fewer people are unemployed.
- *Welfare programs* also increase government spending during downturns and decrease government spending when the economy is doing better.

In short, automatic stabilizers can eliminate recognition lags and implementation lags and thereby alleviate some concerns about the destabilizing effects of fiscal policy.

Crowding-Out

A second challenge in implementing fiscal policy concerns the actual impact of government spending and the multiplier effects. Unfortunately, increases in government spending can lead to decreases in private spending. When government spending substitutes for private spending, the overall change in aggregate demand diminishes. Economists call this effect **crowding-out**. It occurs when private spending falls in response to increases in government spending.

Crowding-out occurs when private spending falls in response to increases in government spending.

For example, say the government starts a new program in which it buys a new laptop computer for every college student in America. (Don't get too excited; this example is just hypothetical.) If the government buys computers for students, students won't buy as many computers for themselves. Now, students might take all the money they saved on computers and spend it on other items, instead. But if they don't—if they put some of the money in savings—then private spending is "crowded out" by government spending. When crowding-out occurs, aggregate demand does not increase as anticipated, and the fiscal policy is less effective.

If the government bought you a new laptop, would you spend your income on another one, too?

Let's look more closely at how crowding-out can work. First, for simplicity, assume that the nation has a balanced government budget and a closed economy (no import or exports). Now suppose the government increases spending by $100 billion but does not raise taxes. This means it must borrow the $100 billion in the loanable funds market. But as we know, every dollar borrowed requires a dollar saved. So when the government borrows $100 billion, the money has to come from $100 billion in savings.

Figure 29.6 illustrates what happens when this government enters the loanable funds market to borrow $100 billion. The graph shows that initially the market is in equilibrium at point A with demand for loans (that is, investment) designated as D_1. The initial interest rate is 5%, and at this rate there is $250 billion worth of savings. This amount of savings funds $250 billion in private borrowing. The table in Figure 29.6 summarizes these initial values in the column labeled "Before stimulus."

Now when the government borrows, the demand for loans increases by $100 billion at all points. This effect is indicated on the graph as a shift from D_1 to D_2. But the new demand for loans changes the equilibrium in the market. The increased demand drives the interest rate up from 5% to 6%, and the new equilibrium quantity of loanable funds increases to $300 billion, shown as point B on the graph. The interest rate rises because of the increase in demand for loans caused by government borrowing.

To demonstrate the overall effects of this new government borrowing, we compare the values of private savings and investment at the two equilibrium points. These are displayed in the table in Figure 29.6. The new equilibrium quantity of loans is $300 billion, but the government has borrowed $100 billion ($G_B$). This means borrowing for private investment spending declines from $250 billion ($I_A$) to $200 billion ($I_B$). Essentially, the higher interest rate discourages some private investment; the government purchases crowd out private investment.

Finally, note that private savings increases from $250 billion ($S_A$) to $300 billion ($S_B$)—that is, by $50 billion—because the higher interest rate (R_B) has caused more individuals to devote more of their income to savings. But if savings rises by $50 billion, consumption must fall by $50 billion. This is a direct

FIGURE 29.6

Crowding-Out in the Loanable Funds Market

Initially, at point A, private savings of $250 billion all becomes private investment of $250 billion. But government borrowing shifts the demand for loans from D_1 to D_2. The new demand for loans leads to equilibrium at point B, with a higher interest rate. At the new equilibrium there is $300 billion in private savings (S_B in the table), but $100 billion goes to the government (G_B) and $200 billion is left for private investment (I_B).

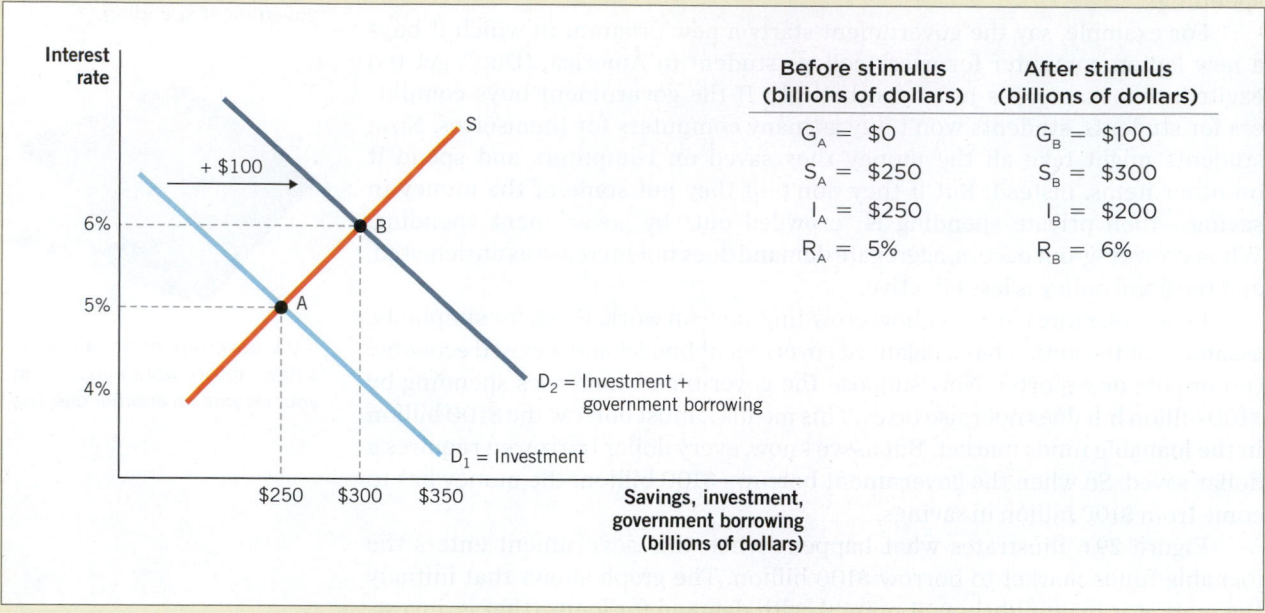

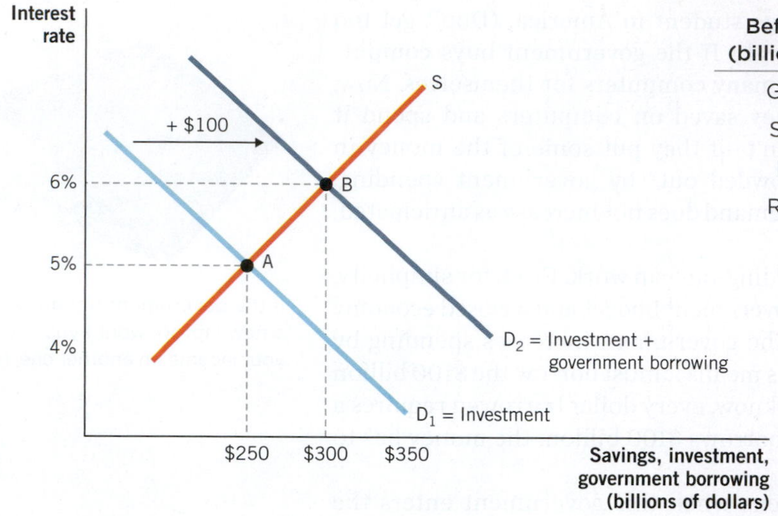

Before stimulus (billions of dollars)	After stimulus (billions of dollars)
$G_A = \$0$	$G_B = \$100$
$S_A = \$250$	$S_B = \$300$
$I_A = \$250$	$I_B = \$200$
$R_A = 5\%$	$R_B = 6\%$

relationship. The end result is that an increase of $100 billion in deficit-financed government spending leads to $100 billion less of private spending—$50 billion from lower private investment and $50 billion from higher savings.

In this example, we have complete crowding-out: every dollar of government spending crowds out a dollar of private spending. In reality, crowding-out may be less than complete, if new funds arrive from overseas or if consumers are encouraged to spend more as a result of the government spending. But this example does illustrate an important consideration of economists regarding the effects of fiscal policy.

ECONOMICS IN THE REAL WORLD

DID GOVERNMENT SPENDING REALLY SURGE IN 2009?

In a February 14, 2011, post on his blog, Nobel Prize–winning economist (and prominent Keynesian) Paul Krugman argued that the increases in federal spending in 2009 were offset by reductions in spending at the state government level. He argued that these reductions effectively put a damper on any potential GDP growth and caused the economy to continue to struggle with high unemployment. According to Krugman, "Once you take state and local cutbacks into account, there was no surge of government spending."

In a sense, what Krugman was identifying is another challenge of fiscal policy and can be seen as a variation of crowding-out. Technically, crowding-out occurs when private individuals substitute government (federal, state, and local) spending in place of their private spending. But Krugman argued that the crowding-out occurred in the government sector. Federal government spending rose, and then state and local government spending fell. Most states were facing budget crises of their own as a result of the recession. Thus, they substituted federal spending for state spending. This strategy helped them to balance their budgets during the recession. But it also meant total government spending did not rise as much as the federal government intended. And this crowding-out may help explain why the 2009 fiscal stimulus failed to push the U.S. economy back to full employment.

Why should states build new highways when the federal government offers to do it for them?

Savings Shifts

Imagine you get a $1,000 check in the mail from the business office at your college. You would probably wonder why you got the check and whether you would have to return it. But you might also get excited and begin thinking about all the goods and services you could buy. How much would you spend, and how much would you save?

Let's consider two different scenarios. First, imagine you receive a $1,000 scholarship after your tuition bill is paid, and you get to use the funds

PRACTICE WHAT YOU KNOW

Crowding-Out: Does Fiscal Policy Lead to More Aggregate Demand?

Imagine that a small country is in recession and the government decides to increase spending. It commissions a very large Adam Smith statue for $50 million. To pay for the statue, the government borrows all of the $50 million. After the government borrows the $50 million, the interest rate rises from 3% to 4% and the equilibrium quantity of loanable funds increases from $500 million to $530 million.

QUESTION: How would you sketch a graph of the loanable funds market representing this scenario? Be sure to indicate on this graph all the changes that take place after the borrowing.

ANSWER: Originally, the market is in equilibrium at point A, with an interest rate of 3% and savings and investment being equal at $500 million. Then the demand for loans increases by $50 million at all points when the government borrows $50 million. This change moves the market to a new equilibrium at point B.

QUESTION: Using the above information and assuming complete crowding-out, what would you predict will happen to C, I, G, and total aggregate demand (AD) in response to the government's action?

Without crowding-out, a newly commissioned statue of economist Adam Smith could stimulate the economy.

(CONTINUED)

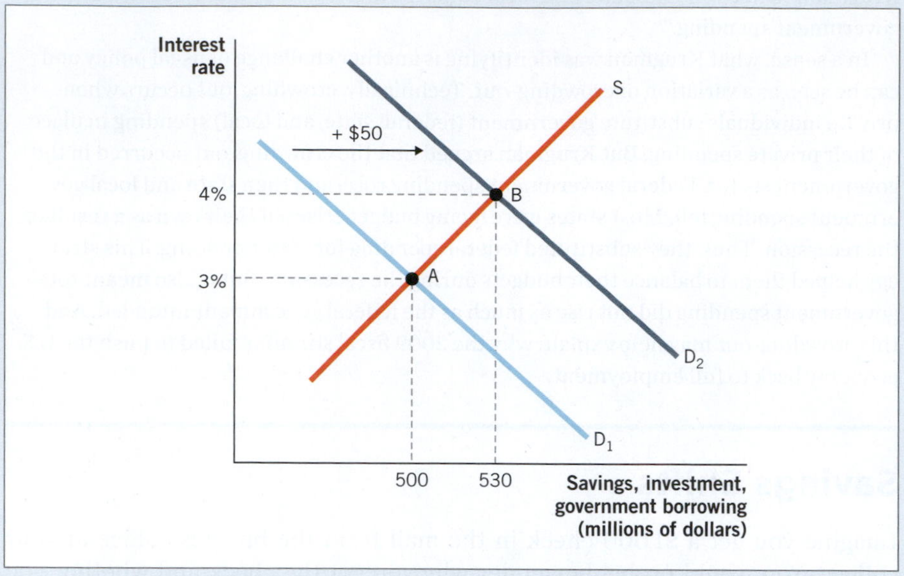

ANSWER: Government spending (G) will increase by $50 million. Total savings will increase from $500 million to $530 million, which means that total savings will increase by $30 million and consumption (C) will fall by $30 million. But because the government is borrowing $50 million of the savings, private investment (I) will fall to $480 million, a decrease of $20 million. All of this means a net change of zero in aggregate demand (AD). These changes are summarized below.

Component	C	I	G	AD
Change (millions of dollars)	−$30	−$20	$50	—

however you like. In that case, you might spend much or all of the $1,000. But now imagine instead that you received the funds in error, and you have to repay them. In this second scenario, you probably wouldn't spend any of the $1,000 you got from the college.

The **new classical critique** of fiscal policy asserts that increases in government spending and decreases in taxes are largely offset by increases in savings.

In some ways, government spending in the economy is similar to the second scenario. New spending today has to be paid for someday, which means that taxes must rise sooner or later. The **new classical critique** of fiscal policy, a model developed in the 1970s by a group of economists including Nobel Prize winners Robert Barro, Robert Lucas, and Thomas Sargent, asserts that increases in government spending and decreases in taxes are largely offset by increases in savings, because people know they'll have to pay higher taxes eventually. But if savings increases, consumption falls, and this outcome mitigates the positive effects of the government spending.

Table 29.2 summarizes the three shortcomings that can diminish the effects of fiscal policy.

TABLE 29.2

Summary of Fiscal Policy Shortcomings

Shortcoming	Summary	Result
Time lags	The effects of fiscal policy may be delayed by lags in recognition, implementation, and impact.	If lags are significant, fiscal policy can be destabilizing and magnify business cycles.
Crowding-out	Government spending can serve as a substitute for private spending.	Even partial crowding-out reduces the impact of fiscal stimulus.
Savings shifts	In response to increases in government spending or lower taxes, people may increase their current savings to help pay for inevitably higher future taxes.	If current savings increases by the entire amount of the federal stimulus, the effects of the stimulus are negated.

What Is Supply-Side Fiscal Policy?

We have considered typical fiscal policy, which focuses squarely on aggregate demand. It is also possible to implement fiscal policy with the intent of affecting the supply side of the economy. In this section, we begin by describing the supply-side perspective and certain popular supply-side policy proposals. We then look more closely at marginal tax rates and consider how changes in tax rates can affect the economy.

Supply-Focused Fiscal Policy in the Coronavirus Recession

In April of 2020, as the COVID-19 spread through the United States, the unemployment rate spiked to 14.7%. However, it came down over the next few months and was back in single-digit territory by August. Most economists attribute the rapid turnaround to government actions that targeted both aggregate demand and aggregate supply.

As we discussed in Chapter 27, the initial economic effects of the virus were primarily on the supply side of the economy: it became more expensive to produce just about anything, as businesses had to incorporate protocols involving masks, social distancing, frequent cleaning and disinfection, and regular COVID-19 testing into their production methods. In that situation, it made sense for the government to try to shore up the supply side of the economy. The use of government spending and taxes for this purpose is called **supply-side fiscal policy**.

Supply-side fiscal policy involves the use of government spending and taxes to affect the production (supply) side of the economy.

Subsidies for college education are a type of supply-side fiscal policy.

The supply side is where decisions are made on what to produce, and how much, given available resources, institutions, and technology. Economic changes that increase production costs for a broad range of suppliers will reduce aggregate supply. The coronavirus made just about everything in the economy—from groceries and gasoline to plane trips and hospital visits—more expensive to produce. That shifted both short- and long-run aggregate supply to the left.

In the spring of 2020, three separate fiscal policy acts were passed on Capitol Hill and signed by President Trump. The total price tag for these was over $2.5 trillion, more than double the cost of any previous U.S. fiscal policy, even after adjustment for inflation. But these spending bills were different from the government's actions during the Great Recession, described earlier. This time, much of the aid was supply-side spending, which went directly to businesses. The major provisions of these acts included:

1. *Small business grants*. The Paycheck Protection Program (PPP) was a $659 billion initiative that extended loans to small businesses to help them survive the shutdown periods. Importantly, these loans were forgivable (they could convert to cash grants) if firms used the funds to retain workers during the downturn. The goal was to minimize layoffs by helping pay workers' wages.
2. *Loans to airlines and other large corporations*. Because firms and households depend heavily on air travel, keeping airlines from failing made sense as a way of speeding the economic recovery. Loans to other big corporations were, like the loans to small businesses, intended to minimize the number of workers laid off.
3. *Hospital aid*. During the pandemic, many hospitals reduced their admittance of nonemergency patients to make room for COVID-19 emergencies. This created a cash-flow problem for hospitals, right when their services were needed most. Federal aid went directly to hospitals to keep them afloat.
4. *State and local government aid*. States, counties, and cities had many additional expenses associated with virus testing and tracing, so they also received needed aid.
5. *Tax rebates*. Households that earned less than $75,000 in 2019 received a tax rebate of $1,200 per single person or $2,400 per couple, and an additional $500 per child.
6. *Unemployment compensation*. In addition to unemployment compensation from existing state programs, laid-off workers received federal benefits in the amount of $600 per week.

Of the six components, the first four focused on the supply side of the economy, while the last two focused on aggregate demand.

Figure 29.7 shows the goal of U.S. fiscal policy in 2020. As we discussed in Chapter 27, the coronavirus pandemic led to declines in SRAS, LRAS, and AD in the year's first few months. In the second quarter alone, real GDP dropped 9%, shown as a decline to Y_{2020} in Figure 29.7. The goal of fiscal policy was to shift aggregate demand and aggregate supply back to their previous levels, even as the global pandemic was still ongoing. This was a huge and expensive undertaking. Still, the fiscal policy certainly helped the economy bounce (partially) back by the end of 2020. In the third quarter of 2020, real GDP rebounded to about $21 trillion, and the unemployment rate fell to 8%.

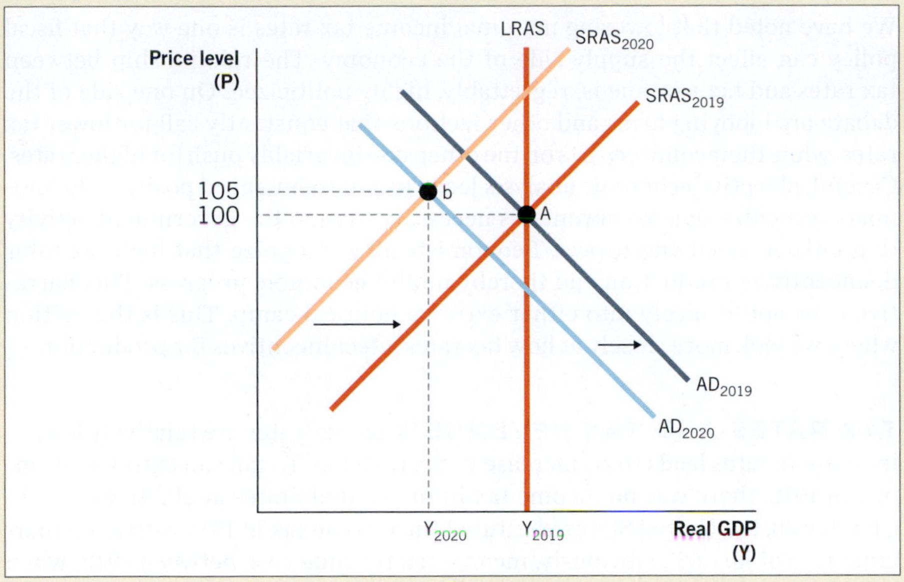

FIGURE 29.7

The Goal of Fiscal Policy in the Coronavirus Recession

Since COVID-19 presented problems on both the demand and supply sides of the economy, fiscal policy was focused on shifting LRAS, SRAS, and AD. The virus had moved the economy from point A, with real GDP Y_{2019}, to point b, lowering GDP to Y_{2020}. With both supply-side and demand-side initiatives, the fiscal policy goal was to move the economy back to Y_{2019}.

Other Supply-Focused Fiscal Policy

Many other fiscal policy initiatives are designed to focus on the supply side of the economy. These include:

1. *Research and development (R&D) tax credits.* Tax breaks are given to firms that spend resources to develop new technology. For example, if an alternative energy firm spends resources on a new lab to develop alternative energy sources, this spending reduces its overall tax bill.
2. *Policies that focus on education.* Subsidies or tax breaks for education expenses are given to help create incentives to invest in education. One example is the Pell Grant, which helps to pay for college expenses. Students receive these grants from the federal government to help them pay for college education. Eventually, education and training increase effective labor resources and thus increase aggregate supply.
3. *Lower corporate profit tax rates.* Lower taxes increase the incentives for corporations to undertake activities that generate more profit.
4. *Lower marginal income tax rates.* Lower income tax rates create incentives for individuals to work harder and produce more, because they keep a larger share of their income. We discuss marginal tax rates in the next section.

Incentives

All of these initiatives share two characteristics. First, they increase incentives for productive activities. Second, each initiative takes time to affect aggregate supply. For example, education subsidies may encourage people to go to college and learn skills useful in the workplace. But the full effect of that education isn't felt until after the education is completed. For this reason, supply-side proposals are generally emphasized as long-run solutions to growth problems.

Marginal Income Tax Rates

Marginal thinking

We have noted that lowering marginal income tax rates is one way that fiscal policy can affect the supply side of the economy. The relationship between tax rates and tax revenue is, regrettably, highly politicized. On one side of the debate are lobbying firms and other factions that constantly call for lower tax rates, while their counterparts on the other side invariably push for higher rates. Careful, objective economic analysis leads to a more nuanced position. Economists recognize that tax revenue is necessary to fund the government activity that citizens need and expect. Economists also recognize that high tax rates disincentivize production and thereby inhibit economic progress. This narrative does not fit nicely into either extreme political camp. This is the section where we look more closely at how tax rates affect incentives for production.

TAX RATES AND TAX REVENUE When tax rates are relatively low, an increase in rates leads to an increase in tax revenue. To take an extreme example: in 1912, there was no income tax in the United States at all. As we saw in Chapter 28, the United States instituted the income tax in 1913 with a top marginal rate of just 6%. Obviously, income tax revenue rose between 1912, when there was no income tax, and 1913, when a modest tax was introduced. At low tax rates, increases in tax rates lead to revenue increases.

But it turns out that if you raise rates too high, tax revenue declines, because the high rates provide negative incentives for production. This means that when tax rates are particularly high, a reduction in tax rates could actually lead to an increase in tax revenue. Tax rate cuts can be creative; that is, they can stimulate work effort, employment, and income and thereby generate *more* income tax revenue for the government.

Consider the following quote:

> The worst deficit comes from a recession. And if we can take the proper action in the proper time, this can be the most important step we can take to prevent another recession. That is the right time to make tax cuts, both for your family budget, and the national budget, resulting from a permanent basic reform and reduction in our rate structure. A creative tax cut, creating more jobs and income and, eventually, more revenue.
>
> —*35th president of the United States*

The president quoted is John F. Kennedy. He made this statement in 1962, when marginal tax rates were as high as 91%. Consider what a 91% marginal tax rate means: these taxpayers keep only 9 cents from an additional dollar's worth of income. Such an astronomical tax rate certainly diminishes incentives for work effort and production! Most economists agree that 91% marginal tax rates stifle economic growth. So although it may seem counterintuitive, it is possible to lower tax rates and increase overall tax revenue.

THE LAFFER CURVE In 1974, University of Chicago professor and economist Arthur Laffer famously tried to illustrate the relationship between tax rates and tax revenue by sketching a drawing on the back of a napkin at dinner. This relationship became known as the Laffer curve. Soon after, it became a centerpiece of Ronald Reagan's presidency in the 1980s and a central component of supply-side economics. Almost since its inception, this curve has been debated.

To understand this curve, let's first clarify the relationship between tax rates and tax revenue. Total income tax revenue depends on the level of income and the tax rate:

$$\text{income tax revenue} = \text{tax rate} \times \text{income}$$

This equation is straightforward. But because human beings react to incentives, it is not always easy to predict how tax revenue will change when tax rates change. The **Laffer curve**, shown in Figure 29.8, illustrates the relationship between tax rates and tax revenue. Notice we have labeled two regions of the Laffer curve. Region I, the blue portion of the curve, illustrates that increasing tax rates leads to increasing tax revenues:

$$\uparrow\text{income tax revenue} = \uparrow\text{tax rate} \times \text{income}$$

But at some point, tax rates become so high that they provide significant disincentives for earning income. This is the case in region II, illustrated by the orange portion of the curve, where increases in the tax rate lead to less tax revenue. Many U.S. taxpayers were in region II in 1962, when some marginal tax rates were above 90% and President Kennedy gave his speech. At this point, an increase in the tax rate reduces income enough (illustrated by the double downward-pointing arrows) that net tax revenue falls:

$$\downarrow\text{income tax revenue} = \uparrow\text{tax rate} \times \downarrow\downarrow\text{income}$$

In region II of the Laffer curve, decreases in the tax rate lead to increases in tax revenue. At the lower rate, people have greater incentives to work and earn more income. Thus, the lower tax rates stimulate the economy and lead to more tax revenue overall.

JFK: Early supply-sider?

The **Laffer curve** is an illustration of the relationship between tax rates and tax revenue.

Incentives

FIGURE 29.8

The Laffer Curve

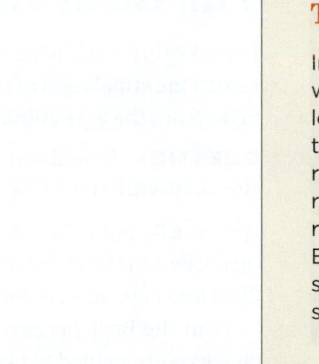

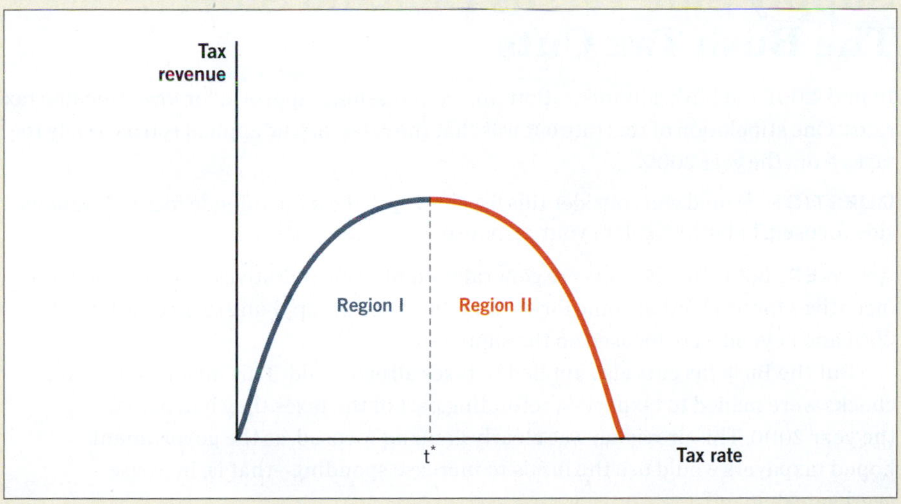

In region I of the Laffer curve, where tax rates are relatively low, increases in tax rates lead to increases in tax revenue. In region II, where tax rates are relatively high, increases in tax rates decrease tax revenue. Economists disagree over the size of t*, the tax rate that separates the regions.

TABLE 29.3

U.S. Income Tax Revenue for Different Income Levels, 1980 and 1991

	Income tax revenue per return (2009 dollars)		
	All taxpayers	**Bottom 50%**	**Top 1%**
1980	$6,954	$1,005	$131,307
1991	6,202	692	153,675

At some specific tax rate, tax revenue is maximized. In Figure 29.8, this rate is labeled t^*. Economists don't know exactly what this amount is, but it seems to be less than 70% in the United States, based on experience from the 1980s. In 1980, the marginal tax rate on the wealthiest Americans was 70%, but then marginal rates fell across all income brackets over the course of the decade. The result was higher tax revenue from the wealthiest Americans (see Table 29.3) even though tax revenue per taxpayer fell overall. Considering all U.S. taxpayers, average tax revenue (adjusted for both inflation and the number of tax returns filed) went from $6,954 to $6,202 between 1980 and 1991. Many analysts point to these figures and see them as proof that the Laffer curve doesn't exist or even that supply-side economics lacks merit. However, at very high rates, the experience of the 1980s shows that rate reductions can lead to higher revenue.

Table 29.3 shows data from the 1980s regarding tax revenue from taxpayers at different income levels. The rate reductions led to less tax revenue overall, because of drops in tax revenue from the many taxpayers who were paying relatively low taxes to begin with. Overall, revenues declined when we adjust for both inflation and population. But for the wealthiest Americans, a rate

PRACTICE WHAT YOU KNOW

With congressional leaders at his side, President Bush signed a law that reduced top income tax rates from 39.6% to 35%.

Supply Side versus Demand Side: The Bush Tax Cuts

In mid-2001, the Bush administration won congressional approval for lower income tax rates. One stipulation of this rate cut was that the rates also be applied retroactively to taxes from the year 2000.

QUESTION: Would you consider this fiscal policy to be demand-side focused, supply-side focused, or both? Explain your response.

ANSWER: Both! Tax rate cuts are generally supply-side initiatives, because they frame incentives for production going forward. So the rate cuts applying to income taxes for 2001 and beyond were focused on the supply side.

But the Bush tax cuts also applied to taxes already paid. This meant that refund checks were mailed to taxpayers, refunding part of the taxes they had paid for the year 2000. This provision was clearly demand focused, as the government hoped taxpayers would use the funds to increase spending—that is, increase aggregate demand.

ECONOMICS for LIFE

Planning for Your Future Taxes

- Recent debt levels will likely lead to higher taxes in the future.
- To reduce your federal tax bill, you can buy municipal bonds.
- You might also want to save more to pay higher future taxes.

The U.S. national debt is currently over $30 trillion, or about $90,000 per person. And it is growing: in 2007 the national debt per person was only $30,000.

What does this mean for you? It means your taxes are going to be higher in the future. All Americans will need to contribute to pay down this large national debt. So taxes in the future will surely be higher, and you should plan accordingly.

In addition, economic growth will likely be lower until the debt is paid down. We know that higher income taxes reduce incentives for production, so it is safe to say that economic growth will be lower until this debt is paid off and taxes can come down again.

However, you can take actions to lower your future tax bills or make them more manageable. First, you probably ought to budget for higher taxes. This may mean saving more now than you would have saved otherwise. Second, in terms of personal investments, you might consider buying securities that provide tax-free income. For example, the interest on municipal bonds (bonds issued by state and local governments) is not federally taxed. These simple steps might turn out to have significant benefits when your future tax bills arrive.

Government spending on highway projects was part of fiscal policy legislated during the Great Recession.

reduction led to an increase in revenue. The takeaway from Table 29.3 is that data from the 1980s confirm the two distinct regions on the Laffer curve. Generally, conservative public figures tend to stress region II, where tax rate reductions lead to increased revenue. Liberals emphasize region I, where tax rate increases lead to more revenue. Recognizing both regions is important for economic policy.

Conclusion

We began the chapter with a recent example of real-life fiscal policy in the United States. Over the next few years, we will be able to see how the 2017 tax cuts actually affected the economy. For sure, the deficit increased. But the growth effects will take some time to work out.

Looking ahead, we turn our attention next to monetary policy. In Chapter 30, we cover money and the Federal Reserve; in Chapter 31, we discuss how monetary policy affects the economy.

ANSWERING *the* BIG QUESTIONS

What is fiscal policy?

- Fiscal policy involves the use of government's budget tools, government spending, and taxes to influence the macroeconomy, often through aggregate demand.
- Countercyclical fiscal policy is designed to counteract business cycle fluctuations by increasing aggregate demand during downturns and decreasing aggregate demand during expansionary periods.

What are the shortcomings of fiscal policy?

- Fiscal policy is subject to three significant lags: a recognition lag, an implementation lag, and an impact lag.
- In addition, crowding-out can diminish the effects of fiscal policy.
- Finally, according to the new classical critique, savings adjustments by private individuals can further diminish the stimulating effects of fiscal policy.

What is supply-side fiscal policy?

- Supply-side fiscal policy involves the use of government spending and taxes to affect the production (supply) side of the economy. This is a long-run view that concentrates on institutional changes.
- A key proposal of supply-side fiscal policy is that lower marginal income tax rates can actually lead to greater tax revenue when tax rates are high.

· CHAPTER PROBLEMS ·

Concepts You Should Know

automatic stabilizers (p. 958)
contractionary fiscal policy (p. 950)
countercyclical fiscal policy (p. 951)
crowding-out (p. 959)
expansionary fiscal policy (p. 947)
fiscal policy (p. 946)
Laffer curve (p. 967)
marginal propensity to consume (MPC) (p. 953)
new classical critique (p. 962)
spending multiplier (p. 954)
supply-side fiscal policy (p. 963)

Questions for Review

1. How are government budget balances affected by countercyclical fiscal policy? Be sure to describe the effects of both expansionary and contractionary fiscal policy.
2. Using the aggregate demand–aggregate supply model, one might argue that the economy will adjust on its own when aggregate demand drops. How does this adjustment work? Why might this adjustment take some time? (If necessary, review Chapter 26.)
3. Explain why the government budget deficit increases during a recession even without countercyclical fiscal policy.
4. Explain the three types of fiscal policy lags. What are automatic stabilizers? Which lags do automatic stabilizers affect?
5. In what circumstances would contractionary fiscal policy be recommended? How might you implement this type of policy? Why would you implement this policy—that is, what are the reasons why it might make sense to use fiscal policy to slow the economy?
6. Many people emphasize just one portion of the Laffer curve and forget that there are actually two sides. First, explain the math behind the positively sloped region of the Laffer curve. That is, explain why an increase in the tax rate sometimes leads to an *increase* in tax revenue. Second, explain the math behind the negatively sloped region of the Laffer curve. That is, explain why an increase in the tax rate sometimes leads to a *decrease* in tax revenue.
7. Assuming that complete crowding-out always holds, what happens to consumption, investment, and interest rates if the government *decreases* borrowing, all else being equal?

Study Problems (*✱ solved at the end of the section*)

1. Explain the difference between typical demand-side fiscal policy and supply-side fiscal policy. For each of the following fiscal policy proposals, determine whether the primary focus is on aggregate demand or aggregate supply:
   a. a $1,000-per-person tax reduction
   b. a 5% reduction in all tax rates
   c. Pell Grants, which are government subsidies for college education
   d. government-sponsored prizes for new scientific discoveries
   e. an increase in unemployment compensation
2. To explore crowding-out, let's set up a simple loanable funds market in initial equilibrium.
   a. Draw a graph showing initial equilibrium in the loanable funds market at $800 million and an interest rate of 4%. Label your initial supply and demand curves as S_1 and D_1.
   b. Now assume that the government increases spending by $100 million that is entirely deficit financed. Show the new equilibrium in the loanable funds market. (*Note:* There is a range of possible numerical answers for this question. You should choose one number and then be sure

the rest of your answer is consistent with this number.)

c. Write the new equilibrium interest rate and quantity of loanable funds in the blanks below:
New interest rate: ______
New quantity of loanable funds: ______

d. If we assume there was no government debt prior to the fiscal stimulus, determine the following new quantities and write them in the blanks below:
Savings: ______
Investment: ______
Government spending: ______

e. How much did private consumption change as a result of the change in the quantity of savings?

3. The new classical critique of activist fiscal policy is theoretically different from the crowding-out critique. Explain the difference by using a graph of the loanable funds market.

4. Let's consider a small nation, Kaitland, in the context of the aggregate demand–aggregate supply model.

a. Kaitland starts off, in the year 2023, in long-run equilibrium with real GDP of $200 billion, an unemployment rate of 4%, and a price level of 100. On a separate sheet of paper, draw the Kaitland economy in long-run equilibrium and be sure to include AD, SRAS, and LRAS curves.

b. In the year 2024, business firm confidence falls significantly. On your previous graph, show how this affects Kaitland's economy. Be sure to clearly indicate any curve shifts, and state clearly how this affects real GDP, unemployment, and the price level.

c. Which two fiscal policy tools can the government use if they wish to increase aggregate demand? How would they specifically use each tool?

d. If we assume no crowding-out, show how the fiscal policy changes from part (c) affect the Kaitland economy.

✱ **5.** Assume that the equilibrium in the loanable funds market is at an interest rate (R) of 3% and the total quantity of loans is $500 billion. In addition, in this initial situation, the government is borrowing $50 billion per year to fund the budget deficit.

a. What is private investment in this initial equilibrium? (It will help to draw a graph of the loanable funds market in this initial equilibrium.)

Now the government increases spending by $200 billion per year and finances this spending completely with additional borrowing.

b. At R = 3%, what would be the quantity demanded of loanable funds?

c. In which direction does the interest rate change to bring the market to equilibrium? Assume that the new equilibrium is at $575 billion and assume complete crowding-out.

d. Determine the exact amount by which each component of GDP changes, assuming no change in net exports.

e. What is the total change in AD from this action?

✱ **6.** Fill in the blanks in the table below. Assume that the MPC is constant over everyone in the economy.

MPC	Spending multiplier	Change in government spending	Change in income
______	5	$100	______
______	2.5	______	–$250
0.5	______	200	______
0.2	______	______	1,000

7. On March 11, 2021, President Biden signed the $1.9 trillion American Rescue Plan (ARP). Assume that the money consisted entirely of cash payments to households.

a. If the economy was initially in recession, what short-run and long-run effects would you expect from the cash infusion into the economy? Specify the predicted changes in real GDP, the unemployment rate, and the price level, all relative to the starting point.

b. What short-run and long-run effects would you expect if the economy was initially at full-employment output?

Solved Problems

5.

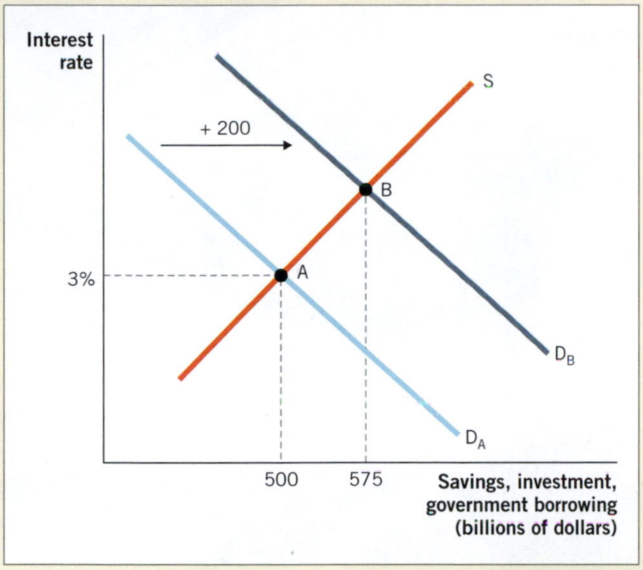

a. The initial equilibrium has an interest rate of 3% and total loans of $500 billion. This equilibrium is pictured as point A in the graph on this page. Because there is a total of $500 billion in loans, but the government is borrowing just $50 billion of this amount, that leaves $450 billion for private investment.

b. The new demand curve is exactly $200 billion to the right of the old demand curve because the government increases the demand for loans by $200 billion at all interest rates. Therefore, at 3%, the new quantity demanded is $700 billion.

c. The interest rate rises to new equilibrium at point B. This increase is normal because at the old interest rate, the quantity demanded exceeds the quantity supplied.

d. Given the new equilibrium at $575 billion, we know that total savings is $575 billion because every dollar borrowed requires a dollar saved. The government is now borrowing $250 billion, which represents an increase in G of +$200 billion. But that leaves just $325 billion for private investment ($575 billion − $250 billion). As a result, I declines by $125 billion from the initial level of $450 billion (see part a). Finally, because total savings was initially $500 billion but is now $575 billion, C (consumption) falls by $75 billion.

e. The change in AD is the sum of the changes in C, I, G, and NX. We assumed no change in NX, but the changes in the others sum to zero (− $75 billion − $125 billion + $200 billion).

6.

MPC	Spending multiplier	Change in government spending	Change in income
0.8	5	$100	*$500*
0.6	2.5	*−100*	−250
0.5	*2*	200	*400*
0.2	*1.25*	*800*	1,000

ONE HUNDRED DOLLARS
KE 39086089 A
100
ONE HUNDRED DOLLARS
100

PART IX

Monetary POLICY

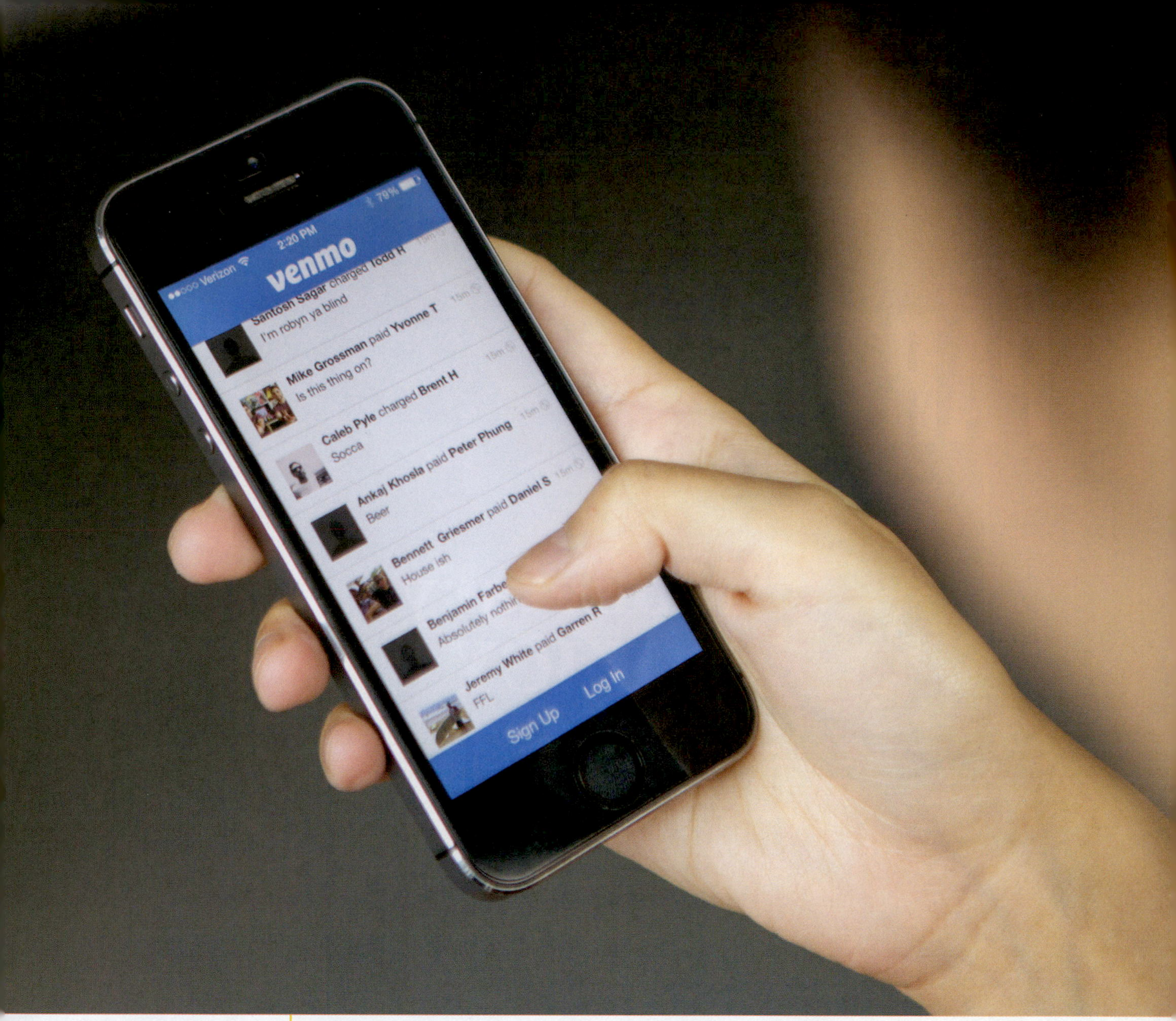

CHAPTER

30

Money and the Federal Reserve

Controlling the Money Supply Is Not as Easy as You Think.

Many people believe that managing the money we use in the economy is simple. After all, there's a fixed amount of paper currency and coins in circulation, and only the government has the authority to print more. But actually, creating money isn't as securely under the government's control as the printing-press model suggests. In fact, individuals and banks, not just in the United States but all around the world, have a hand in determining how many U.S. dollars are coursing around the world economy.

What we use for "money" isn't always paper currency or coins. Just think about your own daily purchases. Most, if not all, of them are paid for with something other than actual cash, right? The prices may be posted in dollars, but you often pay with a debit card, a mobile payment app, or occasionally a personal check.

With a range of options that can be used in purchases, people have a lot more buying power than what's represented by physical currency. This makes it hard to get an exact fix on the size of the money supply.

The last two chapters focused on government budgets and fiscal policy. In this chapter and the next, we turn to the second major category of macroeconomic policy: monetary policy. We begin by looking closely at the definition of money—its functions and its different forms. Because banks

Money is more than just green paper! Venmo (owned by PayPal) is a mobile payment app that can be used to make purchases over the counter and online.

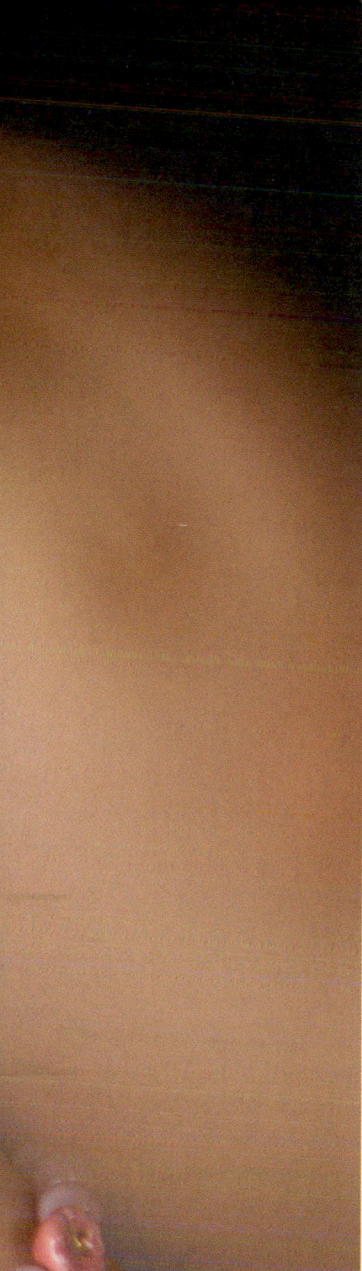

play an integral role in the money supply process, we discuss how they operate and how their decisions affect the amount of money in the economy. Finally, we look at the role of the Federal Reserve System and examine how it oversees our monetary system and the health of the economy. This background provides essential preparation for further discussion of monetary policy in Chapter 31.

· BIG QUESTIONS ·

- What is money?
- How do banks create money?
- How does the Federal Reserve implement monetary policy?

What Is Money?

Currency is the paper bills and coins used to buy goods and services.

Money is any generally accepted means of payment.

A **medium of exchange** is what people trade for goods and services.

What is money? The question may seem odd. After all, we use money all the time, right? Even children know that we use coins and paper bills to buy things like food and clothes (goods) and haircuts and car repairs (services). Those coins and bills constitute **currency**. But people also make many purchases without currency. Our definition of *money* is much broader: **money** is any generally accepted means of payment. In this section, we define the functions of money and then explain how the quantity of money is measured.

Three Functions of Money

Money has three functions: it is a medium of exchange, a unit of account, and a store of value. Let's look at each function.

Money comes in many different colors, shapes, and sizes.

A MEDIUM OF EXCHANGE If you want to buy groceries, you offer money in exchange for them; if you work, you accept money as payment for your labor. Money is a common **medium of exchange**—that is, it is what people trade for goods and services.

Modern economies generally have a government-provided medium of exchange. In the United States, the government provides our dollar currency. But even in economies without government provision, a preferred medium of exchange usually emerges. For example, in colonial Virginia, before there was any government mandate regarding money, tobacco became the accepted medium of exchange. Economist Milton Friedman wrote this about tobacco: "It was the money that the colonists used to buy food, clothing, to pay taxes—even to pay for a bride."

Without money, what would you trade for this coffee and bagel?

Invariably, some medium of exchange evolves in any economy; the primary reason is the inefficiency of barter, which is money's alternative. **Barter** occurs when there is no commonly accepted medium of exchange. It involves individuals trading some good or service they already have for something else they want. If you want food in a barter economy, you must find a grocer who also happens to want whatever you have to trade. Maybe you can offer only your labor services, but the grocer wants a new cash register. In that case, you have to try to find someone who has a cash register and also wants to trade it for your labor. This takes more than a coincidence; it takes a double coincidence. Barter requires a **double coincidence of wants**, in which each party in an exchange transaction happens to have what the other party desires. A double coincidence is pretty unusual, which is why a medium of exchange naturally evolves in any exchange environment.

Barter
involves the trade of a good or service in the absence of a commonly accepted medium of exchange.

A **double coincidence of wants** occurs when each party in an exchange transaction happens to have what the other party desires.

Historically, the first medium of exchange in an economy has been a commodity used to trade for goods and services. **Commodity money** involves the use of an actual good for money. In this situation, the good itself has value apart from its function as money. Examples include gold, silver, and the tobacco of colonial Virginia. But commodities are often inconvenient to carry around. For this and other reasons, money typically evolves into certificates that represent a fixed quantity of the commodity. These certificates become the medium of exchange but are still tied to the commodity, because they can be traded for the actual commodity if the holder demands it.

Commodity money
involves the use of an actual good for money.

Commodity-backed money is money you can exchange for a commodity at a fixed rate. For example, until 1971, U.S. dollars were fixed in value to specific quantities of silver and gold. A $1 U.S. silver certificate looks much like dollar bills in circulation today, but the print along the bottom of the note reads, "One dollar in silver payable to the bearer on demand." Until 1964, we also had commodity coins in the United States. U.S. quarters from 1964 look like the same quarters we use today, but unlike today's they are made of real silver.

Commodity-backed money
is money you can exchange for a commodity at a fixed rate.

While commodity money and commodity-backed money evolve privately in all economies, the type of money used in most modern economies depends on government. In particular, most modern economies make use of fiat money for their medium of exchange. **Fiat money** is money with no value except as the medium of exchange; there is no inherent or intrinsic value to the currency. In the United States, our fiat currency is physically just pieces of green paper, otherwise known as Federal Reserve Notes. This paper has value because the government has mandated that we can use the currency to pay our debts. On U.S. dollar bills, you can read the statement "This note is legal tender for all debts, public and private."

Fiat money
is money with no value except as the medium of exchange; there is no inherent or intrinsic value to the currency.

There are advantages and disadvantages to fiat and commodity monies. On the one hand, commodity-backed money ties the value of the holder's money to something real. If the government is obligated to trade silver for every dollar in circulation, this limits the number of dollars the government can print, which keeps a lid on inflation. Fiat money offers no such constraint on the expansion of the money supply. Rapid monetary expansion and then inflation can occur without a commodity standard that ties the value of money to something real. We have seen this in the past and, unfortunately, still see it today. Inflation in

The money pictured here looks much like our modern money, but the dollar bill is a commodity-backed silver certificate from 1957. At that time, it could be traded for a dollar's worth of actual silver. The quarters and dimes from 1964 are made of real silver.

Turkey hit 50% in early 2022, and until recently, inflation in Venezuela was running at several thousand percent (!) per year.

On the other hand, tying the value of a nation's currency to a commodity is dangerous when the market value of the commodity fluctuates. Imagine how a new discovery of gold affects prices in a nation with gold-backed currency. An increased supply of gold reduces gold prices, and therefore more gold is required in exchange for all other goods and services. This is inflation: the price of everything in terms of the money (gold) rises. This scenario occurred in the mid-fifteenth and mid-seventeenth centuries in Europe as Spanish conquistadors brought back tons of gold from Central and South America. Because a change in the value of a medium of exchange affects the prices of all goods and services in the macroeconomy, it can be risky to tie a currency to a commodity.

A **unit of account** is the measure in which prices are quoted.

A **store of value** is a means for holding wealth.

A UNIT OF ACCOUNT Money also serves as a unit of account. A **unit of account** is the measure in which prices are quoted. Money enables you and someone you do not know to speak a common language. For example, when the cashier says the mangoes you want to buy cost 99 cents each, the cashier is communicating the value of mangoes in a way you understand. Consider a world without an accepted unit of account. In that world, goods would be priced in multiple ways. Theoretically, you might go shopping and find goods priced in terms of any possible currency or even other goods. Imagine how difficult it would be to shop! Using money as a unit of account is so helpful that a standard unit of account generally evolves, even in small economies.

Expressing the value of something in terms of dollars and cents also enables people to make accurate comparisons between items. Thus, money also serves as a measuring stick and recording device. In everyday conversation, we use dollars to measure relative values. How much is your backpack or cell phone worth, or your computer? Your answer is in dollars and cents. You use dollar amounts to keep track of your bank account and to record transactions in a consistent manner.

Thank goodness each of these fruits is priced in a common unit of account.

A STORE OF VALUE Money's third function is as a store of value. A **store of value** is a means for holding wealth. Money has long served as an important store of value. Think of bags of gold coins from the Middle Ages. In both fiction and nonfiction stories, pirates' treasures are generally represented by gold; this precious metal was the vehicle for storing great values. But in modern economies, this function is much less important. Today, we have other options for holding our wealth, many of which offer greater returns than keeping dollar bills in a sock drawer or stuffed under a mattress. We can easily put our dollars into bank accounts or investment accounts that earn interest. These options have caused money's role as a store of value to decline.

If you keep your money in your sock drawer, you incur an opportunity cost of forgone interest from a bank account.

ECONOMICS IN THE REAL WORLD

CRYPTOCURRENCY IS MONEY, TOO

Bitcoin, Ethereum, and other cryptocurrencies have captured the imagination of many people around the globe. Although cryptocurrencies are different from traditional money, in that national governments do not issue them, cryptocurrencies can serve as a medium of exchange. This feature makes them a form of money: people do accept them as payment for goods, services, and debts. You can use bitcoins to buy a game for your Xbox system, pizza from Domino's or Pizza Hut, tools from the Home Depot, or groceries from Whole Foods.

A positive feature of cryptocurrencies is that their value cannot be deliberately manipulated by the government, or by any other entity, for that matter. Instead, a cryptocurrency's value is determined by supply and demand, where the supply is regulated not by a central bank but by a self-maintaining software technology called blockchain. By allowing the supply of Bitcoin to grow only in a very controlled fashion, the blockchain code keeps a tight lid on supply-driven inflation of the currency. In nations where the government currency is not trustworthy, cryptocurrency can provide an alternative that buyers and sellers trust. Bitcoin is very popular in Venezuela, for example.

Owning cryptocurrency is not without risk, however, because the demand side can be unpredictable. And while cryptocurrencies are typically discussed as alternative currencies (as we are doing here), the vast majority of buyers purchase them as a speculative investment. In 2021, the price of 1 bitcoin rose from $29,413 at the start of the year to $64,899 in mid-April. By mid-July, the price had fallen back under $30,000, leaving many disappointed speculators. Some observers see cryptocurrency purchases as a bet on blockchain technology—and believe that it will revolutionize transactions around the globe. But, in the eyes of many, it is another example of speculative investing based on the psychology of crowds.

Dogecoin is a popular cryptocurrency. In 2021, the total market value of all dogecoins was over $27 billion.

Economists watch cryptocurrency markets for two reasons. First, they offer another good example of supply and demand in action, going through wild price changes as demand fluctuates. But we are also curious to see whether alternative currencies flourish in the long term, even while most fiat government currencies are relatively stable. In September of 2021, El Salvador became the first nation to officially embrace Bitcoin as legal tender, alongside the U.S. dollar.

Measuring the Quantity of Money

Now that we have defined the three functions of money, we need to consider how the total amount of money in the economy is measured. As we saw in Chapter 21, the quantity of money in an economy affects the overall price level. In particular, a nation's inflation rate is dependent on the rate of growth of its quantity of money. In addition, in Chapter 31 we'll see that the quantity of money can influence real GDP and unemployment rates. Because

ECONOMICS *in the* MEDIA

The Crypto Bowl

Matt Damon, financial advisor?

The 2022 Super Bowl featured so many ads for cryptocurrency and related services that *Fortune* magazine dubbed the event the "Crypto Bowl." Many of the ads played on viewers' FOMO, or "fear of missing out," if they hadn't already gotten in on the crypto action.

One unintentionally hilarious ad featured Matt Damon comparing crypto investors to adventurers and pioneers like Magellan and the Wright brothers. "Fortune favors the brave," he intoned, as a crew of crypto-astronauts prepared for liftoff. One look at the past ups and downs of, say, Bitcoin will tell you that anyone buying crypto is likely in for a wild ride. Whether fortune will reward the move is anyone's guess. A few online retailers, like Shopify and Overstock.com, have started accepting crypto as payment. At present, though, cryptocurrencies are still mostly a (very) high-risk investment vehicle, not something you'd use to buy coffee or a couch.

Owning cryptocurrency requires keeping track of private "keys"—codes that prove you own the currency. If you lose the codes, or if someone takes the notebook or thumb drive where you keep them, you've lost the money. The bigger risk, however, is that no one knows what will happen with these currencies in the long run. Ads may promote cryptocurrencies as investment opportunities, but the ads are being paid for mostly by people who already own a lot of the currency. These people want the demand to go up so their own holdings increase in value. While stocks and bonds are backed by the performance of the companies that issue them, crypto is backed only by the interest of others wanting it. If the ads stop running, or stop being effective, the value of these new currencies is liable to nosedive.

The invention of the ATM made it harder to justify excluding money in savings from the official money supply.

money has such profound macroeconomic influences, you might think it is important to measure it accurately. Unfortunately, this is not as easy as it once was.

To get a sense of the difficulties of measuring the money supply, think about all the different ways you make purchases. You might hold some currency for emergencies, to make a vending machine purchase or feed a parking meter, or to do laundry. On top of this, you might write checks to pay your rent, tuition, or utilities bills. Moreover, you probably carry a debit card that enables you to withdraw from your savings or checking account. You may buy your morning coffee or your lunch with a mobile payment phone app. You might even use a cryptocurrency for some purchases. To measure the quantity of money in an economy, we must somehow find the total value of all these alternative means people use to buy goods and services. Clearly, currency alone is not enough—people buy things all the time without using currency. Currency is money, but it constitutes only a small part of the total money supply.

Because it is so hard these days to measure the overall amount of money in circulation, the Fed closely monitors interest rates, like the federal funds rate (which we will talk about). Interest rates are the prices of funds in the banking system, so they help the Fed gauge whether there is too little or too much money in the economy. These give an indication of the overall amount of money circulating in the banking system.

M1 AND M2 As we broaden our definition of money beyond currency, we first acknowledge bank deposits on which checks can be written. **Checkable deposits** are deposits in bank accounts from which depositors may make withdrawals by writing checks. These deposits represent purchasing power very similar to currency, because many sellers accept personal checks. Savings deposits are another large category of deposits that count when we measure the money supply, since we easily access these via ATMs or debit cards. Adding checkable deposits and savings deposits to currency gives us a money supply measure known as **M1**.

Checkable deposits are deposits in bank accounts from which depositors may make withdrawals by writing checks.

M1 is the money supply measure composed of currency and checkable deposits.

M2 is a slightly broader money supply measure than M1. M2 includes money market mutual funds and small-denomination time deposits, known as CDs.

At one time, savings deposits were excluded from M1 but included in a broader money supply measure called **M2**. Starting in May 2020, however, savings deposits became part of M1, and so M1 and M2 are now almost identical. The only difference is that M2 adds two minor components: small time deposits and retail money market funds. Figure 30.1 shows M1 and M2 from 2000 through the end of 2021. You can easily spot the point when savings deposits were added to M1.

The key point to remember is that the money supply in an economy includes both currency and bank deposits. Note that credit cards are not part

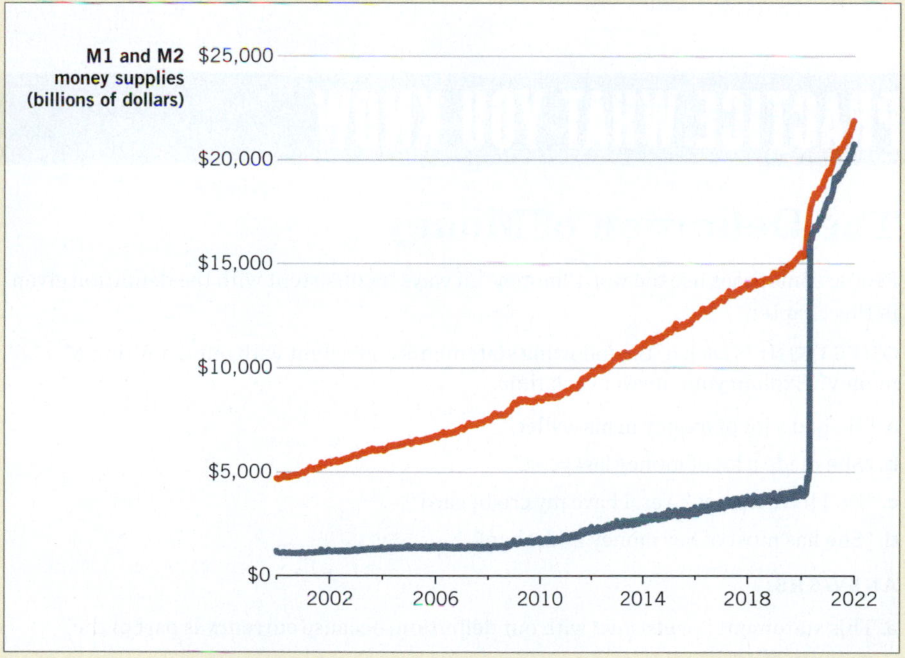

FIGURE 30.1

Measures of the U.S. Money Supply, 2000 through 2021

M1 and M2 are the two most common measures of the money supply. Prior to 2020, M1 included currency and checkable bank deposits. As of 2020, savings deposits are also included in M1. M2 has always included savings deposits, so M1 and M2 are now almost identical.

Source: Federal Reserve, Money Stock Measures.

of the money supply. Purchases made with credit cards involve a loan extended right at the cash register. When the loan is made, a third party is paying for the purchase until the loan is repaid. Because credit card purchases involve the use of borrowed funds, credit cards are not included as part of the money supply.

ECONOMICS IN THE REAL WORLD

THE EVOLUTION OF PRISON MONEY

In the past, cigarettes were often the preferred unit of account and medium of exchange in prisons. This commodity money was useful as currency in addition to its usefulness for smoking. But in 2004 the U.S. government outlawed smoking in federal prisons, and this decision led to the development of a new medium of exchange.

In an October 2008 *Wall Street Journal* article, Justin Scheck reported on one federal facility where cans of mackerel had taken over as the accepted money. According to one prisoner, "It's the coin of the realm." This "bartering" is not legal in federal prisons. Prisoners can lose privileges if they are caught exchanging goods or services for mackerel. Nonetheless, mackerel remains the medium of exchange and the unit of account. For example, haircuts cost about two "macks." The cans of fish also serve as a reliable store of value. Some prisoners even rent lockers from others so they can store their mackerel money.

But while mackerel is popular, it is not the only commodity used as money in federal prisons. In some prisons, protein bars or cans of tuna serve as money. One reason why mackerel is preferred to other alternatives is that each can costs about one dollar—so it's a simple substitute for U.S. currency, which inmates are not allowed to carry.

The evolution of prison money.

PRACTICE WHAT YOU KNOW

This currency is a small part of the M2 money supply, which also includes many bank deposits.

The Definition of Money

People sometimes use the word "money" in ways inconsistent with the definition given in this chapter.

QUESTION: Is each of the following statements consistent with our definition of money? Explain your answer each time.

a. "He had a lot of money in his wallet."

b. "She made a lot of money last year."

c. "Do I have money? Yes, I have my credit card."

d. "She has most of her money in the bank."

ANSWERS:

a. This statement is *consistent* with our definition, because currency is part of the medium of exchange.

(CONTINUED)

b. This statement is *inconsistent* with the definition. It refers to income, not to money.

c. This statement is *inconsistent*. Payment with a credit card requires a loan, so using a credit card is technically not counted in the money supply.

d. This statement is *consistent*. Bank deposits count as money because they represent part of our medium of exchange.

How Do Banks Create Money?

We now have a working definition of money: money includes both currency and deposits at banks. And while private individuals and firms aren't permitted to print currency, private actions do influence the supply of money in the economy, because both private individuals and banks affect deposits. In this section, we explain how banks create money as a by-product of their daily business activity. Note that when we refer to "banks," we are talking about commercial banks, which take in deposits and extend loans. We distinguish commercial banks from investment banks, which serve a different role.

We begin by looking closely at the daily activities at typical banks. After that, we consider how banks influence the money supply.

The Business of Banking

Banks serve two very important roles in the macroeconomy. First, they are middlemen in the market for loanable funds. As we saw in Chapter 23, they provide a way for savers to supply their funds to borrowers without purchasing a financial security. Second, they play a role in creating the supply of money.

To understand how banks create money, let us consider the functions of a bank, illustrated in Figure 30.2. Banks are go-betweens in the market for loans. They are financial intermediaries; that is, they take in deposits and extend loans. Deposits are the primary source of funds, and loans are the primary use of these funds. Banks can be profitable if the interest rate they charge on loans is higher than the interest rate they pay out on deposits.

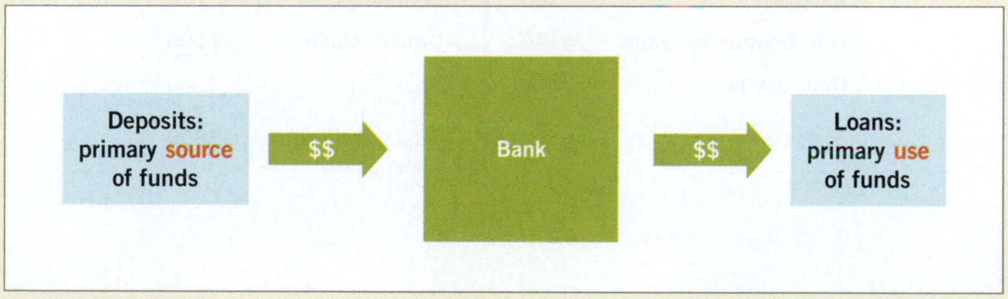

FIGURE 30.2

The Business of Banking: Financial Intermediation

The primary function of commercial banks is financial intermediation: they accept deposits and extend loans.

FIGURE 30.3

Interest Rates on Bank Deposits versus Loans, 1990–2020

Banks charge more interest for loans than they pay for deposits. The difference pays the banks' expenses and produces profits.

Source: FRED data, Federal Reserve Bank of St. Louis. The loan interest rate is the average prime interest rate across the United States; the deposit interest rate is the interest rate on three-month certificates of deposit.

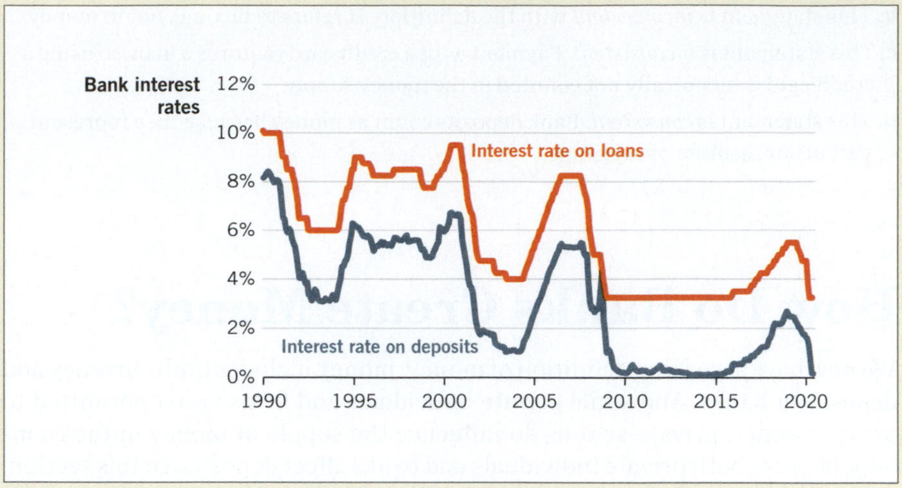

A **balance sheet** is an accounting statement that summarizes a firm's key financial information.

Assets are the items a firm owns.

Figure 30.3 illustrates the gap between interest rates on bank deposits and bank loans for U.S. banks for the period 1990–2020. The two rates go up and down together, but the interest rate on deposits is consistently lower than the interest rate on loans. The difference between the two interest rates helps pay a bank's operating costs and produces profits.

THE BANK'S BALANCE SHEET Information about a bank's financial operations is available in the bank's balance sheet. A **balance sheet** is an accounting statement that summarizes a firm's key financial information. Figure 30.4 shows a hypothetical balance sheet for University Bank. The left side of the balance sheet details the bank's **assets**, which are the items the

FIGURE 30.4

Balance Sheet for University Bank

A bank's balance sheet summarizes its key financial information. The bank's assets are recorded on the left side; this side shows how the bank chooses to use its funds. The sources of the firm's funds are recorded on the right side; this side shows liabilities and owner's equity. The two sides of the balance sheet must match for the financial statement to be balanced.

Assets: Uses of funds (in millions)		Liabilities and owner's equity: Sources of funds (in millions)	
Loans	$400	Deposits	$500
Reserves	$60	Borrowings	$200
U.S. Treasury securities	$140	Owner's equity	$100
Other assets	$200		
Total assets	$800	Total liabilities and equity	$800

firm owns. Assets indicate how the banking firm uses the funds it has raised from various sources. The right side of the balance sheet details the bank's liabilities and owner's equity. **Liabilities** are the financial obligations the firm owes to others. **Owner's equity** (sometimes called *shareholders' equity*) is the difference between the firm's assets and its liabilities. When a firm has more assets than liabilities, it has positive owner's equity. Overall, the right side of the balance sheet identifies the bank's sources of funds.

Liabilities
are the financial obligations a firm owes to others.

Owner's equity
is the difference between a firm's assets and its liabilities.

As you can see, University Bank has extended $400 million in loans. Many of these loans went to firms to fund investment, but some also went to households to purchase homes, cars, and other consumer items. A second important asset held by banks is reserves. **Reserves** are the portion of bank deposits set aside and not loaned out. Reserves include both currency in the bank's vault and funds that the bank holds in deposit at its own bank, the Federal Reserve. Banks also hold U.S. Treasury securities and other government securities as substantial assets in their portfolio. These securities earn interest and carry very low risk. Finally, banks hold other assets, such as physical buildings and furniture.

Reserves
are the portion of bank deposits that are set aside and not loaned out.

Turning to the right side of the balance sheet, we look at the major sources of funds for banks. Banks fund their activities primarily by taking in deposits. In fact, the deposits of typical households are the lifeblood of banks. Banks also borrow from other commercial banks and from the Federal Reserve. The third item on the right side of the balance sheet in Figure 30.4 is the owner's equity in the bank. Because University Bank owns $800 million in total assets but owes only $700 million in liabilities ($500 million in deposits plus $200 million in borrowings), the owners of the bank have $100 million in equity.

In the next section, we look more closely at bank reserves, which play an important role in money creation.

BANK RESERVES Our modern system of banking is a fractional reserve system. **Fractional reserve banking** occurs when banks hold only a fraction of deposits on reserve. The alternative is 100% reserve banking. Banks in a 100% reserve system don't loan out deposits; these banks are essentially just safes, keeping deposits on hand until depositors decide to make a withdrawal.

Fractional reserve banking
occurs when banks hold only a fraction of deposits on reserve.

Figure 30.5 illustrates the process of fractional reserve banking. Deposits come into the banks, and banks send out a portion of these funds in loans. In recent years, U.S. banks have typically loaned out 75 to 85% of their deposits, keeping 15 to 25% on reserve. Banks loan out most of their deposits because, as was already mentioned, collecting interest on loans is how banks cover their costs and earn a profit.

Still, banks do hold some deposits on reserve in order to accommodate withdrawals by their depositors. You'd be pretty unhappy if you tried to make a withdrawal from your bank and it didn't have enough on reserve to honor your request. If word spread that a bank might have difficulty meeting its depositors' withdrawal requests, it might lead to a bank run. A **bank run** occurs when many depositors attempt to withdraw their funds from a bank at the same time.

A **bank run** occurs when many depositors attempt to withdraw their funds from a bank at the same time.

Before 2020, banks were required to hold a certain portion of their deposits in reserve. The required fraction was called the required reserve ratio. For a given bank, the dollar amount of required reserves was required

FIGURE 30.5

Fractional Reserve Banking

In a fractional reserve banking system, banks lend out only a fraction of the deposits they take in. The remainder is set aside as reserves.

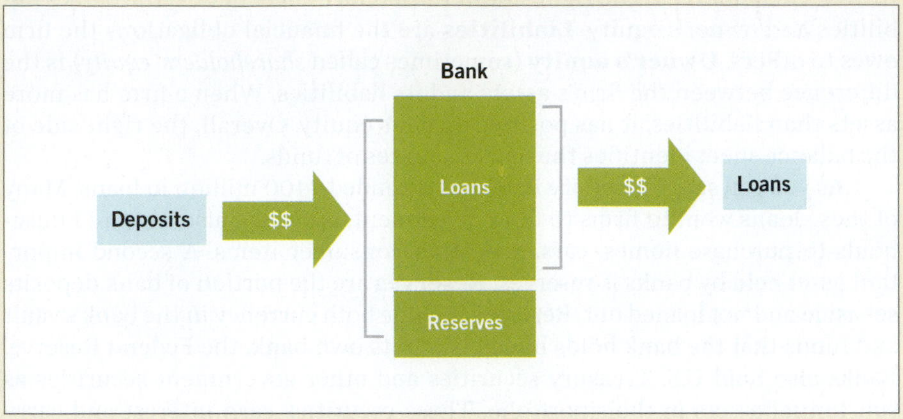

Opportunity cost

determined by multiplying the required reserve ratio by the bank's total amount of deposits. In 2020, the Fed switched to a different tool for encouraging banks to maintain reserves, namely paying banks interest on reserves. We discuss this tool later in the chapter. As for the reserve ratio, it is no longer a requirement but is still a useful concept, as we will see.

THE FDIC AND MORAL HAZARD Because a bank keeps only a fraction of its deposits on reserve, if all depositors try to withdraw their deposits at the same time, the bank will not be able to meet its obligations. But in a typical day, only a small number of deposits are withdrawn. In the past, when word spread that a bank was unstable and perhaps could not meet the demands of depositors—whether this rumor was true or not—depositors would rush to withdraw their funds, leading to a bank run.

During the Great Depression, bank failures became common. From 1929 to 1933, over 9,000 banks failed in the United States alone—more than in any other period in U.S. history. It is clear that many banks were extending loans beyond their ability to collect and pay depositors in a timely manner. As a result, many depositors lost confidence in the banking system. If you became worried about your bank and were not certain you could withdraw your deposits at some later point, wouldn't you run to the bank to get your money out?

This is precisely what happened to many banks during the Great Depression. The Hollywood film classic *It's a Wonderful Life* (1946) captures this situation perfectly. In the movie, the character George Bailey is set to leave on his honeymoon when the financial intermediary he runs is subject to a run. When a depositor asks for his money back, George tells him, "The money's not here. Well, your money's in Joe's house, that's right next to yours. And in the Kennedy house, and Mrs. Macklin's house, and, and a hundred others." This quote summarizes both the beauty and the danger wrapped up in a fractional reserve banking system. Fractional reserve banking allows access to funds by many individuals and firms in an economy, but it can also lead to instability when many depositors demand their funds simultaneously.

After the massive rate of bank failures from 1929 to 1933, the U.S. government instituted federal deposit insurance in 1933 through the Federal Deposit Insurance Corporation (FDIC). Deposit insurance now guarantees that depositors will get their deposits back (up to $250,000) even if their bank goes bankrupt. FDIC insurance greatly decreased the frequency of bank runs. Unfortunately, deposit insurance also created what we call a moral hazard situation. **Moral hazard** is the lack of incentive to guard against risk where one is protected from its consequences. FDIC insurance means that neither banks nor their depositors have an incentive to monitor risk; no matter what happens, they are protected from the consequences of risky behavior.

To end the bank run, George Bailey offers depositors money from his own wallet.

Consider two types of banks in this environment. Type A banks are conservative, take little risk, and earn relatively low returns on their loans. Type A banks make only very safe loans with very little default risk and, consequently, relatively low rates of return. Type A banks rarely fail, but they make relatively low profit and pay relatively low interest rates to their depositors. In contrast, Type B banks take huge risks, hoping to make extremely large returns on their loans. Type B loans carry greater default risk but also pay higher returns. Type B banks often fail, but the lucky ones—the ones that survive—earn very handsome profits and pay high interest rates on their customers' deposits.

Moral hazard
is the lack of incentive to guard against risk where one is protected from its consequences.

Moral hazard draws individual depositors and bankers to type B banking. There is a tremendous upside and no significant downside, because depositors are protected against losses by FDIC insurance. This is the environment in which our modern banks operate, which is why many analysts argue that reserve requirements and other regulations are necessary to help ensure stability in the financial industry—especially given that recessions often start in the financial industry.

ECONOMICS IN THE REAL WORLD

TWENTY-FIRST-CENTURY BANK RUN

For a modern example of a bank run, consider England's Northern Rock Bank, which experienced a bank run in 2007—the first British bank run in over a century. Northern Rock (which is now owned by Virgin Money) had earned revenue valued over $10 billion per year. But extensive losses stemming from investments in mortgage markets led it to near collapse in 2007.

In September of that year, depositors began queuing outside Northern Rock locations because they feared they would not get their deposits back. Eventually, the British government offered deposit insurance of 100% to Northern Rock depositors—but not before much damage had been done. In February 2008, Northern Rock was taken over by the British government because the bank was unable to repay its debts or find a buyer. To make matters worse, there is some evidence that Northern Rock was solvent at the time of the bank run, meaning that stronger deposit insurance could have saved the bank.

In the United States, over 300 banks failed between 2008 and 2011 without experiencing a bank run. (So these banks failed, but the failure did not lead to a bank run.) The individual depositors who funded the risky loans got their money back. So why the bank

Depositors queue outside a Northern Rock Bank location in September 2007.

run in England? The difference is a reflection of the level of deposit insurance offered in the two nations. In England, depositors are insured for 100% of their deposits up to a value of $4,000, then for only 90% of their next $70,000. So British depositors get back a fraction of their deposits up to about $74,000. In contrast, FDIC insurance in the United States offers 100% insurance on the first $250,000.

Creating Money by Multiplying Deposits

We have seen that banks function as financial intermediaries. But as a by-product of their everyday activity, they also create new money. Modern U.S. banks don't mint currency, but they do create new deposits, and deposits are a part of the money supply.

Money deposited in the banking system leads to more money. To see how, let's start with a hypothetical example that involves the Federal Reserve, which supplies the currency in the United States. Let's say that the Federal Reserve decides to increase the money supply in the United States. It prints a single $1,000 bill and drops it out of a helicopter. Let's say you are the lucky person who finds this brand-new $1,000 bill. If you keep the $1,000 in your wallet, then the money supply increases by only $1,000. But if you deposit the new money in a bank, then the bank can use it to create even more money.

Consider what happens if you deposit the $1,000 into a savings or checking account at University Bank. When you deposit the $1,000, it is still part of the money supply, because both currency and bank deposits are counted in the money supply. You don't have the currency anymore, but in your wallet you have a debit card that enables you to access the $1,000 to make purchases. Therefore, the deposit still represents $1,000 worth of the medium of exchange.

But University Bank doesn't keep your $1,000 in reserve; it uses part of your deposit to extend a new loan that earns interest income for the bank. You still have the $1,000 in your account (as a deposit), but someone else receives money from the bank in the form of a loan. Thus, University Bank creates new money by loaning out part of your deposit. You helped the bank in the money creation process because you put your funds into the bank in the first place.

This is just the first step in the money creation process. We'll now explore this process in more detail, utilizing the bank's balance sheet. For this example, we make two simplifying assumptions to help understand the general picture:

Assumption 1: All currency is deposited in banks.

Assumption 2: All banks decide to keep 10% of deposits on reserve.

Neither of these assumptions is completely realistic. But let's work through the example under these conditions, and later we can consider what happens if we relax each assumption.

Consider first how your deposit changes the assets and liabilities of University Bank. The following t-account (an abbreviated version of a firm's balance sheet) summarizes all initial changes to the balance sheet of University Bank when you deposit your new $1,000 (Assumption 1):

UNIVERSITY BANK

Assets		Liabilities and equity	
Reserves	+ $1,000	Deposits	+ $1,000

Under Assumption 2, that banks keep 10% of deposits on reserve, University Bank loans out $900 of your deposit. Perhaps the bank loans this amount to a student named Kaitlyn so she can pay her tuition bill. When University Bank extends the loan to Kaitlyn, the money supply increases by $900. That is, you still have your $1,000 deposit, and Kaitlyn now has $900.

Including your initial deposit and this $900 loan, the balance sheet changes at University Bank are summarized in this t-account:

UNIVERSITY BANK

Assets		Liabilities and equity	
Reserves	+$100	Deposits	+$1,000
Loans	+$900		

Kaitlyn gives her college the $900, and the college then deposits this amount into its own bank, named Township Bank. But the money multiplication process does not end here. Township Bank also (by Assumption 2 again) loans out 90% of the $900, which is $810. This loan creates $810 more in money supply, so total new money is now $1,000 + $900 + $810 = $1,710. Here are the balance sheet changes at Township Bank:

TOWNSHIP BANK

Assets		Liabilities and equity	
Reserves	+$90	Deposits	+$900
Loans	+$810		

You can now see that whenever a bank makes a loan, it creates new money. As long as dollars find their way back into the banking system, banks multiply them into more deposits—which means more money. Table 30.1 summarizes this process of money creation. The initial $1,000 deposit ultimately leads to $10,000 worth of money. When monetary funds are deposited into banks, banks can multiply these deposits; and when they do, they create money.

In the end, the impact on the money supply is a large multiple of the initial increase in money. The exact multiple depends on the **reserve ratio** (rr)

The **reserve ratio** is the portion of deposits that banks keep on reserve.

TABLE 30.1

Money Creation

Assumption 1: All currency is deposited in banks.

Assumption 2: Banks hold 10% of deposits on reserve.

Reserve ratio (rr) = 10%

Initial new money supply = $1,000

Round	Deposit	
1	$1,000	← Initial deposit
2	900	
3	810	
4	729	
•	•	
•	•	
•	•	
Sum	$10,000	← Total money

The **simple money multiplier** is the rate at which banks multiply money when all currency is deposited into banks.

the banks decide to maintain. The rate at which banks multiply money when all currency is deposited into banks (Assumption 1) is called the **simple money multiplier** (m^m). The formula for the simple money multiplier is

(EQUATION 30.1)

$$m^m = \frac{1}{rr}$$

In our example, rr = 0.10, so the multiplier is 1/0.10, which is 10. When the money multiplier is 10, a new $1,000 bill produced by the Federal Reserve can eventually lead to $10,000 in new money.

Of course, in the real world our two assumptions don't always hold. There is a more realistic money multiplier that relaxes the two assumptions. Consider how a real-world money multiplier would compare with the simple money multiplier. First, if people hold on to some currency (relaxing Assumption 1), banks cannot multiply that currency, so the more realistic multiplier is smaller than the simple money multiplier. On the other hand, when banks hold less on reserve (relaxing Assumption 2), more dollars are multiplied, and the real multiplier is larger than the simple version.

Note that the money multiplier process also works in reverse. When funds are withdrawn from the banking system, these are funds that banks cannot multiply. In effect, the money supply contracts.

In 2018, Jerome Powell replaced Janet Yellen as the chair of the Fed's Board of Governors.

How Does the Federal Reserve Implement Monetary Policy?

There's a good chance you've heard of the U.S. Federal Reserve (Fed), even outside economics class. Jerome Powell, the current Chair of the Fed's Board of Governors, is one of the most recognized economic policymakers in the world. And while we've referred to the Fed periodically throughout this text, now it's time to examine it closely.

The Many Jobs of the Federal Reserve

The Fed was established in 1913 as the central bank of the United States. The Fed's primary responsibilities are threefold:

1. *Monetary policy*: The Fed is charged with managing monetary policy so as to promote maximum employment and stable prices effectively.
2. *Central banking*: The Fed serves as a bank for banks, holding their deposits and extending loans to them.
3. *Bank regulation*: The Fed is one of the primary entities charged with ensuring the financial stability of banks.

In this section, we talk about the Fed's role as central bank and bank regulator. We then look at monetary policy in the remainder of the chapter and into the next chapter.

PRACTICE WHAT YOU KNOW

Fractional Reserve Banking: The Buckeye Bank

When banks extend loans, the money supply increases.

Use this balance sheet of the Buckeye Bank to answer the questions below. Assume Buckeye Bank is aiming for 10% of deposits in reserves.

BUCKEYE BANK

Assets		Liabilities and equity	
Reserves	$50,000	Deposits	$200,000
Loans	120,000	Equity	20,000
Treasury securities	50,000		

QUESTION: What is Buckeye's target level of reserves?

ANSWER: Buckeye Bank is aiming for 10% of deposits, which is $20,000.

QUESTION: What is the maximum new loan Buckeye Bank will extend?

ANSWER: Buckeye Bank has $30,000 in extra reserves (reserves beyond its target), so it can extend that total amount in new loans.

QUESTION: How would you rewrite Buckeye Bank's balance sheet, assuming that this loan is made?

ANSWER: The only items that would change are reserves, which would decline by $30,000, and loans, which would increase by $30,000.

BUCKEYE BANK

Assets		Liabilities and equity	
Reserves	$20,000	Deposits	$200,000
Loans	150,000		
Treasury securities	50,000	Equity	20,000

(CONTINUED)

QUESTION: If the Federal Reserve now bought all of Buckeye Bank's Treasury securities, how large a loan could Buckeye now extend while maintaining its targeted reserve ratio of 10%?

ANSWER: Buckeye Bank would now have $50,000 in extra reserves, so it could make a loan in this amount.

QUESTION: What would be the maximum impact on the money supply from this Fed action?

ANSWER: Using the simple money multiplier, we can see that the money supply could grow by as much as $500,000 from this action alone:

$$\$50{,}000 \times m^{m} = \$50{,}000 \times \frac{1}{rr} = \$50{,}000 \times 10 = \$500{,}000$$

CHALLENGE QUESTION: If all banks decide to double their reserve ratios, what happens to the money multiplier?

ANSWER: The money multiplier falls from 10 to just 5. Banks are not multiplying money as many times, since they are holding more aside on reserve.

Federal funds are deposits that private banks hold on reserve at the Federal Reserve.

The Fed is a "central bank"—that is, it acts as a "bank for banks." In its role as central bank, it offers support and stability to the nation's entire banking system. The first component of this role involves the deposits that banks hold at the Fed. **Federal funds** are deposits that private banks hold on reserve at the Fed, and, as of 2008, the Fed pays interest on these deposits. The word "federal" seems to denote that the deposits are government funds, but in fact they are private funds held on deposit at a *federal* agency—the Fed. These deposits are part of the reserves that banks set aside, along with the physical currency in their vaults.

Banks keep reserves at the Fed in part because the Fed clears loans between banks. When banks loan reserves to other banks, these are *federal funds loans*. The federal funds loans are typically very short term (often overnight), and they enable banks to make quick adjustments to their balance sheets. For example, if our theoretical University Bank dips below its desired reserve level, it can approach Township Bank for a short-term loan. If Township Bank happens to have extra reserves, making a short-term loan enables it to earn additional interest. The interest rate that banks charge each other on interbank loans is known as the **federal funds rate**. This rate moves up and down based on the borrowing and lending choices of individual banks. The federal funds rate is generally higher than the interest rate banks earn on their reserves at the Fed.

The **federal funds rate** is the interest rate on loans between private banks. This is the main interest rate that the Fed targets (pushes up and pulls down, depending on economic conditions), because it gives the Fed a strong indicator of the level of money in the economy.

The federal funds rate is one of the most closely monitored interest rates in the world. This is the interest rate that the Fed "targets," for monetary policy. Because the actual quantity of money in the economy is hard to measure, the Fed monitors conditions in the banking system by watching the federal funds rate (among other indicators). In the next section, we'll discuss how the Fed acts to push the federal funds rate up and down, depending on macroeconomic conditions.

FIGURE 30.6

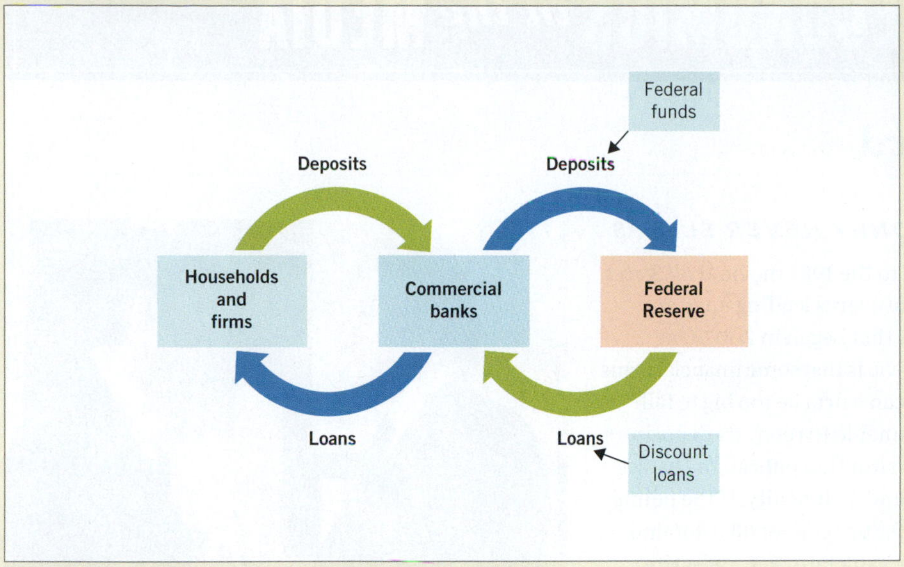

The Federal Reserve as a Central Bank

The Federal Reserve operates as a central bank for commercial banks. Commercial banks make deposits at the Federal Reserve; these deposits are called federal funds. The Federal Reserve also extends loans to commercial banks; these loans are called discount loans.

Figure 30.6 illustrates how the relationship between the Federal Reserve and commercial banks is analogous to the relationship between commercial banks and households and firms. First, households and firms hold deposits at banks, and banks hold deposits at the Fed—these are the federal funds. Second, households and firms take out loans from banks, and banks take out loans from the Fed. The loans from the Fed to the private banks are known as **discount loans**.

Discount loans are loans from the Federal Reserve to private banks.

Discount loans are the vehicle by which the Fed performs its role as "lender of last resort." Given the macroeconomic danger of bank failure, the Fed serves an important role as a backup lender to private banks that find difficulty borrowing elsewhere. The **discount rate** is the interest rate on the discount loans made from the Fed to private banks. The Fed sets this interest rate because it is a loan directly from a branch of the U.S. government to private financial institutions.

The **discount rate** is the interest rate on the discount loans made by the Federal Reserve to private banks.

Discount loans don't often figure prominently in macroeconomics, but in extremely turbulent times, they reassure financial market participants. For example, when many banks were struggling in 2008, financial market participants were assured that troubled banks could rely on the Federal Reserve to fortify failing banks with discount loans. In fact, for the first time in history, other financial firms were allowed to borrow from the Fed. The Fed even extended an $85 billion loan to the insurance company American International Group because it had written insurance policies for financial securities based on failing home mortgages.

The Fed also serves as a regulator of individual banks. The Fed monitors the balance sheets of banks with an eye toward limiting the riskiness of the assets the banks hold. One might ask why banks are subject to this kind of regulation. After all, the government doesn't monitor the riskiness of assets owned by other private firms. However, as we have seen, the interdependent nature of banking

Incentives

ECONOMICS *in the* MEDIA

Moral Hazard

WALL STREET: MONEY NEVER SLEEPS

Gordon Gecko understands moral hazard.

This 2010 film is a sequel to the 1987 movie *Wall Street*. It focuses on the historical events leading up to and during the financial crisis that began in 2007. One recurring theme in the movie is that some financial firms are "too big to fail." How can a firm be too big to fail?

If one bank fails, it is unable to repay its depositors and other creditors. This situation puts all the bank's creditors into similar financial difficulty. If the failing bank is large enough, its failure can set off a domino effect in which bank after bank fails and the entire financial system collapses. If regulators deem a bank too big to fail, they will use government aid to keep the bank afloat.

However, this situation introduces a particularly strong case of moral hazard. After all, banks have incentives to take on risk so they can earn high profits. If we eliminate the possibility of failure by providing government aid, there is almost no downside risk.

In this movie, Gordon Gecko, played by Michael Douglas, defines moral hazard during a public lecture. His definition is this: "When they take your money and then are not responsible for what they do with it."

Gecko is right: when a financial institution is not required to bear the costs of making poor decisions, it is not legally responsible for mishandling its depositors' funds.

firms means that banking problems often spread throughout the entire industry very quickly. In addition, there is the moral hazard problem we discussed earlier: because of deposit insurance, banks and their customers have reduced incentives to monitor the risk of bank assets on their own.

AIG: The first (and last?) insurance company to get a discount loan from the Fed.

Monetary Policy Tools

The Federal Reserve has been actively managing the money supply for over a century. But the last two recessions have changed the way the Fed reacts in times of crisis. In addition, because the money supply is difficult to measure, the Fed generally watches market indicators like the federal funds rate to determine the correct stance for monetary policy.

In this section, we discuss the tools the Fed has used to affect the economy, with emphasis on the primary tools used to combat recent recessions. We begin with a relatively new tool, the interest rate paid on bank reserves.

PRACTICE WHAT YOU KNOW

Federal Reserve Terminology

Let's say the reserves at Buckeye Bank fall below the desired level, so it approaches University Bank for a loan. University Bank agrees to a short-term loan with Buckeye Bank.

QUESTION: What is the name of the funds that private banks like University Bank loan to other private banks (like Buckeye Bank)? What is the interest rate on these loans called?

ANSWER: The funds are called federal funds. The word "federal" makes it sound as if the funds are a loan from the federal government, but they are not. This wording has been adopted because the loan typically takes place through changes in the two banks' accounts at their bank, the Federal Reserve. The interest rate is the federal funds rate.

Loans from the Federal Reserve aren't called federal funds. They're called discount loans.

Now assume that Buckeye Bank has made some particularly troublesome loans (perhaps a lot of high-risk mortgage loans) and that all private parties refuse to lend to Buckeye, which then approaches the Fed for a loan to keep its reserves at the desired level.

QUESTION: What is the name of this type of loan? What is the name of the interest rate charged for this loan?

ANSWER: This is a discount loan, and the interest rate is the discount rate.

INTEREST RATE ON BANK RESERVES Prior to 2008, bank reserves earned no interest. In that era, there were real opportunity costs to holding reserves, because banks could earn interest on loans or by buying financial securities. But in October 2008, the Federal Reserve began paying interest on bank reserves. The rate of interest, known as the **interest on reserve balances (IORB)**, is now an important policy tool. Immediately, banks started holding more reserves. Figure 30.7 shows total reserves in the banking system from 2000 to 2021 (this is the blue area, which goes with the left axis) along with the IORB (on the right axis). Note that the level of reserves prior to October 2008 was essentially zero. You can clearly see the point when the Fed began paying interest on reserves, as reserves climbed immediately.

Interest on reserve balances (IORB)
is the rate of interest paid by the Federal Reserve on bank reserves deposited with the Fed.

Now, the Fed uses this interest rate as its main tool for monetary policy. If the Fed wishes to promote economic activity, it lowers the IORB, as it did in 2020 at the onset of the COVID-19 recession. A reduction in the IORB leads banks to make additional loans, which increases the money supply. This tool can also work in reverse: if the Fed wishes to pull back, it can raise the IORB, causing banks to hold onto more reserves, which dampens the money multiplication process. The Fed did this from 2016 to 2019.

The power of this new tool is still open to debate. As of 2022, banks still held on to significant reserves, even after the interest rate had dropped back down to just 0.15%.

FIGURE 30.7

Bank Reserves and the Interest Rate Paid on Reserves

Total reserves in the banking system (shown as the orange area and measured on the left axis) were essentially zero before the Federal Reserve began paying interest on bank reserves (plotted as the green line and measured on the right axis) in October 2008. During the economic expansion from 2016 to 2019, bank reserves began falling, so the Fed raised the rate of interest on reserve balances (IORB). When the COVID-19 recession began in March 2020, the Fed lowered the IORB to just 0.15%.

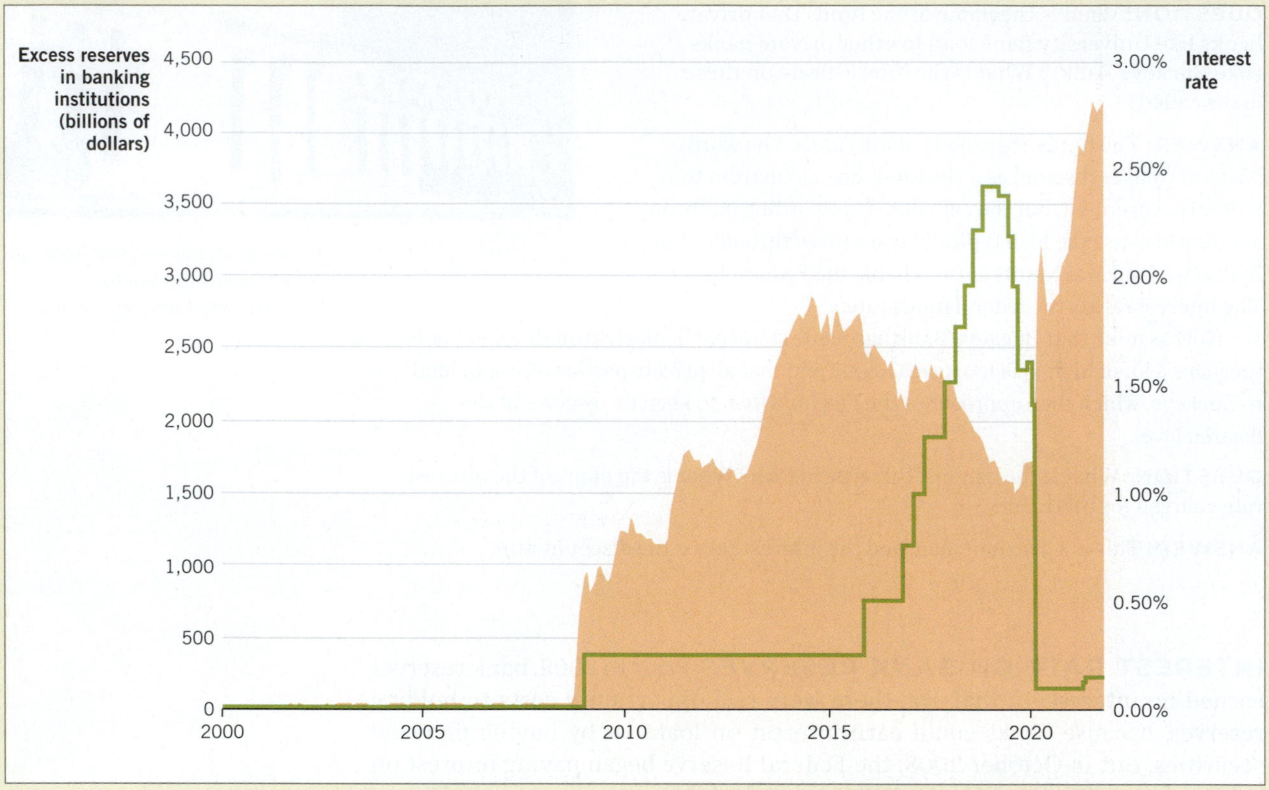

OPEN MARKET OPERATIONS The Fed can also insert money directly into the economy. As a thought experiment, consider the following three possibilities and see if you can guess which is actually used:

1. Drop money out of a helicopter.
2. Distribute $50,000 in new $100 bills to every private bank.
3. Use new money to buy something in the economy.

Open market operations involve the purchase or sale of bonds by a central bank.

If you chose option 3, you are correct. **Open market operations** involve the purchase or sale of bonds by a central bank. When the Fed wants to increase the money supply, it buys securities; in contrast, when it wishes to decrease the money supply, it sells securities. In Chapter 23, we introduced the U.S. Treasury security as a special bond asset. Normal or "traditional" open market operations involve buying and selling short-term (less than one year) Treasury securities.

In principle, the Fed could realize its desired effects through buying any goods and services—real estate, fine art, or, for that matter, tons of coffee and bagels. It would be as if the Fed created a batch of new currency and then went shopping. When it was done shopping, it would leave behind all the new currency in the economy. Whatever it bought during its shopping spree would become an asset on the Fed's balance sheet.

There are at least two good reasons why the Fed chooses the Treasury security market for open market operations. First, the Fed's goal is to get the funds directly into the market for loanable funds. In this way, financial institutions begin lending the new money, and it quickly moves into the economy. Second, a typical day's worth of open market operations might entail as much as $20 billion in purchases. Imagine being the manager of a bagel shop in Washington, D.C., and having the Fed call in a request for $20 billion worth of bagels. That order would be impossible to fill. But the market for U.S. Treasuries is big enough to accommodate this level of purchases seamlessly. The daily volume in the U.S. Treasury market is over $500 billion, so the Fed can buy and sell without difficulty.

Figure 30.8 summarizes how open market operations work. When the Fed buys Treasury securities held by financial institutions (panel [a]), the Fed pays for those bonds using money it creates. The result is more money circulating in the economy, and this shows up as a reduction in the federal funds rate. On the flip side, when the Fed sells bonds to financial institutions (panel [b]), the money it receives in exchange is taken out of the economy, leaving less money in circulation and a higher federal funds rate. In reality, the Fed undertakes open market operations every business day.

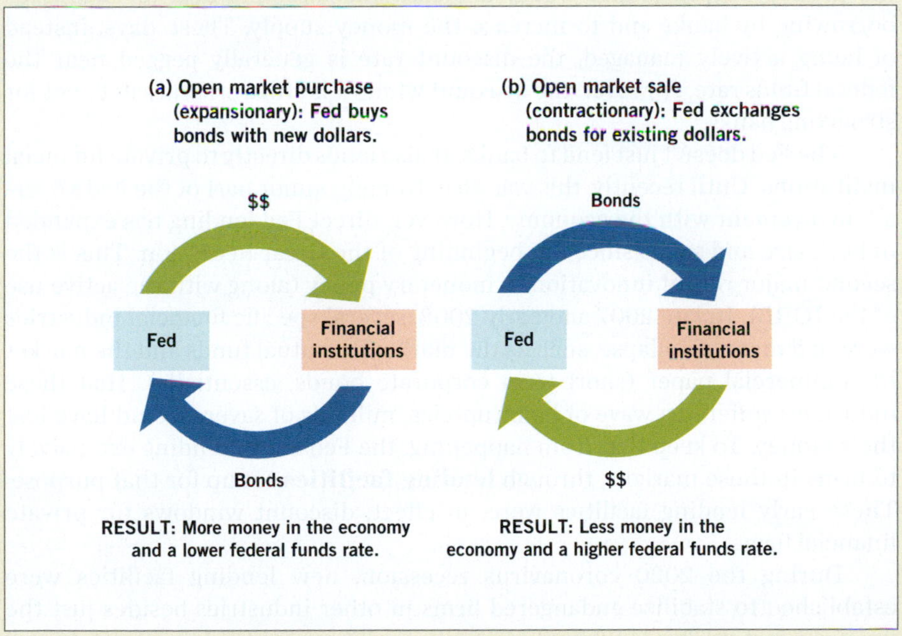
(a) Open market purchase (expansionary): Fed buys bonds with new dollars.
$$
Fed
Financial institutions
Bonds
RESULT: More money in the economy and a lower federal funds rate.
(b) Open market sale (contractionary): Fed exchanges bonds for existing dollars.
Bonds
Fed
Financial institutions
$$
RESULT: Less money in the economy and a higher federal funds rate.

FIGURE 30.8

Open Market Operations

In open market purchases, the Fed buys bonds from financial institutions. This action injects new money directly into financial markets. In open market sales, the Fed sells bonds back to financial institutions. This action takes money out of financial markets.

Typically, it aims to keep market conditions exactly as they were the day before. But the Fed also uses open market operations to increase the money supply to offset recessions.

Starting in 2008, with the economy in the throes of the Great Recession, the Federal Reserve began experimenting with a new variation of open market operations, which has come to be known as *quantitative easing*. Open market operations typically involve buying and selling short-term Treasury securities—that is, bonds that mature in less than a year. In **quantitative easing**, the central bank buys longer-term Treasury securities and other types of securities, specifically targeting certain markets. During the Great Recession, for example, the Fed bought mortgage-backed securities that were considered "toxic assets," meaning assets loaded with risk that could destabilize private markets.

Quantitative easing is the targeted use of open market operations in which the central bank buys securities specifically targeting certain markets.

The quantitative easing programs of the Great Recession injected almost $2 trillion in new funds into targeted sectors of the economy. The reason for this move, unprecedented in size and scope, was that conventional open market securities purchased by the Fed had already pushed the federal funds rate down to zero. Reaching the limits of traditional monetary policy, the Fed had to get inventive. But this new strategy, of targeting particular markets for injections of money, caught on. The Fed decided that loans, too, could be targeted to specific industries. We now turn to that development.

THE DISCOUNT WINDOW AND NEW LENDING FACILITIES

Earlier in this chapter, we discussed the Fed's use of discount loans to support struggling private banks and keep them from failing. The banks obtain these loans at the Fed's **discount window**, as it's called, and the rate the private banks pay on these loans is known as the discount rate. In the past, the Fed would increase the discount rate to discourage borrowing by banks and to decrease the money supply, and it would decrease the discount rate to encourage borrowing by banks and to increase the money supply. These days, instead of being actively managed, the discount rate is generally pegged near the federal funds rate. However, the discount window is still a critical safety net for struggling banks.

The **discount window** is the Fed's tool for extending loans to private banks.

The Fed doesn't just lend to banks. It also lends directly to private financial institutions. Until recently, this was an extremely minor part of the Fed's overall involvement with the economy. However, direct Fed lending has expanded in both size and scope since the beginning of the Great Recession. This is the second major recent innovation in monetary policy (along with the active use of the IORB). In late 2007 and early 2008, several specific financial industries were in danger of collapse, such as the market in mutual funds and the market in commercial paper (short-term corporate bonds, essentially). Had these industries suffered a wave of bankruptcies, millions of savers would have lost their money. To keep that from happening, the Fed began lending extensively to firms in those markets, through **lending facilities** set up for that purpose. These early lending facilities were, in effect, discount windows for private financial firms.

Lending facilities are the Fed's tool for issuing loans to firms in targeted at-risk industries.

During the 2020 coronavirus recession, new lending facilities were established to stabilize endangered firms in other industries besides just the financial sector. The Municipal Liquidity Facility provided loans to state and local governments that had seen spending on unemployed workers go up even as tax revenues went down. A second group of facilities, collectively called the Main Street Lending Program, issued loans to small and medium-sized businesses hit hard by shutdowns and social distancing requirements. The Main Street program also extended loans to hospitals and nonprofits.

Traditional Fed action would have been to increase (or decrease) the money supply for the economy as a whole, to increase (or decrease) aggregate demand. This new monetary policy, carried out via lending facilities, is different. However, the basic concept of lending facilities isn't new at all. It's just an evolution of the discount window, which has been in place since the inception of the Fed in 1913.

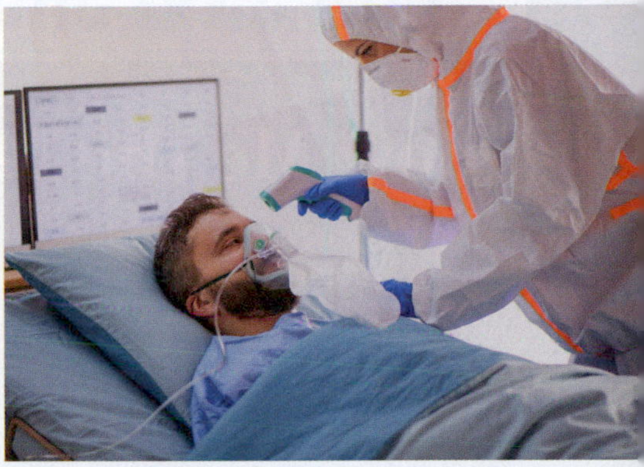

The Fed's new lending facilities helped to sustain hospitals that were hit particularly hard by COVID-19.

RESERVE REQUIREMENTS In the past, the Fed also made use of reserve requirements to administer monetary policy. In March 2020, however, the Fed announced that it would no longer require banks to set aside a portion of deposits on reserve. Historically, though, this was an important tool that the Fed used to affect the money multiplier, and it is still used by many other nations. When the Fed lowered the required reserve ratio, the money multiplier increased. When it raised the required reserve ratio, the money multiplier fell.

For example, consider what would happen if the Fed lowered the required reserve ratio to 5% from 10%. This action alone could have doubled the money multiplier. Lowering the required reserve would mean that banks could loan out a larger portion of their deposits, enabling them to create money by multiplying deposits to a greater extent.

This tool was not as precise or predictable as open market operations. Because small changes in the money multiplier could lead to large swings in the money supply, changing the reserve requirement caused the money supply to change too much. In addition, changing reserve requirements also had unpredictable outcomes because the overall effects depended on the actions of banks. It was possible that the Fed would lower the reserve requirement to 5% and banks would not change their reserves. For these reasons, the reserve requirement had not been used for monetary policy since 1992. In addition, as part of the March 2020 response to the coronavirus crisis, the Fed completely eliminated reserve requirements, hoping this would get banks to lend aggressively.

Table 30.2 summarizes the Fed's monetary policy tools. The tools developed recently are highlighted in orange.

TABLE 30.2

Federal Reserve Tools for Monetary Policy
1. Interest on reserve balances (IORB)
2. Open market operations
Includes quantitative easing
3. Discount window
Includes special lending facilities

DATA SNAPSHOT

Show Me the Money!

The interest rate on reserve balances (IORB) is the Fed's newest monetary policy tool. Generally, when the economy is doing well (the unemployment rate is dropping), the Fed raises the IORB. When the economy is doing poorly (unemployment rates are rising), the Fed lowers the IORB.

IORB and Unemployment Rate

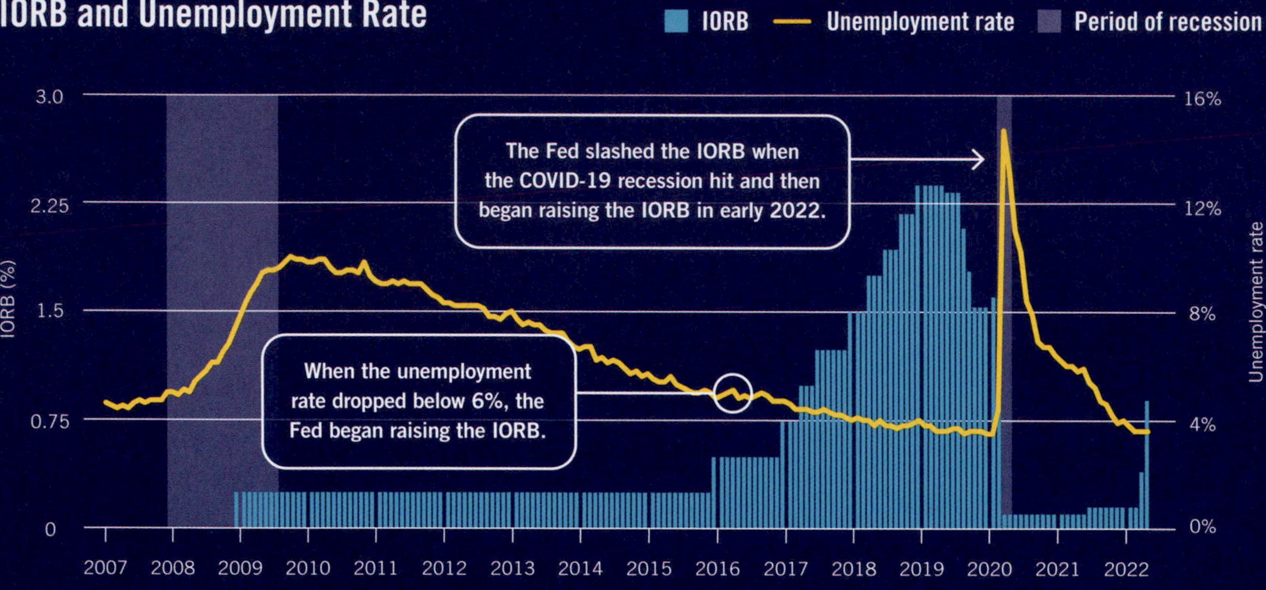

A Timeline of Currency

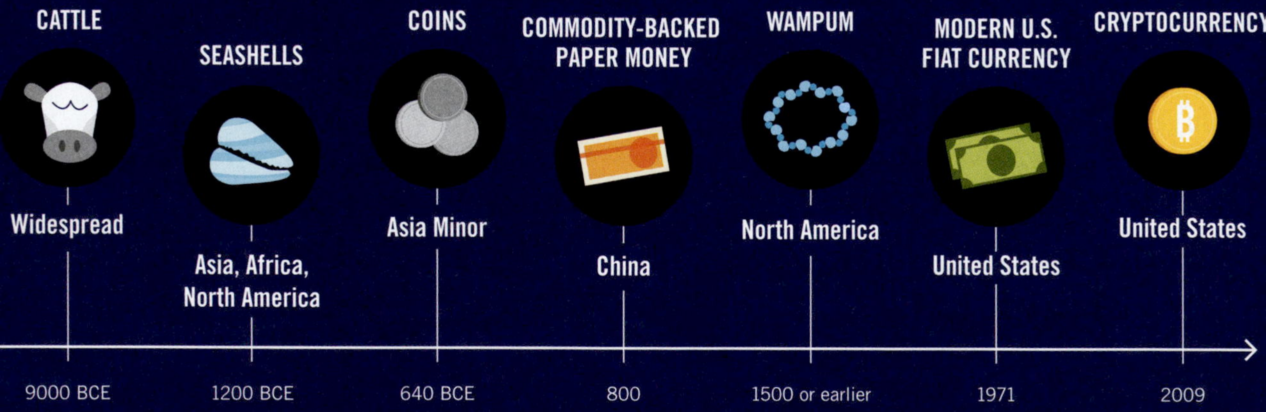

REVIEW QUESTIONS

- When did the Federal Reserve begin paying interest on bank reserves?
- Why did the Fed lower the IORB rate so drastically at the beginning of 2020?

Conclusion

We started this chapter with a common misconception about the supply of money in an economy. Many people believe that it is pretty simple to regulate the quantity of money in an economy. But while currency in modern economies is issued exclusively by government, money also includes bank deposits. Banks expand the money supply when they extend loans, and they contract the money supply when they increase their level of reserves. Even individuals have a significant influence: people like you and me cause the money supply to rise and fall when we change how much currency we hold outside the banking system. Taken together, these facts mean that the Fed's job of monitoring the quantity of money is very difficult. The Fed attempts to expand or contract the money supply, but its efforts may be offset by the actions of banks and individuals.

The material in this chapter sets the stage for a theoretical discussion of monetary policy and the way it affects the economy, which we undertake in the next chapter. ✷

ANSWERING *the* BIG QUESTIONS

What is money?

- Money is primarily the medium of exchange in an economy; it's what people trade for goods and services. Money also functions as a unit of account and a store of value.
- Money includes more than just physical currency; it also includes bank deposits, because people often make purchases with checks or cards that withdraw from their bank accounts.

How do banks create money?

- Banks create money whenever they extend a loan. A new loan represents new purchasing power, while the deposit that backs the loan is also considered money.

How does the Federal Reserve implement monetary policy?

- The Fed has several other tools it can use to control the money supply, including interest paid on bank reserves, open market operations, the discount window and other lending facilities, and the discount rate.

CHAPTER PROBLEMS

Concepts You Should Know

assets (p. 986)
balance sheet (p. 986)
bank run (p. 987)
barter (p. 979)
checkable deposits (p. 983)
commodity-backed money (p. 979)
commodity money (p. 979)
currency (p. 978)
discount loans (p. 995)
discount rate (p. 995)
discount window (p. 1000)
double coincidence of wants (p. 979)
federal funds (p. 994)
federal funds rate (p. 994)
fiat money (p. 979)
fractional reserve banking (p. 987)
Interest on reserve balances (IORB) (p. 997)
lending facilities (p. 1000)
liabilities (p. 987)
M1 (p. 983)
M2 (p. 983)
medium of exchange (p. 978)
money (p. 978)
moral hazard (p. 989)
open market operations (p. 998)
owner's equity (p. 987)
quantitative easing (p. 1000)
reserve ratio (p. 991)
reserves (p. 987)
simple money multiplier (p. 992)
store of value (p. 980)
unit of account (p. 980)

Questions for Review

1. What is the difference between commodity money and fiat money?

2. What are the three functions of money? Which function is the defining characteristic?

3. Suppose you withdraw $100 from your checking account. What impact would this action alone have on the following?

a. the money supply
b. your bank's reserves

4. Why might the actual money multiplier be usually less than the simple money multiplier? Why might it actually be bigger than the simple money multiplier?

5. Why don't banks lend out all of their reserves?

6. How does the Fed increase and decrease the money supply through open market operations?

7. How is the discount rate different from the federal funds rate?

8. Define quantitative easing. How is it different from standard open market operations?

Study Problems (✱ *solved at the end of the section*)

1. Suppose that you take $150 in currency out of your pocket and deposit it in your checking account. Assuming that banks keep 10% of deposits on reserve and no currency is held outside the banking system, what is the largest amount by which the money supply can increase as a result of your action?

2. Consider the balance sheet for Wahoo Bank as presented here.

WAHOO BANK BALANCE SHEET

Assets		Liabilities and equity	
Government securities	$1,600	Liabilities:	
		Checking deposits	$4,000
Reserves	400		
Loans	3,000	Owner's equity	1,000
Total assets	5,000	Total Liablities and Equity	5,000

If Wahoo Bank keeps its reserve ratio at 10%, write the changes to the balance sheet for each of the following scenarios:

a. Bennett withdraws $200 from his checking account.
b. Roland deposits $500 into his checking account.
c. The Fed buys $1,000 in government securities from the bank.
d. The Fed sells $1,500 in government securities to the bank.

3. With a reserve ratio of 10%, which of the following scenarios produces a larger increase in the money supply? Explain why.

a. Maria takes $1,000 from under her mattress and deposits it into a checking account.
b. The Fed purchases $1,000 in government securities from a commercial bank.

4. Using a reserve ratio of 10%, what is the value of government securities the Fed must purchase if it wants to increase the money supply by $2 million?

5. Using a reserve ratio of 10%, imagine $300 is deposited into a checking account. By how much more does the money supply increase if the banks lower their reserve ratio to 7%?

6. Determine whether each of the following is considered standard open market operations or quantitative easing:

a. The Fed buys $100 billion in student-loan-backed securities.
b. The Fed sells $400 billion in short-term Treasury securities.
c. The Fed buys $500 billion in 30-year (long-term) Treasury securities.

* 7. What is the simple money multiplier if the reserve ratio is 15%? If it is 12.5%?

* 8. Suppose the Fed buys $1 million in Treasury securities from a commercial bank. What effect will this action have on the bank's reserves and the money supply? Use a reserve ratio of 10%, and assume all currency is deposited into the banking system.

Solved Problems

7. When the reserve ratio is 15%:

$$m^m = \frac{1}{rr} = \frac{1}{0.15} = 6.67$$

When the reserve ratio is 12.5%:

$$m^m = \frac{1}{rr} = \frac{1}{0.125} = 8$$

8. The immediate result is that the commercial bank will have $1 million in extra reserves, because its deposits did not change. The commercial bank will loan out these extra reserves, and the money multiplier process begins. Under the assumptions of this question, the simple money multiplier applies. Therefore, in the end, $10 million in additional deposits will be created.

CHAPTER

31

Monetary Policy

Central Banks' Control of the Economy Is Anything but Certain.

At times, the U.S. economy seems to hum along with unstoppable success. As a recent example, during the 26-year period from 1982 to 2007, there were just two recessions, and neither was severe or lengthy. During this period, many economists and other observers believed that the business cycle was essentially tamed once and for all. Some credit for this "great moderation" went to Alan Greenspan, the chairman of the board of governors of the Federal Reserve Board during much of this period. Analysts thought that his savvy handling of interest rates and money supply was the key to the sustained economic growth, and that enlightened supervision of central banks was the path to future economic growth throughout the world.

Unfortunately, the stability did not last. The Great Recession, which started in late 2007, plunged the United States into a deep economic downturn. Moreover, the slow recovery after 2009 seemed to underscore the limits of monetary policy during significant downturns, as the Fed's strategies to inject more money into the economy did not cure the problem as easily as some had forecast.

More recently, of course, after another long period of growth, the economy experienced a new shock driven by the spread of the COVID-19 virus. Once again, the Federal Reserve responded with aggressive action and a commitment to support the economy. The hope is that this move will avert a major,

The Federal Reserve plays a powerful role in the world economy, but not as powerful as some people think. Reality has a way of asserting itself, despite the government's best efforts to pretend otherwise.

long-run recession, but it is clear that monetary policy cannot help us circumvent all downturns. In this chapter, we consider how changes in the money supply work their way through the economy. We build on earlier material, drawing on what we learned about the loanable funds market and the aggregate demand–aggregate supply model. We begin by looking at the tools of monetary policy. We then examine how monetary policy affects the economy in the short run. We conclude the chapter by examining why monetary policy can't always turn an economy around.

- BIG QUESTIONS -

- What is the effect of monetary policy in the short run?
- Why doesn't monetary policy always work?
- What is the Phillips curve?

What Is the Effect of Monetary Policy in the Short Run?

Across the globe, when economic growth stagnates and unemployment rises, we often look to the central bank to help the economy. Central banks in most countries use monetary policy to reduce interest rates and make it easier for people and businesses to borrow; this action generates new economic activity to get the economy moving again. In this chapter, we examine how monetary policy effects ripple through the economy.

We begin by considering the immediate, or short-run, effects. Recall the difference between the short run and the long run in macroeconomics. The *long run* is a period of time long enough for all prices to adjust. But in the *short run*, some prices—often the prices of resources such as wages for workers and interest rates for loans—are inflexible.

An Overview of Monetary Policy in the Short Run

To gain some intuition about the macroeconomic results of monetary policy, let's return to an example we talked about in an earlier chapter: your hypothetical college apparel business. Suppose you have one retail location where you sell apparel, and you are considering opening a second. Before you can open a new store, you need to invest in several resources: a physical location, additional inventory, and some labor. You expect the new store to earn the revenue needed to pay for these resources eventually. But you need a loan to expand the business now, so you go to the bank. The bank is willing to grant you a loan, but the interest rate is higher than your expected return on the investment. So you regretfully decide not to open a new location.

But then the central bank decides to expand the money supply and push down interest rates. It may do this by reducing the interest rate on bank reserves, so that banks decide to reduce their reserves and extend more loans in the economy. As a result, interest rates fall at your local bank. You then take out a loan, open the second apparel shop, and hire a few employees.

In this example, monetary policy affects your actions, and your actions affect the macroeconomy. Investment increases because you spend on equipment, inventory, and a physical location. Investment is part of aggregate demand, so aggregate demand increases. As a result of the increase in aggregate demand, real GDP increases and unemployment falls as your output rises and you hire workers. This is what monetary policy can do in the short run: it expands the amount of credit (loanable funds) available and paves the way for economic expansion.

Now let's trace the impact of this kind of monetary policy on the entire macroeconomy. In doing so, we draw heavily on what we have presented in preceding chapters. Here, pulled together from previous chapters, is a short list of concepts we will use (the chapters are identified so you can review as necessary):

1. The Fed uses the interest on reserve balances (IORB) to implement monetary policy. When the IORB falls, banks have an incentive to loan out their reserves, and this then multiplies the money supply and reduces other interest rates (Chapter 30).
2. Lower interest rates increase the quantity of investment demand, just as lower prices increase the quantity demanded in any product market (Chapter 22).
3. Investment is one component of aggregate demand, so changes in investment indicate corresponding changes in aggregate demand (Chapter 26).
4. In the short run, increases in aggregate demand increase output and lower the unemployment rate (Chapter 26).

We have studied each of these concepts separately. Now it is time to put them together for a complete picture of how monetary policy works.

Expansionary Monetary Policy

There are two types of monetary policy: expansionary and contractionary. **Expansionary monetary policy** occurs when a central bank acts to increase the money supply in an effort to stimulate the economy. Traditionally, the Fed expanded the money supply through open-market purchases.

Expansionary monetary policy occurs when a central bank acts to increase the money supply in an effort to stimulate the economy.

Recently, expansionary monetary policy has shifted to lowering the interest on reserve balances (IORB), incentivizing banks to increase lending, which increases the money supply and reduces interest rates.

As we saw in our college apparel store example, expansionary monetary policy increases the funds that banks can use for new loans. Figure 31.1 illustrates

FIGURE 31.1

Expansionary Monetary Policy in the Short Run

(a) When the central bank buys bonds, it injects new funds directly into the loanable funds market. This action increases the supply of loanable funds (S_1 shifts to S_2) and decreases the interest rate from 3% to 2%. The lower interest rate leads to an increase in the quantity of investment demand (D) from $200 billion to $210 billion, which increases aggregate demand (AD). (b) The increase in aggregate demand causes real GDP (Y) to rise from $20 trillion to $20.5 trillion and reduces unemployment (u) in the short run. The general price level also rises to 105 but does not fully adjust in the short run.

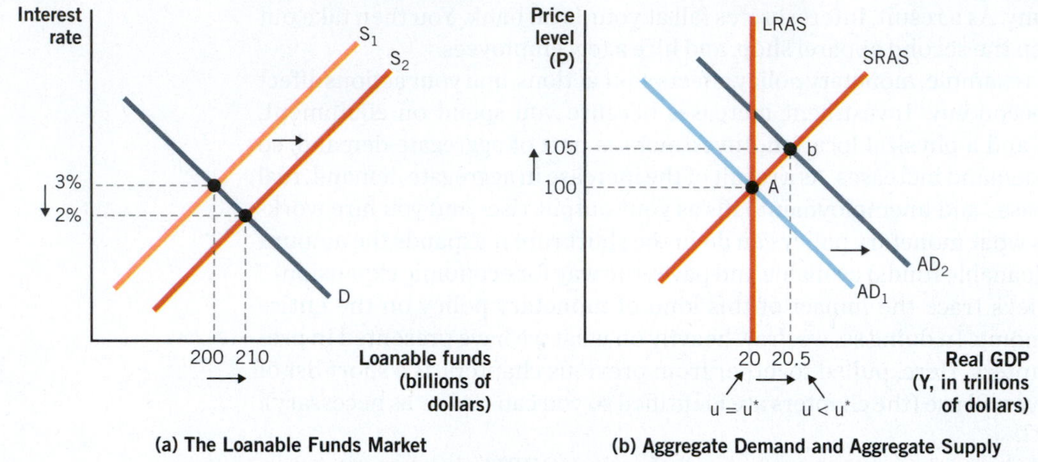

Results summary	Y	u	P
Short run	↑	↓	↑

the short-run effects of expansionary monetary policy in the loanable funds market and on aggregate demand. First, with new funds in the loanable funds market, as pictured in panel (a), the supply of funds increases from S_1 to S_2. This new supply reduces the interest rate from 3% to 2%. At the lower interest rate, firms take more loans for investment, and the quantity demanded of loanable funds increases from $200 billion to $210 billion.

Because investment is a component of aggregate demand, an increase in the quantity of investment demand also increases aggregate demand, as pictured in panel (b) of Figure 31.1. Remember from Chapter 26 that aggregate demand derives from four sources: C, I, G, and NX. When investment (I) increases, aggregate demand increases from AD_1 to AD_2.

In the short run, increases in aggregate demand lead to increases in real GDP. In panel (b) of Figure 31.1, the economy moves from an initial long-run equilibrium at point A to a short-run equilibrium at point b. Real GDP increases from $20 trillion to $20.5 trillion. The increase in GDP leads to more jobs through the increase in aggregate demand; therefore, it also leads to lower unemployment. Finally, the general price level rises from 100 to 105. This price level increase is only partial; in the short run, output prices are more flexible than input prices, which are sticky and do not adjust.

In summary, in the short run, expansionary monetary policy reduces unemployment (u) and increases real GDP (Y). In addition, the overall price level (P) rises somewhat as flexible prices increase in the short run. These results are summarized in the table at the bottom of Figure 31.1.

Before moving on, let's step back and consider the results of the expansion. They seem positive, right? After all, unemployment goes down, and real GDP goes up. This macroeconomic result is consistent with the way monetary policy affected your hypothetical college apparel firm. Real employment and real output expand from the increase in the money supply. However, later in the chapter, we will see that these benefits do not help everyone in the economy.

ECONOMICS IN THE REAL WORLD

MONETARY POLICY IN THE AGE OF THE CORONAVIRUS

The Fed versus COVID-19.

Since its creation, the Fed has squared off against many threats to the American economy. In the first half of 2020, it faced an unexpected new enemy: COVID-19. As this disease forced Americans to stay home and avoid public gatherings, whole sectors of the economy were hit by a massive demand shock. Restaurants, airlines, and sports and entertainment venues all suffered near-total revenue loss and had to lay off workers. On the supply side, automotive plants shut down, movie production companies stopped filming, and colleges and universities closed their campuses. The combined effect of all the economic upheaval was an instant economic contraction.

The Fed responded with lightning speed, using its traditional tools. It cut the **federal funds rate** (the rate banks pay to borrow from each other) target to nearly zero in order to reduce the rates on consumer loans (see Figure 31.2). Remarkably, the Fed also eliminated all reserve requirements, to encourage commercial banks to issue loans, and cut the discount rate to nearly zero. Additionally, the Fed announced it would buy enormous amounts of Treasury bonds and mortgage-backed securities. This amounted to a new round of quantitative easing, the tactic adopted by the Fed during the Great Recession.

The **federal funds rate** is the interest rate on loans between private banks.

The Fed's most surprising action, however, took it into new territory: it added corporate bonds to its mix of asset purchases. The Fed said it would stick to investment-grade bonds and bond funds, but the takeaway message for the markets was that the Fed was ready to do whatever it took to shore up the economy. That included the unprecedented act of lending money directly to large corporations. The Fed even went a step further, saying that it would support lending to smaller businesses as well. Overall, the Fed signaled that it was willing to purchase almost any debt needed "to support smooth market functioning."* These are drastic changes for the U.S. central bank that just 13 years earlier was lending only to commercial banks.

In the Spring of 2022, the Fed responded to rising inflation with a rapid series of increases in the federal funds target rate.

*Board of Governors of the Federal Reserve System, press release, "Federal Reserve Announces Extensive New Measures to Support the Economy," March 23, 2020, https://www.federalreserve.gov/newsevents/pressreleases/monetary20200323b.htm.

REAL VERSUS NOMINAL EFFECTS We have seen that changes in the quantity of money lead to real changes in the economy. You may wonder: if a central bank can create jobs and real GDP by simply increasing the money supply, why would it ever stop? After all, fiat money is just paper! The answer is that

FIGURE 31.2

Expansionary Monetary Policy during Two Recessions

The Fed uses its monetary policy tools to target the federal funds rate, pushing it lower during recessionary periods and raising it to head off potential inflation when the economy is expanding rapidly. From data presented in this graphic, you can see that the Fed dropped the federal funds rate in response to the Great Recession and then again in 2020, at the onset of the coronavirus recession.

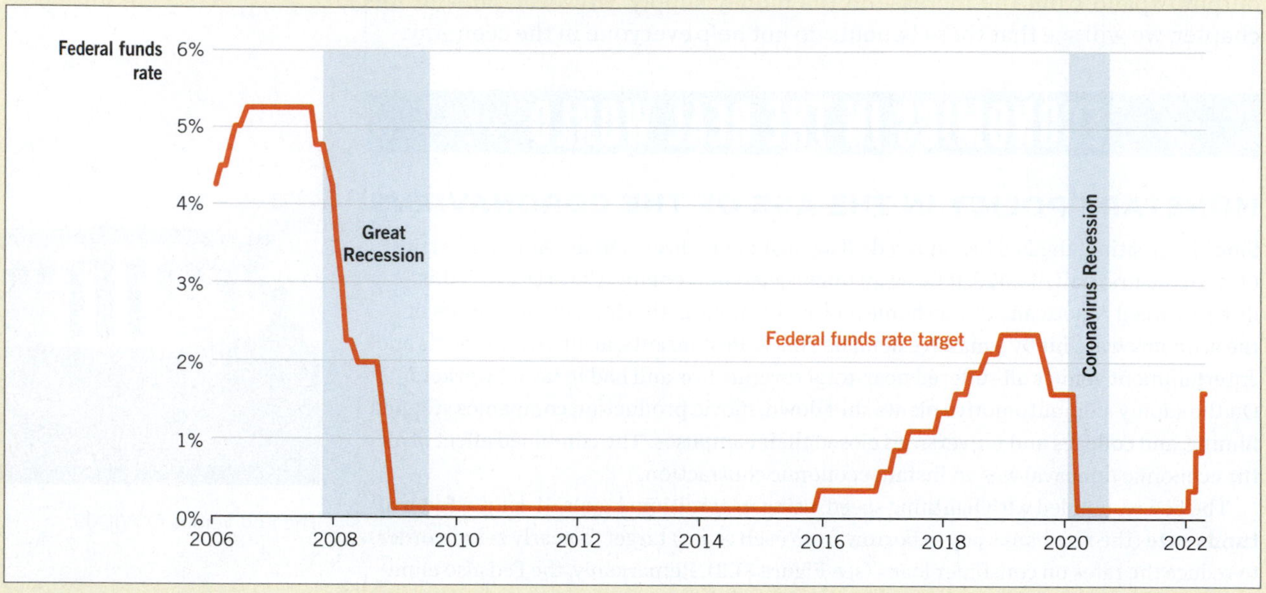

How would you like it if new money entered the economy through backpacks full of currency given to all college students?

while there is a short-run incentive to increase the money supply, these effects wear off in the long run, as prices adjust and then drive down the value of money.

Think of it this way: Let's say the Fed's preferred method of increasing the money supply is to hand all college students backpacks full of newly printed bills. This is a variation on a thought experiment suggested by economist Milton Friedman, involving money dropped from a helicopter. Not a bad idea, right? But let's focus on the macroeconomic effects. Eventually, the new money devalues the entire money supply, because prices rise. But because college students get the money first, you get it before any prices adjust. So these new funds represent an increase in real purchasing power for you. This is why monetary policy can have immediate, real short-run effects: initially, no prices have adjusted. But as prices adjust in the long run, the effects of the new money wear off.

Injecting new money into the economy eventually causes inflation, but inflation doesn't happen right away, and prices do not rise uniformly. During the time that prices are increasing, the value of money is constantly moving downward. Figure 31.3 illustrates the real purchasing power of money as time goes by. Panel (a) shows adjustments to the price level. When new money enters the economy (at time t_0), the price level begins to rise in the short run and then reaches its new level in the long run (at time t_{LR}). Panel (b) shows the value of a dollar relative to these price-level adjustments. When the new money enters the economy, each dollar has its highest value, because prices have not

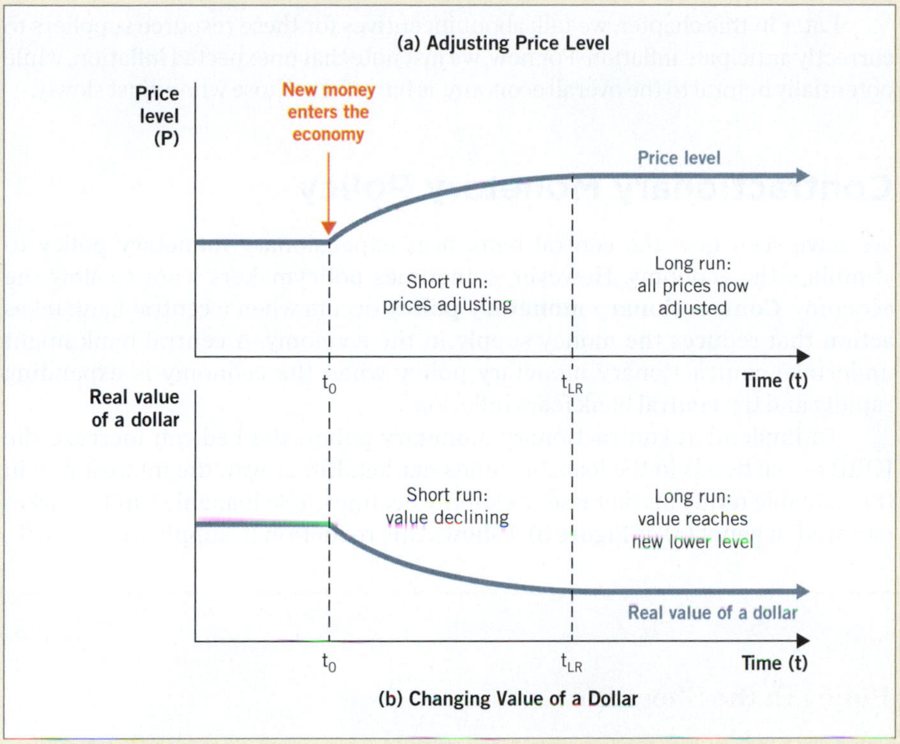

FIGURE 31.3

The Real Value of Money as Prices Adjust

(a) If the central bank increases the money supply at time t_0, the price level begins rising in the short run. In the long run, all prices adjust and the price level reaches its new higher level. (b) As the price level increases, the real value of a dollar declines throughout the short run. In the long run, at t_{LR}, the real value of a dollar reaches a new lower level.

yet adjusted. In the short run, as prices rise, the real purchasing power of each dollar gradually falls. In the long run, all prices adjust, and the real value of each dollar reaches its lower level. At this point, the real effects of the monetary policy dissipate completely.

UNEXPECTED INFLATION HURTS SOME PEOPLE Let's now consider how expansionary monetary policy affects different people across the economy. The basic macroeconomic results, summarized in Figure 31.1, seem very positive: real GDP goes up, the unemployment rate falls, and there is some inflation. Consider that you are living in an economy where these conditions exist. Everywhere you look, the news seems positive, as the media, politicians, and firms focus on the expanding economy. But this action does not help everybody.

For example, consider workers who signed a two-year contract just before the inflation hit the economy. These workers now pay more for goods and services such as groceries, gasoline, education, and health care—yet their wages were set before the inflation occurred. In real terms, these workers experience a pay cut. Monetary policy derives its potency from sticky prices, but if your price (or wage) is stuck, inflation hurts you.

Inflation harms input suppliers that have sticky prices. In addition to workers, lenders (the suppliers of funds used for expansion) are another prominent group harmed when inflation is greater than anticipated. Imagine that you are a banker who extends a loan with an interest rate of 3%, but then the inflation rate turns out to be 5%. The Fisher equation, discussed in Chapter 22, implies that the loan's real interest rate is actually −2%. A negative interest rate definitely harms your bank!

Later in this chapter, we talk about incentives for these resource suppliers to correctly anticipate inflation. For now, we just note that unexpected inflation, while potentially helpful to the overall economy, is harmful to those who adjust slowly.

Contractionary Monetary Policy

Contractionary monetary policy occurs when a central bank acts to decrease the money supply.

We have seen how the central bank uses expansionary monetary policy to stimulate the economy. However, sometimes policymakers want to slow the economy. **Contractionary monetary policy** occurs when a central bank takes action that reduces the money supply in the economy. A central bank might undertake contractionary monetary policy when the economy is expanding rapidly and the central bank fears inflation.

To implement contractionary monetary policy, the Fed can increase the IORB or sell bonds in the loanable funds market. Either way, the interest rate in the loanable funds market rises as supply declines. The loanable funds market pictured in panel (a) of Figure 31.4 shows this reduction in supply from S_1 to S_2.

FIGURE 31.4

Contractionary Monetary Policy in the Short Run

(a) The central bank sells bonds, which pulls funds out of the loanable funds market. This action decreases the supply of loanable funds (S_1 shifts to S_2) and increases the interest rate from 3% to 4%. The higher interest rate leads to a decrease in the quantity of investment demand (D) from \$200 billion to \$190 billion, and this outcome decreases aggregate demand (AD). (b) The decrease in aggregate demand (from AD_1 to AD_2) causes real GDP to decline from \$20 trillion to \$19.5 trillion and induces unemployment in the short run. The general price level also falls to 95 but does not fully adjust in the short run.

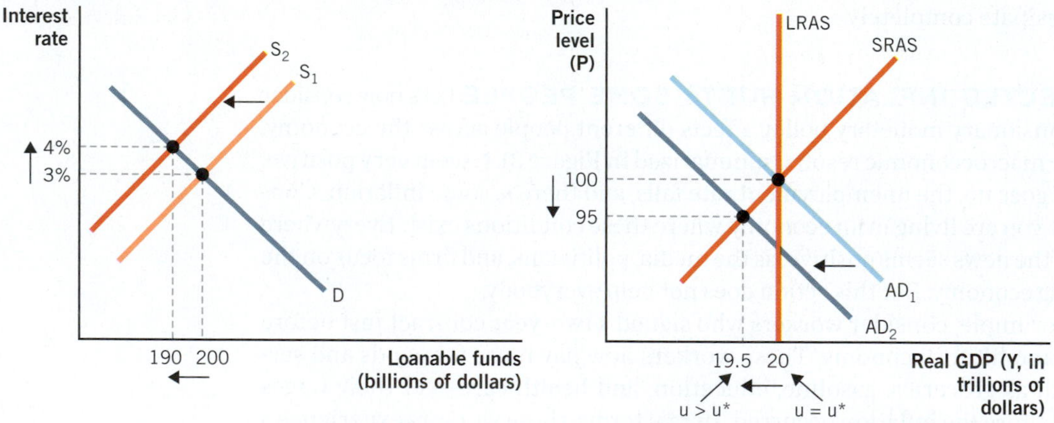

(a) The Loanable Funds Market

(b) Aggregate Demand and Aggregate Supply

Results summary	Y	u	P
Short run	↓	↑	↓

The interest rate rises, and equilibrium investment falls from $200 billion to $190 billion.

When investment falls, aggregate demand falls. Panel (b) of Figure 31.4 illustrates a fall in aggregate demand from AD_1 to AD_2. In the short run, real GDP decreases from $20 trillion to $19.5 trillion, the unemployment rate increases, and the price level decreases.

These short-run results are again the result of fixed resource prices for the firm. A lower money supply leads to downward pressure on prices (P), but sticky resource prices mean that firms cannot adjust their workers' wages or the terms of their loans in the short run. Therefore, firms reduce output and lay off some workers. This is why we see real GDP (Y) falling and the unemployment rate (u) rising. These results are summarized in the table at the bottom of the figure.

ECONOMICS IN THE REAL WORLD

MONETARY POLICY'S CONTRIBUTION TO THE GREAT DEPRESSION

What happens when all these people want to withdraw their funds?

As if monetary policy is not hard enough, consider that the money supply is not completely controlled by a central bank. In Chapter 30, we explained how the actions of private individuals and banks can increase or decrease the money supply via the money multiplier. Banks increase the money supply when they loan out reserves, and they decrease the money supply when they hold more reserves. In addition, individuals like you and me increase the money supply when we deposit funds into bank accounts, and the banks multiply that money by making loans. When we withdraw our funds and hold on to more currency, we decrease the money supply because banks cannot multiply those funds.

Now imagine a scenario with massive bank failures and very little deposit insurance. As more and more banks fail, people withdraw their funds all over the country. While it makes sense that individuals would want to withdraw their money, as people all over the country continue to remove money from banks, the money supply declines significantly. The reduction in the money supply leads to an economic contraction, similar to the scenario we saw in Figure 31.4.

This type of monetary contraction is exactly what happened at the beginning of the Great Depression. From 1929 to 1933, prior to the establishment of federal deposit insurance, over 9,000 banks failed in the United States. Because of these bank failures, people began holding their money outside the banking system. This action contributed to a significant contraction in the money supply. Figure 31.5 shows the money supply prior to and during the Great Depression. After peaking at $676 billion in 1931, the M2 money supply fell to just $564 billion in 1933. This drastic decline was one of the major causes of the Great Depression. In Chapter 27, we referred to policy errors as one of the causes of the decline in aggregate demand that led to the Great Depression. Economists today agree that the Federal Reserve should have done more to offset the decline in the money supply at the onset of the Great Depression. This was perhaps one of the biggest macroeconomic policy errors in U.S. history.

FIGURE 31.5

U.S. Money Supply before and during the Great Depression

The M2 money supply grew to $676 billion in 1931, but then plummeted to $564 billion by 1933. The huge decline in the money supply was a major contributor to the Great Depression. (Values for real money supply are expressed in 2012 dollars.)

Source: U.S. Bureau of the Census, *Historical Statistics of the United States, Colonial Times to 1970.*

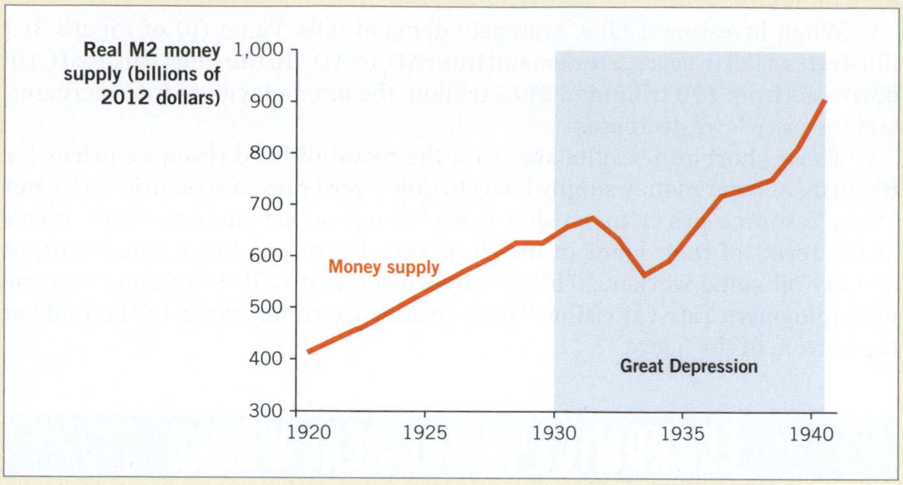

PRACTICE WHAT YOU KNOW

The Federal Open Market Committee is the group that determines monetary policy. It meets once a month.

Expansionary versus Contractionary Monetary Policy: Monetary Policy in the Short Run

QUESTION: In the short run, how does expansionary monetary policy affect real GDP, unemployment, and the price level in the economy?

ANSWER: Real GDP increases, the unemployment rate falls, and the price level rises as all flexible prices adjust.

QUESTION: In the short run, how does contractionary monetary policy affect real GDP, unemployment, and the price level in the economy?

ANSWER: Real GDP decreases, the unemployment rate rises, and the price level falls as all flexible prices adjust.

QUESTION: What real-world circumstance might lead to contractionary monetary policy?

ANSWER: If members of the Federal Open Market Committee at the Federal Reserve thought that inflation was an imminent danger, they might implement contractionary monetary policy.

CHALLENGE QUESTION: What is the interest rate that the Fed influences most directly, and why is this rate a good gauge of the money supply in the economy?

ANSWER: The Fed targets the federal funds rate, which is the rate that banks charge each other for very short-term loans. This interest rate tells the Fed whether the money supply is too tight or too loose. If the federal funds rate rises, the money supply is deemed too tight. If the federal funds rate falls, the money supply is deemed too loose.

Why Doesn't Monetary Policy Always Work?

So far, we have seen that monetary policy can have real effects on the macroeconomy. By shifting aggregate demand, monetary policy can affect real GDP, unemployment, and the price level. But most economists feel that monetary policy is limited in what it can accomplish. In this section, we consider three of these limitations. First, we look at the diminished effects of monetary policy in the long run. Next, we consider how expectations can dampen the effects of monetary policy. Finally, we examine the limitations of monetary policy when economic downturns are caused by shifts in aggregate supply rather than aggregate demand.

Long-Run Adjustments

We have noted that some prices take longer to adjust than others and that the long run is a period long enough for *all* prices to adjust. Output prices can adjust relatively quickly. Think about the output prices at a coffee shop, which are often displayed in chalk behind the cash register; they are easy to change in the short run. In contrast, input prices, such as workers' wages, are often the slowest prices to adjust. After all, wages are sometimes set by contracts; moreover, money illusion (see Chapter 21) can make input suppliers reluctant to lower their prices. But the long run is a period sufficient for all prices to change, even wage contracts, which eventually expire.

Both types of prices affect the decisions made at firms across the economy, and therefore both affect output and unemployment. For example, consider your hypothetical small business producing and selling college apparel. Earlier in this chapter, you secured a loan to open a new retail location because the Fed increased the money supply, which expanded the supply of loanable funds. When you initially received your loan, costs for resources such as workers, equipment, inventory, and a physical plant were relatively low because prices for these resources are sticky and had not yet adjusted. But in the long run, these resource prices adjust. If everything works out well for you, the monetary expansion leads to new demand for your product and you can keep your new store open. But it is also possible that when the prices of resources rise—in the long run—you may not be able to afford them. At that point, with your costs rising, you may have to reduce your output, lay off some workers, and perhaps even close your new retail location. In the long run, as prices adjust throughout the macroeconomy, the stimulating effects of expansionary monetary policy wear off.

Let's see how this process works for the entire economy. Figure 31.6 illustrates long-run macroeconomic adjustments to expansionary monetary policy. As you can see in the graph, expansionary monetary policy shifts aggregate demand from AD_1 to AD_2. This action moves the economy from long-run equilibrium at point A to short-run equilibrium at point b (with a temporary change in real GDP and unemployment). In the long run, as resource prices rise, short-run aggregate supply shifts to the left from $SRAS_1$ to $SRAS_2$, and the economy moves to a new long-run equilibrium at point C. When we compare the new long-run equilibrium to the situation prior to the application of monetary

FIGURE 31.6

Expansionary Monetary Policy in the Long Run

Beginning in equilibrium at point A, an increase in the money supply shifts aggregate demand from AD_1 to AD_2; this action moves the economy to a new short-run equilibrium at point b. Equilibrium at point b is relevant only in the short run, because all prices have not yet adjusted. In the long run, resource prices adjust. This outcome shifts short-run aggregate supply from $SRAS_1$ to $SRAS_2$, and the economy moves to a new long-run equilibrium at point C.

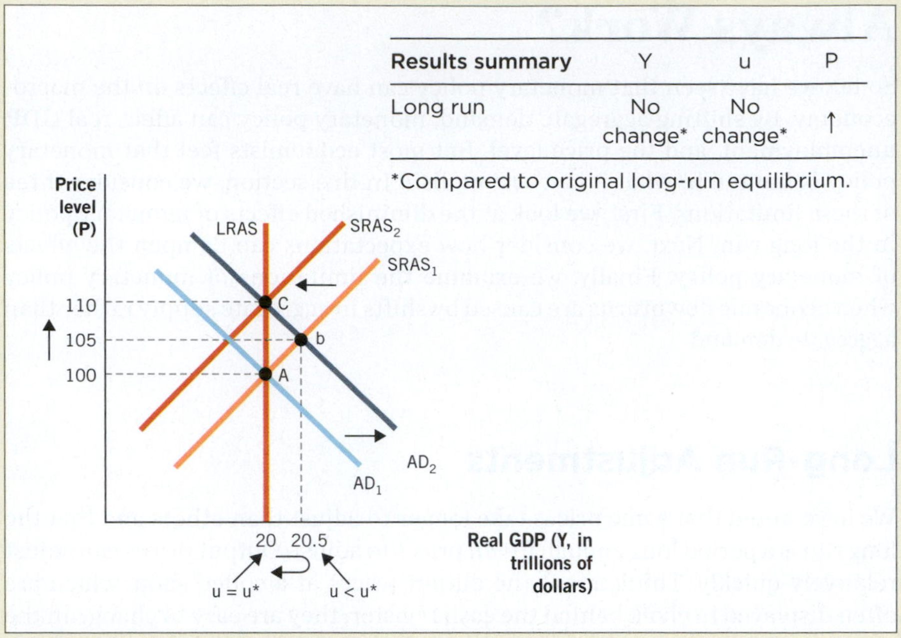

policy, we see that there is no change in real GDP (Y) or unemployment (u), but there is an increase in the price level from 100 to 110.

One important implication of these long-run results is the lack of real economic effects from monetary policy; in the long run, all prices adjust. Therefore, in the long run, monetary policy does not affect real GDP or unemployment. The only predictable result of more money in the economy over the long run is inflation. As we discussed in Chapter 21, the cause of inflation is monetary growth. You now can understand why, in the context of the aggregate demand–aggregate supply model.

From one perspective, our long-run results may seem strange: central banks can't do much in the long run to affect the real economy. However, this statement might also seem logical, since it's possible to increase the money supply by just printing more paper money. But printing more paper money doesn't affect the economy's long-run productivity or its ability to produce; these outcomes are determined by resources, technology, and institutions. The idea that the money supply does not affect real economic variables is known as **monetary neutrality**.

Monetary neutrality is the idea that the money supply does not affect real economic variables.

Given that money is neutral in the long run, why do the Federal Reserve and other central banks employ short-run monetary policy? In fact, many of the substantive debates in macroeconomics focus on the relative importance of the short run versus the long run. Some economists believe it is best to focus on short-run effects, which are very real. After all, during recessions people often lose their jobs, which can be a very painful experience. When the money supply expands, firms can borrow more cheaply and hire more workers. From this perspective, central banks ought to take a very active role in the macroeconomy by increasing the money supply during economic downturns and contracting the money supply during economic expansions. This policy can then potentially smooth out the business cycle.

Other economists discount the short-run expansionary effects of monetary policy and instead focus on the problems of inflation. In Chapter 21, we explored the negative effects of inflation. These include price confusion, wealth redistribution, and uncertainty about future price levels. These by-products of inflation can stifle economic growth.

In the next section, we consider the potency of monetary policy when market participants expect inflation ahead of time.

Adjustments in Expectations

Unexpected inflation harms workers and other resource suppliers who have fixed prices in the short run; therefore, workers normally expect a certain level of inflation and expect to see it reflected by annual pay adjustments or in contractual cost-of-living adjustments that are sometimes tied to inflation rates. The key incentive for anticipating the correct rate of inflation is straightforward: surprise inflation harms people. But when inflation is expected, the real effects on the economy are limited.

Let's look at inflation expectations in the context of the aggregate demand–aggregate supply model. Figure 31.7 shows how monetary expansion affects aggregate demand and aggregate supply when it is expected. Expansionary monetary policy shifts aggregate demand from AD_1 to AD_2. But if this effect is expected, short-run aggregate supply shifts to the left from $SRAS_1$ to $SRAS_2$.

In Chapter 26, we discussed how short-run aggregate supply shifts back when workers and resource suppliers expect higher future prices, because they do not want their real prices to fall. If short-run aggregate supply shifts along with the shift in aggregate demand, the economy goes immediately to

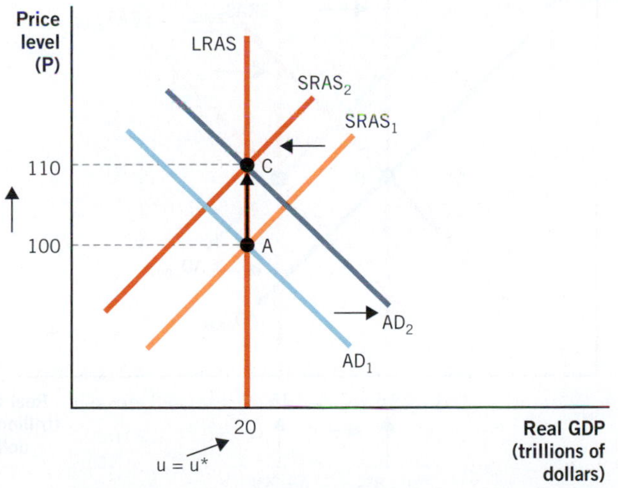

FIGURE 31.7

Completely Expected Monetary Policy

If expansionary monetary policy is expected, short-run aggregate supply shifts along with the shift in aggregate demand, and the economy moves directly from equilibrium at point A to point C. In this case, there are no real effects from the monetary policy, even in the short run. The only lasting change is nominal because the price level rises from 100 to 110.

equilibrium at point C. Therefore, monetary policy has no real effect on the economy—real GDP and unemployment do not change. The only lasting change is nominal, because the price level rises from 100 to 110. Monetary policy has real effects only when some prices are sticky. But if inflation is expected, prices are not sticky; they adjust because people plan on the inflation. To the extent that all prices rise, the effect of monetary policy is limited, even in the short run.

Aggregate Supply Shifts and the Great Recession

We have seen that monetary policy affects the economy by shifting aggregate demand. Thus, if a recession results from reduced aggregate demand, monetary policy can stabilize the economy and return it to higher levels of real GDP and lower unemployment. But not all downturns are a result of aggregate demand shifts. Declines in aggregate supply can also lead to recession. And when supply shifts cause the downturn, monetary policy is less likely to restore the economy to its prerecession conditions.

The Great Recession that began in 2007 seems to have included both shifts of aggregate supply and shifts of aggregate demand. In Chapter 27, we argued that the widespread problems in financial markets at that time negatively affected key institutions in the macroeconomy. Further, new financial regulations restricted banks' ability to lend at levels equal to those in effect prior to 2008. The result was a shift backward in long-run aggregate supply. In addition, as people's real wealth and expected future income levels declined, aggregate demand shifted to the left.

Figure 31.8 shows how the decline in both aggregate demand and aggregate supply might affect the economy. Initially, the economy is in equilibrium

FIGURE 31.8

Aggregate Supply–Induced Recession

Initially, in 2007, the economy is in equilibrium at point A. Then the long-run and short-run aggregate supply curves shift to the left, to $LRAS_{2008}$ and $SRAS_{2008}$. In addition, aggregate demand shifts to the left to AD_{2008}. This combination of shifts takes the economy to a new equilibrium at point B. At point B, monetary policy is limited in its ability to move the economy back to its original level of real GDP because monetary policy affects the economy through aggregate demand.

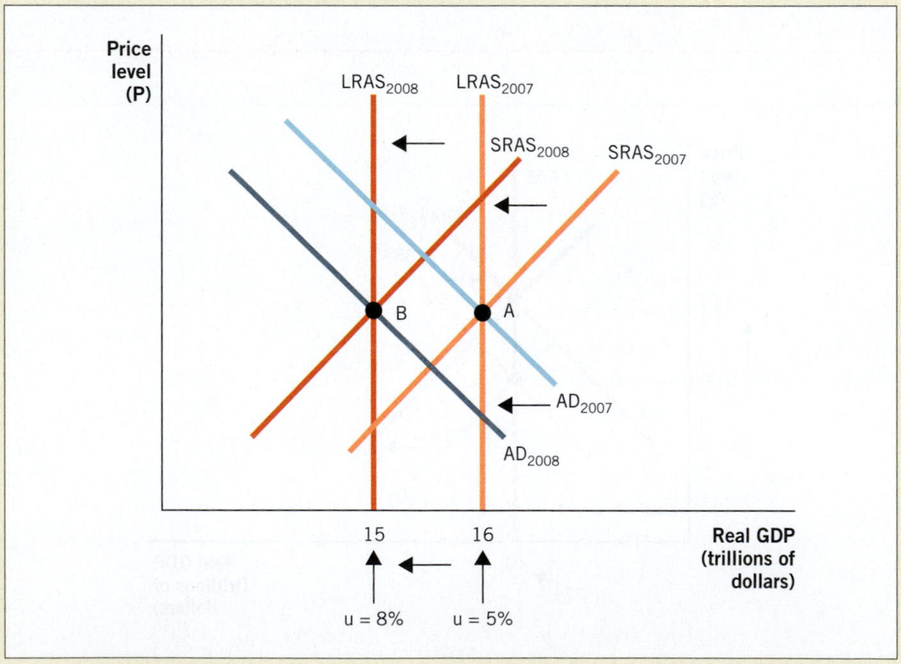

PRACTICE WHAT YOU KNOW

Monetary Policy Isn't Always Effective: Why Couldn't Monetary Policy Pull Us out of the Great Recession?

The Great Recession officially lasted from December 2007 to June 2009. But the effects lingered on for several years thereafter, with slow growth of real GDP and high unemployment rates. These effects all occurred despite several doses of expansionary monetary policy. Not only did the Fed push short-term interest rates to nearly 0%, but it also engaged in several rounds of quantitative easing, purchasing hundreds of billions of dollars' worth of long-term bonds.

QUESTION: What are three possible reasons why monetary policy was not able to restore expansionary growth during and after the Great Recession?

ANSWER:

1. *Monetary policy is ineffective in the long run.* While we don't know the exact length of the short run, all prices certainly had time to adjust by 2010 or 2011, yet the economy was still sluggish. Thus, one possibility is that all prices adjusted, so the effects of monetary policy wore off. This answer alone is probably inadequate, given that the effects of monetary policy were not evident even in the short run.
2. *Monetary policy was expected.* It seems unlikely that monetary policy is much of a surprise nowadays. The Federal Reserve releases official statements after each monetary policy meeting and generally announces the direction it will follow for several months in advance.
3. *The downturn was at least partially due to an aggregate supply shift.* Because monetary policy works through aggregate demand, the effects of monetary policy can be limited if shifts in aggregate supply cause a recession.

at point A, with the aggregate supply and aggregate demand curves from 2007. Then aggregate demand and aggregate supply shift to the left, to the 2008 levels. When this happens, real GDP declines from $16 trillion to $15 trillion, and the unemployment rate rises from 5% to 8%—levels similar to the actual experience during this period. Further, this rise in the unemployment rate was at least partially due to new structural unemployment that raised the natural rate of unemployment.

The dilemma is that at point B, monetary policy is limited in its ability to permanently move output back to its prior level. Even if monetary policy shifts aggregate demand back to AD_{2007}, this shift is not enough to eliminate the recession. Furthermore, as we have stressed throughout this chapter, the effects of monetary policy wear off in the long run.

Thus, in the wake of the Great Recession, the U.S. economy continued to struggle with slow growth and high unemployment, even after significant monetary policy interventions. The bottom line is that monetary policy does not enable us to avoid or fix every economic downturn.

What Is the Phillips Curve?

We have seen that monetary policy can stimulate the economy in the short run. Increasing the money supply increases aggregate demand, which can lead to higher real GDP, lower unemployment, and a higher price level (inflation). The relationship between inflation and unemployment is of particular interest to economists and noneconomists alike; it is at the heart of the debate regarding the power of monetary policy to affect the economy. In this section, we examine this relationship by looking at the Phillips curve.

The Traditional Short-Run Phillips Curve

The **Phillips curve** indicates a short-run negative relationship between inflation and unemployment rates.

In 1958, British economist A. W. Phillips noted a negative relationship between wage inflation and unemployment rates in the United Kingdom. Soon thereafter, U.S. economists Paul Samuelson and Robert Solow extended the analysis to inflation and unemployment rates in the United States. This short-run negative relationship between inflation and unemployment rates became known as the **Phillips curve**. Before looking at Phillips curve data, let's consider the theory behind the Phillips curve in the context of the aggregate demand–aggregate supply model.

Panel (a) of Figure 31.9 shows how unexpected monetary expansion affects the economy in the short run. Initially, with aggregate demand at AD_1 and the

FIGURE 31.9

Aggregate Demand, Aggregate Supply, and the Phillips Curve

(a) This graph shows the effect of unexpected monetary expansion in the short run. Initially, the economy is in equilibrium at point A, with a price level of 100, real GDP of $20 trillion, and an unemployment rate of 5%. Aggregate demand shifts from AD_1 to AD_2, which moves the economy to short-run equilibrium at point b. The move to point b is accompanied by an increase in the inflation rate to 5% (the price level rises from 100 to 105) but a lower unemployment rate of just 3%. (b) Here we see the two equilibrium points in a new graph that plots the negative relationship between inflation and unemployment rates. This graph, known as a Phillips curve, clarifies that higher inflation can lead to lower levels of unemployment in the short run.

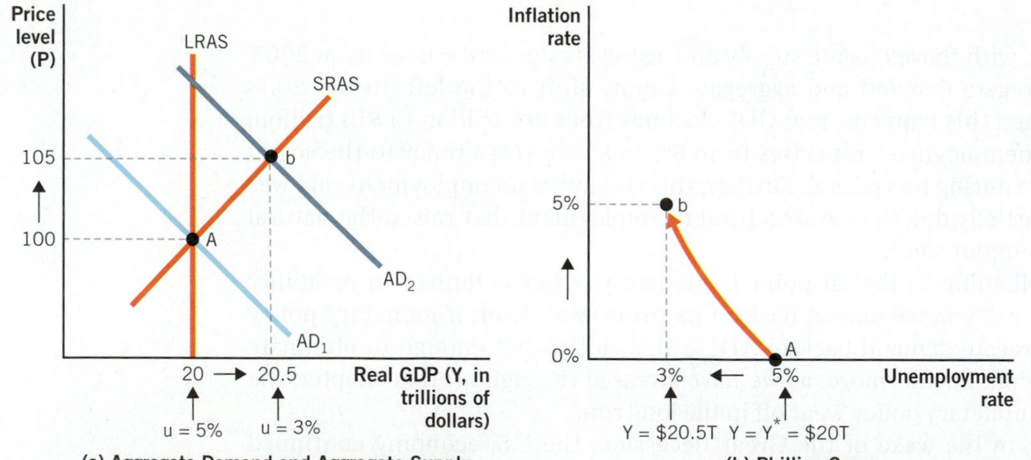

(a) Aggregate Demand and Aggregate Supply

(b) Phillips Curve

price level at 100, the economy is in long-run equilibrium at point A with real GDP (Y) at $20 trillion and the unemployment rate equal to 5%. For this example, we assume the natural rate of unemployment is exactly 5%.

Then expansionary monetary policy shifts aggregate demand to AD_2, which leads to a new short-run equilibrium at point b. Let's focus on the changes to prices and the unemployment rate. The monetary expansion leads to a 5% inflation rate as the price level rises to 105 (indicated in panel b). The unemployment rate drops to 3% as real GDP (Y) expands from $20 trillion to $20.5 trillion. The end result includes both inflation and lower unemployment.

This is the theory behind the Phillips curve relationship: monetary expansion stimulates the economy and brings some inflation, and this outcome reduces the unemployment rate. Similarly, lower inflation is associated with higher unemployment rates. This negative relationship between inflation and unemployment is captured in panel (b) of Figure 31.9, which graphs a Phillips curve. Initially, at point A, the inflation rate is 0% and the unemployment rate is 5%. But when the inflation rate rises to 5%, the unemployment rate drops to 3%.

This negative relationship between inflation and unemployment rates is consistent with Phillips's observations and also with what Samuelson and Solow saw when they plotted historical data. Figure 31.10 plots U.S. inflation and unemployment rates from 1948 to 1969, which includes the period just before and just after the work of Samuelson and Solow. The numerical values plotted represent the years: for example, point 48 represents the year 1948. It is not hard to visualize a Phillips curve relationship in this data: most years with high

FIGURE 31.10

U.S. Inflation and Unemployment Rates, 1948–1969

Data from 1948 to 1969 was very consistent with standard Phillips curve predictions: lower unemployment rates were consistently correlated with higher inflation rates. (Each number in the graph represents a particular year plotted for inflation and unemployment for that year. For example, 51 represents the year 1951, when the inflation rate was about 8% and the unemployment rate was about 3%.)

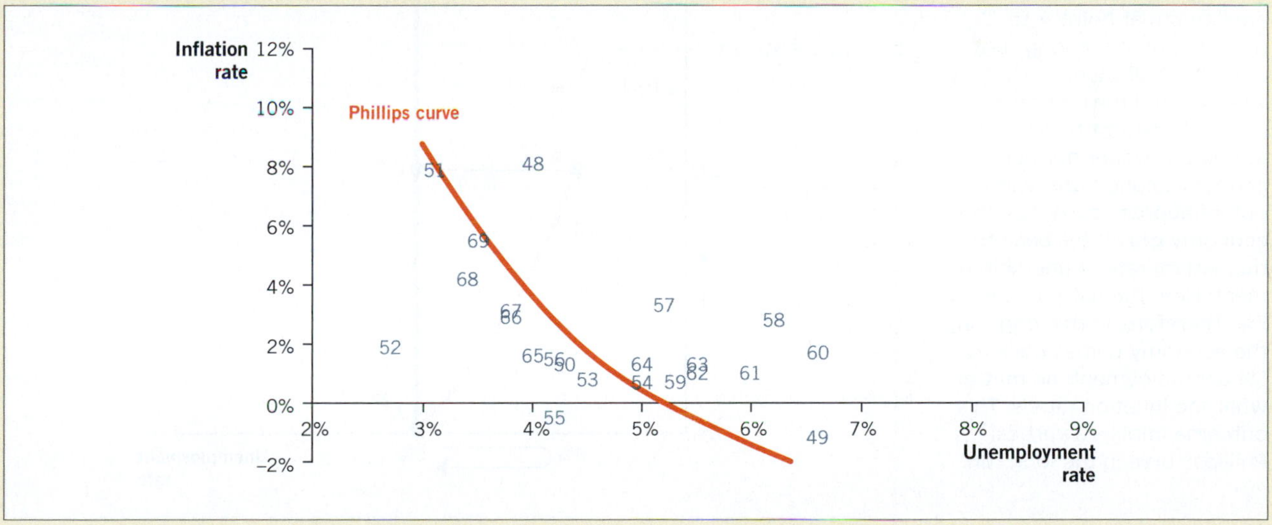

inflation rates had low unemployment rates, while most years with low inflation rates had high unemployment rates.

The Phillips curve implies a powerful role for monetary policy. It implies that a central bank can choose higher or lower unemployment rates simply by adjusting the rate of inflation in an economy. If this is a realistic observation, a central bank can always steer an economy out of recession, simply by creating inflation.

But we have already seen that monetary policy does not always have real effects on the economy. Next we consider the long run, when the real effects of monetary policy wear off. After that, we look at how expectations also mitigate the effects of monetary policy.

The Long-Run Phillips Curve

When all prices are free to adjust, there are no real effects from monetary policy. That is, there are no effects on real GDP or unemployment. Therefore, the long-run Phillips curve looks different from the standard, short-run Phillips curve. Figure 31.11 shows both short-run and long-run Phillips curves. Initially, at point A, there is no inflation in the economy and the unemployment rate is 5%. Then monetary expansion increases the inflation rate to 5%, and the unemployment rate falls to 3% in the short run. This short-run equilibrium is indicated as point b. But when prices adjust in the long run, the unemployment rate returns

FIGURE 31.11

Short-Run and Long-Run Phillips Curves

In the short run, inflation can lead to lower unemployment, moving the economy from equilibrium at point A to point b. But in the long run, the effects of monetary policy wear off and the unemployment rate returns to equilibrium at point C. Under normal economic conditions, without inflationary surprises, the economy gravitates back to the natural rate of unemployment. Here the natural rate is 5%. Therefore, in the long run, the economy comes back to 5% unemployment, no matter what the inflation rate is. This outcome implies a vertical Phillips curve in the long run.

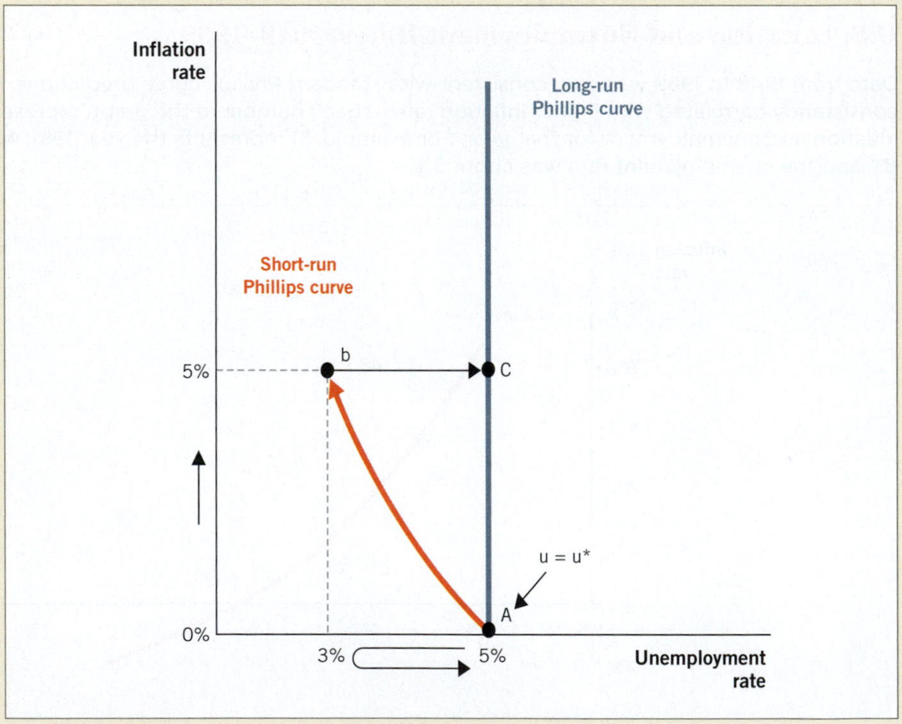

to 5% and the economy moves to a new equilibrium at point C. Inflation is the only result of monetary expansion in the long run.

In Figure 31.11, the unemployment rate is equal to the natural rate (5%) before inflation, and in the long run it returns to the natural rate. Thus, under normal economic conditions, including a scenario with no surprise inflation, we expect the unemployment rate to equal the natural rate ($u = u^*$). Monetary policy can push the unemployment rate down, but only in the short run.

We have also learned that the effects of inflation are dampened or eliminated when inflation is fully expected. We saw this earlier in the context of the aggregate demand–aggregate supply model. Now we look more closely at inflation expectations and how they affect the Phillips curve relationship.

Expectations and the Phillips Curve

We have seen that expected inflation has no real effects on the macroeconomy, even in the short run, because when inflation is expected, all prices adjust. To explore this further, we consider alternative theories of how people form expectations. This topic may seem like one for microeconomics or perhaps even psychology, but it is particularly relevant to monetary policy because the effects of expected inflation are completely different from the effects of unexpected inflation. When inflation is expected, long-term contracts can reflect inflation and mitigate its effects. But when inflation is unexpected, wages and other prices don't adjust immediately, and the result is economic expansion.

ADAPTIVE EXPECTATIONS THEORY In the late 1960s, economists Milton Friedman and Edmund Phelps hypothesized that people adapt their inflation expectations to their prior experience. For example, if the actual inflation rate is consistently 2% year after year, people won't expect 0% inflation; they'll expect 2% inflation. The contributions of Friedman and Phelps came to be known as adaptive expectations. **Adaptive expectations theory** holds that people's expectations of future inflation are based on their most recent experience. If the inflation rate is 5% in 2020, adaptive expectations theory predicts that people will also expect a 5% inflation rate in 2021.

Adaptive expectations theory holds that people's expectations of future inflation are based on their most recent experience.

Consider the hypothetical inflation pattern presented in Table 31.1. The second column shows actual inflation over the course of six years. The inflation rate starts at 0% but then goes up to 2% for two years, then increases to 4%

TABLE 31.1

Adaptive Expectations

Year	Actual inflation rate	Expected inflation rate	Error
2016	0%	—	0%
2017	2	0%	−2
2018	2	2	0
2019	4	2	−2
2020	4	4	0
2021	2	4	2

for two years, and then falls to 2% in the last year. If expectations are adaptive, actual inflation in the current period becomes expected inflation for the future. When actual inflation is expected inflation, there is no error, as indicated in the last column. For example, a 2% actual inflation rate in 2017 means people will expect 2% inflation in the future. So when the actual inflation rate is 2% in 2018, people are not surprised. Adaptive expectations theory predicts that people do not always underestimate inflation.

When the inflation rate *accelerates*, however, people do underestimate inflation. For example, if people experience a 2% inflation rate in 2018, they will expect this level for 2019. But in our example, the rate increases to 4% in 2019, which leads to an error of −2%. Note that it is also possible under adaptive expectations theory to overestimate inflation. Overestimation happens when inflation rates fall. For example, in 2021, people might anticipate a 4% inflation rate because they experienced that level in 2020. If the rate is actually 2%, they overestimate inflation by 2%.

The idea behind adaptive expectations theory is not overly complex, but it revolutionized the way economists think about monetary policy. If expectations adapt, then monetary policy may not have real effects, even in the short run. Expansionary monetary policy can stimulate the economy and reduce unemployment—but only if it is unexpected.

Incentives

This was the insight of Friedman and Phelps. Their basic reasoning was that people are not quite as simpleminded as the basic Phillips curve implies. Given that surprise inflation harms people, they have an incentive to anticipate inflation and, at the very least, learn from past experience. And yet, the data from the 1960s, shown in Figure 31.10, were certainly consistent with the traditional Phillips curve interpretation. But Friedman and Phelps challenged the accepted wisdom in 1968 and predicted that the Phillips curve relationship would not last. In particular, they predicted that high inflation would not always deliver low unemployment—a prediction that proved correct.

Figure 31.12 shows U.S. unemployment and inflation rates for the period 1948 to 1979, with data for the 1970s presented in orange. (As in Figure 31.10, the numerical value represents the year.) Clearly, the 1970s were a difficult decade for the macroeconomy. The prior Phillips curve relationship fell apart—compare Figure 31.12 with Figure 31.10. In the 1970s, inflation was high, and so was unemployment. These macroeconomic conditions are now known as **stagflation**, which is the combination of high unemployment rates and high inflation. The stagflation of the 1970s baffled many economists who believed in the validity of the Phillips curve.

Stagflation
is the combination of high unemployment and high inflation.

RATIONAL EXPECTATIONS THEORY Expectations theory evolved yet again in the 1970s and 1980s, in part because of disenchantment with certain implications of adaptive expectations. For example, according to adaptive expectations theory, market participants consistently underestimate inflation when it is accelerating and overestimate inflation when it is decelerating. Expectations are seemingly always a step behind reality. And these errors are predictable.

Rational expectations theory
holds that people form expectations on the basis of all available information.

Rational expectations theory holds that people form expectations on the basis of all available information. If people form expectations rationally, they use more than just today's current level of inflation to predict next year's. Rational expectations are different from adaptive expectations in that they are forward-looking, while adaptive expectations consider only past experience.

FIGURE 31.12

U.S. Inflation and Unemployment Rates, 1948–1979

The 1970s (data points in orange) showed that it is possible to have both high inflation and high unemployment. This decade proved that policymakers could not rely on a permanent, exploitable downward-sloping Phillips curve.

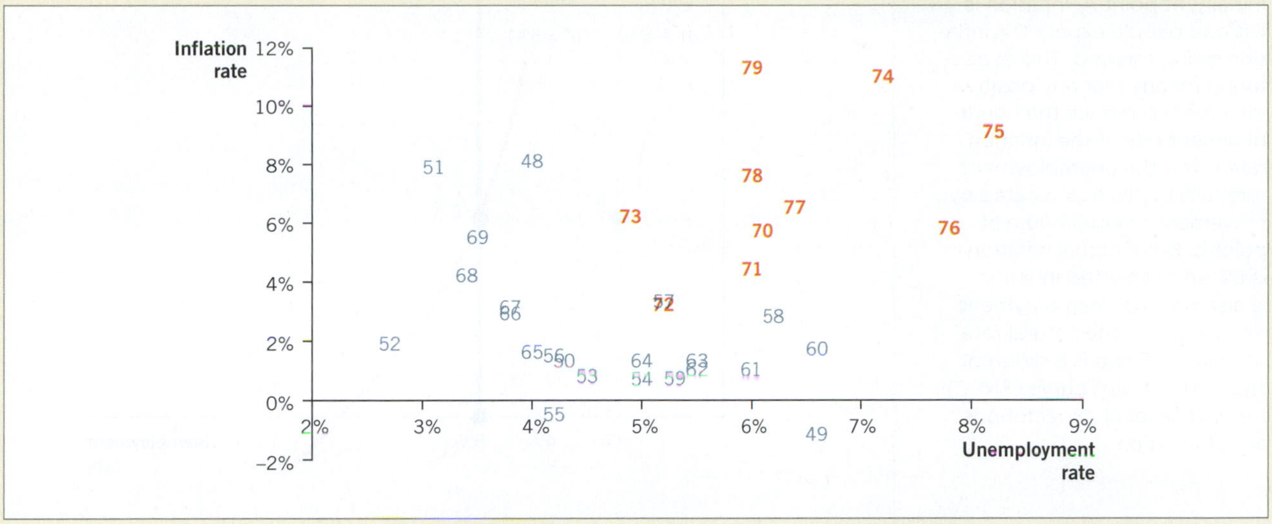

For example, imagine inflation is trending upward. Perhaps the actual inflation rate for three periods is 0%, then 2%, and then 4%. Expectations formed rationally recognize the trend and, looking to the future, predict 6%. This outcome is different from what would occur under adaptive expectations, which would instead imply an expectation of 4% in the fourth period, since that number is consistent with the most recent experience.

Rational expectations theory does not imply that people always predict inflation correctly. No one knows exactly what the level of inflation will be next year. Prediction errors are inevitable. But people are unlikely to underpredict consistently, even when inflation is accelerating. Rational expectations theory identifies prediction errors as random, like the flip of a coin—sometimes positive and sometimes negative.

. . . tick, tock, tick, tock, tick, _____ . . . What comes next?

A Modern View of the Phillips Curve

The short-run Phillips curve is built on the assumption that inflation expectations never adjust. But economists today recognize that the harmful effects of inflation provide an incentive to predict future inflation. Therefore, not all inflation is surprise inflation. And when inflation is not a surprise, it does not affect the unemployment rate. So we need to reconsider how different expectations affect the Phillips curve relationship.

Incentives

Consider a hypothetical economy in which policymakers have never used inflation to try to stimulate the economy. Let's say that the inflation rate is 0%

FIGURE 31.13

The Phillips Curve with Adjusting Expectations

Initially, at point A, inflation is 0% and people expect 0% inflation going forward. This expectation means that any positive inflation will reduce the unemployment rate. If the inflation rate is 5%, the unemployment rate falls to 3%, as indicated by movement to equilibrium at point b. But if actual inflation is 5% and expected inflation is also 5%, the unemployment rate moves to the natural rate at point C. There is a different short-run Phillips curve (SRPC) for each level of expectations about inflation.

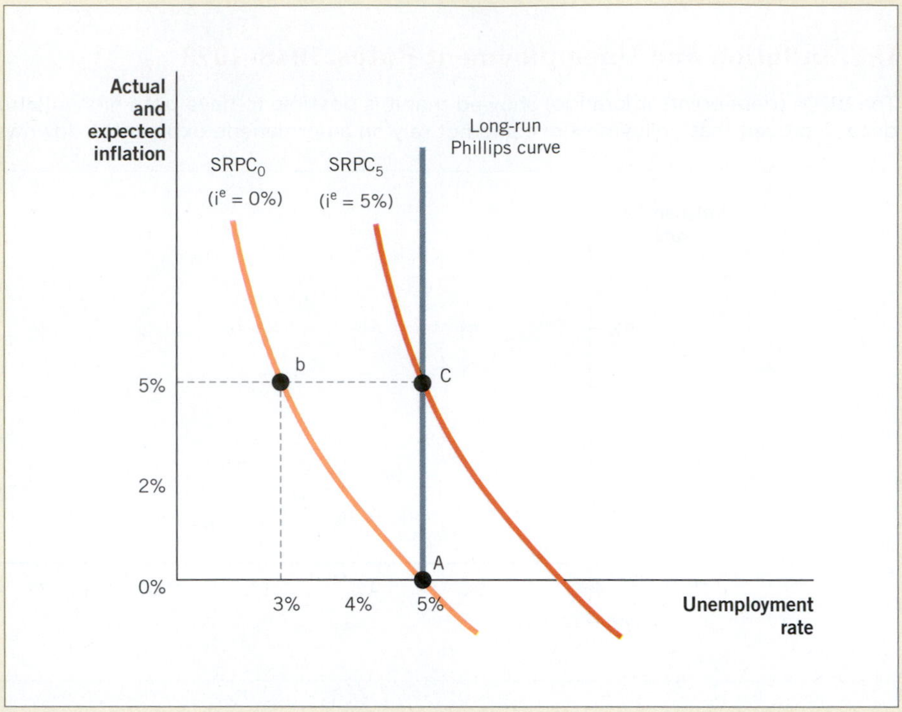

and market participants expect 0% inflation going forward. Figure 31.13 shows this initial situation as point A. Now, if the central bank undertakes policy to raise the inflation rate to 5%, the unemployment rate drops to 3% in the short run. This increase in inflation moves the economy up along the short-run Phillips curve that is labeled $SRPC_0$ (to indicate that expected inflation is 0%: $i^e = 0\%$). The 5% inflation moves the economy to short-run equilibrium at point b on $SRPC_0$.

Now consider what happens if people come to expect a 5% inflation rate. If workers and employers expect 5% inflation, they embed this rate into all long-term contracts. Therefore, when the 5% inflation arrives, it does not stimulate the economy or reduce unemployment. The economy moves to a new equilibrium at point C, which is on $SRPC_5$ (to indicate that expected inflation is now 5%: $i^e = 5\%$). When actual and expected inflation are both 5%, inflation does not reduce the unemployment rate. In summary, the downward-sloping Phillips curve relationship between inflation and unemployment holds only in the short run. In the long run, when expectations adjust, additional inflation does not reduce unemployment.

Figure 31.14 shows unemployment and inflation data from 1948 through 2021. From this complete data set, it seems clear that there is no long-run stable relationship between inflation and unemployment. In fact, the data appear to be randomly distributed. Economists today believe that there are many factors that influence the unemployment rate in the economy, and the inflation rate is just one factor.

FIGURE 31.14

U.S. Inflation and Unemployment Rates, 1948–2021

Data over the long run present a picture of inflation and unemployment rates that looks random. Clearly, the unemployment rate is not always correlated with the inflation rate in the long run.

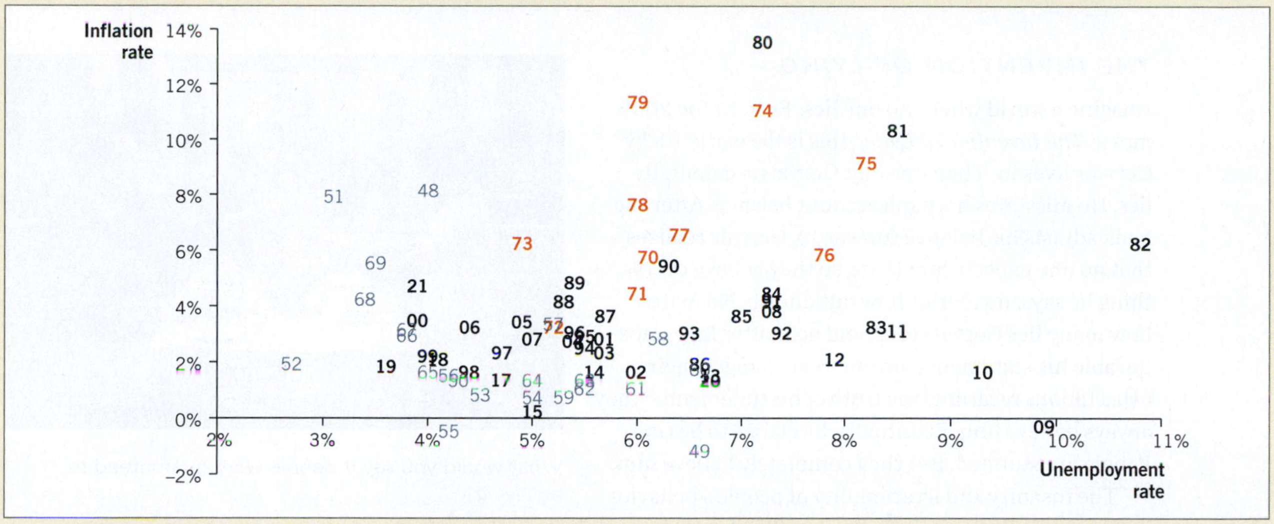

Implications for Monetary Policy

We can now use what we've learned about expectations theory and the Phillips curve to evaluate monetary policy recommendations. **Active monetary policy** involves the strategic use of monetary policy to counteract macroeconomic expansions and contractions. In the 1960s, before the development of expectations theory, monetary policy prescriptions were strictly activist: increase inflation during economic downturns, and reduce inflation when the economy is booming. This policy assumed that the Phillips curve relationship between inflation and unemployment would hold up in the long run.

Active monetary policy involves the strategic use of monetary policy to counteract macroeconomic expansions and contractions.

Modern expectations theory prescribes greater caution. If people anticipate the strategies of the central bank, the power of the monetary policy erodes. If expectations adjust, the optimal monetary policy is to maintain transparency and stability. This conclusion holds if expectations are formed either adaptively or rationally. Let's consider each of these scenarios in turn.

Consider a scenario in which policymakers expand the money supply to decrease the unemployment rate. Say the unemployment rate is clearly above the natural rate, and real GDP is not growing. If expectations are adaptive, inflation reduces the unemployment rate in the short run. Eventually, expectations adjust, and then the central bank needs to increase inflation again just to stay ahead of the adjusting expectations. For monetary policy to succeed in keeping the unemployment rate low, inflation has to accelerate and stay a step ahead of expectations. Essentially, the result is more and more inflation. Worse yet, if the central bank tries to reduce inflation levels, expected inflation then exceeds actual inflation, leading to increased unemployment in the short run. Thus, if

ECONOMICS *in the* MEDIA

Expectations

THE INVENTION OF LYING

Imagine a world where no one lies. Ever. In the 2009 movie *The Invention of Lying*, this is the world Ricky Gervais lives in. Then one day, Gervais accidentally lies. He misstates his bank account balance. After the bank adjusts his balance (upward!), Gervais realizes that no one expects him to lie, so they believe everything he says, no matter how outlandish. No matter how many lies Gervais tells, and no matter how unbelievable his statements, no one ever changes their expectations regarding the truth of his statements—they always believe him. Eventually, he claims to be God. People are stunned. But they completely believe him.

The insanity and irrationality of people's behavior in this movie illustrate exactly how silly it is to continually believe lies that come from the same source. The movie succeeds at being funny because no one in the real world would ever be as gullible or stupid as the people in this movie. In the real world, people would come to expect lies from Gervais. In economics lingo: expectations adjust.

What would you say if people were guaranteed to believe it?

Similarly, in the real world, people come to anticipate inflation when they experience it period after period. It makes no sense to expect 0% inflation if actual inflation has not been 0% for quite some time. In the real world, expectations adjust.

expectations are adaptive, activist monetary policy provides only temporary short-run gains in employment. In the long run, it produces high inflation or unemployment—or both, as it did in the 1970s.

If, instead, expectations are formed rationally, then activist monetary policy may yield no gains whatsoever. Because market participants use all available information when forming inflation expectations, the central bank is unlikely to achieve positive results from activist monetary policy, even in the short run.

Passive monetary policy occurs when central banks purposefully choose only to stabilize money and price levels through monetary policy.

Many economists feel that monetary policy surprise actions should be minimized. **Passive monetary policy** occurs when central banks purposefully choose only to stabilize the money supply and price levels through monetary policy. In particular, passive policy does not seek to use inflation to affect real variables, including unemployment and real GDP. In the United States, the Federal Reserve has moved markedly in this direction since the early 1980s. Ben Bernanke, Janet Yellen, Jerome Powell, and other chairs of the Federal Reserve Board have consistently taken actions that lead to fewer surprises in monetary policy.

ECONOMICS IN THE REAL WORLD

FEDERAL RESERVE PRESS CONFERENCES

In 2011, Ben Bernanke held the first press conference by a Fed chairman specifically to talk about the actions of the Fed's policymaking committee. This was a change in Federal Reserve action that led to a more open and transparent agency. Previously, the Fed merely released carefully worded official statements that often used cryptic language to describe the Fed's outlook for the future.

In the spring of 2011, the economy was struggling to truly emerge from the 2008 recession; unemployment was still over 9%. Yet, in the midst of these economic troubles, the Fed still decided to lay all of its cards on the table. Many observers saw this move as risky. Jacob Goldstein, writing for NPR's *Planet Money* the day before the press conference, explained why it mattered:

> Because everything the head of the Federal Reserve says is a big deal. One offhand comment can send global markets soaring or plunging. And because Fed chairmen, as a general rule, don't give press conferences. They release official statements that are very, very carefully worded. And they appear before Congress. Since the financial crisis, though, the Fed has come under increased scrutiny. The carefully worded statements and congressional appearances weren't carrying the day. So the leaders of the Fed have decided to send the chairman out for press conferences every few months ("to further enhance the clarity and timeliness of the Federal Reserve's monetary policy communication," in Fedspeak).

Bernanke's moves toward greater Fed openness reflected his belief that central bankers ought to be transparent. Both Janet Yellen and Jerome Powell, Bernanke's successors, have continued the press conferences. The move toward transparency reflects the modern view that expectations matter in macroeconomics—whether they are adaptive or rational.

Modern Fed chairs regularly hold press conferences, reflecting the view that transparency is good monetary policy.

DATA SNAPSHOT

Inflation and Unemployment: Is There a Phillips Curve?

If inflation is unexpected, it can reduce unemployment in the short run. But when inflation is expected, it does not reduce unemployment. In the long run, it is difficult to discern any relationship between inflation and unemployment rates. This suggests that the benefits of activist monetary policy may be severely constrained.

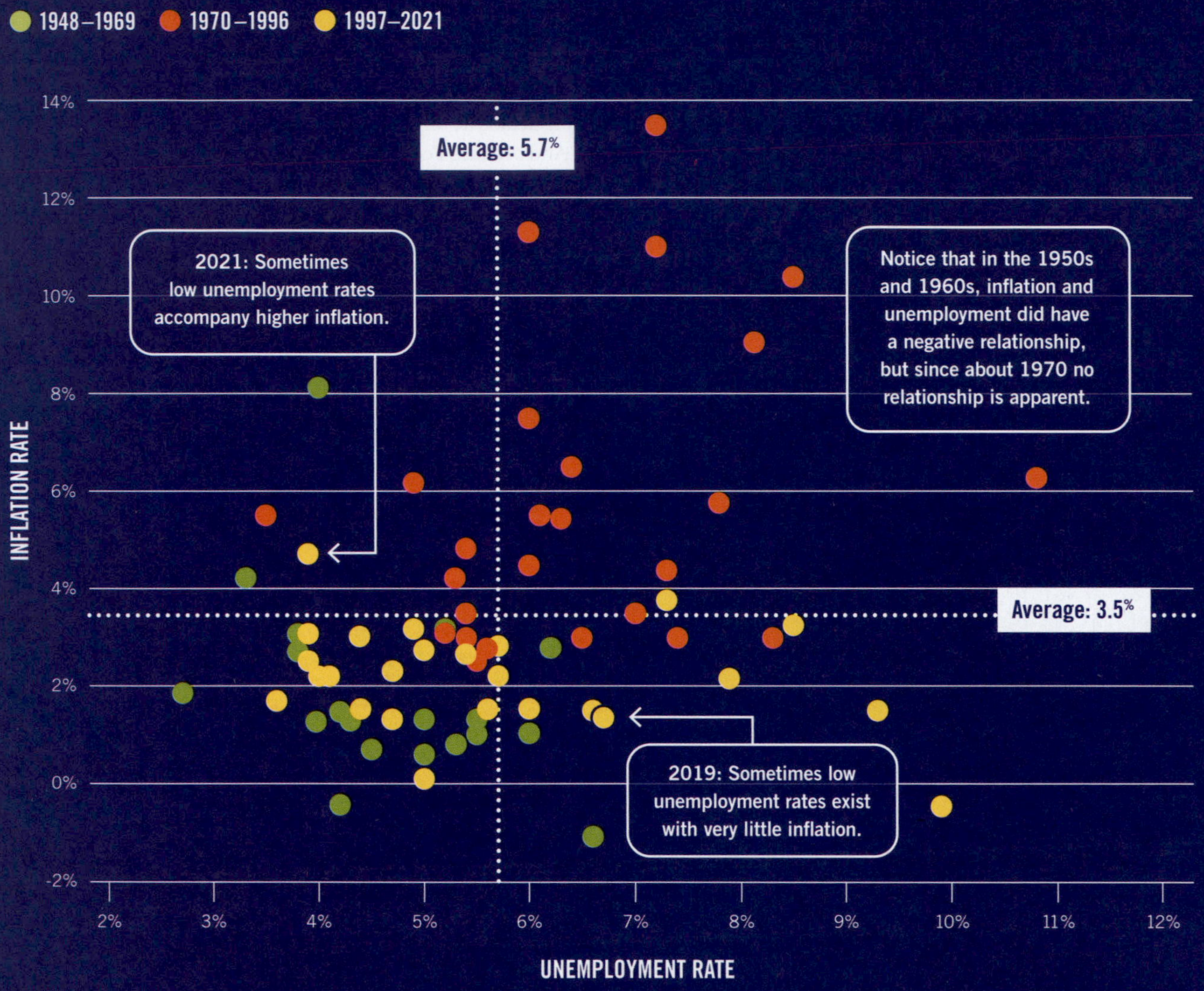

REVIEW QUESTIONS

- Knowing that in the long run inflation is the only result of expansionary monetary policy, why would the government act to increase inflation?
- Can you spot a traditional Phillips Curve in any of the subperiods? If so, which?

PRACTICE WHAT YOU KNOW

Monetary Policy: Expectations

Average unemployment rates in the European Union are about two percentage points higher than those in the United States. Let's consider what might ensue if the European Central Bank (ECB) attempts to use monetary policy to reduce unemployment in Europe. Suppose that in the European economy, all market participants expect a 2% inflation rate but then the European Central Bank (ECB) begins increasing the money supply enough to lead to a 4% inflation rate for a few years.

QUESTION: If expectations are for 2% inflation, what happens to the unemployment rate in the short run?

ANSWER: The unemployment rate falls, because the new inflation is a surprise and it can therefore stimulate the economy.

QUESTION: If expectations are formed adaptively, what happens to the unemployment rate in both the short run and the long run?

ANSWER: The unemployment rate falls in the short run, because the new inflation is different from past experience. In the long run, expectations adapt to the 4% inflation, and all else being equal, the unemployment rises back to its original level (assuming no other changes in the economies).

QUESTION: If expectations are formed rationally, what happens to the unemployment rate in the short run?

ANSWER: If expectations are formed rationally, people understand the incentives of the central bank and therefore may anticipate the expansionary monetary policy. In this case, the unemployment rate does not fall even in the short run.

QUESTION: If the leaders of the ECB held regular press conferences to describe their thinking and their plans for the money supply, how would this affect the influence of inflation on the unemployment rate?

ANSWER: If the ECB leaders were honest and transparent about their deliberations, it would be that much easier for people to form correct expectations about future inflation, which would tend to erase any remaining influence from inflation on unemployment.

The European Central Bank (ECB) undertakes monetary policy on behalf of the 19 nations that use the euro as their currency.

Conclusion

We began this chapter with the observation that central banks can't always control the macroeconomy. If they could, the U.S. economy certainly would not have experienced the sustained downturn that began at the end of 2007. So what can a central bank do? In the short run, if monetary policy is a surprise, a central bank can stimulate the economy and perhaps lessen the effects of a recession. But these results are mitigated when people come to anticipate monetary policy actions.

In the next two chapters, we turn to the international facets of macroeconomics. International trade, exchange rates, and international finance are becoming more important as the world economy becomes ever more integrated. ✷

· ECONOMICS *for* LIFE ·

How to Protect Yourself from Inflation

- Buying stocks or other assets that rise in value with inflation.
- Buying TIPS, which are Treasury securities that automatically adjust for inflation rates.

Gold is not a great long-term investment unless you really fear inflation.

In this chapter, we talked about how inflation harms some people. We also talked about how inflation doesn't harm people if they know it is coming—if it is expected.

If you are worried about inflation harming you, you can protect yourself from its effects. In recent history, U.S. inflation has been low and steady. In this case, inflation doesn't really harm anyone because it is easy to predict. But if you live in a country such as Argentina, where inflation has often been a problem because it has been high and unpredictable, or if you are worried about future inflation in the United States, these tips are for you.

The two types of people most often harmed by inflation are workers with fixed wages and lenders with fixed interest rates. Let's look at how to avoid inflation trouble in both instances.

Let's say you are a worker who is worried about inflation. One way to protect yourself is to avoid committing to long-term wage deals. If you must sign a contract, keep it short in duration. Better yet, include a clause in your contract that stipulates cost-of-living adjustments (COLAs) that are tied to a price index like the CPI. This way, your wages are hedged against future inflation.

But perhaps you are more worried about inflation's effect on your savings or retirement funds. In this case, you are a lender and thus susceptible to fixed interest rates. One way to avoid negative returns is to purchase securities or assets that tend to rise in value along with inflation. Stock prices generally go up with inflation, so you may want to invest more of your retirement funds in stocks rather than bonds. Gold is another asset that tends to appreciate in inflationary times because its value is tied to something real.

However, stocks can be risky, and the long-term returns on gold are historically very low. Thus, you might consider buying Treasury Inflation Protected Securities (TIPS). These are low-risk U.S. Treasury bonds that are indexed to inflation rates, so if inflation goes up, you get a higher rate of return. These bonds guarantee a particular real rate of return, no matter what the rate of inflation.

ANSWERING the BIG QUESTIONS

What is the effect of monetary policy in the short run?

- In the short run, monetary policy can both speed up and slow down the economy.
- Some prices are sticky in the short run. When some prices fail to adjust, changes in the money supply are essentially a change in real financial resources.
- In the short run, expansionary monetary policy can stimulate the economy, increasing real GDP and reducing the unemployment rate.
- In the short run, contractionary monetary policy can slow the economy, which may help to reduce inflation.

Why doesn't monetary policy always work?

- Monetary policy fails to produce real effects under three different circumstances. First, monetary policy has no real effect in the long run because all prices can adjust. Second, if monetary policy is fully anticipated, prices adjust. Finally, if the economy is experiencing shifts in aggregate supply, monetary policy may be unable to restore normal growth, because monetary policy works primarily through aggregate demand.

What is the Phillips curve?

- The Phillips curve is a theoretical negative relationship between inflation and unemployment rates. The modern consensus is that the Phillips curve is a short-run phenomenon that does not hold in the long run.
- The power of inflation to reduce unemployment is directly related to how people's inflation expectations adjust throughout the economy. Modern expectations theory allows for adjusting expectations, which is why most economists now believe that the Phillips curve relationship does not hold in the long run.

CHAPTER PROBLEMS

Concepts You Should Know

active monetary policy (p. 1029)
adaptive expectations theory (p. 1025)
contractionary monetary policy (p. 1014)
expansionary monetary policy (p. 1009)
federal funds rate (p. 1011)
monetary neutrality (p. 1018)
passive monetary policy (p. 1030)
Phillips curve (p. 1022)
rational expectations theory (p. 1026)
stagflation (p. 1026)

Questions for Review

1. Why is it possible to change real economic factors in the short run simply by increasing the money supply?

2. Many people focus on the effect of monetary policy on interest rates in the economy.

  a. Use the loanable funds market to explain how unexpected contractionary monetary policy affects interest rates in the short run.

  b. Now explain how these changes affect aggregate demand and aggregate supply in both the short run and the long run. Also explain the changes in real GDP, the unemployment rate, and the price level.

3. During the economic slowdown that began at the end of 2007, the Federal Reserve used monetary policy to reduce interest rates in the economy. Use what you have learned in this chapter to give a possible explanation as to why the monetary policy failed to restore the economy to long-run equilibrium.

4. Explain why a stable 5% inflation rate can be preferable to one that averages 4% but varies between 1% and 7% regularly.

5. Who is harmed when inflation is less than anticipated? In what ways are they harmed? Who is harmed when inflation is greater than anticipated? In what ways are they harmed?

6. Explain the difference between active and passive monetary policy.

Study Problems *(* solved at the end of the section)*

1. Use the aggregate demand–aggregate supply model to illustrate the downward-sloping relationship between inflation and unemployment rates in the short-run Phillips curve.

2. Suppose the economy is in long-run equilibrium, with real GDP at $19 trillion and the unemployment rate at 5%. Now assume that the central bank unexpectedly *decreases* the money supply by 6%.

  a. Illustrate the short-run effects on the macroeconomy by using the aggregate demand–aggregate supply model. Be sure to indicate the direction of change in real GDP, the price level, and the unemployment rate.

  b. Illustrate the long-run effects on the macroeconomy by using the aggregate demand–aggregate supply model. Again, be sure to indicate the direction of change in real GDP, the price level, and the unemployment rate.

  c. Now assume that this monetary contraction was completely expected. Illustrate both short-run and long-run effects on the macroeconomy by using the aggregate demand–aggregate supply model. Be sure to indicate the direction of change in real GDP, the price level, and the unemployment rate.

3. Suppose the economy is in long-run equilibrium, with real GDP at $19 trillion and the unemployment rate at 5%. Now assume that the central bank *increases* the money supply by 6%.

a. Illustrate the short-run effects on the macroeconomy by using the aggregate demand–aggregate supply model. Be sure to indicate the direction of change in real GDP, the price level, and the unemployment rate.

b. Illustrate the long-run effects on the macroeconomy by using the aggregate demand–aggregate supply model. Again, be sure to indicate the direction of change in real GDP, the price level, and the unemployment rate.

c. Now assume that this monetary expansion was completely expected. Illustrate both short-run and long-run effects on the macroeconomy by using the aggregate demand–aggregate supply model. Be sure to indicate the direction of change in real GDP, the price level, and the unemployment rate.

* **4.** In the past, some people believed that the Federal Reserve routinely expanded the money supply during presidential election years to stimulate the economy and help the incumbent president. For this question, assume that the Fed increases inflation by 3% in every election year.

a. Describe the effect on the economy during election years if market participants expect 0% inflation.

b. Describe the effect on the economy during election years if expectations are formed adaptively.

c. Describe the effect on the economy during election years if expectations are formed rationally.

* **5.** In each of the following scenarios, estimate the unemployment rate in comparison with the natural rate (u^*).

a. Inflation is steady at 2% for two years but then increases to 5% for a year.

b. Inflation is steady at 10% for two years but then decreases to 5% for a year.

c. Inflation is steady at 8% for several years.

d. Inflation is steady at 2% for three years, and then the Fed announces that inflation will be 3% one year later.

6. The following table presents actual inflation rates for a hypothetical nation for 10 years.

Column 1	Column 2
Year	**Actual inflation rate (i)**
Year 1	4%
Year 2	4
Year 3	4
Year 4	6
Year 5	6
Year 6	7
Year 7	6
Year 8	4
Year 9	2
Year 10	1

a. Replicate the table on a separate sheet of paper and leave space for five more columns. Label column 3 "Expected inflation if expectations are adaptive." Fill in this column beginning with year 2.

b. Label column 4 "Unemployment rate if expectations are adaptive." In this column, compare the resulting unemployment rate with the natural rate of unemployment (u^*) using the rule that $u < u^*$ when expected inflation is less than actual inflation, $u > u^*$ when expected inflation is more than actual inflation, and $u = u^*$ when expected inflation is equal to actual inflation.

c. Label column 5 "Random error." To fill in this column, you will need to flip a coin once for each year, beginning in year 2 (nine total coin flips). If the result of your first coin flip is heads, enter a "+1" for year 2, and if the result is tails, enter "−1." Repeat this process for years 3 through 10.

d. Label column 6 "Expected inflation if expectations are rational." For this column, sum together columns 2 and 5. The result is consistent with rational expectations in a world where errors in expectations are common but random.

e. Finally, label column 7 "Unemployment rate if expectations are rational." In this column, compare the resulting unemployment rate with the natural rate of unemployment (u^*) using the rule that $u < u^*$ when expected inflation is less than actual inflation, $u > u^*$ when expected inflation is more than actual inflation, and $u = u^*$ when expected inflation is equal to actual inflation.

Solved Problems

4. a. If people expect 0% inflation, any positive inflation will stimulate the economy and lower the unemployment rate.

b. If people form their inflation expectations adaptively, they will not anticipate inflation in an election year because it would be a break from their recent experience. Therefore, inflation in election years will consistently lower the rate of unemployment.

c. If expectations are formed rationally, then people will consider the incentives of policymakers during election years. Therefore, they will anticipate higher inflation in those years, and the inflation rate will have no effect on the unemployment rate.

5. a. The increase in inflation is likely a surprise, which means that it stimulates the economy and reduces the unemployment rate to a level below the natural rate.

b. The decrease in inflation is likely a surprise, which means that it slows the economy and increases the unemployment rate to a level above the natural rate.

c. Here there are no inflationary surprises, so the inflation rate does not influence the unemployment rate. Therefore, all else being equal, we should expect the unemployment rate to be near the natural rate.

d. Even though the inflation rate increases, it is not a surprise, so all prices have time to adjust. Therefore, all else being equal, we should expect the unemployment rate to be near the natural rate.

BANK NOTE
USD
1-2
USD
5-20
USD
EUR
CNY
JPY
IDR
34.00
34.00
34.00
35.60
4.66
0.2959
0.000139
0.86
0.40
24.09
7.60
7.06
34.66
36.35
0.00
0.3025
0.00
0.00
5.83

PART X

International ECONOMICS

CHAPTER

32

International Trade

Nations Gain through International Trade, Even If They Can Produce Their Goods and Services Domestically.

It's often assumed that, if possible, nations should try to produce their own goods and services rather than trade for them. For many, it seems intuitive that if the United States *can* produce a particular good, the United States *should* produce that good. But way back in Chapter 2, we learned how individuals gain by specializing in the production of certain goods and obtaining other goods through trade, even when the individuals could produce those other goods more efficiently themselves. Here we will see how the same principles apply to trade between nations. This second look at trade will give us a chance to go deeper into the theory.

International trade is greatly facilitated by an invention that gets little fanfare: the stackable shipping container, conceived and developed in the mid-1950s by trucking magnate Malcolm McLean and engineer Keith Tantlinger. Prior to that time, ships had cargo holds. Wooden crates of cargo were loaded individually and meticulously fitted together like a jigsaw puzzle, to maximize the use of interior space. All of this took time, and more time on the unloading end. McLean and Tantlinger's inspired insight was that on- and off-loading time could be reduced

Without the invention of the container ship, getting imports from overseas would be a lot more expensive. Imports come into the United States from all over the globe. But does importing goods from other countries harm our economy?

dramatically by using metal containers of uniform shape and size, and using large cranes to stack the containers, securely locked together, on the decks of specially configured ships, instead of down in the holds.

Today every container is geo-tagged, so manufacturing plants know exactly when the components they need are off-loaded. This arrangement makes just-in-time manufacturing possible. Overall, the "containerization" of shipping reduced costs by approximately 35% compared to the use of cargo holds. The past few decades have seen the volume of trade among the world's nations rise dramatically, though bottlenecks caused by coronavirus-related impacts have shown weaknesses in this model.

To help illustrate the extent of international trade, we begin this chapter with a look at global trade data. We then consider how international trade affects an economy. Finally, we have to reckon with the fact that, despite the theoretical arguments for free trade and the practical advances that make it easy and cheap, not everyone is convinced that free trade is a good idea. So we conclude the chapter by examining trade barriers and the reasons for their existence.

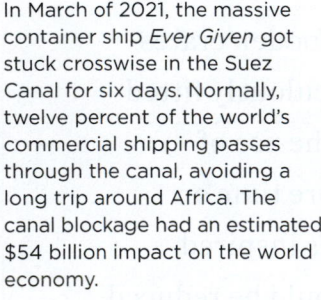

In March of 2021, the massive container ship *Ever Given* got stuck crosswise in the Suez Canal for six days. Normally, twelve percent of the world's commercial shipping passes through the canal, avoiding a long trip around Africa. The canal blockage had an estimated $54 billion impact on the world economy.

· BIG QUESTIONS ·

- Is globalization for real?
- How does international trade help the economy?
- What are the effects of tariffs and quotas?

Is Globalization for Real?

Over the past 75 years, trade among nations all over the world is way up. What this means for you and me is that we can buy fresh Peruvian strawberries (in February!), roses from Kenya, cars from Mexico, and electronics from South Korea. The United States also exports more now than in any earlier era. Imports and exports are both up for other countries, as well, and that means economies around the globe are more and more interdependent. This interdependence is the essence of *globalization,* and it is changing not only what you purchase but also your future job prospects.

Consider a single popular item: the iPhone. Inside the iPhone are parts made in Germany, Japan, Korea, and the United States. The phone is famously "designed by Apple in California," but it is assembled in China. This single item requires thousands of miles of global shipping before anyone ever touches its screen.

The modern trade explosion has occurred for many reasons. Among these are lower shipping and communication costs, reduced trade barriers, and increased specialization in world economies. Total world exports of goods and services are now about one-fourth the size of world GDP. In this section, we look first at the growth in total world trade and then at trends in U.S. trade.

Trade creates value

Growth in World Trade

World trade has grown, but not just in market value. It has also grown as a percentage of total world output. That is, not only are nations trading more, but they are also trading a greater portion of their GDP. Figure 32.1 shows merchandise trade as a percentage of world GDP. This has expanded dramatically, nearly doubling over 50 years, from 11% in 1970 to 21% in 2020.

How many borders does an iPhone cross before it is sold?

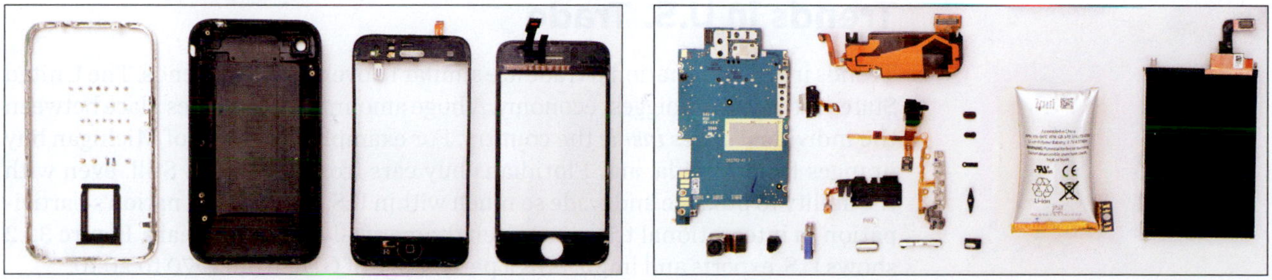

FIGURE 32.1

World Trade as a Percentage of World GDP, 1970–2020

The world's national economies have become more intertwined over the past 50 years. World trade has expanded significantly, and trade has even increased as a share of global GDP. Even with recent declines, total exports as a share of GDP have nearly doubled, from 11% in 1970 to 21% in 2020.

Sources: World Trade Organization; World Bank.

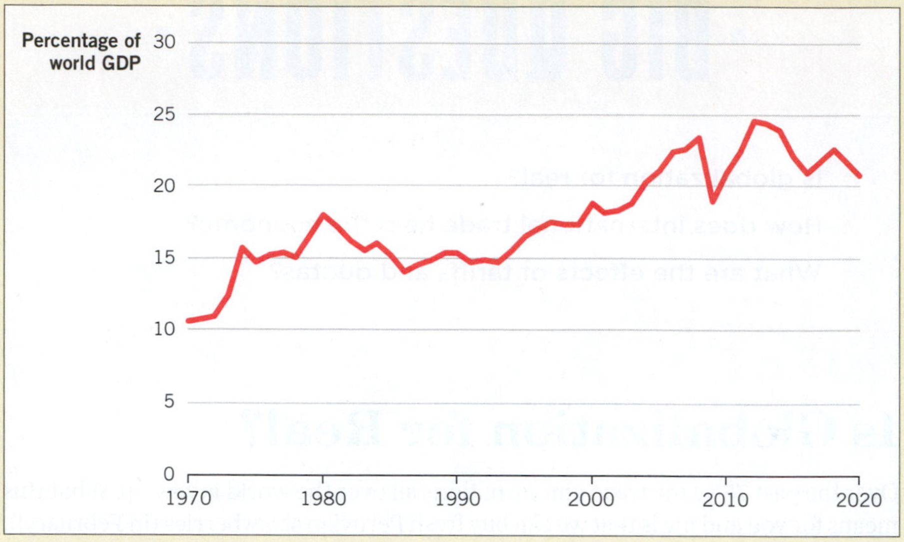

ECONOMICS IN THE REAL WORLD

NICARAGUA IS FOCUSED ON TRADE

Nicaragua, the second-poorest nation in the Western Hemisphere, is trying to escape poverty through international trade. Between 2007 and 2017, its real exports grew from $1.8 billion to $5.3 billion.

Trade with Nicaragua is growing in part because the country has established "free zones," where companies can produce goods for export and avoid standard corporate tax rates. Typical Nicaraguan companies pay a myriad of sales taxes, value-added taxes, corporate profit taxes, and dividend taxes. But these do not apply to output that a company exports to other nations. U.S. companies that have taken advantage of production in these free zones include Levi's, Under Armour, and Nike.

All else equal, market-driven international trade certainly helps nations to prosper. Yet while the free zones are increasing exports, the effect on domestic consumers in Nicaragua may not be entirely positive. Because the goods have to be exported for the manufacturers to take advantage of the tax breaks, there is very little incentive to produce goods for domestic purchase and consumption.

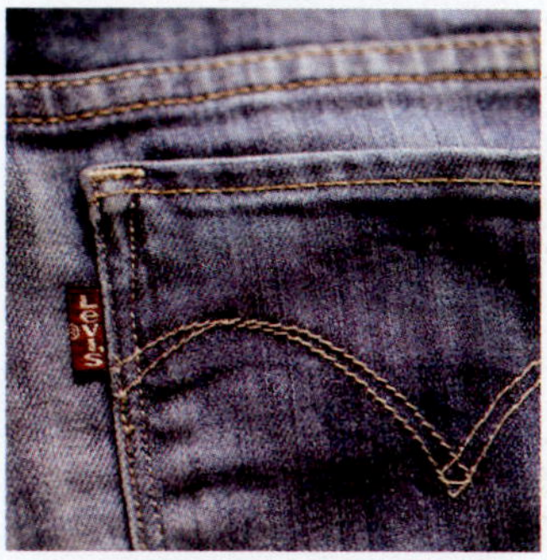

The Levi-Strauss company produces many of its blue jeans in Nicaragua.

Trends in U.S. Trade

Trends in U.S. international trade are similar to overall global trends. The United States is the world's biggest economy. A huge amount of trade takes place between the individual states *inside* the country. For example, residents of Michigan buy oranges from Florida, and Floridians buy cars from Michigan. Still, even with the ability to produce and trade so much within U.S. borders, the nation's participation in international trade has risen dramatically in recent years. Figure 32.2 shows U.S. exports and imports as a percentage of GDP from 1970 to 2020.

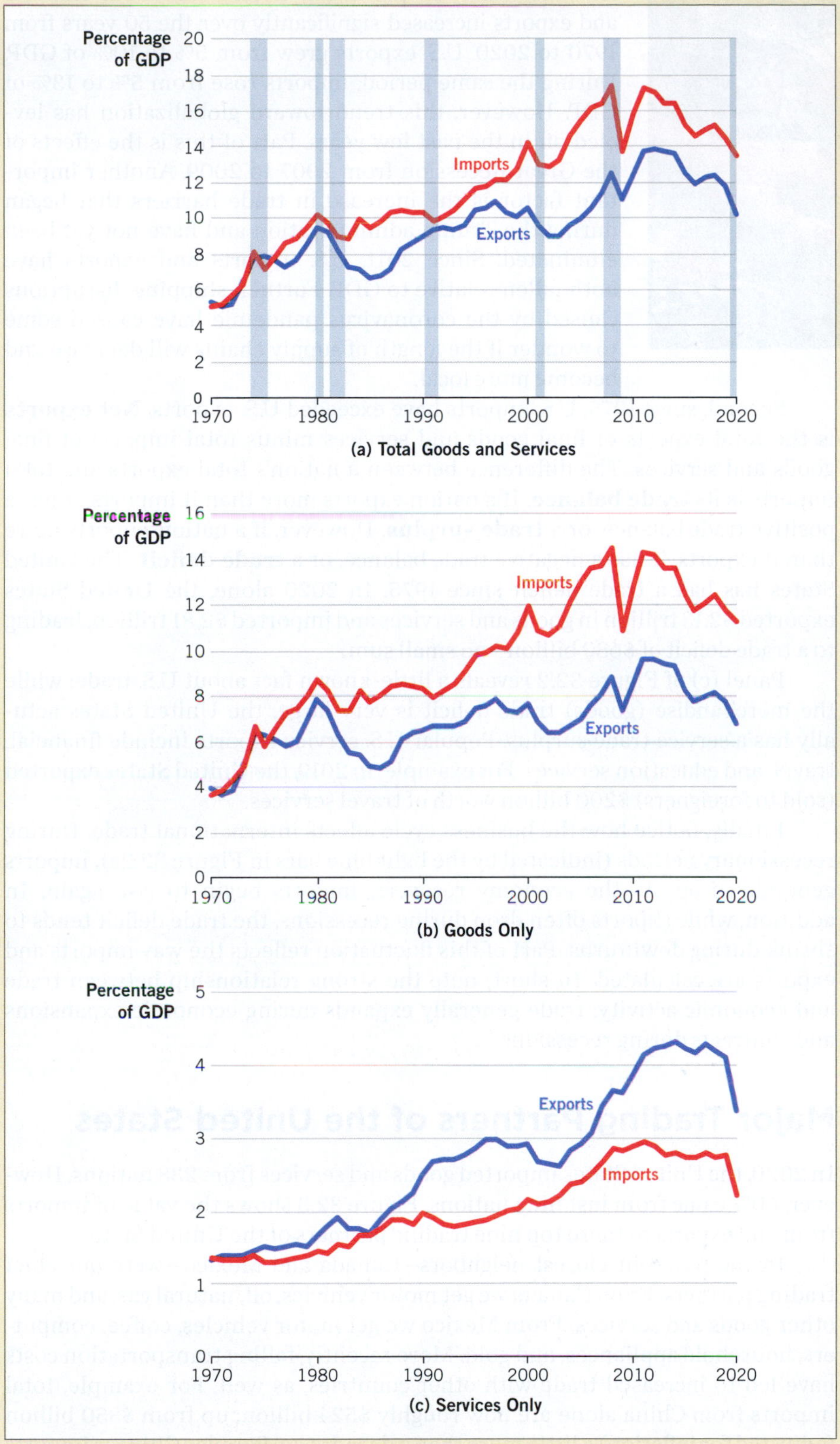

FIGURE 32.2

U.S. Exports and Imports Relative to GDP, 1970–2020 (as a percentage of GDP)

(a) Over the past 50 years, U.S. imports and exports have both increased substantially, even with the decline in both since 2011. The overall U.S. trade balance (imports minus exports) has moved more and more negative. This trade deficit often grows during economic expansions and shrinks during economic recessions, shown as shaded regions. (b) The trade deficit is driven by a merchandise (goods) deficit, and yet, (c) the United States enjoys a trade surplus in services.

Source: U.S. Bureau of Economic Analysis: U.S. International Transactions.

Foreign students who purchase their education in the United States are one type of U.S. service export.

As you look at the data in Figure 32.2, note three features. First, in panel (a), notice that both imports and exports increased significantly over the 50 years from 1970 to 2020. U.S. exports grew from 5% to 10% of GDP. During the same period, imports rose from 5% to 13% of GDP. However, this trend toward globalization has leveled off in the past few years. Part of this is the effects of the Great Recession from 2007 to 2009. Another important factor is the increase in trade barriers that began during the Trump administration and have not yet been eliminated. Since 2011, U.S. imports and exports have both fallen relative to GDP. Further, shipping disruptions caused by the coronavirus pandemic have caused some to wonder if the length of supply chains will decrease and become more local.

Net exports are the total exports of final goods and services minus total imports of final goods and services.

A nation's **trade balance** is the difference between its total exports and total imports.

A **trade surplus** occurs when exports exceed imports, indicating a positive trade balance.

A **trade deficit** occurs when imports exceed exports, indicating a negative trade balance.

Second, since 1975, U.S. imports have exceeded U.S. exports. **Net exports** is the total exports of final goods and services minus total imports of final goods and services. The difference between a nation's total exports and total imports is its **trade balance**. If a nation exports more than it imports, it has a positive trade balance, or a **trade surplus**. However, if a nation imports more than it exports, it has a negative trade balance, or a **trade deficit**. The United States has had a trade deficit since 1975. In 2020 alone, the United States exported $2.13 trillion in goods and services and imported $2.81 trillion, leading to a trade deficit of $680 billion—no small sum.

Panel (c) of Figure 32.2 reveals a little-known fact about U.S. trade: while the merchandise (goods) trade deficit is very large, the United States actually has a service trade surplus. Popular U.S. service exports include financial, travel, and education services. For example, in 2019, the United States exported (sold to foreigners) $200 billion worth of travel services.

Finally, notice how the business cycle affects international trade. During recessionary periods (indicated by the light blue bars in Figure 32.2a), imports generally drop. As the economy recovers, imports begin to rise again. In addition, while exports often drop during recessions, the trade deficit tends to shrink during downturns. Part of this fluctuation reflects the way imports and exports are calculated. In short, note the strong relationship between trade and economic activity: trade generally expands during economic expansions and contracts during recessions.

Major Trading Partners of the United States

In 2020, the United States imported goods and services from 238 nations. However, 60% came from just nine nations. Figure 32.3 shows the value of imports from and exports to these top nine trading partners of the United States.

In the past, our closest neighbors—Canada and Mexico—were our chief trading partners. From Canada we get motor vehicles, oil, natural gas, and many other goods and services. From Mexico we get motor vehicles, coffee, computers, household appliances, and gold. More recently, falling transportation costs have led to increased trade with other countries, as well. For example, total imports from China alone are now roughly $524 billion, up from $350 billion (adjusted for inflation) a little more than a decade ago. Popular Chinese imports include electronics, toys, and clothing.

FIGURE 32.3

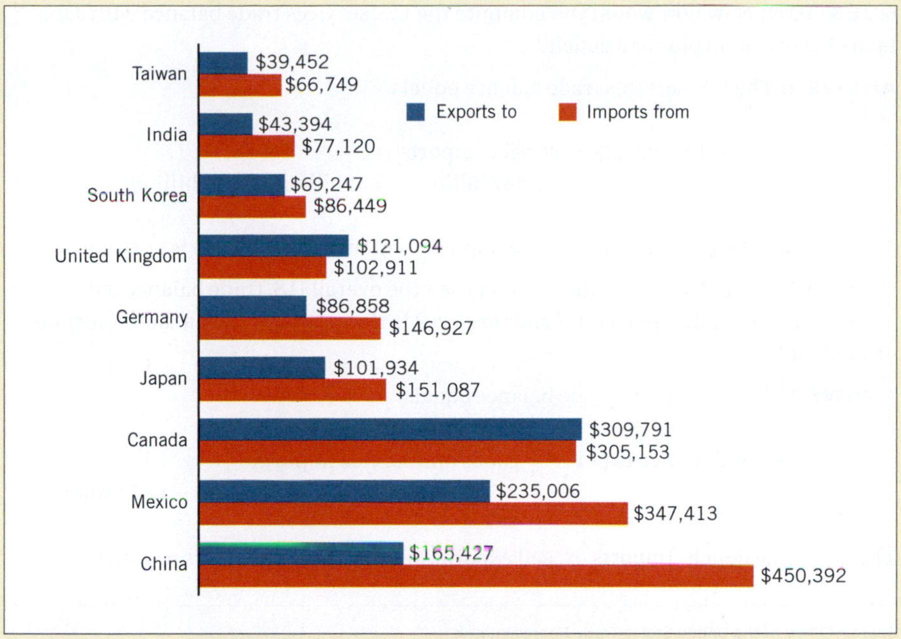

Major Goods Trading Partners of the United States, 2020 (in billions of dollars)

Sixty percent of all U.S. goods imports come from the nine nations shown here. We export more to Canada and Mexico than to other nations, but we import more from China. In 2020, the U.S. trade deficit with China was $300 billion.

Source: U.S. Bureau of Economic Analysis.

PRACTICE WHAT YOU KNOW

Trade in Goods and Services: Deficit or Surplus?

Sony PlayStations are a popular U.S. import from Japan.

The United States imports many goods from Japan, including automobiles, electronics, and medical instruments. But we also export many services to Japan, such as financial and travel services. The table below reflects trade between the United States and Japan in 2014. (All figures are in billions of U.S. dollars.)

	Exports to Japan	Imports from Japan
Goods	$20	$103
Services	47	31

QUESTION: Using the data shown above, how would you compute the U.S. goods trade balance with Japan? Is the balance a surplus or a deficit?

ANSWER: The U.S. goods trade balance equals

$$\text{goods exports} - \text{goods imports}$$
$$= \$20 \text{ billion} - \$103 \text{ billion} = -\$83 \text{ billion}$$

This is a trade deficit. Imports exceed exports, and the trade balance is negative.

(CONTINUED)

QUESTION: Now how would you compute the U.S. services trade balance with Japan? Is the balance a surplus or a deficit?

ANSWER: The U.S. services trade balance equals

$$\text{service exports} - \text{service imports}$$
$$= \$47\text{ billion} - \$31\text{ billion} = \$16\text{ billion}$$

This is a trade surplus. Exports exceed imports, and the trade balance is positive.

QUESTION: Finally, how would you compute the overall U.S. trade balance with Japan, which includes both goods and services? Is this overall trade balance a surplus or a deficit?

ANSWER: The overall U.S. trade balance equals

$$\text{Goods and service exports} - \text{goods and service imports}$$
$$= \$67\text{ billion} - \$134\text{ billion} = -\$67\text{ billion}$$

This is a trade deficit. Imports exceed exports, and the trade balance is negative.

Source: Office of the United States Trade Representative.

In this picture from a dollar store, is there anything that is *not* produced in China?

Canada and Mexico buy the most U.S. exports. To Canada we export cars, car parts, computers, and agricultural products. To Mexico we export cars, car parts, computers, and meat, among many other items. Financial and travel services are major U.S. exports to all our major trading partners.

How Does International Trade Help the Economy?

Trade creates value

In this section, we explain how comparative advantage and specialization make it possible to achieve gains from trade between nations. To keep the analysis simple, we assume that two trading partners—the United States and Mexico—produce only two items, clothes and food. This example will enable us to demonstrate that trade creates value in the absence of any restrictions.

Comparative Advantage

Comparative advantage refers to the situation where an individual, a business, or a country can produce at a lower opportunity cost than a competitor can.

In Chapter 2, we saw that trade creates value and that **comparative advantage** makes the creation of value possible. Gains arise when a nation specializes in production and exchanges its output with a trading partner. In other words, each nation should produce the good it is best at making and trade with other nations for the goods they are best at making. Trade leads to lower costs of production and maximizes the combined output of all nations involved. (Comparative advantage is very important to the discussion that follows. If you don't remember the details of comparative advantage, be sure to review Chapter 2 before proceeding.)

Suppose the United States and Mexico both produce clothing and food. Also assume that the production of one unit of food requires a greater quantity of capital per unit of labor than the production of one unit of clothing (in economics, we say that food is *capital intensive* and clothing is *labor intensive*). Because the United States is generally viewed as abundant in skilled labor but not so much in unskilled labor, while at the same time abundant in capital, it makes sense that it will specialize and produce food. Mexico, which is generally viewed as abundant in unskilled labor, will specialize in clothing.

In Figure 32.4, we see the production possibilities frontier (PPF) for each country when it does *not* specialize and trade. In panel (a), Mexico can produce at any point along its PPF. It can produce 900 million units, or articles, of clothing if it does not make any food, and it can produce 300 million tons of food if it does not make any clothing. Neither extreme is especially desirable because it would mean that Mexico would have to do without either clothing or food. As a result, Mexico will prefer to operate somewhere in between the two extremes. We show Mexico operating along its production possibilities frontier at 450 million articles of clothing and 150 million tons of food. Panel (b) shows that the United States can produce 400 million articles of clothing if it does not

FIGURE 32.4

The Production Possibilities Frontier for Mexico and the United States without Specialization and Trade

(a) Mexico chooses to operate along its production possibilities curve at 450 million articles of clothing and 150 million tons of food. Each ton of food incurs an opportunity cost of three articles of clothing—a food-clothing ratio of 1:3.
(b) The United States chooses to operate along its production possibilities curve at 300 million articles of clothing and 200 million tons of food. Each ton of food incurs an opportunity cost of one-half an article of clothing—a food-clothing ratio of 2:1.

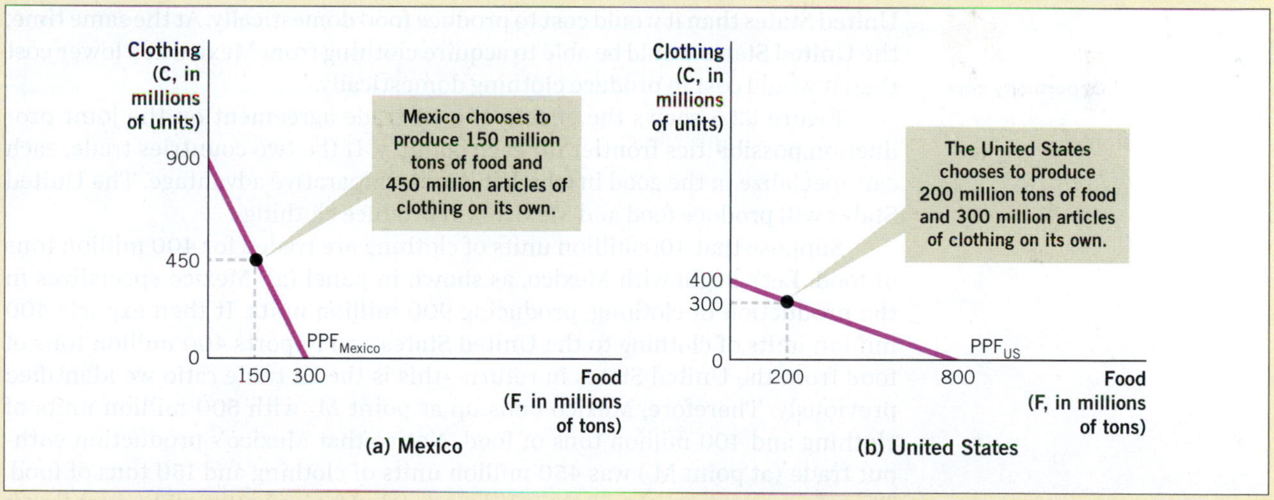

TABLE 32.1

Output and Opportunity Costs for Mexico and the United States

	Chosen output level		Opportunity cost	
	Food (millions of tons)	Clothing (millions of units)	Food (F)	Clothing (C)
Mexico	150	450	3 C	⅓ F
United States	200	300	½ C	2 F

make any food, and it can produce 800 million tons of food if it does not make any clothing. Like Mexico, the United States will prefer to operate somewhere in between—for example, at 300 million articles of clothing and 200 million tons of food.

To see whether gains from trade are able to make both countries better off, we must first examine the opportunity cost that each country faces when making these two goods. In Mexico, producing 150 million tons of food means giving up the production of 450 million articles of clothing (900 − 450 = 450). Thus, each ton of food incurs an opportunity cost of three articles of clothing, yielding a ratio of 150:450, or 1:3, or one ton of food per three articles of clothing. In the United States, producing 200 million tons of food means giving up production of 100 million articles of clothing (400 − 300 = 100). The ratio here is therefore 200:100, or 2:1. (Notice that both ratios are in the format food:clothing.) In the United States, then, a ton of food incurs an opportunity cost of one-half an article of clothing. Table 32.1 shows the initial production choices and the opportunity costs for both nations. Because the United States has a lower opportunity cost of producing food than Mexico, we say that the United States has a comparative advantage in producing food and therefore will specialize in food production.

Opportunity cost

As long as the opportunity cost of the production of the two goods differs between the two countries, as it does here, trade has the potential to benefit both. The key to making trade mutually beneficial in this case is to find a trading ratio between 1:3 and 2:1. For instance, if Mexico and the United States establish a 1:1 trading ratio, Mexico would be able to acquire food at a lower cost from the United States than it would cost to produce food domestically. At the same time, the United States would be able to acquire clothing from Mexico at a lower cost than it would cost to produce clothing domestically.

Opportunity cost

Figure 32.5 shows the effects of a 1:1 trade agreement on the joint production possibilities frontier for each country. If the two countries trade, each can specialize in the good in which it has a comparative advantage. The United States will produce food and Mexico will produce clothing.

Suppose that 400 million units of clothing are traded for 400 million tons of food. Let's begin with Mexico, as shown in panel (a). Mexico specializes in the production of clothing, producing 900 million units. It then exports 400 million units of clothing to the United States and imports 400 million tons of food from the United States in return—this is the 1:1 trade ratio we identified previously. Therefore, Mexico ends up at point M_2 with 500 million units of clothing and 400 million tons of food. Notice that Mexico's production without trade (at point M_1) was 450 million units of clothing and 150 tons of food. Therefore, specialization and trade have made Mexico better off by enabling it to consume 50 million more units of clothing and 250 million more tons of food.

FIGURE 32.5

The Production Possibilities Frontier for Mexico and the United States with Specialization and Trade

(a) After Mexico specializes in clothing and trades with the United States, it is better off by 50 million units of clothing and 250 million tons of food (compare points M_1 and M_2). (b) After the United States specializes in food and trades with Mexico, it is better off by 100 million units of clothing and 200 million tons of food (compare points US_1 and US_2).

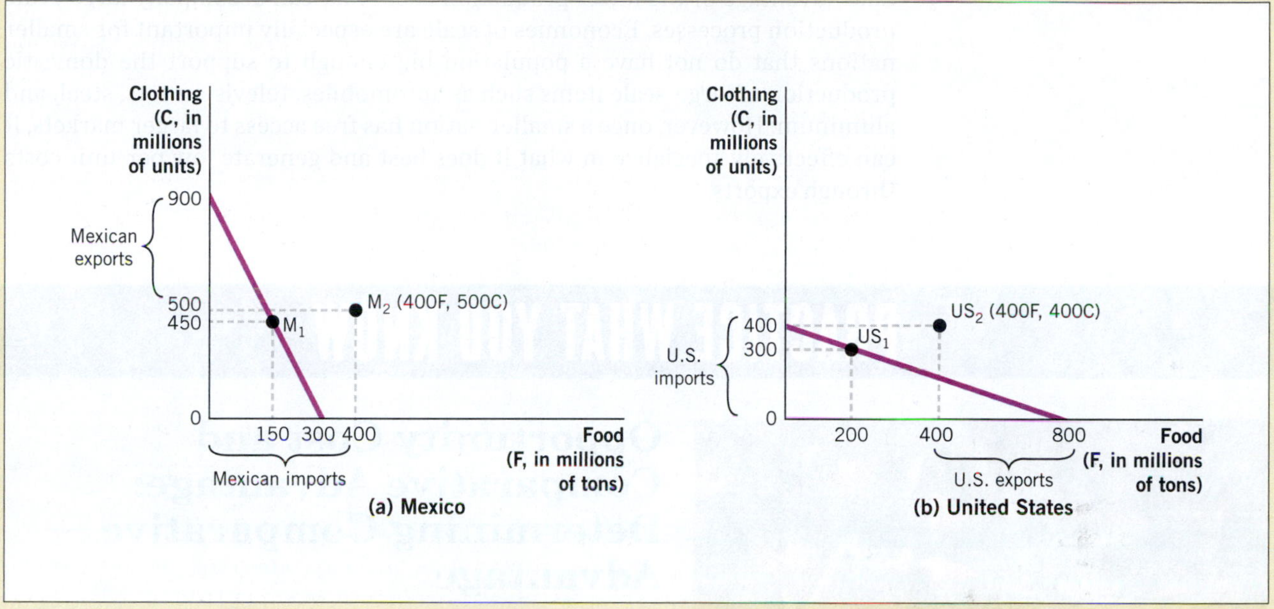

Now let's look at the United States in panel (b). The United States specializes in the production of food, producing 800 million tons. It exports 400 million tons of food to Mexico and imports 400 million units of clothing from Mexico in return. Therefore, the United States ends up at point US_2 with 400 million units of clothing and 400 million tons of food. Notice that U.S. production without trade (at point US_1) was 300 million units of clothing and 200 tons of food. Therefore, specialization and trade have made the United States better off by allowing it to consume 100 million more units of clothing and 200 million more tons of food.

The combined benefits that Mexico and the United States enjoy are even more significant. As we saw in Figure 32.4, when Mexico did not specialize and trade, it chose to make 450 million units of clothing and 150 million tons of food. Without specialization and trade, the United States chose to produce 300 million units of clothing and 200 million tons of food. The combined output without specialization was 750 million units of clothing and 350 million tons of food. However, as we see in Figure 32.5, the joint output with specialization is 900 million units of clothing and 800 million tons of food. In economics, we call this a *positive-sum game* because both players, in this case both countries, win by trading with each other.

Other Advantages of Trade

Although comparative advantage is the biggest reason that many nations trade with other nations, there are other good reasons for nations to engage in trade. In this section, we consider how international trade encourages both economies of scale and increased competition and how these factors can help an economy to grow.

ECONOMIES OF SCALE When a nation specializes its production, it can take advantage of the lower production costs that can accompany large-scale production processes. Economies of scale are especially important for smaller nations that do not have a population big enough to support the domestic production of large-scale items such as automobiles, television sets, steel, and aluminum. However, once a smaller nation has free access to larger markets, it can effectively specialize in what it does best and generate low per-unit costs through exports.

PRACTICE WHAT YOU KNOW

Does China enjoy a comparative advantage in textile production?

Opportunity Cost and Comparative Advantage: Determining Comparative Advantage

U.S. trade with mainland China has exploded in the past decade, with goods imports reaching $467 billion a year and exports up to $124 billion. For the following questions, we consider a hypothetical production possibilities frontier for food and textiles in both China and the United States.

The table below presents daily production possibilities for a typical worker in both China and the United States, assuming that only two kinds of goods are produced in both countries: food and textiles.

Output per worker per day (units)

	Food	Textiles
China	1	2
United States	9	3

QUESTION: What are the opportunity costs of food production for both China and the United States?

ANSWER: The opportunity cost of food production in China is the amount of textile production forgone for a single unit of food output. Because a Chinese worker can produce 2 textile units in a day or 1 unit of food, the opportunity cost of 1 unit of food is 2 textile units.

(CONTINUED)

In the United States, a worker can produce 3 textile units in one day or 9 units of food. Thus, the opportunity cost of 1 unit of food is just $\frac{1}{3}$ textile unit.

QUESTION: What are the opportunity costs of textile production for both China and the United States?

ANSWER: The opportunity cost of textile production in China is the amount of food production forgone for a single textile produced. Because a Chinese worker can produce 1 unit of food in a day or 2 textile units, the opportunity cost of 1 textile unit is $\frac{1}{2}$ unit of food.

In the United States, a worker can produce 9 units of food in one day or 3 textile units. Thus, the opportunity cost of 1 textile unit is 3 units of food.

QUESTION: Which nation has a comparative advantage in food production? Which nation has a comparative advantage in textile production?

ANSWER: The United States has a lower opportunity cost of food production ($\frac{1}{3}$ versus 2 textile units), so it has a comparative advantage in food production. China has a lower opportunity cost of textile production ($\frac{1}{2}$ versus 3 units of food), so it has a comparative advantage in textile production.

In Figures 32.4 and 32.5, the production possibilities frontier is shown as a straight line, which makes the computation of the ratios fairly simple and holds the opportunity cost constant. However, in the real world, access to new markets allows countries to take advantage of economies of scale and therefore lower per-unit costs as production expands. Increased production gives companies the opportunity to economize on distribution costs and marketing and to utilize assembly lines and other forms of automation.

Consider how a small textile company based in Mexico fares under this arrangement. With international trade, the company can expand its sales into the United States—a much larger market. This move creates additional demand, which translates into added sales. A larger volume of sales enables the textile firm's production, marketing, and sales to become more efficient. The firm can purchase fabrics in bulk, expand its distribution network, and use volume advertising.

INCREASED COMPETITION Another largely unseen benefit from trade is increased competition. In fact, increased competition from foreign suppliers forces domestic firms to become more innovative and to compete in terms of both price and quality. Competition also gives consumers more options to choose from, which enables consumers to purchase a broader array of products that better match their needs. For example, many cars are produced in the United States, but foreign automobiles offer U.S. consumers greater variety and help to keep the prices of domestically made cars lower than they would be otherwise.

TRADE AGREEMENTS Gains from trade often spur nations to sign trade agreements, to reduce tariffs and clear the way for mutually beneficial exchange. One prominent example is the North American Free Trade Agreement (NAFTA), which was signed in 1992 by the United States, Canada, and Mexico. NAFTA eliminated many of the barriers to trade that had been erected between the three nations.

When Donald Trump campaigned for president in 2016, he pledged to make trade more fair for the United States. After he became president, his administration renegotiated the terms of NAFTA and signed a new agreement in 2018. The new agreement, called the United States-Mexico-Canada Agreement (USMCA), altered the provisions of NAFTA slightly but also ensured a continuation of trade among the three nations.

Even though trade agreements often stipulate protections for particular industries (most notably, agriculture), they still increase trade between nations. For example, as a result of NAFTA, real U.S. imports and exports of goods with Canada and Mexico have doubled. Between 1993 and 2017, inflation-adjusted exports to Canada rose from $120 billion to $282 billion. Over the same period, inflation-adjusted exports to Mexico grew from $50 billion to $240 billion. The reduction in trade barriers has enabled all three nations to move toward the production of goods and services in which they enjoy a comparative advantage.

The World Trade Organization (WTO) is an international organization that facilitates trade agreements between nations. Created in 1995 by the 123 countries that were then signatories of the General Agreement on Tariffs and Trade, the WTO regulates the trade of various goods and services, including textiles, investment, intellectual property, even agriculture. Moreover, the WTO works to resolve trade disputes. For example, in 2012 the WTO helped to end a 20-year disagreement between Latin American banana exporters and the European Union over a tax on imported bananas.

What Are the Effects of Tariffs and Quotas?

Despite the benefits of free trade, significant trade barriers, such as import taxes, often exist. For example, almost every shoe purchased in the United States is made overseas; but with few exceptions, the U.S. government taxes each pair of shoes that comes across its borders to be sold. For example, a new pair of Nike tennis shoes imported from Vietnam is subject to a 20% import tax. If these shoes are valued at $100, the foreign producer has to pay a $20 tax on them.

Import taxes like those on footwear are not unusual. In this section, we explore two of the most common types of trade barriers: *tariffs* and *quotas*. We then look more closely at common economic and political justifications for **protectionism**, which is a blanket term for governmental actions and policies that restrict or restrain international trade, often with the intent of protecting local businesses and jobs from foreign competition. We close by examining whether or not protectionism is effective.

Protectionism
is a blanket term for governmental actions and policies that restrict or restrain international trade, often with the intent of protecting local businesses and jobs from foreign competition.

Tariffs

Tariffs
are taxes levied on imported goods and services.

Tariffs are taxes levied on imported goods and services. A tariff is paid by the producer of the good when the good arrives in a foreign country. A tariff can be a percentage of the value of the good (called an *ad valorem tax*), a per-unit tax (called a *specific tax*), or a mix of the two. Figure 32.6 illustrates the impact of a per-unit tariff on foreign shoes. To assess how a tariff affects the market price of shoes in the United States, we observe the relationship between domestic demand and domestic supply.

FIGURE 32.6

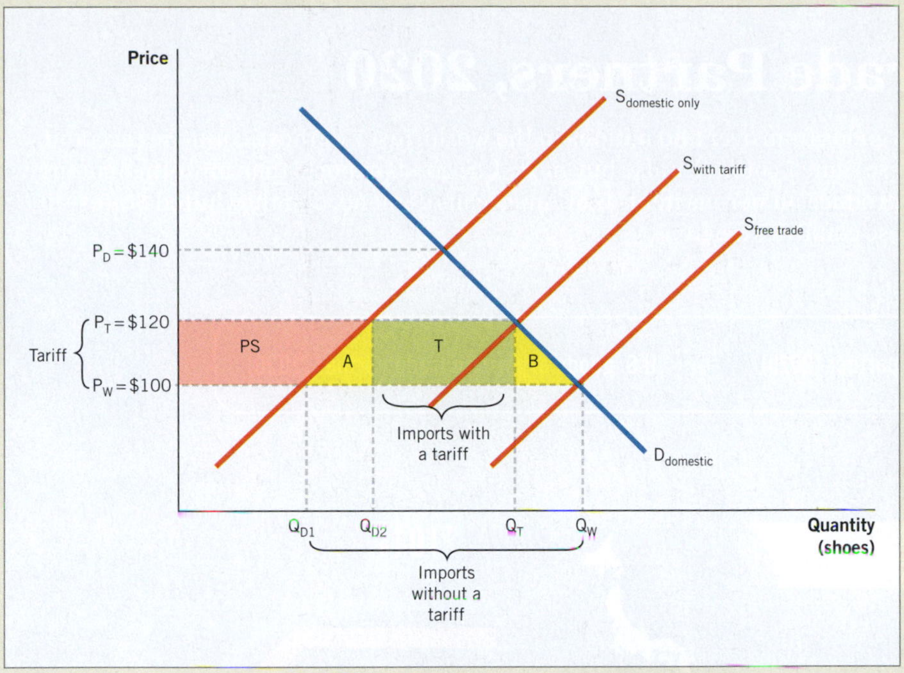

The Impact of a Tariff

Without a tariff, the domestic market is dominated by imports. However, when a tariff is imposed, the price rises and domestic production expands from Q_{D1} to Q_{D2}. At the same time, imports fall to $Q_T - Q_{D2}$. Tariffs also create deadweight loss (shaded areas A and B), revenue for the government (area T), and increased producer surplus for domestic firms (area PS).

We begin by noting that domestic supply ($S_{domestic\ only}$) and domestic demand ($D_{domestic}$) would be in equilibrium at \$140 per pair of shoes. However, this is not the market price if free trade prevails. If trade is unrestricted, imports are free to enter the domestic market, so that supply increases to $S_{free\ trade}$. Now, because trade is unrestricted, domestic producers who might wish to charge a price higher than that charged by foreign producers would find that they could not sell their shoes at that price. As a result, the domestic price (P_D) decreases to the world price (P_W), which is \$100. At \$100, the total quantity demanded is Q_W. Part of this quantity is produced domestically (Q_{D1}), and part is imported from foreign sources ($Q_W - Q_{D1}$).

Now let's see what happens when a tariff of \$20 per pair of shoes is levied. When the country imposes the tariff per pair of shoes, the cost that foreign producers must bear when they export shoes rises by \$20 per pair, the amount of the tariff. Supply decreases to $S_{with\ tariff}$. The tariff pushes the domestic price up from \$100 to \$120 (represented as P_T, reflecting the price with tariff). Foreign producers must pay the tariff, but domestic producers do not have to pay it. One consequence of this situation is that the amount imported drops to $Q_T - Q_{D2}$. At the same time, the amount supplied by domestic producers rises along the domestic-only supply curve from Q_{D1} to Q_{D2}. Because domestic suppliers are now able to charge \$120 and also sell more, they are better off.

We can see this outcome visually by noting that domestic suppliers gain producer surplus equal to the shaded area marked PS. The government also benefits from the tariff revenue, shown as shaded area T. The tariff is a pure transfer from foreign suppliers to the government. In this case, the tariff is \$20 per pair of shoes, so total tax revenue is \$20 times the number of imported pairs of shoes. In addition, there are two areas of deadweight loss, A and B.

DATA SNAPSHOT

Major U.S. Trade Partners, 2020

Though the United States imports goods from over 230 nations in the world, just 7 of those countries account for over 60% of these imports. These same 7 countries also buy more U.S. goods exports than any other country. Clearly, our major trade partners produce numerous items that Americans demand, and the United States produces numerous items that these countries desire.

U.S. goods imports from trade partner (2020) — U.S. goods exports to trade partner (2020)

JAPAN

TOP IMPORTS FROM
- Passenger cars
- Auto parts
- Industrial machines

TOP EXPORTS TO
- Civilian aircraft
- Pharmaceuticals
- Medical equipment

SOUTH KOREA

TOP IMPORTS FROM
- Passenger cars
- Auto parts
- Household goods

TOP EXPORTS TO
- Semiconductors
- Industrial machines
- Civilian aircraft

CHINA

TOP IMPORTS FROM
- Computers
- Household goods
- Apparel

TOP EXPORTS TO
- Soybeans
- Civilian aircraft
- Passenger cars

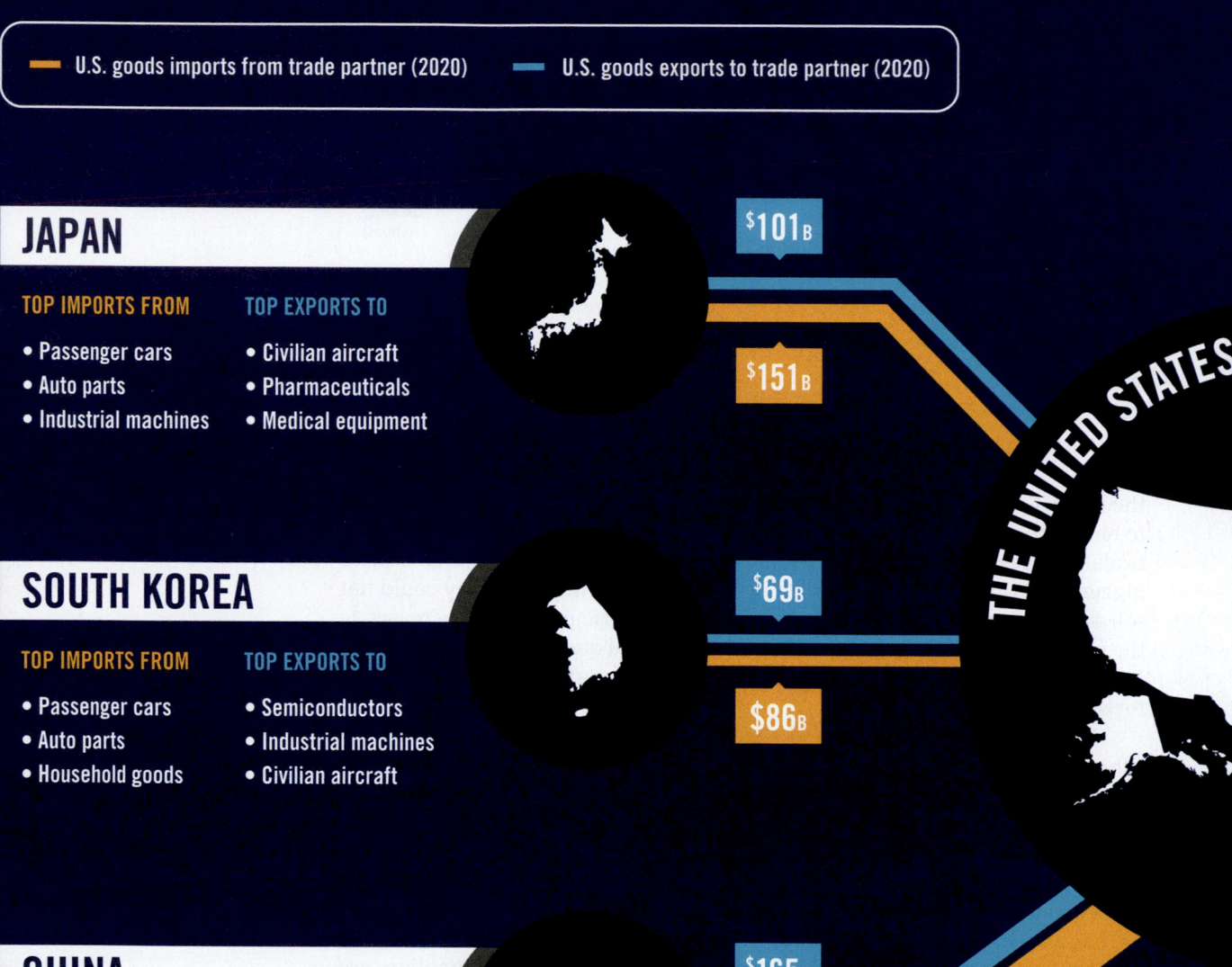

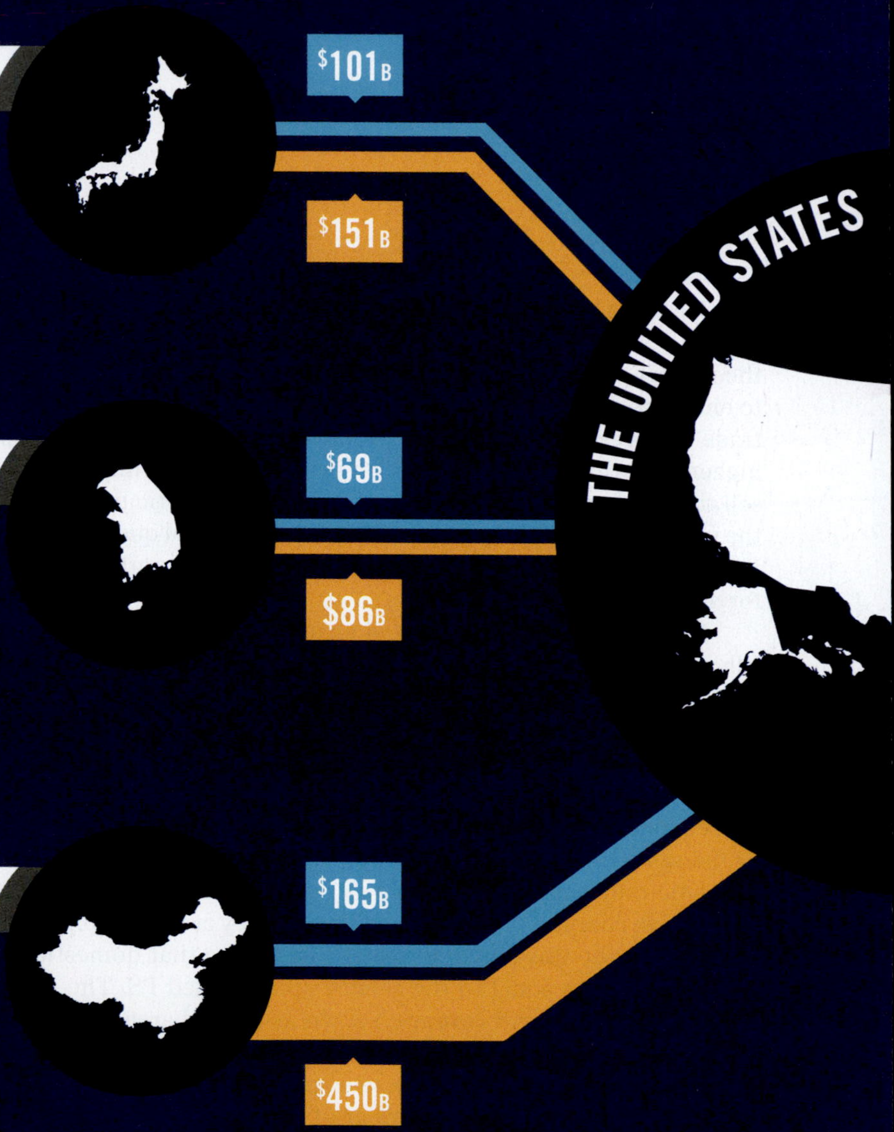

Source: U.S. Bureau of Economic Analysis

REVIEW QUESTIONS

- What U.S. industry generates the most universal demand from our trading partners?
- Based on the list of U.S. imports, how would you finish this sentence? "Americans sure love their ______!"

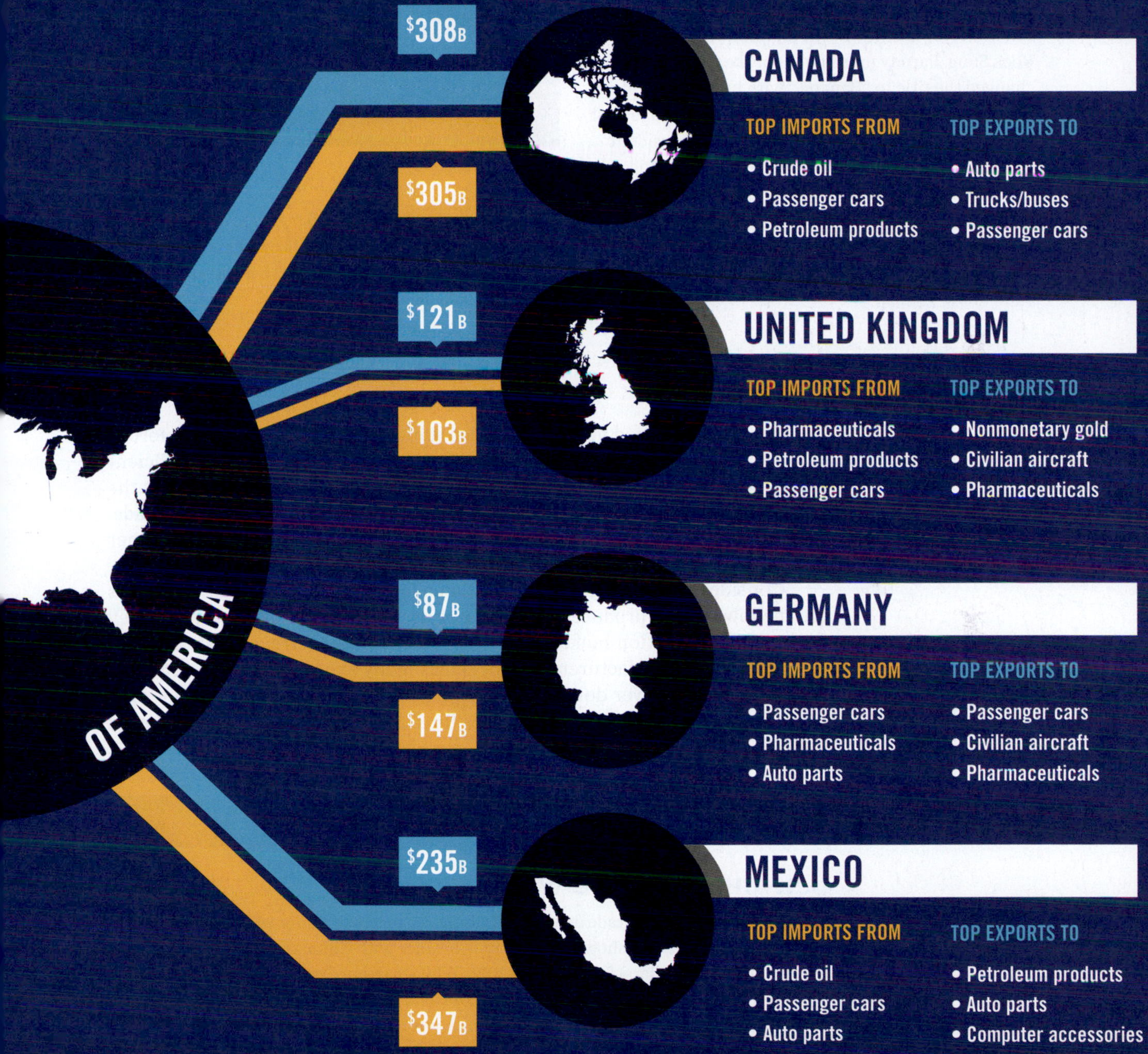

ECONOMICS *in the* MEDIA

Tariffs: A Parody

REMY: "BANANA" (FREE-TRADE "HAVANA" PARODY)

"Havana," recorded by Camila Cabello (with guest vocals by Young Thug) is a very catchy tune that reflects Cabello's Latin roots. In 2018, the song won the American Music Awards for Best Video and Favorite Pop/Rock Song. Parody musician Remy kept the tune but changed the title to "Banana," with lyrics that explain how tariffs would bring back jobs from Havana to East Atlanta. Quite hilariously, Remy plays the president and also all his advisors at a trade policy planning meeting. Each of the advisors weighs in as the song progresses: "Take jobs back from Havana," "Why can't we grow bananas ourselves? They'd taste worse and cost more," and "You'd have to pump in water and heat, dude." If all of this sounds like a bad idea, it is.

THEY SHOULD BE GROWN IN EAST ATLANTA

Placing a tariff on bananas and trying to grow them in the southeast United States is evidence that "We've gone absolutely bananas." Check out the video on YouTube!

Consumers are harmed because the price is higher and some people are forced to switch from foreign brands to domestic shoes. In addition, inefficient domestic producers now get to enter the market. Areas A and B represent the efficiency loss associated with the tariff—or the unrealized gains from trade. The economy as a whole loses from the tariff because the loss in consumer surplus is greater than the gains obtained by producers and the government.

Consider for a moment just how damaging a tariff is. Foreign producers are the lowest-cost producer of shoes, but they are limited in how much they can sell. This situation makes little sense from an import/export standpoint. If foreign shoe manufacturers cannot sell as many shoes in the United States, they will acquire fewer dollars to use in purchasing U.S. exports. So not only does the tariff mean higher shoe prices for U.S. consumers, but it also means fewer sales for U.S. exporters.

ECONOMICS IN THE REAL WORLD

U.S.–CHINA TRADE WAR

Since the 1980s, the U.S. trade deficit with China has increased from $4 billion to about $300 billion. Figure 32.7 shows the U.S. trade balance with China adjusted for inflation (in billions of 2012 dollars) from 2000 to 2020. While both imports and exports have risen over this period, imports have declined since 2015 (and exports have stayed about the same).

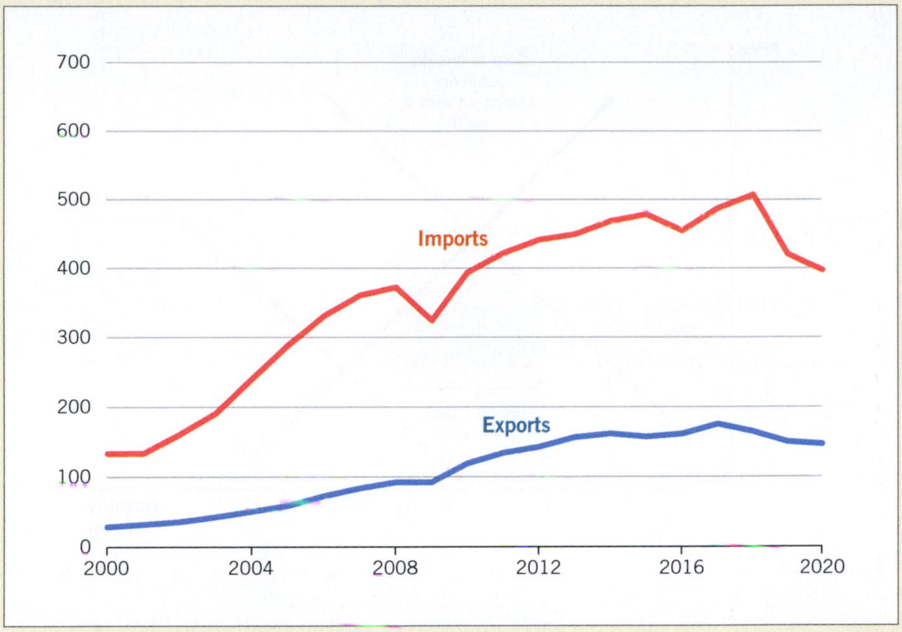

FIGURE 32.7

U.S. Goods and Services Trade with China (Billions of 2012 Dollars)

Since 2000, United States imports and exports of goods and services from China have grown significantly. However, since 2015, imports have fallen while exports have remained constant. This recent change is a direct result of trade restrictions (tariffs) put in place by the Trump administration (and sustained in the Biden administration), followed by retaliatory restrictions from the Chinese government. It will be interesting to see if the new downward trend continues.

Source: Bureau of Economic Analysis.

While this increase in goods for U.S. consumers is viewed positively by economists, the trade deficit is concerning to some in the United States. For example, former President Donald Trump viewed the trade deficit as China taking funds from the United States. In March 2018, Trump said the U.S. "lost $500 billion" a year to China.*

To try to reduce this deficit, President Trump began imposing tariffs on Chinese imports in January of 2018. The first items affected were solar panels, washing machines, steel, and aluminum. China retaliated immediately by imposing tariffs on U.S. aluminum, airplanes, cars, pork, and soybeans. By August of 2018, the list of goods affected had grown into the hundreds. Many tariff levels were initially set at 10%, with later increases to 25%.

Unfortunately, most of the Trump-era tariffs continued into the Biden administration. Economists are generally against tariffs, because they limit the value-creating benefits of trade. Put simply: consumers benefit from additional options.

Trade creates value

*Jim Tankersley, "Trump Hates the Trade Deficit. Most Economists Don't," *New York Times*, March 5, 2018, https://www.nytimes.com/2018/03/05/us/politics/trade-deficit-tariffs-economists-trump.html.

Quotas

Sometimes, instead of taxing imports, governments use import quotas to restrict trade. **Import quotas** are limits on the quantity of products that can be imported into a country. Quotas function like tariffs with one crucial exception: the government does not receive any tax revenue. In the United States today, there are quotas on many products, including milk, tuna, olives, peanuts, cotton, and sugar.

Import quotas are limits on the quantity of products that can be imported into a country.

FIGURE 32.8

The Impact of a Quota

Without a quota, the domestic market is dominated by imports. However, when a quota is imposed, the price rises and domestic production expands from Q_{D1} to Q_{D2}. At the same time, imports fall to $Q_Q - Q_{D2}$. Quotas create deadweight loss (shaded areas A and B), a gain for foreign suppliers (area F), and increased producer surplus for domestic firms (area PS).

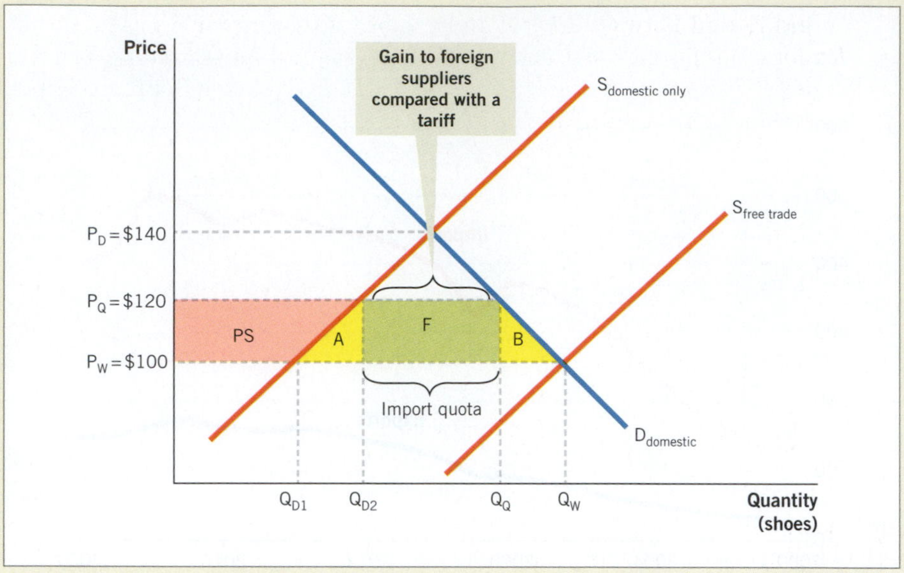

One famous example of quotas comes from the automobile industry in the 1980s and 1990s. During that period, Japan agreed to a "voluntary" quota on the number of vehicles it would export to the United States. Why would any group of firms agree to supply less than it could? The answer involves politics and economics. By voluntarily limiting the quantity they supply, foreign producers avoid having a tariff applied to their goods. Also, because the quantity supplied is somewhat smaller than it would otherwise be, foreign suppliers can charge higher prices. The net result is that a "voluntary" quota makes financial sense if it helps a producing nation to avoid a tariff.

Figure 32.8 shows how a quota placed on foreign-made shoes would work. The figure looks quite similar to Figure 32.6, which is not an accident. If we set the quota amount on foreign shoes equal to the imports after the tariff illustrated in Figure 32.6, the result is exactly the same with one notable exception: the green tariff rectangle, T, in Figure 32.6 has been replaced with a green rectangle, F, which is called the tariff-equivalent quota.

The quota is a strict limit on the number of shoes that may be imported into the United States. This limit pushes up the domestic price of shoes from $100 to $120 (represented as P_Q, reflecting the price under a quota). Because foreign producers must abide by the quota, one consequence is that the amount imported drops to $Q_Q - Q_{D2}$ (where Q_Q represents the total quantity supplied after the imposition of the quota). The smaller amount of imports causes the quantity supplied by domestic producers to rise along the domestic-only supply curve from Q_{D1} to Q_{D2}. Because domestic suppliers are now able to charge $20 more and also sell more, they are better off. We can see this result visually by noting that domestic suppliers gain producer surplus equal to shaded area PS (as we observed in Figure 32.6). As a result, domestic suppliers are indifferent between a tariff and a quota that has the same results. So, like before, there are two areas of deadweight loss, A and B, in which consumers lose because the price is higher and some people are forced to switch from foreign brands to domestic ones.

As you can see by the deadweight loss in shaded areas A and B, a quota results in the same efficiency loss as a tariff. Even though domestic suppliers are indifferent between a tariff and a quota system, foreign producers are not. Under a quota, they are able to keep the revenue generated in the green rectangle, F. Under a tariff, the equivalent rectangle, T, shown in Figure 32.6, is the tax revenue generated by the tariff.

ECONOMICS IN THE REAL WORLD

INEXPENSIVE SHOES FACE THE HIGHEST TARIFFS

Why do cheap imported shoes face such a high tariff?

Overall, U.S. tariffs average less than 2%, but inexpensive shoes face tariffs that are often at least 10 times more than that amount. What makes inexpensive imported shoes so "dangerous"? To help answer this question, a history lesson is in order.

Just 40 years ago, shoe manufacturers in the United States employed 250,000 workers. Today, the number of shoe workers is less than 3,000—and none of those workers assemble cheap shoes. Most of the shoe jobs have moved to low-labor-cost countries. But the shoe tariff, which was enacted to save domestic jobs, remains the same. Not a single sneaker costing less than $3 a pair is made in the United States, so the protection isn't saving any jobs. In contrast, goods such as cashmere sweaters, snakeskin purses, and silk shirts face low or no import tariffs. Other examples range from the 2.5% tariff on cars, tariffs of 4% and 5% for TV sets, and duty (tax)-free treatment for cell phones.

Shoppers who buy their shoes at Walmart and Zappos face the impact of shoe tariffs approaching 50% for the cheapest shoes, about 20% for a pair of name-brand running shoes, and about 9% for designer shoes from Gucci or Prada. This situation has the unintended consequence of passing along the tax burden to those who are least able to afford it.

One could reasonably argue that the shoe tariff is one of the United States' worst taxes. First, it failed to protect the U.S. shoe industry—the shoe jobs disappeared a long time ago. Second, consumers who are poor pay a disproportionate amount of the tax. And third, families with children pay even more because the more feet in a family, the more shoes are needed.

Incentives

Reasons Given for Trade Barriers

Considering all that we have discussed about the gains from trade and the inefficiencies associated with tariffs and quotas, you might be surprised to learn that trade restrictions are quite common. In this section, we consider some of the reasons for the persistence of trade barriers. These include national security, protection of infant industries, retaliation for *dumping*, and favors to special interests.

NATIONAL SECURITY Many people believe that certain industries, such as weapons, energy, and transportation, are vital to our nation's defense. They argue that without the ability to produce its own missiles, firearms, aircraft, and other strategically significant assets, a nation could find itself relying on its

ECONOMICS in the MEDIA

Free Trade

STAR WARS EPISODE I: THE PHANTOM MENACE

Disruptive, barriers to trade are!

The Phantom Menace (1999) is an allegory about peace, prosperity, taxation, and protectionism. As the movie opens, we see the Republic slowly falling apart. Planetary trade has been at the heart of the galactic economy. The central conflict in the movie is the Trade Federation's attempt to enforce its franchise by trying to intimidate a small planet, Naboo, which believes in free trade and peace.

The leader of the Naboo, Queen Amidala, refuses to pursue any path that might start a war. Her country is subjected to an excessive tariff and blockade, so she decides to appeal to the central government for help in ending the trade restrictions. However, she discovers that the Republic's Galactic Senate is ineffectual, so she returns home and prepares to defend her country.

Meanwhile, two Jedi who work for the Republic are sent to broker a deal between Naboo and the Trade Federation, but they get stranded on Tatooine, a desert planet located in the Outer Rim. In the Outer Rim, three necessary ingredients for widespread trade—the rule of law, sound money, and honesty—are missing. As a consequence, when the Jedi try to purchase some new parts for their ship, they find out that no one accepts the credit-based money of the Republic. The Jedi are forced to barter, a process that requires each trader to have exactly what the other wants. This situation results in a complicated negotiation between one of the Jedi and a local parts dealer. The scenes on Tatooine show why institutions, economies of scale, and competition matter so much for trade to succeed.

We encourage you to watch *The Phantom Menace* again with a fresh pair of eyes trained on the economics behind the special effects!

enemies. Thus, people often argue that certain industries should be protected in the interest of national security.

Although it is certainly important for any trade arrangement to consider national security, this argument has been used to justify trade restrictions on goods and services from friendly nations with whom we have active, open trade relations. For example, in 2002, the United States imposed tariffs on steel imports. Some policymakers argued that the steel tariffs were necessary because steel is an essential resource for national security. But, in fact, most imported steel comes from Canada and Brazil, which are traditional allies of the United States.

INFANT INDUSTRIES Another argument in support of steel tariffs in the United States was that the U.S. steel industry needed some time to implement new technologies that would enable it to compete with steel producers in other

PRACTICE WHAT YOU KNOW

Tariffs and Quotas: The Winners and Losers from Trade Barriers

Why would we penalize Chinese tire imports?

We have seen that tariffs definitely affect trade balances. One clear example is the U.S. tariff on Chinese tires that was imposed in 2009. The result of this tariff was a drop in imports of these tires from 13 million tires to just 5.6 million tires in one quarter. In addition, within a year, average radial car tire prices rose by about $8 per tire in the United States; the average price of Chinese tires rose from $30.79 to $37.98, while the average price of tires from all other nations rose from $53.94 to $62.05.

QUESTION: Who were the winners and losers domestically from this tire tariff?

ANSWER: The primary winners are domestic tire makers and the government since it collects the tariffs. The primary losers were U.S. tire consumers, who saw prices rise by about $8 per tire, or $32 for a set of four tires.

CHALLENGE QUESTION: Who would be the winners and losers overseas?

ANSWER: The primary winners were the producers of tires from everywhere except China. Because this tariff was targeted at a single nation, it did not affect tire producers in other nations. Non-Chinese tire producers realized an average of $8 more per tire. The losers were Chinese tire manufacturers.

Source: Gary Clyde Hufbauer and Sean Lowry, "US Tire Tariffs: Saving Few Jobs at High Cost," Policy Brief, Peterson Institute for International Economics, April 9, 2012.

nations. This **infant industry argument** states that domestic industries need trade protection until they are established and able to compete internationally. According to this point of view, once the fledgling industry gains traction and can support itself, the trade restrictions can be removed.

The **infant industry argument** states that domestic industries need trade protection until they are established and able to compete internationally.

However, reality doesn't work this way. Firms that lobby for protection are often operating in an established industry. For example, the steel industry in the United States is over 100 years old. Establishing trade barriers is often politically popular, but finding ways to remove them is politically difficult. There was a time when helping to establish the steel, sugar, cotton, or peanut industries might have made sense based on the argument for helping new industries. But the tariffs that protect those industries have remained, in one form or another, for over 100 years.

RETALIATION FOR DUMPING In 2009, the U.S. government imposed tariffs on radial car tires imported from China. These tariffs began at 35% and then gradually decreased to 25% before being phased out after three years. The argument in support of this tariff was that Chinese tire makers were *dumping* their tires in U.S. markets. **Dumping** occurs when a foreign supplier sells a good below the price it charges in its home country. As the name implies, dumping is often a deliberate effort to gain a foothold in a foreign market. It can also be the result of subsidies within foreign countries.

Dumping occurs when a foreign supplier sells a good below the price it charges in its home country.

ECONOMICS *for* LIFE

The Impact of Tariffs on Domestic Prices

To help you out, we've identified a few of the products with the highest tariffs, to give you a sense of how much the prices of those imports are affected:

- French chocolates—100% tariff
- European truffles—100%
- Sneakers—48%
- Chinese tires—35%

New Balance gets a "kick" out of tariffs on Nike.

The U.S. International Trade Commission (Office of Tariff Affairs and Trade Agreements) is responsible for publishing the applicable tariff rates for all merchandise imported into the United States. If you are interested in digging deeper, the full schedule can be found here: https://hts.usitc.gov/current. But be warned, the entire tariff schedule runs to almost four thousand pages!

From that list, sneakers are the item that most of us own. U.S. tariffs on sneakers benefit New Balance, the last large shoemaker to keep its entire production process stateside. If you have ever wondered why popular brands of shoes such as Nike and Adidas have higher prices, this is part of the reason. Since Nike and most other retailers produce many of their final products outside the United States, they must pay the tariff that protects domestic suppliers such as New Balance, and they pass those costs through to the customer.

In cases of dumping, the WTO allows for special *countervailing duties* to offset the subsidies. Thus, the United States placed a tariff on the imported tires to restore a level playing field. In essence, anytime a foreign entity decides to charge a lower price to penetrate a market, the country that is dumped on is likely to respond by imposing a tariff or quota to protect its domestic industries from foreign takeover. However, retaliation is also problematic. British economist Joan Robinson understood the risks well. She argued that the threat of trade barriers might conceivably work as a negotiation ploy, but when it came to actually enacting a retaliatory tariff, it "would be just as sensible to drop rocks into our harbours because other nations have rocky coasts."*

FAVORS TO SPECIAL INTERESTS The imposition of trade barriers is often referred to as "protection." This term raises the questions *Who is being protected?* and *What are they being protected from?* We have seen that trade barriers drive up domestic prices and lead to a lower quantity of goods or services in the market where the barriers are imposed. This situation does

*Joan Robinson, *Essays in the Theory of Employment* (New York: MacMillan, 1937).

not protect consumers. In fact, tariffs and quotas protect domestic producers from international competition. Steel tariffs were put in place to help domestic steel producers, and tire tariffs were put in place to help domestic tire producers.

When we see trade barriers, the publicly stated reason is generally one of the three reasons we have already discussed: national security, infant industry protection, or retaliation for dumping. But we must also recognize that these barriers may be put in place as a favor to special interest groups that have much to gain at the expense of domestic consumers. For example, as a result of sugar import regulations, U.S. consumers pay twice as much for sugar as the rest of the world does. Thus, while sugar tariffs and quotas protect U.S. sugar producers from international competition, they cost U.S. consumers more than $3 billion in 2014 alone. This outcome represents a special interest gain at the expense of U.S. consumers. If it were a tax transferred from consumers to producers, it would likely not persist. However, this kind of favor doesn't appear in the federal budget.

Conclusion

We began this chapter by rejecting the misconception that nations should not trade for goods and services they can produce for themselves. An analysis of the concept of comparative advantage shows that nations can gain by (1) specializing in the production of goods and services for which they have the lowest opportunity cost and then (2) trading for the other goods and services they wish to consume.

International trade is expanding all over the world. The United States now imports and exports more than at any time in its history. Increased trade is generally positive for all nations involved. However, trade barriers still exist around the globe for various reasons, including national security, the protection of infant industries, retaliation for dumping and subsidies, and favors to special interests. ✷

ANSWERING *the* BIG QUESTIONS

Is globalization for real?

- Over the long run, yes, globalization is very real. Since 1970, world exports have grown from 10% to about 22% of world GDP. For the United States, imports and exports have both grown over the past five decades. However, this trend has slowed and maybe even reversed since about 2010. The Great Recession slowed world trade, and then Trump-era trade restrictions imposed by both the United States and foreign governments slowed it further.

How does international trade help the economy?

- Gains from trade occur when a nation specializes in production and exchanges its output with a trading partner. For this arrangement to work, each nation must produce goods for which it is a low-opportunity-cost producer and then trade them for goods for which it is a high-opportunity-cost producer.
- In addition, trade benefits nations' economies through economies of scale and increased international competition.

What are the effects of tariffs and quotas?

- Protectionism in the form of trade restrictions, such as tariffs and quotas, is common. A tariff is a tax on imports; a quota is a quantity restriction on imports.
- Proponents of trade restrictions often cite the need to protect defense-related industries and fledgling firms and to fend off dumping. But protectionist policies can also serve as political favors to special interest groups.

CHAPTER PROBLEMS

Concepts You Should Know

comparative advantage (p. 1050)
dumping (p. 1065)
import quotas (p. 1061)
infant industry argument (p. 1065)
net exports (p. 1048)
protectionism (p. 1056)
tariffs (p. 1056)
trade balance (p. 1048)
trade deficit (p. 1048)
trade surplus (p. 1048)

Questions for Review

1. What are three problems with trade restrictions? What are three reasons often given in support of trade restrictions?
2. What would happen to the standard of living in the United States if all foreign trade were eliminated?
3. How might a nation's endowment of natural resources, labor, and climate shape the nature of its comparative advantage?
4. Why might foreign producers voluntarily agree to a quota rather than face an imposed tariff?
5. Tariffs reduce the volume of imports. Do tariffs also reduce the volume of exports? Explain your response.

Study Problems (* solved at the end of the section)

1. Consider the following table for the neighboring nations of Quahog and Pawnee. Assume that the opportunity cost of producing each good is constant.

Product	Quahog	Pawnee
Meatballs (per hour)	4,000	2,000
Clams (per hour)	8,000	1,000

   a. What is the opportunity cost of producing meatballs in Quahog? What is the opportunity cost of harvesting clams in Quahog?
   b. What is the opportunity cost of producing meatballs in Pawnee? What is the opportunity cost of producing clams in Pawnee?
   c. Based on your answers in parts (a) and (b), which nation has a comparative advantage in producing meatballs? Which nation has a comparative advantage in producing clams?

2. Suppose that the comparative-cost ratios of two products—mangoes and sardines—are as follows in the hypothetical nations of Mangolia and Sardinia:

   Mangolia: 1 mango = 2 cans of sardines
   Sardinia: 1 mango = 4 cans of sardines

   In what product should each nation specialize? Explain why the terms of trade of 1 mango = 3 cans of sardines would be acceptable to both nations.

3. What are the two trade restriction policies we discussed in this chapter? Who benefits and who loses from each of these policies? What is the new outcome for society?

* 4. Germany and Japan both produce cars and beer. The table below shows production possibilities per worker in each country. For example, one worker in Germany produces 8 cars or 10 cases of beer per week. (For a review of absolute versus comparative advantage, see Chapter 2.)

	Labor force	Cars (C)	Beer (B)
Germany	200	8	10
Japan	100	20	14

   a. Which nation has an absolute advantage in car production? Which one has an absolute advantage in beer production? Explain your answers.
   b. Which nation has a comparative advantage in car production? Which one has a comparative advantage in beer production? Explain your answers.

✷ 5. Continuing with the example given in the previous problem, assume that Germany and Japan produce their own cars and beer and allocate half their labor force to the production of each.

a. What quantities of cars and beer does Germany produce? What quantities does Japan produce?

Now suppose that Germany and Japan produce only the good for which they enjoy a comparative advantage in production. They also agree to trade half of their output for half of what the other country produces.

b. What quantities of cars and beer does Germany produce now? What quantities does Japan produce?

c. What quantities of cars and beer does Germany consume now? What quantities does Japan consume?

d. People often act as if international trade is a zero-sum game, meaning that when one party wins, the other party must lose an equal amount. State this book's foundational principle that contradicts this idea.

✷ 6. Determine whether each statement is true or false.

Developing countries stand to gain from international trade because

a. trade enables them to specialize in producing where they have a comparative advantage.

b. trade gives them access to the greater variety of goods produced abroad.

c. trade subjects their local producers to greater competition.

d. trade allows them to produce larger amounts than they could consume themselves, allowing them to take advantage of increasing returns to scale.

7. Is it possible for a producer to have both an absolute advantage and a comparative advantage?

Solved Problems

4. a. Japan has an absolute advantage in both because $20 > 8$ and $14 > 10$.

b. Japan has a comparative advantage in car production because its opportunity cost is less than Germany's ($0.7 < 1.25$). Germany has a comparative advantage in beer production because its opportunity cost is less than Japan's ($0.8 < 1.43$).

5. a. Germany: (C, B) = (800, 1,000); Japan: (C, B) = (1,000, 700)

b. Germany: (C, B) = (0, 2,000); Japan: (C, B) = (2,000, 0)

c. Germany: (C, B) = (1,000, 1,000); Japan: (C, B) = (1,000, 1,000)

d. Trade creates value for all involved because each party must benefit from the terms of trade or they would not agree to trade.

6. All four statements are true: (a) Trade is built on the concept of specialization and the application of comparative advantage in that process. (b) Trade allows countries to obtain a greater variety of goods and services from abroad than they could produce on their own. (c) Because trade effectively increases the number of potential competitors in the market, local producers are subject to more competition than would exist without trade. (d) When countries export goods, they benefit from being able to access a larger marketplace, which gives them the opportunity to produce at a larger scale than they would without trade.

CHAPTER

33 International Finance

Trade Deficits Do Not Indicate Economic Problems.

Since 1975, the United States has had a trade deficit with the rest of the world—we import more than we export. Many people believe that trade deficits are bad for an economy. After all, it seems unfair that we buy goods from other nations, but they do not buy nearly as many from us. The news media often perpetuate these beliefs by reporting trade deficit data in alarmist tones. The word "deficit" never sounds good. However, economists are not generally bothered by trade deficits. A trade deficit does not indicate economic problems. In fact, a trade deficit usually accompanies a strong and growing economy. A relatively wealthy economy can afford to buy goods and services from all over the world.

In this chapter, we explore the two most important topics in international finance: exchange rates and trade balances. We begin by explaining the determinants of exchange rates in both the short run and the long run, and then we come back to the topic of international trade balances.

New luxury cars, wrapped in protective white plastic, await the next leg of their journey to buyers. These vehicles are made by Jaguar Cars, a British company, to be exported to places like the United States. Overall, far more goods enter the United States than leave it. Is that a bad thing?

· BIG QUESTIONS ·

- Why do exchange rates rise and fall?
- What is purchasing power parity?
- What causes trade deficits?

Why Do Exchange Rates Rise and Fall?

Have you ever tried to buy a foreign currency? Perhaps you've seen exchange rates displayed on a sign at a bank or airport. If so, you've seen national flags and many potentially confusing numbers. An **exchange rate** is the price of foreign currency. This price tells how much a unit of foreign currency costs in terms of another currency. For example, the price of a single Mexican peso in terms of U.S. dollars is about $0.05, or 5 cents. This is the exchange rate between the peso and the dollar.

An **exchange rate** is the price of foreign currency, indicating how much a unit of foreign currency costs in terms of another currency.

A key message from Chapter 32 is that the world economy is becoming ever more integrated: globalization is real and increasing. As more goods and services flow across borders, exchange rates become more important. Exchange rates affect the relative prices of goods and services. Any good that crosses a border requires a foreign currency exchange. For example, the price you pay in the United States for a Samsung television built in South Korea depends on the exchange rate between the U.S. dollar and the won (the currency of South Korea).

Zooming out to the macro view, exchange rates affect the prices of all imports and exports—and therefore GDP. The more integrated the world economy becomes, the more closely economists watch exchange rates because they affect both what nations produce and what they consume.

Are you planning a trip abroad? If so, you'd better figure out how to use signs like this to exchange currency.

CANADA CAD 0.9512 0.8883
CHINA CNY 7.3169 6.0910
EURO EUR 0.6644 0.6100
JAPAN JPY 109.00 102.00
SINGAPORE SGD 1.3712 1.2630
HONG KONG HKD 7.0043 6.4072
NEW ZEALAND NZD 1.1646 1.0675
MYR 3.2536 2.7818

Our approach to exchange rates is straightforward: *exchange rates are prices*. For example, the exchange rate between the U.S. dollar and the won is the dollar price of one won, or the number of dollars required to buy a single won. It is just like the price of other goods we buy. Exchange rates are prices determined in world currency markets. Just as there are global markets where people buy and sell commodities such as sugar, wheat, and roses, there are also world markets, often called *foreign exchange markets*, where people buy and sell currencies.

Exchange rates are determined by the demand for and supply of currency in foreign exchange markets. Thus, if we want to explore the factors that make exchange rates rise and fall, we must consider the factors that affect the demand for and the supply of foreign currency. In this section, we look at some characteristics of foreign exchange markets and then consider the demand for and supply of foreign currency. We will finish up by considering why exchange rates rise and fall.

Characteristics of Foreign Exchange Markets

In a foreign exchange market, the good in question is a foreign currency. Very likely, you've held foreign currency at some point in your life—perhaps because a friend or relative saved some as a souvenir from a trip abroad or perhaps because you were fortunate to vacation or study in a foreign country. The primary reason why people purchase a foreign currency is to buy goods and services produced in the country that uses that currency. Don't lose sight of this simple truth; it is at the core of our entire conversation about exchange rate determination.

The demand for foreign currency is a derived demand. **Derived demand** is demand for a good or service that derives from the demand for another good or service. For example, if you travel to Belgium, you will probably want to buy some chocolate. But first you must buy euros, because the euro is the currency of Belgium. The euro is an unusual currency because it is used by 19 separate European nations, including Belgium, Germany, France, Spain, and Portugal. The demand for euros in world markets is derived from the demand for Belgian chocolate and many other goods, services, and financial assets produced in those 19 nations.

Derived demand is demand for a good or service that derives from the demand for another good or service.

Nowadays it is easier to buy goods in foreign countries by using a credit or debit card; you don't have to physically buy foreign currency. This approach works because your bank or card company is willing to buy the foreign currency for you. To you, it feels like you are paying in U.S. dollars, since you use the same card all over the world and you see deductions from your bank account in dollars. But your bank literally takes dollars from your account and exchanges them for foreign currency so it can pay foreign companies in their own currency. Your bank charges a fee for this service that makes the transaction simpler for you.

EXCHANGE RATES ARE THE PRICE OF FOREIGN CURRENCY

In this section, we look more closely at exchange rates. First, we clarify how exchange rates are quoted; then, we consider how appreciation and depreciation—two new terms—affect exchange rates.

Table 33.1 shows a few selected exchange rates from March 2022. Exchange rates can be viewed from either side of the exchange. For example, the exchange rate between the U.S. dollar and the Chinese yuan can be viewed as either of the following:

1. the number of yuan required to buy one U.S. dollar (¥ per $)
2. the number of U.S. dollars required to buy one yuan ($ per ¥)

While these two rates communicate the same information, they are not usually the same number. Instead, they are reciprocals of each other. We exclusively use the second option—the number of U.S. dollars required to buy one unit of foreign currency. This number is represented in the last column

TABLE 33.1

Exchange Rates between the U.S. Dollar and Other Currencies, March 2022

	Units of foreign currency you can buy with one U.S. dollar	Number of U.S. dollars required to buy one unit of foreign currency
British pound	0.768	1.30
Chinese yuan	6.34	0.158
Euro	0.916	1.09
Indian rupee	76.7	0.0130
Japanese yen	117	0.00851
Mexican peso	20.9	0.0478
South Korean won	1240	0.000809

Source: Google Public Data.

in Table 33.1. We choose this option for consistency; it is the way we quote all other prices. For example, if you walk into Starbucks and look at the prices posted on the wall, they indicate the number of dollars it takes to buy a single coffee drink. Thus, when we quote exchange rates in this textbook, we always specify the number of dollars required to buy a single unit of foreign currency.

If a currency becomes more valuable in world markets, its price rises, and this increase is called an appreciation. **Currency appreciation** occurs when a currency increases in value relative to other currencies. In contrast, **currency depreciation** occurs when a currency decreases in value relative to other currencies. If the dollar depreciates, it is less valuable in world markets.

Currency appreciation occurs when a currency becomes more valuable relative to other currencies.

Currency depreciation occurs when a currency becomes less valuable relative to other currencies.

Figure 33.1 illustrates appreciation and depreciation with the exchange rate between the U.S. dollar and the Chinese yuan. The exchange rate starts at \$0.15. If the exchange rate rises above \$0.15, it takes more dollars to buy yuan,

FIGURE 33.1

Exchange Rates and Currency Appreciation and Depreciation

An exchange rate is the price of a unit of foreign currency. When the exchange rate rises, foreign currency is more expensive, so this is an appreciation of the foreign currency but a depreciation of the domestic currency. When the exchange rate falls, foreign currency is less expensive, so this is a depreciation of the foreign currency but an appreciation of the domestic currency.

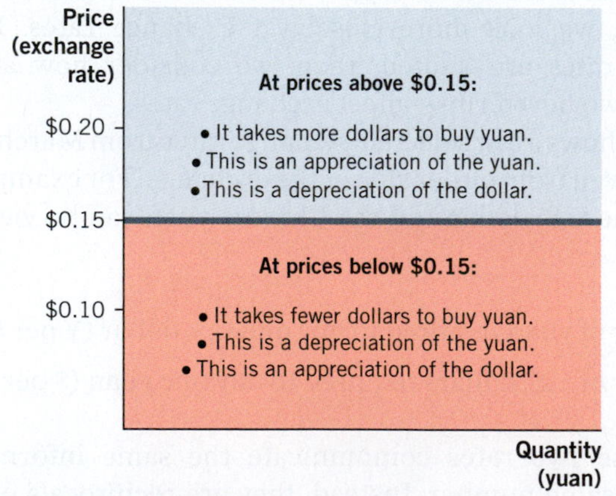

which signals an appreciation of the yuan and a depreciation of the dollar. If, instead, the price falls below $0.15, it takes fewer dollars to buy yuan, which signals a depreciation of the yuan and an appreciation of the dollar.

SOME HISTORICAL PERSPECTIVE When exchange rates rise, foreign currencies become more expensive relative to the dollar. This means that imports become more expensive. But then U.S. exports become less expensive, so foreigners around the globe can afford to buy more U.S. goods and services. These are the reasons why exchange rates are important macroeconomic indicators to watch.

The recent past offers a mixed picture of the world value of the dollar. Figure 33.2 plots exchange rates for the currencies of two different trading partners of the United States: Europe (the euro) and China (the yuan). The vertical axis in each panel measures the dollar price of one unit of the relevant foreign currency. Panel (a) shows the exchange rate with the euro. The euro exchange rate fluctuated wildly over the 17 years pictured, rising from $1.20 to almost $1.60 during the recession year of 2008 but then falling to under $1.10 by 2015. Between 2013 and 2015, the value of the dollar grew significantly. Panel (b) shows a similar story for the yuan over the 15-year period. As the price of yuan climbed, dollars were depreciating. But by 2016, the price of the yuan dropped to less than fifteen cents, indicating a stronger U.S. dollar.

FIGURE 33.2

Two Foreign Exchange Rates, 2004–2021

These exchange rates are reported as the number of U.S. dollars required to purchase a unit of foreign currency. (a) In looking at the euro exchange rate from 2004 to 2021, we see that the price of the euro rose from $1.20 to almost $1.60 but then fell below $1.10 in 2015. (b) The fluctuations in the Chinese yuan exchange rate are much more muted because the Chinese government actively manages this exchange rate. Notice the two flat regions prior to 2011. These are not produced naturally in world markets.

Source: FRED Economic Data, Federal Reserve Bank of St. Louis.

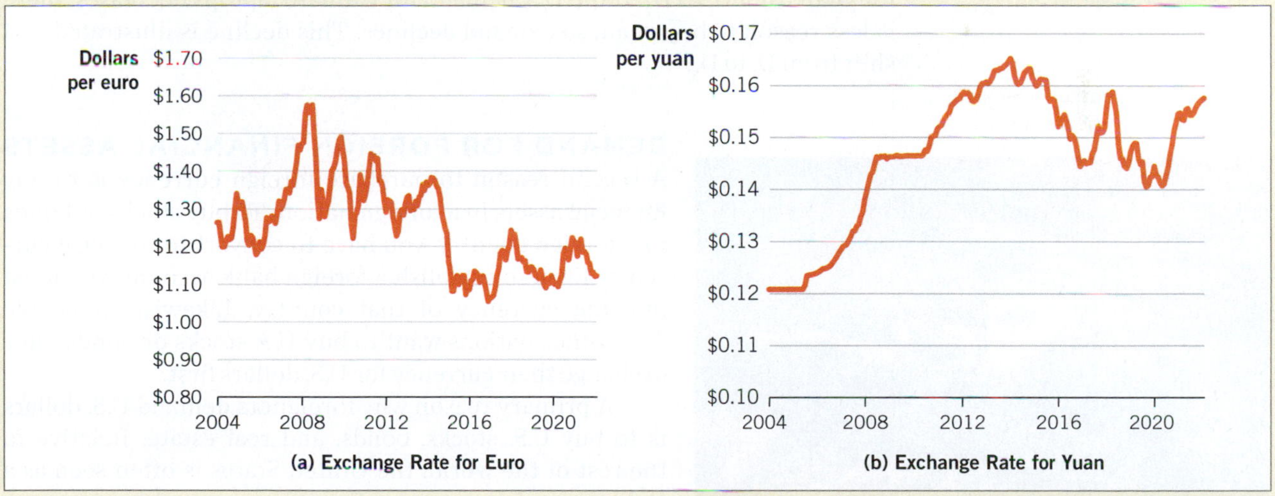

The Demand for Foreign Currency

In this section, we discuss the factors that affect the demand side of the market for foreign currency. We distinguish three primary factors: the price of the currency (the exchange rate), the demand for foreign goods and services, and the demand for foreign financial assets.

PRICE OF FOREIGN CURRENCY (THE EXCHANGE RATE)

The law of demand holds in foreign currency markets. When the price of the yuan falls, goods and services produced in China (like Lenovo laptops) are less expensive relative to goods and services produced in the United States. Therefore, when the price of yuan falls, the quantity of Chinese goods demanded increases. Conversely, when the price of yuan rises, it becomes more expensive to purchase Chinese goods, and quantity demanded falls.

DEMAND FOR FOREIGN GOODS AND SERVICES As we emphasized earlier, people generally purchase foreign currency to buy goods or services produced in foreign countries. Perhaps you are thinking, "I buy goods from other countries without purchasing foreign currency." This is true: you can buy imported TVs, cars, fruits, and clothing without ever touching a coin or bill of foreign currency. But those goods were originally purchased with the foreign currency of the nation where they were produced.

For example, a Lenovo laptop computer is produced in China, but you can buy it on the Internet or in a store in the United States. The workers and factory owners in China are paid in yuan. This means that the business firm that imports the Lenovo laptop from China buys yuan to pay for the product. In short, someone has to buy the foreign currency, even if it is not you. For this reason, the demand for a nation's currency derives from (depends on) the demand for its exports.

When the demand for a nation's exports rises, the demand for its currency rises, too. For example, if the U.S. demand for Chinese laptops increases, the demand for yuan increases at all prices. Figure 33.3 illustrates changes in demand for yuan. An increase in demand for Chinese laptops shifts the demand for yuan from D_1 to D_2. If the U.S. demand for Chinese laptops decreases, there is less reason to buy yuan, so demand declines. This decline is illustrated as a shift from D_1 to D_3.

If you want to snorkel in Mexico, you'd better buy some pesos.

DEMAND FOR FOREIGN FINANCIAL ASSETS

A second reason to purchase foreign currency is to buy financial assets in a foreign nation. To buy stocks or bonds in a foreign country, you have to convert to the local currency. Even to establish a foreign bank account, you must buy the currency of that country. Likewise, if people from other nations want to buy U.S. stocks or bonds, they exchange their currency for U.S. dollars first.

A primary reason why foreigners demand U.S. dollars is to buy U.S. stocks, bonds, and real estate. Relative to the rest of the world, the United States is often seen as a stable, low-risk economy. For this reason, there is a consistent demand for U.S. dollars.

FIGURE 33.3

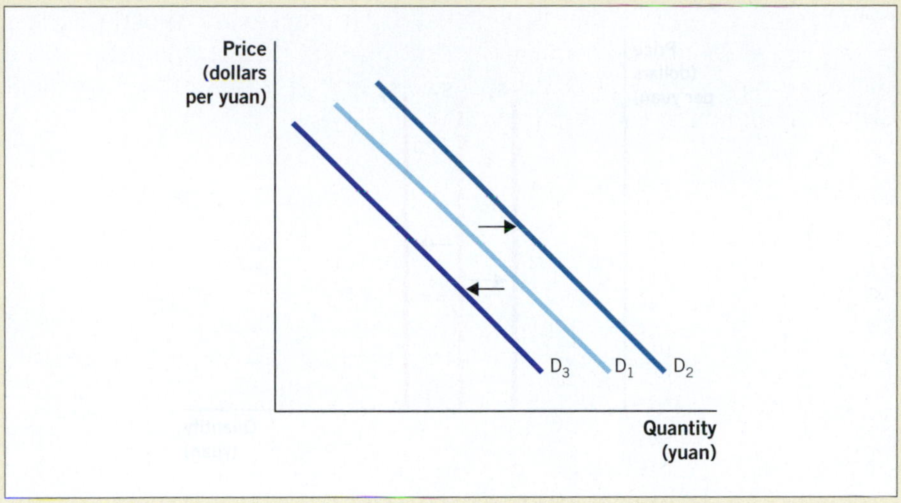

Shifts in the Demand for Foreign Currency

Increases in the demand for foreign currency (D_2) derive from an increased demand for foreign goods and services and/or foreign financial assets. Decreases in the demand for foreign currency (D_3) derive from a decreased demand for foreign goods and services and/or foreign financial assets. Here we illustrate these relationships with the U.S. dollar and the Chinese yuan.

Along these lines, one key factor in foreign exchange markets is interest rates across nations. If interest rates rise in one country (relative to rates in the rest of the world), the demand for its currency increases, since there is a greater demand for the assets with higher returns, all else equal. For example, if interest rates in China rise relative to those in the rest of the world, it means Chinese bonds provide a higher return than previously, and demand rises along with the interest rate. In Figure 33.3, this move is indicated as a shift from D_1 to D_2. When interest rates fall, there is reduced demand for the nation's currency. We see this outcome in Figure 33.3 as a shift from D_1 to D_3.

The Supply of Foreign Currency

In Chapter 30, we discussed fiat currency. This type of currency is printed and supplied by governments. From a market standpoint, it is fixed in quantity at any one time. Governments increase and decrease the supply of fiat currency very often, and when they do, the supply curve shifts, as Figure 33.4 shows. For example, consider the possible actions of the People's Bank of China (PBC), which is the central bank of China, the agency that determines monetary policy for the country. Initially, the supply of yuan is vertical at S_1. If the PBC increases the supply of yuan relative to the supply of dollars, the supply curve shifts outward to S_2. If, instead, the PBC reduces the supply of yuan relative to the supply of dollars, the supply curve shifts in the opposite direction, to S_3.

Applying Our Model of Exchange Rates

In this section, we consider applications of our model of exchange rates. In reality, exchange rates fluctuate daily, and these prices affect the prices of all imports and exports. These fluctuations are the result of shifts in demand, supply, or both. We start with changes in demand.

FIGURE 33.4

Shifts in the Supply of Foreign Currency

The supply of any nation's currency is determined by that nation's government. If the People's Bank of China increases the supply of yuan relative to the supply of dollars, the supply curve shifts from S_1 to S_2. If the supply of yuan decreases relative to the supply of dollars, the curve shifts in the opposite direction, to S_3.

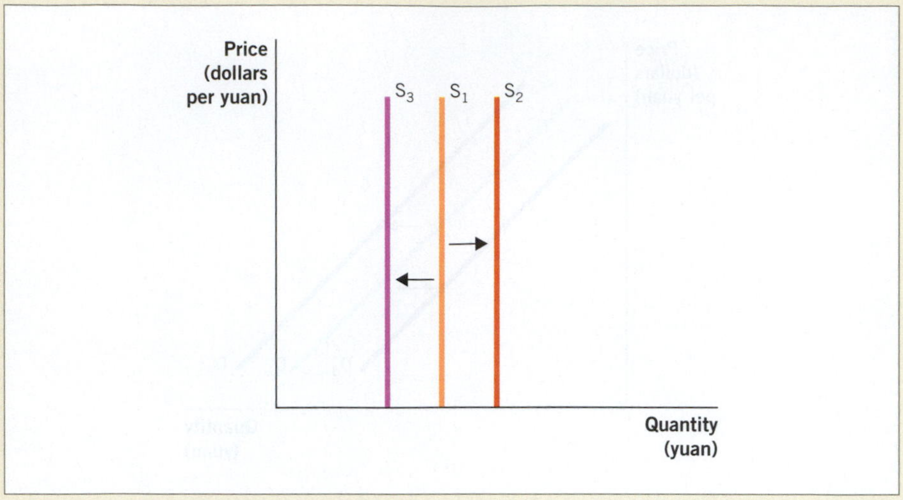

CHANGES IN DEMAND In most of the world, computer shoppers can choose from many varieties; these include Dell (largely produced in the U.S.) and Lenovo (produced in China). In microeconomics, you might study the impact on computer manufacturers from a shift in consumer preferences away from Dells and toward Lenovos. But these kinds of demand changes, which occur quite frequently, also affect the market for foreign currency. For example, if consumer preferences in the United States shift away from Dells and toward Lenovos, the demand for the yuan rises.

Figure 33.5 shows the results of a shift toward Lenovos. Initially, the market (for yuan) is in equilibrium with supply S and demand D_1. The initial equilibrium exchange rate is \$0.15. Then, after U.S. consumers demand more Lenovos, the demand for yuan shifts out to D_2. This shift causes the exchange rate to rise to \$0.20.

If the cause of the shift is an increase in the demand for Chinese financial assets (like Alibaba bonds), the result is the same. Thus, if interest rates in China rise, this signals investors around the globe to buy financial assets in China. The increase in the yuan demand leads to an increase in the exchange rate. The higher exchange rate implies a yuan appreciation and, by comparison, a dollar depreciation. People want more yuan, so its value rises in relation to the dollar.

How are exchange rates affected when consumers choose Lenovo over Dell computers?

If, instead, global demand for goods, services, and financial assets moves away from China and toward the United States, yuan demand falls (shifting to D_3) as people move toward dollars. In this case, the exchange rate falls and the yuan depreciates, while the dollar appreciates.

These shifts in demand occur naturally in a global economy where consumers across different nations choose among products produced in a wide variety of countries. Even just focusing on a single type of good, like cars, we can choose to buy from the United States, Germany,

FIGURE 33.5

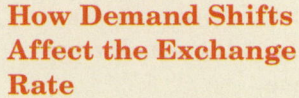

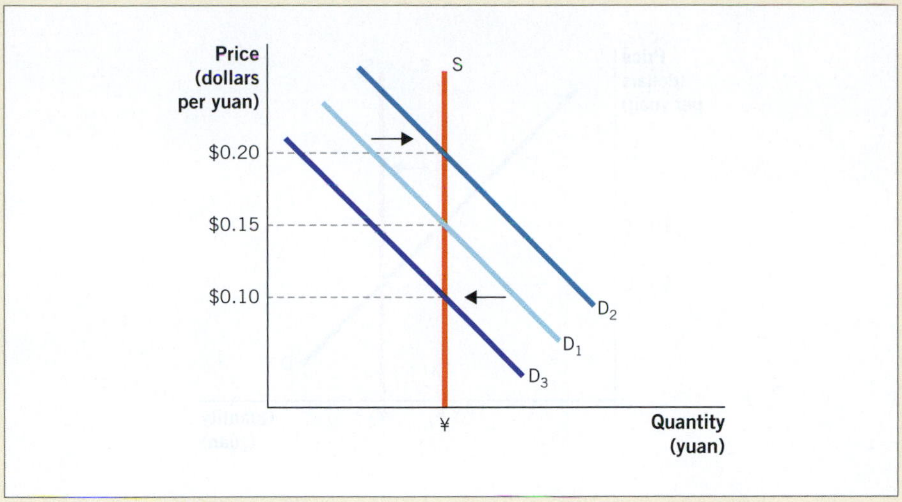

How Demand Shifts Affect the Exchange Rate

An increase in the demand for foreign currency leads to an increase in the exchange rate from $0.15 to $0.20. This signals a depreciation of the U.S. dollar relative to the yuan. A decrease in the demand for foreign currency leads to a decrease in the exchange rate from $0.15 to $0.10. This signals an appreciation of the U.S. dollar relative to the yuan.

Japan, South Korea, the United Kingdom, Canada, and Italy, to name just a few car-producing countries. But as international demanders' product preferences change, exchange rates are affected. Table 33.2 summarizes how shifts in demand affect foreign exchange rates.

However, there are also "unnatural" changes in exchange rates, caused by intentional actions of government monetary authorities all over the globe. To understand these, we look at shifts in currency supply.

CHANGES IN SUPPLY The supply side of currency markets is determined by government. Figure 33.6 illustrates a scenario in which the People's Bank of China (PBC) increases the supply of yuan. This move shifts supply from S_1 to S_2 and causes the exchange rate to fall from $0.15 to $0.10. The drop in the exchange rate means that the yuan depreciates relative to the dollar—a direct result of the increase in yuan supply. The PBC action means there are now more yuan per dollar, so yuan are worth less in relative terms.

The scenario pictured in Figure 33.6 is actually quite common. Government monetary authorities often intervene in markets to drive down their exchange rates. **Exchange rate manipulation** occurs when a national

Exchange rate manipulation occurs when a national government intentionally adjusts its money supply to affect the exchange rate of its currency.

TABLE 33.2

Shifts in Demand for Foreign Currency

Cause	Demand for foreign currency	Exchange rate change
Increase in demand for foreign goods and services or financial assets	Demand increases.	Exchange rate rises.
Decrease in demand for foreign goods and services or financial assets	Demand decreases.	Exchange rate falls.

FIGURE 33.6

How Supply Shifts Affect the Exchange Rate

All else being equal, an increase in the quantity of yuan shifts the supply of yuan to the right, to ¥$_2$. This shift causes the exchange rate to decrease from \$0.15 to \$0.10. Thus, the yuan depreciates and the dollar appreciates.

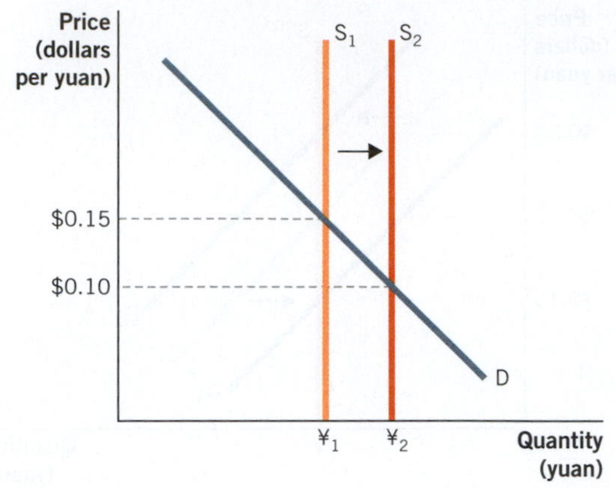

government intentionally adjusts its money supply to affect the exchange rate of its currency.

It may seem odd that a government would take action to purposefully depreciate the value of its own currency. After all, don't we typically want our assets to *appreciate*? If you learned that the value of your car depreciated drastically in the last year, you would not take it as good news. What if the value of your parents' home depreciates; is that good news? No, these are both bad news. However, nations depreciate their own currencies in order to make their exports more affordable to buyers worldwide. When the yuan falls in value, each dollar buys more yuan. And a devalued yuan makes Chinese products more affordable. All else equal, the demand for Chinese products then rises in the United States.

Currency devaluation, by increasing the quantity of currency, can certainly have a short-run impact on aggregate demand. But to see how the currency devaluation affects the overall Chinese economy, we need to consider it in the context of the aggregate demand–aggregate supply model. In Chapter 26, we included the value of domestic currency among the factors that shift aggregate demand. We noted that a decrease in the value of domestic currency (depreciation) causes an increase in aggregate demand.

Let's now consider this observation in the context of our present discussion. If the PBC acts to depreciate the yuan, aggregate demand for Chinese goods and services increases, as shown in Figure 33.7 as a shift from AD_1 to AD_2. In the short run, this shift leads to greater real GDP (Y_1) and lower unemployment in China. This happens because some prices are inflexible in the short run. But when all prices adjust (shifting SRAS from $SRAS_1$ to $SRAS_2$), output returns to its earlier level, leaving only inflation as the result of the increased quantity of yuan—the price level rises from 100 to 110. In the end, yuan are less expensive; but because of inflation, it takes more yuan to buy Chinese goods. In the long run, there are no real effects from the action: the LRAS curve remains at Y^*.

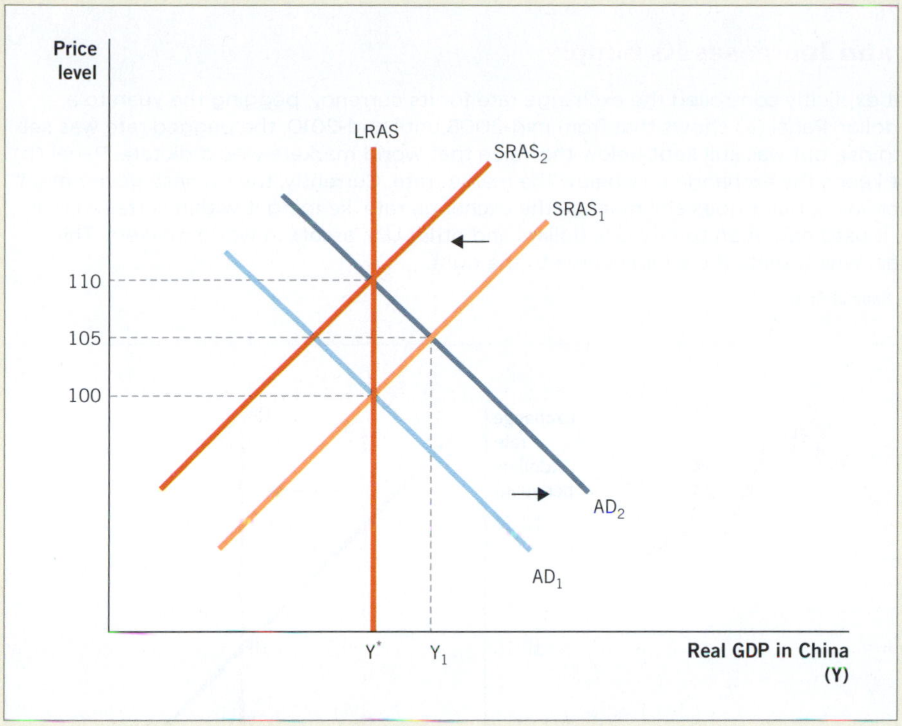

FIGURE 33.7

Increase in Aggregate Demand in China Arising from Yuan Depreciation

A depreciation of the yuan increases aggregate demand for Chinese goods and services. In the short run, real GDP increases and unemployment (not pictured here) decreases due to some sticky prices. In the long run, when prices adjust fully, there are no real effects, just inflation, because the price level rises from 100 to 110.

PEGGING EXCHANGE RATES Panel (a) of Figure 33.8 plots the U.S. dollar exchange rate with the Chinese yuan. Notice the flat period between 2008 and 2010, then the gradual, mostly evenly paced increases after that. This pattern is not due to natural market forces; it is because the Chinese government maintained a pegged exchange rate with the dollar. **Pegged (fixed) exchange rates** are exchange rates fixed at a certain level through the actions of a government. The alternative to pegged exchange rates is flexible exchange rates. **Flexible (floating) exchange rates** are exchange rates determined by the market forces of supply of and demand for currency. Previously in this chapter, our discussions have assumed flexible exchange rates.

Pegged (fixed) exchange rates are exchange rates fixed at a certain level through the actions of a government.

Flexible (floating) exchange rates are exchange rates determined by the supply of and demand for currency.

Many exchange rates today, such as those we have already considered, are flexible. Previously, China explicitly pegged its currency, the yuan, to the U.S. dollar. The yuan was pegged at a value below that which would have prevailed if the exchange rate were flexible; the market-determined rate would have been above $0.160. For instance, the yuan was pegged at $0.147 from 2008 to 2010; this is the flat region in Figure 33.8, panel (a). Nations cannot just pass laws to peg an exchange rate, because world markets are not subject to the laws of individual nations. Instead, the Chinese government maintained its peg by adjusting the supply of yuan made available to world markets. Currently, the Chinese government does not peg the exchange rate at a specific level, but it does still manage the level by keeping it within a range of values.

To decrease the price of the yuan, the Chinese government increased the supply of yuan relative to the supply of dollars. Panel (b) in Figure 33.8

FIGURE 33.8

How China Pegs the Yuan and Increases Its Supply

In the past, the Chinese government explicitly controlled the exchange rate for its currency, pegging the yuan to a particular value relative to the U.S. dollar. Panel (a) shows that from mid-2008 until mid-2010, the pegged rate was set at $0.147; after this, it was allowed to rise but was still kept below the value that world markets would dictate. Panel (b) shows how the Chinese government keeps the exchange rate below the market rate. Currently, the Chinese government doesn't peg the currency to an exact value, but it does still manage the exchange rate, keeping it within certain bands. When it wants to devalue the yuan, it uses new yuan to buy U.S. dollars and other U.S. assets in world markets. This strategy increases the supply of yuan, which shifts the supply curve to the right.

Source: FRED Economic Data, Federal Reserve Bank of St. Louis.

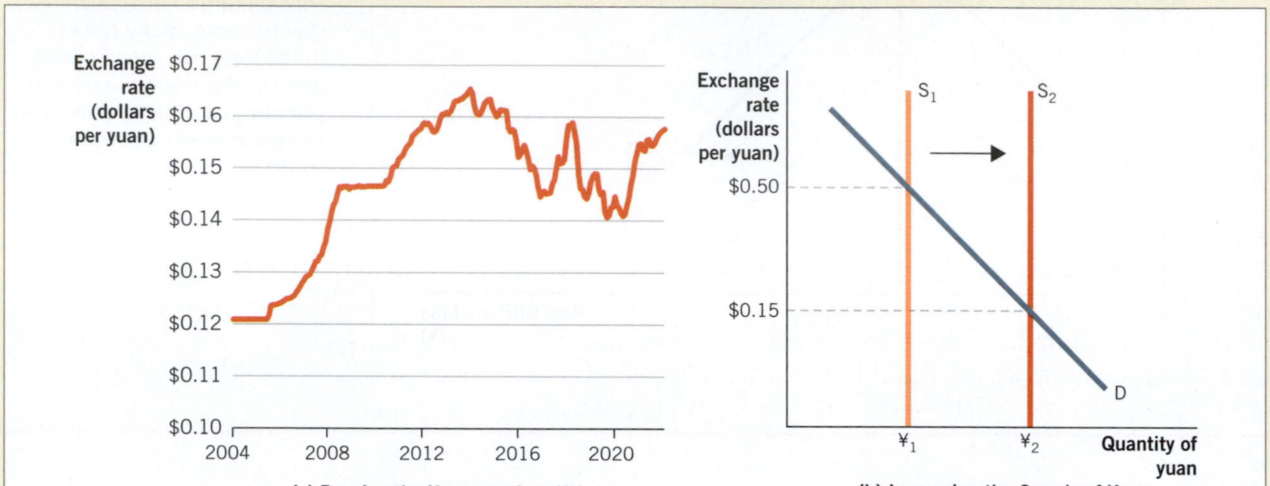

(a) Pegging the Yuan at a Low Value Relative to U.S. Dollars

(b) Increasing the Supply of Yuan Relative to U.S. Dollars

illustrates how an increase in supply drives down the price of the yuan. In practice, when the Chinese government desires a yuan devaluation, it buys U.S. dollars and U.S. Treasury securities in world markets. Notice the word "buy" in the last sentence. That's right: the Chinese government has to buy these, and when it buys them with newly minted yuan, the supply of yuan shifts to the right, to S_2. This action causes the Chinese currency to depreciate. Essentially, the Chinese government is conducting open market operations by purchasing U.S. Treasury securities. Ironically, this is exactly how the U.S. Federal Reserve enacts expansionary monetary policy for the United States.

The Chinese government devalues the yuan so that Chinese goods and services become less expensive on world markets. The government wants Chinese exports to be very affordable because it is trying to build the nation's economy through exports. The Chinese view this as a long-term strategy that will help their economy develop into an industrial economy. Since 2010, the Chinese government has been letting the yuan rise in value, but as the Economics in the Real World feature explains, the Chinese government seems to be having second thoughts.

ECONOMICS IN THE REAL WORLD

CHINESE EXPORT GROWTH SLOWS

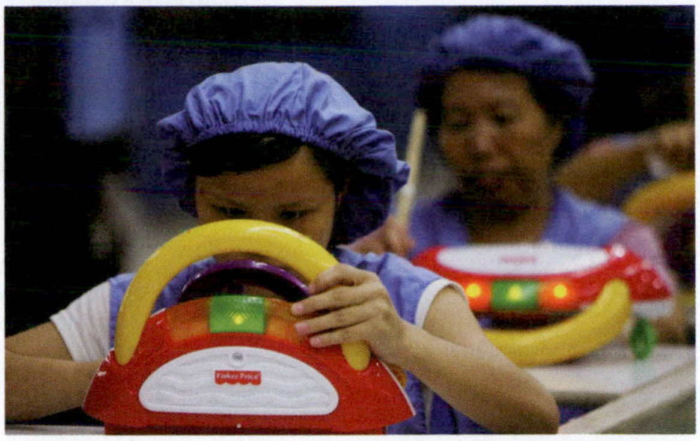

Will the Chinese government continue to keep the value of the yuan down so that Americans can buy these toys at reduced prices?

In August 2015, the Chinese government took action to devalue the yuan, letting the exchange value fall 3% in just two days. The goal of the Chinese government was to cheapen the yuan to make Chinese exports cheaper for Americans and others to buy. The devaluation of the yuan took place while the Chinese economy was struggling to maintain the phenomenal growth of the prior two decades. But many economists question whether continued currency devaluations can lead to sustainable economic growth.

In one sense, it is clear that the Chinese economy has been growing at historically high rates over the past two decades. This fact seems to indicate that the devaluation strategy is helping the Chinese economy overall, not just the export sector. Perhaps this is true, but let's be careful. After all, many other changes have taken place in China over the past two decades. Recall from Chapters 24 and 25 that institutional changes (especially the introduction of private property rights) have significantly altered production incentives in China. Therefore, it is inaccurate to pin China's success on currency devaluation alone.

In addition, the devaluation of the Chinese currency has other side effects. In particular, devaluation harms Chinese workers, who are paid in yuan. When the government devalues the currency, this move effectively gives the workers a real pay cut. Part of the reason why Chinese exports are so inexpensive is that the nation's labor costs are very low. But this is not a positive outcome for the wage earners.

PRACTICE WHAT YOU KNOW

The Bahamian Dollar Is Pegged to the U.S. Dollar

This might not look like three U.S. dollars, but that's basically what it is.

While the Chinese government keeps the dollar–yuan exchange rate artificially low to encourage exports, other nations peg their currency to the dollar to guarantee stability. In fact, as of 2015, there were still dozens of nations that pegged their currency to the U.S. dollar. Not all the exchange rates are held artificially low with their dollar peg.

QUESTION: Assume that the Bahamian government wants to peg its currency to the U.S. dollar at a 1:1 ratio (one U.S. dollar = one Bahamian dollar). But the current exchange rate is at 90 cents (10 cents below the official peg). What must the Bahamian central bank do to return to the $1 exchange rate?

ANSWER: In this case, as illustrated in the graph on the next page, the initial supply and demand curves intersect at $0.90 before the government intervenes to enforce the peg. Thus, the Bahamian central bank should reduce the supply of Bahamian dollars from S_1 to S_2 to increase the exchange rate to $1.00.

(CONTINUED)

CHALLENGE QUESTION: Assume instead that the Bahamian government wants to alter its exchange rate to exactly $0.45, and the current exchange rate is $0.90. What must the Bahamian central bank do to reach a pegged exchange rate of $0.45?

ANSWER: In this case, the Bahamian central bank will need to double the supply of Bahamian dollars in world markets. This will eventually cause the value of the Bahamian dollar to fall by half.

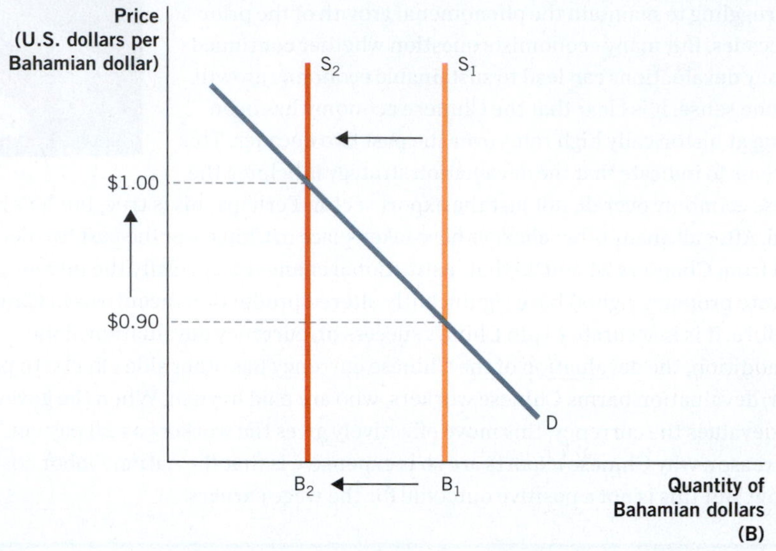

What Is Purchasing Power Parity?

As we have noted, the world economy is becoming ever more integrated. This integration affects both suppliers and demanders of goods and services. Suppliers can often choose where they wish to sell their output, and demanders can often choose where they want to buy their goods and services—even if doing so requires a little extra shipping.

In this section, we discuss the theory of how exchange rates are determined in the long run. We begin by examining how market exchanges determine the price of a particular good at different locations inside a nation. Then we extend this discussion to prices of goods and services in different nations. Finally, we come back and consider limitations to the theory. We begin with the *law of one price*.

The Law of One Price

Let's consider a simplified example of trade within the borders of one country: Florida oranges are consumed in Michigan and many other states. What happens if the price of Florida oranges is different in Michigan and Florida? Figure 33.9 illustrates two different markets for Florida oranges—one in

FIGURE 33.9

The Law of One Price

(a) Initially, the price of a pound of oranges in Florida is $1.80, while (b) the same oranges sell for $2.20 per pound in Michigan. Thus, orange suppliers reduce supply in Florida and increase supply in Michigan. If transportation costs are zero, these supply changes will take place until the price is the same in both locations.

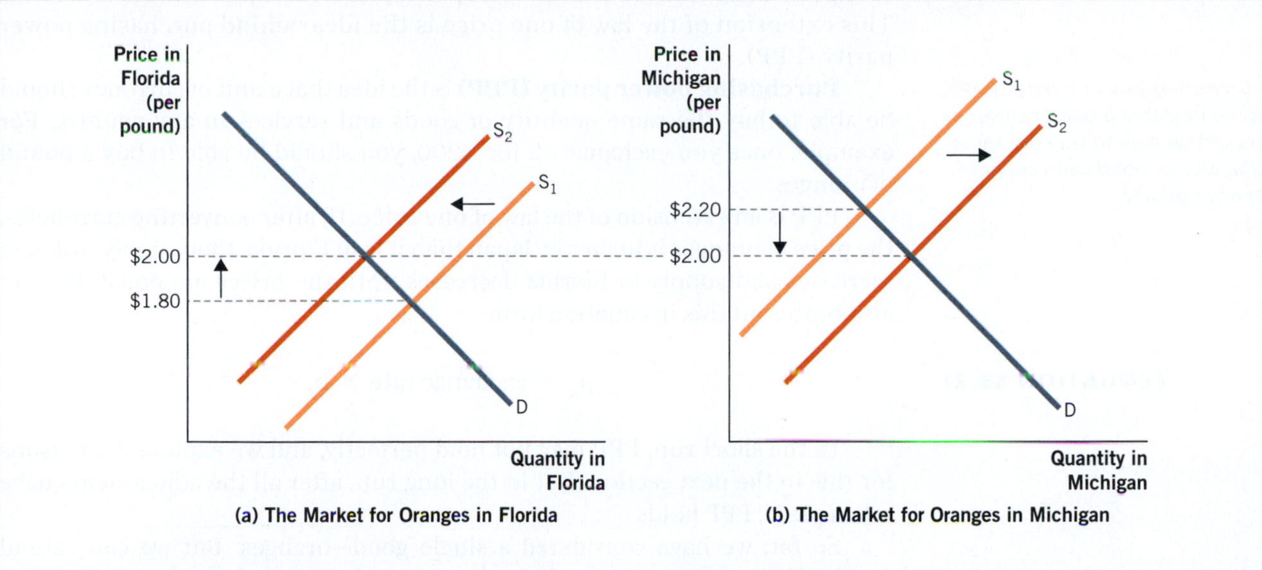

Florida and one in Michigan. Initially, as we see in panel (a), the price of a pound of oranges in Florida is $1.80; as we see in panel (b), the price of a pound of the same oranges in Michigan is $2.20. Assume for now that there are no transportation costs and no trade barriers. In this case, sellers in Florida have an incentive to sell their oranges in Michigan, where the price is 40 cents higher. Thus, the supply in Florida will decline and the supply in Michigan will increase. These supply shifts will lead to an increased price in Florida and a decreased price in Michigan. The adjustment continues until the prices are the same in both locations, at $2.00.

Incentives

This adjustment process is the logic behind the **law of one price**, which says that after accounting for transportation costs and trade barriers, identical goods sold in different locations must sell for the same price. We can state the law of one price in equation form, where p_A is the price of a good in location A and p_B is the price of the same good in location B:

The **law of one price** says that after accounting for transportation costs and trade barriers, identical goods sold in different locations must sell for the same price.

$$p_A = p_B \quad \text{(EQUATION 33.1)}$$

The law of one price also holds across international borders. For example, if Florida oranges are sold in Japan, the price should be the same once we account for the costs of shipping and trade barriers. But when oranges ship across international borders, a new issue arises because different nations generally use different currencies. We take up this issue in the next section.

Purchasing Power Parity and Exchange Rates

In Japan, the medium of exchange is the yen. The exchange rate between the U.S. dollar and the yen is about \$0.01. Therefore, since each yen is worth about a penny, the law of one price implies that it should take about 100 times as many yen to buy oranges in Japan as it does dollars to buy the same oranges in the United States. Thus, if the price of a pound of oranges in the United States is \$2, the price in Japan should be ¥200. This extension of the law of one price is the idea behind purchasing power parity (PPP).

Purchasing power parity (PPP) is the idea that a unit of currency should be able to buy the same quantity of goods and services in any country.

Purchasing power parity (PPP) is the idea that a unit of currency should be able to buy the same quantity of goods and services in any country. For example, once you exchange \$2 for ¥200, you should be able to buy a pound of oranges.

PPP is an extension of the law of one price. If, after converting currencies, the price of oranges is higher in Japan than it is in Florida, then supply to Japan increases and supply in Florida decreases until the prices are equal. We can also represent this in equation form:

(EQUATION 33.2)

$$p_A = \text{exchange rate} \times p_B$$

In the short run, PPP may not hold perfectly, and we explain the reasons for this in the next section. But in the long run, after all the adjustments have taken place, PPP holds.

So far, we have considered a single good—oranges. But we can extend purchasing power parity to all final goods and services in order to derive an important implication regarding exchange rates. If Equation 33.2 holds for all final goods and services, then the price levels (P) in different nations should be related as follows:

(EQUATION 33.3)

$$P_A = \text{exchange rate} \times P_B$$

In Equation 33.3, P_A is the price level in nation A and P_B is the price level in nation B. We can rewrite Equation 33.3 to derive a key implication of PPP:

(EQUATION 33.4)

$$\text{exchange rate} = P_A \div P_B$$

This equation is a direct extension of the law of one price to international trade in all goods and services. We can use Equation 33.4 to learn what causes big swings in exchange rates over time. For example, the exchange rate between the U.S. dollar and the Mexican peso has fallen in recent years, which means that the dollar has appreciated relative to the peso. In 2008, each peso cost approximately \$0.10, but over the next decade, the rate fell by half, to \$0.05. This long-run change reflects shifts in relative price levels of the United States and Mexico. While inflation in the United States averaged just 1.7% from 2008 to 2018, inflation in Mexico for the same period was 4.2% per year. These changing price levels led to an increase in the exchange rate, because $P_{US} \div P_{Mexico}$ increased between 2008 and 2018. Thus, in the long run, exchange rate fluctuations are driven by relative changes in price levels.

ECONOMICS *in the* MEDIA

Impossible Exchange Rates

EUROTRIP

These friends don't have to look far to find a bargain when their dollars are strong relative to the local currency.

In this movie from 2004, four American high school graduates travel to Europe and end up in Bratislava, the capital of Slovakia. They are particularly concerned when they pool their remaining money and find they have just $1.83. But it turns out that the U.S. dollar is extremely valuable in Slovakia. Using this small amount of money, the four friends are able to have an amazing night on the town. At one point, they tip a busboy just 5 cents, but this tip is so valuable that the man promptly retires from his job to enjoy his wealth.

An appreciating and strong U.S. dollar is good news to people who are paid in U.S. dollars. The stronger your home currency, the more you can buy around the globe.

But purchasing power parity means that the kind of wild overvaluation of the dollar we see in *Eurotrip* is not possible in the real world. If the dollar were really this strong in some nation, tourists would flood in with dollars and then drive the prices up to a more reasonable level. The movie's story makes for entertaining theater, but the law of one price and purchasing power parity mean these kinds of bargains can't last long in the real world.

ECONOMICS IN THE REAL WORLD

THE BIG MAC INDEX

Is the price of this McDonald's sandwich the same all over the world?

We have said that purchasing power parity is a condition that should hold in the long run. The British magazine *The Economist* has devised a creative way to test PPP at any given point in time. It compares the price of a McDonald's Big Mac sandwich across many nations. The Big Mac is a good choice because it is roughly the same good all over the world. For example, in December 2021, the price of a Big Mac in the United States was $5.81. Given that the exchange rate between the U.S. dollar and the euro was about $1.12 at that time, we can use Equation 33.2 to find the implied price of the Big Mac in the Euro area:

$$5.81 = 1.12 \times P_{\text{Europe}}$$

Solving for the price in Europe, we find that $5.81 \div 1.12 = 5.19$ euros. In fact, the actual price was 4.42 euros, so it seems that the Big Mac is priced much lower in Europe.

Table 33.3 shows the Big Mac price across seven different nations, along with the price implied by PPP. The first column of numbers gives the actual price of the Big Mac in terms of the domestic currency for each nation. The last column shows the actual price of the Big Mac converted to U.S. dollars using the exchange rate. If PPP held perfectly, the prices in the last column would all be $5.58, the price of a Big Mac in the United States.

In the next section, we examine why PPP might not hold exactly in the short run. One of the key reasons is that the goods must be identical across nations.

Why PPP Does Not Hold Perfectly

When we look at the Big Mac index, we see that PPP does not always hold perfectly. There are five reasons why PPP may not hold in the short run.

First, for the law of one price and PPP to hold, the goods or services sold in different locations must be identical. As Table 33.3 notes, the Indian version of the Big Mac is not even a hamburger; it is a chicken sandwich. Thus, we should not expect the prices to be the same.

Second, some goods and services are not tradable. One example is a haircut. Haircuts in China typically cost less than $5 (and often include a massage), whereas haircuts in the United States almost always cost more than $20. But we cannot import a "haircut produced in China"; you'd have to travel to China to buy that service. Therefore, the supply of foreign haircuts cannot adjust to force PPP to hold. This is the case for all nontradable goods and services.

Third, trade barriers inhibit the trade of goods across some international borders. If goods cannot be traded or if tariffs and quotas add to the costs of trade, then prices will not equalize and PPP will not hold. The higher the trade barriers, the higher the price of the good in the foreign country. For example, tariffs and quotas on Florida oranges imported to Japan would lead to higher prices in Japan than in Florida.

Fourth, shipping costs keep prices from completely equalizing. In fact, higher shipping costs will lead to higher prices of the same good in a foreign nation. The greater the shipping costs, the bigger the difference in prices that can persist.

TABLE 33.3

The Big Mac Index, December 2021

	Actual price in domestic currency	Exchange rate	Price in U.S. dollars
U.S. dollar	5.81	1.00	$5.81
Chinese yuan	24.40	0.157	3.83
Euro	4.42	1.12	4.97
Indian rupee*	190	0.0134	2.55
Japanese yen	390	0.00868	3.38
Mexican peso	69	0.0484	3.34
U.K. pound	3.59	1.33	4.79

Source: https://www.economist.com/big-mac-index.

*In India, the Big Mac is not sold; the closest comparison is with the Maharaja Mac, which substitutes chicken for beef.

PRACTICE WHAT YOU KNOW

The Law of One Price: What Should the Price Be?

BILLY bookcases from Ikea can be shipped all over the world.

The Ikea furniture company sells Swedish bookshelves all over the world. One popular model is called the BILLY bookcase. The 2022 base price for the BILLY bookcase in the United States was \$50, while the price in the United Kingdom was £40.

QUESTION: In 2022, the exchange rate between the U.S. dollar and the British pound sterling was about \$1.33. Using this figure, how would you determine the 2022 price implied by PPP for the BILLY bookcase in the United Kingdom? To be clear, we are asking for the price in British pounds sterling that is equal to the \$50 price in the United States.

ANSWER: From Equation 33.2,

$$\text{price in the United States} = \text{exchange rate} \times \text{price in the United Kingdom}$$

Therefore, substituting in the price in the United States and the exchange rate, we have

$$\$50.00 = \$1.33 \times \text{price in the United Kingdom}$$

Solving this equation, we get

$$\frac{50.00}{1.33} = £37.59$$

QUESTION: The 2022 price implied by PPP was £37.59, while the actual price in the United Kingdom at that time was £40. This is fairly close. What are possible reasons why the price in the United Kingdom was slightly lower than PPP would lead us to expect?

ANSWER: Two reasons seem particularly likely. First, shipping costs to the United Kingdom may have been lower than shipping costs to the United States. In addition, there were likely lower trade barriers across Europe than between Europe and the United States.

Finally, we have emphasized consistently throughout this book that some prices take longer to adjust than others. PPP is a theory about long-run price adjustments across nations, with prices reacting to changes in demand and supply. The theory is by definition a long-run theory, which only holds after all prices have completely adjusted. Therefore, it will not typically hold perfectly in the short run.

In sum, PPP is a theory that teaches us a lot about the level of exchange rates in the long run—why exchange rates rise and fall over long periods of time. But in the real world, given these limitations, PPP typically does not hold perfectly at any point in time.

Your trade deficit with a local lunch spot does not make you worse off.

What Causes Trade Deficits?

At the beginning of this chapter, we noted that many people think trade deficits are harmful. In this section, we consider why this is a misconception. We also look at the specific causes of trade deficits.

A trade deficit means that more goods and services are coming in than are going out. On a micro level, individuals can have trade deficits with other individuals or business firms. Think about your favorite place to eat lunch. Perhaps you go there once a week. You have a trade deficit with that restaurant; unless you also happen to work there, you buy more from the restaurant than the restaurant buys from you. Does this deficit make you worse off, or indicate weakness on your part? No. In fact, the wealthier you are, the more you may eat at your favorite restaurant and thus further increase your trade deficit. If voluntary trade creates a trade deficit for you, it doesn't mean that you are worse off. Remember: trade creates value.

Trade creates value

When we extend this concept to the entire economy, the result is the same: we are not worse off when more goods and services flow in. In fact, historical data reveal that the U.S. trade deficit often increases during periods of economic growth. Figure 33.10 shows the U.S. trade balance (imports/exports) with recessionary periods shaded as vertical blue bars. The solid blue horizontal line is drawn where exports exactly equal imports. As the orange graph line becomes increasingly negative, it indicates a bigger trade deficit. Notice that the trade deficit widens during periods of expansion and shrinks during recessions. The data show us that trade deficits are often a by-product of positive economic periods.

Before we can explore the various causes of trade deficits, we need to discuss more about the accounting of international trade and financial flows. For this we turn to the balance of payments.

Balance of Payments

In this section, we introduce the terminology of international transactions accounts—the accounts used to track transactions that take place across borders. For a while, it may seem like we have left economics to study accounting. But we need to clarify how international transactions are recorded before we can fully explain the causes of trade deficits and surpluses.

The **balance of payments (BOP)** is a record of all payments between one nation and the rest of the world.

The **current account** is the BOP (balance of payments) account that tracks all payments for goods and services, current income from investments, and gifts.

A nation's **balance of payments (BOP)** is a record of payments between that country and the rest of the world. Anytime a payment is made across borders, it is tracked in the BOP. If you buy a car made in Japan, the dollar amount of that transaction is recorded in the balance of payments. If someone from Canada buys shares of stock in a U.S. corporation, that payment is also tracked in the U.S. balance of payments (as well as in Canada's).

The balance of payments is divided into two major accounts: the current account and the capital account. Different types of transactions are entered into each account. The **current account** tracks payments for goods and

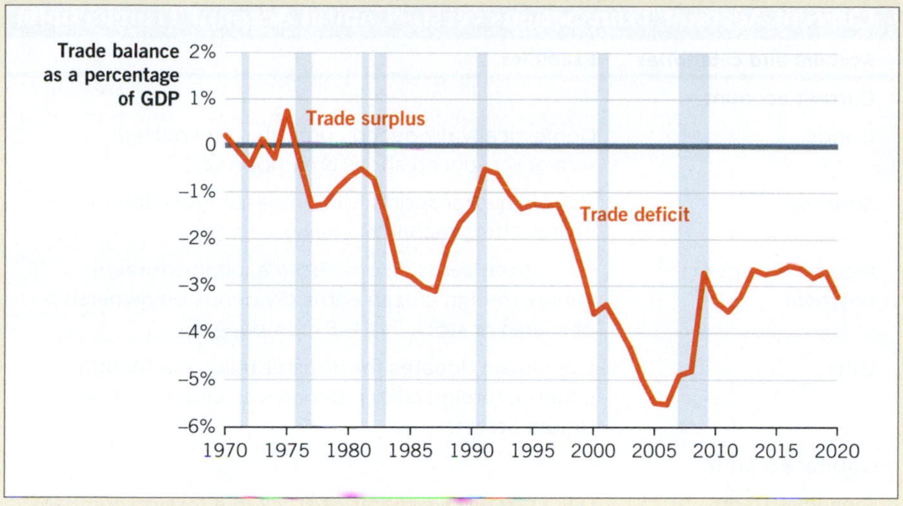

FIGURE 33.10

U.S. Trade Balance and Recessions, 1970–2020

Since 1975, the U.S. trade balance has been a deficit, with the deficit reaching its peak in 2006. The trade deficit typically grows during economic expansions and shrinks during recessions, which are indicated here with vertical blue bars.

Source: U.S. Bureau of Economic Analysis, *U.S. International Transactions.*

services, gifts, and current income from investments. When we import TVs from Japan or strawberries from Peru (goods), when we utilize technical advice from a call center in Mumbai, India (a service), and when we supply international aid to refugees in the Middle East (a gift), these transactions are recorded in the current account.

The **capital account** tracks payments for real and financial assets between nations. When residents of one nation buy financial securities such as stocks and bonds from another nation, these payments are recorded in the capital account. When the Chinese government buys U.S. Treasury securities, this transaction is recorded in the capital account. If someone from the United States deposits funds into a Swiss bank account, this transaction is recorded in the capital account. Even if you trade for the currency of another nation, your transaction is recorded in the capital account.

The **capital account** tracks payments for real and financial assets between nations and extensions of international loans.

Purchases of real assets also enter in the capital account. If you buy a vacation home in Cozumel, Mexico, it counts as an outgoing payment in the capital account. When Signa Holding (an Austrian real estate company) purchased the Chrysler Building in New York City, the transaction was recorded in the capital account as an incoming payment.

Did it hurt the U.S. economy when Signa Holding (an Austrian firm) bought the Chrysler Building in New York City?

Because much of the activity in the capital account is in financial securities, it is sometimes called the *financial account*. Table 33.4 shows the major categories of the current account and the capital account, along with some examples of the types of transactions entered in each.

Table 33.5 shows actual values for the U.S. current and capital accounts in 2020. Goods and services are by far the largest entry in the current account. For this reason, we focus primarily on goods and services when we discuss the current account.

The dollar amounts in this table represent changes in the various accounts during 2020. For example, on the current account side, the data indicate that the United States exported about \$2.1 trillion worth of goods and services but imported about \$2.8 trillion worth. This trade deficit accounts for most of

TABLE 33.4

Current Account Transactions versus Capital Account Transactions

Account and categories	Examples
Current account	
Goods	Domestically produced computer is exported; foreign-produced shoes are imported.
Services	U.S. airline transports foreign passengers; foreign call center offers technical advice.
Income receipt or payment	U.S. citizen earns income from a job in a foreign nation; foreign citizen earns dividends on ownership of shares of stock in a U.S. company.
Gifts	U.S. citizen donates for disaster relief in a foreign country; foreign citizen donates to charity in the United States.
Capital account	
Financial assets	U.S. citizen buys shares of stock in a foreign company; foreign government buys U.S. Treasury securities.
Real assets	U.S. citizen buys a vacation home in another country; foreign citizen buys an office building in the United States.

TABLE 33.5

U.S. Balance of Payments, 2020

Current account (millions of dollars)		Capital account (millions of dollars)	
Goods and services		Real and financial assets	
Exports	$2,134,441	U.S.-owned assets abroad	−$809,323
Imports	−$2,811,125	Foreign-owned assets in United States	$1,456,528
Income			
Receipts	$1,124,201	Net financial derivatives	−$5,780
Payments	−$1,063,612		
Gifts	−$5,488	Statistical discrepancy	−$19,842
Balance	−$621,583		$621,583

Source: United States Bureau of Economic Analysis.

the current account deficit. On the capital account side, U.S. individuals (and government) purchased about $800 billion worth of assets from abroad, but foreigners bought about $1.5 trillion in U.S. assets in 2020. In the short run, statistical discrepancies are common.

An **account deficit** exists when more payments are flowing out of an account than into the account.

When we evaluate the trade balance, we are really focusing on the current account. In fact, when you read about a "trade deficit," you are likely reading about a current account deficit. An **account deficit** exists when more payments are flowing out of an account than into the account. Generally, this means we are importing more goods and services than we are exporting. Table 33.5 shows that the U.S. current account deficit in 2020 was $676,684 ($2,811,125 − $2,134,441) million.

An **account surplus** exists when more payments are flowing into an account than out of the account. Because goods and services constitute most of the current account, a surplus of the current account is driven by a trade surplus. Table 33.5 shows a capital account surplus of $621,583 for the United States in 2020. You will notice that this surplus is the same size as the current account deficit. This is no coincidence, and we explain the relationship in the next section.

Banana imports are recorded with other goods and services in the current account.

THE KEY IDENTITY OF BALANCE OF PAYMENTS To talk about the major causes of trade deficits, we need to clarify the link between the current and capital accounts. Basically, when one of the accounts increases, the other decreases. We begin with an example before we state an important identity.

Let's say you are shopping for a new car, and you decide on a Toyota manufactured in Japan. Let's assume the following:

An **account surplus** exists when more payments are flowing into an account than out of the account.

- Before you buy a Japanese car, the U.S. trade is completely balanced: imports = exports.
- Before you buy the car, the U.S. capital account is also balanced: U.S. ownership of foreign assets = foreign ownership of U.S. assets.
- The car costs $40,000.

Now when you buy the car, there are two sides to the exchange: from your perspective, you are trading dollars for an imported good; from the perspective of Toyota, the company is trading its car for a U.S. financial asset (dollars). Thus, the exchange is recorded twice in the U.S. balance of payments. First, it is recorded as an import in the current account, and it leads to a current account deficit of $40,000. Second, it is recorded as the purchase of U.S. currency, a U.S. financial asset, in the capital account, and this transaction implies a surplus in the capital account of $40,000. These are entries of equal but offsetting magnitude, which is the principle behind the *balance* of payments.

Now we arrive at an important principle with regard to the balance of payments, which we call the *key identity of the balance of payments*: while either account can be in deficit or surplus, together they sum to zero. A positive balance in the current account means there must be a negative balance in the capital account, and vice versa. We can also write this principle in equation form:

$$\text{current account balance} + \text{capital account balance} = 0 \qquad \textbf{(EQUATION 33.5)}$$

Thus, if the current account is in deficit, the capital account is in surplus by the same amount. If the current account is in surplus, the capital account is in deficit by the same amount.

Before moving on, let's consider two other scenarios stemming from our Japanese car example. First, what happens if the new foreign owners of the $40,000 in U.S. currency decide to use it to buy Microsoft software manufactured in the United States? This transaction involves $40,000 worth of U.S. exports, so the current account deficit disappears, as does the capital account surplus.

TABLE 33.6

An Example of Balance of Payments

Example: A U.S. citizen buys a Japanese car for $40,000.

Scenario I: The Japanese company holds on to the $40,000.

U.S. current account:	−$40,000
U.S. capital account:	+ $40,000
Total	0

Scenario II: The Japanese company buys $40,000 worth of U.S.-produced Microsoft software.

U.S. current account:	−$40,000 + $40,000 = 0
U.S. capital account:	+ $40,000 − $40,000 = 0
Total	0

Scenario III: The Japanese company buys $40,000 worth of Microsoft Corporation stock.

U.S. current account:	− $40,000
U.S. capital account:	+ $40,000
Total	0

Finally, what happens if, instead, the Japanese owners of $40,000 in U.S. currency use it to purchase shares of Microsoft stock? In this case, the U.S. current account deficit stays at $40,000 and the capital account surplus stays at $40,000, because the Japanese have simply shifted to a different U.S. financial asset. These three scenarios are summarized in Table 33.6. In all cases, the current account changes are offset by opposite capital account changes.

We can see this identity when we examine actual balance of payments data for a nation. Figure 33.11 illustrates the identity with real historical data from

FIGURE 33.11

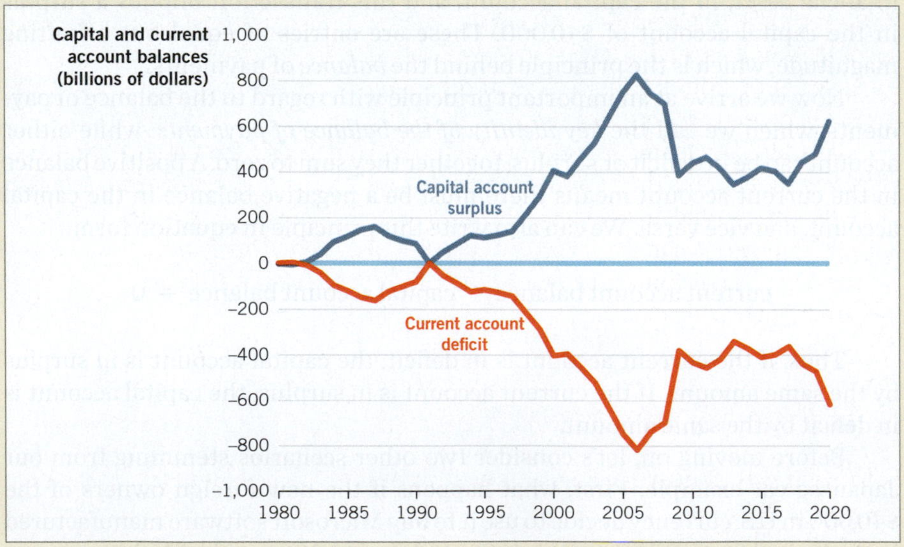

U.S. Current and Capital Account Balances since 1980

The current account and the capital account are essentially mirror images of each other. If we say that the United States has a current account deficit, we are also saying that it has a capital account surplus.

Source: United States Bureau of Economic Analysis.

PRACTICE WHAT YOU KNOW

Current Account versus Capital Account Entries

QUESTION: Would the following international transactions be recorded in the U.S. current account or the capital account?

a. the purchase of a Canadian government bond by a resident of Pennsylvania

b. the sale of a U.S. Treasury bond to a resident of Ontario, Canada

c. the purchase of a condominium in Cancun, Mexico, by a U.S. resident

d. the purchase of a Samsung television by Best Buy (a U.S. company)

e. the purchase of an airplane ticket from United Airlines (a U.S. company) by a resident of Chengdu, China, to come to the United States to attend college

ANSWERS:

a. This would be recorded in the capital account because it is the purchase of a financial asset.

b. This would be recorded in the capital account because it is the sale of a financial asset.

c. This would be recorded in the capital account because it is the purchase of a real asset.

d. This would be recorded in the current account because it is the purchase of a good.

e. This would be recorded in the current account because it is the purchase of a service.

If a foreign student buys a ticket on a U.S. airline, how does this transaction affect the balance of payments?

the United States. The orange line is the U.S. current account balance—clearly in deficit since 1991. Figure 33.11 also plots the balance of the capital account, which is clearly in surplus since 1991. Notice that when the capital account surplus grows, it accompanies a larger current account deficit. As the current account deficit exceeded $800 billion in 2006, the capital account surplus also exceeded $800 billion. The two lines are very close to mirror images, which they should be, based on Equation 33.5.

This identity is important for practical purposes because it shows us that anything that affects the capital account also affects the current account. Thus, if we are interested in the major causes of trade deficits, we need to examine not only what causes a current account deficit to increase but also what causes a capital account surplus to increase, because the two are essentially mirror images.

The Causes of Trade Deficits

People who are concerned about trade deficits often think about trade in terms of fairness. After all, if our economy is buying goods from nations around the globe, shouldn't these nations be buying goods from us? The way we calculate GDP seems to reinforce this point of view. Recall that GDP is the sum of four components—consumption (C), investment (I), government expenditures (G), and net exports (NX):

$$GDP = Y = C + I + G + NX$$

The fourth piece is net exports. All else being equal, the net exports component falls when a nation imports more goods. In this sense, the greater current account deficit implies lower GDP. While that implication might make you think that nations are better off with fewer imports or more exports, you shouldn't jump to this conclusion.

There are several causes of deficits in the current account. Although the United States has consistently had a current account deficit since 1975, the cause has varied over time. We consider three primary causes of current account deficits: strong economic growth, lower personal savings rates, and fiscal policy.

STRONG ECONOMIC GROWTH One cause of current account deficits is strong domestic growth. A nation growing and increasing in wealth relative to the rest of the world is also a nation that can afford to import significant quantities of goods and services.

Think of this first in terms of individuals. Imagine that you open a coffee shop and your business does very well. You earn significant profits, and your personal wealth grows. This new wealth enables you to purchase many goods and services that you would not be able to afford if you were less well off. With your new wealth, you'll likely develop trade deficits with many stores and restaurants in your town. You might even establish trade deficits with ski resorts, golf courses, and car dealerships. Bill Gates has personal trade deficits all over the world simply because he buys large quantities of goods and services.

This scenario also applies to nations. During periods of rapid economic expansion in the United States, our current account deficit has grown. The prime example of this is the late 1990s. Look again at Figure 33.11. In the long growth period during the late 1990s, the economy was growing and the current account deficit was growing as well. U.S. wealth was increasing, which enabled us to afford more imports from around the globe. The reverse occurs during economic downturns. When U.S. wealth falls, we are less able to afford imports, and the current account deficit shrinks.

Bill Gates seems to enjoy his trade deficits.

Certain distinct effects cause the trade deficit to grow during economic expansion. The first is in the current account: wealthy domestic consumers can afford to import more goods and services. The second is in the capital account: growing economies offer higher investment returns, so funds from around the globe flow in to take advantage of high rates of return. Table 33.7 summarizes these two complementary effects.

When an economy is growing rapidly relative to the rest of the world, the firms in that economy are willing to pay more for investment funds. This demand for loanable funds shifts to the right and interest rates increase. Subsequently, international funds flow in to take advantage of these higher interest rates.

To clarify, let's return to the example where your coffee shop business is doing very well. One way to expand your business is to offer shares of stock in the business. People buy this stock, hoping to get in on the financial success of your great new business. The stock purchases represent a capital inflow for your business. It works in exactly the same way for nations that are growing

TABLE 33.7

Why Strong Growth Leads to a Current Account Deficit

Primary account	Explanation	Result
Current account	The growing economy leads to wealthier consumers who import more goods and services from around the world.	Net exports fall, which leads to a greater current account deficit.
Capital account	The growing economy offers greater returns, which attracts international funds for investment.	The capital account surplus increases, which reinforces the greater current account deficit.

relatively quickly: funds from around the globe flow in to take advantage of the high returns.

For a macro example, consider the case of China. In recent years, China has periodically experienced a current account deficit, largely owing to its rapid economic growth. This result seems almost counterintuitive, as the rapid Chinese growth has largely been in the area of manufacturing exports. Yet the income surge has also enabled Chinese citizens to import goods and services from all over the globe. In addition, greater returns have brought an influx of global investment funds. These effects were so strong that by late 2010, China was recording current account deficits.

LOWER PERSONAL SAVINGS RATES A second major cause of current account deficits is low domestic savings rates. When households are not saving much, funds must flow in from overseas to supplement domestic investment.

Let's return to the example of your coffee shop. Your business is doing well, and you are considering expansion. You decide you want to open another location for your coffee shop. If you have been frugal and saved a portion of your income, you can use your own savings to expand the business. However, if you have spent your income, you'll need to rely on the savings of others to pay for your expansion. You'll have to borrow from a bank or issue some bonds or perhaps sell shares of stock in your coffee shop business. The purchase of financial assets in your firm is analogous to capital account purchases in the balance of payments.

We can extend the analysis to a macroeconomy. If individuals and governments save a significant portion of their income, the savings can be used to fund investment. In contrast, if savings falls, investment must be funded with outside sources. In the United States, personal savings rates have dropped significantly since the early 1990s (see Figure 22.8). So while the U.S. economy was growing throughout the 1990s and into the first decade of this century, the necessary financing was coming from savers around the globe. This activity increased the capital account surplus. Of course, any increase in the capital account surplus implies an increase in the current account deficit.

As we discussed in Chapter 22, the influx of funds from around the globe was instrumental in keeping interest rates low in the United States and enabling firms to fund expansion. These funds were critical as U.S. savings rates fell, but they did contribute to the widening current account deficit.

TABLE 33.8

Causes of Current Account Deficits

Cause	Explanation
Rapid domestic growth	Domestic buyers are able to afford imports given the increase in wealth, which widens the current account deficit. At the same time, foreign funds are attracted to higher rates of return in the growing economy, which increases the capital account surplus.
Declining domestic savings	Falling domestic savings leaves a finance gap for investment. The gap is filled with foreign funds, which increases the capital account surplus.
Government budget deficits	Increased government borrowing means greater competition for investment funds. All else being equal, more foreign funds are needed to lend to the government, and this activity widens the capital account surplus.

FISCAL POLICY Large budget deficits also contribute to current account deficits. This is part of the reason for large U.S. current account deficits in the 1980s and then again after 2000. Large government budget deficits devour both domestic and foreign funds. Recall this important principle from Chapter 22: *Every dollar borrowed requires a dollar saved.* So when the U.S. government borrows trillions each year, this is similar to a further reduction in personal savings: the government is using funds that could have been used for private investment.

Domestic savings are not enough to fund the budget deficit. International funds also flow in to fund the budget deficit. The influx of international funds increases the capital account surplus and thus increases the trade deficit.

Table 33.8 summarizes these different causes of trade deficits. The bottom line is that many factors cause trade deficits, some that don't even seem related to goods and services. The past few decades of U.S. experience offer examples of all three. The 1980s was a time of large budget deficits, and the trade deficit widened. Beginning around 1990, personal savings rates fell and the economy grew rapidly; the trade deficit widened, even as the federal government balanced its budget. Finally, in recent years historically large budget deficits have added to the pressure for capital inflows, reducing any prospects for elimination of the trade deficit in the near future.

Conclusion

We began this chapter with the misconception that trade deficits are harmful to an economy. But we have seen that many factors affect a trade balance, and typically a trade deficit means that the domestic economy is actually doing well. Goods and service flows are interrelated with real and financial asset flows. Given this relationship, changes in personal savings rates and government budget deficits can affect trade balances.

We also studied exchange rates in this chapter and considered them as market prices that depend on the supply of and demand for foreign currency. But exchange rates are also subject to manipulation by governments. Depreciating a nation's currency makes its exports less expensive but doesn't always help all the residents of a nation. ✳

ANSWERING the BIG QUESTIONS

Why do exchange rates rise and fall?

- An increase in the exchange rate indicates a depreciation of the domestic currency. The exchange rate increases when there is an increase in demand for foreign goods, services, and financial assets relative to the demand for domestic goods, services, and financial assets.
- The exchange rate also increases when there is a decline in the supply of foreign currency relative to the domestic currency.
- A decrease in the exchange rate indicates an appreciation of the domestic currency. The exchange rate decreases when there is a decrease in demand for foreign goods, services, and financial assets relative to domestic goods, services, and financial assets.
- The exchange rate also falls when there is an increase in the supply of foreign currency relative to the supply of domestic currency.

What is purchasing power parity?

- Purchasing power parity (PPP) is a theory about the determinants of long-run exchange rates. PPP implies that the exchange rate between two nations is determined by a ratio of relative price levels in the two nations. If a nation experiences more inflation than its trading partners do, its exchange rate will rise, indicating a depreciation of its currency.
- PPP is based on the law of one price.

What causes trade deficits?

- Trade deficits are essentially synonymous with current account deficits. As such, they increase when the current account deficit or the capital account surplus increases.
- Economic growth increases the current account deficit as wealthier residents demand more imports. It also works through the capital account as higher rates of return attract foreign funds.
- A second cause of trade deficits is lower personal savings rates.
- A third cause of trade deficits is larger government budget deficits.

CHAPTER PROBLEMS

Concepts You Should Know

account deficit (p. 1094)
account surplus (p. 1095)
balance of payments (BOP) (p. 1092)
capital account (p. 1093)
currency appreciation (p. 1076)
currency depreciation (p. 1076)
current account (p. 1092)
derived demand (p. 1075)
exchange rate (p. 1074)
exchange rate manipulation (p. 1081)
flexible (floating) exchange rates (p. 1083)
law of one price (p. 1087)
pegged (fixed) exchange rates (p. 1083)
purchasing power parity (PPP) (p. 1088)

Questions for Review

1. The United States imports Molson beer from Canada. Assume that Canada and the United States share the same currency and that a bottle of Molson beer costs $2 in Toronto, Canada, but just $1 in Chicago.
   a. What market adjustments will ensue in this case, assuming no shipping costs or trade barriers?
   b. If Canadians like Molson beer more than the residents of the United States do, can a price differential persist? Why or why not?
2. The United States currently has a current account deficit. How would each of the following events affect this deficit, assuming no other changes?
   a. U.S. economic growth slows relative to the rest of the world.
   b. U.S. personal savings rates increase.
   c. U.S. federal budget deficits decline.
   d. Foreign rates of return (in financial assets) rise relative to rates of return in the United States.
3. Why are current account balances generally mirror images of capital account balances?
4. Sometimes, official government reserves are singled out in the balance of payments accounts. For example, when China buys U.S. financial assets (currency and Treasury securities), this purchase is classified as "Official Government Reserves." On which side of the balance of payments should such purchases be reflected—the current account or the capital account? Explain your logic.
5. What are three factors that might make a capital account surplus grow?
6. Is a trade deficit a sign of economic weakness? Why or why not?
7. The rate of inflation in India from 2007 to 2011 was 8%. Over the same period, the inflation rate in the United States was 2.7%.
   a. What is the implication of these inflation rates for the exchange rate between the dollar and the rupee? In particular, does the PPP condition imply a rise or a fall in the exchange rate? Explain your answer.
   b. Is the change in the exchange rate an appreciation or a depreciation of the dollar? Is it an appreciation or a depreciation of the rupee?

Study Problems *(* solved at the end of the section)*

1. If interest rates in India rise relative to interest rates around the world, how is the world value of the rupee affected? Illustrate these effects in the market for rupees.
2. From Chapter 21, we know that the primary cause of inflation is expansion of the money supply. In this chapter, we find an additional side effect of monetary expansion. What is this effect? Use demand and supply of foreign currency to illustrate your answer.
3. Explain the numerical effect on both the U.S. current account and the U.S. capital account from each of these examples.
   a. In the United States, the company Best Buy purchases $1 million worth of TVs from the Samsung corporation, a Korean firm, using U.S.

dollars. In addition, Samsung keeps the U.S. dollars.

b. Best Buy purchases $1 million worth of TVs from the Samsung corporation, using U.S. dollars. Samsung then trades its dollars to a third party for won, the Korean currency.

c. Best Buy trades $1 million for Korean won and then uses the won to buy TVs from Samsung.

4. The price of a dozen roses in the United States is about $30. Use this information, along with the exchange rates given in Table 33.1, to answer the following questions.

a. Assuming that PPP holds perfectly, what is the price of a dozen roses in Turkey? Express your answer in units of Turkish lira.

b. If the actual price in Turkey costs more lira than the answer you found in part (a), how might you account for the discrepancy?

✱ **5.** Explain why the supply curve for foreign currency is vertical. Let's say you return from a trip to Mexico with 1,000 pesos. If you decide to exchange these pesos for dollars, does your action shift the supply of pesos?

✱ **6.** For each of the following transactions, determine whether it will be recorded in the U.S. current account or capital account and whether the entry will be positive or negative.

a. A resident of the United States buys an airplane ticket to England on Virgin Atlantic Airways, a British company.

b. The government of England buys U.S. Treasury securities.

c. A U.S. citizen buys shares of stock in a Chinese corporation.

7. Use our simple model of exchange rates (the market for foreign currency) to determine the effect on the U.S.–Japanese exchange rate from each of the following (assuming no other changes):

a. an increase in Japanese demand for oil produced in the United States

b. an increase in U.S. demand for Japanese real estate

c. an increase in Japanese demand for U.S. Treasury securities

d. a decrease in the supply of Japanese yen relative to U.S. dollars

8. The Canadian dollar is sometimes called a "loonie," because of the figure of a loon (a duck-like bird) engraved on the dollar coin. The exchange rate between the U.S. dollar and the loonie has recently hovered around $0.75, so each loonie costs about seventy-five U.S. cents. Let's start with this exchange rate but then let it fluctuate. Use what you know about the law of one price to fill in the missing information in the table below. (For this question, assume the law of one price holds perfectly.)

Exchange rate	Price level in U.S.	Price level in Canada
$0.75	100	_____
0.80	100	_____
0.50	100	_____
0.75	_____	100
0.80	_____	100
0.50	_____	150
_____	100	150
_____	150	100
_____	100	100

Solved Problems

5. The supply curve is vertical because the supply is completely controlled by the government and does not vary with changes in price. Your exchange does not shift the supply of pesos; only the government can do that. Instead, it signals a reduction in demand for pesos.

6. a. This is a purchase of a service, so it enters the current account. It enters negatively because it is an import; thus, funds are flowing out of the U.S. current account.

b. This is a purchase of financial assets in the United States, so it is entered in the U.S. capital account. The entry is positive because funds are flowing into the capital account.

c. This is a purchase of financial assets abroad, so it enters the U.S. capital account. It enters negatively because funds are flowing out.

GLOSSARY

absolute advantage one producer's ability to make more than another producer with the same quantity of resources

account deficit condition existing when more payments are flowing out of an account than into the account

account surplus condition existing when more payments are flowing into an account than out of the account

accounting profit profit calculated by subtracting the explicit costs from total revenue

active monetary policy the strategic use of monetary policy to counteract macroeconomic expansions and contractions

adaptive expectations theory the theory that people's expectations of future inflation are based on their most recent experience

adverse selection phenomenon existing when one party has information about some aspect of product quality that the other party does not have

aggregate demand is the total demand for final goods and services in an economy

aggregate production function the relationship between all the inputs used in the macroeconomy and the economy's total output (GDP)

aggregate supply the total supply of final goods and services in an economy

antitrust laws laws that attempt to prevent oligopolies from behaving like monopolies

assets the items a firm owns

asymmetric information an imbalance in information that occurs when one party knows more than the other

automatic stabilizers government programs that automatically implement countercyclical fiscal policy in response to economic conditions

average fixed cost (AFC) an amount determined by dividing total fixed cost by the output

average tax rate the total tax paid divided by the amount of taxable income

average total cost (ATC) the sum of average variable cost and average fixed cost

average variable cost (AVC) an amount determined by dividing total variable cost by the output

backward-bending labor supply curve supply curve occurring when workers value additional leisure more than additional income

backward induction in game theory, the process of deducing backward from the end of a scenario to infer a sequence of optimal actions

balance of payments (BOP) a record of all payments between one nation and the rest of the world

balance sheet an accounting statement that summarizes a firm's key financial information

bank run an event occurring when many depositors attempt to withdraw their funds from a bank at the same time

banks private firms that accept deposits and extend loans

barriers to entry restrictions that make it difficult for new firms to enter a market

barter the trade of a good or service in the absence of a commonly accepted medium of exchange

behavioral economics the field of economics that draws on insights from experimental psychology to explore how people make economic decisions

bond a security that represents a debt to be paid

bounded rationality the concept that although decision-makers want a good outcome, either they are not capable of performing the problem solving that traditional economic theory assumes or they are not inclined to do so; also called *limited reasoning*

budget deficit condition occurring when government outlays exceed revenue in a given time period, usually a year

budget surplus condition occurring when government revenue exceeds outlays in a given time period, usually a year

business cycle a short-run fluctuation in economic activity

cap and trade an approach used to curb pollution by creating a system of emissions permits that are traded in an open market

capital account the balance of payments account that tracks payments for real and financial assets between nations and extensions of international loans

capital gains taxes taxes on the gains realized by selling an asset for more than its purchase price

capital goods goods that help produce other valuable goods and services in the future

cartel a group of two or more firms that act in unison

ceteris paribus (*pronounced KETeris PAReebus*) meaning "other things being equal," the concept under which economists examine a change in one variable while holding everything else constant

chained CPI a measure of the consumer price index in which the typical consumer's "basket" of goods and services considered is updated monthly

checkable deposits deposits in bank accounts from which depositors may make withdrawals by writing checks

circular flow diagram a diagram that shows how goods, services, and resources flow through the economy

classical economists economists who stress the importance of aggregate supply and generally believe that the economy can adjust back to full-employment equilibrium on its own

Clayton Act law of 1914 targeting corporate behaviors that reduce competition

club good a good with two characteristics: it is nonrival in consumption and excludable

Coase theorem theorem stating that if there are no barriers to negotiations, and if property rights are fully specified, interested parties will bargain to correct externalities

coinsurance payments a percentage of costs the insured must pay after exceeding the insurance policy's deductible up to the policy's contribution limit

collusion an agreement among rival firms that specifies the price each firm charges and the quantity it produces

commodity-backed money money that can be exchanged for a commodity at a fixed rate

commodity money the use of an actual good for money

common-resource good a good with two characteristics: it is rival in consumption and nonexcludable

comparative advantage the situation where an individual, a business, or a country can produce at a lower opportunity cost than a competitor can

compensating differential the difference in wages offered to offset the desirability or undesirability of a job

competitive market a market in which there are so many buyers and sellers that each has only a small (negligible) impact on the market price and output

complements two goods that are used together; when the price of a complementary good rises, the quantity demanded of that good falls and the demand for the related good goes down

constant returns to scale condition occurring when long-run average total costs remain constant as output expands

consumer goods goods produced for present consumption

consumer optimum the combination of goods and services that maximizes the consumer's utility for a given income or budget

consumer price index (CPI) a measure of the price level based on the consumption patterns of a typical consumer

consumer surplus the difference between the willingness to pay for a good (or service) and the price paid to get it

consumption the purchase of final goods and services by households, excluding new housing

consumption smoothing behavior occurring when people borrow and save to smooth consumption over their lifetime

contractionary fiscal policy a decrease in government spending or increase in taxes to slow economic expansion

contractionary monetary policy a central bank's action to decrease the money supply

convergence the idea that per capita GDPs across nations equalize as nations approach the steady state

copayments fixed amounts the insured must pay when receiving a medical service or filling a prescription

cost-benefit analysis a process that economists use to determine whether the benefits of providing a public good outweigh the costs

countercyclical fiscal policy fiscal policy that seeks to counteract business cycle fluctuations

CPI see *consumer price index*

creative destruction the introduction of new products and technologies that leads to the end of other industries and jobs

cross-price elasticity of demand (E_c) measurement of the percentage change in the quantity demanded of one good to the percentage change in the price of a related good

crowding-out phenomenon occurring when private spending falls in response to increases in government spending

currency the paper bills and coins used to buy goods and services

currency appreciation a currency's increase in value relative to other currencies

currency depreciation a currency's decrease in value relative to other currencies

current account the BOP (balance of payments) account that tracks all payments for goods and services, current income from investments, and gifts

cyclical unemployment unemployment caused by economic downturns

deadweight loss the decrease in economic activity caused by market distortions

decision tree diagram that illustrates all of the possible outcomes in a sequential game

debt the total of all accumulated and unpaid budget deficits

deductibles fixed amounts the insured must pay before most of the policy's benefits can be applied

default risk the risk that the borrower will not pay the face value of a bond on the maturity date

deflation condition occurring when overall prices fall

demand curve a graph of the relationship between the prices in the demand schedule and the quantity demanded at those prices

demand schedule a table that shows the relationship between the price of a good and the quantity demanded

depreciation a fall in the value of a resource over time

derived demand demand for a good or service that derives from the demand for another good or service

diamond-water paradox concept explaining why water, which is essential to life, is inexpensive, while diamonds, which do not sustain life, are expensive

diminishing marginal product phenomenon occurring when the marginal product of an input falls as the quantity of the input rises

diminishing marginal utility condition occurring when marginal utility declines as consumption increases

direct finance activity in the loanable funds market when borrowers go directly to savers for funds

discount loans loans from the Federal Reserve to private banks

discount rate the interest rate on the discount loans made by the Federal Reserve to private banks

discount window the Fed's tool for extending loans to private banks

discouraged workers see *marginally attached workers*

diseconomies of scale condition occurring when long-run average total costs rise as output expands

dissaving withdrawing funds from previously accumulated savings

Dodd-Frank Act the primary regulatory response to the financial turmoil that contributed to the Great Recession

dominant strategy in game theory, a strategy that a player will always prefer, regardless of what his or her opponent chooses

double coincidence of wants condition occurring when each party in an exchange transaction happens to have what the other party desires

dumping behavior occurring when a foreign supplier sells a good below the price it charges in its home country

economic contraction a phase of the business cycle during which economic activity is decreasing

economic expansion a phase of the business cycle during which economic activity is increasing

economic growth the percentage change in real per capita GDP

economic profit profit calculated by subtracting both the explicit costs and the implicit costs from total revenue

economic rent the difference between what a factor of production earns and what it could earn in the next-best alternative

economics the study of how individuals and societies allocate their limited resources to satisfy their practically unlimited wants

economic thinking a purposeful evaluation of the available opportunities to make the best decision possible

economies of scale condition occurring when long-run average total costs decline as output expands

efficiency wages wages higher than equilibrium wages, offered to increase worker productivity

efficient describing an outcome when an allocation of resources maximizes total surplus

efficient scale the output level that minimizes average total cost in the long run

elasticity a measure of the responsiveness of buyers and sellers to changes in price or income

endogenous factors the variables that are inside a model

endogenous growth growth driven by factors inside an economy

endowment effect the principle that once we own something, we value it more

entitlement programs see *mandatory outlays*

equation of exchange an equation that specifies the long-run relationship between the money supply, the price level, real GDP, and the velocity of money

equilibrium condition occurring at the point where the demand curve and the supply curve intersect

equilibrium price the price at which the quantity supplied is equal to the quantity demanded; also known as the *market-clearing price*

equilibrium quantity the withdrawing amount at which the quantity supplied is equal to the quantity demanded

equity (1) the fairness of the distribution of benefits among the members of a society; (2) the part of an asset that you own

excess capacity phenomenon occurring when a firm produces at an output level smaller than the output level needed to minimize average total costs

excess demand see *shortage*

excess supply see *surplus*

exchange rate the price of foreign currency, indicating how much a unit of foreign currency costs in terms of another currency

exchange rate manipulation a national government's intentional adjustment of its money supply to affect the exchange rate of its currency

excise taxes taxes levied on a particular good or service

excludable good a good for which access can be limited to paying customers

exogenous factors the variables that are outside a model

exogenous growth growth that is independent of factors within the economy

expansionary fiscal policy an increase in government spending or decrease in taxes to stimulate the economy toward expansion

expansionary monetary policy a central bank's action to increase the money supply in an effort to stimulate the economy

expected return the anticipated rate of return on a capital investment based on the probabilities of all possible outcomes

explicit costs tangible out-of-pocket expenses

external costs the costs of a market activity imposed on people who are not participants in that market

externalities the costs or benefits of a market activity that affect a third party

face value the bond's value at maturity—the amount due at repayment; also called *par value*

factors of production the inputs (labor, land, and capital) used in producing goods and services

federal funds deposits that private banks hold on reserve at the Federal Reserve

federal funds rate the interest rate on loans between private banks

federal jobless benefits see *unemployment insurance*

fiat money money with no value except as the medium of exchange; there is no inherent or intrinsic value to the currency

final goods goods sold to final users

financial intermediaries firms that help to channel funds from savers to borrowers

fiscal policy the use of the government's budget tools, government spending, and taxes to influence the macroeconomy

Fisher equation equation stating that the real interest rate equals the nominal interest rate minus the inflation rate

fixed costs costs that do not vary with output in the short run; also known as *overhead*

flexible (floating) exchange rates exchange rates determined by the supply of and demand for currency

floating exchange rates see *flexible exchange rates*

fractional reserve banking a system in which banks hold only a fraction of deposits on reserve

framing effect a phenomenon seen when people change their answer depending on how the question is asked (or change their decision depending on how alternatives are presented)

free-rider problem a phenomenon occurring when someone receives a benefit without having to pay for it

frictional unemployment unemployment caused by delays in matching available jobs and workers

full-employment output the economy's output level when the unemployment rate is equal to the natural rate; also called *potential output* or *potential GDP*

gambler's fallacy the belief that recent outcomes are unlikely to be repeated and that outcomes that have not occurred recently are due to happen soon

game theory a branch of mathematics that economists use to analyze the strategic behavior of decision-makers

GDP see *gross domestic product*

GDP deflator a measure of the price level used to calculate real GDP

Gini index a measurement of the income distribution of a country's residents

GNP see *gross national product*

government outlays the part of the government budget that includes both spending and transfer payments

government spending spending by all levels of government on final goods and services

Great Recession the U.S. recession that lasted from December 2007 to June 2009

gross domestic product (GDP) the market value of all final goods and services produced within a country during a specific period

gross national product (GNP) the output produced by workers and resources owned by residents of the nation

hot hand fallacy the belief that random sequences exhibit a positive correlation

human capital the resource represented by the quantity, knowledge, and skills of the workers in an economy

immediate run a period of time when there is no time for consumers to adjust their behavior

imperfect market a market in which either the buyer or the seller can influence the market price

implicit costs the costs of resources already owned, for which no out-of-pocket payment is made

import quotas limits on the quantity of products that can be imported into a country

incentives factors that motivate a person to act or exert effort

incidence the burden of taxation on the party who pays the tax through higher prices, regardless of whom the tax is actually levied on

income effect phenomenon occurring when laborers work fewer hours at higher wages, using their additional income to demand more leisure

income elasticity of demand (E_I) measurement of how a change in income affects spending

income inequality ratio ratio calculated by dividing the top quintile's income percentage by the bottom quintile's income percentage

income mobility the ability of workers to move up or down the economic ladder over time

indirect finance activity in the loanable funds market when savers deposit funds into banks, which then loan these funds to borrowers

infant industry argument the idea that domestic industries need trade protection until they are established and able to compete internationally

inferior good a good for which demand declines as income rises

inflation the growth in the overall level of prices in an economy

in-kind transfers transfers (mostly to the poor) in the form of goods or services instead of cash

inputs the resources (labor, land, capital) used in the production process

institution a significant practice, relationship, or organization in a society; the official and unofficial conditions that shape the environment in which decisions are made

interest rate (1) is a price of loanable funds, quoted as a percentage of the original loan amount; (2) the price a borrower pays to a lender to use the lender's money

interest rate effect effect occurring when a change in the price level leads to a change in interest rates and therefore in the quantity of aggregate demand

interest on reserve balances (IORB) the rate of interest paid by the Federal Reserve on bank reserves deposited with the Fed

intermediate goods goods that firms repackage or bundle with other goods for sale at a later stage

internal costs the costs of a market activity paid only by an individual participant

internalize relating to a firm's handling of externalities, to take into account the external costs (or benefits) to society that occur as a result of their actions

international trade effect effect occurring when a change in the price level leads to a change in the quantity of net exports demanded

intertemporal decision-making planning to do something over a period of time, which requires valuing the present and the future consistently

investment (1) the process of using resources to create or buy new capital; (2) private spending on the tools, plant, and equipment used to produce future output

investor confidence a measure of what firms expect for future economic activity

invisible hand a phrase coined by Adam Smith to refer to the unobservable market forces that guide resources to their highest-valued use

Keynesian economists economists who stress the importance of aggregate demand and generally believe that the economy needs help returning to full-employment equilibrium

labor force those who are already employed or actively seeking work and are part of the work-eligible population

labor force participation rate the percentage of the work-eligible population that is in the labor force

Laffer curve an illustration of the relationship between tax rates and tax revenue

law of demand the law stating that, all other things being equal, quantity demanded falls when the price rises, and rises when the price falls

law of increasing opportunity cost the law stating that the opportunity cost of producing a good rises as a society produces more of it

law of one price the law stating that after accounting for transportation costs and trade barriers, identical goods sold in different locations must sell for the same price

law of supply the law stating that, all other things being equal, the quantity supplied of a good rises when the price of the good rises, and falls when the price of the good falls

law of supply and demand the law stating that the market price of any good will adjust to bring the quantity supplied and the quantity demanded into balance

lending facilities the Fed's tool for issuing loans to firms in targeted at-risk industries

liabilities the financial obligations a firm owes to others

life-cycle wage pattern the predictable effect age has on earnings over the course of a person's working life

limited reasoning see *bounded rationality*

loanable funds market the market where savers supply funds for loans to borrowers

long run (1) in microeconomics, the period of time when consumers make decisions that reflect their long-term wants, needs, or limitations and have time to fully adjust to market conditions; (2) in macroeconomics, a period of time sufficient for all prices to adjust

Lorenz curve a visual representation of the Gini index

loss the result when total revenue is less than total cost

M1 the money supply measure composed of currency and checkable deposits

M2 the money supply measure that includes everything in M1 plus savings deposits, money market mutual funds, and small-denomination time deposits (CDs)

macroeconomic policy governmental acts to influence the macroeconomy

macroeconomics the study of the overall aspects and workings of an economy

mandatory outlays government spending determined by ongoing government programs like Social Security and Medicare; sometimes called *entitlement programs*

marginal cost (MC) the increase in cost that occurs from producing one additional unit of output

marginally attached workers those who are not working, have looked for a job in the past 12 months, and are willing to work, but have not sought employment in the past four weeks; see *discouraged workers*

marginal product the change in output divided by the change in input

marginal product of labor the change in output associated with adding one additional worker

marginal propensity to consume (MPC) the portion of additional income spent on consumption

marginal revenue the change in total revenue a firm receives when it produces one additional unit of output

marginal utility the additional satisfaction derived from consuming one more unit of a good or service

marginal tax rate the tax rate paid on an individual's next dollar of income

marginal thinking the evaluation of whether the benefit of one more unit of something is greater than its cost

market-clearing price see *equilibrium price*

market demand the sum of all the individual quantities demanded by each buyer in the market at each price

market economy an economy in which resources are allocated among households and firms with little or no government interference

market failure condition occurring when there is an inefficient allocation of resources in a market

market power a firm's ability to influence the price of a good or service by exercising control over its demand, supply, or both

markets systems that bring buyers and sellers together to exchange goods and services

market supply the sum of the quantities supplied by each seller in the market at each price

markup the difference between the price the firm charges and the marginal cost of production

maturity date of a bond, the date on which the loan repayment is due

Medicaid a joint federal and state program that helps low-income individuals and households pay for the costs associated with long-term medical care

Medicare a mandated U.S. federal program that funds health care for people age 65 and older

medium of exchange what people trade for goods and services

menu costs the costs of changing prices
microeconomics the study of the individual units that make up the economy
minimum wage the lowest hourly wage rate that firms may legally pay their workers
monetary neutrality the idea that the money supply does not affect real economic variables
monetary policy the government's adjustment of the money supply to influence the macroeconomy
money any generally accepted means of payment
money illusion the interpretation of nominal changes in wages or prices as real changes
monopolistic competition a type of market structure characterized by low barriers to entry, many different firms, and product differentiation
monopoly condition existing when a single company supplies the entire market for a particular good or service
monopoly power a measure of a monopolist's ability to set the price of a good or service
monopsony a situation in which there is only one buyer
moral hazard the lack of incentive to guard against risk where one is protected from its consequences
mutual interdependence a market situation where the actions of one firm have an impact on the price and output of its competitors
Nash equilibrium a phenomenon occurring when all economic decision-makers opt to keep the status quo
natural monopoly the situation that occurs when a single large firm has lower costs than any potential smaller competitor
natural rate of unemployment the typical unemployment rate that occurs when the economy is growing normally
net exports the total exports of final goods and services minus total imports of final goods and services
net investment investment minus depreciation
network externality condition occurring when the number of customers who purchase or use a product influences the quantity demanded
new classical critique the assertion that increases in government spending and decreases in taxes are largely offset by increases in savings
New Growth Theory an approach to long-run growth that focuses on technological change and the incentives fostering innovation inside an economy
nominal GDP GDP measured in current prices and not adjusted for inflation
nominal interest rate the interest rate before it is corrected for inflation; the stated interest rate
nominal wage a worker's wage expressed in current dollars
normal good a good consumers buy more of as income rises, holding all other factors constant
normative statement an opinion that cannot be tested or validated; it describes "what ought to be"
occupational crowding the phenomenon of relegating a group of workers to a narrow range of jobs in the economy
oligopoly a form of market structure that exists when a small number of firms sell a differentiated product in a market with high barriers to entry
open market operations operations involving the purchase or sale of bonds by a central bank
opportunity cost the highest-valued alternative that must be sacrificed to get something else
output the product the firm creates
output effect how a change in price affects the number of customers in a market
outsourcing of labor a firm's shifting of jobs to an outside company, usually overseas, where the cost of labor is lower
overhead see *fixed costs*
owner's equity the difference between a firm's assets and its liabilities
par value see *face value*
passive monetary policy a central bank's use of monetary policy only to stabilize money and price levels
pegged (fixed) exchange rates exchange rates fixed at a certain level through the actions of a government
per capita GDP GDP per person
perfect price discrimination the practice of selling the same good or service at a unique price to every customer
Phillips curve curve indicating a short-run negative relationship between inflation and unemployment rates
positive statement an assertion that can be tested and validated; it describes "what is"
potential GDP see *full-employment output*
potential output see *full-employment output*
poverty rate the percentage of the population whose income is below the poverty threshold
poverty threshold the income level below which a person or family is considered impoverished
PPP see *purchasing power parity*
predatory pricing the practice of a firm deliberately setting their prices below average variable costs with the intent of driving rivals out of the market
preference reversal phenomenon occurring when risk tolerance is not consistent
price ceiling a legally established maximum price for a good or service
price controls an attempt to set prices through government regulations in the market
price effect how a change in price affects the firm's revenue
price elasticity of demand a measure of the responsiveness of quantity demanded to a change in price
price elasticity of supply a measure of the responsiveness of the quantity supplied to a change in price
price floor a legally established minimum price for a good or service
price gouging laws temporary ceilings on the prices that sellers can charge during times of emergency
price leadership phenomenon occurring when a dominant firm in an industry sets the price that maximizes its profits and the smaller firms in the industry follow by setting their prices to match the price leader

price level an index of the average prices of goods and services throughout the economy

price maker a firm with some control over the price it charges

price taker a firm with no control over the price set by the market

priming effect phenomenon occurring when the order of the questions influences the answers

principal-agent problem a situation in which a principal entrusts an agent to complete a task and the agent does not do so in a satisfactory way

prisoner's dilemma a situation in which decision-makers face incentives that make it difficult to achieve mutually beneficial outcomes

private good a good with two characteristics: it is excludable and rival in consumption

private property provision of an exclusive right of ownership that allows for the use, and especially the exchange, of property

private property rights the rights of individuals to own property, to use it in production, and to own the resulting output

producer surplus the difference between the willingness to sell a good (or service) and the price the seller receives

product differentiation the process firms use to make a product more attractive to potential customers

production function the relationship between the inputs a firm uses and the output it creates

production possibilities frontier (PPF) a model that illustrates the combinations of outputs a society can produce if all of its resources are being used efficiently

productivity the effectiveness of effort as measured in terms of the rate of output per unit of input

profit the result when total revenue is higher than total cost

profit-maximizing rule the rule stating that profit maximization occurs when a firm chooses the quantity of output that equates marginal revenue and marginal cost, or MR = MC

progressive income tax system income tax system in which people with higher incomes pay a larger portion of their income in taxes than people with lower incomes do

property rights an owner's ability to exercise control over a resource

prospect theory a theory suggesting that individuals weigh the utilities and risks of gains and losses differently

protectionism a blanket term for governmental actions and policies that restrict or restrain international trade, often with the intent of protecting local businesses and jobs from foreign competition

public goods a good that can be consumed by more than one person, and from which nonpayers are difficult to exclude

purchasing power the value of your income expressed in terms of how much you can afford

purchasing power parity (PPP) the idea that a unit of currency should be able to buy the same quantity of goods and services in any country

quantitative easing the targeted use of open market operations in which the central bank buys securities specifically targeting certain markets

quantity demanded the amount of a good or service that buyers are willing and able to purchase at the current price

quantity supplied the amount of a good or service producers are willing and able to sell at the current price

rational expectations theory the theory that people form expectations on the basis of all available information

real GDP GDP adjusted for changes in prices

real-income effect a change in purchasing power as a result of a change in the price of a good

real interest rate the interest rate corrected for inflation; the rate of return in terms of real purchasing power

real wage the nominal wage adjusted for changes in the price level

recession a short-term economic downturn

rent control a price ceiling that applies to the market for apartment rentals

rent seeking a condition occurring when resources are used to secure monopoly rights through the political process

reserve ratio the portion of deposits that banks keep on reserve

reservation price see *willingness to pay*

reserves the portion of bank deposits that are set aside and not loaned out

resources the inputs used to produce goods and services; also known as *factors of production*

risk-averse people those who prefer a sure thing over a gamble with a higher expected value

risk-neutral people those who choose the highest expected value regardless of the risk

risk-takers those who prefer gambles with lower expected values, and potentially higher winnings, over a sure thing

rival good a good that cannot be enjoyed by more than one person at a time

rule of 70 rule stating that if the annual growth rate of a variable is x%, the size of that variable doubles approximately every 70 ÷ x years

Samaritan's dilemma a situation in which an act of charity creates disincentives for recipients to take care of themselves

savings rate personal saving as a fraction of disposable (after-tax) income

scale the size of the production process

scarcity the inherently limited nature of society's resources, given society's unlimited wants and needs

secondary markets markets in which securities are traded after their first sale

securitization the creation of a new security by combining otherwise separate loan agreements

security a tradable contract that entitles its owner to certain rights

services outputs that provide benefits without producing a tangible product

Sherman Antitrust Act (1890) the first federal law limiting cartels and monopolies

shoe-leather costs the resources that are wasted when people change their behavior to avoid holding money

shortage market condition when the quantity supplied is less than the quantity demanded; also called *excess demand*

short run (1) in microeconomics, the period of time when consumers make decisions that reflect their short-term wants, needs, or limitations and can partially adjust their behavior; (2) in macroeconomics, the period of time in which some prices have not yet adjusted

signals information conveyed by profits and losses about the profitability of various markets

simple money multiplier the rate at which banks multiply money when all currency is deposited into banks

single-payer system government coverage of most health care costs, with citizens paying their share through taxes

social costs the sum of the internal costs and external costs of a market activity

social optimum the price and quantity combination that would exist if there were no externalities

Social Security a U.S. government–administered retirement funding program

social welfare see *total surplus*

specialization the limiting of one's work to a particular area

spending multiplier a formula to determine an equation's effect on spending from an initial change of a given amount

stagflation the combination of high unemployment and high inflation

status quo bias condition existing when decision-makers want to keep things the way they are

steady state the condition of a macroeconomy when there is no new net investment

stocks ownership shares in a firm

store of value a means for holding wealth

strike a work stoppage designed to aid a union's bargaining position

structural unemployment unemployment caused by changes in the industrial makeup (structure) of the economy

subsidy a payment made by the government to encourage the consumption or production of a good or service

substitutes goods that are used in place of each other; when the price of a substitute good rises, the quantity demanded of that good falls and the demand for the related good goes up

substitution effect (1) the decision by laborers to work more hours at higher wages, substituting labor for leisure; (2) a consumer's substitution of a product that has become relatively less expensive as the result of a price change

sunk costs unrecoverable costs that have been incurred as a result of past decisions

supply curve a graph of the relationship between the prices in the supply schedule and the quantity supplied at those prices

supply schedule a table that shows the relationship between the price of a good and the quantity supplied

supply shocks surprise events that change a firm's production costs

supply-side fiscal policy policy that involves the use of government spending and taxes to affect the production (supply) side of the economy

surplus market condition when the quantity supplied is greater than the quantity demanded; also called *excess supply*

switching costs the costs incurred when a consumer changes from one supplier to another

tariffs taxes levied on imported goods and services

technological advancement the introduction of new techniques or methods so that firms can produce more valuable outputs per unit of input

technology the knowledge available for use in production

third-party problem a situation in which those not directly involved in a market activity experience negative or positive externalities

time preferences the fact that people prefer to receive goods and services sooner rather than later

tit-for-tat a long-run strategy that promotes cooperation among participants by mimicking the opponent's most recent decision with repayment in kind

total cost the amount a firm spends to produce and/or sell goods and services

total revenue the amount a firm receives from the sale of goods and services

total surplus the sum of consumer surplus and producer surplus, measuring the well-being of all participants in a market, absent any government intervention; also known as *social welfare*

trade the voluntary exchange of goods and services between two or more parties

trade balance the difference between a nation's total exports and total imports

trade deficit condition occurring when imports exceed exports, indicating a negative trade balance

trade surplus condition occurring when exports exceed imports, indicating a positive trade balance

tragedy of the commons the depletion of a common-resource good

transfer payments payments made to groups or individuals when no good or service is received in return

treasury securities the bonds sold by the U.S. government to pay for the national debt

ultimatum game an economic experiment in which two players decide how to divide a sum of money

underground economies markets in which goods or services are traded illegally

underemployed workers those who have part-time jobs but would prefer to work full-time

unemployment condition occurring when a worker who is not currently employed is searching for a job without success

unemployment insurance a government program that reduces the hardship of joblessness by guaranteeing that unemployed workers receive a percentage of their former income while unemployed; also known as *federal jobless benefits*

unemployment rate the percentage of the labor force that is unemployed

union a group of workers who bargain collectively for better wages and benefits

unit of account the measure in which prices are quoted

util a personal unit of satisfaction used to measure the enjoyment from consumption of a good or service

utility a measure of the level of satisfaction that a consumer enjoys from the consumption of goods and services

value of the marginal product (VMP) the marginal benefit of an input, calculated as the marginal product multiplied by the unit price of the output

variable costs costs that change with the rate of output

velocity of money the number of times a unit of money exchanges hands in a given year

wage discrimination a situation occurring when workers with the same ability as others are not paid the same because of their race, ethnic origin, sex, age, religion, or some other group characteristic

wealth the net value of one's accumulated assets

wealth effect the change in the quantity of aggregate demand that results from wealth changes due to price-level changes

welfare economics the branch of economics that studies how the allocation of resources affects economic well-being

willingness to pay the maximum price a consumer will pay for a good or service; also known as the *reservation price*

willingness to sell the minimum price a seller will accept to sell a good or service

winner-take-all phenomenon occurring when extremely small differences in ability lead to sizable differences in compensation

CREDITS

Text

Page 483: Table 1 reprinted from *The Gender Earnings Gap in the Gig Economy: Evidence from over a Million Rideshare Drivers* by Cody Cook, Rebecca Diamond, Jonathan Hall, John A. List, Paul Oyer, June 7, 2018, Stanford Graduate School of Business. Working Paper No. 3637. Reprinted by permission of the authors.

Photos

FRONT MATTER

Page viii: SabOlga/Shutterstock; **p. ix**: tinotchka/Stockimo/Alamy Stock Photo; **p. xiii**: Gpointstudio/Cultura Creative/Alamy Stock Photo; **p. xvi**: Pressmaster/Shutterstock; **p. xviii**: Stockbroker/MBI/Alamy Stock Photo; **p. xx**: Imaginechina Limited/Alamy Stock Photo; **p. xxiii**: Malcolm Fairman/Alamy Stock Photo; **p. xxvi**: AOC Photo/Alamy Stock Photo; **p. xxvii**: Konstantin Chagin/Shutterstock; **p. xxviii**: stefano baldini/Alamy Stock Photo; **p. 1**: Kara Coppock.

PART I

Page 2: Mira/Alamy Stock Photo.

CHAPTER 1

Page 4: SabOlga/Shutterstock; **p. 6**: mervas/Shutterstock; **p. 8** left: Phang Kim Shan/Dreamstime.com, right: Nguyen Thai/Dreamstime.com; **p. 9**: Reprinted with permission of The Onion. Copyright: © 2013, by Onion, Inc. www.theonion.com; **p. 10**: Leonard Zhukovsky/Shutterstock; **p. 11**: Gordon Donovan/Alamy Stock Photo; **p. 12**: Oscilloscope/Courtesy Everett Collection; **p. 13**: Image provided courtesy of Virginia Polytechnic Institute and State University (Virginia Tech); **p. 14**: Daniel DeSlover/ZUMA Wire/Alamy Live News; **p. 15**: Dirk Mateer; **p. 16** top: ilpo musto/Alamy Stock Photo, bottom: Seanyu/Dreamstime.com; **p. 17**: Debra Gruszecki/Staff/ZUMA Press/Newscom; **p. 20**: Rawpixel.com/Shutterstock; **p. 22**: Theo Wargo/WireImage for Clear Channel/Getty Images.

CHAPTER 2

Page 26: John McGovern/Alamy Stock Photo; **p. 28**: Xyla Foxlin; **p. 29**: Veritasium, Inc.; **p. 31**: Todd Pierson/EFE/Newscom; **p. 32**: Nikolai Sorokin/Dreamstime.com; **p. 33**: Caroline Blumberg/PA Images/Alamy Stock Photo; **p. 39**: Lou-Foto/Alamy; **p. 45**: Photo courtesy of How to Make Everything, LLC; **p. 46**: Philcold/Dreamstime.com; **p. 47**: PG/Bauer-Griffin/GC Images/Getty Images; **p. 48**: CBS Photo Archive/Getty Images; **p. 49** left: Teraberb/Dreamstime.com, right: oneinchpunch/Shutterstock; **p. 51**: ©Open Road Films/Courtesy Everett Collection; **p. 52** top: Monkeybusiness/Dreamstime.com, bottom: MediaWorldImages/Alamy Stock Photo; **p. 53**: Hero Images/Digital Vision/Getty Images.

PART II

Page 70: tinotchka/Stockimo/Alamy Stock Photo.

CHAPTER 3

Page 72: Antons Jevterevs/Alamy Stock Photo; **p. 74**: All Canada Photos/Alamy; **p. 75** top: Walter Bibikow/Danita Delimont/Alamy Stock Photo, bottom: Tpt/Shutterstock; **p. 76**: ESPECIAL/NOTIMEX/Newscom; **p. 77**: Italarico/Shutterstock; **p. 78**: Ian West/PA Images/Alamy Stock Photo; **p. 80** left: Jeffrey Mayer/Pictorial Press Ltd/Alamy Stock Photo, right: Ian West/PA Images/Alamy Stock Photo; **p. 81**: studioM/Depositphotos; **p. 83**: Simon Burt/Alamy Stock Photo; **p. 84**: Marvel Studios/Kobal/Shutterstock; **p. 85** left: Radius Images/Alamy, right: Showface/Dreamstime.com; **p. 90**: Lucian Coman/Dreamstime.com; **p. 92**: AP Photo/Ted S. Warren; **p. 93**: M. BERMAN/Alamy Stock Image; **p. 94**: Stockbyte/Getty Images; **p. 98**: superelaks/Shutterstock; **p. 100**: Jason Davis/Getty Images for HGTV; **p. 101**: Redfin; **p. 111**: Maskot/Alamy Stock Photo; **p. 112**: NOAA.

CHAPTER 4

Page 114: Randy Holmes/ABC via Getty Images; **p. 116**: left to right: Sunflowerr/Shutterstock, dechevm/

Depositphotos, Elymas/Shutterstock; **p. 117**: nejron/Depositphotos; **p. 118** top: Allstar Picture Library/Alamy, bottom: supparsorn/Shutterstock; **p. 119** top: Chris Ryan/OJO Images Ltd/Alamy Stock Photo, bottom: Seanyu/Dreamstime.com; **p. 120** top to bottom: Wisconsinart/Dreamstime.com, Oleksiy Mark/Dreamstime.com, Lisa Thornberg/iStockphoto.com, Arpad Benedek/istockphoto.com; **p. 121**: Used with the permission of Inter IKEA Systems B.V. Photo by Rio Valencerina; **p. 122**: Sonja Flemming/CBS via Getty Images; **p. 124**: BraunS/iStockphoto; **p. 125** top: Rick Rhay/iStockphoto, bottom: Alex Belomlinsky/iStockphoto ; **p. 126**: Wikimedia Commons; **p. 127** clockwise from top left: BraunS/iStockphoto, Rick Rhay/iStockphoto.com, Alex Belomlinsky/iStockphoto, Wikimedia Commons; **p. 128** top to bottom: BraunS/iStockphoto, Wikimedia Commons, Alex Belomlinsky/iStockphoto, Rick Rhay/iStockphoto.com; **p. 133**: Jason Alden/Bloomberg via Getty Images; **p. 134** top: AlexanderLipko/Shutterstock; bottom: Wilf Doyle/Alamy Stock Photo; **p. 137**: Xpogo LLC; **p. 138**: Eliza Snow/iStockphoto.com; **p. 139** top: Design Pics Inc/Alamy Stock Photo; Table 4.4 top to bottom: Svetlana Foote/Dreamstime.com, Steven von Niederhausern/iStockphoto.com, Ragoarts/Dreamstime.com; **p. 140** Table 4.5 clockwise from top left: Steve Shepard/iStockphoto.com, Steve Shepard/iStockphoto .com, Chaoss/Dreamstime.com, Daniel R. Burch/iStockphoto.com, Olga Lyubkina/iStockphoto.com, Ljupco Smokovski/Dreamstime.com; **p. 140** top: Keith Homan/Shutterstock, bottom: W. W. Norton & Co., Inc.; **p. 141**: dotshock/Shutterstock; **p. 142**: Daniel Bendjy/iStockphoto.com; **p. 143** top: Yuri Arcurs/Dreamstime.com; Table 4.6 top to bottom: Yuri Arcurs/Dreamstime.com, jakelv7500/Shutterstock, Julie Feinstein/Dreamstime.com; **p. 145**: George Peters/iStockphoto.com; **p. 146**: Avigator Fortuner/Shutterstock; **p. 148**: GWImages/Shutterstock; **p. 149**: Rich Legg/iStockphoto.com.

CHAPTER 5

Page 154: Giuseppe Masci/Alamy Stock Photo; **p. 157**: Tamara Arranz/©Netflix/Courtesy Everett Collection; **p. 162** top: Matt Baron/Shutterstock, bottom: Halfpoint/Shutterstock; **p. 164** Chuck Place/istockphoto.com; **p. 165** top: Vivian Zink/©NBC/courtesy Everett Collection, bottom: Daniel Kraso_/Alamy Stock Photo; **p. 167** left: PaulVImages/iStockphoto.com, right: Dan Van Den Broeke/Dreamstime.com; **p. 170**: AP Photo/Kiichiro Sato; **p. 171**: Perry van Munster/Alamy Stock Photo; **p. 174**: Uros Petrovic/Dreamstime.com; **p. 177**: glowonconcept/Depositphotos; **p. 178**: apcuk/iStockphoto.com; **p. 182**: Cultura Creative (RF)/Alamy Stock Photo.

CHAPTER 6

Page 188: Federico Parra/AFP/Getty Images; **p. 191** top: Reuters/Carlos Garcia Rawlins/Alamy Stock Photo; Table 6.1 top to bottom: Chhob/Dreamstime.com, Michael Neelon(misc)/Alamy Stock Photo, ermess/Shutterstock.com, Justin Sullivan/Getty Images, BluIz60/Alamy Stock Photo; **p. 192**: ESB Professional/Shutterstock; **p. 195**: Str/EPA/Shutterstock; **p. 196**: Benoit Daoust/Alamy Stock Photo; **p. 197**: Dinodia Photos/Alamy Stock Photo; **p. 198**: Maridav/Alamy Stock Photo; **p. 201** top: Yuri Arcurs/Dreamstime.com, bottom: Steven von Niederhausern/iStockphoto.com; **p. 202** top to bottom: Julie Feinstein/Dreamstime.com, Courtesy of Andrew Le, Chris Graythen/Getty Images; **p. 203**: Anthony Aneese Totah Jr/Dreamstime.com; **p. 205**: Peter Booth/iStockphoto.com; **p. 206**: Goran Bogicevic/Shutterstock; **p. 210** left: calimedia/Shutterstock, right: Kyoungil Jeon/iStockphoto.com; **p. 211**: Robert Churchill/iStockphoto.com; **p. 213**: Howard Greenblatt via Planetpix/Alamy Stock Photo.

CHAPTER 7

Page 218: Greg Taylor/Alamy Stock Photo; **p. 222**: left: Christophe Testi/Dreamstime, right: Jaro68/Shutterstock, bottom: Charlieb34/Dreamstime.com; **p. 224**: wwing/iStock/Getty Images Plus; **p. 225**: Sean Locke/iStockphoto.com; **p. 227** Table 7.2 clockwise from top left: Charlieb34/Dreamstime.com, Jeanette Virginia Goh/Shutterstock, Jonathan Cohen/iStockphoto.com, RiverNorthPhotography/iStockphoto.com, Stef Bennett/Dreamstime.com; Steve Lovegrove/Dreamstime.com; bottom: Roy Morsch/Getty Images; **p. 229**: Prostock-studio/Alamy Stock Photo; **p. 230** left: Suretha Rous/Alamy Stock Photo, right: David Gray/Bloomberg via Getty Images; **p. 231**: AS Food Studio/Shutterstock; **p. 232**: Yaw Niel/Shutterstock; **p. 233** top: The Family Circus © 2006 Bil Keane, Inc. Dist. by King Features Syndicate, Inc., bottom left: Dzmitry Kliapitski/Alamy Stock Photo, bottom right: lightasafeather/e+/Getty Images; **p. 234** Table 7.3 clockwise from top: left: AS Food Studio/Shutterstock, Dzmitry Kliapitski/Alamy Stock Photo, U.S. Navy photo by Mass Communication Specialist 3rd Class John Grandin, lightasafeather/Getty Images; bottom: Oscity/Shutterstock; **p. 235**: Kenneth Sponsler/iStockphoto.com; **p. 236**: stuar/Shutterstock; **p. 237**:

USGS; **p. 239** top: Karl Dolenc/iStockphoto, bottom: The Ocean Cleanup (Handout)/EPA-EFE/Shutterstock; **p. 240**: Stephanie Keith/Polaris/Newscom; **p. 241**: Corine Sciboz/ZUMA Press/Newscom; **p. 242**: Daniel DeSlover/ZUMA Wire/Alamy Live News.

PART III

Page 248: Gpointstudio/Cultura Creative/Alamy Stock Photo.

CHAPTER 8

Page 250: Paul Chinn/San Francisco Chronicle via Getty Images; **p. 252**: Photoshot/Newscom; **p. 253**: Zits © 2002 Zits Partnership, Dist. by King Features Syndicate, Inc.; **p. 256**: YinYang/iStockphoto.com; **p. 257**: ©2018 Disney/Pixar/PictureLux/The Hollywood Archive/Alamy Stock Photo; **p. 258**: Jim West/Alamy Stock Photo; **p. 262**: Kin Man Hui/San Antonio Express-News/ZUMA Press/Newscom; **p. 266**: FOXTROT © (2005) Bill Amend. Reprinted with permission of Andrews McMeel. All rights reserved.; **p. 267**: Photo by Granada/Optomen Tv/A Smith Co/Kobal/Shutterstock; **p. 268**: John Verner/iStockphoto.com; **p. 269** top: Sandra Nicol/iStockphoto.com, bottom: Courtesy of GARY ZVONKOVIC/Zvonkovic Photography; **p. 270** top: wonderlandstock/Alamy Stock Photo; Figure 8.3 top to bottom: Sandra Nicol/iStockphoto.com, wonderlandstock/Alamy Stock Photo, John Verner/iStockphoto.com; **p. 271**: Monty Brinton/CBS via Getty Images; **p. 272**: Liu Tao/FEATURECHINA/Newscom; **p. 273**: RSBPhoto1/Alamy Stock Photo; **p. 274**: Ali Goldstein/©Netflix/courtesy Everett Collection.

CHAPTER 9

Page 280: UfaBizPhoto/Shutterstock; **p. 284**: top to bottom: Neilson Barnard/iStockphoto.com, Manon Ringuette/Dreamstime.com, Raine Vara/Alamy, Russell Shively/iStockphoto.com; **p. 285** top: Michel Porro/Getty Images, bottom: Jochen Tack/Alamy Stock Photo; **p. 286**: ©20th Century Fox. All rights reserved/courtesy Everett Collection; **p. 288**: Michael Shake/Dreamstime.com; **p. 290**: Courtesy of Dirk Mateer; **p. 294**: Chris Farina/Corbis via Getty Images; **p. 295**: Alexandr Mitiuc/Dreamstime.com; **p. 297**: Prostock-studio/Shutterstock; **p. 299** top: Judy Ledbetter/iStockphoto.com, bottom: adrian beesley/iStockphoto.com; **p. 302**: Maria Loginova/Shutterstock; **p. 303**: Photo Still from I Love Lucy-Courtesy of CBS Broadcasting Inc.; **p. 305**: Chrisyates/Dreamstime.com; **p. 306**: MediaPunch/Shutterstock.

CHAPTER 10

Page 312: michael melia/Alamy Stock Photo; **p. 317**: top: Robyn Beck/AFP/Getty Images, bottom: Mediscan/Alamy Stock Photo; **p. 318**: Courtesy of Scott Honea; **p. 319**: Howard Harrison/Alamy; **p. 320**: Paramount Pictures/Album/Newscom; **p. 325**: Sergio Sergo/Shutterstock; **p. 326**: Colonel/Getty Images; **p. 329** left: Ryan McGinnis/Alamy Stock Photo, right: Christopher Capozziello/Zuffa LLC via Getty Images, bottom: Paul Souders/Getty Images; **p. 330** left: jfmdesign/iStockphoto, right: Debbi Smirnoff/iStockphoto.com; **p. 331**: Ursula Coyote/©AMC/Courtesy Everett Collection; **p. 332**: AFP/Getty Images; **p. 335**: John Mutrux/MCT/Newscom.

CHAPTER 11

Page 342: tirc83/Getty Images; **p. 347**: Nieuwland Photography/Alamy Stock Photo; **p. 348**: Tracy Bennett/Mgm/Kobal/Shutterstock; **p. 350**: Weldon Schloneger/Shutterstock; **p. 352**: Cynthia Farmer/Dreamstime.com; **p. 353**: vau902/iStockphoto.com; **p. 355**: CREATISTA/Shutterstock; [**p. 356**: author, no credit] **p. 357** top: Chon Kit Leong/Alamy Stock Photo, bottom: Sharkshock/Shutterstock; **p. 359**: rafapress/Shutterstock; **p. 360**: Uber; **p. 361**: ©Universal/courtesy Everett Collection; **p. 362**: Levis.com.

CHAPTER 12

Page 366: Mike Fanous/Gamma-Rapho via Getty Images; **p. 370** left: swalls/iStockphoto.com, right: Mahmoud Masad/Alamy Stock Photo, bottom: TravelCollection/Alamy Stock Photo; **p. 376**: ShutterWorx/iStockphoto.com; **p. 378** top: CBS Photo Archive/Getty Images, bottom: Monkey Business Images/Dreamstime.com; **p. 379**: Serafino Mozzo/iStockphoto; **p. 380**: Jim Carroll, Druther's DQ Group; **p. 381** top to bottom: wsfurlan/istockphoto.com, Ian Dagnall/Alamy Stock Photo, Stanley Marquardt/Alamy, Moritz Wolf/imageBROKER/Alamy Stock Photo, fewerton/Alamy Stock Photo, Carlos Gawronski/iStockphoto, Felix Choo/Alamy Stock Photo; **p. 383** top: stockcreations/Shutterstock, left: Joao Virissimo/Shutterstock, right: Bernd Juergens/Shutterstock, bottom: PEANUTS ©1966 Peanuts Worldwide LLC. Dist. By Andrews McMeel. Reprinted with permission. All rights reserved.; **p. 387** top: Little Caesars, left: Atm2003/Dreamstime.com, bottom: Pedro Antonio Salaverría Calahorra/Dreamstime.com; **p. 388**: W. W. Norton & Co., Inc.; **p. 389**: digitalreflections/Shutterstock; **p. 390**: Pavel Rodimov/Alamy Stock Photo; **p. 391**: Karlis Dambrans/Shutterstock.

CHAPTER 13

Page 396: Daniel Acker/Bloomberg/Getty Images; p. 399: iStockphoto; **p. 403**: Jack Sullivan/Alamy; **p. 405**: Enrique Shore/Alamy Stock Photo; **p. 408**: Tower of God Animation Partners; **p. 410**: Marvel Studios/Kobal/Shutterstock; **p. 413**: Hagar The Horrible ©2006 King Features Syndicate, Inc., Hearst Holdings, Inc.; **p. 414**: The Evolution of Trust (2017) by Nicky Case: ncase.me/trust; **p. 416**: Nickilford/iStockphoto; **p. 418**: Sanja Bucko/Warner Bros/Kobal/Shutterstock; **p. 419**: Joshua Resnick/Shutterstock; **p. 422**: YvanDube/istockphoto.com; **p. 423**: Richard Levine/Alamy; **p. 424**: Alex Ruhl/Shutterstock; **p. 425** top: Bobby Bank/WireImage/Getty Images, bottom: Sixteen String Jack Prods/Avalon Tv/Kobal/Shutterstock; **p. 426**: Tim Boyle/Bloomberg/Getty Images.

PART IV

Page 432: Pressmaster/Shutterstock.

CHAPTER 14

Page 434: Dean Drobot/Shutterstock; **p. 437** top: Ernesto Diaz/iStockphoto.com, bottom: Monkey Business Images/Shutterstock; **p. 438**: Daniel Laflor/iStockphoto.com; **p. 441**: Valery Sharifulin/ZUMA Press/Newscom; **p. 442** top: South West Images Scotland/Alamy Stock Photo, bottom: Robert Kneschke/Alamy Stock Photo; **p. 443**: ©Walt Disney Studios Motion Pictures/courtesy Everett Collection; **p. 445**: Courtesy Nathan Yau/flowingdata.com; **p. 448** top: Ringo Chiu/ZUMA Wire/Alamy Live News, bottom: Kt/Dreamstime.com; **p. 450**: Phanie/Alamy Stock Photo; **p. 452**: LUCASFILM/AF Archive/Alamy Stock Photo; **p. 453** top: The Protected Art Archive/Alamy, bottom: GRAND AVENUE ©2003 Steve Breen and Mike Thompson. Reprinted by permission of Andrews McMeel for UFS. All rights reserved; **p. 456**: Qilai Shen/In Pictures Ltd./Corbis via Getty Images; **p. 458**: ©Columbia Pictures/courtesy Everett Collection; **p. 459**: MCT/Newscom; **p. 462**: Jasper Juinen/Bloomberg via Getty Images; **p. 463**: jez gunnell/iStockphoto.com.

CHAPTER 15

Page 470: Nicki Dingraudo; **p. 472**: uniball/iStockphoto.com; **p. 474**: Ljupco/iStockphoto.com; **p. 475**: victorhe2002/iStockphoto.com; **p. 476** top: Matthew Simmons/Stringer/WireImage/Getty Images, bottom: Frances Roberts/Alamy Stock Photo; **p. 477** top to bottom: uniball/iStockphoto.com, Stockbyte/Getty Images, victorhe2002/iStockphoto.com, Frances Roberts/Alamy Stock Photo; **p. 478**: LiPo Ching/Bay Area News Group/MCT/Alamy Stock Photo; **p. 479** top: Valerie Shoaps/Cal Sport Media/Alamy Live News, bottom: Westend61 GmbH/Alamy Stock Photo; **p. 480** left to right: Independent Photo Agency Srl/Alamy Stock Photo, Denis Makarenko/Shutterstock, MediaPunch Inc/Alamy Live News; **p. 482**: Tero Vesalainen/Shutterstock; **p. 485**: Stockbroker/MBI/Alamy Stock Photo; **p. 491**: THE BORN LOSER ©Art and Chip Sansom. Reprinted by permission of ANDREWS MCMEEL SYNDICATION for UFS. All rights reserved; **p. 492**: nilgun bostanci/iStockphoto.com; **p. 495** left: from Vox.com video,'Homer Simpson: An economic analysis', September 9th, 2016. Zachary Crockett/Vox Media, Inc. Data source: The Simpsons (seasons 1-27), BLS, Glassdoor; US Census Bureau" https://www.vox.com/2016/9/6/12752476/the-simpsons-homer-midd!e-class, right: TM and Copyright: ©20th Century Fox Film Corp. All rights reserved/Everett Collection; **p. 496**: vdvornyk/iStock/Getty Images Plus; **p. 497**: Nik Merkulov/Shutterstock; **p. 500**: Murray Close/©Lionsgate/Courtesy Everett Collection; **p. 501**: Roberto Serra/Iguana Press/Getty Images; **p. 502**: zhang bo/iStockphoto.com; **p. 503**: Album/Alamy Stock Photo.

PART V

Page 508: Stockbroker/MBI/Alamy Stock Photo.

CHAPTER 16

Page 510: Erik Pendzich/Shutterstock; **p. 513** top: Stephen Walls/iStockphoto.com, bottom: john shepherd/iStockphoto.com; **p. 516**: Mathias Wilson/iStockphoto.com; **p. 517** top: Siren Pictures/Netflix/Album/Alamy Stock Photo; Table 16.1 top to bottom: Christian Degroote/Dreamstime.com, Robert Billstone/iStockphoto.com, Juanmonino/iStockphoto.com, iStockphoto, Stoyan Yotov/Shutterstock, Cal Vornberger/Alamy; **p. 521**: Vividpixels/Dreamstime.com; **p. 522**: South Florida Reporter; **p. 525**: Malcolm Park/Alamy Live News; **p. 526**: Rimma Bondarenko/Alamy Stock Photo; **p. 530**: AiVectors/Shutterstock.com.

CHAPTER 17

Page 544: Photo by CBS via Getty Images; **p. 547**: iofoto/istockphoto.com; **p. 548** top: Jennifer Pitiquen/Dreamstime.com, bottom: Monty Brinton/CBS Photo Archive/Getty Images; **p. 549**: Monty Brinton/CBS via Getty Images; **p. 550**: Photo courtesy of Ulrike Malmendier. ©Edward Caldwell; **p. 551**: Ryan Balderas/iStockphoto.com; **p. 553** top: ©Walt Disney Studios Motion Pictures/Courtesy Everett Collection, bottom:: Filmfoto/Dreamstime.com; **p. 554** top: Marc De Simone/Alamy Stock Photo, bottom: Courtesy of University of Rochester; **p. 555**: MBI/Alamy Stock Photo; **p. 558**: National Science Foundation; **p. 559**: Everett Collection Inc/Alamy; **p. 561** top: Collection Christophel/© Paramount Pictures - MTV Entertainment Studios - Dickhouse Productions - Gorilla Flicks, bottom: Mark Stahl/iStockphoto.com; **p. 562** top: Jason Merritt/FilmMagic/Getty Images, bottom: Alex Slobodkin/iStockphoto.com; **p. 563**: AJR_photo/Shutterstock; **p. 564**: iunewind/Alamy Stock Vector.

CHAPTER 18

Page 568: sokolova_sv/Shutterstock; **p. 571** left: Brooks-Brown/Science Source, right: Mark Kostich/iStockphoto.com; **p. 578**: D Dipasupil/FilmMagic/Getty Images; **p. 580**: Matt Groening/20th Century Fox/Kobal/Shutterstock; **p. 581**: Hero Images Inc./Alamy Stock Photo; **p. 583**: Kathy Hutchins/Shutterstock; **p. 586**: Alina Troeva/Shutterstock; **p. 587**: Jovan Jaric/iStockphoto.com; **p. 589**: Michael Burrell/Alamy Stock Photo; **p. 592**: top: Olekcii Mach/Alamy Stock Photo, **p. 592**: bottom: Vera Cheredova/Alamy Stock Vector/Alamy; **p. 594**: sjscreens/Alamy Stock Photo.

PART VI

Page 600: Imaginechina Limited/Alamy Stock Photo.

CHAPTER 19

Page 602: Robert Melen/Alamy Stock Photo; **p. 605** left: Sailorman/Dreamstime.com, right: Emile Wamsteker/Bloomberg via Getty Images; **p. 606**: Ryan McGinnis/Alamy Stock Photo; **p. 612**: David Zentz/Aurora Photos/Alamy Stock Photo; **p. 613** left: Joe Biafore/iStockphoto.com, right: Michael Shake/Dreamstime.com; **p. 614**: Lee Jae-Won/Nippon News/Aflo Co. Ltd./Alamy Stock Photo; **p. 616**: top: AP Photo/Lee Jin-man, bottom: Sipa via AP Images; **p. 617** top: Kelpfish/Dreamstime.com, bottom: Alexander Kharchenko/Dreamstime.com; **p. 618**: Lezh/iStockphoto.com; **p. 624**: NPR; **p. 625**: Keith Dannemiller/Alamy Stock Photo; **p. 626**: Katja Bone/iStockphoto.com; **p. 628**: Jackstraw22/Dreamstime.com; **p. 629**: Ursula Coyote/©AMC/Courtesy Everett Collection; **p. 633**: kristian sekulic/iStockphoto.com; **p. 634**: michaeljung/Shutterstock; **p. 635**: Bernardo Ramonfaur/Alamy Stock Photo.

CHAPTER 20

Page 642: Tyler Stableford/Getty Images; **p. 646**: Kristoffer Tripplaar/Sipa USA/Alamy; **p. 648**: River-tracks/Dreamstime.com; **p. 649** top: Donald Bowers/Getty Images for Quill.com, bottom: Nabeel Zytoon/Dreamstime.com; **p. 652**: Joe Raedle/Getty Images; **p. 655**: Igor Mojzes/Alamy Stock Photo; **p. 660**: iStockPhoto; **p. 664**: AP Photo/Nam Y. Huh; **p. 665**: Mykola Sosiukin/Alamy Stock Photo.

CHAPTER 21

Page 672: Juan Torres/NurPhoto/Getty Images; **p. 674**: Wang Ying/Xinhua/Alamy Live News; **p. 675**: Reuters/Howard Burditt/Alamy Stock Photo; **p. 676**: Ljupco/iStockphoto.com; **p. 677** top to bottom: Ljupco/iStockphoto.com, AdShooter/iStockphoto.com, hakusan/iStockphoto.com; **p. 678**: S1001/Shutterstock.com; **p. 681** left: alexander kirch/istockphoto.com, right: Yalcin Sonat/Alamy Stock Photo; **p. 683** top to bottom: Stephen Krow/iStockphoto.com, Joe Potato Photo/iStockphoto.com, Michael Neelon(misc)/Alamy, Daniel Bendjy/iStockphoto.com, AVATAR, Zoe Saldana, Sam Worthington (back), 2009. TM Copyright ©20th Century Fox. All rights reserved/Courtesy Everett Collection; **p. 684** top to bottom: ©20th Century-Fox Film Corporation, TM Copyright/courtesy Everett Collection, ©Walt Disney Studios Motion Pictures/©Marvel Studios/Alamy Stock Photo, ©20th Century Fox Film Corp. All rights reserved./Courtesy Everett Collection, Lucasfilm/Bad Robot/Walt Disney Studios/Kobal/Shutterstock, ©Marvel/©Walt Disney Studios Motion Pictures/Courtesy Everett Collection, Amblin/Legendary/Universal/Kobal/Shutterstock, PictureLux/The Hollywood Archive/Disney Enterprises, Inc./Alamy Stock Photo, Marvel Enterprises/Kobal/Shutterstock, ©Universal Pictures/Courtesy Everett Collection, BFA/Walt Disney Studios/Alamy Stock Photo; **p. 685** top to bottom: Selznick/MGM/Kobal/Shutterstock, ©Walt Disney Co./Everett Collection, ©20th Century Fox Film Corp. All rights reserved./Courtesy Everett Collection, ©20th Century-Fox Film Corporation, TM Copyright/courtesy Everett Collection, ©Walt Disney Co./Courtesy Everett Collection, Lucasfilm/Fox/Kobal/Shutterstock, ©Walt Disney Studios Motion Pictures/©Marvel Studios/Alamy Stock Photo, Universal History Archive/Shutterstock,

Universal/Kobal/Shutterstock, ©Walt Disney Studios Motion Pictures/Lucasfilm Ltd./Courtesy Everett Collection; **p. 686**: Jim West/Alamy; **p. 687**: AUSTIN POWERS: THE SPY WHO SHAGGED ME, Mike Myers, 1999, (c) New Line/courtesy Everett Collection; **p. 689**: AP; **p. 690**: Reuters/Kimberly White/Alamy Stock Photo; **p. 692**: Courtesy of Lee Coppock; **p. 695**: Hocus Focus Studio/iStockphoto.com; **p. 696**: George Peters/iStockphoto.com; **p. 701**: Cherry blossom/Shutterstock.

CHAPTER 22

Page 708: Sergey Borisov/Alamy Stock Photo; **p. 712**: Courtesy of Lee Coppock; **p. 713**: Robert Clay/Alamy Stock Photo; **p. 718** top: Yavuz Sariyildiz/shutterstock, bottom: Wesley Thornberry/iStockphoto.com; **p. 722**: Universal Pictures/Courtesy Everett Collection; **p. 724**: Ameer Alhalbi/NurPhoto via Getty Images; **p. 725** top: DeadDuck/iStockphoto.com, bottom: DeadDuck/iStockphoto.com; **p. 726**: SpongeBob Squarepants, 2004, ©Paramount/courtesy Everett Collection; **p. 728**: Feng Li/Getty Images; **p. 731**: creativestockexchange/Shutterstock.com.

CHAPTER 23

Page 736: Alex Segre/Alamy Stock Photo; **p. 740**: Henk Badenhorst/iStockphoto.com; **p. 741**: Anjela30/depositphotos; **p. 747** top: Richard Levine/Alamy Stock Photo, bottom: S. Greg Panosian/iStockPhoto; **p. 749**: Peter Foley/Bloomberg via Getty Images; **p. 752**: Courtesy of The Joe I. Herbstman Memorial Collection of American Finance (tm) www.JIHMC.org; **p. 755**: L A Heusinkveld/Alamy Stock Photo; **p. 756**: Jaap Buitendijk/©Paramount/Courtesy Everett Collection; **p. 757**: Christopher Futcher/iStockphoto.com.

PART VII

Page 762: Malcolm Fairman/Alamy Stock Photo.

CHAPTER 24

Page 764: NASA/ISS Crew Earth Observations Facility and the Earth Science and Remote Sensing Unit, Johnson Space Center; **p. 768**: Irene Abdou/Alamy Stock Photo; **p. 769** left to right: Steven Wynn/iStockphoto.com, INTERFOTO/Alamy Stock Photo, FALKENSTEINFOTO/Alamy Stock Photo, traveler1116/iStockphoto.com, Georgios Kollidas/Shutterstock.com, HultonArchive/iStockphoto.com; **p. 772**: Courtesy of Lee Coppock; **p. 777** top: Monkey Business Images/Shutterstock, bottom: Nicholas Han/Alamy Stock Photo; **p. 778** clockwise from top left: Onepony/Dreamstime.com, Sonya Etchison/Dreamstime.com, Mark Phelan/Detroit Free Press/TNS/Alamy Live News, Cobalt88/Dreamstime.com, ClassicStock/Alamy, Martyn Goddard/Getty Images; **p. 779**: studio157/iStockphoto.com; **p. 782**: Moritz Hager/Photoshot/Newscom; **p. 783**: Chris Ratcliffe/Bloomberg via Getty Images; **p. 784**: David Paul Morris/Bloomberg/Getty Images; **p. 785**: Britta Kasholm-Tengve/iStockphoto.com; **p. 786**: John Warburton Lee/SuperStock; **p. 789** top: STR/AFP/Getty Images, bottom: Nic Bothma/EPA/Shutterstock; **p. 790**: Jacom Stephens/iStockphoto.com; **p. 792**: ©Marvel/©Walt Disney Studios Motion Pictures/Courtesy Everett Collection; **p. 793**: Courtesy of Daniel D. Lee; **p. 794** top: Bryce Vickmark/MIT/UPI/Alamy Live News, bottom: Luke MacGregor/Bloomberg via Getty Images.

CHAPTER 25

Page 800: Alexander Demianchuk/ITAR-TASS News Agency/Alamy Stock Photo; **p. 804** left: Bartosz Hadyniak/iStockphoto.com, right: Klaas Lingbeek-van Kranen/iStockphoto.com; **p. 805**: TM and Copyright ©20th Century Fox Film Corp. All rights reserved. Courtesy: Everett Collection; **p. 807**: Danilo Mongiello/Dreamstime.com; **p. 809**: Stacey Lynn Payne/iStockphoto.com; **p. 811**: Ugurhan Betin/Getty Images; **p. 812**: Carl Juste/Miami Herald/TNS/Alamy Live News; **p. 814** left: tirc83/iStockphoto.com, right: Aleksey Boldin/Alamy Stock Photo; **p. 816**: CB2/ZOB/WENN/Newscom; **p. 817**: Cernan Elias/Alamy Stock Photo; **p. 818:** Chris Boswell/iStockphoto.com; **p. 819** top: Geraint Lewis/Alamy Stock Photo, bottom: PaeguS/Shutterstock; **p. 821** left and right: Carlos Barria/Reuters/Newscom; **p. 825** top: Luis Sandoval Mandujano/iStockphoto.com, bottom: Alptraum/Dreamstime.com; **p. 826**: Jemal Countess/Getty Images.

CHAPTER 26

Page 832: Richard B. Levine/Alamy Stock Photo; **p. 837**: Jason Stitt/Dreamstime.com; **p. 838**: Mike Mareen/Shutterstock; **p. 839**: Marek Uliasz/Alamy Stock Photo; **p. 840** top: EricVega/iStockphoto.com, bottom: Steven Pepple/Dreamstime.com; **p. 842**: Christopher Pillitz/Photonica World/Getty Images; **p. 844** left to right: EricVega/iStockphoto.com, Courtesy of Lee Coppock,Vassiliy Mikhailin/iStockphoto.com; **p. 846**: Justin Sullivan/Getty Images;

p. 847: ©Warner Bros./Pictorial Press Ltd/Alamy Stock Photo; **p. 851** top: Courtesy of Lee Coppock, bottom: Stacey DiFazio/Alamy Stock Photo; **p. 854**: inga spence/Alamy Stock Photo; **p. 858**: ©Warner Bros./ Courtesy Everett Collection; **p. 861**: SAUL LOEB/ AFP/GettyImages; **p. 862**: Hariandi Hafid/SOPA Images/ZUMA Wire/Alamy Live News.

CHAPTER 27

Page 870: Lange, D., photographer. (1936) Migrant agricultural worker's family. Library of Congress, https://www.loc.gov/item/2017762903/; **p. 872**: Kevin Frayer/Getty Images; **p. 874**: ©Walt Disney/ Moviestore Collection LTD/Alamy Stock Photo; **p. 876**: Sueddeutsche Zeitung Photo/Alamy Stock Photo; **p. 877**: Universal History Archive/Getty Images; **p. 880**: Underwood Archives/Getty Images; **p. 884** left: Library of Congress, Prints & Photographs Division, FSA/OWI Collection, LC-DIG-fsa-8a22559, right: Britta Kasholm-Tengve/iStockphoto.com; **p. 885** top: Gumpanat Thavankitdumrong/Alamy Stock Photo, bottom: Getty Images; **p. 891**: Cavan Images/Alamy Stock Photo; **p. 892** left: Sueddeutsche Zeitung Photo/Alamy Stock Photo; right: Album/ Alamy Stock Photo; **p. 898**: JGI/Jamie Grill/Tetra Images, LLC/Alamy Stock Photo; **p. 900**: Wavebreak Media ltd/Alamy Stock Photo; **p. 906**: U.S. Air Force photo/Staff Sgt. James L. Harper Jr.(The appearance of U.S. Department of Defense visual information does not imply or constitute DOD endorsement.); **p. 907**: Ariel Skelley/Digital Vision/Getty Images.

PART VIII

Page 914: AOC Photo/Alamy Stock Photo.

CHAPTER 28

Page 916: Songquan Deng/Alamy Stock Photo; **p. 918**: REUTERS/Jonathan Ernst/Alamy Stock Photo; **p. 920**: U.S. Navy photo by Andy Wolfe courtesy of Lockheed Martin; **p. 921**: wavebreakmedia/ Shutterstock; **p. 922**: svariophoto/iStockphoto.com; **p. 923**: AP Photo; **p. 930**: lucky336/iStockphoto. com; **p. 937**: Shutterstock; **p. 939**: MichaelVi/ depositphotos; **p. 940**: Hero Images Inc./Alamy Stock Photo.

CHAPTER 29

Page 944: Official White House Photo by Adam Schultz; **p. 948**: Reuters/Rick Wilking/Alamy Stock Photo; **p. 948** left: Erin Schaff/POOL/EPA-EFE/ Shutterstock, right: Official White House Photo by Adam Schultz; **p. 953**: eurobanks/Shutterstock.com, **p. 955** top: PAY IT FORWARD, Haley Joel Osment, 2000/Everett Collection, bottom: Raja Rc/Dreamstime.com; **p. 956** top: Charles Trainor Jr./Miami Herald/TNS/Alamy Live News, bottom: Photo by Erik Jepsen; **p. 957**: Louis-Paul St-Onge/iStockphoto. com; **p. 958**: AP Photo/Eric Risberg; **p. 959**: Stephen Krow/iStockphoto.com; **p. 961** top: Bohuslav Mayer/ Dreamstime.com, bottom: Ronnie McMillan/Alamy; **p. 963**: Monkey Business Images/Shutterstock; **p. 967**: NASA; **p. 968**: Reuters/Kevin Lamarque/ Alamy Stock Photo; **p. 969**: AP Photo/Ed Reinke.

PART IX

Page 974: Konstantin Chagin/Shutterstock.

CHAPTER 30

Page 976: Andrew Harrer/Bloomberg via Getty Images; **p. 978**: Yonhap/EPA/Shutterstock; **p. 979**: Charles Islander/iStockphoto.com; **p. 980** left: National Numismatic Collection at the Smithsonian Institution, right: Scottnodine/Dreamstime.com, bottom: Deborah-Maxemow/iStockphoto.com; **p. 981** top: Ken Tannenbaum/iStockphoto.com, bottom: Jiri Hera/Alamy Stock Photo; **p. 982** top: Crypto.com/Youtube, bottom: Baris Simsek/iStockphoto.com; **p. 984** left: PaulVImages/ iStockphoto.com, right: Maurice Crooks/Alamy, bottom: tomas del amo/Alamy; **p. 989**: RKO/Album/Alamy Stock Photo; **p. 990**: Duncan Hale-Sutton/Alamy Stock Photo; **p. 992**: Federal Reserve/Flickr; **p. 993**: Ted Foxx/Alamy Stock Photo; **p. 996** top: TM Copyright ©20th Century Fox Film Corp. All rights reserved. Everett Collection, bottom: Evan El-Amin/Shutterstock; **p. 997**: Uschools University Images/iStockhoto/Getty Images; **p. 1001**: halfpoint/Depositphotos.

CHAPTER 31

Page 1006: Backyard Productions/Alamy Stock Photo; **p. 1011**: Kevin Dietch/UPI/Newscom; **p. 1012**: Dani Simmonds/Alamy; **p. 1015**: Bettmann/ Getty Images; **p. 1016**: Britt Leckman/Federal Reserve/Flickr; **p. 1027**: Almir1968/Dreamstime. com; **p. 1030**: Warner Bros./Courtesy Everett Collection; **p. 1031**: Federal Reserve/Flickr; **p. 1033**: Jackryan89/Dreamstime.com; **p. 1034**: Oleksiy Mark/Dreamstime.com.

PART X

Page 1040: stefano baldini/Alamy Stock Photo.

CHAPTER 32

Page 1042: Flourish (a registered trademark of Canva); **p. 1044**: Suez Canal Authority/Handout via Xinhua/Alamy Stock Photo; **p. 1045** left and right: Phil Crean A/Alamy Stock Photo; **p. 1046**: Aleksandra Yakovleva/iStockphoto.com; **p. 1048**: Craig Hastings/Getty Images; **p. 1049**: Chris Ratcliffe/Bloomberg via Getty Images; **p. 1050**: UrbanZone/Alamy Stock Photo; **p. 1054**: Stephen Shaver/UPI/Shutterstock; **p. 1060**: Reason.com; **p. 1063**: AP Photo/Damian Dovarganes; **p. 1064**: Mary Evans/LUCASFILMS/Ronald Grant/Everett Collection; **p. 1065**: Larry Leung/FeatureChina/Newscom; **p. 1066** left: Sergio Azenha/Alamy Stock Photo, right: 2p2play/Shutterstock.

CHAPTER 33

Page 1072: Solent News/Splash News/Newscom; **p. 1074**: david franklin/iStockphoto.com; **p. 1078**: Patryk Kosmider/iStockphoto.com; **p. 1080**: Will Ireland/Future/Shutterstock; **p. 1085** top: Feng Li/Getty Images, bottom: B.A.E. Inc./Alamy; **p. 1089** top: 2004, © DreamWorks/courtesy Everett Collection, bottom: Niknikopol/Dreamstime.com; **p. 1091**: Alex Segre/Alamy; **p. 1092**: Courtesy of Lee Coppock; **p. 1093**: btrenkel/iStockphoto.com; **p. 1095**: AP Photo/Peter Dejong; **p. 1097**: Chmiel/iStockphot.com; **p. 1098**: Sean Gallup/Getty Images.

INDEX

Note: Page numbers in **boldface** indicate where key terms are defined. Page numbers in *italics* indicate figures or tables.

T